Supply Chain Engineering and Logistics Handbook

Supply Chain Engineering and Logistics Handbook

Inventory and Production Control

Erick C. Jones, PhD

CRC Press
Taylor & Francis Group
Boca Raton London New York

CRC Press is an imprint of the
Taylor & Francis Group, an **informa** business

CRC Press
Taylor & Francis Group
6000 Broken Sound Parkway NW, Suite 300
Boca Raton, FL 33487-2742

First issued in paperback 2021

© 2020 by Taylor & Francis Group, LLC
CRC Press is an imprint of Taylor & Francis Group, an Informa business

No claim to original U.S. Government works

ISBN-13: 978-1-138-06651-9 (hbk)
ISBN-13: 978-1-03-217645-1 (pbk)
DOI: 10.1201/9781315159096

Library of Congress Cataloging-in-Publication Data

Names: Jones, Erick C., author.
Title: Supply chain engineering and logistics handbook : inventory and production control / authored by Erick C. Jones.
Description: Boca Raton : CRC Press, an imprint of Taylor & Francis Group, 2019. | Includes bibliographical references.
Identifiers: LCCN 2019015737| ISBN 9781138066519 (hardback : alk. paper) | ISBN 9781315159096 (ebk.)
Subjects: LCSH: Business logistics—Handbooks, manuals, etc. | Inventory control—Handbooks, manuals, etc.
Classification: LCC HD38.5 .J646 2019 | DDC 658.7—dc23
LC record available at https://lccn.loc.gov/2019015737

Visit the Taylor & Francis Web site at
http://www.taylorandfrancis.com

and the CRC Press Web site at
http://www.crcpress.com

Contents

Part 2   Basic Knowledge for Global Supply Chain Engineering

Preface

With the "Modern SCM for SMOR", we hope to establish concepts and principles by which students, supply chain management, logistics engineers, and operations research and management practitioners and researchers will learn about Modern techniques for Supply Chain Management (SCM) in the Service, Manufacturing, and Operations Research (SMOR) fields. Also, we will expand on how this field is modernizing with concepts with ideas on the internet of things (IoT), Radio Frequency Identification (RFID) and Automatic Identification (AutoID) enabling technologies, and cloud-based collaboration IT technologies that process BIG DATA to optimize the supply chain.

The text is organized into three sections that focus on supply chain (SC) history, how the SC are connected today, and where the SC field is going with current research. The overall intellectual merit of the text is that it introduces a framework similar to sundial that allows an organization to determine where their company may fall on the Supply Chain Technology Scale. The text will describe those who are using more historic technologies, some companies that are using current collaboration tools for connecting their SC to other global supply chains (GSCs), and the SCs that are moving more toward cutting-edge technologies.

Student Learning Outcomes: Upon completion of this course, the student is expected to have demonstrated his/her ability to know and properly use:

1. Forecasting techniques and their applications
2. Aggregate planning techniques for production operations
3. Inventory control management techniques in production operations
4. Scheduling for production operations
5. Push and pull production control systems: material resource planning (MRP) and just-in-time (JIT).

Some features of this book, which make it unique, are that it:

1. Presents a decision model for choosing the best Supply Chain Engineering (SCE) strategies for Service and Manufacturing Operations with respect to Industrial Engineering and Operations Research techniques
2. Presents an economic comparison model for evaluating SCE strategies for manufacturing outsourcing as opposed to keeping operations in house
3. Demonstrates how to integrate automation techniques such as RFID into planning and distribution operations
4. Summative history of multiple Industrial Engineering techniques on manufacturing and service industries that impact the GSCs
5. Case studies of SC inventory reductions using automation from automatic information technology (AIT) and RFID Research from Dr. Jones's RFID Supply Chain Lab
6. Case studies from Industrial Engineering consultants
7. Planning and scheduling classroom theory and problems
8. Transportation and SC classroom theory and problems.

Our overall goal for this text is for it to allow students to learn modern Industrial Engineering used in modern GSC operations, allow military personnel and contractors to learn and use it with respect to SC operations including modern automation Unique Item Identifier (UID) standards, and allow practitioners to learn and integrate the techniques into scheduling and planning operations at all levels, from the strategic GSC level to the tactical scheduler and inventory control levels.

In general, we hope this text will be used as an academic text, practitioner's handbook, and military contractor's guide for using modern SC strategies that inform engineers, managers, and strategic planners and can be used to educate individuals and organizations on how to cost-justify, understand, and implement modern SC strategies, technologies, and large-scale re-engineering initiatives.

MATLAB® is a registered trademark of The MathWorks, Inc. For product information, please contact:

The MathWorks, Inc.
3 Apple Hill Drive
Natick, MA 01760-2098 USA
Tel: 508-647-7000
Fax: 508-647-7001
E-mail: info@mathworks.com
Web: info@mathworks.com

Acknowledgments

This book is the product of many long hours, hard work, and perseverance of not only the author but also the strong team that supported this extensive effort. I wish to acknowledge the many members who contributed to and were inspirational in this effort.

I want to thank first of all God, and my savior, his son Jesus Christ, for giving me the strength and interest to complete this extensive task. Next, I want to thank my family—Erick, Chelsey, Morgan, Christopher, Matthew, Darlene, George, Ranita, Shirley, Malcolm Sr., Felicia, Dwight, and Shelly—for motivating me. I want to thank my graduate students for their enthusiasm to support this project and a few of those who are not referenced in the text: Dhruvi, the real taskmaster; Dhaval; Krishna; Sathish; Pranesh; and Jenish. I also wish to thank my colleagues and staff at the University of Texas at Arlington, including Peter, Dereje, Lynn, Anand, Paul, Ann, Kimetha, and Sandra.

I want to thank my friends and colleagues at the National Science Foundation for providing additional inspiration about the future: Jim, Karen, Dean, Nirmala, Earnestine, Giselle, Susan, Joerg, Criselda, Tierra, Sean, Tyrone, Art, Leroy, James, Talitha, Heather, Andrea, Chi-Chi, Abi, Celeste P., Celeste, Bob, Don, Paige, Bruce, Junhong, Eduardo, Tammie, Khershed, and Latanya. I may have missed someone, but it was great working with everyone.

I want to specially thank all my PhD and master's thesis students for their contribution to the text. I want to express my thanks to Dr. Billy Gray and Dr. Felicia Jefferson for their individual efforts to enhance the text.

Also, I want to thank George and Elizabeth Pickett for the Endowed Professorship at the University of Texas at Arlington; without their generous support, I could not have continued my research in the area and completed this book.

I want to acknowledge all the great companies and representatives I have worked for in the supply chain world over the years, especially Tompkins and Associates; James Tompkins has been a lifelong inspiration. Others include the United Parcel Service, my first engineering job; Academy Sports and Outdoors, my first Engineering Management and Executive Leadership opportunity; and Arthur Anderson, LLP, where I was in leadership at the Executive level. I want to thank my alma mater, both University of Houston, Central, and of course the Aggies, Texas A&M University, College Station. I also want to thank the following professional organizations: the Institute of Industrial and Systems Engineers (IISE), American Society for Engineering Education (ASEE), and American Association for the Advancement of Science (AAAS). I also want to acknowledge the National Academies (NA) and the National Academy of Engineering (NAE) for their inspirational activities that motivate me to keep extending the boundaries of the Grand Challenges.

Thank you
Erick C. Jones

Author

Dr. Erick C. Jones is a noted US Engineering Scientist. His fundamental theory on automated inventory control, quality control, and management has impacted the fields of supply chain management, industrial manufacturing, and industrial and systems engineering. He is the George and Elizabeth Pickett Endowed Professor of Industrial, Manufacturing and Systems Engineering and Associate Dean for Graduate Studies in the College of Engineering at the University of Texas at Arlington (UTA). Jones joined UTA in 2010 after eight years at the University of Nebraska-Lincoln, where he rose to the rank of Associate Professor with Tenure. He served as the Deputy Director of the UT Arlington Homeland Security focused University Center SAVANT, and he serves as the current Director of the (RFID & Auto-ID) RAID labs at UTA.

Dr. Jones's background led him to be invited to *National Science Foundation* (NSF) as Program Officer for the largest Engineering Investment in the country, the Engineering Research Center (ERC). Also given his impact on graduate students he worked in the largest fellowship program in the country: NSF Graduate Research Fellowships Program (GRFP). Until recently, Dr. Jones has served as a rotating Program Director at the **NSF**. His programs included the **GRFP**, the Graduate Research Internship Program (GRIP), and the Workforce Strand of the Education Core Research Program in the Education and Human Resources Directorate. His last NSF detail was as a Program Director for the **ERCs** in the Engineering Directorate. Dr. Jones *was one of only a few* program directors to serve in two NSF Directorates.

Academic background

Dr. Jones graduated from Texas A&M University with a bachelor's degree in industrial engineering in May 1993. He later earned a master's degree from the University of Houston, Houston, Texas, where his thesis was "Turnover of Part-Time Hourly Employees in an Industrial Service Company" under the guidance of Dr. Christopher Chung in May 1996. He further went on to obtain a PhD in industrial engineering from the University of Houston while concurrently working in industry. Under the guidance of his advisor, Dr. Chung, he worked on the topic "A Predictive SPC Model for Determining Cognitive Voluntary Turnover before Physical Departure" and successfully conferred PhD in August 2003.

Industry background

Dr. Jones boasts a broad background that spans both industry and academia. Dr. Jones has held positions in industry that include Industrial Engineering Specialist, Director of Engineering, Consultant and Project Manager, and Executive Manager of a "Big 5" Accounting firm, and Executive Manager for United Parcel Service (UPS), Tompkins Associates, Academy Sports and Outdoors, and Arthur Andersen.

He managed teams and operations as small as 3 people and as large as 500 people. He has managed projects implementing warehouse management systems (WMS) and enterprise resources planning (ERP) system, designing and constructing new facilities, and reengineering Fortune 1000 organizations. Operations managed include strategic systems deployment, teams of large-scale distribution operation, and human resources at an executive level. He is an expert in the field of supply chain optimization, distribution logistics, and inventory control. His contribution has laid foundation for our modern understanding of the Internet of Things (IOT), Blockchain, Radio Frequency Identification (RFID), Auto UD, and Supply Chain Technologies.

Pioneering the RFID technology

In 2003, soon after obtained his PhD degree Dr. Jones moved to academia bringing with him the industrial experience that revolutionized the shape of industrial engineering in further years. His unique background positioned him to develop one of the first and largest academic RFID labs in the country. While working as a newly hired Assistant Professor, Dr. Jones opened the RFID Supply Chain Logistics (RfSCL) lab in Lincoln, Nebraska, to aid in the advances of RFID in automatic data capture technology. The RfSCL goal was to utilize the accepted industry Six Sigma methodologies to define industry problems and, in the process of solving problems, identify and pursue relevant research opportunities. The industry–university focus has led to his lab becoming one of the National Science Foundation's Industry University Cooperatives (NSF I/UCRC) in the Centers for Engineering Logistics and Distribution (CELDi).

His research projects focused majorly on four areas: logistics systems analysis and design, supply chain modeling, material flow design and improvement, and intelligent systems. In the RfSCL, projects were either applied research or theoretical research models. RFID applied research concentrated on areas such as RFID and bar code integration into WMS and ERP systems or RFID in industrial applications such as conveyors which changed the face of logistics.

Theoretical research models for RFID included RFID integration into GPS/GIS or alternate active tag standard development. Supply chain applied research focused on facility/transportation network modeling and RFID and bar code systems integration for inventory. Theoretical research models included mathematical modeling inventory polices and stochastic modeling of supply chain networks.

His students worked on innovative projects like dealing with RFID include embedded RFID license plates (DOT), ROW underground RFID tags (TxDOT), and RFID RTLS (NASA), and corporate supply chain analysis and grain terminal network analysis.

Universal acclaim for the advancements in RFID technology

Dr. Jones continues this research today, which includes a research project that led to RFID being shipped and utilized at NASA on the International Space Station (ISS) in 2013. NASA has deployed its "Project RFID" for use on the ISS, which includes using an RFID reader with both bar coding and RFID capabilities. This was developed in collaborating with Dr. Jones lab (https://blog.atlasrfidstore.com/nasa-rfid-never-lost-space).

Dr. Dwight Mosby, Dr. Jones' former student and current manager at Manager, Payload Operations Director Office at NASA, mentioned "Some astronauts have tweeted from space about the usefulness of the RFID technology."

Six Sigma, quality control, and quality management

Dr. Jones brings industry experience in quality implementations as a former consultant. He is an American Society for Quality (ASQ) Certified Six Sigma Black Belt. He originated and directed a university-level Six Sigma black belt program for several years. The program expanded to a state-level program with an industry and university certification board. He is the Chairman for the International Supply Chain Education Alliance (ISCEA)—Industry Technology Board, Indian Institute of Technology Bombay (IITB) that certifies the training programs, exams and review process for the ISCEA technology RFID supply chain management (RFIDSCM), and Six Sigma programs.

His biggest impact to the day in his opinion remains the implementation of yellow belt certification in developing countries. This enabled the underprivileged students who could not afford to go to college in India, Sri Lanka, and USA to obtain certification in yellow belt, which enhanced their understanding of and paved ways towards the bright industrial careers. Understanding the Pareto Analysis, fish bone diagram and flowcharting enhanced their skills and opportunities for getting hired.

Supply chain management, manufacturing, and industrial engineering

Dr. Erick C. Jones currently works at the University of Texas at Arlington. He is the George and Elizabeth Pickett Endowed Professor of Industrial, Manufacturing and Systems Engineering, and Associate Dean for Graduate Studies in the College of Engineering. In an effort to support the marriage of industry's supply chain needs like automatic identification technology with academia's theoretical applications, he has created a Radio Frequency and Auto Identification Labs (RAID).

Recently, Dr. Jones' interdisciplinary research with chemists and physicists, neuroscientists and surgeons, and bio- and biomedical engineers is leading to *translational and commercial* research for important national programs including the BRAIN initiative, Homeland Security and Safety, and Smart Planet initiatives. His research partnerships range from medical schools, international airports, and international university collaborations.

Academically, Dr. Jones has received over $9 million dollars in funding for academic research projects, from organizations such as NASA, The NSF, Department of Transportation, and US State Department to name a few. Dr. Jones' research activities are *internationally recognized* in the areas of automated data capture using RFID technologies, Quality Control at the Six Sigma level, and Manufacturing Technologies that support the development of "Auto Sensing" technologies. He has published over 165 manuscripts including 3 textbooks. As part of his research efforts, he has advised over 34 master's students and 16 PhD students along with 32 undergraduate research students on sponsored research projects.

Dr. Jones' current focus is on RFID research for the U.S. Department of Transportation, the Department of Defense Transportation Command, and NASA JSC. His research interests include RFID, RTLS, and satellite technology development and testing with respect to inventory control. Other research areas include supply chain logistics, Six Sigma quality engineering management, and knowledge worker turnover.

The purpose of this facility is to support project initiatives like RFID, logistics (supply chain engineering), manufacturing (Six Sigma and Lean initiatives), and information technology (ERP, WMS). The facility's goal is to enhance the industrial engineering field by utilizing some of the research methodologies to provide solutions in the areas of RFID, supply chain logistics, and engineering management. The mission of the RfSCL is "providing integrated solutions in logistics and other data driven environments through automatic data capture, real world prototypes, and analysis." Equipment used in the lab include active and passive tags/readers and software (Matrics, Alien, Samsys, IMPINJ, SERIT), hytrol conveyor, and GCS WMS, HP5555 Mobile Active Reader and Software, RF Code active tags, and SAVI Active Tags and Reader (WMRM/WORM). The methodology utilized for research in the lab is known as DFSS (Design for Six Sigma), which is similar to the Six Sigma DMAIC methodology. The seven steps in this methodology are define, measure, analyze, identify, design, optimize, and verify. The RfSCL team consists of approximately 15 graduate students, with 7 being PhD students and the rest master's students. The RfSCL has received over 40 research awards that have amounted to over $3,067,756. The lab has also received over $1,726,357 in research funding.

Significant work with national organizations

NSF Engineering Research Centers (ERC) Program

From 2016 to 2018, Dr. Jones served as the Program Director, ERC), and ERC Director at Engineering Directorate/Engineering Education Centers of NSF, Arlington, VA. He primarily contributed to the Nanomanufacturing Systems for Mobile Computing and Mobile Energy Technologies (NASCENT), Nanotechnology-Enabled Water Treatment (NEWT), Revolutionizing Metallic Biomaterials (RMB), and Re-Inventing the Nation's Urban Water Infrastructure (RENUWIT) centers.

Dr. Jones was part of a team that revamped the program to Generation 4 research centers where the main elements are Convergent Research and Innovation, positive societal impact, engineering workforce development, the development of a culture of diversity and inclusion, and a focus on value creation within the innovation ecosystem.

NSF Graduate Research Fellowships Program (GRFP)

From 2015 to 2017 Dr. Jones served as the Program Director; GRFP, GRIP, and EHR Core Research (ECR) Workforce Development Strand Lead; and Enabling the Future of Making (MAKER, Lead) at the Education and Human Resources Directorate/Division of Graduate Education department of NSF.

This program recognizes and supports outstanding graduate students in NSF-supported science, technology, engineering, and mathematics disciplines who are pursuing research-based master's and doctoral degrees at accredited United States institutions.

William J. Fulbright Scholar in Mexico 2013

Dr. Jones was awarded an NSF OISE program called International Research Experiences Program in Mexico. During this research he worked with the Monterrey Tech System in Mexico campuses, specifically Queretero. His students did research with global companies including Werner Trucking, Kellogg's, and TRW. The result of this experience is that he was invited to participate in the US State Department William J. Fulbright program to promote Engineering Education in Mexico. He was hosted by Monterrey Tech Queretero and visited schools across Mexico to discuss Engineering Education. He also taught Logistics during the summer in Spanish at Monterrey Tech Queretero.

Aflred P. Sloan Minority PhD Program

Dr. Jones was a APS Minority PhD Scholar while he was a PhD student. He later was awarded a APS Minority PhD Center while at the University of Nebraska-Lincoln, and again while at UT Arlington.

The result of this program yield nine PhD students who were Underrepresented Minorities who completed their doctorate. This represented 100% of the students that were recruited in his program to have completed Dr. Jones is now on the Aflred P. Sloan Minority PhD Scholars Network, SSMN Board.

Textbooks from the Author

Academic Textbooks

1. *Modern Quality for Organizations Using Lean Six Sigma Techniques* by Jones, E. C
   Book description: The next step in the evolution of the organizational quality field, Lean Six Sigma (LSS) has come of age. However, many challenges to using LSS in lieu of, in conjunction with, or integrated with other quality initiatives remain. An update on the current focus of quality management, *Quality Management for Organizations Using Lean Six Sigma Techniques* covers the concepts and principles of LSS and its origins in quality, total quality management (TQM), and statistical process control (SPC), and then explores how it can be integrated into manufacturing, logistics, and health-care operations.

2. *RFID and Auto-ID in Planning and Logistics* by Jones, E. C, and Chung, C.A.
   Book description: As RFID technology is becoming increasingly popular, and the need has arisen to address the challenges and approaches to successful implementation. *RFID and Auto-ID in Planning and Logistics: A Practical Guide for Military UID Applications* presents the concepts for students, military personnel and contractors, and corporate managers to learn about RFID and other automatic information capture technologies, and their integration into planning and logistics functions. The text includes comparisons of RFID with technologies such as bar codes, satellite tags, and global positioning systems, and provides a decision model for choosing the appropriate technology for a given application.

3. *RFID in Logistics* by Jones, E. C, and Chung, C.A.

    Book description: Radio Frequency Identification (RFID) tagging is now mandated by the department of defense and many of the world's largest retailers including Walmart. In order to stay competitive, more than 200,000 manufacturers and suppliers must develop strategies for integrating RFID technologies into their supply chains.

Industrial Handbooks

1. *Tracked, What You Should Know About RFID, Internet of Things, Big Data and Data Security: The Official RFIDSCM Certification Handbook;* **Engineering Version** by Jones, E. C., Gray, B., Wijemanne, M and Bolton, J.
2. *Tracked, What Everyone Should Know About Invisible Inventory, Monitoring and Tracking, The Official RFIDSCM Certification Handbook;* **Engineering Version** by Jones, E. C., Gray, B and Armstrong, H.
3. *The Six Sigma Trap, What you should know about Six Sigma that your company is not telling you: The Official ISCEA CLSSYB Certification Book* by Jones, E. C., and Armstrong, H.A.

Part 1

Understanding Global Supply Chain Engineering

Part I

1

Introduction to the Fourth Industrial Revolution and the Supply Chain

Erick C. Jones

The very substance of the ambitious is merely the shadow of a dream.

William Shakespeare

1.1 Introduction

At the time of writing this book, many people consider we are in the Fourth Industrial Revolution. The World Economic Forum's chairman Klaus Schwab is synonymous for addressing this term along with the use of the terms "second machine age" and "Industry 4.0". The Fourth Industrial Revolution has been generally defined as the connection of physical, digital, and biological systems, also termed cyber-physical systems. This description integrates technologies such as robotics, artificial intelligence, nanotechnology, quantum computing, and biotechnology. These technologies are often associated with Fourth Industrial Revolution terms such as internet of things (IoT), industrial IoT, fifth-generation wireless technologies, additive manufacturing, and autonomous vehicles. At the time of this writing, there is a great deal of buzz on how companies such as Uber and other ride sharing companies, and Tesla, one of the newest car manufacturing companies that focuses on driverless vehicles, have inspired great investment into future technologies.

1.2 Other Industrial Revolutions

1.2.1 First Industrial Revolution

Benchmarking the other industrial revolutions with main events, we can identify the First Industrial Revolution, occurring in the 18th and 19th centuries, with rural, farming, and mostly agrarian communities and/or the population that moved to industrial areas where major urban cities were first created. The primary impact was the creation of steam power from large bodies of water. This period is identified by the use of the steam engine.

1.2.2 Second Industrial Revolution

The Second Industrial Revolution is approximated from the late 1800s through World War I and is generally associated with the expansion of steel, oil and gas, and the discovery of electricity. The driving industry was the railroad industry and what many called the robber barons. Correspondingly, innovations such as the telephone, light bulb, and the internal combustion engine spawned this revolution.

1.2.3 Third Industrial Revolution

The Third Industrial Revolution, which many people would argue that we are still participating in, is called the Digital Revolution. The Digital Revolution is associated with the advancement of technology from analog electronic and mechanical devices to digital devices and technology. The time is approximated as starting during the 1980s when computer giants such as Microsoft, Dell, and Microsoft corporations revolutionized the acceptance and the use of the personal computer, the internet, and other information and communication technologies. Arguably, the foundational building blocks for the Third Industrial Revolution took place during the 1940s, following World War II with large-scale computers used to decode and decipher information at a faster pace and the competitive east versus west race to space.

1.2.4 Fourth Industrial Revolution (Industry 4.0 and Smart Factory)

Again, the Fourth Industrial Revolution builds on the Digital Revolution, representing new ways in which technology becomes embedded within societies and even the human body. In the book *The Fourth Industrial Revolution*, Klaus Schwab describes the fourth revolution as fundamentally different from the previous three, which were characterized mainly by advances in technology; the Fourth Industrial Revolution will advance communication and connectivity rather than hardware technology. Schwab suggests that future technologies have great potential to continue to connect billions of more people to the web, drastically improve the efficiency of businesses and organizations, and help regenerate the natural environment. The Fourth Industrial Revolution is also referred to as Industry 4.0 by the German government and others who see the embodiment of the revolution as smart factory and smart communities.

1.3 Supply Chain Envisioned for the Fourth Industrial Revolution

In the following sections, we describe a sample research project and ideas that exemplify how supply chains (SCs) are planned to be impacted by the Fourth Industrial Revolution.

1.3.1 Understanding the Societal Impacts of a Maker-Based Reverse SC

The recent Maker Movement has spurred a new excitement of moving more STEM-based domestic jobs to the United States. The idea of citizen science having an impact on entrepreneurship, student learning, and increased domestic manufacturing capacity is exhilarating. Though many of these ideas build upon techniques and ideas that stem from advanced manufacturing research breakthroughs, some of these breakthroughs have been apparent in 3D printing, advanced manufacturing, and nanomanufacturing activities. There are also those who believe that soon the research will move into the quantum arena.

For these ideas to be realized, there must be a fundamental re-thinking of optimizing the SC. This project seeks to investigate the ideas that would increase manufacturing capacity through sourcing of domestic production through citizen sciences. We hypothesize that at an "amazon"-like sourcing of local production, capabilities of a maker would provide inputs to demand that would allow for SCs to be re-optimized such that outsourcing is minimized. One such research project was to investigate a framework that allows the idea of how maker-based and citizen science can bring manufacturing capacity back to the United States, exemplified by "ordering" product exemplars from National Science Foundation (NSF)-funded Engineering Research Centers (ERCs) locally. The idea was to optimize the use of the multi-million-dollar centers invested in by the U.S. government.

Utilizing the centers as HUBS to perform citizen science, the representative three main customers, routes, or omnichannel routes in a cyber-manufacturing cloud-based service are direct customer, retailers, and manufacturers. The customer definition can lead to a specific cloud-service application, for example, an open source cloud service can be the focus in customized products. In contrast, if the customer is a manufacturer or a retailer, the focus will be a software with several specifications about the product to ensure high quality of the "neighbor manufacturer" and less variety. Therefore, this framework utilizes Six-Sigma Quality Management as a common business language to understand the kind of information that is going to be required from a cyber-manufacturer cloud-based search engine.

The other aspect to take into consideration is the cloud-based service in the SC that is required and the reverse SC if there is lack of quality or lack of meeting expectations for the customer. In this frame, the visibility is of great importance, especially when the providers are several and growing, to track who the actual provider of the item is. Therefore, the study will include the feasibility of the implementation of a tool like blockchain in the SC of a cyber-manufacturing cloud-based service.

The last aspect to take into consideration is the actual building of a cyber-manufacturing cloud-based search engine pilot. There is open access to the Netflix model using Open Source Software Center, so whoever wants to replicate the model of Netflix can do it. Therefore, the last phase of the project will be using the market study with six-sigma tools, and the study about the visibility and traceability of the goods to construct a pilot of the cyber-manufacturing engine, so that the 3D printing can be more accessible to customers, and increase the number of "neighbor manufacturers".

1.3.1.1 The Big IDEA

This book provides a framework with models that show how 3D printing (targeted Nano/Quantum-based) devices can be domestically sourced. Methods for testing and hopefully creating local resources that provide products, which can reduce the lead time in the SC for the three types of customers, are identified. It also provides a pathway for government-funded ERCs program—seminal program at the NSF as they transition toward sustainability as future domestic manufacturing capacity for the United States.

1.3.1.2 How Does This New Type of SC Improve the World?

Ultimately, this book provides the foundational knowledge to answer questions that will impact the future such as: Will a cyber-manufacturing cloud-based search engine increase the number of 3D printing as a possible conduit to manufacturing being performed in the future in the neighborhoods by normal citizens?

1.3.1.3 Research Goal and Objectives

In order to meet these research goals, we seek to investigate the following research objectives:

1. *Identify the market necessities to be fulfilled by neighbor manufacturers to be tested by ERC centers.*
2. *Determine the performances and challenges of scale-up activities to meet this type of demand using traceability and visibility of the SC.*
3. *Evaluate the break-even, economic, and performance challenges of bringing production back domestically while applying cyber-manufacturing cloud-based search engine pilot.*

1.3.1.4 The Greater Good

The knowledge shared in this book provides a future pathway for domestic workforce careers in advanced manufacturing (Nano/Quantum) using the "neighbor-manufacturer" concept (citizen science) and maker-based products for profit. It also aligns to the U.S. vision of supporting more middle-class jobs based on future technologies. Moreover, the research may connect the idea and expose community, individuals, and students to cloud-based software, advanced modern manufacturing technologies, and IoT technologies such as blockchain. These activities will support the future workforce innovation of the U.S.

1.3.2 Aligning Blockchain-Based SCs to Reduce Food Poisoning in the U.S.

There has been great excitement and confusion about the blockchain. The blockchain is generically a set of standards for automatic detection and identification of hard to track items such as the growth of plant leaves in a food setting. There is great interest by high-ranking parties in the U.S. workforce including industry, academia, and federal agencies on how and when these technologies can be used to impact the society at large. Multiple important stakeholders seek to understand how this disruptive technology can impact SCs. This aligns to a number of corporate and government goals that seek a deep basic fundamental engineering understanding of how technologies can disrupt SCs. This book identifies frameworks and models that impact operations and our ability to understand how society benefits and/or is harmed by this type of technology. We seek to support the research goals with the following specific objectives. The objectives are:

1. Identify clear usages of blockchain in the food and drug SC through different stakeholders' lenses.
2. Investigate SC and logistics engineering optimization models that demonstrate the productive and disruptive impacts on food and drug SCs of critical food sources and drugs.
3. Evaluate the costs to society, organization, and operations from wasted human capital, optimization of performance, and reduction of waste from stakeholders' perspectives.

1.3.2.1 The Big IDEA

The outcomes of these proposed activities are that initial conversations and prioritized models can be discussed and provide a roadmap for research and investment in these areas, and also the understanding to the community on how blockchain will impact the food and drug SCs of the future.

The greater good of these proposed activities is this fundamental understanding on how blockchain is envisioned and can be utilized in society. Also, while conducting the initial research for this textbook, research and industry requests were garnered leading to a greater goal of investigating the impact of this book's framework on educating the future workforce with special emphasis on underrepresented groups.

1.4 National Research Agenda on SC

Given that no text is modern by the time it gets to press, in an attempt to align this text to modern thought, the author sought to align the ideas with current research activities at the national level with respect to global SC activities. This text seeks to provide a modern view on how SC and operations engineering (OE) is viewed in the modern day. The NSF recently revised the concept of Service, Manufacturing, and Operations Research—the traditional fields of Supply Chain Management to be more aligned with modern thought of utilizing the knowledge of SCs to improve society and have societal impacts. At the time I was working at NSF, it was exciting to see the government seek to make SC science more than just models and algorithms but make it more about solving societal problems. The announcement to focus on operations was more to assist the community and included discussions on the importance of SC research, and the second announcement was a call for action to address a societal problem of eliminating illicit SC networks. The announcements are listed below. (See the announcement from the NSF.)

Given this, the focus of our book is not only to support the historical teaching of SC and OE, but also to provide alignment with the new way of looking at SC knowledge.

As such, in this text, we provide examples of usage that impact society in fields including the following and also point the future researchers to projects that were supported by NSF and other agencies.

Historical *concepts* such as optimizing and improving:

Raw Materials

Bill of Materials

Customer Delivery

Transportation and Logistics

Warehousing, Distribution, and 3PL (Third Party Logistics)

New *methods* such as:
Data Science, Big Data, and Artificial Intelligence
Optimization and Simulation
Operations Research and Data Analytics

Operations such as:
Advanced Manufacturing Systems
Public Safety and Security
Healthcare Delivery and Sustainability.

The OE program supports fundamental research on advanced analytical methods for improving operations in complex decision-driven environments.

Analytical methods include, but are not limited to, deterministic and stochastic modeling, optimization, decision and risk analysis, data science, and simulation. I find that understanding the power of the SC and its tools is what makes them both exciting to learn, difficult to apply, and crucial to execute.

Announcement 1
In 2017, the NSF realigned the focus to fit the OE focus; see link: www.nsf.gov/pubs/2017/nsf17051/nsf17051.jsp.

NSF 17-051
Dear Colleague Letter: Announcing Realignment of the Service, Manufacturing, and Operations Research (SMOR) Program and Name Change to the Operations Engineering (OE) Program

February 6, 2017

Dear Colleagues:
The Division of Civil, Mechanical and Manufacturing Innovation (CMMI), within the National Science Foundation's (NSF) Directorate for Engineering (ENG) announces a realignment of the Service, Manufacturing, and Operations Research (SMOR) program effective 15 January, 2017. Consistent with that realignment, the program name has changed to Operations Engineering (OE). The OE program will continue to manage existing awards made through the SMOR program and will continue to support quantitative research that addresses operational methods within the service and manufacturing domains, enterprise planning and operations, and other emerging domains, including the public sector. The SMOR program will no longer accept new proposals.

NEW PROGRAM HIGHLIGHTS
The OE program focuses on fundamental research in quantitative methods strongly motivated by problems that have potential for high impact in engineering applications. Areas of priority for the program include production and advanced manufacturing systems, public safety and security, healthcare delivery, and sustainability. In addition, the program is eager to support impactful research in new and emerging areas, particularly in the deployment of new knowledge to increase productivity and improve service delivery. The program encourages convergence of domain-specific and domain-independent knowledge that can lead to breakthrough, transformative capabilities. Proposed research that is strictly methodological in nature, without addressing the potential for impact in engineered systems, will not be supported in the OE program. Full program details are available at: https://www.nsf.gov/funding/pgm_summ.jsp?pims_id=505202.

OTHER PROGRAMS WITH RELATED INTERESTS
The OE program is not intended as the primary source of funding for research on operational methods in domain areas supported by other NSF programs. Research on operational methods in transportation and infrastructure systems is supported by the Civil Infrastructure Systems (CIS) program in

CMMI. Research on advanced manufacturing processes and cyber-enabled manufacturing is supported within the Advanced Manufacturing Cluster in CMMI. Research on operational methods in energy and power systems is supported by the Energy, Power, Control and Networks (EPCN) program in ECCS. Research on individual and group decision making, management science, and organizational design is supported by the Decision, Risk, and Management Science (DRMS) program in the Social, Behavior, and Economic (SBE) Directorate.

Basic methodological and algorithmic research in optimization may be more appropriate for the Applied Mathematics (AM) program in the Mathematics and Physical Sciences (MPS) Directorate or the Algorithmic Fundamentals (AF) program in the Computer, Information Systems, and Engineering (CISE) Directorate. The OE program is highly supportive of leveraging funds across NSF programs but is not the primary source of funding for purely methodological or algorithmic research.

Investigators are encouraged to discuss proposal ideas with program officers for program fit prior to submission.

Sincerely,
Barry W. Johnson, Ph.D.
Assistant Director (Acting)
Directorate for Engineering

Announcement 2
In 2018, the NSF sought to impact the society by understanding how to disrupt Illicit SCs; see link: www.nsf.gov/pubs/2018/nsf18059/nsf18059.jsp

NSF 18-059
Dear Colleague Letter: Disrupting Operations of Illicit Supply Networks

March 27, 2018

Dear Colleagues:

Illicit supply networks pose profound threats to the health, prosperity, and security of our Nation. These nimble and technologically sophisticated networks traffic enslaved people, illegal weapons, drugs (including opioids), nuclear material, looted antiquities, exotic animal products, and other contraband. These same networks function to funnel illicit profits back to criminal organizations. Illicit supply networks are unencumbered by national boundaries and fuel transnational criminal organizations, with grave consequences for national and international security.

With this Dear Colleague Letter (DCL), the National Science Foundation (NSF) invites proposals to the Operations Engineering program for EArly-concept Grants for Exploratory Research (EAGER) into operational methods to detect, disrupt and disable illicit supply networks. Supplemental funding requests to relevant existing NSF awards and responsive to this DCL are also invited. Such requests also must be responsive to this DCL.

Projects must focus on fundamental research that advances the scientific understanding of the operations of illicit supply networks and methods for their disruption. In recognition of the high importance of broader impacts in NSF research, proposed work must be framed in the context of one or more distinct illicit trafficking environment(s), and must demonstrate domain knowledge of the chosen setting.

While proposals must be responsive to the Operations Engineering program description, given the gravity, scope and complexity of illicit supply networks, submissions from transdisciplinary teams, including operations researchers, are strongly encouraged. Teams may include researchers from the geography and spatial sciences; law and criminal justice; data and computational science; economics; and/or public health communities. In that vein, the benefits and skillsets of the proposed teams, including how they will collaborate, should be articulated.

Representative topics include (but are not limited to) modeling the operational and spatial dynamics of illicit networks; understanding market incentives and mechanisms of illicit networks, including their social, cultural, criminological and legal aspects; innovations in data science and engineering in online space that have the potential to detect and disrupt illicit operations.

EAGER proposals with budgets up to $300,000 or supplemental funding requests s to existing awards up to 20% of the original award budget (but not exceeding $300,000) will be considered. Proposed budgets must be justified by project scope. See the NSF Proposal & Award Policies & Procedures Guide (PAPPG) for guidelines and expectations for these types of proposals. In particular, EAGER proposals must clearly indicate the reason that the proposed work is appropriate for EAGER support.

Interested PIs must contact one of the program officers listed below before submission of their EAGER proposal:

Georgia-Ann Klutke, ENG/CMMI, gaklutke@nsf.gov, (703) 292-2443
Mark Hurwitz, SBE/SES, mhurwitz@nsf.gov, (703) 292-7023
Wendy Nilsen, CISE/IIS, wnilsen@nsf.gov, (703) 292-2568
Antoinette Winklerprins, SBE/BCS, hanwinkle@nsf.gov, (703) 292-7266
Jonathan Leland, SBE/SES, jleland@nsf.gov, (703) 292-7285

EAGER proposals and supplemental funding requests for supplemental funding will be reviewed on an ongoing basis, but should be submitted to the Operations Engineering program in the Civil, Mechanical, and Manufacturing Innovation Division of the Engineering Directorate by May 15, 2018, to be considered for FY 2018 funding. Titles for proposals responding to this DCL should be prefixed with "EAGER: ISN:".

Signed,
Dawn M. Tilbury
Assistant Director, Engineering Directorate

1.4.1 Overall Goals

The focus of this book is to not only support the historical teaching of SC and OE but also provide alignment to the new way of looking at SC knowledge.

We seek to provide examples of usage that impact society in fields including the following and also point the future researchers to projects that were supported by NSF and other agencies.

Historical *concepts* such as optimizing and improving:
Raw Materials
Bill of Materials
Customer Delivery
Transportation and Logistics
Warehousing, Distribution, and 3PL (Third Party Logistics)

New *methods* such as:
Data Science, Big Data, and Artificial Intelligence
Optimization and Simulation
Operations Research and Data Analytics

Operations such as:
Advanced Manufacturing Systems
Public Safety and Security
Healthcare Delivery and Sustainability

The OE program supports fundamental research on advanced analytical methods for improving operations in complex decision-driven environments. Analytical methods include, but are not limited to, deterministic and stochastic modeling, optimization, decision and risk analysis, data science, and simulation.

2

Global Supply Chain Engineering Definitions

Erick C. Jones

Inventory is like the potential power if managed well, if managed poorly it becomes a deadly sin.

Erick C. Jones

2.1 History of Global Supply Chain Management

2.1.1 Introduction

Some of the history of the Supply Chain Engineering Management are routed in scientific management that were pioneered during the Second Industrial Revolution. The foundation of this work is routed in work measurement and time study methods and history. The expansions from these methods are inventory control, manufacturing, just in time theories. Let us look into them in detail.

2.1.2 Motion and Time Studies in a Lean Framework

The concept of Lean evolved from the scientific management. In a physical world, science is defined in terms of time, motion, and space. Thus, the key to scientific management is the minimization of time and motion that will allow organizational goal realization. The goal of any business is to make money (Goldratt, 1984). In order to make more money, organizations employ lean methods such as kanban, just-in-time (JIT), and single-minute exchange of die (SMED) to eliminate the seven wastes. However, the objective of these lean methods is to eliminate waste and increase productivity (Figure 2.1).

Productivity can be broadly defined as the ratio between output and some or all of the resources used to produce the output. Generally, productivity is measured in terms of labor productivity, capital productivity, and material productivity. These productivities, in addition to other management and supply chain factors, contribute to the overall productivity of the organization.

$$\text{Labor productivity} = \frac{\text{Units produced}}{\text{Hours worked}} \qquad (2.1)$$

$$\text{Capital productivity} = \frac{\text{Output}}{\text{Capital input}} \qquad (2.2)$$

$$\text{Material productivity} = \frac{\text{Output}}{\text{Material input}} \qquad (2.3)$$

Over the years, the body of knowledge has evolved to increase productivity of an organization and of the individuals who make up the organization. Time and motion studies focus on the elimination of unnecessary work and design methods that are most effective and suit the person who uses them.

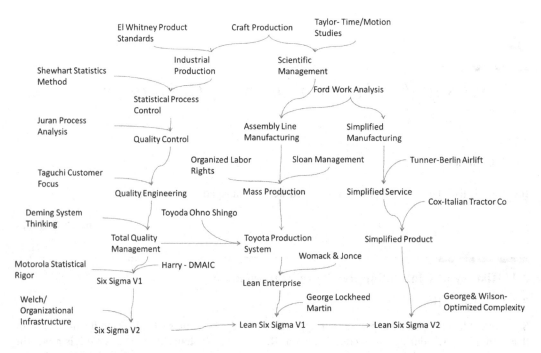

FIGURE 2.1   Evolution of Lean Six Sigma. (Source: Upton and Cox, 2002.)

2.1.3 History of Time and Motion Studies

Fredrick W. Taylor has been generally considered as the father of scientific management. However, time studies were conducted in Europe many years before Taylor's time. In 1760, Jean Rodolphe Perronet, a French engineer, made extensive time studies in manufacturing, while 60 years later, an English economist, Charles W. Babbage, conducted time study in manufacturing. Taylor began his time study work in 1881 at the Midvale Steel Company in Philadelphia. Taylor proposed that the work of each employee be planned out by the management at least 1 day in advance. Workers were to receive complete written instructions describing their tasks in detail and noting the means to accomplish them. Each job was to have a standard time, determined by time studies made by experts. In June 1903, at the Saratoga meeting of the American Society of Mechanical Engineers (ASME), Taylor presented his famous paper *Shop Management* which included the elements of scientific management: time study, standardization of all tools and tasks, use of planning department, use of slide rules and similar time-saving implements, instruction cards for workers, bonuses for successful performance, differential rates, mnemonic systems for classifying products, routing systems, and modern cost systems.

Frank B. Gilbreth and his wife, Lillian M. Gilbreth, were the founders of the modern Motion Study Technique, which may be defined as the study of the body motions used in performing an operation, to improve the operation by eliminating unnecessary motions, simplifying necessary motions, and then establishing the most favorable motion sequence for maximum efficiency. They studied body motions to increase production, reduce fatigue, and instruct operators in the best method of performing an operation. They developed the technique of filming motions to study them, in a technique known as Micromotion Study. In this Micromotion Study, the fundamental element or sub-divisions of an operation are studied by means of a motion picture camera and a timing device which accurately indicates the time intervals on the motion picture film. Additionally, they developed the techniques of cyclegraphic and chronocyclegraphic analyses for studying the motion paths made by an operator. For the cyclegraphic analysis, the path of motion of an operator is recorded by attaching a small electric light bulb to the finger, hand, or other part of the body and photographed, with a still camera which records the path of light as it moves through space. Such a record is called a cyclegraph. Additionally, if an interrupter is placed in the electric circuit with the bulb, and if the light is flashed on quickly and off slowly, the path of the bulb will appear as a dotted line with pear-shaped dots indicating the direction of the motion. The spots of light will be spaced according to the speed of the movement, being widely spaced when the operator moves fast and close together when the movement is slow. From this graph, it is possible to measure accurately time, speed, acceleration, and retardation, and to show direction and the path of motion in three dimensions. Such a record is called a chronocyclegraph.

Carl G. Barth developed a production slide rule for determining the most efficient combinations of speeds and feeds for cutting metals of various hardness, considering the depth of cut, size of tool, and life of the tool. He also investigated the number of foot-pounds of work a worker could do in a day.

Henry Laurence Gantt developed simple graphs that would measure performance while visually showing projected schedules. He invented a wage payment system that rewarded workers for above-standard performance, eliminated any penalty for failure, and offered the boss a bonus for every worker who performed above standard. He emphasized human relations and promoted scientific management as more than an inhuman "speedup" of labor.

2.1.4 Continuous Improvement

Engineers make things, but industrial engineers make things better. In order to make things better, the industrial engineer applies a logical and systematic approach to solve almost any problem. The steps involved are

1. Problem definition
2. Analysis of problem (also known as benchmarking)
3. Search for possible alternatives
4. Evaluation of alternatives
5. Recommendation for action
6. Continuously monitor the action.

Problem Definition: Although we state the definition or formulations of the problem as the first step in the problem-solving procedure, this is often preceded by the problem identification. In most situations, this is accomplished using the Pareto analysis, which uses the concept that the major (80%) part of an activity is accomplished by a minority (20%). Thus, the problem presenting the most opportunity receives the greatest attention. Sometimes, it is better to define a subproblem to address a larger problem depending upon the complexity of the problem.

Analysis of the Problem: The problem definition usually results in a broad statement or definition. Now it becomes necessary to obtain data to understand the root cause and determine how they apply to the problem. The steps involved are

1. Specifications or constraints, including any limits on original capital expenditures.
2. Description of the present method of operation. This might include process charts, flow diagrams, trip frequency diagrams, man and machine charts, operation charts, and SIMO charts.
3. Determination of activities that man probably can do best and those that the machine can do best and man–machine relationships.
4. Re-examination of problems—determination of subproblems.
5. Re-examination of criteria.

Search for Possible Solutions: The basic objective of course is to find the preferred solution that will meet the criteria that have been established. This suggests that several alternative solutions be found and then the preferred solution can be found from the alternatives. However, it is important to ask the question "What is the basic cause that has created the problem?" If the basic cause can be eliminated, then the problem is fixed. Many times, the basic cause cannot be completely eliminated, and one should explore a broad and idealistic view in considering possible solution.

Evaluation of Alternative: With a set of possible solutions to the problem, there is no one correct answer. Often judgmental factors exist that must be considered over the quantitative evaluation in arriving at the preferred solution. It is desirable to select three solutions: (1) the ideal solution, (2) preferred solution for immediate use, and (3) future solution. The evaluation of the alternatives should consider future difficulties such as time and cost to maintain and repair the equipment, the adjustment to widely varying sizes or product mix, the effects of wear and tear of equipment, and the operator.

Recommendation for Action: After the preferred solution has been determined, it is communicated to other persons through written and/or oral reports. The written reports become the standard operating procedure. The oral reports are recommendations made as a presentation with simulation models, charts, diagrams, or working models.

Continuously Monitor the Action: Upon implementing the recommended procedure, the system must be continuously monitored using quality charts and periodic reevaluation of the measurable attributes to ensure the improvements have been made and are still being realized.

2.1.5 Time Study

Time study is used to determine the time required by a qualified and well-trained person working at a normal pace to do a specified task. The difference between motion study and time study is that motion study is largely based on design and time study involves measurement. Standard time for operations is established using time study. Time studies are mostly utilized to establish wage incentives. It is also used to

1. Determine schedules and planning work.
2. Determine standard costs, and as an aid in preparing budgets.
3. Estimate product cost before manufacturing it.
4. Determine machine effectiveness, and as an aid in balancing assembly lines and work done on a conveyor.
5. Determine time standards to be used as a basis for labor cost control.

2.1.6 Time Study Equipment

The equipment needed for time study consists of a timing device and an observation board. The most commonly used equipment are (1) stop watch or electronic time, (2) video camera, and (3) data collector and computer.

2.1.7 Important Definitions

Normal Time: The time required by an average-trained operator to perform a task in the true environment and the normal working pace.

Normal Pace: The pace of an average-trained operator working over an 8 h shift period.

Actual Time: The observed time for an operator to perform a task.

Allowances: The amount of time added to the normal time to provide for body breaks, personal need, unavoidable delays (not within the control of the operator), and fatigue.

The study is completely based on techniques that helps assess the areas of improvement for a worker. It aims at elevating the productivity of a worker and thereby enhancing the efficiency of a process on which the employee is working on. It strives to cultivate comfortable work conditions with safety in mind that motivates the workers. It can be seen that the concept of muda, or waste of lean, thinking is applied here.

Every job is broken down into tasks or the smallest components. The details and timings for each movement are recorded. Thus, a change in a small pocket of work can resonate greatly in terms of overall performance.

2.1.8 Making the Time Study

The exact procedures differ with the operation under study. However, the generic steps in making a time study are as follows:

1. Secure and record information about the operation and operator being studied.
2. Divide the operation into elements and record a complete description of the method.
3. Observe and record the time taken by the operator.
4. Determine the number of cycles to be timed.
5. Rate the operator's performance.
6. Check and calculate that there are sufficient number of cycles.
7. Determine the allowances.
8. Determine the time standard for the operation.

2.1.9 Recording Information about the Operation and Operator

All the information on the top portion of the observation sheet must be filled prior to the study. Otherwise, the study is worthless as a record (Figure 2.2).

2.1.10 Divide the Operation into Its Elements

Timing an entire operation is not practical. Further breaking down the operation into its elements will be beneficial because the elements may be a standard practice for the operation which may be used to establish training programs. Additionally, the time values of the elements will allow the establishment of the standard time. An operator may not work at the same tempo throughout the cycle and need to give a proper rating for each of these elements of an operation. There are certain rules in establishing the elements of an operation prior to the study. These rules are as follows:

1. The element should be as short in duration as can be accurately timed.
2. Handling time should be separated from machine time.
3. Constant elements should be separated from variable elements.

Each element should be concisely recorded in the space provided on the sheet.

2.1.11 Recording the Time

There are three common methods of reading stopwatches: (1) continuous timing, (2) repetitive timing, and (3) accumulative timing.

In the continuous method of timing, the observer starts the watch at the beginning of the first element and permits it to run continuously during the study. The observer notes the readings at the end of each element and records it in the observation sheet.

In the repetitive method, the watch is reset to zero at the end of each element. This method gives the direct time without any calculations as required in continuous timing.

In the accumulative method, the direct reading of the time for each element is with the use of two stopwatches. The stopwatches are set up in a way that when the first stopwatch is started, the second stopwatch is stopped and vice versa.

In recent days, the operations are videotaped. The videotape is further analyzed using video editing software such as Multimedia Video Task Analysis (MVTA) and Adobe Premier. These software packages provide accurate time measurements based on frame rate and the time stamp on the tape.

OBSERVATION SHEET													
SHEET 1 OF 1 SHEETS					**DATE**								
OPERATION					**OP.NO.**								
PART NAME					**PART NO.**								
MACHINE NAME					**MACH.NO.**								
OPERATOR'S NAME & NO.					**MALE** ☐ **FEMALE** ☐								
EXPERIENCE ON JOB					**MATERIAL**								
FOREMAN					**DEPT.NO.**								

BEGIN	FINISH	ELAPSED	UNITS FINISHED		ACTUAL TIME PER 100		NO. MACHINES OPERATED		

ELEMENTS		SPEED	FEED		1	2	3	4	5	6	7	8	9	10	SELECTED TIME
1.				T R											
2.				T R											
3.				T R											
4.				T R											
5.				T R											
6.				T R											
7.				T R											
8.				T R											
9.				T R											
10.	(1)			T R											
11.	(2)			T R											
12.	(3)			T R											
13.	(4)			T R											
14.	(5)			T R											
15.	(6)			T R											
16.	(7)			T R											
17.	(8)			T R											
18.				T R											

SELECTED TIME	RATING	NORMAL TIME	TOTAL ALLOWANCE	STANDARD TIME

SKETCH OF COMPONETS:	TOOLS.JIGS.GAUGES:
	TIMED BY:

FIGURE 2.2 Time study observation sheet.

2.1.12 Number of Cycles to Be Timed

The time required to perform the elements of an operation may be expected to vary slightly from cycle to cycle. As time study is a sampling process, a greater number of observations will converge the time results of the representative activity. The number of observations can be computed using the variation formula:

$$\sigma_{\bar{x}} = \frac{\sigma'}{\sqrt{N}} \tag{2.4}$$

where
  $\sigma_{\bar{x}}$ = Standard deviation of averages
  σ' = Standard deviation for a given element (generally obtained using quality control methods)
  N = Actual number of observations of the element

2.1.13 Rating an Operator

Rating is the process during which the time study analyst compares the speed or tempo as normal performance using his/her judgment. This rating is the most difficult step in time study. It is a common practice to establish the rating using frequency distributions. In many situations, the rating is established using a sample population. However, there are other types of rating which are seldom used:

1. Skill and effort rating
2. Westinghouse system of rating
3. Synthetic rating
4. Objective rating
5. Physiological evaluation of performance level
6. Performance rating (commonly used in USA).

After the rating has been established, the normal time is calculated as

$$\text{Normal time} = \text{Selected time} \times \frac{\text{Rating in percent}}{100} \tag{2.5}$$

2.1.14 Determine the Allowances and Standard Time

The normal time for an operation does not contain any allowances. However, the operator can take time-outs for personal needs, for rest, and for reason beyond his/her control. These allowances are included to establish the standard time.

$$\text{Standard time} = \text{Normal time} + (\text{Normal time} \times \text{Allowances in percent}) \tag{2.6}$$

2.1.15 Types of Time Study

The different studies that need to be performed to improve productivity, eliminating waste, include

- Direct time study
- Time study standard data
- Predetermined time systems
- Predetermined time systems standard data
- Work sampling.

The direct time study is a work measurement method where the actual time is measured by observing the task and the operator using a stopwatch. The measured time is later modified to provide the allowances. However, this study may be complicated with complex tasks. Oftentimes, a task element may be repeated across several operations. A direct time study is not a feasible solution to this method. As a cost-saving activity, organizations study such repetitive task elements to create a standard data file. This standard time data may be defined as the normal time values obtained from direct time measurement from a similar operation earlier. The challenge with this method is the cost associated with generating standard data.

In many situations, set jobs or tasks, when broken down to finer elements, may consist of the combination of the same task elements. In such situations, the predetermined times can be calculated by adding the time required to perform individual times.

Changes such as simplification, rearranging the order of task completion, and analyzing various profitable combinations can be brought into use. The quality of work life is the priority, and in doing so, the motion study is the predecessor to the time study. Designs of workstations to reduce unnecessary stress and movement deterrent to the work culture can be incorporated.

Some of the techniques for motion study or study of work methods are

- Process charts
- Flow diagrams
- Multiactivity charts
- Flow patters
- Workstation design
- Operations analysis chart
- Predetermined time standards system (PTSS), etc.

2.1.16 Methods-Time Measurement

"Methods-Time Measurement is a procedure which analyzes any manual operation or method into the basic motions required to perform it and assigns to each motion a predetermined time standard which is determined by the nature of the motion and the conditions under which it is made".

The predetermined motion time standard systems such as MTM-1, MTM-2, MTM-UAS, MTM-MEK, MTM-B, Maynard Operation Sequence Techniques (MOST), and MODAPTS have been used in establishing labor rates in industry by quantifying the amount of time required to perform specific tasks.

2.1.17 Time Studies and Human Factors

One of the goals of time and motion studies is to make the work as easy and satisfying for the operator as possible. Human factors are the field of industrial engineering which focuses on people to enhance functional effectiveness and maintain or enhance human health, safety, and satisfaction. In order to enhance human welfare, it is necessary to evaluate the human–machine system from a physiological perspective and the environment in which the person functions. Extensive research (Gnaneswaran et al., 2008, 2011, 2013) is being conducted to address the issues relating to fatigue based on hours of work, rest periods, lighting, heating, ventilation, noise, vibration, and psychology.

Using these tools, changes can occur by the following:

- Process Time: Gilbreths' process charts that help answer the 5 Whys by charting the flow of processes.
- Improving operations performance through operations charts from the mapping of work patterns in order to analyze various motions and reduce cycle time and setup time.
- Worker ergonomics and safety must be considered for consistent performance results.

These tools bring about changes like (Stewart and Swaffield, 2008)

- Team and singular performances for every time element are measured to remove elements that do not contribute value.
- Inevitable delay due to fatigue and breaks are allocated for improved pace. The measurement of this amount of time is called work sampling.
- Standardization for future.
- Implementing SMED.

We can thus use motion and time studies to measure performance by line balancing, visual inspection, work sampling, and reporting scores through Scoreboarding (Stewart and Swaffield, 2008).

2.1.18 Challenges with Time Study

There are no specific limitations with time study. However, there are challenges with unions and the improper training for the time study analyst. Traditionally, time study has been taught in an undergraduate level. However, many graduate students do not get the correct training in performing time studies in their curriculum. Time and motion studies are a staple of any industrial engineering curriculum.

2.1.19 Economic Tools

Tools from the realm of economics are taken for the cost-benefit type of analysis of projects. Timely estimation of costs that might be incurred and forecast performance for allowing decisions by sponsors to undertake such projects is to be done before initiation. However, it is mostly done after completion.
  It requires the implementation of the following steps:

- Estimate parameters in the project that contribute to costs called as cost factors
- Express performance improvements in terms of profits
- Evaluate total profit or loss
- Provide suggestions for areas of improvement.

We will now identify tools required for assessment of the net profits. It must be noted that any form of income is termed as positive cash flow and any form of cost incurred or price paid is negative cash flow.

1. Return on Assets (ROA):
   It is defined as the ratio of net positive in flow of cash and the total value of resources utilized for the project:

$$ROA = \frac{\text{Net positive cash flow}}{\text{Total assets}} \qquad (2.7)$$

(Source: CSSBB, 2007)

2. Return on Investment (ROI):
   The ratio of net positive cash flow and the investment allocated for the project:

$$ROI = \frac{\text{Net income}}{\text{Investment}} \qquad (2.8)$$

(Source: CSSBB, 2007)

3. Net Present Value (NPV):

$$NPV = \sum_{j=0}^{n} \frac{X_j}{(1+k)^j} \qquad (2.9)$$

The equation for calculating the NPV is shown above where X_j represents the net cash flow for the year j, n is the number of years considered for the cash flow, and k is minimum acceptable rate of return (MARR) value which is nothing but the minimum acceptable rate of return, which is dependent on the type of cash flow. The decision criterion when using NPV as a tool is if NPV has a value above zero, then the project is approved.

4. Internal Rate of Return (IRR): It is the discount rate for which the NPV is zero or the net cash flow after applying this MARR interest rate is zero. It is given by the following equation:

$$0 = \sum_{j=0}^{n} \frac{X_j}{(1+i)^j} \qquad (2.10)$$

Here, "i" represents the IRR. Many iterations are done before arriving at this rate, and for projects, it is normally expected to lie in the range of 5%–25%. The decision criterion for projects is that IRR must be greater than ROI (CSSBB, 2007).

5. Payback Period:
   It is the number of years required to level out the incoming cash flow with outgoing negative cash flow. It can be calculated using the following equation:

$$0 = \sum_{j=0}^{p} X_j \qquad (2.11)$$

It, however, has disadvantages as it does not consider the time value of money nor the cash flows which may be positive after this period. It is useful while comparing projects for which module gives faster ROI.

The decision criterion is usually 1–2 years of payback period and is compared to the set limit for all projects undertaken by the organization for approval (Quality Council of Indiana, Inc., 2007).

2.1.20 Evaluating Quality Costs

Quality costs are the costs incurred when quality is not added to the product or service and to re-insert value to the item. It is not the cost of creation of value that is important for improving quality.

Costs of quality are categorized as cost of poor quality (COPQ) and cost of good quality (isixsigma, 2009).

2.1.21 COGQ: Cost of Good Quality

It is incurred while preventing the loss of quality due to not confirming to specifications. They are of the following types:

1. Appraisal costs are the costs associated with evaluating products or services for performance and its conformance to specifications. It includes price for testing and resources for testing: equipment and personnel and calibration.
2. Cost of prevention of processes leads to poor quality. By following these activities, the cost of prevention increases:
   - New product review
   - Quality planning
   - Supplier capability surveys
   - Process capability evaluations
   - Quality improvement team meetings

- Quality improvement projects
- Quality education and training (isixsigma) (American Society for Quality).

2.1.22 Cost of Poor Quality

It involves the cost incurred to overhaul and refurbish the product to meet requirements. These are of the following types:

- Cost of internal failure
- Cost of external failure

Traditional quality costs are supposed to be tangible, and they are incurred on following activities and are due to internal failures:

- Rework
- Warranty
- Scrap production
- When rejects are made
- Processing again.

If the quality of the product were intact and as intended, these costs can be avoided.

Additionally, there are costs incurred which are intangible or difficult to measure, and these are due to external failures:

- More setups
- Expediting costs
- Lost sales
- Late delivery
- Loss of customer loyalty
- Excessive inventory
- Long cycle times
- Engineering change orders (American Society for Quality).

2.1.23 Total Quality Costs

The summation of all quality costs represents the loss in sales and income due to failure to meet customer requirements as a result of sub-standard quality.

2.1.24 Conclusion

Average COPQ is said to be approximately 15% of sales.

If we don't aim higher than that, we will continue to eat the COPQ—which translates to 15% of sales. As you can see here, this results in a great deal of lost opportunity to the business—most of which has been difficult to measure in the past. Recouping those costs, and reinvesting them in ways that help our business grow and succeed, is critical to future success. Six Sigma is an important means to that end to this loss and is one that is a major step forward from traditional continuous improvement activities.

With Six Sigma, product and service excellence is identified, measured, and benchmarked. Then, defects are eliminated so that we can deliver customer success and business value—which translates to growth. It involves relentless problem-solving on specific projects that bring the most value to the business and to customers.

Before approval of a project, such costs must be calculated and preventive measures must be taken.

2.1.25 Inventory Control Basics

Inventory amount and size decisions are traditionally driven by the costs of maintaining inventories and costs of being out of stock. Operations managers seek to maintain inventory levels that minimize the total cost of both.

In this section, we discuss closed-loop inventory control. The approaches discussed here are relatively unsophisticated. There is a large amount of information available in other academic texts along with consultative materials available in industry. We will discuss certain aspects of inventory control theory so that the impact that radio frequency identification (RFID) technologies can be recognized.

2.1.26 Inventory Carrying Costs

Inventory carrying costs fall into several categories. They include the following:

1. Storage costs are the costs associated with occupying space in a storeroom, warehouse, or distribution center (DC). Inventory costs such as insurance for fire, flood, and theft are included in the expense of storing goods.
2. Theft or inventory shrinkage identifies when more items are recorded entering warehouses than leaving.
3. Obsolescence describes when items in an inventory eventually become out of date.
4. Depreciation or deterioration of inventory as a function of time, not usage.
5. Interest refers to the interest charges for the money invested in inventories. Oftentimes, this represents the investment into company inventories as opposed to money that can be invested in other investments.
6. Taxes refer to when inventories are taxed. Traditionally, the tax is derived on the basis of the inventory on hand on a certain date. Most companies make a concentrated effort to have inventory present on that day to be as low as possible.
7. Carrying costs include inventory tax, and costs associated with avoiding or evading the inventory taxes.
    a. Consider products such as fresh produce which may deteriorate in only a few days. The depreciation portion of a produce company's carrying costs might be as high as 50% per day. Other products depreciate completely given their expiration dates including products such as dairy products, drugs, bread, some soft drinks, and camera film. For these products, the rate of depreciation can be calculated because expired products that are unsold must be removed from the shelf.
    b. Specialized inventory costs are related to pets and livestock which have costs related to being watered and fed. Security cost for high-value items such as computer chips may increase inventory carrying costs.
    c. Inventory carrying charges are expressed as a percentage of the inventory's value, and a widely cited estimate is that carrying costs approximate 25% per year of a product's value (Table 2.1).

Opportunity costs are not traditionally included in most carrying costs calculations. Most companies must consider the trade-off of holding inventory against the having inventory to meet the fluctuations of customer demand.

2.1.27 Stock-Out Costs

Stock-out refers to the event that occurs when an item is out of stock when a customer wants to buy the item. Stock-out costs are difficult to determine and oftentimes effect customer satisfaction. The difficulty of determining cost that is lost due to stock-outs is that it requires a good understanding

TABLE 2.1

Component Breakdown of the 25% Figure

Insurance	0.25%
Storage facilities	0.25
Taxes	0.50
Transportation	0.50
Handling costs	2.50
Depreciation	5.00
Interest	6.00
Obsolescence	10.00
Total	25.00%

Source: Adapted from Alford, L. P., and Bangs, J. R. (eds.), *Production Handbook*, New York: Ronald, 1955, 396–397.

of company customer behavior. Customer can have many varied reactions to stock-outs. We suggest that the responses can be placed into three categories:

- Future sale
- Lost sale
- Loss of customer.

Consider a set of 500 customers who experienced stock-outs for a given product. The three types of customers' responses may suggest of the 500 customers, 50 will return as a future sale, 325 customers may go to another store which represents a lost sell, and 125 customers may never return to the company. The percentages represented by future sale, lost sale, and loss of the customer are 10%, 65%, and 25%, respectively. These percentages can be considered probabilities of the events taking place and can be used to determine the average cost of a stock-out.

The following table illustrates the procedure. Each cost is multiplied by the likelihood that it will occur, and the results are added. A delayed sale has no cost because the customer is brand loyal and purchases the product when it is again available. The lost sale alternative results in loss of the profit that would have been made on the customer's purchase. The lost customer situation is the worst. The customer tries the competitor's product and prefers it to the product originally requested. The customer is lost, and the cost involved is that of developing a new brand-loyal customer. These costs are usually determined by a firms' marketing department, but we use the suggested numbers for demonstration purposes (Table 2.2).

2.1.28 Safety Stocks

Firms usually maintain **safety stocks** or excess inventory in order to prevent an excessive number of stock-outs. Analysis is required in order to minimize the amount of safety stock and to determine the optimum level of safety stocks. This is illustrated in Table 2.3.

TABLE 2.2

Determination of the Average Cost of a Stock-Out

Alternative	Loss	Probability	Average Cost
1. Brand-loyal customer	$0.00	0.10	$0.00
2. Switches and comes back	$37.00	0.65	$24.05
3. Lost customer	$1,200.00	0.25	$300.00
Average cost of a stock-out.		1.00	$324.05

TABLE 2.3

Safety Level Analysis

Number of Units of Safety Stock	Total Value of Safety Stock ($480 per Unit)	25% Annual Carrying Cost	Carrying Cost of Incremental Safety Stock	Number of Additional Orders Filled	Additional Stock-out Costs Avoided
10	$4,800	$1,200	$1,200	20	$6,481.00
20	9,600	2,400	1,200	16	5,184.80
30	14,400	3,600	1,200	12	3,888.60
40	19,200	4,800	1,200	8	2,592.40
50	24,000	6,000	1,200	6	1,944.30
60	28,800	7,200	1,200	4	1,296.20
70	33,600	8,400	1,200	3	972.15

We consider this example to demonstrate safety stock analysis. Consider that goods must be ordered from a wholesaler in multiples of 10. The carrying cost of an additional or marginal 10 units is $1,200. However, by stocking an additional 10 units of safety stock and maintaining it throughout the year, the firm is able to prevent 20 stock-outs. The average cost of a stock-out has already been determined to be $324.05. We derive that saving 20 stock-outs saves the firm $6,481.00 ($324.05 × 20). In this case, the savings justify the investment costs. Next, we consider an alternative that maintains a safety stock throughout the year of 20 units. This adds $1,200 to the costs but prevents 16 additional stock-outs from occurring, thereby saving $5,184.80.

The optimum quantity of safety stock is 60 units. With this quantity, the carrying cost of 10 additional units is $1,200, but $1,296.20 is saved. If the safety stocks are increased from 60 to 70 units, the additional carrying cost is again $1,200, while the savings are only *$972.15*. We conclude that the firm would be more profitable by permitting three stock-outs to occur each year. Note that these concerns determine a level of customer service.

Safety stocks indicates that a firm will attempt to meet customer demand for out-of-stock items. Many firms choose not to maintain safety stock due to the high carrying cost for inventory. Some mass merchandisers do not replace many items given their profit margins and the fact that customers are not loyal to buying at that firm. In these situations, customer behavior is to buy a complete set of items and/or fixtures needed to complete a project. They understand that the merchandiser may not have that product in the future. This is evidenced in popular "closeout" stores such as Big Lots and Hobby Lobby in which the firm buys large quantities of a product and sells it at a discount. When the product is sold out, there is no expectation of that product appearing at the store in the future.

2.1.29 Economic Order Quantity

Safety stock level is the minimum inventory a firm tries to keep on hand. Commonly, determining the inventory level, how they should be reordered, and how much should be ordered each time are determined by the economic order quantity (EOQ). We will provide a brief overview of EOQ. Further reading is available in academic texts that discuss operation and production planning.

The typical inventory order size problem can be dealt with calculating the proper order size based on minimizing the total of two costs: (1) the costs of carrying the inventory, which are in direct proportion to the size of the order that will arrive; and (2) the costs of ordering, which mainly involve the paperwork associated with handling each order, irrespective of its size. Consider if there were no inventory carrying costs, customers would hold inventory and avoid reordering. If there were no costs associated with ordering, one would place orders continually and maintain no inventory at all, aside from safety stocks. Figure 2.3 shows the two costs on a graph and indicates the point at which they are minimized.

Mathematically, the EOQ is determined using this formula:

$$EOQ = \sqrt{\frac{2AB}{I}}$$

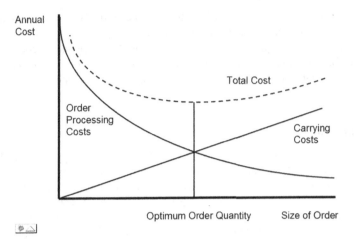

FIGURE 2.3 Determining EOQ by use of a graph.

where

EOQ = The most economic order size, in dollars
A = Annual usage, in dollars
B = Company costs per order of placing the order
I = Carrying costs of the inventory (expressed as an annual percentage)

If $1,000 of an item is used each year, if the order costs are $25 per order submitted, and if carrying costs are 20%, what is the EOQ?

$$EOQ = \sqrt{\frac{2 \times 1,000 \times 25}{0.20}} = \sqrt{250,000} = \$500 \text{ order size}$$

Because of the assumption of even outward flow of goods, inventory carrying costs are applied to one half the order size that would be the average inventory on hand as illustrated in Table 2.4.

EOQs, once calculated, may not be the same as the lot sizes that the product is bought and sold at a company. EOQs can also be calculated in terms of the number of units that should be ordered. The formula is

$$EOQ = \sqrt{\frac{2(\text{Annual use in number of units}) (\text{Cost of placing an order})}{\text{Annual carrying cost per item per year}}}$$

Assume that an item in Table 2.4 example costs $5. Substituting numbers in the new formula yields

$$EOQ = \sqrt{\frac{2 \times 1,000 \times 25}{0.20}} = \sqrt{\frac{10,000}{1}} = 100 \text{ units}$$

TABLE 2.4

EOQ Calculations

Number of Orders per Year	Order Size	Ordering Cost	Carrying Cost of Average Inventory in Stock	Total Cost
1	$1,000	$125	$100	$125
2	500	50	50	100
3	333	75	33	108
4	250	100	25	125
5	200	125	20	145

The earlier EOQ formula and Table 2.4 showed that $500 was the best order size, and because the product is priced at $5.00 per unit, the answer is the same.

The simple EOQ formulation just given does not take into large volume discounts. We can review Table 2.4 and visualize how discounts would have an impact on total costs as the figures. By imputing different values into the table horizontally, volume discounts can be evaluated and marketed to increase future business.

2.1.30 Inventory Flows

In the previous section, we utilize the figures from the EOQ and the safety stock calculations as analysis tools. We cannot utilize these same calculations to determine inventory policy. We must first take the given information and use it to develop an **inventory flow** diagram. Assume that the EOQ in this instance has been determined to be 120 units, that the safety stock level is 60 units, that average demand is 30 units per day, and that the replenishment or order cycle is 2 days. On day 1 (in the following figure), an EOQ of 120 units arrives (Figure 2.4).

We will consider a common inventory flow diagram suggested in other texts. Consider the following, total inventory (point A) is 180 units (one EOQ plus 60 units of safety stock). Demand is steady at 30 units per day. On day 3, total inventory has declined to 120 units (point B), which is the reorder point, because it takes 2 days to receive an order and during this time, 60 units would be sold. If the inventory policy mandates that safety stock is not to be used under normal circumstances, reordering at 120 units means that 60 units (safety stock) will be on hand 2 days later when the EOQ arrives. The EOQ of 120 units arrives at point C, and then, total inventory increases to 180 units at point D.

If the rate of sales doubles to 60 units per day, the reorder point is hit at 120 units (point E), and an additional EOQ is ordered. However, it will not arrive for 2 days. A day after the reordering, the regular inventory is exhausted, and at point F, the safety stock is starting to be used. At point G, the EOQ arrives just as the safety stock is about to be exhausted. If the EOQ arrived later than day 8, a stock-out would have occurred. The new EOQ boosts the inventory to 120 units, which is also the reorder point. Therefore, at point H, another EOQ is ordered. Starting on day 8, the demand settles back to the old average of 30 units per day.

If it appeared that the demand rate of 60 units per day was going to become the average demand rate, the EOQ will need to be recalculated. Recall that a basic input into the EOQ formula is annual sales of the product. If this number changes, then the EOQ must be determined again.

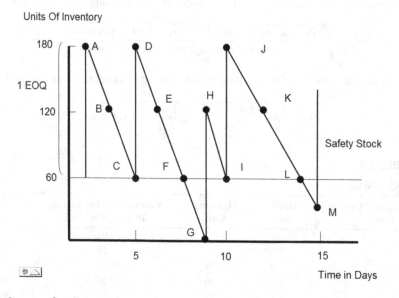

FIGURE 2.4   Inventory flow diagram.

Starting at point H, demand is again 30 units per day. The next EOQ arrives on schedule at point I, and total inventory increases to 180 units at point J. The reorder point is at 120 units, and an EOQ is ordered on day 12. Demand stays constant, but the transportation mode delivering the EOQ is delayed 1 day. Instead of arriving on day 14, it arrives on day 15. Safety stock is entered at point L on day 14. A stock-out is again prevented because the EOQ arrives at point M. Note that safety stock protects against two problem areas: increased rate of demand and an increased replenishment cycle.

When an EOQ is used, as illustrated in Figure 2.4, the time between orders varies. The normal time between orders was 4 days, but when sales doubled, the time between orders was only 2 days. One requirement for the effective utilization of an EOQ is that the level of inventory in the system must be monitored constantly. The ability of RFID to allow for this type of monitoring holds great promise for using EOQ theories more effectively. Then, when the reorder point is hit, an EOQ is ordered. With the advent of computerization, many firms have the capability to constantly monitor their inventory and hence have the option of using an EOQ system. A reorder point for each item can be established in the computer's memory, so it can indicate when the stock has been depleted to a point where a new order should be placed. The integration of RFID will allow for middle wear, decision support, and execution systems to transmit the purchase order to the vendor electronically.

A variation of the EOQ method is the *fixed-order quantity* method, used in repetitive purchases of the same commodity. This method can be initiated with RFID technologies triggering the reorder points. An example would be when a materials' retailer located in China buys product by the barge load (approximately 1,000 tons per load). The retailer would wait until its product is out of stock before ordering another barge load. RFID would enable this type of activity by triggering the point-of-sale (POS) checkout counter system to order the next lot of products from the China manufacturer directly. Tying the technical knowledge of the quantity to order with the automatic information capture of RFID will provide tremendous value in the future.

2.1.31 Fixed-Order-Interval System

An alternative inventory concept that is also commonly used is known as the fixed-order-interval system. In this system, EOQs are not used; instead, orders are placed at fixed intervals, such as every 3 days or twice a month. In the EOQ system, the time interval fluctuates, with the order size remaining the same. In fixed-interval systems, the opposite holds and order sizes may vary.

Fixed-interval systems are used in many situations. One situation is when the firm does not maintain automatically updated stock levels. Such firms are manually checked to verify the levels of all items and determine which stocks are running low. This task is assigned on a regular basis and may be laborious. Another situation is when vendors offer the firm significant discounts if it will place its orders at certain fixed-time intervals. Because the discounts are greater than the advantages of using the EOQ system, the fixed-interval ordering system is utilized. Further, an additional condition is when the firm buys free on board (FOB) origin and tries to utilize its private trucking fleet whenever possible. If one of the firm's trucks travels empty in one direction without freight, commonly called deadheads, from a point near a supply source back to the firm's plant on a regular basis, the firm may decide to buy FOB origin and carry supplies in its own truck.

The fixed-order-interval system is commonly used with a safety stock inventory. It usually requires more safety stock than the EOQ system because the EOQ system requires constant monitoring of its inventory levels. In an EOQ system, if sales start to increase, the reorder point will be moved to an earlier time and a new order for an EOQ system needs to be placed. Stock-outs can still take place, but only during the restocking cycle after the new order has been placed. With the fixed-order-interval system, the inventory levels are not monitored and a stock-out can occur during both the order cycle and the time before order placement.

Most fixed-order-interval systems do borrow one element from EOQ systems. Next to each bin or slot in the warehouse is a barcode, card, or indicator that will allow for determination of the minimum quantity for that product. When the order pickers note that the stocks have been reduced to this level, they notify their supervisor, who decides whether the reorder should occur immediately or on the next scheduled date.

Cyclical buying is a very specialized form of fixed-interval ordering. This practice occurs in the women's fashion industry, in which retailers place their orders directly with the manufacturer for each season's fashions, and there is almost no possibility of reordering. Another example is a grocery retailer's purchase of Halloween pumpkins or Christmas trees.

2.1.32 JIT Inventory Systems

An inventory system that has received widespread attention is the JIT system. The concept is related to the fixed-order-interval system, and customers place orders with their suppliers on set schedules that frequently involve daily or hourly deliveries. In comparison to the EOQ system, the concept is based on the assumption that ordering costs are negligible; hence, firms order frequently to minimize inventory holding costs. In JIT systems, inventory is kept at a minimum because the processes create perpetual motion and continuous movement.

In addition to the JIT inventory systems, there are several other, more traditional systems for replenishing inventory stocks. Nearly, all inventory systems require some formal stock-level monitoring capability. In practice today, the JIT systems may be incorporated into execution systems that are stand-alone, which are often termed best of breed or within a larger enterprise wide system. Software applications that create perpetual motions and execution include warehouse management systems (WMSs), transportation management systems (TMS), and order management systems (OMS).

2.1.33 RFID and Inventory Control

Some researchers suggest that operational labor can be reduced in distribution operations by as much as 30%. AT Kearney (2004), a notable supply chain consulting firm, suggests that labor savings of 7.5% are possible from reduction inventory cycle counting by using RFID. Distribution inbound receiving along with inventory cycle counting inventory reductions was recognized by Accenture Consulting (Lacey, 2005). Other researchers have reported savings in stocking and retail checkout operations (Chappel et al., 2002).

Opportunities in which RFID passive implementations can save money in operations in the future include

- Automatic replenishment from reserve stocking area
- Safety-stock reduction
- Automatic picking and stocking routing
- Automatic order generation from current inventory availability.

2.1.34 Automatic Replenishment

Optimizing replenishments within warehouse or DCs (replenish primary picking locations, cross-docking, and kitting operations), within retail operations (replenish shelves from the back room to the retail floor), and within the supply chain (replenish or stock inventory between different nodes in the supply chain) are the practical applications for implementing RFID.

2.1.35 Safety-Stock Reduction

Researchers have investigated inventory control models and their impact on safety stock. Some research suggests transactional errors lead to variability in planning and inflate the need for safety stock. Transaction errors create excess inventory due to miscounting of inventory and buffer stock becomes necessary to meet service for these errors. The buffer stock for errors and the excess stock maintained due to the bullwhip effect created by inventory timing create a large amount of excess inventory (Lee et al., 2005, Kok and Shang, 2004).

So commonly, the optimal amount of inventory ordered traditionally derived by the EOQ or that includes a reorder component is represented by a continuous review (Q, R) system. Oftentimes, to

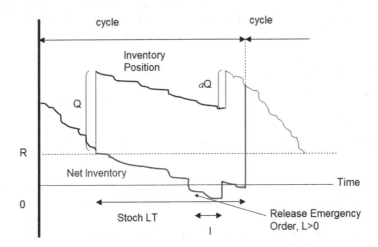

FIGURE 2.5 RFID continuous review application model. (Source: Lee and Ozer, 2005.)

account for the scheduling and lack of real-time information, an adjusted periodic review system is used which includes safety-stock inventory. Recently, researchers have addressed how RFID can influence the amount of inventory (Lee and Ozer, 2005, Gauker, 2006). Consider the following model from Lee et al. (2005):

1. Here, lead time is defined as placing an emergent order $q(q = \alpha Q, \alpha < 1)$ at any time point b based on RFID real-time information as l, and cost to place the emergent order is $k(l)$.
2. l is much less than the lead time of the regular order (Q). Additionally, the probability the emergent order will arrive before the regular order to be $p(l)$ if the regular order is already on its way and an emergent order is released anyway.
3. Moreover, assume that expected total cost associated with inventory position IP and RFID reading point b without releasing emergent order is $C_0(IP, b)$ and the according total cost with emergent order release is $C_1(IP, b)$.
4. So, we can compare the two different costs under periodic review without RFID implementation and continuous review with given RFID real-time information in order to decide whether an emergent order should be placed (Figure 2.5).

$$C_1(IP, b) = K(l) + P(l) * C_0(IP, b) + (1 - P(l)) * C_0(IP + q, b)$$

Other researchers such as Gauzkler (2006) utilize similar continuous review application models to determine inventory levels in a real-time manner. In summary, current research models suggest that inventory can be reduced using RFID technologies due to the fact that their real-time data capture abilities allow for common periodic models to move closer to the theoretical optimal continuous review models. The largest challenge is moving this theory to practice. Currently, in order for this model to work in practice, a fixed infrastructure of antennas and readers is in place at the operational level. This would, in reality, cost operations more in process redesign than the theoretical inventory reduction savings.

2.1.36 Picking and Routing

Using RFID technology, such as real-time locator systems, the promise of capitalizing on employee location information and inventory status to optimize employees' order picking and stocking routes can be realized. This use of RFID builds on picking routes and stocking strategies commonly used in WMS.

An RFID system's ability to provide real-time information will further help optimize order picking schedules. The opportunities to reduce labor cost in these activities may be realized, and the significance in labor savings may be large. Labor reduction of 20% for picking and stocking labor is commonly mentioned by users of WMSs that employ these types of algorithms.

2.1.37 Order Batching of Waves

Using RFID to group orders, commonly called waves, is automatically based on the latest inventory availability. The opportunity to use inventory as it is being received at the dock for immediate shipments can be utilized, dramatically reducing labor for stocking, replenishment, and picking. This theory, commonly called cross-docking, requires a considerable amount of receiving labor to be realized. The promise of RFID will truly enable this one of many opportunities to effectively organize, group, and fulfill orders automatically.

Next, the importance of order wave batching is critical in high-speed operations, but inventory inaccuracies can reduce the quality of these batching of orders and reduce their effectiveness. Specifically, in order management modules of WMSs or enterprise resource planning (ERP) systems, the order bid processes within the software schema orders compete against one another for resources to meet their specific goals, described as the bid process in the negotiation schema. The real-time ability of RFID to provide inventory accuracy and identify secondary location of the inventory immediately can improve the accuracy of the wave batches.

2.1.38 Summary

In summary, the contribution of RFID systems to closed-loop distribution logistics can produce significant contributions in three areas: (1) inventory reduction with respect to safety-stock reduction, (2) optimization of order grouping and releases, and (3) labor reduction with respect to picking and stocking labor.

The real benefit of RFID will be based on its ability to provide the inventory accuracy benefits of current technologies such as barcodes and translate the non-line of sight benefits into inventory savings. The areas that will be investigated in the future from a closed-loop perspective in distribution operations, including the aforementioned areas, are listed below:

1. Physical and cycle inventory counts
2. Inventory replenishment
3. Order picking
4. Inventory stocking
5. Order cross-docking
6. Order kitting
7. Many other common distribution operations.

The realization of these savings will more than likely result as RFID is integrated into common execution software, such as WMS, LES, and TMS, quantifying labor savings.

We previously discussed the benefits of RFID technology as a closed-loop systems framework. Traditional automatic identification systems are closed loop in the fact that they are static and traditionally are used within one tier of the supply chain. Consider a tote barcode or pallet tag that is used within a company's DC or between other DCs. Rarely is this barcode integrated between other unknown partners or even the customer to evaluate the history of that unit load, as opposed to a system in which information is passed from one intelligent automatic identification technology to another.

Consider each technology acting as an intelligent agent. So, if a customer desires to know the history of a product, the universal product code (UPC) transfers information to a barcode, which transfers information to a passive RFID tag, which transfers information to an active RFID tag, and which passes information to a Global Positioning System (GPS). This daisy chain type of interlinking provides an open-loop concept that provides all potential players a look into the supply chain's effective visibility. This nesting of Auto ID technologies may be an intermediate step to profitability for most intermediate RFID implementations. We next consider a framework that describes these types of technologies.

Review Questions

Question 138: Variances from budget for a project:

A. Are used to focus corrective action efforts

B. Are the difference between planned and actual

C. Indicate the project manager did a poor job of controlling costs

D. Are usually expressed in standard deviation units from the norm

  (a) A B

  (b) B C D

  (c) C D

  (d) A B C D

Answer: A

Question 139: Project benefits which should be included in a benefit-cost analysis are:

A. Increased profits

B. Improved process capability

C. Increased defects

D. Reduced warranty claims

  (a) A B C

  (b) A C D

  (c) A B D

  (d) A B C D

Solution: D. Project cost-benefit analysis is a comparison to determine if the project will be (or was) worthwhile. It is used as a management tool to determine if approval should be given for the project go-ahead. The sequence for performing it includes identifying and expressing project benefits, identifying and estimating cost factors, and calculating net project gain (loss).

Question 140: Quality cost analysis has shown that appraisal costs are apparently too high in relation to sales. Which of the following actions would NOT be considered in pursuing this problem?

  (a) Work sampling in inspection and test areas

  (b) Adding inspectors to reduce scrap cost

  (c) Pareto analysis of quality costs

  (d) Considering the elimination of some test operations

Solution: B. Six Sigma is all about financial benefits. A good quality cost system is an important part of the Six Sigma infrastructure and critical to good process management. Appraisal costs associated with the efforts required for inspection, testing, confirmation, approving plans, or cost incurred for product quality audits. All the costs that are borne in conjunction with quality measurement, management, and planning are included under appraisal costs.

Question 141: If the project IRR is estimated at 11% and:

A. The company cost of capital is 10%

B. The company cost of capital is 12%

C. Funds are limited, and another project will yield 14%

D. Funds are unlimited, and another project will yield 14%

The project will be approved only when:

(a) A C are true

(b) A D are true

(c) B C are true

(d) B D are true

Answer: B

2.2 GSC Engineering Supply Chain Planning Levels

2.2.1 Introduction

In the following section, we demonstrate the Global Supply Chain (GSL) Engineering Framework. The squares represent the planning phases: strategic, intermediary, and tactical. The below diagram demonstrates the research and assessments performed at the different planning stages which include supply chain network design decisions, transportation policies, and inventory control policies. The decision flow indicates that oftentimes decisions are made from a top-down decision policy.

The right side of the diagram represents the validation and applications at these levels which include facility location optimization decisions, transportation optimization, and inventory management. The information flow indicates that optimization takes place in a bottom-up manner given that actual or real-world data has to be used as opposed to abstract scenarios, and at the base level, the real information has to flow from operations for executive management to make optimized decisions.

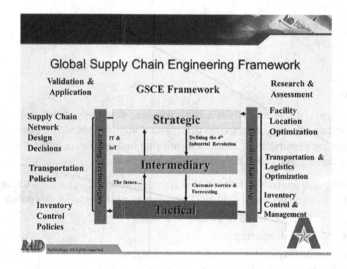

2.3 Global Supply Chain Engineering Planning
Supports Operational Optimization

The problems encountered in the design and operations of complex logistics networks need to be solved at three levels: *tactical*, *intermediary*, and *strategic*. At a strategic level, a company must answer numerous design questions such as

1. How many facilities need to be built or leased

2. Where to build or lease them

3. The customers served by a facility
4. What segments of the transportation network to outsource to third-party logistics (TPL) companies
5. What segments to retain in-house
6. How many trucks to own.

Because these factors are continuously changing, the company also must determine at an intermediate-term and short-term (tactical) level:

1. How many and what transshipment points to operate
2. How many trucks to maintain.
3. Driver staffing requirements, route selection, inventory positions, reorder points, etc.

Different operations may seek to minimize their cost, or maximize their profit, and pass on inefficiencies to the next operation. For example, in our framework, a warehouse manager making a tactical-level decision may seek to minimize receiving labor and create a large queue of inbound trailers (an intermediate-level decision) to wait for unloading. Also, a transportation manager (intermediate) may set trailer load plans that require each trailer to occupy a facility dock door, inevitably creating the need for a larger facility (strategic-level decision). The bullwhip effect on inventory is demonstrated by excess inventory in warehouses (tactical) due to lack of confidence in forecasts given by corporate sales (strategic). We now review the levels in more detail.

2.3.1 Tactical Level

At the tactical level using real-time data provided by automation such as RFID, Internet on Things (IoT), and other cyber-enabled systems will mean on-demand availability of the most current information. Most pundits suggest that there will be a major impact on dynamic inventory replenishment for manufacturing and warehousing operations. The use of technologies is often confined to closed-loop passive systems. The ability for information to be used in an open system that provides information throughout the different levels provides unique opportunities.

As information captured is integrated into an open system, external and internal disturbances can be evaluated. Internal disturbances are caused by breakdowns in company-managed assets; external disturbances are caused by factors beyond the organization control such as hurricanes, major snowstorms, tornados, earthquakes, and significant disruptions in fuel supply.

Due to the fact that current information is available on-demand, it is possible to develop intelligent agent-based, real-time decision support systems to dynamically re-align supply chain planning such as adjusting the transportation network or opening temporary facilities.

2.3.2 Intermediate Level

As we discuss intermediate-level planning, we are commonly referring to transportation planning. The main effect is for cyber-enabled systems and automation real-time capabilities to reorganize transportation operations. We introduce transportation in the supply chain in the next section to provide background.

2.3.2.1 Transportation Strategy

As a supply chain driver, transportation has a large impact on customer responsiveness and operational efficiency. Faster transportation allows a supply chain to be more responsive but reduces its efficiency. The type of transportation a company uses also affects the inventory and facility locations in the supply chain. The role of transportation in a company's competitive strategy is determined by the target customers. Customers who demand a high level of responsiveness, and are willing to pay for the responsiveness, allow a company to use transportation responsively. Conversely, if the customer base is price-sensitive, then the company can use transportation to lower the cost of the product at the expense of responsiveness. Because a company may use transportation to increase responsiveness or efficiency, the optimal decision for the company means finding the right balance between the two.

2.3.2.2 Common Transportation Decisions

The transportation design is the collection of transportation modes, locations, and routes used for shipment. Decision on transportation from a supply source will be directed to the customer or will go through intermediate consolidation points. Design decisions also include whether multiple supply or demand points will be included in a single run or not. Also, companies must decide on the set of transportation modes that will be used.

2.3.2.3 Transportation Mode

The mode of transportation describes how a product is moved from one location in the supply chain network to another. Companies can choose between air, truck, rail, sea, and pipeline as modes of transport for products. Each mode has different characteristics with respect to the speed, size of shipments (parcels, cases, pallet, full trucks, railcar, and containers), cost of shipping, and flexibility that lead companies to choose one particular mode over the others. Typical measurement for transportation operations includes the following metrics:

- **Average inbound transportation cost** is the cost of bringing product into a facility as a percentage of sales or cost of goods sold (COGS). Cost can be measured per unit brought in, but is typically included in COGS. It is useful to separate this cost by supplier.
- **Average incoming shipment size** measures the average number of units or dollars in each incoming shipment at a facility.
- **Average inbound transportation cost per shipment** measures the average transportation cost of each incoming delivery. Along with the incoming shipment size, the metric identifies opportunities for greater economies of scale in inbound transportation.
- **Average outbound transportation cost** measures the cost of sending a product out of a facility to the customer. Cost should be measured per unit shipped, oftentimes measured as a percentage of sales. It is useful to separate this metric by customer.
- **Average outbound shipment size** measures the average number of units or dollars on each outbound shipment at a facility.
- **Average outbound transportation cost per shipment** measures the average transportation cost of each outgoing delivery.
- **Fraction transported by mode** measures the fraction of transportation (in units or dollars) using each mode of transportation. This metric can be used to estimate if certain modes are overused or underutilized.

2.3.2.4 Intermediate-Level Summary

The fundamental trade-off for transportation is between the cost of transporting a given product (efficiency) and the speed with which that product is transported (responsiveness). Using fast modes of transport raises responsiveness and transportation cost but lowers the inventory holding cost.

2.3.3 Strategic Level

Technologies such as barcodes, RFID, and GPS can affect strategic-level planning in the form of location of facilities. The impact of automatic identification technologies is envisioned to have large reduction of inventory and labor such that the number of facilities can be reduced. It also models for dynamically erecting temporary buildings and portable facilities based on demand shifts. The previous concepts of open-loop nesting of automatic data capture technologies with automation and effective communication would support these types of operations. From a closed-loop perspective, this idea can be achieved on a smaller scale with the common passive RFID Electronic Product Code (EPC) protocols that are being standardized and accepted. The open-loop concept may be achieved in the future with this standardization and adoption of protocols. This type of mobile supply chain is the future using cyber-enabled technologies.

We provide a brief overview of facilities planning and consideration next.

2.3.3.1 Facilities Strategy

The locations to or from which the inventory is transported. This includes within a facility where inventory can be transformed into another state during manufacturing, stored in warehousing, and selected for customers in order fulfillment operations. External facilities determine how to profitably fulfill customer orders using transportation and effective inventory location.

Strategies such as using economies of scale when a product is manufactured or stored in only one location; this centralization increases efficiency. The cost savings may reduce responsiveness, as many of a company's customers may be located far from the production facility. On the other hand, locating facilities close to customers increases the number of facilities needed and consequently reduces efficiency.

2.3.3.2 Facilities Decisions

Decisions regarding facilities include the following.

2.3.3.2.1 Facility Function

Production facilities designs are based on whether they accommodate production operations that are dedicated or a combination of the two. Flexible designs can accommodate many types of products but are often less efficient, whereas facilities designed for dedicated products are more efficient. Also, designs distinguish whether a product will support a product focus or a functional focus. A product-focused facility performs considerable functions such as fabrication and assembly when producing a single product.

Warehouses and DCs must design facilities to accommodate a cross-docking or storage strategy. Cross-docking facilities designs accommodate for inbound trucks from suppliers to be unloaded, broken down into smaller lots, and re-loaded onto outbound store-bound trucks. For storage facilities design, decisions about reserve storage, primary picking location, and replenishment from reserve storage to primary picking location must be made.

2.3.3.2.2 Location

Facility location is commonly a trade-off here on whether to centralize in order to gain economies of scale or to decentralize to become more responsive by being closer to the customer. Economic factors including quality of workers, cost of workers, cost of facility, availability of infrastructure, proximity to customers, the location of that firm's other facilities, tax effects, and other strategic factors are important prior to final decisions.

2.3.3.2.3 Capacity

Facility capacity determines flexibility and to respond to wide swings in the demand. Excess capacity will likely be less efficient per unit of product it produces than one with high utilization; however, it will have the ability to respond to demand fluctuations. Common metrics include

- **Capacity** is the maximum amount a facility can store or process.
- **Utilization** is the percent of capacity that is currently being used in the facility.
- **Production cycle time is** the time required to process a unit if there are no delays at any stage.

- **Actual average cycle time** is the average actual time taken for all units processed over a specified duration such as a week or a month.
- **Cycle time efficiency** is the ratio of the theoretical flow time to the actual average flow time.
- **Product variety** is the number of products processed in a facility
- **Top 80/20 analysis** is the percent of total volume processed by a facility that comes from the top 20% stock keeping units (SKUs) or customers. An 80/20 outcome in which the top 20% contribute 80% volume indicates likely benefits from focusing the facility where separate processes are used to process the top 20% and the remaining 80%, generally referred to as Pareto analysis.
- **Process down time** is the percent of time that the facility was processing units, being set up to process units, unavailable because it was down, or idle because it had no units to process.
- **Average production batch size** is the average quantity produced in each production batch.
- **Production service level** is the percent of production orders completed on time and in full.

2.4 Cyber-Enabled Best Practices for Success

In this chapter, we have reviewed many insights and concepts that will allow the logistics engineers, industrial engineers, and operations managers to understand the opportunities and challenges with using cyber-enabled technologies. Some of the best practices for implementing systems include

1. Understand the need for implementation
   a. Mandates and compliance with customer
   b. Strategic cost reductions
   c. Perform a SWOT analysis to review integration into company operations
   d. Strengths, weaknesses, opportunities, and threats.
2. Identify the process and operation that cyber-enabled and or IoT system implementations will be most cost-effective. Generally, the higher up the supply chain that it is implemented the more cost-effective, also the greater the complexity of the implementation.
3. Create a prototype implementation in the identified operation.
4. Test and evaluate the prototype.
5. Improve the prototype.
6. Re-test the prototype.
7. Roll out the RFID system to operations.

2.4.1 Summary of Planning Levels Usage in Current AI and Cyber-Enabled Systems

In summary, we describe how future cyber-enabled systems such as RFID can support information in the supply chain by enabling visibility. This visibility enhances supply partners' ability to optimize inventory, orders, raw materials, and delivery points. Automatic identification or Auto ID technologies such as RFID into a common cyber-enabled and Artificial Intelligent nomenclature created by standardized technology protocols will provide large supply chain savings.

We introduce a planning structure that provides opportunities at different levels to reduce inventory costs with more effective labor policies, more effective scheduling, and the reduction of expensive assets such as facilities transportation containers. The ability for technologies to provide timely information and visibility into the supply chain is based on three aspects: cyber-enabled technologies that include automatic data capture, real-time information, and real-time location status. This information can be used by the engineer (traditionally industrial) to provide successful cyber-enabled technology initiatives including RFID, AI, and other Big Data initiatives.

2.5 Information Use in the Supply Chain

In this section, we discuss how Global Supply Chain Engineering supports

- Information use in the supply chain
- Open- and closed-loop systems as an intelligent agent
- Real-time item visibility that facilitates inventory control
- Supply chain planning and operational optimization
- Organizational improvement with best practices.

In this text, we discuss how captured information influences supply chain performance with data analysis, inventory management, transportation, and supply chain visibility.

1. Data analysis includes the evaluations concerning facilities, inventory, transportation, costs, prices, and customers throughout the supply chain.
2. Inventory management includes raw materials, work in process (WIP), and finished goods within a supply chain. Changing inventory policies can affect the supply chain's efficiency and responsiveness.
3. Transportation visibility provides information about inventory transported from point to point in the supply chain. Transportation includes many combinations of modes and routes, each with its own performance characteristics. Transportation modes have a large impact on supply chain responsiveness and cost.
4. Supply chain visibility provides information including status updates that allow for evaluation of the physical locations in the supply chain network where product is stored, assembled, or fabricated. The two major types of facilities are production sites and storage sites. The location, capacity, and flexibility of facilities have a significant impact on the supply chain's performance

In this section, we discuss the role that information plays in the supply chain, as well as key information-related decisions that supply chain managers must make.

2.5.1 Data Analysis and Information Gathering

Data analysis and information gathering affect every part of the supply chain. Information gathering affects a supply chain in many different ways. Consider the following:

1. Information serves as the connection between various stages of supply chain, allowing them to coordinate and maximize total supply chain profitability.
2. Information is important to the daily operations of each stage in the supply chain. Consider a production scheduling system that uses information on demand to create schedules that allow a factory to produce the right products at the right time. A WMS uses information to create visibility of the warehouse's inventory. The company can then use this information to determine whether new orders can be filled.
3. Information is an important driver that companies have used to become more responsive and efficient. The growth of the importance of information technology is due to the fact that it has effectively improved business. Though information can support efficiencies if integrated too aggressively, it can result into costly decisions, such as expensive software system implementations. Organizations should ask and decide what information is necessary for reducing cost and improving their responsiveness within a supply chain.

2.5.2 Push and Pull Operational Strategies

Different types of operational strategies require different types of information. Push systems are associated with material requirements planning (MRP) systems that use master production schedules to create schedules for suppliers with part types, quantities, and delivery dates.

Pull systems are associated with kanban systems, which fulfill only the necessary requirements from actual customer demand.

For practical use, they require the latest information on actual demand. Modern execution systems such as WMSs, and TMS, and related execution modules in ERP systems use these strategies in their programmed logic. The effectiveness of these types of systems is predicated on timeliness of the collected information. RFID, barcodes, and other automatic identification systems allow these types of systems to effectively reduce operational costs.

2.5.3 Supply Chain Coordination

Data collection allows supply chain coordination to occur when all stages of a supply chain work toward the objective of maximizing total supply chain profitability based on shared information. Lack of coordination can result in a significant loss of supply chain profit. Coordination among different stages in a supply chain requires each stage to share appropriate information with other stages.

2.5.4 Forecasting and Aggregate Planning

Timely information creates more accurate forecasting about what future demand and conditions will be. Obtaining forecasting information frequently means using sophisticated techniques to estimate future sales or market conditions. Managers must decide how they will make forecasts and to what extent they will rely on forecasts to make decisions. Companies often use forecasts both on a tactical level to schedule production and on a strategic level to determine whether to build new plants or even whether to enter a new market.

Once a company creates a forecast, the company needs a plan to act on the forecast. Aggregate planning transforms forecasts into plans of activity to satisfy the projected demand. A key decision managers face is how to collaborate on aggregate planning throughout the entire supply chain. The aggregate plan becomes a critical piece of information to be shared across the supply chain because it affects both the demand on a firm's suppliers and the supply to its customers.

2.5.5 RFID and Other Enabling Technologies

Many technologies along with RFID exist to share and analyze information in the supply chain. Some of these technologies include the following.

2.5.6 EDI Business Transmissions

Electronic data interchange (EDI) refers to the electronic transmission of standard business documents in a predetermined format from one company's business computer to its trading partners' computer (Cannon, 1999). EDI relies on two standards, ANSI and EDIFACT, to ensure standardized business communication. EDI allows a firm to transmit information, such as POS demand for information, purchase orders, and inventory status information, to users within the firm and to customers and trading partners. EDI systems have been implemented generally by larger firms because of the expense it requires for dedicated software and advanced hardware.

The Internet has critical advantages of EDI with respect to information sharing. The Internet conveys much more information and therefore offers much more visibility than EDI. Better visibility improves decisions across the supply chain. Internet communication among stages in the supply chain is also easier because a standard infrastructure (the World Wide Web) already exists. Thanks to the Internet, e-commerce has become a major force in the supply chain.

2.5.7 Web-Based Application Systems

The use of the web for both business to consumer (B2C) and business to business (B2B) is growing quickly. The web will have significant implications for supply chain management (SCM) in the coming years. Thomas Freidman, a leader on political thought, mentions that the web is allowing for small companies to compete with large companies in both B2C and B2B transactions using the web. Unlike the failed dot-bomb companies in the early 20th century, well-thought-out small businesses are now able to compete by leveraging web-based transactions. Many software firms offer web-based systems. Some advantages web-based supply chain systems provide include
Unlimited access with web access

1. A common platform unlike the complexity of EDI
2. Cost-effective implementation.

Because many firms are concerned with Internet security, some prefer the complex EDI protocols which provide more extensive security than do web-based systems. However, given the new web-based EDI protocol standards and the cost implications, the web-based systems will begin to replace EDI systems in the coming years.

2.5.7.1 Business Operations Systems

ERP systems provide the transactional tracking and global visibility of information from within a company and across its supply chain. The real-time information helps a supply chain to improve the quality of its operational decisions. ERP systems keep track of the information, whereas the Internet provides one method with which to view this information.

SCM software uses the information in ERP systems to provide analytical decision to support in addition to the visibility of information. ERP systems show a company what is going on, while SCM systems help a company decide what it should do.

2.5.7.2 Overall Trade-Off: Responsiveness vs. Efficiency

Good information can help a firm improve both its responsiveness and efficiency. The information driver is used to improve the performance of other drivers, and the use of information is based on the strategic position the other drivers support. Accurate information can help a firm improve efficiency by decreasing inventory and transportation costs. Accurate information can improve responsiveness by helping a supply chain better match supply and demand.

Common literature suggests that we are living in the "information age". The availability of information in many sources that appear in academic publications, trade journals, magazines, newsletters, blogs, e-magazines, and so on is introduced every day. The explosion of information availability on the web due to web search companies such as Yahoo, Google, and Microsoft allows people to perform web searches for information on almost anything.

Supply chains information provides the organization strategic advantage over competition and is key running a business efficiently and effectively in an ever-changing and more complex environment. Information plays a key role in the management of the supply chain as evidenced in such uses for forecasts, aggregate manpower planning, and customer inquiries.

Concepts such as JIT manufacturing and delivery, vendor-managed inventory (VMI), and crossdocking require timely information within the supply chain. JIT uses timely information to optimize the scheduling of deliveries or manufacturing in such a way to minimize inventories. The VMI concept allowed vendors to review information from a supplier and order only what is needed in specific time period which allowed them reduce ordering excess inventory. These concepts leverage the concept of information in the supply chain. In the next section, we describe some of the concepts for leveraging information in the supply chain. This will introduce the bullwhip effect, which is general term that describes the inefficiencies realized in supply chain operations with imperfect information. We will discuss the determinants and current ways information can offset these inefficiencies including electronic commerce, web-based systems, and RFID.

2.5.8 e-Commerce and Technology

Electronic commerce or e-commerce refers to a technology that allows businesses to operate a common transaction that was traditionally performed on a paper-based system, but is now performed electronically. They include EDI, e-mail, electronic funds transfers, electronic publishing, image processing, electronic bulletin boards, blogs, Internet voice mail, Internet video meetings, mp3 sharing, shared databases, POS barcode systems in supermarkets, and all manners of web-based business systems.

Some well-known companies such as General Electric Corporation, one of the world's largest diversified manufacturers of a wide variety of products, use web-based transactions systems and EDI as a regular part of its business practices in most divisions. Other companies use EDI, Internet-based systems, electronic forecasting, and WMSs to gain competitiveness.

During the last few years of the 20th century, initial public offering of stock for a company (IPOs) of the "dot-com" companies were occurring almost every day and their share prices rose steadily, even though many of these companies had customers. These "pure play" e-tailers, which represented Internet-based retailers without traditional brick and mortar operations, have all but disappeared. One that survived and thrived is Amazon.com. Amazon has significantly expanded their product line and is one of the few successful "pure play" e-tailers that survived the dot-com bust. One of the authors who was a consultant during the time of the e-tailer craze recalls that the main failure was the real lack of a business plan and focusing on developing a "killer app" or creative front-end software and websites as their major objective. Some of the primary portals (Yahoo and Google, for example) require big money to allow direct access to an e-commerce site. These failed e-tailers were also referred to as "dot-bomb" companies instead of "dot-com" companies.

A new phenomenon derived from these companies' failures, which was recently documented by Thomas Friedman in his landmark text *The World Is Flat*, is that smarter versions of these e-businesses initiatives are re-appearing and competing against larger companies in local markets domestically and internationally. Most profits for Internet activities are business-to-business web-based systems accounts. They represent a much greater share of the e-commerce marketplace than to web-based retailers.

2.5.9 RFID as a Part of the Information Supply Chain

RFID tags are emerging as the barcodes of the future. As we discussed in the earlier chapters, bar codes have become common in retailing but were only accepted in mass in 1985. The expectation is that though active RFID tags were commercially viable in 1973 and utilized in toll roads and animal tracking in the mid-1980s, passive tags were arguably commercially viable in 2005 with mass acceptance in logistics expected by 2010. This emerging technology may have one of the fastest technology acceptance rates in history.

Common applications include (1) EZ Pass for paying bridge or highway tolls, (2) tagging of library books in some libraries, and (3) tagging of cargo containers at most of the world's ports. Reconciling shipments against bill-of-landings or packing and customer orders can be performed succinctly and accurately, eliminating the need to perform these functions manually. Beyond these, the supply chain RFID technologies have broader applications such as emergency human identification for finding abducted children in Mexico, or mountain climbers in Colorado who may become lost in an avalanche. Such applications of RFID technology benefits are taunted, yet fiercely debated as to how they may threaten individual rights and privacy. In the application chapters, details of these applications and their challenges are discussed. We now further detail how RFID technologies provide information strategically to allow organizations to improve operational effectiveness.

2.5.10 RFID as an Intelligent Agent System

Because of the differing automatic identification technologies such as barcode, RFID passive, RFID active, surface acoustic wave (SAW) tags, and sensor tags, they must be integrated for use in the supply chain. We suggest using RFID technologies as an intelligent agent system (IAS) that supports real-time decision support systems as solution for this integration challenge.

The idea of an intelligent agent is pervasive control system frameworks. Control frameworks can be classified as hierarchical, heterarchical, and hybrid (Shukla and Chen, 1996, Heragu et al., 2002). We consider RFID tags that have a master–slave relationship that exists between higher and lower levels in a hierarchical automatic identification framework. An operational example would be using barcodes affixed to cartons to write information to passive RFID pallet tags. The information is passed to the next highest unit load, case to pallet level with each technology acting as independent systems. This is similar to the control system concept in which response to input data is passed up the chain of command, higher-level controllers pass down command data for execution by the lower-level controllers. In control systems, this theory works well when there is little interference between the technologies; RFID integration does present this problem (Szelke and Kerr, 1994, Brussel et al., 1998). We will refer to this type of system as open system. A heterarchical framework is present when there are interactions between the lower-level controllers, and we permit these to engage in one-on-one communication, assuming there is no hierarchy or higher-level controller. For RFID systems, this represents the use of reading tags on a common protocol, such as the EPC Global passive standard where multiple readers can read standardized tags. We refer to this type of system in our text as a closed system. Hybrid frameworks (Heragu et al., 2002, Brussell et al., 1998, Maturana et al., 1999, Ottaway and Burns, 2000, Tawegoum et al., 1994) discuss how these frameworks capture the benefits of hierarchical and heterarchical frameworks while avoiding their pitfalls. For RFID technologies to work with other Auto ID technologies in the short run, this type of approach will be necessary to realize organizational savings.

A practical example of how the integration of multiple RFID technologies that operate at different frequencies can be modeled in control frameworks so that real-time information can be used to determine an inventory policy is given as follows: a high-frequency (HF) 13.56 passive tag is used to track retail over-the-counter drugs at the item level, ultra-high-frequency (UHF) 915 MHz passive RFID tags can be used to track inventory at the case and pallet-level inventory, and UHF 303 MHz active tags track the status of inventory on tractor trailers. Popular industrial literature assumes that linking information with relational databases provides real-time information on the status at the item level (i.e., the active tag can show the status of the drugs because the tags were relationally linked as they moved up in container level).

The flaws in this assumption may be that different technologies have different error rates in scanning validation and human error of integrating these relations, such as database programming, and the technologies do not have common standards. The current mandate from Wal-Mart encompasses only one standard, the Electronic Product Code (EPC) global standard for Generation 1 and 2 UHF 856–915 MHz passive tags.

Further, this EPC global standard is currently accepted in the United States but has not been completely adopted by other countries. Also, current Food and Drug Administration (FDA) initiatives for over-the-counter drug tracking incorporate the 13.56 MHz RFID tags. The lack of understanding of how the mixed RFID technologies will have negative impacts, such as higher error rates and lower productivity, provides a gap that I seek to investigate during this research project. One of the authors identified this gap when testing technologies NASA ISS. The most operationally valid solutions included multiple RFID technologies (Jones and Chung, 2006).

2.5.11 Summary of Cyber-Enabled Systems, AI, and Auto-identification as Information Enablers

This section provides us with an understanding of key technologies, how all the technologies differ, and how they can be integrated to work for operational effectiveness. This will allow WMS algorithm such as "bucket brigades" calculations, picking route optimization, and other effective system updates that will improve operations. Further insights on safety-stock minimization, customer order optimization, and pick/stock labor minimization will be effected and discussed later in the text.

2.5.12 AI, Big Data, and Barcodes and RFID Provide Timely Visibility in Logistics

Artificial Intelligence, Big Data, and barcodes and RFID support information in the supply chain by enabling visibility. The concept of visibility describes the ability for anyone, including customers, to have access to inventory, orders, raw materials, and delivery points at any time. Visibility is currently provided by a mixture of automatic identification or Auto ID technologies such as barcodes, smart labels, ISBN, and UPC codes along with others. The opportunity for RFID is that it uses non-line of sight scanning and the integration of the aforementioned Auto ID identifiers into RFID nomenclature, and a demand for standardized technology protocols will provide large supply chain savings.

The real-time nature of RFID is considered a benefit and currently a challenge. The benefit is that you have the latest information to make the best decisions; the drawback is that the amount of data currently presents a data storage problem for operational systems.

Better visibility provides reduced inventory, labor and assets management using inventory policies, scheduling, and decision support system information. This is exemplified by

- RFID supports reduced inventory costs with more effective labor policies.
- RFID supports labor reduction with more effective scheduling.
- RFID supports the reduction of expensive assets such as facilities, trucks, containers, and railroad time because of more accurate information in decision support systems.

The ability for RFID to provide timely information and visibility into the supply chain is based on three components of RFID technologies. They are

1. Automatic data capture
2. Real-time information
3. Real-time location system.

The RFID-enabling technologies diagram represents these components as interconnecting orbits.

The Figure 2.1 also shows how IoT technologies such as RFID support timely information in the supply chain by enabling information to be accessed faster. This implies faster decisions can be made, which produces operational optimization that can be effectively repeated. In Figure 2.1, the boxes represent the enabling technologies and provide information flow. The ability to allow resident information collected automatically in real time that leads to faster more effective decisions is where cyber-enabled systems show future promise. Business costs are reduced as operations become more productive by reducing labor, transportation, and facility cost of moving inventory in the supply chain.

Many organizations see the benefit of using cyber-enabled systems is that they can effectively manipulate inventory. Inventory exists in the supply chain because of the variance between supply and demand. This variance is necessary for manufacturers where it is economical to manufacture in large lot quantities and then store for future sales. The variance is also present in retail stores where inventory is held for future customer demand. Oftentimes, businesses suggest that inventory is a marketing vehicle creating demand by passing customers. The main role for inventory plays is to satisfy customer demand by providing product available when the customers want it. Another significant role that inventory plays is to reduce cost by exploiting economies of scale that may exist during production and distribution. Given that it is suggested to have such a large impact on inventory, we will present some relevant information on inventory in the supply chain.

2.6 Inventory in the Supply Chain

Inventory is held throughout the supply chain in the form of raw materials, WIP, and finished goods. Inventory is a major source of costs in a supply chain and impacts customer responsiveness and eventually customer satisfaction. Inventory also has a significant impact on the material flow time in a supply chain. Material flow time is the time that elapses between the points at which material enters the supply chain to the point at which it exits. For a supply chain, throughput is the rate at which sales occur. If inventory is represented by I, flow time by T, and throughput by D, the three can be related using Little's law as follows:

$$I = DT$$

For example, if the flow time of an auto-assembly process is 10 h and the throughput is 50 units an hour, Little's law tells us that the inventory is $50 \times 10 = 500$ units. If we were able to reduce inventory to 250 units while holding throughput constant, we would reduce our flow time to 5 h (250/50). We note that in this relationship, inventory and throughput must have constant units. One can see that those inventory and flow times are related and that throughput is often determined by customer demand. The goal of many operations is to reduce amount of inventory needed without increasing cost or reducing responsiveness.

2.7 Business Responsiveness

Inventory plays a significant role in a firm's responsiveness. Inventory decisions may require strategies that locate inventory close to the customer or by locating a main warehouse centrally, or by locating stocking DCs seasonally using a centralized stocking concept. Each strategy has trade-offs that need to be evaluated by each organization's goals. Some of the goals involve:

- Cycle inventory
- Safety inventory
- Seasonal inventory
- Level of product availability
- Inventory-related metrics.

2.7.1 Cycle Inventory

Cycle inventory is defined as the average amount of inventory used to satisfy demand between receipts of supplier shipments. The size of the cycle inventory is a result of the production, transportation, or purchase of material in large lots. Companies produce or purchase in large lots to exploit economies of scale in the production, transportation, or purchase process. With the increase in lot size, however, also comes an increase in carrying costs.

2.7.2 Safety Inventory

Safety inventory is inventory held in case demand exceeds expectations; it is held to counter uncertainty. Because demand is uncertain and may exceed expectations, however, companies hold safety inventory to satisfy an unexpectedly high demand. If a company does not have enough inventory, they may lose sales and profit. Thus, choosing safety inventory involves making a trade-off between the costs of having too much inventory and the costs of losing sales due to not having enough inventory.

2.7.3 Seasonal Inventory

Seasonal inventory is additional inventory stored to counter predictable variability in demand due to a given repeatable period. Companies using seasonal inventory build up inventory in periods of low demand and store it for periods of high demand when they will not have the capacity to produce all that is demanded. The trade-off for organizations is determining how much seasonal inventory to build, in other words the cost of carrying the additional seasonal inventory vs. the cost of having a more flexible production rate.

2.7.4 Level of Product Availability

Level of product availability is the amount of demand that is available from products currently in non-committed inventory. A high level of product availability provides a high level of responsiveness, but increases cost because inventory has to be held with no prior commitment or order, and oftentimes, this excess inventory is held but rarely used. In contrast, a low level of product availability lowers inventory holding cost but results in customer failure and loss current and future sales. The basic trade-off when determining the level of product availability is between the cost of inventory to increase product availability and the loss from not satisfying customers.

2.7.5 Inventory-Related Metrics

Often given the importance of inventory, data is collected and assessed in order to ensure proper management. Some common metrics are described as follows:

- Average inventory measures the average number of inventory in dollars or units over a time period such as days, months, and years.
- Obsolete inventory products with more than a specified number of days of inventory identify the products for which the firm is carrying a high level of inventory.
- Average safety inventory measures the average amount of inventory on hand when a replenishment order arrives. Average safety inventory should be measured by SKU in both units and days of demand. It can be estimated by averaging over time the minimum inventory on hand in each replenishment cycle.
- Seasonal inventory measures the amount of both cycle and safety inventories that are purchased solely due to seasonal changes in demand
- Fill rate measures the fraction of orders/demand that was met on time from inventory.
- Percent of time out of stock measures the fraction of time that a particular SKU had zero inventory.

There are underlying trade-offs that organizations make with regard to inventory decisions between responsiveness and inventory costs. Increasing inventory generally makes the supply chain more responsive to the customer. A higher level of inventory also facilitates a reduction in production and transportation costs because of improved economies of scale in both functions. This choice, however, increases inventory holding cost. Moreover, these inventory costs in the supply chain can be greatly affected by a lack of supply chain coordination, commonly referred to as the bullwhip effect.

2.7.6 The Bullwhip Effect

The bullwhip effect has been evaluated by both practitioners and academics. Chopra and Meindl (2007) provides a brief history of the bullwhip effect. The problem was identified when Proctor & Gamble (P&G) were studying replenishment patterns for one of their best-selling products. They recognized there was a greater variability between (1) orders placed by distributors against retail stores sales and (2) against requested materials from suppliers. Given that the product had consistent demand over the years, the large discrepancy was not expected. P&G coined the term "bullwhip" effect for this phenomenon. It also has been referred to as the "whiplash" or "whipsaw" effect. Other organization such as HP experienced the bullwhip effect in patterns of sales for products such as printers.

Many researchers and practitioners have attempted to discover the origins of this effect due to the fact that it creates excess cost in the form of inventory in the supply chain. Some believe when working with demand that is constant and highly predictable that effect is produced when companies order products in batch quantities at operational supply chain levels is what creates the effect.

The grocery industry, which exhibits this type of demand, sought to reduce the bullwhip effect with an efficient consumer response (ECR) initiative in which the food delivery supply chain would reduce a projected excess of 100 days of inventory from the supply chain. The stated goal of the ECR initiative was to save $30 billion annually by reducing the bullwhip effect in food delivery logistics (Crawford, 2004).

Some causes' solutions that may reduce the effects of the bullwhip effect on demand forecasting, order batching, price fluctuations and creative order gamin are suggested by researchers (Chopra and Meindl, 2007, Lee, Padmanabhan, and Whang, 1997).

They include sharing of information, supplier alignment, stable price structure, and incentives to prevent gaming. First, the sharing of information from all parties from common data such as POS data creates forecasts on these data. Other techniques include EDI as it is commonly described. EDI and other web-based exchange formats provide a means for integrating information between company software platforms.

Second, supplier alignment allows for the coordination of pricing, transportation, and inventory planning efforts operations in the supply chain.

Fixed costs, which create order batching behavior and economies of scale costs such as transportation, can be limited with real-time information. Things such as smaller batch lot quantities and effective transportation scheduling are allowed by information that provides alignment. Another trend encouraging small batch ordering is the outsourcing of logistics to third parties. Logistics companies can consolidate loads from multiple suppliers. Logistics outsourcing to companies such as UPS Supply Chain Solutions is expanding rapidly.

Third, supplier pricing is designed to motivate customers to buy in large batches and store items for future use. This behavior is called price stabilization and is designed to reduce sales demand variation. This is evident when comparing retailers that run frequent promotions with warehouse stores that offer everyday low pricing. The warehouse stores have more stable demand than do department stores in which promotional sales account for most of their business. Finally, exaggeration of orders to manipulate pricing is often referred to as gaming and can be affected dramatically by information. These order forecasts can be smoothed using past demand, not sales forecasting.

2.8 Summary

In summary, the effective use of information to manage inventory can counteract the bullwhip effect created by partners in the supply chain acting in their own best interests. The need for information timely can be supported by cyber-enabled and automation technologies; of course, I am a big fan of using RFID-based technologies.

Technologies like RFID provide an opportunity to reduce the uncertainty leading to the bullwhip effect through more real-time information. Given the costs of holding excess inventory in capital, obsolescence (or spoilage), handling costs, occupancy costs, pilferage, damage, taxes, and insurance, it may be worthwhile to use real-time information in evaluating inventory reduction.

End of Chapter Questions

1. What are the three planning levels for Global Supply Chain Engineering?
2. What are the four types of participants that make up a supply chain?
3. At what level is inventory control policies planned?
4. What are the three components of inventory control for enabling technologies RFID Logistics?
5. What does EOQ represent?
6. What two forms of inventory are buffered with continuous review models?
7. Which buffer does EOQ address?
8. Which buffer does safety-stock address?

9. Weekly demand for Lego at a Wal-Mart store is normally distributed with a mean of 2,500 boxes and a standard deviation of 500. The replenishment lead time is 2 weeks. Assuming a continuous review replenishment policy, evaluate the safety inventory that the store should carry to achieve a customer stock level (CSL) of 90%.

10. Carbon fiber seat posts are consumed by a bicycle manufacturing factory at a fairly steady rate of 100 per week. The seat posts cost the factory $35.00 each. It costs the plant $125 to initiate an order, and holding costs are based on an annual interest rate of 20%. Determine the optimal number of seat posts for the plant to purchase and the time between orders. (Use the EOQ formula.)

11. Weekly demand for Lego at a Wal-Mart store is normally distributed with a mean of 2,500 boxes and a standard deviation of 500. The replenishment lead time is 2 weeks, and the store manager has decided to review inventory every 4 weeks. Assuming a periodic review replenishment policy, evaluate the safety inventory that the store should carry to provide a CSL of 90%. Evaluate the OUL for such a policy.

12. What two replenishment policies are associated with inventory control?
13. What are two impacts of RFID on inventory control?
14. What are two impacts of RFID on transportation?
15. Give two reasons to use the anechoic chamber for RFID.
16. What are the steps of RFID design for six sigma-research (DFSSR)?
17. Describe how order scheduling impacts labor and the effect RFID can have on minimizing this process.

REFERENCES

Atmel. *Antenna Matching for UHF - RFID Transponder ICs.* Heilbronn: Atmel Corporation, 2005, 1–11.
Brussel, H. V., Wyns, J., Valckenaers, P., Bongaert, L., and Peeters, P. (1998). Reference architecture for holonic manufacturing systems: PROSA. *Computers in Industry*, 37, 255–274.
Cannon, J. P., and Perreault, W. D., Jr. (November 1999). Buyer-seller relationships in business markets. *Journal of Marketing Research*, 36 (No. 4), 439–460.
Chappell, G., Durdan, D., Gilbert, G., Ginsburg, L., Smith, J., and Tobolski, J. (2002). Auto-ID on delivery: The value of Auto-ID technology in the retail supply chain, Auto-ID Center, November 1, www.autoid-center.org.
Chopra, S., and Meindl, P. *Supply Chain Management: Strategy, Planning, and Operation.* Upper Saddle River, NJ: Prentice-Hall, 2007.
Clampitt, H. G. *RFID.* 1st ed. Houston, TX: PWD Group Inc., 2006, 1–280.
Crawford, J. C. (October 2004). Book review. *Journal of Product Innovation Management*, 21 (6), 438–439.
CSSBB. https://asq.org/cert/six-sigma-black-belt. 2007.
Department of Trade and Industry. *The History of Quality.* 1 December 2012.
Foster, S. T. *Managing Quality: Integrating the Supply Chain.* Upper Saddle River, NJ: Pearson Prentice Hall, 2007. Print.
Gaukler, G. M., Seifert, R. W. Chapter 2, Applications of RFID in supply chains. In: *Trends in Supply Chain Design and Management*, Jung H., Jeong B., and Chen F. F. (eds) Springer Series in Advanced Manufacturing. London: Springer-Verlag, 2007, pp. 29–48.
Gnaneswaran, V., Jones, E. C., and Bishu, R. R. Endurance limit for periodontal scaling task. Submitted August 2011, Accepted August 2012. *International Journal of Industrial Ergonomics*.
Gnaneswaran, V., Madhunuri, B., and Bishu, R. R. (2008). A study of latex and vinyl gloves: Performance versus allergy protection properties. *International Journal of Industrial Ergonomics*, 38 (2), 171–181.
Gnaneswaran, V., Jones, E. C., and Bishu, R. R. (January 2013). Development of force-endurance models for simulated scaling task. *International Journal of Industrial Ergonomics*, 43 (1), 31–39.
Goldratt, E. M., and Cox, J. *The Goal: A Process of Ongoing Improvement.* London: Routledge, 1984.
Grover, M. P. *Work Systems and the Methods, Measurement, and Management of Work.* Upper Saddle River, NJ: Pearson Prentice Hall, 2007. Print.

Heragu, S. S., Graves, R. J., Byung-In, K., St Onge, A. (September 2002). Intelligent agent based framework for manufacturing systems control. *IEEE Transactions on Systems, Man, and Cybernetics-Part A: Systems and Humans*, 32 (5), 560–573.

History of Time and Motion Study, http://ie.emu.edu.tr/development/dosyalar/%7Be_A-az3-Enu%7DCH3.pdf.

isixsigma. Highlights from the 2009 Energy Forum. www.isixsigma.com/community/blogs/highlights-2009-energy-forum/. 2009.

Jones, E. C., and Chung, C. A. (March 2006). A methodology for measuring engineering knowledge worker productivity. *Engineering Management Journal*, 18 (1), 32–29.

Kearney, A. T. (2004). RFID/EPC: Managing the transition (2004–2007). Research analysis report.

Kök, G., and Shang, K. (April 2007). Inspection and replenishment policies for systems with inventory record inaccuracy. *Manufacturing & Service Operations Management*, 9 (2), 185–205.

Lacy, S. (January 2005). RFID: Plenty of mixed signals. *Business Week Online*.

Lee, H. L., Padmanabhan, V., and Whang, S. (1997). Information distortion in a supply chain: The bullwhip effect. *Management Science*, 43, 546–558.

Lee, Y. *Antenna Circuit Design for RFID Applications*. Microchip Technology Inc., 2003, 1–50. 10 September 2006 www.microchip.com/downloads/en/AppNotes/00710c.pdf#search=%22antenna%20design%20RFID%22.

Lee, C. C., and Chu, W. H. J. (February 2004). Who should control inventory in a supply chain?. *European Journal of Operational Research*, 164, 158–172.

Lee, H., and Özer, Ö. (January 2009). Unlocking the value of RFID. *Production and Operations Management*, 16 (1), 40–64.

Maturana, F., Shen, W., and Norrie, D. H. (1999). MetaMorph: An adaptive agent-based architecture for intelligent manufacturing. *International Journal of Production Research*, 37 (10), 2159–2174.

Nikitin, P. V., and Rao, K. V. S. (2005). Power reflection coefficient analysis for complex impedances in RFID tag design. *IEEE Transactions on Microwave Theory and Techniques*, 53, 2721–2724. 15 September 2006.

Olsson, T. Research. Electronics Design Division. 2004. Sweeden University. 18 September 2006. www.itm.mh.se/forskning/elektronik/research/groups/system/rfid.htm.

Ottaway, T. A., and Burns, J. R. (2000). An adaptive production control system utilizing agent technology. *International Journal of Production Research*, 38 (4), 721–737.

Quality Council of Indiana, Inc. *Certified Six Sigma Black Belt Primer*. West Terre Haute, IN: Quality Council of Indiana, 2007. Print.

Rao, S., and Lam, S. F. (2005). Antenna design for UHF RFID tags: A review and a practical application. *IEEE Transactions on Antennas and Propagation*, 53, 3870–3876. 8 September 2006.

Rao, K., Nikitin, P. V., and Lam, S. F. *Impedance Matching Concepts in RFID Transponder Design*. Everett, WA: Intermec Technologies Corporation, 1–4.

Sanford, J. R. *Antenna Design Considerations for RFID Applications*. Cushcraft Corporation, 1–5. 13 September 2006 www.cushcraft.com/comm/support/pdf/Antenna%20Design%20for%20RFID%20app.pdf#search=%22antenna%20design%20RFID%22.

Shukla, C. S., and Chen, F. F. (December 1996). The state of the art in intelligent real-time FMS control: A comprehensive survey. *Journal of Intelligent Manufacturing*, 7 (6), 441–455.

Stewart, M. B., and Swaffield, J. K. (February 2008). The other margin: Do minimum wages cause working hours adjustments for low-wage workers?. Economica, 75 (297), 148–167.

Sure, P. The silver ink printed antenna. In *The World of RFID*, 2005, 70–72.

Szelke, E., and Kerr, R. M. (1994). Knowledge-based reactive scheduling. *Production Planning & Control: The Management of Operations*, 5 (2), 124–145.

Tawegoum, R., Castelain, E., and Gentina, J. C. (1994). Hierarchical and dynamic production control in flexible manufacturing systems. *Robotics and Computer-Integrated Manufacturing*, 11 (4), 327–334.

Vuong, T.-P., and Beroulle, V. Antennas for RFID tags. *Joint sOc-EUSAI Conference*, Grenoble, 2005, 19–22.

3

Evaluating the Impact of Sustainability and Pipeline Quality on the Global Crude Oil Supply Chain

Erick C. Jones and Sunny Paraskumar Jain

The efficiency curve model is modified to compare crude oil supply chain among Indonesia, Russia, and Colombia based on oil transportation distances and associated cost, refinery costs, and the costs associated with refinery sustainability and pipeline quality shown in *Modeling the Supply Chain* (Author: Shapiro). However, this model was originally used to determine the optimal locations of distribution centers (DCs) based on transportation cost and the capacity of the DCs, and was modified to allow the use of different costs associated with the quality condition of the pipeline and the costs of sustaining an environmentally friendly facility. This case used to optimize the total cost of oil supply chain for Indonesia, Russia, and Colombia. We seek to extend our previous supply chain model, which represent the outbound oil supply chain for Indonesia. The outputs of this chapter are efficiency curves that show how the costs of pipeline quality and facility sustainability affect the overall costs of the oil industry of Indonesia, Russia, and Colombia.

3.1 Introduction

3.1.1 The U.S. Dependency on Foreign Oil

The United States import oil from different countries, which is essential to sustain American people's necessity based on current situation. The United States imported about 7.7 MMbd of crude oil, and 2.1 MMbd of petroleum liquids and refined products in 2013. The United States also exported 3.6 MMbd of crude oil and petroleum products (very little was crude oil), which made the United States a net exporter of petroleum liquids and refined products. Net imports of crude oil and petroleum products (imports minus exports) averaged 6.2 MMbd and accounted for 33% of U.S. total petroleum consumption in 2013, the lowest level since 1986. U.S. dependence on imported petroleum has declined since peaking in 2005.

This trend is the result of a variety of factors including a decline in consumption and shifts in supply patterns. The economic downturn following the financial crisis of 2008, efficiency improvements, changes in consumer behavior, and patterns of economic growth all contributed to the decline in petroleum consumption. Additionally, the increased use of domestic biofuels (ethanol and biodiesel), and strong gains in domestic production of crude oil and natural gas plant liquids expanded domestic supplies and reduced the need for imports.

The current U.S. sources for oil are not limited to politically stable countries, but it majorly relies on Canada & OPEC member Saudi Arabia. There is a concern about the impact to the U.S. economy if Canada or Saudi Arabia decides to manipulate demand and possibly stops exporting oil to the United States. The dependence on foreign oil does not present strategic challenges to the United States and that it does not negatively affect the nation's economy and national security. This dependency has had a large impact on the U.S. foreign policy and continues to influence international relationships. Today, the consideration is more in regards as to which foreign oil sources are the most challenging and what steps could be taken by the U.S. government to help alleviate these challenges.

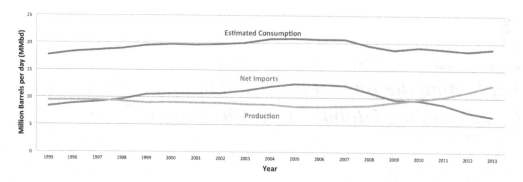

FIGURE 3.1   U.S. petroleum and other liquid production, estimated consumption, and net imports from 1995 to 2013. (Preliminary Data U.S. EIA October 2014.)

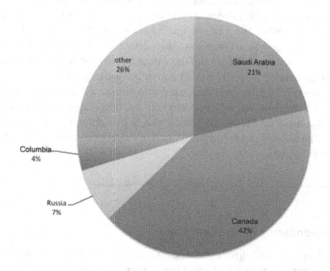

FIGURE 3.2   U.S. net imports of crude oil and petroleum products from Saudi Arabia, Canada, Russia, and Colombia in 2013. (Preliminary Data: U.S. EIA, October 2014.)

3.1.1.1 Problem Statement

The U.S. EIA stated that the United States consumed an estimated 18.96 million barrels per day (MMbd) of petroleum products and produced 12.31 MMbd of crude oil and petroleum products during 2013. Therefore, the U.S. net imports of crude oil and petroleum products equaled 6.57 MMbd, making the United States dependent on foreign oil—see Figure 3.1 [U.S. EIA].

Most of the imports came from the western hemisphere. The western hemisphere including North, South, and Central America, the Caribbean, and the U.S. territories; and the Persian Gulf countries such as Iraq, Kuwait, Qatar, Saudi Arabia, and United Arab Emirates exported 55.8% and 31.8%, respectively, of crude oil and petroleum products to the United States in 2013. Oil from Canada and Saudi Arabia accounted for 42% and 21%, respectively, of the U.S. crude oil and petroleum products imports, resulting in those countries representing the top two foreign oil sources for the United States in 2013—see Figure 3.2.

3.2 Research Significance

This is problematic due to the fact that 21% of the U.S. net crude oil and petroleum products imports come from one country, Saudi Arabia, which threatens U.S. homeland security by leaving the United States susceptible to Middle Eastern manipulation. While the United States does import a larger percentage of crude oil and petroleum products from Canada, Canada is considered an ally due to treaties signed during World War II and during the Cold War.

According to U.S. EIA, oil from Russia and Colombia is approximately 7% and 4% of the U.S. crude oil and petroleum product, respectively (see Figure 1.2).

The significance of this research is to seek impacts of the U.S. dependency on foreign oil problems by introducing a mixed-integer programming (MIP) model that identifies how other nations such as Indonesia, Russia, and Colombia can be more efficient in their crude oil supply chain and produce more crude oil products for export. This model was built with respect to the trade-off between crude oil supply chain quality, sustainable environmental incentives, and supply chain costs. Furthermore, the broader impact is how investments into other countries crude oil supply chains can be quantified and optimized and how countries such as Indonesia can be identified as possible candidates for investment for future global crude oil needs. This chapter hypothesizes that the crude oil supply chain quality will impact the crude oil supply chain costs. Additionally, the environmental sustainability will have an impact on crude oil supply chain costs and suggests that the crude oil supply chains of each of these countries will dictate their ability to produce crude oil for export. The overall objective is to investigate a MIP model that supports decisions about providing economic and environmental incentives to improve the supply chain quality of crude oil so that it becomes more cost-effective for the United States to import crude oil from other nations as opposed to other global sources.

3.3 Research Questions and Hypothesis

The U.S. government, crude oil refining companies, and other stake holders find it necessary to invest infrastructure and to buy crude oil from other nation to accomplish the requirement of the United States. Therefore, this dissertation attempt to answer the following global question: "When is it economically benefit to invest in supply chain of crude oil for given nation?" This question hypothesizes that the pipeline quality and sustainability will impact the supply chain cost and suggest that the crude oil supply chain for given nation will dictate their ability to be an ideal candidate for investment.

3.4 Research Purposes

The goal of the most of companies is to maximize profit and shareholder value. In the oil industry, to maximize of shareholder value, the value of oil resources should be maximized through managing production, exploration, and development activities to assure a functioning market (Pirog, 2007). Reserve replacement and ability to expand production and sales to meet demand are important activities to ensure the long-term feasibility of company. Technical efficiency is required to minimize cost and to improve performance and environmental integrity.

The management of the company organizing production to accomplish goal helps to make profit in current as well as future time. Management makes investment decision to raise company's rate of return and to increase the profitability.

A majority of government operate their national oil companies, so these companies do not follow stakeholder value maximization model. They have to compete with governmentally mandated objectives to maximize the value of the company. These companies have pressure to maximize the flow of fund to national treasuries.

There are several examples of unsuccessful deals between national oil companies in which the outcome was not able to meet expectations like "China and Iran" and "China and Saudi Arabia".

Furthermore, the broader impact is how investments into other countries crude oil supply chains can be quantified and optimized, and how countries such as Russia/Colombia can be identified as possible candidates for investment for future global crude oil needs. This chapter hypothesizes that the crude oil supply chain quality will impact the crude oil supply chain costs. Additionally, the environmental sustainability will have an impact on crude oil supply chain costs and suggests that the crude oil supply chains of each of these countries will dictate their ability to produce crude oil for export. The overall objective is to investigate a MIP model that supports decisions about providing economic and environmental incentives to improve the supply chain quality of crude oil, specifically in Russia/Colombia so that it becomes more cost-effective for the United States to import crude oil from Russia/Colombia as opposed to other global sources.

3.5 Background

3.5.1 Crude Oil and Petroleum Product

3.5.1.1 Crude Oil Formation

Crude oil, commonly known as petroleum, was formed from the remains of animals and plants (called biomass) that lived many years ago. Over many years, the biomass was covered by layers of mud, silt, and sand that formed into sedimentary rock. Geologic heat and the pressure of the overlying rock turned the biomass into a hydrocarbon-rich liquid that we call crude oil, and eventually forced it into porous rock strata called reservoirs. Oil reserves cannot be reproduced because it needs millions of years to form. That's why crude oil is called non-renewable energy source. There are also formations or deposits of hydrocarbon-saturated sands and shale where geologic conditions have not been sufficient to turn the hydrocarbons into liquid.

Crude oil is a liquid found within the Earth comprised of hydrocarbons, organic compounds, and small amounts of metal. While hydrocarbons are usually the primary component of crude oil, their composition can vary from 50% to 97% depending on the type of crude oil and how it is extracted. Organic compounds such as nitrogen, oxygen, and sulfur typically make up between 6% and 10% of crude oil, while metals such as copper, nickel, vanadium, and iron account for less than 1% of the total composition.

3.5.1.2 Crude Oil Exploration

Petroleum has been used since ancient time. Geologists observe rock structure and its characteristics to determine the oil reservoir. According to E-tech international, oil exploration and production processes consist of five main processes (Figure 3.3).

3.5.1.3 Exploration

Oil and gas exploration is the discovery for hydrocarbon deposits (oil and gas) underneath the Earth's surface by petroleum geologists and geophysicists. It contains locating oil and gas reservoirs using primarily seismic surveys and drilling wells.

Exploration is an expensive, high-risk operation because it costs millions of dollars and every one out of three wells, on average, contains hydrocarbons. Therefore, companies have to drill multiple wells in one area before finding an oil or gas, which can take several years.

During exploration drilling, information about the rocks and fluids (water, gas, and oil) and samples are collected from the well which leads to following information:

- Whether there are any hydrocarbons at that location
- How much oil or gas might be present
- What depth the oil or gas occurs at.

FIGURE 3.3   Crude oil exploration process.

Exploration activities can also be risky because of

- The location—remote or difficult terrain, or a sensitive ecosystem.
- Safety—people can have accidents while obtaining seismic surveys or drilling wells, even though safety is always a top priority.

3.5.1.4 Appraisal

If a company is successful with their exploration drilling and makes an oil or gas discovery, then they move into the appraisal phase of the lifecycle. The purpose of this phase is to reduce the uncertainty about the size of the oil or gas field and its properties.

During appraisal, more wells are drilled to collect information and samples from the reservoir. Another seismic survey might also be acquired in order to better image the reservoir. These activities can take several more years and cost tens to hundreds of millions of dollars.

More seismic surveys and wells help petroleum geologists; geophysicists and reservoir engineers understand the reservoir better. For example, they try to find out whether rock or fluid properties change away from the discovery well, how much oil or gas might be in the reservoir, and how fast oil or gas will move through the reservoir.

The appraisal stage is successful if a company decides that the oil or gas field can be developed. One risk that companies face is even after investing time and money in the appraisal stage, they might not find a way to develop the field safely, profitably, and responsibly (in terms of communities and the environment).

3.5.1.5 Development

The development stage takes place after successful appraisal and before full-scale production. The main activities (and people involved) are

- To form a plan to develop the oil or gas field, including how many wells need to be drilled to produce the oil or gas (geologists, geophysicists, and reservoir engineers)
- To decide the best design for the production wells (drilling engineers)
- To decide what production facilities are required to process the oil/gas before it is sent to a refinery or customer (facilities engineers)
- To decide what the best export route might be for the oil and gas (logistics engineers).

Executing the development plan involves drilling engineers who drill the first phase of production wells and project engineers who build the planned facilities. Many thousands of people can be involved in building production facilities, and safety is a top priority. The risk of accidents is highest in this phase because of the number of people involved at construction sites.

It costs hundreds of millions, sometimes billions of dollars and typically 5–10 years to develop an oil or gas field, depending on the location, size and complexity of the facilities, and the number of wells needed. Onshore developments are typically much cheaper than offshore developments.

No oil or gas field will be developed unless the company believes that they will make enough money to pay back their exploration, appraisal and development costs, as well as profit from selling the hydrocarbons. Even more importantly, developments will only happen if the communities or ecosystems affected can be protected.

3.5.1.6 Production

Production is the phase during which hydrocarbons are extracted from an oil or gas field and the first money (or revenue) comes from selling the oil or gas. After a number of years, the revenue exceeds the company's investment, and they begin to make a profit.

Production can last several years up to 40 years, depending on the size of the oil or gas field and how expensive it is to keep the wells and production facilities running. Every year, millions of dollars will be spent on operating and maintaining the field. Safe production operations are critical; otherwise, companies risk harming people or the damaging the environment, e.g., through an oil spill or explosion.

Operators work in shifts to keep production going. Engineers will usually be located full time at the production facilities in order to operate and maintain them. Reservoir engineers will check on the health and performance of the field to plan how best to maintain production. Additional wells might need to be drilled or the production facilities improved to maximize recovery of the oil or gas.

3.5.1.7 Decommissioning

Decommissioning is the term used for removing the production facilities and restoring oil and gas sites that are no longer profitable. The term is usually used to refer to offshore facilities. Offshore oil and gas platforms can be vast structures requiring large amounts of materials in their construction. By bringing the facilities onshore for dismantling and disposal, these materials can be reclaimed.

Decommissioning involves removing not only the main platform but also pipelines and cables. The aim is to reduce the risk to the marine environment and to reuse or recycle materials. In the majority of cases, all equipment is removed, and the site returned to its condition before development began. Some installations can be reused as oil and gas facilities at another location or reused in place for another purpose (e.g., as a wind farm or aid to navigation). Occasionally, part of the platform may be left in place because they benefit the marine environment, e.g., steel legs of tension leg platforms that are used to create artificial reefs in the Gulf of Mexico.

Project, logistics, and environmental engineers will be involved in decommissioning a production facility. This vital step takes several years and many millions of dollars. Government requirements and community views will be taken on board during decommissioning.

3.5.1.8 Crude Oil Extraction

Extracting oil and natural gas from oil field isn't as simple as just drilling and completing a well. Crude oil extraction process consists of three recovery process (see Figure 3.4).

3.5.1.8.1 Primary Recovery

When an oil field is first produced, the oil typically is recovered as a result of expansion of reservoir fluids which are naturally pressured within the producing formation. The only natural force present to

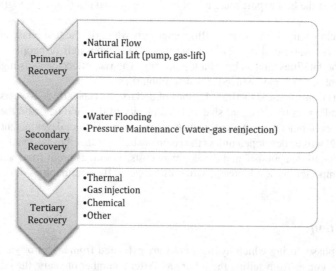

FIGURE 3.4 Crude oil extraction process.

move the oil through the reservoir rock to the well bore is the pressure differential between the higher pressure in the rock formation and the lower pressure in the producing well bore. Various types of pumps are often used to reduce pressure in the well bore, thereby increasing the pressure differential. At the same time, there are many factors that act to impede the flow of oil, depending on the nature of the formation and fluid properties, such as pressure, permeability, viscosity, and water saturation. This stage of production, referred to as "primary recovery", recovers only a small fraction of the oil originally in place in a producing formation, typically ranging from 10% to 25%.

Primary recovery first relies on underground pressure to drive fluids to the surface. When the pressure falls, artificial lift technologies, such as pumps, are used help bring more fluids to the surface. In some situations, natural gas is pumped back down the well underneath the oil. The gas expands, pushing the oil to the surface. Gas lift technology is often used in offshore facilities. Primary recovery often taps up to 15% of the oil in a deposit.

3.5.1.9 Secondary Recovery

After the primary recovery phase, many, but not all, oil fields respond positively to "secondary recovery" techniques in which external fluids are injected into a reservoir to increase reservoir pressure and to displace oil toward the well bore. Secondary recovery techniques often result in increases in production and reserves the abovementioned primary recovery. Waterflooding, a form of secondary recovery, works by repressuring a reservoir through water injection and "sweeping" or pushing oil to producing well bores. Through waterflooding, water injection replaces the loss of reservoir pressure caused by the primary production of oil and gas, which is often referred to as "pressure depletion" or "reservoir voidage". The degree to which reservoir voidage has been replaced through water injection is known as "reservoir fill up" or simply as "fill up". A reservoir which has had all of the produced fluids replaced by injection is at 100% fill up. In general, peak oil production from a waterflood typically occurs at 100% fill up. Estimating the percentage of fill up which has occurred, or when a reservoir is 100% filled up, is subject to a wide variety of engineering and geologic uncertainties. As a result of the water used in a waterflood, produced fluids contain both water and oil, with the relative amount of water increasing over time. Surface equipment is used to separate the oil from the water, with the oil going to pipelines or holding tanks for sale and the water being recycled to the injection facilities. In general, in the Mid-Continent Region, a secondary recovery process may produce an additional 10%–20% of the oil originally in place in a reservoir.

3.5.1.10 Tertiary Recovery

A third stage of oil recovery is called "tertiary recovery". In addition to maintaining reservoir pressure, this type of recovery seeks to alter the properties of the oil in ways that facilitate additional production. The three major types of tertiary recovery are chemical flooding, thermal recovery (such as a steam flood), and miscible displacement involving carbon dioxide (CO_2), hydrocarbon, or nitrogen injection.

Thermal recovery entails injecting steam into the formation. The heat from the steam makes the oil flow more easily, and the increased pressure forces it to the surface.

Gas injection uses either miscible or immiscible gases. Miscible gasses dissolve CO_2, propane, methane, or other gasses in the oil to lower its viscosity and increase flow. Immiscible gasses do not mix with the oil, but increase pressure in the "gas cap" in a reservoir to drive additional oil to the well bore.

Chemical flooding involves mixing dense, water-soluble polymers with water and injecting the mixture into the field. The water pushes the oil out of the formation and into the well bore.

We are currently field testing new technologies in chemical flooding on some of our properties. If successful, this testing may lead to reserve and production increases in the future. Any future tertiary development programs and subsequent capital expenditures would be contingent upon commercial viability established by successful pilot testing. At this time, there are no estimated reserves or production associated with tertiary recovery projects assigned to our properties. We will continue to review future opportunities for growth through the use of various tertiary recovery techniques.

3.5.2 Oil Refinery and Transportation

A crude oil refinery is a group of industrial facilities that turns crude oil and other inputs into finished petroleum products. A refinery's capacity refers to the maximum amount of crude oil designed to flow into the distillation unit of a refinery, also known as the crude unit.

3.5.2.1 Crude Oil Distillation

Crude oil is unprocessed oil, which comes out of a ground. Refineries process crude oil into many different petroleum products. These products include gasoline, diesel fuel, jet fuel, and asphalt. The most basic refining process separates crude oil into its various components. The various components of crude oil have different sizes, weights, and boiling temperatures. The process is very complex and involves both chemical reactions and physical separations. Crude oil is composed of thousands of different molecules. It would be nearly impossible to isolate every molecule and make finished products from each molecule. Chemists and engineers deal with this problem by isolating mixtures of molecules according to the mixture's boiling point range. Crude oil is heated and put into a distillation tower (a still) where different hydrocarbon components are boiled off and recovered as they condense at different temperatures (see Figure 3.5).

The major products of crude oil according to its specific temperature are as follows (Table 3.1).

3.5.2.2 Crude Oil Transportation

Oil transportation is a major industry in and of itself, with a range of transportation options available, depending on the situation at hand. The most important methods include pipeline, rail, barge, and truck. Transportation and storage in the oil and gas industry concern to the movement of crude oil from the oil fields (where oil has been discovered) to petroleum refineries (where the oil is further processed) to storage areas, where the petroleum products are stored for distribution and emergency reserves.

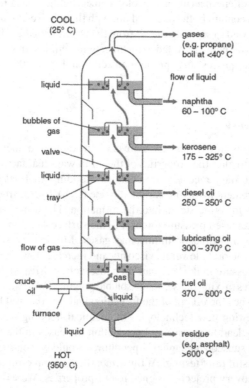

FIGURE 3.5 Crude oil distillation process.

TABLE 3.1

Crude Oil Products

Product Name	Boiling Range (°C)	State	Uses
Petroleum gas	40	Gas	Used for heating, cooking
Naphtha	60–100	Gas	Intermediate that will be processed more to make gasoline
Gasoline	40–205	Liquid	Motor fuel
Kerosene	175–325	Liquid	Fuel for jet engine and tractors
Diesel oil	250–350	Liquid	Used for diesel fuel and heating oil
Lubricating oil	300–370	Liquid	Used for motor oil, grease, and other lubricant
Fuel oil	370–600	Liquid	Used for industrial fuel
Residuals	Above 600	Solid	Coke, asphalt, tar, waxes, etc.

Advances in exploration and production have helped to locate and recover a supply of oil and natural gas from major reserves across the globe. At the same time, demand for petroleum-based products has grown in every corner of the world. But supply and demand are rarely concentrated in the same place. Transportation therefore is vital to ensuring the reliable and affordable flow of petroleum we all count on to fuel our cars, heat our homes, and improve the quality of our lives.

There are four modes of transportation associated with crude oil.

3.5.2.2.1 Ship and Barge

Oil tankers ships are used for oil transport overseas or from sea to shore. Tankers can carry huge amounts of oil, and they have the flexibility of being able to transport to a variety of locations, whereas pipelines have fixed networks and limited ranges. As the name implies, tankers store large quantities of oil in enormous tanks on the ship.

Unlike oil tankers ship, barges are used to transport oil in barrels. This allows for easy loading and unloading of measured units of oil.

Advantage of ship and barge:

- Capitalizes on existing infrastructure for receiving marine shipment at coastal refineries

Disadvantage of ship and barge:

- Impact of day–to-day unconventional crude transit still unknown, instead vessel traffic.

3.5.2.2.2 Pipeline

Oil pipelines are the most efficient means of transporting oil. They can handle enormous amounts of oil day in and day out with very little human interaction, and they can cover enormous distances.

Advantages of pipelines:

- Cost-effective form of transit for producer
- Income incentives for landowners.

Disadvantages of pipeline

- Distraction to agriculture and other land uses from construction and operation
- Difficulties associated with land restoration.

3.5.2.2.3 Rail

Trains are useful for transporting large amounts of oil over land and can generally reach a wider network of locations than oil pipelines can.

Advantages of rail:

- Increased flexibility for producer and refiner
- Infrastructural benefit.

Disadvantage of rail:

- Crowding out rail network access by other industries
- Functionality and safety can be affected by adverse weather.

3.5.2.2.4 Truck

Trucks are the most limited oil transportation method in terms of storage capacity, but they have the greatest flexibility in potential destinations. This means trucks are often the last step in the transport process, delivering oil, and refined petroleum products to their intended storage destinations.

Advantage of truck:

- Ideal for short distance but can be used for long hauls.

Disadvantage of truck:

- Road traffic congestion and infrastructure damage.

3.5.2.3 Crude Oil Waste

The United States Environmental Protection Agency (EPA) classifies crude oil waste into following two categories: (1) exempt and (2) non-exempt wastes.

The EPA defines exempt wastes as follows:

"Wastes that are generated before the end point of primary field operations are exempt. The term end point of initial product separation means the point at which crude oil leaves the last vessel in the tank battery associated with the wells. This tank battery separates crude oil from the produced water and/or gas".

With respect to crude oil, primary field operations include activities occurring at or near the wellhead and before the point where the oil is transferred from an individual field facility or a centrally located facility to a carrier for transport to a refinery or a refiner.

Primary field operations include exploration, development, and the primary, secondary, and tertiary production of oil or gas. Crude oil processing, such as water separation, de-emulsifying, degassing, and storage at tank batteries associated with a specific well or wells, are examples of primary field operations. Furthermore, because natural gas often requires processing to remove water and other impurities prior to entering the sales line, gas plants are considered to be part of production operations regardless of their location with respect to the wellhead.

List of exempt and non-exempt for crude oil E&P

Exempt waste

- Produced water
- Drilling fluids
- Drill cuttings
- Rig wash
- Drilling fluids and cuttings from offshore operations disposed of onshore
- Geothermal production fluids
- Hydrogen sulfide abatement wastes from geothermal energy production
- Well completion, treatment, and stimulation fluids
- Basic sediment, water, and other tank bottoms from storage facilities that hold product and exempt waste

- Accumulated materials such as hydrocarbons, solids, sands, and emulsion from production separators, fluid treating vessels, and production impoundments
- Pit sludge's and contaminated bottoms from storage or disposal of exempt wastes
- Gas plant dehydration wastes, including glycol-based compounds, glycol filters, and filter media
- backwash and molecular sieves
- Workover wastes
- Cooling tower blowdown
- Gas plant sweetening wastes for sulfur removal, including amines, amine filters, amine filter media, backwash, precipitated amine sludge, iron sponge, and hydrogen sulfide scrubber liquid and sludge
- Spent filters, filter media, and backwash (assuming the filter itself is not hazardous and the residue in it is from an exempt waste stream)
- Pipe scale, hydrocarbon solids, hydrates, and other deposits removed from piping and equipment prior to transportation
- Produced sand
- Packing fluids
- Hydrocarbon-bearing soil
- Pigging wastes from gathering lines
- Wastes from subsurface gas storage and retrieval
- Constituents removed from produced water before it is injected or otherwise disposed of
- Liquid hydrocarbons removed from the production stream but not from oil refining
- Gases from the production stream, such as hydrogen sulfide and carbon dioxide, and volatilized hydrocarbons
- Materials ejected from a producing well during blowdown
- Waste crude oil from primary field operations
- Light organics volatilized from exempt wastes in reserve pits, impoundments, or production equipment

Non-exempt waste

- Unused fracturing fluids or acids
- Gas plant cooling tower cleaning wastes
- Painting wastes
- Waste solvents
- Oil and gas service company wastes such as empty drums, drum reinstate, sandblast media, painting wastes, spent solvents, spilled chemicals, and waste acids
- Vacuum truck and drum reinstate from trucks and drums transporting or containing non-exempt waste
- Refinery wastes
- Liquid and solid wastes generated by crude oil and tank bottom reclaimers
- Used equipment lubricating oils
- Waste compressor oil, filters, and blowdown
- Used hydraulic fluids
- Waste in transportation pipeline related pits (except with approval by NDDH)
- Caustic or acid cleaners
- Boiler cleaning wastes
- Boiler scrubber fluids, sludge, and ash

- Incinerator ash
- Laboratory wastes
- Sanitary wastes
- Pesticide wastes
- Radioactive tracer wastes
- Drums insulation and miscellaneous solids.

3.5.2.4 Pipeline Quality Factors

Pipelines are not part of primary field operations; thus, oil wastes that are generated by pipelines are non-exempt. Failure of a pipeline segment caused by accidental excavation damage is an example of non-exempt wastes, which will result in oil companies paying fines to the EPA as well as settlements to clean the surrounding environment. This pipeline segment failure is chosen as the sampling plan of supply chain quality-level performance.

Table 3.2 shows summary of various causes for pipeline failure.

Pipeline quality affects the transportation cost for crude oil. Cause-and-effect diagram for pipeline loss is shown in Figure 3.6.

3.5.2.5 Refinery Sustainability

Globalization has resulted in pressure on multinational firms to improve environmental performance. In order to achieve improvement in environmental performance, a company must integrate its environmental management strategies, while maintaining production quality and cost goals, into the supply

TABLE 3.2

Causes for Pipeline Failure

Type of Failure	Causes
Mechanical failure	Construction, material, and structural
Corrosion	Internal, external
Operational failure	System, human
Third-party activity	Accidental, malicious, incidental
Natural hazard	Subsidence, flooding, earthquake, etc.

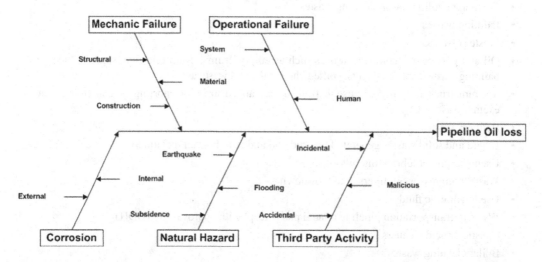

FIGURE 3.6   Cause-and-effect diagram for pipeline loss.

chain, which includes all of the operational lifecycle stages such as unique partnerships with suppliers. Environmental sustainability has been defined as "meeting the needs of the present without compromising the ability of the future generations to meet their needs" [UN Document].

For oil companies, the concept of sustainability is most appropriately used when evaluating their business strategies. Sustainability concerns are to the degree of which they will not only reduce negative impacts on the natural environment through their operations but also invest in business practices that promote policies to make wide-reaching progress toward sustainable development. In the industry, the operations of oil companies are examined for their impact on the surrounding environment annually. To distinguish from the above definition of sustainability, environmentally conscious operations are referred to as green operations. However, green operations are not necessarily sustainable in the long run, but minimizing the negative impact of operational processes is still environmentally conscious. Company operations deal with energy usage necessary for operating refineries, emissions, and waste. Meanwhile, sustainability of the products deals with oil, natural gas, and possible alternatives to fossil fuels.

In the oil industry exploration and production processes, sustainability involves the products, and as such, the petroleum industry itself is environmentally unsustainable because like all fossil fuels, oil is a limited resource. Some risks of accidental spills of oil have the potential to pollute water, contaminate soil, harm species, and affect livelihoods.

Oil companies need to plan all major operations in advance and manage their costs during the supply chain to improve the profit margin. Sustainability that associated with oil companies' processes or products will have positive and negative impacts on the supply chain costs. An example of the negative impact is certainly the tragic British Petroleum (BP) drill explosion and oil spill in 2010, which impacted nature and animals in the Gulf of Mexico. This accident resulted in damaging the environment as well as costing BP a settlement of billions of dollars. On contrary, an example of the positive impact is the ability to be capable of reserving the productivity of oil itself as a natural resource asset, which leads to supply chain costs savings.

Unlike the quality metrics, which focused on pipelines performance, this research considers refining process as a good candidate to determine its sustainability metrics. Refinery is a complex process. Oil refineries essentially serve as the second stage in the production process following the actual extraction by oil rigs. The first step in the refining process is distillation where crude oil is heated at extreme temperatures to separate the different hydrocarbons. The refining sector of the oil industry has significantly affected the crude oil global marketplace due to the demand growth of petroleum products. As the petroleum products demand increases, the demand for conversion capacity increases. Refineries affect supply chain profit margins such that refineries' variable costs vary on the petroleum products demand.

There are two sustainability factors that are considered for refineries performance. The first factor is the refining operations, which deal with energy usage necessary for operating refineries, emissions, and waste. The second factor is the refining products, which deal with oil to fossil fuels. Refining processes that deal with energy usage are chosen as environmental sustainability according to the performance-sampling plan.

3.5.3 Oil Industry

3.5.3.1 Russia

The petroleum industry in Russia is one of the largest industries in the world. Russia was the third-largest producer of liquid fuels in 2012, following the United States and Saudi Arabia. Russia's proven oil reserves were 80 billion barrels as of January 2013, according to the *Oil and Gas Journal*. In 2012, Russia produced an estimated 10.4 MMbd of total liquids (of which 9.9 MMbd was crude oil), and it consumed roughly 3.2 MMbd. Russia exported over 7 MMbd in 2012, including roughly 5 MMbd of crude oil and the remainder in products.

Most of Russia's oil production continues to originate in West Siberia, notably from the Priobskoye and Samotlor fields. Approximately 62% of oil produced from West Siberia region, while nearly 22% oil produced from the Urals-Volga region. The use of more advanced technologies and the application of improved recovery techniques are resulting in increased oil output from existing oil deposits.

Fields in the Western Siberian Basin produce the majority of Russia's oil, with developments at the Samotlor (TNK-BP) and Priobskoye (Rosneft) fields extracting more than 750,000 and 800,000 bd, respectively. Russian firms govern the region, although foreign companies, notably Shell, have secured access to production in Western Siberia as well.

West Siberia is Russia's main oil-producing region, accounting for around 6.4 MMbd of liquids production, nearly two-thirds of Russia's total production. While this region is mature, West Siberian production potential is still significant but will depend on improving production economics at fields that are more complex and that contain a significant portion of remaining reserves. The two largest oil fields in West Siberia are North Priobskoye and Samotlor, which account for about 20% of West Siberian production. Urengoy is the largest gas field in the region.

Urals-Volga was the largest producing region of the Soviet Union until the late 1970s, when it was surpassed by Western Siberia. Today, this region is a distant-second producing region, accounting for about 22% of Russia's total output. The giant Romashkinskoye field (discovered in 1948) is the largest in the region. Tatneft operates it. While the field reached its peak production level sometime in the late 1970s, it likely will continue to produce until at least 2030, according to Wood Mackenzie.

The potential oil reserves of Eastern Siberia, the Russian Arctic, the northern Caspian Sea, and Sakhalin Island are attracting attention.

Russian companies are also expanding into the Arctic and Eastern Siberian regions, prompted on by tax holidays and lower oil export tariffs. While several new fields have come online since 2009, bringing additional fields into production will take time and may require an improved oil tax system from the government.

Russia has 40 oil refineries with a total crude oil distillation capacity of 5.5 MMbd, according to *Oil and Gas Journal*. Rosneft, the largest refinery operator, has a crude distillation capacity of 1.3 MMbd and operates Russia's largest refinery, the Angarsk facility. LUKoil is the second-largest operator of refineries in Russia with a crude distillation capacity of 1 MMbd.

In 2012, Russia exported approximately 7.4 MMbd of total liquid fuels, with 5 MMbd of crude oil and 2.4 MMbd of petroleum products. The majority (79%) of Russia's crude oil exports went to European countries (including Eastern Europe), particularly Germany, the Netherlands, and Poland. Around 18% of Russia's crude oil exports were destined for Asia, while the remainder went mostly to the Americas. Russia's crude oil exports to North America and South America have been largely displaced by increases in crude oil production in the United States, Canada, and, to a lesser extent, Brazil, Colombia, and other countries on the continent. More than 80% of Russia's oil is exported via the Transneft pipeline system, and the remainder is shipped via rail and on vessels that load at independently owned terminals.

Russia has an extensive domestic distribution and export pipeline network. Russia's pipeline network is nearly completely owned and run by the state-run Transneft, which transports about 88% of all crude oil and about 27% of oil products produced in Russia. These pipelines include a number of domestic pipeline networks, pipelines that transport oil to export terminals such as Novorossiysk on the Black Sea and Primorsk on the Baltic Sea, as well as a number of export pipelines that deliver oil to western European markets. Russian export pipelines include Druzhba, Baltic Pipeline System, North-West Pipeline System, Tengiz-Novorossiysk, and Baku-Novorossiysk. All of these pipelines, with the exception of the Tengiz-Novorossiysk, are Transneft-controlled.

3.5.3.2 Colombia

Colombia produced 969,000 barrels per day (bd) of oil in 2012, up 61% from the 604,000 bd produced in 2008. EIA estimates that oil production in 2013 to be just over 1 MMbd and expects this rising trend to continue. The Ministry of Mines and Energy reported that Colombian production is expected to reach 1.3 MMbd by 2020. Colombia consumed 287,000 bd in 2012, allowing the country to export most of its oil production.

Colombia's oil production has increased since 2008 because of increased exploration and development. New exploration and development were spurred by regulatory reform.

Much of Colombia's crude oil production occurs in the Andes foothills and the eastern Amazonian jungles. Meta department, in central Colombia, is also an important production area, predominately of heavy crude oil. Its Llanos basin contains the Rubiales oilfield, the largest producing oil field in the country.

The largest producing oil field in the country is the Rubiales heavy oil field, located in Meta department, and operated by partners Pacific Rubiales and Ecopetrol. Low levels of production began at Rubiales in the late 1980s, but increasing investment and the completion of a new pipeline have allowed production rates to rise in recent years. Gross production at Rubiales exceeded 177,000 bd in 2012, up from 37,000 bd in 2008. Other large oil fields include Cano Limon, Castilla, and Cupiagua.

Colombia has six major oil pipelines, four of which connect production fields to the Caribbean export terminal at Covenas. These include the 500-mile Ocensa pipeline, which has the capacity to transport 650,000 bd from the Cusiana/Cupiagua area; the 460-mile, 220,000 bd-capacity Cano Limon pipeline; and the smaller Alto Magdalena and Colombia Oil pipelines. The Llanos Orientales pipeline came online in late 2009, linking the Rubiales field to the Ocensa pipeline, with a capacity of 340,000 bd. The sixth pipeline, the TransAndino, has a capacity of 190,000 bd and transports crude from Colombia's Orito field in the Putumayo basin to Colombia's Pacific port at Tumaco linking to Ecuador.

3.6 Research Methodology

3.6.1 Research Objective and Hypothesis

This research generates MIP baseline models and a proficient frontier curve, which include sampling plans for both pipeline quality and refinery sustainability performance, to evaluate the quality and sustainability for Russia and Colombia. This research utilizes Microsoft Excel Solver to solve for optimal solutions.

There are two primary research questions that we have to achieve in this section:

Research Objective 1: What is the impact of pipeline quality on crude oil supply chain efficiency?
Research Objective 2: What is the impact of sustainability on crude oil supply chain efficiency?

This chapter evaluates whether or not the crude oil sustainability and pipeline quality impact the crude oil supply chain cost. To evaluate the impact, we introduce two sets of hypothesis, which help to answer the research question. In statistical hypothesis testing, two hypotheses are compared. These are called the null hypothesis and the alternative hypothesis. The null hypothesis is the hypothesis that states that there is no relation between the phenomena whose relation is under investigation, or at least not of the form given by the alternative hypothesis. The alternative hypothesis, as the name suggests, is the alternative to the null hypothesis: it states that there *is* some kind of relation. The alternative hypothesis may take several forms, depending on the nature of the hypothesized relation; in particular, it can be two-sided (e.g., there is *some* effect, in a yet unknown direction) or one-sided (the direction of the hypothesized relation, positive or negative, is fixed in advance).

These two hypotheses statement are stated as follows:

Hypothesis Statement for Objective # 1
Null Hypothesis
   H_0: The crude oil pipeline quality will not impact the supply chain cost.
Alternative Hypothesis
   H_a: The crude oil pipeline quality will impact the supply chain cost.
Decision Rule
   Reject H_0 if supply chain cost variation is greater than 15%.
Hypothesis Statement for Objective # 2
Null Hypothesis
   H_0: The environmental sustainability will not impact the supply chain cost.
Alternative Hypothesis
   H_a: The environmental sustainability will impact the supply chain cost.
Decision Rule
Reject H_0 if supply chain cost variation is greater than 15%.

3.6.2 Research Criteria and Approach

In this research, the DC model shown in Shapiro's book is utilized to show optimal locations to place DCs based on transportation distances and the size of the DCs. The model was worked in Microsoft Excel and used GRG nonlinear engine in Solver to solve the objective function. To achieve research objective, we introduce three specific objectives:

Specific Objective 1. Evaluate the supply chain factors that determine pipeline quality of crude oil production

Specific Objective 2. Evaluate the supply chain factors that determine Sustainability of crude oil production

Specific Objective 3. Evaluate the economic impacts of quality and sustainability on operational strategies in supplier network.

To satisfy these three specific objectives, we approach several steps.

3.6.2.1 Phase 1

In this phase, we introduce steps to achieve Specific Objective 1. "Evaluate the supply chain factors that determine pipeline quality of crude oil production".

Step 1—Questionnaire development
- Conduct a survey to observe different level of pipeline quality and loss associated with it (Figure 3.7).

Step 2—Evaluate the performance level for quality
- From the survey, evaluate the level of quality required to satisfy Specific Objective 1. Table 3.3 shows the performance level for pipeline quality.

3.6.2.2 Phase 2

In this phase, we introduce steps to achieve Specific Objective 2. "Evaluate the supply chain factors that determine Sustainability of crude oil production".

Step 3—Questionnaire development
- Conduct a detailed study for all the refinery of Russia and Colombia to check its sustainability with respect to process and product.
- Following questions need to be answered to get detailed report.
    1. What's the energy consumption for proceed?
    2. Is the product environmental safe and nonhazardous?
    3. Do the company have any recycling process?
    4. Do they have any safety rules for employees?
    5. Usage of environment-friendly material.

Step 4—Evaluate the performance level for sustainability
With the help of detail study regarding refinery sustainability, we evaluate the following level of performance for refinery sustainability to satisfy Specific Objective 2.
Table 3.4 shows the performance level for refinery sustainability.

3.6.2.3 Phase 3

In this phase, we introduce steps to achieve Specific Objective 3. Evaluate the economic impacts of quality and sustainability on operational strategies in supplier network.

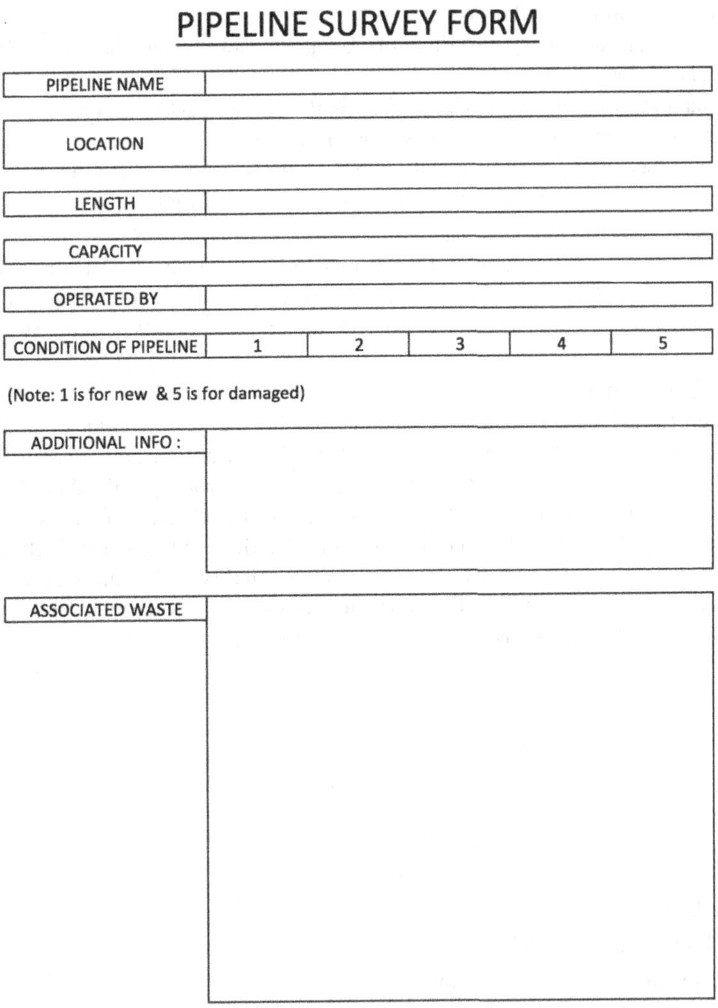

PIPELINE SURVEY FORM

PIPELINE NAME	

LOCATION	

LENGTH	

CAPACITY	

OPERATED BY	

CONDITION OF PIPELINE	1	2	3	4	5

(Note: 1 is for new & 5 is for damaged)

ADDITIONAL INFO :	

ASSOCIATED WASTE	

FIGURE 3.7 Pipeline survey form.

TABLE 3.3

Pipeline Quality Performance Level

Quality Level	Pipeline Quality Description
1	Damaged and causing non-exempt waste
2 (base)	Good condition and causing little non-exempt waste
3	New and not causing non-exempt waste

TABLE 3.4

Refinery Sustainability Performance Level

Sustainability Level	Refinery Sustainability Description
1	High energy usage consumption
2 (base)	Medium energy usage consumption
3	Low energy usage consumption

Step 5—Selection of oil field and refinery

With the help of quality and sustainability level, we choose following oil field and refinery for Russia and Colombia.

For Russia and Colombia, we select only two oil fields for each location. To extend the size, we introduce small and large oil field at all the location (Table 3.5).

For refinery selection, we select only some of the most important refinery. Russia and Colombia have so many refineries with wide range of choice (Table 3.6).

Step 6—Generate Scenario to collect data

According to oil fields location and performance level criteria, we have a total of 24 scenarios for Russia and Colombia. Each scenario represents the data set for oil fields according to the performance level of given selection criteria like pipeline quality or refinery sustainability (Table 3.7).

Step 7—Generate the model.

In this step, the DC model example printed in *Modeling the Supply Chain* textbook by Shapiro is used to show ideal locations for DCs which depends on transportation distances, associated transportation cost, and the capacity of the DCs. The model was optimized in Microsoft Excel and used GRG nonlinear engine in Solver to maximize the objective function. The objective function was solved based on the oil transportation cost, the fixed costs for pipeline quality and refinery efficiency, and the variable costs for pipeline quality and refinery efficiency. Several scenarios were run that varied the transportation and variable costs in order to compare how pipeline quality and refinery sustainability impact the supply chain costs.

Objective Function

$$\text{Max } Z: \sum_{i \to 4} A_{ij}X_{ij}Y_{ij} + \sum_{i \to 4} B_{ij}Y_{ij} + \sum_{i \to 4} C_{ij}X_{ij}Y_{ij}$$

where

A_{ij} = Transportation costs from field i to refinery j
B_{ij} = Fixed costs from field i to refinery j
C_{ij} = Sustainability costs from field i to refinery j
i = The oil field from where the oil originates

TABLE 3.5

Oil Field Numbering

i	Russia	Colombia
1	Samotlor—large	Rubiales—large
2	Samotlor—small	Rubiales—small
3	Priobskoye—large	Cano Limon—large
4	Priobskoye—small	Cano Limon—small

TABLE 3.6

Refinery Numbering

j	Russia	Colombia
1	Angarsk	Barrancabermeja
2	Achinsk	Cartagena
3	Tuapse	Apiay
4	Syzran	Orito
5	Kuibyshev	Tibu
6	Novokuibyshevsk	-

TABLE 3.7

Scenarios Summary

Country	Oil Field Location	Sampling Plan	Performance Level	Scenario
Russia	Samotlor	Pipeline quality	1	1
			2 (base)	2
			3	3
		Refinery sustainability	1	4
			2 (base)	5
			3	6
	Priobskoye	Pipeline quality	1	7
			2 (base)	8
			3	9
		Refinery sustainability	1	10
			2 (base)	11
			3	12
Colombia	Rubiales	Pipeline quality	1	13
			2 (base)	14
			3	15
		Refinery sustainability	1	16
			2 (base)	17
			3	18
	Cano Limon	Pipeline quality	1	19
			2 (base)	20
			3	21
		Refinery sustainability	1	22
			2 (base)	23
			3	24

j = The refinery to where the oil is shipped and processed
X_{ij} = The number of barrels of oil shipped from field i to refinery j
Y_{ij} = The binary selection of moving oil from field i to refinery j

Constraints

1. Capacity Constraint

   In the capacity constraint, number of barrels shipped from oil field to refinery must be less than refinery capacity.

$$\sum_{i \to 4} X_{ij} \le D_j$$

where D_j is the capacity of refinery j.

2. Selection Constraint

   The selection of the refineries used at each location was constrained using a binary constraint. The fact that only one refinery would be used at each location, the sum of the two constraints needed to be less than or equal to 1 in order to work in Solver. These equations are

$$Y_{1j} + Y_{2j} \le 1$$

$$Y_{3j} + Y_{4j} \le 1$$

Step 8—Data Collection

   Crude oil supply chain quality data are collected from the Organization of the Petroleum Exporting Countries (OPEC) public databases, the U.S. EIA website, Russian oil company

(Rosneft Corp), Russian oil transportation company (Transneft piping), and Colombian oil company (Ecopetrol). The U.S. EIA and the U.S. EPA websites are used to collect data for sustainability.

Data set includes the oil transportation cost, distance, the fixed costs, and the variable costs.

Step 9—Optimize the Model

The model was optimized in Microsoft Excel and used GRG nonlinear engine in Solver to maximize the objective function. Find total cost for all the 24 scenarios depend on pipeline quality and sustainability.

3.7 Results

To get the optimum solution, we have to run the model with all 24 scenarios. Following are the results for each scenario. After getting the result for all 24 scenarios, we will do hypothesis testing to achieve research objective.

3.7.1 Scenario 1

Scenario 1 describes the pipeline quality level 1 for Samotlor oil field in Russia.

If pipeline quality level is 1 (damaged and causing non-exempt waste), its transportation cost increases.

Table 3.8 shows the distance (km) and unit cost (ruble per hundred barrel) from Samotlor oil field to refineries.

Table 3.9 shows the fixed cost and sustainability cost associated with refinery for Scenario 1.

Run the scenario with Excel using GRG nonlinear, we obtain the total value is 9.11117E + 11.

3.7.2 Scenario 2

Scenario 2 describes the pipeline quality level 2 for Samotlor oil field in Russia.

If pipeline quality level is 2 (good condition and causing little non-exempt waste), its transportation cost remains standard. We considered this model as a base model.

TABLE 3.8

Transportation Distance and Cost (Scenario 1)

From/To		Angarsk	Achinsk	Tuapse	Syzran	Kuibyshev	Novokuibyshevsk
Samotlor	Distance	1,175	596	1,916	1,171	384	1,127
	Cost	2.53	3.18	2.41	2.57	3.49	2.78
Priobskoye	Distance	876	312	2,058	1,382	178	1,326
	Cost	2.69	4.12	1.96	2.41	4.69	2.48

TABLE 3.9

Fixed and Sustainability Cost (Scenario 1)

		Angarsk	Achinsk	Tuapse	Syzran	Kuibyshev	Novokuibyshevsk
Samotlor—large	Fixed cost	189,000	123,000	132,000	151,000	143,000	149,000
	Sustainability cost	139	111	128	119	102	99
Samotlor—small	Fixed cost	129,000	97,000	101,000	139,000	136,000	142,000
	Sustainability cost	113	99	119	107	97	94
Priobskoye—large	Fixed cost	176,000	104,000	128,000	147,000	141,000	145,000
	Sustainability cost	127	102	121	127	111	98
Priobskoye—small	Fixed cost	103,000	89,000	99,000	136,000	133,000	136,000
	Sustainability cost	103	95	111	114	92	95

TABLE 3.10

Transportation Distance and Cost (Scenario 2)

From/To		Angarsk	Achinsk	Tuapse	Syzran	Kuibyshev	Novokuibyshevsk
Samotlor	Distance	1,175	596	1,916	1,171	384	1,127
	Cost	2.13	2.78	2.01	2.17	309	2.38
Priobskoye	Distance	876	312	2,058	1,382	178	1,326
	Cost	2.69	4.12	1.96	2.41	4.69	2.48

Table 3.10 shows the distance (km) and unit cost (ruble per hundred barrel) from Samotlor oil field to refineries.

Table 3.11 shows the fixed cost and sustainability cost associated with refinery for Scenario 2.

Run the scenario with Excel using GRG nonlinear, we obtain the total value is 5.84768E + 11.

3.7.3 Scenario 3

Scenario 3 describes the pipeline quality level 3 for Samotlor oil field in Russia.

If pipeline quality level is 3 (new condition and not causing non-exempt waste), its transportation cost remains lower than base model.

Table 3.12 shows the distance (km) and unit cost (ruble per hundred barrel) from Samotlor oil field to refineries.

Table 3.13 shows the fixed cost and sustainability cost associated with refinery for Scenario 3.

Run the scenario with Excel using GRG nonlinear, we obtain the total value is 7.84129E + 11.

3.7.4 Scenario 4

Scenario 4 describes the sustainability level 1 from Samotlor oil field in Russia.

If refinery sustainability level is 1 (high energy usage consumption), its sustainability cost increases.

Table 3.14 shows the distance (km) and unit cost (ruble per hundred barrel) from Samotlor oil field to refineries.

TABLE 3.11

Fixed and Sustainability Cost (Scenario 2)

		Angarsk	Achinsk	Tuapse	Syzran	Kuibyshev	Novokuibyshevsk
Samotlor—large	Fixed cost	189,000	123,000	132,000	151,000	143,000	149,000
	Sustainability cost	139	111	128	119	102	99
Samotlor—small	Fixed cost	129,000	97,000	101,000	139,000	136,000	142,000
	Sustainability cost	113	99	119	107	97	94
Priobskoye—large	Fixed cost	176,000	104,000	128,000	147,000	141,000	145,000
	Sustainability cost	127	102	121	127	111	98
Priobskoye—small	Fixed cost	103,000	89,000	99,000	136,000	133,000	136,000
	Sustainability cost	103	95	111	114	92	95

TABLE 3.12

Transportation Distance and Cost (Scenario 3)

From/To		Angarsk	Achinsk	Tuapse	Syzran	Kuibyshev	Novokuibyshevsk
Samotlor	Distance	1,175	596	1,916	1,171	384	1,127
	Cost	1.73	2.38	1.61	1.77	2.69	1.98
Priobskoye	Distance	876	312	2,058	1,382	178	1,326
	Cost	2.69	4.12	1.96	2.41	4.69	2.48

TABLE 3.13

Fixed and Sustainability Cost (Scenario 3)

		Angarsk	Achinsk	Tuapse	Syzran	Kuibyshev	Novokuibyshevsk
Samotlor—large	Fixed cost	189,000	123,000	132,000	151,000	143,000	149,000
	Sustainability cost	139	111	128	119	102	99
Samotlor—small	Fixed cost	129,000	97,000	101,000	139,000	136,000	142,000
	Sustainability cost	113	99	119	107	97	94
Priobskoye—large	Fixed cost	176,000	104,000	128,000	147,000	141,000	145,000
	Sustainability cost	127	102	121	127	111	98
Priobskoye—small	Fixed cost	103,000	89,000	99,000	136,000	133,000	136,000
	Sustainability cost	103	95	111	114	92	95

TABLE 3.14

Transportation Distance and Cost (Scenario 4)

From/To		Angarsk	Achinsk	Tuapse	Syzran	Kuibyshev	Novokuibyshevsk
Samotlor	Distance	1,175	596	1,916	1,171	384	1,127
	Cost	2.13	2.78	2.01	2.14	3.09	2.38
Priobskoye	Distance	876	312	2,058	1,382	178	1,326
	Cost	2.69	4.12	1.96	2.41	4.69	2.48

TABLE 3.15

Fixed and Sustainability Cost (Scenario 4)

		Angarsk	Achinsk	Tuapse	Syzran	Kuibyshev	Novokuibyshevsk
Samotlor—large	Fixed cost	189,000	123,000	132,000	151,000	143,000	149,000
	Sustainability cost	159	131	148	139	122	119
Samotlor—small	Fixed cost	129,000	97,000	101,000	139,000	136,000	142,000
	Sustainability cost	133	119	139	127	117	114
Priobskoye—large	Fixed cost	176,000	104,000	128,000	147,000	141,000	145,000
	Sustainability cost	127	102	121	127	111	98
Priobskoye—small	Fixed cost	103,000	89,000	99,000	136,000	133,000	136,000
	Sustainability cost	103	95	111	114	92	95

Table 3.15 shows the fixed cost and sustainability cost associated with oil field for scenario 4. Run the scenario with Excel using GRG nonlinear, we obtain the total value is 8.3641E + 11.

3.7.5 Scenario 5

Scenario 5 describes the sustainability level 2 from Samotlor oil field in Russia.

If refinery sustainability level is 2 (medium energy usage consumption), its sustainability cost remains normal. We considered this model as a base model.

Table 3.16 shows the distance (km) and unit cost (ruble per hundred barrel) from Samotlor oil field to refineries.

Table 3.17 shows the fixed cost and sustainability cost associated with oil field for Scenario 4.

Run the scenario with Excel using GRG nonlinear, we obtain the total value is 5.84768E + 11.

3.7.6 Scenario 6

Scenario 6 describes the sustainability level 3 from Samotlor oil field in Russia.

If refinery sustainability level is 3 (low energy usage consumption), its sustainability cost decreases.

Table 3.18 shows the distance (km) and unit cost (ruble per hundred barrel) from Samotlor oil field to refineries.

Table 3.19 shows the fixed cost and sustainability cost associated with oil field for Scenario 6.

Run the scenario with Excel using GRG nonlinear, we obtain the total value is 8.29875E + 11.

3.7.7 Scenario 7

Scenario 7 describes the pipeline quality level 1 for Priobskoye oil field in Russia.

If pipeline quality level is 1 (damaged and causing non-exempt waste), its transportation cost increases.

TABLE 3.16

Transportation Distance and Cost (Scenario 5)

From/To		Angarsk	Achinsk	Tuapse	Syzran	Kuibyshev	Novokuibyshevsk
Samotlor	Distance	1,175	596	1,916	1,171	384	1,127
	Cost	2.13	2.78	2.01	2.14	3.09	2.38
Priobskoye	Distance	876	312	2,058	1,382	178	1,326
	Cost	2.69	4.12	1.96	2.41	4.69	2.48

TABLE 3.17

Fixed and Sustainability Cost (Scenario 5)

		Angarsk	Achinsk	Tuapse	Syzran	Kuibyshev	Novokuibyshevsk
Samotlor—large	Fixed cost	189,000	123,000	132,000	151,000	143,000	149,000
	Sustainability cost	139	111	128	119	102	99
Samotlor—small	Fixed cost	129,000	97,000	101,000	139,000	136,000	142,000
	Sustainability cost	113	99	119	107	97	94
Priobskoye—large	Fixed cost	176,000	104,000	128,000	147,000	141,000	145,000
	Sustainability cost	127	102	121	127	111	98
Priobskoye—small	Fixed cost	103,000	89,000	99,000	136,000	133,000	136,000
	Sustainability cost	103	95	111	114	92	95

TABLE 3.18

Transportation Distance and Cost (Scenario 6)

From/To		Angarsk	Achinsk	Tuapse	Syzran	Kuibyshev	Novokuibyshevsk
Samotlor	Distance	1,175	596	1,916	1,171	384	1,127
	Cost	2.13	2.78	2.01	2.14	3.09	2.38
Priobskoye	Distance	876	312	2,058	1,382	178	1,326
	Cost	2.69	4.12	1.96	2.41	4.69	2.48

TABLE 3.19

Fixed and Sustainability Cost (Scenario 6)

		Angarsk	Achinsk	Tuapse	Syzran	Kuibyshev	Novokuibyshevsk
Samotlor—large	Fixed cost	189,000	123,000	132,000	151,000	143,000	149,000
	Sustainability cost	119	91	108	99	82	79
Samotlor—small	Fixed cost	129,000	97,000	101,000	139,000	136,000	142,000
	Sustainability cost	93	79	99	87	77	74
Priobskoye—large	Fixed cost	176,000	104,000	128,000	147,000	141,000	145,000
	Sustainability cost	127	102	121	127	111	98
Priobskoye—small	Fixed cost	103,000	89,000	99,000	136,000	133,000	136,000
	Sustainability cost	103	95	111	114	92	95

Table 3.20 shows the distance (km) and unit cost (ruble per hundred barrel) from Priobskoye oil field to refineries.

Table 3.21 shows the fixed cost and sustainability cost associated with refinery for Scenario 7.

Run the scenario with Excel using GRG nonlinear, we obtain the total value is 9.17049E + 11.

3.7.8 Scenario 8

Scenario 8 describes the pipeline quality level 2 for Priobskoye oil field in Russia.

If pipeline quality level is 2 (good condition and causing little non-exempt waste), its transportation cost remains standard. We considered this model as a base model.

Table 3.22 shows the distance (km) and unit cost (ruble per hundred barrel) from Priobskoye oil field to refineries.

Table 3.23 shows the fixed cost and sustainability cost associated with refinery for Scenario 8.

Run the scenario with Excel using GRG nonlinear, we obtain the total value is 5.84768E + 11.

3.7.9 Scenario 9

Scenario 9 describes the pipeline quality level 3 for Priobskoye oil field in Russia.

If pipeline quality level is 3 (new condition and not causing non-exempt waste), its transportation cost remains lower than base model.

TABLE 3.20

Transportation Distance and Cost (Scenario 7)

From/To		Angarsk	Achinsk	Tuapse	Syzran	Kuibyshev	Novokuibyshevsk
Samotlor	Distance	1,175	596	1,916	1,171	384	1,127
	Cost	2.13	2.78	2.01	2.17	3.09	2.38
Priobskoye	Distance	876	312	2,058	1,382	178	1,326
	Cost	3.09	4.52	2.36	2.81	5.09	2.88

TABLE 3.21

Fixed and Sustainability Cost (Scenario 7)

		Angarsk	Achinsk	Tuapse	Syzran	Kuibyshev	Novokuibyshevsk
Samotlor—large	Fixed cost	189,000	123,000	132,000	151,000	143,000	149,000
	Sustainability cost	139	111	128	119	102	99
Samotlor—small	Fixed cost	129,000	97,000	101,000	139,000	136,000	142,000
	Sustainability cost	113	99	119	107	97	94
Priobskoye—large	Fixed cost	176,000	104,000	128,000	147,000	141,000	145,000
	Sustainability cost	127	102	121	127	111	98
Priobskoye—small	Fixed cost	103,000	89,000	99,000	136,000	133,000	136,000
	Sustainability cost	103	95	111	114	92	95

TABLE 3.22

Transportation Distance and Cost (Scenario 8)

From/To		Angarsk	Achinsk	Tuapse	Syzran	Kuibyshev	Novokuibyshevsk
Samotlor	Distance	1,175	596	1,916	1,171	384	1,127
	Cost	2.13	2.78	2.01	2.17	309	2.38
Priobskoye	Distance	876	312	2,058	1,382	178	1,326
	Cost	2.69	4.12	1.96	2.41	4.69	2.48

Table 3.24 shows the distance (km) and unit cost (ruble per hundred barrel) from Priobskoye oil field to refineries.

Table 3.25 shows the fixed cost and sustainability cost associated with refinery for Scenario 9.

Run the scenario with Excel using GRG nonlinear, we obtain the total value is 7.49348E + 11.

3.7.10 Scenario 10

Scenario 10 describes the sustainability level 1 from Priobskoye oil field in Russia.

If refinery sustainability level is 1 (high energy usage consumption), its sustainability cost increases.

Table 3.26 shows the distance (km) and unit cost (ruble per hundred barrel) from Priobskoye oil field to refineries.

Table 3.27 shows the fixed cost and sustainability cost associated with oil field for Scenario 10.

Run the scenario with Excel using GRG nonlinear, we obtain the total value is 8.36077E + 11.

3.7.11 Scenario 11

Scenario 11 describes the sustainability level 2 from Priobskoye oil field in Russia.

TABLE 3.23

Fixed and Sustainability Cost (Scenario 8)

		Angarsk	Achinsk	Tuapse	Syzran	Kuibyshev	Novokuibyshevsk
Samotlor—large	Fixed cost	189,000	123,000	132,000	151,000	143,000	149,000
	Sustainability cost	139	111	128	119	102	99
Samotlor—small	Fixed cost	129,000	97,000	101,000	139,000	136,000	142,000
	Sustainability cost	113	99	119	107	97	94
Priobskoye—large	Fixed cost	176,000	104,000	128,000	147,000	141,000	145,000
	Sustainability cost	127	102	121	127	111	98
Priobskoye—small	Fixed cost	103,000	89,000	99,000	136,000	133,000	136,000
	Sustainability cost	103	95	111	114	92	95

TABLE 3.24

Transportation Distance and Cost (Scenario 9)

From/To		Angarsk	Achinsk	Tuapse	Syzran	Kuibyshev	Novokuibyshevsk
Samotlor	Distance	1,175	596	1,916	1,171	384	1,127
	Cost	2.13	2.78	2.01	2.17	3.09	2.38
Priobskoye	Distance	876	312	2,058	1,382	178	1,326
	Cost	2.29	3.72	1.56	2.01	4.29	2.08

TABLE 3.25

Fixed and Sustainability Cost (Scenario 9)

		Angarsk	Achinsk	Tuapse	Syzran	Kuibyshev	Novokuibyshevsk
Samotlor—large	Fixed cost	189,000	123,000	132,000	151,000	143,000	149,000
	Sustainability cost	139	111	128	119	102	99
Samotlor—small	Fixed cost	129,000	97,000	101,000	139,000	136,000	142,000
	Sustainability cost	113	99	119	107	97	94
Priobskoye—large	Fixed cost	176,000	104,000	128,000	147,000	141,000	145,000
	Sustainability cost	127	102	121	127	111	98
Priobskoye—small	Fixed cost	103,000	89,000	99,000	136,000	133,000	136,000
	Sustainability cost	103	95	111	114	92	95

If refinery sustainability level is 2 (medium energy usage consumption), its sustainability cost remains normal. We considered this model as a base model.

Table 3.28 shows the distance (km) and unit cost (ruble per hundred barrel) from Priobskoye oil field to refineries.

Table 3.29 shows the fixed cost and sustainability cost associated with oil field for Scenario 11.

Run the scenario with Excel using GRG nonlinear, we obtain the total value is 5.84768E + 11.

TABLE 3.26

Transportation Distance and Cost (Scenario 10)

From/To		Angarsk	Achinsk	Tuapse	Syzran	Kuibyshev	Novokuibyshevsk
Samotlor	Distance	1,175	596	1,916	1,171	384	1,127
	Cost	2.13	2.78	2.01	2.14	3.09	2.38
Priobskoye	Distance	876	312	2,058	1,382	178	1,326
	Cost	2.69	4.12	1.96	2.41	4.69	2.48

TABLE 3.27

Fixed and Sustainability Cost (Scenario 10)

		Angarsk	Achinsk	Tuapse	Syzran	Kuibyshev	Novokuibyshevsk
Samotlor—large	Fixed cost	189,000	123,000	132,000	151,000	143,000	149,000
	Sustainability cost	139	111	128	119	102	99
Samotlor—small	Fixed cost	129,000	97,000	101,000	139,000	136,000	142,000
	Sustainability cost	113	99	119	107	97	94
Priobskoye—large	Fixed cost	176,000	104,000	128,000	147,000	141,000	145,000
	Sustainability cost	147	122	141	147	131	118
Priobskoye—small	Fixed cost	103,000	89,000	99,000	136,000	133,000	136,000
	Sustainability cost	123	115	131	134	112	115

TABLE 3.28

Transportation Distance and Cost (Scenario 11)

From/To		Angarsk	Achinsk	Tuapse	Syzran	Kuibyshev	Novokuibyshevsk
Samotlor	Distance	1,175	596	1,916	1,171	384	1,127
	Cost	2.13	2.78	2.01	2.14	3.09	2.38
Priobskoye	Distance	876	312	2,058	1,382	178	1,326
	Cost	2.69	4.12	1.96	2.41	4.69	2.48

TABLE 3.29

Fixed and Sustainability Cost (Scenario 11)

		Angarsk	Achinsk	Tuapse	Syzran	Kuibyshev	Novokuibyshevsk
Samotlor—large	Fixed cost	189,000	123,000	132,000	151,000	143,000	149,000
	Sustainability cost	139	111	128	119	102	99
Samotlor—small	Fixed cost	129,000	97,000	101,000	139,000	136,000	142,000
	Sustainability cost	113	99	119	107	97	94
Priobskoye—large	Fixed cost	176,000	104,000	128,000	147,000	141,000	145,000
	Sustainability cost	127	102	121	127	111	98
Priobskoye—small	Fixed cost	103,000	89,000	99,000	136,000	133,000	136,000
	Sustainability cost	103	95	111	114	92	95

3.7.12 Scenario 12

Scenario 12 describes the sustainability level 3 from Priobskoye oil field in Russia.

If refinery sustainability level is 3 (low energy usage consumption), its sustainability cost decreases.

Table 3.30 shows the distance (km) and unit cost (ruble per hundred barrel) from Priobskoye oil field to refineries.

Table 3.31 shows the fixed cost and sustainability cost associated with oil field for Scenario 12.

Run the scenario with Excel using GRG nonlinear, we obtain the total value is 8.30213E + 11.

3.7.13 Scenario 13

Scenario 13 describes the pipeline quality level 1 for Rubiales oil field in Colombia.

If pipeline quality level is 1 (damaged and causing non-exempt waste), its transportation cost increases.

Table 3.32 shows the distance (km) and unit cost (peso per barrel) from Rubiales oil field to refineries.

Table 3.33 shows the fixed cost and sustainability cost associated with refinery for Scenario 13.

Run the scenario with Excel using GRG nonlinear, we obtain the total value is 3.6274E + 8.

3.7.14 Scenario 14

Scenario 14 describes the pipeline quality level 2 for Rubiales oil field in Colombia.

If pipeline quality level is 2 (good condition and causing little non-exempt waste), its transportation cost remains standard. We considered this model as a base model.

TABLE 3.30

Transportation Distance and Cost (Scenario 12)

From/To		Angarsk	Achinsk	Tuapse	Syzran	Kuibyshev	Novokuibyshevsk
Samotlor	Distance	1,175	596	1,916	1,171	384	1,127
	Cost	2.13	2.78	2.01	2.14	3.09	2.38
Priobskoye	Distance	876	312	2,058	1,382	178	1,326
	Cost	2.69	4.12	1.96	2.41	4.69	2.48

TABLE 3.31

Fixed and Sustainability Cost (Scenario 12)

		Angarsk	Achinsk	Tuapse	Syzran	Kuibyshev	Novokuibyshevsk
Samotlor—large	Fixed cost	189,000	123,000	132,000	151,000	143,000	149,000
	Sustainability cost	139	111	128	119	102	99
Samotlor—small	Fixed cost	129,000	97,000	101,000	139,000	136,000	142,000
	Sustainability cost	113	99	119	107	97	94
Priobskoye—large	Fixed Cost	176,000	104,000	128,000	147,000	141,000	145,000
	Sustainability cost	107	82	101	107	91	78
Priobskoye—small	Fixed cost	103,000	89,000	99,000	136,000	133,000	136,000
	Sustainability cost	83	75	91	94	72	75

TABLE 3.32

Transportation Distance and Cost (Scenario 13)

From/To		Barrancabermeja	Cartagena	Apjay	Orito	Tibu
Rubiales	Distance	248	507	86	380	335
	Cost	3.32	2.65	4.95	2.76	2.91
Cano Limon	Distance	300	556	98	315	401
	Cost	2.12	1.94	3.28	2.14	2.43

Table 3.34 shows the distance (km) and unit cost (peso per barrel) from Rubiales oil field to refineries. Table 3.35 shows the fixed cost and sustainability cost associated with refinery for Scenario 14. Run the scenario with Excel using GRG nonlinear, we obtain the total value is 3.4201E + 8.

3.7.15 Scenario 15

Scenario 15 describes the pipeline quality level 3 for Rubiales oil field in Colombia.

If pipeline quality level is 3 (new condition and not causing non-exempt waste), its transportation cost remains lower than base model.

Table 3.36 shows the distance (km) and unit cost (peso per barrel) from Rubiales oil field to refineries. Table 3.37 shows the fixed cost and sustainability cost associated with refinery for Scenario 15. Run the scenario with Excel using GRG nonlinear, we obtain the total value is 3.2398E + 8.

3.7.16 Scenario 16

Scenario 16 describes the sustainability level 1 from Rubiales oil field in Colombia.

If refinery sustainability level is 1 (high energy usage consumption), its sustainability cost increases.

TABLE 3.33

Fixed and Sustainability Cost (Scenario 13)

		Barrancabermeja	Cartagena	Apjay	Orito	Tibu
Rubiales—large	Fixed cost	183,000	188,000	149,000	120,000	131,000
	Sustainability cost	127	114	91	101	106
Rubiales—small	Fixed cost	178,000	185,000	143,000	114,000	129,000
	Sustainability cost	113	109	88	97	97
Cano Limon—large	Fixed cost	165,000	173,000	143,000	116,000	129,000
	Sustainability cost	138	125	86	98	102
Cano Limon—small	Fixed cost	158,000	166,000	136,000	111,000	125,000
	Sustainability cost	124	119	79	95	92

TABLE 3.34

Transportation Distance and Cost (Scenario 14)

From/To		Barrancabermeja	Cartagena	Apjay	Orito	Tibu
Rubiales	Distance	248	507	86	380	335
	Cost	3.14	2.42	4.78	2.59	2.79
Cano Limon	Distance	300	556	98	315	401
	Cost	2.12	1.94	3.28	2.14	2.43

TABLE 3.35

Fixed and Sustainability Cost (Scenario 14)

		Barrancabermeja	Cartagena	Apjay	Orito	Tibu
Rubiales—large	Fixed cost	183,000	188,000	149,000	120,000	131,000
	Sustainability cost	127	114	91	101	106
Rubiales—small	Fixed cost	178,000	185,000	143,000	114,000	129,000
	Sustainability cost	113	109	88	97	97
Cano Limon—large	Fixed cost	165,000	173,000	143,000	116,000	129,000
	Sustainability cost	138	125	86	98	102
Cano Limon—small	Fixed cost	158,000	166,000	136,000	111,000	125,000
	Sustainability cost	124	119	79	95	92

TABLE 3.36

Transportation Distance and Cost (Scenario 15)

From/To		Barrancabermeja	Cartagena	Apjay	Orito	Tibu
Rubiales	Distance	248	507	86	380	335
	Cost	2.99	2.21	4.53	2.46	2.63
Cano Limon	Distance	300	556	98	315	401
	Cost	2.12	1.94	3.28	2.14	2.43

TABLE 3.37

Fixed and Sustainability Cost (Scenario 15)

		Barrancabermeja	Cartagena	Apjay	Orito	Tibu
Rubiales—large	Fixed cost	183,000	188,000	149,000	120,000	131,000
	Sustainability cost	127	114	91	101	106
Rubiales—small	Fixed cost	178,000	185,000	143,000	114,000	129,000
	Sustainability cost	113	109	88	97	97
Cano Limon—large	Fixed cost	165,000	173,000	143,000	116,000	129,000
	Sustainability cost	138	125	86	98	102
Cano Limon—small	Fixed cost	158,000	166,000	136,000	111,000	125,000
	Sustainability cost	124	119	79	95	92

TABLE 3.38

Transportation Distance and Cost (Scenario 16)

From/To		Barrancabermeja	Cartagena	Apjay	Orito	Tibu
Rubiales	Distance	248	507	86	380	335
	Cost	3.14	2.42	4.78	2.59	2.79
Cano Limon	Distance	300	556	98	315	401
	Cost	2.12	1.94	3.28	2.14	2.43

TABLE 3.39

Fixed and Sustainability Cost (Scenario 16)

		Barrancabermeja	Cartagena	Apjay	Orito	Tibu
Rubiales—large	Fixed cost	183,000	188,000	149,000	120,000	131,000
	Sustainability cost	145	131	105	113	117
Rubiales—small	Fixed cost	178,000	185,000	143,000	114,000	129,000
	Sustainability cost	139	124	96	101	104
Cano Limon—large	Fixed cost	165,000	173,000	143,000	116,000	129,000
	Sustainability cost	138	125	86	98	102
Cano Limon—small	Fixed cost	158,000	166,000	136,000	111,000	125,000
	Sustainability cost	124	119	79	95	92

Table 3.38 shows the distance (km) and unit cost (peso per barrel) from Rubiales oil field to refineries. Table 3.39 shows the fixed cost and sustainability cost associated with refinery for Scenario 16. Run the scenario with Excel using GRG nonlinear, we obtain the total value is 3.4796E + 8.

3.7.17 Scenario 17

Scenario 17 describes the sustainability level 2 from Rubiales oil field in Colombia.

If refinery sustainability level is 2 (medium energy usage consumption), its sustainability cost remains normal. We considered this model as a base model.

Table 3.40 shows the distance (km) and unit cost (peso per barrel) from Rubiales oil field to refineries.
Table 3.41 shows the fixed cost and sustainability cost associated with refinery for Scenario 17.
Run the scenario with Excel using GRG nonlinear, we obtain the total value is 3.4201E + 8.

3.7.18 Scenario 18

Scenario 18 describes the sustainability level 3 from Rubiales oil field in Colombia.
If refinery sustainability level is 3 (low energy usage consumption), its sustainability cost decreases.
Table 3.42 shows the distance (km) and unit cost (peso per barrel) from Rubiales oil field to refineries.
Table 3.43 shows the fixed cost and sustainability cost associated with refinery for Scenario 18.
Run the scenario with Excel using GRG nonlinear, we obtain the total value is 3.3942E + 8.

3.7.19 Scenario 19

Scenario 19 describes the pipeline quality level 1 for Cano Limon oil field in Colombia.
If pipeline quality level is 1 (damaged and causing non-exempt waste), its transportation cost increases.
Table 3.44 shows the distance (km) and unit cost (peso per barrel) from Cano Limon oil field to refineries.

TABLE 3.40

Transportation Distance and Cost (Scenario 17)

From/To		Barrancabermeja	Cartagena	Apjay	Orito	Tibu
Rubiales	Distance	248	507	86	380	335
	Cost	3.14	2.42	4.78	2.59	2.79
Cano Limon	Distance	300	556	98	315	401
	Cost	2.12	1.94	3.28	2.14	2.43

TABLE 3.41

Fixed and Sustainability Cost (Scenario 17)

		Barrancabermeja	Cartagena	Apjay	Orito	Tibu
Rubiales—large	Fixed cost	183,000	188,000	149,000	120,000	131,000
	Sustainability cost	127	114	91	101	106
Rubiales—small	Fixed cost	178,000	185,000	143,000	114,000	129,000
	Sustainability cost	113	109	88	97	97
Cano Limon—large	Fixed cost	165,000	173,000	143,000	116,000	129,000
	Sustainability cost	138	125	86	98	102
Cano Limon—small	Fixed cost	158,000	166,000	136,000	111,000	125,000
	Sustainability cost	124	119	79	95	92

TABLE 3.42

Transportation Distance and Cost (Scenario 18)

From/To		Barrancabermeja	Cartagena	Apjay	Orito	Tibu
Rubiales	Distance	248	507	86	380	335
	Cost	3.14	2.42	4.78	2.59	2.79
Cano Limon	Distance	300	556	98	315	401
	Cost	2.12	1.94	3.28	2.14	2.43

Table 3.45 shows the fixed cost and sustainability cost associated with refinery for Scenario 19. Run the scenario with Excel using GRG nonlinear, we obtain the total value is 3.4213E + 8.

3.7.20 Scenario 20

Scenario 20 describes the pipeline quality level 2 for Cano Limon oil field in Colombia.

If pipeline quality level is 2 (good condition and causing little non-exempt waste), its transportation cost remains standard. We considered this model as a base model.

Table 3.46 shows the distance (km) and unit cost (peso per barrel) from Cano Limon oil field to refineries.

TABLE 3.43

Fixed and Sustainability Cost (Scenario 18)

		Barrancabermeja	Cartagena	Apjay	Orito	Tibu
Rubiales—large	Fixed cost	183,000	188,000	149,000	120,000	131,000
	Sustainability cost	119	107	86	97	101
Rubiales—small	Fixed cost	178,000	185,000	143,000	114,000	129,000
	Sustainability cost	109	101	78	89	93
Cano Limon—large	Fixed cost	165,000	173,000	143,000	116,000	129,000
	Sustainability cost	138	125	86	98	102
Cano Limon—small	Fixed cost	158,000	166,000	136,000	111,000	125,000
	Sustainability cost	124	119	79	95	92

TABLE 3.44

Transportation Distance and Cost (Scenario 19)

From/To		Barrancabermeja	Cartagena	Apjay	Orito	Tibu
Rubiales	Distance	248	507	86	380	335
	Cost	3.14	2.42	4.78	2.59	2.79
Cano Limon	Distance	300	556	98	315	401
	Cost	2.31	2.11	3.46	2.43	2.59

TABLE 3.45

Fixed and Sustainability Cost (Scenario 19)

		Barrancabermeja	Cartagena	Apjay	Orito	Tibu
Rubiales—large	Fixed cost	183,000	188,000	149,000	120,000	131,000
	Sustainability cost	127	114	91	101	106
Rubiales—small	Fixed cost	178,000	185,000	143,000	114,000	129,000
	Sustainability cost	113	109	88	97	97
Cano Limon—large	Fixed cost	165,000	173,000	143,000	116,000	129,000
	Sustainability cost	138	125	86	98	102
Cano Limon—small	Fixed cost	158,000	166,000	136,000	111,000	125,000
	Sustainability cost	124	119	79	95	92

TABLE 3.46

Transportation Distance and Cost (Scenario 20)

From/To		Barrancabermeja	Cartagena	Apjay	Orito	Tibu
Rubiales	Distance	248	507	86	380	335
	Cost	3.14	2.42	4.78	2.59	2.79
Cano Limon	Distance	300	556	98	315	401
	Cost	2.12	1.94	3.28	2.14	2.43

Table 3.47 shows the fixed cost and sustainability cost associated with refinery for Scenario 20. Run the scenario with Excel using GRG nonlinear, we obtain the total value is 3.4201E + 8.

3.7.21 Scenario 21

Scenario 21 describes the pipeline quality level 3 for Cano Limon oil field in Colombia.

If pipeline quality level is 3 (new condition and not causing non-exempt waste), its transportation cost remains lower than base model.

Table 3.48 shows the distance (km) and unit cost (peso per barrel) from Cano Limon oil field to refineries.

Table 3.49 shows the fixed cost and sustainability cost associated with refinery for Scenario 21.

Run the scenario with Excel using GRG nonlinear, we obtain the total value is 3.4190E + 8.

3.7.22 Scenario 22

Scenario 22 describes the sustainability level 1 from Cano Limon oil field in Colombia.

If refinery sustainability level is 1 (high energy usage consumption), its sustainability cost increases.

TABLE 3.47

Fixed and Sustainability Cost (Scenario 20)

		Barrancabermeja	Cartagena	Apjay	Orito	Tibu
Rubiales—large	Fixed cost	183,000	188,000	149,000	120,000	131,000
	Sustainability cost	127	114	91	101	106
Rubiales—small	Fixed cost	178,000	185,000	143,000	114,000	129,000
	Sustainability cost	113	109	88	97	97
Cano Limon—large	Fixed cost	165,000	173,000	143,000	116,000	129,000
	Sustainability cost	138	125	86	98	102
Cano Limon—small	Fixed cost	158,000	166,000	136,000	111,000	125,000
	Sustainability cost	124	119	79	95	92

TABLE 3.48

Transportation Distance and Cost (Scenario 21)

From/To		Barrancabermeja	Cartagena	Apjay	Orito	Tibu
Rubiales	Distance	248	507	86	380	335
	Cost	3.14	2.42	4.78	2.59	2.79
Cano Limon	Distance	300	556	98	315	401
	Cost	1.98	1.75	3.02	1.99	2.27

TABLE 3.49

Fixed and Sustainability Cost (Scenario 21)

		Barrancabermeja	Cartagena	Apjay	Orito	Tibu
Rubiales—large	Fixed cost	183,000	188,000	149,000	120,000	131,000
	Sustainability cost	127	114	91	101	106
Rubiales—small	Fixed cost	178,000	185,000	143,000	114,000	129,000
	Sustainability cost	113	109	88	97	97
Cano Limon—large	Fixed cost	165,000	173,000	143,000	116,000	129,000
	Sustainability cost	138	125	86	98	102
Cano Limon—small	Fixed cost	158,000	166,000	136,000	111,000	125,000
	Sustainability cost	124	119	79	95	92

Table 3.50 shows the distance (km) and unit cost (peso per barrel) from Cano Limon oil field to refineries.
Table 3.51 shows the fixed cost and sustainability cost associated with refinery for Scenario 22.
Run the scenario with Excel using GRG nonlinear, we obtain the total value is 3.4204E + 8.

3.7.23 Scenario 23

Scenario 23 describes the sustainability level 2 from Cano Limon oil field in Colombia.

If refinery sustainability level is 2 (medium energy usage consumption), its sustainability cost remains normal. We considered this model as a base model.

Table 3.52 shows the distance (km) and unit cost (peso per barrel) from Cano Limon oil field to refineries.

Table 3.53 shows the fixed cost and sustainability cost associated with refinery for Scenario 23.
Run the scenario with Excel using GRG nonlinear, we obtain the total value is 3.4201E + 8.

3.7.24 Scenario 24

Scenario 24 describes the sustainability level 3 from Cano Limon oil field in Colombia.

If refinery sustainability level is 3 (low energy usage consumption), its sustainability cost decreases.
Table 3.54 shows the distance (km) and unit cost (peso per barrel) from Cano Limon oil field to refineries.
Table 3.55 shows the fixed cost and sustainability cost associated with refinery for Scenario 24.
Run the scenario with Excel using GRG nonlinear, we obtain the total value is 3.4200E + 8.

TABLE 3.50

Transportation Distance and Cost (Scenario 22)

From/To		Barrancabermeja	Cartagena	Apjay	Orito	Tibu
Rubiales	Distance	248	507	86	380	335
	Cost	3.14	2.42	4.78	2.59	2.79
Cano Limon	Distance	300	556	98	315	401
	Cost	2.12	1.94	3.28	2.14	2.43

TABLE 3.51

Fixed and Sustainability Cost (Scenario 22)

		Barrancabermeja	Cartagena	Apjay	Orito	Tibu
Rubiales—large	Fixed cost	183,000	188,000	149,000	120,000	131,000
	Sustainability cost	127	114	91	101	106
Rubiales—small	Fixed cost	178,000	185,000	143,000	114,000	129,000
	Sustainability cost	113	109	88	97	97
Cano Limon—large	Fixed cost	165,000	173,000	143,000	116,000	129,000
	Sustainability cost	151	144	98	112	119
Cano Limon—small	Fixed cost	158,000	166,000	136,000	111,000	125,000
	Sustainability cost	146	135	91	101	105

TABLE 3.52

Transportation Distance and Cost (Scenario 23)

From/To		Barrancabermeja	Cartagena	Apjay	Orito	Tibu
Rubiales	Distance	248	507	86	380	335
	Cost	3.14	2.42	4.78	2.59	2.79
Cano Limon	Distance	300	556	98	315	401
	Cost	2.12	1.94	3.28	2.14	2.43

TABLE 3.53

Fixed and Sustainability Cost (Scenario 23)

		Barrancabermeja	Cartagena	Apjay	Orito	Tibu
Rubiales—large	Fixed cost	183,000	188,000	149,000	120,000	131,000
	Sustainability cost	127	114	91	101	106
Rubiales—small	Fixed cost	178,000	185,000	143,000	114,000	129,000
	Sustainability cost	113	109	88	97	97
Cano Limon—large	Fixed cost	165,000	173,000	143,000	116,000	129,000
	Sustainability cost	138	125	86	98	102
Cano Limon—small	Fixed cost	158,000	166,000	136,000	111,000	125,000
	Sustainability cost	124	119	79	95	92

TABLE 3.54

Transportation Distance and Cost (Scenario 24)

From/To		Barrancabermeja	Cartagena	Apjay	Orito	Tibu
Rubiales	Distance	248	507	86	380	335
	Cost	3.14	2.42	4.78	2.59	2.79
Cano Limon	Distance	300	556	98	315	401
	Cost	2.12	1.94	3.28	2.14	2.43

TABLE 3.55

Fixed and Sustainability Cost (Scenario 24)

		Barrancabermeja	Cartagena	Apjay	Orito	Tibu
Rubiales—large	Fixed cost	183,000	188,000	149,000	120,000	131,000
	Sustainability cost	127	114	91	101	106
Rubiales—small	Fixed cost	178,000	185,000	143,000	114,000	129,000
	Sustainability cost	113	109	88	97	97
Cano Limon—large	Fixed cost	165,000	173,000	143,000	116,000	129,000
	Sustainability cost	131	119	82	91	95
Cano Limon—small	Fixed cost	158,000	166,000	136,000	111,000	125,000
	Sustainability cost	119	107	69	82	83

3.8 Conclusion

There are three expected results from this research:

1. We expected to reject our H_0 with respect to predefined hypothesis that the crude oil supply chain quality and sustainability impact crude oil supply chain costs.
2. We expected the crude oil supply chain quality level to impact the supply chain cost model by more than 15%.
3. We expected the crude oil supply chain sustainability factor to impact the supply chain cost model by more than 15%.

The optimum solution for all the 24 scenarios provides enough information for eight efficiency curves (Figures 3.8–3.15; Tables 3.56–3.64).

TABLE 3.56

Samotlor—Pipeline Quality

Scenario	Quality Level	Total Cost
1	1	9.11117E + 11
2	2 (base)	5.84768E + 11
3	3	7.84129E + 11

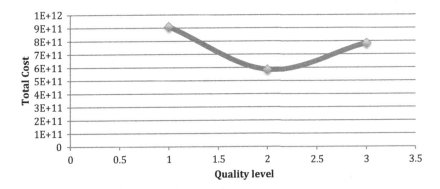

FIGURE 3.8   Samotlor—pipeline quality.

TABLE 3.57

Samotlor—Refinery Sustainability

Scenario	Sustainability Level	Total Cost
4	1	8.3641E + 11
5	2 (base)	5.84768E + 11
6	3	8.29875E + 11

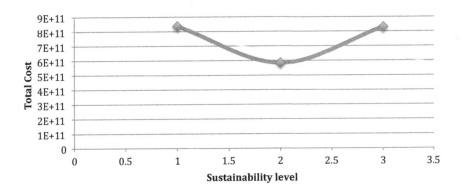

FIGURE 3.9   Samotlor—refinery sustainability.

TABLE 3.58

Priobskoye—Pipeline Quality

Scenario	Quality Level	Total Cost
7	1	9.17049E + 11
8	2 (base)	5.84768E + 11
9	3	7.49348E + 11

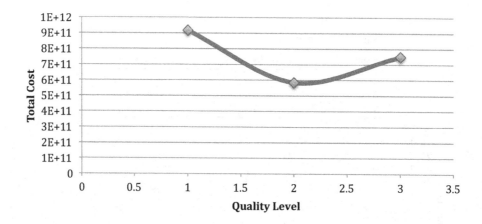

FIGURE 3.10 Priobskoye—pipeline quality.

TABLE 3.59

Priobskoye—Refinery Sustainability

Scenario	Sustainability Level	Total Cost
10	1	8.36077E + 11
11	2 (base)	5.84768E + 11
12	3	8.30213E + 11

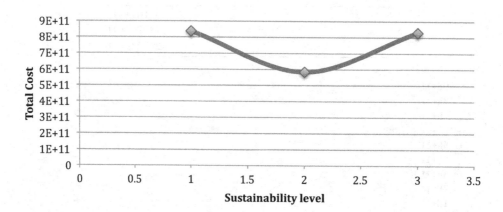

FIGURE 3.11 Priobskoye—refinery sustainability.

TABLE 3.60

Rubiales—Pipeline Quality

Scenario	Quality Level	Total Cost
13	1	3.6274E + 8
14	2 (base)	3.4201E + 8
15	3	3.2398E + 8

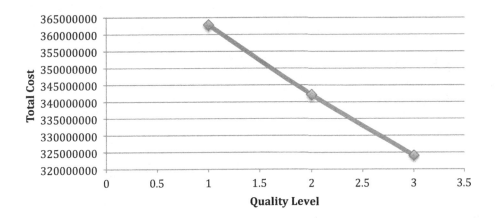

FIGURE 3.12 Rubiales—pipeline quality.

TABLE 3.61

Rubiales—Refinery Sustainability

Scenario	Sustainability Level	Total Cost
16	1	3.4796E + 8
17	2 (base)	3.4201E + 8
18	3	3.3942E + 8

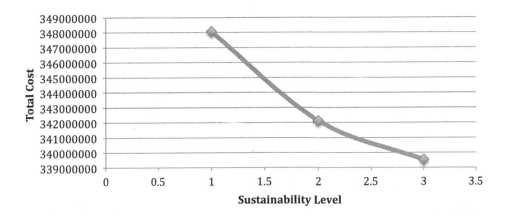

FIGURE 3.13 Rubiales—refinery sustainability.

TABLE 3.62

Cano Limon—Pipeline Quality

Scenario	Quality Level	Total Cost
19	1	3.4212E + 8
20	2 (base)	3.4201E + 8
21	3	3.4190E + 8

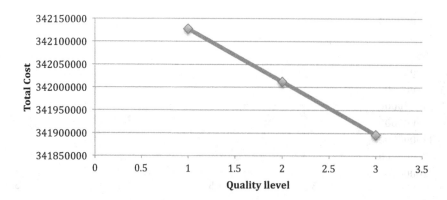

FIGURE 3.14   Cano Limon —pipeline quality.

TABLE 3.63

Cano Limon—Refinery Sustainability

Scenario	Sustainability Level	Total Cost
22	1	$3.4204E + 8$
23	2 (base)	$3.4201E + 8$
24	3	$3.4199E + 8$

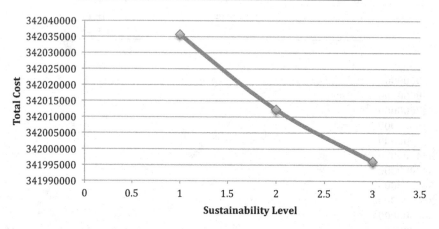

FIGURE 3.15   Cano Limon—refinery sustainability.

TABLE 3.64

Cost Variation by Percentage

	Russia		Colombia	
	Samotlor	**Priobskoye**	**Rubiales**	**Cano Limon**
Pipeline quality	34%	28%	6%	4%
Refinery sustainability	42%	42%	2%	1%

From the above efficiency curves, we have to find cost variation for each case and perform hypothesis testing. In order to reject each hypothesis, the model needed to show that both the pipeline quality and refinery sustainability changed the total supply chain cost by 15%.

Table 3.64 shows cost variation by percentage for Russia and Colombia with respect to pipeline quality and refinery sustainability level.

For Russia, cost variation is more than 15% in both the cases, so we have to reject null hypothesis. In other world, pipeline quality and refinery sustainability will impact the supply chain cost.

For Colombia, cost variation is less than 15% in both the cases, so we fail to reject null hypothesis. In other world, pipeline quality and refinery sustainability will not impact the supply chain cost.

3.8.1 Limitation

There are some expected limitations for this research such as the availability of data and scope of the research. The U.S. EIA provides copious amounts of useful data for the U.S. oil industry. There are certain limitations for the data collection of the Russia and Indonesian oil industry due to lack of information.

3.8.2 Future Work

The importance of the proposed research is a comparison of pipeline quality and environmental sustainability on supply chain cost for Russia and Colombia. The broader impacts of the proposed research are how investments into other countries' crude oil supply chains can be quantified and optimized; exporting countries such as Russia and Colombia can be considered as possible candidates for investment for future global needs.

The scope of this research is to extend the research for Indonesia Oil Supply Chain and use the methodology for Russia and Colombia. This scope is already broad enough considering the nature of supply chain activities on both countries. Future work can be conducted as the continuation of this research, which uses the proposed model that includes other countries and adds more variables as type of oil transportation and some other add-on value factors.

Appendix 3.A: U.S. Petroleum and Other Liquids Production, Estimated Consumption, and Net Imports (1995–2013) (million barrels per day)

Year	Production	Estimated Consumption	Net Imports
1995	9.39989315	17.72458904	8.32469589
1996	9.44454918	18.3089071	8.86435792
1997	9.46093973	18.62030411	9.15936438
1998	9.27800548	18.91714521	9.63913973
1999	8.9934137	19.51933973	10.52592603
2000	9.05777596	19.70107923	10.64330327
2001	8.95700822	19.64870685	10.69169863
2002	8.99843288	19.76130685	10.76287397
2003	8.76583288	20.03350685	11.26767397
2004	8.72242077	20.73115574	12.00873497
2005	8.32468767	20.80215616	12.47746849
2006	8.31616438	20.68741918	12.3712548
2007	8.46932055	20.68038082	12.21106027
2008	8.56359563	19.49796721	10.93437158
2009	9.13379726	18.77139726	9.6376
2010	9.68453151	19.18012877	9.49559726
2011	10.13620821	18.88207397	8.74586576
2012	11.11735507	18.49021585	7.37286078
2013	12.31197483	18.88679944	6.57482461

Source: Preliminary Data U.S. EIA October 2014, web.

Appendix 3.B: U.S. Net Imports of Crude Oil and Petroleum Products from Saudi Arabia, Canada, Russia, and Colombia (2004–2014) (thousand barrels per day)

Year	Net Imports	Saudi Arabia	Canada	Russia	Colombia
2004	12,097	1,557	1,980	298	173
2005	12,549	1,536	2,001	410	188
2006	12,390	1,462	2,194	368	149
2007	12,036	1,483	2,266	413	148
2008	11,114	1,529	2,229	464	181
2009	9,667	1,003	2,257	562	240
2010	9,441	1,096	2,302	612	300
2011	8,450	1,193	2,377	624	371
2012	7,393	1,364	2,530	477	358
2013	6,237	1,326	2,593	460	273
2014	5,041	1,162	2,586	327	174

Source: Preliminary Data U.S. EIA October 2014, web.

Appendix 3.C: Russia Crude Oil Production, Consumption, and Net Exports (1992–2013) (thousand barrels per day)

Year	Crude Oil Production	Consumption	Estimated Net Export
1992	7,631.929	4,423.1588	3,395.5581
1993	6,730	3,750.4598	3,200.5467
1994	6,135	3,178.9824	3,127.8767
1995	5,995	2,976.1331	3,196.3559
1996	5,850	2,619.4548	3,397.1023
1997	5,920	2,562.4824	3,538.608
1998	5,854	2,488.6083	3,581.0568
1999	6,078.948	2,537.6239	3,774.6924
2000	6,479.202	2,578.4981	4,145.1408
2001	6,917	2,590.2318	4,569.503
2002	7,408.173	2,636.4088	5,022.4824
2003	8,132.1988	2,681.8629	5,852.9157
2004	8,804.7077	2,750.8139	6,522.9565
2005	9,043.0822	2,785.1365	6,726.1051
2006	9,247.2055	2,803.4681	6,928.8821
2007	9,437.0634	2,885.101	7,053.0811
2008	9,356.7836	2,981.919	6,893.1139
2009	9,495.3649	2,888.534	7,161.0184
2010	9,694.1145	3,134.8999	7,158.9405
2011	9,773.5178	3,352.108	7,057.955
2012	9,921.6093	3,395.109	7,199.6916
2013	10,053.8438	3,515.143	7,248.5994

Source: U.S. Energy Information Administration.

Appendix 3.D: Colombia Crude Oil Production, Consumption, and Net Exports (1990–2013) (thousand barrels per day)

Year	Crude Oil Production	Consumption	Estimated Net Export
1990	440	208.9058	245.0924
1991	419	209.8785	219.8971
1992	433	232.5302	212.2805
1993	456	240.2192	227.1003
1994	450	244.4073	218.0097
1995	585	250.6331	346.421
1996	622.9645	278.1295	363.924
1997	652	286.5139	378.8357
1998	732.518	289.02	456.9996
1999	816	282	548.194
2000	690.5765	277.4874	426.6286
2001	625	271.1817	365.6424
2002	576.9397	256.1985	332.0776
2003	540.733	265.3557	289.3206
2004	528.7613	267.5158	274.4406
2005	525.7931	270.7081	269.9784
2006	531.0385	276.9701	271.3819
2007	531.1352	270.1889	275.9195
2008	588.3567	265.2192	338.4548
2009	670.6457	259.6515	430.6252
2010	785.5262	269.883	536.0068
2011	914.2544	294.2727	644.2705
2012	944.2186	304	665.0549
2013	1,003.2463	306	722.4737

Source: U.S. Energy Information Administration.

REFERENCES

Achebe, C.H. Analysis of oil pipeline failure in oil and gas industries in the Niger delta area of Nigeria. www.iaeng.org/publications.

Agbaeze, K.N. Petroleum pipe leakages PPMC report for chief officers mandatory courses. 026 Lagos (2000).

Austria. Organization of the petroleum exporting countries (OPEC). World Oil Outlook 2012. Vienna: WOO. Web. (2012).

BERA Journal, issue 5/6: Winter 2005/Spring 2006 Updated July 2013 (www.loc.gov/rr/business/BERA/issue5/transportation.html).

Bjorklund, M., et al. Performance measurements in the greening of supply chains. *Supply Chain Management: An International Journal*, 17, No. 1, 29–39, 2012.

Blackburn, J. Designing and managing sustainable closed-loop supply chains. Ongoing project funded by the National Science Foundation (NSF). Award Abstract: 0531661. 1 July 2005–31 December 2005.

Bozon, I. Uncertainty and volatility in today's energy system: Stability, security, and sustainability through mutual interdependence. *Journal of Petroleum Technology*, 47, March 2006.

Chima, C.M. Supply-chain management issues in the oil and gas industry. *Journal of Business and Economic Research*, 5, No. 6, 27–36, June 2007.

Chopra, S., and Meindl, P. *Supply Chain Management: Strategy, Planning, & Operation*. Upper Saddle River, NJ: Prentice Hall, 2007.

Colombia's Oil Production Company. www.ecopetrol.com.

Gray, B., Jones, E., Weatheron, Y., Sunarto, R., and Armstrong, H. Utilizing pipeline quality and facility sustainability to optimize crude oil supply chains. *International Journal of Supply Chain Management*, 2, 9–16, December 2013.

Herran, A., et al. A mathematical model for planning transportation of multiple petroleum products in a multipipeline system. *Computers & Chemical Engineering*, 34, 401–413, 2010.

Hong, W. Optimal sampling plans in supply chains with endogenous product quality. Ongoing project funded by the National Science Foundation (NSF). Award Abstract: 1030233. 15 August 2010–31 July 2013.

Hussain, R., Assavapokee, T., and Khumawala, B. Supply chain management in the petroleum industry: Challenges and opportunities. *International Journal of Global Logistics & Supply Chain Management*, 1, 2, 90–97, November 1, 2006.

LUKoil to lose the lead soon. Rosneft will become Russia's leading oil producer in 2007, Analytical department of RIA RosBusinessConsulting.

Meixell, M.J. and Gargeya, V.B. Global supply chain design: A literature review and critique, transportation research Part E. *Logistics and Transportation Review*, 41, 531–550, 2005.

MirHassani, S.A. An operational planning model for petroleum products logistics under uncertainty. *Applied Mathematics and Computation*, 196, 744–751, 2008.

MirHassani, S.A., and Ghorbanalizadeh, M. The multiproduct pipeline scheduling system. *Applied Mathematics and Computation*, 56, 891–897, 2008.

Moffat, D., and Linden, O. Perception and reality: Assessing priorities for sustainable development in the Niger Delta, AMBIO. *Journal of Human Environment*, 24, Nos. 7–8, 527–538, 1995.

Muriel, A., and Simchi-Levi, D. *Supply Chain Design and Planning - Applications of Optimization Techniques for Strategic and Tactical Models*. North Holland: Design, Coordination and Operation, 2004.

Pirog, R. *The Role of National Oil Companies in the International Oil Market*. Washington, DC: Congressional Research Service (CRS), pp. 1–17, 21 August 2007.

Platts, K.W., and Song, N. Overseas sourcing decisions – The total cost of sourcing from China. *Supply Chain Management: An International Journal*, 15, No. 4, 320–331, 2010.

Rejowski, R., and Pinto, J.M. A novel continuous time representation for scheduling of pipeline systems with pumping yield rate constraints. *Computers & Chemical Engineering*, 32, 1042–1066, 2008.

Rejowski, R., and Pinto, J.M. An MILP formulation for the scheduling of multiproduct pipeline systems. *Brazilian Journal of Chemical Engineering*, 19, 467–474, 2002.

Rejowski, R., and Pinto, J.M. Efficient MILP formulations and valid cuts for multiproduct pipeline scheduling. *Computers & Chemical Engineering*, 28, 1511–1528, 2004.

Rejowski, R., and Pinto, J.M. Scheduling of a multiproduct pipeline systems. *Computers & Chemical Engineering*, 27, 1229–1246, 2003.

Reynolds, L. Seven dangerous (and surprising) side effects of the U.S. Dependency on Foreign Oil. The American Surveyor: A Foot in the Past … An Eye to the Future. 4 August 2010: 1.

Rodrigo, B.F., et al. Multi-objective stochastic supply chain modeling to evaluate tradeoffs between profit and quality. *International Journals Production Economics*, 127, 292–299, 2010.

Russia's Oil Production Company. Rosneft. www.rosneft.com.

Russia's Oil Transportation Corporation. www.transneft.com.

Russian Oil Output Climbed 1.2 Percent in 2009 Bloomberg Retrieved on 2 January 2010.

Sanchez, C.M., and McKinley, W. Environmental regulatory influence and product innovation: The contingency effects of organizational characteristics. *Journal of Engineering and Technology Management*, 15, No. 4, 257–278, 1998.

Shapiro, J.F. *Modeling the Supply Chain*. Belmont: Thomson Higher Education, 2007.

Szidarovszky, F., et al. *Techniques for Multi-Objective Decision Making in Systems Management*. 1st Ed. Vol. 2. West Lafayette: Elsevier, 1986.

Trench, C.J. How pipelines make the oil market work – Their networks, operation and regulation. Association of Oil Pipe Lines and American Petroleum Institute Pipeline Committee. (2001): 1–20.

UN Documents, *Our Common Future*, Chapter 2: Towards sustainable development, www.un-documents.net/ocf-02.htm, 13-02-2013.

United States. E-Tech International. *Overview of the Oil and Gas Exploration and Production Process.* New Mexico: Environmental Management in Oil and Gas Exploration and Production, 2012.

United States. Environmental Protection Agency (EPA). *Exemption of Oil and Gas Exploration and Production Wastes from Federal Hazardous Waste Regulation.* Washington: Oil Pipeline, 1993.

United States. The American Petroleum Institute (API). *Pipeline 101.* Washington: Crude Oil, 2010.

United States. The American Petroleum Institute (API). *Understanding Today's Crude Oil and Product Markets.* Washington: Crude Oil, 2006.

United States. The American Petroleum Institute (API). *Voluntary Sustainability Reporting Guidance 2010.* Washington: Environmental Performance, 2012.

United States. The National Energy Education Development (NEED) Project. *Petroleum.* Virginia: Petroleum, 2012.

United States. U.S. Energy Information Administration (U.S.EIA). *Indonesia.* Washington: Frequently Asked Questions, 2012.

United States. U.S. Energy Information Administration (U.S.EIA). *Oil: Crude and Petroleum Products Explained.* Washington: GPO, 2012.

United States. U.S. Energy Information Administration (U.S.EIA). *OPEC Countries.* Washington: Frequently Asked Questions, 2012.

United States. U.S. Energy Information Administration (U.S.EIA). *PADD Regions Enable Regional Analysis of Petroleum Product Supply and Movement.* Washington: Frequently Asked Questions, 2012.

United States. U.S. Energy Information Administration (U.S.EIA). *What are the Major Sources and Users of Energy in the United States?* Washington: Frequently Asked Questions, 2012.

United States. U.S. Energy Information Administration (U.S.EIA). *What are the Products and Uses of Petroleum?* Washington: Frequently Asked Questions, 2012.

United States. U.S. Energy Information Administration (U.S.EIA). *World Oil Transit Chokepoints.* Washington: Frequently Asked Questions, 2012.

Unites states. U.S. Energy Information Administration (U.S. EIA). Russia Analysis brief, 2014.

Unites states. U.S. Energy Information Administration (U.S. EIA). Colombia Analysis brief, 2014.

Van den Heever, S.A., and Grossmann, I.E. An iterative aggregation/disaggregation approach for the solution of a mixed-integer non linear oil field infrastructure planning model. *Industrial & Engineering Chemistry Research*, 39, 1955–1971, 2000.

Varna, S., Wadhwa, S., and Deshmukh, S.G. Evaluating petroleum supply chain performance: Application of analytical hierarchy process to balanced scorecard. *Asia Pacific Journal of Marketing and Logistics*, 20, 3, 343–356, 2008.

What is Crude Oil? A Detailed Explanation on this Essential Fossil Fuel by Editorial dept. July 24, 2009) (www.oilprice.com).

Part 2

Basic Knowledge for Global Supply Chain Engineering

4

Forecasting in Global Supply Chain Engineering

If you can't describe what you are doing in a process you don't know what you are doing.

W. Edwards Deming

4.1 Forecasting

Forecasting is the process of predicting the future. The two functional areas of the firm that make the most use of forecasting methods are marketing and production. Marketing typically forecasts sales for both new and existing product lines. Sales forecasts are used by the production department for operations planning. Can all events be accurately forecasted? The answer is clearly no. Games of chance played at casinos are random. By tipping the probabilities in its favor, the house is always guaranteed to win over the long term. There is evidence that daily prices of stocks follow a purely random process, much like a coin-flipping experiment. Studies have shown that professional money managers rarely outperform stock portfolios generated purely at random. In production and operations management, we are primarily interested in forecasting product demand. Because demand is likely to be random in most circumstances, can forecasting methods provide any value? In most cases, the answer is yes. Although some portions of the demand process may be unpredictable, other portions may be predictable. Trends, cycles, and seasonal variation may be present, all of which give us an advantage over trying to predict the outcome of a coin toss. In this chapter, we consider methods for predicting future values of a series based on past observations.

4.1.1 The Time Horizon in Forecasting

We may classify forecasting problems along several dimensions. One is the time horizon. Figure 4.1 is a schematic showing the three time horizons associated with forecasting and typical forecasting problems encountered in operations planning associated with each. Short-term forecasting is crucial for day-to-day planning. Short-term forecasts, typically measured in days or weeks, are required for inventory management, production plans that may be derived from a materials requirement planning system, and resource requirements planning. Shift scheduling may require forecasts of workers' availabilities and preferences.

The immediate term is measured in weeks or months. Sales patterns for product families, requirements and availabilities of workers, and resource requirements are typical intermediate-term forecasting problems encountered in operations management.

Long-term production and manufacturing decisions are part of the firm's overall manufacturing strategy. One example is long-term planning of capacity needs. When demands are expected to increase, the firm must plan for the construction of new facilities and/or the retrofitting of existing facilities with new technologies. Capacity planning decisions may require downsizing in some circumstances.

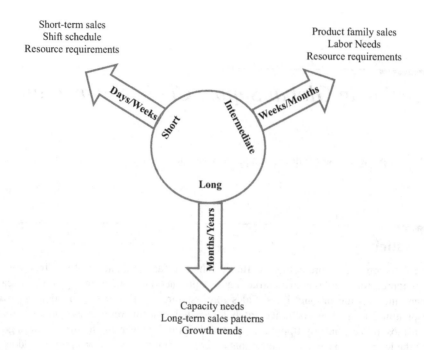

FIGURE 4.1   Forecast horizons in operations planning.

4.1.2 Characteristics of Forecasts

1. *They are usually wrong.* Resource requirements and production schedules may require modifications if the forecast of demand proves to be inaccurate. The planning system should be sufficiently robust to be able to react to unanticipated forecast errors.

2. *A good forecast is more than a single number.* A good forecast also includes some measure of the anticipated forecast error. This could be in the form of a range or an error measure such as the variance of the distribution of the forecast error.

3. *Aggregate forecasts are more accurate.* Recall from statistics that the variance of the average of a collection of independent identically distributed random variables is lower than the variance of each of the random variables; that is, the variance of the sample mean is smaller than the population variance. This same phenomenon is true in forecasting as well. On a percentage basis, the error made in forecasting sales for an entire product line is generally less than the error made in forecasting sales for an individual item.

4. The longer the forecast horizon, the less accurate the forecast will be.

5. *Forecasts should not be used to the exclusion of known information.* A particular technique may result in reasonably accurate forecasts in most circumstances. However, there may be information available concerning the future demand that is not presented in the past history of the series.

4.1.3 Subjective Forecasting Models

We classify forecasting methods as either **subjective** or **objective**. A subjective forecasting method is based on human judgment. There are several techniques for soliciting opinions for forecasting purposes.

1. *Sales force composites.* In forecasting product demand, a good source of subjective information is the company sales force. The sales force has direct contact with consumers and is therefore in a good position to see changes in their preferences. To develop a sales force composite forecast, members of the sales force submit sales estimates of the products they will sell in the coming

year. These estimates might be individual numbers or several numbers, such as pessimistic, most likely, and optimistic estimates. Sales managers would then be responsible for aggregating individual estimates to arrive at overall forecasts for each geographic region or product group. Sales force composites may be inaccurate when compensation of sales personnel is based on meeting a quota. In that case, there is more clearly an incentive for the sales force to lowball its estimates.

2. *Customer surveys.* Customer surveys can signal future trends and shifting preference patterns. To be effective, however, surveys and sampling plans must be carefully designed to guarantee that the resulting data are statistically unbiased and representative of the customer base. Poorly designed questionnaires or an invalid sampling scheme may result in the wrong conclusions.

3. *Jury of executive opinion.* When there is no past history, with new products, expert opinion may be the only source of information for preparing forecasts. For new product planning, opinions of personnel in the functional areas of marketing, finance, and production should be solicited. Combining individual forecasts may be done in several ways. One is to have the individual responsible for preparing the forecast interview. The executives directly develop a forecast for the results of the interviews. Another is to require the executives to meet as a group and come to a consensus.

4. *The Delphi method.* The Delphi method, like the jury of executive opinion method, is based on soliciting the opinions of experts. The difference lies in the manner in which individual opinions are combined. This method attempts to eliminate some of the inherent shortcomings of group dynamics, in which the personalities of some group members overshadow those of other members. This method requires a group of experts to express their opinions, preferably by individual sample survey. The opinions are then compiled, and a summary of the results is returned to the experts, with special attention to these opinions that are significantly different from the group averages. The experts are asked if they wish to reconsider their original opinions in light of the group response. The process is repeated until (ideally) an overall group consensus is reached. This method has advantages and disadvantages. Its primary advantage is that it provides a means of assessing individual opinion without the usual concerns of personal interactions. On the negative side, the method is highly sensitive to the care in the formulation of the questionnaire. Because discussions are intentionally excluded from the process, the experts have no mechanism for resolving ambiguous questions. Furthermore, it is not necessarily true that a group consensus will ever be reached.

4.1.4 Objective Forecasting Methods

Objective forecasting methods are those in which the forecast is derived from an analysis of data. A **time series** method is one that uses only past values of the phenomenon we are predicting. **Causal models** are ones that use data from sources other than the series being predicted; that is, there may be other variables with values that are *linked* in some way to what is being forecasted. We discuss these first.

4.1.5 Causal Models

Let Y represent the phenomenon we wish to forecast and $X_1, X_2, ..., X_n$ be n variables that we believe to be related to Y. Then the causal model is one in which the forecast for Y is some function of these variables, say

$$Y = f(X_1, X_2, ..., X_n).$$

Econometric models are special causal models in which the relationship between Y and $(X_1, X_2, ..., X_n)$ is linear. That is,

$$Y = \alpha_0 + \alpha_1 X_1 + \alpha_2 X_2 + \cdots + \alpha_n X_n$$

for some constants $(\alpha_1, ..., \alpha_n)$. The method of least squares is most commonly used to find estimators for the constants.

Let us consider a simple example of a causal forecasting model. A realtor is trying to estimate his income for the succeeding year. In the past, he has found that his income is close to being proportional to the total number of housing sales in his territory. He also has noticed that there has typically been a close relationship between housing sales and interest rates for home mortgages. He might construct a model for the form

$$Y_t = \alpha_0 + \alpha_1 X_{t-1},$$

where Y is the number of sales in year t and X_{t-1} is the interest rate in year $t-1$. Based on past data, he would then determine the least squares estimators are currently $\alpha_0 = 385.7$ and $\alpha_1 = -1.878$. Hence, the estimated relationship between home sales and mortgage rates is

$$Y_t = 385.7 - 1.878 X_{t-1},$$

where X_{t-1}, the previous year's interest rate, is expressed as a decimal. Then, if the current mortgage interest rate is 10%, the model would predict that the number of sales the following year in his territory would be $385.7 - 187.8 = 197.9$ or about 198 houses sold.

Causal models of this type are common for predicting economic phenomena such as the GNP (gross national product) and the GDP (gross domestic product). Both MIT and the Wharton School of Business at the University of Pennsylvania have developed large-scale econometric models for making these predictions. Econometric prediction models are typically used by the economics and finance arms of the firm to forecast values of macroeconomic variables. Time series methods are more commonly used for operations planning applications.

4.1.6 Time Series Methods

Time series methods are often called naïve methods, as they require no information other than the past values of the variable being predicted. *Time series* is just a fancy term for a collection of observations of some economic or physical phenomenon drawn at discrete points in time, usually equally spaced. The idea is that information can be inferred from the pattern of past observations and can be used to forecast future values of the series.

In time series analysis, we attempt to isolate the patterns that arise most often. These include the following:

1. *Trend.* Trend refers to the tendency of a time series to exhibit a stable pattern of growth or decline. We distinguish between linear trend (the pattern described by a straight line) and non-linear trend (the pattern described by a nonlinear function, such as a quadratic or exponential curve). When the pattern of trend is not specified, it is generally understood to be linear.

2. *Seasonality.* A seasonal pattern is one that repeats at fixed intervals. In time series, we generally think of the pattern repeating every year, although daily, weekly, and monthly seasonal patterns are common as well. Fashion wear, ice cream, and heating oil exhibit a yearly seasonal pattern. Consumption of electricity exhibits a strong daily seasonal pattern.

3. *Cycles.* Cyclic variation is similar to seasonality, except that the length and the magnitude of the cycle may vary. One associates cycles with long-term economic variations (i.e., business cycles) that may be present in addition to seasonal fluctuations.

4. *Randomness.* A pure random series is one in which there is no recognizable pattern to the data. One can generate patterns purely at random that often appear to have structure. An example of this is the methodology of stock market chartists who impose forms on random patterns of stock market price data. On the other side of the coin, data that appear to be random could have a very definite structure. Truly random data that fluctuate around a fixed mean form what is called a horizontal pattern (Figure 4.2).

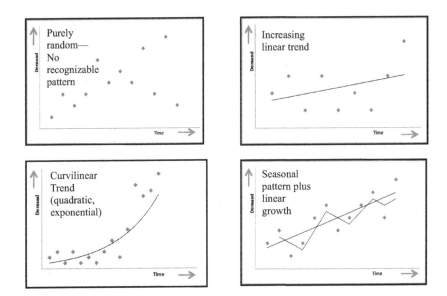

FIGURE 4.2   Time series patterns.

4.1.7 Notation Conventions

Define $D_1, D_2, ..., D_t, ...$ as the observed values of demand during periods 1, 2, ..., t, ... We will assume throughout that $(D_t, t \geq 1)$ is the time series we would like to predict. Furthermore, we will assume that if we are forecasting in period t, then we have observed $D_t, D_{t-1}, ...$ but have not observed D_{t+1}.

Define F_t as the forecast made *for* period t in period $t - 1$. That is, it is the forecast made at the end of period $t - 1$ after having observed $D_{t-1}, D_{t-2}, ...$ but before observing D_t. For now, we will assume that forecasts are one-step-ahead forecasts; that is, they are made for the demand in the next period.

Finally, note that a time series forecast is obtained by applying some set of weights to past data. That is,

$$F_t = \sum_{i=0}^{\infty} \propto_n D_{t-n}$$

4.1.8 Evaluating Forecasts

Define the forecast error in period t, e_t, as the difference between the forecast value for that period and the actual demand for that period. For multiple-step-ahead forecasts,

$$e_t = F_{t-\tau,t} - D_t,$$

and for one-step-ahead forecasts,

$$e_t = F_t - D_t$$

Let $e_1, e_2, ..., e_n$ be the forecast errors observed over n periods. Two common measures of forecast accuracy during these n periods are the mean absolute deviation (MAD) and the mean squared error (MSE), given by the following formulas:

$$\text{MAD} = (1/n) \sum_{i=1}^{n} |e_i|$$

$$\text{MSE} = (1/n)\sum_{i=1}^{n} e_i^{2}$$

Note that the MSE is similar to the variance of a random sample. The MAD is often the preferred method of measuring the forecast error because it does not require squaring. Furthermore, when forecast errors are normally distributed, as is generally assumed, an estimate of the standard deviation of the forecast error, σ_e, is given by 1.25 times the MAD.

Though the MAD and the MSE are the two most common measures of forecast accuracy, other measures are used as well. One that is not dependent on the magnitude of the values of demand is known as the mean absolute percentage error (MAPE) and is given by the formula

$$\text{MAPE} = \left[\left(\frac{1}{n}\right)\sum_{i=1}^{n}\left|\frac{e_i}{D_t}\right|\right] \times 100$$

A desirable property of forecasts is that they should be unbiased. Mathematically, that means that $E(e_i) = 0$. One way of tracking a forecast method is to graph the values of the forecast error e_i over time. If the method is unbiased, forecast errors should fluctuate randomly above and below zero. An example is presented in Figure 4.3.

An alternative to a graphical method is to compute the cumulative sum of the forecast errors, $\sum e_i$. If the value of this sum deviates too far from zero (either above or below), it is an indication that the forecasting method is biased. Statistical control charts also are used to identify unusually large values of the forecast error.

4.1.9 Methods for Forecasting Stationary Series

In this section, we will discuss two popular techniques, moving averages and exponential smoothing, for forecasting stationary time series. A stationary time series is one in which each observation can be represented by a constant plus a random fluctuation. In symbols,

$$D_t = \mu + \varepsilon_t,$$

where μ is an unknown constant corresponding to the mean of the series and ε_t is a random error with mean zero and variance σ^2.

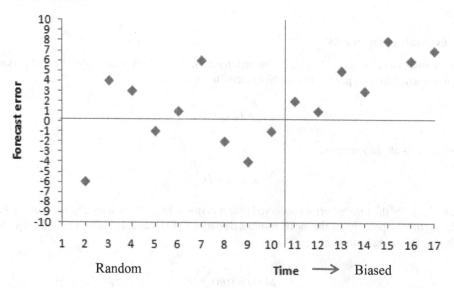

FIGURE 4.3 Forecast errors over time.

The methods we consider in this section are more precisely known as single or simple exponential smoothing and single or simple moving averages. In addition, single moving averages also include weighted moving averages, which we do not discuss. For convenience, we will not use the modifiers *single* and *simple* in what follows. The meaning of the terms will be clear from the context.

4.1.9.1 Moving Averages

A simple but popular forecasting method is the method of moving averages. A moving average of order N is simply the arithmetic average of the most recent N observations. For the time being, we restrict attention to one-step-ahead forecasts. Then F_t, the forecast made in period $t-1$ for period t, is given by

$$F_t = (1/N) \sum_{i=t-N}^{t-1} D_i = \left(\frac{1}{N}\right)(D_{t-1} + D_{t-2} + \cdots + D_{t-N})$$

In words, this says that the mean of the N most recent observations is used as the forecast for the next period. We will use the notation MA(N) for N-period moving averages.

An apparent disadvantage of the moving-average technique is that one must recompute the average of the last N observations each time a new demand observation becomes available. For a large N, this could be tedious. However, recalculation of the full N-period average is not necessary every period, since

$$F_{t+1} = (1/N) \sum_{i=t-N+1}^{t} D_i = \left(\frac{1}{N}\right)\left[D_t + \sum_{i=t-N+1}^{t} D_i + D_{t-N}\right]$$

$$= F_t + (1/N)[D_t - D_{t-N}]$$

This means that for one-step-ahead forecasting, we need only to compute the difference between the most recent demand and the demand of N periods old in order to update the forecast. However, we still need to keep track of all N past observations. Why?

4.1.9.2 Moving Average Lags Behind the Trend

Consider a demand process in which there is a definite trend. For example, suppose that the observed demand is 2, 4, 6, 8, 10, 12, 14, 16, 18, 20, 22, 24. Consider the one-step-ahead MA(3) and MA(6) forecasts for:

Period	Demand	MA(3)	MA(6)
1	2		
2	4		
3	6		
4	8	4	
5	10	6	
6	12	8	
7	14	10	7
8	16	12	9
9	18	14	11
10	20	16	13
11	22	18	15
12	24	20	17

The demand and the forecasts for the respective periods are pictured in Figure 4.4. Notice that both the MA(3) and the MA(6) forecasts lag behind the trend.

MA(6) has a greater lag. This implies that the use of simple moving averages is not an appropriate forecasting method when there is a trend in the series.

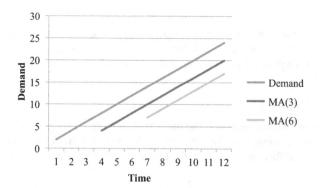

FIGURE 4.4 Moving average forecasts lag behind the trend.

4.1.9.3 Exponential Smoothing

Another very popular forecasting method for stationary time series is exponential smoothing. The current forecast is the weighted average of the last forecast and the current value of demand. That is,

New forecast = α(Current observation of demand) + $(1 - \alpha)$ (Last forecast).

In symbols,

$$F_t = \alpha D_{t-1} + (1 - \alpha)F_{t-1},$$

where $0 < \alpha \leq 1$ is the smoothing constant, which determines the relative weight placed on the current observation of demand. Interpret $(1 - \alpha)$ as the weight placed on past observations of demand. By a simple rearrangement of terms, the exponential smoothing equation for F_t can be written as

$$F_t = F_{t-1} - \alpha\left(F_{t-1} - D_{t-1}\right)$$
$$= F_{t-1} - \alpha e_{t-1}$$

Written this way, we see that exponential smoothing can be interpreted as follows: the forecast in any period t is the forecast in period $t - 1$ minus some fraction of the observed forecast error in period $t - 1$. Notice that if we forecast high in period $t - 1$, e_{t-1} is positive and the adjustment is to decrease the forecast. Similarly, if we forecast low in period $t - 1$, the error is negative, and the adjustment is to increase the current forecast.

As before, F_t is the one-step-ahead forecast for period t made in period $t - 1$. Notice that since

$$F_t = \alpha D_{t-1} + (1 - \alpha)F_{t-1},$$

we can substitute the above to obtain

$$F_t = \alpha D_{t-1} + \alpha(1 - \alpha)D_{t-2} + (1 - \alpha)^2 F_{t-2}$$

We can now substitute for F_{t-2} in the same fashion. If we continue in this way, we obtain the infinite expansion for F_t

$$F_t = \sum_{i=0}^{\infty} \alpha(1 - \alpha)^i D_{t-i-1} = \sum_{i=0}^{\infty} \alpha_i D_{t-i-1},$$

where the weights are $\alpha_0 > \alpha_1 > \alpha_2 > \cdots > \alpha_i = \alpha(1 - \alpha)^i$, and

$$\sum_{i=0}^{\infty} \alpha_i = \sum_{i=0}^{\infty} \alpha(1-\alpha)^i = \alpha \sum_{i=0}^{\infty} (1-\alpha)^i = \alpha \times \frac{1}{1[1-(1-\alpha)]} = 1$$

Hence, exponential smoothing applies a declining set of weights to all past data.

In fact, we could fit the continuous exponential curve $g(i) = \alpha \exp(-\alpha i)$ to these weights, which is why the method is called exponential smoothing. The smoothing constant α plays essentially the same role here as the value of N does in moving averages. If α is large, more weight is placed on the current observation of demand and less weight on past observations, which results in forecasts that will react quickly to changes in the demand pattern but may have much greater variation from period to period. If α is small, then more weight is placed on past data and the forecasts are more stable.

When using an automatic forecasting technique to predict demand for a production applications table, forecasts (i.e., forecasts that do not vary a great deal from period to period) are very desirable. Demand forecasts are used as the starting point for production planning and scheduling. Substantial revision in these forecasts can wreak havoc with employee work schedules, component bills of materials, and external purchase orders. For this reason, a value of α between 0.1 and 0.2 is generally recommended for chase orders.

Notice that the exponential smoothing equation also can be written in the form

$$F_t = F_{t-1} - \alpha \left(F_{t-1} - D_{t-1} \right) = F_{t-1} - \alpha e_{t-1}$$

In this form, we see that exponential smoothing adjusts the previous forecast by a fraction of the previous forecast error to obtain the current forecast.

Multiple-step-ahead forecasts are handled the same way for simple exponential smoothing as for moving averages; that is, the one-step-ahead and the multiple-step-ahead forecasts are the same.

The derivation of the mean and variance can be found of the forecast error for both moving averages and exponential smoothing in terms of the variance of each individual observation, assuming that the underlying demand process is stationary. This derivation demonstrates that both methods are unbiased; that is, the expected value of the forecast error is zero. Furthermore, by equating the expressions for the variances of the forecast error, one obtains the same relationship between α and N as by equating the average age of data. This means that if both exponential smoothing and moving averages are used to predict the same stationary demand pattern, forecast errors are normally distributed, and $\alpha = 2/(N+1)$, then both methods will have exactly the same distribution of forecast errors. (However, this does not mean that the forecasts obtained by the two methods are the same.)

4.1.9.4 Multiple-Step-Ahead Forecasts

Thus far, we have talked only about one-step-ahead forecasts. That is, we have assumed that a forecast in period t is for the demand in period $t + 1$. However, there are cases where we are interested in making a forecast for more than one step ahead. For example, a retailer planning for the Christmas season might need to make a forecast for December sales in June in order to have enough time to prepare. Since the underlying model assumed for both moving averages and exponential smoothing is stationary (i.e., not changing in time), the one-step-ahead and multiple-step-ahead forecasts for moving averages and exponential smoothing are the same. That is, a forecast made in June for July sales is the same as a forecast made in June for December sales. (In the case of the retailer, the assumption of stationarity would probably be wrong, since December sales would likely be greater than a typical month's sales. That would suggest that these methods would *not* be appropriate in this case.)

4.1.9.5 Comparison of Exponential Smoothing and Moving Averages

There are several similarities and several differences between exponential smoothing and moving averages.

4.1.9.5.1 Similarities

1. Both methods are derived with the assumption that the underlying demand process is stationary (i.e., it can be represented by a constant plus a random fluctuation with zero mean).
2. Both methods depend on the specification of a single parameter. For moving averages, the parameter is N, the number of periods in the moving average, and for exponential smoothing the parameter is α, the smoothing constant. Small values of N or large values of α result in forecasts that put greater weight on current data, and large values of N and small values of α put greater weight on past data. Small N and large α may be more responsive to changes in the demand process but will result in forecast errors with higher variance.
3. Both methods will lag behind a trend if one exists.
4. When $\alpha = 2/(N + 1)$, both methods have the same distribution of forecast error. This means that they should have roughly the same level of accuracy, but it does *not* mean that they will give the same forecasts.

4.1.9.5.2 Differences

1. The exponential smoothing forecast is a weighted average of *all* past data points (as long as the smoothing constant is strictly less than 1). The moving-average forecast is a weighted average of only the last N periods of data. This can be an important advantage of moving averages. An outlier (an observation that is not representative of the sample population) is washed out of the moving-average forecast N periods but remains forever in the exponential smoothing forecast.
2. In order to use moving averages, one must save all N past data points. In order to use exponential smoothing, one need only save the last forecast. This is the most significant advantage of the exponential smoothing method and one reason for its popularity in practice. This issue is less important today than it has been, as the cost of information storage has decreased enormously in recent years. However, it is still easier to manage a system that requires less data. It is primarily for this reason that exponential smoothing appears to be more popular than moving averages for production-planning applications.

4.1.10 Trend-Based Methods

Both exponential smoothing and moving-average forecasts will lag behind a trend if one exists. We will consider two forecasting methods that specifically account for trends in the data: regression analysis and Holt's method. Regression analysis is a method that fits a straight line to a set of data. Holt's method is a type of double exponential smoothing that allows for simultaneous smoothing on the series and on the trend.

4.1.10.1 Regression Analysis

Let $(x_1, y_1), (x_2, y_2), ..., (x_n, y_n)$ be n paired data points for the two variables X and Y. Assume that y_i is the observed value of Y when x_i is the observed value of X. Refer to Y as the dependent variable and X as the independent variable. A relationship exists between X and Y that can be represented by the straight line

$$\hat{Y} = a + bX$$

Interpret Y as the predicted value of Y. The goal is to find the values of a and b so that the line $\hat{Y} = a + bX$ gives the best fit of the data. The values of a and b are chosen so that the sum of the squared distances between the regression line and the data points is minimized (see Figures 4.5 and 4.7).

When applying regression analysis to the forecasting problem, the independent variable often corresponds to time and the dependent variable to the series to be forecasted. Assume that $D_1, D_2, ..., D_n$ are the values of the demand at times 1, 2, ..., n. The optimal values of a and b are given by

$$b = \frac{S_{xy}}{S_{xx}}$$

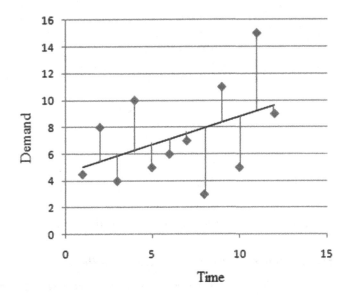

FIGURE 4.5 An example of a regression line.

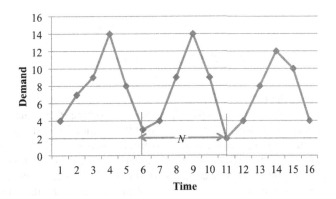

FIGURE 4.6 A seasonal demand series.

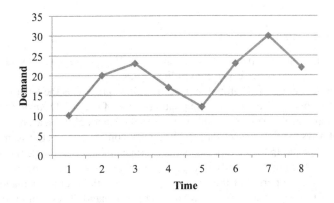

FIGURE 4.7 Demand history for example.

and

$$a = \bar{D} - b(n+1)/2,$$

where

$$S_{xy} = n\sum_{i=1}^{n} iD_i - \frac{n(n+1)}{2}\sum_{i=1}^{n} D_i,$$

$$S_{xx} = \frac{n^2(n+1)(2n+1)}{6} - \frac{n^2(n+1)^2}{4},$$

and $\bar{D}$ is the arithmetic average of the observed demands during periods 1, 2, ... , n.

4.1.10.2 Double Exponential Smoothing Using Holt's Method

Holt's method is a type of double exponential smoothing designed to track time series with linear trend. The method requires the specification of two smoothing constants, α and β, and uses two smoothing equations: one for the value of the series (the intercept) and the other for the trend (the slope). The equations are

$$S_t = \alpha D_t + (1-\alpha)(S_{t-1} + G_{t-1}),$$

$$G_t = \beta(S_t - S_{t-1}) + (1-\beta)G_{t-1}$$

Interpret S_t as the value of the intercept at time t and G_t as the value of the slope at time t. The first equation is very similar to that used for simple exponential smoothing. When the most current observation of demand, D_t, becomes available, it is averaged with the prior forecast of the current demand, which is the previous intercept, S_{t-1}, plus 1 times the previous slope, G_{t-1}. The second equation can be explained as follows. Our new estimate of the intercept, S_t, causes us to revise our estimate of the slope to $S_t - S_{t-1}$. This value is then averaged with the previous estimate of the slope, G_{t-1}. The smoothing constants may be the same, but for most applications, more stability is given to the slope estimate (implying $\beta \leq \alpha$).

The τ-step-ahead forecast made in period t, which is denoted by $F_{t,t+\tau}$ is given by

$$F_{t,t+\tau} = S_t + \tau G_\tau$$

4.1.11 Methods for Seasonal Series

A seasonal series is one that has a pattern that repeats every N periods for some value of N (which is at least 3) (Figure 4.6). A typical series is pictured in Figure 4.8.

We refer to the number of periods before the pattern begins to repeat as the length of the season (N in the picture). Note that this is different from the popular usage of the word *season* as a time of year. In order to use a seasonal model, one must be able to specify the length of the season.

There are several ways to represent seasonality. The most common way is to assume that there exists a set of multipliers. This multiplier, c_t, represents the average amount that the demand in the tth period of the season is above or below the overall average. For example, if $c_3 = 1.25$ and $c_5 = 60$, then, on average, the demand in the third period of the season is 25% above the average demand and the demand in the fifth period of the season is 40% below the average demand. These multipliers are known as seasonal factors.

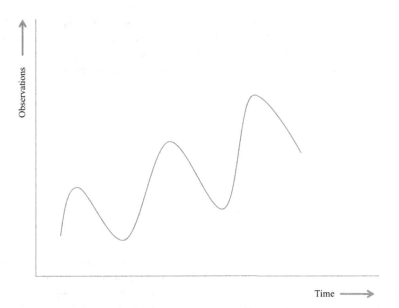

FIGURE 4.8 Seasonal series with increasing trend.

4.1.12 Seasonal Factors for Stationary Series

This method is very simple for computing factors for a time series with seasonal variation and no trend. It requires a minimum of two seasons of data. The method is as follows:

1. Compute the sample mean of all the data.
2. Divide each observation by the sample mean. This gives seasonal factors for each period of observed data.
3. Average the factors for like periods within each season. That is, average all the factors corresponding to the first period of the season, and so on. The resulting averages are the N seasonal factors. They will always add to exactly N.

4.1.13 Seasonal Decomposition Using Moving Averages

This method is more accurate when there is also a trend and requires a minimum of two seasons of data. It is a slightly more complex method for estimating seasonal factors and requires the computation of N-period moving averages, where N is the length of the season. This method is best illustrated by the example below.

Suppose that the original demand history of a certain item for the past eight quarters is given by 10, 20, 26, 17, 12, 23, 30, 22. The graph of this demand series is given in Figure 4.7.

The picture suggests that these data represent two seasons, with each season being four periods long. The next step is to compute all four-period moving averages. This gives

Period	Demand	MA(4)
1	10	
2	20	
3	26	
4	17	18.25
5	12	18.75
6	23	19.50
7	30	20.50
8	22	21.75

Next, the moving averages must be "centered". The moving average 18.25 is computed by averaging the demand for periods 1, 2, 3, and 4. The center of these numbers is 2.5. The next average of 18.75 corresponds to periods 2, 3, 4, and 5. The center of these numbers is 3.5. We repeat this process for the remaining averages and locate them in the centered positions in the following way.

Period	Demand	MA(4)	Centered
1	10		
2	20		18.25
3	26		18.75
4	17	18.25	19.50
5	12	18.75	20.50
6	23	19.50	21.75
7	30	20.50	
8	22	21.75	

Had N been odd instead of even, the centered values would have occurred on periods instead of between periods. (For example, for $N = 5$ the first MA(5) value is centered at period 3.)

Next, we must get these centered values back "on" periods. To do so, we average adjacent values. Averaging 18.25 and 18.75 gives 18.5, which corresponds to the average of periods 2.5 and 3.5, which is 3. Repeating this process for the other centered values gives centered moving averages for periods 4, 5, and 6 as well.

The next step is to obtain values for periods 1, 2, 7, and 8. In order to obtain values for periods 1 and 2, we average the values for periods 3 and 4, and to obtain values for periods 7 and 8, we average the values for periods 5 and 6. In this way, we obtain a centered moving average for each period in which we have an observation of demand.

(A) Period	(B) Demand	(C) Centered MA	(B/C) Ratio
1	10	18.81	0.532
2	20	18.81	1.063
3	26	18.50	1.405
4	17	19.125	0.888
5	12	20.00	0.600
6	23	21.125	1.089
7	30	20.56	1.463
8	22	20.56	1.070

Once we have obtained the centered moving average for each period, we form the ratio of the demand for that period over the centered MA. These values, reported in the fourth column above, are estimates of the seasonal factors for each period. The next step is to form the average of the factors that correspond to the same periods of each season. As we have exactly two seasons of data, we average $(0.532 + 0.600)/2 = 0.566$, $(1.063 + 1.089)/2 = 1.076$, $(1.405 + 1.463)/2 = 1.434$, and $(0.888 + 1.070)/2 = 0.979$. In this case, this procedure yields exactly four seasonal factors. In general, it will result in exactly N seasonal factors.

Finally, we must be sure that the sum of the seasonal factors is exactly N, or exactly 4 for this example. We find $0.566 + 1.076 + 1.434 + 0.979 = 4.055$. In order to make the sum equal to exactly 4, we multiply each factor by $4/4.055 = 0.9864$. The final seasonal factors are

Period	Factor
1	0.588
2	1.061
3	1.415
4	0.966

The sum of these final seasonal factors is exactly 4. Based on the given data, these factors tell us that, on average, the first quarter of each year results in sales that are about 45% below the yearly average, the second quarter in sales that are about 6% above the yearly average, and so on. The next step in the process is to *divide* each observation by the appropriate seasonal factor in order to obtain the de-seasonalized demand.

(A) Period	(B) Factor	De-seasonalized Demand (A/B)
10	0.588	17.92
20	1.061	18.85
26	1.415	18.39
17	0.966	17.60
12	0.588	21.50
23	1.061	21.68
30	1.415	21.22
22	0.966	22.77

The de-seasonalized series will still contain all components of the signal of the original series except for seasonality. A forecast can now be made based on the de-seasonalized demand, which must be "re-seasonalized" by multiplying by the appropriate seasonal factor.

As an example, suppose that we were using a 6-month moving average to forecast the de-seasonalized series. The average of the last six observations is 20.52. This number is then multiplied by the appropriate seasonal factor to obtain factors of future demand. The forecast for period 9 is $(20.52)(0.5580) = 11.45$, for period 10 is $(20.52)(1.061) = 21.77$, and so on.

However, because the de-seasonalized series exhibits a trend, it would be more appropriate to apply a trend-based method such as Holt's method or regression analysis to the de-seasonalized series. If we use regression analysis, we obtain the least squares fit of the data as $D_t = 16.8 + 0.7092t$. Suppose that we are interested in 9 through 12. Substituting t equals 9 through 12 into the regression equation gives the forecasts of the de-seasonalized series for the following year as 23.18, 23.89, 24.60, and 25.31. Each of these forecasts obtained by this method for the following year (periods 9 through 12) is, respectively, 12.93, 25.35, 34.81, and 24.45.

4.1.14 Winter's Method for Seasonal Problems

The moving-average method described above can be used to predict a seasonal series with or without a trend. However, as new data becomes available, the method requires that all seasonal factors be recalculated from scratch. Winter's method is a type of triple exponential smoothing, and this has the important advantages of being easy to update as new data becomes available.

We assume a model of the form

$$D_t = (\mu + G_t)c_t + \varepsilon_t$$

Interpret μ as the base signal or intercept at time $t = 0$ excluding seasonality, G as the trend or slope component, c_t, as the multiplicative seasonal component in period t, and finally ε, as the error term. Because the seasonal factor multiplies both the base level and the trend term, we are assuming that the underlying series has a form similar to that pictured in Figure 4.8.

Again, assume that the length of the season is exactly N periods and that the seasonal factors are the same each season and have the property Σc_{t-N}. Three exponential smoothing equations are used each period to update estimates of de-seasonalized series, the seasonal factors, and the trend. These equations may have different smoothing constants, which we will label α, β, and γ.

1. *The series.* The current level of the de-seasonalized series, S_t, is given by

$$S_t = \alpha\left(D_t/c_{t-N}\right) + (1-\alpha)\left(S_{t-1} + G_{t-1}\right)$$

Notice what this equation does. By dividing by the appropriate seasonal factor, we are de-seasonalizing the newest demand observation. This is then averaged with the current forecast for the de-seasonalized series, as in Holt's method.

2. *The trend.* The trend is updated in a fashion similar to Holt's method.

$$G_t = \beta\left(S_t - S_{t-1}\right) + (1-\beta)G_{t-1}$$

3. The seasonal factors.

$$c_t = \gamma\left(D_t/S_t\right) + (1-\gamma)c_{t-N}$$

The ratio of the most recent demand observation over the current estimate of the de-seasonalized demand gives the current estimate of the seasonal factor. This is then averaged with the previous best estimate of the seasonal factor, c_{t-N}. Each time that a seasonal factor is updated, it is necessary to norm the most recent N factors to add to N.

Finally, the forecast made in period t for any future period $t+1$ is given by

$$F_{t,t+\tau} = \left(S_t + \tau G_t\right)c_{t+\tau-N}$$

Note that this forecasting equation assumes that $t \le N$. If $N < \tau \le 2N$, the appropriate seasonal factor would be $c_{t+\tau-2N}$; if $2N < \tau \le 3N$, the appropriate seasonal factor would be $c_{t+\tau-3N}$; and so on.

4.1.14.1 Initialization Procedure

In order to get the method started, we need to obtain initial estimates for the series, the slope, and the seasonal factors. Winter's suggests that a minimum of two seasons of data be available for initialization. Let us assume that exactly two seasons of data are available, that is, $2N$ data points. Suppose that the current period is $t = 0$, so that the past observations are labeled $D_{-2N+1}, D_{-2N+2}, \ldots, D_0$.

1. Calculate the sample means for the two separate seasons of data.

$$V_1 = \frac{1}{N}\sum_{j=-2N+1}^{-N} D_j$$

$$V_2 = \frac{1}{N}\sum_{j=-N+1}^{0} D_j$$

2. Define $G_0 = (V_2 - V_1)/N$ as the initial slope estimate. If $m > 2$ seasons of data are available for initialization, then compute $V_1, \ldots, V_m$ as above and define $G_0 = (V_m - V_1)/[(m-1)N]$. If we locate V_1 at the center of the first season of data (at period $(-3N+1)/2$) and V_2 at the center of the second season of data (at period $(-N+1)/2$), then G_0 is simply the slope of the line connecting V_1 and V_2 (refer to Figures 4.9 and 4.11).

3. Set $S_0 = V_2 + G_0[(N-1)/2]$. This estimates the value of the series at time $t = 0$. Note that S_0 is the value assumed by the line connecting V_1 and V_2 (see Figure 4.11).

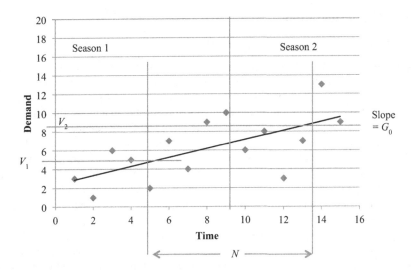

FIGURE 4.9　Initialization for Winter's method.

4.

   a. The initial seasonal factors are computed for each period in which data are available and then averaged to obtain one set of seasonal factors. The initial seasonal factors are obtained by dividing each of the initial observations by the corresponding point along the line connecting V_1 and V_2. This can be done graphically or by using the following formula:

$$c_t = \frac{D_t}{V_i - \left[\dfrac{(N+1)}{2} - j\right]G_0} \quad \text{for} - 2N + 1 \le t \le 0,$$

where $i = 1$ for the first season, $i = 2$ for the second season, and j is the period of the season. That is, $j = 1$ for $t = -2N + 1$ and $t = -N + 1$; $j = 2$ for $t = -2N + 2$ and $t = -N + 2$, and so on.

   b. Average the seasonal factors. Assuming exactly two seasons of initial data, we obtain

$$c_{-N+1} = \frac{c_{-2N+1} + c_{-N+1}}{2}, \ldots, c_0 = \frac{c_{-N} + c_0}{2}$$

   c. Normalize the seasonal factors.

$$C_j = \left[\frac{c_j}{\displaystyle\sum_{i=0}^{-N+1} c_i}\right] \circ N \quad \text{for} -N + 1 \le j \le 0$$

The initialization procedure discussed above is the one suggested by Winter's. It is not the only means of initializing the system. Seasonal factors could be determined by the method of moving averages. Another alternative would be to fit a linear regression to the baseline data and use the resulting slope and intercept values, as was done in Holt's method, to obtain S_0 and G_0. The seasonal factors would be obtained by dividing each demand observation in the baseline period by the corresponding value on the regression line, averaging like periods, and norming. The actual values of the initial estimates of the intercept, the slope, and the seasonal factors will be similar no matter which initialization scheme is employed.

4.1.15 Practical Considerations

4.1.15.1 Model Identification and Monitoring

Determining the proper model depends on the characteristics of the history of observations and on the context in which the forecasts are required. When historical data are available, they should be examined carefully in order to determine if obvious patterns exist, such as trend or seasonal fluctuations. Usually, these patterns can be spotted by graphing the data. Statistical tests, such as significance of regression, can be used to verify the existence of a trend, for example. Identifying complex relationships requires more sophisticated methods. The *Sample autocorrelation function* can reveal intricate relationships that simple graphical methods cannot. The Box–Jenkins methodology is based on identifying the appropriate model from an examination of the autocorrelation structure. The Box–Jenkins methods require substantial past history (at least 72 data points are recommended) and separate model identification and optimization for each series considered. Judging from the literature, such methods are really used in production applications.

Once a model has been chosen, forecasts should be monitored regularly to see if the model is appropriate or if some unforeseen change has occurred in the series. As we indicated, a forecasting method should not be biased. That is, the expected value of the forecast error should be zero. In addition to the methods mentioned, one means of monitoring the bias is the *tracking signal* developed by Trigg in the early 1960s. Following earlier notation, let e_t be the observed error in period t and $|e_t|$ the absolute value of the observed error. The smoothed values of the error and the absolute error are given by

$$E_t = \beta e_t + (1 - \beta)E_{t-1},$$

$$M_t = \beta|e_t| + (1 - \beta)M_{t-1}$$

The tracking signal is the ratio

$$T_t = \left| \frac{E_t}{M_t} \right|$$

If forecasts are unbiased, the smoothed error E_t should be small compared to the smoothed absolute error M_t. Hence, a large value of the tracking signal indicates biased forecasts, which suggest that the forecasting model is inappropriate. The value of T_t that signals a significant bias depends on the smoothing constant β. For example, Trigg claims that a value of T_t exceeding 0.51 indicates nonrandom errors for a β of 0.1. The tracking signal also can be used directly as a variable smoothing constant.

4.1.15.2 Simple vs. Complex Time Series Methods

Literature suggests that the simplest methods are often as accurate as sophisticated ones. A more sophisticated forecasting method is one that requires the estimation of a larger number of parameters from the data. Trouble can arise when these parameters are estimated incorrectly. To give some idea of the nature of this problem, consider a comparison of simple moving averages and regression analysis for the following series 7, 12, 9, 23, 27. Suppose that we are interested in forecasting at the end of period 5 for the demand in period 15 (i.e., we require $F_{5,15}$). The five-period moving-average forecast made at the end of period 5 is 15.6, and this would be the forecast for period 15. The least squares fit of the data is $D_t = 0.3 + 5.1t$. Substituting $t = 15$, we obtain the regression forecast of 76.8. In Figure 4.10, we picture the realization of the demand through period 15. Notice what has happened. The apparent trend that existed in the first five periods was extrapolated in period 15 by the regression equation. However, there really was no significant trend in this particular case. The more complex model gave significantly poorer results for the long-term forecast.

There is some evidence that the arithmetic average of forecasts obtained from the different methods is more accurate than a single method. This is perhaps because often a single method is unable to capture the underlying signal in the data and different models capture different aspects of the signal.

What do these observations tell us about the application of forecasting techniques to production planning? At the aggregate level of planning, forecast accuracy is extremely important, and multiple-step-ahead

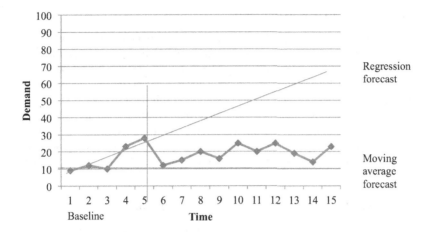

FIGURE 4.10 The difficulty with long-term forecasts.

forecasts play an integral role in the planning of workforce and production levels. For that reason, blind reliance on time series methods is not advised at this level. At a lower level in the system, such as routine inventory management for spare parts, the use of simple time series methods, such as moving averages or exponential smoothing, makes a great deal of sense. At the individual item level, short-term forecasts for a large number of these items are required, and monitoring the forecast for each item is impractical at best. The risk of severe errors is minimized if simple methods are used.

4.1.16 Overview of Advanced Topics in Forecasting

4.1.16.1 Box–Jenkins Methods

A popular advanced time series technique is the *Box–Jenkins method*, which exploits possible dependencies among values of the series from period to period. Accounting for these dependencies can often substantially improve forecasts.

For example, suppose a company has instituted a sales incentive system that provides a bonus for the employee with the best improvement in bookings from one month to the next. With such an incentive in place, a month of poor sales is often followed by a month of good sales. Similarly, a month of good sales would usually be followed by a lull. This means that sales in consecutive months tend to be negatively correlated. This information can be used to improve sales forecasts.

Autocorrelation is the correlation (i.e., degree of dependency) among values of observed data separated by a fixed number of periods. In the example above, we would say that the series has a negative autocorrelation of order one. If high values tend to be followed by high values, the autocorrelation of order one is positive. We can also measure autocorrelations of order greater than one. For example, if low values tend to be followed by low values two periods later, then the series exhibits a positive autocorrelation of order two. To use these methods, one determines sample autocorrelations from the data for one period of separation, two periods of separation, and so on.

The most general Box–Jenkins model is known as the *ARIMA* (autoregressive integrated moving average) model. Autoregressive processes and moving-average processes (different from the previous moving average models) are two models of time series with autocorrelation. The term *integrated* refers to differencing. First-order differencing means deriving a new series that is equal to the first differences of successive values of the original series. Differencing is a means of eliminating trend and polynomial growth.

Developing the proper form of the model requires a deep understanding of these processes. One must employ sophisticated mathematical techniques to estimate the model's parameters. Furthermore, to obtain a reasonable estimate for the autocorrelation function, one must have a substantial history of observations. At least 72 data points are recommended. The payoff is that under the right circumstances, these methods can significantly outperform simpler ones.

4.1.16.2 Simulation as a Forecasting Tool

Computer simulation is a powerful technique for tackling complex problems. A computer simulation is a description of a problem reduced to a computer program. The program is designed to recreate the key aspects of the dynamics of a real situation. When a problem is too complex to model mathematically, simulation is a popular alternative. By rerunning the program under different starting conditions and/or different scenarios, one can, by a kind of trial-and-error process, discover the best strategy for managing a system.

Simulation is a common tool for modeling manufacturing planning problems such as complex material flow problems in the plan. It is less commonly used as a forecasting tool and can recommend the optimal timing and pricing of new product introductions by incorporating forecasts of component availability and price changes, fluctuating demand for a given feature or price, and the impact of rival models.

4.1.16.3 Forecasting Demand in the Presence of Lost Sales

Retailers rely heavily on forecasting. Basic items (items that don't change appreciably from season to season, such as men's dress shirts) generally have substantial sales history, arguing for the use of times series methods to forecast demand. However, there is an important difference between what is observed and what one wants to forecast. The goal is to forecast *demand*, but one only observes *sales*. Suppose a customer wants to buy a blouse in a certain size and color and finds it's not available on the shelf. She will most likely leave the store and try to find the product somewhere else. This is known as a lost sale. The difficulty is that most retailers have no way to track lost sales. Thus, they observe sales but need to estimate demand.

As an example, consider an item that is restocked to 10 units at the beginning of each week. Suppose that over the past 15 weeks the sales history for the item was 7, 5, 10, 10, 8, 3, 6, 10, 10, 9, 5, 0, 10, 10, 4. Consider those weeks in which sales were 10 units. What were the demands in those weeks? The answer is that we don't know. We only know that it was *at least* 10. If you computed the sample mean and sample variance of these numbers, they would underestimate the true mean and variance of demand.

How does one go about forecasting demand in this situation? In the parlance of classical statistics, this is known as a censored sample. That means that we know the values of demand for only a portion of the sample. For the other portion of the sample, we know only a lower bound on the demand. Special statistical methods that incorporate censoring give significantly improved estimates of the population mean and variance in this case. These methods can be embedded into sequential forecast schemes, such as exponential smoothing, to provide significantly improved forecasts.

To see how dramatic this difference can be, consider a situation in which the true weekly demand for a product is a normal random variable with mean 100 and standard deviation 30. Suppose that items are stocked up to 110 units at the start of each week. Exponential smoothing is used to obtain two sets of forecasts: the first accounts for lost sales (includes censoring) and the second does not (does not including censoring). Figures 4.13 and 4.14 show the estimators for the mean and the standard deviation with and without censoring. Notice the severe low bias when lost sales are ignored in both cases. That means that by not correctly accounting for the difference between sales and demand, one underestimates both the mean and the variance of the demand. Since both the mean and the variance of demand are inputs for determine optimal stocking levels, these levels could be severely underestimated.

4.2 Aggregate Planning

4.2.1 Introduction to Aggregate Planning

In 2009, Hopp et al. described aggregate planning as macro production planning and addresses the problem of deciding how many employees the firm should retain and the quantity and the mix of products to be produced. Examples include when airlines must plan staffing levels for flight attendants and pilots or when hospitals plan staffing levels for nurses. For military operations, planning the correct number of personnel is crucial. These strategies can be considered for both logistics personnel and other strategic planning challenges.

Aggregate planning strategies are an important, fundamental part of an organization strategy or a military mission. Planning strategies may include reducing costs by making frequent changes in the size and/or composition of the personnel.

If a military operation must provide a service or produce a product, aggregate planning begins with the forecasting of demand. Demand forecasting depends on the general strategy the organization may have toward personnel and commitments to personnel.

There are many texts that describe aggregate planning or macro planning. We utilize many common ideas and strategies that are common to this academic field. One of the most comprehensive descriptions of these techniques is described in Factory Physics. We utilize some of these examples and descriptions to provide an overview of the topic.

Demand forecasts are never exact due to the fact there are always random components of the demand that cannot be predicted in advance. For education purposes, the aggregate planning methodologies discussed in this chapter assume that demand is deterministic or known. This assumption is made in order to allow us to focus on the methods, not on the advanced statistics, required for stochastic prediction.

In-house production means some components might be purchased from outside suppliers, but the primary product is produced by the organization. This idea has historically been associated with Henry Ford, one of the first American manufacturers to design a manufacturing process by owning a stand of rubber trees so he would not have to purchase rubber for tires.

This model is changing organizations that are seeking more flexibility by outsourcing the manufacturing operations; in other words, in the work performed on a subcontract basis in the late 2000s, Hopp et al. suggested that aggregate planning involves competing objectives. One objective is to react quickly to anticipated changes in demand, which would require making frequent and potentially large changes in the size of the labor force or a chase strategy. This may be cost effective but could be a poor long-run business strategy. Workers who are laid off may not be available when business turns around. For this reason, the organization may seek the goal of retaining a stable workforce. However, this strategy often results in large buildups of inventory during periods of low demand. Service firms may incur substantial debt to meet payrolls in slow periods. A third objective is to develop a production plan for the firm that maximizes profit over the planning horizon subject to constraints on capacity. When profit maximization is the primary objective, explicit costs of making changes must be factored into the decision process.

Aggregate planning methodology is designed to translate demand forecasts into a blueprint for planning staffing and production levels for the firm over a predetermined planning horizon. Aggregate planning methodology is not limited to top-level planning. Although generally considered to be a macro planning tool for determining overall workforce and production levels, large companies may find aggregate planning useful at the plant level as well. Production planning may be viewed as a hierarchical process in which purchasing, production, and staffing decisions must be made at several levels in the firm. Aggregate planning methods may be applied at almost any level, although the concept is one of managing groups of items rather than single items.

We utilize examples from Hopp to demonstrate several techniques for determining aggregate plans. Some of these are approximate and some are optimal. We hope to convey to the reader our understanding of the issues involved in aggregate planning, a knowledge of the basic tools available for providing solutions, and an appreciation of the difficulties associated with implementing aggregate plans in the real world.

4.2.2 Aggregate Units of Production

The aggregate planning approach is predicted on the existence of an aggregate unit of production. When the types of items produced are similar, an aggregate production unit can correspond to an "average" item, but if many different types of items are produced, it would be more appropriate to consider aggregate units in terms of weight (tons of steel), volume (gallons of gasoline), amount of work required (worker-years of programming time), or dollar value (value of inventory in dollars). What the appropriate aggregating scheme should be is not always obvious. It depends on the context of the particular planning problem and the level of aggregation required.

Example 4.1

A plant manager working for a large national appliance firm is considering implementing an aggregate planning system to determine the workforce and production levels in his plant. This particular plant produces six models of washing machines. The characteristics of the machines are

Model Number	Number of Worker-Hours Required to Produce	Selling Price ($)
A5532	4.2	285
K4242	4.9	345
L9898	5.1	395
L3800	5.2	425
M2624	5.4	525
M3880	5.8	725

The plant manager must decide on the particular aggregation scheme to use. One possibility is to define an aggregate unit as one dollar of output. Unfortunately, the selling prices of the various models of washing machines are not consistent with the number of worker-hours required to produce them. The ratio of the selling price divided by the worker-hours is $67.86 for A5532 and $125.00 for M3880. (The company bases its pricing on the fact that the less expensive models have a higher sales volume.) The manager notices that the percentages of the total number of sales for these six models have been fairly constant, with values of 32% for A5532, 21% for K4242, 17% for L9898, 14% for L3800, 10% for M2624, and 6% for M3880. He decides to define an aggregate unit of production as a fictitious washing machine requiring $(0.32)(4.2) + (0.21)(4.9) + (0.17)(5.1) + (0.14)(5.2) + (0.10)(5.4) + (0.06)(5.8) = 4.856$ hours of labor time. He can obtain sales forecasts for aggregate production units in essentially the same way by multiplying the appropriate fractions by the forecasts for unit sales of each type of machine.

The approach used by the plant manager in Example 4.1 was possible because of the relative similarity of the products produced. However, defining an aggregate unit of production at a higher level of the firm is more difficult. In cases in which the firm produces a large variety of products, a natural aggregate unit is sales dollars. Although, as we saw in the example, this will not necessarily translate to the same number of units of production for each item, it will generally provide a good approximation for planning at the highest level of a firm that produces a diverse product line.

Aggregate planning (and the associated problem of disaggregating the aggregate plans or converting them into detailed master schedules) is closely related to hierarchical production planning (HPP) championed by Hax and Meal (1975). HPP considers workforce sizes and production rates at a variety of levels of the firm as opposed to simply the top level, as in aggregate planning. For aggregate planning purposes, Hax and Meal recommend the following hierarchy:

1. *Items.* These are the final products to be delivered to the customer. An item is often referred to as an SKU (for stock keeping unit) and represents the finest level of detail in the product structure.

2. *Families.* These are defined as a group of items that share a common manufacturing setup cost.

3. *Types.* Types are groups of families with production quantities that are determined by a single aggregate production plan.

In the example above, items would correspond to individual models of washing machines. A family might be all washing machines, and a type might be large appliances. The Hax–Meal aggregation scheme will not necessarily work in every situation. In general, the aggregation method should be consistent with the firm's organizational structure and product line.

In Figure 4.11, we present a schematic of the aggregate planning function and its place in the hierarchy of production planning decisions.

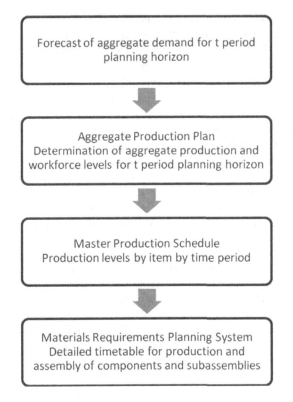

FIGURE 4.11 The hierarchy of production planning decisions.

4.2.3 Overview of the Aggregate Planning Problem

Having now defined the appropriate aggregate unit for the level of the firm for which an aggregate plan is to be determined, we assume that there exists a forecast of the demand for a specified planning horizon, expressed in terms of aggregate production units. Let $D_1, D_2, \dots, D_T$ be the demand forecasts for the next T planning periods. In most applications, a planning period is a month, although aggregate plans can be developed for other periods of time, such as weeks, quarters, or years. An important feature of aggregate planning is that the demands are treated as known constants (i.e., the forecast error is assumed to be zero). The reasons for making this assumption will be discussed below.

The goal of aggregate planning is to determine aggregate production quantities and the levels of resources required to achieve these production goals. In practice, this translates to finding the number of workers that should be employed and the number of aggregate units to be produced in each of the planning periods $1, 2, \dots, T$. The objective of aggregate planning is to balance the advantages of producing to meet demand as closely as possible against the disruptions caused by changing the levels of production and/or the workforce levels.

The primary issues related to the aggregate planning problem include

1. *Smoothing.* Smoothing refers to costs that result from changing production and workforce levels from one period to the next. Two of the key components of smoothing costs are the costs that result from hiring and firing workers. Aggregate planning methodology requires the specification of these costs, which may be difficult to estimate. Firing workers could have far-reaching consequences and costs that may be difficult to evaluate. Firms that hire and fire frequently develop a poor public image. This could adversely affect sales and discourage potential employees from joining the company. Furthermore, workers that are laid off might not simply wait around for business to pick up. Firing workers can have a detrimental effect on the future size of the labor

force if those workers obtain employment in other industries. Finally, most companies are simply not at liberty to hire and fire at will. Labor agreements restrict the freedom of management to freely alter workforce levels. However, it is still valuable for management to be aware of the cost trade-offs associated with varying workforce levels and the attendant savings in inventory costs.

2. *Bottleneck problems.* We use the term *bottleneck* to refer to the inability of the system to respond to sudden changes in demand as a result of capacity restrictions. For example, a bottleneck could arise when the forecast for demand in 1 month is unusually high and the plant does not have sufficient capacity to meet that demand. A breakdown of a vital piece of equipment also could result in a bottleneck.

3. *Planning horizon.* The number of periods for which the demand is to be forecasted, and hence the number of periods for which workforce and inventory levels are to be determined, must be specified in advance. The choice of the value of the forecast horizon, T, can be significant in determining the usefulness of the aggregate plan. If T is too small, then current decisions indicated by the aggregate plan could be incorrect. Another issue involving the planning horizon is the *end-of-horizon* effect. For example, the aggregate plan might recommend that the inventory at the end of the horizon be drawn to zero in order to minimize holding costs. This could be a poor strategy, especially if demand increases at that time. (However, this particular problem can be avoided by adding a constraint specifying minimum ending inventory levels.)

   In practice, rolling schedules are almost always used. This means that at the time of the next decision, a new forecast of demand is appended to the former forecasts and old forecasts might be revised to reflect new information. The new aggregate plan may recommend different production and workforce levels for the current period than were recommended one period ago. When only the decisions for the current planning period need to be implemented immediately, the schedule should be viewed as dynamic rather than static.

   Although rolling schedules are common, it is possible that because of production lead times, the schedule must be frozen for a certain number of planning periods. This means that decisions over some collection of future periods cannot be altered. The most direct means of dealing with frozen horizons is simply to label as period 1 the first period in which decisions are not frozen.

4. *Treatment of demand.* As noted above, aggregate planning methodology requires the assumption that demand is known with certainty. This is simultaneously a weakness and a strength of the approach. It is weakness because it ignores the possibility (and, in fact, likelihood) of forecast errors. It is virtually a certainty that demand forecasts are wrong. Aggregate planning does not provide any buffer against unanticipated forecast errors. However, most inventory models that allow for random demand require that the average demand be constant over time. Aggregate planning allows the manager to focus on the systematic changes that are generally not present in models that assume random demand. By assuming deterministic demand, the effects of seasonal fluctuations and business cycles can be incorporated into the planning function.

4.2.4 Costs in Aggregate Planning

As with most of the optimization problems considered in production management, the goal of the analysis is to choose the aggregate plan that minimizes cost. It is important to identify and measure those specific costs that are affected by the planning decision.

1. *Smoothing costs.* Smoothing costs are those costs that accrue as a result of changing the production levels from one period to the next. In the aggregate planning context, the most salient smoothing cost is the cost of changing the size of the workforce. Increasing the size of the workforce requires time and expense to advertise positions, interview prospective employees, and train new hires. Decreasing the size of the workforce means that workers must be laid off. Severance pay is thus one cost of decreasing the size of the workforce. Other costs, somewhat harder to measure, are (1) the costs of a decline in worker morale that may result and (2) the potential for decreasing the size of the labor pool in the future, as workers who are laid off acquire jobs with other firms or in other industries.

Most of the models that we consider assume that the costs of increasing and decreasing the size of the workforce are linear functions of the number of employees that are hired or fired. That is, there is a constant dollar amount charged for each employee hired or fired. The assumption of linearity is probably reasonable up to a point. As the supply of labor becomes scarce, there may be additional costs required to hire more workers, and the costs of laying off workers may go up substantially if the number of workers laid off is too large. A typical cost function for changing the size of the workforce appears in Figure 4.12.

2. *Holding costs.* Holding costs are the costs that accrue as a result of having capital tied up in inventory. If the firm can decrease its inventory, the money saved could be invested elsewhere with a return that will vary with the industry and with the specific company. Holding costs are almost always assumed to be linear in the number of units being held at a particular point in time. We will assume for the purposes of the aggregate planning analysis that the holding cost is expressed in terms of dollars per unit held per planning period. We also will assume that holding costs are charged against the inventory remaining on hand at the *end* of the planning period. This assumption is made for convenience only. Holding costs could be charged against starting inventory or average inventory as well.

3. *Shortage costs.* Holding costs are charged against the aggregate inventory as long as it is positive. In some situations, it may be necessary to incur shortages which are represented by negative level of inventory. Shortages can occur when forecasted demand exceeds the capacity of the production facility or when demands are higher than anticipated. For the purposes of aggregate planning, it is generally assumed that excess demand is backlogged and filled in a future period. In a highly competitive situation, however, it is possible that excess demand is lost and the customer goes elsewhere. This case, which is known as lost sales, is more appropriate in the management of single items and is more common in a retail than in a manufacturing context.

   As with holding costs, shortage costs are generally assumed to be linear. Convex functions also can accurately describe shortage costs, but linear functions seem to be the most common. Figure 4.13 shows a typical holding/shortage cost function.

4. *Regular time costs.* These costs involve the cost of producing one unit of output during regular working hours. Included in this category are the actual payroll costs of regular employees working on regular time, the direct and indirect costs of materials, and other manufacturing expenses. When all production is carried out on regular time, regular payroll costs become a

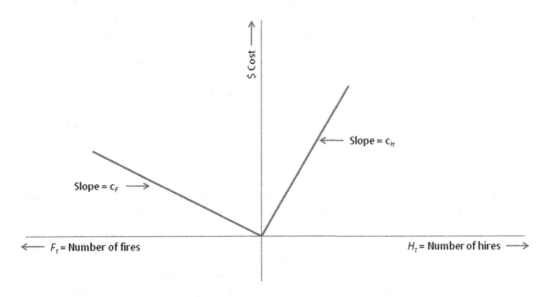

FIGURE 4.12 Cost of changing the size of the workforce.

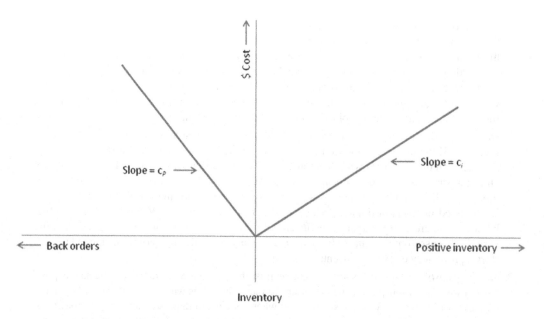

FIGURE 4.13 Holding costs and backorder costs.

"sunk cost", because the number of units produced must equal the number of units demanded over any planning horizon of sufficient length. If there is no overtime or worker idle time, regular payroll costs do not have to be included in the evaluation of different strategies.

5. *Overtime and subcontracting costs.* Overtime and subcontracting costs are the costs of production of units not produced on regular time. Overtime refers to production by regular time employees beyond the normal work day, and subcontracting refers to the production of items by an outside supplier. Again, it is generally assumed that both of these costs are linear.

6. *Idle time costs.* The complete formulation of the aggregate planning problem also includes a cost for underutilization of the workforce or idle time. In most contexts, the idle time cost is zero, as the direct costs of idle time would be taken into account in labor costs and lower production levels. However, idle time could have other consequences for the firm. For example, if the aggregate units are input to another process, idle time on the line could result in higher costs to the subsequent process. In such cases, one would explicitly include a positive idle cost.

When planning is done at a relatively high level of the firm, the effects of intangible factors are more pronounced. Any solution to the aggregate planning problem obtained from a cost-based model must be considered carefully in the context of company policy. An optimal solution to a mathematical model might result in a policy that requires frequent hiring and firing of personnel. Such a policy may be infeasible because of prior contract agreements or undesirable because of the potential negative effects on the firm's public image.

4.2.4.1 A Prototype Problem

One can obtain adequate solutions for many aggregate planning problems by hand or by using relatively straightforward graphical techniques. Linear programming is a means of obtaining (nearly) optimal solutions. We illustrate the different solution techniques with the following example.

Example 4.2

Densepack is to plan workforce and production levels for the 6-month period from January to June. The firm produces a line of disk drives for mainframe computers that are plug compatible with several computers produced by major manufacturers. Forecast demands over the next

6 months for a particular line of drives produced in the Milpitas, California, plant are 1,280, 640, 1,200, 2,000, and 1,400. There are currently (end of December) 300 workers employed in the Milpitas plant. Ending inventory in December is expected to be 500 units, and the firm would like to have 600 units on hand at the end of June.

There are several ways to incorporate the starting and ending inventory constraints into the formulation. The most convenient is simply to modify the values of the predicted demand. Define net predicted demand in period 1 as the predicted demand minus initial inventory. If there is a minimum ending inventory constraint, this amount should be added to the demand in period T. Minimum buffer inventories also can be handled by modifying the predicted demand. If there is a minimum buffer inventory in every period, this amount should be added to the first period's demand. If there is a minimum buffer inventory in only one period, this amount should be added to that period's demand and subtracted from the next period's demand. Actual ending inventories should be computed using the original demand pattern, however.

Returning to Example 4.2, we define the net predicted demand for January as 780(1,280 − 500) and the net predicted demand for June as 2,000(1,400 + 600). By considering net demand, we may make the simplifying assumption that starting and ending inventories are both zero. The net predicted demand and the net cumulative demand for the 6 months from January to June are as follows:

Month	Net Predicted Demand	Net Cumulative Demand
January	780	780
February	640	1,420
March	900	2,320
April	1,200	3,520
May	2,000	5,520
June	2,000	7,520

The cumulative net demand is pictured in Figure 4.4. A production plan is the specification of the production levels for each month. If shortages are not permitted, then cumulative production must be at least as great as cumulative demand each period. In addition to the cumulative net demand, Figure 4.14 also shows one feasible production plan.

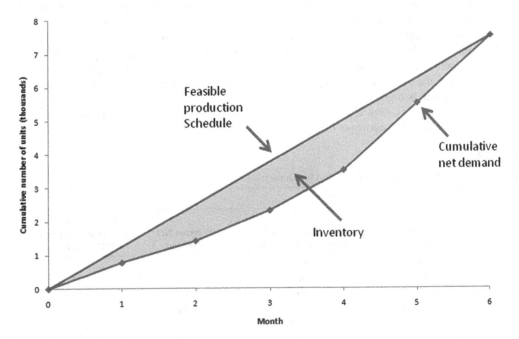

FIGURE 4.14   A feasible aggregate plan for Densepack.

In order to illustrate the cost trade-offs of various production plans, we will assume in the example that there are only three costs to be considered: cost of hiring workers, cost of firing workers, and cost of holding inventory. Define

$$C_H = \text{Cost of hiring one worker} = \$500,$$

$$C_F = \text{Cost of firing one worker} = \$1,000,$$

$$C_I = \text{Cost of holding one unit of inventory for 1 month} = \$80.$$

We require a means of translating aggregate production in units to workforce levels. Because not all months have an equal number of working days, we will use a day as an indivisible unit of measure and define

$$K = \text{Number of aggregate units produced by one worker in 1 day}.$$

In the past, the plant manager observed that over 22 working days, with the workforce level constant at 76 workers, the firm produced 245 disk drives. That means that on average the production rate was 245/22 = 11.1364 drives per day when there were 76 workers employed at the plant. It follows that one worker produced an average of 11.1364/76 = 0.14653 drive in 1 day. Hence, $K = 0.14653$ for this example.

We will evaluate two alternative plans for managing the workforce that represents two essentially opposite management strategies. Plan 1 is to change the workforce each month in order to produce enough units to most closely match the demand pattern. This is known as a *zero inventory plan*. Plan 2 is to maintain the minimum constant workforce necessary to satisfy the net demand. This is known as the *constant workforce plan*.

4.2.4.2 Evaluation of a Chase Strategy (Zero Inventory Plan)

In this section, we will develop a production plan for Densepack that minimizes the levels of inventory the firm must hold during the 6-month planning horizon. Table 4.1 summarizes the input information for the calculations and shows the minimum number of workers required in each month.

One obtains the entries in the final column of Table 4.1, the minimum number of workers required each month, by dividing the forecasted net demand by the number of units produced per worker. The value of this ratio is then rounded *upward* to the next higher integer. We must round upward to guarantee that shortages do not occur. As an example, consider the month of January. Forming the ratio 780/2.931 gives 266.12, which is rounded up to 267 workers. The number of working days each month depends upon a variety of factors, such as paid holidays and worker schedules. The reduced number of days in June is due to a planned shutdown of the plant in the last week of June.

TABLE 4.1

Initial Calculations for Zero Inventory Plan for Densepack

A	B	C	D	E
Month	Number of Working Days	Number of Units Produced per Worker (B × 0.14653)	Forecast Net Demand	Minimum Number of Workers Required (D/C rounded up)
January	20	2.931	780	266
February	24	3.517	640	182
March	18	2.638	900	341
April	26	3.810	1,200	315
May	22	3.224	2,000	620
June	15	2.198	2,000	910

TABLE 4.2

Zero Inventory Aggregate Plan for Densepack

A	B	C	D	E	F	G	H	I
Month	Number of Workers	Number Hired	Number Fired	Number of Units per Worker	Number of Units Produced (B × E)	Cumulative Production	Cumulative Net Demand	Ending Inventory (G – H)
January	267		33	2,931	783	783	780	3
February	182		85	3,517	640	1,423	1,420	3
March	342	160		2,638	902	2,325	2,320	5
April	315		27	3,810	1,200	3,525	3,520	5
May	621	306		3,224	2,002	5,527	5,520	7
June	910	289		2,198	2,000	7,527	7,520	7
Totals		755	145					30

Recall that the number of workers employed at the end of December is 300. Hiring and firing workers each month to match forecast demand as closely as possible results in the aggregate plan given in Table 4.2. The number of units produced each month (column F in Table 4.2) is obtained by the formula

Number of units produced =

Number of workers × Average number of aggregate units produced in a month by a single worker

and rounded to the nearest integer.

The total cost of this production plan is obtained by multiplying the totals at the bottom of Table 4.2 by the appropriate costs. For this example, the total cost of hiring, firing, holding is $(755)(500) + (145)(1,000) + (30) (80) = \$524,900$. This cost must now be adjusted to include the cost of holding for the ending inventory of 600 units, which was netted out of the demand for June. Hence, the total cost of this plan is $524,900 + (600) (80) = \$572,900$. Note that the initial inventory of 500 units does not enter into the calculations because it will be netted out during the month of January.

It is usually impossible to achieve zero inventory at the end of each planning period because it is not possible to employ a fractional number of workers. For this reason, there will almost always be some inventory remaining at the end of each period in addition to the inventory required to be on hand at the end of the planning horizon.

It is possible that ending inventory in one or more periods could build up to a point where the size of the workforce could be reduced by one or more workers. In this example, there is sufficient inventory on hand to reduce the workforce by one worker in the months of both March and May. Check that the resulting plan hires a total of 753 workers and fires a total of 144 workers and has a total of only 13 units of inventory. The cost of this modified plan comes to $569,540.

4.2.4.3 Evaluation of the Constant Workforce Plan

Now assume that the goal is to eliminate completely the need for hiring and firing during the planning horizon. In order to guarantee that shortages do not occur in any period, it is necessary to compute the minimum workforce required for *every* month in the planning horizon. For January, the net cumulative demand is 780, and there are 2,931 units produced per worker, resulting in a minimum workforce of 267 in January. There are exactly $2,931 + 3,517 = 6,448$ units produced per worker in January and February combined, which have a cumulative demand of 1,420. Hence, $1,420/6,448 = 220.22 \approx 221$ workers are required to cover both January and February. Continuing to form the ratios of the cumulative net demand and the cumulative number of units produced per worker for each month in the horizon results in Table 4.3.

The minimum number of workers required for the entire 6-month planning period is the maximum entry in column D in Table 4.3, which is 411 workers. It is only a coincidence that the maximum ratio occurred in the final period.

TABLE 4.3

Computation of the Minimum Workforce Required by Densepack

A	B	C	D
Month	Cumulative Net Demand	Cumulative Number of Units Produced per Worker	Ratio B/C (rounded up)
January	780	2.931	267
February	1,420	6,448	221
March	2,320	9,086	256
April	3,520	12,896	273
May	5,520	16,120	243
June	7,520	18,318	411

TABLE 4.4

Inventory Levels for Constant Workforce Schedule

A	B	C	D	E	F
Month	Number of Units Produced per Worker	Monthly Production (B × 411)	Cumulative Production	Cumulative Net Demand	Ending Inventory (D − E)
January	2,931	1,205	1,205	780	425
February	3,517	1,445	2,650	1,420	1,230
March	2,638	1,084	3,734	2,320	1,414
April	3,810	1,566	5,300	3,520	1,780
May	3,224	1,325	6,625	5,520	1,105
June	2,198	903	7,528	7,520	8
Total					5,962

Because there are 300 workers employed at the end of December, the constant workforce plan requires hiring 111 workers at the beginning of January. No further hiring and firing of workers are required. The inventory levels that result from a constant workforce of 411 workers appear in Table 4.4. The monthly production levels in column C of the table are obtained by multiplying the number of units produced per worker each month by the fixed workforce size of 411 workers. The total of the ending inventory levels is 5,962 + 600 = 6,562. (Recall that 600 units were netted out of the demand for June.) Hence, the total inventory cost of the plan is (6.562)(80) = \$524,960. To this we add the cost of increasing the workforce from 300 to 411 in January, which is (111)(500) = \$55,500 giving a total cost of this plan of \$580,460. This is somewhat higher than the cost of the zero inventory plan, which was \$569,540. However, because costs of the two plans are close, it is likely that the company would prefer the constant workforce plan in order to avoid any unaccounted costs of making frequent changes in the workforce.

4.2.4.4 Mixed Strategies and Additional Constraints

The zero inventory plan and constant workforce strategies treated above are pure strategies: they are designed to achieve one objective. With more flexibility, small modifications can result in dramatically lower costs. One might question the interest in manual calculations considering the aggregate planning problems can be formulated and solved optimally by linear programming.

Manual calculations enhance intuition and understanding. Computers are dumb. It is easy to overlook a critical constraint or objective when using a computer. It's important to have a feel for the right solution before solving a problem on a computer, so that glaring mistakes are obvious. An important skill, largely ignored these days, is being able to do a ballpark calculation in one's head before pulling out the calculator or computer.

Figure 4.4 shows the constant workforce strategy for Densepack. The hatched area represents the inventory carried in each month. Suppose we allow a single change in the production rate during the 6 months. Can you identify a strategy from the figure that substantially reduces inventory without permitting shortages?

Graphically, the problem is to cover the cumulative net demand curve with two straight lines, rather than one straight line. This can be accomplished by driving the net inventory to zero at the end of period 4 (April). To do so, we need to produce enough in each of the months January through April to meet the cumulative net demand each month. That means we need to produce 3,520/4 = 880 units in each of the first 4 months. In Figure 4.4, the line connecting the origin to the cumulative net demand in April lies wholly above the cumulative net demand curve for the prior months. If the graph is accurate, that means that there should be no shortages occurring in these months. The May and June production is then set to 2,000, exactly matching the net demand in these months. With this policy we obtain

Month	Cumulative Net Demand	Cumulative Production
January	780	880
February	1,420	1,760
March	2,320	2,640
April	3,520	3,520
May	5,520	5,520
June	7,520	7,520

As we will see in the next section, this policy turns out to be optimal for the Densepack problem.

The graphical solution method also can be used when additional constraints are present. For example, suppose that the production capacity of the plant is only 1,800 units per month. Then the policy above is infeasible in May and June. In this case, the constraint means that the slope of the cumulative production curve is bounded by 1,800. One solution in this case would be to produce 980 in each of the first 4 months and 1,800 units in each of the last 2 months. Another constraint might be that the maximum change from one month to the next be more than 750 units. Suggest a production plan to meet this constraint.

There are few examples of constraints that might arise in using aggregate planning methodology. As the constraints become more complex, finding good solutions graphically becomes more difficult. Fortunately, most constraints of this nature can be incorporated easily into the linear programming formulations of aggregate planning problems.

4.2.5 Solution of Aggregate Planning Problems by Linear Programming

Linear programming is a term used to describe a general class of optimization problems. The objective is to determine values of n nonnegative real variables in order to maximize or minimize a linear function of these variables that is subject to m linear constraints of these variables. The primary advantage in formulating a problem as a linear program is that optimal solutions can be found very efficiently by the simplex method.

When all cost functions are linear, there is a linear programming formulation of the general aggregate planning problem. Because of the efficiency of commercial linear programming codes, this means that (essentially) optimal solutions can be obtained for very large problems.

4.2.5.1 Cost Parameters and Given Information

The following values are assumed to be known:

c_H = Cost of hiring one worker

c_F = Cost of firing one worker

c_I = Cost of holding one unit of stock for one period

c_R = Cost of producing one unit of stock for one period

c_O = Incremental cost of producing one unit on overtime

c_U = Idle cost per unit of production

c_S = Cost to subcontract one unit of production

n_t = Number of production days in period t

K = Number of aggregate units produced by one worker in 1 day

I_0 = Initial inventory on hand at the start of the planning horizon

D_t = Forecast of demand in period t.

The cost parameters also may be time dependent; that is, they may change with t. Time-dependent cost parameters could be useful for modeling changes in the costs of hiring or firing due, for example, to shortages in the labor pool, or changes in the costs of production and/or storage due to shortages in the supply of resources, or changes in interest rates.

4.2.5.2 Problem Variables

The following are the problem variables:

W_t = Workforce level in period t

P_t = Production level in period t

I_t = Inventory level in period t

H_t = Number of workers hired in period t

F_t = Number of workers fired in period t

O_t = Overtime production in units

U_t = Worker idle time in units ("undertime")

S_t = Number of units subcontracted from outside.

The overtime and idle time variables are determined in the following way. The term Kn_t represents the number of units produced by one worker in period t, so that Kn_tW_t would be the number of units produced by the entire workforce in period t. However, we do not require that $Kn_tW_t = P_t$. If $P_t > Kn_tW_t$, then the number of units produced exceeds what the workforce can produce on regular time. This means that the difference is being produced on overtime, so that the number of units produced on overtime is exactly $O_t = P_t - Kn_tW_t$. If $P_t < Kn_tW_t$, then the workforce is producing less than it should be on regular time, which means that there is worker idle time. The idle time is measured in units of production rather than in time and is given by $U_t = Kn_tW_t - P_t$.

4.2.5.3 Problem Constraints

Three sets of constraints are required for the linear programming formulation. They are included to ensure that conservation of labor and conservation of units are satisfied.

1. Conservation of workforce constraints.

$$\underset{\text{Number of workers in } t}{W_t} = \underset{\text{Number of workers in } t-1}{W_{t-1}} + \underset{\text{Number hired in } t}{H_t} - \underset{\text{Number fired in } t}{F_t} \quad \text{for } 1 \le t \le T$$

2. Conservation of units constraints.

$$\underset{\text{Inventory in } t}{I_t} = \underset{\text{Inventory in } t-1}{I_{t-1}} + \underset{\text{Number of units produced in } t}{P_t} - \underset{\text{Number of units subcontracted in } t}{S_t} - \underset{\text{Demand in } t}{D_t} \quad \text{for } 1 \le t \le T$$

3. Constraints relating production levels to workforce levels.

$$\underset{\text{Number of units produced in } t}{P_t} = \underset{\text{Number of units produced by regular workforce in } t-1}{Kn_t W_t}$$

$$+ \underset{\text{Number of units produced on overtime in } t}{O_t} - \underset{\text{Number of units idle production in } t}{U_t} \qquad \text{for } 1 \leq t \leq T$$

In addition to these constraints, linear programming requires that all problem variables be nonnegative. These constraints and the nonnegativity constraints are the minimum that must be present in any formulation. Notice that (1), (2), and (3) constitute $3T$ constraints, rather than 3 constraints, where T is the length of the forecast horizon.

The formulation also requires specification of the initial inventory, I_0, and the initial workforce, W_0, and may include specification of the ending inventory in the final period, I_T.

The objective function includes all of the costs defined above. The linear programming formulation is to choose values of the problem variables W_t, P_t, I_t, H_t, F_t, O_t, U_t, and S_t to

$$\text{Minimize} \sum_{t=1}^{T} \left(c_H H_t + c_F F_t + c_I I_t + c_R P_t + c_O O_t + c_U U_t + c_S S_t \right)$$

subject to

$$W_t = W_{t-1} + H_t - F_t \qquad \text{for } 1 \leq t \leq T \qquad \text{(A)}$$
$$\text{(conservation of workforce)},$$

$$P_t = Kn_t W_t + H_t - F_t \qquad \text{for } 1 \leq t \leq T \qquad \text{(B)}$$
$$\text{(production and workforce)}$$

$$I_t = I_{t-1} + P_t + S_t - D_t \qquad \text{for } 1 \leq t \leq T \quad \text{(inventory balance)} \qquad \text{(C)}$$

$$H_t, F_t, I_t, O_t, U_t, S_t, W_t, P_t \geq 0 \quad \text{(non-negativity)} \qquad \text{(D)}$$

plus any additional constraints that define the values of starting inventory, starting workforce, ending inventory, or any other variables with values that are fixed in advance.

4.2.5.4 Rounding the Variables

In general, the optimal values of the problem variables will not be integers. However, fractional values for many of the variables do not make sense. These variables include the size of the workforce, the number of workers hired each period, and the number of workers fired each period and also may include the number of units produced each period. (It is possible that fractional numbers of units could be produced in some applications.) One way to deal with this problem is to require in advance that some or all of the problem variables assume only integer values. Unfortunately, this makes the solution algorithm considerably more complex. The resulting problem, known as an integer linear programming problem, requires much more computational effort to solve than does ordinary linear programming. For a moderate-sized problem, solving the problem as an integer linear program is certainly a reasonable alternative.

If an integer programming code is unavailable or if the problem is simply too large to solve by integer programming, linear programming still provides a workable solution. However, after the linear programming solution is obtained, some of the problem variables must be rounded to integer values.

Simply rounding off each variable to the closest integer may lead to an infeasible solution and/or one in which production and workforce levels are inconsistent. It is not obvious what the best way to round the variables is. We recommend the following conservative approach: round the values of the numbers of workers in each period t to W_t, the next larger integer. Once the values of W_t are determined, the values of the other variables, H_t, F_t, and P_t can be found along with the cost of the resulting plan.

Conservative rounding will always result in a feasible solution but will rarely give the optimal solution. The conservative solution generally can be improved by trial-and-error experimentation.

There is no guarantee that if a problem can be formulated as a linear program, the final solution makes sense in the context of the problem. In the aggregate planning problem, it does not make sense that there should be both overtime production and idle time in the same period, and it does not make sense that workers should be hired and fired in the same period. This means that either one or both of the variables O_t and U_t must be zero and either one or both of the variables H_t and F_t must be zero for each t, $1 \leq t \leq T$. This requirement can be included explicitly in the problem formulation by adding the constraints

$$O_t U_t = 0 \quad \text{for } 1 \leq t \leq T,$$

$$H_t F_t = 0 \quad \text{for } 1 \leq t \leq T,$$

since if the product of two variables is zero, it means that at least one must be zero. Unfortunately, these constraints are not linear, as they involve a product of problem variables. However, it turns out that it is not necessary to explicitly include these constraints, because the optimal solution to a linear programming problem always occurs at an extreme point of the feasible region. It can be shown that every extreme point solution automatically has this property. If this were not the case, the linear programming solution would be meaningless.

4.2.5.5 Extensions

Linear programming also can be used to solve somewhat more general versions of the aggregate planning problem. Uncertainty of demand can be accounted for indirectly by assuming that there is a minimum buffer inventory B, each period. In that case, we would include the constraints

$$I_t \geq B_t \quad \text{for } 1 \leq t \leq T$$

The constants B_t would have to be specified in advance. Upper bounds on the number of workers hired and the number of workers fired each period could be included in a similar way. Capacity constraints on the amount of production each period could easily be represented by the set of constraints:

$$I_t \geq B_t \quad \text{for } 1 \leq t \leq T$$

The linear programming formulation above assumed that inventory levels would never go negative. However, in some cases it might be desirable or even necessary to allow demand to exceed supply, for example, if forecast demand exceeded production capacity over some set of planning periods. In order to treat backlogging of excess demand, the inventory I_t must be expressed as the difference between two nonnegative variables, say I_t^+ and I_t^-, satisfying

$$I_t = I_t^+ - I_t^-,$$

$$I_t^+ \geq 0, I_t^- \geq 0$$

The holding cost would now be charged against I_t^+ and the penalty cost for back orders (say c_p) I_t^-. However, notice that for the solution to be sensible, it must be true that I_t^+ and I_t^- are not both positive in the same period t. As with the overtime and idle time and the hiring and firing variables, the properties of linear programming will guarantee that this holds without having explicitly included the constraint $I_t^+ I_t^- = 0$ in the formulation.

In the development of the linear programming model, we stated the requirement that all the cost functions must be linear. This is not strictly correct. Linear programming can also be used when the cost functions are *convex piecewise-linear functions*.

A convex function is one with an increasing slope. A piecewise-linear function is one that is composed of straight lines that have increasing slopes. A typical example is presented in Figure 4.15.

In practice, it is likely that some or all of the cost functions for aggregate planning are convex. For example, if Figure 4.17 represents the cost of hiring workers, then the marginal cost of hiring one additional worker increases with the number of workers that have already been hired. This is probably more accurate than assuming that the cost of hiring one additional worker is a constant independent of the number of workers previously hired. As more workers are hired, the available labor pool shrinks, and more effort must be expended to hire the remaining available workers.

In order to see exactly how convex piecewise-linear functions would be incorporated into the linear programming formulation, we will consider a very simple case. Suppose that the cost of hiring new workers is represented by the function pictured in Figure 4.16. According to the figure, it costs c_{H1} to hire each worker until H^* workers are hired, and it costs c_{H2} for each worker hired beyond H^* workers, with $c_{H1} < c_{H2}$. The variable H_1, the number of workers hired in period T, must be expressed as the sum of two variables:

$$H_t = H_{1t} + H_{2t}$$

Interpret H_{1t} as the number of workers hired up to H^* and H_{2t} as the number of workers hired beyond H^* in period t. The cost of hiring is now represented in the objective function as

$$\sum_{t=1}^{T}(c_{H1}H_{1t} + c_{H2}H_{2t}),$$

and the additional constraints

$$H_t = H_{1t} + H_{2t}$$

$$0 \le H_{1t} \le H^*$$

$$0 \le H_{2t}$$

must also be included.

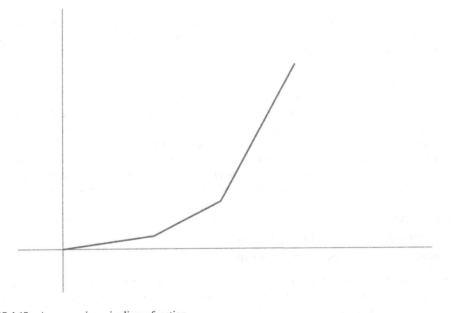

FIGURE 4.15 A convex piecewise linear function.

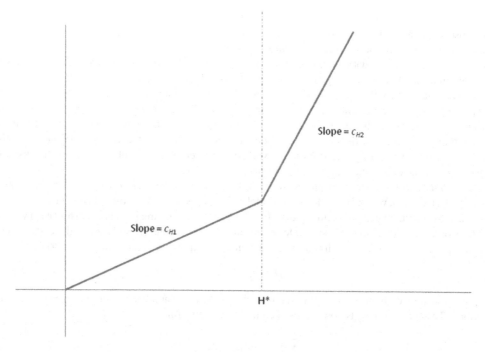

FIGURE 4.16   Convex piecewise linear hiring cost function.

In order for the final solution to make sense, it can never be the case that $H_{1t} < H^*$ and $H_{2t} > 0$ for some *t*. (Why?) However, because linear programming searches for the minimum cost solution, it will force H_{1t} to its maximum value before allowing H_{2t} to become positive, since $c_{H1} < c_{H2}$. This is the reason that the cost functions must be convex. This approach can easily be extended to more than two linear segments and to any of the other cost functions present in the objective function. The technique is known as separable convex programming and is discussed in greater detail in Hillier and Lieberman (1990).

4.2.5.6 Other Solution Methods

Bowman (1956) suggested a transportation formulation of the aggregate planning problem when back orders are not permitted. Several authors have explored solving aggregate planning problems with specially tailored algorithms. These algorithms could be faster for solving large aggregate planning problems than a general linear programming code such as LINDO. In addition, some of these formulations allow for certain types of nonlinear costs. For example, if there are economics of scale in production, the production cost function is likely to be a concave function of the number of units produced. Concave cost functions are not as amenable to linear programming formulations as convex functions. We believe that a general-purpose linear programming package is sufficient for most reasonable-sized problems that one is likely to encounter in the real world. However, the reader should be aware that there are alternative solution techniques that could be more efficient for large problems and could provide solutions when some of the cost functions are nonlinear. A paper that details a transportation-type procedure more efficient than the simplex method for solving aggregate planning problems is Erenguc and Tufekci (1988).

4.3 Solving Aggregate Planning Problems by Linear Programming: An Example

We will demonstrate the use of linear programming by finding the optimal solution to Example 4.1. As there is no subcontracting, overtime, or idle time allowed, and the cost coefficients are constant with respect to time, the objective function is simply

$$\text{Minimize}\left(500 \sum_{t=1}^{6} H_t + 1{,}000 \sum_{t=1}^{6} F_t + 80 \sum_{t=1}^{6} I_t \right)$$

The boundary conditions comprise the specifications of the initial inventory of 500 units, the initial workforce of 300 workers, and the ending inventory of 600 units. These are best handled by including a separate additional constraint for each boundary condition.

The constraints are obtained by substituting $t = 1, \ldots, 6$ into Equations (A), (B), and (C). The full set of constraints expressed in standard linear programming format (with all problem variables on the left-hand side and nonnegative constants on the right-hand side) is as follows:

$$W_1 - W_0 - H_1 + F_1 = 0$$

$$W_2 - W_1 - H_2 + F_2 = 0$$

$$W_3 - W_2 - H_3 + F_3 = 0 \tag{A}$$

$$W_4 - W_3 - H_4 + F_4 = 0$$

$$W_5 - W_4 - H_5 + F_5 = 0$$

$$W_6 - W_5 - H_6 + F_6 = 0$$

$$P_1 - I_1 - I_0 = 1{,}280$$

$$P_2 - I_2 - I_1 = 640$$

$$P_3 - I_3 - I_2 = 900 \tag{B}$$

$$P_4 - I_4 - I_3 = 1{,}200$$

$$P_5 - I_5 - I_4 = 2{,}000$$

$$P_6 - I_6 - I_5 = 1{,}400$$

$$P_1 - 2.931W_1 = 0$$

$$P_2 - 3.517W_2 = 0$$

$$P_3 - 2.638W_3 = 0 \tag{C}$$

$$P_4 - 3.810W_4 = 0$$

$$P_5 - 3.224W_5 = 0$$

$$P_6 - 2.198W_6 = 0$$

$$W_1, \ldots, W_6, P_1, \ldots, P_6, I_1, \ldots, I_6, H_1, \ldots, H_6 \geq 0 \tag{D}$$

$$W_1 = 300$$

$$I_0 = 500 \tag{E}$$

$$I_6 = 600$$

TABLE 4.5

Aggregate Plan for Densepack Obtained from Rounding the Linear Programming Solution

A	B	C	D	E	F	G	H	I
Month	Number of Workers	Number Hired	Number Fired	Number of Units per Worker	Number of Units Produced (B × E)	Cumulative Production	Cumulative Net Demand	Ending Inventory (G – H)
January	273		27	2,931	800	800	780	20
February	273			3,517	960	1,760	1,420	340
March	273			2,638	720	2,480	2,320	160
April	273			3,810	1,040	3,520	3,520	0
May	738	465		3,224	2,379	5,899	5,520	379
June	738			2,198	1,622	7,521	7,520	1
Totals		465	27					900

We have solved this linear program using the LINDO system developed by Schrage (1984). The output of the LINDO program is given in Table 4.5. In the supplement on linear programming, we also treat solving linear programs with Excel. The Excel Solver, of course, gives the same results. The value of the objective function at the optimal solution is $379,320.90, which is *considerably* less than that achieved with either the zero inventory plan or the constant workforce plan. However, this cost is based on fractional values of the variables. The actual cost will be slightly higher after rounding.

Following the rounding procedure recommended earlier, we will round all the values of W_t to the next higher integer. That gives $W_1 = \ldots = W_4 = 273$ and $W_5 = W_6 = 738$. This determines the values of the other problem variables. This means that the firm should fire 27 workers in January and hire 465 workers in May. The complete solution is given in Table 4.6.

TABLE 4.6

LP Optimum Found at Step 24 Objective
Function Value 1) 379,320.900

Variable	Value	Reduced Cost
H_1	0.000000	1500.000000
H_2	0.000000	791.378100
H_3	0.000000	222.439900
H_4	0.000000	6.736023
H_5	464.782300	0.000000
H_6	0.000000	192.750300
F_1	27.047150	0.000000
F_2	0.000000	708.621900
F_3	0.000000	1,277.560000
F_4	0.000000	1,493.264000
F_5	0.000000	1,500.000000
F_6	0.000000	1,307.250000
W_0	300.000000	0.000000
W_1	272.952900	0.000000
W_2	272.952900	0.000000
W_3	272.952900	0.000000
W_4	272.952900	0.000000
W_5	737.735200	0.000000
W_6	737.735200	0.000000

(Continued)

TABLE 4.6 (Continued)

LP Optimum Found at Step 24 Objective
Function Value 1) 379,320.900

Variable	Value	Reduced Cost
I_0	500.000000	0.000000
I_1	20.024820	0.000000
I_2	340.000000	0.000000
I_3	160.049800	0.000000
I_4	0.000000	18.445950
I_5	378.458200	0.000000
I_6	600.000000	0.000000
P_1	800.024800	0.000000
P_2	959.975200	0.000000
P_3	720.049600	0.000000
P_4	1,039.950000	0.000000
P_5	2,378.458000	0.000000
P_6	1,621.542000	0.000000

Again, because column H in Table 4.6 corresponds to net demand, we add the 600 units of ending inventory in June, giving a total inventory of 900 + 600 = 1,500 units. Hence, the total cost of this plan is (500)(465) + (1,000)(27) + (80)(1,500) = \$379,500, which represents a substantial savings over both the zero inventory plan and the constant workforce plan.

The results of the linear programming analysis suggest another plan that might be more suitable for the company. Because the optimal strategy is to decrease the workforce in January and build it back up again in May, a reasonable alternative might be to not fire the 27 workers in January and to hire fewer workers in May. In this case, the most efficient method for finding the correct number of workers to hire in May is to simply re-solve the linear program, but without the variables $F_1, \ldots, F_6$, as no firing of workers means that these variables are forced to zero (if you wish to avoid re-entering the problem into the computer, simply append the old formulation with the constraints $F_1 = 0, F_2 = 0, \ldots, F_6 = 0$). The optimal number of workers to hire in May turns out to be 374 if no workers are fired, and the cost of the plan is approximately \$386,120. This is only slightly more expensive than the optimal plan and has the important advantage of not requiring the firing of any workers.

4.4 The Linear Decision Rule

An interesting alternative approach to solving the aggregate planning problem has been suggested by Holt, Modigliani, Muth, and Simon (1960). They assume that all of the relevant costs, including inventory costs and the costs of changing production levels and numbers of workers, are represented by quadratic functions. That is, the total cost over the T-period planning horizon can be written in the form

$$\sum_{t=1}^{T} \left[c_1 W_t + c_2 \left(W_t - W(t-1) \right)^2 + c_3 \left(P_t - Kn_t W_t \right)^2 + c_4 P_t + c_5 \left(I_t - c_6 \right)^2 \right]$$

subject to

$$I_t = I_{t-1} + P_t - D_t \quad \text{for } 1 \le t \le T$$

The values of the constants $c_1, c_2, \ldots, c_6$ must be determined for each particular application. Expressing the cost functions as quadratic functions rather than simple linear functions has some advantages over the linear programming approach. As quadratic functions are differentiable, the standard rules of calculus can be used to determine optimal solutions. The optimal solution will occur where the first partial derivatives with respect to each of the problem variables are zero. When quadratic functions are differentiated, they yield first-order equations (linear equations), which are easy to solve. Also, quadratic functions give a more accurate approximation to general nonlinear functions than to linear functions. (Any nonlinear function may be approximated by a Taylor series expansion in which the first two terms yield a quadratic approximation.)

However, the quadratic approach also has one serious disadvantage. It is that quadratic functions (i.e., parabolas) are symmetric (see Figure 4.17). Hence, the cost of hiring a given number of workers must be the same as the cost of firing the same number of workers, and the cost of producing a given number of units on overtime must be the same as the cost attached to the same number of units of worker idle time. The problem can be overcome somewhat by not setting the center of symmetry of the cost function at zero, but the basic problem of symmetry still prevails.

The most appealing feature of this approach is the simple form of the optimal policy. For example, the optimal production level in period t, P_t, has the form

$$P_t = \sum_{n=0}^{K} \left(a_n D_{t+n} + b W_{t-1} + c I_{t-1} + d \right)$$

The terms a_n, b, c, and d are constants that depend on the cost parameters; W_t has a similar form. The computational advantages of the linear decision rule are less important now than they were when this analysis was first done because of the widespread availability of computers today. Because linear programming provides a much more flexible framework for formulating aggregate planning problems, and reasonably large linear programs can be solved even on personal computers, one would have to conclude that linear programming is a preferable solution technique.

It should be recognized, however, that the text by Holt, Modigliani, Muth, and Simon represents a landmark work in the application of quantitative methods to production planning problems. The authors developed a solution method that results in a set of formulas that are easy to implement, and they actually undertook the implementation of the method. The work details the application of the approach to a large manufacturer of household paints in the Pittsburgh area. The analysis was actually implemented in the company, but a subsequent visit to the firm indicated that serious problems arose when the linear decision rule was followed, primarily because of the firm's policy of not firing workers when the model indicated that they should be fired.

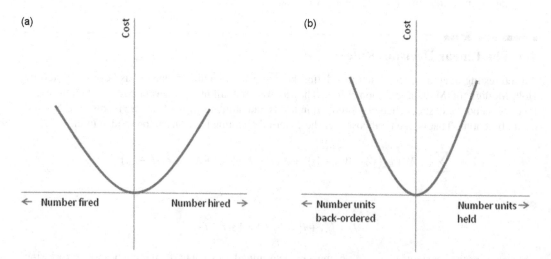

FIGURE 4.17 Quadratic cost functions used in deriving the linear decision rule. (a) Cost of changing workforce levels. (b) Cost of changing inventory levels.

4.4.1 Modeling Management Behavior

Bowman (1963) developed an interesting technique for aggregate planning that should be applicable to other types of problems as well. His idea is to construct a sensible model for controlling production levels and fit the parameters of the model as closely as possible to the actual prior decisions made by management. In this way, the model reflects the judgment and the experience of managers and avoids a number of the problems that arise when using more traditional modeling methods. One such problem is determining the accuracy of the assumptions required by the model. Another problem that is avoided is the need to determine values of input parameters that could be difficult to measure.

Let us consider the problem of producing a single product over T planning periods. Suppose that $D_1, \ldots, D_T$ are the forecasts of demand for the next T periods and that production levels $P_1, \ldots, P_T$ must be determined. The simplest reasonable decision rule is

$$P_t = D_t \quad \text{for } 1 \le t \le T$$

Trying to match production exactly to demand will generally result in a production schedule that is too erratic. Production smoothing can be accomplished using a decision rule of the form

$$P_t = D_t + \alpha(P_{t-1} - D_t),$$

where α is a smoothing factor for production having the property $0 \le \alpha \le 1$. When α equals zero, this rule is identical to the one above. When $\alpha - 1$, the production in period t is exactly the same as the production in period $t - 1$. The choice of α provides a means of placing a relative weight on matching production with demand versus holding production constant from period to period.

In addition to smoothing production, the firm also might be interested in keeping inventory levels near some target level, say I_N. A model that can smooth both inventory and production simultaneously is

$$P_t = D_t + \alpha(P_{t-1} - D_t) + \beta(I_N - I_{t-1}),$$

where $0 \le \beta \le 1$ measures the relative weight placed on smoothing of inventory.

Finally, the model should incorporate demand forecasts. In this way, production levels can be increased or decreased in anticipation of a change in the pattern of demands. A rule that includes smoothing of production and inventory as well as forecasts of future demand is

$$P_t = \sum_{i=t}^{t+n} a_{t-i+1} D_i + \alpha(P_{t-1} - D_t) + \beta(I_N - I_{t-1})$$

The decision rule is arrived at by a straightforward common-sense analysis of what a good production rule should be. It is interesting to note how similar this rule is to the linear decision rule discussed in the previous section, which was derived from a mathematical model. Undoubtedly, the previous work on the linear decision rule inspired the form of this rule. It is often the case that the most valuable feature of a model is indicating the best *form* of an optimal strategy, not necessarily the best strategy itself.

The particular model for P_t requires determination of $a_1, \ldots, a_n, \alpha, \beta$, and I_N. Bowman suggests that the values of these parameters be determined by retrospectively observing the system for a reasonable period of time and fitting the parameters to the actual history of management actions during that time using a technique such as least squares. In this way, the model becomes a reflection of past management behavior.

Bowman compares the actual experience of a number of companies with the experience that they would have had using his approach and shows that in most cases there would have been a substantial cost reduction. The model merely emulates management behavior, so why would it outperform actual management experience? The theory is that a model derived in this manner is a reflection of management making rational decisions, as most of the time the system is stable. However, if a sudden unusual event occurs, such as a much-higher-than-anticipated demand or a sudden decline in productive capacity due, for example, to the breakdown of a machine or the loss of key personnel, it is likely that many managers would tend to overreact. However, the model would recommend production levels that are consistent for making decisions that would keep management from panicking in an unusual situation. Although the approach is conceptually appealing, there are few reports in the literature of successful implementation of such a technique.

4.4.2 Disaggregating Aggregate Plans

Aggregate planning can be done at several levels, but it is always the case that an aggregate plan corresponds to some grouping of items. These groupings can vary in size from several items, composing a product family, to the entire line of items produced by the firm. In either case, ensuring that the aggregate plan and the master production schedules for the individual items are consistent could be an issue. When aggregate plans are the result of combining or aggregating individual item plans, disaggregation is straightforward. However, aggregate planning provides a top-down management perspective, and for that reason aggregate plans are not generally the result of a bottom-up aggregation of single-item master production schedules. A firm concerned with providing consistency between the aggregate plan and the individual item production schedules would need to develop a disaggregation scheme consistent with the definition of an aggregate unit and with the organizational structure of the firm.

It is not clear that coordinating the production schedules for individual items with the aggregate plan is a serious issue in all circumstances. Aggregate planning may be viewed primarily as a means of determining gross workforce levels over a specified planning horizon. Aggregate units may be a fictitious construct designed only to develop a meaningful representation of the overall sales activity of the firm. When this is the case, the detailed planning of individual item production plans can be treated as a separate problem that must be solved subject to the constraints determined by the size of the workforce.

However, if an aggregate unit of production does correspond to an actual item, or is determined using a hierarchical planning structure such as the one discussed earlier in the chapter (items, families, and types), it is important that the master production schedule and the aggregate plan be consistent. The problem of breaking down an aggregate plan into a master schedule by item has received little attention. Individual companies are probably dealing with the problem in ways that suit their specific production systems and organizational structures, but few general approaches to the problem have been developed.

A general scheme for dealing with the disaggregation issue that is consistent with the grouping of items into families and families into types has been championed by a group of researchers from MIT. The methods are discussed in detail in Hax and Candea (1984). We present a very brief overview of their approach.

Suppose that X^* represents the number of aggregate units of production of a given type indicated by the aggregate plan for the next immediate planning period. One computes the number of units of family j to be produced, Y_j, by solving the following mathematical programming problem:

$$\text{Minimize} \sum_{j=1}^{J} \frac{K_j \lambda_j}{Y_j}$$

subject to

$$\sum_{j=1}^{J} Y_j = X^*$$

and

$$a_j \leq Y_j \leq b_j \quad \text{for } 1 \leq j \leq J,$$

where K_j is the setup cost for family j and λ_j is the annual demand for family j. The constants a_j and b_j are upper and lower bounds on the number of units of each family that can be produced. The term $K_j \lambda_j / Y_j$ is the average annual setup cost for family j. Hence, it follows that the objective function represents the total average annual setup cost for all of the families constituting this particular type. Holding cost is ignored at this level, because the objective function for the aggregate planning model that resulted in X^* is assumed to have included holding costs. The justification for using only the first-period results of the aggregate plan is that schedules are generated on a rolling horizon basis. As new information becomes available each period, the old schedules are revised and updated.

A number of feasibility issues need to be addressed before the family run sizes Y_j are further disaggregated into lots for individual items. The objective is to schedule the lots for individual items within a family so that they run out at the scheduled setup time for the family. In this way, items within the same family can be produced within the same production setup.

The concept of disaggregating the aggregate plan along organizational lines in a fashion that is consistent with the aggregation scheme is an appealing one. Whether or not the methods discussed in this section provide a workable link between aggregate plans and detailed item schedules remains to be seen.

Another approach to the disaggregation problem has been explored by Chung and Krajewski (1984). They develop a mathematical programming formulation of the problem. Inputs to the program include aggregate plans for each product family. This includes setup time, setup status, total production level for the family, inventory level, workforce level, overtime, and regular time availability. The goal of the analysis is to specify lot sizes and timing of production runs for each individual item, consistent with the aggregate information for the product family. Although such a formulation provides a potential link between the aggregate plan and the master production schedule, the resulting mathematical program requires many inputs and can result in a very large mixed integer problem that could be very time consuming to solve. For these reasons, firms are unlikely to use such methods when there are large numbers of individual items in each product family.

4.4.3 Production Planning on a Global Scale

Globalization of manufacturing operations is commonplace. Many major corporations are now classified as multinationals; manufacturing and distribution activities routinely cross international borders. With the globalization of both sources of production and markets, firms must rethink production planning strategies. One issue explored in this chapter was smoothing of production plans over time; costs of increasing or decreasing workforce levels (and, hence, production levels) play a major role in the optimization of any aggregate plan. When formulating global production strategies, other smoothing issues arise. Exchange rates, costs of direct labor, and tax structure are just some of the differences among countries that must be factored into a global strategy.

Why the increased interest in global operations? In short, cost and competitiveness. According to McGrath and Bequillard (1989):

> The benefits of a properly executed international manufacturing strategy can be very substantial. A well developed strategy can have a direct impact on the financial performance and ultimately be reflected in increased profitability. In the electronic industry, there are examples of companies attributing 5% to 15% reduction in cost of goods sold, 10% to 20% increase in sales, 50% to 150% improvement in asset utilization, and 30% to 100% increase in inventory turnover to their internationalization of manufacturing.

Cohen et al. (1989) outline some of the issues that a firm must consider when planning production levels on a worldwide basis. These include the following:

- In order to achieve the kinds of economics of scale required to be competitive today, multinational plants and vendors must be managed as a global system.
- Duties and tariffs are based on material flows. Their impact must be factored into decisions regarding shipments of raw material, intermediate product, and finished product across national boundaries.
- Exchange rates fluctuate randomly and affect production costs and pricing decisions in countries where the product is produced and sold.
- Corporate tax rates vary widely from one country to another.
- Global sourcing must take into account longer lead times, lower unit costs, and access to new technologies.

- Strategies for market penetration, local content rules, and quotas constrain product flow across borders.
- Product designs may vary by national market.
- Centralized control of multinational enterprises creates difficulties for several reasons, and decentralized control requires coordination.
- Cultural, language, and skill differences can be significant.

Determining optimal globalized manufacturing strategies is clearly a daunting problem for any multinational firm. One can formulate and solve mathematical models similar to the linear programming formulations of the aggregate planning models presented in this chapter, but the results of these models must always be balanced against judgment and experience. Cohen et al. (1989) consider such a model. They assume multiple products, plants, markets, raw materials, vendors, vendor supply contract alternatives, time periods, and countries. Their formulation is a large-scale mixed integer, nonlinear program.

One issue not treated in their model is that of exchange rate fluctuations and their effect on both pricing and production planning. Pricing, in particular, is traditionally done by adding a markup to unit costs in the home market. This completely ignores the issue of exchange rate fluctuations and can lead to unreasonable prices in some countries. For example, this issue has arisen at Caterpillar Tractor. In this case, dealers all over the world were billed in U.S. dollars based on U.S. production costs. When the dollar was strong relative to other currencies, retail prices charged to overseas customers were not competitive in local markets. Caterpillar found themselves losing market share abroad as a result. In the early 1980s, the firm switched to a locally competitive pricing strategy to counteract this problem.

The notion that manufacturing capacity can be used as a hedge against exchange rate fluctuations has been explored by several researchers. Kogut and Kulatilaka (1994), for example, develop a mathematical model for determining when it is optimal to switch production from one location to another. Since the cost of switching is assumed to be positive, there must be sufficiently large difference in exchange rates before switching is recommended. As an example, they consider a situation where a firm can produce its product in either the United States or Germany. If production is currently being done in one location, the model provides a means of determining if it is economical to switch locations based on the relative strengths of the deutschmark and dollar. While such models are in the early stages of development, they provide a means of rationalizing international production planning strategies. Similar issues were also explored by Huchzermier and Cohen in 1996.

4.4.4 Practical Considerations

Aggregate planning can be a valuable aid in planning production and manpower levels for a company and provides a means of absorbing demand fluctuations by smoothing workforce and production levels. There are a number of advantages for planning on the aggregate level over the detail level. One is that the cost of preparing forecasts and determining productivity and cost parameters on an individual item basis can be prohibitive. The cost of data collection and input is probably a more significant drawback of large-scale mathematical programming formulations of detailed production plans than in the cost of actually performing the computations. A second advantage of aggregate planning is the relative improvement in forecast accuracy that can be achieved by aggregating items. Aggregate forecasts are generally more accurate than individual forecasts. Finally, an aggregate planning framework allows the manager to see the "big picture" and not be unduly influenced by specifics.

With all these advantages, one would think that aggregate planning would have an important place in the planning of the production activities of most companies. However, this does not appear to be the case. There are number of reasons for the lack of interest in aggregate planning methodology. First is the difficulty of properly defining an aggregate unit of production. There appears to be no simple way of specifying how individual items should be aggregated that will work in all situations. Second, once an aggregating scheme is developed, cost estimates and demand forecasts for aggregate units are required. It is difficult enough to obtain accurate cost and demand information for real units. Obtaining such information on an aggregate basis could be considerably more difficult, depending on the aggregation scheme that is used. Third, aggregate planning models rarely reflect the political and operational realities of the environment in which the company is operating. Assuming that workforce levels can be changed easily is probably not very realistic for most companies. Finally, as Silver and Peterson (1985) suggest, managers do not want to rely on a mathematical model for answers to the extremely sensitive and important issues that are addressed in this analysis.

Another issue is whether or not the goals of aggregate planning analysis can be achieved through methods other than those discussed in this chapter. Schwarz and Johnson (1978) claim that the cost savings achieved using a linear decision rule for aggregate planning could be obtained by improved management of the aggregate inventory alone. They substantiate their hypothesis using the data reported in Holt, Modigliani, Muth, and Simon (1960) and show that for the case of the paint company virtually all of the cost savings of the linear decision rule were a result of increasing the buffer inventory and not of making major changes in the size of the labor force. Better inventory management could return a large portion of the benefits that a company might realize with aggregate planning.

Even with this long list of disadvantages, the mathematical models discussed in this chapter can, and should, serve as an aid to production planners. Although optimal solutions to a mathematical model may not be true optimal solutions to the problem that they address, they do provide insight and could reveal alternatives that would not otherwise be evident.

REFERENCES

Bowman, E.H. Production scheduling by the transportation method of linear programming. *Operations Research* 4 (1956), 100–103.

Bowman, E.H. Consistency and optimality in managerial decision making. *Management Science* 9 (1963), 310–321.

Chung, C., and L.J. Krajewski. Planning horizons for master production scheduling. *Journal of Operations Management* 4 (August 1984), 389–406.

Cohen, M.A., M.L. Fisher, and J. Jaikurmar. International manufacturing and distribution networks, In *Managing International Manufacturing*, ed. K. Ferdows, pp. 67–93. Amsterdam: North Holland, 1989.

Erenguc, S., and S. Tufekci. A transportation type aggregate production model with bounds on inventory and backordering. *European Journal of Operations Research* 35 (1988), 414–425.

Hax, A.C., and D. Candea. *Production and Inventory Management*. Englewood Cliffs, NJ: Prentice Hall, 1984.

Hax, A.C., and H.C. Meal. Hierarchical integration of production planning and scheduling. In *TIMS Studies in Management Science*. Volume 1. *Logistics*, ed. M. Geisler, pp. 53–69. New York: Elsevier, 1975.

Hillier, F.S., and G.J. Lieberman. *Introduction to Operations Research*. 5th ed. San Francisco: Holden Day, 1990.

Holt, C.C., F. Modigliani, J.F. Muth, and H.A. Simon. *Planning Production, Inventories, and Workforce*. Englewood Cliffs, NJ: Prentice hall, 1960.

Kogut, B., and N. Kulatilaka. Operating flexibility, global manufacturing, and the option value of a multinational network. *Management Science* 40 (1994), 123–139.

McGrath, M.E., and R.B. Bequillard. International manufacturing strategies and infrastructural considerations in the electronics industry. In *Managing International Manufacturing*, ed. K Ferdows, pp. 23–40. Amsterdam: North Holland, 1989.

Schrage, L. *Linear, Integer, and Quadratic Programming with LINDO*. Palo Alto, CA: Scientific Press, 1984.

Schwarz, L.B., and R.E. Johnson. An appraisal of the empirical performance of the linear decision rule for aggregate planning. *Management Science* 24 (1978), 844–849.

Silver, E.A., and R. Peterson. *Decision Systems for Inventory Management and Production Planning*. 2nd ed. New York: John Wiley & Sons, 1985.

5

Inventory Control

Erick C. Jones

History is important because I believe lessons are repeated until they are learned.

Erick C. Jones

Inventory amount and size decisions are traditionally driven by the costs of maintaining inventories and costs of being out of stock. Operations managers seek to maintain inventory levels that minimize the total cost of both.

In this section, we discuss closed-loop inventory control. The approaches discussed here are relatively unsophisticated. There is a large amount of information available in other academic texts, along with consultative materials available in industry. We will discuss certain aspects of inventory control theory so that the impact that radio frequency identification (RFID) technologies have can be recognized.

5.1 Inventory Carrying Costs

Inventory carrying costs fall into several categories. They include the following:

1. Storage costs are the costs associated with occupying space in a storeroom, warehouse, or distribution center. Inventory costs such as insurance for fire, flood, and theft are included in the expense of storing goods.
2. Theft or inventory shrinkage identifies when more items are recorded entering warehouses than leaving.
3. Obsolescence describes when items in an inventory eventually become out of date.
4. Depreciation or deterioration of inventory as a function of time, not usage.
5. Interest refers to the interest charges for the money invested in inventories. Oftentimes, this represents the investment into company inventories, as opposed to money that can be invested in other investments.
6. Taxes refer to when inventories are taxed. Traditionally the tax is derived on the basis of the inventory on hand on a certain date. Most companies make a concentrated effort to have inventory present on that day to be as low as possible.
7. Carrying costs include inventory tax, and costs associated with avoiding or evading the inventory taxes.
   a. Consider products such as fresh produce which may deteriorate in only a few days. The depreciation portion of a produce company's carrying costs might be as high as 50% per day. Other products depreciate completely given their expiration dates including products such as dairy products, drugs, bread, some soft drinks, and camera film. For these products, the rate of depreciation can be calculated because expired products that are unsold must be removed from the shelf.

TABLE 5.1

Component Breakdown of the 25% Figure

Insurance	0.25%
Storage facilities	0.25
Taxes	0.50
Transportation	0.50
Handling costs	2.50
Depreciation	5.00
Interest	6.00
Obsolescence	10.00
Total	25.00%

Source: Adapted from L. P. Alford and J. R. Bangs (eds.), *Production Handbook* (New York: Ronald, 1955), pp. 396–397.

b. Specialized inventory costs are related to pets and livestock which have costs related to being watered and fed. Security cost for high-value items such as computer chips may increase inventory carrying costs.

c. Inventory carrying charges are expressed as a percentage of the inventory's value, and widely cited estimate is that carrying costs approximate 25% per year of a product's value (Table 5.1).

Opportunity costs are not traditionally included in most carrying costs calculations. Most companies must consider the trade-off of holding inventory against the having inventory to meet the fluctuations of customer demand.

5.1.1 Stock-Out Costs

Stock-out refers to the event that occurs when an item is out of stock when a customer wants to buy the item. Stock-out costs are difficult to determine and oftentimes effect customer satisfaction. The difficulty of determining cost that is lost due to stock-outs is that it requires a good understanding of company's customer behavior. Customer can have many varied reactions to stock-outs. We suggest that the responses can be placed into three categories:

• Future sale
• Lost sale
• Loss of customer.

Consider a set of 500 customers who experienced stock-outs for a given product. The three types of customers responses may suggest of the 500 customers, 50 will return as a future sale, 325 customers may go to another store which represents a lost sell, and 125 customers may never return to the company. The percentages represented by future sale, lost sale, and loss of the customer are 10%, 65%, and 25%, respectively. These percentages can be considered probabilities of the events taking place and can be used to determine the average cost of a stock-out.

Table 5.2 illustrates the procedure. Each cost is multiplied by the likelihood that it will occur, and the results are added. A delayed sale has no cost because the customer is brand loyal and purchases the product when it is again available. The lost sale alternative results in loss of the profit that would have been made on the customer's purchase. The lost customer situation is the worst. The customer tries the competitor's product and prefers it to the product originally requested. The customer is lost, and the cost involved is that of developing a new, brand-loyal customer. These costs

TABLE 5.2

Determination of the Average Cost of a Stock-Out

Alternative	Loss	Probability	Average Cost
1. Brand-loyal customer	$0.00	0.10	$0.00
2. Switches and comes back	$37.00	0.65	$24.05
3. Lost customer	$1,200.00	0.25	$300.00
Average cost of a stock-out.		1.00	$324.05

are usually determined by a firms marketing department, but we use the suggested numbers for demonstration purposes.

5.1.2 Safety Stocks

Firms usually maintain **safety stocks** or excess inventory in order to prevent an excessive number of stock-outs. Analysis is required in order to minimize the amount of safety stock and to determine the optimum level of safety stock. This is illustrated in Table 5.3.

We consider this example to demonstrate safety-stock analysis. Consider that goods must be ordered from a wholesaler in multiples of 10. The carrying cost of an additional or marginal 10 units is $1,200. However, by stocking an additional 10 units of safety stock and maintaining it throughout the year, the firm is able to prevent 20 stock-outs. The average cost of a stock-out has already been determined to be $324.05. We derive that saving 20 stock-outs saves the firm $6,481.00 ($324.05 × 20). In this case, the savings justify the investment costs. Next, we consider an alternative that maintains a safety stock throughout the year of 20 units. This adds $1,200 to the costs but prevents 16 additional stock-outs from occurring, thereby saving $5,184.80.

The optimum quantity of safety stock is 60 units. With this quantity, the carrying cost of 10 additional units is $1,200, but $1,296.20 is saved. If the safety stocks are increased from 60 to 70 units, the additional carrying cost is again $1,200, while the savings are only *$972.15*. We conclude that the firm would be more profitable by permitting three stock-outs to occur each year. Note that these concerns determine a level of customer service.

Safety stocks indicate that a firm will attempt to meet customer demand for out-of-stock items. Many firms choose not to maintain safety stock due to the high carrying cost for inventory. Some mass merchandisers do not replace many items given their profit margins and the fact that customers are not loyal to buying at that firm. In these situations, customer behavior is to buy a complete set of items and/or fixtures needed to complete a project. They understand that the merchandiser may not have that product in the future. This is evidenced in popular "closeout" stores such as Big Lots and Hobby Lobby in which

TABLE 5.3

Safety Level Analysis

Number of Units of Safety Stock	Total Value of Safety Stock ($480 per Unit)	25% Annual Carrying Cost	Carrying Cost of Incremental Safety Stock	Number of Additional Orders Filled	Additional Stock-out Costs Avoided
10	$4,800	$1,200	$1,200	20	$6,481.00
20	9,600	2,400	1,200	16	5,184.80
30	14,400	3,600	1,200	12	3,888.60
40	19,200	4,800	1,200	8	2,592.40
50	24,000	6,000	1,200	6	1,944.30
60	28,800	7,200	1,200	4	1,296.20
70	33,600	8,400	1,200	3	972.15

the firm buys large quantities of a product and sells it at a discount. When the product is sold out, there is no expectation of that product appearing at the store in the future.

5.1.3 Economic Order Quantity

Safety stock level is the minimum inventory a firm tries to keep on hand. Commonly, determining the inventory level, how they should be reordered, and how much should be ordered each time are determined by the economic order quantity (EOQ). We will provide a brief overview of EOQ. Further reading is available in academic texts that discuss operation and production planning.

The typical inventory order size problem can be dealt with calculating the proper order size based on minimizing the total of two costs: (1) the costs of carrying the inventory, which are in direct proportion to the size of the order that will arrive; and (2) the costs of ordering, which mainly involve the paperwork associated with handling each order, irrespective of its size. Consider if there were no inventory carrying costs, customers would hold inventory and avoid reordering. If there were no costs associated with ordering, one would place orders continually and maintain no inventory at all, aside from safety stocks.

Mathematically, the EOQ is determined using this formula:

$$EOQ = \sqrt{\frac{2AB}{I}}$$

where
  EOQ = The most economic order size, in dollars
  A = Annual usage, in dollars
  B = Company costs per order of placing the order
  I = Carrying costs of the inventory (expressed as an annual percentage)

If $1,000 of an item is used each year, if the order costs are *$25* per order submitted, and if carrying costs are 20%, what is the EOQ?

$$EOQ = \sqrt{\frac{2 \times 1,000 \times 25}{0.20}} = \sqrt{250,000} = \$500 \text{ order size}$$

Because of the assumption of even outward flow of goods, inventory carrying costs are applied to one half the order size that would be the average inventory on hand, as illustrated in Table 5.4.

EOQs, once calculated, may not be the same as the lot sizes that the product is bought and sold at a company. EOQs can also be calculated in terms of the number of units that should be ordered. The formula is

$$EOQ = \sqrt{\frac{2(\text{Annual use in number of units}) (\text{Cost of placing an order})}{\text{Annual carrying cost per item per year}}}$$

Assume that an item in Table 5.4, for example, costs *$5*. Substituting numbers in the new formula yields

$$EOQ = \sqrt{\frac{2 \times 1,000 \times 25}{0.20}} = \sqrt{\frac{10,000}{1}} = 100 \text{ units}$$

The earlier EOQ formula and Table 5.4 showed that $500 was the best order size, and because the product is priced at $5.00 per unit, the answer is the same.

The simple EOQ formulation just given does not take into large volume discounts. We can review Table 5.4 and visualize how discounts would have an impact on total costs as the figures. By imputing different values into the table horizontally, volume discounts can be evaluated and marketed to increase future business.

TABLE 5.4

EOQ Calculations

Number of Orders per Year	Order Size	Ordering Cost	Carrying Cost of Average Inventory in Stock	Total Cost
1	$1,000	$125	$100	$125
2	500	50	50	100
3	333	75	33	108
4	250	100	25	125
5	200	125	20	145

5.2 Inventory Flows

In the previous section, we utilize the figures from the EOQ and the safety-stock calculations as an analysis tool. We cannot utilize these same calculations to determine inventory policy. We must first take the given information and use it to develop an **inventory flow** diagram. Assume that the EOQ, in this instance, has been determined to be 120 units, that the safety stock level is 60 units, that average demand is 30 units per day, and that the replenishment or order cycle is 2 days. On day 1 (in the Figure 5.1), an EOQ of 120 units arrives.

We will consider a common inventory flow diagram suggested in other texts. Consider the following, total inventory (point A) is 180 units (one EOQ plus 60 units of safety stock). Demand is steady at 30 units per day. On day 3, total inventory has declined to 120 units (point B), which is the reorder point, because it takes 2 days to receive an order and during this time, 60 units would be sold. If the inventory policy mandates that safety stock is not to be used under normal circumstances, reordering at 120 units means that 60 units (safety stock) will be on hand 2 days later when the EOQ arrives. The EOQ of 120 units arrives at point C, and then, total inventory increases to 180 units at point D.

If the rate of sales doubles to 60 units per day, the reorder point is hit at 120 units (point E), and an additional EOQ is ordered. However, it will not arrive for 2 days. A day after the reordering, the regular inventory is exhausted, and at point F, the safety stock is starting to be used. At point G, the EOQ

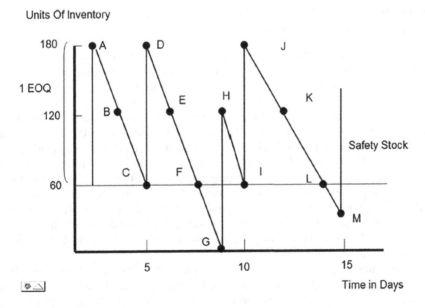

FIGURE 5.1 Inventory flow diagram.

arrives just as the safety stock is about to be exhausted. If the EOQ arrived later than day 8, a stock-out would have occurred. The new EOQ boosts the inventory to 120 units, which is also the reorder point. Therefore, at point H, another EOQ is ordered. Starting on day 8, the demand settles back to the old average of 30 units per day.

If it appeared that the demand rate of 60 units per day was going to become the average demand rate, the EOQ will need to be recalculated. Recall that a basic input into the EOQ formula is annual sales of the product. If this number changes, then the EOQ must be determined again.

Starting at point H, demand is again 30 units per day. The next EOQ arrives on schedule at point I, and total inventory increases to 180 units at point J. The reorder point is at 120 units, and an EOQ is ordered on day 12. Demand stays constant, but the transportation mode delivering the EOQ is delayed one day. Instead of arriving on day 14, it arrives on day 15. Safety stock is entered at point L on day 14. A stock-out is again prevented because the EOQ arrives at point M. Note that safety stock protects against two problem areas: increased rate of demand and an increased replenishment cycle.

When an EOQ is used, as illustrated in Figure 5.1, the time between orders varies. The normal time between orders was 4 days, but when sales doubled, the time between orders was only 2 days. One requirement for the effective utilization of an EOQ is that the level of inventory in the system must be monitored constantly. The ability of RFID to allow for this type of monitoring holds great promise for using EOQ theories more effectively. Then, when the reorder point is hit, an EOQ is ordered. With the advent of computerization, many firms have the capability to constantly monitor their inventory and hence have the option of using an EOQ system. A reorder point for each item can be established in the computer's memory, so it can indicate when the stock has been depleted to a point where a new order should be placed. The integration of RFID will allow for middle wear, decision support, and execution systems to transmit the purchase order to the vendor electronically.

A variation of the EOQ method is the *fixed-order quantity* method, used in repetitive purchases of the same commodity. This method can be initiated with RFID technologies, triggering the reorder points. An example would be when a materials' retailer located in China buys product by the barge load (approximately 1,000 tons per load). The retailer would wait until its product is out of stock before ordering another barge load. RFID would enable this type of activity by triggering the point-of-sale (POS) checkout counter system to order the next lot of products from the China manufacturer directly. Tying the technical knowledge of the quantity to order with the automatic information capture of RFID will provide tremendous value in the future.

5.3 Fixed-Order-Interval System

An alternative inventory concept that is also commonly used is known as the fixed-order-interval system. In this system, EOQs are not used; instead, orders are placed at fixed intervals, such as every 3 days or twice a month. In the EOQ system, the time interval fluctuates, with the order size remaining the same. In fixed-interval systems, the opposite holds, and order sizes may vary.

Fixed-interval systems are used in many situations. One situation is when the firm does not maintain automatically updated stock levels. Such firms are manually checked to verify the levels of all items and determine which stocks are running low. This task is assigned on a regular basis and may be laborious. Another situation is when vendors offer the firm significant discounts if it will place its orders at certain fixed-time intervals. Because the discounts are greater than the advantages of using the EOQ system, the fixed-interval ordering system is utilized. Further, an additional condition is when the firm buys free on board (FOB) origin and tries to utilize its private trucking fleet whenever possible. If one of the firm's trucks travels empty in one direction without freight, commonly called deadheads, from a point near a supply source back to the firm's plant on a regular basis, the firm may decide to buy FOB origin and carry supplies in its own truck.

The fixed-order-interval system is commonly used with a safety-stock inventory. It usually requires more safety stock than the EOQ system because the EOQ system requires constant monitoring of its inventory levels. In an EOQ system, if sales start to increase, the reorder point will be moved to an earlier time and a new order for an EOQ system needs to be placed. Stock-outs can still take place, but only during the restocking cycle after the new order has been placed. With the fixed-order-interval system, the inventory levels are not monitored and a stock-out can occur during both the order cycle and the time before order placement.

Most fixed-order-interval systems do borrow one element from EOQ systems. Next to each bin or slot in the warehouse is a barcode, card, or indicator that will allow for determination of the minimum quantity for that product. When the order pickers note that the stocks have been reduced to this level, they notify their supervisor, who decides whether the reorder should occur immediately or on the next scheduled date.

Cyclical buying is a very specialized form of fixed-interval ordering. This practice occurs in the women's fashion industry, in which retailers place their orders directly with the manufacturer for each season's fashions, and there is almost no possibility of reordering. Another example is a grocery retailer's purchase of Halloween pumpkins or Christmas trees.

5.4 Just-in-Time Inventory Systems

An inventory system that has received widespread attention is the just-in-time (JIT) system. The concept is related to the fixed-order-interval system, and customers place orders with their suppliers on set schedules that frequently involve daily or hourly deliveries. In comparison to the EOQ system, the concept is based on the assumption that ordering costs are negligible; hence, firms order frequently to minimize inventory holding costs. In JIT systems, inventory is kept at a minimum because the processes create perpetual motion and continuous movement.

In addition to the JIT inventory systems, there are several other, more traditional systems for replenishing inventory stocks. Nearly, all inventory systems require some formal stock-level monitoring capability. In practice today, the JIT systems may be incorporated into execution systems that are stand-alone, which are often termed best of breed or within a larger enterprise-wide system. Software applications that create perpetual motions and execution include warehouse management systems (WMS), transportation management systems (TMS), and order management systems (OMS).

5.5 RFID and Inventory Control

Some researchers suggest that operational labor can be reduced in distribution operations by as much as 30%. Kearney (2004), a notable supply chain consulting firm, suggests that labor savings of 7.5% are possible from reduction inventory cycle counting by using RFID. Distribution inbound receiving along with inventory cycle counting inventory reductions was recognized by Accenture Consulting. Other researchers have reported savings in stocking and retail checkout operations (Chappel et al., 2002).

Opportunities in which RFID passive implementations can save money in operations in the future include

- Automatic replenishment from reserve stocking area
- Safety-stock reduction
- Automatic picking and stocking routing
- Automatic order generation from current inventory availability.

5.6 Automatic Replenishment

Optimizing replenishments within warehouse or distribution centers (replenish primary picking locations, cross-docking, and kitting operations), within retail operations (replenish shelves from the back room to the retail floor), and within the supply chain (replenish or stock inventory between different nodes in the supply chain) are the practical applications for implementing RFID.

5.7 Safety-Stock Reduction

Researchers have investigated inventory control models and their impact on safety stock. Some research suggests transactional errors lead to variability in planning and inflate the need for safety stock. Transaction errors create excess inventory due to miscounting of inventory, and buffer stock becomes necessary to meet service for these errors. The buffer stock for errors and the excess stock maintained due to the bullwhip effect created by inventory timing create a large amount of excess inventory (Kok and Shang, 2007).

So commonly, the optimal amount of inventory ordered traditionally derived by the EOQ or that includes a reorder component is represented by a continuous review (Q, R) system. Oftentimes, to account for the scheduling and lack of real-time information, an adjusted periodic-review system is used which includes safety-stock inventory. Recently, researchers have addressed how RFID can influence the amount of inventory. Consider the following model from Lee et al. (2005).

1. Here, lead time is defined as placing an emergent order $q(q = \alpha Q, \alpha < 1)$ at any time point b based on RFID real-time information as l, and cost to place the emergent order is $k(l)$.
2. l is much less than the lead time of the regular order (Q). Additionally, the probability the emergent order will arrive before the regular order to be $p(l)$ if the regular order is already on its way and an emergent order is released anyway.
3. Moreover, assume that expected total cost associated with inventory position IP and RFID reading point b without releasing emergent order is $C_0(IP, b)$ and the according total cost with emergent order release is $C_1(IP, b)$.
4. So, we can compare the two different costs under periodic review without RFID implementation and continuous review with given RFID real-time information in order to decide whether an emergent order should be placed.

$$C_1(IP, b) = K(l) + P(l) * C_0(IP, b) + (1 - P(l)) * C_0(IP + q, b)$$

Other researchers such as utilize similar continuous review application models to determine inventory levels in a real-time manner. In summary, current research models suggest that inventory can be reduced using RFID technologies due to the fact that their real-time data capture abilities allow for common periodic models to move closer to the theoretical optimal continuous review models. The largest challenge is moving this theory to practice. Currently, in order for this model to work in practice, a fixed infrastructure of antennas and readers is in place at the operational level. This would, in reality, cost operations more in process redesign than the theoretical inventory reduction savings.

5.8 Picking and Routing

Using RFID technology, such as real-time locator systems, the promise of capitalizing on employee location information and inventory status to optimize employees order picking and stocking routes can be realized. This use of RFID builds on picking routes and stocking strategies commonly used in WMS.

An RFID system's ability to provide real-time information will further help optimize order picking schedules. The opportunities to reduce labor cost in these activities may be realized, and the significance in labor savings may be large. Labor reduction of 20% for picking and stocking labor is commonly mentioned by users of WMS that employ these types of algorithms.

5.9 Order Batching of Waves

Using RFID to group orders, commonly called waves, is automatically based on the latest inventory availability. The opportunity to use inventory as it is being received at the dock for immediate shipments can be utilized, dramatically reducing labor for stocking, replenishment, and picking. This theory, commonly called cross-docking, requires a considerable amount of receiving labor to be realized. The promise of RFID will truly enable this one of many opportunities to effectively organize, group, and fulfill orders automatically.

Next, the importance of order wave batching is critical in high-speed operations, but inventory inaccuracies can reduce the quality of these batching of orders and reduce their effectiveness. Specifically, in order management modules of WMS or enterprise resource system (ERP), the order bid processes within the software schema orders compete against one another for resources to meet their specific goals, described as the bid process in the negotiation schema. The real-time ability of RFID to provide inventory accuracy and identify secondary location of the inventory immediately can improve the accuracy of the wave batches.

5.10 Summary

In summary, the contribution of RFID systems to closed-loop distribution logistics can produce significant contributions in three areas: (1) inventory reduction with respect to safety-stock reduction, (2) optimization of order grouping and releases, and (3) labor reduction with respect to picking and stocking labor.

The real benefit of RFID will be based on its ability to provide the inventory accuracy benefits of current technologies such as barcodes and translate the non-line of sight benefits into inventory savings. The areas that will be investigated in the future from a closed-loop perspective in distribution operations, including the aforementioned areas, are listed below:

1. Physical and cycle inventory counts
2. Inventory replenishment
3. Order picking
4. Inventory stocking
5. Order cross-docking
6. Order kitting
7. Many other common distribution operations.

The realization of these savings will more than likely result as RFID is integrated into common execution software, such as WMS, LES, and TMS, quantifying labor savings.

We previously discussed the benefits of RFID technology as a closed-loop systems framework. Traditional automatic identification systems are closed loop in the fact that they are static and traditionally are used within one tier of the supply chain. Consider a tote barcode or pallet tag that is used within a company's distribution center or between other distribution centers. Rarely is this barcode integrated between other unknown partners or even the customer to evaluate the history of that unit load, as opposed to a system in which information is passed from one intelligent automatic identification technology to another.

Consider each technology acting as an intelligent agent. So, if a customer desires to know the history of a product, the UPC transfers information to a barcode, which transfers information to a passive RFID tag, which transfers information to an active RFID tag, and which passes information to a Global Positioning System (GPS). This daisy chain type of interlinking provides an open loop concept that provides all potential players a look into the supply chain's effective visibility. This nesting of Auto ID technologies may be an intermediate step to profitability for most intermediate RFID implementations. We next consider a framework that describes these types of technologies.

REFERENCES

Atali, A., Lee, H. L., & Özer, Ö. (2005). If the inventory manager knew: Value of RFID under imperfect inventory information. Technical report, Stanford University, Stanford, CA.

Chappell, G., Durdan, D., Gilbert, G., Ginsburg, L., Smith, J., & Tobolski, J. (2002). *Auto-ID on Delivery: The Value of Auto-ID Technology in the Retail Supply Chain*. Accenture White Paper.

Gaukler, G., Seifert, R., Hausman, W. H. (2004). Item-level RFID in the retail supply chain. To appear in *Production and Operations Management*.

Kearney, A. T. (2004). Meeting the retail RFID mandate: A discussion of the issues facing CPG companies. Technical report, A. T. Kearney, Inc.

Kök, A. G., & Shang, K. (2007). Inspection and replenishment policies for systems with inventory record inaccuracy. *Manufacturing and Service Operations Management*, 9, 185–205.

6

ERP Systems

Erick C. Jones and Gowthaman Anantakrishnan

You can beat a team of individuals with great talent with a talented team that has a system.

Erick C. Jones

6.1 Research Summary

Organizations continuously seek effective ways to conduct their business and operations by employing various techniques and tools. Enterprise resource planning (ERP) is an important tool that has been in practice by organizations for more than a couple of decades. By 2013, the ERP world market size has reached $24.5 billion. ERP is a suite of integrated applications or software for business management that stores the data from every stage of business operations (inventory, production planning, cost and development, etc.) in a centralized database. The data stored in ERP are used in various business decisions like purchasing raw materials, delivery date determination, lead time for delivery date, etc. The accuracy rate of the data should be very high to avoid making incorrect business decisions. Data accuracy is affected the most by manual errors and update intervals. The aim of this research is to reduce the manual errors and provide real-time data updates by integrating AutoID technologies with the ERP system. Systems, applications, and products in data processing (SAP) system is chosen as the test ERP system because it is the most popular system and holds the majority of the market share.

This research evaluates the impact of the AutoID technologies on the ERP system data accuracy and reliability by two different approaches. In the first approach, the impact on accuracy and reliability is evaluated by comparing the traditional manual data entry methods and AutoID technologies' accuracy and reliability. In the second approach, mathematical model representing the perceived impact of data from different warehouse areas on the ERP systems data accuracy is built by developing a survey and collecting the answers from various SAP business champions. Regression analysis will be used to analyze the data collected. The specific aims of these approaches are provided below.

Specific Aim 1: Evaluate the observed perspective of the warehouse areas' impact on ERP system data accuracy.
The methods and approach envisioned for this research include regression analysis on the data to develop a mathematical model to represent the effects of warehouse areas (finished good product inventory (FI), raw material inventory (RI), packaging material inventory (PI), storage location (SL), and delivery planning) on ERP data accuracy. A survey will be developed to measure the impact of AutoID on overall ERP and its functional areas. This survey will be answered by AutoID and ERP users from various levels within the organizations. The data collected will be analyzed using regression to provide an impact model. Software used are Minitab, SAS, Microsoft Excel, and ERP system.

Specific Aim 2: Evaluate the performance impact of manual entry, barcode, and radio frequency identification (RFID) on ERP.
The methods and approach envisioned for this research are to evaluate the accuracy and reliability of the data entered into the ERP system by the manual entry, barcode, and RFID. In the manual entry method, the data are entered into the ERP system using different personnel for each trial. The personnel chosen

will have various experience levels and different age groups. In the barcode method, the inventories are tracked using the barcode. The ERP system will be integrated with barcode reader, and as the product is read by the barcode scanner, the data are captured and entered into the ERP system directly. In the RFID methodology, instead of barcode, RFID will be used. The experiment is repeated with different volumes of inventories, different product sizes and types, and different intervals of time. Data collected are analyzed by using analysis of variance (ANOVA). Software used are Minitab, SAS, Microsoft Excel, and ERP system.

Specific Aim 3: Evaluate the economic impact of AutoID on ERP.

The methods and approach envisioned for this research include calculating the return on investment (ROI) analysis. ROI is the ratio of the gains from the investment and cost of investment to the cost of the investment. The gains in the investment on AutoID is calculated by identifying the cost saved in terms of reducing excess inventory cost, reduction in loss of business due to fewer inventories, and impact on customer satisfaction. The impact on customer satisfaction is measured by developing a survey and requesting the customers to participate in the survey. The target customers will be the customers affected by delay in shipment. These customers will be grouped based on the number of times the orders have been delayed. The cost of the investment includes the cost of the hardware, software, and labor required for integrating AutoID with ERP. Software used are Minitab, SAS, Microsoft Excel, and ERP system.

6.2 Background and Introduction

This dissertation is the foundation for a future proposal to PD 13–1786 (National Science Foundation proposal to the CMMI Division for the MES group for announcement 1786). ERP systems provide information about any operations within the organization to anybody with the right credentials. The information provided covers all aspects of an organization (manufacturing, supply chain, sales, services, etc.). The investment in software and hardware for ERP systems is well over $15 billion per year and additional $10 billion in professional services (Davenport and Thomas, 2000). Various critical business decisions are made based on the data available in the ERP system. Some examples of these decisions are purchasing the raw materials, production schedule, customer credit decision, etc. The data stored in the ERP system should have high accuracy; inaccurate data will lead to bad decision-making eventually hurting the company in terms of money, customer satisfaction, etc. Therefore, it is necessary to maintain accurate data to avoid these types of situations. Inventory level tracking is one of the areas most affected by the inaccurate data and inadequate tracking system.

Traditionally, the inventory levels are counted manually for each product line at the end of the manufacturing shift or end of the day. The data are then entered into the ERP system manually or through mass upload of data sheet. There is a high possibility of error in the data collected and entered into the ERP system. Recent advances in AutoID capture technologies like RFID and barcode are greatly increasing the accuracy of the data collected. These technologies are also integrated with ERP directly to decrease the human error in manual data entry (Chiu et al., 2011). In this research, accuracy and reliability impacts of AutoID technologies on an ERP system will be evaluated.

6.2.1 Current Research in this Area

This research is timely in that other funded research has explored this for warehouse management integration with ERP, using RFID to track inventory management. Given all these researches, we seek to evaluate the performance and economic impact of AutoID on ERP systems. This research is necessary because the traditional ERP systems are insufficient to integrate different stakeholders such as customers, suppliers, and other business parties, especially when they are out of the company premises (Chiu et al., 2011).

There are various research efforts to improve the ERP performance, but there is not enough research on using AutoID with ERP. In this research, the impacts of economics and performance of using AutoID with ERP are evaluated, which is inadequately studied before. The remainder of this chapter is organized as follows. First, background and related work are provided. Then, the research question, hypothesis, and objective are discussed. Next, data collection technique and statistical methodologies employed to analyze the data are listed. Expected results are discussed next. Finally, current limitations and future research are discussed.

6.2.2 Relevant Background and Definitions

This research is based on three foundation areas namely ERP, inventory control, and AutoID technologies.

6.2.3 Evolution of ERP System

In a manufacturing environment, the quantity of each finished product to be manufactured in each planning period is specified by the master production schedule (MPS). The required quantity of the finished product can be achieved only when the number of parts and raw materials required for each finished product is available. To achieve this goal, many production planning and control techniques were used in MPS. Material resource planning (MRP) is one such tool which was adopted during 1970 due to the distinction between independent and dependent demand items. The MRP is used to plan and create purchase orders for the raw materials and components for the final product based on the required quantity of the final product in a planning period.

MRP evolved continuously in subsequent years to include various business functions. In early 1980, MRP developed into a company-wide system virtually, planning and controlling all the organization resources from a material planning and control system. Since this concept is different from the basic concept of MRP, Wight (1984) gave a new term MRP II referring to manufacturing resources planning. In addition to integrating manufacturing functions like production, marketing, and financing, MRP II also integrated other functions like personnel, engineering, and purchasing into the planning system. Since the MRP II is a company-wide system, this enabled it to have a simulator built in to simulate various business and production scenarios to the organization. These simulations helped organizations to save huge cost and time efforts by providing information about various scenarios in advance even before the real production began. The overview of the MRP II system is shown in Figure 6.1.

In the beginning of 1988, the ERP systems evolved from MRP II systems as Dow Chemical Company purchased the ERP module from SAP AG of Germany (Schaaf, 1999). Gartner Group of Stamford, Connecticut, USA used the term "enterprise resource planning" to describe the system designed to plan and schedule all resources of an enterprise. Thus, the main difference is that MRP II focuses on internal

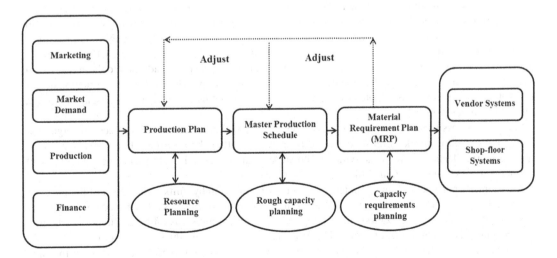

FIGURE 6.1 A general MRP II system flow.

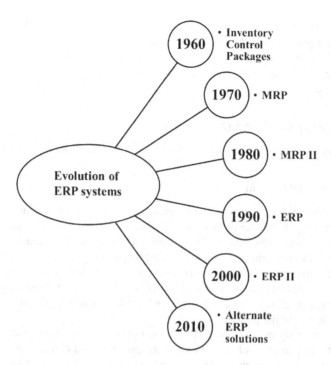

FIGURE 6.2 Evolution of ERP systems.

resources planning, while the ERP systems also focus on planning and scheduling supplier resources. However, the terms MRP II and ERP were used interchangeably during 1988–1994. The evolution of ERP systems is shown in Figure 6.2. The recognition of ERP systems as a stand-alone system was pioneered when the SAP AG in 1994 released the *R*/3. The *R*/3 release also shifted the technology platform to UNIX-based client–server architecture from mainframe. Many companies began to invest heavily in the SAP in the succeeding years. A generic ERP system is illustrated in Figure 6.2.

6.2.4 Overview of ERP System

A suite of software modules comprise the ERP system. Each module is responsible for a separate business function or a group of separate business functions. An overview of an ERP system is given in Figure 6.3. There are four main functional areas of operations in most of the companies, namely marketing and sales (M/S), supply chain management (SCM), accounting and finance (A/F), and human resources (HR). The main functions of these areas are shown in Table 6.1. In addition to these functional areas, there are also other modules like customer relation service, warehouse module, project management, etc. These modules are adopted by the organizations depending on the requirements, affordability, and various other criteria.

Various business functions are comprised in these functional areas of operation. Recently, organizations have started to think in terms of business processes rather than business functions. A business process is a collection of input activities to create an output desired by the customer. Examples of business processes are shown in Table 6.2.

A customer's perspective can be understood by the organization by thinking in terms of the business process. The customer interacts with different functional areas of business, from placing an order to receiving the product. Organizations must integrate these functional areas efficiently to provide quality service and satisfaction to the customer. The information about the product specifications, inventories, prices, and promotional information must also be shared accurately and efficiently between the integrated functional areas.

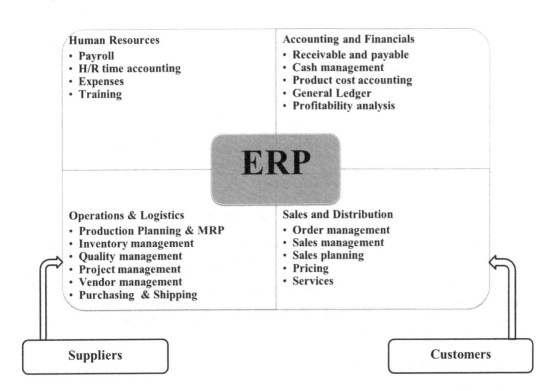

FIGURE 6.3 Overview of an ERP system.

TABLE 6.1

Main Functions of Functional Areas

M/S	SCM
Develop products: Interact with the customer and market and gather the requirements for the features needed to be added in the next iteration of the existing product or fix issues or develop a complete new product.	**Manufacturing:** Manufacture the product that is required.
Determine pricing: Determine the cost for the products based on the market and features in the products.	**Purchasing:** Purchase the raw materials and raw components required to manufacture the final products.
Promote products to customers: Create promotional materials, contact customers and organizations, conduct seminars to educate the potential customers about the products.	
Interact with customers: Customer surveys, keep track of returning customers.	
Sales: Keep track of the sales, credit for each repeat customers, etc.	
Sales Forecasts: Analyze the historical sales data and provide forecast about the required sales in different markets in different seasons.	

A/F	HR
Sales: Track the sales of any product or service sold by the organization. Analyze the information to provide profitability of the products.	Recruit, train, evaluate and compensate the employee.
Raw material purchase: Track the purchase of raw materials, components, or services needed to manufacture the final product.	
Payroll: Pay and track the employees' compensation.	
Receipt: Issue receipt of cash to the customers.	

6.2.5 ERP Information System

ERP system software modules, in addition to integrating the functional areas, also share and transfer the information efficiently (Hicks and Stecke, 1995). All the information is stored in a centralized database, providing the same information across all modules and avoiding multiple entries.

TABLE 6.2

Example of Business Process

Input	Functional Area Responsible for Input	Process	Output
Request to purchase product	Marketing and sales	Sales order	Order is generated
Financial help for purchase	A/F	Arranging financing in-house	Customer finances through the company
Technical support	M/S	24-h help line available	Customer's technical query is resolved
Fulfillment of order	SCM	Shipping and delivery	Customer receives the product

Source: Book: *Concepts in Enterprise Resource Planning*, 2006.

6.2.6 Information System in Marketing and Sales (M/S)

The information in M/S starts from when a customer places an order. These orders are received by M/S by telephone, email, fax, web, etc. The information is shared with SCM for production planning purposes, with accounting for billing purposes, and with HR for hiring sales force, legal requirements, and other purposes. Analyzing the sales order data can provide valuable information about sales trends helping in business decision making. An example is that the sales trend of a product can be used in evaluating marketing efforts and determining sales force strategies. One other example is that the information can be used in determining product price.

6.2.7 Information System in SCM

SCM shares and receives information between the other functional areas. The organization develops a production plan to meet the final product requirement that is obtained by the sales data from the M/S (both projected and actual). The planning for internal resources includes the plan for manufacturing capacities, allocating overtime, additional work force, etc. The plan for the external resources includes raw materials, service, and any other additional components required. The inaccurate forecast may result in two scenarios. The first scenario is excess finished good products or raw materials. This results in loss of money associated with the storage of the excess inventory, and in some cases, the product might pass the expiry date, depreciation value, be out of style, etc. The second scenario is less finished good product or raw materials, also known as stock-out. In this scenario, the company may lose potential business because of customer's decision to find a different source, damaged relationship between the company and the customer, less customer satisfaction, etc.

6.2.8 Information System in A/F

A/F shares and receives information between the other functional areas. A/F keeps track of the accounts receivable for each sales order and cash receipts issued to the customers at the time of payment and accounts payable for the each purchase order for the raw materials, components, and services. Based on all these data, they prepare various reports about the profitability and organization's financial situation. A/F receives sales data from M/S, production and inventory data from SCM, and payroll and benefit data from HR. M/S accesses customer credit determined by A/F for credit approval when an order is placed. Invalid accounts can lead to the approval of credit for the high-risk customers, which, in turn, leads to the loss of money. In some other cases, M/S personnel can deny the credit for a high-value customer, thereby damaging the relationship between customer and the company.

6.2.8 Information System in HR

HR shares and receives information between the other functional areas. HR determines the workforce requirements like the number of employees (to meet the production plan from SCM and other functional areas), type of skills required, compensation, training, benefits, etc. To determine all these requirements, HR needs accurate information from all the functional areas.

6.2.9 ERP Implementation

The investment in software and hardware for ERP systems is well over \$15 billion per year world over and additional \$10 billion in professional services (Davenport and Thomas, 2000). Because of the huge cost, not all firms adopt all the modules of the ERP. The firms that can afford it adopt entire ERP modules (Chalmers, 1999). Smaller firms adopt few components of each module (Ferman, 1999). Customers and suppliers can access the authorized information over a secured network through an external communication interface (Figure 6.4).

6.2.10 ERP System Selection

Davenport and Thomas (1998) estimated that 50%–75% of the U.S. firms suffer failure to a certain degree in implementing advanced manufacturing technology. An ERP system is a very complicated system imposing its own logic on organization strategy and culture. The majority of the implementation failure occurs when the ERP specifications and organizations requirements are mismatched. Therefore, it is very important to perform a careful ERP system selection process. Most of the ERP systems are similar only with minor differences. Research indicates that 80%–90% of the ERP systems are same across various organizations and only 10%–20% vary due to the customization for the organization need (Langdoc, 1998; Ptak, 1999; Langenwalter, 2000). Therefore, the organization should identify the critical business needs and desired features to select the suitable ERP system. There are two methods available for the selection of the ERP system (Umble et al., 2003). One method is to focus on the information technology infrastructure to implement the overall business strategy. This method is usually employed by the companies of large size to have a centralized data and control. Companies of small and medium sizes employ a method in which the ERP system is customized to match the specific functions and business process to increase operation efficiency, reduce costs, and manage business easily (Krupp, 1998; Ptak and Schragenheim, 2003).

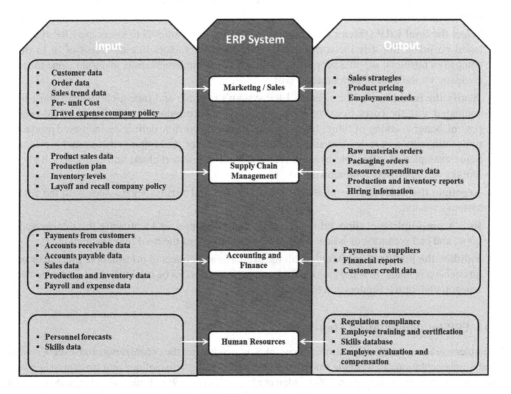

FIGURE 6.4   Input information and output from the ERP modules.

Based on the previous researches by Langenwalter (2000), Minahan (1998), and Oden et al. (1993), the following are the recommended steps in selection process:

1. **Create the vision:** Define the organization objectives, strategy, and mission. Identify the critical and executive level users to examine, identify, and redesign the business process. This ensures the required buy-in from all levels of the organization. In case of multiple plants and sites, the team should include participants from all the plants and sites. Clearly define the reasons for ERP system implementation. Once the approval from the top management is obtained for the vision, broadcast it throughout the organization.

2. **Create a feature and function list:** A team with experience in both ERP systems and company process should identify the required features and functions of the software to support the company vision and functional areas. The business managers should map the existing business processes and map the processes to the best ERP application model.

3. **Create a software candidate list:** The ERP system choices can be narrowed down by industry type and size. The systems that can closely meet the organization requirements need to be selected. Communicating with the users of the ERP can also help to narrow down the list.

4. **Narrow the field to four to six candidates:** This is accomplished by analyzing each ERP system's strength and weakness and performing goodness of fit test.

5. **Create the request for proposal (RFP):** RFP contains the function and feature list describing the company needs in each functional area or department and the "outer wrapper", consisting of the terms and conditions, instructions to the supplier, supplier response forms, and so forth.

6. **Review the proposal:** The strength and weakness of the system are considered in the review. Request additional information when the provided information is unclear or not sufficient.

7. **Select two or three finalists:** It is a good practice to select more than one finalist at this stage.

8. **Request for a demonstration from the finalist**: In order to understand and select the best ERP system, all the critical business from all levels of management should be present for the demonstrations.

9. **Select the final ERP system:** General tendency of the companies is to select the ERP system based on prize. But it is recommended to consider other factors like closeness of fit to the company's business, supplier support, flexibility, ease of implementation, and total value to the company vs. the total implementation cost.

10. **Justify the investment:** The selected ERP system's tangible and intangible benefits must be compared with the costs. Some of the tangible benefits are reduced costs, improved material control, better visibility of future requirements, increased on-time deliveries, increased productivity, elimination of redundant and contradictory databases, and improved customer services. Some examples of intangible benefits are substantially reduced chaos and confusion, higher morale, and improved communications.

11. **Negotiate the contract:** Negotiate the price, service, and various legal issues with the ERP system's vendor.

12. **Run a pre-implementation pilot:** The pilot can be helpful in identifying the unexpected, good, and bad scenarios or issues. This can be used to adjust the final implementation.

13. **Validate the justification:** Based on all the available and collected information, final go or no go decision is made. In some cases, a different ERP system can be selected, the contract can be renegotiated, or the vendors can be changed.

6.2.11 ERP Implementation Steps

ERP implementation can be either simple or complex, depending on the organization and level of customization. Implementation can be made smoother and easier by using a disciplined and structured approach. Various researchers (Langenwalter, 2000; Oden et al., 1993; Ptak, 1999; Ptak and Schragenheim, 2000) have compiled the following recommended steps in ERP implementation process:

1. **Review the pre-implementation process to date:** First step is to verify that all the critical implementation success factors are in place. Also verify that the system selection process is completed satisfactorily.

2. **Install and test any new hardware:** Before the real implementation, perform a test on the hardware to verify that it is capable of supporting the software, provides smoother operations, and meets the required performance.

3. **Install the software and perform the computer room pilot:** After installing the software, a technical person should test the software to make sure the software is installed correctly.

4. **Attend system training:** The in-house developers and users must attend the training to learn operation of the systems, features, transactions, etc.

5. **Train on the conference room pilot:** A mock-up business environment, from the order input to shipping the product to customer, is created to perform pilot and understand the system.

6. **Establish security and necessary permission:** All the user authorizations and permissions for the required data must be implemented during the room pilot.

7. **Ensure that all data bridges are sufficiently robust and the data are sufficiently accurate:** The data obtained from the legacy system should have high-level accuracy in order to convince the users to trust the new system.

8. **Document policies and procedure:** Document policies like formatting, authorization for creating, editing, and deleting the document should be created and clearly established.

9. **Bring the ERP system online for entire organization in a single or phased approach:** In a single approach, the whole company is brought into the new system. This may result in shutdown for 1 or 2 weeks. In the phased approach, ERP systems are brought online one module, plant, and product sequentially. The first implementation can be used to adjust or modify the next implementation.

10. **Celebrate:** This is an important step in the implementation process because it recognizes the milestone achievement and also demonstrates the project importance

11. **Improve continually:** The initial implementation may not address all the scenarios; some scenarios may arise after the implementation. Therefore, the system must be improved continuously.

6.2.12 ERP Implementation Success

A successful implementation of the ERP system depends on the viewpoints of the people evaluating the implementation. ERP implantation team identifies the implementation as success when the project is completed within budget and within the project timeline. The ERP system end users identify the success based on the smooth operations of the system. Management identifies the success when the predetermined goals are achieved and the business is improved (Somers and Nelson, 2004; Zhang et al., 2005). The success of the ERP can be measured through two approaches using objective financial measures like profit figure and company cost (Dezdar and Sulaiman, 2011) or self-reported subjective measures (Nah et al., 2007; Bradley, 2008; Muscatello and Chen, 2008; Sawah et al., 2008). The most popular approach is using financial measures, but it is difficult to quantify the benefits and impacts (Wu and Wang, 2007) and isolate the ERP effect and other variables affecting the performance of organization (Chien and Tsaur, 2007).

Researches indicate that there are five main non-financial criteria used to measure the ERP success. Table 6.3 shows the five non-financial criteria some researchers used in their research.

6.2.13 Factors Affecting Successful ERP Implementation

There are many factors that affect the success of ERP system implementation. Many researchers have identified various factors that are responsible for failure or success of the ERP implementation (Zhang et al., 2005). For example, Somers and Nelson (2004) have identified 22 critical factors,

TABLE 6.3

Five Non-financial Criteria Some Researchers Used

Project management success like "time, budget, and predetermined goals"	Kamhawi (2007)
DeLone and McLean's (1992, 2003) success models	Chien and Tsaur (2007), Fan and Fang (2006)
Technology Acceptance Model (TAM) developed by Davis and Sampson (1986)	Dezdar and Sulaiman (2011)
User satisfaction	Wu and Wang (2007)
Combination of the above	Bradley (2008), Chien et al. (2007), Nah et al. (2007), Ramayah et al. (2007), Sawah et al. (2008), Wang and Chen (2006), Zhang et al. (2005)

Al-Mashari et al. (2003) identified 12 critical factors, Umble et al. (2003) categorized these factors into 10 categories, and Dezdar and Sulaiman (2009) categorized the factors into 17 categories. The following are the most important and prominent factors that affect the success of ERP implementation: clear understanding of strategic goals, commitment by top management, excellent project management, organization change management, a great implementation team, data accuracy, extensive education and training, focused performance measures, and multi-site issues.

1. **Clear understanding of strategic goals:**

   Key people throughout the company who can provide a clear and strategic vision of the company should be identified. With their help, strategic goals to improve customer satisfaction, provide more responsibilities to employees and facilitate the long-term suppliers should established. The goals must be defined clearly along with the expectations and deliverables. The organization must provide a clear reason for the ERP system implementation and critical business needs (Krupp, 1998; Latamore, 1999; Schragenheim, 2000; Travis, 1999).

2. **Commitment by top management:**

   ERP implementation can be successful only when there is a strong leadership, top management commitment, and participation (Wilder and Davis, 1998; Laughlin, 1999; Oden et al., 1993; Sherrard (1998). It is important to have an executive management planning committee with clear knowledge of ERP that supports the demands, payback, and costs of the implementation (Umble et al., 2003). In addition to the committee, the project should be led by a champion who is highly respected and in an executive level position (Maxwell, 1999).

3. **Excellent project management:**

   An excellent project management includes a clear objective definition, good work and resource plan, and accurate tracking of project (Wilder and Davis, 1998; Laughlin, 1999; Oden et al., 1993; Sherrard, 1998). An unclear objective definition may lead to "scope creep which increase the budget, impeding the project progress and creating complication in implementation" (Wilder and Davis, 1998; Laughlin, 1999; Minahan, 1998). The project plan schedules should be more aggressive but achievable (Laughlin, 1999).

4. **Organization change management:**

   The legacy structure and processes of an organization may not be compatible with the ERP system structure, tools, and types of information. Thus, re-engineering or developing of existing business process or new business process respectively may be required to support the organization goals while implementing ERP systems (Minahan,1998). Organization control may need to be realigned to support the redesign of the business process. The realignment affects most of the organization's functional areas and social systems. This, in turn, can result in significant modification in organizational structures, policies, processes, and employees (Umble et al., 2003).

   Many of the executives view ERP implementation as a software implementation to address a technological challenge. But executives fail to understand that ERP can fundamentally change the business process of an organization. This is a major issue faced by the ERP implementation.

The ERP implementation must be driven by the business and its requirements, not to address a technological challenge (Chew et al., 1991; Minahan, 1998). Inadequate preparation of employees in the organization for these changes may lead to denial, resistance, and chaos. These can all be avoided by preparing the employees to embrace change.

5. **A great implementation team:**

The implementation team should comprise personnel who are skilled, with great reputation, flexibility, and past accomplishments. The team should be able to make critical decisions without interruption and in constant communication with the management team (Wilder and Davis, 1998; Laughlin, 1999; Minahan, 1998; Sherrard, 1998). The team is also responsible for creating project plan, determining the project schedule, assigning responsibilities, determining due dates, and maintaining availability of the required resources.

6. **Data accuracy:**

Data accuracy is one of the important requirements since the data is shared throughout the integrated functional areas of ERP. When inaccurate information is entered in one functional area, it also affects all other areas. Therefore, the data entry personnel should be well educated about the importance of the data accuracy and also be trained to enter the accurate data (Stedman, 1999; Stein, 1999). Additional training to adopt the new system not to work around the system must be provided. Employees must be convinced by educational seminars to commit to the new system. Further to support the commitment, old systems must be removed. Employees tend to use the old system if they exist with the new system (Hutchins, 1998).

7. **Extensive education and training:**

The most recognized critical factor for the success of ERP implementation is the education and training of the user. The training enables the users to implement the system more efficiently with a standard operating procedure; without training, user may invent a separate procedure to operate the system (Schragenheim, 2000). In order for the training to succeed, the users should be trained early in the implementation process most likely before the implementation starts. The reports indicate that assigning 10%–15% of the entire project budget for the training results in 80% success rate of the implementation (Okrent and McCaskey, 1999; Volwer, 1999).

The users are expected to use the system efficiently after the training and education, but much of the learning comes from the hands-on experience. Hence, there should be a permanent contact for the users to help with the issues they face and to monitor the user. Regular interactions with the users are required to identify the issues with the system and encourage the users to share the knowledge learned by hands-on experience and increase the system familiarity (Travis, 1999).

8. **Focused performance measures:**

Performance measures must be constructed accurately and efficiently to indicate system performance. It should also be designed to encourage the employee's behaviors by all individuals and functions. These measures include on-time deliveries, customer order-to-ship time, inventory turns, gross profit margin, vendor performance, inventory turns, etc. (Umble et al., 2003). For the success of system implementation, compensation should be tied with the system implementation. When compensation and implementation are not tied together, the bonuses and raises will be paid even if the system is not implemented leading to the failure of the implementation. The goals must be clearly defined, and the realistic expectations from the vendor, implementation team, and management should be set. When the goals are not achieved, the concerned team or individual should be provided with the assistance or replaced. The individual or team should be rewarded in a visible way when they meet the goals within the allocated time. The system should be measured and monitored continuously for successful operation (Hutchins, 1998).

9. **Multi-site issues:**

There are many concerns regarding the multi-site implementations, and addressing these concerns can increase the success rate of the ERP implementation. The level of autonomy for each site mainly depends on the two factors namely the degree of remote site process and product consistency and degree of need to control and access the information, system setup, and usage through a centralized system. Another affecting factor is the degree of capability for the remote site to tune the system for unique situations. The issue in this situation is the difference between organization culture and the individual site's local culture. Both the organization culture and local optimization of the system have their own advantages. Optimizing the system for the organizational culture provides the ability to move products and people around the sites more effectively and consolidate the data across all the sites easily. Local optimization results in effective and efficient operations and reduction in costs.

Another issue is whether to implement it in all sites simultaneously or one site at a time. Many companies prefer to implement the ERP system in all sites in order to recover from the investments as soon as possible. But the recommended approach is to select a site to do a pilot implementation. The results from the pilot implementation help to make a decision to further proceed with entire project due to the success or cancel the project due to the failure. Furthermore, the lessons learned from the pilot implementation can make further implementation more smooth and efficient (Umble et al., 2003).

6.2.14 ERP Implementation Success Rate

ERP provides many benefits to different business depending on the ERP module adopted by the firm. One of the common and main benefits is ability to integrate business processes (Brakely, 1999; Davenport and Thomas, 1998, 2000). Customer satisfaction can also be greatly improved by adopting ERP. For example, NEC Technologies increased order processing and invoicing speed and quick customer-service response times by adopting the ERP systems (Michel, 1997). ERP is also effective in reducing inventory costs, improving efficiency, and increasing profitability (Appleton, 1997; Brakely, 1999). Manufacturing lead times can also be reduced by adopting ERP (Goodpasture, 1995). Other potential benefits of ERP include reduction in inventory, decrease in working capital, readily available information about customer requirements and needs, and integrated system enabling user to view and manage the vendors and customers as an integrated whole.

Despite all the benefits of ERP systems, not all the firms adopted have successful implementation. The failure rates of ERP systems remain in 67%–90% range (Calogero, 2000; Shore, 2005). 65% of the ERP implementations result in overrun in cost and scheduling with an average of 178% and 230% respectively and the rest of 35% being cancelled (Amid, Moloagh, and Ravasan, 2012). According to a survey, the percentage of ERP implementation failure to provide the anticipated benefits is 70% (Wang et al., 2007). Many surveys indicate that even in the best situations, ERP system integration fails to produce the desired results (Liao et al., 2007). Many reports are available showing that ERP has failed in well-known organizations like Hershey, FoxMeyer, Nike, etc. Failure of ERP implementation will result in loss of investments leading to bankruptcy (Cotteleer, 2002). FoxMeyer Drug ($5 billion pharmaceutical company) claimed that the reason for their bankruptcy was that their ERP system was creating shipments with excess products for incorrect orders (Bicknell, 1998; Boudette, 1999).

Despite all these case studies, there are no unique definitions existing for ERP system implementation failures or success (Chen, 2001). Various researchers have classified the reasons behind failure or success based on their own viewpoint, but in general, they can be classified into two categories (Al-Turkia, 2011). The failures in first category are defined as failures to achieve the implementation goals like integrating organizational information, better decision making, improving inter-organizational communications, and decreasing operational bottlenecks (Hsu and Chen, 2004; Spathis, and Ananiadis, 2005; Olhager and Selldin, 2003). Achieving these goals is defined as success.

In the second category, different levels of failures or success are considered, and definitions are provided for the each level. Heeks (2002) classified the success or failure into three categories as shown in Figure 6.5. Gargeya and Brady (2005) later classified the level of failure into two levels, namely complete failure and partial failure. The cancellation of a project or omission from project before full implementation is considered to be complete failure. Increase in implementation costs from the initial estimation, extended project period, non-compliance of implemented processes with agreed ones, not achieving goals and not meeting the required return on investment (ROI) or user satisfaction are considered to be partial failures (Figure 6.5).

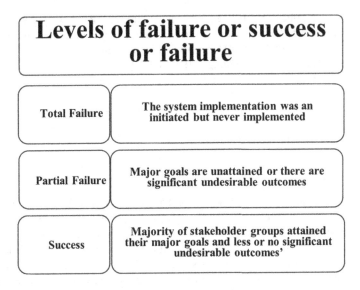

Levels of failure or success or failure

Total Failure	The system implementation was an initiated but never implemented
Partial Failure	Major goals are unattained or there are significant undesirable outcomes
Success	Majority of stakeholder groups attained their major goals and less or no significant undesirable outcomes'

FIGURE 6.5 Level of failure or success by Heeks (2002).

6.2.15 Improving ERP Data Quality Using AutoID

The invention of the barcode in 1954 marked the beginning of the AutoID (Schuster et al., 2004). It received recognition in 1974, and the industries start to adopt the technology and develop the standards (Haberman, 2001). Many firms benefited from barcode in automatic data capture for raw materials, work in process (WIP), and finished goods. It also improved data accuracy by decreasing the human error and reduced amount of labor required for many business transactions. Later advance in AutoID enabled to track the inventories wirelessly providing the infrastructure capable of new levels of interconnectivity (Dinning and Schuster, 2003). Schuster et al. (2004) indicated that these AutoID technologies will have an important impact on ERP system. American Production and Inventory Control Society (APICS) conducted a survey in 2004 for determining the main reason for implementing the AutoID technologies. The results are given in Table 6.4.

The AutoID technology includes open protocols and standard for data codes and formats, tags and readers, and IT infrastructure interfaces. This enables interoperating between the components (hardware or software) that are obtained from various vendors. The flexibility provides the organization to choose the systems that best fit its needs and the ERP system that the organization has in use or plans to use.

Data is collected by the proximity optical scanning in barcode method, and the data is updated in ERP in batch mode. This has a drawback of configuring fully automatic data collection points and true

TABLE 6.4

APICS Survey

What Is Your Main Goal in Implementing an AutoID Solution?	
Improve inventory accuracy	55%
Trading partner requirement	13%
Increase inventory turns	10%
Reduce out-of-stock situation	9%
Enhance supplier relationship	9%
Improve fill rates	4%
Sample size 658 respondents	
Survey conducted online, April 2004	

Source: Schuster, Scharfeld, and Kar (2004).

high-speed, which in turn affects the timeliness of inputs into the ERP system. AutoID not only does not have these drawbacks, but also enables real-time streaming data, processing, filtering, and response (Schuster and Koh, 2004). A simple AutoID system is illustrated in Figure 6.9. The data capture techniques used in material requirements planning (MRP), manufacturing resource planning (MRPII), the current ERP systems, and ERP with AutoID systems and their advantages and disadvantages are shown in Table 6.5.

In a supply chain environment, billions of items need to be tracked and maintained. This requires a comprehensive information technology infract structure to handle the huge volume of data generated by these items. AutoID provides the required infrastructure by utilizing RFID.

6.2.16 RFID History

The existence of RFID technologies has been traced back to pre-World War II era (Jones and Chung, 2007). Radar, discovered by Sir Robert Alexander Watson-Watt (1935), is used to track the aircraft by the allies and axis during the war. The major drawback was that the planes could not be distinguished between friend and foe. Further research by Watson-Watt led to the development of identify friend or foe (IFF) system to identify the friend or foe. This was considered as the first active RFID system (Jones and Chung, 2007). The aircraft is identified as friendly when the on-board transmitter receives the signals from the radar station and signals back.

In the 1950s and 1960s, the development in radar and radio frequency (RF) communication systems provided a new application, a way to identify the objects remotely. Many stores began using this application of the RF system as an anti-theft system. This anti-theft system uses a single bit tag, either on or off. The bit is deactivated when the product price is paid and product is allowed to leave the store. The reader will read the products with tags that are not deactivated and alert the authorities, thereby preventing any unpaid products from leaving the store.

Los Alamos National Laboratory in the 1970s developed a system to track nuclear materials at the request of the United States Department of Energy (Jones and Chung, 2007). The concept of the system is to have a transponder in each truck and readers at the gates of the facilities. This system was later commercialized by the former Los Alamos scientists in the mid-1980s to develop automated toll payment systems. Today these systems are more commonly used all over the world.

In the 1970s, Los Alamos investigated animal tracking efforts using microwave systems. The main focus was to track the medical history for the cows. This ensures that all the cows receive the correct dosage. Later, in the 1980s, a passive RFID system with 125-kHz radio waves along with transponder in a glass enclosure injected under the cow ears was developed by Los Alamos. Similar researches are also conducted in Europe using inductive technology (Jones and Chung, 2007).

In the 1980s in the U.S., the applications of RFID were focused on transportation, personnel, and animals. The focus in Europe was on animals, industrial, and business applications. During the 1980s, various other countries namely Italy, Spain, Portugal, and Norway also started to employ RFID in their toll

TABLE 6.5

Comparison of Data Capture Technologies

	MRP (1960s)	MRPII (1980s)	ERP (1990s)	ERP + AutoID (2004)
Data Capture	Manual	Barcode + Manual	Barcode + Manual	RFID
Data Type	SKU code	SKU code	SKU code or item serial number	Mass serialization—a serial number for each item or component
Pro/Con	Improved planning capabilities, limited data available, accuracy problem	Speedy collection of data and improved accuracy, batch mode, delay in updates	Standardized collection of data, some lot control, limited serial number control, lack of middleware, mature technology	Granular data at serial number level, middleware to manage serial numbers, common standards, real time, initial stages of development, technology to read tags must be refined

Source: Schuster, Scharfeld, and Kar (2004).

roads (Jones and Chung, 2007). In the U.S., Container Handling Cooperative Program and Association of American Railroads were supporting the use of RFID in the tolls. The first commercial application of the RFID in tolls began in Norway in 1987. The U.S. followed next in using RFID in toll in Dallas North Turnpike in 1989. New York and New Jersey port authority began the practice of using RFID for the buses travelling through the Lincoln Tunnel.

By the 1990s, electronic tolls using RFID were widely in use throughout the U.S. In Oklahoma in 1991, an open highway electronic tolling system was opened, eliminating the need for cameras and barriers and the vehicles to travel through the toll at highway speed. In 1992, Harris County Toll Road Authority installed the combined system of traffic management and toll collection. The tag was used in Harris County toll (Table 6.6).

6.2.17 RFID Components Overview

A high-level RFID system requires the following components: tags (one tag is embedded in each object that needs to be tracked), one or more antennas (installed in the locations where the tags need to be read when they pass through the location), and a reader (all the antennas are attached to the reader).

6.2.18 Tags

Tags are embedded into each object, boxes, pallets, containers, etc. of the final product that needed to be tracked. The tags come in various shapes and sizes; the organization has to choose the tag that fits its need. The tag's primary function is to transmit the information stored in the tag to the rest of RFID system. The tags can be classified with respect to power sources, frequencies, writing capabilities, tag components, tag costs, and tag generations (Jones and Chung, 2007).

6.2.18.1 Power Sources

All tags require power to operate and communicate with antenna. The tags are classified into three types based on their power sources. They are active tags, passive tags and semi-passive tags. The tag type chosen for the RFID system drives the selection of the other RFID components.

6.2.18.2 Passive Tags

In passive tags, there is no individual power source. The tag is powered by the electromagnetic power obtained from the antenna. The elimination of the power source made the passive tags less expensive, with simple design and long shelf life. It also has a drawback in the form of limited range. The tag has to be in the close proximity of the antenna in order to obtain the required power for transmitting the signal.

6.2.18.3 Active Tags

Active tags have an on-board power source through a small battery with additional circuitry to provide a long read range. Integrating the battery with the tag requires a plastic enclosure for both safety and design purposes. These additional requirements of the active tags increase their cost considerably when

TABLE 6.6

A Brief History of the RFID System

1940s	1960s	1980s	1990s	Today
• WWII Friend or Foe	• EAS	• Railcar Tagging	• Security Access & Control	• Low cast tags
		• Animal Tracking	• Highway Toll Passes	• IT infrastructure
			• Vehicle immobilization systems	

Source: Schuster, Scharfeld, and Kar (2004).

compared to passive tags. Another disadvantage is that the huge sizes of the tags prevent them from adhering to the product using an adhesive layer. They usually prefer to track pallets or containers. Active tags will be in a sleep mode until they enter the RFID system interrogation zone. This will reduce the battery usage and prolong the battery life. Advanced active tags can be integrated with other systems like satellite communication system or global positioning system (GPS) for various purposes.

6.2.18.4 Semi-active Tag

Semi-active tags are designed to have features of both passive and active tags. The on-board power source is used to power the tag's circuitry, but for communication purposes, it uses electromagnetic field power from the antenna. Therefore, these tag types will have long read range compared to passive tags but smaller size and less effective cost compared to active tags. Additionally, the power source is also used to power sensors to monitor environmental conditions like humidity and temperature.

6.2.18.5 Surface Acoustic Wave (SAW)

Active and passive tags use semiconductor physics concept to generate the power required for the operation. In surface acoustic wave (SAW), tags receive the wave from the reader and convert them on the surface of the chip into nanoscale surface acoustic waves. These waves are then encoded into a unique pulse train, converted back into wave and transmitted back to the reader. Since the SAW tags do not require DC power to operate, they provide long read range. They also measure the temperature by calculating the distance between the reader and the tag. The general operating temperature range is −100°C to 200°C.

6.2.18.6 SAW RFID Tags

SAW tags are passive in nature but operate on a different theory compared to typical RFID tags. The common tags generate power for operation based on semiconductor physics. In SAW tags, the incoming waves are converted on the chip surface into acoustic waves. The acoustic waves are then encoded into unique pulse train and transmitted back to the reader antenna. This also allows the measuring of temperature by calculating the difference between tag and the reader distances. The operating temperature range of the SAW tags is between −100°C and 200°C.

6.2.18.7 Tag Frequencies

Different frequency ranges on which the tags normally operate are provided in Table 6.7. For specialization operations, active tags may use microwave frequencies. The selection of the operating frequencies depends on the materials that are used in the product or the packaging materials tracked by the tags. This is because the strength of the RFs can be reduced either by reflecting or absorbing depending on the metals or liquid respectively present in the system. This results in decrease in operating range and power required to activate the tag.

6.2.18.8 Writing Capabilities

The tag stores the information in any one of the following formats: ASCII, hex characters, or decimal characters. The tags are classified into three types based on the writing capabilities of these data.

Read Only: The data stored in these types of tags can be only be read, not altered. The data are stored in the tag by the manufacture, and the data are provided either by the purchaser or by the manufacturer. An example is E-Z pass tags, in which the tag data are usually numbers, and these numbers are associated to a vehicle.

Write Once, Read Many (WORM): The purchasers are provided with opportunity to enter the data into this type of tags. But once the data is entered, they cannot be altered or erased which means if incorrect information is entered, the tag becomes invalid.

Read/Write: The tag data can be programmed and reprogrammed as many times as the purchaser requires in this type of tags. This allows the purchaser to correct the tag data if incorrect information is entered.

Tag Components: The minimum components of any type of tags are integrated circuitry chip, an antenna, and a substrate or tag housing. Additional components like battery and specialized integrated components are added to monitor temperature, humidity, vibration, or various other environment conditions.

Tag Integrated Circuitry: It contains the data, logic to decode the reader RF signal, and code the data needs to transmit back to the reader. Passive tags are capable of transmitting 96 bits of data, whereas the active tags are limited by the integrated component's capability.

Tag Antennas: The tag antenna receives the RF signals from the reader antenna and passes it to the integrated circuitry. The integrated circuitry response is then transmitted back to the reader antenna by the tag antenna. The tag frequency determines the configuration of the antenna. Linear-shaped antennas are used in ultra-high-frequency (UHF) tags, and coil-shaped antennas are used for high-frequency (HF) tags. The greater read range of tag is directly proportional to the tag sizes. The antenna size determines the capability of absorbing and transmitting the RF signals. Some common antenna designs are illustrated in Figure 6.6.

Tag Substrate or Tag Housing: Tag housing serves a dual purpose: front surface provides the housing to the tag components, and the back surface provides adhesive surface to attach the tag to the item. Thin plastics are one of the common materials used for the tag housing.

6.2.19 Antennas

An antenna in the RFID system is used for receiving and transmitting the RF signals from and to the tag by the reader. A single antenna can be used when the angle of the tag and reader is always constant like manufacturing applications. In situations where the angle varies all the time, multiple antenna are required. The tag read accuracy increases with the increased number of antennas. Generally, an antenna is enclosed by a rectangle-shaped plastic housing to provide protection against the damage, environmental hazards, etc. The housing also serves as a means to attach the antenna to the position.

6.2.20 Reader and Scanners

Reader: The reader receives the data stored in the tag through antenna and transmits back to the middleware software installed in a host computer. The general location of the readers in a manufacturing environment is on top of the conveyor or as portal in the loading docks.

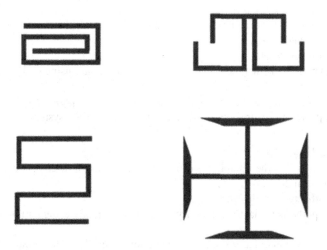

FIGURE 6.6 Common Tag antenna designs (Jones and Chung, 2007).

Scanner: In a situation where the material has to be scanned away from the mounted reader, like scanning the individual item during picking and packing, a scanner can be used. The user can carry the scanner anywhere in the warehouse to verify the RFID data of the interested items. In some cases, they are also mounted on the mobile equipment such as a forklift. The scanner verifies the RFID data wirelessly by communicating with the middleware installed in a host computer. A commonly used scanner is illustrated in Figure 6.6.

6.3 Research Question, Hypothesis, and Objectives

The overall research goal is to evaluate the impacts of AutoID on ERP data accuracy and reliability. Three research questions are proposed to achieve this main goal.

Research question 1: What is the observed perspective of impact of AutoID on ERP system?
Hypothesis 1:
Null hypothesis: $\beta_1 = \beta_2 = \beta_3 = \beta_4 = \beta_5 = 0$
The null hypothesis is that all the independent variables (logistics handling (LH), SL, FI, RI, and PI) have no effect on the dependent variable (accuracy).
Alternative hypothesis: $\beta_j \neq 0$
The alternative hypothesis is that at least one of the independent variables affects the accuracy.
The null hypothesis is rejected at α level 0.05. Rejecting the null hypothesis means that at least one of the independent variables contributes to the model indicating that the ERP data accuracy is indeed affected by the one of the dependent variables.

Research question 2: Do the AutoID technologies have an economic impact on the ERP system?
Hypothesis 2:
Null hypothesis: Net present value (NPV) ≤ 0
The null hypothesis is that the NPV of implementing RFID into ERP is less than zero and does not have positive economic impact.
Alternative hypothesis: NPV > 0
The alternative hypothesis is that the NPV of implementing RFID into ERP is greater than zero and has positive economic impact.
The null hypothesis is rejected at α level 0.05. Rejection of null hypothesis means that the implementing RFID into ERP has positive economic impact.

Research question 3: Do the AutoID technologies increase the accuracy and reliability of the ERP system data?
Hypothesis 3:
Null hypothesis: $\beta_1 = \beta_2 = \beta_3 = 0$
The null hypothesis is that the accuracy of the data is same in all three data entry methods namely manual entry, barcode, and RFID.
Alternative hypothesis: $\beta_3 > \beta_2 > \beta_1$
The alternative hypothesis is that the accuracy of the data is greater using RFID than the barcode and the manual entry.
The null hypothesis is rejected at α level 0.05. Rejection of null hypothesis means that using AutoID technology does improve the accuracy of the data entered into the ERP system.

Hypothesis 4:
Null hypothesis: $\beta_1 = \beta_2 = \beta_3 = 0$
The null hypothesis is that the reliability of the data is same in all three data entry methods namely manual entry, barcode, and RFID.
Alternative hypothesis: $\beta_3 = \beta_2 = \beta_1$
The alternative hypothesis is that the reliability of the data is greater using RFID than the barcode and the manual entry.
The null hypothesis is rejected at α level 0.05. Rejection of null hypothesis means that using AutoID technology does improve the reliability of the data entered into the ERP system.

6.4 Research Methodology and Data Collection

Specific objective 1: Evaluate the perceived impact of warehouse data on ERP system data accuracy.

By interview with the various ERP specialists and users, warehouse specialists and users, three main warehouse data that might affect the ERP data accuracy were identified; they are LH, SL, and inventory (FI, RI, and PI).

LH: LH includes tracking, locating, managing the movement, and storage of the inventory. Inadequate system can lead to incorrect data about the inventory location and quantity resulting in the excess inventory, less inventory, in some cases the expiration of the finished good products, etc.

SL: The percentage of storing the materials or finished products in invalid location is high when humans are involved. The design and selection of the SL can also attribute these errors. These errors directly affect the ERP data accuracy of material SL.

Inventory: The invalid quantity of the finished good products, raw materials, and storage materials affects the accuracy of the ERP data. The invalid inventory data cause monetary loss to any organization.

A survey (Appendix A) was developed to measure the impact of the following warehouse areas: LH, SL, FI, RI, and PI on ERP data accuracy. The survey was filled by ERP users and business personnel. Regression analysis is performed on the data collected (Carmienke et al., 2013). The dependent variable (y) is the ERP data accuracy, and independent variables are

X_1—LH
X_2—SL
X_3—FI
X_4—RI
X_5—PI

A matrix scatter plot is plotted between the dependent variable and independent variables and among the independent variables to identify the correlation effects. The scatter plot also helps to identify the potential complications like x and y outliers, multicollinearity. A preliminary model is then developed for the dependent and independent variables. An example of the preliminary model is provided in Eq. (6.1):

$$\bar{y} = \beta_0 + \beta_1 x_1 - \beta_2 x_2 + \beta_3 x_3 - \beta_4 x_4 + \beta_5 x_5$$

(6.1)

Example of the fitted model

where
- $\bar{y}$ is the dependent variable
- $x_1, x_2, x_3, x_4,$ and x_5 are the independent variables
- β_0 is the y intercept

The model is tested for the normality, multicollinearity, outliers, inflation of the outliers, and variance. Then, based on the test results, the best model is selected using backward deletion model and best subset models. The final model is then again tested for the normality, multicollinearity, outliers, inflation of the outliers, and variance.

Specific objective 2: Evaluate the economic impact of AutoID on ERP.

The cash inflow and outflow for 5 years are calculated. Using the cash flow, the NPV is calculated to determine whether the project is economically viable. NPV is calculated using the formula

$$\text{NPV} = \frac{R_t}{(1+i)^t}$$

where

t—the time of the cash flow

i—the discount rate (the rate of return that could be earned on an investment in the financial markets with similar risk)

R_t—the net cash flow, i.e., cash inflow – cash outflow, at time t.

Specific objective 3: Evaluate the accuracy and reliability impact of manual entry, barcode, and RFID on ERP (Figure 6.7).

In manual data entry method, the user collects the data about the inventory and enters into the ERP. The data are collected by manual count of the inventory. The experiment is repeated by the different product types (metallic, plastic, carbon based). Then accuracy of the data entered into ERP system is calculated. The experiment is repeated using barcode and by the RFID. The concept of AutoID integration with ERP is illustrated in Figure 6.7. The experiment setup for the accuracy and reliability of manual entry is shown in Tables 6.8 and 6.9. The same experiment setup is also used for accuracy and reliability measurement using the barcode and RFID.

The data collected are analyzed using analysis of variance (ANOVA) (Khaled and Hayam, 2013; Upadhyay et al., 2013). A t test for independent samples could also be used to arrive at the same conclusion. However, ANOVA is a much more flexible and powerful technique that can be applied to much more complex research issues. One important reason for using ANOVA methods rather than multiple two-group studies analyzed via t tests is that the former method is more efficient, and with fewer observations more information is obtained. There is another advantage of ANOVA over simple t tests: ANOVA can detect interaction effects between variables and, therefore, is used to test more complex hypotheses about reality. The ANOVA table is calculated using the equations given in Table 6.10.

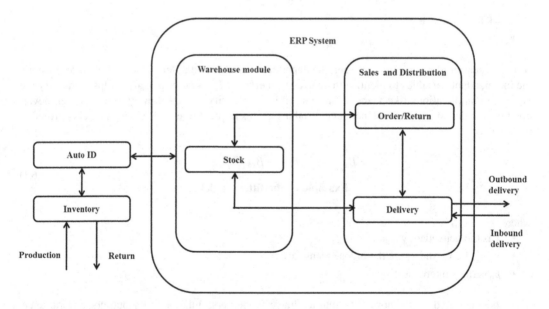

FIGURE 6.7   Concept of AutoID integration with ERP.

TABLE 6.7

Tag Operating Frequency Ranges

Frequency	High Frequency (HF)	Ultra High Frequency (UHF)
Range	13.56 MHz	902–928 MHz Or 2,400–2,500 MHz

TABLE 6.8

Experiment Setup for Manual Entry Accuracy

	Experimental Group 1	Experimental Group 2	Experimental Group 3
Manual Entry	Metallic	Plastic	Carbon based
Mean			

TABLE 6.9

Experiment Setup for Manual Entry Reliability

	Experimental Group 1	Experimental Group 2	Experimental Group 3
Manual Entry	Metallic	Plastic	Carbon based
Mean			

TABLE 6.10

ANOVA Table

Source	Degrees of Freedom (DF)	Sum of Squares (SS)	Mean of Squares (MS = SS/DF)	F	p-Value
Model	$p - 1$	SSR	MSR = SSM/DFM	F^*	$P[F_{p-1,\,n-p}] >$ observed F^*
Error	$n - p$	SSE	MSE = SSE/DFE		
Total	$n - 1$	SSTO	SST/DFT		

- p is probability value
- n is the degrees of freedom.
- SSR is the regression sum of squares.
- SSE is the error sum of squares.
- MSR is the mean square of regression.
- MSE is the mean square for error.
- F^* is the F-statistic.

The ERP system SAP is selected as the test bed because the majority of the market share is owned by SAP (Columbus, 2014) (Figure 6.8).

6.5 Results

6.5.1 Regression Analysis

The response variable (Y) measured in this research is the ERP data accuracy (AC) score ranging from 1 to 10. All the predictor variables are measured in rating from 1 to 10 [1 being the lowest and 10 being the highest]. All the predictor variables are given below:

X_1—LH
X_2—SL
X_3—FI
X_4—RI
X_5—PI.

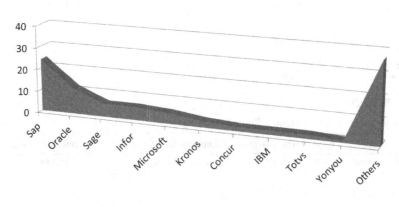

World Wide ERP Software Market Share in 2013
Market Size: $25.4B

■ Market Share in %

FIGURE 6.8   2013 SAP market shares.

6.5.2 Matrix Scatter Plot (Figure 6.9)

The matrix scatter plot shown in Figure 6.9 provides scatter plots in relation to the AC score of all five of the X variables listed in Section 6.5.1. In addition, the five variables are also provided in scatter plots amongst each other; thus by looking at the rows and columns, one can determine which combination they are looking at. The top row correlates AC score vs. LH, SL, FI, RI, and PI. These plots demonstrate that LH, SL, FI, RI, and PI seem to have a correlation with the accuracy.

6.5.3 Response–Predictor Pairwise Correlations

The plot between the predictor variable LH and response variable AC has an upward trend indicating there is strong correlation between them. The plot between the other predictor variables (SL, FI, RI, and PI) and response variable AC has a slight upward trend indicating weaker correlation between them.

6.5.4 Predictor–Predictor Pairwise Correlation

All the plots have empty space, but in a perfect situation, this plot will be filled.

LH rating vs. SL: The plot indicates a slight upward trend indicating that these variables may be correlated.

LH vs. FI: The plot indicates a slight upward trend indicating that these variables may be correlated.

LH vs. RI: The plot indicates a slight upward trend indicating that these variables may be correlated.

LH vs. PI: The plot indicates a slight upward trend indicating that these variables may be correlated.

SL rating vs. FI: The plot indicates a slight upward trend indicating that these variables may be correlated.

SL vs. RI: The plot indicates a slight upward trend indicating that these variables may be correlated.

SL vs. PI: The plot indicates a slight upward trend indicating that these variables may be correlated.

FI vs. RI: The plot indicates a slight upward trend indicating that these variables may be correlated.

FI vs. PI: The plot indicates a slight upward trend indicating that these variables may be correlated.

RI vs. PI: The plot indicates a slight upward trend indicating that these variables may be correlated (Table 6.11).

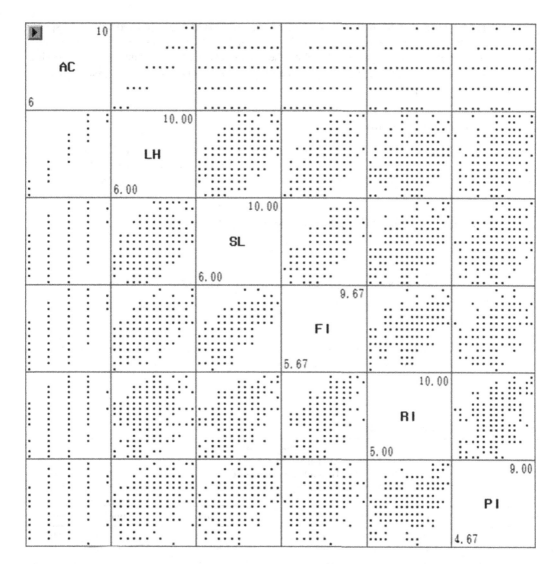

FIGURE 6.9 Scatter plot between predictor variable and response variable.

TABLE 6.11

Pearson Correlation

	AC	LH	SL	FI	RI	PI

Pearson Correlation Coefficients, N = 468

	AC	LH	SL	FI	RI	PI
AC	1.00000	0.93232	0.47476	0.54312	0.31627	0.40891
LH	0.93232	1.00000	0.46507	0.54418	0.29723	0.40883
SL	0.47476	0.46507	1.00000	0.63349	0.44032	0.41019
FI	0.54312	0.54418	0.63349	1.00000	0.48690	0.45971
RI	0.31627	0.29723	0.44032	0.48690	1.00000	0.49848
PI	0.40891	0.40883	0.41019	0.45971	0.49848	1.00000

The values in Table 6.11 indicate that the predictor variable LH is highly correlated with the response variable AC. And the predictor variables SL, FI, RI, and PI have low correlation with the response variable AC. These results agree with the scatter plot. The values between the dependent variables are less than 0.7. This indicates that there may be some multicollinearity between these variables. This also matches with the scatter plot.

6.5.5 Potential Complications

Curvilinearity and high multicollinearity do not exist in the data. The plot between AC score (response variable) and the predictor variables (LH, SL, FI, RI, and PI) may have few outliers in y direction. The predictor and predictor plots (LH, SL, FI, RI, and PI) have few outliers in the x direction.

6.5.6 Preliminary Multiple Linear Regression Model Analysis

Preliminary model is

$$\hat{y} = 0.13862 + 0.89616x_1 + 0.03095x_2 + 0.02330x_3 + 0.01559x_4 + 0.009932x_5$$

(6.2)

Preliminary model

The intercept *0.13862* indicates the value of the AC when the values of LH, SL, FI, RI, and PI are 0. The ANOVA and parameter estimates are shown in Tables 6.12 and 6.13.

TABLE 6.12

ANOVA Table for the Preliminary Model

		The REG Procedure Model: MODEL 1 Dependent Variable: AC			
		ANOVA			
Source	DF	Sum of Squares	Mean Square	F Value	Pr > F
Model	5	286.77947	57.35589	631.49	<0.0001
Error	462	41.96198	0.09088		
Corrected Total	467	328.74145			
Root MSE		0.30137	R^2	0.8724	
Dependent Mean		7.75427	Adj R^2	0.8710	
Coeff Var		3.88656			

TABLE 6.13

Parameter Estimates for the Preliminary Model

Variable	DF	Parameter Estimate	Standard Error	t Value	Pr > |t|	Variance Inflation
Intercept	1	0.13862	0.16528	0.84	0.4021	0
LH	1	0.89616	0.02056	43.59	<0.0001	1.52967
SL	1	0.03095	0.02186	1.42	0.1574	1.80594
FI	1	0.02330	0.02713	0.86	0.3910	2.11503
RI	1	0.01559	0.01518	1.03	0.3052	1.53611
PI	1	0.00932	0.02018	0.46	0.6445	1.52679

The slope *0.89616* indicates the increase in the mean AC score when there is unit increase in the LH.
The slope *0.03095* indicates the increase in the mean AC score when there is unit increase in the SL.
The slope *0.02330* indicates the increase in the mean AC score when there is unit increase in the FI.
The slope *0.01559* indicates the increase in the mean AC score when there is unit increase in the RI.
The slope *0.009932* indicates the increase in the mean AC score when there is unit increase in the PI.

6.5.7 Correlation

The correlation coefficients between all predictors are lesser than the cutoff value 0.7. This indicates there is a correlation between these factors. The correlation interpretation and their respective r values are provided in Table 6.11. The SAS analysis is shown in Tables 6.14 and 6.15.

TABLE 6.14

Predictor Variables and r Values for Preliminary Model

Predictor Variable	Predictor Variable	r Value	Correlation
LH	SL	$r_{12} = 0.465$	Somewhat positively correlated.
LH	FI	$r_{13} = 0.544$	Somewhat positively correlated.
LH	RI	$r_{14} = 0.297$	May be positively correlated.
LH	PI	$r_{15} = 0.409$	Somewhat positively correlated.
SL	FI	$r_{23} = 0.633$	Somewhat positively correlated.
SL	RI	$r_{24} = 0.440$	Somewhat positively correlated.
SL	PI	$r_{25} = 0.410$	Somewhat positively correlated.
FI	RI	$r_{34} = 0.487$	Somewhat positively correlated.
FI	PI	$r_{35} = 0.460$	Somewhat positively correlated.
RI	PI	$r_{45} = 0.498$	Somewhat positively correlated.

TABLE 6.15

SAS Output for the Correlation

The CORR Procedure					
Six Variables	**AC**	**LH**	**SL**	**FI**	**RI**	**PI**
Simple Statistics					
Variable	**N**	**Mean**	**Std. Dev.**	**Sum**	**Minimum**	**Maximum**
AC	468	7.75427	0.83901	3629	6.00000	10.00000
LH	468	7.82173	0.83900	3661	6.00000	10.00000
SL	468	7.86220	0.85751	3680	6.00000	10.00000
FI	468	7.67024	0.74748	3590	5.67000	9.67000
RI	468	7.64746	1.13829	3579	5.00000	10.00000
PI	468	6.96374	0.85383	3259	4.67000	9.000000
Pearson Correlation Coefficients, N = 468					
	AC	**LH**	**SL**	**FL**	**RI**	**PI**
AC	1.00000	0.93232	0.47476	0.54312	0.31627	0.40891
LH	0.93232	1.00000	0.46507	0.54418	0.29723	0.40883
SL	0.47476	0.46507	1.00000	0.63349	0.44032	0.41019
FL	0.54312	0.54418	0.63349	1.00000	0.48690	0.45971
RI	0.31627	0.29723	0.44032	0.48690	1.00000	0.49848
PI	0.40891	0.40883	0.41019	0.45971	0.49848	1.00000

6.5.8 Model Assumption

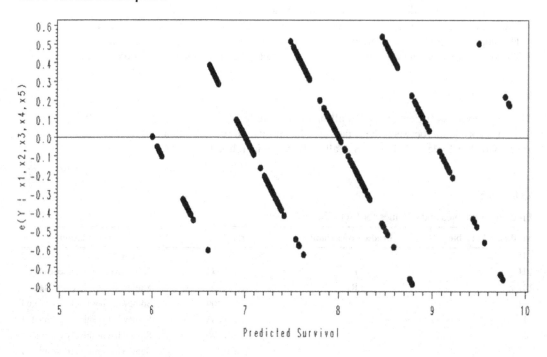

6.5.8.1 Residuals (e) vs. ŷ

The following plot indicates that the data points are not randomly distributed; therefore the linear model assumption may not be resaonable. There is a funnel shape indicating the variance is not constant.

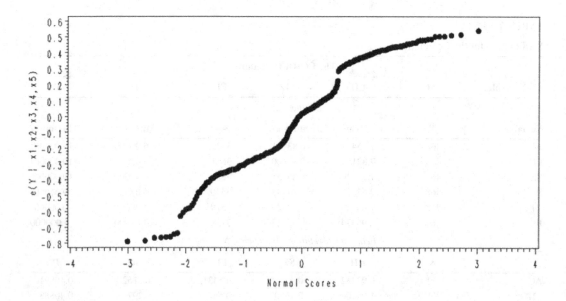

6.5.8.2 Normal Probability Plot

The distribution of the residuals has shorter tails (on both sides) than the normal distribution. Normality is violated.

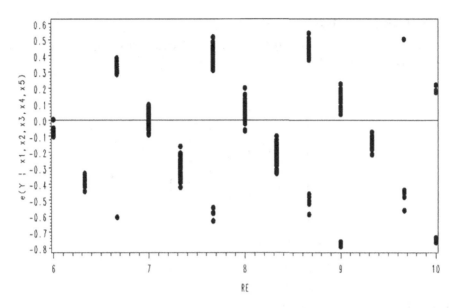

6.5.8.3 Residuals (e) vs. Reliability (x₁)

There is no curvature indicating current multiple linear regression (MLR) form may be reasonable. There are no y outliers; there may be some x outliers when $x = 6$ and 10.

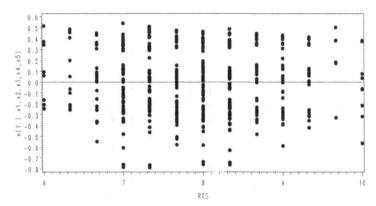

6.5.8.4 Residuals (e) vs. Responsiveness (x₂)

There is no curvature indicating current MLR form may be reasonable. There are no y and x outliers.

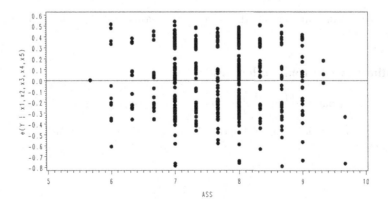

6.5.8.5 *Residuals (e) vs. Assurance (x₃)*

There is no curvature indicating current MLR form may be reasonable. There are no y outliers, but there may be some x outliers when x is <6 and >9.

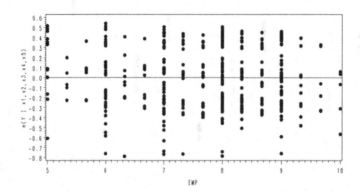

6.5.8.6 *Residuals (e) vs. Empathy (x₄)*

There is no curvature, indicating current MLR form may be reasonable. There are no y outliers; there may be some x outliers when $x = 6$ and 10.

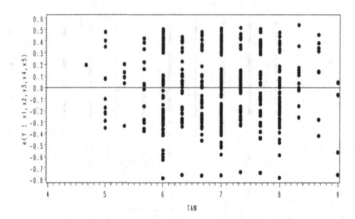

6.5.8.7 *Residuals (e) vs. Tangible (x₅)*

There is no curvature indicating current MLR form may be reasonable. There are no y outliers; there may be some x outliers when $x < 5$.

6.5.9 *y* Outliers (Bonferroni Outlier Test)

Cutoff values for the y outlier $t\left(\left(1 - \dfrac{\alpha}{2n}\right), n - p - 1\right) = t(0.9998931624, 462) = 3.73195$. The $|t_i|$ values greater than 3.73195 are considered as the y outlier. None of the $|t_i|$ values are greater than the cutoff value 3.73195 indicating they are no y outliers.

Obs	RE	RES	ASS	EMP	TAN	SQ	yhat	e	tres	cookdi	hii	dffitsi	enrm
1	8.33	7.67	8.00	6.33	7.00	8	8.19130	-0.19130	-0.63765	.000619822	0.009063	-0.06094	-0.40420
2	7.33	8.67	7.00	6.67	6.67	7	7.30502	-0.30502	-1.01937	.002495204	0.014203	-0.12236	-1.01481
3	7.67	9.33	8.33	6.00	7.33	8	7.65684	0.34316	1.15361	.005866103	0.025766	0.18767	0.81168
4	8.00	8.67	7.00	6.67	6.67	8	7.90545	0.09455	0.31598	.000239658	0.014198	0.03788	0.32410
5	7.33	8.33	7.33	6.00	7.00	7	7.29482	-0.29482	-0.98470	.002138209	0.013058	-0.11326	-0.97099
6	8.33	7.33	7.00	6.00	7.00	8	8.15234	-0.15234	-0.50848	.000514603	0.011801	-0.05552	-0.30161
7	7.00	7.67	6.67	5.67	6.00	7	6.94882	0.05118	0.17087	.000060229	0.012226	0.01899	0.15316
8	8.00	8.00	8.00	7.00	7.00	8	7.91623	0.08377	0.27858	.000056177	0.004324	0.01834	0.28485
9	8.33	7.33	7.67	6.67	6.33	8	8.17214	-0.17214	-0.57339	.000420783	0.007621	-0.05021	-0.34675
10	7.33	8.33	8.00	7.00	7.33	7	7.32909	-0.32909	-1.09667	.001732919	0.008571	-0.10199	-1.12889
11	7.00	7.00	6.67	5.67	6.00	7	6.92808	0.07192	0.23977	.000091384	0.009447	0.02339	0.23501
12	8.33	8.33	8.00	7.00	7.00	8	8.22217	-0.22217	-0.73912	.000475655	0.005197	-0.05340	-0.52963
13	7.33	7.33	7.00	6.00	6.00	7	7.24686	-0.24686	-0.82208	.000817625	0.007207	-0.07002	-0.68418
14	8.33	8.33	8.00	7.00	6.00	8	8.21286	-0.21286	-0.70970	.000814373	0.009608	-0.06986	-0.48699
15	9.00	9.00	8.67	8.00	7.00	9	8.87453	0.12547	0.41836	.000287084	0.009746	0.04147	0.45113
16	9.67	9.67	8.67	8.00	7.00	10	9.49570	0.50430	1.69023	.009663251	0.019891	0.24128	2.25672
17	8.00	8.00	7.33	6.67	6.67	8	7.89240	0.10760	0.35799	.000114554	0.005334	0.02619	0.37532
18	7.67	7.67	7.67	6.00	6.00	7	7.57769	-0.57769	-1.92571	.005733187	0.009191	-0.18602	-1.92745
19	8.33	8.33	7.67	7.00	7.33	8	8.21756	-0.21756	-0.72409	.000532673	0.006059	-0.05650	-0.50515
20	8.00	8.00	9.00	7.00	7.33	8	7.94260	0.05740	0.19220	.000112316	0.017916	0.02593	0.17487
21	8.67	8.67	9.00	8.00	7.33	9	8.57935	0.42065	1.40277	.003298538	0.009958	0.14083	1.41717
22	8.00	8.00	7.67	7.00	6.67	8	7.90546	0.09454	0.31424	.000058515	0.003543	0.01872	0.31846
23	9.00	9.00	8.67	8.00	7.67	9	8.88078	0.11922	0.39730	.000226186	0.008525	0.03681	0.42169
24	7.67	8.33	8.33	7.00	6.00	7	7.62908	-0.62908	-2.09974	.008742665	0.011758	-0.22988	-2.08754
25	8.67	7.67	8.67	7.00	7.00	8	8.52205	-0.52205	-1.74425	.007073471	0.013758	-0.20647	-1.83344
26	7.67	8.33	8.33	7.00	7.67	8	7.64464	0.35536	1.18544	.002511872	0.010611	0.12282	0.89648
27	8.00	8.67	7.33	6.00	6.00	8	7.89645	0.10355	0.34642	.000331365	0.016297	0.04455	0.35244
28	9.00	10.00	9.00	8.67	7.00	9	8.92362	0.07638	0.25589	.000212211	0.019074	0.03565	0.25708
29	8.33	10.00	9.00	8.00	7.33	8	8.31582	-0.31582	-1.05814	.003649862	0.019183	-0.14800	-1.08929
30	8.33	9.00	8.33	7.67	7.00	8	8.26104	-0.26104	-0.86932	.000915708	0.007218	-0.07410	-0.78955
31	9.67	8.33	8.33	7.00	7.67	9	9.43696	-0.43696	-1.46217	.006068427	0.016745	-0.19105	-1.66138
32	8.00	9.00	8.00	7.00	6.67	8	7.94411	0.05589	0.18641	.000059004	0.010085	0.01880	0.16943
33	8.67	10.00	9.00	8.00	7.00	9	8.61744	0.38256	1.28197	.005462373	0.019553	0.18116	1.08929
34	9.00	9.33	8.33	8.00	7.33	9	8.87990	0.12010	0.40064	.000287659	0.010639	0.04151	0.43931
35	9.00	8.00	8.33	7.00	6.67	9	8.81700	0.18300	0.61060	.000693701	0.011040	0.06447	0.57326
36	8.33	9.00	8.67	7.67	7.33	8	8.27204	-0.27204	-0.90653	.001176691	0.008518	-0.08401	-0.84181
37	7.67	8.33	8.67	6.00	6.00	8	7.62141	0.37859	1.27076	.006277433	0.022792	0.19420	1.07965
38	8.33	8.33	8.67	7.00	7.67	8	8.24402	-0.24402	-0.81447	.001304956	0.011665	-0.08845	-0.65737
39	7.33	9.33	8.00	7.00	6.67	7	7.35389	-0.35389	-1.18465	.004156062	0.017458	-0.15798	-1.33444
40	8.33	7.33	8.67	6.33	7.67	8	8.20263	-0.20263	-0.68032	.001840207	0.023300	-0.10502	-0.44521

6.5.10 *x* Outliers

The leverage value (the highest h_{ii} value) is 0.042413.

To check the *x* outliers, the h_{ii} values should be less than $\dfrac{2p}{n} = ((2*6)/468) = 0.025641$.

Values h_{ii} at observations 3, 50, 56, 58, 88, 91, 94, 112, 206, 237, 259, 263, 272, 279, 307, 309, 312, 334, and 459 are greater than 0.025641. This clearly indicates the values at these observations are *x* outliers.

6.5.11 Influence

The cutoff value for the degrees of freedom for Beta (DFBETAS) is $2/(\sqrt{n}) = 2/(\sqrt{(468)}) = 0.092450033$. Since DFBETAS for all the outliers are less than the cutoff values, the values at both the *x* and *y* outliers are not influential.

		DFBETAS—Cutoff Value—0.0042735					
Observation	*x* Outlier	Intercept	RE	RES	ASS	EMP	TAN
3	Yes	*−0.0355*	*−0.0654*	**0.11**	0.0396	*−0.1417*	0.0459
50	Yes	**0.0048**	*−0.0254*	0.0166	*−0.0167*	0.0118	0.0169
56	Yes	0.1896	*−0.2582*	0.1533	*−0.1839*	0.1519	0.0203
58	Yes	*−0.0066*	**0.062**	*−0.0383*	0.0303	*−0.0365*	*−0.0275*
88	Yes	*−0.0388*	*−0.0622*	**0.0511**	*0.0031*	*−0.1015*	**0.1389**

(Continued)

| Observation | x Outlier | DFBETAS—Cutoff Value—0.0042735 | | | | | |
		Intercept	RE	RES	ASS	EMP	TAN
91	Yes	*−0.1035*	*−0.0128*	**0.0517**	**0.0598**	*−0.0595*	**0.0398**
94	Yes	**0.2013**	*−0.2998*	**0.1237**	**0.1363**	*−0.0597*	*−0.2094*
112	Yes	*−0.0531*	**0.0895**	*0.0038*	**0.0251**	**0.0505**	*−0.1201*
206	Yes	**0.0207**	**0.016**	*−0.0169*	*−0.0021*	*−0.0053*	*−0.0155*
237	Yes	**0.0171**	*−0.0516*	*−0.0125*	**0.0179**	*−0.0412*	**0.0593**
259	Yes	**0.0773**	*−0.0657*	**0.0057**	**0.1033**	*−0.1061*	*−0.0825*
263	Yes	**0.0654**	*−0.0631*	**0.1119**	*−0.0115*	*−0.114*	*−0.0251*
272	Yes	*−0.0181*	*−0.0277*	**0.0259**	*−0.0156*	**0.016**	**0.0296**
279	Yes	**0.0549**	*−0.1808*	**0.1998**	*−0.278*	**0.1462**	**0.1765**
307	Yes	*0.002716*	**0.009154**	**0.0329**	**1.0476**	*0.0017*	*0.0009*
309	Yes	**0.5161**	**1.7449**	**0.0326**	**1.0066**	**0.3202**	*0.00176*
312	Yes	*−0.0695*	*−0.234*	**0.0318**	**1.0456**	*−0.0424*	*−0.0164*
334	Yes	*0.0009*	**0.0671**	*−0.004*	**0.0092**	**0.0441**	*−0.12*
459	Yes	*−0.0228*	*−0.0495*	*−0.0079*	**0.0325**	*−0.0475*	**0.0815**

Bold values—above the cutoff values.
Italic values—below the cutoff values.

6.5.12 DFFITS

The cutoff value for the degrees of freedom for FITS (DFFITS) is $2\left(\sqrt{(p/n)}\right) = 2\left(\sqrt{(2/468)}\right) = 0.13074409$. DFFITS for all the variables at the outliers are lesser than the cutoff values at these observations. This indicates that the observations at the x outliers are not influential.

6.5.13 Cooks Distance

If the $d_{ii} > F(0.50, 1,461)$, it indicates that the outliers are influential. But from the SAS output, it is clear that is not the case indicating that the outliers are not influential.

6.5.14 Inflation

Since max variance for IF $(VIF)_k = 2.11503$ is <5 and average $(VIF) = 1.702708$ is not much bigger than 1, we conclude that serious multicollinearity is not a problem.

Parameter Estimates

Variable	DF	Parameter Estimate	Standard Error	t Value	Pr > |t|	Variance Inflation
Intercept	1	0.13862	0.16528	0.84	0.4021	0
LH	1	0.89616	0.02056	43.59	<.0001	1.52967
SL	1	0.03095	0.02186	1.42	0.1574	1.80594
FI	1	0.02330	0.02713	0.86	0.3910	2.11503
RI	1	0.01559	0.01518	1.03	0.3052	1.53611
PI	1	0.00932	0.02018	0.46	0.6445	1.52679

6.5.15 Modified Levene Test

The Modified Levene test is performed by dividing the data into two groups based on the median of that.

```
                         The TTEST Procedure

                            Statistics

                    Lower CL              Upper CL  Lower CL            Upper CL
 Variable  group    N    Mean    Mean       Mean    Std Dev  Std Dev   Std Dev  Std Err
    d          1   219  0.2449  0.2652     0.2856    0.1396   0.1527    0.1685   0.0103
    d          2   249  0.2138  0.2362     0.2587    0.1653   0.1798    0.1972   0.0114
    d     Diff (1-2)        -0.002   0.029     0.0595    0.1576   0.1677    0.1792   0.0155

                            T-Tests

        Variable   Method         Variances    DF    t Value   Pr > |t|
           d       Pooled         Equal        466     1.87     0.0628
           d       Satterthwaite  Unequal      465     1.88     0.0601

                      Equality of Variances

        Variable   Method      Num DF    Den DF    F Value   Pr > F
           d       Folded F      248       218      1.39     0.0135
```

6.5.15.1 t-Test for Variance Constant Check

H_0: Variance is constant.

H_a: Variance is not constant.

Decision rule: p-Value (t-test) <0.05

$p = 0.0135 < p = 0.05$. Therefore, reject the H_0.

This indicates that the variance is not constant for the preliminary model. This agrees with the plot.

	e	enrm
e e(Y | x1,x2,x3,x4,x5)	**1.00000**	**0.98175**

6.5.15.2 Normality Test

$C(\alpha = 0.01, n = 468) = 0.982$ (Since the value at $n = 100$ is almost 1, we take $n = 100$)

$\rho = 0.982 < 0.985$.

Assumption of normality is violated at alpha level of 0.01.

Further, this assumption of non-normal data can be argued that the violation occurring at the third decimal place can be treated as a normal data which may be an artifact of the experiment of data collection process. For this reason, the data can be assumed as a normal data for further computations and does not warrant transformations. This conclusion has been made by looking at the residual plots of the independent variables which indicate a random pattern.

Therefore, the preliminary model is

$$\hat{y} = 0.13862 + 0.89616x_1 + 0.03095x_2 + 0.02330x_3 + 0.01559x_4 + 0.009932x_5$$

The regression coefficients can be interpreted as the unit change in the predictor variable increases the unit change in the dependent variable. For example, per unit change in LH increases the accuracy by 0.13862, when all other predictor variables are held constant. Similarly per unit changes in SL, FI, RI, and PI increase the accuracy by 0.89616, 0.02330, 0.01559, and 0.009932, respectively, while other predictor variables are held constant.

6.5.16 Analysis of Variance

The coefficient of Multiple Determination R^2 is a measure of goodness-of-fit of linear regression. It has a value of 0.8724 which implies 87.24% of variation in the accuracy is explained by the predictor variables LH, SL, FI, RI, and PI. This is a good value as high values of R^2 are desired.

Analysis of Variance

Source	DF	Sum of Squares	Mean Square	F Value	Pr > F
Model	5	286.77947	57.35589	631.49	<.0001
Error	462	41.96198	0.09083		
Corrected Total	467	328.74145			

Root MSE	0.30137	R-Square	0.8724
Dependent Mean	7.75427	Adj R-Sq	0.8710
Coeff Var	3.88656		

Parameter Estimates

Variable	DF	Parameter Estimate	Standard Error	t Value	Pr > |t|	Variance Inflation
Intercept	1	0.13862	0.16528	0.84	0.4021	0
RE	1	0.89616	0.02056	43.59	<.0001	1.52967
RES	1	0.03095	0.02186	1.42	0.1574	1.80594
ASS	1	0.02330	0.02713	0.86	0.3910	2.11503
EMP	1	0.01559	0.01518	1.03	0.3052	1.53611
TAN	1	0.00932	0.02018	0.46	0.6445	1.52679

p-Values for the variable Tangible rating are high. This indicates that this variable has less significance in the model.

The predictor variable reliability rating has the lowest p-value, indicating that this variable is the most significant in the model.

The next significant predictor variable is Responsiveness followed by Empathy and Assurance, based on their p-value.

F-test on the significance of regression

At $\alpha = .05$ and for $n = 468$

$F(0.95,4,125) = 2.233274717$

$F^* = 57.35589/0.09083 = 631.4641638 > 2.44417$. Therefore, the regression is significant.

6.5.16.1 *Exploration of Interaction Term*

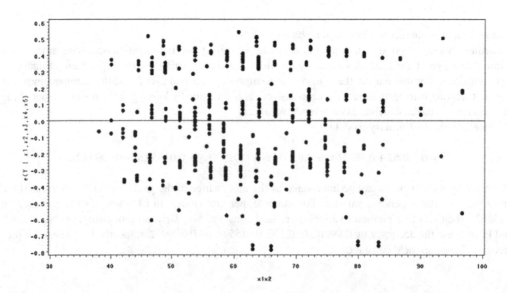

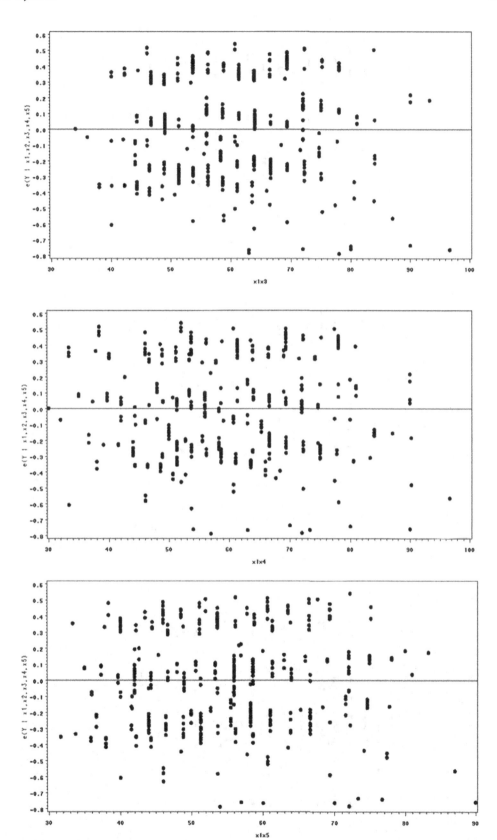

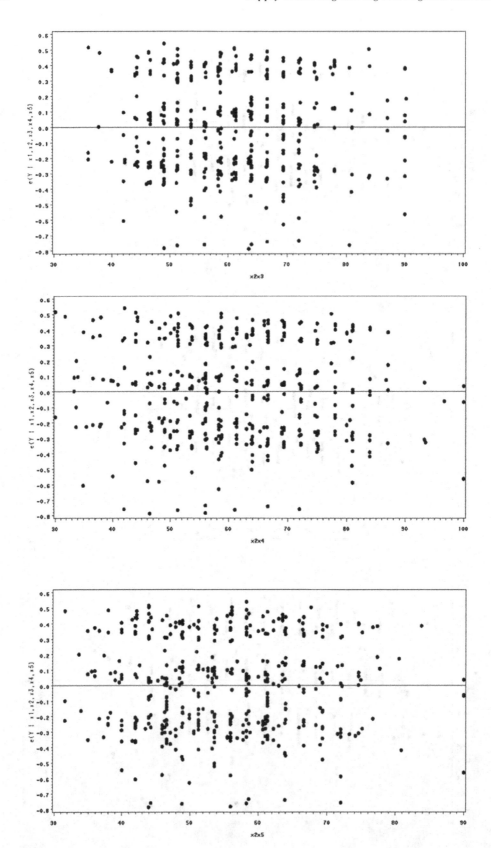

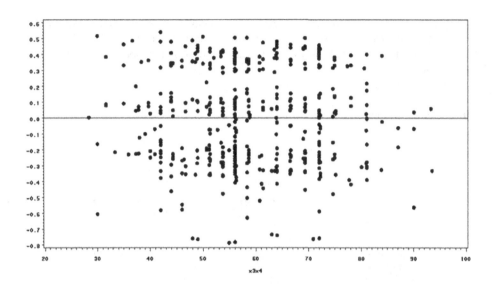

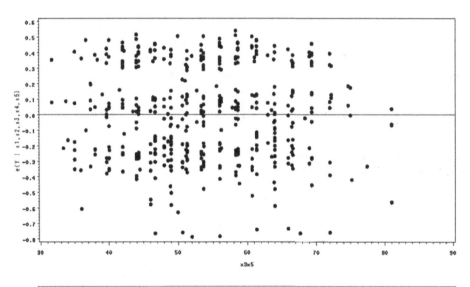

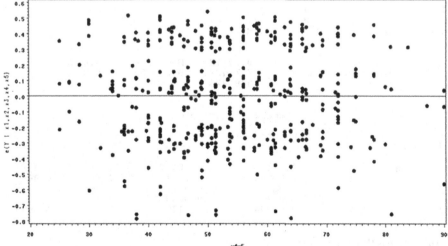

The possibility of adding interaction terms to the regression model can be verified by the partial regression plots. The plots indicate that there are no trends in any of the interactions. Therefore, we can conclude that there is no need to consider any of the interaction terms in the model.

Model Search:

Backward Deletion Method:

The $\alpha = 0.10$ is chosen.

Step 0: The initial full model will be as follows.

```
                          Analysis of Variance

                                  Sum of            Mean
Source                 DF        Squares          Square     F Value    Pr > F

Model                   5      286.77947        57.35589     631.49     <.0001
Error                 462       41.96198         0.09083
Corrected Total       467      328.74145


                Root MSE              0.30137    R-Square     0.8724
                Dependent Mean        7.75427    Adj R-Sq     0.8710
                Coeff Var             3.88656
```

```
                          Parameter Estimates

                    Parameter       Standard                            Variance
Variable     DF      Estimate          Error    t Value    Pr > |t|    Inflation

Intercept     1       0.13862        0.16528       0.84      0.4021            0
LH            1       0.89616        0.02056      43.59      <.0001      1.52967
SL            1       0.03095        0.02186       1.42      0.1574      1.80594
FI            1       0.02330        0.02713       0.86      0.3910      2.11503
RI            1       0.01559        0.01518       1.03      0.3052      1.53611
PI            1       0.00932        0.02018       0.46      0.6445      1.52679
```

The variable PI has the highest p-value.

Step 1: Model with the variable PI removed

```
                        The REG Procedure
                          Model: MODEL1
                     Dependent Variable: AC

                          Analysis of Variance

                                  Sum of            Mean
Source                 DF        Squares          Square     F Value    Pr > F

Model                   4      286.76011        71.69003     790.65     <.0001
Error                 463       41.98134         0.09067
Corrected Total       467      328.74145


                Root MSE              0.30112    R-Square     0.8723
                Dependent Mean        7.75427    Adj R-Sq     0.8712
                Coeff Var             3.88326
```

```
                          Parameter Estimates

                    Parameter       Standard
Variable     DF      Estimate          Error    t Value    Pr > |t|

Intercept     1       0.15374        0.16187       0.95      0.3427
LH            1       0.89801        0.02015      44.58      <.0001
SL            1       0.03174        0.02177       1.46      0.1455
FI            1       0.02474        0.02693       0.92      0.3588
RI            1       0.01794        0.01429       1.26      0.2099
```

The variable FI has the highest p-value.

Step 2: Model with the variable FI removed

```
                          The REG Procedure
                            Model: MODEL1
                       Dependent Variable: AC

                        Analysis of Variance

                                Sum of          Mean
Source                    DF    Squares         Square      F Value    Pr > F

Model                      3   286.68361       95.56120     1054.27    <.0001
Error                    464    42.05784        0.09064
Corrected Total          467   328.74145


              Root MSE                0.30107    R-Square     0.8721
              Dependent Mean          7.75427    Adj R-Sq     0.8712
              Coeff Var               3.88261


                        Parameter Estimates

                       Parameter       Standard
Variable        DF     Estimate          Error     t Value    Pr > |t|

Intercept        1      0.19764         0.15462      1.28      0.2018
LH               1      0.90445         0.01889     47.89      <.0001
SL               1      0.04035         0.01965      2.05      0.0406
RI               1      0.02159         0.01372      1.57      0.1164
```

The variable RI has the highest p-value.
Step 3: Model with the variable RI removed

```
                          The REG Procedure
                            Model: MODEL1
                       Dependent Variable: AC

                        Analysis of Variance

                                Sum of          Mean
    Source                DF    Squares         Square      F Value    Pr > F

    Model                  2   286.45936      143.22968     1575.18    <.0001
    Error                465    42.28210        0.09093
    Corrected Total      467   328.74145


              Root MSE                0.30154    R-Square     0.8714
              Dependent Mean          7.75427    Adj R-Sq     0.8708
              Coeff Var               3.88876


                        Parameter Estimates

                Parameter     Standard                                       Variance
Variable   DF   Estimate       Error    t Value   Pr > |t|    Tolerance     Inflation

Intercept   1    0.24887       0.15139    1.64     0.1009                         0
LH          1    0.90790       0.01879   48.33     <.0001     0.78371       1.27598
SL          1    0.05139       0.01838    2.80     0.0054     0.78371       1.27598
```

All the p-values are less than $\alpha = 0.10$, i.e., the model is significant at $\alpha = 0.10$. This is the potentially good model provided by the backward deletion method. The maximum variance inflation factor for each variable is not greater than 5, and average (VIF) = 1.27598 is not bigger than 1. Therefore, multicollinearity is not a problem.

The potentially good model is

$$\hat{y} = 0.24887 + 0.90790 x_1 + 0.05139 x_2$$

Stepwise:
The best model by the stepwise method is

$$\hat{y} = 0.46185 + 0.93233 x_1$$

All the p-values are less than $\alpha = 0.10$, i.e., the model is significant at $\alpha = 0.10$. The maximum variance inflation factor for each variable are not greater than 5, and average (VIF) = 1 is not bigger than 1. Therefore, multicollinearity is not a problem.

Variable LH Entered: R-Square = 0.8692 and C(p) = 9.3500

Analysis of Variance

Source	DF	Sum of Squares	Mean Square	F Value	Pr > F
Model	1	285.74858	285.74858	3097.23	<.0001
Error	466	42.99287	0.09226		
Corrected Total	467	328.74145			

Variable	Parameter Estimate	Standard Error	Type II SS	F Value	Pr > F
Intercept	0.46185	0.13178	1.13313	12.28	0.0005
LH	0.93233	0.01675	285.74858	3097.23	<.0001

Best Subsets:

Number in Model	Adjusted R-Square	R-Square	C(p)	AIC	SBC	Variables in Model
1	0.8689	0.8692	9.3500	-1113.3191	-1105.02216	LH
1	0.2935	0.2950	2087.770	-324.8761	-316.57911	FI

Number in Model	Adjusted R-Square	R-Square	C(p)	AIC	SBC	Variables in Model
2	0.8708	0.8714	3.5244	-1119.1209	-1106.67552	LH SL
2	0.8705	0.8710	4.7711	-1117.8693	-1105.42394	LH FI

Since the above adjusted R^2 levels off and also $c(p)$ is close to $p = 3$, the model with LH and SL is a potential good model.

Number in Model	Adjusted R-Square	R-Square	C(p)	AIC	SBC	Variables in Model
3	0.8712	0.8721	3.0554	-1119.6097	-1103.01582	LH SL RI
3	0.8710	0.8719	3.7869	-1118.8710	-1102.27715	LH SL FI

Since the above adjusted R^2 levels off and also $c(p)$ is close to $p = 3$, the model with LH, SL, and RI is a potential good model. It also contains the minimum value for average inventory cost (AIC) and savings before costs (SBC).

Number in Model	Adjusted R-Square	R-Square	C(p)	AIC	SBC	Variables in Model
4	0.8712	0.8723	4.2131	-1118.4617	-1097.71939	LH SL FI RI
4	0.8710	0.8722	4.7372	-1117.9314	-1097.18908	LH SL RI PI

Number in Model	Adjusted R-Square	R-Square	C(p)	AIC	SBC	Variables in Model
5	0.8710	0.8724	6.0000	-1116.6776	-1091.78678	LH SL FI RI PI

Potential Good models by Best Subsets:

The first potential good model is $\hat{y} = 0.24887 + 0.90790x_1 + 0.05139x_2$. The maximum variance inflation factor for each variable is not greater than 5, and average (VIF) = 1.27598 is not bigger than 1. Therefore, multicollinearity is not a problem.

Parameter Estimates

Variable	DF	Parameter Estimate	Standard Error	t Value	Pr > |t|	Tolerance	Variance Inflation
Intercept	1	0.24887	0.15139	1.64	0.1009	.	0
LH	1	0.90790	0.01879	48.33	<.0001	0.78371	1.27598
SL	1	0.05139	0.01838	2.80	0.0054	0.78371	1.27598

The second potential good model is $\hat{y} = 0.19764 + 0.90445x_1 + 0.04035x_2 + 0.02159x_4$. The maximum variance inflation factor for each variable is not greater than 5, and average (VIF) = 1.33794 is not bigger than 1. Therefore, multicollinearity is not a problem. But this model has an insignificant predictor, so it cannot be a candidate.

Parameter Estimates

Variable	DF	Parameter Estimate	Standard Error	t Value	Pr > |t|
Intercept	1	0.19764	0.15462	1.28	0.2018
LH	1	0.90445	0.01889	47.89	<.0001
SL	1	0.04035	0.01965	2.05	0.0406
RI	1	0.02159	0.01372	1.57	0.1164

Best Models:

Model 1 : $\hat{y} = 0.46185 + 0.93233x_1$ (from stepwise)

Model 2 : $\hat{y} = 0.24887 + 0.90790x_1 + 0.05139x_2$ (from best subsets)

Model Selection:

Model 1: $\hat{y} = 0.46185 + 0.93233x_1$ (model with LH)

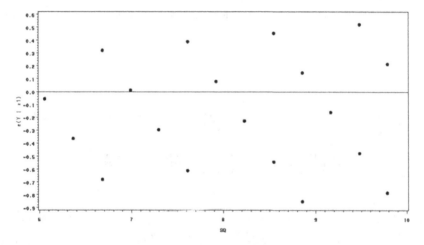

There is no funnel shape indicating the variance is constant.

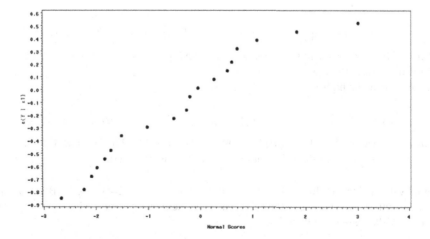

Normal plot has right tail. Normality might be reasonable.

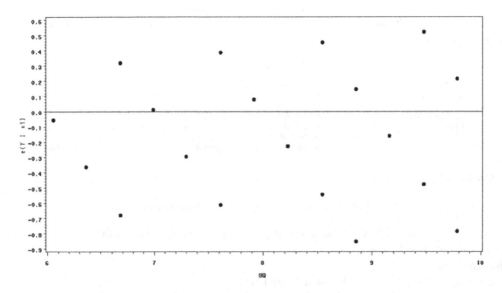

There is no curvature indicating current MLR form may be reasonable. There are no *x* or *y* outliers.

```
                              The REG Procedure
                                Model: MODEL1
                          Dependent Variable: AC

                            Analysis of Variance

                                    Sum of          Mean
        Source            DF       Squares        Square    F Value    Pr > F

        Model              1     285.74858     285.74858    3097.23    <.0001
        Error            466      42.99287       0.09226
        Corrected Total  467     328.74145


               Root MSE              0.30374    R-Square     0.8692
               Dependent Mean       7.75427    Adj R-Sq     0.8689
               Coeff Var            3.91710


                            Parameter Estimates

                    Parameter     Standard                               Variance
  Variable    DF    Estimate         Error    t Value    Pr > |t|    Tolerance    Inflation

  Intercept    1     0.46185       0.13178       3.50      0.0005           .            0
  LH           1     0.93233       0.01675      55.65      <.0001     1.00000      1.00000
```

y Outlier:

Cutoff value for the *y* outlier $t\left(\left(1-\dfrac{\alpha}{2n}\right), n-p-1\right) = t(0.9998931624, 466) = 3.73169$. The $|t_i|$ values greater than 3.73169 are considered as the *y* outliers. None of the $|t_i|$ values are greater than the cutoff value 3.73195 indicating they are no *y* outliers.

The leverage value (the highest h_{ii} value) is 0.042413.

x Outlier:

To check the *x* outliers, the h_{ii} values should be less than $\dfrac{2p}{n} = ((2*1)/468) = 0.0042735$.

Values h_{ii} at observations 87, 94, 99, 101, 107, 109, 110, 111, 118, 190, 220, 261, and 425 are greater than 0.042413. This clearly indicates the values at these observations are *x* outliers.

Inflation

The cutoff value for the **DFBETAS** is $2/\left(\sqrt{n}\right) = 2/\left(\sqrt{(468)}\right) = 0.092450033$. DFBETAS for all the variables at the outliers are lesser than the cutoff values at these observations. This shows that the observations at the *x* outliers are not influential.

DFFITS

The cutoff value for the DFFITS is $2\left(\sqrt{(p/n)}\right) = 2/\left(\sqrt{(2/468)}\right) = 0.13074409$. DFFITS for all the variables at the outliers are lesser than the cutoff values at these observations. This indicates that the observations at the x outliers are not influential.

Cooks Distance

If the $d_{ii} > F(0.50, 1,466)$, it indicates that the outliers are influential. But from the SAS output, it is clear that is not the case indicating that the outliers are not influential.

Variance Inflation

Since max $(VIF)_k$ 1 < 5 and average $(VIF) = 1$ is equal to 1, conclude that serious multicollinearity is not a problem.

Model 2: $\hat{y} = 0.24887 + 0.90790x_1 + 0.05139x_2$ (model with LH and SL)

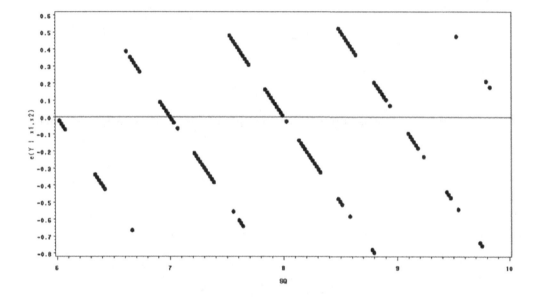

There is no funnel shape indicating the variance is constant.

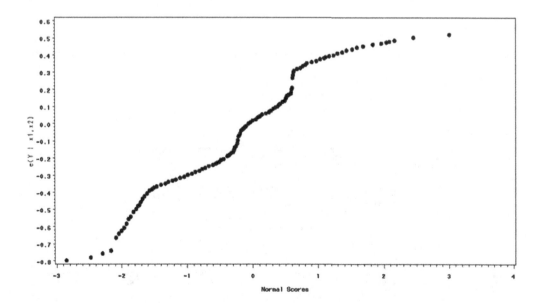

Normal plot has right tail. Normality is violated.

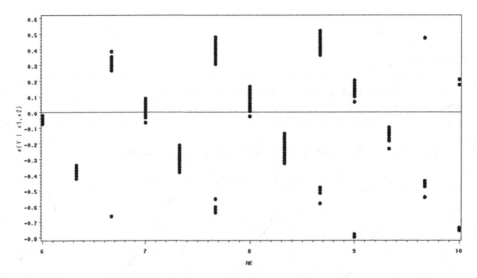

There is no curvature indicating current MLR form may be reasonable. There are no *x* or *y* outliers.

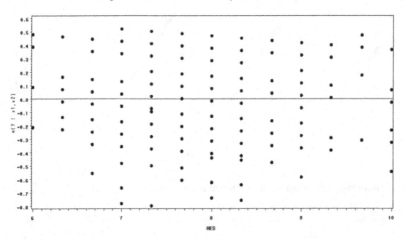

There is no curvature indicating current MLR form may be reasonable. There are no *x* or *y* outliers.

```
                          The REG Procedure
                            Model: MODEL1
                        Dependent Variable: AC

                          Analysis of Variance

                                    Sum of          Mean
        Source              DF      Squares        Square    F Value    Pr > F

        Model                2    286.45936     143.22968    1575.18    <.0001
        Error              465     42.28210       0.09093
        Corrected Total    467    328.74145


                   Root MSE            0.30154    R-Square     0.8714
                   Dependent Mean      7.75427    Adj R-Sq     0.8708
                   Coeff Var           3.88876


                          Parameter Estimates

                     Parameter     Standard                                   Variance
   Variable    DF     Estimate       Error    t Value    Pr > |t|   Tolerance   Inflation

   Intercept    1      0.24887      0.15139       1.64     0.1009                       0
   LH           1      0.90790      0.01879      48.33     <.0001     0.78371     1.27598
   SL           1      0.05139      0.01838       2.80     0.0054     0.78371     1.27598
```

y Outlier:

Cutoff value for the y outlier $t\left(\left(1 - \dfrac{\alpha}{2n}\right), n - p - 1\right) = t(0.9998931624, 466) = 3.73169$. The $|t_i|$ values greater than 3.73169 are considered as the y outlier. None of the $|t_i|$ values are greater than the cutoff value 3.73195 indicating they are no y outliers.

x Outlier:

The leverage value (the highest h_{ii} value) is 0.042413.

To check the x outliers, the h_{ii} values should be less than $\dfrac{2p}{n} = ((2*2)/468) = 0.008547$.

Values h_{ii} at observations 7, 38, 51, 56, 83, 122, 149, 168, 198, 218, 239, 241, 342, 357, 382, and 418 are greater than 0.042413. This clearly indicates the values at these observations are x outliers.

Inflation

The cutoff value for the DFBETAS is $2/\left(\sqrt{n}\right) = 2/\left(\sqrt{(468)}\right) = 0.092450033$. DFBETAS for all the variables at the outliers are lesser than the cutoff values at these observations. This shows that the observations at the x outliers are not influential.

DFFITS

The cutoff value for the DFFITS is $2\left(\sqrt{(p/n)}\right) = 2/\left(\sqrt{(2/468)}\right) = 0.13074409$. DFFITS for all the variables at the outliers are lesser than the cutoff values at these observations. This indicates that the observations at the x outliers are not influential.

Variance Inflation

Since max $(\text{VIF})_k$ 1.27598 < 5 and average $(\text{VIF}) = 1.27598$ is less than 1, conclude that serious multicollinearity is not a problem.

Model Comparison:

The variations between the two potential models are minimal. The chosen model is one with the variable reliability rating. This model has less number of x outliers. The R^2 is also higher, which is desired. Also the slope for the predictor variable (LH) of the chosen model is higher than the slope of the other models' predictor variables (LH and SL). This indicates that the predictor variable (LH) in the chosen model has more impact on the predictor variables (LH and SL) on the accuracy. Therefore, the chosen model is

$$\hat{y} = 0.46185 + 0.93233x_1$$

Final MLR Model:

$$\hat{y} = 0.46185 + 0.93233x_1$$

The intercept 0.46185 indicates the score of the accuracy when the rating for reliability is 0.

The slope *0.93233* indicates the increase in accuracy when there is a unit increase in the reliability rating.

The REG Procedure
Model: MODEL1
Dependent Variable: AC

Analysis of Variance

Source	DF	Sum of Squares	Mean Square	F Value	Pr > F
Model	1	285.74858	285.74858	3097.23	<.0001
Error	466	42.99287	0.09226		
Corrected Total	467	328.74145			

Root MSE	0.30374	R-Square	0.8692	
Dependent Mean	7.75427	Adj R-Sq	0.8689	
Coeff Var	3.91710			

Parameter Estimates

Variable	DF	Parameter Estimate	Standard Error	t Value	Pr > |t|	Tolerance	Variance Inflation
Intercept	1	0.46185	0.13178	3.50	0.0005	.	0
LH	1	0.93233	0.01675	55.65	<.0001	1.00000	1.00000

The R^2 is 0.8692 which is close to 1 indicating that the model is reasonable.

Joint confidence intervals (CIs) for parameters β_1

$b_1 = 0.93233$ and $\{b_1\} = 0.01675$

At $\alpha = 10$

$B = t(1 - \alpha/2g; n - p) = t(1 - 0.10/2(1); 468 - 2) = t(0.95, 466) = 1.64813$

CI for $\beta_1 = 0.93233 \pm (1.64813*0.01675) = (0.9599, 0.9047)$

With confidence coefficient of 0.90, we can conclude that the slope accuracy lies between the 0.9599 and 0.9047.

Inferences for x_h:

We are interested in finding out the mean response of accuracy at which the reliability rating is at its highest value. We choose the following value because the reliability score is highest.

Accuracy	LH
10	10

CI at x_h:

CI is (9.2387, 9.8374). 90% CI for the service quality was developed with the lower limit 9.2387 and upper limit 9.8374.

Confidence Band:

$$W = \sqrt{p * F(1 - \alpha, p, n - p)} = \sqrt{2 * 2.314} = 4.628$$

$F(0.9, 2, 466) = 2.314$

Two-sided confidence band is (7.6233, 10.4624). 90% prediction interval for the service quality was developed with the lower limit 7.6233 and upper limit 10.4624.

Prediction Interval (PI)

PI is (8.9317, 9.9374). 90% prediction interval for the service quality was developed with the lower limit 8.9317 and upper limit 9.9374.

Specific objective 2:

Initial cost for manual data entry involves labor wage; for barcode and RFID, it includes implementation cost and equipment cost.

	Manual Data Entry	Barcode	RFID
Initial cost	$55,000		

Economic Analysis:

The cash flow for 5 years is provided in the below table. The required annual rate of return is 12%.

Year	All Cash Out	All Cash In	Net Cash Flow
Year 0	890,000.00		
Year 1	0.00	250,000.00	250,000.00
Year 2	0.00	250,000.00	250,000.00
Year 3	0.00	250,000.00	250,000.00
Year 4	0.00	250,000.00	250,000.00
Year 5	0.00	250,000.00	250,000.00

The NPV is calculated as $11,194.05 using the NPV formula. The NPV value profile is provided in the below table.

| NPV Profile | | |
Annual RRR (Discount) (%)	+NPV: Accept	−NPV: Reject
5	192,369	
6	163,091	
7	135,049	
8	108,178	
9	82,413	
10	57,697	
11	33,974	
12	11,194	
13	−10,692	−10,692
14	−31,730	−31,730
15	−51,961	−51,961
16	−71,427	−71,427
17	−90,163	−−90,163
18	−108,207	−108,207
19	−125,591	−125,591
20	−142,347	−142,347
21	−158,504	−158,504
22	−174,090	−174,090
23	−189,132	−189,132
24	−203,654	−203,654
25	−217,680	−217,680

From the table hurdle rate, the rate at which the NPV reduces below zero is identified as 12%. The NPV is graphically represented as shown in the figure below.

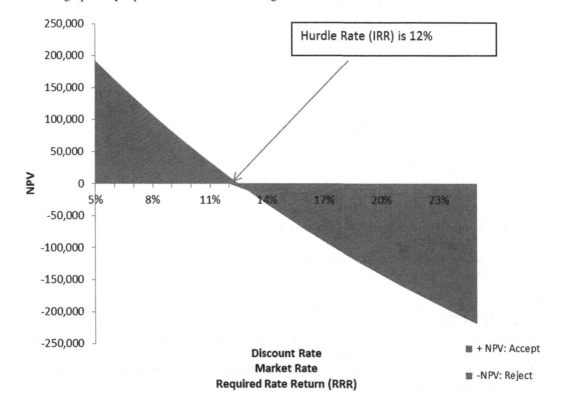

6.6 Conclusion

Hypothesis 1:
  Reject the null hypothesis: $\beta_1 = \beta_2 = \beta_3 = \beta_4 = \beta_5 = 0$
From the regression model, it is clear that β_1, β_2, β_3, β_4, and β_5 are all not zero. The regression model clearly suggests the dependent variable LH affects the accuracy of the ERP data; therefore, the null hypothesis is rejected. This suggests that the method or the system employed in the material handling affects the accuracy of the ERP data. The accuracy of the data can be improved by implementing robust material handling systems like RFID system and various other systems. Employing the RFID as material handling system also provides additional advantage like live inventory update and SL identification, can monitor environment conditions required for certain products, etc.
  Hypothesis 2:
  Reject the null hypothesis: NPV ≤ 0
The NPV calculated is positive value; therefore, the null hypothesis is rejected. The hurdle rate (IRR, internal rate of return) 12% is within the acceptable rate. This clearly indicates that implementing RFID for the data entry into the ERP system is economically justified and has an economic impact on the organizations.

6.7 Limitations and Future Research

The variables identified in this research may not be applicable for all types of industries. Further analysis requires using cluster method and statistical quality approach. The economic analysis is done using only one product line. Adding additional product lines may alter the results. Furthermore, some of the data used are simulated due to the restricted access and may vary when using the real data.

The future research is to develop and evaluate an interface between the RFID and ERP system to enter the data from RFID directly into ERP systems. Then compare the manual data entry and the RFID interface data entry to identify the impact of these systems on the ERP data accuracy.

Appendix 6.A: Survey

(1 being the lowest and 10 being the highest)

1. Rate how the LH affects the ERP data accuracy
   1 2 3 4 5 6 7 8 9 10
2. Rate how the SL affects the ERP data accuracy
   1 2 3 4 5 6 7 8 9 10
3. Rate how the FI affects the ERP data accuracy
   1 2 3 4 5 6 7 8 9 10
4. Rate how the RI affects the ERP data accuracy
   1 2 3 4 5 6 7 8 9 10
5. Rate how the PI affects the ERP data accuracy
   1 2 3 4 5 6 7 8 9 10.

REFERENCES

Al-Mashari, M., Al-Mudimigh, A., & Zairi, M. (2003). Enterprise resource planning: A taxonomy of critical factors. *European Journal of Operational Research*, 146, 352–364.
Al-Turkia, U. M. (2011). An exploratory study of ERP implementation in Saudi Arabia. *Production Planning & Control: The Management of Operations*, 22(4), 403–414.

Amid, A., Moalagh, M., & Ravasan, A. Z. (2012). Identification and classification of ERP critical failure factors in Iranian industries. *Information Systems*, 37(3), 227–237.

Appleton, E. (1997). How to survive ERP. *Datamation*, 43(3), 50–53.

Bicknell, D. (1998). SAP to fight drug firm's $500M suit over R/3 collapse, *Computer Weekly*, 3 September, 3.

Boudette, N. E. (1999). Europe's SAP scrambles to stem big glitches—Software giant to tighten its watch after Snafus at Whirlpool, Hershey. *Wall Street Journal*, 5, A25–A26.

Bradley, J. (2008). Management based critical success factors in the implementation of enterprise resource planning systems. *International Journal of Accounting Information Systems*, 9(3), 175–200.

Brakely, H. (1999). What makes ERP effective? *Manufacturing Systems*, 17(3), 120.

Calogero, B. (2000, June). Who is to blame for ERP failure? *Sun Server Magazine*.

Carmienke, S., Freitag, M. H., Pischon, T., Schlattmann, P., Fankhaenel, T., Goebel, H., & Gensichen, J. (2013). General and abdominal obesity parameters and their combination in relation to mortality: A systematic review and meta-regression analysis. *European Journal of Clinical Nutrition*, 67, 573–585.

Chalmers, R. (1999). Small manufacturers seek best ERP fit. *Manufacturing Engineering*, 123(4), 42–48.

Chen, I. J. (2001). Planning for ERP systems: Analysis and future trend. *Business Process Management Journal*, 7(5), 374–386.

Chew, B. W., Leonard-Barton, D., & Bohn, R. E. (1991). Beating Murphys law. *Sloan Management Review*, 5, 16.

Chien, S.-W., & Tsaur, S.-M. (2007). Investigating the success of ERP systems: Case studies in three Taiwanese high-tech industries. *Computers in Industry*, 58, 783–93.

Chien, S.-W., Hu, C., Reimers, K., & Lin, J.-S. (2007). The influence of centrifugal and centripetal forces on ERP project success in small and medium-sized enterprises in China and Taiwan. *International Journal of Production Economics*, 107(2), 380–396.

Chiu, D. K., Mark, K. P., Kafeza, E., & Wong, T. P. (2001). Enhancing ERP system with RFID: Logistic process integration and exception handling. *International Journal of Systems and Service-Oriented Engineering*, 2(3), 17.

Columbus, L. (2014, May 2). Gartner's ERP market share update shows the future of cloud ERP is now. Retrieved from www.forbes.com: www.forbes.com/sites/louiscolumbus/2014/05/12/gartners-erp-market-share-update-shows-the-future-of-cloud-erp-is-now/.

Cotteleer, M. J. (2002). ERP: Payoffs and Pitfalls. (S. J. Johnston, Interviewer) Harvard Business School Working Knowledge.

Davenport, D., & Thomas, H. (1998). Putting the enterprise into the enterprise system. *Harvard Business*, 8(25), 121–131.

Davenport, D., & Thomas, H. (2000). *Mission Critical: Realizing the Promise of Enterprise Systems*. Boston, MA: Harvard Business School Publishing.

Davis, J. C., & Sampson, R. J. (1986). *Statistics and Data Analysis in Geology*. Vol. 646. New York: Wiley.

DeLone, W. H., & McLean, E. R. (1992). Information systems success: The quest for the dependent variable. *Information Systems Research*, 3(1), 60–95.

Delone, W. H., & McLean, E. R. (2003). The DeLone and McLean model of information systems success: A ten-year update. *Journal of Management Information Systems*, 19(4), 9–30.

Dezdar, S., & Sulaiman, A. (2009). Successful enterprise resource planning implementation: Axonomy of critical factors. *Industrial Management & Data Systems*, 109(8), 1037–1052.

Dezdar, S., & Sulaiman, A. (2011). The influence of organizational factors on successful ERP implementation. *Management Decision*, 49(6), 911–926.

Dinning, M., & Schuster, E.W. (2003). Fighting friction. *APICS–The Performance Advantage*, 13(2), 27–31.

Ellen F. Monk, Bret J. Wagner, *Concepts in Enterprise Resource Planning*, Thomson Course Technology, 2006.

Fan, J., & Fang, K. (2006). ERP implementation and information systems success: A test of DeLone and McLean's model. *Portland International Center for Management*, (pp. 1272–1280). Istanbul.

Ferman, J. (1999). Strategies for successful ERP connections. *Manufacturing Engineering*, 123(4), 48–60.

GAO: www.gao.gov/products/GAO-13-279SP.

Gargeya, V. B., & Brady, C. (2005). Success and failure factors of adopting SAP in ERP system implementation. *Business Process Management Journal*, 11(5), 501–516.

Goodpasture, V. (1995). Easton steps up to the plate. *Manufacturing Systems*, 13(9), 58–64.

Haberman, A. (2001). *Twenty-Five Years Behind Bars*. Cambridge, MA: Harvard University Press.

Heeks, R. (2002). Information systems and developing countries: Failure, success, and local improvisations. *The Information Society: An International Journal*, 18(2), 101–112.

Hicks, D. A., & Stecke, K. E. (1995). The ERP maze: Enterprise resource planning and other production and inventory control software. *IIE Solutions*, 27(8), 12.

Hsu, L.-L., & Chen, M. (2004). Impacts of ERP systems on the integrated-interaction performance of manufacturing and marketing. *Industrial Management & Data Systems*, 104(1), 42–55.

Hutchins, H. (1998). 7 key elements of a successful implementation and 8 mistakes you will make anyway. *APICS 1998 International Conference Proceedings*, (pp. 356–358). Falls Church, VA.

Jones, E. E., & Chung, C. A. (2007). *RFID in Logistics A Practical Introduction*. New York: CRC Press.

Kamhawi, E. M. (2007). Critical factors for implementation success of ERP systems: An empirical investigation from Bahrain. *International Journal of Enterprise Information Systems*, 3(2), 34–49.

Khaled, E., & Hayam, W. (2013). Reinvestigating the relationship between ownership structure and inventory management: A corporate governance perspective. *International Journal of Production Economics*, 143(1), 207–218.

Krupp, J. (1998). Transition to ERP implementation. *APICS–The Performance Advantage*, 8, 36–39.

Langdoc, S. (1998). ERP reality check for scared CIOs. *PC Week*, 15(38), 88.

Langenwalter, G. A. (2000). *Enterprise Resources Planning and Beyond: Integrating Your Entire Organization*. Boca Raton, FL: St. Lucie Press.

Latamore, G. (1999). Flexibility fuels the ERP evolution. *APICS–The Performance Advantage*, 44–50.

Laughlin, S. P. (1999). An ERP game plan. *Journal of Business*, 20, 32–37.

Liao, X., Li, Y., & Lu, B. (2007). A model for selecting an ERP system based on linguistic information processing. *Information Systems*, 32(7), 1005–1017.

Maxwell, K. (1999). Executive study assesses current state of ERP in paper industry. *Pulp and Paper*, 73(10), 39–43.

Michel, R. (1997). The quicker the better. *Manufacturing Systems*, 15, 26A–26A.

Minahan, T. (1998). Enterprise resource planning. *Purchasing*, 16, 112–117.

Monk, E. F., & Wagner, B. J. (2006). *Concepts in Enterprise Resource Planning*. Mason, OH: Thomson Course Technology.

Muscatello, J. R., & Chen, I. J. (2008). Enterprise Resource Planning (ERP) implementations: Theory and practice. *International Journal of Enterprise Information Systems*, 4(No. 1), 63–78.

Nah, F. F. H., Islam, Z., & Tan, M. (2007). Empirical assessment of factors influencing success of enterprise resource planning implementations. *Journal of Database Management*, 18(4), 26–50.

Oden, H., Langenwalter, G., & Lucier, R. (1993). *Handbook of Material and Capacity Requirements Planning*. New York: McGraw Hill.

Okrent, M., & McCaskey, D. (1999). Catching the ERP second wave. *APICS—The Performance Advantage*.

Olhager, J., & Selldin, E. (2003). Enterprise resource planning survey of Swedish manufacturing firms. *European Journal of Operational Research*, 146(2), 365–373.

Ptak, C. A. (1999). ERP implementation-surefire steps to success ERP World Proceedings. *ERP World Proceedings*. Retrieved from www.erpworld.org/conference/erpe-99/proceedings.

Ptak, C. A., & Schragenheim, E. (2000). *ERP: Tools, Techniques, and Applications for Integrating the Supply Chain*. Boca Raton, FL: St. Lucie Press.

Ptak, C. A., & Schragenheim, E. (2003). *ERP: Tools, Techniques, and Applications for Integrating the Supply Chain*. Boca Raton, FL: CRC Press.

Ramayah, T., Roy, M. H., Arokiasamy, S., Zbib, I., & Ahmed, Z. U. (2007). Critical success factors for successful implementation of enterprise resource planning systems in manufacturing organizations. *International Journal of Business Information Systems*, 2(3), 276–297.

Sawah, S. E., Tharwat, A. A., & Rasmy, M. H. (2008). A quantitative model to predict the Egyptian ERP implementation success index. *Business Process Management Journal*, 14(3), 288–306.

Schaaf, D. (1999). Where ERP leads, training follows. *Training*, 36(No. 5), ET14–ET18.

Schragenheim, E. (2000). When ERP worlds collide. *APICS–The Performance Advantage*, 55–57.

Schuster, E. W., & Koh, R. (2004). To track and trace. *APICS – The Performance*, 14(2), 34–38.

Schuster, E. W., Scharfeld, T. A., Kar, P., Brock, D., & Allen, S. (2004). The prospects for improving ERP data quality using auto-ID. *Cutter IT Journal: Information Technology and the Pursuit of Quality*, 2, 1.

Sherrard, R. (1998). Enterprise resource planning is not for the unprepared. *ERP World Proceedings*. San Francisco, CA.

Shore, B. (2005). Failure rates in global ITS projects and the leadership challenge. *Journal of Global Information Technology Management*, 8(3), 1–6.

Small, M. H., & Yasin, M. M. (1997). Advanced manufacturing technology: Implementation policy and performance. *Journal of Operations Management*, 15, 349–370.

Somers, T. M., & Nelson, K. G. (2004). A taxonomy of players and activities across the ERP project life cycle. *Information & Management*, 41, 257–278.

Spathis, C., & Ananiadis, J. (2005). Assessing the benefits of using an enterprise system in accounting information and management. *Journal of Enterprise Information Management*, 18(2), 195–210.

Stedman, C. (1999). ERP can magnify errors. *Computerworld*, 19, 1.

Stein, T. (1999). Making ERP add up - companies that implemented enterprise resource planning systems with little regard to the return on investment are starting to look for quantifiable results. *Information Week*, 24, 59.

Travis, D. (1999). Selecting ERP. *APICS–The Performance Advantage*, 37–39.

Trefis Team. (2014, January 6). Key trends impacting ERP software revenues for SAP in 2014, *Forbes.com*.

Umble, J. E., Haft, R. R., & Umble, M. M. (2003). Enterprise resource planning: Implementation procedures and critical success factors. *European Journal of Operational Research*, 146, 241–257.

Upadhyay, V. V., Tewari, P. C., & Gupta, A. (2013). Evaluation of vendor managed inventory elements in manufacturing sector using ANOVA technique. *IUP Journal of Supply Chain Management*, 10(2), 54–72.

Volwer, J. (1999). Learning in the play pit. *Computer Weekly*, 27, 34.

Wang, E. T. G., & Chen, J. H. F. (2006). Effects of internal support and consultant quality on the consulting process and ERP system quality. *Decision Support Systems*, 42(2), 1029–1041.

Wang, E. T., Chia-Lin Lin, C., Jiang, J. J., & Klein, G. (2007). Improving enterprise resource planning (ERP) fit to organizational process through knowledge transfer. *International Journal of Information Management*, 27(3), 200–212.

Wang, S. -W., Chen, W. -H., Ong, C. -S., Liu, L., and Chuang, Y.-W. (2006). RFID application in hospitals: A case study on a demonstration RFID project in a Taiwan hospital. *Proceedings of the 39th Hawaii International Conference on System Sciences (HICSS'06)*, (p. 184a). Track 8. Kauia, HI.

Wight, O. W. (1984). *Manufacturing Resource Planning: MRP II: Unlocking America's Productivity Potential*. New York: John Wiley & Sons.

Wilder, C., & Davis, B. (1998). False starts strong finishes. *Informationweek*, 711, 41–46.

Wu, J.-H., & Wang, Y.-M. (2007). Measuring ERP success: The key-users' viewpoint of the ERP to produce a viable IS in the organization. *Computers in Human Behavior*, 23(3), 1582–1596.

Zhang, Z., Lee, M. K., Huang, P., Zhang, L., & Huang, X. (2005). A framework of ERP systems implementation success in China: An empirical study. *International Journal of Production Economics*, 98, 56–80.

7

Logistics in Global Supply Chain Engineering

Erick C. Jones

The line between disorder and order lies in logistics….

Sun Tzu

7.1 Logistics

7.1.1 Introduction

In this chapter, we discuss how radio frequency identification (RFID) supports

- Information use in the supply chain
- Open- and closed-loop systems as an intelligent agent
- Real-time item visibility that facilitates inventory control
- Supply chain planning and operational optimization
- Organizational improvement with best practices.

7.1.2 RFID Supports Information Use in the Supply Chain

In this text, we discuss how RFID-captured information influences supply chain performance with data analysis, inventory management, transportation, and supply chain visibility (Wehking et al. 2006).

1. **Data analysis** includes the evaluations concerning facilities, inventory, transportation, costs, prices, and customers throughout the supply chain (Carbon 2000).
2. **Inventory management** includes raw materials, work in process, and finished goods within a supply chain. Changing inventory policies can affect the supply chain's efficiency and responsiveness.
3. **Transportation visibility** provides information about inventory transported from point to point in the supply chain. Transportation includes many combinations of modes and routes, each with its own performance characteristics. Transportation modes have a large impact on supply chain responsiveness and cost.
4. **Supply chain visibility** provides information including status updates that allow for evaluation of the physical locations in the supply chain network where a product is stored, assembled, or fabricated. The two major types of facilities are production sites and storage sites. The location, capacity, and flexibility of facilities have a significant impact on the supply chain's performance

In this section, we discuss the role that information plays in the supply chain, as well as key information-related decisions that supply chain managers must make.

7.1.3 Data Analysis and Information Gathering

Data analysis and information gathering affect every part of the supply chain. Information gathering affects a supply chain in many different ways. Consider the following:

1. Information serves as the connection between various stages of supply chain, allowing them to coordinate and maximize total supply chain profitability.
2. Information is important to the daily operations of each stage in the supply chain. Consider a production scheduling system that uses information on demand to create schedules that allow a factory to produce the right products at the right time. A warehouse management system (WMS) uses information to create visibility of the warehouse's inventory. The company can then use this information to determine whether new orders can be filled.
3. Information is an important driver that companies have used to become more responsive and efficient. The growth of the importance of information technology is due to the fact that it has effectively improved business. Though information can support efficiencies, if integrated too aggressively, it can result in costly decisions such as expensive software system implementations. Organizations should ask and decide what information is necessary for reducing cost and improving their responsiveness within a supply chain.

7.1.4 Push and Pull Operational Strategies

Different types of operational strategies require different types of information. Push systems are associated with *material requirements planning* (MRP) systems that use master production schedules to create schedules for suppliers with part types, quantities, and delivery dates.

Pull systems are associated with kanban systems which fulfill only the necessary requirements from actual customer demand.

For practical use, they require the latest information on actual demand. Modern execution systems such as WMSs, transportation management systems (TMS), and related execution modules in enterprise resource planning (ERP) systems use these strategies in their programmed logic. The effectiveness of these types of systems is predicated on timeliness of the collected information. RFID, barcodes, and other automatic identification systems allow these types of systems to effectively reduce operational costs.

7.1.5 Supply Chain Coordination

Data collection allows supply chain coordination to occur when all stages of a supply chain work toward the objective of maximizing total supply chain profitability based on shared information. Lack of coordination can result in a significant loss of supply chain profit. Coordination among different stages in a supply chain requires each stage to share appropriate information with other stages.

7.1.6 Forecasting and Aggregate Planning

Timely information creates more accurate forecasting about what future demand and conditions will be. Obtaining forecasting information frequently means using sophisticated techniques to estimate future sales or market conditions. Managers must decide how they will make forecasts and to what extent they will rely on forecasts to make decisions. Companies often use forecasts both on a tactical level to schedule production and on a strategic level to determine whether to build new plants or even whether to enter a new market.

Once a company creates a forecast, it needs a plan to act on the forecast. Aggregate planning transforms forecasts into plans of activity to satisfy the projected demand. A key decision managers face is how to collaborate on aggregate planning throughout the entire supply chain. The aggregate plan becomes a critical piece of information to be shared across the supply chain because it affects both the demand on a firm's suppliers and the supply to its customers.

7.1.6.1 RFID and Other Enabling Technologies

Many technologies along with RFID exist to share and analyze information in the supply chain. Some of these technologies include the following.

7.1.6.1.1 EDI Business Transmissions

Electronic data interchange (EDI) refers to the electronic transmission of standard business documents in a predetermined format from one company's business computer to its trading partner's computer. The two standards EDI relies on to ensure standardized business communication are ANSI and EDIFACT. EDI allows a firm to transmit information, such as point-of-sale (POS) demand for information, purchase orders, and inventory status information, to users within the firm and to customers and trading partners. EDI systems have been implemented generally by larger firms because of the expense it requires for dedicated software and advanced hardware.

The Internet has critical advantages of EDI with respect to information sharing. The Internet conveys much more information, and therefore, offers much more visibility than EDI. Better visibility improves decisions across the supply chain. Internet communication among stages in the supply chain is also easier because a standard infrastructure (the World Wide Web) already exists. Thanks to the Internet, e-commerce has become a major force in the supply chain.

7.1.6.1.2 Web-Based Application Systems

The use of the web for both business to consumer (B2C) and business to business (B2B) is growing quickly. The web will have significant implications for supply chain management (SCM) in the coming years. Thomas Freidman, a leader on political thought, mentions that the web is allowing for small companies to compete with large companies in both B2C and B2B transactions using the web. Unlike the failed dot-bomb companies in the early 20th century, now, well-thought-out small businesses are able to compete by leveraging web-based transactions.

Many software firms offer web-based systems. Some advantages web-based supply chain systems provide include

1. Unlimited access with web access
2. Common platform unlike the complexity of EDI
3. Cost-effective implementation.

Because many firms are concerned with Internet security, some prefer the complex EDI protocols which provide more extensive security than do web-based systems. However, given the new web-based EDI protocol standards and the cost implications, the web-based systems will begin to replace EDI systems in the coming years.

7.1.6.1.3 Business Operations Systems

ERP systems provide the transactional tracking and global visibility of information from within a company and across its supply chain. The real-time information helps a supply chain to improve the quality of its operational decisions. ERP systems keep track of the information, whereas the Internet provides one method with which to view this information.

SCM software uses the information in ERP systems to provide analytical decision to support in addition to the visibility of information. ERP systems show a company what is going on, while SCM systems help a company decide what it should do.

7.1.7 Overall Trade-Off: Responsiveness vs. Efficiency

Good information can help a firm improve both its responsiveness and efficiency. The information driver is used to improve the performance of other drivers, and the use of information is based on the strategic position the other drivers support. Accurate information can help a firm improve efficiency by decreasing inventory and transportation costs. Accurate information can improve responsiveness by helping a supply chain better match supply and demand.

Common literature suggests that we are living in the "information age". The availability of information in many sources that appear in academic publications, trade journals, magazines, newsletters, blogs, e-magazines, and so on is introduced every day. The explosion of information availability on the web due to web search companies such as Yahoo, Google, and Microsoft allows people to perform web searches for information on almost anything.

A supply chain's information provides the organization with a strategic advantage over competition and is key to running a business efficiently and effectively in an ever-changing and more complex environment. Information plays a key role in the management of the supply chain as evidenced in such uses for forecasts, aggregate manpower planning, and customer inquiries.

Concepts such as just-in-time (JIT) manufacturing and delivery, vendor-managed inventory (VMI), and cross-docking require timely information within the supply chain. JIT uses timely information to optimize the scheduling of deliveries or manufacturing in such a way to minimize inventories. The VMI concept allows vendors to review information from a supplier and order only what is needed in specific time periods, which allows them reduce ordering excess inventory. These concepts leverage the concept of information in the supply chain. In the next section, we describe some of the concepts for leveraging information in the supply chain. Then, we will introduce the bullwhip effect, which is a general term that describes the inefficiencies realized in supply chain operations with imperfect information. We will discuss the determinants and current ways information can offset these inefficiencies, including electronic commerce, web-based systems, and RFID.

7.1.8 e-Commerce and Technology

Electronic commerce or e-commerce refers to a technology that allows businesses to operate a common transaction that was traditionally performed on a paper-based system, but is now performed electronically. They include EDI, e-mail, electronic funds transfers, electronic publishing, image processing, electronic bulletin boards, blogs, Internet voice mail, Internet video meetings, mp3 sharing, shared databases, POS barcode systems in supermarkets, and all manners of web-based business systems.

Some well-known companies such as General Electric Corporation, one of the world's largest diversified manufacturers of a wide variety of products, uses web-based transactions systems and EDI as a regular part of its business practices in most divisions. Other companies use EDI, Internet-based systems, electronic forecasting, and WMSs to gain competitiveness.

During the last few years of the 20th century, Initial Public Offering of company stock (IPOs) of the "dot-com" companies were occurring almost every day and their share prices rose steadily, even though many of these companies had customers. These "pure play" e-tailers, which represented Internet-based retailers without traditional brick and mortar operations, have all but disappeared. One that survived and thrived is Amazon.com. Amazon has significantly expanded their product line and is one of the few successful "pure play" e-tailers that survived the dot-com bust. One of the authors who was a consultant during the time of the e-tailer craze recalls that the main failure was the real lack of a business plan and focusing on developing a "killer app" or creative front-end software and websites as their major objective. Some of the primary portals (Yahoo and Google, for example) require big money to allow direct access to an e-commerce site. These failed e-tailers were also referred to as "dot-bomb" companies instead of "dot-com" companies.

A new phenomenon derived from these companies' failures, which was recently documented by Thomas Friedman in his landmark text "The World is Flat", is that smarter versions of these e-businesses' initiatives are re-appearing and competing against larger companies in local markets domestically and internationally. Most profits for Internet activities are business-to-business web-based systems accounts. They represent a much greater share of the electronic commerce marketplace than web-based retailers.

7.1.9 RFID as Part of the Information Supply Chain

RFID tags are emerging as the barcodes of the future. As we discussed in the earlier chapters, bar codes have become common in retailing but were only accepted in mass in 1985. The expectation is that though active RFID tags were commercially viable in 1973 and utilized in toll roads an animal tracking in the mid-1980s, passive tags were arguably commercially viable in 2005, with mass acceptance in logistics expected by 2010. This emerging technology may have one of the fastest technology acceptance rates in history.

Common applications include (1) EZ Pass for paying bridge or highway tolls, (2) tagging of library books in some libraries, and (3) tagging of cargo containers at most of the world's ports. Reconciling shipments against bill-of-landings or packing and customer orders can be performed succinctly and accurately, eliminating the need to perform these functions manually. Beyond the supply chain, RFID technologies have broader applications, such as emergency human identification for finding abducted children in Mexico or mountain climbers in Colorado who may become lost in an avalanche. Such applications of RFID technology benefits are taunted, yet fiercely debated as to how they may threaten individual rights and privacy. In the application chapters, details of these applications and their challenges are discussed. We now further detail how RFID technologies provide information strategically to allow organizations to improve operational effectiveness.

7.1.10 RFID as an Intelligent Agent System

Because of the differing automatic identification technologies such as barcode, RFID passive, RFID active, SAW tags, and sensor tags, they must be integrated for use in the supply chain. We suggest using RFID technologies as an intelligent agent system (IAS) that supports real-time decision support systems as solution for this integration challenge.

The idea of an intelligent agent is pervasive control system frameworks. Control frameworks can be classified as *hierarchical*, *heterarchical*, and *hybrid*. We consider RFID tags that have a master–slave relationship that exists between higher and lower levels in a *hierarchical* automatic identification framework. An operational example would be using barcodes affixed to cartons to write information to passive RFID pallet tags. The information is passed to the next highest unit load, case to pallet level with each technology acting as independent systems. This is similar to the control system concept in which response to input data is passed up the chain of command, higher-level controllers pass down command data for execution by the lower-level controllers. In control systems, this theory works well when there is little interference between the technologies; RFID integration does present this problem. We will refer to this type of system as open system. A *heterarchical* framework is present when interactions between the lower-level controllers and permit these to engage in one-on-one communication assuming there is no hierarchy or higher-level controller. For RFID systems, this represents the use of reading tags on a common protocol, such as the EPC Global passive standard where multiple readers can read standardized tags. We refer to this type of system in our text as a closed system. *Hybrid* frameworks discuss how these frameworks capture the benefits of hierarchical and heterarchical frameworks while avoiding their pitfalls. For RFID technologies to work with other Auto ID technologies in the short run, this type of approach will be necessary to realize organizational savings.

A practical example of how the integration of multiple RFID technologies that operate at different frequencies can be modeled in control frameworks so that real-time information can be used to determine an inventory policy is given as follows: a high-frequency (HF) 13.56 passive tag is used to track retail over-the-counter drugs at the item level, ultra-high-frequency (UHF) 915 MHz passive RFID tags can be used to track inventory at the case and pallet level inventory, and UHF 303 MHz active tags track the status of inventory on tractor trailers. Popular industrial literature assumes that linking information with relational databases provides real-time information on the status at the item level (i.e., the active tag can show the status of the drugs because the tags were relationally linked as they moved up in container level).

The flaws in this assumption may be that different technologies have different error rates in scanning validation and human error of integrating these relations, such as database programming, and the technologies do not have common standards. The current mandate from Wal-Mart encompasses only one standard, the Electronic Product Code (EPC) global standard for Generation 1 and 2 UHF 856–915 MHz passive tags.

Further, this EPC global standard is currently accepted in the United States but has not been completely adopted by other countries. Also, current Food and Drug Administration (FDA) initiatives for over-the-counter drug tracking incorporate the 13.56 MHz RFID tags. The lack of understanding of how the mixed RFID technologies will have negative impacts such as higher error rates and lower productivity provides a gap that I seek to investigate during this research project. One of the authors identified this gap when testing technologies NASA ISS. The most operationally valid solutions included multiple RFID technologies.

7.1.11 Summary of RFID and Information Enablers

This section provides us with an understanding of key technologies, how all the technologies differ, and how they can be integrated to work for operational effectiveness. This will allow WMS algorithm such as "bucket brigades" calculations, picking route optimization, and other effective system updates that will improve operations. Further insights on safety stock minimization, customer order optimization, and pick/stock labor minimization will be affected and discussed later in the text.

7.1.12 RFID Provides Timely Visibility in Logistics

RFID supports information in the supply chain by enabling visibility. The concept of visibility describes the ability for anyone, including customers, who have access to inventory, orders, raw materials, and delivery points at any time. Visibility is currently provided by a mixture of automatic identification or Auto ID technologies such as barcodes, smart labels, ISBN, and UPC codes along with others. The opportunity for RFID is its non-line of sight scanning ability and the integration of the aforementioned Auto ID identifiers into RFID nomenclature, and push for standardized technology protocols will provide large supply chain savings.

The real-time nature of RFID is considered a benefit and currently a challenge. The benefit is that you have the latest information to make the best decisions; the drawback is that the amount of data currently presents a data storage problem for operational systems.

Better visibility provides reduced inventory, labor and assets management using inventory policies, scheduling, and decision support system information. This is exemplified by

- RFID supports reduced inventory costs with more effective labor policies.
- RFID supports labor reduction with more effective scheduling.
- RFID supports the reduction of expensive assets such as facilities, trucks, containers, and railroad time because of more accurate information in decision support systems.

The ability for RFID to provide timely information and visibility into the supply chain is based on three components of RFID technologies. They are

1. Automatic data capture
2. Real-time information
3. Real-time location system.

RFID supports timely information in the supply chain by enabling information to be accessed faster. This implies that faster decisions can be made, which produces operational optimization that can be effectively repeated (Banerjee et al. 1997). The ability to allow resident information collected automatically in real time that leads to faster more effective decisions is where RFID shows future promise. Business costs are reduced as operations become more productive by reducing labor, transportation, and facility cost of moving inventory in the supply chain.

Many organizations look at the benefit of using RFID that they can effectively manipulate inventory. Inventory exists in the supply chain because of the variance between supply and demand. This variance is necessary for manufacturers where it is economical to manufacture in large lot quantities and then store items for future sales. The variance is also present in retail stores where inventory is held for future customer demand. Oftentimes, businesses suggest that inventory is a marketing vehicle creating demand by passing customers. The main role for inventory plays is to satisfy customer demand by providing a product when the customers want it. Another significant role that inventory plays is to reduce cost by exploiting economies of scale that may exist during production and distribution. Given that it is suggested to have such a large impact on inventory, we will present some relevant information on inventory in the supply chain.

7.1.13 Inventory in the Supply Chain

Inventory is held throughout the supply chain in the form of raw materials, work-in-process (WIP), and finished goods. Inventory is a major source of costs in a supply chain and impacts customer responsiveness and eventually customer satisfaction. Inventory also has a significant impact on the material flow time in a supply chain. Material flow time is the time that elapses between the points at which material enters the supply chain to the point at which it exits. For a supply chain, throughput is the rate at which sales occur. If inventory is represented by I, flow time by T, and throughput by D, the three can be related using Little's law as follows:

$$I = DT$$

For example, if the flow time of an auto assembly process is 10 h and the throughput is 50 units an hour, Little's law tells us that the inventory is $50 \times 10 = 500$ units. If we were able to reduce inventory to 250 units while holding throughput constant, we would reduce our flow time to 5 h (250/50). We note that in this relationship, inventory and throughput must have constant units. One can see that those inventory and flow times are related and that throughput is often determined by customer demand. The goal of many operations is to reduce amount of inventory needed without increasing cost or reducing responsiveness.

7.1.14 Business Responsiveness

Inventory plays a significant role in a firm's responsiveness. Inventory decisions may require strategies that locate inventory close to the customer or by locating a main warehouse centrally, or by locating stocking distribution centers seasonally using a centralized stocking concept. Each strategy has trade-offs that need to be evaluated by each organization's goals. Some of the goals involve

- Cycle inventory
- Safety inventory
- Seasonal inventory
- Level of product availability
- Inventory-related metrics.

7.1.14.1 Cycle Inventory

Cycle inventory is defined as the average amount of inventory used to satisfy demand between receipts of supplier shipments. The size of the cycle inventory is a result of the production, transportation, or purchase of material in large lots. Companies produce or purchase in large lots to exploit economies of scale in the production, transportation, or purchase process. With the increase in lot size, however, also comes an increase in carrying costs.

7.1.14.2 Safety Inventory

Safety inventory is inventory held in case demand exceeds expectations; it is held to counter uncertainty. Because demand is uncertain and may exceed expectations, however, companies hold safety inventory to satisfy an unexpectedly high demand. If a company does not have enough inventory, they may lose sales and profit. Thus, choosing safety inventory involves making a trade-off between the costs of having too much inventory and the costs of losing sales due to not having enough inventory.

7.1.14.3 Seasonal Inventory

Seasonal inventory is additional inventory stored to counter predictable variability in demand due to a given repeatable period. Companies using seasonal inventory build up inventory in periods of low demand and store it for periods of high demand when they will not have the capacity to produce all that is demanded. The trade-off for organizations is determining how much seasonal inventory to build, in other words the cost of carrying the additional seasonal inventory vs. the cost of having a more flexible production rate.

7.1.14.4 Level of Product Availability

Level of product availability is the amount of demand that is available from products currently in non-committed inventory. A high level of product availability provides a high level of responsiveness, but increases cost because inventory has to be held with no prior commitment or order, and oftentimes, this excess inventory is held but rarely used. In contrast, a low level of product availability lowers inventory holding cost but results in customer failure and loss current and future sales. The basic trade-off when determining the level of product availability is between the cost of inventory to increase product availability and the loss from not satisfying customers.

7.1.14.5 Inventory-Related Metrics

Often given the importance of inventory, data is collected and assessed in order to ensure proper management. Some common metrics are described below:

- *Average inventory* measures the average number of inventory in dollars or units over a time period such as days, months, and years.
- *Obsolete inventory* products with more than a specified number of days of inventory identify the products for which the firm is carrying a high level of inventory.
- *Average safety inventory* measures the average amount of inventory on hand when a replenishment order arrives. Average safety inventory should be measured by stock keeping unit (SKU) in both units and days of demand. It can be estimated by averaging over time the minimum inventory on hand in each replenishment cycle.
- *Seasonal inventory* measures the amount of both cycle and safety inventory that is purchased solely due to seasonal changes in demand.
- *Fill rate* measures the fraction of orders/demand that was met on time from inventory.
- *Percent of time out of stock* measures the fraction of time that a particular SKU had zero inventory.

There are underlying trade-offs that organizations make with regard to inventory decisions between responsiveness and inventory costs. Increasing inventory generally makes the supply chain more responsive to the customer. A higher level of inventory also facilitates a reduction in production and transportation costs because of improved economies of scale in both functions. This choice, however, increases inventory holding cost. Moreover, these inventory costs in the supply chain can be greatly affected by a lack of supply chain coordination, commonly referred to as the bullwhip effect.

7.1.15 The Bullwhip Effect

The bullwhip effect has been evaluated by both practitioners and academics. Chopra (2006) provides a brief history of the bullwhip effect. The problem was identified when Proctor & Gamble (P&G) were studying replenishment patterns for one of their best-selling products. They recognized there was greater variability between (1) orders placed by distributors against retail stores sales and (2) against requested materials from suppliers. Given that the product had consistent demand over the years, the large discrepancy was not expected. P&G coined the term "bullwhip" effect for this phenomenon. It also has been referred to as the "whiplash" or "whipsaw" effect. Other organization such as HP experienced the bullwhip effect in patterns of sales for products such as printers.

Many researchers and practitioners have attempted to discover the origins of this effect due to the fact that it creates excess cost in the form of inventory in the supply chain. Some believe when working with demand that is constant and highly predictable that effect is produced when companies order products in batch quantities at operational supply chain levels is what creates the effect.

The grocery industry, which exhibits this type of demand, sought to reduce the bullwhip effect with an efficient consumer response (ECR) initiative in which the food delivery supply chain would reduce a projected excess of 100 days of inventory from the supply chain. The stated goal of the ECR initiative was to save $30 billion annually by reducing the bullwhip effect in food delivery logistics.

Some causes' solutions that may reduce the effects of the bullwhip effect on demand forecasting, order batching, price fluctuations, and creative order gamin are suggested by researchers.

They include sharing of information, supplier alignment, stable price structure, and incentives to prevent gaming. First, the sharing of information from all parties from common data such as a POS data creates forecasts on these data. Other techniques include EDI or EDI as it is commonly described. EDI and other web-based exchange formats provide a means for integrating information between company software platforms.

Second, supplier alignment allows for the coordination of pricing, transportation, and inventory planning efforts operations in the supply chain.

Fixed costs, which create order batching behavior and economies of scale costs such as transportation, can be limited with real-time information. Things such as smaller batch lot quantities and effective transportation scheduling are allowed by information that provides alignment. Another trend encouraging small batch ordering is the outsourcing of logistics to third parties. Logistics companies can consolidate loads from multiple suppliers. Logistics outsourcing to companies such as UPS Supply Chain Solutions is expanding rapidly.

Third, supplier pricing is designed to motivate customers to buy in large batches and store items for future use. This behavior called price stabilization and is designed to reduce sales demand variation. This is evident when comparing a retailer that runs frequent promotions with warehouse stores that offer everyday low pricing. The warehouse stores have more stable demand than do department stores in which promotional sales account for most of their business. Finally, exaggeration of orders to manipulate pricing is often referred to as gaming and can be affected dramatically by information. These order forecasts can be smoothed using past demand, not sales forecasting.

7.2 Summary

In summary, the effective use of information to manage inventory can counteract the bullwhip effect created by partners in the supply chain acting in their own best interests. The need for information timely can be supported by RFID technologies.

RFID technologies provide an opportunity to reduce the uncertainty leading to the bullwhip effect through more real-time information. Given the costs of holding excess inventory in capital, obsolescence (or spoilage), handling costs, occupancy costs, pilferage, damage, taxes, and insurance, it may be worthwhile to use real-time information in evaluating inventory reduction.

End of Chapter Questions

1. What are the five components of the EPC Air Interface Standard?
2. What are three advantages of the Gen 2 protocol for RFID tags?

3. What are the three planning levels for RFID in logistics?
4. What are the four types of participants that make up a supply chain?
5. At what level is inventory control in RFID logistics planned?
6. What are the three components of inventory control for RFID logistics?
7. What does EOQ represent?
8. What two forms of inventory are buffered with continuous review models?
9. Which buffer does EOQ address?
10. Which buffer does safety stock address?
11. Weekly demand for Lego at a Wal-Mart store is normally distributed with a mean of 2,500 boxes and a standard deviation of 500. The replenishment lead time is 2 weeks. Assuming a continuous review replenishment policy, evaluate the safety inventory that the store should carry to achieve a customer stock level (CSL) of 90% (Gotsman and Koren 2005).
12. Carbon fiber seat posts are consumed by a bicycle manufacturing factory at a fairly steady rate of 100 per week. The seat posts cost the factory $35.00 each. It costs the plant $125 to initiate an order, and holding costs are based on an annual interest rate of 20%. Determine the optimal number of seat posts for the plant to purchase and the time between orders. (Use the economic order quantity (EOQ) formula.)
13. Weekly demand for Lego at a Wal-Mart store is normally distributed with a mean of 2,500 boxes and a standard deviation of 500. The replenishment lead time is 2 weeks, and the store manager has decided to review inventory every 4 weeks. Assuming a periodic review replenishment policy, evaluate the safety inventory that the store should carry to provide a CSL of 90%. Evaluate the OUL for such a policy.
14. What two replenishment policies are associated with inventory control?
15. What are two impacts of RFID on inventory control?
16. What are two impacts of RFID on transportation?
17. Give two reasons to use the anechoic chamber for RFID.
18. What are the steps of RFID design for Six Sigma-research (DFSSR)?
19. Describe how order scheduling impacts labor and the effect RFID can have on minimizing this process.

7.3 Facilities Layout

7.3.1 Optimizing RFID Portal Locations in Distribution Using Systematic Layout Planning

7.3.2 Introduction

The manufacturing facility layout design (FLD) has been discussed by a number of researchers (Tompkins et al. 1996). Continuous improvement has been achieved through the use of simulation and computer-aided programs for designing facilities in actual manufacturing and warehouse environments. However, FLD still is a complex and broad area that cuts across several specialized disciplines. Basically, the facility layout problem is to determine the "most efficient" arrangement of cells or functional departments subject to flow and capital constraints imposed by the original layout, management, and site requirements.

The optimum solution for these facility layout problems is not only controlled by numerical function, but more depends on the accepted baseline of the application of site and relevant requirements. Therefore, the solution for each single layout problem should not be single solution with the optimum result based on the ratio of each function department and its weight value. Most of the research on facility layout utilizes the classical concept about classification of layout problem by either the quadratic assignment problem (QAP) or a large-scale mixed-integer programming (MIP) problem, whereas nonlinear programming (NLP) formulations have been solved by numerical methods, by simulated annealing or by genetic algorithm approaches. MIP formulations have been solved by ad hoc interactive designer reasoning or by reducing the MIP to a linear programming optimization problem either by qualitative reasoning or, once again, by ad hoc interactive designer reasoning, and by genetic approach. Although integer and non-integer problems have solved complicated layout problems which are two-dimensional (2D) with flow and capital consideration, particular situations and single case problems may have to be evaluated in other ways.

RFID facility layouts with warehouse applications introduce a new type of parameter to the traditional FLD problem. The following sections illustrate the differences.

Muther (1979) developed a layout procedure known as systematic layout planning (SLP). It uses as its foundation the activity relationship chart which described in the facility layout process. SLP is based on input data and an understanding of the roles and relationships between activities, a material flow analysis (from-to-chart), and an activity relationship analysis (activity relationship chart). This analysis results in a relationship diagram. The next two steps involve the determination of the amount of space to be assigned to each activity. Based on modifying considerations and practical limitations, a number of layout alternatives are developed and evaluated. The SLP procedure can be used sequentially to develop first a block layout and then a detailed layout for each planning department. The following example discusses the application of SLP with an RFID warehouse design procedure.

7.4 Modeling Procedure

7.4.1 Phase 1: Multi-objective RF Warehouse Architecture

The overall RFID Warehouse Implementing System includes three main parts: RFID edge layer, RFID physical layer, and enterprise integration network. The RFID physical layer is the connection of other two layers. The RFID system is designed to process streams of tag or sensor data coming from one or more readers. The edge layer has the capability to filter and aggregate data prior to sending it to a requesting application. For example, an action (tag read) is triggered when the object moves or a new object comes into the reader's view. The RFID edge servers filter and collect the tag data at each individual site and send it over the Internet to the third layer—enterprise integration layer. The localized data is identified by moving actions and stationary actions separately which divide the RFID reading type to portal door distribution process within limited range and mobile reader inventory checking. The fundamental tenet of warehouse portal distribution system is that they must be able to accommodate changes that may occur on a network. The portal devices provide real-time, positioning access capabilities to user communities, delivering and searching personal data. It allows external customer and partner accessing with data protection and securely access.

We can now divide the RFID warehouse system into three parts as we discussed before, the physical layer, the logic layer, and the system integration layer. Each layer has different components depending on what functions the RFID system needs. By understanding the flow in the warehouse, we can determine the types of tag and antennas needed in the warehouse.

Basically, the RFID implementation in any process has two to three layers. The physical layer produces log events for radio frequency (RF) sensor during process executions. Logic layer records the log events-related data including filter and integrate functions. The analysis of the physical layer activity has been discussed in facility layout research. The difference between previous research with RFID facility layout is that the data flow should be added as a factor that influences the RFID warehouse efficiency and performance.

First, the production process was its own upstream and downstream flow. Each department and activity function has multiple interactions with the others which layout are defined by traditional facility layout algorithm. For any given department, the overall workflow for sites and how and where the functional part fits into it. But for RFID warehouse, the labeling function part is substituted by 2D portal door with installed antenna.

7.4.2 Phase 2: Data Environment Analysis

The data flow through the distribution process in warehouse is one of the design components of RFID warehouse layout. The goal of such activity is to define the input and output data in order to confirm the efficiency of data flow and its physical flow. Data standards standardize data formats and data organization to ensure that the required data can be smoothly exchanged within the supply chain. Both the workflow and data flow are generated by production flow from physical layer to logical layer. All the data through picking to distributing process are generated by RFID equipment including the tags on each pallet or antenna on the portal. Therefore, the location of RFID equipment has influential power on accuracy of distribution process which will form the individual data flow according to the workflow. The location of RFID antenna, we call it sensor in this chapter, will be discussed in this chapter. First, the "sensor" is used to refer to a device which is connected, via network or RF communication medium, to other sensor devices in the network. The location of sensors in the warehouse relates to either its environment or data traffic flow itself which is detected by fixed antenna on portal door. Similarly, the data flow will be employed by sensors specifically in the picking entrance portal and distributing portal. Therefore, the data traffic through two portal doors and its layout will be our consideration in this chapter. We will discuss the other communication between the nodes in warehouse in the future work. In order to measure the accuracy and efficiency of RFID performance in warehouse, we are using ratio to evaluate the relationship of performance and efficiency of RFID readability which is equal to the simple relationship between input and output data which will be related to regression analysis to show fair performance:

$$\sigma_r = \alpha_I / \beta_O \tag{7.1}$$

where

$$\sigma_r = \text{Ratio}; \ \alpha_I = \text{Input}; \ \beta_O = \text{Output}$$

However, this ratio only gives an average performance for RFID readability. The components of input require the precise data to evaluate the environment and performance. But we measure the benchmark of the performance used to compare the different input data and data flow. For example, the different amounts of workflow reflect the different data flow in warehouse, but the benchmark gives us a reliable data to measure different warehouse environment and workflow.

The statistical power analysis estimates the power of the workflow to detect a meaningful effect, given product flow size, significance level, and standardized effect size. Product flow size analysis determines the product flow size required to get a significant result, given statistical power, test size, and standardized effect size. These analyses examine the sensitivity of statistical power and product flow size to other components, enabling researchers to efficiently use the research resources. According to the power of the data analysis, we know the workflow during distribution process can be too low or too high, which will influence the capital loss for warehouse. If sample size is too large, time and resources will be wasted, often for minimal gain. For the benchmark as we discussed before, we used GPOWER, high-precision power analysis software, to determine the product flow size we needed so that we can draw a powerful conclusion. The inputs of GPOWER for determining the flow size in linear multiple regression model are effect size, the alpha level, power value, and the number of predictors. GPOWER uses f as a measure of effect size, which has relationship with R (coefficient of determination: the total proportion of the dependent variable variability that is explained by predicted variables) as the below equation described:

$$f^2 = \frac{R^2}{1 - R^2} \tag{7.2}$$

In this experiment, we used $f = 1.5$ ($R = 0.6$), and we used alpha value (0.05), power value (0.90), and the number of predictors (4) as other three inputs. Special considerations should be addressed when setting up an RFID system with multiple interrogators that have overlapping interrogation zones. For instance, a pair of reader in portal door interrogation zone may interrogate multiple tags in a dynamic environment.

The concept of interrogation will be abstracted as "read zone" as for the practical and real environment reason in the following content. By considering the warehouse environment requirement for RFID application in distribution process, the portal door RF read zone will be limited in some ranges between dock equipment and RF interrogation range. The ranges of RF antenna (portal) and physical range of dock door layout can be described as n—vertex graph $G(V = \{1, \dots, n\}, E)$, and for each edge—its Euclidean "length". Denote a 2D layout of the graph where the coordinates of vertex are. In the non-noisy version of the problem, we know that there exists a layout of the antennas that realizes the given edge lengths. Our goal is then to reproduce this layout. Fortunately, there is additional information which we may exploit to eliminate spurious solutions to the layout problem—we know that the graph is a complete description of the close antennas. Consequently, the distance between each two nonadjacent antennas should be greater than some constant r, which is larger than the longest edge. This can further constrain the search space and eliminate most undesired solutions. Formally, we may pose our problem as follows:

Layout problem is given in a graph $G(V = \{1, \dots, n\}, E)$, and for each edge—its Euclidean "length", find an optimal layout () (is the location of the antenna i), which satisfies for all—$i \neq j$:

$$\|p_i - p_j\| = l_{ij} \quad \text{if } \langle i, j \rangle \in E \tag{7.3}$$

$$\|p_i - p_j\| > R \quad \text{if } \langle i, j \rangle \notin E \tag{7.4}$$

where

$$R = \max_{\langle i,j \rangle \in E} l_{ij}$$

An optimal layout is similar to that generated by common force-directed graph drawing algorithms that place adjacent nodes closely while separating nonadjacent nodes. Therefore, we may estimate the distances between nonadjacent antennas and then give constructive suggestions to minimize the blind spot within the reachable zone.

The interrogation zone from a pair of antennas gives us a visual description for the range we calculated in formulae 7.3 and 7.4. The center red zone means the high readability zone for 2 in. from each side of portal door. The accuracy deduced with the increasing distance from tag to each side of the portal. Estimating an antenna's physical coordinates according to the feature and requirement of RFID and warehouse system. The data that antenna is reported should be accompanied with an indication of where in space that data was reported. The bandwidth and limitations of antenna network made it necessary for the data location coordinates of physical location of portal door in warehouse. In many cases, location itself gives the range of data that should be sensed—localization drives the need for RFID antennas network in warehouse and distribution process, which is able to locate the items and tagged parts. In addition, the accuracy of geographic routing and graph algorithms bring the next step to validate the portal and other function parts in warehouse (Table 7.1).

TABLE 7.1

Minimum Maneuvering Distance between the Back of the Dock Leveler and the Beginning of the Staging Area and Recommended Dock Staging Dimensions (Thompkins, 1982)

Equipment Used	Distance (ft)	Item	Dimension (ft)
None (manual)	5	Served road width	
Hand truck		**One-way traffic**	12
Two wheel	6	**Two-way**	24
Four wheel	8	**Gate openings, Vehicles only**	
Hand lift (jack)	8	**One-way traffic**	16
Narrow aisle truck	10	**Two-way**	28
Lift truck	12	**Gate openings, vehicles + pedestrians**	
Tow tractor	14	**One-way**	22
		Two-way	34

The design of portal door and the layout of RFID antennas combined both frequency interrogation and physical portal length so that the tagged pallets will be tracked and the employed frequency from antenna can record the data with moving tags.

7.5 Layout Improvement Alternatives and Numerical Results

Relying on the basis of implementation and RF facility layout principle, the facility layout algorithm will follow the baseline model we discussed above. Therefore, the qualitative algorithm is deployed to analyze the overall function parts. The layout algorithm continues to develop the relationship between each function parts including warehouse layout and RFID distributing zone. Because of the limitation of the RFID interrogation zone, we consider the correlated to the RF facility layout.

7.6 Computer-Aided Program Algorithm Approach (BLOCPLAN)

The program generates and evaluates block-type layouts in response to user-supplied data. It is used for single story layouts. BLOCPLAN uses a "banding" procedure to develop layouts. This permits a large range of possible layouts for a problem. For a nine-department problem, the number of possible layouts is close to 20 million, and for a 15-department layout, there are more than 2.6 X 1013 possibilities. Each department will also be rectangular in shape. The structure that holds the departments will also be rectangular in shape, and the user may select the length/width ratio of the structure.

7.6.1 Relationship Data

BLOCPLAN uses the relationship codes described by Muther in *Systematic Layout Planning*, (Muther, 1973, CBI Publishing, Boston, Mass). Each sub-procedure we discussed in SLP flowchart shows that the functional departments are defined by the material flow. We take one of the typical warehouses as an example; for BLOCPLAN, they use adjacencies for one type of layout analysis. We define the departments as picking/receiving, storing, inspecting, forward picking, sorting, shipping, and dock to dock. The difference between classic warehouse layout algorithm using BLOCPLAN- and RFID-applied warehouse is the consideration of adjacent function zone separated for the reason of interfaces between sensors. For instance, the picking, forward picking, shipping, and dock to dock zone are considerably separated according to the amount of product flow.

7.7 Discussion and Conclusion

The use of RFID systems in both existing and new facilities requires rethinking traditional layout approaches. This is necessitated by the need to take into consideration the department relationship requirements added by RFID system components. What may have previously been an optimal facility layout may no longer be optimal.

This chapter describes a layout methodology that takes an integrating multi-objective architectural approach involving data environment analysis, and RFID interrogation zone optimization. The effectiveness of the resulting layouts can be evaluated using facility layout software such as BLOCPLAN for Windows.

REFERENCES

Banerjee, P., Zhou, Y., and Montreuel, B. (1997), Genetically assisted optimization of cell layout and material flow path skeleton, *IIE Transactions*, 29(4), 277–291.

Carbon, T. A. (2000), Measuring efficiency of semiconductor manufacturing operations using data envelopment analysis (DEA), *IEEE SEMI Advanced Semiconductor Manufacturing Conference*, Boston, MA.

Gotsman, C., and Koren, Y. (2005), Distributed graph layout for sensor networks. In J. Pach (ed) *Lecture Notes in Computer Science (LNCS)*, 3383, pp. 273–284, 2004. Berlin: Springer-Verlag.

Muther, R. (1973), *Systematic Layout Planning*, Boston, MA: CBI Publishing.

Tompkins, J. A., White, J. A., Bozer, Y. A., Frazelle, E. H., Tanchoco, J. M. A., and Trevino, J. (1996), *Facility Planning*, 2nd edition. New York: Wiley.

Wehking, K., Seeger, F., and Kummer, S. (2006), RFID transponders: Link between information and material flows. How reliable are identification procedures?, *Logistics Journal*. doi:10.2195/lj_ref_wehking_e_042006.

Part 3

Research Design in Global Supply Chain Engineering

8

Analyzing Variability

Erick C. Jones

Management by best seller is often explored rather than using the timeless principles of scientific management.

Erick C. Jones

8.1 Introduction to Lean Six Sigma Levels

This chapter provides foundational knowledge and approaches to measuring the variability of processes in Global Supply Engineering. In this text, we introduce the varying levels of analysis by contextualizing the Lean Six Sigma levels of the student. In general, the yellow belt level refers to undergraduate students, green belt is correlated to Master's students and/or advanced engineering undergraduate students with exposure to advanced statistics (industrial engineering, operations management, and operations engineering), and black belt is synonymous to PhD students, graduate engineering students, and industrial experts with extensive training or experiences.

8.2 Introduction

Analyze is the important phase in the Lean Six Sigma process steps of Define, Measure, Analyze, Improve, and Control. These steps are also referred to as DMAIC. Having the metrics established and measured, and also having identified the key process input variables that affect the key process output variables, the analyze phase utilizes different statistical and hypothesis testing tools to quantify the data obtained in measure to be used in later phases, i.e., improve and control. The analyze phase is classified as the following:

- Measuring and modeling relationships between variables
- Hypothesis testing
- Additional analysis methods.

These methods utilize tools which are discussed later in the chapter based on belt certifications.

8.3 Establishing Baseline

The purpose of establishing baseline is to quantify the performance level of "little y" that was zeroed down in measure. The main objectives are to determine and document the baseline overall process performance and the baseline potential process capability. The baseline results should consist of Z-scores (both long term and short term) for the baseline process and also the confidence interval estimates. It is nothing but the targets and specifications identified in the previous phase of Measure. Hence, this step of the project produces estimates of baseline (i.e., current) process performance for the process output(s). Confidence intervals for those estimates are determined to bind their imprecision. Additional process mapping also documents the configuration of the process that generates the output of interest. We require a greater detailed understanding of the process operations and flow than was needed at the outset of the project.

Improvement of any process requires the precise understanding of the current process. Hence, baseline is established to measure and report the ability of the current process to perform to the required levels of target and specification. Baseline is the current state of the process (its basis or starting point) before beginning the Six Sigma process improvement project. Baseline refers to both

- Current overall process performance
- Current potential process capability.

Before initiating the process improvements, it is vital for any belt-certified member to understand how the process is performing. Establishing the current process performance includes estimation of current defect rates, defective rates, overall and stepwise yields, mean outputs, and output variances. Generally, the baseline process metrics will be the following for any processes:

- Defects, defectives, and related metrics
- Six Sigma process metrics and Z-scores
  - Overall process performance
  - Potential process capability
- Related quality engineering process performance metrics
- Process output yield and related metrics.

Hence, the Six Sigma metrics can be defined and examined in terms of Z-scores by combining process statistics and customer targets and specifications. In the process, the distinction between short-term and long-term variations will also be considered to arrive at the metrics of overall process performance and potential process capability.

8.4 Baseline Performance Metrics

8.4.1 Counting "Defects" or "Defectives"

Examples:

- Specific sizes of new product not available at the market introduction date (number not available/number planned)
- Errors in test requests submitted for road test evaluation (number of requests with errors/total number planned) or (total number of errors on all requests/total number of "opportunities for error" on all requests).

8.4.2 Measuring Characteristic or Variable

Examples:

- The cycle time, in seconds, to evaluate the uniformity characteristics of a tire
- The viscosity of a polymer
- The length of a conveyor belt.

8.4.3 Baseline Process Metrics

Baseline process metrics quantify the ability of the current process to meet specifications. There are two primary baseline process metrics:

- Overall Process Performance—a measure of overall, or "long-term", process results
  - Estimated from summary statistics using all the data
  - Resulting Z-score reported as Zlong-term or ZLT.
- Potential Process Capability—a measure of within-group, or "short-term", process potential
  - Estimated from data subdivided into rational sets or subgroups
  - Resulting Z-score reported as Zshort-term or ZST.

The estimation of baseline process metrics is given as follows:

- Gather data about the process output, *y*
  - Retain process-associated information "tags"
  - No special data handling or follow-up.
- Analyze the data
  - Calculate summary statistics
  - Look at process behavior.
- Calculate the 6s performance metrics
  - Overall process performance, ZLT
  - Potential process capability, ZST.

The baseline process metrics can be classified as discrete and continuous outputs. The background on this topic was discussed in the previous chapter, and the reader can also read the appendix. This section provides us with the different discrete and continuous data and its mode of measurements.

8.4.4 Discrete Outputs

Discrete data gives only certain specific values possible. Following are some of the examples:

Pass?	(yes, no)
Color?	(black, gray, white)
Grade?	(A, B, C, D, F)
Opinion rating?	(good, OK, poor)

Each question above has only one particular distinct value possible. The two common discrete output variables are tabulated as follows:

Defective	(yes or no)
Defect	(type-1, type-2, type-C, *etc.*)

The definitions of "Defective and Defect" is given below:

- **Defective**—Any unit with one or more defects.
- **Defect**—An imperfection, blemish, non-conformance. Any instance where the product or service fails to meet a specific requirement. One unit of output may contain more than one defect.

The most commonly encountered process output "Defects" are defect of output quality, defect of process cycle time, and defect of process cost component. Hence, it is not possible to assess process performance without the assessment of when the process meets, and does not meet, the customer requirements (i.e., knowing what constitutes the Defects and the Defectives). Therefore, the project teams, the sponsor, the process owner, etc. must know and agree upon the critical, measurable process output characteristic(s), as well as the relevant targets and specifications. To count and measure the defects and defectives, the following terminologies are important to be known.

A unit is a specified quantity of process output, the basis for process performance analysis. Units are operationally defined to count Defects and Defectives, and the rational definition varies by situation. Some examples of a unit are Lot, Container (truck trailer, pallet, box), Piece (tire, bale, belt, document), and Time (shift, day, week, month).

Opportunity is any property of the process output (product or service) or the process that is or can be chosen for improvement based on the inputs from Define and Measure. Some examples of opportunities are product opportunities such as parts, features, and materials; and process opportunities such as machines, procedures, and tools. The terminologies about discrete data are being made clear; the important part is to know the procedure for determining performance statistics for discrete data.

- Count the number of defects or defectives.
- Determine the total number of "opportunities for defect" or "opportunities for defective".
- Calculate the ratio of defects (or defectives) to opportunities. The ratio may be expressed as a percentage, parts per million, and defects per million opportunities.
- Determine the Z-score that is equivalent to the ratio just calculated (Figure 8.1).

The following example will demonstrate these steps in detail for better understanding. There are a number of tires provided for inspection for testing. The question is to find how many are blemished tires?

Note: A blemish is the presence of any of six different conditions (coded as D, B, P, G, R, and F). It is possible for the sidewall to have more than one of these conditions.

The specification for Figure 8.1 is "no blemishes on the tire sidewall". Since the process output has a stated specification of a quality characteristic, "no blemishes", it can be evaluated for Defects (and Defectives). The tire is the Unit of interest in this example; each tire is one unit of output. The "non-serial side" of each tire is carefully examined for the presence of six different blemishes, coded as D, B, P, G, R, and F. Once again consider the same example for blemishes on tires and blemishes on the tires but with defects.

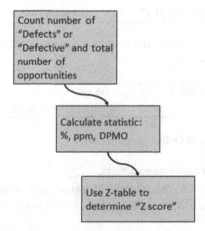

FIGURE 8.1   Baseline statistics for discrete data.

To perform the first step in the baseline statistics, the defective and defect levels are to be counted by performing the following questionnaire:

- Defective Level
  - What is the unit? How many units are there?
  - What is a Defective? How many defectives? What is the DPMO?
- Defect Level
  - What is the Defect? How many defects? How many Defects/Unit [dpu]?
  - What is the Opportunity? How many Opportunities per Unit?
  - How many Defects/million Opportunities [DPMO]?

Counting the Units with defects (3) shows three **defectives** in the five units or 60% defective. This can also be expressed as 600,000 "defects per million opportunities". "Counting the **defects** (7) gives seven defects for five units". But there is more than one "opportunity for defect" for each unit. In this case, there are six opportunities per unit. There are five units (NSS sides of five tires), so there are 30 opportunities for defects. Seven defects were observed, so there are 7/30 or 0.233 defects per opportunity. Expressed in terms of "defects per million opportunities", this is 233,000 DPMO. The description of a process in which the inputs and outputs are predominantly data or information, rather than a physical product, is called transactional process. Order entry and claims processing are examples of transactional processes. In the above example, the process output is a test request. Six quality characteristics have been identified and the target is defined—"no errors in critical fields". The test request is the "unit of interest". Each request is checked for conformance to the six different information requirements (Figure 8.2).

An error is defined as missing or incorrect information corresponding to any of six different information fields entered in test requests (coded as D, B, P, G, R, and F). It is possible for one request to have more than one of these "defects". "Five test requests" are reviewed (in the actual project, the number was over 200, but let's keep it simple for now). Counting the Units (Requests) with defects shows three **defectives** in the five units or 60% defective. This can also be expressed as 600,000 "defects per million opportunities". Counting the **defects** gives seven defects for five units. But there is more than one "opportunity for defect" for each unit. In this case, there are six opportunities per unit. There are five units, so there are 30 opportunities for defects. Seven defects were observed, so there are 7/30 or 0.233 defects per opportunity. Expressed in terms of "defects per million opportunities", this is 233,000 DPMO.

We now have process output samples that have been graded for "defective" or "not defective". But the output attribute (little y) is unknown, and also the defect is unknown. All that is known is that the discrete attribute grading was done with a validated measurement system. The "defective" units were "taped" at the time that Lot samples were graded and the Unit is either the production Lot or a pallet of tires representing that Lot. Thus, there are 20 Units in the process output sample, and three of them are clearly indicated as Defective. Seventeen of the units are not defective, so there is an estimate of 0.85 proportion conforming or 85% yield.

Process output pass/fail rates can be expressed in many ways. The basic measurement is the observed raw count. Here are some other pass/fail expressions and their units, along with corresponding values for our example (Table 8.1).

TEST REQUST FORM		
REQUESTOR		
DEVELOPMENT CODE		
BLOCKING CONDITION		
PERFORMANCE STANDARD		
GRADIENT		
FUNCTIONAL TESTS		

FIGURE 8.2 Test request form.

TABLE 8.1

Discrete Process Output Metrics

	Pass	Fail
Raw counts	17	3
Percentages	85	15
Proportions	0.85	0.15
Fractions	17/20	3/20
Ratios	17:3	5.7:1
Parts per million [ppm]	850,000	150,000

Proportion Conforming	Rt. Tail	Percent Out	PPM	Z-score
0.50	0.50	50%	500,000	0.000
0.55	0.45	45%	450,000	0.126
0.60	0.40	40%	400,000	0.253
0.65	0.35	35%	350,000	0.385
0.70	0.30	30%	300,000	0.524
0.75	0.25	25%	250,000	0.674
0.80	0.20	20%	200,000	0.842
0.85	0.15	15%	150,000	1.036
0.90	0.10	10%	100,000	1.282
0.91	0.09	9%	90,000	1.341
0.92	0.08	8%	80,000	1.405
0.93	0.07	7%	70,000	1.476
0.94	0.06	6%	60,000	1.555
0.95	0.05	5%	50,000	1.645
0.96	0.04	4%	40,000	1.751
0.97	0.03	3%	30,000	1.881
0.98	0.03	3%	25,000	1.960
0.98	0.02	2%	20,000	2.054
0.99	0.01	1%	10,000	2.326

FIGURE 8.3   Converting yield, % Defective, DPMO, etc., Z-score.

Process "yield" can be a useful metric, depending on its basis and definition. It is an aggregate measure of pass rate. The complement to process yield is Process Defective or Defect Rate. You may often see these rates expressed as [ppm] or [PPM]. PPM is identical to DPMO when there is one opportunity per unit.

The spreadsheet below shows the cumulative probability value as a function of the Z-value or Z-score. In figure 8.4, the spreadsheet table provides a quick way to look up the approximate value of Z-score for a given process output. The required information needed, to look up a Z-score, is an observed or estimated process yield (proportion conforming). Conversely, one can also use the complement of process yield, i.e., the proportion of nonconforming process output (Figures 8.3 and 8.4).

As the Six Sigma culture grows within the business organization, it will become more common to hear process performance referred to in terms of Z-score. The spreadsheet table can be used to quickly convert to the process yield, PPM, etc. given a stated Z-score. For example, the process yield corresponding to a Z-score of 3.0 is about 99.83 [%] by visual interpolation. The process defective rate corresponding to a Z-score of 3.0 is approximately 1,700 [ppm], again by visual interpolation (Figure 8.5).

The process performance can be evaluated using several approaches. In the first approach, we assess performance using Lot as the unit of process output. Further, we will measure the process output using a discrete quality variable—DEFECTIVE STATUS; this output variable has two possible values: "Defective" and "Not-Defective". The tabulated observations of discrete process output values for the 20 Lots are shown in Figure 8.5. The table displays output values of "yes" and "no". For our analysis, we will usually code this type of discrete values (i.e., textual values) in a Minitab worksheet with numeric values, such as "1" and "0" in this case.

8.4.5 Process Capability for Binomial Process Outputs

Binomial data are usually associated with recording the **number of defective** items out of the **total number** of items sampled. For example, if you are a manufacturer, you might have a go/no-go gauge

FIGURE 8.4   Converting Z-score to yield.

Lot	Defective?	Lot	Defective?
1	yes	11	no
2	no	12	no
3	no	13	no
4	no	14	yes
5	no	15	no
6	yes	16	no
7	no	17	no
8	yes	18	no
9	no	19	no
10	yes	20	yes

FIGURE 8.5   Overall performance, by Defective Lots.

that determines whether an item is defective or not. You could then record the number of items that were failed by the gauge and the total number of items inspected. Or, you could record the number of people who call in sick on a particular day, and the number of people scheduled to work that day. These examples could be modeled by a binomial distribution if the following conditions are met:

- Each item is the result of identical conditions.
- Each item can result in one of two possible outcomes ("success/failure", "go/no-go", etc.).
- The probability of a success (or failure) is constant for each item.
- The outcomes of the items are independent of each other.

8.4.6 Process Capability for Poisson Process Output

The **Poisson** distribution characterizes data for which you can only count the nonconformities that exist—it is impossible to count nonconformities that do not exist. The Poisson distribution characterizes defects data, which are nonconformities that affect part of a product or service but that do not render the product or service unusable.

- The data are counts of discrete events (defects) that occur within a finite area of opportunity.
- The defects occur independently of each other.
- There is an equal opportunity for the occurrence of defects.
- The defects occur rarely (when compared to what could be).

Now for one set of data, three different values of overall performance (Z-score) are available and the question is which metric is correct.

- Defectives, with Lot as the Unit: $Z_{LT} = 0.5$
- Defectives, with Tire as the Unit: $Z_{LT} = 2.3$
- Defects, with six Opportunities per Tire: $Z_{LT} = 2.8$.

The correct metric depends on the nature of the project, and whichever approach is chosen, stick with it throughout the project.

- Defectives/Lot:
  - (+) Historic data generally more available
  - (−) Cannot improve process via defectives if multiple defects.
- Defects/Tire:
  - (−) Historic data generally less available
  - (+) Can better identify source(s) of defect, to target solution(s).

Hence, with the above-illustrated example, the overall process performance for discrete outputs can be conducted by the following steps:

- Choose appropriate test measurement and level of detail, i.e., Defectives, Total Defects, or Specific Defect(s).
- Choose Unit to measure, e.g., a tire, a pallet of tires, and an order of tires; a service order, a service hour, and a service form.
- Decide which segments, groups, types, regions, etc., to include in the study.
- Conduct the study; collect the data.
  - *Important*: If you will collect data specifically for the 6s project, gather data for as many process-related elements as practically/economically reasonable.
- Analyze process data.
  - Use either binomial (pass/fail counts) or Poisson (rates) capability analysis.
- Report the DPMO and the Z-score, with their confidence limits.

8.4.7 Continuous Outputs

Continuous outputs are within a given interval, any real value possible (at least in theory), and some of the examples are temperature; time, mass, pressure, viscosity, etc. Continuous data sets provide descriptive statistics, sample mean, and sample standard deviation (Figure 8.6).

The typical plot for continuous data is given in Figure 8.7.

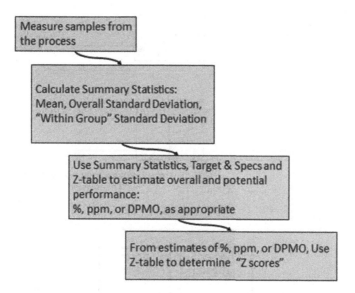

FIGURE 8.6 Baseline statistics for continuous data.

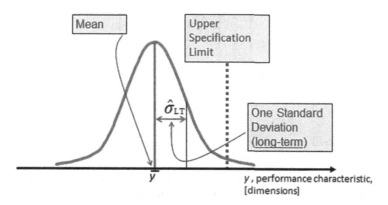

FIGURE 8.7 Continuous data.

The metrics for continuous data is also established by means of Z-scores. Z-scores are the process performance metrics to report for both overall process performance (Z_{LT}) and potential process capability (Z_{ST}). The subscript LT is for long-term project and ST id for short-term project. The computation of the overall process performance metric, Z_{LT}, is simple algebra. It is a mere substitution of the proper specification limit, and the long-term process mean and standard deviation.

Calculation of one-sided Z-scores: Figure 8.8 shows the one-sided Z-score calculation.

The practice of adding 1.5 to the overall process performance (Z_{LT}) is completely arbitrary. The assumption is that process performance will have smaller variance over "short term" than overall (long term). With a smaller magnitude for S_{ST} than S_{LT}, more standard deviations can now fit between the process mean and specification limit. In fact, the popular "add 1.5 units to Z_{LT} to estimate Z_{ST} rule of thumb is a special case!" Here's one scenario when this would be a good estimation method:

- Measured $Z_{LT} = 4.5$
- Measured $Z_{ST} = 6.0$
  - Or independent of mean and specs
- $S_{ST} = 0.75\ S_{LT}$ (approximately) and measured $S_{LT}^2 \sim 2S_{ST}^2$.

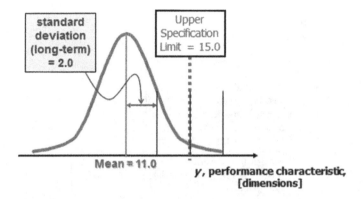

FIGURE 8.8   One-sided Z-score.

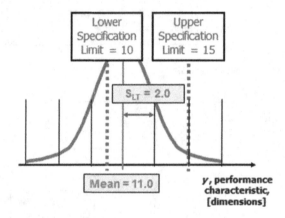

FIGURE 8.9   Calculation of two-sided Z-score.

Calculation of two-sided Z-score: Figure 8.9 shows the calculation for two-sided Z-score.

Here is the extension to the initial, one-sided specification process output example, as promised above. Conceptually, we add the individual probabilities of nonconforming process output (from the two tails) into a total nonconforming proportion.

The mechanics used to compute the overall process performance metric (Z_{LT} or Z_{bench}), for processes with two-sided specifications, are

- Compute the predicted probability of the nonconforming output in the lower tail.
- Compute the predicted probability of the nonconforming output in the upper tail.
- Sum the individual probabilities for a total predicted probability of non-conformance.
- Convert the total probability to a Z-score.

8.4.8 Process Capability Analysis for Normal Process Outputs

It is known that process output will not be normally distributed. Regarding the non-normality of the data, there are methods that can be used to normalize certain outputs, e.g., Box-Cox transformation. However, no ordinary methods are available to normalize bimodal data. The bimodal process output suggests that different sources of variation exist within the process. If the previous methods to assess process stability such as process behavior charts are used, the output will be unstable and non-normal. At this point, the initial process capability analysis can be considered as a gross estimate of overall performance only.

The baseline report is sometimes called the process scorecard. The actual overall process performance is reported, with both the Z-score (Z_{LT} or Z_{bench}) and the DPMO shown. The above section provides the computations of only the process capability. The next section focuses on "short-term" performance, i.e., potential process capability.

8.4.8.1 Potential Process Capability

Overall process performance metric, or "long-term" performance, includes variance across all observed output. Overall data can be stratified, or grouped, into shorter time periods or other rational subgroups. Calculation based on the performance within subgroups will give us an estimate of the potential capability of the process. "Within-group" variation also referred to as "short-term" variation. Estimates of short-term variation are critical in determining baseline potential process capability. Figure 8.10 shows rational subgrouping.

In the estimation of potential process capability, there is a need to hypothesize a "rational subgroup" by which to stratify, or group, the overall process output results. There are three general classes of rational subgrouping, or variation, though any rational difference/factor can be used:

- Positional (location): Variation within a single unit or across a unit with many parts, e.g., variation from district to district, machine to machine, and operator to operator.
- Sequential: Variation among consecutive pieces, batches, groups, etc. For example, variation from step to step.
- Temporal (time): Variation within short time spans, e.g., shift to shift and week to week.

Each subgroup contains multiple elements such that an estimation of within-(sub)group variation is possible.

8.4.9 Short-Term Variation

- The purpose of obtaining an estimate of "short-term" variation is to get an estimate of the capability of the process.
- The total—or overall—variation includes all sources for variability.

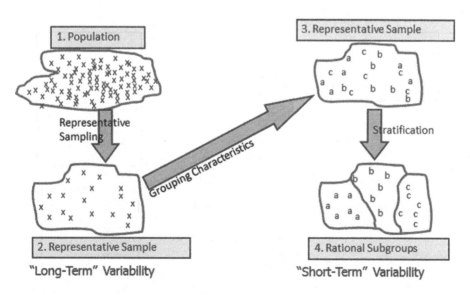

FIGURE 8.10   Rational subgrouping.

- Based on your knowledge of the process, identify various ways to stratify or "slice" the overall data.
- As the description "short-term" implies, one way is to look at shorter slices of time.
- But time is not the only way to group the data, as shown in Figures 8.11–8.13.

In the distribution in Figure 8.10 represents the result of merely shifting the mean outputs from all subgroups (the five individual lines) to the overall mean. This outcome does not require reducing the lines' individual variances. But there is even greater opportunity for improvement than shown in this diagram, if the means can be shifted to the process target. The difference between the Z_{LT} (overall process performance) and Z_{ST} (potential process capability) is called Z_{shift}.

$$Z_{shift} = Z_{ST} - Z_{LT} \qquad (8.1)$$

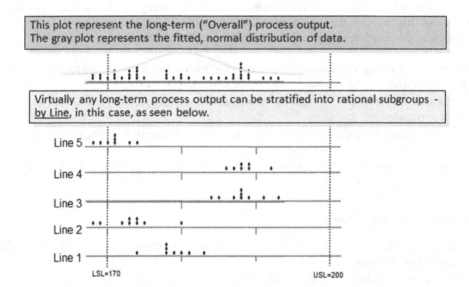

FIGURE 8.11 Long-term variation.

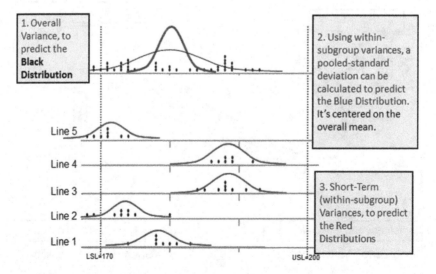

FIGURE 8.12 Determination of short-term variation.

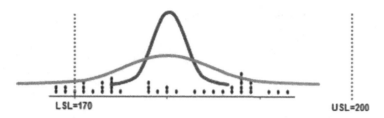

FIGURE 8.13 Short-term (within subgroup) variation.

"Long-term" data are segmented by some rational factor to compute the "short-term" variability. An estimate of "short-term" standard deviation for a three-subgroup variation is given by

$$\sigma_{ST} = \sqrt{\frac{\sigma_{ST1}^2 + \sigma_{ST2}^2 + \sigma_{ST3}^2}{3}} \tag{8.2}$$

The short-term (or within-group) standard deviation is the basis for the estimate of potential process capability. This simple formula for the short-term standard deviation holds true when subgroup sizes are equal. When not equal, a more general formula for "pooled standard deviation" is used. The pooled standard deviation is a weighted average of the subgroups' standard deviations and is given by

$$S_p^2 = \frac{(n_1 - 1)S_1^2 + (n_2 - 1)S_2^2 + (n_3 - 1)S_3^2}{(n_1 - 1) + (n_2 - 1) + (n_3 - 1)} \tag{8.3}$$

Based on the above insight, tools are available to analyze the data. Those tools are categorized and explained based on different belts below.

8.5 Analysis Tools

8.5.1 Cause-and-Effect Diagram (Fishbone Diagram)

Cause-and-effect or fishbone diagrams are an effective team-based tool which can be used to determine the potential root cause of a problem.

A cause-and-effect diagram helps in the following ways:

- Breaks the problem down into many bits.
- Displays all possible causes in a graphical manner.
- Maybe also called fishbone, 4-M, or Ishikawa diagram.
- Shows the interaction of various causes.
- Follows the idea of brainstorming when ideas are to be generated.

A fishbone session may be divided into three sessions:

1. Prioritizing
2. Brainstorming
3. Action plans development.

The problem statement is identified, and brainstorming for the categories is done. The next step would be the prioritization of the problem causes; polling is often used. The three most probable causes are encircled from the action plan development. The 4-M (manpower, machine, method, and materials) version of the fishbone diagram is usually sufficient. The expanded version must be occasionally used. In a

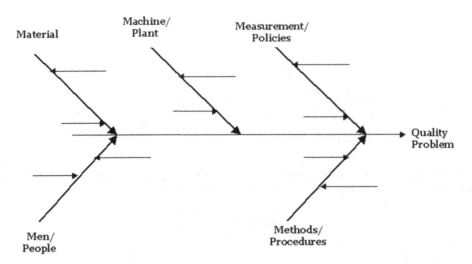

FIGURE 8.14   Fishbone 5-M and E example.

lab environment, measurement is the key. During the discussion of brown grass in the lawn, environment is important. A 5-M and E schematic is shown in Figure 8.14.

Figure 8.15 shows an example of a cause-and-effect diagram, and the 5-M and E concept of determining and solving the causes for a quality problem.

For additional examples of cause-and-effect or Ishikawa diagram, refer to *Guide to Quality Control* (1982) by Ishikawa K.

8.5.2 Fault Tree Analysis

Fault tree analysis (FTA) is a method which systematically defines an event that is unique and undesirable, and determines all possible reasons or failure which could cause the event to occur. This event might constitute the top event in a fault tree diagram and generally is used to represent the complete failure of the product. In comparison with Failure Mode and Effects Analysis (FMEA), FTA is a faster and easier method of analysis because its focus is on a selected group of all possible system failures, especially those that could cause a catastrophic event. FMEA works in a sequential manner through all events that could cause possible system failures, regardless of how severe they could be.

On proper application, FTA becomes a very useful tool during initial product design phase and also an evaluation tool for performing preliminary design modifications. Several potential uses of FTA can be as follows:

- Performing the functional analysis of highly complex systems
- Performing the evaluation of subsystem events on top event
- Performing the evaluation of safety requirements and specifications
- System reliability evaluation
- Potential design and safety hazards identification
- Simplification of troubleshooting and maintenance
- Logically removing the causes of an observed failure.

FTA over FMEA when

- Safety of public, operation, and maintenance is the first priority.
- Identification of a small number of differentiated events can be done.

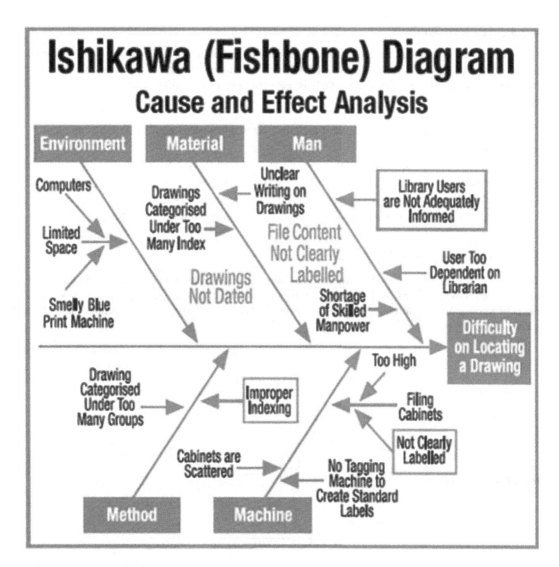

Ishikawa (Fishbone) Diagram
Cause and Effect Analysis

Environment

Computers

Limited Space

Smelly Blue Print Machine

Material

Drawings Categorised Under Too Many Index

Drawings Not Dated

Man

Unclear Writing on Drawings

File Content Not Clearly Labelled

Library Users are Not Adequately Informed

User Too Dependent on Librarian

Shortage of Skilled Manpower

Difficulty on Locating a Drawing

Drawing Categorised Under Too Many Groups

Improper Indexing

Too High

Filing Cabinets

Not Clearly Labelled

Cabinets are Scattered

No Tagging Machine to Create Standard Labels

Method

Machine

FIGURE 8.15 Actual fishbone example.

- Critical importance to the completion of functional profile is given.
- Errors by humans and software provide a high potential of failure.
- Quantified risk evaluation is the primary concern.
- Highly complex or highly interconnected product functionality.
- Once initiated product is not repairable.

FMEA over FTA when

- The top events are limited to a small number.
- There is a feasibility for multiple potentially successful functional profiles.
- Determining the possible failure modes is important.
- Software intervention or little human involvement in product functionality.

Reliability Toolkit (1993)

8.5.3 Fault Tree Symbols

FTA employs the logic gates concept for the determination of reliability of a system. Assessing potential system failure modes can also be done using FTA. There are many FTA symbols which are broken down into two main categories: event and gate symbols. Few examples of the various FTA symbols are shown below:

- Basic event: This is the lowest level of fault that one would wish to study. It is used as an input to logic gate (Figure 8.16).
- Fault event: It contains a description of the lower level fault (Figure 8.17).
- Initiator event: It is an external event that is used to initiate the process (Figure 8.18).
- "OR" gate: The output occurs only when one input event occurs (Figure 8.19).
- "AND" gate: The output event occurs only both input events occur (Figure 8.20).

8.5.4 Root Cause Analysis

The responsibility of root cause determination is usually given to a team or an individual to fix the deficit or correct it. Some problems might be very complex and difficult to solve. In other cases, the solution might be known, but time might be required to solve it. Table 8.2 shows the proposed actions that can be taken to solve the problem.

FIGURE 8.16   Basic event

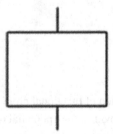

FIGURE 8.17   Fault event

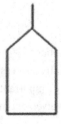

FIGURE 8.18   Initiator event

FIGURE 8.19   "OR" gate

FIGURE 8.20   "AND" gate

TABLE 8.2

Corrective Actions—Short and Long Terms

Situation	Immediate Action	Intermediate Action	Root Cause Action
The dam leaks	Plugging the dam	Patching the dam	Determining the cause of leak so it does not repeat again.
Oversized parts	Critical inspection	Installing an oversized kick out device in line	Analysis of the process and taking the actions to eliminate the production of oversized parts.

8.5.5 Subjective Tools

- Ask why two times
- Brainstorming
- Analysis of the process flow
- Problem-solving systematically
- Plan Do Check Act
- Nominal group technique
- Ishikawa diagrams
- Six thinking hats
- FMEA or FTA
- Employing of teams.

8.6 Analytical Tools

- Data collection
- Pareto charts

- Regression analysis
- Check sheets
- Process capability analysis
- Portioning of variation
- Subgrouping of data
- Simple trials
- Analytical tests or hypothesis tests
- Control charts.

When a permanent corrective action is determined, the management must determine if the root cause analysis has been performed to its full extent, if the corrective action is satisfactory to remove all the failures, and if the corrective action is reliable and maintainable.

8.6.1 5 Whys

The 5 Whys approach to determining the root cause analysis may also be described as asking the question "why?" five times. It is generally attributed to a Japanese method to root cause analysis. The following is an example of 5 Whys.

Symptoms: the customer shipment was not delivered on time.

1. Why?—Die stamping press broke down resulting in running out of parts,
2. Why?—Lack of scheduled maintenance of the press for a period of three months,
3. Why?—Reduction of maintenance department staff from 6 to 8.
4. Why?—Maintenance department budget shot up due to overtime costs and the General Manager required a reduction in costs of overtime for all overhead support departments.
5. Why?—Removal of unnecessary spending by the CEO because company was not reaching profit goals. So, the root cause was the CEO being worried about getting fired for poor profit performance.

There is nothing magical about 5 Whys. In fact, the root cause may be determined during the third or fourth why itself. In other cases, one may need to go beyond the 5 Whys to determine the root cause.

8.6.2 5 W's and H

The 5W's and H approach to root cause analysis is described by asking the questions Who? What? When? Why? Where? and How? The 5W's and H approach is an old method used by reporters of newspapers in asking questions to get the full story. In the quality context, responses to these questions can be organized into a fishbone diagram or a cause-and-effect diagram. In some cases, this same basic method is simply referred to as 5Ws. Note that the order of W's varies, depending upon the problem. The technique looks at the problem from more than one viewpoint in order to include information as much as possible that might be needed to determine the problem.

Question 88: When testing equal variances should I use Bartlett's test (or the F-test) or Levene's test? Solution (Section 14.3.4): Bartlett's test and the F-test are sensitive to the normality assumption. Levene's test is robust to the normality assumption. So, if your data are continuous and normally distributed, use Bartlett's test (or the F-test). If your data are continuous, but not necessarily normally distributed, use Levene's test.

Note: An F-test replaces Bartlett's test when there are only two groups.

8.7 Review Questions

Question 89: (Analyze/improve) Which of the following measures of variability is NOT dependent on the exact value of every measurement?

(a) Variance
(b) Range
(c) Standard deviation
(d) Mean deviation

Answer: B—Section 16.9.1

Solution: B. The range method is a simple way to quantify the combined repeatability and reproducibility of a measurement system. It computes the total measurement system variability and allows the total measurement system variability to be separated into repeatability, reproducibility, and part variation.

8.8 Understanding Hypotheses

8.8.1 Entitlement

It helps in finding out how process could be improved further from results through previously discussed methods. Finding entitlement by three approaches for current process performance is the key. Entitlement is defined as **"the best that the existing processes can perform, often intermittently, and for only short periods of time"**.

This definition implies that some empirical evidence of process output exists for the current process. The intermittent nature of entitlement usually indicates that certain process output subgroups are produced by certain process conditions or states that do not exist continuously, throughout the entire process system. When we have empirical measurements for rational subgroups, we can test for differences in performance. These could be differences in output mean as well as output variance. The tests are called hypothesis tests.

We can also look externally or internally for other empirical evidence of entitlement for the existing process. Internal benchmarking looks for data from within the organization, say an operation with the same process. External benchmarking would look at other companies using the same process. Benchmarking can also identify "best-in-class", the best process performance to produce the same process output. Finding out the Design Intent to determine theoretical potential is the third approach. We look into understanding hypotheses testing by looking at the types of errors.

8.8.2 Types of Errors

Errors are to be considered before making conclusions from results of tests. There are two types of possible errors:

- Type I: This type of error occurs when the null hypothesis is rejected though it is true. Producer's risk is defined this way, and the probability of this risk is termed by a variable alpha (α) and $0 < \alpha < 1$.
- Type II: This type of error occurs when the null hypothesis is not rejected when it is false. Consumer's error is defined this way, and the probability of this risk is termed by a variable (β) and $0 < \beta < 1$.

The level of risk that the recipient is willing to undertake is decided upon and is used to arrive at results. Of course, smaller values of α and β, i.e., smaller risk, are desirable. However, it is observed that if you reduce α, β increases. We must find a trade-off region to work with. Also, if we deal with large data points, the risk reduces considerably. To understand risks better, let us consider this simple situation. We make (and accept) decisions based upon incomplete knowledge all the time. Examples of such decisions with incomplete knowledge are

- Judge or jury verdict in a legal proceeding
- Referee's ruling in a professional sports game
- Hypothesis testing of sample means or other statistics.

All decisions based upon sample observations risk reaching an incorrect conclusion even if we had perfect measurements and used perfect judgment due to finite sample size (a form of incomplete knowledge). The only decisions made without risk are those in which complete knowledge is available, assuming perfect judgment is exercised. We accept that no person has complete knowledge from a finite sample from a large population.

Hypothesis testing is our interest in decision-making. Decisions are almost always made with respect to a null hypothesis (H_0) of "no difference". The alternative hypothesis (H_a) can only be supported with sufficient evidence to overturn (i.e., reject) the assumption of the null. In baseball, the umpire's assumption is that the base runners are "no different than 'safe'". This is the null hypothesis of baseball. Only when there is clear evidence to reject the null hypothesis, can the umpire rule that the runner is "not safe". Unfortunately, the umpire does not have complete knowledge. For instance, he can only view the play from one point or perspective, and only at "full speed". As instant video replays often show (from different angles or in slow motion), the umpire's decisions are not always perfect.

Alpha (α) risk is the probability that a sample mean is found by chance to be in the tail of the distribution, while the sample distribution is, in fact, the same as the true population distribution. This could cause a type I error, that is, rejecting the null hypothesis when it is actually true. Again, alpha risk is the risk of thinking that the sample is from a population that is d units away from the reference distribution when, in fact, it is actually from the reference distribution. Delta is the minimum difference that the experimenter wants to detect. The possibility of this being the true difference between the means and still going undetected is the beta risk. One way to increase our chance of detecting the difference is to accept a greater risk.

Critical Difference (δ): Minimum practical difference you need to detect based on financial or technical consequence, to make a good decision. Type II error (β risk) is the probability of missing a difference of size δ.

$$\delta \text{ (delta)} = \text{The difference between } m_o \,\&\, m_1 \text{ that we desire to detect.}$$

The experimenter needs to decide how small a difference (δ) he needs to detect, before the testing or experiment since after the test, you already know whether or not you found a significant effect! With enough samples, even very small differences can be detected. The experimenter should have an idea of the minimum size of the difference he would like to detect in the experiment. The probability of there being a difference of this size and of not noticing the difference in the hypothesis test is beta. The "power" of a statistical test is the test's probability of detecting a critical difference of size δ (Figure 8.21).

This graphical presentation of the data suggests that there is a difference between the two lines' output performance. Six Sigma principles require, however, that quantitative evidence be evaluated by quantitative methods (statistics!) in order to make that decision. The difference in the lines' outputs for this example might be intuitively obvious to you, but what if the difference is not so (visibly) apparent? (Figure 8.22).

This illustrates the difficulty in using visual, intuitive weighting to make decisions: what if there were more observations, what if there were fewer, how large does the difference really need to be, etc.

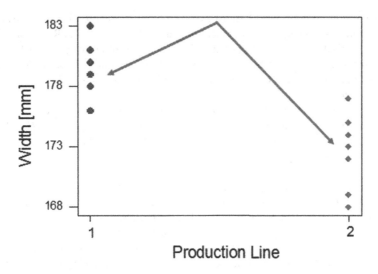

FIGURE 8.21 Example 1.

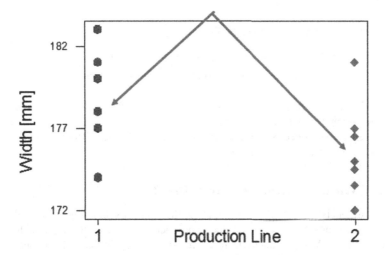

FIGURE 8.22 Example 2.

There are two mistakes that can be made in answering the question as to whether the lines being compared are really different:

- You decide that there is a difference between the two lines, but there really is no difference.
- You decide that there is no difference between the two lines, but there really is a difference.

In general, the same two mistakes can be made in any comparative decision of this sort (i.e., a binomial equal/not-equal, greater/not-greater, yes/no, etc. decision). We will revisit this idea in the next section of this module.

8.8.3 Hypothesis Testing

Hypothesis testing is the analysis based on the observed data points to reach a conjecture in the decision-making process. Here, an assumption is made on a statistical parameter, and this is asserted to be true by comparing the results with the data. A statistical procedure is to **decide** whether there are **differences** among data sets being **compared**, with a predetermined level of confidence. Rejection of a hypothesis means that there is a small probability of obtaining the sample, i.e., refuting the theory based on information observed, when in fact, the hypothesis is true (Myers). It is relevant to the topics discussed in the following pages. But before we start a discussion on the application of this technique, we must understand the terminology in terms of statistics.

Hypothesis testing is analogous to a legal trial. In the U.S. legal system, a person begins the trial presumed innocent (really, presumed "not guilty"). That is the null hypothesis (H_o)! The prosecutor accuses the defendant of being "guilty", the alternative hypothesis (H_a). Similarly, we always judge with respect to the null of "not guilty": reject the null (found "guilty") or cannot reject the null (found "not guilty").

There are risks of two incorrect verdicts present in every trial. First, there's the risk of convicting an innocent man (risk of **rejecting** a null hypothesis that describes the **truth**). The second is the risk of letting a guilty man goes free (risk of **accepting** the null hypothesis that is **false**). In the U.S. court example, the risk or probability of convicting an innocent person (*a* or alpha) is deemed of critical concern. This system is based on the belief that it's much more evil to convict an innocent man than to let a guilty man go free. To minimize the risk of convicting the innocent, very strong evidence is required to decide "guilty". To put it in hypothesis testing terms, we want to be as close as possible to 99.99% certain that we will not convict the innocent.

8.8.3.1 U.S. Legal System Hypothesis Tests

H_o: Defendant is Not Guilty (presumed "innocent"; no different than any other)

H_a: Defendant is Guilty (evidence beyond reasonable doubt to reject innocence).

The two risks on incorrect verdict are β, which is setting a guilty person free (*failing to reject H_o when H_a is true*), and α, which is convicting an innocent person (*i.e., rejecting H_o when it is true*).

In technical practice, there's been similar aversion to falsely declaring "difference found", (thus small a), but it's often been at expense of (large, unknown) *b*!

8.8.4 Why and When Are Hypothesis Tests Used?

Hypothesis tests are decision aids. They do not make the decisions, but they aid in making good decisions in uncertain situations. Say that you produce a product on a number of lines, and the overall performance has not been good. You calculated the mean and standard deviation of the output its conformance (or non-conformance) to the customer specifications. A process improvement project is begun on one of the lines, and management wants to know whether the new process is indeed better than the old (upgrading the other lines would be a substantial capital cost).

Hypothesis testing would be used to decide whether the performance of the "improved" line is statistically different (i.e., better) than the old way of doing things, given the risk (uncertainty) the business is willing to take.

Remember: Six Sigma uses data-based decision-making. The hypothesis test is the statistical test to determine whether there are real differences between data sets.

Hypothesis tests always compare two mutually exclusive (contradictory) hypotheses.

8.8.4.1 Null Hypothesis

The null hypothesis (H_o) says, "There is no difference between the two sets. If you think there is, you've got to prove it". It is the formal statement against which experimental evidence is tallied. Its source is the overall problem that it addresses. A null hypothesis, H_o, can be rejected or failed to accept. The statement that a hypothesis is accepted is never used as it is ambiguous and against the belief that there is not enough evidence to support the statement due to unavoidable circumstances. With enough data, it is decided that we have failed to reject a null hypothesis statement. The null hypothesis (denoted H_0) is referred to as "H-naught". Null hypotheses are almost always set up to be "straw men". We generally hope or expect to disprove or "knock over" the null hypothesis.

8.8.4.2 Alternate Hypothesis

The alternative hypothesis (H_a) says, "There is a difference between the two sets of data". The alternative hypothesis (denoted as H_a) is sometimes referred to as "the research hypothesis". The alternative hypothesis describes the situation that we hope or expect to "prove" or demonstrate as "the truth" (Figure 8.23).
For the **mean width—production line** example, above:

- Null (H_o): There is no difference between average widths (i.e., the averages are equal: $Avg_1 = Avg_2$).
- Alternative (H_a): There is a difference in average widths (i.e., the averages are not equal: $Avg_1 \neq Avg_2$).
"If p is low, the null must go".

This little ditty is useful to some people in remembering which hypothesis to accept or reject.

8.8.5 Translation

"If the p-value is less than our chosen (a) value for the significance level {typically, $a = 0.05$} then one *can reject the Null* hypothesis. Therefore, there is a 'statistically significant' difference between samples".
"If the p-value is greater than our chosen value for the significance level {typically, $a = 0.05$} then one *cannot reject the Null* hypothesis".
Other forms of the alternative hypothesis are called as one-sided tests. We use them when we want to test whether one sample mean is greater than (or less than) another, e.g.,

- Are Region One's sales less than Region Two's?
- Is the chemical process yield improved with the new catalyst?

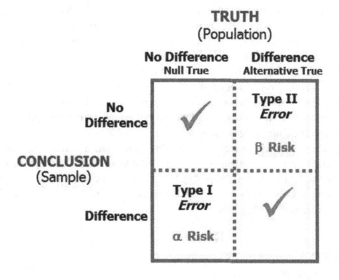

FIGURE 8.23 General hypothesis testing.

In these situations, the alternative hypotheses are no longer "not equal to ($\neq$)", but "less than (<)" or "greater than (>)".

- H_a: Region One < Region Two
- H_a: Yield New > Yield Old.

The alternative hypothesis says, "There is a difference", and it could be one of the following:

- Samples are **not equal** (we used this H_a in example, above).
- Sample one is **greater than** sample two.
- Sample one is **less than** sample two.

In hypothesis testing, we "stack the deck" in favor of the null hypothesis. Evidence is required to reject the null hypothesis, i.e., to conclude that there really is a difference.

It brings us to a discussion on one-sided and two-sided tests.

- If the value of risk is placed at one side of the test, then it is termed as a one-sided test. It is also termed as one-tailed test.
- If the population has shifted on either direction, then it is termed as a two-sided test. It is also termed as two-tailed test.

The "equal/not-equal" test is called a "two-sided" test, because it doesn't matter whether the difference is greater than zero or less. The "greater than" or "less than" tests are called "**one-sided**" tests. It should be noted that the null hypothesis almost always remains the same. It states, "There is no difference" between the groups being compared for the statistic of interest. We could get "tricky" with the null hypothesis and use a non-zero test mean to test whether the difference in means was some specified (non-zero) value. For example,

- H_o: $(\text{Avg}_1 - \text{Avg}_2) = 3$
- H_a: $(\text{Avg}_1 - \text{Avg}_2) \neq 3$.

The major difference in the report of one-sided test results is in the statement of the 95% confidence interval for the means' difference. In the one-sided test, the 95% CI is a single lower bound on the difference. Let us consider an example, the lower CI bound is +0.10. We can be 95% confident that the difference between means is no less than +0.10. The best estimate for the means' difference is +3.19, and the minimum estimate for the difference is also positive (+0.10); since the confidence interval of means' difference does not include the value of 0.00, we conclude that there is a difference in the direction indicated by the alternative hypothesis (i.e., ">").

In other words, any test has risk associated with it. This risk (α) determines the level of confidence which is $(1 - \alpha)$. Thus, it determines the critical value of test statistic. The two-sided test uses the alternative hypothesis that states that the two sets of data are **not equal**. In the one-sided test, the alternative hypothesis is either **greater than or less than.**

The examples above required comparing two samples against one another (i.e., "two-sample t-tests"). However, some situations require comparing a single sample against a "known" (or reference) value. Thus, in **one-sample** t-tests, we are not comparing two samples, but we compare a single sample against the reference. One-sample tests can be one-sided tests (equal vs. greater than, or equal vs. less than) as well as two-sided tests (equal vs. not equal).

Examples:

- Comparing a sample against a historical mean
- Comparing a sample against an industry standard
- Comparing a sample against a claim or goal.

The one-sample *t*-test compares sample results against a known historical mean or a standard of some kind. If we have a specific goal or claim to compare a sample against, we also use the one-sided test.

Now we try an Exercise: Accounts receivable (A/R) Six Sigma Project Process output (A/R as percent of sales) for the 12-month baseline period averaged 24%. Benchmarking resources indicate that "best-in-class" performance (A/R as percent of sales) in similar businesses is no greater than 18%. The region manager agrees that receivables are not below 18%, but says that, considering month-to-month fluctuations, the results are not "significantly above 18%"and "the trend shows that we should be fewer than 18% soon".

- What one-sample test could you perform to test the manager's hypothesis?
- How could you test the manager's claim about the "trend"?
- What are your conclusions?

Solution: Always consider this question: What are you trying to prove with your hypothesis test? In step 5, we must determine the entitlement for the existing process. In this particular example, we are trying to develop statistical evidence as to whether the baseline A/R process output (accounts receivable, as percent of sales) is above the industry standard. If the "industry standard" process and the baseline process are comparable, and the claim of "industry standard" is accurate, we may have achieved entitlement performance already. Use the one-sided, one-sample *t*-test.

Exercise 2: (Continuation) Process results (A/R as percent of sales) during the six months after implementation of a process change (trial) showed reduction of A/R from 24% to 20.5%. If the difference is real, the payback would be good; however, the proposed process changes would also be costly to implement. Review the data. What are your conclusions and recommendation(s)?

Solution: Again, think about what it is you are trying to prove. In this example, we are trying to develop statistical proof that the new method causes the accounts receivables to be lower than the current method. Use the two-sample *t*-test. The alternative hypothesis should be greater than current method.

The value of β is large if $\mu = \mu_o$ and small if μ is largely skewed from μ_o. To construct a power curve $1 - \beta$ is plotted against alternatives of μ (Certified Six Sigma Black Belt (CSBB)). There is gain in power if α is low and also when sample size increases. $1 - \beta$ is the probability of rejecting the null hypothesis given the null hypothesis is false. It is evident that sample size is dependent on risks, variance, and minimum value to be measured ($\mu - \mu_o$).

8.8.6 Chi-Squared Test

The goodness-of-fit (GOF) test using the chi-square distribution is used as a technique for modeling and analyzing the $y = f(x)$ relationship when both the y and the $x(s)$ are discrete. The test determines whether two discrete variables are associated, i.e., whether the distribution of observations for one variable differs depending on the category of the second variable. The data are usually displayed in table form, and the results are often called cross-tabulations. The statistical conclusions drawn from the *p*-values are the same as in the other analytical methods. We always attempt to characterize process output characteristics with continuous data because of their greater power.

There are often situations in which all process data are discrete, and this test is appropriate in those cases. As part of the retail sales process, the sales representatives are instructed to obtain certain buyer information. The information can be used to provide follow-up information and reminders to the buyer. The Black Belt (BB) project is focused on improving the compliance to this instruction. The BB pulls records from the five sales regions. While the processes are the same, sample size from the regions varies. It is desirable to predict whether the number of faults (an order missing the needed information) occurs at a similar rate across all five regions. Since both input (Region) and output (Fault/No-Fault) are discrete, the chi-squared test is appropriate. Since we know the total number of opportunities and the number of faults, we can easily calculate the expected number of non-faults. The expected number of non-faults is simply (# of Opps) − (Expected No. of Faults). The expected number of non-faults can also be calculated based upon the expected proportion of non-faults in the same manner that we previously calculated the expected number of faults.

$$SS = \left(f_o - f_e\right)^2 \big/ f_e \tag{8.4}$$

From the SS information, chi-squared is easily calculated:

$$\chi^2 = SS_{\text{faults}} + SS_{\text{non-faults}} \tag{8.5}$$

8.8.7 Analysis of Variance

Analysis of variance (ANOVA) is a statistical procedure for testing whether there is a significant difference among MEANS of multiple subsets of data. The one-way ANOVA is an extension of t-test.

- t-Test compares two means.
- One-way ANOVA compares multiple means.

8.8.8 p-Value

The p-value (P) tells you whether the various level means are significantly different from each other: If P is less than or equal to the significance (a) level chosen, one or more means are significantly different.

As with other inferential statistics tests, we also compare the confidence intervals for the various "levels" or subgroup samples. The two-line ANOVA test clearly shows the non-overlapping confidence intervals around the sample means: further confirmation of the difference between means. The significant p-value in the one-way ANOVA does not indicate that all the lines have different means. The correct interpretation is that there is a statistically significant difference between one (or more) of the lines and the others.

8.8.9 Tukey's Method

Tukey's method compares the means for each pair of factor levels using a family error rate (often called family-wise error rate) to control the rate of type I error. The family error rate is the probability of making one or more type I errors for the entire set of comparisons. Tukey's method adjusts the error rate for individual comparisons (individual error rate), based on the family error rate you choose.

8.8.10 Fisher's Least Significant Difference

Fisher's lease significant difference (LSD) method compares the means for each pair of factor levels using the individual error rate you select. Note that the family error rate, which is the probability of making one or more type I errors for the entire set of comparisons, will be higher than the error rate for each individual comparison.

Review Questions

Question 90: When testing equal variances, should I use Bartlett's test (or the F-test) or Levene's test?

Solution: Bartlett's test and the F-test are sensitive to the normality assumption. Levene's test is robust to the normality assumption. So, if your data are continuous and normally distributed, use Bartlett's test (or the F-test). If your data are continuous, but not necessarily normally distributed, use Levene's test.

Note: An F-test replaces Bartlett's test when there are only two groups.

Overall performance is calculated by using the standard deviation of the entire sample (no subgrouping). The potential capability is calculated by using the pooled standard deviation of the rational subgroups. To study more about ANOVA, refer the previous chapter.

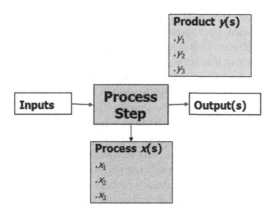

FIGURE 8.24 *x-y* Process map.

8.9 *x-y* Process Map

Deliverables of lean project is to identify Areas of Opportunity. Area of opportunities are listed as follows:

- Rework
- Time traps
- Redundant work
- Unnecessary work.

Identify real value-added, business value-added, and non-value-added activities. Processes are identified and taken on the quick success.

The *x-y* process map shows the inputs and output(s) for the major process steps. The *x-y* process map is the foundation for the further work of deliverables for lean project. The *x-y* process map is shown in Figure 8.24.

x-y process map is the input for FMEA. With the failure mode analysis, it is possible to determine variation throughout the time series. The next step will be analyzing data with respect to data type that is continuous or discrete. Using the information data, *x-y* relationship is generated. Potential *x(s)* is determined with the result obtained from the generated *x-y* relationship.

Let us consider an example for *x-y* process map for the tire used in the trick. The inside surface of the finished tire and the liner should have a uniform appearance, with the impression of the curing bladder over the entire surface. Irregular surface appears when the bladder impression is missing. Although it is not an indication of a performance problem with the tire, customers will not accept any tire with this condition.

Major steps for process inputs and outputs for each step are determined. It is essential to analyze the process. Use the observations and the knowledge of process experts, the front-line people doing the work. To get an accurate picture of the process as it actually operates today, the above process is essential. The *x-y* map can also be documented in spreadsheet form. In this format, it is easy to transfer the results of the *x-y* map to FMEA.

8.10 Failure Mode and Effect Analysis

FMEA is an indispensable tool in identification and prioritization of the *x(s)*. The FMEA helps to identify potential failure modes at each step of the process that may affect the critical to quality. FMEA provides vital information to reliability engineer, design engineer, and other tools to analyze the subsystem and system and other things that cause potential failure mode. For each failure mode, the downstream effects and upstream causes are identified. Each failure mode may have multiple potential causes, and each failure mode may have multiple effects. This is an important qualification. Then, the probability of failure mode that will occur and the effect it will create on rest of the system is analyzed. The new technique is known as FMECA (failure modes, effects, and criticality analysis). Criticality can be analyzed by rating it for each process at each step. FMEA is generally used to identify all possible failure modes, effects, and causes associated with a product or process. In a Six Sigma project, the application is narrowed to only those elements related to the project $y(s)$ (Quality Council of Indiana, Inc., 2007).

Map the process and identify the major steps (about 3–6) of the process. This step is already completed this in the x-y map. The next step is to identify the quality characteristics of each step. The quality characteristics measure how well the function is being performed. A function is an intended purpose of the product or process. These are the $y(s)$ of the x-y process map. In a manufacturing process, quality characteristics could include dimensions, weight, color, and surface finish. In a service or transactional process, examples could include response time and completed fields of an order.

Potential failure modes, or categories of failure, can then be identified by describing the way in which process steps fail to meet the function required. Failure modes fall into one of five possible failure categories:

- Complete failure
- Partial failure
- Intermittent failure
- Failure over time
- Over-performance of function.

Failure mode is a non-conformance at each specific step. Use the process steps from the x-y map as the process steps of the FMEA. Use the $y(s)$ from the x-y map to define the potential failure modes in the FMEA. There can—and generally will—be multiple failure modes for each element or activity (Figure 8.25).

Process Step	Potential Failure Modes	Effect of Failure	S E V	Cause of Failure	O C C	Current Controls	D E T	R P N
Build Bands	Lamination ridges							
	Liner damage							
	Inner contamination							
Build 1st Stage Carcass	Roller imprint							
	Torn liner							
Build 2nd Stage Carcass	Cold carcass							
	Carcass sags							
Prepare for Cure	Bladder not in full contact with liner							
	Holding pressure too low							

FIGURE 8.25 Potential failure mode.

Process Step	Potential Failure Modes	Effect of Failure	S E V	Cause of Failure	O C C	Current Controls	D E T	R P N
Build Bands	Lamination ridges	Forms void to trap air						
	Liner damage	Forms void to trap air						
	Inner contamination	Low component tack						
Build 1st Stage Carcass	Roller imprint	Small voids trap air						
	Torn liner	Slit traps air						
Build 2nd Stage Carcass	Cold carcass	Resists bladder forces						
	Carcass sags	Resists bladder forces						
Prepare for Cure	Bladder not in full contact with liner	Air between bladder and liner						
	Holding pressure too low	Bladder pulls away from liner						

FIGURE 8.26 Effects of failure.

The next step in the FMEA process is to identify potential downstream consequences when the failure mode occurs. This should be a team brainstorming activity. After consequences have been identified, they must be fit into the FMEA model as effects. It is assumed that failure mode effects always occur when the failure mode occurs. There may be multiple failure effects for each element or activity. An assessment of the severity of the effect of the potential failure mode is made. Severity applies to the specific effect only. For a given effect and given customer, the severity rating doesn't change (Figure 8.26).

8.11 Failure Mode and Effect Analysis Process Steps

Failure mode and effect analysis process steps are shown as follows:

- FMEA number: Unique numbering is provided for log controlling purpose. It is assigned by the reliability team for tracking purposes.
- Part number, part name, and other appropriate description are provided.
- Design responsibility is assigned to each department.
- Job will be assigned to a person for the preparation of failure mode and effect analysis.
- Provide time information to the FMEA and prepare any revision if it is required at any level.
- The part number or subsystem number that is being analyzed needs to be specified.
- Component function is studied thoroughly.
- Potential failure mode is analyzed.
- Potential effects of failure mode are also analyzed.
- Causes for the failure effects are studied.
- Appropriate control measures are sorted to avoid the failure from occurring (Quality Council of Indiana, Inc., 2007) (Figure 8.27).

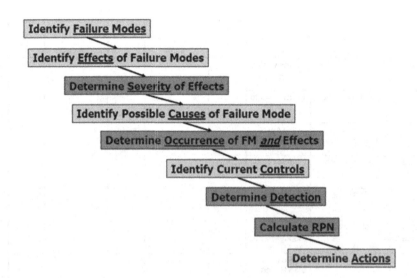

FIGURE 8.27   FMEA process steps.

8.12 Risk Assessment and RPN

Major step involved risk assessment and Risk Priority Number (RPN) are listed as follows:

- RPN can be determined by the following equation. This number is the product of indices of probability of failure that it occurs, severity of the effect of the failure, and measure of effectiveness of the current control:

$$\text{Risk Priority Number} = P \times S \times D \tag{8.6}$$

- Probability of failure of failure mode that will occur is denoted by the letter P. Values are assigned from 1 to 10. If the value is 1, there is no chance of failure to occur, and if the value is 10, there is high possibility of occurrence.
- Severity of the failure effects on the subsystem if the failure effects is denoted by the letter S.
- D denotes the effectiveness of the current control to determine the weakness. This index is numbered from 1 to 10. If the value is 1, then it denotes the highest possibility of getting affected by the failure. If the value is 10, then it denotes the product will make it to final production without detection.
- All decisions are based on the RPN.
- Separate column is provided to note the steps to be taken to reduce the risk (Quality Council of Indiana, Inc., 2007)

8.13 Types of FMEA

There are four types of FMEA:

- Design FMEA
- Process FMEA
- System FMEA
- Functional FMEA.

Process Step	Potential Failure Modes	Effect of Failure	S E V	Cause of Failure	O C C	Current Controls	D E T	R P N
Prepare for Cure	Bladder not in full contact with liner	Air between bladder and liner	8	Toe vents plugged	2	Operator inspection	4	64
		Air between bladder and liner	8	Bladder position off-center	5	Operator judgement	5	200
		Air between bladder and liner	8	Low shaping pressure	5	Pressure gauge	4	160
		Air between bladder and liner	8	Incomplete air purge	8	Operator judgement	8	512
		Air between bladder and liner	8	Holding air pressure too low	7	Pressure gauge	4	224
		Air between bladder and liner	8	Insufficient spray on bladder	4	Operator judgement	4	128
		Air between bladder and liner	8	Cold bladder	4	Operator judgement	5	160
	Holding pressure too low	Bladder pulls away from liner	7	Air line removed too soon	5	Operator practice	4	140
		Bladder pulls away from liner	7	Line pressure drops	2	Pressure gauge	5	70
		Bladder pulls away from liner	7	Air leaks from bladder assembly	4	Pressure gauge	5	140

FIGURE 8.28 Calculation risk priority number.

Design FMEA: FMEA is performed at the design level of the product/ services. The aim of this process is to determine how failure mode affects the system and what are the steps to reduce the failure effects. This process is done before the product is released before the manufacturing phase.

Process FMEA: This type of FMEA is done to the manufacturing and production process. This process is done during quality phase during the production. All possible failures during the manufacturing process are accounted and described in this type.

System FMEA: All the part level FMEA will be merged to form the whole system. As the system goes to the downstream, more failure modes are taken into account.

Functional FMEA: This focuses on the functional attribute of the system. This concentrates more on performance of each part rather than the specific part attributes of the part (Quality Council of Indiana, Inc., 2007).

Review Questions

Question 91: A Six Sigma improvement team may be required to analyze customer data in order to define a project or the results of an improvement. Which of the following tools could be employed?

A. Statistical tests
B. Line graphs
C. Matrix diagrams
D. Pareto analysis

(a) A B D
(b) A C D
(c) B C D
(d) A B C D

Answer: D

Question 92: A null hypothesis requires several assumptions, a basic one of which is:

(a) That variables are independent

(b) That the confidence interval is 2 standard deviations

(c) That the sample size is adequate

(d) That the variables are dependent

Answer: D

Question 93: A graphical display of the total percentage of results below a certain measurement value is called a:

(a) Cumulative distribution function

(b) Histogram

(c) Probability density function

(d) Expected value

Answer: A

Question 94: If the probability of a car starting on a cold morning is 0.6, and we have two such cars, what is the probability of at least one of the cars starting on a cold morning?

(a) 0.36

(b) 0.60

(c) 0.84

(d) 0.81

Answer: Need calculation

Question 95: Which table should be used to determine a confidence interval on the mean when the standard deviation is not known and the sample size is 10?

(a) F

(b) X squared

(c) t

(d) z

Answer: C

Question 96: A null hypothesis requires several assumptions, a basic one of which is:

(a) That variables are independent

(b) That the confidence interval is 2 standard deviations

(c) That the sample size is adequate

(d) That the variables are dependent

Answer: D

Question 97: One would normally describe recorded values reflecting length, volume, and time as:

I. Measurable

II. Discrete

III. Continuous

IV. Variable

    (a) I, II, III, and IV

    (b) II and IV only

    (c) I, III, and IV

    (d) I and III only

Answer: C

Solution: C. The values of length, volume, and time are always discrete and never continuous.

8.14 Multi-vari Studies, Process Capability, and Regression

Tools used in black belt are multi-vari studies, process capability, and regression.

8.14.1 Multi-vari Studies

Multi-vari charts are a visual way of representing variation through a series of charts. Multi-vari literally means many variables. It is graphical tool for investigating the effect of up to four variables on the output of interest. Multi-vari analysis can be used to study uncontrolled noise variation with the intent being to reduce or eliminate the variation due to noise. The content of the chart is evolved over time. Multi-vari study is statistical process control; it is used to track variables such as temperature or pressure. It uses discrete input data. It also concentrates on historical data.

A key assumption of testing with numerical data is that the data is the same across all points but often will vary across the sample. When any measurement is taken, for example, let us assume that we are measuring temperature of a cross section of the furnace, and the temperature of the cross section of the furnace will vary depending on where the measurement is taken. It also varies for different thicknesses of the part. In that case, a multi-vari chart is a very useful tool for analyzing the variable. Minitab is the tool which is used for representing the variation in data set. The graphical representation of the data generated in Minitab can quickly identify major sources of variation or noise in the data for further investigation. These charts are used to determine the consistency or stability of a process. It consists of series of vertical lines along a time frame. The length of each line determines the range of values in sample size. Multi-vari sampling plan procedures are listed as follows:

- Choose the process and characteristics that need to be analyzed.
- Choose appropriate sample size and time frequency.
- Build tabulation sheet to record values and time for each sample set.
- Plot multi-vari chart with measured value on the vertical scale and time along horizontal axis.
- Join the observed values with appropriate lines.
- Analyze the chart for variation with sample to sample, data set over the time.
- It may be necessary to do more studies on areas where there is maximum variation.
- It may be mandatory to repeat the multi-vari study to verify results (Quality Council of Indiana, Inc., 2007).

Data is analyzed to determine potential relationships between key process input variables, the $x(s)$, and key process output variables, $y(s)$. It should help identify main sources of variation. It should also be helpful to think sources of variation as positional, sequential, or temporal variables, or factors.

Three categories of variation are positional, sequential, and temporal. Understanding these categories of variation is very helpful when submitting the data for analysis and designing data collection.

Positional (location): In case of positional variation within a single unit or across a unit with many parts. In other words, variation can be represented within the piece.

Sequential (order): Variation is observed in sequential among consecutive pieces, batches, groups, etc. Variation is from step to step and is observed from piece to piece.

Temporal (time): Variation in temporal is over short time span against long time span. It is used to track time-related changes. Examples of temporal are shift-to-shift and week-to-week.

8.14.1.1 Advantages of Multi-vari chart

- In multi-vari charts, variation can be represented within the piece.
- Variation is also observed from piece to piece.

- It is used to track time-related changes.
- It helps in reducing variation by determining the areas of excessive variation. It also helps to identify areas which do not have excessive variation (Quality Council of Indiana, Inc., 2007).

8.14.1.2 Characteristics of Multi-vari Chart

The quality characteristics are measured at two extremes; measurements are drawn as the lowest and highest values over a time frame. Quality characteristics are represented by three attributes of interest that are given in three horizontal panels. These characteristics are

- Piece-to-piece variability
- Time-to-time variability
- Variability on a single piece.

Multi-vari chart can be used while analyzing furnace temperature, flow of river, and rolled steel thickness. Temperature rises when the measurement is close to the heat source in case of furnace temperature. Flow is slower when it is measured closer to the land. The actual thickness may vary across the sample. Variation is achieved within the piece where the part is tapered and thin in the middle; variation can occur over time and is repeated over time. Variation in the sample is shown by the line length. Variation from sample to sample is represented by the vertical lines (Figure 8.29).

To represent a multi-vari chart, a sample set is taken and plotted from the highest value to lowest value. Variation will be established by a vertical line. Thickness is measured at four points across the width as shown in Figure 8.30. Figures 8.31 and 8.32 illustrate excessive variability within plate and less variability.

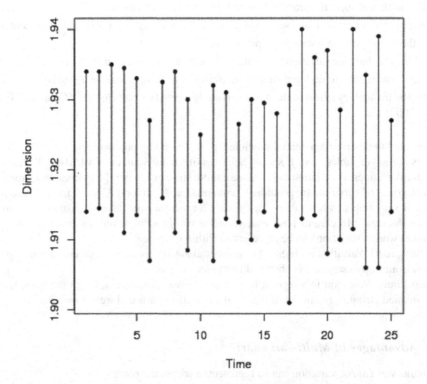

FIGURE 8.29   Multi-vari chart example (http://r-resources.massey.ac.nz/161325examples/examples66x.png).

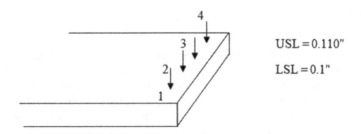

FIGURE 8.30 Multi-vari measurement of a plastic plate (Quality Council of Indiana, Inc., 2007.)

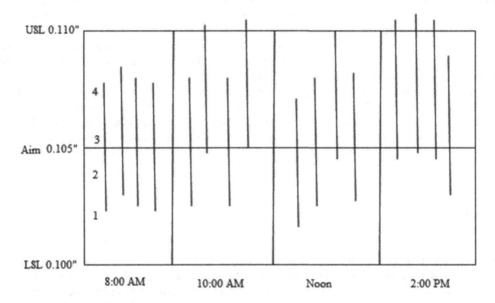

FIGURE 8.31 Excessive variability within piece (Quality Council of Indiana, Inc., 2007.)

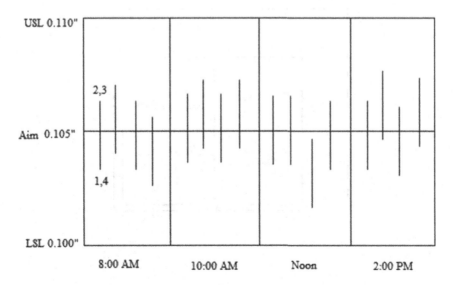

FIGURE 8.32 Less variability within piece (Quality Council of Indiana, Inc., 2007.)

8.15 Regression

After accounting for variation, it requires sorting through the many inputs $x(s)$ that could be driving the output response (s) of interest, $y(s)$. We need to accurately and efficiently identify the inputs that have the greatest effect on our outputs so that we can focus the business resources where we will get the greatest project benefit. Main aim of the analysis is to identify importance of x-y relationship. The two-by-two matrix presented here is a useful reference when determining the proper statistical tool to employ based upon the data types of a given project. Knowing the data types for the input and output under study, use the table to help select the applicable statistical tool. The goal in developing transfer functions is not simply to describe the data collected; rather, it is to develop a model that can be used to accurately predict future outcomes. Amidst all the statistical tools, it is easy to forget the bigger goal—we want to understand our processes so completely that we are able to control not only during the project but well into the future (Figure 8.33).

Regression analysis is probably the most widely used technique in modeling and data analysis. In the term "simple regression", the word "simple" refers to the fact that there is a single independent (x) variable used to predict the value of the output variable, y. This differentiates simple regression from "multiple regression", in which multiple input variables (conceivably many $x(s)$) are used to predict the value of y. The term "linear" simply means a transfer function that is composed of input variables that are only raised to the first power. (Recall that $x^1 = x$.) In the case of simple (a single x) linear regression, the function is a straight, one-dimensional line. The familiar convention for the equation of a straight line is

$$y = mx + b \tag{8.7}$$

where
    m is the slope.
    y is the intercept.

Simple regression is the technique to model and analyze relationship between a continuous response variable, y, and one continuous predictor variable, x. Simple linear regression produces a model of an output's behavior. Statistical significance of the modeled relationship between y and x is described quantitatively by the p-value. The value of y is expressed, as a linear function of the value of x, by the transfer function which is defined as

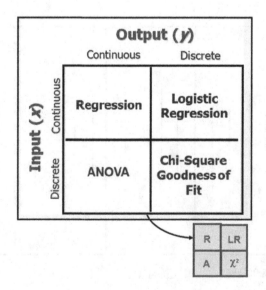

FIGURE 8.33 Statistical tools for analysis.

$$y = \beta_0 + \beta_1 x_1 + \varepsilon \qquad (8.8)$$

y is the predicted response or dependent variable.
x_1 is the predictor or independent variable.
β_0 and β_1 are the regression coefficients for the transfer function.
β_0 is the y intercept of regression line.
β_1 is the slope of the regression line.
ε is an error term.

Assume an analysis of a constant variable. Gather data that summarizes it according to the constant variable. An equation can be developed according to the function of the variable using simple regression. Note that both the input and output variables are continuous, indicating that we are able to apply regression for the analysis.

TABLE 8.3

Study Time and Performance

Student	Study Time (h)	Test Results (%)
1	60	67
2	40	61
3	50	73
4	65	80
5	35	60
6	40	55
7	50	62
8	30	50
9	45	61
10	55	70

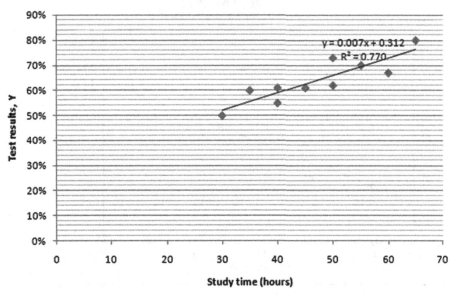

FIGURE 8.34 Plot for scatter.

Let us consider analysis of student individual study time and individual test performance. The table shows the data points for the study time and test performance. Data points in the table are plotted as a graph, which is known as a scatter plot. In this case, the plot consists of study time in horizontal scale or x axis and test results in the vertical scale or y axis. Observe that y increases as x increases. One technique for predicting equations relating x and y is to place a ruler on the data points and move it through them; if it passes through the majority of the points, it is considered a best-fit line. Judging from the "look" of the data, we suspect that a relationship exists. We could estimate the form of the relationship by drawing a visually "best-fit" straight line through the data points (Table 8.3 and Figure 8.34).

8.16 Fitted Line Plot

The fitted line plot figure will show the scatter plot, the best-fit line, and other useful information about the relationship between the two variables. In the case of a fitted line plot, we will examine options that provide a visualization of the predictive power of a regression. Using Minitab, a fitted line plot can be generated based upon the data that minimizes the distances between the points and the line. Notice that the output also provided the regression equation, as well as values for R-squared and R-squared (adjusted), but no p-value. In generating the fitted line plot or the graph of the best regression equation, it is the sum of the squared distances from each actual observation (the plotted points) to the fitted line that are minimized (Figure 8.35).

The p-value gives an indication of the significance of the coefficients. The R-square value is a measure of how well the model fits the data; it gives the "percent of total variance" that is "explained" by the model. The R-square (adjusted) "discounts" R-square when there is too much complexity in the model. It provides a better indication as to how well the regression will fit future data. A red line in the plot represents the confidence interval of the regression line. The red confidence interval lines represent the area where we are 95% confident that the actual regression line falls. Green line indicates the confidence interval for the prediction of an individual part. The green predictive interval represents the area where we are 95% confident that future values predicted by the regression will fall (Figure 8.36).

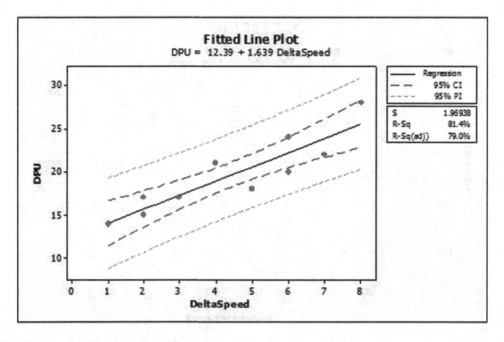

FIGURE 8.35 Fitted line plot.

```
Regression Analysis: DPU versus DeltaSpeed

The regression equation is
DPU = 12.4 + 1.64 DeltaSpeed

Predictor          Coef      SE Coef          T          P
Constant         12.389        1.370       9.04      0.000
DeltaSpeed       1.6389       0.2774       5.91      0.000

S = 1.969       R-Sq = 81.4%      R-Sq(adj) = 79.0%

Analysis of Variance
Source              DF            SS          MS          F          P
Regression           1        135.37      135.37      34.90      0.000
Residual Error       8         31.03        3.88
Total                9        166.40
```

FIGURE 8.36 Regression output.

8.17 Residuals

In fitting a line to observed data, the "residual" is the model error. Its magnitude is the vertical distance between the observed value and the predicted value (the fitted line). Residuals can be analyzed to provide information about the model, including non-normality of errors, non-random variation of errors, non-constant variability of errors, and non-linear relationships.

Normal Plot of Residuals: This type of residual normally forms a straight line.

Histogram of Residuals: It should appear roughly normal symmetric with one peak. Bars located away from the main group (outliers) may indicate unusual observations.

Chart of Residuals: Any out-of-control points should be investigated as indications of a non-random pattern in the data that may be the results of special cause variation.

Residuals vs. Fits: If points appear to form a curve, there may be evidence of non-linear relationships. If the spread (variability) of the data points increases or decreases with the fits, the data may have non-constant variance (Figure 8.37).

8.18 Multiple Regression

Multiple regression is a technique for modeling and analyzing the relationship among a continuous response variable, y, and more than one continuous input variable, $x(s)$. y is expressed, as a function of the $x(s)$, by the transfer function developed from the observed data:

$$y = \beta_0 + \beta_1 x_1 + \beta_2 x_2 + \cdots + \beta_k x_k + \varepsilon \tag{8.9}$$

where
y is the predicted response, or output, variable.
$x_1, x_2, \ldots, x_k$ are the predictor, or input, variables.
$\beta_0, \beta_1, \beta_2, \ldots, \beta_k$ are the regression coefficients (constants).
ε is the error term.

The statistical significance of the regression equation is again determined by the p-value. The topic of multiple regressions covers a range of techniques that can be used to investigate possible

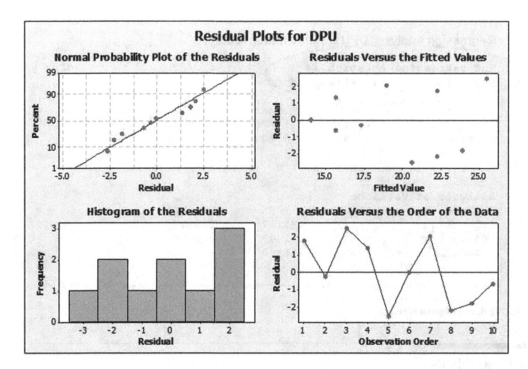

FIGURE 8.37   Interpreting residual.

relationships between a response variable and two or more potential $x(s)$. A p-value is computed for each input variable, x_i, to determine the statistical strength it contributes to predicting the value of the response, y. Only the significant factors are kept in the prediction equation—the trivial $x(s)$ are dropped from the model.

Best subsets regression is an iterative process that examines potential models with one predictor, then two, then three, and so on, through a model that includes all possible predictors. The best subsets regression identifies the best models (prediction equations) for various numbers of predictors. Only models with the highest R-squared values are retained in the analysis. Model selection is made based upon the Minitab output. A good model should have

- High R-squared
- High adjusted R-squared
- A C-p metric value that is approximately equal to the number of predictors in the specified model
- A low s (s is the standard deviation of the error term in the model).

Many potential $x(s)$ can be screened simultaneously. There is a danger when the $x(s)$ included are correlated with each other (called multi co-linearity). This risk is minimized with techniques such as best subsets regression and stepwise regression. Discrete variables, e.g., operator and method, can be sometimes be coded (1–2–3, 0–1, etc.) for use as logical, quasi-continuous variables. As always, correlation does not prove causation.

8.19 Simple Linear Regression Model

The simple linear regression model has a straight line that represents a set of n data points in a manner such that the sum of the squared residuals of the model is as small as possible. The slope of the fitted line

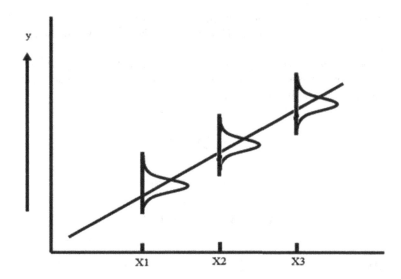

FIGURE 8.38 Simple linear regression model illustrating variation in *y* with respect to *x*.

between will be equal to correlation between y and x modified by the ratio of standard deviation of the given variable. The mathematical equation for the simple regression model is given as follows:

$$y = \beta_0 + \beta_1 x \tag{8.10}$$

where β_0 is the *y* intercept when $x = 0$, and β_1 represents the slope of the line (Quality Council of Indiana, Inc., 2007). The *x* axis does not tend to zero such that *y* intercept looks to be very high. The actual value of random error will be the difference between the observed value of *y* and the mean value of *y* with the specified value of *x*. The main assumption for the observation value of *y* changes in a random manner and has a normal probability distribution for the given *x* value (Figure 8.38).

A probabilistic model equation for the observed value is given as

$$y = (\text{Mean value of } y \text{ with respect to the } x \text{ value}) + \text{Random error} \tag{8.11}$$

$$y = \beta_0 + \beta_1 x + \varepsilon \tag{8.12}$$

y is the predicted response or dependent variable.
x_1 is the predictor or independent variable.
β_0 and β_1 are the regression coefficients for the transfer function.
β_0 is the *y* intercept of regression line.
β_1 is the slope of regression line.

8.20 The Method of Least Squares

The method of linear equation is used to approximate sets which have more equations than unknown variables. The statistical method of determining the best-fit straight line is, in many aspects, the best method if one fits a line by eye. The goal is to reduce the deviations of the points from the lines. It denotes the predicted value of *y* determined from the fitted line as ŷ.

$$\hat{y} = \beta_0 + \beta_1 x \tag{8.13}$$

where β_0 and β_1 represent the estimates of β_0 and β_1, respectively (Figure 8.39).

One should determine the meaning of best if we want to reduce the deviation of points in choosing the best-fitting line.

The principle of least square is nothing, but the best-fit criterion of goodness used to reduce the sum of squares of the deviation of the observed values of y from those predicted. A mathematical expression shown below reduces the sum of the squared errors:

$$\text{SSE} = \sum_{i=1}^{n} (y - \hat{y})^2 \tag{8.14}$$

Substituting the value of $\hat{y}$ in Eq. 14.8, we obtain an altered equation:

$$\text{SSE} = \sum_{i=1}^{n} \left[y - (\beta_0 + \beta_1 x) \right]^2 \tag{8.15}$$

The least squared estimators of β_0 and β_1 are estimated as

$$S_x^2 = \sum_{i=1}^{n} X_i^2 - \left\{ \left[\sum_{i=1}^{n} X_i^2 \right] \Big/ n \right\} \tag{8.16}$$

$$S_{xy} = \sum_{i=1}^{n} X_i \bullet Y_i - \left(\left\{ \left[\sum_{i=1}^{n} X_i \right] \bullet \left[\sum_{i=1}^{n} Y_i \right] \Big/ n \right\} \right) \tag{8.17}$$

$$\beta_1 = S_{xy} \big/ S_x^2 \tag{8.18}$$

$$-\beta_0 = y - \beta_1 X \tag{8.19}$$

Once β_0 and β_1 are computed, substitute the values into the equation of a line to obtain the least squares on regression line (Quality Council of Indiana, Inc., 2007).

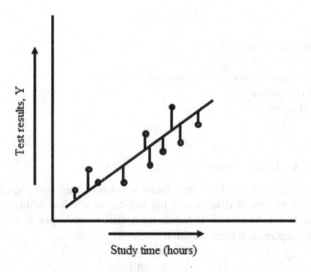

FIGURE 8.39 Method of least squares illustrating test results vs. study time.

Note:

- Things to be noted are to be careful of rounding errors. The calculation should have a minimum of six significant digits in estimating the sum of squares of deviations.
- Plot the data against the model to ensure accurate modeling, and do not project outside of regression line. If it does not provide a reasonable fit for the given data set, then there is a calculation error.
- Do not project outside the regression line.

8.21 Logistics Regression

Logistic regression is a technique for modeling and analyzing the $y = f(x)$ relationship when the y is attribute (usually binary, but multiple ordinal responses are also acceptable) and the $x(s)$ are continuous. Logistic regression relates single dependent variable to more independent variable. It is similar to that of regular linear regression since it has regression coefficients, residuals, and predicted value. In case of linear regression, it is assumed that response variable is continuous, whereas in case of logistic regression, response variable is continuous. Logistic regression is not used as often as ANOVA or regression, as the emphasis in Six Sigma is to find $y(s)$ that are continuous variable. Since the response is generally binary, a logistic transformation is performed to prevent the possibility of negative probabilities as outcomes. The statistical conclusions are drawn from logistic regression. *P*-values are no different than when using the other analytical methods. Ordinary least squares approach is used to determine the regression coefficient for linear regression, and maximum-likelihood estimation is used to determine the regression coefficient for logistic regression.

Logistic regression is used to provide information about analysis of the two values of interest, that is, good or bad, vote or not vote, pass or fail, enlist or not enlist, yes or no. Since a logistic regression model takes only the value of 0 and 1, it is also known as binary regression model. The general equation for logistic regression is given as

$$y = b_0 + b_1 x_1 + e \tag{8.20}$$

where $y_i = 0, 1$.

Transfer function before logistic transformation:

$$p = \alpha + \beta_1 x_1 + \cdots + \beta_k x_k \tag{8.21}$$

where p = the predicted probability of an outcome

The probability of the results can be computed in this certain category by the given mathematical formula:

$$p = 1/(1 + e^{-y}) = e^y/(1 + e^y) = 1/[1 + e^{-(b_0 + b_1 x_1)}] \tag{8.22}$$

This equation is similar to that of linear regression equation model, but the regression model uses a different equation to calculate b coefficient values. Since the right side of the transfer function could be less than 0 (or greater than 1) for certain values of $x_1, \ldots, x_k$, predicted probabilities of less than 0 or greater than 1 could be obtained, which is impossible. This is why the logistic transformation of p is used as the dependent variable:

$$\log(p) = \ln \frac{p}{1 - p} = \alpha + \beta_1 x_1 + \cdots + \beta_k x_k \tag{8.23}$$

It can also be expressed as

$$p = \left(e^{\alpha + \beta_1 x_1 + \cdots + \beta_x k_x}\right) / \left(1 + e^{\alpha + \beta_1 x_1 + \cdots + \beta_x k_x}\right) \tag{8.24}$$

Let us consider the example of the piping problem. In this case, the effect of temperature on leaks is analyzed. The predictor (x) or input is joint temperature, and it is a continuous variable. The output (y)

is joint leaks in this case. There are only two possible outcomes: "leaks" and "no leaks"; this accounts for 100% of all possible results. Data were collected from 24 launches prior to the challenger. The data in Figures 8.40 and 8.41 illustrates the analysis of whether the temperature is the predictor of leaks.

8.22 Process Capability Analysis

Process capability analysis provides us with the information of the natural process variation with respect to the customers' specifications. Previously, the setting of targets, specifications, and its measurements were studied. This section tells us where the current processes or their variations stand with respect to customers' requirements. A capable process is the one in which all natural variation fits within the customers' target range. The process variation is compared with the engineering or specification tolerances to check the suitability of the process. It is also important for the process to be stable before performing the analysis, and hence, it is always performed after the control charts. The process capability analysis has three basic steps (Quality Council of Indiana, Inc., 2007):

- Planning for collecting data
- Collecting data
- Plotting and analyzing results.

The process capability is carried out in order to reduce the variability of the process so that conformity occurs with the customers' targets. When the natural process limits are compared with engineering or specifications range, the following actions are performed:

- Do nothing.
- Change the specifications.

JointTemp	Incidents	JointStatus	StatusCode
52	3	Leak	1
56	1	Leak	1
58	1	Leak	1
63	1	Leak	1
70	1	Leak	1
70	1	Leak	1
75	2	Leak	1
66	0	OK	0
67	0	OK	0
67	0	OK	0
67	0	OK	0
68	0	OK	0
69	0	OK	0
70	0	OK	0
70	0	OK	0
72	0	OK	0
73	0	OK	0
75	0	OK	0
76	0	OK	0
76	0	OK	0
78	0	OK	0
79	0	OK	0
80	0	OK	0
81	0	OK	0

FIGURE 8.40 Illustration of logistic regression example.

```
Binary Logistic Regression: StatusCode versus JointTemp

Link Function:  Logit
Response Information
Variable  Value         Count
StatusCo  1                 7   (Event)
          0                17
          Total           24

Logistic Regression Table
                                                Odds          95% CI
Predictor        Coef    SE Coef      z     P   Ratio    Lower    Upper
Constant       15.048      7.278   2.07 0.039
JointTem      -0.2325     0.1066  -2.18 0.029    0.79     0.64     0.98

Log-Likelihood = -10.144
Test that all slopes are zero: G = 8.687, DF = 1, P-Value = 0.003

Goodness-of-Fit Tests
Method           Chi-Square    DF       P
Pearson              11.238    15   0.736
Deviance             11.969    15   0.681
Hosmer-Lemeshow       6.898     8   0.548
```

FIGURE 8.41   Results of logistic regression.

- Center the processes.
- Reduce variability.
- Accept the losses.

The identification of characteristics and its specifications based on customers' perspective has already been discussed, and the data collection for the same was discussed in green belt section. The important task is to develop sampling plans. The knowledge of sampling and its probability distributions is widely required here. The process capability indices are usually calculated based on probability distributions and generally classified as normal and non-normal distributions.

Process capability is carried out for three categories: (1) the process that is currently running and is in control. The data from control chart can be utilized for analysis. (2) Analysis of new processes. Pilot run can used to evaluate the capability analysis. (3) Process capabilities carried out to improve the process. The analysis can be performed by using the design of experiments (DOE). The DOE gives optimum values which provide minimum variations.

8.23 Process Capability for Normal Distribution

If the process is said to be stable over time, with only common causes of variation, then it follows normal distribution (AIAG, 1995). This text provides us with information for process capability analysis with normal distribution data. When process capability with only common causes of variation is plotted, a bell-shaped curve is obtained, corresponding to normal distribution. The area outside the specification is given by the Z value:

$$Z_{\text{lower}} = \frac{\bar{X} - \text{LSL}}{S} \tag{8.25}$$

$$Z_{\text{upper}} = \frac{\text{USL} - \bar{X}}{S} \tag{8.26}$$

The Z transformation formula is

$$Z = \frac{X - \mu}{\sigma} \tag{8.27}$$

where
  X: Data value
  μ: Mean
  σ: Standard deviation.

The Z value, hence, gives the number of standard deviations away from the mean and standard normal table that can be used to find the area under the curve, which gives the probability of occurrences. This book, as mentioned earlier, assumes that the reader is well aware of the concepts in probability.

8.24 Process Capability Indices

The process capability is determined by means of sigma and indices. The capability index can be defined as C_P

$$C_P = \frac{\text{USL} - \text{LSL}}{6\sigma_R} \tag{8.28}$$

$C_p > 1.33$; the process is capable.
$C_p = 1.00–1.33$; the process is capable with tight control.
$C_p < $ The process is incapable.

The capability ratio is defined as

$$C_R = \frac{6\sigma_R}{(\text{USL} - \text{LSL})} \tag{8.29}$$

$C_R < 0.75$; the process is capable.
$C_R = 0.75–1.00$; the process is capable with tight control.
$C_R > $ the process is incapable.

The ratio between the smallest answer is

$$C_{pk} = \frac{\text{USL} - \bar{X}}{3\sigma_R} \text{ (or) } \frac{\bar{X} - \text{LSL}}{3\sigma_R} \tag{8.30}$$

C_{pm} index is based on Taguchi index, which concentrates on centering the process toward its target, given as

$$C_{pm} = \frac{\text{USL} - \text{LSL}}{6\sqrt{(\mu - T)^2 + \sigma^2}} \tag{8.31}$$

where
  USL: Upper specification limit
  LSL: Lower specification limit
  T: Target value
  μ: Process mean
  σ: Process standard deviation.

8.25 Process Performance

The process performance is estimated with the help of sigma estimate. The sigma estimate is given by

$$\sigma_i = \frac{\sum (X - \bar{X})^2}{(n-1)} \tag{8.32}$$

σ_i is a measure of total data sigma.
  The performance index is defined as (Figure 8.42)

$$P_p = \frac{\text{USL} - \text{LSL}}{6\sigma_i} \tag{8.33}$$

The performance ratio is given by

$$P_R = \frac{6\sigma_i}{(\text{USL} - \text{LSL})} \tag{8.34}$$

The ratio giving the smallest answer between is (Figure 8.43)

$$P_{pk} = \frac{\text{USL} - \bar{X}}{3\sigma_i} \text{ or } \frac{\bar{X} - \text{LSL}}{3\sigma_i} \tag{8.35}$$

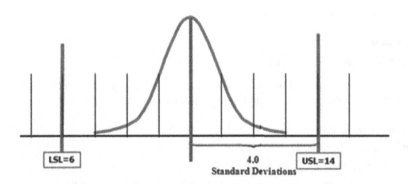

FIGURE 8.42 Performance index.

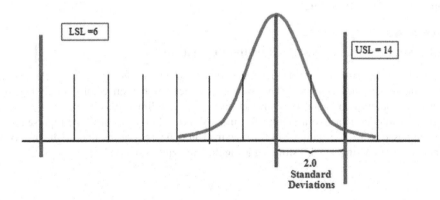

FIGURE 8.43 Process performance index.

8.26 Process Performance Metrics

The process performance indices are calculated based on the measurements of the systems. The common process performance metrics are discussed here.

The Six Sigma metrics are given by

Total Opportunities, TO = TOP = $U \times O$

Defects per unit, DPU = D/U also = $-\ln (Y)$

Defects per normalized unit = $-\ln (Y_{norm})$

Defects per opportunity, DPO = DPU/O = D/UO

Defects per million opp., DPMO = DPO $\times 10^6$

where Defects = D, Units = U, Opportunities for a defect = O, yield = Y

Yield relationships are given by

- Probability of a unit containing X flaws: $P(x) = \dfrac{e^{-DPU}DPU^X}{X!}$

- First pass yield, $Y = FPY = e^{-DPU}$

- Defects per unit, DPU $= -\ln(Y)$

- Rolled throughput yield, $Y_n = RTY = \prod_{i=1}^{n} Y_i$

- Normalized yield number of steps, $Y_{norm} = \sqrt[n]{RTY}$

- Total defects per unit, TDPU $= -\ln(Y_n)$

8.27 Rolled Throughput Yield

Rolled throughput yield is defined as the cumulative calculation of yield or defects through multiple process steps. The following steps are followed for determining the Rolled Through per Yield (RTY):

- Calculate the yield for each step and the resulting RTY.
- The RTY for a process will be the baseline metric.
- Revisit the project scope.
- Significant differences in individual yields can suggest improvement opportunities.

RTY = yield of step 1*yield of step 2*yield of step 3

Example: RTY = 0.90*0.86*0.92*0.65

8.28 Chi-Squared Analysis of Contingency Tables

Coefficient of contingency is an objective methodology used for the analysis of chi-squared test. It measures the dependency level between any two attributes. Higher values of C imply higher degree of relationship. The optimal values of C are determined by the dimensions of the matrix of attributes derived from arranging data into a tabular forming (Merkin, 2001). An attribute representing a row/column is supposed to have the number of traits equivalent to degrees of freedom of the matrix of data.

The coefficient of contingency is estimated using the following equation:

$$C = \sqrt{\chi^2 / (N + \chi^2)}$$

Review Questions

Question 98: Advantages of Gantt charts include:
   A. The charts are easy to understand
   B. The details of activities are easily displayed
   C. Each bar represents a single activity
   D. Estimates of optimistic, most likely, and pessimistic times are included
   (a) A, B, and D
   (b) A and C
   (c) A, C, and D
   (d) A and B

Answer: B

Solution: B. Other advantages are that it is simple to change the chart, the chart can be constructed with minimal data, and program task progress vs. date is shown.

Question 99: Which of the following distributions does NOT require the use of the natural logarithmic base for probability calculations?
   (a) Weibull
   (b) Normal
   (c) Binomial
   (d) Poisson

Answer: C

Solution: C. Binomial distribution is one of the several distributions used to model discrete data. It is used to model situations having only two possible outcomes, usually labeled as success or failure.

Question 100: Let X be any random variable with mean u and standard deviation s. Take a random sample of size n. As n increases and as a result of the central limit theorem,
   (a) The distribution of the sum Sn = X1 + X2 + $\cdots$ + Xn approaches a normal distribution with mean u and standard deviation $s/\sqrt{n}$.
   (b) The distribution of Sn = X1 + X2 + $\cdots$ + Xn approaches a normal distribution with mean u and standard deviation $s/\sqrt{n}$.
   (c) The distribution of the population mean approaches a normal distribution with mean u and standard deviation of $s/\sqrt{n}$.
   (d) The distribution of X approaches a normal distribution with mean u and standard deviation $s/\sqrt{N}$.

Answer: C

Solution: C. The significance of the central limit theorem on control charts is that the distribution of sample means approaches a normal distribution.

Question 101: A number resulting from the manipulation of some raw data according to certain specified procedures is called:
   (a) A constant
   (b) A population
   (c) A statistic
   (d) A parameter

Answer: C

Question 102: Variation in the shape parameter for the Weibull distribution can, in turn, create all of the following distribution shapes EXCEPT:

(a) Normal

(b) Rayleigh

(c) Exponential

(d) Hypergeometric

Solution: D. The shape factor is what gives the Weibull distribution its flexibility. The variance of the distribution decreases as the value of the shape parameter increases. Shape factor = 1 is identical to exponential distribution, shape factor = 2 is identical to Rayleigh distribution, and shape factor between 3 and 4 approximates the normal distribution.

Question 103: One would normally describe recorded values reflecting length, volume, and time as

I. Measurable

II. Discrete

III. Continuous

IV. Variable

    (a) I, II, III, and IV

    (b) II and IV only

    (c) I, III, and IV

    (d) I and III only

Question 104: Sampling plans are routinely selected based on their:

I. Validity

II. Known risks

III. Applicability

    (a) I, II, and III

    (b) II and III only

    (c) I only

    (d) I and II only

Answer: A

Question 105: What is the most widespread use of the F distribution?

(a) To test for equality of variances from two normal populations

(b) To make decisions and construct confidence intervals by summing the square of normal random variables

(c) To model discrete data when the population size is small compared to the sample size

(d) To compensate for error in the estimated standard deviation for small sample size

Answer: A

Question 106: Identify the three types of check sheets commonly used to record counted, measured, and locational data:

I. Measles charts

II. Attribute lists

III. Recording check sheets

IV. Checklists

V. Variable lists

    (a) I, III, and IV only

    (b) III, IV, and V only

(c) II, III, and IV only

(d) II, III, and V only

Answer: A

Question 107: In performing an analysis of variance for a single factor experiment, a fundamental assumption which is made is that the factor:

(a) Means are equal

(b) Means are unequal

(c) Variances are equal

(d) Variances are unequal

Answer: C

Question 108: One-way analysis of variance is most similar in its objectives to:

(a) A test for equality of two population means

(b) A test for equality of two sample proportions

(c) A test of a population mean

(d) A chi-squared test for independence

Answer: A

Question 109: Three trainees were given the same Lot of 50 pieces and asked to classify them as defective or non-defective, with the following results:

Defective 17 30 25

Non-defective 33 20 25

In determining whether or not there is a difference in the ability of the three trainees to properly classify the parts, which of the following statements is (are) true?

I. The chi-square calculated value is 6.9

II. Using a level of significance of .050, the critical value of the chi-square is 5.99

III. Since the obtained chi-square is greater than 5.99, we reject the null hypothesis

(a) I, II, and III

(b) I only

(c) I and II only

(d) II only

Answer: A

Question 110: The fundamental equation of analysis of variance may express the idea that:

(a) The total standard deviation is equal to the sum of the standard deviation for the treatment effect plus the standard deviation of the random error

(b) A basic population model can be constructed to represent the behavior of the experimentation

(c) The total sum of squares of deviations from the grand mean is equal to the sum of squares of deviations among treatment means and the grand mean plus the sum of squares of deviation within treatments

(d) The degrees of freedom are not additive

Answer: C. With ANOVA, the variations in response measurement are partitioned into components that reflect the effects of one or more independent variables. The variability of a set of measurements is proportional to the sum of squares of deviations used to calculate the variance.

Question 112: In non-parametric statistics:

I. No assumptions are made concerning the distribution from which the samples are taken

II. The parameters of the distribution do not relate to the parameters of the sample

III. The sample and the distribution must have no parameters in common

(a) II only

(b) III only

(c) II and III only

(d) I only

Answer: D. The non-parametric techniques of hypothesis testing are applicable for many quality engineering problems and projects. The non-parametric tests are often called "distribution-free" since they make no assumption regarding the population distribution. Non-parametric tests may be applied ranking tests in which data is not specific in any continuous sense, but are simply ranks.

Question 113: If an investigator were interested in performing a hypothesis test of the equality of population medians, which of the following would NOT be an option?

(a) Mann–Whitney test

(b) Levene's test

(c) Kruskal–Wallis test

(d) Mood's median test

Answer: B. Levene's test is used to test null hypothesis in which multiple population variances (corresponding to multiple samples) are equal. It determines whether a set of k samples have equal variances. Equal variances across samples are called homogeneity of variances.

Question 114: When evaluating data for GOF to suspected distributions, which of the following statements are true?

  I. Most distributions have the same degree of freedom

 II. The chi-squared test can be used for hypothesis testing

III. In all cases, the data is divided into cells

(a) I and II only

(b) I, II, and III only

(c) II and III only

(d) I and III only

Answer: C. GOF tests are part of a class of procedures that are structured in cell. The degree of freedom for each distribution is different.

Question 115: In a single factor analysis of variance, the assumption of homogeneity of variances applies to:

(a) The variances within the treatment groups

(b) The variances of the treatment groups

(c) The total variance

(d) All of the above

Answer: B. The pooled standard deviation of within treatments variation can be considered the process capability sigma of individual measurements. It is the variation within measurements which would still remain if the difference among treatment means were eliminated.

Question 116: If an investigator were interested in performing a hypothesis test of the equality of population medians, which of the following would NOT be an option?

(a) Mann–Whitney test

(b) Levene's test

(c) Kruskal–Wallis test

(d) Mood's median test

Answer: B. The range method is a simple way to quantify the combined repeatability and reproducibility of a measurement system. It computes the total measurement system variability and allows the total measurement system variability to be separated into repeatability, reproducibility, and part variation.

REFERENCES

AIAG, et al. *Statistical Process Control (SPC): Reference Manual.* Southfield, MI: Automotive Industry Action Group, 1995. Print.

Ishikawa, K. *Guide to Quality Control.* Tokyo: Asian Productivity Organization 1982.

Merkin, B. Eleven ways to look at chi-squared coefficient for contingency tables. *The American Statistician* (2001): 55, 111–120. Print.

Quality Council of Indiana, Inc. *Certified Six Sigma Black Belt Primer.* West Terre Haute, IN: Quality Council of Indiana, Inc., 2007. Print.

9

How Total Quality Management and Lean Six Sigma Drove Need for Supply Chain Integration

Erick C. Jones

Let all things be done decently and in order.

Corinthians I

9.1 Introduction

Most economists would agree that for a country such as the United States to remain a strong economic power, its manufacturing sectors must remain competitive. Often, domestic economic conditions, such as the national trade deficit, are linked to the countries' manufacturing competitiveness. Given that trade is driven by customers' willingness to pay for products and services and many studies suggest that customers would pay more for a better quality of product, quality is an important factor for driving trade in the United States. In this chapter, we hope to provide an overview of defining quality. Section one of this book will follow the "Quality Trail" as seen below. Figure 9.1 shows that everything that has been established in quality management (QM) will lead to Lean Six Sigma (LSS).

9.1.1 Quality

How Quality Is Defined
The Merriam-Webster dictionary defines quality in several ways including (1) peculiar and essential character, (2) a degree of excellence, (3) superiority in kind, (4) a distinguishing attribute, and (5) an acquired skill. These definitions range from describing products to describing people. Our focus will be mainly on describing products and services. We will define quality in this text by taking several approaches that are consistent with historical engineering themes. Though there may be other approaches that can be applied to defining quality, Garvin's (1984) approach is generally accepted in engineering. The five approaches to quality include global or transcendent, product-based, user-based, manufacturing-based, and value-based approaches.

Global Approach
The global approach to quality is a very generic view of quality. It is often difficult for companies to analyze and/or measure subjectively. It is generally described as "good enough" or it "gets the job done"

FIGURE 9.1 The quality trail.

when described by customers. Often, this type of quality is further defined by companies as good enough not to get sued. In other words, if no one is defining this as bad quality, then it must be good quality.

Product-Based Approach
The product-based approach to quality is related to defining a product's attributes. Attributes or features that customers find more desirable would define the product as having higher quality. Often companies determine the higher quality attribute by defining what they are willing to pay more money for. For example, a car with leather seats and a high-end radio system would be considered higher quality than a car with cloth seats and no radio.

User-Based Approach
The user-based approach to quality is related to users defining the features and attributes they consider important. One of the more important quality gurus, Joseph Juran (1998), defines quality as "fitness for use" as defined by the user. In other words, the users and their expectations of the product determine quality. This is further clarified that different users may use the product in different ways, and a high-quality product must possess multiple elements that "fit" different uses effectively.

Manufacturing-Based Approach
The manufacturing-based approach to quality is related to meeting engineering specifications in order to meet quality standards. This is generally the most comfortable definition for engineers in defining quality in that it is specific, measurable, and objective. Unfortunately, meeting engineering specifications does not always ensure higher sales from finicky customers. This approach is generally attributed to Crosby's "conformance to requirements" concept (1979). The concepts describe a set of requirements that must be met in a manner required by specifications or standards. Generally, if these specifications are not met, then the product is considered non-compliant and defective. Every distinct non-compliant attribute is considered a defect.

Value-Based Approach
The value-based approach to quality is related to the market driving quality. It builds on the fact that consumers pay higher prices for better quality products. The general idea is that the market value determines the quality of the product. There are attributes that are associated with the value-based approach. These attributes are generally associated with Garvin (1984) and include (1) performance, (2) features, (3) reliability, (4) conformance, (5) durability, (6) serviceability, (7) aesthetics, and (8) perceived quality.

Performance
The performance attribute refers to product's primary operating characteristics. It describes the ability for a product to meet its intended purpose, for example, the ability for a car to operate on a freeway by accelerating into and out of traffic as opposed to the car radio's ability to play. The primary purpose of the car is its performance on the road.

Features
The feature attribute describes the "nice to haves" or the "bells and whistles" of a product. An example would be extra food and drinks for first class flight passengers, hand-free phone syncing inside a car, and automatic shut off motion sensors on big screen televisions. Often, these features determine mean higher quality to consumers and drive the sell for many products.

Reliability
The reliability attribute describes the probability of a product's failing within a specified period of time. Oftentimes, this attribute is associated with a product's name brand. For example, American cars were perceived to have the propensity not to perform consistently over their useful designed lives and were considered lower quality than Japanese cars. Reliability in manufacturing literature is generally measured with the following terms: MTFF (mean time to first failure) and MTBF (mean time between failures).

Conformance
The conformance attribute is described as the degree to which a product's design and operating characteristics meet pre-established standards.

It involves

1. Internal elements (inside the factory): conformance is measured commonly by the number of defects (proportion of all units that fail to meet specifications and so require rework or repair)
2. External elements (outside the factory): conformance is measured commonly by the number of repairs under warranty.

Durability

The durability attribute is described as the measure of product life, defined in two dimensions:

1. Technically: durability is the amount of use one gets from a product before it physically deteriorates and the repair is not possible (i.e., after so many hours of use, the filament of a light bulb burns up and the bulb must be replaced).
2. Economically: durability is the amount of use one gets from a product before it breaks down, and the repair is possible. The product's life is determined by repair costs, personal valuations of time and inconveniences, losses due to downtime, and other economic variables.

Serviceability

The serviceability attribute is described as the speed, courtesy, and competence of the repair service. Objective and subjective views play a role in defining *serviceability*.

Aesthetics

The aesthetic attribute is described as how a product looks, feels, sounds, tastes, or smells (appearance and impression): *quality* is viewed as the combination of these attributes that best match the consumer preferences.

Perceived Quality

The perceived quality attribute is described as how consumers feel as they use the product. The concepts of durability and reliability are related to how consumers feel about a product. It is implied that a product that fails frequently (low durability) is likely to be scrapped earlier than one that is more reliable. Consumers, if financially able to make a choice, would choose the product with higher durability as a means to choose a product with higher quality.

This myriad of attributes also further defines the differences among the five traditional approaches to *quality*, previously explained. Each of the approaches focuses implicitly on different attributes and dimensions of quality: for example, the product-based approach encompasses the concepts on performance, features, and durability; the user-based approach describes aesthetics and perceived quality; and the most commonly focused upon in the concept for Six Sigma is the manufacturing-based approach, which includes the ideas of conformance and reliability. The efforts toward improvements in these measures are normally viewed as translating directly into quality gains (objective measures of quality). They are less likely to reflect individual preferences.

9.2 Perspectives on Quality

What Do Organizational Departments or Functions Think about Quality?

Functional Perspectives on Quality

Organizational quality may mean different things to different organizational functions. Each function has lensed the specific tasks for their function and then translates how quality impacts those tasks. Typical functions that are impacted by quality include Engineering, Operations, Executive Management, Marketing, Financial, and Human Resources. Each function will have a differing view on quality and its effect on their functional goals in the organization.

Engineering Perspective on Quality

A critical perspective, and one that our book focuses upon generally, is the engineering perspective. Engineers generally seek to apply scientific and mathematical problem-solving skills and models to business and industrial problems. They generally focus on seeking solutions related to product and process design and/or redesign. Product design engineering involves activities associated with developing a product from concept development to final design and implementation. This also includes product redesign that involves continuously improving current products. In product design and redesign, quality is an important component, and with better designs, engineers seek to produce high-quality products. Process design is generally inferred in product redesign and new product design. The idea of integrating quality into the process is the general theme in most quality theories. The idea is that if you have processes that support high-quality components and sub-components, then products will have high quality.

Operations Perspective on Quality

The operations planning and management view of quality is rooted in the engineering approach. Like engineers, operations managers, planners, and schedulers are tasked with optimizing product and process design. In contrast to traditional engineering, operations researchers and some specialized industrial engineers focus on decision modeling rather than focusing on the technical (traditional engineering) aspects of these activities, and they concentrate on the management, specifically, best decisions and policies to execute these activities. Operations management has developed into an integrative field, combining concepts from engineering, operations research, organizational theory, organizational behavior, and strategic management.

Systems Perspective

Operations management, in conjunction with industrial and systems engineers, utilizes a systems view to address quality problems that support modern QM thinking. The systems view involves the understanding that product quality is the result of the interactions of several variables such as machines, labor, procedures, planning, and management.

Executive Management Perspective on Quality

Executive management is tasked with managing the investments that support organizational strategic objectives. We define strategy as the planning processes used by an organization to achieve a set of long-term goals. The strategic objectives must be understandable and executable in terms of goals, policies, and plans to achieve quality improvement. In some organizations, it is more traditional for quality-related strategic planning to be treated separately from firm-level strategic planning. It is more common for organizations to integrate strategic planning and include QM into the firm's business practices.

The ultimate goal of strategic quality planning is to aid an organization to achieve sustainable competitive advantage, market share, and returns for its investors. Research shows that quality is still one of the major concerns for CEOs of the larger organizations.

Marketing Perspective on Quality

Marketing efforts are often focused on managing the public's perception of quality. This may include focusing on customer relationship management, including attention to delivering value to the customer. The tools for influencing customer perceptions of quality are primarily price and advertising. The marketing perspective primarily focuses on the end customer's perspective of the product. Customer service surveys are important mediums in assessing quality.

Financial Perspective on Quality

One of the most commonly asked questions about QM is "will it pay us financial benefits?" The financial perspective relies more on quantified, measurable, result-oriented thinking. W. Edwards Deming made the first theoretical attempt to link quality improvements to financial results through the "Deming Value Chain". Later, Juran mentioned that management would always ask the question "will it make us money?" This has led to the concept in quality described as the law of diminishing marginal returns.

According to this law, there is a point at which investments in quality improvement will become uneconomical. According to the quadratic economic quality level model, higher levels of quality will result in higher expenditures. This view is at odds with the ethic of continual improvement. Some suggest that this is the main distinction between traditional quality program concepts and LSS initiatives. The focus of deriving the firm return or the intrinsic value that will be received by performing with quality as opposed to a firm seeking to do continual improvement on an ongoing basis has been a point of distinction.

Human Resources Perspective on Quality

Understanding the human resources perspective on quality is difficult and necessary because of the fact that implementing quality without the commitment of employees brings disastrous results. This perspective of quality generally encompasses several concepts, which include but are not limited to Employee Empowerment, Organizational Design, Job Analysis, and 360-Degree Evaluation.

Employee Empowerment—Empowering employees involves moving decision making to the lowest level in the organization.

Organizational Design—Human resources managers are involved in many aspects of organizational design, such as the design of reward systems, pay systems, organizational structure, compensation, training mechanisms, and employee grievance arbitration.

Job Analysis—Involves collecting detailed information about a particular job.

360-Degree Evaluation—A performance measurement system in which an employee's peers, supervisors, and subordinates are involved in evaluating the worker's performance.

9.3 TQM and Quality Overview

There have been many different terms that refer to an integrative philosophy of management that seeks continuously improving the quality of the firm's products and internal processes which include TQM, QM, and corporate quality to name a few (Ahire, 1997). The most prominent of these names, the author suggests, is TQM.

TQM also promotes the idea that the organization and all of its employees support the idea of continuous improvement, and this integrative approach translates into high-quality products. The idea that the quality of products and processes is the responsibility of everyone in the organization including management, the workforce, and suppliers is prescribed. Cua et al. (2001) identified nine common TQM practices:

1. Cross-functional product design
2. Process management
3. Supplier QM
4. Customer involvement
5. Information and feedback
6. Committed leadership
7. Strategic planning
8. Cross-functional training
9. Employee involvement.

The TQM concepts and practices were developed by U.S. quality gurus. An interesting fact about these gurus or consultants was that they initially had few believers in these concepts in the United States. On the other hand, Japan was struggling with perception of low-quality goods originating from their country as whole. After Japanese companies had great success with these principles, many of these gurus became well known. In fact, the Japanese highest honor for a company is named after one of the U.S. gurus. The premier annual prize for manufacturing excellence in Japan is the Deming Award. The U.S. gurus who were recognized for their ideas in Japan were mainly W. Edwards Deming, Joseph M. Juran, and Armand V. Feigenbaum. There are others, but these are the ones who made the main contributions that also extend into LSS concepts. Other contributors to LSS methodologies were Philip B. Crosby and Kaoru Ishikawa.

9.3.1 How Does an Organization Teach, Train, and Attain Quality?

The Implementation of Quality

There are generally two ways to implement quality organizationally. One approach is to take the attitude that quality is integrated into all firm functions, policies, and procedures. Another approach is to implement quality on an "as needed" function. The "as needed" approach seeks to add quality as a means to improve profits through a highly specialized team. Generally, companies have performed both approaches. The companies maintain acceptable quality throughout their operations to have acceptable products in the market. Later, they use quality teams, lean initiatives, and Six Sigma teams to improve quality when necessary to make products more competitive in the marketplace.

The Integrated Approach

The integrated approach to quality is generally associated with a concept called the three spheres of quality. It is implied that the conceptual areas of quality are integrated throughout a firm's policies, procedures, and products.

Three Spheres of Quality

The three spheres of quality originated by Juran refer to quality control (QC), quality assurance (QA), and QM. Often, activities in one sphere could also be completed in another sphere and are subject to the interpretation of how the activities support the firms' needs.

Quality Control (QC)—QC focuses upon providing analysis, identifying relationships and causes of variation that create lower quality. QC generally refers to the following activities:

- Monitoring process capability and stability
- Measuring process performance
- Reducing process variability
- Optimizing processes to nominal measures
- Performing acceptance sampling
- Developing and maintaining control charts.

Quality Assurance (QA)—QA focuses on testing and researching activities to guarantee that products meet specification and perform as advertised. QA activities are related to the following:

- Failure mode and effects analysis
- Concurrent engineering
- Experimental design
- Process improvements
- Design team formation and management
- Off-line experimentation
- Reliability/durability product testing.

Quality Management (QM)—QM describes the management processes that overarch and tie together the completions, control, and transitioning of quality activities. QM activities include the following:

- Planning for quality improvement
- Creating a quality organizational culture
- Providing leadership and support
- Providing training and retraining
- Designing an organizational system that reinforces quality ideals
- Providing employee recognition
- Facilitating organizational communication.

9.4 What If Quality Is Too Expensive to Justify?

"As Needed" Implementation of Quality

The "as needed" implementation of quality throughout the firm includes the concept that is based on what does the customer perceive as quality: if the customer does not want to pay for it, then excessive quality is not necessary. This concept drives the thought that activities that do not support the customer's view of quality are non-value activities or wasted efforts in the firm. Minimizing these activities, or making processes "lean", is supported by this implementation approach and also using specialized teams such as Six Sigma teams to identify a process that the customer and/or financial motivations have suggested need to be improved and yield higher quality to improve the firm's bottom line.

Also, this implementation is influenced by international markets and customers who may have differing preferences between cultures and countries. This drives how countries influence quality.

Limitation of Quality Measures

Quality is difficult to measure and often organizationally difficult to justify in traditional accounting terms such as return on investment (ROI). The timing between quality initiatives and the cost savings creates difficulty in justifying quality investments. Generally hidden costs, which usually are not accounted for, are the main drivers for quality investment. Understanding the cost of quality (COQ) is one of the main reasons that modern LSS techniques have replaced other quality initiatives. Six Sigma focuses upon the COQ.

9.4.1 How Can the COQ Be Justified?

Cost of Quality

After World War II, many quality departments emerged globally because of the fact that several countries' infrastructures were destroyed in the war. In order to make competitive products for export, these companies had to change the poor-quality image of their goods. Quality initiatives in various organizations across the world began, such as Deming helping Japanese companies. Many companies discovered quality was the root cause of their economic performance, sometimes in a negative way. For instance, IBM instilled a zero-defect policy, and their economic performance did not improve. Juran addressed the concept of Quality Costs in the first *Quality Control Handbook* (1951). It described that the losses due to defects were equal to the costs of QC.

Traditional COQ

Conformance costs are costs that are incurred to ensure manufactured products or delivered services conform to specifications. Conformance costs are made up of the following:

1. Prevention costs, activities related to prevention of defects
2. Appraisal costs, activities related to measuring and evaluating the product or service.
3. Nonconformance costs are the prices paid when they do not conform to a customer's requirement. Nonconformance costs are made of internal failure costs, failures incurred prior to shipment to customer, and external failure costs, costs discovered after shipment or service delivery.
   a. Internal failure costs can be remedied by using rework, identifying amount of scrap produced, reinspection, and retesting, to name a few.
   b. External failure costs can be remedied by investigating customer complaints, inspecting warranties, and repairs.

Caveats are the direct tradeoffs between conformance and nonconformance expenditures that are economically difficult to measure. Some of the main issues with the hypothetical COQ concepts include the following:

- COQ reports do not provide specific actions.

- COQ calculations do not capture all of the costs, and multiple tasks may count the same savings multiple times leading to corporate accounting inaccuracies.
- Accounting conventions such as capital spending and rules for defining period and product cost render COQ of little use for evaluating a quality program.

9.4.2 Who Started Quality and What Ideas Did They Contribute?

Quality Philosophers, Gurus, and Contributors

William E. Deming

Deming is often considered the father of modern quality. Deming, a U.S. quality consultant who had limited success with American businesses, introduced quality principles to more accepting Japanese manufacturers on a large-scale post World War II. Many of Deming's principles and ideals are the foundation of quality initiatives today. He utilized some of the concepts identified with Shewart such as control charts into his philosophies in his research. Other notable ideas include Keiretsu partnerships with suppliers as precursors to vendor managed inventory and partnerships of today. He also introduced concepts of common and special causes of manufacturing defects. He described the idea of seeking profound knowledge to make breakthrough improvements in quality and manufacturing efficiency. Moreover, he had organization understand and appreciated what we describe as "system thinking", theories on process variation, and organizational knowledge management and information retention. The idea of understanding the psychology of the employee was a major contribution. This concept is realized in what his overarching philosophies described as the 14 points are. Deming's 14 points are based on three principles: constancy of purpose, continual improvement, cooperation between factions. Deming believed in 14 points of quality:

1. Create constancy of purpose.
2. Adopt the new philosophy.
3. Cease inspection, require evidence.
4. Improve the quality of supplies.
5. Continuously improve production.
6. Train and educate all employees.
7. Supervisors must help people.
8. Drive out fear.
9. Eliminate boundaries.
10. Eliminate use of slogans.
11. Eliminate numerical standards.
12. Let people be proud of their work.
13. Encourage self-improvement.
14. Commit to ever-improving quality.

Another contribution that directly relates to Six Sigma techniques was that Deming was the first guru to theoretically attempt to link quality improvements to financial results. It was described as the "Deming Value Chain".

Joseph M. Juran

Juran followed Deming in Japan and was mainly known for using the Quality Trilogy (planning, control, and improvement). He also originated the three spheres of quality: QC, QA, and QM. Juran (1998) defined quality's "fitness for use" as defined by the user. In other words, the users and the expectations that they have on the product determines quality. This is further clarified that different users may use the product in different ways, and a high-quality product must possess multiple elements that "fit" different uses effectively.

He also contributed to the LSS ideas of financially quantifying quality improvements. To support this idea, he introduced ideas such as decreasing chronic waste, limiting rework, and minimizing the COQ. He is known for mentioning that management will always ask the question "will it make us money?" This has led to the concept in quality described as the law of diminishing marginal returns extended the idea of the COQ.

Philip B. Crosby

Crosby focused on improving preventing approaches which would reduce quality appraisal tradeoff. He is also widely recognized for his creation of the management maturity grid. This approach is generally attributed to **Crosby's** "conformance to requirements" concept (1979). The concept describes a set of requirements that must be met in a manner required by specifications or standards. Generally, if these specifications are not met, then the product is considered non-compliant and defective.

Armand V. Feigenbaum

Feigenbaum believes that an organization should be excellence driven rather than defect driven, as well as adjusting the view of the organization to match that of the customer. Feigenbaum in essence says Excellence-driven rather a defect-driven, a view defined by the customer.

Garvin's (1984) approach is generally accepted in engineering. The five approaches to quality include global or transcendent, product-based, user-based, manufacturing-based, and value-based approaches.

Ishikawa

Ishikawa perfected the cause and effect diagram. He also believed the customer defines the quality definition the organization believes in. He was also a pioneer in quality circles and teamwork to improve quality.

Taguchi

Taguchi created the loss function and focused on improving quality in design with the reduction of noise in the forms of system design, parameter design, and tolerance design.

Japanese Contributions to Quality

Japan has many contributions to the art of QM, most notably, lean production. Two views emerge that pertain to lean. The first view of lean is a philosophical view of waste reduction. This view asserts that anything in the process that does not add value for the customer should be eliminated. The second view of lean is a systems view, stating the Just In Time (JIT) is a group of techniques or systems focused on optimizing quality processes. Other contributions include Visibility, In-Process Inspection, 5S, and emphasizing teamwork and quality circles.

Japanese quality is the quality belief and methods the Japanese used post World War II to present day. They are as follows:

Fitness to Standard—Ingrained in management to have quality over profit.

PDCA Style—Plan-Do-Check-Act (Shewart Charts).

Fitness to Use—Understand customer needs.

Fitness to Cost—High quality, low cost.

Fitness to Latent Requirement—Discover customer needs before they do (Kano Diagram).

Hoshin-Kanri—Vertical deployment of TQM strategy.

9.4.3 How Is Quality Rewarded and Enforced Globally?

Quality Awards

Quality Awards and Standards are driven by how the country was improved through its business enterprises and how their businesses are perceived globally. The awards are usually named after famous individuals who contributed to business successes of companies in the country.

The Deming Prize

The Deming Prize for quality was established in 1951 by the Japanese Union of Scientists and Engineers (JUSE). There are three categories for awards: Application Prize for Division, Application Prize for Small Business, and the Quality Control Award for Factory. Judging is based on several criteria: policy, organization, and operations; collecting and using information; analysis; planning for the future; education and training; QA, quality effects, standardization, and control. Contrary to the Malcolm Baldrige award, there is no limit on the number of companies that can receive the award in a given year. The Deming Prize is much more focused on processes than the Baldrige award.

Malcolm Baldrige National Quality Award (MBNQA)

The Malcolm Baldrige National Quality Award (MBNQA) was created be the federal government to award companies and organizations that held the highest standard for quality success. The award is open to small and large firms in manufacturing and service sectors. It is, however, not open to public-sector and nonprofit entities. Each year, two winners are selected for each category, limiting the number of winners per year to 6. The award is based off of seven criteria: Senior Executive Leadership, Information and Analysis, Strategic Quality Planning, Human Resource Development and Management, Management Process of Control, Quality and Operational Results, and Customer Focus and Satisfaction. The criteria focus on business results. Companies must show outstanding results in the listed areas to win. The means of obtaining the results do not follow any given format and are adaptive to each hopeful organization (Figure 9.2).

The Baldrige selection process is thorough and exact to ensure the most deserving and qualified firm is selected. The first step is eligibility determination. The completed application is sent to the National Institute of Standards and Technology (NIST). The application is reviewed by examiners and then by judges, who will determine whether the application will be given a consensus score by the examiners. Firms that are granted Baldrige site visits sometimes refer to themselves as "Baldrige Qualified". The site visit consists of a team of four to six examiners visiting a company over a period not to exceed one week. One of the most important outcomes is examiner feedback. For more information on the Malcolm Baldrige award, visit *www.NIST.gov*.

European Quality Award

Much like the MBNQA, Europe issues the European Quality Award every year to the most accomplished applicant. There is also a second-level award given to all of the organizations that met the award criteria.

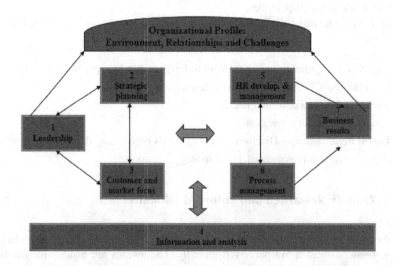

FIGURE 9.2 Baldrige award framework.

9.4.4 Quality Standards

ISO 9000

ISO (International Organization of Standardization) 9000 is a quality initiative that is widely used across the world. There are 12 member countries that work together to eliminate separate standards. ISO 9000 is currently used by 91 countries, and that number grows yearly. Additionally, there are three levels of audit robustness: ISO 9001, 9002, and 9003. ISO 9000 is the basic set of requirements for a Total Quality Management System (TQMS).

The current ISO standard is ISO 9000:2008, 2008 being the year of the latest update in the standardization. The focus of ISO 9000:2000 is for companies to document their quality systems in a series of manuals to facilitate trade through supplier conformance. There are two standards that follow ISO 9000 which are ISO 9001 and ISO 9004. ISO 9001 is used for internal implementation and contractual purposes. ISO 9004 is used for standardizing continuous improvement and enhancing overall performance. ISO is based on several underlying QM principles: customer focus, leadership, involvement of people, process approach, systems approach to management, continual improvement, factual approach to decision making, and mutually beneficial supplier relationship. Registering for ISO 9000:2008 is thorough and the steps are listed below.

1. Inquiry—Client contacts registrars to investigate the terms for registration and makes a selection.
2. Contract with registrar—Registration steps are determined, and a price is negotiated. A pre-assessment or gap analysis may be done.
3. Phase 1 audit—Registrar performs an onsite audit of the documented quality system against the applicable standard.
4. Certification audit—Every element of the ISO 9000 standard is audited several times during the registration process. During each 3-year period, 100% of the organization is audited.
5. Process audits (optional)—The client may choose business processes for auditing to the applicable standard, allowing the client to learn and experience the registrar's auditing methods.
6. Final certification audit—Once the client's documented quality system has met the applicable standard, the registrar will conduct an audit to determine the system's effective implementation.
7. Rolling certification (surveillance) audits—The registrar returns on either 6 month or annual cycle. Sometimes referred to as surveillance audits.

ISO 14000 and 14001

ISO 14000 is a series of standards that provide guidelines and compliance standards for environmental compliance. ISO 14001 is the compliance standard for ISO 14000, which focuses on environmental management systems. Both of the standards use the same approach as ISO 9000:2008 in several of the focus areas but direct the standardization to environmental compliance.

To find out more about the International Organization of Standardization, visit www.iso.org.

9.5 Integrating TQM with LSS Techniques

Many organizations emphasize quality as a means to stay competitive in the marketplace. Over the long run, they view having a reputation of high quality as representing future market share for new customers and maintaining market share for existing customers over their lifetime. Further improving quality can provide long-term financial savings, such as scrap and rework reduction. We associate these quality savings as long-term savings that are difficult to quantity. One method to quantify quality is the initiative known as Six Sigma. The label "Six Sigma" originates from statistical terminology. Wherein, Sigma represents standard deviation. The probability of falling within plus or minus Six Sigma on a normal Curve is 0.9999966, which is more commonly represented as a defect rate of 3.4 parts per million

(Zhang et al., 2012; qtd. in Jayakumar and Jones, 2004). This level of quality is seen as the goal in most Six Sigma initiatives.

LSS is a methodology that allows organizations to "maximize shareholder value by the fastest rate of improvement in customer satisfaction, cost, quality, process, speed, and invested capital". It is a combination of well-known waste elimination and process improvement techniques of lean manufacturing and Six Sigma (Zhang et al., 2012). LSS is a well-structured, theory-based methodology to improve performances, develop effective leadership, customer satisfaction, and bottom-line results (Jones and Garza, 2010; Zhang et al., 2012). Together, lean manufacturing and Six Sigma become more powerful and eliminate the cons of each approach (Zhang et al., 2012). There are several approaches that can be utilized by LSS such as DMAIC, DMADV, or IDOV. The Define Measure, Analyze, Improve, and Control (DMAIC) methodology utilized by Six Sigma is employed to reduce the resources wasted within existing processes. To design a new product to be Six Sigma quality, the Design for Six Sigma (DFSS) approach is needed; this process operates on either the Define, Measure, Analyze, Design, and Verify (DMADV) or IDOV (Identify, Design, Optimize, and Validate) methodology (Jones, Riley and Battieste, 2010).

9.5.1 Will LSS Really Work?

As various QA methods are being developed and discarded, TQM through Six Sigma is becoming popular. The goal of TQM and Six Sigma is to identify the poor quality immediately during the production process, rather than spending time to inspect the finished product. The quality of the manufacturing process determines the quality of a finished product. In the supply chain, it is not always possible to control the manufacturing process for incoming materials, especially for outside suppliers. In this instance, quality can only be measured by the percentage of defective goods received from the suppliers. In order to more effectively manage the supply chain, companies must choose suppliers that will produce quality materials without a substantial price tag.

Sigma stands for the Greek symbol σ that designates a standard deviation in statistics. Six refers to the number of standard deviations from a mean the specifications should be. Six Sigma began at Motorola in 1982 as an effort to reduce costs and improve quality. It now involves planning, organization, training, human resources planning, and pay-for-knowledge. It requires both organizational and individual cooperation to achieve a goal.

A process that is so well understood and controlled that six standard deviations will fit between the average output and the specific limit. Main purposes of using Six Sigma process are listed below:

- To deal with a world of declining product prices
- To compete successfully with the best companies in the world
- To establish standard language and approaches across functions and across businesses
- To develop the next generation of leaders
- To establish standard language and approaches across functions and across businesses
- To develop the next generation of leaders.

Honeywell invites key customers to participate in their black belt and other education programs. GE provides on-site service to assist customers in solving their problems. GE customers feel the difference of implementing the Six Sigma. They have more than 3,000 Six Sigma projects underway in the airline industry which will achieve $400 million in savings for the customers. This service to the customers will improve the long-term relationships.

9.5.2 How Can I Integrate LSS into the Operations throughout My Supply Chain?

Operations phase is expected to begin once the LSS methodologies are implemented, i.e., the change in processes, network, and outlook of the organization has been accepted. The following steps could be followed to integrate LSS into the operations (Devane, 2004):

1. Executives must accept their roles and responsibilities and be able to set priorities.
2. Leaders must consider newly established expectations while evaluating performance. Those who ignore these new values must be discarded from the functional team.
3. Periodic reviews of efforts toward improvement and sustainability in the new framework with accurate data representing financial impact must be recorded.
4. Active management must support the project lead by the new perspective of LSS with proper training and feedback sessions.
5. Gain in cash flows need not be excessively emphasized as the net result of improvement. Encouragement through awards of quality and recognition is best for creating motivation in employees.
6. All goals must tally with the organization's overall mission and strategic plan for steering into the future successfully.
7. Cross-functional team exchanges are encouraged while keeping boundaries of each team intact. This is considered to be the job of the manager.
8. The organizational human resource structure must be flexible enough to incorporate such transformations.
9. The new methods must be publicized by the management who must be supportive of the change to encourage other employees to accept them.
10. Financial contribution must always be sought after.

9.6 Voice of the Customer

Voice of the customers (VOC) can be classified as the following topics:

- Customer identification
- Customer feedback
- Customer requirements.

Customer Identification:
The concept of Six Sigma was evolved for the customers. In an organization, everything starts and ends with customers. The customers' expectations and needs are set as quality. The customers expect performance, reliability, value for their money, and on time delivery (Harry and Schroeder, 2000). The customers are not necessarily the ones who ultimately buy the product, but LSS concepts evolved in such a way that the operator in the next station is the customer. The primary customer of the process will or should have the highest impact on the process (Pande, Neuman, and Cavanagh, 2000). The define phase concentrates on defining the primary customers who make most of the revenues for the organization. Every business has many potential customers, and the customers have their own business criteria. The organization considers cost, quality, features, and availability factors for weighing the potential customers. The cost, quality, features and availability factors (CQFA) value grid helps the organization succeed in one way or the other. To define the customers and to analyze customer data is very much required, and obtaining wrong customer data can cause a flaw (Pande, Neuman, and Cavanagh, 2000). Hence, customer data is vital. To have proper customer data, customer surveys are required without pitfalls, so the organization or the company can produce and design product for the right market, i.e., the right customers. Hence in any market, the customers can constitute

- Current, happy customers
- Current, unhappy customers
- Lost customers
- Competitor's customers
- Prospective customers.

Any organization must want to work in any of the above-mentioned customers to improve their market, which is nothing but customer retention and customer loyalty which is discussed in detail later in the chapter. In order to obtain the right customer data, the following methods are to be followed (Eckes, 2001):

- Surveys
- Focus groups
- Interviews
- Complaint systems
- Market research
- Shopper programs.

The traditional methods of obtaining customer data are as follows:

- Targeted and multi-level surveys
- Targeted and multi-level interviews
- Customer scorecards
- Data warehousing
- Customer audits
- Supplier audits
- Quality function deployment (QFD).

As mentioned earlier, various belts are certified to follow and implement Six Sigma methodologies. The challenge lies in getting as many valuable data as possible. Hence, in belt certifications, the apt tools to use for defining customers are taught and discussed later in the chapter. Also, the certified belt users help in defining and distinguishing the internal and external customers who are important to that particular project in an organization. This helps the sponsors or the executive management to understand the basic customers better and work toward effective deliverables for the customers.

Internal customers:
Internal customers are those in the company who is affected by the product or service as it is being generated. The internal customers are often forgotten in the process of concentrating on the process to satisfy the external customers. The concept of LSS is to involve every employee and make him/her responsible for the process. This affects employee satisfaction and involvement on a positive scale which on the other hand affects the customer satisfaction. For employee satisfaction, sound communication is important which can be improved by (Lowenstein, 1995)

- Company newsletters
- Story boards
- Team meetings
- Staff meetings.

To involve employees in a better and effective way, training and education by black belts are very important. The black belts and master black belts are vested with a crucial responsibility of selecting right people for the Six Sigma methodology. The process is called stakeholder analysis. When Six Sigma projects are initiated, there might be resistance from the people involved for the proposed change. It is obvious for the resistance to arise. No matter how brilliant the idea and how obvious the benefits, any effort to change something will trigger resistance. People have many different reasons to resist change, often quite legitimate. Resistance may take many different forms, depending on the perspective, position, and personality of the person. Resistance to change is one of the most frequent reasons why projects ultimately fail. Hence, sponsors and black belts are left with no option but to accept the resistance.

The success lies in using this resistance as an opportunity to improve the proposed methodology more effectively. The stakeholder analysis is performed by the following:

- Identify key stakeholders of the project
- Identify current level of support/resistance
- Define needed level of support
- In case of gaps, develop strategy how to move each stakeholder to the needed level of support.

The first and foremost step is to identify the key stakeholders of the projects. The question "who are the key stake holders?" is very crucial and can possibly be answered by the following:

- Owners of the process
- Anyone contributing to the process
- Anyone affected by the process
- Those who benefit from process output
- All who see themselves as stakeholders.

The next step is assessing the commitment of the stakeholders for the proposed project. If the stakeholders have a hidden agenda, it is important to resolve it before the commencement of the project (Figures 9.3–9.5).

The stakeholder analysis can be refined by performing two-dimensional stakeholder analyses. The refinement is done by adding the power/influence dimension. This gives the black belts a map showing where people stand regarding the project and helps in focusing on the efforts for the project. Some people may be opposed to the change but have little influence on the success/failure of your project. The goal is to move everyone with success/failure influence toward positive or least neutral. The success/failure influence of those who remain stubbornly opposed must be minimized. The two-dimensional stakeholder analyses are illustrated in Figures 9.6 and 9.7.

External Customers:
External customers are not part of the organization but are impacted by it. External customers play a crucial role as they make most of the money. The external customers can be end users, intermediate customers, and impacted parties. End users are the customers who buy the product for own utility. The intermediate customers are those who buy the product and then resell. Retailers, distributors, and wholesalers are all some of the entities of intermediate customers. Impacted parties are those who did not actually buy the product but are impacted by it. The define phase concentrates mostly on identifying the external customers, and it is more complex. In the following sections, the identification customers

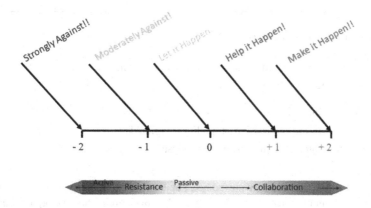

FIGURE 9.3 Stakeholder commitment.

Key Stakeholder	What is Valued by the Key Stakeholder	Commitment X (present level) / O (required level)					Recommended Actions
		-2	-1	0	+1	+2	
Executive						X⊙	
TTL		X──────────→⊙					
BTM		X───────→⊙					
Production Director				X→⊙			
Purchasing Mgr				⊙	X		
Finance Mgr			X→⊙				

X   Current Stakeholder position

⊙   Where the Stakeholder needs to be

FIGURE 9.4   Stakeholder commitment.

TBM-Uptime - Stakeholder Analysis							
Key Stakeholder	What is valued by the Key Stakeholder	Commitment (X) present level / (0) required level					Recommended Actions
		-2	-1	0	1	2	
Plant Manager	He gives strong support, he is also the sponsor of the project					X 0	
Production Manager	He will give support, because he will get benefit, but he may be influenced by the BT Managers			X ──→ 0			He will be involved during the next meetings.
QTEC Manager	He will give support, because he will get benefit in view of waste, but he one of his Technology Mgrs is involved in the project as Black/Green Belt					X 0	
Production Control Manager	His support is required if trials are required (later in the project). If we can improve the uptime he will get benefit from the project		X ──────→ 0				"Some evening discussions"
BTM Truck	If we improve the situation he will get benefit. But he may loose the possibility to hide some of his own problems (DANGEROUS)		X ────────────→ 0				Involve him before "starting" of the project. Small meeting before project launch. Always try to get informations about his feeling (during walk-over to parking etc.).

FIGURE 9.5   Stakeholder analysis—example.

and data analysis are discussed based on the belt certifications. The external customers in general can be identified by the following questions:

- Are the customers interested in lowest possible price?
- Are the customers interested in highest quality imaginable?
- Are the customers interested in sparing no expense?

Customer service:

Customer service is an important entity nowadays. The best way to identify and retain customers is by providing the best customer service. The following can be considered when the organization is trying to improve its customer service:

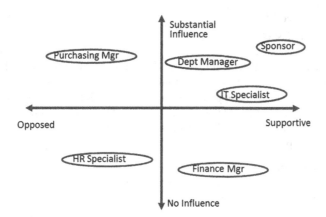

FIGURE 9.6 Two-dimensional analyses.

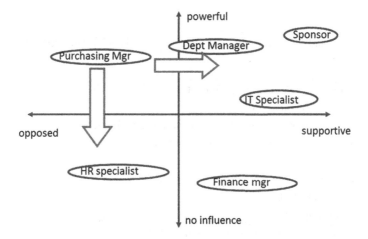

FIGURE 9.7 Two-dimensional analyses with movement.

- Listen to customer
- Define service strategy
- Set performance standards
- Select and train employees
- Recognize and reward accomplishments.

The above-stated points are very vital because of about 70% of the customers who are not willing to buy the product; it is not because of the quality of the product but due to service quality. The information from non-customers is also important because there will be a better feedback about the product in the negative scale which can be used as an opportunity to improve the product.

Customer retention and loyalty:
Most of the organizations concentrate on acquiring new customer base, but the cost of retaining a current customer is only one-fourth of cost of acquiring a new customer. It has been found that the current customer is five times worth than a new customer. The life cycle of customers can be defined in five stages:

- Acquisition—High cost
- Retention—Cost ¼ of acquisition
- Attrition—Enthusiasm fades as dissatisfaction increases

- Defection—Loss of customer
- Reacquisition—Highest cost.

The company must make efficient steps in retaining the customers. The customers buy happiness from not just the products and services. The happy customers are known as "apostles", who spread goodwill about the product. The effects of unhappy customers are more adverse, and they are coined the term "terrorists" and spread negative message about the product. The customer loyalty is measured not on bulk purchase but on repeated purchase. The customer retention grows loyal customers. The customers must now be seen as loyal partners.

Customer metrics selection:
Metrics are usually developed in the measure phase, but metrics in the define phase are established measures of customers. The primary metrics are

- Suppliers
- Internal process
- Customers.

The basic metrics are quality, cycle time, cost, value, and labor. The nine dimensions of quality are (Garvin, 1988) as follows:

- Performance: Primary features of the product
- Features: Secondary features added to the product
- Conformance: Obtaining a product that meets fit, form, and function
- Reliability: The dynamic quality of a product over time
- Durability: Useful life
- Service: Ease of repair
- Response: Human interface
- Aesthetics: Product appearance
- Reputation: Based on past performance (Figure 9.8).

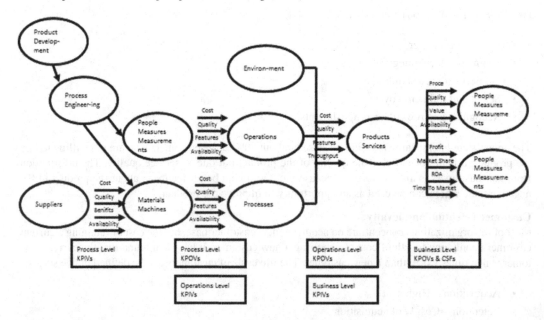

FIGURE 9.8 Process performance metrics.

Customer data collection:
As mentioned earlier, feedback data from the customer is important for analysis. When collecting data, it is important to know the various levels in the organization which get affected. The levels can broadly be classified as follows:

- Business level
- Process level
- Operations level.

The customers and their impacts are provided in Table 9.1.

Customer surveys:
Better understanding of customer satisfaction is done through customer surveys. The customer survey sample sizes and frequency will have significant cost implications. The customer survey should be within the available resources, and the need for change is the environment. The most often used tool for customer surveys is L-type matrix. The matrix uses numbers 1–10, corresponding to very dissatisfied to very satisfied. The surveys can be developed in questionnaire form with 25–30 questions (Figure 9.9).

Customer data analysis:
The data collected through surveys and feedback is used for analyzing the customers' changing attitudes over a period of time. This helps an organization to constantly meet the customer requirements without losing the goodwill of the customers. The tools utilized are described below.

Line graph:
The line graph shows the discrete or continuous features of the product over a period of time. The charts help in finding the changes and visually determines whether the products are same, worse, or better. A discrete chart is illustrated in Figure 9.10.

TABLE 9.1

Customer Data Collection

	Business Level	**Operational Level**	**Process Level**
Customers	• Shareholders • Top management	• Whoever purchased the product (External) • Whoever manages the product (Internal)	• Employees "next" in the process • Any employee affected
Interests	Financial data • Stock price • Market share • Earnings • ROI	• Work-in-process (WIP) • Sigma level • Throughput • Yield • Operational effectiveness (External)	• Key Process Variables (KPVs) • Job satisfaction • Advancement fairness • Pay • Training
Time frame	• Quarterly • Annually	• Daily or weekly (Internal)	• Hours (production rates)

	Customer Satisfaction									
	Very Dissatisfied					Very Satisfied				
Task	1	2	3	4	5	6	7	8	9	10
On Schedule										
Good Product										
Friendly										
Prompt										

FIGURE 9.9 L-type matrix.

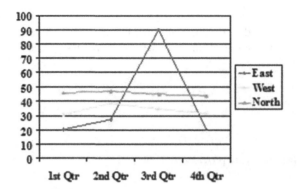

FIGURE 9.10   Line chart.

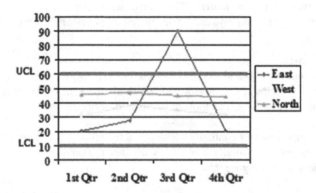

FIGURE 9.11   Control chart.

Customer	Defect Type								Totals
	A	B	C	D	E	F	G	H	
1		12	1	12	12	1	3		42
2	5			9	12				26
3	3	5		6	13			2	29
4	1	2	3	5	8			3	22
5	1			7	9	1	1	5	24
6	2	5	6	9	1			1	24
Totals	13	24	10	48	55	2	4	11	167

FIGURE 9.12   Matrix diagram.

Control charts:
Control charts are used in order to determine the variation of the product's feature. The calculation of control limits provides an advantage over line charts. An attribute chart is illustrated in Figure 9.11.

Matrix diagrams:
A variety of matrix diagrams can be used for examination of customer defects. The data from matrix diagram can be used for project selection. The matrix diagram is illustrated in Figure 9.12.

Voice of customers:
Good understanding of the needs of the customer is critical to the survival of most companies. VOC actually enables the organization to

- Make decisions on products and services
- Identify product features and specifications
- Focus on improvement plans
- Develop baseline metrics on customer satisfaction
- Identify customer satisfaction drivers.

Understanding and listening to the VOC are very important for any company. There are various tools to perform this, and they are discussed in the later sections according to the belt certifications.

Methods of hearing the VOC:
Passive Techniques:

- Existing data (customer complaints, phone logs, sales reps' reports)
- Advantages (low cost, historical comparison, data available)
- Disadvantages (depend on customer to communicate)

Active Techniques:

- Require going to the customer (interviews, direct observations, surveys)
- Advantages (deeper understanding, target audiences)
- Disadvantages (data not available, resources required)

Process to understand VOC:

- Plan
    - Understand the purpose of VOC process and its alignment with business objectives
    - Identify customers to be studied and prepare questions
- Gather Data
    - Gather VOC data
- Understand VOC
    - Translate customer language into business requirements and metrics
- Deploy
    - Take action based upon the VOC.

Critical to Quality:
This tool actually focuses on the key metrics of customer satisfaction. A critical to quality (CTQ) tree will translate the initial customer requirements to numerical or quantified requirements for the product or service. The creation of the CTQ tree involves the following steps:

- Identify the customer
- Identify the customer's need
- Identify the set of basic requirements of the customer
- Progress further with more levels as needed
- Validate the requirements with the customer.

The tools for analyzing the VOC differ based on belt certifications and are discussed accordingly in the later sections of the chapter.

Project charter and teams:
The define step involves a team and its sponsors reaching an agreement on what the project is and what the goal to be achieved from them is. Presuming that the project charter is already in place, the most

important function of define is for the team to decide what they have to accomplish and confirm their understanding with the sponsorship. The sponsor and team should agree on the following:

- Decide and determine what the problem is and the agreement on the problem: which customers will be affected, what their "voices" are saying, how the current process or outcome fails to meet their needs, and so on and so forth.
- The link of the project between corporate strategy and its expected contribution to ROI.
- Decide on the boundaries of the project
- Know what indicators or metrics are used for the evaluation of the success of the project.

In service environments, the last two points that are mentioned above often prove particularly more important. When the process that has to be done is studied and mapped out, then deciding the start and end points of the project becomes a simple matter. Most services have not been mapped prior to improvement; there is often an argument between the team and the sponsors in the early stages of the project improvement as the team creates a SIPOC (suppliers, inputs, process, outputs, customers) or value stream map and then the direction to identify exactly what they should include as part of their project and what they shouldn't.

Setting Project Boundaries:
Projects that are too big will end up with floundering teams who have trouble finishing in a reasonable frame of time. Choose a small or insignificant one, and you'll never convince anyone that Six Sigma is worth the investment. Projects that do not significantly contribute to financial payback will cause everyone from line managers to the senior executives to quickly lose interest. Another concern to be considered when we think about project boundaries is the level of the certification the employees possess. During their training period, black belts work on a project of limited scope only. The metrics for success in the define phase might be as follows:

- Customer satisfaction, to make sure all customer segments are represented
- Speed/lead time
- The team to determine the defects and opportunities for improvement, to have a sigma-level improvement
- How the above processes will help financially.

There are two key issues in Define:

- Making sure the right people are on the bus. The decision should be determined by not only the kind of people that are representative of the work area(s) affected by the project and that possess the knowledge, experience, and training that help the team reach the project goals, but also by an evaluation of the dynamics of the team.
- It is important to make sure that everyone in the team is starting from the same point and have the same goals from the project. This includes all the members of team, belt certified professionals, champions, black belts, and the other staff who are working for the process but might not be part of the team.

Of course, granting authority to employees doesn't guarantee that people will work together or necessarily achieve all the lofty goals that are espoused in this approach. Many issues surround empowerment and teamwork that must be addressed. These issues range from operations and behavior to organizational design. For example, if the existing culture does not reward this type of activity, it is doubtful that participatory approaches will work until the cultural issues are resolved. However, using teams can lead to cultural changes that facilitate improvement. This chapter focuses on the issues related to managing projects and teams to help make the transition succeed.

From a behavioral perspective, empowerment is a tool to enhance organizational learning. Organizational learning implies change in organizational behavior in a way that improves performance.

This type of learning takes place through a network of interrelated components. These components include teamwork, strategies, structures, cultures, systems, and their interactions. Cooperative learning relies on an open culture where no one feels threatened to expose opinions or beliefs—a culture where individuals can engage in learning, questioning, and not remain constrained by "taboos" or existing norms. This strategy includes continuous improvement projects as a governing principle for all team members.

Project charter:
The project charter is represented in the following four areas:

- Content of the charter
- Negotiation of the charter
- Project management
- Project measures.

Content of the charter:
The development of a charter is a vital element for establishing an improvement team. The charter is a document that defines the team's mission, the boundaries of the project, the consequences, and the time frame. It is usually the top management that creates the charter and presents it to the teams, or the teams can also create a charter and present it to the top management and obtain their approval. Either way, the top managements are responsible for giving the team the support and direction needed for working.

It begins with creating a purpose statement. This may be a single- or double-line statement explaining the purpose of formation of the team. The purpose statement should be in correlation with the organization's vision and mission statements. The objective to be achieved should also be defined in this purpose statement.

The objective should be defined in such a way that it can be measured. The scope or the boundaries of the project should also be given in the project charter. This is to determine the organizational limit within which a team is permitted to operate. Time delaying and energy draining can be prevented if the boundaries of the project are defined.

Teams are supposed to know what is expected of them. The team has the permission, authority, and blessing from the various levels of management to operate, conduct research, consider and implement changes that may be of need for the process. A charter provides the following advantages:

- Confusion elimination
- Determines the subject boundaries
- Areas that are not to be addressed
- Determines the deliverable
- Provides a basis for the team to set a goal
- Authorizes the team to collect relevant data

A team project charter should contain the following:

- The financial impact
- Problem definition
- Scope or boundary of the project
- Goal statement
- Role of team members
- Milestones or deliverables
- Resources required.

Financial impact:
This is a short summary of the reason for carrying out the project. It will normally involve quality, cost, or delivery of a product with a financial justification. There are four basic activities:

- Design of a new product
- Redesign of an existing product
- Design of a new process
- Redesign of an existing process.

A common problem for most companies is the lack of measurement of the impact. A project improvement team should carry out whatever project is in accordance with financial department justification guidelines. For example, if the existing quality defect rate is at 5,000 defects per million opportunities, the possible justification is a reduction to 250 defects per million opportunities with a cost savings of $1,000,000 (Eckes, 2001). The advantages and shortcomings of the project should be looked into. There should be an involvement of the entire organization, if necessary, to determine the key costs and their resources for a successful project. Projects that do not provide financial augmentation should be eliminated right away.

A common problem for many projects is the lack of a company impact measurement. For example, if the existing quality defect rate is at 5,000 defects per million opportunities, the possible justification is a reduction to 250 defects per million opportunities with a cost savings of $1,000,000.

Problem statement:
A problem statement will give a detailed statement on the issue that has to be improved. The problem statement should be crafted such that it describes as much as it can such as for how long the problem has been there, how it has affected the business, what the gap in performance and the measurable item that might be affected is. The problem statement should not be such that it makes one jump to conclusions. A sample problem statement would be "The ABC Company, in 2007, has experienced a 25% drop in sales, with a 40% drop in net profit". The problem statement should contain a reference to a baseline measure for guidance. The collection of good data and process performance measurements will provide a picture of the areas in the company that need improvement the most. In addition, the foundation of the work will provide a measure for other teams working on other projects as well.

Goal statement:
The goal statement is created and agreed to by the team and the champion. The goal is hoped to be attained in a 120- or 160-day period. According to the Six Sigma metric, it is required to have 50% reduction in some initial metric, for example, reducing the collectibles from 120 to 60 days and reducing the scrap from 25% to 2.5%. One of the most efficient ways of formulating the goal statement is theory of constraints.

Step 1: Identify
Concentrating on a non-constraint resource would not increase the throughput (the rate at which money comes into the system through sales) because there would not be an increase in the number of orders fulfilled. There might be local gains, but if the material ends up waiting longer somewhere else, there will be no global benefit.

- In order to manage a constraint (bottleneck), it is first necessary to identify it.
- Constraint (bottleneck): resource whose capacity is less than the demand.
- This knowledge helps determine where an increase in "productivity" would lead to increased profits.
- To increase throughput, flow through the constraint must be increased.

Step 2: Exploit

- Once the constraint is identified, the next step is to focus on how to get more output within the existing capacity limitations.

- Because the constraint is what limits the system's throughput, we have to make it work to the maximum.

Step 3: Subordinate
Subordination usually involves significant changes to current (and generally long established) ways of doing things at the non-constraint resources.

- Subordinate the non-bottlenecks to the system constraint.
- All the other components of the system must work so as to guarantee full-speed functioning of the constraint.

Step 4: Elevate
After the constraint is identified, the available capacity is exploited, and the non-constraint resources have been subordinated, the next step is to determine if the output of the constraint is enough to supply market demand. If so, there is no need at this time to "elevate" because this process is no longer the constraint of the system. In that case, the market would be the constraint, and the theory of constraints (TOC) thinking process should be used to develop a marketing solution.

- If, after fully exploiting this process, it still cannot produce enough output to meet demand, it is necessary to find more capacity by "elevating" the constraint.

Step 5: Go back to Step 1

- Once the output of the constraint is no longer the factor that limits the rate of fulfilling orders, it is no longer the constraint.
- Step 5 is to go back to Step 1 and identify the new constraint—because there always is one. The five-step process is then repeated.

Milestones or deliverables:
A well-organized project is bound to have set of short-term goals or deliverables that are used to keep the project on track and help bring it to completion. It has been pointed out that the initial team projects should be at the 120-day length. Only half of the project time is supposed to be allocated to define and measure phases. Assigning teams and the right kind of people for the project is very important. The success rate of the project decreases as the length of time assigned to complete the task increases. A typical milestone chart might be as follows:

- Day 0: start team activities.
- Day 1: start the define portion of the project.
- Day 3: begin the measure portion of the project.
- Day 80: start the analysis phase of the project.
- Day 120: start the improvement phase of the project.
- Day 160: bulk of project control elements are in progress.

Resources required for a project are very important to be noted and detailed down. Typical resources might be as follows:

- Qualified people
- Machine time
- Machinery
- Lab or office space
- Phones and faxes

- Computer equipment
- Utilities.

The Six Sigma define phase should provide the top management the following information:

1. Importance of carrying out the project
2. Goal of the project
3. Skills of the champion and other leaders
4. Boundaries of the project
5. The key process
6. Metrics
7. Customer requirements.

Charter negotiation:
The team to the top management can present the project charter. However, the project team might be closer to the actual facts through another approach toward the problem. So, there are bound to be charter negotiations. They might be as follows:

- Objectives—change in the design or final product due to customer feedback.
- Scope—boundaries the organization I providing might require further expansion. Requirement for more people to carry out the project.
- Resources—requirement of more resources. A complete accurate requirement of resources can never be provided. Management may be required to prioritize certain resources beyond the team's control.
- Project transition—the transition of a project to normal company controls might require a time extension.
- Project closure—project closure date might be required to be moved up because of diverse events or changes in customer preference.

Project management and its benefits:
Project managers are hired by most organizations to ensure that complexities of a project move in an organized fashion and make the proper transitions in a timely and economical manner. The type of "matrix management" has proved very effective in providing deliverables on time. The project management roles and responsibilities are to include the following:

- Leading the cross-functional team
- Possessing excellent communication skills and ability to convey the message clearly
- Schedule meeting to check progress at regular intervals
- Sustaining the team and its motivation
- Development of a detailed project plan
- Letting the team know the benefits of the project to all the share holders
- Tracking of the progress of the tasks and deliverables
- Maintaining flow of information between financial and information management.

Projects need charters, plans, and boundaries. A project may be selected from a broad range of areas including

- Customer feedback
- Improvement in process capabilities
- Cost reduction chances

- Defects reduction
- Employing lean principles
- Growth in market share
- Reduction in cycle times
- Improvement in services.

The project should be consistent with the strategies of the company for survival and/or growth. The project should rather be specific.

Project measures:
It should be noted that the vital project measurements are hard to decide until the project charter and its processes are not complete. The accurate selection of project measures ensures the overall success of Six Sigma implementation. Since most projects deal with time and money issues, most project measures will also be related to time and money. The project measures provide information, which is required to analyze and improve the business process, as well as manage and evaluate the impact of the Six Sigma project. After a list of activities of the project is prepared, the budget of the project is determined. During the project, the actual costs are collected as inputs and used as inputs to determine the estimated costs. The project manager or the team leader compares the revised estimated costs with the actual costs and determines the progress of the project. A project should be reasonable, attainable, and based on estimates of the tasks to be accomplished.

The various revenue factors included in the analysis are

- Income from additional sales generated due to the revised cost of the product and the changes in the quality, features, availability to the customer
- Reduced number of defects, scrap, returns, warranty claims, cost of poor quality, poor market phase.

Cost factors included in the budget are

- Labor cost
- Administrative expenses
- Equipment costs
- Subcontracted work
- Overheads
- Contingency funds.

The timing of the revenues and costs also plays a very important role. Sometimes the revenues projected to be obtained might not be obtained because the funds were not available in the right time frame. The precision and detail of the project-planning phase play a very important role in the success of the project. The costs associated with each project are obtained based on historical data, quotes, standard rates, or similar activities performed previously. Estimates of project revenues are described based on four types of measurements:

- Budget—the plan of the total costs and cash inflows expressed in dollar amounts for the project. The plan also includes timing of the revenues and costs and a cost benefit analysis
- Forecast—the predicted total revenues and costs, adjusting to include the actual information at the point of completion of project
- Actual—revenues and costs that have actually occurred for the project
- Variance—the difference between the budgeted and actual revenues and costs. A positive variance shows the project will be favorable, while a negative variance shows that a loss will be incurred.

Teams:
Flattening Hierarchies for Improved Effectiveness: Along with emphasis on teamwork and empowerment, there has been a move toward flattening hierarchies in organizations. Led by consultants such as Tom Peters and others, top managers have eliminated layers of bureaucratic managers in order to improve communication and simplify work. Having many layers of management can have the effect of increasing the time required to perform work. For example, it has been reported that in the 1980s, one of the largest automobile manufacturers in the United States required 6 months to determine its standard colors for office phones. Probably this decision required many meetings and proper authorization. However, such decisions need to be made. The time required to make this decision was excessive.

Too many layers of management also can impede creativity, stifle initiative, and make empowerment impossible. With fewer layers of management, companies tend to rely more on teams. When Lee Iacocca took the reins at Chrysler Corp., one of his first acts was to eliminate several levels of management. Iacocca credits this move with making other needed changes easier within the organization.

Team Leader Roles and Responsibilities:
Quality professionals are unanimous; to be successful in achieving teamwork and participation, strong leadership both at the company level and within the team is essential. However, what is not always clear is what it means to be an effective team leader. We know that leaders are responsible for setting the team direction and seeking future opportunities for the team. Leaders reinforce values and provide a system for achieving desired goals. Leaders establish expectations for high levels of performance, customer focus, and continuous learning. Leaders are responsible for communicating effectively for evaluating organizational performance and for providing feedback concerning such performance.

An important aspect of leadership is the organization's preparedness to follow the leadership. The best general is probably not going to be successful if the troops are not well trained or prepared. Hersey and Blanchard propose a theory called a situational leadership model that clarifies the interrelation between employee preparedness and effectiveness of leadership. According to Hersey and Blanchard, situational leadership is based on interplay among the following:

- The amount of guidance and direction a leader gives (task behavior)
- The amount of socioeconomic support a leader provides (relationship behavior)
- The readiness level that followers exhibit in performing a specific task, function, or objective.

Therefore, if team members are trained and prepared so that they are "task ready", leadership will be more effective. Readiness, in this context, is the "extent to which a follower has the ability and willingness to accomplish a specific task". Readiness is a function of two variables. These are ability and technical skills and self-confidence in one's abilities. Therefore, effective leadership helps employees become competent and instills confidence in employees that they can do the job.

As it relates to QM, leadership is especially difficult. Leaders are told that they should empower employees. To many leaders, this implies laissez-faire or hands-off approach to management. In other words, many leaders feel that they are to provide resources but that they should not be involved in overly controlling employee behavior. Although the literature contains examples of companies that have been successful in delegating authority to this extent, QM is not a vehicle by which leaders abdicate their responsibility.

In most organizations, employees want leaders who provide clear direction, necessary information, and feedback on performance, insight, and ideas. Skilled team leaders need to demonstrate this ability to lead. The single most important attribute of companies with failed QM programs is a lack of leadership. A close second is poor communication, which is related to leadership. Effective leaders are people who are able to provide visions, ideas, and motivation to others to achieve the greater good.

Besides team leaders, there are a variety of roles that individuals occupy in teams. Also, team roles can be defined functionally. Often, teams require different functional talents such as management, human resources, engineering, operations, accounting, marketing, management information systems, and others. In these cases, the managers overseeing the project help to identify the talents needed and then search for the team members to provide these talents (Figure 9.13).

Considerations   Considerations

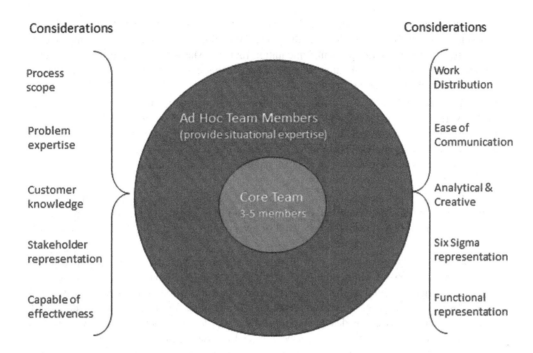

Process
scope

Problem
expertise

Customer
knowledge

Stakeholder
representation

Capable of
effectiveness

Work
Distribution

Ease of
Communication

Analytical &
Creative

Six Sigma
representation

Functional
representation

FIGURE 9.13 The core and *ad hoc* team.

Team Formation and Evolution:
The way a team is formed depends—to an extent—on the objectives or goals of the team. Regardless of the type of team your firm employs, teams experience different stages of development. These stages include the following: Forming, where the team is composed and the objective for the team is set; Storming, where the team members begin to get to know each other and agreements have not yet been made that facilitate smooth interaction between team members; norming, where the team becomes cohesively developed and performing, where a mutually supportive, steady state is achieved. And in successful projects, the final stage is mourning, where the team members regret the ending of the project and breaking up of the team.

Team Rules: During the norming stage, teams develop ground rules. Such ground rules can forestall conflict. It is often useful to establish ground rules for a team to be functional. If a team is functional, individual participation enhances the group's effectiveness. If the team is dysfunctional, such participation reduces the effectiveness of the group. Acts of commission include talking behind the backs of other team members or otherwise acting out one's feelings. There are also acts of omission in such passive aggressive behavior as forgetting to attend meetings or withholding information. Counteractive behavior improves the group's effectiveness by negating dysfunctional behavior. Counteractive behavior can be enacted by either the team, the facilitator, the team manager, or even the offending individual.

Types of teams:
At the point, we will pause to define the various types of teams that are used in improving quality. Continuous process improvement often requires small teams that are segmented by work areas. Projects with multiple departments in a company require cross-functional teams. Large projects require teams with large budgets and multiple members. Smaller projects, such as "formulating a preventive maintenance plan for oiling the metal lathes", probably will require a much smaller team. In the following sections, we list and define a number of teams.

1. **Process Improvement Teams**: Process improvement teams are teams that work to improve processes and customer service. These teams may work under the direction of management or may be self-directed. In either case, the process improvement teams are involved in some or all

of the following activities: identifying opportunities for improvement, prioritizing opportunities, selecting projects, gathering data, analyzing data, making recommendations, implementing change, and conducting post-implementation reviews. Many process improvement teams are on outgrowth of quality-related training. These teams use the basic tools and the PDCA cycle to effect change relating to processes.

2. **Cross-Functional Teams**: Cross-functional teams enlist people from a variety of functional groups within the firm. In the real world, problems often cut across functional borders. As a result, problem-solving teams are needed that include people from a variety of functions. These cross-functional teams often work on higher-level strategic issues that involve multiple functions. Such teams often work on macro level, quality-related problems such as communication or redesigning company-wide processes.

3. **Tiger Teams**: A Tiger team is a high-powered team assigned to work on a specific problem for a limited amount of time. These teams are often used in re-engineering efforts or in projects where a specific problem needs to be solved in a very short period of time. The work is very intense and has only a limited duration.

4. **Natural Work Groups**: Natural work groups are teams organized around a common product, customer, or service. Many times, these teams are cross-functional and include marketers, researchers, engineers, and producers. The objective of natural work groups includes tasks such as increasing responsiveness to customers and market demand. In order to implement natural work groups are improved job design and improved work life for employees. The key elemental impact of natural work groups is to improve service by focusing work units in an organization on the customer. A by-product is improved communication with customers. Often a natural work group will be established for a specific customer.

5. **Self-Directed Work Teams**: A self-directed work team is a team chartered to work on projects identified by team members themselves. There is little managerial oversight except to establish the teams and fund their activities. Self-directed teams are identified as either little S or big S teams. Little S self-directed work teams are made up of employees empowered to identify opportunities for improvement, select improvement projects, and complete implementation. Big S self-directed teams are involved in managing the different functions of the company without a traditional management structure. These types of teams contain totally self-directed employees who make decisions concerning benefits, finances, pay, processes, customers, and all the other aspects of running the business. Often big S self-directed work teams hold partial ownership of the companies they work for so that they participate in the benefits of their teamwork.

   Technology and Teams: New tools for teamwork are constantly emerging. Also, team effectiveness is a precursor to project task performance. Integrated Information Systems (IS) tools involve integrated information systems such as computer aided design (CAD)/computer aided manufacturing (CAM) and computer integrated manufacturing (CIM). This aids in achieving improvement in efficiency and effectiveness. Process technology is used in helping to improve task performance. Process standardization methods such as the tools of quality and customer input methods complete the model. This model amplifies that more and more, team effectiveness is assisted by integrated tolls and technologies, and the impact of technology should increase. As software becomes cheaper and easier to use, more tools will be used by everyone involved with the project.

6. **Virtual Teams**: The term "virtual teams" is emerging as more companies become "virtual organizations", loosely knit consortia that produce products and services. Virtual teams are teams that rarely or never physically meet, except in electronic meetings using group decision software. Among virtual organizations, projects often cross organizational boundaries. Today, Internet and Intranet-based applications called team ware are emerging that allow us to access the World Wide Web and build a team, share ideas, hold virtual meetings, brainstorm, keep schedules, and archive past results with people in far-flung locations around the world. Hectic schedules and the difficulty in finding convenient times to meet to solve problems will make teams of this type more important in the future.

Implementing teams:

The teams in our examples have something in common. The performance of the team is essential to their individual success, and in some cases, even lives hang in the balance. If the National Association for Stock Car Auto Racing (NASCAR) team performs ineffectively, the driver loses. If the Massachusetts General Hospital team is ineffective, people die. If The Navy's Sea, Air and Land Forces (SEALs) don't function properly, lives are lost and the mission fails. How do we engender this sense of urgency in quality improvement teams? How do we create a momentum or team ethic that will help us beat the odds and be successful? Accomplishing this often requires facilitation and team building. Facilitation is helping or aiding teams by maintaining a process orientation and focusing the group. Team Building is accomplished by following a process that identifies roles for team members and then helps them to become competent in achieving those roles.

The role of the facilitator is very important in managing teams, particularly when team members have little experience with teamwork. The role of the facilitator is to make it easy for the group to know where it is going, know why it wants to get there, know how to get there, and know what it is going to do next. A facilitator focuses the group on the process it must follow. Successful facilitation does not mean that the group always achieves its desired results. The facilitator is responsible for ensuring that the team follows a meaningful and effective process to achieve its objectives.

How is this accomplished? The facilitator should plan how the group will work through a task, help the group stay on track and be productive, draw out quiet members, discourage monopolizing, help develop clear and shared understanding, watch body language and verbal cues, and help the group achieve closure. Again, facilitators must remain neutral on content. Facilitators cannot take sides or positions on important areas of disagreement. However, facilitators should help key members reach points of agreement. Effective meeting management is an important skill for a facilitator of quality improvement teams. Often quality improvement involves a series of meetings of team members who meet to brainstorm, perform root-cause analysis, and carry out other activities. Tools for successful meeting management include an agenda, predetermined objectives for the meeting, a process for running the meeting, processes for voting, and development of an action plan using these tools requires outstanding communication skills as well as human relations skills. The steps required for planning a meeting are

- Defining an agenda
- Developing meeting objectives
- Designing the agenda activity outline
- Using process techniques (Figure 9.14).

Structured processes, a set of rules for managing meetings, work well in conducting meetings. It is paradoxical that structured processes are inhibiting, time consuming, and unnatural—which is why they

Date: Time:

In Attendance:

    Project Sponsor(s), Black Belt, Core Team Members, Master Black Belt

Agenda:

      – Review Business Case for the project

      – Review and discuss Project Charter

      – Develop team-behavior contract

      – Develop Project Plan, including team information and project schedule

Assignments:

What   Who   By When

Next Meeting:

FIGURE 9.14 Meeting notes.

work. Why do we use processes in meetings? The answers are clear. We wish meetings to stay focused, to involve deeper exploration, to separate creative from evaluative activities, to provide objective ground rules' defensiveness, and to separate the person from the idea.

Tools such as flip charts, sticky dots, whiteboards, and sticky notes are used commonly in structured process activities. The focus of team meetings moves from clarifying to generating ideas, to evaluating ideas, and to action planning. Some of the techniques, such as silent voting and idea writing, help team members reach consensus rapidly.

Another useful meeting management tool that was pioneered by Hewlett Packard is the "parking lot". The parking lot is a flip chart or whiteboard where topics that are off the subject are parked with the agreement that these topics will be candidates for next meeting's agenda. At the end of the meeting, the group agrees on the agenda for the following meeting, and the parking lot is erased.

Conflict resolution in Teams: As people work closely together in teams, conflicts arise. Conflict resolution is a hugely important topic for team leaders and members. Conflicts are endemic to all kinds of team projects. Using team processes, assumptions are questioned, change is brainstormed, and cultures are challenged. This type of creative activity results in possible conflict. It is claimed that team leaders and project managers spend more than 20% of their time resolving conflict. If this is true, then conflict resolution resounds as one of the very important underdiscussed topics in team building.

There are many sources of conflict. Some conflicts are internal, such as personality conflicts or rivalries, or external, such as disagreements over reward systems, scarce resources, lines of authority, or functional differentiation. Teams bring together individuals from a variety of cultures, backgrounds, and functional areas of expertise. Being on a team can create confusion for individuals and insecurity as members are taken out of their comfort zones. It is interesting to note that these are also some of the reasons for teams to be successful. Some organizational causes of differences are more insidious: faulty attribution, faulty communication, or grudges and prejudice. Four recognizable stages occur in the conflict resolution process:

- Frustration. People are at odds, and competition or aggression ensues.
- Conceptualization and orientation. Opponents identify the issues that need to be resolved.
- Interaction. Team members discuss and air the problems.
- Outcome. The problem is resolved.

One of the things a leader must be able to do is manage conflict in the organization. In order to foster a wee-run workplace, leaders must be able to resolve conflict effectively in the organizations. Leaders resolve conflict in a variety of ways:

- Passive conflict resolution: Some managers and leaders ignore conflict. This is probably the most common approach to working out conflict. There may be positive reasons for this approach. The leader may prefer that subordinates work things out themselves. Or the conflict may be minor and will take care of itself over time. Leader feels that some issues are small enough to not merit micromanagement.
- Win–win: Leaders might seek solutions to problems that satisfy both sides of a conflict by providing win–win scenarios. One form of this is called balancing demands for the participants. This happens when the manager determines what each person in the conflict wants as an outcome and looks for solutions that can satisfy the needs of both parties.
- Structured problem solving: Conflicts can be resolved in a fact-based manner by gathering data regarding the problem and having the data analyzed by a disinterested observer to add weight to the claims of one of the conflicting parties.
- Confronting conflict: At times, it is best to confront the conflict and use active listening techniques to help subordinates resolve conflicts. This provides a means for coming to a solution of the conflict.

- Choosing a winner: In some cases, where the differences between the parties in the conflict are great, the leader may choose a winner of the conflict and develop a plan of action for conflict resolution between parties.
- Selecting a better alternative: Sometimes there is an alternative neither of the parties to the conflict has considered. The leader then asks the conflicting parties to pursue an alternative plan of action.
- Preventing conflict: Skilled leaders use different techniques to create an environment that is relatively free of conflict. These approaches are more strategic in nature and involve organizational design fundamentals. By carefully defining goals, rewards, communication systems, coordination, and the nature of competition in a firm, conflict can be reduced or eliminated. Conflicts often are the results of the reward systems in the firm. A systems approach will focus attention on organizational design rather than individual interactions.

9.7 Project Tracking

Project management is an essential process in establishing a scheduled plan and allocating available resources judiciously. The strings of activities that constitute a project are to be monitored for straying off the timeline for its proper implementation. Thus, the objective of a project is adhered to utilizing the allocated resources within time and cost constraints at the desired level of performance to reach specified goal. The phases of project management include:

- Planning
- Scheduling
- Controlling.

Tracking is the controlling phase of project management to ensure the requirements of the undergoing project are met. It involves an exercise of making rightful decisions:

- Identifying sources of bottlenecks
- Delegating duties
- Choosing the right tradeoffs
- Measuring results against expected outcomes
- Applying timely corrective plans
- Establishing tolerance level in timeline
- Future developments to current work
- Efficient communication and continuous tracking (Figure 9.15).

Work breakdown structure (WBS):
It is a descriptive document on the constitution of the project, the assigned responsibilities for each work group. Each responsibility is converted to a string of activities and further broken down to subtasks or elements that are set to motion by a team. From subtask to activity, each responsibility has a constricting time frame which should be flexible enough to accommodate variations in implementation. Interrelationships between predecessor events and following events are to be streamlined and scheduled. Offsetting is required to avoid losses by arranging for a safety stock of resources and to accommodate any increase in cost incurred. However, the deadlines are fixed in nature. For adherence to such fixed time requirements resources have to be fixed and aplenty. There should be arrangements for coordinating between different elements in the organization that source their equipment, material, etc. from the same pool. Seamless scheduling becomes essential for parallel tasks with slack time. Planning for such

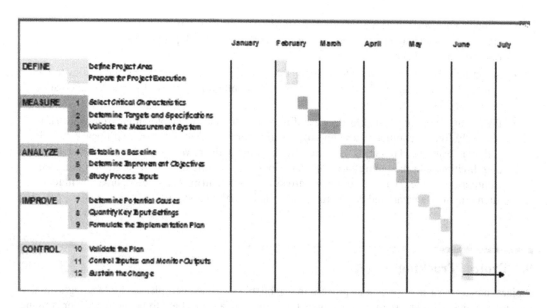

FIGURE 9.15 Project timeline.

activities requires tools that can recognize the amounts of resources, time and calculate costs. These include the following:

1. Program evaluation and review technique (PERT)
2. Critical path method (CPM)
3. Gantt Chart.

The WBS is useful to pull out relevant activities and the investment required. As is evident, these tools are helpful for the analyze phase in the Six Sigma process which we shall review in detail later.

The network planning rules are based on these tools and they are

- All activities must begin on completion of preceding events.
- Logicality of event precedence is implied using arrows.
- The direct event connection can be established through only one activity.
- Network must begin and end at single events.
- Event numbers must be unique.

The PERT and CPM tools are similar except that CPM is activity oriented and PERT is event oriented. Gantt Charts are representation of activities or events against time. It must be kept in mind the purpose, frequency, method (written reports, summary, and forms), prioritizing amongst random events, feedback loops, and contingency plans. The feedback loop has the methods for contingency measures. It is an autogenerated control plan. Success or failure is to be measured against

- The fulfillment of goals
- Adherence to time limits
- Boundary variance
- Utilization index of resources.

A properly executed plan must have a high rate of success for all these measures. Contingency plans must be at no extra costs and wastage of resources. Unanticipated events and complexity of project that pose challenges in terms of better technologies are not acceptable excuses for occurrence of failures. Performance standards for results are set high, and issues must be resolved justifiably by the team leader to maintain the schedule for the given budget levels.

Unit of measurements for the timeline is specified as days, weeks, months, etc. according to convenience. Methods for controlling range from planning and monitoring use manual methods like paper, graph, and markers to software.

Advantages of manual methods are

- Easy to use
- Apt for scheduling
- Reduced cost
- Customizable
- Flexible to needs
- Hands-on feel of status.

Advantages of computer software are

- Monitors random events
- Impact of alternatives
- Detailed project status reports
- Automatic calculation of time frames
- Easy reporting
- Quicker generation of summaries
- Plan is in real time
- Automated data collection activities.

Milestones Reporting:
Significant events in the project timeline are termed as milestones. They help keep pace with the project schedule and in reporting the progress and status level of the project. They act as a decision to point to proceed with the project state. Presentations are made at these pit stops to check for further bottlenecks expected. Plans for dealing with the conditions that arise due to these potential setbacks are discussed. The time is already set during the project-planning phase as to which activity can be termed as an important milestone. For any well-managed project, a set of stages or milestones are used to keep the project on track and to help bring a project to completion. Only half of the project would be allocated to define and measure stages.

Project report:
The project report is a progress summary that states the performance vs. the anticipated benefits and costs incurred with the budget planned initially. Also, the tasks completed against the level of milestone are analyzed for status. The postmortem analysis is the next step that gives what went wrong and is used as a base for building and improving on further plans. Benefit from effective processes.

Document Archiving:
Document archiving is documenting the data, the source of materials, process parameters, and reports generated during the project. The organization of these files must be coherent and have special storage conditions.

These are

- Security with special access
- Retrievability
- Protection from damage

- Traceability of these documents using indicators
- Duplication of files for safety
- Using reliable mediums.

9.8 Tools Used in Yellow Belt

Tools used in yellow belt are SMART objective, SIPOC, and translation of VOC to CTQ.

SMART objective:
The objectives framed by the organization should follow SMART way so that the company can thrive to achieve the goal. SMART is defined in Table 9.2.

SIPOC:
SIPOC is expanded as suppliers, inputs, process, outputs, customers. SIPOC is a high-level process map with four to seven steps displayed. The following steps should be followed to develop the SIPOC:

- Have the team to create the process map.
- The process may have four to five key steps.
- List the output of the process.
- List the customers of the output of the process.
- List the inputs of the process.
- List the suppliers of the process.
- Identify some preliminary requirements of the customers.

Involve the team leader, champion, and other stakeholders for verification of the project (Figure 9.16).

- Suppliers: Suppliers are the provider of inputs to your process.
- Inputs: Inputs are the materials, resources, or data required to execute your process.
- Process: Process is defined as a structured set of activities that transform a set of inputs into specified outputs.
- Outputs: Outputs are products or services that result from the process.
- Customers: The recipients of the process output.

TABLE 9.2

SMART Objective

Specific	The objective needs to be more specific and clearly identify the issue.
Measurable	It is possible to measure whether the objective has been achieved.
Achievable	The objective should be achievable.
Relevant	The objective should be relevant to company's strategy.
Timed	There should be a target date for completion.

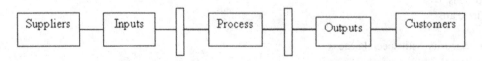

FIGURE 9.16   SIPOC process.

VOC in yellow belt:

The primary driver for any Six Sigma initiative is the VOC. Market trends trigger the performance of any system. These two factors are the strategy for any system that initiates Six Sigma. For any firm to be successful, they need to understand what the customer requires from the company's product or services. VOC can be defined by following three terms:

- Customer needs
- Customer perception
- Customer attributes.

The attributes which drive toward the achievement of specific goals are defined as the customer needs. The customer's opinion to evaluate the product or services in a favorable manner or unfavorable manner is defined as the customer attributes. The manner in which the customer presumes and interprets about a company is known as customer perception.

Companies work on these attributes to attract the purchasers. They look into the primary function as well as the needs, wants, and expectations of the product to achieve high serviceable level. They develop product or services based on following functions:

- Service levels that favorably influence customer attitudes
- Advertising objectives that positively impact customer perceptions
- Product specifications that meet customer needs.

Primary targets for any firm are increase in market share and revenue growth. For this purpose, firm should identify a strategy for retaining the current customer base and acquisition of new customer base. The firm should not only listen to their own customer's requirement but they should also get information from the customers who are currently in business services with their competitors. This enables to increase market share and revenue growth. If the company does only VOC, it loses its chance of attracting its competitor's customer.

Strategic use of Six Sigma is to process the value gap. Value gaps can either be closed or can be increased to that of competitors. Value gaps can be customized based on VOC and competitor's customer. Inputs from this process can be used for changes in strategy, and they should be incorporated into the system. It is not helpful only to determine the changes in value stream map if the inputs obtained from the above process are not incorporated into the information system.

Various sources of VOC in yellow belt are listed below:

- Internal quality metrics—rework, scrap
- Customer complaints
- Customer inspection meetings
- Telephone calls
- Performance relative to alternatives
- Failure analysis (FAL) reports/feedback
- Questionnaires
- Personal visits
- Surveys
- Focus groups
- Interviews.

VOC can be analyzed by two methods. The first method is to tabulate all the expectations from the product or services by the firm. This analysis is done from the customer's perspective. All the defects in the product or services are tabulated in the flip chart. The second method is to analyze the product or services individually. The facilitator is responsible to translate the results in flip chart. Then the details about results are discussed by having a meeting among the team.

VOC can be assessed based on two techniques: qualitative research and quantitative research. Qualitative research is done to obtain results to obtain customer perception. Qualitative research is based on structured questions. Quantitative research is also called as survey research. This method is used for collecting data from the customer. This quantifies the customer's expectations, perceptions and requirements, etc.

A primary target or metrics for any firm is to achieve customer satisfaction. A customer requires highest possible quality for a product for emotional commitment toward the firm. The customer is not solely concerned about the tradeoff between price and quality. Customer satisfaction parameters can be measured by analyzing all the attributes till the product is purchased by the customer.

Value is also considered to be the parameter for customer satisfaction. Suppose if customer is willing to pay high for getting a quality product, then the price is sublimed in this process, and quality takes first place in this condition. Hence, the value of the product should be considered as an important parameter for the customer's satisfaction.

Critical to Quality:
CTQ: any measurable product or service characteristic that is important to the customer from the customer's point of view. This tool actually focuses on the key metrics of customer satisfaction. A CTQ tree will translate the initial customer requirements to numerical or quantified requirements for the product or service.

Translation of VOC to CTQ
VOC drives the firm to achieve customer perception and needs. Critical to quality quantifies the VOC. VOC should be clearly studied, and following steps need to be analyzed:

- Customer needs
- Define the metric
- Target
- Specification/tolerance limit.

VOC is analyzed thoroughly, and detailed sketches for the customer's needs, metrics, and targets are charted out.

- Customer needs: Customer needs is defined as the attribute that drives the firm to a specific goal. It also specifies about consistent delivery against agreement.
- Define the metric: Metric is defined as the difference in the number of days between the customer request date and actual date received.
- Target: Target should be thriving to achieve zero metric.
- Tolerance limit: Tolerance limit specifies 1 or 2 days ahead are behind the metric (Figure 9.17).

Basic insights from this process are specified below.

- It is impossible to measure whether some customer needs are being met. In those cases, find an alternative to measure such that it will specify whether the customer's satisfaction is achieved.
- Target value is the point at which the customer is most satisfied.

VOC	Customer need	Define the metric	CTQ Target	CTQ tolerance

FIGURE 9.17   Translation of VOC to CTQ.

- Customer satisfaction level becomes unstable if the value goes above or below the target value.
- Tolerance is the point between the customer's satisfaction and dissatisfaction.
- CTQ has no impacts on the capacity of the process.

Review Questions

Question 29: A work schematic that details the relationship between inputs, processes, outputs, customers, and feedback is called

   (a) A subsystem
   (b) A SIPOC diagram
   (c) A system diagram
   (d) An activity network diagram.

Answer: B

Question 30: On a process flow diagram, the component that indicates a need for correction is called

   (a) Input
   (b) SIPOC
   (c) Feedback
   (d) Output.

Answer: C

Question 31: Any business process is composed of three main levels for the purpose of Six Sigma strategy development. Which of the following is NOT included?

   (a) Operations
   (b) Process
   (c) Shareholder
   (d) Business.

Answer: C

Question 32: The process map known as SIPOC provides team members an understanding of the process. It is a view of the process taken at

   (a) The customer's perspective
   (b) Floor level
   (c) A very detailed level
   (d) A very high level.

Answer: D

Solution: SIPOC is the abbreviation of suppliers, inputs, process, outputs, customers. SIPOC is a high-level process map with four to seven steps displayed. The following steps should be followed to develop the SIPOC.

Question 33: The SIPOC process map stands for suppliers, inputs, process, outputs, and customers. It provides a view of the process that contains steps. How many steps does the process contain approximately?

   (a) 21–40
   (b) 4–7
   (c) 8–15
   (d) 16–20.

Answer: B—SIPOC is the abbreviation of suppliers, inputs, process, outputs, customers. SIPOC is a high-level process map with four to seven steps displayed. The following steps should be followed to develop the SIPOC.

Question 34: A work schematic that details the relationship between inputs, processes, outputs, customers and feedback is called

(a) A subsystem

(b) A SIPOC diagram

(c) A system diagram

(d) An activity network diagram.

Answer: None

Question 35: The team's charter describes the team's

(a) Meeting dates, milestones, and targets

(b) Leader, facilitator, recorder, and timekeeper

(c) Mission, scope, and objectives

(d) Members, sponsors, and facilitators.

Answer: C

Solution: The charter is a document that defines the team's mission, the boundaries of the project, the consequences, and the time frame.

Question 36: One advantage of project management is that it does NOT require

(a) Planning

(b) People

(c) Objectives

(d) Unlimited resources.

Answer: D

The phases of project management include planning, scheduling, and controlling.

Question 37: The project charter will be useful in many ways, including

(a) Ensuring the team members will support the charter

(b) Permitting the team leader to develop milestones from it

(c) Assuring the champion will assign responsible team members

(d) Providing a consistent target for the team.

Answer: D

Question 38: A commonly reported problem with Six Sigma projects deal with

(a) A desire to complete projects on time

(b) A failure to complete any project charter documentation

(c) A lack of business impact for the company

(d) A requirement that projects must be at least $100,000 in value.

Answer: C

Question 40: The relevant stakeholders in an important project would typically include all of the following EXCEPT

(a) Owners and stockholders

(b) Potential suppliers

(c) Potential competitors

(d) Hourly employees.

Answer: C

Solution: C. The question "who are the key stake holders?" is very crucial and can possibly be answered from the following:

- Owners of the process
- Anyone contributing to the process
- Anyone affected by the process
- Those who benefit from process output.

Question 40: Upper management typically supports the team process best by

A. Reinforcing positive team results
B. Punishing negative team members
C. Providing direction and support
D. Allowing teams to establish the company's mission statement.

Solution: B. Besides these two, management supports team process by ensuring a constancy of purpose, sharing business results, giving people a sense of mission, and developing a realistic and integrated plan.

Question 41: Upper management typically supports the team process best by

A. Reinforcing positive team results
B. Punishing negative team members
C. Providing direction and support
D. Allowing teams to establish the company's mission statement
   (a) A
   (b) A and C
   (c) A, B, and C
   (d) A, B, C, and D.

Answer: D

Question 42: Team success is most dependent on which of the following?
   (a) The team leader
   (b) Team members having full knowledge of the fishbone technique
   (c) Active support by mid-managers
   (d) Policy support by top management.

Solution: D. Initial team projects should be at the 120-day length. Assigning teams for an initial project with lengths of more than 160 days will lower the anticipated success rate.
Answer: D

Question 43: The term variables can be described in the following way:
   (a) A definable attribute or characteristic of a product
   (b) A quality which is absent in a product in one or more specifications
   (c) A quality which can assume several (more than two) values
   (d) A quality which can be absent or present in a product.

Answer: C

Question 46: A customer satisfaction program has started on the right foot. It has gone very well for the last year or so. The company should

A. Look to improve the program, with new customer input
B. Do nothing with the program; it's not broken

C. Form a manager's group to add new wrinkles to the program

    (a) A

    (b) B and C

    (c) B

    (d) C.

Solution: A. Look to improve the program, with new customer input.

9.9 Tools Used in Green Belt

The tools used in green belt are Pareto diagrams, benchmarking, brainstorming processes, thought process maps, process mapping, and value stream mapping (VSM).

Pareto diagrams:
The Pareto diagrams are used to prioritize problems so that the major problems can be identified. The diagrams are used to

- Analyze a problem from a new perspective
- Focus attention on problems in priority order
- Compare data changes during different time periods
- Provide a basis for the construction of a cumulative line
- Prioritize problems
- Segregate the significant problems from the insignificant problems.

Pareto analysis is based on 80-20 rule. Dr. Juran states that 80% of the problems come from 20% of causes. Pareto analysis is used to segregate vital few problems with trivial many problems. For the Six Sigma professionals, it is important to identify the most important opportunity for improvement in order to get large returns from the project.

A Pareto chart is similar to histogram. A histogram is a graphical interpretation of the distributed data in a quantitative manner into a class. A Pareto chart is the frequency bar chart which represents quantified data by quantitative characteristics. Steps for constructing Pareto chart are

- Choose the subject for the chart. The subject can be anything which can be causing problems to any particular line or any product.
- Identify the data that needs to be collected. Identify if percentage or cost or quantity is going to be tracked.
- Collect data related to the quality issues. The quality issues are collected over the time period.
- Use check sheet as the input to collect data. Gather the total number of defects and non-conformities in each category.
- Based on the information from the check sheet, calculate the percentage of total non-conformities.
- Specify the cost incurred for the defects or non-conformities.
- Plot the data setting up scale for chart.
- The x-axis represents the subject of study usually non-conformities or defects or items of interest. The y-axis represents the number of defects, number of occurrences, percentage, or cost incurred per category.
- Draw the chart by organizing the data in descending order, that is, data from the largest category to the smallest category.
- The last step is to analyze the chart. Check for the largest bar; it represents the vital few problems.

Benchmarking:
Any enterprise should know their strongest competitors on a process-by-process basis. Sometimes it is necessary to look outside the industry to find good benchmarking data. Six Sigma firms often compare their performance with other companies in order to improve their performance in the marketplace. The company compares its standards with the best practices of other companies. Benchmarking is done by visual judgment by the reviewers, documentation, and interviews with people who are directly involved.

With the above inputs about the comparisons, the company identifies the steps for the improvement for their own performance. Areas where benchmarking can be done for an organization are listed below:

- Procedures
- Processes
- Quality improvement efforts
- Marketing
- Operational strategies.

Another type of benchmarking is by investigating the effectiveness of the system implemented by the company with its designed performance level. This is known as effectiveness benchmarking.

The third type of benchmarking is known as continuous benchmarking. This enables continuous improvement as the vital feature for an organization. This also puts day-to-day improvement as a pavement for continuous improvement. Areas where continuous benchmarking can be done are listed below:

- Operations
- Procedures
- Processes
- Performance
- Project
- Strategies.

Benchmarking is done by the following sequence.

1. Determine Current Practices
   - Select problem area.
   - Identify key performance factors.
   - Understand own processes and the processes of others.
   - Select performance criteria based on needs and priorities.
2. Identify Best Practices
   - Measure the performance within the organization.
   - Determine the leaders in the critical areas.
   - Find an internal or external organization to benchmark.
3. Analyze Best Practices
   - Visit the organization as a benchmark partner.
   - Collect information and data of the benchmark leader.
   - Evaluate and compare current practices with the benchmark.
4. Model Best Practices
   - Drive improvement changes to advance performance.
   - Extend performance breakthroughs within the organization.

- Incorporate new information in the business decision making.
- Share results with benchmark partner.
- Seek other benchmark leaders for further improvement.

5. Repeat

Examples of benchmarking:

- Customer satisfaction
- Actual customer desires
- Current competition
- Best in related industries
- Best in the world.

Benchmarking process provides a path for continuous improvement process. Information provided can be used to investigate root causes and reduce variation in the process followed (Figure 9.18).

Thought process map:
Purpose of thought process map is to document questions and decisions made during Six Sigma project. Thought process map helps to assure that questions raised during project are not ignored. This tool is used for evaluating the document. It is also used for updating the document during the course of the project.

   Thought process map is used to raise questions as the black belt works through the project, and it also concentrates on assumptions underlying the questions. It also provides answers to those questions and methods to answer the questions.

Value Stream Mapping:
VSM is a lean tool which is used to determine the non-value-added activities and also used to eliminate those activities to reduce the cost associated with those processes. Activities are analyzed, and investigation of their purpose is done. Various questions associated with VSM are given below:

- Whether the activities are required
- Whether the activities are performed efficiently
- Whether the activities give useful results (Figure 9.19).

1. Determine the service process:
   In determining the types of service activities, it is best to start with the end process. End work product will be consumed by the customer. Six Sigma professionals will do mapping by this process.

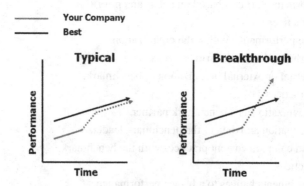

FIGURE 9.18   Benchmarking.

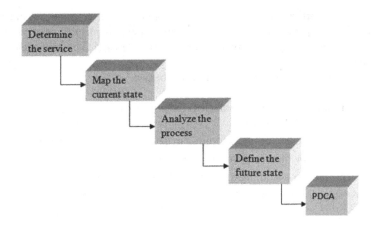

FIGURE 9.19   VSM.

2. Map the current state:
   Starting with the end process in a system, Six Sigma professionals will follow the below listed guidelines.
   - Begin with physical activation.
   - Follow the sequential work order.
   - Map the process in backward flow.
   - Document the data obtained. Document the physical flow of information. Determine the actual start and end times, and based on these values, calculate the cycle time.
   - Map the entire flow of work sequence.

3. Analyze the process:
   Value stream process analysis consists of cycle time measurements, slack time at each level of the value stream, quantification of resources required to produce the product, actual time taken. Additional information like rework, processes with high bottlenecks, and excessive accuracy are checked for the process. If the wasteful activities are determined, the following four techniques are used to reduce the costs. In activity elimination, if the activity is not used to achieve the required customer service level, then stop performing that process. Activity sharing is concerned about exploiting the advantage of economies of scale. Combine processes in efficient manner for effective operation of the services. Activity reduction reduces the time and other resources involved in that particular activity by scaling back the activity. If there is voluminous amount of data involved in the value stream, there is a possibility for automation.

4. Define the future state:
   The future state value stream map is the altered workflow by making the activities and process lean. This improves the efficiency of the system. Each member in the team individually recommends process modification, activity changes, structural changes, technological improvements. These inputs will serve as the communication tool for the improved solution with its benefits.

Process Mapping:
Process maps are a vital tool in green belt which provide clear insight about how process and activities are carried in an organization. Process maps are the graphical tool which represent each process in pictorial representation. Creating the process maps helps the Six Sigma team to understand current processes and also aids in improving the current process. When the modification is made to the processes, process maps are a useful tool in communicating the proposed changes to the process in the system.

Process maps use flowcharts and flow diagrams. Flowcharts are an effective means of communication medium which can be easily understood. Team members can clearly identify what can be done to the process at each level. Non-value-added activities present in the process can be easily determined and can be separated from the process.

Steps involved in constructing process maps are given below:

- Determine the process limits: In order to chart the process, it is essential to determine the start of the process and end of the process.
- Define the process steps: Use of brainstorming to determine the steps for new process.
- Sort the steps in order by their occurrence in the process.
- Place those steps in order according to the symbols and create a chart.
- Evaluate those steps for efficiency and problems (Figures 9.20 and 9.21).

Brainstorming:

To determine the root cause of the problems, a Six Sigma improvement team looks into brainstorming as the input to resolve. The need for brainstorming is to develop the use of opportunities, problems, and ideas from the team. Each member present in the team needs to participate. Brainstorming enables the team members to generate different ideas that will suit the certain process. Effective brainstorming involves the recording of all ideas developed during the brainstorming session. The leader should facilitate everyone in the team to participate during the course of brainstorming. Brainstorming involves no negativism, no criticism, and no evaluation of ideas.

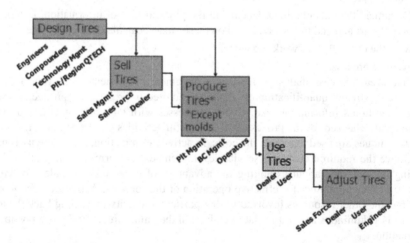

FIGURE 9.20   Process mapping.

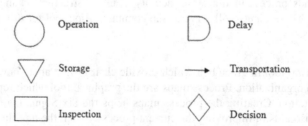

FIGURE 9.21   Symbols used for process mapping.

Review Questions

Question 46: Benchmarking should be done in the following sequence:

A. Measure competitive performance

B. Implement significant improvement

C. Understand your own process

D. Identify improvement criteria

   (a) A C D B

   (b) C D A B

   (c) D C B A

   (d) A B C D

Answer: B

Question 47: A graphical display of the total percentage of results below a certain measurement value is called a

   (a) Cumulative distribution function

   (b) Histogram

   (c) Probability density function

   (d) Expected value

Answer: A

Question 48: Which of the following are principal reasons for utilizing process mapping?

A. To identify where unnecessary complexity exists

B. To visualize the process quickly

C. To eliminate the total planning process

D. To assist in work simplification

   (a) A and B

   (b) A, B, and C

   (c) A, B, and D

   (d) A, B, C, and D

Answer: C

Question 49: A SWOT analysis is an easy way for a company to evaluate itself and plan a strategy. A key concern is

   (a) Lack of resources

   (b) Situation changing over time

   (c) Lack of objectivity in the analysis

   (d) Lack of planned change

Solution: C. SWOT is expanded as Strengths, Weaknesses, Opportunities, and Threats. This is an objective analysis.

Question 50: Which of the following process mapping symbols would NOT be associated with a decision point?

   (a) Hexagon

   (b) Square

   (c) Triangle

   (d) Diamond

Answer: B

Solution: B. Square represents process. Hexagon represents decision or preparation. Diamond represents decision.

Question 51: Process flow improvement steps normally do NOT include

A. Asking why we do it this way

B. Asking what would make it "perfect"

C. Analyzing each step in detail

D. The use of Pareto diagrams

E. A comparison with processes different than your own

    (a) A and E

    (b) D

    (c) C

    (d) B and D

Answer: D

Solution: D. Pareto charts are traditionally used for purposes like market segmentation. They are data analysis tools.

Question 53: How should the value of a customer best be measured?

    (a) Retention length

    (b) Current volume contribution

    (c) Loyalty

    (d) Lifetime worth

Answer: D

Solution: D. The value of a loyal customer is not measured on the basis of one gigantic purchase but rather on his/her lifetime worth. Loyal customers account for a high proportion of sales and profit growth. Customer retention generates repeat sales, and it is cheaper to retain customers.

Question 54: The organization's customer service program can be enhanced in many ways. One of the ways would be

    (a) Restrict access to customer data

    (b) Utilize employee involvement

    (c) Provide better procedures for customer service personnel

    (d) Have supervisors available to answer more questions

Answer: C

Solution: C. The following can be considered when the organization is trying to improve its customer service:

- Listen to customer
- Define service strategy
- Set performance standards
- Select and train employees
- Recognize and reward accomplishments

The above-stated points are very vital because of about 70% of the customers who are not willing to buy the product; it is not because of the quality of the product but due to service quality.

Question 55: Ideally, customer feedback should satisfy organization needs such as

A. Identifying customer requirements

B. Fulfilling ISO 9000 requirements

C. Spotting upcoming trends

D. Having data for analysis
- (a) A and C only
- (b) A, B, C, and D
- (c) B and C only
- (d) A only

Answer: D

Solution: D. The data collected through surveys and feedback is used for analyzing the customers' changing attitude over a period of time. This helps organization to constantly meet the customer requirements without losing the goodwill of the customers.

Question 56: Flowcharting of activities and systems is most helpful in detecting
- I. Inappropriate use of resources
- II. Deficiencies in the organizational structure
- III. Holes or gaps in the control system
- IV. Improper use of statistical methods
  - (a) I and III only
  - (b) I, II and IV only
  - (c) I and II only
  - (d) I only

Answer: A

Solution: A. A flowchart can describe the sequence of the products, paper work, administrative procedures, containers, and operator actions. Flowcharting is the initial step for process improvement for the Six Sigma team. Team members can clearly identify what could be done to the process at each level. Non-value-added activities present in the process can be easily determined and can be separated from the process.

Question 57: Understanding customer needs is a constant requirement for organizations. Customer data and information is often collected in various amounts. The organization should resolve to
- A. Use more proactive approaches
- B. Focus on improvement plans
- C. Identify customer satisfaction drivers
- D. Sort out the unneeded customer data
  - (a) A, B, C, and D
  - (b) A only
  - (c) B and C
  - (d) A, B, and C

Answer: A

Solution: A. Good understanding of the needs of the customer is critical to the survival of most companies. VOC actually enables the organization to

- Make decision on products and services
- Identify product features and specifications
- Focus on improvement plans
- Develop baseline metrics on customer satisfaction
- Identify customer satisfaction drivers

Question 58: Which hierarchy of needs does customer expectations follow, from low to high?
- A. Expected
- B. Basic

   C. Unanticipated

   D. Desired

     (a) B A C D

     (b) C A B D

     (c) D B A C

     (d) A B C D

Answer: A

Solution: A. The customer generally follows a hierarchy of needs: Basic, Expected, Unanticipated, and Desired.

Question 59: The benefits of market segmentation include

  (a) Finishing a consistent marketing plan

  (b) Providing uniform product manufacturing

  (c) Spotting market trends

  (d) Generating high-volume, low-cost production

Question 61: In the preparation of a project, efforts should be made to identify and involve various parties affected by the planned changes. These other parties are known as

  (a) Stakeholders

  (b) Champions

  (c) Team leaders

  (d) Process owners

Answer: A

Solution: A. Internal customers are those in the company who are affected by the product or service as it is being generated. The black belts and master black belts are vested with a crucial responsibility of selecting right people for the Six Sigma methodology. The process is called stakeholder analysis. The stakeholder analysis is performed by the following steps:

• Identify key stakeholders of the project.
• Identify current level of support/resistance.
• Define needed level of support.
• In case of gaps, develop strategy on how to move each stakeholder to the needed level of support.

Question 64: EVOP is

  (a) Evolutionary Operations

  (b) Environmental Operating Procedure

  (c) Experimental Variation on Operations or Processes

  (d) Exploratory Variable Operation Process

Answer: B

9.10 Black Belt

9.10.1 Kano Model

The Kano model can also be referred to as the Kano analysis. It used for the analysis of the requirements of the customer. Noriki Kano is a Japanese engineer and consultant whose work is being employed by Japanese and American engineers for analysis. It is based on three categories as follows.

- Dissatisfiers (basic requirements)

  The expectations of the customer involve these basic requirements as a part of the total package. If these requirements cannot be completed, the customer will not be satisfied. For example, an American travelling to China will expect to have travelling facilities like in America. There is let-down because travel facilities cannot be as good all over the world. It was noted that the Americans found the travel facilities to China were as good as those in America during the Beijing Olympics.

- Beijing Olympics

  The more the requirements of the customer are met, the more pleased is the customer. The tourist taking a tour to the Caribbean on a cruise expects a week of entertainment, food, and relaxation at a reasonable price. The more the personal attention given to the tourist, the happier the tourist is. This makes the travel experience a great one for the crew and staff as well.

- Delighters

  These are the features or the services that are provided to the customer which are beyond the expectations of the customer. For tennis, it would be great if a customer could meet the tennis players when he purchases a ticket at the U.S. open, not just get sunburned and watch a thrilling match. Imagine meeting these players for lunch and also having to watch the match. This would be a delighter.

  Competition to provide the best to the customer is constantly increasing the basic expectations of the customer. The standards of a happy customer are rising. What was once considered to be a delighter will soon become a basic satisfier to the customer. It is important for companies to know the changing needs of the customer and move to improve their performance.

Improvement projects, most of the time, are selected between the satisfier and delighter categories. Most companies in a competitive environment would not stay long enough to tackle a basic issue (Pande, Neuman, and Cavanagh, 2000; Rath and Strong, 2000) (Figure 9.22).

9.10.2 Quality Function Deployment

QFD is a tool that is sometimes referred to as the VOC or house of quality. It is defined as the tool that determines the customers' wants and needs and converts them into technical characteristics.

The technical characteristics are taken care by the company through the design function, or better still, through a team which is cross functional and includes domains of sales, marketing, design engineering, manufacturing engineering, and operations. The basic goal of this activity is to ensure the product or service is focused on meeting the customer's needs and requirements. It is a tool which is to be used for

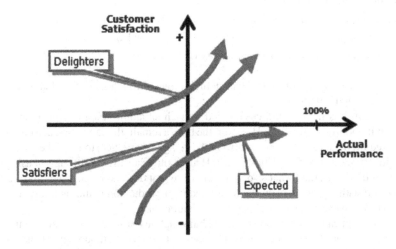

FIGURE 9.22 Kano model.

the entire organization. It is flexible and customizable for the wish of the customer and also functions well for products that are manufactured and in the service industry.

QFD saw its first application in the KOBE shipyards in 1972 by Yoji Akao and his team. It met great success and was introduced to America by Don Clausing in the mid-1980s. Various companies in America have applied the principles of QFD to their product design process. Hauser and Clausing (1988) provide an illustration concerning the position of the emergency-parking brake for a sports car. Engineering initially wanted to place the brake between the seat and the door, but this caused a problem for the women driver wearing a skirt. Could she get out gracefully? Would this eventually cause dissatisfaction?

As an advantage of QFD, we can learn that Toyota and Honda reduced the new product cycle times to about 2½–3 years by means of QFD. The carmakers were on a cycle time of 5 years. QFD could be considered as a concurrent engineering tool.

It provides a graphic method of expressing relationships between customer's wants and design features. It is a matrix that lists the attributes and customer's requirements, and compares them to the features of the design.

The customer's collection of wants and expectations are expressed through the available methods to most organizations: surveys, focus groups, interviews, trade shows, hot lines, etc. The house of quality is a technique used to organize the data. The house of quality is called so because of the image used in the construction. The use of matrices is the key to building the house. The primary matrix shows the relationship between the requirements of the customer and the design features and requirements.

The construction of the house is shown below:

- The left side comprises the needs and wants of the customer.
- The ceiling has the design features and technical requirements.
- The right side contains the priorities of the customer.
- The foundation contains the benchmarking, target values.
- The roof of the house contains the matrix describing the relationship between design features (Figure 9.23).

The possible benefits of using QFD are it

- Creates a customer focuses environment
- Reduces the cycle time of the process
- Uses engineering methods that are concurrent
- Reduces design to manufacture costs
- Increases communication through teams that are cross functional
- Creates data for proper documentation of engineering knowledge
- Prioritizes requirements and improves quality (Figure 9.24).

Cascaded matrices are used to propagate the customer's voice through more detailed parts of the design and solution stages (Figure 9.25).

The house of quality is flexible and customized to each situation. Each organization has their own guidelines that will modify Figure 9.25. However, the basics remain the same, to reach out to the customer's needs and requirements and to be proactive in the design of products to meet the customer's needs.

After the primary design characteristics are set, Hauser and Clausing (1988) suggest using the "how's" from the house of quality as the "what's" of another house that depicts the detailed product design. This process is repeated with a process planning house and then production planning house. In this way, the VOC is carried through every stage from design to manufacturing.

While it is easy to get caught up in the process of building the house of quality and feeding in the date, one should not lose sight of the objectives of the house of quality methodology. Hauser and Clausing (1988) state that QFD is a kind of map with concepts that provides the means for inter-functional planning

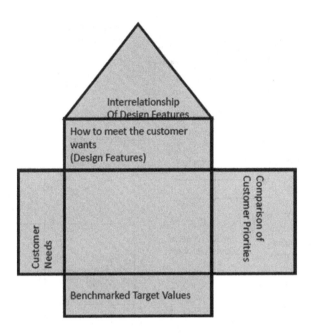

FIGURE 9.23   House of quality.

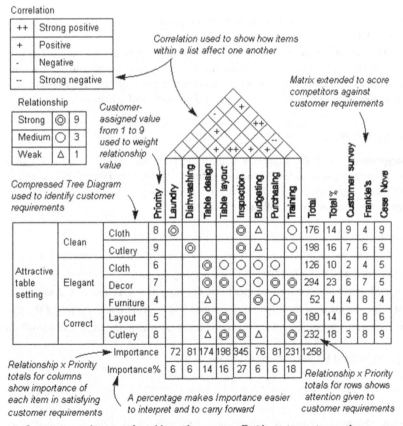

Customer requirements for table-setting versus effort in restaurant procedures

FIGURE 9.24   Example for house of quality.

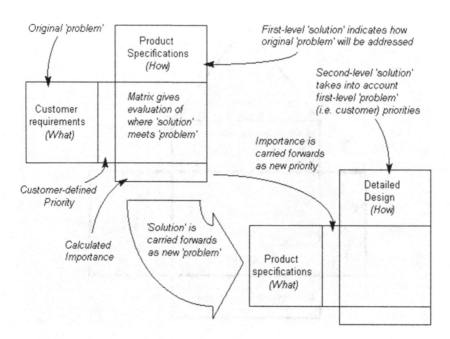

FIGURE 9.25   Hypothetical black belt house of quality.

and communications. The principle benefit of QFD is quality in-house. It gets people thinking in the right directions and thinking together.

The VOC, both internal and external, is presented in the form of house of quality. The various organization groups—engineering, marketing, manufacturing, and so on—are able to see the effect of design and planning changes to maintain and keep the customer happy, and effect of costs and engineering characteristics in the development of new or improved products and services.

9.10.3 Affinity Diagram

An affinity diagram is one of the tools that is used in black belt. Affinity diagrams are used for the purpose of organizing data and ideas. Affinity diagram is used for organizing inputs obtained from the brainstorming into groups based on the relationship and analysis.

Affinity diagrams are used for the following purposes:

- Refining the successful thinking to generate more volume of idea
- Sorting the ideas based on different groups according to the relationship in notes or cards
- Generating idea which is apart from typical meeting
- Organizing inputs obtained from proper brainstorming as a large number of ideas
- Summarizing the ideas according to their groups and figuring out the depth of the problem
- Raising issues and questions, reviewing them, and prioritizing the ideas and recording them.

The following can be used for performing affinity diagrams:

1. Preparation of Affinity Diagram
   - Clarify the theme.
   - Theme should be written as a short, clear, "well-scrubbed" sentence, stated as a question that is fairly specific, e.g., "What are issues surrounding implementation of business plan?"
   - Warm up.

- Hold an open discussion on the theme for a total of five minutes.
- Time is allocated equally among the participants.

2. (a) Write the Cards
   - Card Writing
     - Initially, plan for about 20–25 cards, allocated equally among the participants.
     - Each member records idea on a self-stick note.
     - No talking while writing cards.
   - Hints
     - Responses should not be solutions.
     - Express associated problems or weaknesses.
   - Checklist
     - One idea per card.
     - Complete sentence—in the form of a statement, not a question.

2. (b) Scrub the Cards:
   - Team leader reads each note to the group.
   - If the card is not clear to all, edit as needed.
   - Repeat until all cards are scrubbed.
   - Place all of the "scrubbed" notes randomly onto a flip chart.
   - Checklist.
   - Cards are at a low level of abstraction.
   - Each card represents only one idea.
   - The cards answer the question given in the theme.
   - Everyone understands the specific (concrete) meaning of the card.
   - Note: Approximately 1/3–1/2 of the time you will spend in your LP session should be spent scrubbing cards.

3. First-Level Grouping:
   - With everyone standing at the chart, the team silently arranges notes into 5–10 related groupings based on similar meanings.
   - Keep the clusters to 3–5 notes.
   - Some cards may not fit in any group—leave them by themselves.
   - If a note keeps getting moved from cluster to cluster, it's OK to create a duplicate.

4. Write Titles:
   - The team writes a title header card for each cluster of notes to convey their meaning.
   - Hints
     - Purpose of titles is to extract the essential thought of the group of cards.
     - Title should not be simply addition of the thoughts of cards in the group.
     - Avoid overgeneralization—the title should only be one level of abstraction above the group.

5. Finish the Affinity Diagram:
   - Draw the affinity diagram connecting all finalized title header cards with their groupings (Figures 9.26–9.29).

9.10.4 Interrelationship Diagram

The Interrelationship Diagram is a tool used to prioritize those issues with the greatest impact. The Interrelationship diagram aids in making distinctions between causes (or drivers) and effects

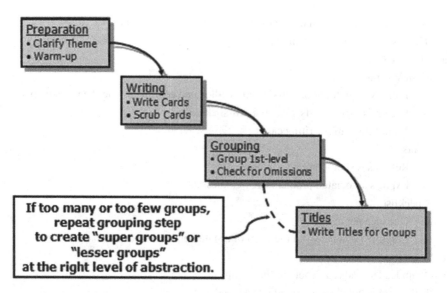

FIGURE 9.26 Affinity diagram.

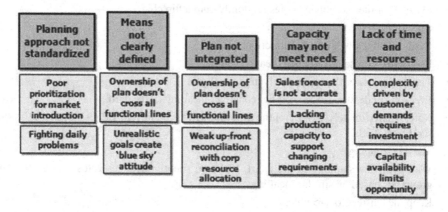

FIGURE 9.27 Affinity diagram for business plan.

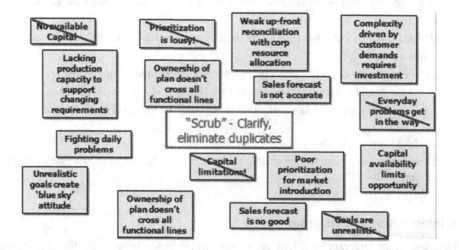

FIGURE 9.28 Generate ideas for affinity diagram.

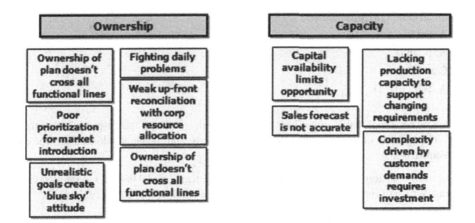

FIGURE 9.29 Identification of groupings.

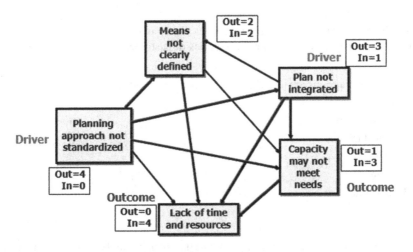

FIGURE 9.30 Interrelationship diagram.

(or outcomes). The affinity diagram is used to identify the key underlying issues of a problem. Main purpose of this tool is for better understanding of relationships between complex issues.

Main uses of this tool are

- To identify or select Six Sigma project area
- To identify key drivers that influence customer needs
- To identify less significant drivers that do not greatly influence customer needs (Figure 9.30).

Review Questions

Question 67: The initial construction of several matrices to display a QFD involves the building of a "house of quality". The sidewalls normally depict

A. Customer needs

B. Customer competitive assessment

C. Design features

    D. Technical competitive assessment
        (a) A and B
        (b) A, B, and C
        (c) C and D
        (d) A, B, C, and D
Answer: A

Solution: A. QFD is a tool that is sometimes referred to as the "voice of the customer" or as the "house of quality". The left side of the house has the customer needs, and the right side contains the customer priorities (comparisons).

Question 68: A new customer satisfaction tool known as the Kano model is used for analyzing customer requirements. Which of the following are NOT considered a Kano model category?
    (a) Moments of truth
    (b) Delighters
    (c) Satisfiers
    (d) Dissatisfiers
Answer: A

Solution: A. The Kano model is also referred to as Kano analysis. It is used to analyze customer requirements. The model is based on three categories of customer needs: dissatisfiers, satisfiers, and delighters.

Question 69: Affinity diagrams are useful tools to help analyze and solve
    A. Unfamiliar problems
    B. Structured problems
    C. Mathematical models
        (a) B only
        (b) A, B, and C
        (c) B and C only
        (d) A only
Answer: D

Solution: D. The use of affinity diagrams is a technique that an individual or team can employ for problem solving. Unfamiliar problems may represent difficulties to the group. This technique is beneficial for new and complex problems.

Question 70: If the interaction roof of a house of quality uses a numeric scale (instead of alphabetic), what data type would be displayed?
    (a) Nominal
    (b) Ratio
    (c) Ordinal
    (d) Interval
Answer: B

Question 71: In QFD, which of the following steps should occur before proceeding to the other steps?
    (a) Perform customer competitive assessment
    (b) Conduct technical competitive assessment
    (c) Determine the customer needs
    (d) Assess the technical design features required
Answer: C

Appendix: A Relationship between Six Sigma and Malcolm Baldrige Quality Award

Abstract
In this chapter, we make a case for how the implementation of the Six Sigma Process Improvement Methodology may result in the achievement of the Malcolm Baldrige National Quality Award (MBNQA) for companies. Our approach is focused on integrating the Six Sigma Process Improvement Methodology Six Sigma implementation within the Baldrige model. While the Baldrige model constitutes the overarching perspective of overall quality of a firm, implementing Six Sigma helps firms to achieve the requirements of the Baldrige criteria. In that regard, Six Sigma and the Baldrige model are complementary. It is expected that firms need to implement both the Baldrige model and Six Sigma to achieve higher levels of quality and performance.

The Baldrige Model for Quality

Despite being described as a "badge of honor" (Dow et al., 1999), the MBNQA is much more than a quality award for an organization. Garvin (1991) described it as "The most important catalyst for transforming American Business". Furthermore, Juran (1994) argues that the MBNQA is a helpful model for getting into world-class quality. MBNQA has been primarily used as a framework for business improvement rather than as an award for quality. The Baldrige model consists of seven categories as follows:

1. Leadership
2. Strategic Planning
3. Customer and Market Focus
4. Measurement, Analysis, and Knowledge Management
5. Human Resource Focus
6. Process Management
7. Business Results.

MBNQA is not only used as a model for QM implementation, but can also be helpful as a self-assessment tool, providing a framework for continuous business process improvement. Figure 9.31 shows the framework for the MBNQA. The framework has evolved over time (since 1988) to address the challenges of the dynamic business environment and has progressed as a comprehensive, integrated system for overall organizational performance management. It has also been used as a guideline for organizations to achieve higher levels of quality (NIST, 2005).

Six Sigma Methodology

According to Feld and Stone (2002), Six Sigma is a data-driven philosophy used to drive management decisions and actions across an organization. Caulcutt (2001) indicates that Six Sigma reduces waste, increases customer satisfaction, and improves processes with a considerable focus on financially measurable results. For the purpose of this chapter, Six Sigma is defined as the relentless pursuit of process variation reduction and breakthrough improvements that increase customer satisfaction and impact the bottom line (Rasis et al., 2002a,b).

A popular framework for implementing a Six Sigma methodology is the DMAIC process. Define, Measure, Analyze, Improve, and Control (DMAIC) are the key processes of a standard framework for the **SSPIM** approach and are shown in Figure 9.32.

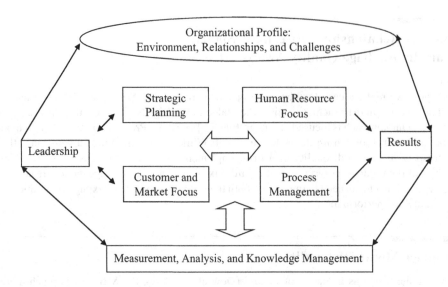

FIGURE 9.31 Baldrige criteria for performance excellence framework: a systems perspective. (Source: www.quality. nist.gov.)

FIGURE 9.32 DMAIC framework.

According to Jing and Li (2004), the psychology of this approach is that key process input variables are narrowed down to a vital few with the idea that having control of the vital few will allow for good control of the whole picture. DMAIC is widely used when a product or process is already in existence but performing inadequately. It is a management strategy that seeks to make an organization more effective and efficient. DMAIC focuses on eliminating unproductive steps, developing and applying new metrics, and using technology to drive improvement (De Feo and Barnard, 2004). Six Sigma has a strategic component aimed at not only developing commitment to it, but also active involvement of higher management. That strategic component is the responsibility of management to identify the key processes of their organization, measure their effectiveness and efficiency, and initiate improvements of the worst performing processes. We need to recognize that while the Baldrige model tends to address the system or the enterprise-wide improvement, Six Sigma attempts to produce micro-level or specific improvement. We believe that firms can achieve higher levels of performance in the Baldrige criteria through implementing Six Sigma projects within the company that focus on the key criteria addressed within the Baldrige model.

The Baldrige Model and Six Sigma

We found that the goal of the SSPIM is to reduce variation in the product/service/process in dimensions (characteristics) that are essential for customer satisfaction. To do so, firms need to analyze their products, processes, and services and determine the variables that affect customer satisfaction. The experience of Motorola with Six Sigma helped the company to win the Baldrige award in 1988. According to Sumberg (2005), the SSPIM quality laid the foundation for Motorola to be the first company to win the Baldrige award. We hypothesize that the linkage between these two initiatives may provide a strong indicator to business success as evidenced by the success of Motorola.

The advantage of the Baldrige model to other quality improvement systems (e.g., TQM and PDCA) revolves around the systems approach within the Baldrige model. The Baldrige model specifically addresses the areas companies need to concentrate on to improve their performance. In addition, it should be noted that the Baldrige model is a self-assessment model. Companies can use the Baldrige model to assess their performance over time, identify their strengths and weaknesses, and focus on the areas that need improvement. This valuable feedback mechanism in the Baldrige model makes it attractive to the majority of companies to use it as a tool to improve their performance over time. In summary, we argue that the Baldrige model is a better choice for companies in their never-ending journey for excellence in quality.

We can incorporate Six Sigma methodology to the Baldrige model. Byrne and Norris (2003) explain how Six Sigma methodology and the Baldrige model are related. They state that "Baldrige provides the framework, Six Sigma the methodology". Six Sigma proponents argue that winning quality awards, improving quality, and increasing customer satisfaction are achieved through the Six Sigma methodology (Douglas and Erwin, 2000). We need to clarify that while the Baldrige model is typically applied at the enterprise level, Six Sigma is deployed as a number of independent projects (throughout the enterprise). Accordingly, by implementing Six Sigma methodology (as independent projects) within the Baldrige model, firms can achieve higher operational performance and efficiency (through Six Sigma projects) while operating under the guidelines and the framework of the Baldrige criteria. It that regard, the two approaches are complementary. The DMAIC cycle of the SSPIM can be employed as a practical tool for addressing the requirement in each category within the Baldrige framework. We can correlate that the Baldrige model assists in defining the goals and objectives and Six Sigma provides the techniques and tactics to achieve these objectives.

The integration of the SSPIM with QM systems is getting more attention in recent years. Lupan et al. (2005) addressed the relationship between Six Sigma and the ISO 9001:2000 quality system. They proposed a strategy for the implementation of the SSPIM as an improvement solution for the ISO 9001:2000. Their approach was focused on the integration of the DMAIC cycle with the PDCA process approach in ISO 9001:2000. Similar to ISO 9001:2000, we suggest that SSPIM can be effectively integrated into the Baldrige model. We also want to suggest the benefits of integrating Six Sigma to the Baldrige model are that it provides a more verifiable cost savings to companies and has the ability to gain greater acceptance due to the popularity among companies from the bottom-line cost reductions. We suggest that integration of traditionally Six Sigma standards, such as projects, should demonstrate a minimum of $100,000 earning before interest and taxes (EBIT) provides further validation that Baldrige companies are successful organizations.

In comparison with the other popularized quality certification initiative ISO 9001:2000 quality system, we suggest that the Baldrige model has more specific criteria which help in defining quality-related projects in a more effective way. The criteria for the Baldrige model have been clearly stated and described. Furthermore, in the Baldrige model, firms need to achieve business performance as well as customer satisfaction. While ISO 2004:2000 (a guideline document to ISO 9001:2000 for performance improvement) emphasizes the effectiveness of a QM system on organizational performance, it does not provide any practical procedure to improve the overall performance of the organization. Rather, it mainly focuses on the overall quality of the firm with respect to customer satisfaction. The Baldrige model offers a broader view of quality, where it relates quality to customer satisfaction and business results (performance). The ISO 9001:2000 "aims to enhance [customer] satisfaction through the effective application of the [quality] system" (section 1.1b of ISO 9001:2000) while the focus of the Baldrige model is on performance excellence for the entire organization in an overall management framework—which includes both quality and business performance (NIST, 2002). This could lead one to conclude that ISO 9001:2000 was designed to document organizational procedures in contrast to Baldrige model which is designed to evaluate, measure, and critique an organizational performance. We suggest that Six Sigma is a better theoretical and real-world fit with the Baldrige award than other quality initiatives such as the ISO 9001:2000.

Implementing Six Sigma within the Baldrige Model
Our approach for implementing the SSPIM within the Baldrige model is consistent with the approach Lupan et al. (2005) have taken to relate Six Sigma with ISO 9001:2000. According to this approach, the implementation of the Baldrige model would mean

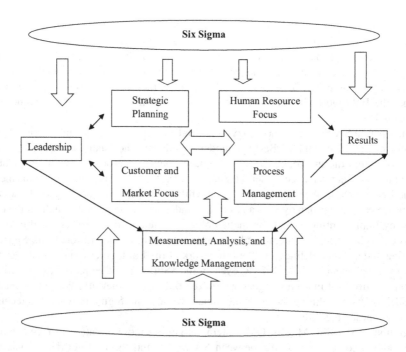

FIGURE 9.33 An integrative approach to Six Sigma implementation in the Baldrige model.

- a focus on performance excellence for the entire organization in an overall management framework
- identifying and tracking all-important organizational results: customer satisfaction, product/service, financial, human resource, and organizational effectiveness.

We need to recognize that while the Baldrige model does not provide any specific methodology, tool, or technique that can be incorporated, it does offer general guidelines. As such, we believe that the SSPIM is a practical, appropriate, and useful tool that can be used to make the Baldrige model goals into more operational measures.

Accordingly, we may apply Six Sigma methodology on each of the seven Baldrige categories to evaluate it after Six Sigma is implemented, compare that with the level of the category before, and asses the improvement we have made in the Baldrige model. In this respect, while companies are using the Baldrige criteria as a self-assessment tool for evaluating the overall quality of the firm (with respect to the requirement of the Baldrige model), improving the enterprise-wide quality level could be achieved through different Six Sigma projects.

The major difference is that Six Sigma projects may not be independent; rather, they are all focusing on achieving higher levels of quality set by the Baldrige criteria. Figure 9.33 shows the integration of Six Sigma into the Baldrige model. In this integrative approach, SSPIM is used to improve each category of the Baldrige model. Depending upon the constraints or requirement of the organization, SSPIM can be implemented separately on each category or simultaneously.

Integrating Six Sigma with the Baldrige Model

The proposed integrative Six Sigma and Baldrige model is based on the following principles:

- The Six Sigma methodology is linked with the Baldrige model. In fact, it becomes part of the Baldrige model (and not separate from it) for achieving performance excellence. Such a performance requirement is set by top management. After the establishment of such goals (which need to be aligned with the requirements of the Baldrige model), SSPIM is used to improve processes and meet quality objectives.

- SSPIM can be applied to all types of the projects, processes, and products. The selection, administration, and control mechanisms are directed by the top management.
- The Baldrige self-assessment includes both the assessment of each of the seven categories, in the Baldrige model, as well as the efficiency and effectiveness of the SSPIM. Such an approach toward quality ensures that the company is gaining benefit from implementing the SSPIM.
- The proposed model for the integrative Six Sigma–Baldrige framework is capable of addressing the core values of the Baldrige model. Through the focus of the SSPIM on management by fact (data analysis and statistics) and goal setting (focus on results), the Baldrige core values—visionary leadership, customer-driven excellence, organizational and personal learning, valuing employees and partners, agility, focus on the future, managing for innovation, social responsibility, and systems perspective—can be addressed.

The Case for Motorola

To show how the principles described in this chapter can be applied in a real-world setting, we provide an example from a company that has effectively implemented Six Sigma and has won the Baldrige award twice: Motorola.

Motorola's success rests on integrating QM initiatives with statistical QC tools and techniques. Having been influenced by Japanese management practices at one of the previously owned Motorola's plants, Quasar, Motorola's management learned how to improve the quality of their products. Under Motorola's leadership, Quasar was losing market share to foreign competitors that sold products of better quality and lower cost. In 1974, Motorola sold Quasar to a Japanese consumer electronic company, Matsushima. Under Japanese management, the factory made drastic improvements in the quality of its products, producing TV sets with 1/20th the number of defects that were made under Motorola's management. It was interesting to note that Matsushima was using the same workforce, technology, and design as Motorola. After a visit to the factory, Motorola's management realized that such surprising results could be achieved when an organization is focused on processes, people, and quality (ICFAI Center for Management Research: http://icmr.icfai.org/casestudies.catalogue.Operatios/OPER050.htm). In other words, they found that it is the quality system which leads a company to produce the products of higher quality. They also realized that in order to improve the quality of their products, they need to change their focus of quality improvement from product attributes to operational procedures.

This shift in thinking about quality within Motorola resulted in an emphasis in the systems approach, the interactions between different processes within the organization, and their overall impact on performance. By focusing on management (leadership), people (human resource management), process (process management), flow of information (information, analysis, and knowledge management), VOC (customer and market focus), and commitment to higher product quality (strategic planning), Motorola was successful in reducing the defect rate in its process to the Six Sigma level (3.4 defects per million). Such a dramatic improvement could not be achieved by just focusing on process management using statistical QC tools and techniques. Rather, as evidenced by the Quasar case, it is the result of improvement in all aspects of organization—leadership, strategic planning, customer and market focus, measurement, analysis and knowledge management, human resource focus, and process management—that led to achieving higher level of performance, which coincidently are the criteria of the Baldrige model.

In the current stage, Six Sigma and the Baldrige model have commonalities. With reference to the Baldrige criteria, Six Sigma is directly related to customer focus and satisfaction; process management; and information, analysis, and knowledge management. They have been partially integrated now. The challenge is how to implement Six Sigma in areas such as leadership, strategic planning, and human resource management to achieve a full integration. We have the following recommendations for the full integration of Six Sigma within the Baldrige model.

Leadership and Six Sigma: Six Sigma projects can be effectively defined to enhance the quality of the leadership in an organization. In that regard, the feedback from the Baldrige model can be used as a base to define Six Sigma projects with focus on leadership development. Companies can assess how their leaders lead and how they should lead—both come from the Baldrige model. Then, they can develop Six Sigma projects that aim at meeting the desired leadership goals. Developing leadership standards can be a useful tool. Motorola has its own "4e's + Always 1" leadership standard which addresses key leadership characteristics: (1) envision: developing vision, strategies, and a viable plan to achieve them; (2) energize: create an environment for employees to excel and innovate; (3) edge: make tough, effective, and timely decisions; (4) execute: achieve results in a timely manner; and (5) ethics and character: conduct business practices professionally and ethically. Companies that do not integrate their leadership within Six Sigma projects are subject to failure in achieving their desired outcome from Six Sigma projects. Honeywell was astute enough to understand that it needed to integrate its SSPIM initiative with the organizational leadership (Carter et al., 2005).

Human Resource Management and Six Sigma: The feedback from the Baldrige self-assessment can be used to identify potential Six Sigma projects focusing particularly on human resource development. In addition, the SSPIM enhances organizational knowledge base through training and systematic learning. But the impact of the SSPIM on human resource development goes beyond that. "There are hundreds of human resources issues that should be addressed when you begin Six Sigma", says David Silverstein, CEO and president of Breakthrough Management Group, a Six Sigma consulting firm based in Longmont, Colorado. This includes developing a plan for delivery of Six Sigma training, preparing human resource teams for their role in Six Sigma, and creating and implementing a communication strategy that will keep the organization informed about Six Sigma achievements. "The human resources team controls the history and the culture of the company", he says. "They are a vital part of the system that supports Six Sigma", Silverstein says. At Lockheed Martin, an interview with Six Sigma personnel identified a few behaviors that were critical to the success of Six Sigma. Most of these behaviors were crucial conversations—such as slow rate of response in employee needs, observing unproductive practices, and attention given by top management to the problems—that enabled Six Sigma projects to progress or stalled them depending upon how these behaviors were handled (Carter et al., 2005).

Strategic Planning and Six Sigma: Honeywell was another company that successfully implemented the SSPIM within the entire organization. Honeywell developed a new generation of Six Sigma which was called Six Sigma Plus. This initiative was primarily a quality strategy which was developed through the merger of Allied Signal and Honeywell in 1999. In Six Sigma Plus, Honeywell focused on key strategic objectives: providing more value to its customer though empowering the employees; improving its processes, products, and services; and capitalizing on e-Business. In fact, Honeywell's Six Sigma Plus program was focusing on implementing high-impact projects consistent with its strategic planning. It employed a rigorous project selection process which was in line with the company's overall strategic plan.

The above are just a few examples of the link between Six Sigma and the Baldrige model. As noted, the link between the SSPIM and the Baldrige model has been already established in categories such as process management; customer and market focus; and information, analysis, and knowledge management. Companies can achieve significant improvement in their Six Sigma projects if they fully integrate it with the Baldrige model.

Conclusion

Organizations try to implement the Baldrige model as a means for achieving business excellence. The seven categories within the Baldrige model are integrated and related with the purpose of addressing business challenges so that companies can be competitive in the dynamic business environment. However, the Baldrige model does not provide any tool or technique that can be used by the firm for achieving desired performance and/or quality objectives.

Six Sigma is a practical methodology for reducing cost, improving quality, and fostering continuous improvement in the product/process. Because Six Sigma originated through quality, it provides time-tested tools that have enabled continuous improvement for organizations such as GE and Motorola that leads to better performance. Also, it has been widely used by companies which are seeking to achieve higher level of customer satisfaction and profitability. This research suggests that due to Six Sigma's previous acceptance by other companies, the ability to produce bottom-line savings, and its foundations in quality, it would be a strong addition to the Baldrige model. Furthermore, we need to notice that one of the requirements of the Baldrige model is achieving business results.

Finally, we need to notice that one of the requirements of the Baldrige model is achieving better performance levels. We believe that integrating the SSPIM into the Baldrige model not only helps firms achieve higher levels of performance and customer satisfaction in each category of the Baldrige model, but also provides them with a useful methodology for pursuing quality and performance level set by the Baldrige model.

REFERENCES

Ahire, S. L. 1997. Management science- total quality management interfaces: An integrative framework. *Interfaces*, 27 (6), 91–105.

Byrne, G., and Norris, B. May 2003. Drive Baldrige level performance. *Six Sigma Forum Magazine*, 13–21.

Carter, L., Ulrich, D., and Goldsmith, M. 2005. *Best Practices in Leadership Development and Organization Change*, Pfeiffer Publisher, John Wiley and Sons, San Francisco, CA.

Caulcutt, R. 2001. Why is Six Sigma so successful? *Journal of Applied Statistics*, 28 (3&4), 301–306.

Crosby, P. B. 1979. *Quality Is Free: The Art of Making Quality Certain*, McGraw-Hill, New York.

Cua, K. O., McKone, K. E., and Schroeder, R. G. 2001. Relationships between implementation of TQM, JIT, and TPM and manufacturing performance. *Journal of Operations Management*, 19 (6), 675–694.

De Feo, J., and Barnard, W. 2004. *Juran Institute's Six Sigma: Breakthrough and Beyond*, McGraw-Hill, New York.

Devane, T. 2004. *Integrating Lean Six Sigma and High Performance Organizations Leading the Charge toward Dramatic, Rapid and Sustainable Improvement*, Pfeiffer An imprint of Wiley, San Francisco, CA. Print.

Does, R., Van den Huvel, E., De Mast, J., and Bisgaard, S. 2002. Comparing non-manufacturing with traditional applications of Six Sigma. *Quality Engineering*, 15 (1), 177–182.

Douglas, P. C., and Erwin, J. March/April 2000. Six Sigma focus on total customer satisfaction. *The Journal for Quality & Participation*, 45–49.

Dow, D., Samson, D., and Ford, S. 1999. Exploding the myth: do all quality management practices contribute to superior quality performance? *Production and Operations Management*, 8 (1), 1–27.

Drucker, P. F., ed. 1986. *Managing for Results: Economic Tasks and Risk-Taking Decisions*, Harper & Row, New York. Print.

Eckes, G., ed. 2001. *The Six Sigma Revolution*, John Wiley & Sons, New York. Print.

Feld, K. and Stone, W. 2002. Using Six Sigma to change and measure improvement. *Performance Improvement*, 41 (9), 20–26.

Flynn, B. B., and Saladin, B. 2001. Further evidence on the validity of the theoretical models underlying the Baldrige criteria. *Journal of Operations Management*, 19 (3), 617–652.

Gale, S. F. May 2003. Building frameworks for Six Sigma success - Case studies – Quality management philosophy, Workforce.

Garvin, D. A. November–December 1987. Competing on the eight dimensions of quality. *Harvard Business Review*, 101–109.

Garvin, D., ed. 1988. *Managing Quality: The Strategic and Competitive Edge*, The Free Press, New York. Print.

Garvin, D. A. 1991. How the Baldrige award really works. *Harvard Business Review*, 69 (6), 80–93.

Harry, M., and Schroeder, R. 2000. *Six Sigma, the Breakthrough Management Strategy*, Currency/Doubleday, New York.

Hauser, J. R., and Clausing, D. May–June 1988. The house of quality. *The Harvard Business Review*. Print.

Jing, G., and Li, N. February 2004. Claiming Six Sigma, *Industrial Engineer*, 37–39.

Jones, E. C., and Garza, A. 2010. Six-Sigma deployment success according shareholder value. *Proceedings of the 2010 Institute of Industrial Engineers Annual Conference*. Ed. Print.

Jones, E. C., Riley, M. W, and Battieste, T. The value of industrial engineers in lean Six Sigma organizations. *Proceedings of the 2010 Industrial Engineering Research Conference*. Ed. Johnson, A., and Millers, J. Print.

Juran, J. M. 1994. The upcoming century for quality. *Quality Progress*, 27 (8), 29–37.

Juran, J. 1998. *Juran's Quality Control Handbook*, 5th edn, McGraw-Hill, New York.

Lowenstein, M. 1995. *Customer Retention*, ASQC Quality Press, Milwaukee, WI. Print.

Lupan, R., Bacivarof, I. C., Kobi, A., and Robledo, C. 2005. A relationship between Six Sigma and ISO 9000:2000. *Quality Engineering*, 17, 1–7.

Narasimhan, J., and Jones, E. C. Reduction in the variation of welding process using the operational six-sigma methodology. *Proceedings of the 2004 Industrial Engineering Research Conference*. Ed. Houston, TX. Print.

National Institute of Standards and Technology (NIST), Baldrige criteria quality program. 2002. Baldrige, Six Sigma, & ISO: Understanding your options, CEO issue sheet, www.quality.nist.gov/.

National Institute of Standards and Technology (NIST), Baldrige criteria quality program. 2005. www.quality. nist.gov/Business-Criteria.htm.

Pande, P. S., Neuman, R. P., and Cavanagh, R. R. eds. 2000. *The Six Sigma Way*, McGraw-Hill, New York. Print.

Rasis, D., Gitlow, H., and Popovich, E. 2002a, Paper organizers international: A fictitious Six Sigma green belt case study 1. *Quality Engineering*, 15 (1), 127–145.

Rasis, D., Gitlow, H., and Popovich, E. 2002b. Paper organizers international: A fictitious Six Sigma green belt case study 2. *Quality Engineering*, 15 (2), 259–274.

Rath, and Strong, eds. 2000. *Rath & Strong's Six Sigma Pocket Guide*, Rath & Strong Management Consultants, Lexington, MA. Print.

Sumberg, B. B. February 2005. Linking business needs and lessons learned to education. *Training & Development*, 70.

Zhang, Q., et al. 2012. Lean Six Sigma: A literature review. *Interdisciplinary Journal of Contemporary Research in Business*, 3 (10): 599–605. Print.

10

A Relationship between Six Sigma and Malcolm Baldrige Quality Award

Mellat-Parast M. and Erick C. Jones

Continuous improvement is better than delayed perfection.

Mark Twain

10.1 Introduction

The Malcolm Baldrige National Quality Award (MBNQA) has evolved from a means of recognizing the best quality management practices to a comprehensive framework for world-class performance, where it is widely used as a model for process improvement (Flynn and Saladin, 2001). Companies strive to achieve higher quality of products and/or services and enhance their profitability through implementing the Baldrige criteria. Interestingly, these criteria are well established by the Six Sigma Process Improvement Method (SSPIM).

While the Baldrige criteria and the SSPIM have followed different development paths, they have the same roots. The U.S. Congress established the MBNQA in 1987 to enhance U.S. competitiveness by promoting quality awareness, recognizing the quality and business excellence of U.S. companies, and publicizing the successful performance of these companies. On the other hand, the SSPIM was developed by Motorola in the late 1980s as an improvement initiative focused on quality (Feld and Stone, 2002). However, both originated from quality management philosophies and attempt to enhance performance, increase profitability, and improve quality. Accordingly, it is worth investigating how the Baldrige criteria and the SSPIM might be related to each other.

The purpose of this chapter is to investigate the relationship between the SSPIM and the Baldrige model. We use the Baldrige framework as a generic model for process improvement within an organization. We refer to the SSPIM from a management point of view—as a number of independent projects within a firm—in order to link it to the implementation of the Baldrige model (Lupan et al., 2005). We argue that it is possible to implement Six Sigma philosophies within the Baldrige framework and integrate it with the overall quality system of the organization.

10.2 The Baldrige Model for Quality

Despite being described as a "badge of honor" (Dow et al., 1999), the MBNQA is much more than quality award for an organization. Garvin (1991) described it as "The most important catalyst for transforming American Business." Furthermore, Juran (1994) argues that the MBNQA is a helpful model for getting into world-class quality. MBNQA has been primarily used as a framework for business improvement rather than as an award for quality. The Baldrige model consists of seven categories as follows:

1. Leadership
2. Strategic planning

3. Customer and market focus

4. Measurement, analysis, and knowledge management

5. Human resource focus

6. Process management

7. Business results.

MBNQA is not only used as a model for quality management implementation, but can also be helpful as a self-assessment tool, providing a framework for continuous business process improvement. Figure 9.31 shows the framework for the MBNQA. The framework has evolved over time (since 1988) to address the challenges of the dynamic business environment and has been progressed as a comprehensive, integrated system for overall organizational performance management. It has also been used as a guideline for organizations to achieve higher levels of quality (NIST, 2005).

10.3 Six Sigma Methodology

According to Feld and Stone (2002), Six Sigma is a data-driven philosophy used to drive management decisions and actions across an organization. Caulcutt (2001) indicates that Six Sigma reduces waste, increases customer satisfaction, and improves processes with a considerable focus on financially measurable results. For the purpose of this chapter, Six Sigma is defined as the relentless pursuit of process variation reduction and breakthrough improvements that increase customer satisfaction and impact the bottom line (Rasis et al., 2002).

A popular framework for implementing a Six Sigma methodology is the DMAIC process. Define, Measure, Analyze, Improve, and Control (DMAIC) are the key processes of a standard framework for the **SSPIM** approach.

According to Jing and Li (2004), the psychology of this approach is that key process input variables are narrowed down to a vital few with the idea that having control of the vital few will allow for good control of the whole picture. DMAIC is widely used when a product or process is already in existence but performing inadequately. It is a management strategy that seeks to make an organization more effective and efficient. DMAIC focuses on eliminating unproductive steps, developing and applying new metrics, and using technology to drive improvement (De Feo and Barnard, 2004). Six Sigma has a strategic component aimed at not only developing commitment to it, but also active involvement of higher management. That strategic component is the responsibility of management to identify the key processes of their organization, measure their effectiveness and efficiency, and initiate improvements of the worst performing processes. We need to recognize that while the Baldrige model tends to address the system or the enterprise-wide improvement, Six Sigma attempts to produce micro-level or specific improvement. We believe that firms can achieve higher levels of performance in the Baldrige criteria through implementing Six Sigma projects within the company that focuses on the key criteria addressed within the Baldrige model.

10.4 The Baldrige Model and Six Sigma

We found that the goal of the SSPIM is to reduce variation in the product/service/process in dimensions (characteristics) that are essential for customer satisfaction. To do so, firms need to analyze their products, processes, and services and determine the variables that affect customer satisfaction. The experience of Motorola with Six Sigma helped the company to win the Baldrige award in 1988. According to Sumberg (2005), the SSPIM quality laid the foundation for Motorola to be the first company to win the Baldrige award. We hypothesize that the linkage between these two initiatives may provide a strong indicator to business success as evidenced by the success of Motorola.

The advantage of the Baldrige model to other quality improvement systems (e.g., total quality management (TQM) and PDCA (Plan, Do, Check, and Action)) revolves around the systems approach within the Baldrige model. The Baldrige model specifically addresses the areas companies need to concentrate on to improve their performance. In addition, it should be noted that the Baldrige model is a self-assessment model. Companies can use the Baldrige model to assess their performance over time, identify their strengths and weaknesses, and focus on the areas that need improvement. This valuable feedback mechanism in the Baldrige model makes it attractive to the majority of companies to use it as a tool to improve their performance over time. In summary, we argue that the Baldrige model is a better choice for companies in their never-ending journey for excellence in quality.

We can incorporate Six Sigma methodology to the Baldrige model. Byrne and Norris (2003) explain how Six Sigma methodology and the Baldrige model are related. They state that "Baldrige provides the framework, Six Sigma the methodology." Six Sigma proponents argue that winning quality awards, improving quality, and increasing customer satisfaction is achieved through the Six Sigma methodology (Douglas and Erwin, 2000). We need to clarify that while the Baldrige model is typically applied at the enterprise level, Six Sigma is deployed as a number of independent projects (throughout the enterprise). Accordingly, by implementing Six Sigma methodology (as independent projects) within the Baldrige model, firms can achieve higher operational performance and efficiency (through Six Sigma projects) while operating under the guidelines and the framework of the Baldrige criteria. In that regard, the two approaches are complementary. The DMAIC cycle of the SSPIM can be employed as a practical tool for addressing the requirement in each category within the Baldrige framework. We can correlate that the Baldridge model assists in defining the goals and objectives and Six Sigma provides the techniques and tactics to achieve these objectives.

The integration of the SSPIM with quality management systems is getting more attention in recent years. Lupan et al. (2005) addressed the relationship between Six Sigma and the ISO 9001:2000 quality system. They proposed a strategy for the implementation of the SSPIM as an improvement solution for the ISO 9001:2000. Their approach was focused on the integration of the DMAIC cycle with the PDCA process approach in ISO 9001:2000. Similar to ISO 9001:2000, we suggest that SSPIM can be effectively integrated into the Baldrige model. We also want to suggest the benefits of integrating Six Sigma to the Baldrige model that it provides a more verifiable cost savings to companies and has the ability to gain greater acceptance due to the popularity among companies from the bottom-line cost reductions. We suggest that integration of traditionally Six Sigma standards, such as projects, should demonstrate a minimum of $100,000 earning before interest and taxes (EBIT) provides further validation that Baldridge companies are successful organizations.

In comparison with the other popularized quality certification initiative ISO 9001:2000 quality system, we suggest that the Baldrige model has more specific criteria which helps in defining quality-related projects in more effective way. The criteria for the Baldrige model have been clearly stated and described. Furthermore, in the Baldrige model, firms need to achieve business performance as well as customer satisfaction. While ISO 2004:2000 (a guideline document to ISO 9001:2000 for performance improvement) emphasizes the effectiveness of a quality management system on organizational performance, it does not provide any practical procedure to improve the overall performance of the organization. Rather, it mainly focuses on the overall quality of the firm with respect to customer satisfaction. The Baldrige model offers a broader view of quality, where it relates quality to customer satisfaction and business results (performance). The ISO 9001:2000 "aims to enhance [customer] satisfaction through the effective application of the [quality] system" (section 1.1b of ISO 9001:2000), while the focus of the Baldrige model is on performance excellence for the entire organization in an overall management framework—which includes both quality and business performance (NIST, 2002). This could lead one to conclude that ISO 9001:2000 was designed to document organizational procedures in contrast to Baldridge which is designed to evaluate, measure, and critique an organizational performance. We suggest that Six Sigma is a better theoretical and real-world fit with the Baldridge award than other quality initiatives such as the ISO 9001:2000.

10.5 Implementing Six Sigma within the Baldrige Model

Our approach for implementing the SSPIM within the Baldrige model is consistent with the approach Lupan et al. (2005) have taken to relate Six Sigma with ISO 9001:2000. According to this approach, the implementation of the Baldrige model would mean

- A focus on performance excellence for the entire organization in an overall management framework.
- Identifying and tracking all-important organizational results: customer satisfaction, product/service, financial, human resource, and organizational effectiveness.

We need to recognize that while the Baldrige model does not provide any specific methodology, tool, or technique that can be incorporated, it does offer general guidelines. As such, we believe that the SSPIM is a practical, appropriate, and useful tool that can be used to make the Baldrige model goals into more operational measures.

Accordingly, we may apply Six Sigma methodology on each of the seven Baldrige categories to evaluate it after Six Sigma is implemented, compare that with the level of the category before, and assess the improvement we have made in the Baldrige model. In this respect, while companies are using the Baldrige criteria as a self-assessment tool for evaluating the overall quality of the firm (with respect to the requirement of the Baldrige model), improving the enterprise-wide quality level could be achieved through different Six Sigma projects.

The major difference is that Six Sigma projects may not be independent; rather, they are all focusing on achieving higher levels of quality set by the Baldrige criteria. Figure 9.33 shows the integration of Six Sigma into the Baldrige model. In this integrative approach, SSPIM is used to improve each category of the Baldrige model. Depending upon the constraints or requirement of the organization, SSPIM can be implemented separately on each category or simultaneously.

10.6 Integrating Six Sigma with the Baldrige Model

The proposed integrative Six Sigma and Baldrige model is based on the following principles:

- The Six Sigma methodology is linked with the Baldrige model. In fact, it becomes part of the Baldrige model (and not separate from it) for achieving performance excellence. Such a performance requirement is set by top management. After the establishment of such goals (which need to be aligned with the requirements of the Baldrige model), SSPIM is used to improve processes and meet quality objectives.
- SSPIM can be applied to all types of the projects, processes, and products. The selection, administration, and control mechanisms are directed by the top management.
- The Baldrige self-assessment includes both the assessment of each of the seven categories, in the Baldrige model, as well as the efficiency and effectiveness of the SSPIM. Such an approach towards quality ensures that the company is gaining benefit from implementing the SSPIM.
- The proposed model for the integrative Six Sigma–Baldrige framework is capable of addressing the core values of the Baldrige model. Through the focus of the SSPIM on management by fact (data analysis and statistics) and goal setting (focus on results), the Baldrige core values—visionary leadership, customer-driven excellence, organizational and personal learning, valuing employees and partners, agility, focus on the future, managing for innovation, social responsibility, and systems perspective—can be addressed.

10.7 The Case for Motorola

To show how the principles described in this chapter can be applied in a real-world setting, we provide an example from a company that has effectively implemented Six Sigma and has won the Baldrige award twice: Motorola.

Motorola's success rests on integrating quality management initiatives with statistical quality control tools and techniques. Having been influenced by Japanese management practices at one of the previously owned Motorola's plants: Quasar, Motorola's management, learned how to improve the quality of their products. Under Motorola's leadership, Quasar was losing market share to foreign competitors that sold products of better quality and lower cost. In 1974, Motorola sold Quasar to a Japanese consumer electronics company, Matsushima. Under Japanese management, the factory made drastic improvements in the quality of its products, producing TV sets with 1/20th the number of defects that were made under Motorola's management. It was interesting to note that Matsushima was using the same workforce, technology, and design as Motorola. After a visit to the factory, Motorola's management realized that such surprising results could be achieved when an organization is focused on processes, people, and quality (ICFAI Center for Management Research: http://icmr.icfai.org/casestudies.catalogue.Operatios/OPER050.htm). In other words, they found that it is the quality system that leads a company to produce higher quality of products. They also realized that in order to improve the quality of their products, they need to change their focus of quality improvement from product attributes to operational procedures.

This shift in thinking about quality within Motorola resulted in an emphasis in the systems approach, the interactions between different processes within the organization, and their overall impact on performance. By focusing on management (leadership), people (human resource management), process (process management), flow of information (information, analysis, and knowledge management), voice of customers (customer and market focus), and commitment to higher product quality (strategic planning), Motorola was successful in reducing the defect rate in its process to the Six Sigma level (3.4 defects per millions). Such a dramatic improvement could not be achieved by just focusing on process management using statistical quality control tools and techniques. Rather, as evidenced by the Quasar case, it is the result of improvement in all aspects of organization: leadership, strategic planning, customer and market focus, measurement, analysis and knowledge management, human resource focus, and process management led to achieving higher level of performance, which coincidently are the criteria of the Baldrige model.

In its current stage, Six Sigma and the Baldrige model have commonalities. With reference to the Baldrige criteria, Six Sigma is directly related to customer focus and satisfaction, process management, and information, analysis, and knowledge management. They have been partially integrated now. The challenge is how to implement Six Sigma in areas such as leadership, strategic planning, and human resource management to achieve a full integration. We have the recommendations for the full integration of Six Sigma within the Baldrige model:

Leadership and Six Sigma: Six Sigma projects can be effectively defined to enhance the quality of the leadership in an organization. In that regard, the feedback from the Baldrige model can be used as a base to define Six Sigma projects with focus on leadership development. Companies can assess how their leaders lead and how they should lead—both come from the Baldrige model. Then, they can develop Six Sigma projects that aim at meeting the desired leadership goals. Developing leadership standards can be a useful tool. Motorola has its own "4e's+Always 1" leadership standard which addresses key leadership characteristics: (1) envision—developing vision, strategies, and a viable plan to achieve them; (2) energize—create an environment for employees to excel and innovate; (3) edge—make tough, effective, and timely decisions; (4) execute—achieve results in a timely manner; and (5) ethics and character—conduct business practices professionally and ethically. Companies that do not integrate their leadership within Six Sigma projects are subject to failure in achieving their desired outcome from Six Sigma project. Honeywell was astute enough to understand that it needed to integrate its SSPIM initiative with the organizational leadership (Carter et al., 2005).

Human Resource Management and Six Sigma: The feedback from the Baldrige self-assessment can be used to identify potential Six Sigma projects focusing particularly on human resource development. In addition, the SSPIM enhances organizational knowledge base through training and systematic learning. But the impact of the SSPIM on human resource development goes beyond that. "There are hundreds of human resources issues that should be addressed when you begin Six Sigma", says David Silverstein, CEO and president of Breakthrough Management Group, a Six Sigma consulting firm based in Longmont, Colorado. This includes developing a plan for delivery of Six Sigma training, preparing human resource teams for their role in Six Sigma, and creating and implementing a communication strategy that will keep the organization informed about Six Sigma achievements. "The human resources team controls the history and the culture of the company," he says. "They are a vital part of the system that supports Six Sigma," says Silverstein. At Lockheed Martin, an interview with Six Sigma personnel identified a few behaviors that were critical to the success of Six Sigma. Most of these behaviors were crucial conversations—such as slow rate of response in employee needs, observing unproductive practices, and attention given by top management to the problems—that enable Six Sigma projects to progress or stalled them depending upon how these behaviors were handled (Carter et al., 2005).

Strategic Planning and Six Sigma: Honeywell was another company that successfully implemented the SSPIM within the entire organization. Honeywell developed a new generation of Six Sigma which was called Six Sigma plus. This initiative was primarily a quality strategy which was developed through the merger of Allied Signal and Honeywell in 1999. In Six Sigma Plus, Honeywell focused on key strategic objectives: providing more value to its customer through empowering the employees, improving its processes, products, and services, and capitalizing on e-Business. In fact, Honeywell's Six Sigma Plus program was focusing on implementing high-impact projects consistent with its strategic planning. It employed rigorous project selection process which was in line with the company's overall strategic plan.

The above are just a few examples of the link between Six Sigma and the Baldrige model. As noted, the link between the SSPIM and the Baldrige model has been already established in categories such as process management, customer and market focus, and information, analysis, and knowledge management. Companies can achieve significant improvement in their Six Sigma projects if they fully integrate it with the Baldrige model.

10.8 Conclusion

Organizations try to implement the Baldrige model as a means for achieving business excellence. The seven categories within the Baldrige model are integrated and related to the purpose of addressing business challenges so that companies can be competitive in the dynamic business environment. However, the Baldrige model does not provide any tool or technique that can be used by the firm for achieving desired performance and/or quality objectives.

Six Sigma is a practical methodology for reducing cost, improving quality, and fostering continuous improvement in the product/process. Because Six Sigma originated through quality, it provides time-tested tools that have enabled continuous improvement for organizations such as GE and Motorola that lead to better performance. Also, it has been widely used by companies which are looking to achieve higher level of customer satisfaction and profitability. This research suggests that due to Six Sigma's previous acceptance by other companies, the ability to produce bottom-line savings, and its foundations in quality, it would be a strong addition to the Baldrige model. Furthermore, we need to notice that one of the requirements of the Baldrige model in business results.

Finally, we need to notice that one of the requirements of the Baldrige model is achieving better performance levels. We believe that integrating the SSPIM into the Baldrige model not only helps firms achieve higher levels of performance and customer satisfaction in each category of the Baldrige model, but also provides them with a useful methodology for pursuing quality and performance level set by the Baldrige model.

REFERENCES

Byrne, G. and Norris, B. (May 2003) Drive Baldrige level performance, *Six Sigma Forum Magazine*, 2, 13–21.
Carter, L., Ulrich, D., and Goldsmith, M. (2005) *Best Practices in Leadership Development and Organization Change*, Pfeiffer Publisher, John Wiley and Sons, San Francisco, CA.
Caulcutt, R. (2001) Why is Six Sigma so successful? *Journal of Applied Statistics*, 28 (3&4), 301–306.
De Feo, J. and Barnard, W. (2004) *Juran Institute's Six Sigma: Breakthrough and Beyond*, McGraw-Hill, New York.
Does, R., Van den Huvel, E., De Mast J., and Bisgaard, S. (2002) Comparing non-manufacturing with traditional applications of six sigma, *Quality Engineering*, 15 (1), 177–182.
Douglas, P.C. and Erwin, J. (March/April 2000) Six Sigma focus on total customer satisfaction, *The Journal for Quality & Participation*, 23, 45–49.

Dow, D., Samson, D., and Ford, S. (1999) Exploding the myth: Do all quality management practices contribute to superior quality performance? *Production and Operations Management*, 8 (1), 1–27.

Feld, K. and Stone, W. (2002) Using six sigma to change and measure improvement, *Performance Improvement*, 41 (9), 20–26.

Flynn, B.B. and Saladin, B. (2001) Further evidence on the validity of the theoretical models underlying the Baldrige criteria, *Journal of Operations Management*, 19 (3), 617–652.

Gale, S.F. (May 2003) Building frameworks for Six Sigma success—Case Studies—Quality management philosophy, *Workforce*.

Garvin, D.A. (1991) How the Baldrige award really works, *Harvard Business Review*, 69 (6), 80–93.

Jing, G. and Li, N. (February 2004) Claiming six sigma, *Industrial Engineer*, 36, 37–39.

Juran, J.M. (1994) The upcoming century for quality, *Quality Progress*, 27 (8), 29–37.

Lupan, R., Bacivarof, I.C., Kobi, A., and Robledo, C. (2005) A relationship between Six Sigma and ISO 9000:2000, *Quality Engineering*, 17, 1–7.

National Institute of Standards and Technology (NIST), Baldrige Criteria Quality Program (2005) www.quality.nist.gov/Business-Criteria.htm.

National Institute of Standards and Technology (NIST), Baldrige Criteria Quality Program (2002) Baldrige, Six Sigma, & ISO: Understanding your options, CEO issue sheet, www.quality.nist.gov/.

Rasis, D., Gitlow, H., and Popovich, E. (2002) Paper organizers international: A fictitious six sigma green belt case study 1, *Quality Engineering*, 15 (1), 127–145.

Rasis, D., Gitlow, H., and Popovich, E. (2002) Paper organizers international: A fictitious six sigma green belt case study 2, *Quality Engineering*, 15 (2), 259–274.

Sumberg, B.B. (February 2005) Linking business needs and lessons learned to education, *Training & Development*, 70.

11

Evaluating Increasing Hospital Closure Rates in U.S.: A Model Framework and Lean Six Sigma Deployment Approach for Quality Improvement Initiatives to Prevent Further Closures in Rural and Disadvantaged Locations

Soma Sekar Balasubramanian and Erick C. Jones

Progress is impossible without change; and those who cannot change their minds cannot change anything.

George Bernard Shaw

11.1 Introduction

11.1.1 Overview

The U.S. is witnessing huge reforms and changes in healthcare industry at recent times. The recent reform enacted in 2010 is believed to have changed the landscape of the healthcare system in the country. The federal government's initiatives to improve the current healthcare scenario in the country are reflected from the expansion of Medicaid, establishing Health Insurance Marketplaces, with the intention of expanding health insurance coverage for economically challenged and common man alike. Since then, a record number of people got themselves newly insured as the Medicaid program is intended to cover 17 million newly insured people. As of 2014, about 8.02 million people enrolled through State exchanges 5.02 million people enrolled for Medicaid (Mangan). Other important changes contained within the reform include the transition from traditional fee-for-service reimbursements to value-based ones by targeting quality of hospital care. Several new programs, such as the Hospital Readmission Reduction Program (HRRP) and Hospital Value Based Purchasing Program (HVBP), were implemented to improve the patient outcomes and reduce unnecessary healthcare costs by penalizing and reducing reimbursements for hospitals that do not perform on par with other hospitals nationwide.

In sharp contrast to the above healthcare industry events, which tend to make us believe that the country's healthcare situation is on an upward improving trend, there are some serious issues and concerns that are simultaneously happening at present, which need some immediate attention. One important formidable issue is the hospital closures that are happening around the country in recent years. In a country where half of the population are from rural areas, 79 rural hospitals have closed since 2010 until this date, and 673 hospitals are on the verge of closing (Daly).

11.1.2 Impacts of Rural Hospital Closures

Although the number of hospitals closed so far may look small, the closure of a hospital in a rural area might have far more complications than we would expect. The number of hospitals serving a county or a town in rural areas is very low compared to urban ones. When a hospital halts its service, the patients must travel very long distances to find the next nearest hospital for care. The situation becomes even

347

worse when the patient has a medical emergency, such as a heart attack, stroke, etc. There have been reports already surfaced on the casualties of patients who lost their lives due to traveling long distances for treatment (Lieb, Walters). The problems caused by rural hospitals closing do not stop here. Hospitals have been one of the major revenue yielding businesses in rural areas, as they are often one of the biggest and highest-paying employers in those areas. When they close, they have a domino effect on the other local businesses (Walters). Hospitals of varying sizes and capabilities are being closed permanently or converted to emergency and outpatient clinics. In some hospitals, vital processes are temporarily affected, disrupting the care being given to the patients. The majority of the time, hospitals are closed due to financial distress. In many cases, when a hospital gets hit with the revenue, its economic condition deteriorates as time progresses, and the management tend to lay off its staff and are forced to operate with limited resources. Eventually, the hospital is shut down once for all.

11.2 Purpose of this Research

Hospital closures, in many instances, have been viewed in a perspective such that the factors associated with it are external to the hospital that affect closures. This research incorporates and evaluates the factors which are present within the hospitals that affect closures. It also focuses on hospital closures in disadvantaged locations and suggests ways to prevent closure problems all together in the future. Given the changes and decisions contained within Protection and Affordable Care Act (PPACA) to improve quality of care such as transitioning from traditional fee-for-service to value-based reimbursements, it is more likely that the changes may have affected the rural hospitals as even a 3% of the reimbursement cut can translate into hundreds of thousands of dollars and many hospitals operate on a negative operating margin. (Average operating margin for rural hospitals is −11%.) In this situation, the hospitals are under tremendous scrutiny on the quality of care given to patients and increased pressure to improve their care processes for retaining their complete reimbursements and avoiding penalties. Patients are enabled to make informed decisions about choosing caregivers, thereby forcing the hospitals to make improvements to stay competitive and attract patients. Thus, it is imperative to understand the baseline status of rural hospitals on their performance levels and provide solutions to prevent further closures in the future. The second section of this research provides remedial strategies for hospitals by improving processes through the deployment of Lean Six Sigma (LSS) projects. By implementing the projects, the cost savings achieved will help to alleviate the risks and prevent further closures in the future.

11.3 Research Objectives

The research objectives for this research are divided into three parts. First, we aim to identify the factors that are involved in closures in recent years. Second, we will evaluate if the factors might have contributed to the risk of closures. The third objective illustrates an action plan in the form of deploying LSS projects to avoid closure problems in the future. Each research objective is explained in detail hereunder.

Research Objective 1: Identify the Hospital Closure Risk Factors based on Economic and Operational Importance

Hospital closures occur all the time. Several factors play a role to bring a hospital's operations to stop. But in recent years since 2010, the rate of rural hospital closures in the U.S. has been steadily increasing until now. At the same time, the country's healthcare industry experienced several changes due to the healthcare reform that was amended in 2010. Hence, the first objective is to find out the reasons behind rising rate of hospital closures in such a way to correlate with the reform changes. In addition, other potential closure factors are identified for further evaluation. In this part of the research, factors are classified into two categories, namely financial and operational factors. Factors that are external to the hospital that may cause the risk of closure of hospitals are named as financial factors, and factors that are internal to the hospital, i.e., factors that are responsible by the hospital, are named as operational factors (Figure 11.1).

FIGURE 11.1   Hospital closure risk factors classification.

Research Objective 2: Evaluate the Hospital Closure Risk Factors to Determine the Likelihood of Causing the Risk of Closure
In research objective 2, the factors identified in the previous research objective are evaluated by creating a predictive model using statistical methods to see if they cause the hospital closures. The factors are evaluated individually based on operational importance, financial importance, and finally as a combined model of both.

The gains attained from this component of the research is a model that the hospitals can use to evaluate themselves against the performance on certain core measures, which can potentially cause the risk of closures. By knowing their standing on the performances, it will help the hospitals to make quick decisions and plans to improve their performance levels to alleviate the risks. Also, the model will influence the state officials to make changes for any policy decisions such as expanding Medicaid so that the rate of uninsured can be reduced, thereby mitigating the risk of closures to some extent.

Research Objective 3: Deployment and Evaluation of Quality Improvement Initiatives
As mentioned above, to prevent further hospitals from closing in the future, hospitals need to make some quick decisions to save themselves from closing its doors. At this time, one of the rational decisions to overcome this situation is to create some improvement action plans to reduce costs, improve revenue and profit. One of the enablers to make improvement initiatives is by deploying LSS in hospitals.

In this component of the research, LSS projects are identified and their corresponding cost savings are quantified. The projects are then selected with an objective of maximizing cost savings to be deployed in the hospitals, including hospitals in disadvantaged locations, within an enterprise system. By doing it, the deployed projects are expected to generate cost savings for hospitals, thereby reducing the financial vulnerability of the hospitals, making the hospitals self-sufficient enough to manage their operations. In the long run, it will enable hospitals to attract more patients, thus creating more revenue opportunities and thus become more financially capable. It will also provide immunity to larger extent that any policy decisions or the adverse conditions that prevail outside the hospital will not affect it.

11.4 Background

This chapter is organized such that the first three sections discuss the changes and events that have happened since the Healthcare Reform was enacted in 2010. The following section discusses literature studies on research performed that is similar to this research.

11.4.1 Transitioning from Fee-for-Service to Value-Based Reimbursements

As mentioned earlier, with the new reform in place, hospital reimbursements are being transitioned to value-based ones on performance rather than the traditional fee-for-service in which the hospitals and physicians were paid based on the number of services and time spent irrespective of the outcome of the treatment. The Centers for Medicare and Medicaid (CMS) in fact has made some decisive initiatives to

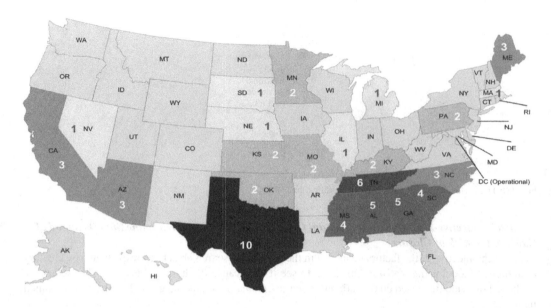

FIGURE 11.2 Rural hospital closures around the US since 2010–2016. *Note*: Updated March 2016.

tie in 30% of the payments to Accountable Care Organization (ACO) or bundled payments by 2016 and reach 50% in 2018, as well as 85% of all traditional Medicare payments will be tied in to quality or value by 2016 and 90% by 2018 through HVBP and HRRP (Brown) (Figure 11.2).

The underlying reason for the transition is to bring changes to the way the care is delivered in order to avoid adverse patient outcomes and expensive unnecessary patient's hospital stay and treatment. The transition from the fee-for-service reimbursement system to one based on value is one of the greatest financial challenges health systems currently face (Brown and Crapo). Those hospitals that will not be able to perform on par as hospitals that excel in processes would be in trouble and will face financial problems. Some of the initiatives such as the HVBP, ACO, bundled payment, clinical integration are already in place to make the transition happen. In order to asses a hospital's performance, proper measures need to be in place, and for many years, providers must have submitted quality measures for programs such as Hospital Inpatient Quality Reporting (IQR) System, Hospital Outpatient Quality Reporting, and Physician Quality Reporting System. The value-based reimbursements and HRRPs will rely heavily on hospital's performance levels on those measures (Figure 11.3).

The next two sections illustrate two important programs that decide the reimbursement decisions based on hospitals' performances.

11.4.2 Hospital Value-Based Purchasing

One of the initiatives to tie in quality with reimbursements is the HVBP, which was enacted in Section 3001(a) of the Affordable Care Act. HVBP is based on the performances of the hospitals on the hospital quality data reporting infrastructure developed for the Hospital IQR Program. The Total Performance Score (TPS) is calculated for hospitals based on their performances on a set of measures from the IQR program. The HVBP includes several measures on different domains, including selective Processes of Care measures (Processes of Care Domain), Patient Satisfaction surveys (Hospital Consumer Assessment of Healthcare Providers and Systems (HCAHPS) Domain), Mortality rates (Outcome Domain), and Medicare Spending per Beneficiary (Efficiency Domain). CMS has designed to fund this program through reduction from participating hospitals' Diagnosis-Related Group (DRG) payments for the applicable first year. Hospitals can earn back the deducted amount in equal, greater, or even lesser amount depending on their TPS. The scheduled DRG deductions commenced in 2013 with 1%, 1.25% in 2014, 1.5% in 2015, 1.75% in 2016 and reached 2% in 2017 (Table 11.1).

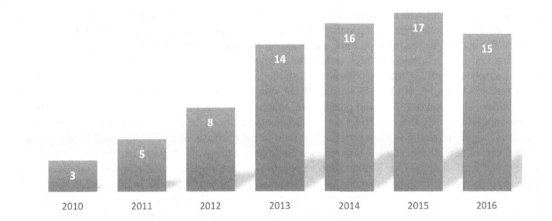

FIGURE 11.3 Rural hospital closures by year. *Note*: Data for 2016 year is from January to October.

TABLE 11.1

Rural Hospital Closures by State from 2010 to 2016

S. No.	State	Number of Hospitals Closed
1.	Alabama	5
2.	Arizona	3
3.	California	3
4.	Georgia	6
5.	Illinois	1
6.	Kansas	2
7.	Kentucky	4
8.	Maine	3
9.	Massachusetts	1
10.	Michigan	1
11.	Minnesota	2
12.	Mississippi	5
13.	Missouri	3
14.	Nebraska	1
15.	Nevada	1
16.	North Carolina	3
17.	Ohio	2
18.	Oklahoma	4
19.	Pennsylvania	2
20.	South Carolina	4
21.	South Dakota	1
22.	Tennessee	8
23.	Texas	11
24.	Virginia	1
25.	Wisconsin	1

Note: Updated October 2016.

11.4.3 Hospital Readmission Penalties and Implications

One of the other performance measurement programs to tie in quality with reimbursement from CMS is the HRRP, where the hospitals are penalized for excess readmissions for the diagnosis within a 30-day period. The acceptable readmission rates are based on averages calculated at national level, and those hospitals that have readmissions higher than the accepted level are penalized up to 3% starting FY 2015. Launched in 2012, CMS fined hospitals with the maximum penalty of 1% in FY 2013, 2% in FY 2014, and 3% during FY 2015. CMS started HRRP with three measures on health conditions including heart failure (HF), heart attack, and pneumonia. Now the measures also include Chronic Obstructive Pulmonary Disease (COPD) and Hip/Knee replacement conditions. In 2013, 18% of Medicare patients, which is roughly around 2 million patients, returned to the hospitals within 30 days with an estimated annual cost of $26 billion, and $17 billion alone could have been avoided (Rau). During the same year, CMS fined 2,213 hospitals for $280 million in penalties, which represents 0.3% of the total Medicare base payment, with 276 hospitals receiving a maximum of 1% penalty (Brown). In 2014, 2,225 hospitals were penalized for $227 million which represents 0.2% of the total Medicare base payment with 1074 hospitals receiving the maximum penalty of 2%. A total of 1,371 hospitals received lower penalties, and the average penalty decreased from 0.42% to 0.38% for year 2015. 2,610 hospitals were assessed for penalties with the average penalty increasing from 0.38% to 0.63% with 39 hospitals receiving a maximum penalty of 3%, and the total fine amount was estimated to be $428 million.

As we can see from the above data, the second year had a drop in the total penalty amount, but again it seems to a rise again in fine amounts for year 2015. It may be because two new measures are added in 2015. It is also important to note that even though a hospital has improved from previous years in terms of reducing the readmissions rate, the hospital is still penalized if the readmissions are above the acceptable level, i.e., perform poorly compared to other hospitals.

Despite the growing concerns that the Medicare and Medicaid funding pays well below the actual costs of care, the readmission penalties should add a big burden on top of the existing problems which the hospitals are experiencing so far. Rural hospitals are not an exception here as well as they depend on 45% of the Medicare payments for their total annual income, and there are already closures reported due to the reimbursement cuts (Janney). Also, rural areas usually tend to have poor and less educated residents with a lack of primary care physician for which it is expected to exacerbate the situation, and avoiding penalty with those conditions is out of hands for the treating hospitals.

Hospitals discharging patients have already taken measures to curb the returning patients within a 30-day window. Hospitals have invested in transitional care activities such as discharge follow-up, reconciling medications, partnering with other local hospitals or care facilities, and performing follow-up phone calls (Bradley et al. 444–450). Some hospitals care for returning patients without readmitting them overnight so that Medicare does not count their cases, while some other hospitals are replacing perfunctory discharge plans by giving patients paper instructions and giving medications which they cannot afford. Some hospitals even send the nurses to patient's home to ensure the patients are taking care of themselves (Rau). While big hospitals can afford to manage the above-mentioned services to avoid patients coming back, it is almost certain that small and financially strained hospitals may not have the resources available to manage the patients once they leave the hospital. Also, the above stopgap arrangements may work for a while, but there is a need for a solution that will last forever.

An important note that must be considered here is that in years 2013 and 2014, the majority of the hospitals that were punished were the ones serving low-income patients in which 77% of the hospitals with the highest share of low-income patients were penalized for excessive readmission during the first year versus just 36% of hospitals with fewest poor patients. Also, The Medicare Payment Advisory Commission (MedPAC) found that the hospitals that serve the destitute people are the ones who have the highest number of readmissions. Some experts believe that the safety-net hospitals that treat the underprivileged patients should not be assumed the same as other hospitals considering socioeconomic status of safety-net hospitals since those are more vulnerable to receive more penalties than others due to the nature of patients they treat. A review conducted by the University of Texas has found that patients who are elderly, minority, poorly educated, poor, smokers and the non-compliant (among others) have high readmission rates. These socioeconomic factors are not controllable by hospitals and are not taken into consideration in penalty calculations (Soumerai and Koppel). The safety net hospital patients are more prone to challenges in taking care of their health. The MedPAC has in fact urged the government to compare hospitals of equal status when assessing penalties. While the bills are pending in both houses of Congress that would make Medicare consider the socioeconomic status of a hospital's patients while calculating fines, the Obama administration has raised concern that assuming safety-net hospitals will do poorer in avoiding readmissions might encourage them to lower expectations for the quality of care for low-income patients (Rau).

There is evidently some severe backlash from certain section of the industry for the HRRP. While efforts for improving quality and reducing costs are imperative, some alternative arrangements needs to be made to last the improvements efforts forever without harming the existing structures of healthcare. Some researchers argue that rather than penalizing hospitals for readmissions that they cannot prevent, they should fund proven and efficient strategies.

11.4.4 Reduction of Disproportionate Share Hospital (DSH) Payments

The safety-net hospitals are predominantly used by the uninsured, poor, and people who cannot afford care. When these patients visit the hospital, and are unable to pay, it becomes a bad debt for the caring hospital. Furthermore, by law, when a patient ends up in an emergency care, regardless of the patient's ability to pay, the hospital must provide treatment for the patient until they become stabilized or eventually die. In those scenarios, it again becomes a debt for hospitals, and it may have to take care of those costs by themselves.

Before, when the PPACA was in place, the federal government made some special arrangements to deal with the above kind of situations by having a program known as "Disproportionate Share Hospital (DSH) Payments". By this program, funds are allotted to hospitals for covering the unmet expenses to prevent further financial strain. But after the PPACA program was implemented, funds from the DSH program were reduced by about $546 million in 2014, $1.25 billion in 2015 compared to 2014, and further $1.2 billion reduction in 2016 compared to 2015 (American Hospital Association). The underlying basis for the reduction of funds is that since Medicaid has been expanded for many new patients along with the PPACA, the government assumes that the previously uninsured people would now be covered by Medicaid, thereby increasing the revenue of the hospitals, and hence the uncompensated costs would eventually come down. But unfortunately, not all the 50 states have accepted to expand the PPACA in their states, and some states had declined the federal mandate. States can have a respite until the DSH payments are being paid to hospitals, but once it is stopped, the condition of hospitals will be even worse.

Along with the DSH payments, these small hospitals have been historically supported to provide care despite their low operating margins by charity donations and other support from respective state government. However, the changes in the health reform seem to have affected those funding sources by either reducing them or completely stopping them.

11.4.5 States Declining Medicaid

In spite of the unfavorable events after the implementation of PPACA, some states have already declined the expansion of Medicaid. As of September 2016, 19 states have declined the expansion of Medicaid, leaving 4.5 million people uninsured (Garfield). The refusal came only after a Supreme Court's ruling. In 2012, the court upheld the constitutionality of the PPACA's mandate of requiring the majority of people to have minimum health insurance coverage starting 2014 (Figure 11.4).

States that accepted to expand the Medicaid program have implemented it through the joint efforts of the federal and state governments. From 2014 until 2019, the federal government would pay most of the cost of the expansion up to 100%, and by 2020, the states would be responsible for paying 10% of its costs.

According to a study from RAND Corporation, the cost of expanding Medicaid is lower than the expense for providing uncompensated care to uninsured residents after the implementation of PPACA. The RAND study also reveals that an estimation of 19,000 deaths would occur annually if the states

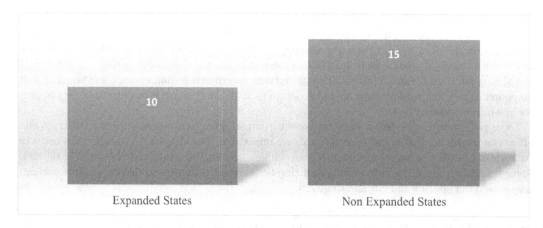

FIGURE 11.4 Medicaid expanded and non-expanded states experiencing closures in the U.S. since 2010.

would not expand Medicaid. Another study from University of North Carolina reveals that the number of hospitals closed are more in the states which did not expand Medicaid than the ones which expanded. But on a different note, there is a shift in the revenue mix. This is seen by the commercial reimbursements decreasing in number over the years and the government reimbursements increasing for those same years (Figure 11.5).

The change in revenue mix impacts a hospital's bottom line because the reimbursements from Medicare and Medicaid are not equivalent with the reimbursements from the private insurance payers. It may also make us think that the hospitals with a good revenue mix from private and government reimbursements may escape this financial crunch and only the hospitals that depend on government reimbursements for the majority of their revenue will face difficulties.

The PPACA supporters, as well the state representatives from states which implemented PPACA, have their own contention of accepting and rejecting the Medicaid expansion. The proponents believe the PPACA will (1) alleviate the uncompensated costs, the burden which the hospitals and the states are managing; (2) reduce costs; (3) reduce the burden on the taxpayers who are generally obligated to cover the uncompensated costs by paying special taxes in some states; (4) create jobs when the hospitals start picking up patients on primary care, thereby causing an increase in demand for workers and creating new opportunities; (5) lessen the costs of burden due to uncompensated care; and (6) improve patient outcome.

Alternatively, the states that rejected the PPACA have their own contentions as well. Some of the important states that rejected the expansion include Florida and Texas and, surprisingly, Texas is the

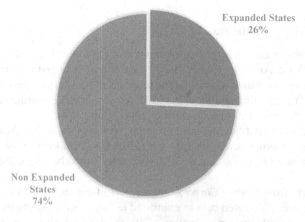

FIGURE 11.5 Percentage of hospitals closed in medicaid expanded and non-expanded states.

state which has the highest number of uninsured patients. Rick Scott, the Governor of Florida, contends that the PPACA would only strain the state budget and it can only be implemented after raising taxes. Also, the permanent relief would be achieved only after sorting out ways to reduce healthcare costs and expand job opportunities for people to afford private insurances.

Although some states do not choose to expand Medicaid, their state residents will still be subjected to taxes, fees, and other revenue provisions of the PPACA and have the big chance of losing the funds allotted for the Medicaid payments. Despite this, some states have made some alternative arrangements to expand Medicaid by using the amounts earmarked for Medicaid to pay for private insurance (Turner and Roy). Whatever decision the states decide to either accept or reject the expansion, the bottom line is that the common people are the ones who will benefit or suffer with their state representative's decision.

In the following sections, the factors identified based on the background study will be further discussed in detail.

11.4.6 Hospital Closure—Discussion of Operational Importance Factors

Traditionally, hospital closures are associated with many external factors that cause financial instability for hospitals. It is true to a great extent that the conditions that exist near the hospitals have a big influence in deciding hospitals' abilities to stay and offer care services, especially in rural areas. But in recent times, hospitals' internal operational characteristics have been under severe scrutiny with new programs in place through the healthcare reform. Hospitals operating on "RED", i.e., on negative margin will financially strain further with reimbursement cuts and penalties as these reimbursement deductions can be translated into hundreds of thousands of dollars which the hospitals cannot afford to lose. This is not desirable, as losing reimbursements will most likely worsen their situation and catalyze the closure decisions.

On this juncture, there is little to no evidence so far on the association with the quality of care provided by the hospitals and likelihood of hospitals to get closed. Spade and Strickland (38–39), in their paper titled "Rural Hospitals Face Many Challenges in Transitioning to Value-Based Care", described the struggle of small non-profit hospitals since changes were brought to the healthcare payment systems to value-based ones, and, in effect, the authors have mentioned that balancing finances will be difficult at this time, so hospital leaders will have to make difficult decisions regarding it. Also, to overcome the changes, hospitals must innovate, restructure, become more efficient, and continuously improve care to protect community safety net. The authors also predicted mergers, shared service partnerships, realignment of services toward outpatient and ambulatory care, conversions of acute care hospitals into community-focused healthcare organizations and in some cases, closure of hospitals with additional reimbursement cuts. Previously, Ly et al. (1291–1296), in their research, identified the relation between the hospitals' margins and the quality of care, as well as hospitals' margins and change of status (closures, mergers, etc.). This research has found that the hospitals in the top 10% of operating margin had higher summary performance indicator score for HF and pneumonia conditions when compared with the hospitals at the bottom 10% of operating margin. The above results are the same for the readmissions as well, so the hospitals with top 10% of operating margin had a lower readmission rate for acute myocardial infarction (AMI) and HF conditions when compared with the hospitals at the bottom 10% of operating margin. This research also found that the hospitals with low operating margins tend to close, merge, and get acquired.

Hung et al. evaluated the rural and urban differences in the proportion of hospitals that received readmission penalties, as well as the differences in rural and urban hospitals' conditions. Specifically, readmission rates were analyzed, and it was found that rural hospitals were penalized more than the urban hospitals, and that both rural and urban hospitals in communities with fewer primary care physicians, low family incomes, low education levels, and higher proportions of people over 65 are more likely to be penalized.

Goldman and Dudley (112–127) studied the rural and urban hospital differences in adherence to ten hospital compare measures on AMI, HF, and community acquired pneumonia (CAP). They found that the rural hospitals had low adherence in six AMI and HF measures.

11.4.7 Hospital Closure—Discussion of Financial Importance Factors

Several factors play a role in bringing a hospital to the brink of stopping its operations. The major influencing reason the hospitals close is that they are no longer financially viable to provide care for the patients. When a hospital is not able to yield revenue to surpass or even match the costs incurred, it becomes difficult for it to continue its services. Many hospitals in rural areas operate as non-profit hospitals, making little to no profits, and in many cases, they operate on negative margins and sustain just for the sake of having healthcare coverage for rural patients.

Traditionally, rural areas are usually said to have low population density, which affects the hospital utilization rate. There were 34 hospitals that closed in 2013 that had an occupancy rate of 34% compared to 48% in the nearest open hospital (Peck). Also, in a comparison with urban hospitals, in 2013, for hospitals with less than 100 beds, the occupancy rates for rural hospitals was 37%, while the rates for urban hospitals was 63% ("Rural Hospitals Continue to Struggle"). There have been several hospitals closed or converted into ambulatory, outpatient care and emergency care centers due to low occupancy rates (Evans). The other reasons for low occupancy rates are due to the peoples' perception that the quality of care in rural hospitals is low, so they travel to their nearest urban hospital. Many rural hospitals tend not to have a good payer mix, with majority of the patients having Medicare insurance, which is believed to pay not to match the costs incurred by the hospitals. These circumstances prevent hospitals from making profits and instead are pushed to financial difficulties.

Kaufman et al. (35–43) researched rural hospital closures and identified factors negatively affecting the operating margin. Thompson et al. examined how the Medicaid expansion affected insurance coverage in rural areas and how it would differ if each state tried to expand Medicaid. Research has found that the number of uninsured populations has considerably decreased after expansion, and the states which did not expand Medicaid will likely have little to no medical coverage.

Getting covered with health insurance is quintessential both for patients and for hospitals. It helps the patients to avoid paying the hefty sum of treatment costs and only allows them to pay very little up front for the care. It protects hospitals from caring for disproportionate numbers of patients who are unable to pay for their care and ending up with bad debt. It is evident from the above research that many hospitals in rural areas, especially in the states that did not expand Medicaid, may likely to suffer from loss of revenue given the poverty conditions in rural areas and more number of people without health insurance.

The other relevant research from Reiter et al. (1721–1729) focused on the uncompensated care provided by hospitals in rural and urban areas and more importantly found the differences between states that expanded Medicaid and the ones that refused expansion. In this research, hospitals have been classified as Critical Access Hospitals (CAHs) and other rural hospitals for both types of states (states that expanded Medicaid and states that did not expand). The authors have calculated the total uncompensated costs as a sum of unmet costs due to Medicaid, Children's Medical Insurance Program (CHIP), unreimbursed costs of other indigent care, bad-debt expense, and charity care costs. The results from their research show that the total uncompensated care costs are higher in states that expanded Medicaid, but the uncompensated costs that were incurred only due to uninsured and under-insured patients were higher in the states that did not expand Medicaid. The authors' overall research suggests that the hospitals in the states that did not expand Medicaid are more financially vulnerable and have more financial pressure and losses. As the DSH payment reduction is planned to be reduced in the forthcoming years, the states that did not expand Medicaid will likely struggle more with a greater number of hospital closures. The reduction was planned in such a way that the uncompensated costs will reduce because of Medicaid expansion. But since few states opted out of expansion, the uncompensated costs' burden will remain the same in those states. The scheduled DSH payment reductions will be in effect for all states irrespective of the expansion of Medicaid thus affecting more rural hospitals in non-expansion states.

The presence of particular races, such as disadvantaged or Hispanic, is believed to affect the closure of hospitals. Hsia and Shen (1912–1920) earlier studied the trauma center closures and how they disproportionately burden the vulnerable populations. They both studied the trauma centers that were closed between 2001 and 2007 with an objective to determine if the driving distance for socioeconomically disadvantaged, racial, and ethnic minorities to the nearest trauma center improved or deteriorated. Their studies reveal that by 2007, 69 million of population had to travel further to the nearest trauma center than they did in 2001. This deterioration in geographical access has been more acute in communities where disadvantaged populations live. This study also reveals that rural communities have a higher risk of experiencing declines in geographical access than urban communities. While this research informs us that more trauma centers have been closed in disadvantaged areas, it is yet to know the association between disadvantaged population and hospital closures.

The research by Bazzoli et al. (129–150) evaluated the closure of "safety net hospitals" (which are predominantly used to treat low-income, poor, and uninsured patients) and its effects on uninsured, Medicaid patients, and racial/ethnic communities. Their research results suggest that certain groups of uninsured and Medicaid patients experienced greater disruptions in care, especially the Hispanic uninsured and Medicaid women hospitalized for births. Here, same as disadvantaged population in earlier research, the relation between closure and Hispanic population is not yet known, although it can be inferred that there may be a relation between presence of large Hispanic population and hospital closures.

Project Selection and Prioritization plays a vital role in successful deployment of LSS initiatives in a company. Considerable attention must be paid to make careful evaluation of projects for the initiatives to be successful.

Antony and Banuelas (20–27) identified success factors for effective Six Sigma implementation: (1) management involvement and commitment; (2) cultural change; (3) organization infrastructure; (4) training; (5) project management skills; (6) project prioritization and selection, reviews, and tracking; (7) understanding the Six Sigma methodology, tools, and techniques; (8) linking Six Sigma to business strategy; (9) linking Six Sigma to customer; (10) linking Six Sigma to human resources; and (11) linking Six Sigma to suppliers. These factors were to be critical factors for the Six Sigma project implementation to be effective.

Antony (1006–1013) did a comparative study between manufacturing and service processes from Six Sigma perspective and noted project selection process should follow voice of the customer, voice of the process, and voice of the strategic business goals. The author also suggests some guidelines for selecting Six Sigma projects as follows: (1) linking to strategic business plan and organizational goals; (2) sense of urgency; (3) selecting projects which can be completed in six months; (4) projects to be clear, succinct, specific, achievable, realistic, and measurable; (5) projects to have support and approval of senior management; (6) project deliverables in terms of their impact on one or more critical characteristics such as critical to quality (CTQ), critical to cost, and critical to delivery; and (7) project selection based on good metrics.

Yang and Hsieh (7594–7603) proposed a Six Sigma project selection method using national quality award criteria and evaluating strategic criteria using Delphi fuzzy multiple criteria decision-making method. Kumar et al. (669–686) focused on the importance of project selection process and its role on successful deployment of Six Sigma. They proposed a hybrid methodology to select projects using analytical hierarchical process and project desirability matrix. Büyüközkan and Öztürkcan (5835–5847) proposed a combined Analytical Network Process (ANP) and Decision Making Trial and Evaluation Laboratory (DEMATEL) to identify and prioritize critical Six Sigma projects.

Dinesh Kumar et al. (419–441) proposed to identify Six Sigma projects using Data Envelopment Analysis (DEA) to maximize the benefit for the organization. The authors used inputs and outputs for Six Sigma projects, which were then analyzed using DEA to select the projects. Hu et al. (6611–6625) developed a multiple objective formulation using a goal programming approach for project portfolio selection in manufacturing companies. Padhy and Sahu (1091–1102) developed a two-staged methodology for project portfolio selection. In the first step, a real option analysis for evaluating the value of the project to improve management flexibility and in the second step, a zero-one linear programming model for selecting and scheduling an optimal project portfolio based on organization's objectives and constraints was proposed.

11.5 Methodology

This first section of the Research Methodology illustrates the detailed steps under each of the three research objectives.

11.5.1 Research Objectives and Specific Steps

Research Objective #1
  Identify Hospital Enterprise System (HES) Closure Factors based on Operational and Economic Importance.

  Step 1: Identify the HES closure factors
  Step 2: Identify the factors that cause the risk of hospital closures based on financial importance
  Step 3: Identify the factors that cause the risk of hospital closures based on operational importance.

Research Objective #2
  Evaluate the HES Closure Risk Factors to Determine the Likelihood of Causing Closures.

  Step 4: Use statistical methods to evaluate the factors to cause risk of closures based on operational importance
  Step 5: Use statistical methods to evaluate the factors to cause risk of closures based on financial importance
  Step 6: Use statistical methods to evaluate the factors to cause risk of closures based on combined methods.

Research Objective #3
  Deployment and Evaluation of Quality Improvement Initiatives.

  Step 7: Identify LSS projects to be implemented in hospitals throughout the HES
  Step 8: Select identified projects based on maximizing cost savings
  Step 9: Run scenario 2 by adding disadvantaged location factor to the model
  Step 10: Select projects to optimize cost savings
  Step 11: Evaluate the benefits for the HES.

In the following sections, each research objective is discussed further in detail.

Research Objective 1: Identifying the Hospital Closure Risk Factors based on Economic and Operational Importance

During the background research, a comprehensive search for hospital closure risk factors was performed from journal literatures, online and print news article reports, televised news reports from prominent journals such as Wall Street Journal, Huffington Post, etc., as well as other social media and print resources. Several factors were found that caused the risk of closures; especially, recent literatures, news reports, and articles highlighted shrinking Medicare reimbursements and other financial assistances over the few years as one of the primary reasons for closures although they did not exactly pinpoint the exact factors that drove those decisions to reduce financial reimbursements to hospitals. Other factors such as market competition, presence of certain race, etc. were also identified which might be the reasons for hospital closures.

As discussed earlier, based on the factors that were identified, it was determined that the closure risk factors can be categorized into two divisions, namely operational importance and financial importance.

Research Objective 2: Evaluating the Risk Factors to Determine the Likelihood of Causing Closures

The goal is to understand the closed rural hospitals in recent times and create a model to predict hospital closures, i.e., to identify the independent predictors.

The response variable in the model is a binary variable, i.e., closed/not closed. For this purpose, a Logistic Regression Model is used to relate the binary dependent variables with the independent continuous variables.

11.5.2 Data Collection

Operational importance factors were collected from Hospital Compare website, a portal which has information on quality of care of Medicare-certified hospitals, which was created as a joint initiative between Medicare and Hospital Quality Alliance. Hospital Compare provides information on how well the hospitals provide recommended care on various constructs including processes of care measures and outcome measures for multiple health conditions such as heart attack, HF, pneumonia, surgery, and other complications to their patients so that the patients can make informed decisions about healthcare. The Federal programs such as HRRP, HVBP, etc. use Hospital Compare measures' data for making decisions regarding penalties and payment reductions based on the performance of the hospitals on those measures.

Financial importance data were collected from Area Resource File, which contains county, state, and national database files.

11.5.3 Discussion of Independent Predictor Variables

11.5.3.1 Operational Importance Model

The objective of the operational importance model is to evaluate hospital performances on core measures that that determine penalties, reimbursement cuts, and incentives based on the appropriate performances of the hospitals. Further, this model will provide a framework for hospitals to target the core measure processes to improve and realize the benefits. Based on HRRP and HVBP, several measures for prominent health conditions including heart attack, HF, and pneumonia as well as several patient experience survey measures were identified.

The HRRP measures include readmissions for heart attack, HF, and pneumonia conditions.

The HVBP contains (1) process of care measures including discharge instructions for HF patients (HF-1), blood culture performed in the emergency department prior to initial antibiotic received in hospital (PN-3B), initial antibiotic selection for CAP in immunocompetent patients (PN-6), which are critical such that those selective processes can prevent adverse patient events, and (2) outcome of care measures, which is believed as an indicator for the poor quality of care provided by the hospitals and includes mortality rates for heart attack, HF, and pneumonia. The HCAHPS measures are typically a survey of patient satisfaction based on their experiences during the hospital stay. Measures such as doctor communication, nurse communication, pain management, hospital cleanliness, explanations on medications given, discharge instructions, and patient's recommendation for the hospital are being used (Tables 11.2–11.4).

TABLE 11.2

Hospital Readmission Reduction Program Measures

Variable	Variable Description
HFR	30-day readmission rate for HF condition
Pneumonia Readmission	30-day readmission rate for pneumonia condition

TABLE 11.3

Hospital Acquired Condition Reduction Program Measures

Variable	Variable Description
Blood Infection	Central Line Associated Blood Stream Infections (CLABSI)

TABLE 11.4

Hospital Value Based Purchasing Program Measures

Variable	Variable Description
HF_1	Discharge instructions for HF patients
PN_3B	Blood culture performed in the emergency department prior to initial antibiotic received in hospital
PN_6	Initial antibiotic selection for CAP in immunocompetent patients
Pneumonia Mortality	30-day pneumonia mortality rates
No Doctor Communication	Percentage of patients who reported that their doctors "Sometimes" or "Never" communicated well
No Nurse Communication	Percentage of patients who reported that their nurses "Sometimes" or "Never" communicated well
No Pain Management	Percentage of patients who reported that their pain was "Sometimes" or "Never" well controlled
No Post Recovery Info	Percentage of patients who reported that they were not given information about what to do during their recovery at home
No Patient Recommendation	Percentage of patients who reported NO they would not recommend the hospital
No Immediate Help	Percentage of patients who reported that they "Sometimes" or "Never" received help as soon as they wanted
No Medication Instructions	Percentage of patients who reported that staff "Sometimes" or "Never" explained about medicines before giving it to them

11.5.4 Discussion of Processes of Care Measure Variables

a. PN-3B (Blood culture performed in the emergency department prior to initial antibiotic received in hospital)

This is a pneumonia process of care measure which focuses on treatment provided to emergency department patients prior to admission orders. Specifically, it targets the initial emergency room blood culture performed prior to the first dose of antibiotics. The reason for importance of this measure is that it is vital to determine the type of bacteria, virus, or fungi for administering the right antibiotics. A higher rate of blood culture performed indicates that hospital provides higher level of care to patients.

b. PN-6 (Initial antibiotic selection for CAP in immunocompetent patients)

The PN-6 is, again, a pneumonia process of care measure which focuses on providing initial antibiotic treatment for pneumonia patients. The reason of importance of this measure is to treat the pneumonia patients with appropriate antibiotic(s). A higher rate of antibiotics given to the patients indicates that hospitals provide higher level of care to patients. Failure to provide right antibiotic(s) results in prolonged length of stay for patients and increased costs for hospitals.

c. HF-1 (Discharge instructions)

The HF-1 is a HF measure which aims HF patients or caregivers to be provided with discharge instructions or educational material during discharge or during the hospital stay. The instructions provide information on activity level, diet, discharge medications, follow-up medication, etc. It is estimated that about 4.7 million persons have HF conditions in the country, and failure to give patients with complete discharge instructions results in higher rates of readmissions.

In order to improve patient outcomes and reduce healthcare costs, this measure is given foremost importance in reimbursement decisions such as in HVBPs.

11.5.5 Outcome of Care Measures

a. 30-day Readmission Rate

Hospital 30-day readmission measures are unplanned readmissions, in which patients return to the hospital for the same diagnosis within 30-day period after discharge. In general, it is believed that one of the ways to improve quality and reduce healthcare costs is to avoid the unplanned 30-day readmissions and that hospitals which have higher than normal readmissions will be penalized for poor quality with the HRRP. Rate of readmission penalties increased from 2% to 3% recently, and rural hospitals depend on 45% of their annual revenue from Medicare. With penalties consuming up critical hospital reimbursements, it is highly likely that the hospitals will be financially stressed and will increase the risk of closure.

b. 30-day Mortality Rate

30-day mortality rates are estimates of deaths within 30 days of a hospital admission, for patients hospitalized with one of several medical conditions or surgical procedures. The mortality rate measures indicate if the hospitals are doing well in preventing complications, educating patients on their care needs, and helping patients to make smooth transition from hospital to home or another type of care facility. This measure is an important factor since it is one of the measures used in HVBP in which a higher performance on this measure will yield incentives and bad performance will result in reduced reimbursements.

11.5.6 HCAHPS Measure

The HCAHPS measure is an initiative to provide a standardized survey instrument and data collection methodology for measuring patient's perspectives on hospital care. It contains a core set of questions that can be combined with a broader, customized set of hospital-specific items. These surveys are designed to produce comparable data on the patient's perspective of care that allows objective and meaningful comparisons between hospitals on domains that are important to hospitals. The HCAHPS survey measures are used in HVBP as well which will enable hospitals to earn incentives for good patient perception of care and hospital or reduced reimbursements for poor patient satisfaction scores.

11.5.6.1 Financial Importance Model

The objective of the financial importance model is to underscore the importance of certain factors that can prove detrimental for the functioning of vulnerable hospitals and how states can leverage the healthcare reform to address those factors. With 74% of the rural hospitals closed in the country from the states that did not expand Medicaid, this financial importance model will help the states' authorities to reconsider their decision on to whether they can expand Medicaid to give health coverage for the needy populations. If not, all factors can be addressed now. Few vital factors, such as hospitals located in areas where many people live without health insurance and have low income such that they cannot afford proper care, can be addressed. Provisions are made in the reforms to tackle these concerns such that they give health coverage for these specific populations thereby reducing the financial problems faced by the hospitals and hence reducing the risk of hospitals getting closed in the future (Figure 11.6).

11.5.6.2 Discussion of Financial Importance Variables

a. High Uninsured Population

The presence of many uninsured populations in a hospital locality is a major threat for hospitals. Big proportions of insured people may force hospitals to provide large uncompensated costs, and rural areas usually tend to have poor and uninsured people who cannot afford care.

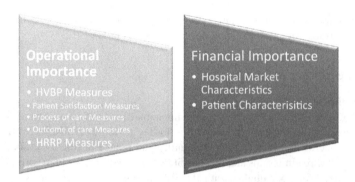

FIGURE 11.6   Operational and financial importance variables.

Two-thirds of the uninsured people live in states that did not expand Medicaid, and identifying it may help in future policy decisions for the coverage of uninsured people (Newkirk).

b. Number of Hospitals

High market share is a threat for hospital existence as more the number of hospitals in a given locality, more the risk of hospitals to lose revenue from the patients. In recent years after reform, patients can make informed decisions to choose a provider based on the performance of hospitals in the past. Hospitals will need to vie for attracting patients without losing to competitors. Although hospitals are sparsely located in rural areas, this factor still poses a threat for the closure of hospitals.

c. Median Household Income

Median household income in a given hospital locality may indicate the characteristics of the patient population that lives. In general opinion, patients with higher household income may have better insurance coverage such as third party or private insurance coverage so that hospitals get better reimbursements and less chances for hospitals to incur uncompensated costs. On the contrary, patients with low household income may have little or inadequate health coverage, which may be a financial burden for hospitals to treat such patients.

d. Population Estimate

It is a well-known fact that rural areas tend to have low population density compared to urban areas. Rural hospitals suffer from lack of revenue due to low patient volumes and occupancy rates. So, if hospitals are located in areas with low population density, it is more likely that the hospital will have low patient revenue and hence will cause the risk of driving the hospital to closure compared to areas with high population densities which may increase revenue and profit, and hence, the chances of survival are more.

e. Race

Race is one of the market characteristic variables that would be of the interest in this study. Previous research has identified that the emergency departments are more likely to be closed in disadvantaged locations (Hsia et al.). The comparison of open and closed hospitals in this research will identify if there would be any association between the presence of a particular race and the risk of closure of a hospital. It can be noted that the Hispanic and African American ethnicity contributes to 43% total uninsured population in U.S. ("Uninsured Rates for the Nonelderly by Race/Ethnicity"). Thus, chances of providing uncompensated care are more.

If this factor proves to be a reason for closure, it would also confirm the notion that the hospitals located in disadvantaged locations are left unnoticed by the hospital management for any improvement initiatives and would have greater chances of closure, which causes increasing disparities for the disadvantaged population than making any initiatives to save these hospitals.

Research Objective 3: Deployment and Evaluation of Quality Improvement Initiatives

The goal of research objective 3 is to deploy quality improvement initiatives such as LSS management techniques at hospitals and evaluate how the improvements will reduce and prevent the risk of closures in the future in rural and disadvantaged locations. At this phase, a hospital system encompassing three hospitals is identified for the study (Figure 11.7).

Improvement initiatives in the form of LSS projects are deployed at these hospitals to realize the cost saving benefits attained at the enterprise level. The inclusion of hospital at the disadvantaged location will make sure that the hospital management will serve the population on those locations. The first step for the deployment initiatives is to identify LSS projects that can be implemented in the above hospitals. To do so, a complete search for LSS project implementations at hospitals was performed from journal literatures, magazine reports from American Society for Quality, Institute of Industrial and Systems Engineers, etc. to identify various information such as the project type (process(es) targeted), quantified savings from the project results, investment amount, tools used, personnel type used (yellow belts, green belts, black belts), duration of the project, etc. At this stage, the project opportunities (target process(es)) identified from literature are assumed to be identified from the hospitals within the enterprise system identified above. Quantified cost savings data was adjusted for inflation to 2016 dollar value using Consumer Price Index Inflation Calculator from Bureau of Labor Statistics. The data for investment costs for majority of the projects was not available from the literature. Hence, the investment data was created using the cost savings data based on the Return on Investment (ROI) approach. Based on literature study, Six Sigma's ROI was estimated between 2:1 and 3:1. Hence, the investment cost of each project was randomly chosen between a range of 1/2 and 1/3 of cost savings from the corresponding project (Figures 11.8 and 11.9).

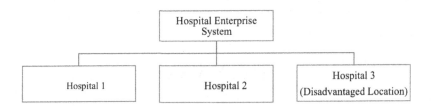

FIGURE 11.7 HES model—stage 1.

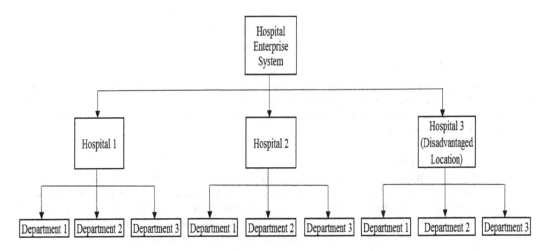

FIGURE 11.8 HES model—stage 2.

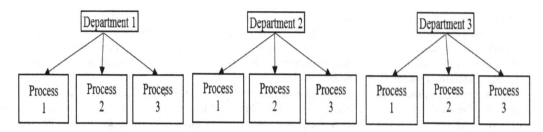

FIGURE 11.9   HES model—stage 3.

The second step is the selection of projects to be deployed on pilot basis in the hospitals from the master list of projects identified from the previous step. A 0–1 integer linear programming (Knapsack) model is proposed for the project selection approach with an objective of maximizing cost savings associated with the selected projects. Two scenarios are developed for maximizing cost savings modeling approach. In the first scenario, projects are selected from either one of the three hospitals, which will maximize savings for the HES. In the second scenario, the third hospital is assumed to belong from a disadvantaged location, and a factor is added to the model such that a certain minimum set of core measure projects are implemented in the disadvantaged hospital so that the hospital can improve its performance on core measures to avoid penalties and reimbursement cuts, reduce costs, and develop opportunities for revenue.

11.5.6.2.1 Model Assumptions

If cost savings is in the range between $0 and $100,000, the project is a yellow belt project.
   If cost savings is in the range between $100,000 and $250,000, the project is a green belt project.
   If cost savings is above $250,000, the project is a black belt project.

11.5.6.2.2 Model Objective Function

$$\text{Max } Z = \sum_{i=1}^{n} \sum_{j=1}^{m} X_{ij} S_{ij}$$

Here, S_{ij} is the expected cost savings by executing project i in hospital j.
   X_{ij} is the binary decision variable if the project i is selected in hospital j $\forall_i = 1,2,3 \ldots$ n, $\forall_j = 1,2,3$.

$$X_{ij} = \begin{cases} 1 & \text{if project } i \text{ is selected in hospital } j \\ 0 & \text{if project } i \text{ is not selected in hospital } j \end{cases}$$

11.5.6.2.3 Model Constraints—Scenario 1

In the following sections, the constraints for the model are discussed such that the projects are implemented in all three hospitals, with three project types, yellow belt, green belt and black belt projects. There is a limit for investment that the hospital enterprise management can allot for the overall project deployment which is set at $1 M.

   a. Project Diversity Constraint
      Project diversity constraint refers to types of Six Sigma projects available such as yellow belt, green belt, and black belt projects. Implementing yellow belt and green belt projects during the deployment phase will help organizations to realize benefits in a short span of time and get the trust from management as well as stakeholders. Hence, a minimum set of yellow belt and green belt projects are implemented in the initial phase of the deployment and is given by following constraints
      The constraint for implementing a minimum set of yellow belt projects is given by

$$\sum_{i=1}^{n}\sum_{j=1}^{m} X_{ij}y_{ij} \leq Y_{ij},$$

where y_{ij} is a binary parameter which decides if ith project implemented in hospital j is a yellow belt project. Y_{ij} is the minimum set of yellow belt projects that needs to be implemented in the pilot phase.

Likewise, the constraint for implementing a minimum set of green belt projects is given by

$$\sum_{i=1}^{n}\sum_{j=1}^{m} X_{ij}g_{ij} \leq G_{ij},$$

where g_{ij} is a binary parameter which decides if ith project implemented in hospital j is a green belt project. G_{ij} is the minimum set of green belt projects that needs to be implemented in the pilot phase.

b. Project Investment Constraint

The constraint for the model to maximize savings within the given investment is given by

$$\sum_{i=1}^{n}\sum_{j=1}^{m} X_{ij}b_{ij} \leq B$$

Here b_{ij} is the investment required to implement project i in hospital j, and B is the maximum allowable investment available.

11.5.6.2.4 Model Constraints—Scenario 2

a. Disadvantaged Location Factor

As discussed above, a disadvantaged location factor is added to the model in scenario 2 by mandatory implementation of a set of core measure projects and is given by

$X_{33} = 1$
$X_{23} = 1$
$X_{13} = 1$

Here, X_{33}, X_{23}, and X_{13} are project 3 in hospital 3, project 2 in hospital 3, and project 1 in hospital 3, respectively.

b. Black Belt Resource Constraint

There is a limit in the number of black belts that the hospital system can use for implementing projects due to limited budget constraints. Hence, the constraint is given by

$$\sum_{i=1}^{n}\sum_{j=1}^{m} X_{ij}a_{ij} \leq A_{ij},$$

where a_{ij} is a binary parameter which decides if ith project implemented in hospital j is a black belt project. A_{ij} is the maximum number of available black belt resources.

c. Project Investment Constraint

The constraint for the model to maximize savings within the given investment is given by

$$\sum_{i=1}^{n}\sum_{j=1}^{m} X_{ij}b_{ij} \leq B$$

Here b_{ij} is the investment required to implement project i in hospital j, and B is the maximum allowable investment available.

11.5.7 Research Hypothesis

Research question: What factors have caused the risk of hospital closures in rural locations and can strategic process improvement initiatives alleviate and prevent further closure of hospitals in the future including in areas of disadvantaged population who need the most help?

The following sections illustrate the research hypotheses for research objectives 2 and 3.

Research Objective 2:
Independent Variables: Predictors outlined in financial and operational importance
   Dependent Variable: Hospital closed/not closed
   Null Hypothesis: None of the independent variables affect the probability that the dependent variable will be hospital closed or not closed. This implies that $\beta_1, \beta_2, ..., \beta_n$ are all zero and that only β_0 differs from zero.

$$(H_0): \beta_j = 0 \text{ for all } j$$

Alternative Hypothesis: At least one of the independent variables affects the probability that the dependent variable will be closed or not closed. This implies that $\beta_1, \beta_2, ..., \beta_n$ are all not zero.

$$(H_a): \beta_j \neq 0 \text{ for at least one } j$$

Rejection Criteria: There are no significant factors to predict closure or no closure

Research Objective 3:
Null Hypothesis (H_0): Deployment of LSS process improvement initiatives will not improve the financial status of hospitals to alleviate and prevent the closure risk of hospitals.
   Alternative Hypothesis (H_a): Deployment of LSS process improvement initiatives will improve financial statuses of hospitals to alleviate and prevent the closure risk.

11.6 Analysis/Results

11.6.1 Statistical Analysis for Predicting Closures

11.6.1.1 Overview

The objective of the specific objective 2 is to evaluate the factors that cause the risk of rural hospital closures in the recent times. Although hospital closures occur from time to time over the years, in this research, the hospitals that were closed between 2010 and 2016 were considered since the healthcare industry started witnessing reforms and policy changes from that year. Since then, the number of hospital closures increased year by year till date in a dramatic fashion. Hence, it makes sense to study the hospitals that were closed only in this time frame to understand the phenomenon behind the closure of hospitals. Between 2012 and 2016, 63 rural hospitals have been closed around the country and have been used for statistical analysis purposes. Although the hospital closures continued until October 2016, the cutoff was set by early 2016 (March). For logistic regression modeling purposes, we have considered 400 open hospitals to be compared with the closed hospitals (Table 11.5).

The data was segregated into two groups, tagged as "training" and "testing" data sets in which the training data set will contain 80% of the total data and testing data set will contain 20% of the data. While the training data set was used for model formation purposes, the testing data set was used for model validation purposes.

11.6.2 Missing Value Analysis

When data was collected for the model variables, it was not available for some hospitals. Appropriately handling missing values is critical for building the model and making conclusions from it. Here, missing values are replaced by hospital closure percentage-based imputation (Table 11.6).

TABLE 11.5

Closed and Open Hospitals Data

Closed hospital (Total)	63
Open hospital (Total)	400
Training data (Closed)	55
Training data (Open)	315
Testing data (Closed)	8
Testing data (Open)	85

TABLE 11.6

Sample Calculation Table for Missing Values (Pneumonia Readmission)

Group	Min	Max	Average	No. of Closed	Closed %	No. of Open	Open %	Total	Total %
1			18.94	14	48.3	15	51.72	29	6.26
2	14.3	16.9	16.24	3	3.75	77	96.25	80	17.30
3	17	17.6	17.31	8	8.7	84	91.3	92	19.9
4	17.7	18.4	18.08	10	11.8	75	88.24	85	18.40
5	18.5	19.5	18.94	18	20.00	72	80.00	90	19.40
6	19.6	24.2	20.70	10	11.5	77	88.51	87	18.80

For closure percentage-based imputation, the data set has been divided into groups or bins, including a separate group for missing values. Then, the hospital closure percentage for the missing value group is compared with the other groups. The missing values are replaced by the average value of a group which has the closure percentage closest to that of the missing value group's closure percentage. Per Table 11.6, about 6% of the hospitals have missing data for the Pneumonia Readmission variable, and hence the variable data has been divided into groups in order to impute missing values. From the table, the closure percentage of missing value group (group 1) is 48.3%, and the closest closure percentage from other groups here is 20% from group 5. Hence, the average value of pneumonia readmission is 18.94 from group 5 and is replaced as the missing value for group 1.

11.6.3 Descriptive Statistics Analysis

a. PN_3B Measure (blood culture performed in the emergency department prior to initial antibiotic received in hospital)

The median percentage of PN_3B process compliance for closed hospitals is 82% with a standard deviation of 10.5. The spread of values is considerably large ranging from 60% up to 100%, which may indicate some lapses in care compliance for this process measure among closed hospitals. Also, most of the closed hospitals have compliance rate around 82% denoting that many hospitals are not fully compliant with the measure. The distribution of the data from the histogram indicates that the data is clearly not normal (Figure 11.10).

Mann–Whitney–Wilcoxon Test

Test Hypothesis:

H_0: Population distribution of closed hospital group = Population distribution of open hospital group
PN_3B Process measure will not affect hospital closure status

H_1: Population distribution of closed hospital group ≠ Population distribution of open hospital group
PN_3B Process measure will affect hospital closure status

Rejection Criteria: At 0.05 significance level, reject null hypothesis if p-value is <0.005 and fail to reject null hypothesis if p-value is >0.005

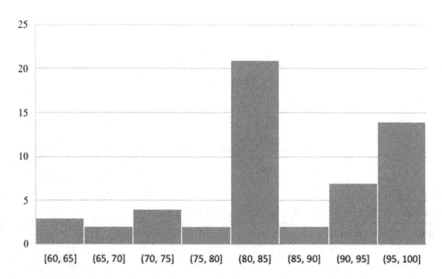

FIGURE 11.10 Histogram for PN_3B process measure.

Results:

Closed_Open	N	Mean Score	Normal Approximation	
			Z	−5.4893
PN_3B_O	315	198.155556	One-Sided Pr < Z	<0.0001
PN_3B_C	55	113.018182	Two-Sided Pr > |Z|	<0.0001

Average scores used for ties

Conclusion:

At $p < 0.0001$, there is an evidence of association between PN_3B process measure and closure of hospitals, i.e., PN_3B process measure affects closure of hospitals.

11.6.4 PN_3B vs. Logit Analysis

A different form of bivariate analysis is to plot the independent variables against the raw logits which is commonly used in logistic regression. It is performed to understand the independent variable (IV) and dependent variable (DV) relationships and provides meaningful information on the associations which can be used later in the logit model. By graphing the logits of closure against the independent variable, the IV and DV relationship is analyzed by the direction and form of association between the likelihood of closure and IV. It is done by grouping each independent variable into bins (ranking the observations), and corresponding mean for each bin is calculated. The raw logits are then plotted against the means for each bin.

The plot for PN_3B vs. the raw logits displays a downward negative trend, although not much linear, still exhibiting an association such that as the percentage of compliance with PN_3B process increases, the likelihood of closure decreases. It also tends to make a conclusion that the variable may contribute to the model. The increase in PN_3B process measure will likely reduce the financial pressures for hospitals by avoiding reimbursement cuts and creating revenue opportunities by bringing incentives for performing well on this measure, thereby reducing the overall risk of hospital closure (Figure 11.11).

     b. PN_6 Measure (initial antibiotic selection for CAP in immunocompetent patients)

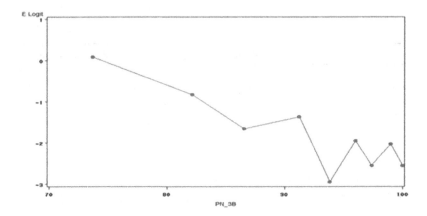

FIGURE 11.11 Trend analysis for PN_3B measure.

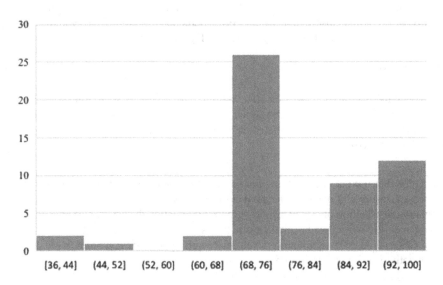

FIGURE 11.12 Histogram for PN_6 process measure.

This variable denotes the compliance measure for pneumonia condition. As the compliance rate of this measure increases, the risk of hospital closure decreases. The distribution of data shows that the data is not normal. The closures occurred for hospitals with a compliance range between 36% and 100%, but the hospitals with the percentage of compliance of about 72% experienced most closures, which also indicates that many closed hospitals are not fully compliant with this process measure (Figure 11.12).

Mann–Whitney–Wilcoxon Test

Test Hypothesis:

H_0: Population distribution of closed hospital group = Population distribution of open hospital group PN_6 Process measure will not affect hospital closure status

H_1: Population distribution of closed hospital group ≠ Population distribution of open hospital group PN_6 Process measure will affect hospital closure status

Rejection Criteria: At 0.05 significance level, reject null hypothesis if p-value is <0.005 and fail to reject null hypothesis if p-value is >0.005

Results:

Closed_Open	N	Mean Score	Normal Approximation	
			Z	−5.5651
PN_6_O	315	198.392063	One-Sided Pr < Z	<.0001
PN_6_C	55	111.663636	Two-Sided Pr > |Z|	<.0001

Average scores used for ties

Conclusion:
At $p < 0.0001$, there is an evidence of association between PN_6 process measure and closure of hospitals, i.e., PN_6 process measure affects closure of hospitals.

11.6.5 PN_6 vs. Logit Analysis

The graphical analysis of the PN_6 variable and the logits shows an overall downtrend which indicates the association of PN_6 and closure of hospitals. As the percentage of compliance with the PN_6 process measure increases, the likelihood of closure decreases (Figure 11.13).

   c. HF Readmission:

The closed hospitals' readmission rates for HF condition have relatively small range of 9.3% with many closed hospitals having the median readmissions rate of 27%. The distribution of the HF readmission (HFR) data is clearly not normally distributed on the histogram (Figure 11.14).
   Mann–Whitney–Wilcoxon Test

Test Hypothesis:
   H_0: Population distribution of closed hospital group = Population distribution of open hospital group
   HFR process measure will not affect hospital closure status
   H_1: Population distribution of closed hospital group ≠ Population distribution of open hospital group
   HF process measure will affect hospital closure status
   Rejection Criteria: At 0.05 significance level, reject null hypothesis if p-value is <0.005 and fail to reject null hypothesis if p-value is >0.005

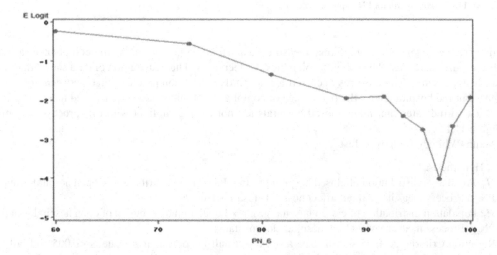

FIGURE 11.13   Trend analysis for PN_6 process measure.

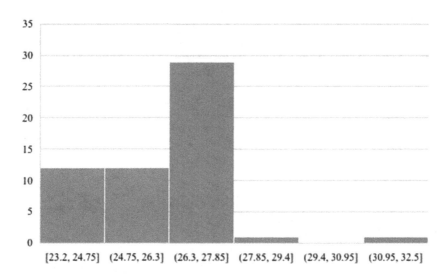

FIGURE 11.14 Histogram for HFR process measure.

Results:

Closed_Open	N	Mean Score	Normal Approximation	
			Z	5.3115
HFR_O	315	173.168254	One-Sided Pr > Z	<.0001
HFR_C	55	256.127273	Two-Sided Pr > |Z|	<.0001

Average Scores used for ties

Conclusion:

At $p < 0.0001$, there is an evidence of association between HFR process measure and closure of hospitals, i.e., HFR process measure affects closure of hospitals.

11.6.6 HFR vs. Logit Analysis

From the logit vs. HFR plot, a positive upward trend is observed, although not completely linear, which indicates that as the HFR level increases, the odds of closure increase as well, which informs us that this variable may contribute to the model. Hospitals with higher percentages of readmissions than the national average will be penalized, causing them financial problems. Hence, as the rate of readmissions increases, the likelihood of closure also increases (Figure 11.15).

d. Number of Hospitals

By looking at the distribution, the data is clearly not normal. The number of hospitals present in the same county as closed hospitals ranges from a minimum of 1 to maximum of 7 (Figure 11.16).

Mann–Whitney–Wilcoxon Test

Test Hypothesis:

H_0: Population distribution of closed hospital group = Population distribution of open hospital group
Number of Hospitals will not affect hospital closure status

H_1: Population distribution of closed hospital group ≠ Population distribution of open hospital group
Number of Hospitals will affect hospital closure status

Rejection Criteria: At 0.05 significance level, reject null hypothesis if p-value is <0.005 and fail to reject null hypothesis if p-value is >0.005

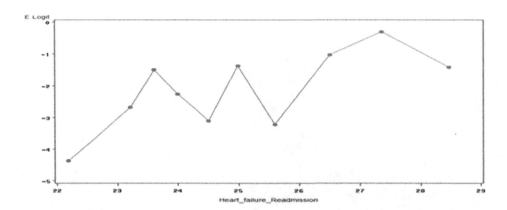

FIGURE 11.15   Trend analysis for HFR process measure.

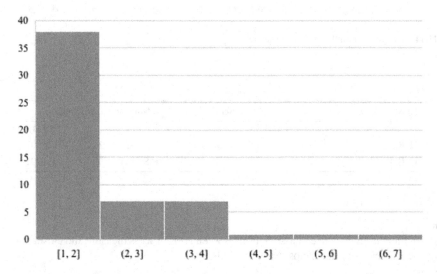

FIGURE 11.16   Histogram for Number of Hospitals.

Results:

Closed_Open	N	Mean Score	Normal Approximation	
No. of Hospitals_O	315	177.677778	Z	3.8821
No. of Hospitals_C	55	230.300000	One-Sided Pr > Z	<.0001
			Two-Sided Pr > |Z|	<0.0001

Average scores used for ties

Conclusion:
At $p < 0.0001$, there is evidence of association between Number of Hospitals and closure of hospitals, i.e., Number of Hospitals affects closure of hospitals.

11.6.7 Number of Hospitals vs. Logit Analysis

The logit plotted against the Number of Hospitals variable displays an almost straight positive trend such that as the Number of Hospitals increases, the odds of closure increase. This is true to large extent, since

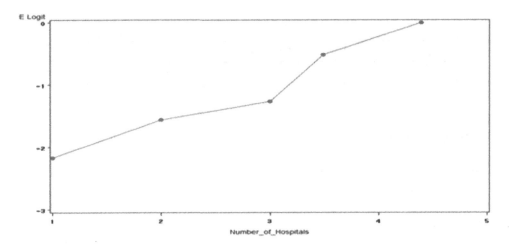

FIGURE 11.17 Trend analysis for Number of Hospitals.

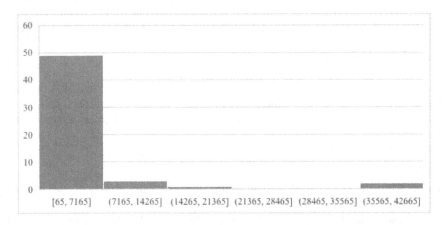

FIGURE 11.18 Histogram for Hispanic Population.

as the Number of Hospitals in each area increases, the competition among hospitals increases, and hence more likely, the hospitals lose revenue (Figure 11.17).

e. Hispanic Population

From the data distribution for closed hospitals' Hispanic population, it looks like the data is heavily skewed to the right. The calculated range for the Hispanic population data is 39,262 with a median value of 1,444. Thereby, only looking at the above two parameters, it suggests that the data is widely spread, but many closed hospitals have the population living nearby up to 7,165 (Figure 11.18).

Mann–Whitney–Wilcoxon Test

Test Hypothesis:

H_0: Population distribution of closed hospital group = Population distribution of open hospital group
Hispanic Population will not affect hospital closure status

H_1: Population distribution of closed hospital group ≠ Population distribution of open hospital group
Hispanic Population will affect hospital closure status

Rejection Criteria: At 0.05 significance level, reject null hypothesis if p-value is <0.005 and fail to reject null hypothesis if p-value is >0.005

Results:

Closed_Open	N	Mean Score	Normal Approximation	
			Z	0.9080
0	315	183.388889	One-Sided Pr > Z	0.1820
1	55	197.590909	Two-Sided Pr > |Z|	0.3639

Average scores used for ties

Conclusion:

At $p = 0.3639$, there is no evidence of association between Hispanic Population and closure of hospitals, i.e., Hispanic Population will not affect closure of hospitals.

11.6.8 Hispanic Population vs. Logit Analysis

The logit vs. Hispanic Population does not show any positive or negative relationship, but it does show that the data points are clustered with many data points at the beginning and the data is sporadically distributed as the population increases, which is an indication of skewness present in the overall distribution of closed and open hospitals. The absence of the trend suggests that there may not be any relationship between the independent and the dependent variables and the variable will not contribute to the model (Figure 11.19).

    f. Disadvantaged Population

The disadvantaged population residing near the close hospitals range from 46 to 22,293 in which having the population strength of up to 4,446 experienced maximum number of closures (Figure 11.20). Also, by looking at the above distribution, the data is clearly not normal and indicates some skewness might be present.

    Mann–Whitney–Wilcoxon Test

Test Hypothesis:

    H_0: Population distribution of closed hospital group = Population distribution of open hospital group
    Disadvantaged Population will not affect hospital closure status
    H_1: Population distribution of closed hospital group ≠ Population distribution of open hospital group
    Disadvantaged Population will affect hospital closure status
    Rejection Criteria: At 0.05 significance level, reject null hypothesis if p-value is <0.005 and fail to reject null hypothesis if p-value is >0.005

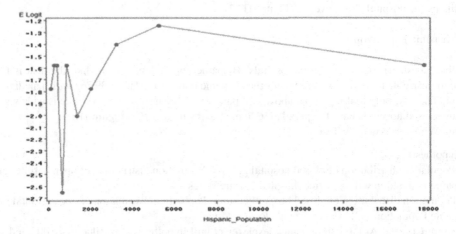

FIGURE 11.19   Trend analysis for Hispanic Population.

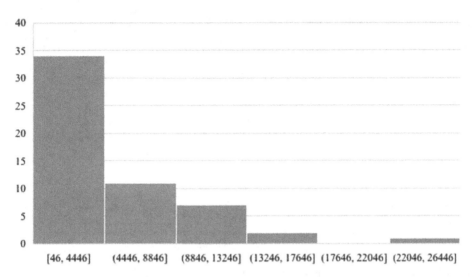

FIGURE 11.20 Histogram for Disadvantaged Population.

Results:

Closed_Open	N	Mean Score	Normal Approximation	
			Z	4.2071
0	315	175.726984	One-Sided Pr > Z	<0.0001
1	55	241.472727	Two-Sided Pr > |Z|	<0.0001

Average scores used for ties

Conclusion:
At $p < 0.0001$, there is an evidence of association between Disadvantaged Population and closure of hospitals, i.e., Disadvantaged Population affects closure of hospitals.

11.6.9 Disadvantaged Population vs. Logit Analysis

The logits vs. Disadvantaged Population shows an overall upward trend although lightly skewed at the beginning (Figure 11.21). The indication of an upward trend suggests that the disadvantaged population may contribute to the model.

11.6.10 Categorical Classification of Continuous Predictor Variables

The overall data distribution of Disadvantaged Population and Hispanic Population for open and closed hospitals is highly skewed to the right, i.e., positively skewed. The calculated skewnesses for Disadvantaged Population and Hispanic Population are 3.93 and 3.85, the standard errors are 307.88 and 309.36, and median values are 983 and 1071, respectively. The relatively larger values of skewness and standard error suggest that it would lead to biased results. For variables of this high skewness and standard error, the continuous data can be converted to categorized ones to better understand the data. Hence, the categorical variable is created using the median values of both the variables. Table 11.7 shows the data is categorized such that one data group is less than 1,000 and another group is greater than or equal to 1,000.

For modeling purposes, the categorized variable will be used. However, a model created using raw data will be compared with the model using categorized variable for comparison and evaluation purposes.

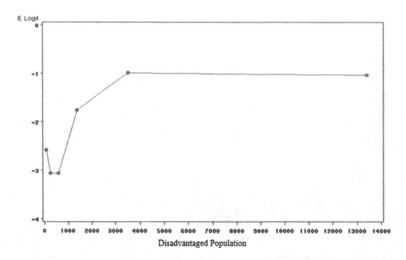

FIGURE 11.21   Trend analysis for Disadvantaged Population.

TABLE 11.7

Categorical Classification of Continuous Predictor Variables

Disadvantaged Population	Hispanic Population
Disadvantaged Population_1 < 1,000	Hispanic Population_1 < 1,000
Disadvantaged Population_2 ≥ 1,000	Hispanic Population_2 ≥ 1,000

11.6.11 Log Transformation of Continuous Predictor Variables

Although the skewness for population estimate and median household income is not relatively very high (2.68 and 1.98, respectively), the standard errors are very high (435.94 and 1901.28, respectively). A log transformation will help to reduce the standard error as well as the skewness, which will help improve the predictive ability of the median household income and population estimate variables on the dependent variable.

Table 11.8 shows the results of skewness and standard error after completing log transformation. Evidently, the standard error and skewness have considerably been reduced. The following normality plots for Median Household Income and Population Estimate also show the before and after scenarios of log transformation of the two variables which depict improved normality. The above two log-transformed variables will be used for modeling purposes (Table 11.8; Figures 11.22 and 11.23).

For comparison and evaluation purposes, the preferred model using the log-transformed variables will again be compared with the model using the raw data.

11.6.12 Correlation Analysis

The correlation analysis is performed to quantify the strength of any linear relationship between the independent variables. The matrix plot in Figure 11.24 shows a positive correlation among the three

TABLE 11.8

Log-Transformed Results for Continuous Predictor Variables

Variable	Standard Error	Skewness
Median Household Income_L	0.01	0.4
Population Estimate_L	0.04	−0.42

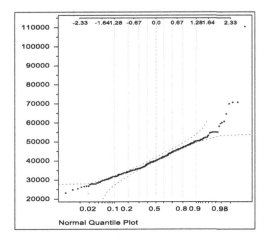
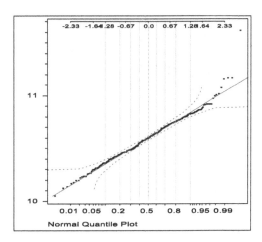

FIGURE 11.22 Normal quantile plot for Median Household Income before and after log transformation.

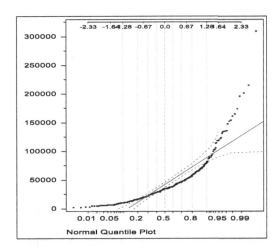
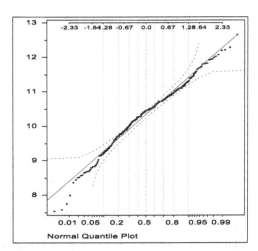

FIGURE 11.23 Normal quantile plot for Population Estimate before and after log transformation.

variables—No Patient Recommendation and No Immediate Help, No Patient Recommendation and No Nurse Communication, and No Immediate Help and No Nurse Communication.

	No Patient Recommendation	No Immediate Help
No Immediate Help	r = 0.816	
	p = 0.000	
No Nurse Communication	r = 0.880	r = 0.865
	p = 0.000	p = 0.000

The results from the correlation analysis above show that the correlation between No Patient Recommendation and No Immediate Help is 0.816, No Patient Recommendation and No Nurse Communication is 0.880, and No Nurse Communication and No Immediate Help is 0.860 (Figure 11.24).

A positive higher correlation value closer to 1 indicates that a strong relationship exists between two independent variables such that the increase in value of one variable increases the value of the other variable as well. The correlation values of 0.816, 0.880, and 0.865 indicate that the variables are related

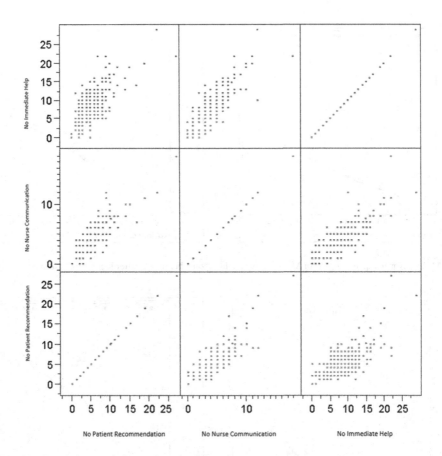

FIGURE 11.24 Correlation matrix for continuous predictors.

fairly strongly with each other. The corresponding p values are all less than 0.05 which indicates that the correlations are significant.

Multicollinearity could be a potential issue due to high correlations between No Patient Recommendation, No Immediate Help, and No Nurse Communication. The presence of multicollinearity will lead to high-standard errors and will make it harder to reject the null hypothesis.

Running regression models with potentially correlated variables may confirm the presence of multicollinearity. A Variation Inflation Factor (VIF) value >5 indicates the presence of multicollinearity.

In the following sections, a series of models was run with all possible combinations of potential correlated variables to check for multicollinearity problem.

11.6.12.1 Multicollinearity Check Model 1

Variable	DF	Parameter Estimate	Standard Error	Pr > |t|	Variance Inflation
Intercept	1	0.02029	0.04110	0.6218	0
No Patient Recommendation	1	0.02993	0.01089	0.0063	4.69098
No Nurse Communication	1	−0.04526	0.01802	0.0125	6.21364
No Immediate Help	1	0.01737	0.00780	0.0266	4.19253

The results from the above model show the VIF for No Nurse Communication variable is >5, and for the other two variables, No Patient Recommendation and No Immediate Help have VIF value <5. Looking at this model shows that multicollinearity will have influence in the model in the presence of No Nurse

Communication variable. Further, in the correlation analysis, the highest correlated value is 0.880 between No Nurse Communication and No Patient Recommendation.

11.6.12.2 Multicollinearity Check Model 2

Variable	DF	Parameter Estimate	Standard Error	Pr > |t|	Variance Inflation
Intercept	1	0.04873	0.03927	0.2155	0
No Patient Recommendation	1	0.03552	0.01065	0.0009	4.44143
No Nurse Communication	1	−0.02384	0.01532	0.1205	4.44143

The VIF for No Patient Recommendation and No Nurse Communication is 4.44143 which is <5, so multicollinearity will not be a problem with the presence of the above two variables in the model.

11.6.12.3 Multicollinearity Check Model 3

Variable	DF	Parameter Estimate	Standard Error	Pr > |t|	Variance Inflation
Intercept	1	0.01107	0.04133	0.7890	0
No Nurse Communication	1	−0.01549	0.01453	0.2872	3.96950
No Immediate Help	1	0.02232	0.00766	0.0038	3.96950

The VIF values for No Nurse Communication and No Immediate help are <5, and hence multicollinearity will not be an issue with the presence of the above two variables.

11.6.12.4 Multicollinearity Check Model 4

Variable	DF	Parameter Estimate	Standard Error	Pr > |t|	Variance Inflation
Intercept	1	0.00171	0.04072	0.9665	0
No Patient Recommendation	1	0.01350	0.00876	0.1244	2.99677
No Immediate Help	1	0.00690	0.00665	0.2996	2.99677

The VIF values of No Patient Recommendation and No Immediate Help are <5 (2.99677), which are the least VIF values among other trials for multicollinearity check. Also, the correlation analysis performed on the above variables resulted in 0.816, which is again the least among all. Multicollinearity will not be an issue with the presence of above two variables.

From the correlation analysis and multicollinearity check using the VIF values, the variable No Nurse Communication seems to cause multicollinearity problems and hence will be removed from the model.

11.6.13 Model Formation

11.6.13.1 Financial Importance Model (Model 1)

Response Variable: 1-Closed, 0-Open
   Method: Backward Elimination Procedure
   Begin Backward Selection Procedure
   Step 0: The following effects are entered.
   Intercept
   Number of Hospitals
   Percent Uninsured
   Median Household Income_L

Population Estimate_L
Disadvantage Population_2
Hispanic Population_2

Model Fit Statistics		
Criterion	Intercept Only	Intercept and Covariates
AIC	313.065	263.798
SC	316.978	291.193
−2 Log L	311.065	249.798

Testing Global Null Hypothesis: BETA=0			
Test	Chi-Square	DF	Pr > ChiSq
Likelihood Ratio	61.2665	6	<0.0001
Score	58.9224	6	<0.0001
Wald	44.6712	6	<0.0001

Step 1: Effect Hispanic_Population_2 is removed.

Model Fit Statistics		
Criterion	Intercept Only	Intercept and Covariates
AIC	313.065	262.703
SC	316.978	286.185
−2 Log L	311.065	250.703

Testing Global Null Hypothesis: BETA=0			
Test	Chi-Square	DF	Pr > ChiSq
Likelihood Ratio	60.3613	5	<0.0001
Score	58.2898	5	<0.0001
Wald	44.0156	5	<0.0001

Residual Chi-Square Test		
Chi-Square	DF	Pr > ChiSq
0.9039	1	0.3417

Step 2: Effect Median Household Income_L is removed

Model Fit Statistics		
Criterion	Intercept Only	Intercept and Covariates
AIC	313.065	264.393
SC	316.978	283.960
−2 Log L	311.065	254.393

Testing Global Null Hypothesis: BETA=0			
Test	Chi-Square	DF	Pr > ChiSq
Likelihood Ratio	56.6719	4	<0.0001
Score	55.7189	4	<0.0001
Wald	42.0130	4	<0.0001

Residual Chi-Square Test		
Chi-Square	DF	Pr > ChiSq
4.5212	2	0.1043

Note: No additional effects met the 0.05 significance level for removal from the model.

Summary of Backward Elimination					
Step	Effect Removed	DF	Number In	Wald Chi-Square	Pr > ChiSq
1	Hispanic_Population_2	1	5	0.8995	0.3429
2	Median Household Income_L	1	4	3.5579	0.0593

Analysis of Maximum Likelihood Estimates					
Parameter	DF	Estimate	Standard Error	Wald Chi-Square	Pr > ChiSq
Intercept	1	2.0667	2.4028	0.7398	0.3897
Number of Hospitals	1	1.0191	0.1913	28.3871	<0.0001
Percent Uninsured	1	0.0934	0.0375	6.2026	0.0128
Population Estimate_L	1	−0.8064	0.2406	11.2334	0.0008
Disadvantaged Population_2	1	1.5406	0.3875	15.8069	<0.0001

Odds Ratio Estimates		
Effect	Point Estimate	95% Wald Confidence Limits
Number of Hospitals	2.771	1.905 4.031
Percent Uninsured	1.098	1.020 1.182
Population Estimate_L	0.446	0.279 0.715
Disadvantaged Population_2	4.667	2.184 9.974

Association of Predicted Probabilities and Observed Responses			
Percent Concordant	80.6	Somers' D	0.616
Percent Discordant	19.0	Gamma	0.618
Percent Tied	0.3	Tau-a	0.156
Pairs	17325	c	0.808

Hosmer and Lemeshow Goodness-of-Fit Test		
Chi-Square	DF	Pr > ChiSq
14.3560	8	0.0729

--END OF MODEL 1--

TABLE 11.9

Summary of Significant Predictors for Financial Model

Variable	Coefficient	Wald Chi-Square
Number of Hospitals	1.0191	28.3871
Percent Uninsured	0.0934	6.2026
Disadvantaged Population_2	1.5406	15.8069
Population Estimate	−0.8064	11.2234

From model 1 results, at 95% confidence level, variables Number of Hospitals, Percent Uninsured Population Estimate_L, and Disadvantaged Population_2 are significant ($p < 0.05$). These variables will be used in the combined model along with the significant variables from operational importance model to create model 3 for predicting closures.

The goodness-of-fit test (Hosmer and Lemeshow) results with $p > 0.05$ show that the model is acceptable and the model adequately fits the data.

Table 11.9 summarizes the significant predictors which cause hospital closures that are external to the hospital, i.e., factors that are externally present outside the hospital to affect closures.

By looking at this financial importance model alone and analyzing the odds ratio estimates, we will have some crucial information for the financial importance model.

From the odds ratio analysis,

The odds ratio for Number of Hospitals is 2.771. In percentage terms, an increase in the number of hospitals in a county increases the odds of closure by 177%.

The odds ratio for Percent Uninsured is 1.098. In percentage terms, an increase of 1% uninsured population in a county increases the odds of closure by 9.8%.

The odds of closure of hospitals in Disadvantaged_Population_2 locality over the odds of closure of hospitals in Disadvantaged_Population_1 locality are 4.667. It means hospitals in disadvantaged locations where the population is greater than equal to 1,000 are more likely to be closed in comparison with hospitals in disadvantaged locations where population is less than 1,000. In percentage terms, odds of closure of hospitals in Disadvantaged_Population_2 locality is 367% higher than hospitals in Disadvantaged_Population_1 area.

The odds ratio for a Population Estimate of 0.446 indicates that a unit increase in population decreases the risk of closure by 55.4%.

11.6.13.1.1 Model 1 Check without Transformation and Categorical Classification

In order to evaluate model 1 without log transformation for Median Household Income and Population Estimate and without creating categorical classification for Disadvantaged Population and Hispanic Population, analysis on model 1 will be performed only using only the raw data. The following are the analysis results from the raw data of model 1.

Analysis of Maximum Likelihood Estimates					
Parameter	DF	Estimate	Standard Error	Wald Chi-Square	Pr > ChiSq
Intercept	1	−1.7722	1.4106	1.5784	0.2090
Number of Hospitals	1	0.8686	0.1599	29.4976	<0.0001
Percent Uninsured	1	0.0914	0.0379	5.8176	0.0159
Median Household Income	1	−0.00008	0.000027	9.3188	0.0023

Odds Ratio Estimates			
Effect	Point Estimate	95% Wald Confidence Limits	
Number of Hospitals	2.384	1.742	3.261
Percent Uninsured	1.096	1.017	1.180
Median Household Income	1.000	1.000	1.000

Association of Predicted Probabilities and Observed Responses			
Percent Concordant	79.9	Somers' D	0.603
Percent Discordant	19.7	Gamma	0.605
Percent Tied	0.4	Tau-a	0.153
Pairs	17325	*c*	0.801

From the analysis above, it is noted that the results are different when compared to the analysis results that were done using transformation and creating categorical classification of variables. At 95% confidence level, there are three predictors which are significant ($p < 0.05$). Among them, predictor Median Household Income will not make much contribution to the model since the coefficient is almost zero, and also the odds ratio of 1 suggests that the variable neither predicts closure nor opening of hospitals. Also, the Percent Concordant and the Somers' D values which indicate the accuracy of the model is relatively less compared to the model using transformed and categorized variables. Effectively, two variables Number of Hospitals and Percent Uninsured predict hospital closure using raw data for model 1, but the model 1 formed using transformed and categorized variables has four variables, which can predict closure. Thus, the preferred model using transformation of Median Household Income and Population Estimate as well as categorization of Hispanic Population and Disadvantaged Population proved to be better to form model 1 in comparison to forming the model using the raw data.

11.6.13.1.2 Model 1 Check with Variables Categorized vs. Log Transformation

To reduce high-standard error as well to reduce skewness for Disadvantaged Population and Hispanic Population, the other option is to do a log transformation for those variables. Although creating categorical variables has resulted in better results in comparison to forming model using raw data, a model created by log transforming Hispanic Population and Disadvantaged Population can be compared with that of the categorized ones to choose a better alternative. The following analysis results show Model 1 after Disadvantaged Population and Hispanic Population have been log transformed.

Analysis of Maximum Likelihood Estimates					
Parameter	DF	Estimate	Standard Error	Wald Chi-Square	Pr > ChiSq
Intercept	1	2.0498	2.4369	0.7075	0.4003
Number of Hospitals	1	1.0445	0.1923	29.5040	<0.0001
Percent Uninsured	1	0.0779	0.0384	4.1153	0.0425
Population Estimate_L	1	−0.9802	0.2650	13.6827	0.0002
Disadvantaged_Population_L	1	0.4191	0.1106	14.3533	0.0002

Association of Predicted Probabilities and Observed Responses			
Percent Concordant	80.1	Somers' D	0.605
Percent Discordant	19.5	Gamma	0.608
Percent Tied	0.4	Tau-a	0.154
Pairs	17325	*c*	0.803

Odds Ratio Estimates			
Effect	Point Estimate	95% Wald Confidence Limits	
Number of Hospitals	2.842	1.950	4.143
Percent Uninsured	1.081	1.003	1.165
Population Estimate_L	0.375	0.223	0.631
Disadvantaged Population_L	1.521	1.224	1.889

From the above analysis, in comparison with the original preferred model using categorization of Disadvantaged Population and Hispanic Population variables, the predictors remain the same for model 1. Also, from the analysis, although the Percent Concordant does not vary much from the original preferred model with a difference of 0.5, there is a difference in Somers' D value of 1.1, which suggests categorization of Hispanic Population and Disadvantaged Population is a better option in comparison with log transformation of those two variables.

11.6.13.2 Operational Importance Model (Model 2)

Response Variable: 1-Closed, 0-Open
  Method: Backward Elimination Procedure
  Begin Backward Selection Procedure
  Step 0: The following effects are entered.
  Intercept, Pneumonia Readmission, HFR, No Patient Recommendation, No Pain Management, Blood Infection, No Doctor Communication, Pneumonia Mortality, PN_3B, PN_6, HF_1, No Medication Instructions, No Post Discharge Info, No Immediate help.

Model Fit Statistics		
Criterion	Intercept Only	Intercept and Covariates
AIC	313.065	267.604
SC	316.978	318.480
−2 Log L	311.065	241.604

Testing Global Null Hypothesis: BETA=0			
Test	Chi-Square	DF	Pr > ChiSq
Likelihood Ratio	69.4627	13	<0.0001
Score	73.3234	13	<0.0001
Wald	50.8580	13	<0.0001

Step 1: Effect No Doctor Communication is removed.

Residual Chi-Square Test		
Chi-Square	DF	Pr > ChiSq
0.0022	1	0.9630

Step 2: Effect No Patient Recommendation is removed.

Model Fit Statistics		
Criterion	Intercept Only	Intercept and Covariates
AIC	313.065	265.625
SC	316.978	312.587
−2 Log L	311.065	241.625

Testing Global Null Hypothesis: BETA=0			
Test	Chi-Square	DF	Pr > ChiSq
Likelihood Ratio	69.4395	11	<0.0001
Score	73.2913	11	<0.0001
Wald	51.0508	11	<0.0001

Residual Chi-Square Test		
Chi-Square	DF	Pr > ChiSq
0.0231	2	0.9885

Step 3: Effect No Post Discharge Info is removed.

Model Fit Statistics		
Criterion	Intercept Only	Intercept and Covariates
AIC	313.065	263.653
SC	316.978	306.701
−2 Log L	311.065	241.653

Testing Global Null Hypothesis: BETA=0			
Test	Chi-Square	DF	Pr > ChiSq
Likelihood ratio	69.4121	10	<0.0001
Score	73.2878	10	<0.0001
Wald	51.0637	10	<0.0001

Residual Chi-Square Test		
Chi-Square	DF	Pr > ChiSq
0.0507	3	0.9970

Step 4: Effect HF_1 is removed.

Model Fit Statistics		
Criterion	Intercept Only	Intercept and Covariates
AIC	313.065	261.686
SC	316.978	300.821
−2 Log L	311.065	241.686

Testing Global Null Hypothesis: BETA=0			
Test	Chi-Square	DF	Pr > ChiSq
Likelihood Ratio	69.3787	9	<0.0001
Score	73.1031	9	<0.0001
Wald	51.0269	9	<0.0001

Step 5: Effect Pneumonia Mortality is removed.

Model Fit Statistics		
Criterion	Intercept Only	Intercept and Covariates
AIC	313.065	259.946
SC	316.978	295.167
−2 Log L	311.065	241.946

Residual Chi-Square Test		
Chi-Square	DF	Pr > ChiSq
0.0841	4	0.9991

Testing Global Null Hypothesis: BETA=0			
Test	Chi-Square	DF	Pr > ChiSq
Likelihood ratio	69.1190	8	<0.0001
Score	72.4408	8	<0.0001
Wald	50.3679	8	<0.0001

Residual Chi-Square Test		
Chi-Square	DF	Pr > ChiSq
0.3408	5	0.9968

Step 6: Effect No Immediate Help is removed.

Model Fit Statistics		
Criterion	Intercept Only	Intercept and Covariates
AIC	313.065	258.237
SC	316.978	289.545
−2 Log L	311.065	242.237

Testing Global Null Hypothesis: BETA=0			
Test	Chi-Square	DF	Pr > ChiSq
Likelihood Ratio	68.8278	7	<0.0001
Score	72.0345	7	<0.0001
Wald	50.5920	7	<0.0001

Residual Chi-Square Test		
Chi-Square	DF	Pr > ChiSq
1.2539	7	0.9896

Step 7: Effect Blood Infection is removed.

Model Fit Statistics		
Criterion	Intercept Only	Intercept and Covariates
AIC	313.065	256.979
SC	316.978	284.374
−2 Log L	311.065	242.979

Testing Global Null Hypothesis: BETA=0			
Test	Chi-Square	DF	Pr > ChiSq
Likelihood Ratio	68.0857	6	<0.0001
Score	71.9088	6	<0.0001
Wald	50.7251	6	<0.0001

Residual Chi-Square Test		
Chi-Square	DF	Pr > ChiSq
0.6195	6	0.9961

Step 8: Effect No Medication Instructions is removed.

Model Fit Statistics		
Criterion	Intercept Only	Intercept and Covariates
AIC	313.065	256.253
SC	316.978	279.734
−2 Log L	311.065	244.253

Testing Global Null Hypothesis: BETA=0			
Test	Chi-Square	DF	Pr > ChiSq
Likelihood Ratio	66.8117	5	<0.0001
Score	70.6248	5	<0.0001
Wald	51.0656	5	<0.0001

Residual Chi-Square Test		
Chi-Square	DF	Pr > ChiSq
2.4613	8	0.9635

Step 9: Effect Pneumonia Readmission is removed.

Model Fit Statistics		
Criterion	Intercept Only	Intercept and Covariates
AIC	313.065	256.020
SC	316.978	275.587
−2 Log L	311.065	246.020

Testing Global Null Hypothesis: BETA=0			
Test	Chi-Square	DF	Pr > ChiSq
Likelihood Ratio	65.0452	4	<0.0001
Score	69.1947	4	<0.0001
Wald	50.7083	4	<0.0001

Residual Chi-Square Test		
Chi-Square	DF	Pr > ChiSq
4.2310	9	0.8956

Step 10: Effect No Pain Management is removed.

Model Fit Statistics		
Criterion	Intercept Only	Intercept and Covariates
AIC	313.065	257.014
SC	316.978	272.668
−2 Log L	311.065	249.014

Testing Global Null Hypothesis: BETA=0			
Test	Chi-Square	DF	Pr > ChiSq
Likelihood Ratio	62.0509	3	<0.0001
Score	66.4705	3	<0.0001
Wald	49.8094	3	<0.0001

Residual Chi-Square Test		
Chi-Square	DF	Pr > ChiSq
7.1506	10	0.7112

Note: No additional effects met the 0.05 significance level for removal from the model.

Step	Effect Removed	DF	Number In	Wald Chi-Square	Pr > ChiSq
1	No Doctor Communication	1	12	0.0022	0.9630
2	No Patient Recommendation	1	11	0.0210	0.8847
3	No Post Discharge Info	1	10	0.0276	0.8682
4	HF_1	1	9	0.0335	0.8547
5	Pneumonia Mortality	1	8	0.2567	0.6124
6	No Immediate Help	1	7	0.2870	0.5922
7	Blood Infection	1	6	0.6050	0.4367
8	No Medication Instructions	1	5	1.2738	0.2591
9	Pneumonia Readmission	1	4	1.7782	0.1824
10	No Pain Management	1	3	2.9216	0.0874

Analysis of Maximum Likelihood Estimates					
Parameter	DF	Estimate	Standard Error	Wald Chi-Square	Pr > ChiSq
Intercept	1	−1.8583	3.1837	0.3407	0.5594
HFR	1	0.3407	0.0934	13.3002	0.0003
PN_3B	1	−0.0640	0.0235	7.4492	0.0063
PN_6	1	−0.0331	0.0162	4.1700	0.0411

Odds Ratio Estimates		
Effect	**Point Estimate**	**95% Wald Confidence Limits**
HFR	1.406	1.171	1.688
PN_3B	0.938	0.896	0.982
PN_6	0.967	0.937	0.999

Association of Predicted Probabilities and Observed Responses			
Percent Concordant	77.7	Somers' D	0.572
Percent Discordant	20.5	Gamma	0.582
Percent Tied	1.8	Tau-a	0.145
Pairs	17325	c	0.786

Hosmer and Lemeshow Goodness-of-Fit Test		
Chi-Square	**DF**	**Pr > ChiSq**
6.2737	8	0.6166

TABLE 11.10

Summary of Significant Predictors for Operational Model

Variable	Coefficient	Wald Chi-Square
PN_3B	−0.0640	7.4492
HFR	0.3407	13.3002
PN_6	−0.0331	4.170

At 0.05 significance level, HFR, PN_3B, and PN_6 variables are significant. These variables will be used along with the significant variables from the financial importance model to be used in the final model to predict hospital closures.

The goodness-of-fit test (Hosmer and Lemeshow) results show that the model is acceptable ($p > 0.05$) and the model adequately describes the data.

Odds Ratio Estimates Evaluation:

The odds ratio for HFR is 1.046. In percentage terms, a 1% increase in HFR will increase the odds of closure by 4.6%.

The odds ratio for PN_6 is 0.938. A 1% increase in PN_6 compliance reduces the odds of closure by 6.2%.

The odds ratio for PN_3B is 0.967. A 1% increase in PN_3B compliance reduces the odds of closure by 3.3% (Table 11.10).

11.6.13.3 *Final Model—Combination of Financial and Operational Importance Models (Model 3)*

Response Variable: 1-Closed, 0-Open
   Method: Backward Elimination Procedure
   Begin Backward Selection Procedure
   Step 0: The following effects are entered.
   Intercept
   HFR
   PN_6
   PN_3B
   Number of Hospitals
   Percent Uninsured

Population Estimate_L
Disadvantaged Population_2

Model Fit Statistics		
Criterion	Intercept Only	Intercept and Covariates
AIC	313.065	222.557
SC	316.978	253.865
−2 Log L	311.065	206.557

Testing Global Null Hypothesis: BETA=0			
Test	Chi-Square	DF	Pr > ChiSq
Likelihood ratio	104.5077	7	<0.0001
Score	102.9263	7	<0.0001
Wald	59.8501	7	<0.0001

Step 1: Effect Population Estimate Log is removed.

Model Fit Statistics		
Criterion	Intercept Only	Intercept and Covariates
AIC	313.065	220.651
SC	316.978	248.045
−2 Log L	311.065	206.651

Testing Global Null Hypothesis: BETA=0			
Test	Chi-Square	DF	Pr > ChiSq
Likelihood Ratio	104.4142	6	<0.0001
Score	102.8075	6	<0.0001
Wald	59.8243	6	<0.0001

Residual Chi-Square Test		
Chi-Square	DF	Pr > ChiSq
0.0939	1	0.7593

Step 2: Effect Percent Uninsured is removed.

Model Fit Statistics		
Criterion	Intercept Only	Intercept and Covariates
AIC	313.065	219.200
SC	316.978	242.681
−2 Log L	311.065	207.200

Testing Global Null Hypothesis: BETA=0			
Test	Chi-Square	DF	Pr > ChiSq
Likelihood Ratio	103.8653	5	<0.0001
Score	102.6700	5	<0.0001
Wald	59.3377	5	<0.0001

Residual Chi-Square Test		
Chi-Square	DF	Pr > ChiSq
0.6392	2	0.7264

Note: No additional effects met the 0.05 significance level for removal from the model.

Summary of Backward Elimination					
Step	Effect Removed	DF	Number In	Wald Chi-Square	Pr > ChiSq
1	Population Estimate_L	1	6	0.0938	0.7594
2	Percent Uninsured	1	5	0.5471	0.4595

Analysis of Maximum Likelihood Estimates					
Parameter	DF	Estimate	Standard Error	Wald Chi-Square	Pr > ChiSq
Intercept	1	−3.3947	3.4837	0.9495	0.3298
HFR	1	0.3848	0.1023	14.1574	0.0002
PN_6	1	−0.0535	0.0185	8.3754	0.0038
PN_3B	1	−0.0646	0.0272	5.6445	0.0175
Number of Hospitals	1	0.5967	0.1685	12.5426	0.0004
Disadvantaged Population_2	1	1.8700	0.4208	19.7484	<0.0001

Odds Ratio Estimates			
Effect	Point Estimate	95% Wald Confidence Limits	
HFR	1.469	1.202	1.795
PN_6	0.948	0.914	0.983
PN_3B	0.937	0.889	0.989
Number of Hospitals	1.816	1.305	2.527
Disadvantaged Population_2	6.488	2.844	14.802

Association of Predicted Probabilities and Observed Responses			
Percent Concordant	86.9	Somers' D	0.741
Percent Discordant	12.8	Gamma	0.743
Percent Tied	0.3	Tau-a	0.188
Pairs	17325	c	0.870

Hosmer and Lemeshow Goodness-of-Fit Test		
Chi-Square	DF	Pr > ChiSq
8.2114	8	0.4131

At 95% confidence level, variables PN_3B, PN_6, HFR, Disadvantaged Population_2, and Number of Hospitals are significant ($p < 0.05$). This combined model from financial importance and operational importance variables will be used for final model formation to predict the closure of rural hospitals.

The goodness-of-fit test (Hosmer and Lemeshow) yields a significant p-value of 0.0879, which is >0.05, implying that the model is acceptable and fits the data well.

The concordance percentage (87.6%) and the Somers' D value (75.4%) are high relative to low discordance (12.1%), which indicates the observed pairs predict a higher probability of an event of closure.

Odds Ratio Estimates Evaluation:

The odds ratio for HFR is 1.469. A HF Hone percent increase in HFR will increase the risk of closure by 46.9%.

The odds ratio for PN_6 is 0.948. In percentage terms, a 1% increase in PN_6 compliance reduces the odds of closure by 5.2%.

The odds ratio for PN_3B is 0.937. In percentage terms, a 1% increase in PN_3B compliance reduces the odds of closure by 6.3%.

The odds ratio for Number of Hospitals is 1.816. An increase of one hospital in a county increases the odds of closure by 81.6%.

The odds ratio of closure of hospitals in Disadvantaged_Population_2 locality over in Disadvantaged_Population_1 locality is 6.488. In percentage terms, odds ratio of closure of hospitals located where disadvantaged population of greater than or equal to 1,000 reside is 548.8% higher than that of hospitals located where disadvantaged population of less than 1,000 reside (Table 11.11).

11.6.13.4 Model Formation for Predicting Hospital Closures

Natural log of odds ratio is equivalent to linear function of independent variables. The antilog of the logit function will allow us to find the estimated regression equation:

$$\text{Logit}(p) = \ln\left(\frac{p}{1-p}\right) = \beta_0 + \beta_1 x_1 + \beta_2 x_2 + \ldots + \beta_k x_k,$$

where β_0 = Intercept term

$\beta_1, \beta_2, \ldots, \beta_k$ are estimated parameters

$x_1, x_2, \ldots, x_k$ are the independent variables.

$$\left(\frac{p}{1-p}\right) = e^{\beta_0 + \beta_1 x_1 + \beta_2 x_2 + \cdots + \beta_k x_k}$$

Solving for p

$$\Rightarrow p = \frac{e^{\beta_0 + \beta_1 x_1 + \beta_2 x_2 + \cdots + \beta_k x_k}}{1 + e^{\beta_0 + \beta_1 x_1 + \beta_2 x_2 + \cdots + \beta_k x_k}}$$

TABLE 11.11

Summary of Significant Predictors for Final Model

Variable	Estimates	Wald Chi-Square
Number of Hospitals	0.5967	12.5426
PN_3B	−0.0646	5.6445
PN_6	−0.0535	8.3754
HFR	0.3848	14.1574
Disadvantage Population_2	1.87	19.7484

The estimated regression equation is given by

$$\hat{p} = \frac{e^{-3.3947-0.0646\text{PN3B}-0.0535\text{PN6}+0.5967\text{NOH}+1.87\text{DP2}+0.38\text{HFR}}}{1+e^{-3.3947-0.0646\text{PN3B}-0.0535\text{PN6}+0.5967\text{NOH}+1.87\text{DP2}+0.38\text{HFR}}},$$

where
   NOH—Number of Hospitals
   DP2—Disadvantaged Population_2
   HFR—Heart Failure Readmission
   PN3B—PN_3B
   PN6—PN_6

11.6.13.4.1 Sample Calculation for Predicted Probability

To validate the model formed above for its predictive capability, a random observation is chosen, and the predicted probability will be manually calculated and be compared with the model system calculated predicted probability. Finally, the probability will then be compared with the cutoff probability to see where the predicted probability lies, i.e., in the closure group or in the non-closure group, and hence the model's predictive ability will be determined. Here, observation 157 is chosen, and the system generated predicted probability is 0.115.

Let the above probability be compared with the manually calculated predicted probability using the variable parameters and the estimated regression equation as shown below.

   PN_3B = 92; PN_6 = 85; Number of Hospitals = 1; Disadvantaged Population = 1; HFR = 24.4.

$$\hat{p} = \frac{e^{-3.3947-0.0646(92)-0.0535(85)+0.5967(1)+1.87(1)+0.38(24.4)}}{1+e^{-3.3947-0.0646(92)-0.0535(85)+0.5967(1)+1.87(1)+0.38(24.4)}}$$

$$= \frac{e^{-2.1467}}{1+e^{-2.1467}} = \frac{0.11687}{1+0.11687} = 0.10464$$

Hence, $\hat{p} = 0.10464$.

The predicted probability calculated using the estimated regression equation is 0.10464 with a difference of 0.01 from the calculated probability value of 0.115. This calculated value is lesser than the cutoff probability value of 0.157 (details on calculating the cutoff probability is explained in the model validation part), which means that this observation will be in the non-closure (open) hospital group. This is true for the fact that this hospital originally was an open hospital. Hence, the model was correct in its prediction.

11.6.14 Model Validation

11.6.14.1 Overview

For model validation purposes, a series of diagnostics tests were performed to primarily evaluate the model's discrimination ability. A model's discriminatory power refers to the capability of the model to discriminate closures and non-closures.

11.6.14.2 Kolmogorov–Smirnov Statistic

The Kolmogorov–Smirnov (K–S) test is one such measure to evaluate the differences in two distribution functions and test if the logistic model discriminates between closure and non-closure. It is a measure that identifies the maximum separation distance between the cumulative distribution function (CDF) of positive and negative distributions known as K–S Statistic. To calculate the K–S Statistic, ten deciles are created; the percentages of closure and non-closure are calculated for each corresponding decile. Finally, cumulative percentages of closures and non-closures are calculated. The difference of the cumulative percentages of closure and non-closure for each decile is calculated. The K–S Statistic is identified by the largest difference between the cumulative percentages of closure and non-closure.

For the training data, the K–S Statistic is 60.9% which occurs at the third decile, which is an acceptable determination level of model reliability. The results also satisfy the K–S Statistic guidelines such that the K–S Statistic value should be between 40 and 70. Similarly, the K–S Statistic was calculated for the testing data and resulted in 54.1% which is acceptable again per K–S Statistic guidelines (Table 11.12; Figures 11.25 and 11.26).

11.6.14.3 Receiver Operating Characteristic (ROC) Curve

Another way to determine the discriminatory ability of the model is by using Sensitivity and Specificity. Sensitivity is the probability of predicting closure when closure is the predicted outcome, and Specificity is the probability of predicting non-closure when non-closure is the predicted outcome.

TABLE 11.12

K–S Statistics Table for Training Data

Decile	Closure	Non-Closure	% of all Closures	% of all Non-Closure	Cum. % Closure	Cum. % Non-Closure	K–S Statistic (%)
~10%	26	11	47.3	3.5	47.3	3.5	43.8
~20%	12	25	21.8	7.9	69.1	11.4	57.7
~30%	7	30	12.7	9.5	81.8	21.0	60.9
~40%	2	35	3.6	11.1	85.5	32.1	53.4
~50%	1	36	1.8	11.4	87.3	43.5	43.8
~60%	4	33	7.3	10.5	94.5	54.0	40.6
~70%	1	36	1.8	11.4	96.4	65.4	31.0
~80%	2	35	3.6	11.1	100.0	76.5	23.5
~90%	0	37	0.0	11.7	100.0	88.3	11.7
~100%	0	37	0.0	11.7	100.0	100.0	0.0
Totals	55	315				KS	60.9

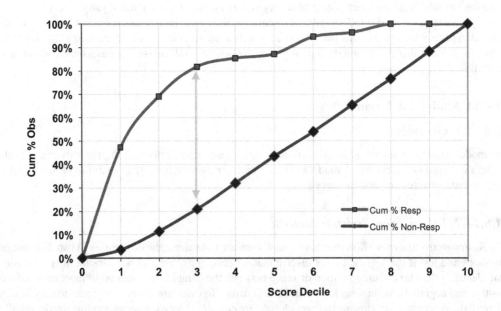

FIGURE 11.25 K–S graph for model formation data.

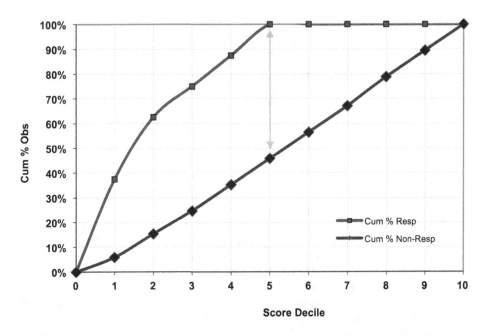

FIGURE 11.26 K–S graph for model validation data.

Hosmer and Lemeshow suggested a method to create a classification table by selecting the cutoff point at which the Sensitivity and Specificity are equal (Mernard). So, a cutoff point is chosen, when the Sensitivity and Specificity are equal. Figure 11.27 shows the Sensitivity and Specificity curves when they are plotted from 1 (100%) to 0 (0%) and 0 (0%) to 1 (100%), respectively. The point where the two curves meet is where the Sensitivity and Specificity are equal and is chosen as the cutoff point. A classification table is created based on this cutoff value (Figure 11.27; Table 11.13).

From the analysis table, when $p = 0.157$, the Sensitivity and Specificity are equal to 0.81 and approximately equal to 0.81, respectively.

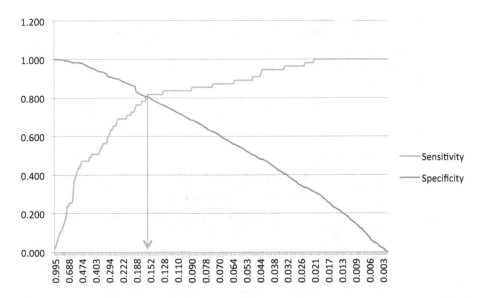

FIGURE 11.27 Sensitivity and Specificity cutoff point graph.

TABLE 11.13

Sensitivity and Specificity Cutoff Point Summary Table

Probability	No. of Correctly Predicted Events	No. of Correctly Predicted Nonevents	No. of Nonevents Predicted as Events	No. of Events Predicted as Nonevents	Sensitivity	Specificity	1-Specificity
0.157	45	254	61	10	0.81	0.806	0.193651

11.6.14.3.1 Classification and ROC Testing for Model Formation Data

Table 11.14 is a classification table created using the training data. The purpose is to determine how well the model could correctly classify closure and non-closure.

The classification results show the model correctly classified 45 hospitals as closed and incorrectly classified 10 as closed, i.e., the model correctly predicted closure of about 81%. Classification table also shows that the model correctly predicted non-closure of about 81% by correctly classifying 254 hospitals as closed and incorrectly classifying 61 hospitals as non-closure. For both cases, the higher the value, the better the model's ability for classification.

Sensitivity and Specificity may also be used as a basis for calculating a measure of explained variation (Mernard). Here, the Sensitivity is plotted on the y-axis, and 1-Specificity is plotted on the x-axis generating a curve known as ROC curve. The accuracy of the model is the ability of itself to correctly discriminate closures and non-closures. One measure of accuracy is the area under the curve (AUC). In general, the higher the area under the ROC curve, better is the model to correctly classify events (Closure and Non-closure).

By Hosmer and Lemeshow's general rules for interpreting AUC values, the following guidelines are given (Figure 11.28).

AUC = 0.5 (No Discrimination)

$0.7 \leq$ AUC < 0.8 (Acceptable Discrimination)

$0.8 \leq$ AUC < 0.9 (Excellent Discrimination)

AUC ≥ 0.9 (Outstanding Discrimination)

Association of Predicted Probabilities and Observed Responses			
Percent Concordant	86.9	Somers' D	0.741
Percent Discordant	12.8	Gamma	0.743
Percent Tied	0.3	Tau-a	0.188
Pairs	17325	c	0.870

TABLE 11.14

Classification Table for Model Formation Data

Training Data-Classification Table			
	Closed-1, Open-0		Total
Closed-1, Open-0	0	1	
0	254	10	271
1	61	45	99
Total	315	55	370

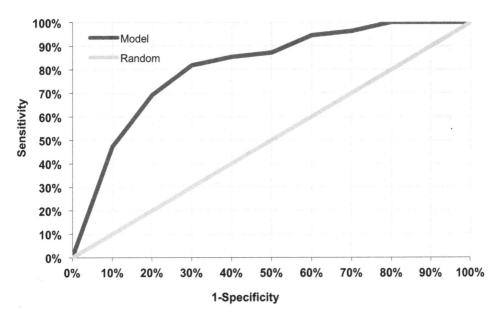

FIGURE 11.28 ROC curve for model formation data.

The AUC is given by the c-statistic from the table which is 0.87 or 87%. In terms of its discriminatory power in accordance with the above guidelines, the model's discriminatory power is excellent.

11.6.14.3.2 Classification and ROC Testing for Validation Data

A classification table for the validation data was created using the p-value equal to 0.157, and the results are shown in Table 11.15.

From the classification table for the validation data, the model correctly classified five hospitals as closed and incorrectly classified three as closed, i.e., the sensitivity is 62.5%. Also, the model correctly classified 64 hospitals as non-closure and incorrectly classified 18 as non-closure, and hence the specificity of the model is 75%. The overall accuracy of the model is 74%. An ROC curve plotted for the validation model using Sensitivity and 1-Specificity is shown below.

The area under the ROC curve is 85% given by the c-statistic, which implies the model's discriminatory ability is excellent.

The AUCs for model formation and validation are 87% and 85%, respectively, which are approximately in the same range, and have suggested that both models are performing well in terms of classifying closure events and non-closure events respectively (Figure 11.29).

TABLE 11.15

Classification Table for Model Validation Data

	Validation Data-Classification Table		
	Closed-1, Open-0		Total
Closed-1, Open-0	0	1	
0	64	3	72
1	18	5	21
Total	85	8	93

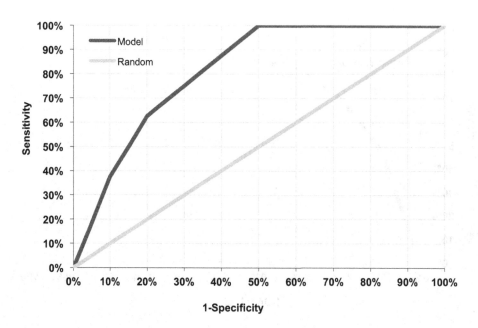

FIGURE 11.29   ROC curve for model validation data.

Association of Predicted Probabilities and Observed Responses			
Percent Concordant	82.1	Somers' D	0.642
Percent Discordant	17.9	Gamma	0.645
Percent Tied	0	Tau-a	0.158
Pairs	680	c	0.85

11.6.14.4 Deployment and Evaluation of LSS Project Initiatives

11.6.14.4.1 Scenario 1 Results

Different scenarios were run by adjusting the yellow belt, green belt, and black belt project types. As discussed in the methodology section, the idea is to limit the black belt resources due to limited resources available on the same. Also, having a minimum number of yellow belt and green belt projects will ensure the effectiveness of Six Sigma will be realized soon to instill belief in the management and stakeholders.

The model parameters for scenario 1 were set such that there are at least three yellow belt projects and two green belt projects implemented during the pilot phase (Table 11.16).

In effect, the model for scenario 1 resulted with a cost savings of $2,838,871 with an investment of $999,576. In total, eight projects were chosen, in which four projects were chosen from hospital 2 and four projects were chosen from hospital 3. Among them, two yellow belt and two black belt projects were chosen from hospital 2, and one yellow belt, two green belt, and one black belt project were chosen from hospital 3. Table 11.7 depicts the results in detail.

TABLE 11.16

Model Parameters Table

Scenario: 1		Scenario: 2	
Y_{ij}	3		
G_{ij}	2	A	3
B	$1,000,000	B	$1,000,000

TABLE 11.17

Scenario 1—Model Results Summary

Total maximized cost savings	$2,838,871
Total investment cost	$999,576
Total number of projects selected	8
Number of yellow belt projects selected	3
Number of green belt projects selected	2
Number of black belt projects selected	3

11.6.14.4.2 Scenario 2 Results

The model parameters for scenario 2 were set such that the number of black belt projects will not exceed 3 since the three core measure projects identified in hospital 3 have two black belt projects among them. The model for scenario 2 resulted with a cost savings of $2,624,783. In total, seven projects were selected from hospitals 2 and 3 among which two yellow belt and one black belt project were selected from hospital 2 and two green belt and two black belt projects were chosen from hospital 3. The three core measure projects from hospital 3 include two black belt and one green belt project. The total investment for the project was $998,465. Table 11.18 depicts the results in detail.

11.6.14.4.3 Net Present Value Comparison of LSS Projects
Deployment Decision and No Action

Net Present Value (NPV) method can be used to evaluate project implementation decision vs. no action taken option using the costs of two alternatives (Jones et al. 285–303). Here, a hypothetical operating cost of $12 M is used for the NPV analysis to compare alternatives between deploying LSS projects and no action taken option. The analysis is performed in both scenarios discussed above. An interest rate of 12% and a time period of 3 years are used for comparing alternatives.

Scenario 1:

$$NPV_{no\ action} = \$12,000,000\left(P/A\ 12\%,3\right)$$

$$= \$12,000,000(0.712)$$

$$= \$8,544,000$$

$$NPV_{LSS\ deployment} = \$999,576 + \$9,161,129\left(P/A\ 12\%,3\right)$$

$$= \$999,576 + 6,522,723.85$$

$$= \$7,522,300$$

From the above NPV analysis, the comparison between deploying LSS projects and no action option results with a cost difference of $1,021,700. Hence, deploying LSS projects is a better option for the hospital.

TABLE 11.18

Scenario 2—Model Results Summary

Total maximized cost savings	$2,624,783
Total investment cost	$998,465
Total number of projects selected	7
Number of yellow belt projects selected	2
Number of green belt projects selected	2
Number of black belt projects selected	3

Scenario 2:

$$\text{NPV}_{\text{no action}} = \$12,000,000\left(\text{P/A } 12\%,3\right)$$

$$= \$12,000,000(0.712)$$

$$= \$8,544,000$$

$$\text{NPV}_{\text{LSS deployment}} = \$998,465 + \$937,5217\left(\text{P/A } 12\%,3\right)$$

$$= \$998,465 + \$6,675,154.5$$

$$= \$7,673,620$$

The NPV analysis for scenario 2 results with a cost difference of \$870,380, and hence, deploying LSS projects will benefit the hospital system.

Conclusion:

Although the cost savings realized from implementing LSS projects will not eliminate the closure risks in one sweep, the initial savings from the pilot phase of implementation will alleviate the risks to some degree. Also, by focusing on improving core measure processes, hospitals can avoid unnecessary costs due to poor quality (sample calculations in the Appendix) as well as avoid penalties and can leverage the programs such as HVBP to receive incentives for good quality of care. As more projects are implemented in the later phases, by strategically implementing projects based on the needs, the hospitals can achieve cost savings, generate additional revenues, and improve the profit margin, thus eliminating the closure issues.

11.7 Contribution to the Body of Knowledge

IE 5300—RFID in Logistics

The lab experiments performed in this course helped in experimentally studying and conducting research.

IE 5303—Quality Systems

Understanding the concepts of quality, the tools, and the methodology used for quality improvement.

IE 5304—Engineering Economy

Understanding the economics is vital for this project. Cost reduction, improving revenue and profit are the key for the hospitals to prevent closures in the future.

IE 5320—Enterprise Engineering Methods

Understanding Hospital Enterprise as a system with the complex nature of processes and activities involved and identifying key stakeholders involved at different levels of the processes.

IE 5342—Metrics and Measurements

Standardizing care and other related processes will help hospitals in achieving efficiency and generate additional revenue yielding opportunities.

11.8 Conclusions and Discussions

11.8.1 Conclusions

The motivation behind this project is the wave of rural closures happening since 2010 on an increasing trend till date around the country. The project started with background study of closures occurring throughout the country but majority of the closures happening in the southern region of the country (Texas being the state with the maximum number of closures).

The background research gave an idea that the variables identified can be classified as Operational Importance and Financial Importance variables to analyze separately. The statistical analysis that was performed on the potential variables resulted with five significant predictors in total, among which three variables are from operational importance model and two are from financial importance model to be significant in predicting hospital closures. The model validation analysis proved the model to be accurately predicting closures with a discriminatory capabilities of 87% and 85% using model formation and model validation data, respectively.

The analyses from research objective 2 show that there are some lapses in care existing within the hospitals, which may lead to their closure. For instance, the variable HFR is proved to predict closure, meaning closed hospitals do not adequately take steps to prevent patients coming back within 30 days for the same diagnosis, which results in unnecessary costs as well as more likelihood of receiving penalties.

The results from the LSS deployment show that hospitals can bring the present situation in control when they start making changes within their system. The savings realized from the quality improvement efforts through LSS during the pilot phase should bring in confidence and improved morale among the top management and employees alike. Although the initial cost savings will not completely change the financial status and eliminate risks for the hospitals, in the long run, identifying and implementing more projects based on the needs of the patients, needs of business goals, and needs of the process will bring in transformation of the enterprise to achieve operational excellence. The transformation may attract more patients and create a win–win situation for the hospitals to save costs by improving quality as well as gain revenue by improving utilization rate and patient volume which has been long-standing issue for rural hospitals. The improvement efforts should also be able to provide immunity to hospitals to some extent against poor socioeconomic conditions in hospital's vicinity as well as any policy changes in the future that may hamper the existence of these hospitals. The inclusion of hospitals in disadvantaged locations for strategic improvements will make sure that the patients that depend on those hospitals will get adequate and timely care.

11.8.2 Limitations

Many literatures lacked cost savings data associated with Six Sigma projects.

Although data couldn't be collected from open and closed hospitals for confidentiality reasons, the publicly made available data, specifically, the comparison data of process performance of hospitals was attainable.

11.8.3 Future Work

This study has unveiled several future opportunities for research in this area. Projects can be planned to be implemented on a multi-phase basis if more feasible projects could be identified. Also, hospitals can target to have a good project mix by targeting efficiency to reduce costs, improve bottom line savings as well as projects which will focus on patient satisfaction, which will help rural hospitals to get the trust from patients and may translate into hard and soft savings.

This research has opened the avenue for improvements in hospitals located in disadvantaged locations. Hospitals in disadvantaged locations can develop strategies to attain process improvements throughout the hospital to attract more patients and thereby improve revenue and profit.

The other potential future research is related to policy decisions, such as analyzing the pros and cons if the states who have not expanded Medicaid yet will change their decision to expand in the near future.

APPENDIX 11.A: Predicted Probabilities

S. No.	Probability	S. No.	Probability	S. No.	Probability	S. No.	Probability
1	0.045474	36	0.006633	71	0.403086	106	0.151757
2	0.031347	37	0.005563	72	0.107878	107	0.599678
3	0.170528	38	0.002678	73	0.264548	108	0.040923
4	0.065235	39	0.141782	74	0.063556	109	0.039872
5	0.013524	40	0.110254	75	0.404734	110	0.459233
6	0.062943	41	0.187571	76	0.019558	111	0.075023
7	0.209116	42	0.109493	77	0.02248	112	0.114413
8	0.026538	43	0.095033	78	0.617078	113	0.460231
9	0.006555	44	0.006394	79	0.873406	114	0.915913
10	0.187571	45	0.039665	80	0.73123	115	0.003605
11	0.053484	46	0.077891	81	0.437394	116	0.007192
12	0.013353	47	0.010104	82	0.187571	117	0.017225
13	0.015263	48	0.538668	83	0.146304	118	0.138459
14	0.008157	49	0.003166	84	0.207953	119	0.040736
15	0.00374	50	0.004804	85	0.200823	120	0.295436
16	0.187571	51	0.215333	86	0.050887	121	0.009974
17	0.090487	52	0.038511	87	0.281351	122	0.455628
18	0.599678	53	0.070087	88	0.065686	123	0.086065
19	0.146272	54	0.003905	89	0.295436	124	0.006061
20	0.044895	55	0.070418	90	0.040612	125	0.006933
21	0.067735	56	0.007084	91	0.109385	126	0.011096
22	0.240097	57	0.044291	92	0.056538	127	0.005648
23	0.418124	58	0.002741	93	0.09364	128	0.032456
24	0.542687	59	0.157611	94	0.087648	129	0.008152
25	0.005352	60	0.105138	95	0.01073	130	0.089826
26	0.868915	61	0.027272	96	0.033276	131	0.118151
27	0.046131	62	0.076675	97	0.140882	132	0.400522
28	0.006392	63	0.831685	98	0.033163	133	0.619628
29	0.00495	64	0.024658	99	0.091988	134	0.024106
30	0.064161	65	0.007018	100	0.053478	135	0.016535
31	0.106308	66	0.058775	101	0.011148	136	0.066869
32	0.754781	67	0.021326	102	0.029959	137	0.432323
33	0.067735	68	0.008971	103	0.004053	138	0.00445
34	0.373152	69	0.037357	104	0.012534	139	0.599678
35	0.010584	70	0.014094	105	0.092547	140	0.295436

S. No.	Probability	S. No.	Probability	S. No.	Probability	S. No.	Probability
141	0.019957	176	0.373424	211	0.038441	246	0.069658
142	0.388566	177	0.015669	212	0.015266	247	0.057748
143	0.127745	178	0.023819	213	0.050135	248	0.599678
144	0.023924	179	0.183736	214	0.030578	249	0.442808
145	0.140447	180	0.010905	215	0.035103	250	0.353565
146	0.026262	181	0.885007	216	0.432323	251	0.008918
147	0.546696	182	0.505351	217	0.066658	252	0.022361

(Continued)

S. No.	Probability	S. No.	Probability	S. No.	Probability	S. No.	Probability
148	0.018107	183	0.128412	218	0.018641	253	0.044845
149	0.069758	184	0.038378	219	0.06789	254	0.042828
150	0.189625	185	0.111722	220	0.036346	255	0.047694
151	0.276304	186	0.295436	221	0.087174	256	0.865521
152	0.016895	187	0.015745	222	0.014939	257	0.124903
153	0.156914	188	0.116748	223	0.074817	258	0.015405
154	0.036515	189	0.028324	224	0.599678	259	0.012904
155	0.054881	190	0.139169	225	0.032297	260	0.872538
156	0.115587	191	0.187571	226	0.130977	261	0.021879
157	0.02366	192	0.995437	227	0.088619	262	0.083953
158	0.170474	193	0.026005	228	0.008738	263	0.189134
159	0.069582	194	0.003941	229	0.008748	264	0.045762
160	0.007805	195	0.05008	230	0.047194	265	0.015457
161	0.018165	196	0.010908	231	0.063591	266	0.003345
162	0.293537	197	0.02044	232	0.187571	267	0.005265
163	0.295436	198	0.00945	233	0.011426	268	0.009864
164	0.040131	199	0.220842	234	0.031747	269	0.73123
165	0.214058	200	0.640265	235	0.097598	270	0.033018
166	0.164123	201	0.0357	236	0.382828	271	0.25088
167	0.515363	202	0.208354	237	0.005449	272	0.030013
168	0.078067	203	0.42678	238	0.041278	273	0.029784
169	0.041585	204	0.007747	239	0.224837	274	0.017506
170	0.020874	205	0.070536	240	0.016673	275	0.03726
171	0.550378	206	0.027346	241	0.007118	276	0.035761
172	0.168576	207	0.687669	242	0.007689	277	0.010605
173	0.065434	208	0.167228	243	0.063699	278	0.002619
174	0.078044	209	0.866069	244	0.003038	279	0.266747
175	0.333246	210	0.056929	245	0.007447	280	0.13281

S. No.	Probability	S. No.	Probability	S. No.	Probability
281	0.124447	311	0.970365	341	0.039823
282	0.013004	312	0.091642	342	0.087899
283	0.202824	313	0.011198	343	0.12259
284	0.066457	314	0.163218	344	0.075304
285	0.275293	315	0.030326	345	0.020097
286	0.032505	316	0.032105	346	0.076675
287	0.0708	317	0.323028	347	0.073083
288	0.187571	318	0.031406	348	0.002005
289	0.05466	319	0.003799	349	0.222387
290	0.030886	320	0.295436	350	0.678622
291	0.012591	321	0.021675	351	0.006596
292	0.088296	322	0.021241	352	0.071015
293	0.062684	323	0.012117	353	0.005662
294	0.425411	324	0.028998	354	0.23635
295	0.171554	325	0.19683	355	0.018708
296	0.010779	326	0.73123	356	0.187571
297	0.007214	327	0.831685	357	0.01509
298	0.050552	328	0.311437	358	0.473672
299	0.016827	329	0.471444	359	0.153672

(*Continued*)

S. No.	Probability	S. No.	Probability	S. No.	Probability
300	0.057341	330	0.051478	360	0.231533
301	0.00998	331	0.006134	361	0.272247
302	0.138862	332	0.053039	362	0.021386
303	0.002833	333	0.012804	363	0.060124
304	0.187571	334	0.077687	364	0.043681
305	0.187571	335	0.030863	365	0.082658
306	0.026365	336	0.144452	366	0.120885
307	0.081123	337	0.043887	367	0.016911
308	0.115362	338	0.019527	368	0.322757
309	0.025624	339	0.005244	369	0.157329
310	0.026508	340	0.130176	370	0.013772

APPENDIX 11.B: Area under the ROC Curve Calculation

11.B.1 Model Formation Data

Approx. Score %-ile	Closures	Non-Closures	Response Rate (%)	% of all Closures	% of all Non-Closures	Cum. % Closures	Cum. % Non-Closures	Gini Calc.
~10%	26	11	70.3	47.3	3.5	47.3	3.5	0.0083
~20%	12	25	32.4	21.8	7.9	69.1	11.4	0.0462
~30%	7	30	18.9	12.7	9.5	81.8	21.0	0.0719
~40%	2	35	5.4	3.6	11.1	85.5	32.1	0.0929
~50%	1	36	2.7	1.8	11.4	87.3	43.5	0.0987
~60%	4	33	10.8	7.3	10.5	94.5	54.0	0.0952
~70%	1	36	2.7	1.8	11.4	96.4	65.4	0.1091
~80%	2	35	5.4	3.6	11.1	100.0	76.5	0.1091
~90%	0	37	0.0	0.0	11.7	100.0	88.3	0.1175
~100%	0	37	0.0	0.0	11.7	100.0	100.0	0.1175
Totals	55	315	14.86					87%

11.B.2 Model Validation Data

Approx. Score %-ile	Closures	Non-Closures	Response Rate (%)	% of all Closures	% of all Non-Closures	Cum. % Closures	Cum. % Non-Closures	Gini Calc.
~10%	3	5	37.5	37.5	5.9	37.5	5.9	0.0110
~20%	2	8	20.0	25.0	9.4	62.5	15.3	0.0471
~30%	1	8	11.1	12.5	9.4	75.0	24.7	0.0647
~40%	1	9	10.0	12.5	10.6	87.5	35.3	0.0860
~50%	1	9	10.0	12.5	10.6	100.0	45.9	0.0993
~60%	0	9	0.0	0.0	10.6	100.0	56.5	0.1059
~70%	0	9	0.0	0.0	10.6	100.0	67.1	0.1059
~80%	0	10	0.0	0.0	11.8	100.0	78.8	0.1176
~90%	0	9	0.0	0.0	10.6	100.0	89.4	0.1059
~100%	0	9	0.0	0.0	10.6	100.0	100.0	0.1059
Totals	8	85	8.6					85%

APPENDIX 11.C: Cost of Quality Sample Calculations

Pneumonia PN 6—selection of initial appropriate antibiotics	
Non-adherence with this standard is likely to cause increased length of stay	
Estimate that non-adherence will likely increase the length of stay by 1 day	
Estimated average cost per stay	$12,000
Estimated length of stay	5.3 days
Average cost per day	$2,264
Number of patients who were not given initial appropriate antibiotics	75
Total cost for non-adherence	$169,800
HF-1 (discharge instructions)	
Non-adherence with this standard is likely to cause readmissions	
Estimate that non-adherence will likely cause readmissions by 12%	
Estimated average cost per stay	$12,000
Number of patients who are likely to be readmitted	14
Total cost for non-adherence	$168,000

REFERENCES

Advisory.com. CMS: The 2,225 Hospitals that Will Pay Readmissions Penalties Next Year. N.p., 2013. Web. 30 Aug. 2015.

Advisory.com. CMS: The 2,610 Hospitals Facing Readmission Penalties this Year. N.p., 2014. Web. 31 Aug. 2015.

Antony, Jiju. Six Sigma in the UK Service Organisations: Results from a Pilot Survey. *Managerial Auditing Journal* 19.8 (2004): 1006–1013. Web.

Antony, Jiju, and Ricardo Banuelas. Key Ingredients for the Effective Implementation of Six Sigma Program. *Measuring Business Excellence* 6.4 (2002): 20–27. Web.

Barnet, Shannon. 20 Hospital Closures, Bankruptcies So Far in 2014. *Beckershospitalreview.com*. N.p., 2014. Web. 31 Oct. 2015.

Bazzoli, Gloria J. et al. The Effects of Safety Net Hospital Closures and Conversions on Patient Travel Distance to Hospital Services. *Health Services Research* 47.1pt1 (2011): 129–150. Web.

Blount, Thor. Accountable Care Organizations and Medicare Shared Savings Program. *Accountable Care Organizations and Medicare Shared Savings Program*. Zanebenefits, 2013. Web. 31 Oct. 2015.

Bls.gov. CPI Inflation Calculator. Web. 28 Nov. 2016.

Bradley, E.H. et al. Hospital Strategies Associated With 30-Day Readmission Rates for Patients With Heart Failure. *Circulation: Cardiovascular Quality and Outcomes* 6.4 (2013): 444–450. Web.

Brown, Bobbi. Best Way to Run a Hospital Readmissions Reduction Program. *Healthcatalyst.com*. Web. 30 Aug. 2015.

Brown, Bobbi. Value-Based Purchasing: Why Your Timeline Just Got Shorter. *Healthcatalyst.com*. Web. 31 Oct. 2015.

Brown, Bobbi, and Jared Crapo. Key to Transitioning from Fee-for-Service to Value-Based. *Healthcatalyst.com*. N.p., 2014. Web. 30 Aug. 2015.

Büyüközkan, Gülçin, and Demet Öztürkcan. An Integrated Analytic Approach for Six Sigma Project Selection. *Expert Systems with Applications* 37.8 (2010): 5835–5847. Web.

Daly, Rich. 673 Rural Hospitals Vulnerable to Closure: Analysis. *Healthcare Business News*. N.p., 2016. Web. 24 Nov. 2016.

Demko, Paul. As Rural Hospitals Struggle, Solutions Sought to Preserve Healthcare Access. *Modern Healthcare*. N.p., 2015. Web. 31 Oct. 2015.

Dinesh Kumar, U. et al. Six Sigma Project Selection Using Data Envelopment Analysis. *The TQM Magazine* 19.5 (2007): 419–441. Web.

Evans, Melanie. Hospitals Face Closures As "A New Day in Healthcare" Dawns. *Modern Healthcare*. N.p., 2015. Web. 18 Nov. 2016.

Garfield, Rachel. The Coverage Gap: Uninsured Poor Adults in States that Do Not Expand Medicaid. *Kaiser Family Foundation*. N.p., 2016. Web. 29 Nov. 2016.

Gold, Jenny. Accountable Care Organizations, Explained. *Kaiser Health News*. N.p., 2015. Web. 31 Oct. 2015.

Goldman, L. Elizabeth, and R. Adams Dudley. United States Rural Hospital Quality in the Hospital Compare Database—Accounting for Hospital Characteristics. *Health Policy* 87.1 (2008): 112–127. Web.

Hsia, R.Y.-J., and Y.-C. Shen. Rising Closures of Hospital Trauma Centers Disproportionately Burden Vulnerable Populations. *Health Affairs* 30.10 (2011): 1912–1920. Web.

Hsia, Renee Y., Arthur L. Kellermann, and Yu-Chu Shen. Factors Associated With Closures of Emergency Departments in the United States. *JAMA* 305.19 (2011): N.p. Web.

Hu, G. et al. A Multi-Objective Model for Project Portfolio Selection to Implement Lean and Six Sigma Concepts. *International Journal of Production Research* 46.23 (2008): 6611–6625. Web.

Hung, Peiyin, Michelle Casey, and Ira Moscovice. *Which Rural And Urban Hospitals Have Received Readmission Penalties Over Time?* University of Minnesota Rural Health Research Center, 2015. Print.

Janney, Cristina. Small Rural Hospitals Face Big Changes under the Affordable Care Act. *Journal Star*. N.p., 2014. Web. 30 Aug. 2015.

Jones, Erick C. et al. Case Study: The Engineering Economics of RFID in Specialized Manufacturing. *The Engineering Economist* 52.3 (2007): 285–303. Web.

Kaufman, Brystana et al. The Rising Rate of Rural Hospital Closures. *The Journal of Rural health*. N.p., 2015. Web. 6 Nov. 2015.

Kff.org. Uninsured Rates For The Nonelderly By Race/Ethnicity. N.p., 2015. Web. 31 Oct. 2015.

Kumar, Maneesh, Jiju Antony, and Byung Rae Cho. Project Selection and its Impact on the Successful Deployment of Six Sigma. *Business Process Management Journal* 15.5 (2009): 669–686. Web.

Lieb, David. More Rural Hospitals Closing. *jems.com*. N.p., 2015. Web. 30 Aug. 2015.

Lillie-Blanton, Marsha et al. Rural and Urban Hospital Closures, 1985–1988: Operating and Environmental Characteristics that Affect Risk. *Inquiry* 29.3 (1992): 332–344. Web.

Ly, Dan P., Ashish K. Jha, and Arnold M. Epstein. The Association Between Hospital Margins, Quality of Care, and Closure or Other Change in Operating Status. *Journal of General Internal Medicine* 26.11 (2011): 1291–1296. Web.

Mangan, Dan. Latest Score: Obamacare Enrolls 8.02 Million By April 19. *CNBC*. N.p., 2014. Web. 27 Nov. 2016.

Medicare *DSH*. American Hospital Association, 2015. Print.

Medicare.gov. Hospital Readmission Reduction Program. N.p., 2015. Web. 30 Aug. 2015.

Menard, Scott W. *Logistic Regression*. 1st ed. Los Angeles, CA: SAGE, 2010. Print.

NC Rural Health Research Program. 79 Rural Hospital Closures: January 2010–Present. N.p., 2015. Web. 31 Oct. 2015.

Newkirk, Vann. The Affordable Care Act and Insurance Coverage in Rural Areas. *Kff.org*. N.p., 2014. Web. 5 Nov. 2015.

Padhy, R.K., and S. Sahu. A Real Option Based Six Sigma Project Evaluation and Selection Model. *International Journal of Project Management* 29.8 (2011): 1091–1102. Web.

Peck, Andrea. More Hospitals Closed Due to Empty Beds As Providers Succeed in Reducing Hospital Admissions: Pathologists Should Respond Outpatient/Outreach Services. *Darkdaily.com*. N.p., 2015. Web. 21 Nov. 2016.

Qualitynet.org. Payments- Hospital Value Based Purchasing. N.p., 2015. Web. 31 Oct. 2015

RAND Corporation. Expanding Medicaid Is Best Financial Option for States. N.p., 2013. Web. 30 Aug. 2015.

Rau, Jordan. Medicare Fines 2,610 Hospitals for Excess Readmissions. *Medpagetoday.com*. N.p., 2014. Web. 30 Aug. 2015.

Rau, Jordan. Medicare Fines 2,610 Hospitals in Third Round of Readmission Penalties. *Kaiser Health News*. N.p., 2014. Web. 30 Aug. 2015.

Reforming Health Blog. Are Readmission Penalties Unfair to Safety Net Hospitals?. N.p., 2014. Web. 30 Aug. 2015.

Reiter, K.L., M. Noles, and G.H. Pink. Uncompensated Care Burden May Mean Financial Vulnerability for Rural Hospitals in States that Did Not Expand Medicaid. *Health Affairs* 34.10 (2015): 1721–1729. Web.

Rural Hospitals Continue to Struggle. *Medical Research Consultants*. Web. 18 Nov. 2016.

Soumerai, Stephen, and Ross Koppel. An Obamacare Penalty on Hospitals. *Wall Street Journal*. N.p., 2013. Web. 31 Aug. 2015.

Spade, Jeffrey S., and Stephanie C. Strickland. Rural Hospitals Face Many Challenges in Transitioning to Value-Based Care. *North Carolina Medical Journal* 76.1 (2015): 38–39. Web.

Support.minitab.com. ROC (Receiver Operating Characteristic) Curve – Minitab. N.p., 2016. Web. 18 Nov. 2016.

The Henry J. Kaiser Family Foundation. A Guide to the Supreme Court's Decision on the ACA's Medicaid Expansion. 1 Aug. 2012. Web. 2015.

Thompson, Kristie, Brystana Kaufman, and Mark Holmes. *How Does Medicaid Expansion Affect Insurance Coverage Of Rural Populations?* North Carolina Rural Health Research Program, 2014. Print.

Turner, Grace-Marie, and Avik Roy. Why States Should Not Expand Medicaid. *Galen Institute.* N.p., 2013. Web. 30 Aug. 2015.

Walters, Edgar. Rural Hospitals Struggle to Keep their Doors Open. *texastribune.org.* N.p., 2015. Web. 30 Aug. 2015.

Yang, Taho, and Chiung-Hsi Hsieh. Six-Sigma Project Selection Using National Quality Award Criteria and Delphi Fuzzy Multiple Criteria Decision-Making Method. *Expert Systems with Applications* 36.4 (2009): 7594–7603. Web.

12

TQM Case Study

Erick C. Jones

12.1 Introduction

Technical organizations often face the challenge of aligning their supply chain (SC). The technical manager faces challenges in coordinating data collection and analysis efforts to evaluate the SC in a cost-effective manner. In some organizations, it may be prudent to utilize current technical personnel to perform this analysis. Oftentimes companies consider utilizing costly software and consultants prior to using their in-house resources. Allowing the technical manager to utilize an internal team to provide an analysis is more cost effective for several reasons.

1. Data collected will be utilized again if consultants are deemed necessary.
2. The in-house team will understand the implications of solutions that the model may provide and can make adjustments for reality.
3. Simplified assumptions can be agreed upon by internal stakeholders.
4. The project will prepare personnel for change.
5. The project provides a cost-effective solution.

Also, this study will reveal if your SC network may be too complex to model using simply the Excel solver prior to investing in an extensive study. Though it is very important to perform SC analysis, many companies cannot justify the use of expensive software and consultant to perform these analyses continually. The technical manager can provide good solutions by creating this type of study.

Previously, a project team of students from the University of Nebraska-Lincoln and personnel from the City began a Six Sigma Project to reduce obsolete inventory. The SC consisted of a network of warehouses, storerooms, suppliers, and the internal end user who represented the customer. During the Six Sigma process improvement study, the team determined that customer service needs were not being met, obsolete inventory was being driven by purchasing behavior, and that facility costs could be reduced with facility consolidations. The team analyzed the SC network of the city's Public Works Department using modeling techniques to recommend which warehouses could be consolidated. Based on recommendations, 96,000 ft² could be reduced, and gross of $ 3.5M would be saved over 5 years not including taxes and depreciation. This represents a cost reduction of 25%.

12.2 Background

A technical manager's goal when locating facilities and allocating inventory should maximize the overall profitability of the resulting SC network while providing customers with adequate service. Traditionally, revenues come from the sale of product, and costs arise from facilities, labor, transportation, material, and inventory holding. Ideally, profits after tariffs and taxes should be maximized when designing a SC network. In this scenario, the city government does not pay taxes or collect revenues, so their goals were to minimize overall operating cost and still be responsive to the customer.

Trade-offs must be made by the technical managers during network design. For example, building many facilities to serve local markets reduces transportation cost and provides fast response time, but it increases the facility and inventory costs incurred by the firm. Technical managers can use network design models in two different situations. First, those models are used to decide on locations where facilities will be established and the capacity assigned to each facility. Second, these models are used to assign current demand to the available facilities and identify lanes along which product will be transported. Managers must consider this decision at least on an annual demand basis, prices, and tariff charge. In both cases, the goal is to maximize the profit while satisfying customer needs. The following information must be available before the design decisions can be made:

1. Location of supply sources and markets
2. Location of potential sites
3. Demand forecast by market
4. Facility, labor, and material cost by site
5. Transportation costs between each pair of sites
6. Inventory costs by site as well as a function of quantity
7. Sales price of product in different regions
8. Taxes and tariffs as product is moved between locations
9. Desired response time and other service factors (Chopra and Meindl 2004).

Given this information, a choice of model type can be made. Previous literature highlights some general models that have differing goals. Each model has differing objectives; the models that were considered for this study were the Capacitated Plant Location Model and the Gravity Location Model. The Capacitated Plant Location Model seeks to minimize the total cost of the current SC network; the problem is formulated into an integer program. The Gravity Location Model's goal is to locate an optimal location based on cost inputs. Beyond optimization models, the technical manager could build a simulation of their SC.

In this study, we chose to use the Capacitated Plant Location Model (Chopra and Meindl 2004) in order to determine the minimal number of facilities that could hold inventory and meet customer demand. In our study, the City has chosen to consolidate warehouse facilities. Management is questioning whether all 12 facilities are necessary. They have assigned a SC Team of University of Nebraska-Lincoln and City personnel to study the network for the Public Works operations and identify the warehouses that can be closed. The goal is to formulate the model to minimize total costs taking into account costs, taxes, and duties by location. Given the taxes and duties do not vary between various locations, and that the city does not pay taxes, the team decided to use the existing facility locations and allocate demand to the open warehouses to minimize the total cost of facilities, transportation, and inventory.

12.2.1 The Capacitated Plant Location Model

The capacitated plant location network optimization model requires the following inputs:

N = number of potential locations
M = number of demand points
D_i = annual demand from market i
K_i = potential capacity of plant i
F_i = annualized fixed cost of keeping factory i open
C_{ij} = cost of producing and shipping one unit from factory i to marker j (cost includes production inventory, transportation, and duties)
and the following decision variables:
Y_i = 1 if plant is open, 0 otherwise
X_{ij} = quantity shipped from factory i to market j.

The problem is formulated as the following integer program

$$\text{Min}\left(\sum_{i=1}^{n} F_i Y_i + \sum_{i=1}^{n} \sum_{j=1}^{m} C_{ij} X_{ij}\right)$$

subject to

$$\sum_{i=1}^{m} X_{ij} D_{ij} \quad \text{for } j = 1 \ldots m \tag{12.1}$$

$$\sum_{j=1}^{n} X_{ij} \le K_i Y_i \quad \text{for } i = 1 \ldots n \tag{12.2}$$

$$Y_i \in (0,1) \quad \text{for } i = 1 \ldots n \tag{12.3}$$

The objective function minimizes the total cost (fixed + variable) of setting up and operating the network. The constraint in Eq. 5.1 requires that the demand at each facility market be satisfied. The constraint in Eq. 5.2 states that no plant can supply more than its capacity. (Capacity is 0 if closed and K_i if it is open. The product of the terms $K_i Y_i$ captures this effect.) The constraint in Eq. 5.3 enforces that each plant is either open ($Y_i = 1$) or closed ($Y_i = 0$). The solution will identify the plants that are to be kept open, their capacity, and the allocation of regional demand to these plants. The model is solved using the Solver tool in Excel (Chopra and Meindl 2004).

12.3 Network Modeling Steps Incorporated into a Six Sigma Service Project

The typical Six Sigma DMAIC approach was used with the addition of a network model within the Analyze phase. DMAIC stands for Define, Measure, Analyze, Improve, and Control. These are the steps in a standard improvement model for a Six Sigma-directed project.

12.3.1 Define

The main work in the Define phase is for the team to complete an analysis of what the project should accomplish and to confirm their understanding with their sponsor(s). They should agree on the problem, understand the project's link to corporate strategy and its expected contribution to return on investment capital, agree on the project boundaries, and know what indicators or metrics will be used to evaluate success. The last two issues often prove particularly important in service environments (George 2003). The problem defined for this project was to reduce obsolete inventory.

12.3.2 Measure

One of the major advances of Six Sigma is its *demand* for data-driven management. Most other improvement methodologies tended to dive from identifying a project into Improve without sufficient data to really understand the underlying causes of the problem. The Measure phase is Six Sigma's stage for data collection and "measuring" the problem. This phase is generally broken into several steps, including establish baselines, observe the process, and collect data (George 2003). The measure of success was reducing the percent of obsolete inventory in the SC.

12.3.3 Analyze

The purpose of the Analyze phase is to make sense of all the information and data collected in Measure. A challenge to all teams is *sticking to the data* and not just using their own experience and opinions to make conclusions about the root causes (George 2003). There are many tools available in the Analyze phase, including network modeling. Network models provide a rich and robust framework for combining data, relationships, and forecast from descriptive models. They provide managers with broad and deep insights into effective plans, which are based on the company's decision options, goals, commitments, and resource constraints (Shapiro 2001). After using regression analysis and design of experiment analysis, the team chose to use SC optimization for a more robust solution.

The network model used within this project followed several steps including:

1. Collect Input Data and Establish Baseline.
2. Set Optimization Constraints.
3. Run Alternatives with the Capacitated Plant Location Model (Chopra and Meindl 2004).
4. Show Alternatives in Revenue, Savings, and Customer Service.
5. Select an Alternative.

These steps led to an alternative that minimized the cost of the SC. This alternative then directs the tasks within the Improve stage.

12.3.4 Improve

The sole purpose of the Improve phase is to make changes in a process that will eliminate the defects, waste, costs, etc. that are linked to the customer needs identified in the Define stage (George 2003). The Improve stage differs for every Six Sigma project. The common theme is that the improvements should be centered on the largest issues found in the Analyze phase. The recommendations for consolidating facilities (the SC model recommended) and using a more robust criterion for eliminating outdated inventory were recommended for the improvement.

12.3.5 Control

The purpose of Control is to make sure that any gains made will be preserved, until and unless new knowledge and data show that there is an even better way to operate the process. The team must address how to share what they learned with the process owner and ensure that everyone working on the process is trained in using any new, documented procedures. Six areas of Control are critical: document the improved process, turn the results into dollars, verify maintenance of gains continually, install an automatic monitoring system, pilot the implementation, and develop a control plan. Key performance indicators were identified to be tracked with Statistical Process Control charts for the following year. This is further elaborated in the results section.

The DMAIC process with the Capacitated Plant Location Model in the Analyze phase was utilized to study the City of Houston's Public Works Warehousing Operations.

12.4 Case Description

12.4.1 Organizational Description

The organization used for this case study is a city in Southwest United States, Public Works, Materials Management Branch (MMB). The MMB is responsible for the processing and coordination of all procurement and contract-related activities as well as warehousing and distribution of all general inventory items for the department.

The branch facilitates purchases ranging from pipes for restoration of sewer lines to computers and traffic signs. To promptly obtain goods and services, the department utilizes in excess of 800 commodity and service contracts. The branch is divided into three functional sections: Procurement, Contract Management, and Warehousing and Distribution. This study was centered on the Warehousing and Distribution section.

The MMB has the responsibility for Warehousing and Distribution of general and automotive inventory items, from cradle to grave, for the department. Two central depots serve as staging locations for inventory that is distributed to a network of ten general supply warehouses, nine automotive warehouses, and many storerooms located throughout the City. The inventory consists of a variety of items, e.g., pipe, valves, fittings, office, janitorial supplies, etc.

12.4.2 Project Description

The MMB had been audited in previous years, and the audits identified opportunities for improvement in the warehousing operations. The audits identified excess obsolete inventory, need to evaluate standard operating procedures, and labor productivity. Obsolete inventory is defined as inventory that has not had any requests for disbursement for over one year.

The current system contains 12 warehouses and 28 storerooms with an ongoing cost of $14.94M. Upon inspection, it was estimated that the warehouses have a maximum of 30% space utilization. The current SC is shown in Figure 12.1. Public Works owned $10.1M of inventory within the MMB warehouses. The inventory that was deemed as obsolete was valued at $3.6M or 35% of the total inventory.

The modeling steps were followed to complete the analysis.

1. Collect Input Data and Establish Baseline
   The current SC information was collected to form the input data for the network model. The inputs included costs for electricity, gas, data lines, and labor. Also, holding and transportation costs were estimated for each facility. The warehouses do not pay taxes or water costs since they are in a city building, so information as to lost water sales and lost taxes was also captured and used in the cost equations.

2. Set Optimization Constraints
   The optimization constraints included the size limitations of each facility and the future demand at each facility. The facility size was collected from operations. The future demand on inventory was estimated to be the same as last year's value.

3. Run Alternatives with the Capacitated Plant Location Model (Chopra and Meindl 2004)
   The costs and data that were collected in steps 1 and 2 of the modeling were input into Chopra's model in Excel and the Solver Add-In was utilized to run alternatives of the least cost model.

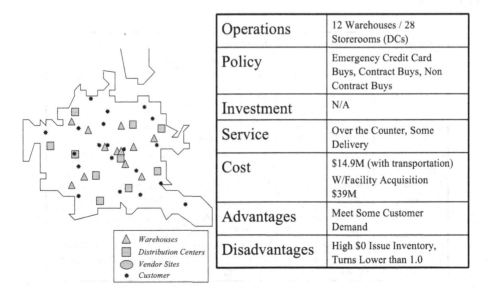

Operations	12 Warehouses / 28 Storerooms (DCs)
Policy	Emergency Credit Card Buys, Contract Buys, Non Contract Buys
Investment	N/A
Service	Over the Counter, Some Delivery
Cost	$14.9M (with transportation) W/Facility Acquisition $39M
Advantages	Meet Some Customer Demand
Disadvantages	High $0 Issue Inventory, Turns Lower than 1.0

△ Warehouses
▢ Distribution Centers
◯ Vendor Sites
✳ Customer

FIGURE 12.1 Current SC description.

4. Show Alternatives in Revenue, Savings, and Customer Service

The different alternatives were then evaluated for revenue and savings with a return on investment (ROI) calculation assuming the project had a 5-year life. The customer service provided in each alternative was evaluated by a team from operations.

5. Select an Alternative

The optimal solution contains two warehouses, which are centrally located as shown in Figure 12.2. This gives a reduction of 96,000 ft^2 which translates into $3.5M over 5 years. This solution will increase the space utilization to 65% and reduce the obsolete inventory to 10% of the total value held within the warehouses.

As the city moves to the optimized model, the Control phase of DMAIC will keep the improvements in place and running smoothly. The metrics that are given to continue the control are the Key Performance Indicators (KPIs) given in Figure 12.3. These should be measured and tracked utilizing Statistical Process Control (SPC). This data could then be used to repeat an optimization in the future.

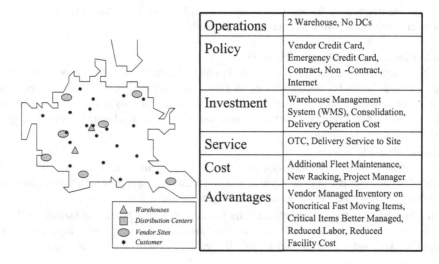

Operations	2 Warehouse, No DCs
Policy	Vendor Credit Card, Emergency Credit Card, Contract, Non -Contract, Internet
Investment	Warehouse Management System (WMS), Consolidation, Delivery Operation Cost
Service	OTC, Delivery Service to Site
Cost	Additional Fleet Maintenance, New Racking, Project Manager
Advantages	Vendor Managed Inventory on Noncritical Fast Moving Items, Critical Items Better Managed, Reduced Labor, Reduced Facility Cost

△ *Warehouses*
▣ *Distribution Centers*
⬭ *Vendor Sites*
✴ *Customer*

FIGURE 12.2 Optimized SC.

Category	Metric	Definition
Service	Turns	Annual $ Issued Divided by Average
Service	% Obsolete Inventory	# of Commodity Codes (CC) that have not been Issued for over 1 Year Divided by the Total # of CCs
Cost	Cost / Pick	Total Labor Cost Divided by Total # of Picks
Cost	Cost / Order	Total Labor Cost Divided by Total # of Orders
Asset Management	Facility Utilization	# of Pallet Positions Utilized vs. Available
Future		
Transportation	Shipments / Division	Track the Number of Deliveries to Site for Each Division
Inventory	Velocity	Annual Revenue / Daily Overhead
Labor	% Productivity by Area / Task	Divide Actual Labor Hours by the Efficiency Standard for the Task and Track by Employee
Labor	Picks / Hour	Number of Pick Issues and Divide by Pick Labor Hours
Purchasing	PCard Spend by Category	PCard Spend by Contract, Non-Contract, and Emergency Usage vs. Total PCard Spend

FIGURE 12.3 Key performance indicators.

12.4.3 Lessons Learned

The lessons learned included model complexity changes and challenges and limitations which could be better met. The model complexity was chosen to reflect a first look at the SC and a simple optimization. A more complex model may have been used if better original data had been available. The data that was available could not be validated because it came from the enterprise resource planning (ERP) system which was antiquated. The model was validated with site tours and sampling for volumetric data. We note that the model is only as good as the data it is provided. A common term is "garbage in" to a model, and you get "garbage out". If a more complex model was utilized, software other than Excel would be needed as well as consultants.

It was difficult to reach agreement between divisions on what part of the cost data can be incorporated as reduced costs. For example, the portion of overall utility costs can be equated to warehouse space versus the other uses of the buildings today, and the percent of value can be used for holding cost because the city does not pay taxes and does not invest excess monies.

12.5 Implications for the Technical Manager

A technical manager should use this article to better understand their own first steps in SC optimization projects. This information should encourage the manager to begin to look at their information internally, before hiring a consulting team. The first look may give a viable answer that can be implemented for increased efficiencies and savings.

A technical manager can gather internal data and then use the methods in Excel Solver to create the appropriate SC model. The specific steps for using Excel can be found in different references; we recommend the steps outlined by Chopra. The technical manager can justify many good solutions for the SC by further using current technical personnel. This may provide another tool for the technical manager to justify his technical staff. If the internal team does not solve the problem, or the manager is ready for a second look at the issue, a consultant can be hired with very little lost to the company.

This study provided an overall method for performing continuous improvement projects using the Six Sigma methodology. Further, this study shows how in the Analyze stage, a technical manager can perform a SC analysis on current operations. The technical manager can use this study as a guide for both.

12.6 Conclusions

This chapter details a quick and relatively inexpensive way to perform an analysis for SC savings opportunities. The major benefit is that you utilize internal personnel who have been already budgeted for and may have a better understanding of operations than outside consultants. Also, the initial study may be modeled using existing spreadsheets before more costly software and consulting options are explored.

This simple analysis may not replace a complex SC analysis using some of the more advanced software which incorporates the CPLEX and ILOG modeling engines. These software companies allow for more constraints than the less powerful spreadsheet will allow. They have claimed to have 20%–50% more optimized results that may translate into more cost savings. This is contingent if consultants can better interpret data, future business strategies, and evaluate logistics networks including transportation traffic patterns.

From the case study application, we identified a workable set of challenges with lessons learned that can be valuable to organization when modeling the SC. The technical manager and his team can be a valuable asset when doing both continuous improvement projects and providing valuable SC modeling expertise.

REFERENCES

Bowersox, Donald J., David J. Closs, and M. Bixby Cooper, *Supply Chain Logistics Management*, Boston, MA: McGraw-Hill/Irwin (2002).

Chopra, Sunil, and Peter Meindl, *Supply Chain Management*, Upper Saddle River, NJ: Pearson Prentice Hall (2004).

George, Michael L., *Lean Six Sigma*, New York: McGraw-Hill (2002).

George, Michael L., *Lean Six Sigma for Service*, New York: McGraw-Hill (2003).

Johnson, James C., Donald F. Wood, Daniel L. Wardlow, and Paul R. Murphy Jr., *Contemporary Logistics*, Upper Saddle River, NJ: Prentice Hall (1999).

Kotnour, T.G., S. Barton, J. Jennings and R.D. Bridges, "Understanding and Leading Large-Scale Change at the Kennedy Space Center," *Engineering Management Journal*, 10:2 (1998), 17–21.

Kotnour, T.G., J. Matkovich and R. Ellison, "Establishing a Change Infrastructure through Teams," *Engineering Management Journal*, 11:3 (1999), 25–30.

Leach, Frederick J., and Jerry D. Westbrook, "Motivation and Job Satisfaction in One Government and Development Environment," *Engineering Management Journal*, 12:4 (December 2000), 3–9.

Michealson, Herbert B., *How to Write and Publish Engineering Papers and Reports*, iSi Press (1982).

Shapiro, Jeremy F., *Modeling the Supply Chain*, Boston, MA: Cengage Learning, Inc. (2001).

Turnquist, Mark A., and Linda K. Nozick, "A Nonlinear Optimization Model of Time and Resource Allocation Decisions in Projects with Uncertainty," *Engineering Management Journal*, 16:1 (March 2004), 40–49.

Vof, Stefan, and David L. Woodruff, *Introduction to Computational Optimization Models for Production Planning in a Supply Chain*, Berlin: Springer (2003).

Yoon, Chang and Harris Makatsoris, "Supply Chain Modeling Using Simulation," *International Journal of Simulation*, 2:1 (2004), 24–30.

Part 4

Technology in Global Supply Chain Engineering

13

The Internet of Things (IoT) Technologies and the Tracking of Supply Chain Assets

Erick C. Jones

In God We Trust. All Others Must Bring Data.

W. Edwards Deming

13.1 Introduction to AIT Technologies

Generally, in order to utilize technology effectively, one should initially understand it. Radio frequency identification (RFID) technologies fall into a group of technologies described as automatic information technologies (AITs), which are complex entities that can be utilized in many ways. Military operators will have to use knowledge, insight, and creativity to make effective decisions on how and when to use these systems. Two of these pervasive technologies RFID and barcodes are considered in this text. Due to this fact, this chapter describes the AITs and provides a historical perspective on barcodes and RFID technologies. The perspective provided will help military personnel and contractors, and other managers envision an organized plan that supports effective decisions and can be gained by reviewing historical events.

13.2 Automatic Information Technologies

In this text when we describe AITs, we describe a group of technologies that are generally associated with automatic data capture (ADC) in both military and commercial applications. Other technologies may be included as AITs, but we present a list that this text focuses upon.

The AIT/ADC includes:

1. Barcodes (Linear/2D/3D)
2. RFID (Active/Passive/Semi-Passive)
3. Radio Frequency Data Capture (RFDC)
4. Real-Time Location Systems (RTLSs)
5. Satellite tags/global positioning system (GPS) (Not in Diagram)
6. Microelectromechanical system (MEMS)
7. Contact Memory Buttons
8. Biometrics
9. Common Access Card
10. Optical Character Recognition (OCR).

With such a large variety of technologies to choose from, it is important for one to consider that the strategic purpose or operational requirements should drive the technology that is chosen. The technology

FIGURE 13.1   AIT Jigsaw.

should not be chosen based upon technical bias. Below is a brief description of each technology. We first generally describe the technologies. We will then describe commonly accepted definitions. In this text, we utilize a leading authority on automatic identification (AutoID), Advanced Integrated Manufacturing (AIM), for defining these common ADC technologies (Figure 13.1).

13.2.1 AIM Global

AIM is the industry association and worldwide authority on AutoID and data collection technologies. AIM members are providers and users of technologies, systems, and services that capture, manage, and integrate accurate data into larger information systems that improve processes enterprise-wide. Serving members in 43 countries for 35 years, the association has developed key technical specifications and guidelines that support the use of AutoID and mobile IT solutions.

AIM actively supports the development of technology standards, guidelines, and best practices through its Technical Symbology Committee (TSC) and RFID Experts Group (REG), as well as through participation at the industry, national (American National Standards Institute (ANSI), and international (International Organization of Standardization (ISO)) levels.

AIM has an active educational and government relations focus, providing accurate and unbiased information on data collection technologies and the markets they serve. For more information about AIM and its members and services, please visit www.aimglobal.org or www.rfid.org.

13.2.2 Barcodes

Generally, a barcode is an optically read representation of data in the form of lines and spacing of parallel lines. The line forms are generally categorized as one-dimensional (1D) barcodes. Other representations include geometric patterns such as dots, squares, and hexagons and are categorized as two-dimensional (2D) matrix codes. The codes are read by barcode readers that recognize the patterns. We have included Direct Part Marking (DPM) and Electronic Article Surveillance (EAS) samples for barcoding.

13.2.3 Direct Part Marking

DPM is a technology used to produce two different surface conditions on an item. These markings can be created by laser etching, molding, peening, etc. Traditional print quality measures are based on the assumption that there will be a measurable difference between dark and light elements of a symbol. Because DPM symbols frequently do not have sufficient contrast between elements intended to be dark and light, it is often necessary to provide specialized lighting in order to produce highlights or shadows in order to distinguish the various elements of the symbol. AIM Global shows examples of these technologies via their website.

13.2.4 DPM Quality Guidelines Document

Acknowledging that current ISO print quality specifications for matrix symbologies and 2D print quality are not exactly suited for DPM symbol evaluation, an ad-hoc committee under the supervision of the AIM Technical Symbology Committee developed a guideline to act as a bridge between the existing specifications and the DPM environment in order to provide a standardized image-based measurement method for DPM that is predictive of scanner performance.

The document describes modifications which are to be considered in conjunction with the symbol quality methodology defined in ISO/IEC 15415 and 2D symbology specifications. It defines alternative illumination conditions, modifications to the measurement and grading of certain parameters, and the reporting the grading results.

13.2.5 Electronic Article Surveillance

EAS is a technology used to identify items as they pass through a gated area. Typically, this identification is used to alert someone of the unauthorized removal of items from a store, library, or data center.

There are several types of EAS systems. In each case, the EAS tag or label is affixed to an item. The tag is then deactivated when the item is purchased (or legally borrowed) at the checkout desk. When the item is moved through the gates (usually at a door to the premises), the gate is able to sense if the tag is active or deactivated and sound an alarm if necessary.

EAS systems are used where there is a chance of theft from small items to large. By placing an EAS tag on an item, it is not necessary to hide the item behind locked doors which makes it easier for the consumer to review the product.

Today's EAS source tagging, where the tag is built into the product at the point of manufacture or packaging, has become commonplace. This makes the labeling of goods unnecessary, saving time and money at the store.

13.3 Radio Frequency Identification

RFID is a generic term that is used to describe a system that transmits the identity (in the form of a unique serial number) of an object or person wirelessly, using radio waves. It's grouped under the broad category of AutoID technologies. RFID is in use all around us. If you have ever chipped your pet with an ID tag, used EZPass through a tollbooth, or paid for gas using SpeedPass, you've used RFID. In addition, RFID is increasingly used with biometric technologies for security. Unlike ubiquitous UPC barcode technology, RFID technology does not require contact or line of sight for communication. RFID data can be read through the human body, clothing, and non-metallic materials.

13.3.1 Components

A RFID system consists of the following main components:

- An antenna or coil
- A transceiver (with decoder) also referred to as a reader
- A transponder (RFID tag) electronically programmed with unique information (generally the electronic product code (EPC))
- Host computer System with a database to store the RFID reads
- Transceiver software and logic (often called Edgeware).

The *antenna* emits radio signals to wake up or excite the tag; it may in the same signal be able to read and write data to it.

- The reader emits radio waves in ranges of anywhere from one inch to 100 ft or more, depending upon its power output and the tag frequency. When a tag maneuvers through the correct electromagnetic zone which has the same frequency, it detects the reader's activation signal.
- The reader decodes the data encoded in the RFID tags integrated circuit, and the data is passed to the host computer for processing.

The purpose of an RFID system is to enable data to be transmitted by a portable device, called a tag, which is read by an RFID reader and processed according to the needs of a particular application. The data transmitted by the tag may provide identification or location information or specifics about the product tagged, such as price, color, date of purchase, etc. RFID technology has been used by thousands of companies for a decade or more. RFID quickly gained attention because of its ability to track moving objects. As the technology is refined, more pervasive—and invasive—uses for RFID tags are in the works.

Most manufacturers of RFID tags create the tags with microchip attached to a radio antenna mounted on a substrate. The chip generally stores generally 2 kB of data. To retrieve the data stored on an RFID tag, you need a reader. A typical reader is a device that has one or more antennas that emit radio waves and receive signals back from the tag. The reader then passes the information in digital form to a computer system.

13.3.2 Radio Frequency Data Capture

Radio frequency transmission has been with us since Guglielmo Marconi first demonstrated wireless communications a century ago. Within 30–40 years of Marconi's discovery, radios had become a fixture in nearly every U.S. household. However, it has been only within the last half-dozen years that wireless data transmission has come into its own in a business environment.

RFDC first appeared in warehouses and distribution centers as an enabling technology for automatic identification and data capture (AIDC) implementations, where hardwiring was unfeasible and/or real-time updating of the host database was critical. Early applications typically ran on PCs or controllers, scattered throughout a facility, which were interfaced to what was essentially a batch-oriented host. Those early systems were costly, quirky, and limited in transaction processing. However, they often made ADC a reality in environments where hardwired systems were impossible. Further, RFDC offered certain advantages over hardwired AIDC systems—interactivity and real-time updates of inventory, shipments, or manufacturing applications—that companies could turn to their own competitive advantage.

Technology improvements kept pace with RFDC's steady growth, so that present-day RFDC-based systems provide powerful, sophisticated, and reliable wireless solutions for a wide variety of both local-area and wide-area networked applications.

Five frequently cited benefits to using Radio Frequency Data Communication are increased database accuracy at all times, reduced paperwork, real-time operations, higher productivity, and shorter order response times.

13.3.3 Real Time Locating System

Real-time visibility into exact locations of containers and cargo has never been as important as today with increased movement of cargo from offshore, the need to move it quickly to final destinations, and new security requirements. Today's wireless technology provides critical visibility into supply chain (SC) activities, delivering benefits to carriers, shippers, and customers.

RTLSs are fully automated systems that continually monitor the locations of assets and personnel. An RTLS solution typically utilizes battery-operated radio tags and a cellular locating system to detect the presence and location of the tags. The locating system is usually deployed as a matrix of locating devices that are installed at a spacing of anywhere from 50 to 1,000 ft. These locating devices determine the locations of the radio tags.

The systems continually update the database with current tag locations as frequently as every several seconds or as infrequently as every few hours for items that seldom move. The frequency of tag location updates may have implications for the number of tags that can be deployed and the battery life of the tag. In typical applications, systems can track thousands of tags simultaneously, and the average tag battery life can be 5 or more years.

13.3.4 Satellite Tags with GPS

GPS consist of a series of satellites orbiting the Earth and receivers. GPS works by calculating the distances from a receiver to a number of satellites. With each distance between a receiver and satellite, the number of possible locations is narrowed down, until there is only one possible location. A receiver must calculate its distance from at least three satellites to determine a location on the surface of the Earth. However, four satellites are usually used to increase the location accuracy. This process of location would be controlled by the positioning module of GPS. An average GPS positioning and navigation system would also have the following modules:

- Digital Map Database
- Map Matching
- Route Planning and Guidance
- Human–Machine Interface
- Wireless Communication.

There are three positioning technologies that can be used: radio wave-based positioning, dead reckoning, and signpost. The use of GPS for navigation can have direct and indirect impacts on Intelligent Transportation Systems. GPS navigation systems can provide information about local surroundings. Also, emergency personnel can be provided with a precise location for situations, thus reducing response times. Asset tracking is one of the most popular uses of GPS. One of the limitations of GPS is that receivers cannot communicate with satellites when indoors.

13.3.5 Microelectromechanical SYSTEM

MEMS is a micro-electromechanical, micro-electro-mechanical, or microelectromechanical system that is very small and merges at the nanoscale or *nanoelectromechanical system* (NEMS) and other *nano-technology*. A good resource MEMSNET, an information resource for the MEMS and Nanotechnology development community further describes MEMS "as *micromachines* (in Japan), or Micro Systems Technology—MST (in Europe)". MEMSs are separate and distinct from the hypothetical vision of *molecular nanotechnology* or *molecular electronics*. MEMSs are made up of components between 1 and 100 μm in size (i.e., 0.001–0.1 mm), and MEMS devices generally range in size from 20 μm (20 millionths of a meter) to a millimeter. "The promise that is available for MEMS is that together with silicon-based microelectronics and micromachining technology, the popularized idea of a computer system-on-a-chip is feasible." MEMSNET provides some futuristic ideas such as "Microelectronic integrated circuits can be thought of as the 'brains' of a system and MEMS augments this decision-making capability with 'eyes' and 'arms', to allow microsystems to sense and control the environment. Sensors gather information from the environment through measuring mechanical, thermal, biological, chemical, optical, and magnetic phenomena. The electronics then process the information derived from the sensors and through some decision making capability direct the actuators to respond by moving, positioning, regulating, pumping, and filtering, thereby controlling the environment for some desired outcome or purpose. Because MEMS devices are manufactured using batch fabrication techniques similar to those used for integrated circuits, unprecedented levels of functionality, reliability, and sophistication can be placed on a small silicon chip at a relatively low cost" (www.memsnet.org/mems/what-is.html).

13.3.6 Contact Memory Buttons

13.3.6.1 Contact Memory

Contact memory technology is ideal for use in harsh industrial applications and in situations that would render barcodes unreadable or impractical. Buttons can mark hazardous and radioactive waste for long-term storage, track the maintenance of airplane brakes, and store repair diagrams. Attached to the ears of livestock, buttons track the animals from birth through processing, and carry data on feed and antibiotic use. Contact memory technology is well suited to guard tour and access control applications in which users can access secure areas conveniently. Versatile touch/button technology can be used in healthcare to create records and match mothers and newborns or to track items along an assembly line and to store manufacturing history.

13.3.6.2 Biometrics

Biometrics are automated methods of recognizing a person based on a physiological or behavioral characteristic. Among the features measured are face, fingerprints, hand geometry, handwriting, iris, retinal, vein, and voice.

Biometric technologies are becoming the foundation of an extensive array of highly secure identification and personal verification solutions. As the level of security breaches and transaction fraud increases, the need for highly secure identification and personal verification technologies is becoming apparent.

The need for biometrics can be found in federal, state and local governments, in the military, and in commercial applications. Enterprise-wide network security infrastructures, government IDs, secure electronic banking, investing and other financial transactions, retail sales, law enforcement, and health and social services are already benefiting from these technologies. Biometric-based authentication applications include workstation, network, and domain access, single sign-on, application logon, data protection, remote access to resources, transaction security and Web security. Trust in these electronic transactions is essential to the healthy growth of the global economy. Utilized alone or integrated with other technologies such as smart cards, encryption keys, and digital signatures, biometrics are set to pervade nearly all aspects of the economy and our daily lives. Utilizing biometrics for personal authentication is becoming convenient and considerably more accurate than current methods (such as the utilization of passwords or PINs). This is because biometrics:

- Links the event to a particular individual (a password or token may be used by someone other than the authorized user)
- Is convenient (nothing to carry or remember)
- Accurate (it provides for positive authentication)
- Can provide an audit trail
- Is becoming socially acceptable and cost effective.

13.3.6.3 Common Access Cards

When we use the term "card technologies" or "smart cards", what do we mean? The easy answer is—any technology that can be placed on a card. Typically, we think of our credit or bank card, but there are other sizes and materials used for different applications. The card can be made of plastic (polyester, PVC, or some other materials) or paper or even some amalgamation of materials. The common point is that the card is used to provide "access" to something, and it includes some form of AIDC technology.

There are currently three main technologies we think of when we mention card technologies:

- Magnetic stripe
- Smart cards
- Optical cards.

Other technologies can be put on cards as well (such as barcodes, touch memory, etc.). Often the card will have printing on it, which may involve technologies such as Dye Diffusion Thermal Transfer (D2T2) direct-to-card printing.

13.3.6.4 Optical Character Recognition

Optical Character Recognition (OCR) is used in high-volume financial applications such as payment processing, check reconciliation, and billing. It is also commonly used for high-volume document management in the insurance and healthcare industries. The technology is frequently found in libraries, publishing houses, and wherever printed text must be entered into a computer. OCR is also used in heavy-duty manufacturing environments for reading direct-marked, human-readable part numbers. The pharmaceuticals industry uses a variation of OCR called optical character verification (OCV) to assure that critical human-readable lot and date numbers cannot be misread.

13.3.6.5 Optical Mark Recognition

Optical Mark Recognition (OMR) is used for standardized testing as well as course enrollment and attendance in education. Human resource departments across industries use OMR for applications such as benefits enrollment, employee testing, change of employee status, payroll deductions, and user training. Healthcare providers use the technology for registration and surveys, and medical labs use it for patient evaluations and tracking supply orders and lab services. OMR is also used for time and attendance, labor tracking, inventory management, voting applications, exit surveys, polling, and all manner of questionnaires and evaluation studies. Because it is easy to use and cost effective for opinion tracking, the technology has become a tool for on-location and direct-mail marketing.

13.3.6.6 Machine Vision

Traditional machine vision systems continue to be used for quality inspection, gauging, and robotic assembly in the automotive, electronics, aerospace, healthcare, and metal industries among others. These systems may also incorporate barcode reading. The next generation of 2D dedicated vision-based scanners are being used for quality control, work in process (WIP), and high-speed sortation in industries such as electronics, automotive, and mail and package delivery. The pharmaceutical industry is also using 2D scanning systems to reconcile packaging, inserts, and labels on their packaging lines in order to satisfy the FDA's Current Good Manufacturing Practice (CGMP) regulations.

13.3.6.7 Voice

Voice recognition is commonly used in the automotive industry for various manufacturing and inspection applications. It is also used in warehousing and distribution to track material movement in real time, in the transportation industry for receiving and transporting shipments, in laboratory work, and in inspection and quality control applications across all industries.

13.3.6.8 Magnetic Ink Character Recognition

Magnetic Ink Character Recognition (MICR) is most commonly used to encode and read information on checks and bank drafts to speed clearing and sorting. It is also effective for uncovering fraud, such as color copies of payroll checks or hand-altered characters on a check, both of which are easily detected by the absence of magnetic ink. Fast clearing and sorting, as well as fraud detection, benefits customers, financial institutions, and retail establishments.

Though this s a long list of AITs, it is not comprehensive due to the fact that other technologies are becoming available as this book is being published and distributed. For this book's purposes, we focus upon three main technologies: barcodes, RFID/RTLS technologies, and satellite technologies.

13.3.7 History of RFID

A sense of history in RFID is important for the following reasons. Some RFID technologies have stood the test of time and have become more pervasive in the SC. Other RFID technologies have been utilized in other industries such as animal tracking and present unique advantages. The convergence of RFID systems has been theorized to create innovations in current industries and led to the creation of new industries. Given that the history of RFID is integrated with the history of other ADC devices such as barcodes, we approach chronicling RFID history in following ways.

First, we investigate the development of data acquisition device usage in the distribution and logistics. Second, we overlay the development history of RFID technologies for SC activities. Finally, we introduce future plans for RFID technologies in logistics operations.

The roots of RFID technology can be traced back to World War II (WWII). The radar, which had been discovered in 1935 by Scottish physicist Sir Robert Alexander Watson-Watt, was utilized by all combatants in the war (Germans, Japanese, Americans, and British) to identify aircraft, but there was no unique identification for the aircraft. The main problem with radar was there was no way to identify which planes belonged to the enemy and which were a country's own planes returning from a mission.

The Germans discovered that if pilots rolled their planes as they returned to base, it would change the radio signal reflected back. This crude method alerted the radar crew on the ground that these were German planes and not Allied aircraft. This plane "roll" created a uniquely identifiable signal that acted in essence as a unique reflected signal. This principle is what the base's passive RFID systems are based upon.

Later, Watson-Watt headed a secret project by the British to develop the first active identify friend or foe (IFF) system. A transmitter was placed on each British plane. When the transmitter received signals from radar stations on the ground, it began broadcasting a signal back that identified the aircraft as friendly. RFID works on this same basic concept. A signal is sent to a transponder which wakes up and either reflects back a signal (passive system) or broadcasts a signal (active system).

Advances in radar and radio frequency (RF) communication systems continued through the 1950s and 1960s. Scientists and academics in the United States, Europe, and Japan did research and presented papers explaining how RF energy could be used to identify objects remotely.

Companies began commercializing anti-theft systems that used radio waves to determine whether an item had been paid for or not. EAS tags are still used in retail packaging today at retailers such as JC Penney and SEARS in which they use a 1-bit tag. The bit is either on or off. When someone pays for the item, a cashier deactivates the tag and the bit is turned off, and a person can leave the store. In contrast, if the person doesn't pay and tries to walk out of the store, readers at the door detect the tag and sound an alarm.

13.3.8 Prior to IFF

Though many focus on the WWII as the beginning of RFID development, we will explore other events that contribute to theoretical understanding of RFID technologies. Given that some of the RFID technologies do not include passive, active, and semi-active technologies, we provide other historical events that will allow the student to investigate and create investigative thought on RFID technologies.

Many scientists believe at the beginning of time that electromagnetic energy created the universe often referred to as the "Big Bang" Theory. Due to the fact that most RFID technologies use electromagnetic energy as the source of energy, this Big Bang may be considered the beginning of RFID technologies. Benjamin Franklin explored electromagnetism with his experiments in electricity in the 1700s. In the 1800s, Michael Faraday and James Maxwell contributed theories on electricity and relationship of light and magnetic fields on electromagnetic energy respectively. Michael Faraday, English scientist, explored relationship of light, radio waves, and electromagnetic energy. In 1864, James Maxwell, Scottish physicist, published theory on electromagnetic fields which concluded that electric and magnetic energies travel in transverse waves moving at the speed of light.

Later in the 1800s, in1887, Heinrich Rudolf Hertz, German physicist, confirmed Maxwell's theories and added theories about electromagnetic waves (radio waves) which showed as long transverse waves that travel at the speed of light and can be reflected, refracted, and polarized like light. Also, Hertz was the first credited for transmitting and receiving radio waves, and his demonstrations were later duplicated by Aleksander Popov of Russia. Another key breakthrough for radio transmission was when Guglielmo Marconi successfully transmitted a radiotelegraphy across the Atlantic Ocean.

Now in the 20th century we have in 1906 Ernst F.W. Alexanderson discover the first continuous wave (CW) radio generation and transmission of radio signals which signaled the beginning of modern radio communications where all aspects of radio waves controlled.

The Manhattan project at Los Alamos Scientific Laboratory in 1922 was attributed to the birth of the radar detection. The project described how the radar sends radio waves for detecting and locating an object by the reflection of the radio waves. The refection can determine the position and speed of an object. Given that RFID is a combination of radio broadcast technology and radar, the convergence of these disciplines allowed for future RFID development. Scottish physicist Sir Robert Alexander Watson-Watt was considered to be the inventor of the modern radar system in 1935.

In 1945, historians theorize that the first known device may have been invented by Thermin as a reporting espionage tool for the Russian Government in 1945, the device was the first "bug" or covert listening device. This device was the first to use inducted energy from radio waves of one frequency to transmit an audio signal to another. This made the device difficult to detect, as it did not radiate any signal unless it was being remotely powered and listened to, and endowed it with (potentially) unlimited operational life.

This bug was embedded in a two-foot wooden replica of the Great Seal of the United States and presented to the American ambassador in Moscow, Averell Harriman, by Russian schoolchildren in 1946. This is currently on display at the National Security Agency (NSA), National Cryptologic Museum. The bug hung prominently for years, at least part of the time in the ambassador's study, before a tiny microphone was found in the eagle by a professional bug sweeper using a marta kit, which happened to catch a signal from it while it was being used.

During George F. Kennan's ambassadorship in 1952, a routine security check discovered that the seal contained a microphone and a resonant cavity which could be stimulated from an outside radio signal. George Kennan's memoirs describe the event. In a theme now familiar, Kennan relates that Spaso House had been redecorated under Soviet supervision, without the presence of any American supervisors, giving them opportunity "to perfect their wiring of the house." "The ordinary, standard devices for the detection of electronic eavesdropping revealed nothing at all", but technicians decided to check again, in case our detection methods were out of date. The novelty of the Great Seal bug, which was hung over the desk of our Ambassador to Moscow, was its simplicity. It was a simple resonate chamber, with the front wall that moved and changed the dimensions of the chamber when sound waves struck it. It had no power pack, wires, and no batteries. An ultra-high-frequency signal beamed to it from a van parked near the building was reflected from the bug, after being modulated by sound waves from conversations striking the bug's diaphragm.

13.3.9 How the Great Bug Seal Worked

The Ultimate Spy Book by H. Keith Melton further details how the Great Bug Seal worked. It features a bald eagle, beneath whose beak the Soviets had drilled holes to allow sound to reach the device. Western experts were perplexed on how the device, also known as the "Thing", worked, because it had neither batteries nor electrical circuits. Peter Wright of British intelligence discovered how it operated and later produced a copy of the device for use by both British and American intelligence. The thing was initiated when a radio beam aimed at the antenna from a source outside of the building was sent. Then the sound wave struck the diaphragm causing variations in the amount of space (and the capacitance) between it and the tuning post plate. These variations altered the charge on the antenna, creating modulations in the reflected radio beam. These were picked up and interpreted by the receiver.

13.3.10 Research on RFID

One of the first works exploring RFID was the paper by Harry Stockman, entitled "Communication by Means of Reflected Power" (Proceedings of the IRE, pp. 1196–1204, October 1948). This transcript discussed the basic problems of researching "reflected-power" communication but discussed the usage of the technology. It also predicted that "…considerable research and development work has to be done before the remaining basic problems in reflected-power communication are solved, and before the field of useful applications is explored". For this prediction to become valid, advances in transistor technologies, integrated circuits, microprocessor, development of communication networks, and computing power had to happen over the next 30 years would spur cost economics of RFID-type technologies.

Also, in the 1950s other technical developments in radio and radar along with the IFF exploration of long-range transponder systems for identification include FL Vernon's "Application of the microwave homodyne" and DB Harris's "Radio transmission systems with Modula table passive transponder". These developments also led to future patents for RFID technology.

13.3.11 In the 20th Century

In the 1960s, RF Harrington studied the electromagnetic theory related to RFID papers, "Field Measurements using active scatterers", "Theory of loaded scatterers" in 1963–1964, Robert Richardson's "Remotely activated radio frequency powered devices" in 1963, Otto Rittenbacks's "Communication by radar beams" in 1969, HH Vogelmans's "Passive data transmission techniques utilizing radar beams" in 1968, and JP Vindings's "Interrogator-responder identification system" in 1967.

Commercial Activities were beginning in the 1960s. Sensormatic and Checkpoint were founded in the late 1960s. Other companies such as Knogo developed EAS equipment to counter theft using 1-bit tags. Fundamentally, the presence or absence of a tag was detected, and the tags were made inexpensively and could provide effective anti-theft measures. Most of these systems used microwave or inductive technology. This EAS technology was the first widespread use of RFID technology.

13.3.12 The First RFID Patents

The first U.S. patents for RFID tags were from Mario W. Cardullo and Charles Watson in 1973. Mario W. Cardullo received the first U.S. patent for an active RFID tag with rewritable memory on January 23, 1973. That same year, Charles Walton, a California entrepreneur, received a patent for a passive transponder used to unlock a door without a key. The electronic door lock operated with a card that communicated with an embedded transponder that communicated a signal to a reader near the door. When the reader detected a valid identity number stored within the RFID tag, the reader unlocked the door. Walton licensed the technology to lock makers and other similar companies.

The testing of these technologies was still relevant when one of the authors worked for United Parcel Services (UPS) in the early 1990's in the Strategic Systems Group. Unfortunately, the reliability and the cost effectiveness were not viable even 20 years later at a company as successful as UPS.

13.3.13 Toll Road and Animal Tracking

Also in the 1970s, Los Alamos National Laboratory at the request of the United States Energy Department developed a system for tracking nuclear materials. Scientists developed the idea of putting a transponder in a truck and readers at the gates of secure facilities. The gate's antenna would wake up the transponder in the truck, which would respond with an ID and potentially other data, such as the driver's ID then the gate would automatically open.

There was a realization on how RFID technologies specifically electronic vehicle identification could change transportation. This was evidenced in the transportation efforts including work at Los Alamos and by the International Bridge and Turnpike and Tunnel Association (IBTTA) and the U.S. Federal Highway Administration. Unfortunately, the IBTTA and U.S. Federal Highway Administration held a conference in 1973 and concluded that there is no national interest in developing a standard for electronic vehicle identification. The late 1970s is when companies realized the potential commercial aspects of RFID, companies such as Identronix a spin-off from Los Alamos Scientific Lab, Amtech, who later became part of Intermec and Transcore were developed.

Later in the mid-1980s, this type of system was commercialized when former Los Alamos scientists left and formed companies which developed automated toll payment systems. These systems have become widely used on roads, bridges, and tunnels around the world. Organizations such as the Port Authority of New York and New Jersey tested electronic toll collection systems built by General Electric, Westinghouse, Philips, and Glenayre.

Also in the 1970's, animal tracking efforts were initially investigated using microwave systems at Los Alamos and using inductive technologies in Europe. Animal ID was pursued in Europe by Alfa Laval, Nedeap, and others.

Other forward moving occurrences in the 1970's included the use of modulated backscatter. In 1975, Alfred Koelle, Steven Depp, and Robert Freyman introduced the transcript "Short-range radio-telemetry for electronic identification using modulated backscatter", which is the foundation for current RFID passive tags. Other events include the development of the Raytheon's "Raytag" along with other events from Radio Corporation of America (RCA) and Fairchild in RFID development. Richard Klensch of RCA developed the "Electronic identification system" in 1975, and Sterzer of RCA developed an "Electronic license plate for motor vehicles" in 1977. Thomas Meyers and Ashley Leigh of the Fairchild organization developed "Passive encoding microwave transponder" in 1978.

In the 1980s, RFID history documents many commercial implementations. The most common implementations in the United States were for transportation, personnel, and animals. In Europe, interests were in short-range systems for animals and industrial and business applications. Toll roads in Italy, France, Spain, Portugal, and Norway were equipped with RFID. The USA Association of American Railroads and the Container Handling Cooperative Program were active with RFID initiatives. Though testing of RFID for collecting tolls had been going on for many years, the first commercial application began in Europe in 1987 in Norway. This was followed quickly in the United States by the Dallas North Turnpike in 1989. Port Authority of New York and New Jersey began commercial operation of RFID for buses going through the Lincoln Tunnel. RFID was finding a home with electronic toll collection.

Also Los Alamos was requested by the Agricultural Department to develop passive RFID tags to track cows. The goal was to facilitate the tracking of the amount of hormones and medicines that were administered to cows when they were ill. The challenge of ensuring that each cow received the correct dosage was having multiple economic factors. Los Alamos came up with a passive RFID system that used 125 kHz radio waves. A transponder encapsulated in glass is injected under the cow's skin or is attached to an identification tag. The transponder draws energy from the reader and reflects back a modulated signal to the reader using a technique known as backscatter. This system is still used in cows around the world today.

These low-frequency transponders were also put in cards and used to control the access to buildings.

Over time, companies commercialized 125 kHz systems. Later other companies developed systems that operate on higher radio spectrum to high frequency (13.56 MHz). This frequency was chosen because it was unregulated and unused in most parts of the world. This frequency offered greater range and faster data transfer rates. Companies in Europe began using it to track reusable containers and other assets. The 13.56 MHz frequency RFID systems are used for access control, payment systems (Mobile Speed pass), contactless smart cards, and as an anti-theft device in cars. The cars have a reader in the steering column that reads the passive RFID tag in the plastic housing around the key. The car is rendered disabled if the ID number it is programmed to look for is not found.

In the early 1990s, IBM engineers developed and patented an ultra-high-frequency (UHF) RFID system which offers longer read ranges—20 ft under good conditions and faster data transfer. IBM did some early pilots with Wal-Mart but never commercialized this technology, but IBM ran into financial trouble in the mid-1990s and sold its patents to Intermec, a material handling systems provider. Intermec has been installed in numerous different applications, from warehouse tracking to farming. Intermec invested in this future technology due to the fact that at the time it was expensive because of the low volume of sales and lack of international standards.

Also in 1990s, electronic toll collection using RFID technologies expanded to wide-scale deployment of electronic toll collection in the United States. Open highway electronic tolling system opened in Oklahoma in 1991 in which cars pass scanning points at highway speeds (no need for cameras or barriers). The world's first combined toll collection and traffic management system was installed in the

Houston area by the Harris County Toll Road Authority in 1992. Both of the authors personally were able to witness the construction of the toll road in Houston.

Later, the Kansas turnpike used a system based on the Title 21 Standard which allows usage by other states such as Georgia who also used the same standard. The Title 21 Standard was designed to have a multi-protocol capability in electronic toll collection applications. Also, in the Northeastern United States, seven regional toll agencies formed the E-Z Pass Interagency Group (IAG) in 1990 to develop a regionally compatible electronic toll collection system. Also, toll tags were integrated for multi-use applications in parking garages, toll booths, gated communities, and business campuses; an example would be the Dallas TollTag.

The development of computer engineering technology which allowed microwave Schottky diodes fabricated on a regular Complementary metal–oxide–semiconductor (CMOS) integrated circuit permitted the construction of the microwave RFID tags. These tags contained a single circuit, which previously had been limited to inductively coupled RFID transponders, thus allowing for cheaper active tags and readers.

Federal Communications Commission (FCC) allocated a spectrum in 5.9 GHz band for expansion of intelligent transportation systems, which will spur more RFID development and applications. RFID systems have been installed in numerous different applications, from warehouse tracking to farming. But the technology was expensive at the time due to the low volume of sales and the lack of open, international standards.

13.3.14 Development of Cost-Effective Protocol

In early 1999, when the Uniform Code Council (UCC), EAN International, Proctor & Gamble, and Gillette established the AutoID center at the Massachusetts Institute of Technology (MIT). Two research professors, David Brock and Sanjay Sarma, initiated the idea of integrating low-cost RFID tags on to products in order to track them through the SC. Their idea of transmitting a unique number from the RFID tag in order to keep the cost of the technology cost effective was novel. The idea of using a simple microchip that stored very little information as opposed to using a more complex chip that may require batteries and require more memory allowed for the cost-effective implementation of the idea. Data associated with the serial number on the tag would be stored in a database that would be accessible over the Internet.

Sarma and Brock changed the way people used RFID in the SC. Previously, RFID tags were considered mobile databases that contained information about the product, case, pallet, or container on which they were attached. Sarma and Brock promoted the idea of RFID as an associating networking technology that linked objects to databases through the Internet through the tag. This was an important change to businesses because this enabled the idea of visibility. For example, a manufacturer could automatically let a business partner know when a shipment was leaving the dock at a manufacturing facility or warehouse, and a retailer could automatically let the manufacturer know when the goods arrived.

Between 1999 and 2003, the AutoID center gained industry acceptance of the passive RFID tagging system with the support of more than 100 large end-user companies, the U.S. Department of Defense, and RFID vendors. AutoID research labs were opened in Australia, the United Kingdom, Switzerland, Japan, and China. The AutoID center is credited with developing two air interface protocols (Class 1 and Class 0), the EPC numbering scheme, and a network architecture for associating data on an RFID tag. The technology was licensed to the UCC in 2003. The UCC created EPCglobal organization as a joint venture between the AutoID center and EAN International in order to commercialize EPC technology. The AutoID center closed its doors in October 2003, and its research responsibilities were passed on to AutoID labs.

The industry support is evidenced in the fact that some of the biggest retailers in the world—Albertsons, Metro, Target, Tesco, Wal-Mart—and the U.S. Department of Defense have initiated plans to use EPC technology to track goods in their SC. The pharmaceutical, tire, defense, and other industries are also moving to adopt the technology. EPCglobal ratified a second-generation standard in December 2004 in order to compensate for some of the shortcomings of the first-generation technologies improving challenges such as read distance and better integration between vendor products.

13.3.15 Overview of Passive and Active RFID Technologies

An RFID system consists of a reader, tags, and an air interface. The reader, also known as an interrogator, sends out a signal through an antenna. This signal is usually in the form of an electromagnetic wave. Because the signal is in the form of an electromagnetic wave, a direct line of sight is not needed to read the information on the tag. This is a major advantage of RFID. The signal is received by the tag, and a response signal is sent back to the reader. This response signal contains a unique identifier associated with tag. The response signal can be powered in two ways corresponding to the type of tag. Passive tags utilize the energy of the original signal to send a response signal back to the reader. Passive tags have a limited amount of energy to power the response signal. Therefore, the amount of information transmitted by a passive tag is fairly small: quite similar to the information carried in a barcode.

Active and semi-active tags use energy from an attached battery to power the response signal. The use of the embedded battery allows the response signal to contain more information and travel farther. The reader receives the response signal, decodes it, and sends that information to a database. Often the information in the response signal is connected to additional information in the database.

RFID technology can be used throughout the SC in order to promote visibility. This visibility helps coordinate actions between entities in the SC. Figure 13.2 shows the relationships within the SC that can be affected by the implementation of the RFID technologies. An example of RFID implementation is the use of active tags for detecting tampering and monitoring security of maritime containers. Those types of tags also have the tracking advantages of RFID and can be used to improve operations management.

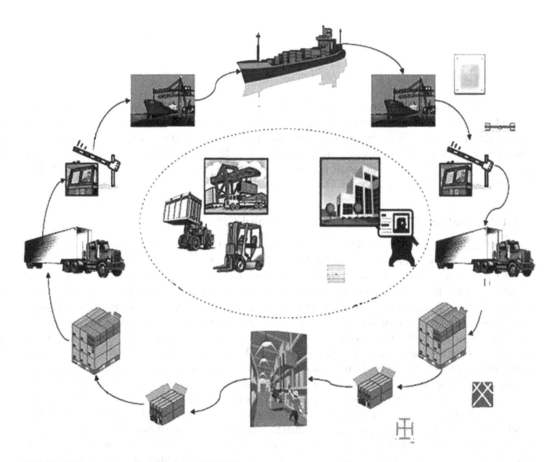

FIGURE 13.2 Integrated supply chain with RFID.

13.4 Global Positioning System

The Navistar Global Positioning System also referred to as GPS has three components:

1. A constellation of satellites orbiting approximately 20,000 km above the earth.

    There are approximately 27 satellites transmitting ranging signals on frequencies in the microwave ranges in the radio spectrum. The transmission frequencies range from 1 to 10 GHz. Most point-to-point services offered today use the frequency bandwidths of (1) 5.92–6.425 GHz for transmission from earth to satellite called uplink, (2) 3.7–4.2 GHz for transmission from satellite to earth called downlink.

2. Ground control monitor stations which control uplink to the satellites.

3. Receivers for the users. There are both Civil and Military users.

In general, the GPS consists of a series of satellites orbiting the Earth and receivers. GPS works by calculating the distances from a receiver to a number of satellites. With each distance between a receiver and satellite, the number of possible locations is narrowed down, until there is only one possible location. A receiver must calculate its distance from at least three satellites to determine a location on the surface of the Earth. However, four satellites are usually used to increase the location accuracy. This process of location would be controlled by the positioning module of GPS. A GPS positioning and navigation system has the following modules:

- Digital Map Database
- Map Matching
- Route Planning and Guidance
- Human–Machine Interface
- Wireless Communication.

There are three positioning technologies that can be used: radio wave-based positioning, dead reckoning, and signpost. The use of GPS for navigation can have direct and indirect impacts on Intelligent Transportation Systems. GPS navigation systems can provide information about local surroundings. Also, emergency personnel can be provided with a precise location for situations, thus reducing response times. Asset tracking is one of the most popular uses of GPS. One of the limitations of GPS is that receivers cannot communicate with satellites when indoors.

13.4.1 Integration of Real-Time Technologies and GPS

RFID and GPS are emerging technologies that will allow for real-time data collection to assist with decision support in supply chain management (SCM). RFID has a wide variety of applications. Some examples of RFID uses are library checkout stations, automatic car toll tags, animal identification tags, and inventory systems. Real-time data collected using RFID allows an SC to synchronize reorder points and other data. Real-time information can also be used to design and operate logistical systems on a real-time basis. GPS is currently used solely as a means to locate equipment and derive navigation directions.

An RFID system consists of a reader, tags, and an air interface. The reader, also known as an interrogator, sends out a signal through an antenna. This signal is usually in the form of an electromagnetic wave. Because the signal is in the form of an electromagnetic wave, a direct line of sight is not needed to read the information on the tag. This is a major advantage of RFID. The signal is received by the tag, and a response signal is sent back to the reader. This response signal contains a unique identifier associated with tag. The response signal can be powered in two ways corresponding to the type of tag. Passive tags utilize the energy of the original signal to send a response signal back to the reader. Passive tags have a limited amount of energy to power the response signal. Therefore, the amount of information transmitted by a passive tag is fairly small: quite similar to the information carried in a barcode.

Active and semi-active tags use energy from an attached battery to power the response signal. The use of the embedded battery allows the response signal to contain more information and travel farther. The reader receives the response signal, decodes it, and sends that information to a database. Often the information in the response signal is connected to additional information in the database.

GPS consist of a series of satellites orbiting the Earth and receivers. GPS works by calculating the distances from a receiver to a number of satellites. With each distance between a receiver and satellite, the number of possible locations is narrowed down, until there is only one possible location. A receiver must calculate its distance from at least three satellites to determine a location on the surface of the Earth. However, four satellites are usually used to increase the location accuracy [2]. This process of location would be controlled by the positioning module of GPS. An average GPS positioning and navigation system would also have the following modules:

- Digital Map Database
- Map Matching
- Route Planning and Guidance
- Human–Machine Interface
- Wireless Communication.

There are three positioning technologies that can be used: radio wave-based positioning, dead reckoning, and signpost. The use of GPS for navigation can have direct and indirect impacts on Intelligent Transportation Systems. GPS navigation systems can provide information about local surroundings. Also, emergency personnel can be provided with a precise location for situations, thus reducing response times. Asset tracking is one of the most popular uses of GPS. One of the limitations of GPS is that receivers cannot communicate with satellites when indoors.

RFID and GPS are radio wave-based technologies that are currently used by many organizations. RFID is primarily used in inventory and material handling processes. Tags are placed on items. When these items pass by checkpoints where readers are located, the tag is read, and the appropriate action can be taken. Real-time inventory can be kept by monitoring tag reads at strategic points like loading docks. RFID can also be useful in material handling. Items on a conveyor can be diverted at the appropriate times based on the information received from the RFID tag. GPS is primarily used to track assets such as vehicles and other expensive equipment. For example, if a truck breaks down, it is possible to locate the truck and get the shipment moving again in the fraction of the time it would take with a GPS receiver.

Current applications of RFID and GPS systems have allowed for more effective tracking of inventory and assets. These technologies can be used in conjunction, but the data has to be captured and written to a database to be correlated to other tags or receivers. If these technologies can be combined to produce hybrid systems, greater gains can be achieved. One focus of research is the nesting of GPS receivers and various RFID tag types. If tags and receivers were able to communicate with one another, even more accurate real-time data collection could be achieved during transportation. This would also reduce equipment costs, because fewer readers would be required.

If these technologies can be nested, it would allow the information in a barcode or a passive RFID tag to be collected by an active tag. This information could then be combined with the information contained within the active tag and transferred to a GPS receiver. The GPS receiver could then send not only its location but all of the information about the cargo being shipped. A possible application of this nested technology approach would be in the railroad industry. Currently, there two passive RFID tags attached to the sides of all rail cars in the United States. In addition, most railroads are using GPS receivers to track locomotives. If nesting became possible, implementation would be easy in this case. Active tags could be used to capture the information correlated to the cargo in all of the rail cars and transmit it to the GPS receiver and thus to the inventory databases.

In addition to nesting technologies, more advanced tags can be developed to allow more detailed data collection. Tags that utilize sensors to capture and write data to the tag are being developed. Some tags have been developed but are still very unreliable. These sensor tags could be used to monitor physical parameters, like temperature and humidity, as well as security parameters. The main problem faced by these passive sensor tags is the limited power supply. The sensor cannot use any energy while outside the range of the reader. Also, the amount of energy available while in read range is very small. This limits possible measurement techniques. With these sensor tags, perishable goods could be monitored to guard against possible safety issues. This could include salmonella outbreaks caused by frozen chicken reaching too high of temperatures for too long and medications being held at temperatures that reduce potency.

13.4.2 Conclusion

Technologies are being used to allow real-time data collection. This allows for more dynamic SCM systems that are able to adjust to varying market and environmental conditions. RFID and GPS facilitate this dynamic SCM. RFID allows for up-to-date inventory levels and, when combined with GPS, can provide a means of tracking inventory as it moves from supplier to customer through the SC. New technologies are being developed to further the amount of information to decision support systems for SCM.

13.5 RTLS

Current RTLSs are typically active systems (using battery-operated tags) to detect presence and location within a 2D coordinate system (XY position only, not height). The license-free frequency ranges are most popular (300–433 MHz) and in particular the 2.45 GHz. At this frequency range, time of flight is efficient, and many RTLSs are based on WiFi, Bluetooth, or Zigbee which occupy this frequency band. Most or all of these current RTLSs rely on the signal strength as an indicator for distance approximation. Other systems use active RFID, infrared, ultrasound, ultra wide band (UWB), or a combination of them to perform the localization.

Below are a subset of the RTLSs that are generally based on the aforementioned procedure.

13.5.1 WiFi RTLS

The Ekahau company is currently incorporating an RTLS using an existing WiFi (802.11) network. The system works by using Received Signal Strength Indicator (RSSI) between multiple access points throughout the tracking area. This provides accuracy indoors of 3–9 ft. The system does not cause any interference to the existing network traffic because the tag communicates only about 60 bytes of data per location update. The tags are active and require a 4–6 V power source. The tags have built in accelerometers and can be configured to report location any time it is moved. Many other companies have previously employed versions of a WiFi RTLS system into operations which has created a great amount of interest due to the fact that these location systems can be incorporated into existing networks.

13.5.2 Active RFID RTLS

RF code has combined active RFID and infrared (IR) in an RTLS implementation.

The system has a read range of up to 10 m.

13.5.2.1 UWB

Multispectral Solutions, Inc. incorporated UWB into an RTLS system based on triangulation ranging. These active tags use time of flight measurements and can achieve location accuracy within 10–30 cm. The read ranges are also around 200 m (Line of Sight (LOS) and about 50 m indoors through obstructions.

13.5.3 Passive RFID RTLS

An approach was used which was able to achieve an accuracy of 0.6 m using a Bayesian statistical method on readings collected from multiple RFID readers. This was accomplished without exploiting any prior information about the location, orientation, or power delivered to the tag.

13.6 Differences in Using RFID, RTLS, and GPS

RFID and GPS are radio wave-based technologies that are currently used by many organizations. RFID is primarily used in inventory and material handling processes. Tags are placed on items. When these items pass by checkpoints where readers are located, the tag is read, and the appropriate action can be taken. Real-time inventory can be kept by monitoring tag reads at strategic points like loading docks. RFID can also be useful in material handling. Items on a conveyor can be diverted at the appropriate times based on the information received from the RFID tag.

RTLS is generally considered similar to GPS or vice versa in that they both use localization algorithms to triangulate positions. Technically GPS can be considered a satellite-based RTLS. The main difference for non-satellite-based RTLSs is that they mainly operate indoors. On the contrary, GPS is traditionally used for outside position location. Also, some RTLSs are considered more accurate than GPS in outdoor conditions, but the main limitation is the need for infrastructure.

GPS is primarily used to track assets such as vehicles and other expensive equipment. For example, if a truck breaks down, it is possible to locate the truck and get the shipment moving again in the fraction of the time it would take without a GPS receiver.

13.6.1 Trend to Integrated AIT Applications

Recently, there has been some confusion by SC managers between the objectives for using RFID technologies and GPS. To add to the confusion, the marketing of the technologies by different vendors has made it difficult for many organizations to decide which technology is best for their operations. Though each technology has different operational objectives, the association of these technologies as ADC technologies have led many to believe the benefits of the technologies are interchangeable. Recently, some manufacturers have created technologies that have integrated both technologies so that their benefits can be leveraged.

Current applications of RFID and GPS systems have allowed for more effective tracking of inventory and assets. These technologies can be used in conjunction, but the data has to be captured and written to a database to be correlated to other tags or receivers. If these technologies can be combined to produce hybrid systems, greater gains can be achieved.

One focus of research is the nesting of GPS receivers and various RFID tag types. If tags and receivers were able to communicate with one another, even more accurate real-time data collection could be achieved during transportation. This would also reduce equipment costs, because fewer readers would be required. The concept of requirement layers for determining the required technology is demonstrated in Figure 13.2. These layers were developed by Bob Kenney at SAVi Technologies (Lockheed Martin) and based off of the following ideas:

- ISO has grouped SC goods into logistic unit hierarchy.
- Objects in each layer are handled differently and have different requirements for each part of the SC.
- Necessitates different requirements for each layer.

If these technologies can be nested, it would allow the information in a barcode or a passive RFID tag to be collected by an active tag. This information could then be combined with the information contained within the active tag and transferred to a GPS receiver. The GPS receiver could then send not only its location but all of the information about the cargo being shipped. This concept was demonstrated earlier and shown in Figure 13.2.

A possible application of this nested technology approach would be in the railroad industry. Currently, there are two passive RFID tags attached to the sides of all rail cars in the United States. In addition, most railroads are using GPS receivers to track locomotives. If nesting became possible, implementation would be easy in this case. Active tags could be used to capture the information correlated to the cargo in all of the rail cars and transmit it to the GPS receiver and thus to the inventory databases.

An application that has recently been developed is demonstrated by the Dow and Chemtrec Company. This application was created to incorporate a tag that uses GPS, RFID, and sensors to track hazardous materials on railcars. The goal of the application was for constant monitoring of hazardous material conditions for railcars. The technology was based on RFID tags required by the American Association of Railroad RFID initiative (Automatic Equipment Identification (AEI)) since the 1970s.

In addition to nesting technologies, more advanced tags can be developed to allow more detailed data collection. Tags that utilize sensors to capture and write data to the tag are being developed. Some tags have been developed but are still very unreliable. These sensor tags could be used to monitor physical parameters, like temperature and humidity, as well as security parameters. The main problem faced by these passive sensor tags is the limited power supply. The sensor cannot use any energy while outside the range of the reader. Also, the amount of energy available while in read range is very small. This limits possible measurement techniques. With these sensor tags, perishable goods could be monitored to guard against possible safety issues. This could include salmonella outbreaks caused by frozen chicken reaching too high of temperatures for too long and medications being held at temperatures that reduce potency.

An example of a tag that captures sensor data and transmits using GPS technologies is the Hammer tag system. This system provides for the creation of a Personal Digital Assistant (PDA) that can write both image and geospatial location data to active RFID tags that can be later captured and integrated into a geographical information system (GIS). The main use was to capture information for geological digs.

Other applications include nesting the RFID and GPS technologies for use with maritime container applications to offset the shortcomings of the different technologies.

The combination of GPS and active RFID tags on marine cargo containers allows for location of maritime containers using RFID-based RTLS that utilizes wireless access points. In the event the RFID wireless access points are not available, the device switches to a GPS-based RTLS. This system design was created to improve the challenges and system limitations of the RFID RTLS system that are caused by the operational conditions of marine ports.

Other scenarios for this type of nesting technologies include military use.

A satellite-based RFID service is described by an OrbitOne application. This GPS tag utilizes a battery powered active RFID tag to capture information at predetermined times in challenging military environments. The information capture through RFID interrogation is later transmitted via LEO (low earth orbit)-based satellites.

Another application utilizes the nesting concept of RFID, GPMS, and GPS for tracking gas distribution in gas tankers. This RFID-based system creates a device which contains an active RFID reader that captures active tag information from tanker gas valves. As the gas valve is opened, the active tag associated with the valve transmits a signal to the active RFID tag reader or interrogator. Later the RFID tag reader transmits information to a general packet radio service (GPRS) connection located in a computer system on-board the tanker's trailer cab. Finally, this GPRS transmits information to operations through a GPS. Another example of this nested GPS and active RFID system includes the Unipart system which is used for traditional SC operations as a means to tracking inventory on tractor trailers.

13.6.2 Summary

Technologies are being used to allow real-time data collection. This allows for more dynamic SCM systems that are able to adjust to varying market and environmental conditions. RFID and GPS facilitate this dynamic SCM. RFID allows for up-to-date inventory levels and, when combined with GPS, can provide a means of tracking inventory as it moves from supplier to customer through the SC. New technologies are being developed to further the amount of information to decision support systems for SCM.

Some technologies can be used to make real-time adjustments to the SC. Those adjustments could be due to many events such as manpower shortages or equipment breakdowns. For example, if a problem occurs to a truck or the road conditions change due to weather, the system, supplied with this updated information, should be able to make the necessary corrections to the transportation routes of other trucks to compensate for the truck failure. This system would be very useful during natural disasters.

With real-time information, the system would reallocate transportation and production to a place that would be the optimum solution. This kind of modeling would reduce the response time for such events from months or weeks to days or hours. This system can also be expanded to urban transportation within a city or long distances.

13.7 Automation in Warehousing

13.7.1 Introduction

It is important to discuss software when we describe RFID and operations such as warehousing. Since the mid-1990s, warehousing and other operations have become computerized. To realize any benefit from technologies such as RFID, operations must be computerized. In this section, we describe the different types of systems that allow for efficient operations. Because software and middleware are the most important pieces of an RFID solution, these packages are needed to make use of information collected by RFID technology with all the other systems operating in the warehouse: warehouse management systems (WMSs), transportation management systems (TMSs), event management systems, order management systems (OMSs), and enterprise resource planning (ERP) systems.

The ability to capture, store, rationalize, and integrate information captured by RFID technology, including product information, location, volume, and transactional data, allows organizations to more efficiently pick/pack, ship, route, track, and distribute materials. This operational improvement can result in lower inventory levels and improved labor and equipment productivity. Integrating the information from RFID tags into an ERP system allows alerts to be sent that pre-set conditions have occurred such as inventory max–min levels have been realized. System standards and compatibility problems can result in expensive software implementation process. Standards are currently being developed at EPCglobal.

13.7.2 Warehouse Applications

Manhattan Associates, the largest WMS vendor, has built its business by implementing software that allows for warehousing best practices. Bobby Collins, Senior Vice President (SVP) of national accounts, suggests that the warehousing problems drive efficiencies and costs in most large and small companies. He describes that WMS implementations seek to drive value by solving the warehousing problems. The top ten warehousing problems are as follows:

- Inventory accuracy
- Space utilization
- Picking information
- Slotting
- Order picking
- Order accuracy
- Returns
- Vendor coordination
- Performance reporting
- Strategic planning.

Warehousing is a requirement of a successful business. Warehousing delivers customer satisfaction. When implementing WMSs, a standard implementation process includes the following master planning methodology:

- Document current warehouse operations
- Determine future requirements over the planning horizon

- Identify and document deficiencies in the existing warehouse
- Identify and document alternative warehouse plans
- Qualitative and quantitative evaluation of alternatives
- Select and specify a plan
- Detail planning
- Implementation.

In the following sections, we provide a brief overview of relevant warehousing operations and how RFID may support improvements in these areas. Also in the text, there is an overall presentation of warehousing and WMS donated by Global Concepts on best practices for warehousing and WMS to further describe usage improving warehousing operations.

13.7.3 Receiving

RFID technology eliminates the need to physically check the bill of lading and/or the packing slip during the receiving process in a warehouse. This represents a significant labor reduction and inventory accuracy improvement in most operations. RFID can alert most WMSs to indicate if a product needs a cross-dock movement. Cross-docking is the process in which product received can be identified as an immediate need to fulfill an order and is immediately loaded into outbound trailers to fulfill the order. This cross-docking process reduces the labor and time to store, replenish, pick, pack, and ship a product. The system requirement consists of a WMS interfacing with an OMS to determine if this product is needed so that a task can be created to ship the product "across the dock" to the outbound dock so the order can be completed and placed on the waiting vehicle. RFID makes the identification of these types of immediate need orders easy and possible more reliably than traditional barcode scanning.

If using a conveyor receiving process or conveyor in general, RFID provides greater efficiencies by eliminating the need to ensure that cases/items are placed properly on the conveyor so that the barcode can be read accurately. RFID allows for accurate reads regardless of product position, resulting in fewer reading errors.

13.7.4 Storage

RFID system can eliminate the need to scan the barcode on the pallet and at the storage, replenishment, and picking locations for the different types of storage racks. RFID scanners can continuously scan locations using WMS specification and create task from identification of inventory inaccuracies. Since the RFID tags can be read from anywhere, products and pallets do not have to be placed in specific or assigned locations such as the golden zone illustrated in Figure 13.3. Material handling principles such as using random storage locations system, minimizing honeycombing, and replenishing to fast picking zones can be realized.

13.7.5 Pick/Pack

RFID readers can be integrated with the WMS to validate that the correct items and amounts are picked and measure productivity in the warehouse.

13.7.6 Shipping

An RFID reader can confirm that each item is placed onto the correct outbound vehicle, which can improve the accuracy of the shipping process. This verification can be made as the product moves through the portal to the outbound dock door. RFID allows for an automatic check of the items loaded into the trailer against the bill of lading. Using RFID readers or portals at exits of the facility and employee areas ensures that all items leaving the building are accounted for.

FIGURE 13.3 Golden zone concept.

13.7.7 Reliability

The reliability of the RFID tags is a problem with many pilot implementations. Currently, RFID accuracy for Walmart implementations has averaged between 70% and 75%. General problems including problems with accuracy are related to multiple reads and no reads because of readers inadvertently scanning adjacent products and/or double scanning the same product. Others include products containing metal or liquids that will reflect, respectively, the signal from the RFID scanner. Metal racking systems could also pose a problem of reflected signals. Additional problems occur with data overload from the high-speed movements of products. "No reads" create a unique problem or RFID technology at the present. With barcode technology, the reader can detect if it did not read a barcode. With RFID technology, a "no read" goes undetected.

13.7.8 IT Infrastructure Issues

One of the major concerns is the potential bandwidth requirement or an RFID system capturing all the available data from every RFID tag in a given warehouse. The potential volume of information from real-time scans moving between multiple applications or every single case or pallet in a warehouse can easily overwhelm even the most robust information system. Hewlett Packard uses RFID in its facilities in Memphis, Tennessee; Chester, Virginia; and Sao Paulo, Brazil. These sites generate 1–5 TB of data a day. Therefore, organizations must analyze the potential data from an RFID tag and determine what information needs to be captured in real time and what information can wait for a batch update. The information systems also need to be robust enough to handle the speed increases associated with a successful RFID implementation. Shorter scanning intervals, faster product movements, and shorter order cycle times must be handled without sacrificing system integrity.

Other problems include the differences between storing UPC barcodes, which are 11 digits, and storing RFID serial numbers, or EPCs, which are 13 digits. The UCC, a standards body for the retail and manufacturing industries, states that their Sunrise 2005 initiative requires all U.S. and Canadian companies to be capable of scanning and processing up to 14-digit barcodes by January 2005.

Slap and ship RFID implementation approach requires a minimal amount of investment to slap tags onto a subset of outgoing shipments to comply with the current mandates. The second approach relies on larger investments to develop an internal capacity that impacts the SC upstream, in an effort to both comply with mandates and capture operational efficiencies from RFID.

The slap and ship approach is driven by the mentality that RFID is a cost of doing business due to the mandates set forth by both Walmart and the US Department of Defense (DoD). Organizations employing this strategy are not looking for a short- or long-term Return on Failure (ROF) on their investment; they are only concerned with being compliant with their customers so that they are able to continue doing business. This approach oftentimes is just as costly as a well-thought-out long-term strategy to use the technology. Most pundits suggest that the second approach should be utilized in order to increase business efficiency. The next section provides some implementation examples in which the companies sought to integrate RFID into operations.

13.7.9 RFID Warehouse Implementation Examples

The following are examples of RFID system implementations in various companies in different business sectors.

13.7.9.1 Gillette

In January 2003, Gillette bought 500 million Class I EPC tags from Alien Technology. Gillette has been using the order to tag all pallets and cases of women razors. Gillette worked with its WMS and TMS provider, Provia, to ensure that the RFID information can be integrated into the appropriate systems. Below is an explanation of how Gillette has incorporated the tags into their processes.

13.7.9.2 International Paper

International Paper, the world's largest paper and forest products company, went live with their first fully automated RFID warehouse tracking system in August 2003. The use of truck-mounted RFID readers and proprietary tracking technology provides forklift operators with execution task information. The elimination RFID portals in tracking inventory movement for the use of mobile forklifts truly integrating RFID in operations have provided more efficiency.

13.7.9.3 Proctor & Gamble

Proctor & Gamble performed a pilot project in which they used RFID at an international manufacturing plant in Spain to send pallets to domestic operations. Results indicated this was a cost-effective way to implement RFID tagging.

Case Study

RELATED BACKGROUND TO ADC, RFID, MILITARY, OR LOGISTICS

Military logisticians can use RFID technology to track troop movement as they use different modes of transportation. For example, they may use a bus to get to the military base, a carrier to get to the next port, a train in an international country, and possibly a tank as they are in theater. We look at a simple example of how one public transportation agency uses RFID technology to support data analysis of passenger demand.

In 2008, gas prices peaked, and Metropolitan Transit saw a record increase in the number of passengers it served. To avoid spending a small fortune on gas, local residents began to take the train for their daily commute to work. Over the past year, passenger use of the trains has fluctuated with gas prices and economic conditions. Methods for tracking passenger counts have been manual, leaving room for error. Variability in passenger usage has made it more difficult to determine if the variability in count was due to an error or due to actual changes in usage. In addition, Metropolitan Transit is facing its own budget cuts and is looking at potentially reducing the number of trains it runs.

To more accurately provide trains based on passenger demand, Metropolitan Transit has launched a new fare collection system that uses smart card technology to collect data as passengers enter and exit the train station. With the new fare collection system up and running, Metropolitan Transit is ready to begin analyzing passenger demand.

Prior to boarding a train, passengers can load a one-way or round-trip fare onto a plastic card that looks similar to a credit card but has an embedded RFID microchip. To enter and exit the train station, passengers tap the card to a card reader that records the station location, time of day, and type of fare loaded on the card.

METHODS AND RELATED MODELS

The data set for the first month of operations since the launch of the new smart card system has been collected and is ready for analysis. The passenger demand, D, followed a uniform distribution $D_{min} = 200$ and $D_{max} = 400$. The supply of trains can now be calculated with the Newsvendor model by using the number of passenger seats to determine the number of trains needed. Each train has 50 seats. The optimal quantity, q, using the newsvendor model is

$$q = F^{-1}\left(\frac{p-c}{p}\right),$$

where F^{-1} is the inverse cumulative distribution function of D, with price, p, and cost, c.

SAMPLE PROBLEM

Metropolitan Transit assumes that there is a cost, c, and a price, p, for each seat on the train. Assume that the price is the passenger fare for one trip: $p = 2$ [$/passenger seat] and the cost of each seat on a train running along the route is $c = 1$ [$/passenger seat]. The optimal quantity of passenger seats is calculated as

$$q_{opt} = F^{-1}\left(\frac{2-1}{2}\right) = F^{-1}(0.5) = D_{min} + (D_{max} - D_{min}) * 0.5 = 300$$

Therefore, the optimal number of trains that Metropolitan Transit should send out is six trains.

CONCLUSION

RFID technology provides a method to more accurately gather data on how passengers interact with a system. As passengers register their smart cards with identifying information, Metropolitan Transit can also adjust other components of its transportation system as passengers move from train to bus to commuter bus.

14

Evaluating the Impacts of the Internet of Things to Reduce Runway Incursions

Samuel Innanore Okate and Erick C. Jones

14.1 Introduction

14.1.1 What Is a Runway Incursion

The Federal Aviation Administration (FAA) is a government agency of the U.S. Department of Transportation which is tasked with the regulation, safety, and oversight of civil aviation within the United States. Moreover, the FAA is responsible for the operation and development of the National Airspace System (NAS), including promoting safety initiatives that support a safe and efficient aerospace system. In 2007, the FAA adopted the definition of a runway incursion from the International Civil Aviation Organization (ICAO) as "any occurrence at an aerodrome involving the incorrect presence of an aircraft, vehicle or person on the protected area of a surface designated for the landing and takeoff of aircraft" (Federal Aviation Administration, June 2015).

14.1.1.1 Runway Incursion Classifications

In efforts to prevent runway incursions, it is necessary to understand the "how" of a runway incursion by the different classification types of an occurrence. Runway incursions can be classified into three types of surface events defined as vehicle and pedestrian deviation (VPD), pilot deviations (PDs), and operational incidents (OIs). According to the National Runway Safety Report 2015–2017, a VPD takes place when there is any entry or movement on the movement area or safety area by a vehicle (including aircraft operated by a non-pilot or an aircraft being towed) or a pedestrian that has not been authorized by Air Traffic Control (ATC) (Federal Aviation Administration, 2016). The National Runway Safety Reports also define a PD as any action of a pilot that infringes any federal aviation regulation and defines an OI to be a surface event attributed to ATC action or inaction (Federal Aviation Administration, 2016). In the event of a runway incursion, the occurrence can also be classified by the severity of the event. Runway incursions can be classified into four categories in terms of severity (Figure 14.1; Table 14.1).

An accident is defined as an incursion that leads to a collision. Runway incursions are one of the most crucial issues in airport safety and security management.

14.1.2 Why is there a Need for Runway Incursion Research

In December of 2015 at Mumbai airport, an airport technician died after a fatal accident occurred where the worker was sucked into the engine of an Air India plane in preparation from being taxied out to take off (Mullen & Singh, 2015). Could this fatal accident have been avoided? This accident is an example of a runway incursion. Approximately, one runway incursion occurs each day in the United States, and the potential for a catastrophic accident is "unacceptable", according to the FAA's risk/severity matrix [2]. At its extreme, runway incursions have been identified to be able to cause hundreds of deaths in a single air traffic accident [2]. With these alarming statistics, it is no secret why runway safety is one of the most

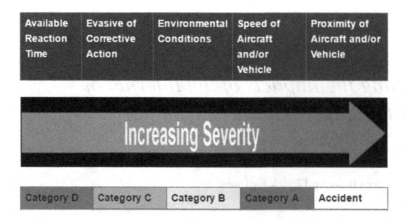

FIGURE 14.1   Classification of runway incursions by increasing severity (Transportation, 2015).

TABLE 14.1

Severity Type Definition

Category A	A serious incident where a collision was barely avoided.
Category B	An incident where there is a significant potential for collision and timely critical corrective or evasive reaction is necessary to avoid a collision.
Category C	An incident characterized by sufficient time and/or distance to circumvent a collision.
Category D	An incorrect presence of a single vehicle/person/aircraft on the protected area of a surface designated for the landing and takeoff of aircraft but with little or no risk of a collision.

Source: Federal Aviation Administration, June 2015.

crucial issues in aviation safety. The likelihood for runway incursions grows exponentially as a function of air traffic growth within the U.S. National Airspace System (NAS) [2].

From Figure 14.2, it is clear that runway incursion rates are increasing per fiscal year. One should also note that the data for FY 2016 is through July 19, 2016 and, at present, at a high rate with six months of the year left. At this pace, it is projected to surpass the FY 2015 totals. With these increasing rates,

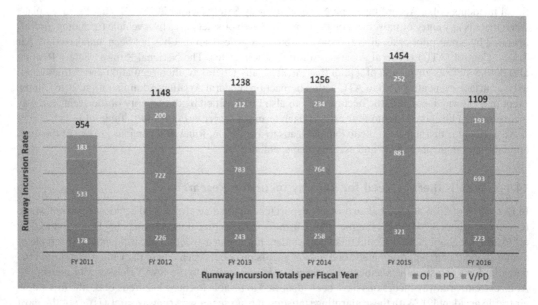

FIGURE 14.2   Runway incursion totals fiscal year 2011 to fiscal year 2016.

runway incursion research for prevention is of the utmost importance. The key element into preventing runway incursions and increasing runway safety is to know why and how the occurrence happened in the first place. Runway incursions are a problematic area in aviation safety, which comes to no surprise why this is a national and international problem.

14.2 Purpose of This Research

This research seeks to enhance the safety on the Air Operations Area (AOA) by investigating the use of automated technology to reduce the potential of a runway incursion event caused by VPD, PDs, OIs, and other occurrences. Moreover, this research seeks to use statistical analysis to examine human causal elements (HCEs), also called human factor errors, which may have played a crucial role in "why" the occurrence took place. Understanding the underlying root causes in why an incursion event took place can lead to the development of numerous technological advancements to assist the workers in performing their job safely and reliably. Moreover, reducing the number of runway incursions can lead to less delays on the runway, which in turn leads to more revenue for the airport to invest in various technologies to improve safety. The overall purpose of this research aims to reduce an occurrence of a runway incursion by exploring a framework that leverages automated technology, investigates human factor errors, and looks at the economic feasibility of using that technology. In addition to the use of automated technology and understanding the economic feasibility, this research seeks to reduce runway incursions by understanding "why" runway incursions occur, "how" they occur, and the legal ramifications in terms of liability "when" they occur.

Outcomes of this research have potential benefit to the long-term growth of civil aviation and Commercial Space Transportation. This research explores a framework to prevent runway incursions and increase safety in the aviation industry, while furthering knowledge and understanding on a broad front of emerging technologies. Furthermore, the hope of this research is that it will bring forth learning, growth, and improvement to a vital area in the aviation industry.

14.3 Research Objectives

The overall objective of this research is to investigate a framework that leverages automated technology, Radio Frequency Identification (RFID), and Zigbee technologies in particular, human causal factors, data analytics and a legal repository of information surrounding a runway incursion incident, and employee training and a decision support system for the purposes of reducing runway incursions. In the first stage of the framework, it is necessary to define and investigate HCEs in effort to understand their roles in "why" the incursion took place. Also, in the first stage of the framework, it is necessary to investigate the types of runway incursions that occur in effort to understand "how" runway incursions happen. The outcome of this will be to develop a device that can reside on a worker or can be mounted in a worker vehicle and provide audible, visual, and vibrating alerts to the employee that alerts them of their location when they are approaching a hazardous zone or encroaching a runway incursion boundary zone. The second stage of the framework will provide data analytics and a legal information repository surrounding the issue of runway incursions in terms of liability when a severe incursion takes place. The last stage of the framework will be to utilize the data analytics and develop an employee training and decision support system that will facilitate the reduction of runway incursion events (Figure 14.3).

This research will focus on the first and second stages of the runway incursion reduction framework as our overall objective of this research at this point. Investigating stage 3 of this framework will be future work of this research. The first and second stages of this research will investigate two research questions. The first question is, "Do HCEs have a significant relationship with runway incursion rates?" The second research question is, "Can automated technologies platform be utilized to reduce the occurrence of a runway incursion?" The research questions will be addressed by the following three research objectives:

Future Work

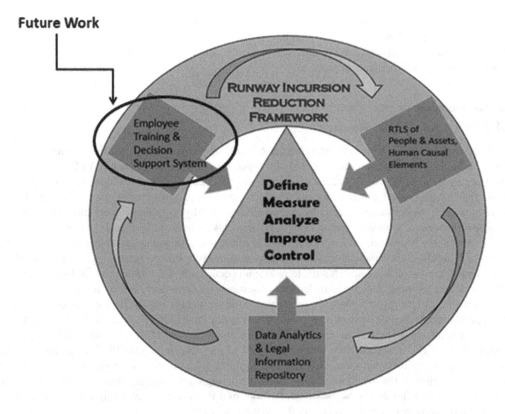

FIGURE 14.3   Runway incursion reduction framework.

Research Objective #1: Evaluate HCEs that contribute to runway incursions on the AOA at an airport.

Research Objective #2: Determine system architecture configuration for maximum reliability. Develop runway incursion detection module. Perform an operational demonstration with selected personnel.

Research Objective #3: Perform economic analysis and evaluate the financial impacts with other solutions. Evaluate the impacts of different automated technologies. Determine the best automated technology to use. Determine legal aspect of runway incursion in terms of liability.

The research problem we wish to investigate is the likelihood of increasing runway safety and minimizing the risk of runway incursions through the use of automated technologies. Furthermore, we wish to increase the body of knowledge and understanding into why runway incursions happen and the legal risks associated when they happen. The innovation of this research is that it proposes a framework to utilize automated technologies to alert workers for the purpose of minimizing runway incursion incidents and enhancing the safety on the AOA. The proposed system utilizes RFID technologies integrated with Zigbee technologies to alert technicians when they enter into aircraft movement areas and aircraft non-movement areas that required authorization as a part of safety concerns to minimize any forms of runway incursions.

The intellectual merit of this dissertation is that it builds upon modern automation technologies in the effort of enhancing the safety and security in an AOA. These technologies can be applied both in vehicle, on ramp operations, and on the airport operations airfield, which can be easily carried by people or placed in an operations vehicle that may accidentally enter the prohibited area. Furthermore, this research seeks to enhance the understanding of how a runway incursion happens, why it happens, and the legal ramifications when it happens.

The broader impact of this research is that it provides an opportunity for engineering students to apply their knowledge in multidisciplinary field, including industrial engineering science and software engineering science to solve real problems that airports all over the world face on a daily basis.

14.4 Organization of this Dissertation

This dissertation is organized in a manner that is consistent with the five-point engineering format of introduction, background, methodology, results, and conclusion.

Section 14.1 is the introduction where the definition of runway incursion is introduced. Furthermore, Section 14.2 discusses why runway incursion research is needed and why it is relevant at every airport around the world. In addition, the introduction discusses the purpose of this research and how automated technology could be one avenue to reduce this problem area in aviation safety. Moreover, the research objectives of this research are discussed.

Section 14.5 sets in motion the background of the dissertation that includes the purpose of runway safety, runway safety data collection and analysis, and relevant funded projects. It also discusses the literature review of human factors, Internet of Things (IoT) definition and applications, RFID technologies, Zigbee technologies, and aviation law.

Section 14.6 discusses the research problem and defines the research methodology to be used is this dissertation. Furthermore, this section discusses the research questions, research objectives and tasks, and hypotheses.

Section 14.8 discusses and interprets the results of the experiment. Moreover, Minitab outputs, statistical data, and the economic viabilities of various technologies are discussed.

Section 14.8 is also the conclusion of the dissertation, which discusses the summary of the experiments and the outcomes of the research objectives. Furthermore, this section will discuss the limitations and future work of the research.

14.5 Background

14.5.1 Runway Safety

The sector of aviation is a very important industry to the U.S. economy. In 2012, the civil aviation sector led to $1.5 trillion in economic activity, sustained 11.8 million jobs which generated $459.4 billion in earnings (U.S. Department of Transportation, January 2015). The aviation industry relies heavily on the safe operations of the National Airspace System (NAS). The FAA is tasked with managing the safety of the NAS. The FAA's mission is to maintain the safest and most efficient aerospace system in the world. The FAA has stated that runway safety is one of their top priorities, which encapsulates pilots, air traffic controllers, and airport vehicle drivers and workers [8]. Runway safety is described as having a safe flight from the moment the flight starts when it leaves the gate and takes off until the flight lands and taxis back to the gate and is concluded [7]. This problem of runway incursions is a national and international problem. The Flight Safety Foundation, an aviation safety research organization, has estimated that ground accidents worldwide cost air carriers $10 billion annually, including costs associated with injuries and fatalities and other indirect costs such as canceled flights.

14.5.1.1 Runway Safety Metrics

The FAA is constantly working toward improving safety performance by recognizing and finding new ways to manage safety risks. For the purpose of monitoring these safety risks, the National Runway Safety Report 2013–2014 states that runway safety is measured by three different metrics:

- Rate of Seriousness of Runway Incursion
- Severity of Runway Incursion
- Types of Runway Incursion.

These three metrics helps the FAA quantify and measure runway incursion data in terms of occurrence and location.

Figure 14.4 displays runway incursion data from fiscal year of 2013 and 2014 separated by category type. From this figure, we see that of the runway incursions taking place in 2013 and 2014, most of the occurrences were of categories C and D.

According to the National Runway Safety Report 2013–2014, Figure 14.5 displays all the regions for the fiscal year 2013 in the nation and calculates the total for runway incursions per region in terms of the number of occurrences per classification type and annual rate for that region.

Figure 14.6 displays all the regions for the fiscal year 2014 in the nation and calculates the total for runway incursions per region in terms of the number of occurrences per classification type and annual rate for that region.

In 2013–2014, approximately 60% of runway incursions were attributed to PDs, 20% were attributed to OIs, and 20% were attributed to VPDs [9]. Runway incursions, along with their associated risks and efforts for reduction and prevention, have been studied intensively. The Commercial Aviation Safety Team (CAST) is a group of key aviation stakeholders working collectively to lead the national and international aviation community to the highest levels of global commercial aviation safety [9]. The FAA has implemented several CAST safety improvements, a Safety Management System (SMS), and a Runway Incursion Mitigation (RIM) program in efforts to reduce the occurrence of a runway incursion.

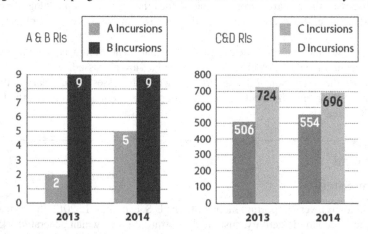

FIGURE 14.4   Runway incursion per category FY 2014 and FY 2014 (Federal Aviation Administration, June 2015).

	Operational Incidents	Pilot Deviations	Vehicle/ Pedestrian Deviations	Other**	Total	Annual RI Rate*
AAL (Alaskan)	13	16	12	1	42	51
ACE (Central)	3	31	3	0	37	24
AEA (Eastern)	25	68	21	0	114	19
AGL (Great Lakes)	47	88	36	1	172	27
ANE (New England)	7	30	7	0	44	24
ANM (Northwest Mountain)	28	68	25	0	121	27
ASO (Southern)	53	154	23	1	231	21
ASW (Southwest)	27	104	41	0	172	27
AWP (Western Pacific)	40	224	43	1	308	28
TOTALS	**243**	**783**	**211**	**4**	**1241**	**248**

* Annual RI Rate — Calculated for all RIs. RI events per million operations.
** Other — Events that meet the criteria of an RI though do not fit within the primary types (emergencies, equipment failures, etc.).

FIGURE 14.5   2013 Runway incursion totals by type (Federal Aviation Administration, June 2015).

	Operational Incidents	Pilot Deviations	Vehicle/ Pedestrian Deviations	Other**	Total	Annual RI Rate*
AAL (Alaskan)	6	30	17	0	53	66
ACE (Central)	6	12	6	0	24	16
AEA (Eastern)	67	59	31	1	158	26
AGL (Great Lakes)	37	77	23	2	139	22
ANE (New England)	6	11	5	0	22	12
ANM (Northwest Mountain)	21	68	21	0	110	24
ASO (Southern)	41	147	31	3	222	20
ASW (Southwest)	25	116	43	1	185	29
AWP (Western Pacific)	49	244	57	1	351	31
TOTALS	**258**	**764**	**234**	**8**	**1264**	**246**

* Annual RI Rate — Calculated for all RIs. RI events per million operations.
** Other — Events that meet the criteria of an RI though do not fit within the primary types (emergencies, equipment failures, etc.).

FIGURE 14.6   2014 Runway incursion totals by type (Federal Aviation Administration, June 2015).

14.5.1.2 Runway Safety Data Collection

The FAA uses various databases and reporting systems that allow different personnel at all levels to get a deeper look into safety data to have a better understanding of runway safety issues. One of the newly implemented systems for critical runway safety data is called the Comprehensive Electronic Data and Analysis Reporting (CEDAR) system. The CEDAR system is currently being used in place of the old the manual safety event reporting system used for record keeping, documenting, collecting, and processing safety event reporting in air traffic facilities (Federal Aviation Administration, 2016). Another database that the FAA uses is the Airport Facility Directory. This directory gives information on various hot spots at airports all over the nation sorted by region. The FAA defines a "hot spot" as being a position on the airport movement area where heightened attention by pilots and airport vehicle drivers is required because that location has a history of potential risk of a runway incursion (U.S. Department of Transportation FAA, May 2016). Identifying these spots makes it easier for pilots and ground workers to be more aware and alert for the potential of an incursion event.

14.5.1.2.1 Runway Incursion Databases

The FAA has also developed a system that allows users to look at safety data from numerous databases in one place. The name of this system is the Aviation Safety Information Analysis and Sharing (ASIAS) System. The ASIAS system allows users to perform queries over multiple databases. Various databases within ASIAS include FAA Accident and Incident Data Systems (AIDS), NASA Aviation Safety and Reporting System (ASRS), National Transportation Safety Board (NTSB) Aviation Accident and Incident Data, just to name a few. In this research, most of the runway incursion rates data due to HCEs will be used from the ASRS. The ASRS is a program that collects voluntarily submitted aviation safety incident/situation reports from pilots, controllers, and others [4]. The purpose of the ASRS is to collect, analyze, and respond to voluntarily submitted aviation safety incident reports in order to lessen the likelihood of aviation accidents [4]. ASRS data are used for three main purposes:

1. Identifying deficiencies and discrepancies in the NAS so that these can be remedied by appropriate authorities [4]
2. Supporting policy formulation and planning for, and improvements to, the NAS [4]
3. Strengthening the foundation of aviation human factors safety research [4].

14.5.1.3 Runway Safety Programs

The FAA has employed various programs to improve runway safety. Order 7050.1b is a directive handbook that is used by the Air Traffic Organization (ATO) Safety and Technical Training staff to adhere to the FAA's long-term goal of improving runway safety by reducing the number of runway incursions and their associated incidents. The ATO Safety and Technical Training office serves as a central point for all of the runway safety efforts made by the FAA. Its primary role is to develop a National Runway Safety Plan that aids them in a wide-ranging strategy to implement runway safety. Various programs range from runway safety action plans to regional and local runway safety plans.

14.5.1.4 Similar Research and Relevant Funded Projects

The FAA is constantly looking into different emerging technologies to help improve the area of runway safety. A current technology that the FAA has installed at 35 of the busiest U.S. airports is the Airport Surface Detection Equipment, Model X, otherwise known as the ASDE-X. This runway incursion technology uses surveillance sensors, surface movement radars to display aircrafts' positions on the Air Operation Area, and Safety Logic, which is a detection and alerting technology that uses complex algorithms to alert controllers of a potential incursion with aircrafts and/or vehicles (Ranieri, 2016). The difference from this researched technology and the one aforementioned in this dissertation is that ASDE-X only provides alerts to the air traffic controllers and not the vehicle drivers.

The FAA has funded runway safety research that has led to the testing and new deployment of technology of other measures [18]. During fiscal year of 2006, FAA spent about 3.5 million on runway incursion prevention research at the William J Hughes Technical Center [18]. Runway safety, runway incursions in particular, is a topic in aviation safety that continuously researches ways to mitigate risks associated with hazards on the runway. Another funded research project on runway safety was employed at the Miami International Airport. The Transportation Security Administration funded the 3.1 million dollar project for a Runway Incursion Detection System. This Runway Incursion Detection System integrated ground-based radar, high-resolution digital cameras, and target-analytics software for the purpose of detecting and verifying runway and taxiway incursions [19]. The benefits of this new system are that it provides a faster and more reliable way of detection and verification of these runway and taxiway incursions [19]. Correspondingly, the FAA recently announced that it will fund $11 million through the Airport Improvement Program (AIP) to eight U.S. airports for risks pertaining to runway incursions to reduce occurrences by funding projects that are used to mitigate incursion hazards (Sadler, 2015).

14.5.2 Human Factors

When talking about runway safety, runway incursions in particular, it is essential to discuss human factors. Approximately, over two-thirds of all aviation accidents and incidents have their roots in human performance errors (Federal Aviation Administration, 2011). Most aviation accidents are caused by human error instead of a mechanical failure of the equipment. The term "human factor" has become gradually more popular in the aviation industry. Human factors are primarily concerned with the integration of technology and humans and how this interaction can successfully sustain a safe flying environment. Human factors can be classified into several disciplines from clinical psychology, medical science to computer science and safety engineering. For the purpose of this dissertation, we will discuss human factors from an aviation industry standpoint. Human error can be defined as an error or operational mistake made by a human. Because of the fact that we as human beings are not perfect, error in work performance is bound to occur. The key is learning about it and finding new ways through technology to address it. Figure 14.7 is a list of human factor errors that affect the aviation industry.

It is important to note that this list is not exhaustive. The FAA has employed numerous human factor specialists that work in the Aviation Safety (AVS) organization to improve the impact of human error in aviation systems. They perform their duties by developing regulations, guidance, and procedures that support the certification of pilots, mechanics, and other aviation workers.

FIGURE 14.7   Human factor errors that effect aviation industry.

14.5.2.1 *Visual and Auditory Performance*

Another part of human factors that is of concern in this dissertation is the visual and auditory performance. This information is of interest because we would like to know the auditory level and type of visual indicator the runway incursion device should be equipped with to provide the worker with an adequate visual and auditory alert that can be seen and heard. Auditory and visual stimuli account for more than 95% of the way a person receives information (Groover, 2007). It comes to no surprise that vision is the most important of the five basic human senses. Light is what stimulates the eyes, which comes from electromagnetic radiant energy that is within the visible spectrum (Groover, 2007). In knowing this, it is very important that the appropriate color of light be used on the device that is within the visible spectrum to effectively alert the worker. Furthermore, it is essential that the auditory alert on the runway incursion detection device is loud enough to alert the worker, even in the presence of background noise. The average human being with no hearing defects can perceive sound frequencies in the range of approximately 20–20,000 Hz, with normal conversation frequencies lying in the range of 500–3,000 Hz (Cambell & Bagshaw, 2002). Moreover, the auditory environment can have a significant effect on the worker. Two major factors that play into the auditory environment are intensity of the noise and the duration of exposure to the noise source (Groover, 2007). It is important that we assess the noise environment of the worker so that a reliable detection device can be produced.

14.5.3 Communication Technologies

Target Tech define communication technology as, "…an umbrella term that includes any communication device or application, encompassing: radio, television, cellular phones, computer and network hardware and software, satellite systems and so on, as well as the various services and applications associated with them, such as videoconferencing and distance learning" (Rouse, 2016). There have been several projects and developments in communication technology regarding the aviation industry that have been employed in order to mitigate the risk of a runway incursion event, no matter the severity. Within this chapter, we will investigate IoT, RFID, and Zigbee technologies.

14.5.3.1 *Internet of Things*

The IoT is a technological solution we can employ to help reduce these occurrences of runway incursions. When we talk about IoT, it can be defined in several different ways. However, at the root of all the definitions for IoT, IoT can be defined as, "the network of physical objects or 'things' embedded with electronics, software, sensors, and network connectivity, which enables these objects to collect and exchange data" [16]. Taking a deeper look into the definition, let's take a closer look at the term "internet" which everyone can identify with as being a system of communication networks that connects individuals to have all encompassing knowledge at their fingertips. When we talk about "things", this can be people, devices, sensors, phones, and the list could be endless. However, when we combine these two terms, we talk about a world where everything is connected, for example, being able to close your garage door from the comfort of your office or being able to send your doctor real-time health information at the touch of a button. The IoT is a phenomena that is rapidly growing and finding more widespread use on a daily basis. Just as any other industry, we can expand IoT into the aviation industry to assist with real-time data for the purpose of supporting the safety aspect of aviation. RFID was known as one of the early technologies for the development of IoT; however, of late, wireless sensor networks and Bluetooth-enabled technology have assisted the advancement of the IoT trend (Buyya & Vahid, 2016). In order to implement a reliable use of IoT, we look to RFID technology integrated with Zigbee technologies.

14.5.3.2 RFID Technology

RFID is a communication technology that has been around for over 80 years. RFID is most commonly used for tracking and identification of various assets and unique objects by way of the movement of radio waves of information from point to point (Clampitt & Jones, 2006). Early on, RFID was used in the military for the purpose of detecting certain aircrafts and determining whether that aircraft was a friend or foe. As time went on, RFID was used in the toll tag industry, tracking animals, and heavily used in the supply chain industry. Now RFID is used across numerous industries with several different applications.

14.5.3.2.1 RFID Theory

RFID uses radio frequency (RF) electromagnetic fields to transfer data wirelessly for the purpose of identifying, detecting, and tracking tags attached to various objects. An RFID system is made of a tag, reader, antenna, and a host computer and software system. The basis of how RFID works is that it uses electromagnetic waves as a communication medium between the reader and the tag. As the tag enters the reader's zone, the reader excites the tag allowing the antenna to send these signals back to the reader (Clampitt & Jones, 2006). Figure 14.8 gives an overview of this operation.

The reliability of the tags being able to read and send information to reader depends on a number of factors. Different factors include the tag type, distance, environment, and its frequency band of use. The various frequency bands that RFID operates in include low-frequency (LF), high-frequency (HF),

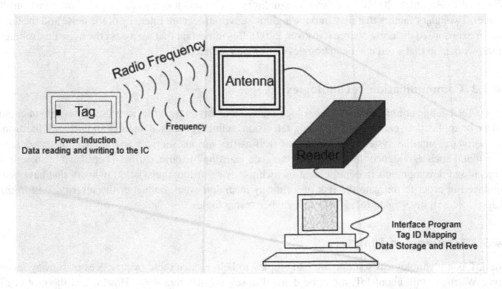

FIGURE 14.8 RFID operation.

and ultra-high-frequency (UHF) bands. Figures 14.9 and 14.10 describe the more and less common frequencies used in RFID.

14.5.3.2.2 RFID Tag Types

There are two main RFID tag types: passive tags and active tags. Passive tags do not have a battery on board; therefore, it relies on the energy of the reader to wake up and excite the tag to begin the information sharing process. Between passive and active tags, passive tags are the least costly. Consequently, passive tags do not have a long read range as the active tags do. However, they do have a lower installation, infrastructure, and maintenance cost. Active tags have a battery on board used to power the tag and respond to the reader. Because of this, active tags have a longer read range and higher accuracy. Subsequently, they are more expensive than passive tags. Another tag type is what's known as a semi-active tag. This tag type is of newer technology which combines the best of both tag types. Semi-active tags come equipped with the on-board battery; however, it uses the reader's energy to respond back. Generally, a semi-active tag lasts longer than active tags and has a higher accuracy rate and read range than passive tags. A semi-active tag is also cheaper than an active tag.

14.5.3.3 Zigbee Technologies

Zigbee is the name of a specification for a pool of high-level communication protocols using small, low-power digital radios based on the IEEE 802.15.4 standard for wireless personal area networks (WPANs) that is proposed to be cheaper and simpler than other WPANs such as Bluetooth [17]. We choose to integrate Zigbee technologies with RIFD because it is targeted at RF applications which require a low data rate, long battery life, and secure networking [17]. Zigbee and RFID are two wireless technologies that have each developed multitudes of applications independent of each other [1]. Each of these technologies

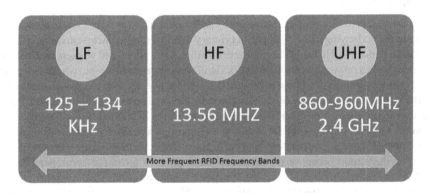

FIGURE 14.9 More frequent RFID frequency bands.

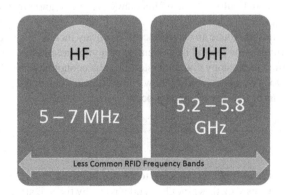

FIGURE 14.10 Less common RFID frequency bands.

has benefits, with Zigbee supporting advanced sensor networks and RFID suitable for low-power wireless tracking of people and assets [1]. With the integration of these two technologies, it is possible to create a Zigbee mesh network with integrated active RFID tracking capability—one in which RFID tags within the network can communicate with each other [1]. We will employ an RFID system integrated with Zigbee technologies that will send audible, visual, and vibrating alerts that warn personnel and contractors of their location when they are approaching or when they are in a hazardous zone in efforts to reduce the occurrence of a runway incursion event.

14.5.4 Aviation Law

Aviation law is the type of law that deals with air travel and the accompanying legal and business aspects associated therein (Wikipedia Foundation Inc., 2016). Federal and state governments are the regulating bodies for aviation law. However, since the terrorist attacks that happened on September 11, 2001, Congress enacted the Aviation and Transportation Security Act of 2001, which now has aviation mostly governed by federal law (Cornell University Law School, 2016). With over 4,000 airports in the country, most of them are owned by governments. Since aviation law is a topic that spans across all other law subjects like property law, contracts, torts, and criminal law, to name a few, aviation law can be considered a diminutive course for all other legal industries (Larsen, Sweeny, & Gillick, 2006). For the purpose of this research, it would be helpful to know what happens when an accident takes place and who is liable. Since this problem of runway incursions is a national and international problem of significance, it would be helpful to provide legal research to the airport legal community surrounding such occurrences that would be beneficial to the airport owners, operators, and airport workers in providing information surrounding legal issues and airport-related law.

14.5.5 Chapter Summary

Furthermore, we seek to reduce runway incursions by understanding "why" a runway incursion takes place by investigating the underlying causes that play a primary role in a runway incursion event. These underlying causes can be defined as HCEs. HCEs are the errors that ATC, pilots, and workers routinely make that have a direct impact in a runway incursion event [7]. Gaining an understanding into why these runway incursions happen will give us insight on how to prevent them. Moreover, we seek to use statistical analysis and determine if a significant relationship exists between the HCEs and an event of an incursion. Furthermore, we attempt to determine which HCE has the highest impact on the likelihood of an occurrence.

Additionally, when there is an aircraft accident, the question arises of whether or not the airport is liable for the related damages associated with the accident. The question arises whether the liability is being placed on the airport owner or the actual operator, pilot, or air traffic controller, who may have played a role in the runway incursion incident. We plan to explore various case laws surrounding severe runway incursion incidents in efforts to understand the liability ownership of these severe incursions and put these results of our findings in a repository database to create one shared location to be accessed by anyone who has a need for such information such as lawyers, pilots, and air traffic controllers to keep them informed when such an event arises.

Overall, this research aims to reduce an occurrence of a runway incursion by exploring our framework that will bring forth learning, growth, and improvement to a vital area in the aviation industry. In addition to the use of automated technology and understanding the economic feasibility, this research seeks to reduce runway incursions by understanding how runway incursions occur, why they occur, and the legal ramifications in terms of liability when they occur.

14.6 Methodology

The significance of this research is that we seek to contribute to the body of knowledge and understanding of the various reasons why these incidents take place by investigating the HCEs and what role they played in an incursion. Furthermore, we seek to develop a prototype that will allow technicians to easily carry the device on person or mounted in a vehicle, for both indoor and outdoor environments, including while driving on the AOA. Moreover, we seek to investigate the legal ramifications when a runway incursion takes place by researching case laws and, at its extreme, the legal ramifications when loss of life occurs. With regard to the significance of this research, the next logical research questions that we seek to investigate are, "Do HCEs have a significant relationship with runway incursion rates?" and furthermore, "Can automated technologies platform be utilized to reduce the occurrence of a runway incursion?" We investigate these questions by exploring a framework that evaluates the relationships between HCEs and runway incursions and uses RFID and Zigbee technologies for the purpose of developing a device that alerts technicians if they are approaching a boundary on the AOA that will cause an incursion incident.

14.6.1 Research Approach

We will use Design for Six Sigma Research (DFSS-R) methodology for our problem-solving approach developed by Dr. Erick C. Jones in 2006. This framework is based on a common operational theme that requires development teams to plan, predict, and perform (3P). The DFSS-R process steps are as follows: Define, Measure, Analyze, Identify, Design, Optimize, and Verify [11]. In the Define step, a clear problem definition is defined. Next, the Measure step sets up accurate metrics through various statistical analysis techniques. In the Analyze step, we want to asses and analyze the current situation. Next, we want to identify relevant technology. After this has been identified, our next step is to design new technology from our current knowledge. Our next step within the methodology is to optimize our new technology by testing it in a live environment and improve any drawbacks. After this is done, we want to validate the technology in a live situation. The DFSS-R process steps are organized within the 3P framework in Figure 14.11.

For this research, we have separated our specific task into 3P framework in Table 14.2.

14.6.2 Research Questions and Hypotheses

There are two primary research questions that will be investigated. As stated earlier, the research questions that of are interest are, "Do HCEs have a significant relationship with runway incursion rates?" and furthermore, "Can automated technologies platform be utilized to reduce the occurrence of a runway

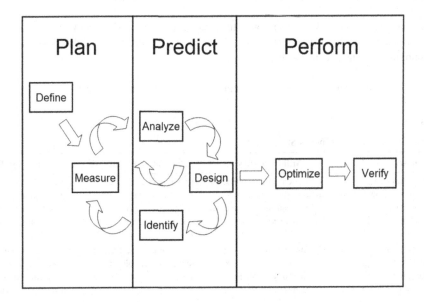

FIGURE 14.11 DFSS-R methodology.

TABLE 14.2

3P's Methodology with Specific Tasks

Plan	Define	*Task 1*
		Task 2
		Task 3
	Measure	*Task 4*
		Task 5
		Task 6
		Task 7
		Task 8
		Task 16
Predict	Analyze	*Task 1*
	Identify	*Task 2*
	Design	*Task 3*
		Task 4
		Task 9
		Task 10
		Task 11
Perform	Optimize	*Task 12*
	Verify	*Task 13*

incursion?" To explore these research questions, hypothesis testing will be used. The hypotheses associated with these research questions are given below.

Research Question #1 Hypothesis Statement:

Null Hypothesis
H_o: There is not a significant relationship between HCEs and runway incursion rates.
Alternative Hypothesis
H_a: There is a significant relationship between HCEs and runway incursion rates.
Decision Rule: Reject H_o if the p-value from the main effect is less than the 0.05 significance level.
Research Question #2 Hypothesis Statement:
Null Hypothesis
H_o: Automated technology system is not reliable to reduce runway incursion incidents.
Alternative Hypothesis
H_a: Automated technology system is reliable to reduce runway incursion incidents.
Decision Rule: Reject H_o if main effects for linear model of statistical reliability show p-value less than the 0.05 significance level.

The research questions and hypothesis statements are summarized in Table 14.3.

TABLE 14.3

Research Questions and Hypotheses Statements

Research Questions	Null Hypothesis	Alternative Hypothesis	Decision Rule
Research Question #1 Do human causal elements have a significant relationship with runway incursion rates?	H_o: There is not a significant relationship between human causal elements and runway incursion rates.	H_a: There is a significant relationship between human causal elements and runway incursion rates.	Reject H_o if the p-value from the main effect is less than the 0.05 significance level.
Research Question #2 Can automated technologies platform be utilized to reduce the occurrence of a runway incursion?	H_o: Automated technology system is not reliable to reduce runway incursion incidents.	H_a: Automated technology system is reliable to reduce runway incursion incidents.	Reject H_o if main effect for linear model of statistical reliability shows p-value less than the 0.05 significance level.

14.6.3 Research Objectives and Specific Tasks

The overall objective is to investigate a framework that can reduce runway incursion occurrences by evaluating the influence of HCEs, evaluating the impact of automated systems that can be tested on a device, investigating economic justification, and providing some legal information surrounding the topic of liability of an occurrence (Table 14.4). The research objectives associated with the specific task and methods are as follows.

Research Objective 1: Evaluate HCEs that contribute to runway incursions on the AOA at an airport.

Task 1—Evaluate the runway incursion incidents for 2014–2015 in the United States by region.

The first step for task 1 of this research was to examine the statistics for the regional runway incursion totals for 2014–2015 on the FAA Runway Safety website. Upon doing this, the observed data was categorized into a table by runway incursion totals by incident type for each region. It is of interest to know whether or not these runway incursions are dependent or independent of location. We want to know this to verify that the data distributions of the runway incursion totals by region that we have observed are not by chance. Intuitively, we would think that runway incursion rates would be dependent on region. To verify this, we used chi-squared test of independence to test the probability of independence. The two-way chi-squared test and hypothesis testing parameters for this are as follows.

$$\chi^2 = \sum_{i=1}^{n}\sum_{j=1}^{k} \frac{\left(O_{i,j} - E_{i,j}\right)^2}{E_{i,j}},$$

where

$O_{i,j}$ = observed value for cell i, j

$E_{i,j}$ = expected value for cell i, j

n = number of rows for incident type

k = number of columns for region

TABLE 14.4

Research Objectives and Tasks

Research Objective 1: Evaluate human causal elements that impact safety on the AOA.
Task 1—Evaluate the runway incursion incidents for 2014–2015 in the United States by region.
Task 2—Determine specific region, state, and airports to evaluate runway incursion rates and human causal elements.
Task 3—Investigate the NASA's ASRS database using ASIAS for selected airports for runway incursions events from 2014 to 2015 and identify top five most common human causal elements.
Task 4—Determine which of the human causal elements have the most impact on runway incursion rates.
Research Objective 2: Determine system architecture configuration for maximum reliability. Develop runway incursion detection module. Perform an operational demonstration with selected personnel.
Task 5—Establish a baseline and configuration method and set up accurate metrics for experiment.
Task 6—Determine and procure all equipment needed to develop incursion detection module.
Task 7—Identify persons of contact at airport and confirm their understanding of the project and agree on project boundaries.
Task 8—Conduct site visits.
Task 9—Identify two major "hotspots" at airport to implement testing of technology.
Task 10—Install the system, and test a prototype to ensure workability of system.
Task 11—Conduct reliability experiments.
Task 12—Perform an operational demonstration with selected personnel, and use feedback for updates.
Task 13—Redefine prototype, and improve design to develop final product.
Research Objective 3: Perform economic analysis, and evaluate the financial impacts with other solutions. Evaluate the impacts of different automated technologies. Determine the best automated technology to use. Determine legal aspect of runway incursion in terms of liability.
Task 14—Calculate NPV for runway incursion prevention system and other solutions.
Task 15—Calculate ROI for runway incursion prevention system.
Task 16—Investigate various case laws surrounding serious runway incursion incidents.

Null hypothesis:

    H_0: Incursion incident and Region are independent.

Alternative Hypothesis:

    H_a: Incursion incident and Region are not independent.

    Decision Rule: Reject H_0 if *p*-value is less than 0.05 significance level.

    Task 2—Determine specific region, state, and airports to evaluate runway incursion rates and HCEs.

After we determined whether or not the runway incursion data is dependent or independent of location, we chose to look at the runway incursion rates in the Southwest (ASW) region in the state of Texas. This location was chosen because the research is being done in this region. However, this can be expanded to any region. We researched all airports in the state of Texas for the purpose of identifying the top airports in Texas which accounted for most of the runway incursion incidents. Once this was determined, we performed another chi-squared test of independence to determine if runway incursion incidents are dependent on or independent of airport. Again, intuitively, we would assume that these runway incursion rates would be dependent on airport. However, we perform this statistical test to verify this relationship. The two-way chi-squared test and hypothesis testing parameters for this are as follows.

$$\chi^2 = \sum_{i=1}^{n}\sum_{j=1}^{k} \frac{\left(O_{i,\,j} - E_{i,\,j}\right)^2}{E_{i,\,j}},$$

where

    $O_{i,j}$ = observed value for cell i, j

    $E_{i,j}$ = expected value for cell i, j

    n = number of rows for incident type

    k = number of columns for airport

Null hypothesis:

    H_0: Incursion incident and airport are independent.

Alternative Hypothesis:

    H_a: Incursion incident and airport are not independent.

    Decision Rule: Reject H_0 if *p*-value is less than 0.05 significance level.

    Task 3—Investigate the NASA's ASRS database using ASIAS for selected airports for runway incursions events from 2014 to 2015, and identify top five most common HCEs.

Next, the task was to go to the ASIAS website and search the NASA's ASRS database for all the runway incursion incidents reported for the top five airports in Texas that account for most of the runway incursion events in Texas. Within the ASIAS database, ASRS allows the individual to sort runway incursion incidents by airport and a range of dates. Each report has its ASRS access number, as well as event date, contributing factors of the event (HCEs), environmental conditions, and a narrative of the reported incident per the individuals involved in the event. For each airport, all reports in the range of January 1, 2014–December 31, 2015 were examined. The output for the report examination was the contributing factor in terms of the HCE or elements that played a role in the incursion event. At that juncture, these HCEs were arranged in an Excel file and sorted by airport, ASRS access number, and the primary and secondary contributing factors for the event. Once in the Excel file, the HCEs were arranged by the sort and filter function in order to analyze the data and count which were the top five elements for the five airports. After this, this data was arranged into a table sorted by airport and top five HCEs in efforts to perform statistical analysis on the data. In order to analyze the data, we utilized a complete block design with airports being the blocking factor h and the HCEs being the treatments τ. The linear model formulation for the complete block design is as follows.

$$Y_{hi} = \mu_{..} + \theta_h + \tau_i + \varepsilon_{hi}, \varepsilon_{hi} \sim N\left(0, \sigma^2\right),$$

$$\text{for } h = 1,\ldots,b; \quad i = 1,\ldots,v,$$

where

Y_{hi} is the random variable response representing the measurement on treatment i observed in block h, and ε_{hi} is the associated random error

$\mu_{..}$ is the overall mean

θ_h is the blocking factor on the response

τ_i is the treatment effect on the response

$$H_o: \tau_1 = \tau_2 = \tau_3 = \tau_4 = \tau_5.$$

H_a: At least two of the τ_i differ.

Decision Rule: Reject H_o if $\dfrac{msT}{msE} > F_{v-1,bv-v-v+1,\infty}$.

It is a reasonable assumption to make that the blocks and the treatments do not interact. We used analysis of variance (ANOVA) to analyze the data.

Task 4—Determine which of the HCEs have the most impact on runway incursion rates.

From the output of our general linear model, we determined which of these HCEs had the most impact on the runway incursion rates.

Research Objective 2: Determine system architecture configuration for maximum reliability. Develop runway incursion detection module. Perform an operational demonstration with selected personnel.

Task 5—Establish a baseline and configuration method, and set up accurate metrics for experiment.

For our task 5, we wanted to establish our baseline and configurations by conducting two experiments. The first experiment tested our theoretical reliability of the runway incursion detection system and considered two different configurations for the antennas that will give us maximum readability for the automated devices to collect data. The second experiment was to test our outside environment in terms of noise level in dB at our respective areas close to where a runway incursion can occur. Our methodology for our experiments to test the reliability and the noise factor followed the format below.

14.7 Experimental Procedure

For our experiments, we worked with both University of Texas at Arlington RAID Labs to conduct our simulation of the reliability of the device and with the FAA air traffic controllers, air traffic management, and technical operations technicians to collect the noise levels out on the AOA surrounding the sites where the proposed system will be integrated. The following are steps of our experiment's procedure:

1. Problem Definition

    In this section, we defined our problem definition for the experiment and conducted site visits and spoke to various personnel regarding the input variables of the simulation model, the output variables, and factors that are of interest.

2. Model Definition

    The model definition was based on the factors including their levels for our experiment. For the reliability experiment, we looked at three factors: antenna configuration with two levels: configuration 1 and configuration 2; distance with three levels: 5, 15, and 25 ft; and device location with three levels: pocket, armband, and waist. For the noise factor experiment, we looked at two factors: sites with two levels: site 1 and site 2 and day with seven levels: Monday, Tuesday, Wednesday, Thursday, Friday, Saturday, and Sunday. The model is a multivariate response linear model. The experimental design was decided in this section.

3. Experiments

    After the model definition and experimental design, the experiments were conducted.

4. Statistical Analysis

    The analysis started with the preliminary analysis of the model assumptions. From there, we conducted the ANOVA. Lastly, we investigated the analysis of effects of the model.

14.8 Results and Conclusions

After the analysis, the final linear model and the results of the experiment were analyzed.

Task 6—Determine all equipment needed to develop incursion detection module.

This task allowed us to look into everything that would be necessary to develop the runway incursion detection module, as well as what it would take to procure the necessary parts.

Task 7—Identify persons of contact at airport, and confirm their understanding of the project, and agree on project boundaries.

Next, it was necessary for us to contact the appropriate individuals in the FAA who worked at the Dallas/Fort Worth Airport. The personnel we contacted were air traffic tower control management, air traffic controllers, and system specialist technicians.

Task 8—Conduct site visits.

Once we made the appropriate contacts, we scheduled times we can meet and talk to various personnel about the project, as well as conduct specific site visits on the AOA where we collected the noise level data.

Task 9—Identify two major "hotspots" at airport to implement testing of technology.

Through informal interviews with air traffic management, air traffic tower controllers, and system specialist technicians, it was determined where a runway incursion would mostly take place and where heightened attention of air traffic controllers and drivers on the AOA is needed; in this case, the system technicians should have equipment that needs to work throughout the AOA.

Task 10—Install the system, and test a prototype to ensure workability of system.

Theoretically, we wanted to install the system on the AOA at the hotspots, but due to regulations from the Dallas/Fort Worth Airport, before installing any new technology it has to go through the proper chain of command and then get approved by Dallas/Fort Worth Airport officials, which is a very lengthy process. So, we ran a simulated reliability experiment with the device at University of Texas at Arlington RAIDS lab. However, we got approval to get the dB noise levels on the AOA for the respective hotspots and surrounding area.

Task 11—Conduct the experiments.

The procedures for experiment 1 and experiment 2 are as follows.

14.8.1 Experiment 1 Procedure

Problem Definition:

For the first experiment, we wanted to test the reliability of the device to be able to accurately and effectively have the proper read reliability for the automated devices once in the interrogator zone of the system. We wanted to know what distance, antenna configuration, and position of the device would give us a maximum response. The system's reliability was established by read rate and signal strength.

Model Definition:

   I. *Experiment 1: System Reliability*

     A. Factors

       1. Factor 1: Antenna configuration with two levels (configuration 1, configuration 2)

       2. Factor 2: Distance with three levels (5, 15, 25 ft)

       3. Factor 3: Position of the device with three levels (pocket, arm, and waist)

B. Response variables
1. Read rate
2. Signal strength

Experiment:

We employed a three full factorial design with $r = 3$ replications (Table 14.5).
The design layout was as follows:

Three Factor Complete Factorial Experiment Layout with Three Replications
Factor 1 = Antenna Configuration—Two levels: Configuration 1 = 1, Configuration 2 = 2
Factor 2 = Distance—Three levels: 5ft = 1, 15 ft = 2, 25 ft = 3
Factor 3 = Tag Location—Three levels: Pocket = 1, Armband = 2, Waist = 3

Randomization of the experiment was performed using Minitab. The randomized data collection table is provided in the Appendix A.

TABLE 14.5

Experiment 1 Coded Layout

N	Factor 1	Factor 2	Factor 3
1	1	1	1
2	1	1	2
3	1	1	3
4	1	2	1
5	1	2	2
6	1	2	3
7	1	3	1
8	1	3	2
9	1	3	3
10	2	1	1
11	2	1	2
12	2	1	3
13	2	2	1
14	2	2	2
15	2	2	3
16	2	3	1
17	2	3	2
18	2	3	3
19	1	1	1
20	1	1	2
21	1	1	3
22	1	2	1
23	1	2	2
24	1	2	3
25	1	3	1
26	1	3	2
27	1	3	3
28	2	1	1
29	2	1	2
30	2	1	3
31	2	2	1

(Continued)

TABLE 14.5 (*Continued*)

Experiment 1 Coded Layout

N	Factor 1	Factor 2	Factor 3
32	2	2	2
33	2	2	3
34	2	3	1
35	2	3	2
36	2	3	3
37	1	1	1
38	1	1	2
39	1	1	3
40	1	2	1
41	1	2	2
42	1	2	3
43	1	3	1
44	1	3	2
45	1	3	3
46	2	1	1
47	2	1	2
48	2	1	3
49	2	2	1
50	2	2	2
51	2	2	3
52	2	3	1
53	2	3	2
54	2	3	3

The linear model formulation is as follows:

$$Y_{ijkt} = \mu_{...} + \alpha_i + \beta_j + \gamma_k + (\alpha\beta)_{ij} + (\alpha\gamma)_{ik} + (\beta\gamma)_{jk} + (\alpha\beta\gamma)_{ijk} + \varepsilon_{ijkt}$$

$$for\ i = 1,\ldots,a,\ j = 1,\ldots,b,\ k = 1,\ldots,c,\ and\ t = 1,\ldots,r.$$

ε_{ijkt} are *iid* $N(0,\sigma^2)$, and Z is the number of response variables.

Y_{ijkt} = *t*th response observed for *trt* (*i, j, k*)

$\mu_{...}$ = the overall mean

α_i = the effect on the response due to *i*th level of factor 1

β_j = the effect on the response due to *j*th level of factor 2

γ_k = the effect on the response due to *k*th level of factor 3

$(\alpha\beta)_{ij}$ = the interaction effect in *i*th and *j*th levels of factors 1 and 2

$(\alpha\gamma)_{ik}$ = the interaction effect in the *i*th and *k*th levels of factors 1 and 3

$(\beta\gamma)_{jk}$ = the interaction effect in the *j*th and *k*th levels of factors 2 and 3

$(\alpha\beta\gamma)_{ijk}$ = the interaction effect in *i*th, *j*th, and *k*th levels of factors 1, 2, and 3

Statistical Analysis:

The statistical analysis was conducted using Minitab.

Results and Conclusions:

The results and conclusion of this experiment are talked about in Chapters 4 and 5.

14.8.2 Experiment Procedure: 2

Problem Definition:

For experiment 2, we tested the outside noise level at two sites of the FAA technician and where the proposed system will be installed. We wanted to investigate the dB noise level because we wanted to know what the acceptable level for the persons carrying the device should be so that they may hear it effectively.

Model Definition:

II. *Experiment 2: Environment Noise Level*
  A. Factors
    1. Factor 1: Site with two levels (site 1, site 2)
    2. Factor 2: Days with seven levels (Mon, Tue, Wed, Thu, Fri, Sat, Sun)
  B. Response Variable
    1. dB level

Experiment:

We employed a two full factorial design with $r = 2$ replications.
The design layout is in Table 14.6.

Two Factor Complete Factorial Experiment Layout with Two Replications

Factor 1 = Sites—two levels—Site 1 = 1, Site 2 = 2

Factor 2 = Days—seven levels—Mon = 1, Tue = 2, Wed = 3, Thu = 4, Fri = 5, Sat = 6, Sun = 7

TABLE 14.6

Experiment 2 Coded Layout

N	Factor 1	Factor 2
1	1	1
2	1	2
3	1	3
4	1	4
5	1	5
6	1	6
7	1	7
8	2	1
9	2	2
10	2	3
11	2	4
12	2	5
13	2	6
14	2	7
15	1	1
16	1	2
17	1	3
18	1	4
19	1	5
20	1	6
21	1	7
22	2	1
23	2	2

(Continued)

TABLE 14.6 (*Continued*)

Experiment 2 Coded Layout

N	Factor 1	Factor 2
24	2	3
25	2	4
26	2	5
27	2	6
28	2	7

Randomization of the experiment was performed using Minitab. The randomized data collection table is provided in the Appendix A.

The linear model formulation is as follows:

for $i = 1, \ldots, a, j = 1, \ldots, b, k = 1, \ldots, c$, and $t = 1, \ldots, r$.

ε_{ijt} are *iid* $N(0, \sigma^2)$.

$Y_{ijt} = t$th response observed for *trt* (i, j)

$\mu_{..} =$ the overall mean

$\alpha_i =$ the effect on the response due to the ith level of factor 1

$\beta_j =$ the effect on the response due to the jth level of factor 2

$(\alpha\beta)_{ij} =$ the interaction effect in ith and jth levels of factors 1 and 2

Statistical Analysis:

The statistical analysis was conducted using Statistical Analysis Software (SAS) and Minitab.

Results and Conclusions:

The results and conclusion of this experiment are talked about in Chapters 4 and 5.

Task 12—Perform an operational demonstration with selected personnel, and use feedback for updates.

This task is now a future task once we are able to win a grant and get approved through the proper channels to carry this research full-scale and apply it at an airport.

Task 13—Redefine prototype and improve design to develop final product.

This task is now a future task once we are able to win a grant and get approved through the proper channels to carry this research full-scale and apply it at an airport.

Research Objective 3: Perform economic analysis and evaluate the financial impacts with other solutions. Evaluate the impacts of different automated technologies. Determine the best automated technology to use. Determine legal aspect of runway incursion in terms of liability.

Task 14—Calculate net present value (NPV) for runway incursion prevention system and other solutions.

Though the main concern of this dissertation was to investigate our runway incursion prevention system, this task had us look into the cost and NPV of employing such a system. Furthermore, we wanted to investigate other solutions that would achieve the similar goals as our system. Moreover, we wanted to see the cost of these other solutions and compare them to our system cost to confirm the economic viability of choosing such a solution.

Task 15—Calculate return on investment (ROI) for runway incursion prevention system.

After the NPV was calculated, we felt it important to know what our ROI would be if an airport or organization decided to invest into implementing this research.

Task 16—Investigate various case laws surrounding serious runway incursion incidents.

For this task, we researched various books and journals to see what the outcome in terms of liability was when a serious accident took place.

The *overall objective of this research* is to investigate a framework that leverages an RFID integrated with Zigbee location system (real-time location system (RTLS)) and human causal factors, data analytics and legal repository of information surrounding a runway incursion incident, and employee training and a decision support system. In the first stage of the framework, we want to define and correlate the HCEs and investigate what role they play in runway incursion rates. Also in the first stage of the framework, we will develop a working prototype that can reside on device and provide audible, visual, and vibrating alerts to the employee and that alerts them of their location when they are approaching a hazardous zone or are in one. In the second stage of the framework, we want to provide data analytics and legal information repository surrounding the issue of runway incursions in terms of liability when a severe incursion takes place. We *hypothesize* that there is a statistically significant relationship between human causal elements and runway incursions rates. We also *hypothesize* that the prototype is capable of alerting FAA technicians when they enter into protected areas that require authorization and presenting safety and security hazards in a reliable way.

14.8.3 Location of Experiments and Equipment Used

14.8.3.1 Results

This section discusses the results obtained from the analysis performed on the data from the research objectives using Excel, SAS, and Minitab.

14.8.3.1.1 Research Question 1 Results

Research Objective #1: Evaluate human causal elements that contribute to runway incursions on the AOA at an airport.

From our first task, we wanted to evaluate the runway incursion data for all of the regions in the United States by incident type. For this, we used a chi-squared test of independence to see if our runway incursion incidents are dependent or independent of region. The observed data is in Table 14.7, and the expected data is in Table 14.8.

H_o: Incident type and region are independent.

H_a: Incident type and region are not independent.

Chi-Sq = 101.902, DF = 16, p-value = 0.000

Conclusion: Reject the null hypothesis, and conclude that there is a relationship between incident type and region.

Since we have a p-value of practically zero and a high chi-square statistic, it is safe to say that runway incursion incidents are dependent on the region. This conclusion was somewhat intuitive; however, we proved our assumption by performing the chi-squared test. Subsequently, incidents are dependent on a specific region. Next, we chose the ASO Southern region, airports in Texas in particular, to further evaluate

TABLE 14.7

Observed Incursion Incident vs. Region

FY 2014–2015	AAL Alaska	ACE Central	AEA Eastern	AGL Great Lakes	ANE New England	ANM Northwest Mountain	ASO Southern	ASW Southwest	AWP Western Pacific	Total
OI	16	15	113	80	24	46	103	51	131	579
PD	64	30	137	183	33	146	315	237	500	1645
VPD	30	10	52	66	9	43	69	85	122	486
Total	110	55	302	329	66	235	487	373	753	2710

TABLE 14.8

Expected Incursion Incident vs. Region

FY 2014–2015	AAL Alaska	ACE Central	AEA Eastern	AGL Great Lakes	ANE New England	ANM Northwest Mountain	ASO Southern	ASW Southwest	AWP Western Pacific	Total
OI	23	12	65	80	14	50	104	80	161	579
PD	67	33	183	183	40	143	296	226	457	1645
VPD	20	10	52	54	12	42	87	67	135	486
Total	110	55	302	329	66	235	487	373	753	2710

our research question. Of the 117 airports in Texas, we looked at the top five airports that accounted for 51% of the total runway incursion rates for the state of Texas. Based on the statistics from the FAA Runway Safety Office, the top five airports were Dallas/Fort Worth (DFW), Dallas Love Field (DAL), George Bush Intercontinental (IAH), David Wayne Hooks Memorial (DWH), and Hobby Airport (HOU). For this, we used a chi-squared test of independence to see if our runway incursion incidents are dependent or independent of airport. The observed data is in Table 14.9, and the expected data is in Table 14.10.

H_0: Incident type and airports are independent.

H_a: Incident type and airports are not independent.

Chi-Sq = 52.001, DF = 8, p-value = 0.000

Two cells with expected counts less than 5.

Conclusion: Reject the null hypothesis, and conclude that there is an association between incident type and airports.

Since we have a p-value of practically zero, it is safe to say that runway incursion incidents are dependent on the particular airport as well. Again, this conclusion was somewhat intuitive based on our previous determination of location by region; however, we statistically proved our assumption by performing the chi-squared test. Subsequently, incidents are dependent on a specific region. Again, since we are located in Texas, and we know statistically that incursion incidents are dependent on airport, we further investigated our research question using these top five airports in Texas. Table 14.11 describes the distribution of incursion incidents that were attributed to these top human causal elements for these five airports. Our data was analyzed using a complete block design with airports as the blocking factor (Tables 14.12–14.16).

Based on our ANOVA results, we have a calculated F-value ratio of 8.09. Since our table value of $F_{4,16}$ is 5.85, we would reject the null hypothesis and conclude that at least two of the treatments, human causal elements, differ and have a different effect on the response, incursion incident rate. Furthermore, we can support our findings by examining our p-value. Since we have a p-value of 0.0009, we can also reject the null hypothesis since our level of significance of 0.05 is larger (Table 14.17).

TABLE 14.9

Observed Incursion Incident vs. TX Airport

FY 2014–2015	DFW	DAL	IAH	DWH	HOU	Total
OI	19	0	11	2	3	35
PD	15	26	6	38	14	99
VPD	8	7	3	17	5	40
Total	42	33	20	57	22	174

TABLE 14.10

Expected Incursion Incident vs. TX Airport

FY 2014–2015	DFW	DAL	IAH	DWH	HOU	Total
OI	8	7	4	12	4	35
PD	24	19	11	32	13	99
VPD	10	7	5	13	5	40
Total	42	33	20	57	22	174

TABLE 14.11

Runway Incursion Events Contributed to Human Causal Element per Airport

Airport 2014–2015	Distraction	Workload	Situational Awareness	Miscommunication	Confusion
DFW	5	27	36	10	12
DAL	3	10	19	6	5
IAH	3	16	29	9	9
DWH	1	1	4	2	1
HOU	1	2	8	1	3

TABLE 14.12

Descriptive Statistics for Human Causal Elements

Human Causal Element	N	Mean Rates	Standard Deviation Rate
Distraction = 1	5	2.6	1.6733201
Workload = 2	5	11.2	10.7563934
Situational awareness = 3	5	19.2	13.5535973
Miscommunication = 4	5	5.6	4.0373258
Confusion = 5	5	6	4.4721360

TABLE 14.13

Factor Information for Complete Block Design

Factor	Levels	Values
HCE	5	1, 2, 3, 4, 5
Airport	5	1, 2, 3, 4, 5

TABLE 14.14

ANOVA Results for Complete Block Design Model

Source	DF	SS	MS	F-Value	p-Value
Model	8	1784.880000	223.110000	8.48	0.0002
Error	16	420.960000	26.310000		
Corrected total	24	2205.840000			

TABLE 14.15

ANOVA Results Type I SS

Source	DF	Type I SS	MS	F-Value	p-Value
HCE	4	851.8400000	212.9600000	8.09	0.0009
Airport	4	933.0400000	233.2600000	8.87	0.0006

TABLE 14.16

ANOVA Results Type III SS

Source	DF	Type III SS	MS	F-Value	p-Value
HCE	4	851.8400000	212.9600000	8.09	0.0009
Airport	4	933.0400000	233.2600000	8.87	0.0006

TABLE 14.17

Model Summary

R-Square	Coefficient of Variation	Root MSE	Rates Mean
80.91%	57.50367	5.129327	8.92000

Also, examining good our R-square we can see that our data fits our model respectably well.

Figure 14.12 shows the box plot of the distribution of runway incursion rates by each human causal element. Again, distraction = 1, workload = 2, situational awareness = 3, miscommunication = 4, and confusion = 5. The box plot shows the mean and the quartiles for each human causal element. We see that the means for the incursion rates due to situational awareness and workload is very different from the other human causal elements (Tables 14.18–14.21).

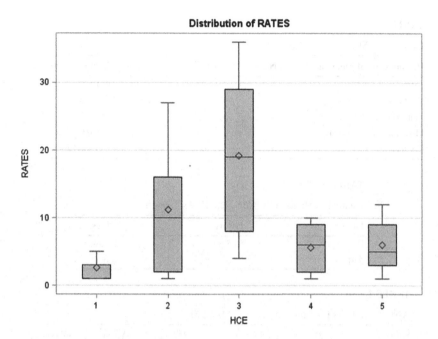

FIGURE 14.12   Box plot distribution of runway incursion rates by human causal element.

TABLE 14.18

Least Squares Means Adjustment for Multiple Comparisons: Tukey

HCEs	Rates LS Mean	LS Mean Number
Distraction = 1	2.6	1
Workload = 2	11.2	2
Situational awareness = 3	19.2	3
Miscommunication = 4	5.6	4
Confusion = 5	6	5

TABLE 14.19

Least Square Means for Effect of HCE

i/j	1	2	3	4	5
1		0.1073	0.0008	0.8832	0.8295
2	0.1073		0.1481	0.4466	0.5164
3	0.0008	0.1481		0.0054	0.0069
4	0.8832	0.4466	0.0054		0.9999
5	0.8295	0.5164	0.0069	0.9999	

Note: LS Mean (i) = LS Mean (j), and dependent variable is Rates.

TABLE 14.20

LS Mean with 95% Confident Limits

HCEs	Rates LS Mean	95% Confidence Limits
Distraction = 1	2.600000	(−2.262861, 7.462861)
Workload = 2	11.200000	(6.337139, 16.062861)
Situational awareness = 3	19.200000	(14.337139, 24.062861)
Miscommunication = 4	5.600000	(0.737139, 10.462861)
Confusion = 5	6.000000	(1.137139, 10.862861)

TABLE 14.21

Tukey's Simultaneous 95% Confidence Limits

i	j	Difference Between Means	Simultaneous 95% Confidence Limits for LS Mean (i) – LS Mean (j)
1	2	−8.6	(−18.538775, 1.338775)
1	3	−16.6	(−26.538775, −6.661225)
1	4	−3.0	(−12.938775, −12.938775)
1	5	−3.4	(−13.338775, −13.338775)
2	3	−8.0	(−17.938775, 1.938775)
2	4	5.6	(−4.338775, 15.538775)
2	5	5.2	(−4.738775, 15.138775)
3	4	13.6	(3.661225, 23.538775)
3	5	13.2	(3.261225, 23.138775)
4	5	−0.4	(−10.338775, 9.538775)

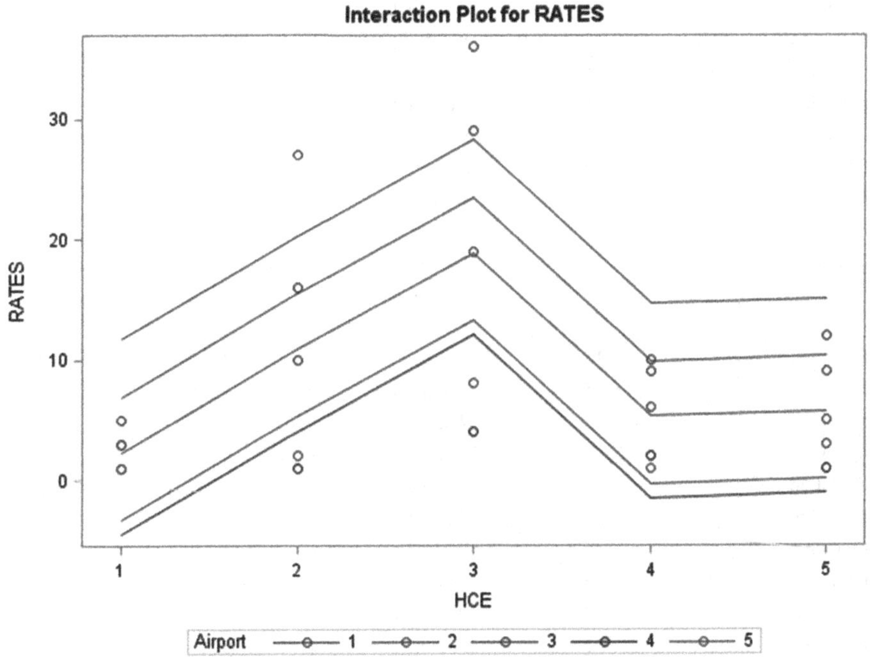

FIGURE 14.13 Interaction plot for human causal elements and airports.

After examination of Tukey's simultaneous 95% confidence limits, we see that pairs 1 and 4, 1 and 5, 3 and 4, and 3 and 5 do not contain zero in their confidence interval. This means that these pairs have statistically different means. The other pairs are considered similar. Furthermore, since all observations follow the same pattern in Figure 4.2, it confirms our initial assumption that there is no interaction between the block and the treatments. The interaction plots for rates are in Figure 14.13.

14.8.3.1.2 Research Question 2 Results

Research Objective #2: Develop runway incursion detection module and perform an operational demonstration with selected personnel. Determine system architecture configuration for maximum reliability.

Experiment 1: System Reliability

Because of limitations of installing actual equipment on AOA, test will be done based on reliability testing of device in terms of read rate and signal strength (Tables 14.22 and 14.23).

TABLE 14.22

Experiment 1 Output Table with Decoded Factors and Responses

Factor 1 Antenna Configuration	Factor 2 Distance (ft)	Factor 3 Tag Location	Response 1 Signal Strength (dBm)	Response 2 Read Rate (Reads/s)
Configuration 1	5	Pocket	−62	2.5
Configuration 1	5	Armband	−57	2.2
Configuration 1	5	Waist	−58	1.3
Configuration 1	15	Pocket	−63	2.8
Configuration 1	15	Armband	−60	3.1
Configuration 1	15	Waist	−65	3.2
Configuration 1	25	Pocket	−67	2.6
Configuration 1	25	Armband	−64	2.9
Configuration 1	25	Waist	−68	2.1
Configuration 2	5	Pocket	−59	3.3
Configuration 2	5	Armband	−57	3.2
Configuration 2	5	Waist	−58	1.5
Configuration 2	15	Pocket	−61	2.0
Configuration 2	15	Armband	−60	2.7
Configuration 2	15	Waist	−63	2.2
Configuration 2	25	Pocket	−65	1.3
Configuration 2	25	Armband	−62	1.5
Configuration 2	25	Waist	−63	0.9
Configuration 1	5	Pocket	−60	2.6
Configuration 1	5	Armband	−55	2.1
Configuration 1	5	Waist	−59	1.7
Configuration 1	15	Pocket	−62	2.4
Configuration 1	15	Armband	−61	3.0
Configuration 1	15	Waist	−68	2.9
Configuration 1	25	Pocket	−66	2.3
Configuration 1	25	Armband	−63	2.8
Configuration 1	25	Waist	−69	2.0
Configuration 2	5	Pocket	−57	3.0
Configuration 2	5	Armband	−55	3.6
Configuration 2	5	Waist	−59	2.0
Configuration 2	15	Pocket	−60	2.1
Configuration 2	15	Armband	−62	2.9
Configuration 2	15	Waist	−65	2.3
Configuration 2	25	Pocket	−66	1.5
Configuration 2	25	Armband	−61	1.9
Configuration 2	25	Waist	−65	1.3
Configuration 1	5	Pocket	−63	2.7
Configuration 1	5	Armband	−58	2.9
Configuration 1	5	Waist	−59	1.8
Configuration 1	15	Pocket	−64	2.9

(Continued)

TABLE 14.22 (*Continued*)

Experiment 1 Output Table with Decoded Factors and Responses

Factor 1 Antenna Configuration	Factor 2 Distance (ft)	Factor 3 Tag Location	Response 1 Signal Strength (dBm)	Response 2 Read Rate (Reads/s)
Configuration 1	15	Armband	−59	3.0
Configuration 1	15	Waist	−66	2.0
Configuration 1	25	Pocket	−67	2.4
Configuration 1	25	Armband	−63	2.8
Configuration 1	25	Waist	−69	1.3
Configuration 2	5	Pocket	−57	3.6
Configuration 2	5	Armband	−55	3.7
Configuration 2	5	Waist	−56	2.3
Configuration 2	15	Pocket	−60	2.4
Configuration 2	15	Armband	−59	2.7
Configuration 2	15	Waist	−62	2.2
Configuration 2	25	Pocket	−64	1.7
Configuration 2	25	Armband	−61	1.9
Configuration 2	25	Waist	−64	1.2

TABLE 14.23

Factor Information with Levels for Experiment 1

Factor	Type	Levels	Values
Antenna configuration (Ant Conf)	Fixed	2	1, 2
Distance	Fixed	3	1, 2, 3
Device position (Dev Pos)	Fixed	3	1, 2, 3

Source	DF	Seq SS	Adj SS	Adj MS	F-Value	p-Value
Ant Conf	1	64.463	64			
Distance	2	428.037				
Dev Pos	2	127.148				
Ant Conf*Distance	2	2.581				
Ant Conf*Dev Pos	2	11.370				
Distance*Dev Conf	4	34.963				
Ant Conf*Dist*Dev Pos	4	15.852				
Error	36	45.333				
Total	53	729.648				

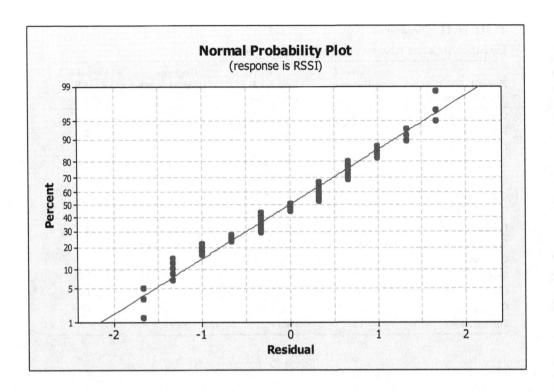

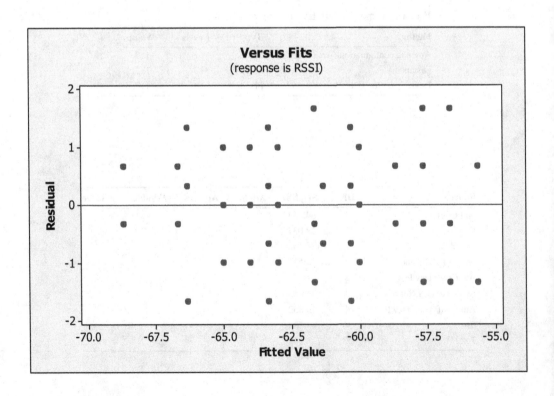

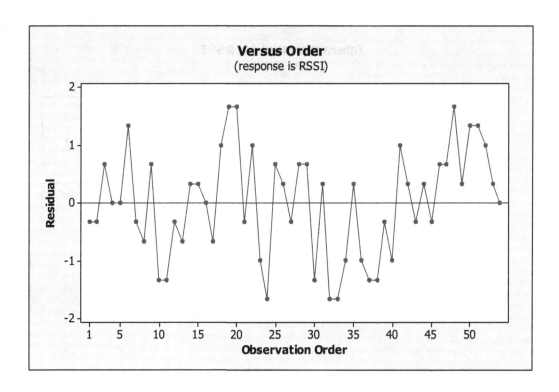

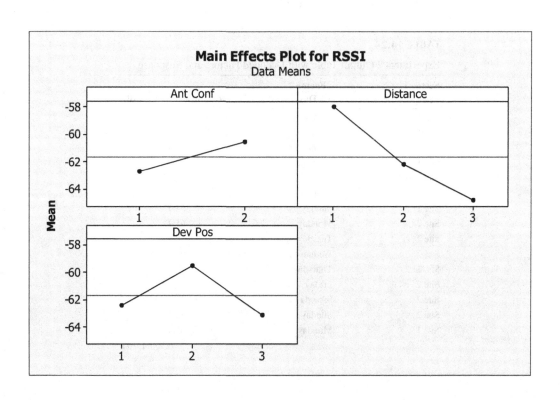

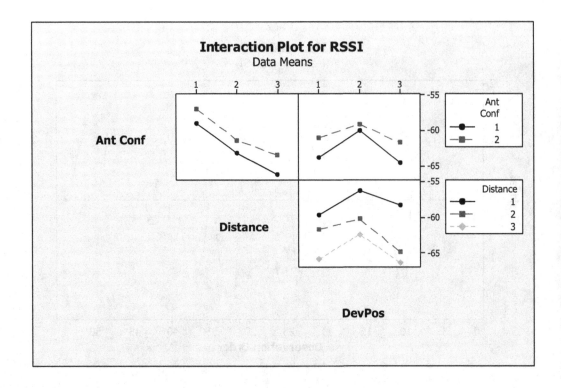

Experiment 2: Environment Noise Levels (Table 14.24)

TABLE 14.24

Experiment 2 Output Table with Decoded Factors and Response

Factor 1 Site	Factor 2 Day	Response Average (dB)
Site 1	Monday	57.6
Site 1	Tuesday	53.4
Site 1	Wednesday	55.4
Site 1	Thursday	52.9
Site 1	Friday	54.3
Site 1	Saturday	56.6
Site 1	Sunday	52.3
Site 2	Monday	61.2
Site 2	Tuesday	58.3
Site 2	Wednesday	54.3
Site 2	Thursday	55.9
Site 2	Friday	53.9
Site 2	Saturday	58.7
Site 2	Sunday	60.2
Site 1	Monday	53.4

(Continued)

TABLE 14.24 (*Continued*)

Experiment 2 Output Table with Decoded Factors and Response

Factor 1 Site	Factor 2 Day	Response Average (dB)
Site 1	Tuesday	54.9
Site 1	Wednesday	52.6
Site 1	Thursday	56.2
Site 1	Friday	55.3
Site 1	Saturday	56.9
Site 1	Sunday	53.2
Site 2	Monday	56.8
Site 2	Tuesday	59.3
Site 2	Wednesday	61.3
Site 2	Thursday	58.9
Site 2	Friday	57.6
Site 2	Saturday	57.9
Site 2	Sunday	59.4

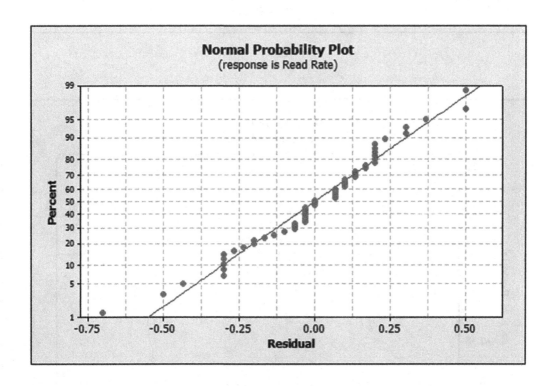

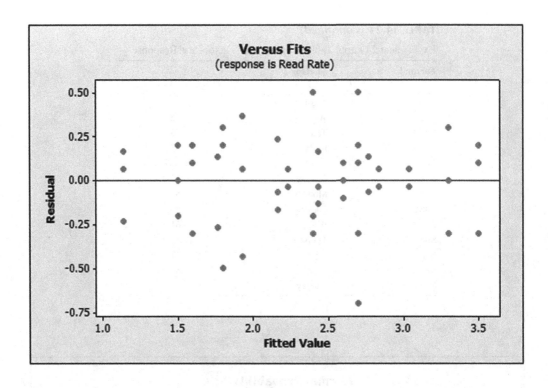

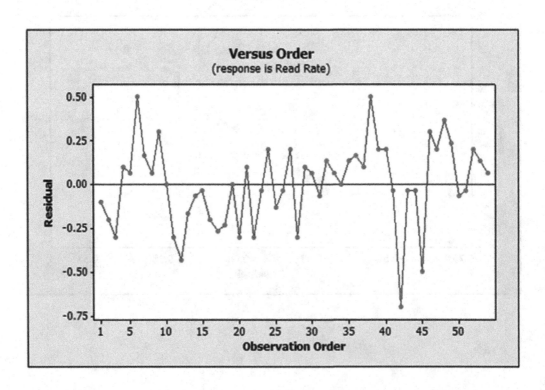

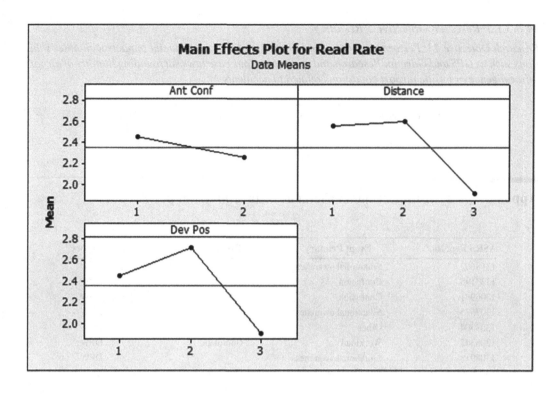

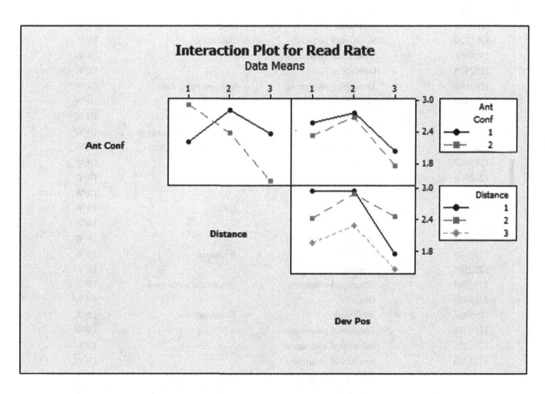

14.8.3.1.3 Research Objective 3 Results

Research Objective #3: Perform economic analysis and evaluate the financial impacts with other solutions such as GPS and Garmin. Research and analyze various case laws surrounding liability of airport for negligence or unsafe airport conditions related to accidents

Decision Criteria	RFID	RFID and Zigbee	GPS
NPV			

Appendix 14.A: Human Causal Element Data Collection per Airport

ASRS Rep. No.	Event Primary	Event Contributing	Airport
1318602	Situational awareness		DFW
1322198	Confusion		DFW
1306991	Confusion		DFW
1307525	Situational awareness		DFW
1308304	Other		DFW
1308342	Workload	Confusion	DFW
1308918	Situational awareness		DFW
1312889	Situational awareness	Confusion	DFW
1313001	Situational awareness	Miscommunication	DFW
1300243	Situational awareness		DFW
1300748	Workload	Distraction	DFW
1301720	Situational awareness	Confusion	DFW
1304801	Situational awareness		DFW
1292925	Distraction		DFW
1293168	Situational awareness	Miscommunication	DFW
1293864	Situational awareness		DFW
1297464	Confusion	Miscommunication	DFW
1284259	Time pressure	Situational awareness	DFW
1284304	Time pressure	Situational awareness	DFW
1285669	Other		DFW
1286504	Other		DFW
1286573	Workload		DFW
1289683	Workload	Other	DFW
1276702	Other		DFW
1276955	Situational awareness		DFW
1279745	Workload	Workload	DFW
1282589	Training		DFW
1283584	Situational awareness	Situational awareness	DFW
1283699	Other		DFW
1268324	Workload	Workload	DFW
1269078	Situational awareness		DFW
1271231	Situational awareness		DFW
1271446	Situational awareness		DFW
1271867	Situational awareness	Situational awareness	DFW
1272529	Workload	Workload	DFW

(Continued)

ASRS Rep. No.	Event Primary	Event Contributing	Airport
1273805	Workload	Workload	DFW
1273854	Other		DFW
1274489	Other		DFW
1259252	Time pressure		DFW
1266437	Other		DFW
1266438	Human–machine interface		DFW
1254520	Situational awareness		DFW
1254923	Workload		DFW
1256687	Miscommunication		DFW
1258312	Workload		DFW
1258349	Other		DFW
1245605	Workload		DFW
1245641	Distraction		DFW
1246187	Other		DFW
1246454	Situational awareness		DFW
1246791	Other		DFW
1247457	Confusion		DFW
1247464	Confusion		DFW
1247781	Situational awareness		DFW
1249434	Situational awareness		DFW
1241381	Other		DFW
1229708	Workload	Workload	DFW
1231304	Situational awareness	Situational awareness	DFW
1232738	Situational awareness		DFW
1235321	Workload	Workload	DFW
1236080	Situational awareness	Situational awareness	DFW
1238005	Situational awareness		DFW
1227038		Situational awareness	DFW
1228645	Workload		DFW
1214992	Other		DFW
1215270	Other		DFW
1215488	Workload		DFW
1216908	Situational awareness		DFW
1218429	Situational awareness		DFW
1219495	Workload		DFW
1221365	Miscommunication		DFW
1207796	Situational awareness		DFW
1209253	Miscommunication		DFW
1211415	Other		DFW
1211416	Human–machine interface	Confusion	DFW
1214122	Workload		DFW
1205119	Other		DFW
1205132	Situational awareness		DFW
1206526	Situational awareness	Situational awareness	DFW
1207473	Troubleshooting		DFW
1202663	Workload		DFW
1186006	Other		DFW
1187848	Workload		DFW
1191087	Situational awareness		DFW

(Continued)

ASRS Rep. No.	Event Primary	Event Contributing	Airport
1176977	Distraction		DFW
1177750	Other		DFW
1181206	Training		DFW
1182315	Confusion		DFW
1168197	Other		DFW
1166840	Time pressure		DFW
1167352	Other		DFW
1167363	Workload		DFW
1167442	Training		DFW
1167841	Distraction		DFW
1158665	Workload		DFW
1141859	Miscommunication		DFW

2014–2015

#	ASRS Acesn Nbr	Event Primary	Event Contrib	Airport
1	1153171	Workload		DAL
2	1162104	Confusion		DAL
3	1163517	Distraction	Distraction	DAL
4	1164386	Workload	Workload	DAL
5	1172499	Workload		DAL
6	1183922	Confusion		DAL
7	1193541	Situational awareness		DAL
8	1195640	Situational awareness		DAL
9	1205167	Other/unknown		DAL
10	1205170	Workload		DAL
11	1205219	Situational awareness		DAL
12	1215138	Situational awareness		DAL
13	1217141	Situational awareness		DAL
14	1218110	Human–machine interface		DAL
15	1218188	Human–machine interface		DAL
16	1227401	Training/qualification		DAL
17	1229437	Situational awareness		DAL
18	1230564	Distraction		DAL
19	1234287	Workload	Workload	DAL
20	1234930	Situational awareness		DAL
21	1238465	Situational awareness	Communication breakdown	DAL
22	1243605	Confusion		DAL
23	1245486	Confusion	Confusion	DAL
24	1246382	Situational awareness		DAL
25	1268232	Workload		DAL
26	1268639	Other/unknown		DAL
27	1274296	Situational awareness		DAL
28	1281127	Workload		DAL
29	1283070	Situational awareness		DAL
30	1291622	Training/qualification	Workload	DAL
31	1291630	Human–machine interface		DAL
32	1294257	Situational awareness		DAL
33	1297343	Situational awareness		DAL

(Continued)

2014–2015

#	ASRS Acesn Nbr	Event Primary	Event Contrib	Airport
34	1299971	Situational awareness		DAL
35	1300884	Situational awareness	Situational awareness	DAL
36	1308700	Situational awareness		DAL
37	1309262	Situational awareness		DAL
38	1310746	Situational awareness		DAL
39	1319541	Training/qualification		DAL
1	1145172	Troubleshooting		IAH
2	1149118	Situational awareness		IAH
3	1170897	Confusion	Confusion	IAH
4	1176567	Situational awareness		IAH
5	1177592	Workload	Workload	IAH
6	1177609	Workload		IAH
7	1177884	Workload		IAH
8	1177967	Human–machine interface		IAH
9	1177972	Confusion		IAH
10	1177994	Training/qualification		IAH
11	1178017	Human–machine interface		IAH
12	1178276	Time pressure	Time pressure	IAH
13	1179710	Human–machine interface		IAH
14	1180935	Confusion		IAH
15	1183317	Distraction		IAH
16	1184912	Workload		IAH
17	1185220	Human–machine interface		IAH
18	1185233	Training/qualification		IAH
19	1186944	Time pressure	Workload	IAH
20	1187998	Distraction	Distraction	IAH
21	1188003	Situational awareness		IAH
22	1188720	Situational awareness		IAH
23	1192434	Human–machine interface		IAH
24	1196111	Training/qualification		IAH
25	1196904	Human–machine interface		IAH
26	1199064	Time pressure		IAH
27	1200599	Human–machine interface		IAH
28	1201653	Workload		IAH
29	1201665	Training/qualification		IAH
30	1203381	Situational awareness	Communication breakdown	IAH
31	1204865	Time pressure		IAH
32	1205460	Situational awareness		IAH
33	1205918	Workload		IAH
34	1210787	Situational awareness		IAH
35	1210930	Situational awareness		IAH
36	1212230	Training/qualification		IAH
37	1215426	Situational awareness	Situational awareness	IAH
38	1219374	Confusion		IAH
39	1222500	Other/unknown		IAH
40	1224652	Confusion		IAH
41	1226218	Training/qualification		IAH
42	1228204	Situational awareness	Situational awareness	IAH

(Continued)

2014–2015

#	ASRS Acesn Nbr	Event Primary	Event Contrib	Airport
43	1237574	Situational awareness		IAH
44	1237636	Human–machine interface	Human–machine interface	IAH
45	1239359	Situational awareness		IAH
46	1240349	Communication breakdown	Situational awareness	IAH
47	1242132	Fatigue		IAH
48	1242670	Training/qualification		IAH
49	1244495	Training/qualification		IAH
50	1244717	Time pressure		IAH
51	1245533	Other/unknown		IAH
52	1246649	Communication breakdown		IAH
53	1247669	Other/unknown		IAH
54	1259251	Workload		IAH
55	1259761	Workload		IAH
56	1260500	Situational awareness		IAH
57	1263786	Fatigue		IAH
58	1264970	Confusion		IAH
59	1265502	Workload	Workload	IAH
60	1266526	Situational awareness		IAH
61	1269051	Human–machine interface		IAH
62	1269969	Training/qualification		IAH
63	1271194	Human–machine interface		IAH
64	1275667	Workload	Workload	IAH
65	1277581	Training/qualification		IAH
66	1277678	Situational awareness		IAH
67	1278319	Situational awareness		IAH
68	1278868	Communication breakdown		IAH
69	1281161	Communication breakdown		IAH
70	1284590	Time pressure		IAH
71	1287754	Situational awareness	Situational awareness	IAH
72	1289395	Situational awareness	Workload	IAH
73	1291626	Confusion	Troubleshooting	IAH
74	1293693	Situational awareness	Situational awareness	IAH
75	1294251	Situational awareness		IAH
76	1297245	Situational awareness		IAH
77	1301946	Situational awareness		IAH
78	1309867	Confusion	Situational awareness	IAH
79	1309869	Workload		IAH
80	1311541	Situational awareness		IAH
1	1181991	Situational awareness		DWH
2	1197457	Communication breakdown	Confusion	DWH
3	1204727	Training/workload		DWH
4	1249539	Situational awareness		DWH
5	1254273	Distraction		DWH
6	1259320	Situational awareness		DWH
7	1274130	Communication breakdown		DWH
8	1310021	Situational awareness		DWH

(*Continued*)

2014–2015

#	ASRS Acesn Nbr	Event Primary	Event Contrib	Airport
1	1142978	Confusion		HOU
2	1147335	Training/workload		HOU
3	1175261	Situational awareness	Training/qualification	HOU
4	1176618	Workload		HOU
5	1185701	Physiological/other		HOU
6	1206403	Situational awareness		HOU
7	1211917	Situational awareness		HOU
8	1227427	Physiological/confusion		HOU
9	1228435	Other/unknown		HOU
10	1238470	Situational awareness		HOU
11	1244548	Troubleshooting		HOU
12	1256817	Human–machine interface/distraction		HOU
13	1282383	Training/qualification		HOU
14	1305477	Situational awareness	Situational awareness	HOU
15	1312818	Confusion		HOU
16	1312861	Communication breakdown		HOU
17	1315699	Situational awareness	Situational awareness	HOU

REFERENCES

Buyya, R., & Vahid, A. D. (May 2016). *Internet of Things: Principles and Paradigms*. Elsevier Science.

Cambell, R., & Bagshaw, M. (2002). *Human Performance and Limitations in Aviation*. Malden, MA: Blackwell Science Ltd.

Clampitt, H. G., & Jones, E. C. (2006). The RFID Certification Textbook. PWD Group.

Cornell Univeristy Law School. (2016). *Legal Information Institute*. Retrieved from Cornell University Law School: www.law.cornell.edu/wex/aviation

Federal Aviation Administration. (2011). AMT Handbook Addendum Human Factors. Retrieved from Federal Aviation Administration: www.faa.gov/regulations_policies/handbooks_manuals/aircraft/media/AMT_Handbook_Addendum_Human_Factors.pdf

Federal Aviation Administration. (June 2015). *National Runway Safety Report 2013–2014*. Washington, DC.

Federal Aviation Administration. (2016). *National Runway Safety Plan 2015–2017*. Washington DC: ATO Safety and Technical Training.

Groover, M. P. (2007). *Work Systems and the Methods, Measurment, and Management of Work*. Uppper Saddle River, NJ: Prentice Hall.

Larsen, P. B., Sweeny, J. C., & Gillick, J. E. (2006). *Aviation Law: Cases, Laws and Related Sources*. New York: Transnational Publisher's Inc.

Mullen, J., & Singh, H. S. (2015, December 17). Air India employee dies after being sucked into plane engine at airport. Retrieved from CNN: www.cnn.com/2015/12/17/asia/air-india-engineer-sucked-into-plane-engine/

Ranieri, A. (2016). Aiport Surface Detection Equipment Model X Safe Airport Traffic under all Weather Conditions. Retrieved from SAAB Solutions: http://saab.com/security/air-traffic-management/air-traffic-management/asde-x/

Rouse, M. (2016). Definition of ICT. Retrieved from Tech Target: http://searchcio.techtarget.com/definition/ICT-information-and-communications-technology-or-technologies

Sadler, K. (2015, September 22). Funding for U.S. airports at risk from runway incursions. Retrieved from International Airport Review: www.internationalairportreview.com/20526/airport-news/funding-for-u-s-airports-at-risk-from-runway-incursions/

U.S. Department of Transportation. (2015, April 21). Runway Safety. Retrieved from Federal Aviation Administration: www.faa.gov/airports/runway_safety/news/runway_incursions/

U.S. Department of Transportation. (January 2015). *The Economic Impact on Civil Aviation on the U.S. Economy.* Washighton, DC: Federal Aviation Administration Communications.

U.S. Department of Transportation FAA. (May 2016). Runway Safety Hot Spots List. Retrieved from Federal Aviation Administration: www.faa.gov/airports/runway_safety/hotspots/hotspots_list/

Wikipedia Foundation Inc. (2016, August 12). Aviation Law. Retrieved from Wikipedia the Free Encylopedia: https://en.wikipedia.org/wiki/Aviation_law

15

A Methodology to Evaluate Obsolete Inventory in Healthcare

Erick C. Jones and Rama K. Thummalapalli

The most dangerous kind of waste is the waste we do not recognize.

Shigeo Shingo

15.1 Introduction

The supply chain (SC) costs of any organization contribute the major part of the investments. The investments in SC must be monitored continuously, and some improvement decisions to optimize the SC can yield positive strategic results. Savings from the implementations of these strategic decisions can be utilized in the overall improvement of the organization. The focus of this research problem is continuous improvement recommendations for managing inventory costs in healthcare facility. These improvements can be achieved by a decision tool developed from this research. The SC includes warehouses and storerooms, purchasing and distribution practices, and end customer defined as personnel who order supplies from the warehouses.

The scope of the research is to lead the overall continuous improvement efforts in the SC which includes analysis of current processes, problem quantification, and documentation of relevant best practices (including typical SC facility types and amount inventory held).

From the literature review of an article by DeScioli and Byrnes (2001), the SC must enable this strategy by:

- Ensuring product availability
- Minimizing storage space
- Reducing material handling time and costs for all medical staff (nurses, pharmacists, physicians)
- Minimizing non-liquid assets (inventory) and maximize the value added tasks.

The improvement criteria based on research objectives are:

- Utilizing ABC inventory analysis to categorize important inventory for setting inventory policy
- Utilizing available data metrics created in order to measure scope of inventory costs to the warehouse
- Comparison of relevant metrics evaluated for ease of use to show "hard evidence" of problems
- Utilizing optimization techniques and current SC costs to derive most cost efficient types of warehouses for the organization.

The major anticipated benefits of this research are:

- Reduction of SC logistics cost of distribution of products
- Improvement in inventory control

- Improvement in warehousing functions such as reduced travel time, improved inventory accuracy and fill rate, and improvement in the management of item cube utilization
- Identification of relevant systems needed to support better inventory visibility at the warehouse.

Effective use of resources does not always correlate to reduction of resources that are currently available. In many organizations, some of the services deploy more resources than they intend to use or deploy lesser resources than the required service levels, thus creating an imbalance in the overall services. The decision to develop a plan for the effective usage of resources must be developed strategically by top-level management with the inputs from middle and lower level management. The theory or principles of resource management or material management are integrated into supply chain management (SCM) or sometimes also referred to as logistics management.

Creating an effective SC with respect to the strategy and the nature of any organization is the primary area of improvement and often considered as quick hits for improvement (Figure 15.1).

The design of SCs is very complex and must satisfy many federal and institutional regulations. The SC products in an organization consist of high-cost and low-cost items that may be perishable and at times non-perishable and products that are consumed at varying demand rates. The demand for products depends on various customer requests. In addition, there are highly critical and non-critical items. SCs have to be constructed such that they can handle products with all combinations of high criticality, low volume, high cost, and perishable goods. An organization's size, geographic location, diversification, and various specializations all affect the nature of its service level, and, hence, the requirements of its SC. Likewise, each department/division within an organization is unique. The variety of products and demand of those products, for example in a healthcare facility, vary greatly from an emergency room to a cardiac laboratory to a primary clinic.

Therefore, the optimal SC in one area of a particular hospital may not be necessarily the best solution for another area in that hospital or in any other hospital. Nor should the SC policy for a particular product within an area be identical to that of other products in the same area. For that reason, this study focuses on developing an SC decision criterion within a healthcare organization that can improve the standard operation procedures (SOPs). That is, the SC developed for a particular product should reflect the nature of that product; for example, different products may require different quantity levels on hand. The research proposes that a healthcare organization should develop its SC for a specific warehouse based on the demand level and perishability, variability, physical size, criticality, and product's unit cost. Thus, a healthcare organization requires a dynamic SC policy in order to achieve its mission and goals of service to patients without incurring prohibitive costs.

The continuous improvement process is initiated by understanding the process and the product flow from the distributors (or manufacturer's) shipping dock to the points of care but does not address the SC design elements at the distributor or manufacturer. Improvement of SC indicates an improvement in the inventory levels. Inventory level is an indicator of investments of an organization, and holding inventory consumes space and requires resources to maintain and protect them from damages. In this process of

Supply Chain Definition

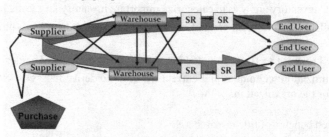

Procurement ⟶ Supplier ⟶ Warehouse ⟶ Stock Room(SR) ⟶ End User

FIGURE 15.1 SC in an organization.

holding inventory, some of the product inventory may become obsolete and useless. From the discussion above, it can be noted that inventory is the crucial component of healthcare organization and it must be handled carefully.

15.2 Background

The theory of SC and inventory control can be dated back to the early 19th century. Inventory theory has been studied by many researchers, and they have developed a logical and theoretical methodology to understand the importance of inventory and how important it was to have accurate information of inventory on hand and not to have any inventory on hand (also called as Just In Time (JIT) methodology). The process of determining the safety stock and having sufficient inventory on hand has been termed as "economic order quantity" (EOQ). EOQ was first derived by F. W. Harris. The EOQ concept has been at the core of inventory theory and has been widely used. Apart from evolution of EOQ, the level of quantity in inventory for sudden change in product demand is known as the buffer stock.

Classical buffer-stock principles date back to 1934 when R. H. Wilson advanced the reorder-point concept, in which he suggested the reorder-point concept must be used in combination with the Harris EOQ formula (Wilson 1934). Wilson presented the ideal ordering point for each stocked item as "the least number of units on the shelves, when a restocking order is started, which will prevent the item from running out of stock more often than is desirable for efficient operation". That least number of units includes enough stock to cover the usual lead time, plus a safety or buffer stock for uncertainty. In 2004, Nicole DeHoratius observed from nearly 370,000 inventory records from 37 stores of one retailer that 65% of the records were inaccurate. That is, the recorded inventory level of an item fails to match the quantity found in the store. Figure 15.2 explains an example of SC model with suppliers, distributors, manufacturers, wholesalers, retailers/customers. The next section presents a detailed background review of the concept of EOQ.

15.2.1 EOQ Models

EOQ is essentially an accounting formula that determines the point at which the combination of order costs and inventory carrying costs are the least. The result is the most cost-effective quantity of products to order. In purchasing, this is known as the order quantity; in manufacturing, it is known as the

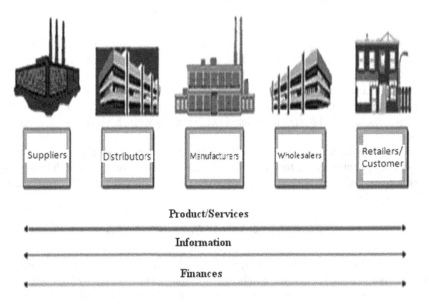

FIGURE 15.2 The layout of SC.

production lot size. In an article by Rogers and Tsubakitani (1991), the focus was on finding the optimal par levels for the lower echelons to minimize penalty costs subjected to the maximum inventory investment across all lower echelons being constrained by a budgeted value. The article provides a methodology that can determine the optimal par levels by a critical ratio (for the newsboy model) adjusted by the Lagrange multiplier related to the budget constraint. Sinha and Matta (1991) analyzed a multi-product system where they focused on minimizing holding costs at both echelon levels plus penalty costs at the lower echelon level. Their results indicate that par level at the lower echelon level is determined by the critical ratio while the par level for the upper echelon is determined by a search of the holding cost function at that level. Detailed explanation about two-echelon and one-echelon SC model has been provided in the later part of this chapter.

Schonberger and Andriessen (1982) illustrate the trade-offs associated with decreasing the setup cost in the classical EOQ model. One of the objectives of this paper is to establish a framework for studying those trade-offs. A research survey conducted by J. E. Holsenback in 2007 demonstrates the necessity of accurately measuring and monitoring inventory holding costs (IHCs). The study further demonstrates that knowledge of the underlying statistical pattern of supply and demand variations can significantly improve forecasting and impact the appropriate levels of safety stock inventory in a variety of industries. IHC assumes that it is linearly proportional to the amount of inventory held, when the rate itself very well may decay (or increase) with increasing quantities. In fact, IHC may change from one accounting period to the next. Failure to accurately determine IHC and use this cost to make decisions fails to recognize that inventory can represent one-third to one-half of a company's assets.

A company with a 36% IHC will pay for the inventory twice in slightly more than 2 years: once to purchase it and a second time to carry it for about 25 months. Hence, it seems problematic that nearly one-half of companies do not use IHC to make their inventory management decisions. The IHC affects profitability and may affect a company's business plan in terms of make-buy, or make-to-order/make-to-stock, as well as other top-level decisions (IOMA, Dec. 2002). While EOQ may not apply to every inventory situation, most organizations will find it beneficial in at least some aspect of their operation. Anytime you have repetitive purchasing or planning of an item, EOQ should be considered. Obvious applications for EOQ are purchase-to-stock distributors and make-to-stock manufacturers; however, make-to-order manufacturers should also consider EOQ when they have multiple orders or release dates for the same items and when planning components and sub-assemblies.

$$EOQ = \frac{\sqrt{2*\text{Annual usage in units*order cost}}}{\sqrt{\text{Annual carrying cost}}}$$

The inputs for calculating EOQ are annual usage, ordering costs, carrying costs, and miscellaneous costs. The values for order cost and carrying cost should be evaluated at least once per year taking into account any changes in interest rates, storage costs, and operational costs. A related calculation is the total annual cost calculation.

Ordering costs are the sum of the fixed costs that are incurred each time an item is ordered. These costs are not associated with the quantity ordered but primarily with physical activities required to process the order.

In research thesis by DeScioli and Byrnes (2001), the main objective of the research was to develop an inventory policy to optimize the total material management costs associated with inventory carrying costs, ordering costs, and stock-out costs. For any given product, the total cost, TC, can be expressed by the formula listed below:

$$TC = (I_{avg} * C_c) + (A * N_O) + (CS_O * NS_O)$$

I_{avg} is the average inventory, C_c is the carrying cost, A is the ordering cost, N_O is the number of orders, CS_O is the stock-out cost, and NS_O is the number of stock-outs. The research by DeScioli compares four SC policies and investigates the efficiency of each of the four SCs based on carrying cost, total inventory cost, ordering cost, and shortage costs.

15.2.1.1 Carrying Cost

Figure 15.3 shows the breakdown of different costs into categories that would be classified under carrying costs. Carrying cost sometimes is also referred as holding cost. It is the cost associated by having inventory on hand and primarily comprises of the factors that are associated with the dollars invested for having sufficient inventory on hand and storing inventory safely in the warehouses.

EOQ calculations and optimizations have been explained by Piasecki (2001) as, if the cost does not change based upon the quantity of inventory on hand, it should not be included in carrying cost. In the EOQ formula, carrying cost is represented as the annual cost per average on hand inventory unit. Major costs of high inventory include increased rent expense and handling costs, greater product damage, more frequent product obsolescence, and longer delay in noticing quality errors. For most products, the annual carrying cost of inventory is an astounding 20%–40% of the materials cost. Many businesses underestimate the carrying cost of inventory. They calculate carrying cost based on the borrowing cost of money alone. Other factors can outweigh this cost. The following are the primary components of carrying cost explained in detail.

15.2.1.1.1 Capital Costs

If you had to borrow money to pay for your inventory, the interest rate would be part of the carrying cost. If you did not borrow on the inventory, but have loans on other capital items, you can use the interest rate on those loans since a reduction in inventory would free up money that could be used to pay these loans. If by some miracle you are debt free, you would need to determine how much you could make if the money was invested.

15.2.1.1.2 Insurance

Since insurance costs are directly related to the total value of the inventory, these costs would also be included in carrying cost.

15.2.1.1.3 Taxes

If you are required to pay any taxes on the value of your inventory, they should also be included in carrying cost.

15.2.1.1.4 Storage Costs

Errors in calculating storage costs are common in EOQ implementations. Generally companies consider all costs associated with the warehouse and divide it by the average inventory to determine a storage cost percentage for the EOQ calculations. This tends to include costs that are not directly affected by the inventory levels and does not compensate for storage characteristics. Carrying costs for the purpose of the EOQ calculation should only include costs that are variable based upon inventory levels.

Apart from the above-explained costs, SC and warehouses incur additional costs such as fleet control, security, depreciation, utilities, and other costs.

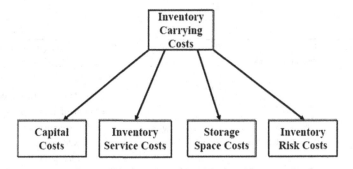

FIGURE 15.3 Inventory cost breakdown (REM Associates).

15.2.1.2 Safety Stock

The amount of safety stock inventory (SSI) that a firm invests out of the total inventory costs is a measure of the relative uncertainty of the product demand, component supply, or both. Where demand and supply are maintained constant (such as in JIT systems), SSI can be minimized. Most manufacturing firms exhibit variable demand and fairly determinable supply. Agricultural and fishing type firms, on the other hand exhibit fairly predictable demand of products.

Safety stocks of these different industry types have manifested themselves with the items on the shelf, silos of grain, fish farms, and frozen foods. Supply and demand can be described by statistical distributions such as normal, chi-square, and Poisson. Therefore, in order to quantify the safety stock of a product, which is a function of the distribution of its supply and demand, it is necessary to understand the statistical nature of both supply and demand separately, since they may exhibit different behaviors. Table 15.1 explains the statistical nature of demand and lead time of various inventory models.

> Even though the effect of the IHC upon the EOQ is smoothed by taking its square root, nothing smoothes out its impact when it is drastically underestimated and applied to an unnecessary excess of inventory. It is evident from the studies presented that IHC should be painstakingly measured, and routinely monitored for accuracy, especially in an economy that shows as many macroeconomic swings as have been exhibited in recent years. Safety in SSI means knowing the up-to-date variability of supply and demand, as these are the key components to formulating SSI. Since not all demand and supply distributions are alike, knowing the underlying statistical pattern of these variations have been shown to significantly improve forecasting and the levels of inventory in every kind of industry. Armed with these lessons of analysis, inventory managers should demonstrate more expertise in defining actual values for these quantities, and less reliance upon age-old, arbitrary estimates.
>
> *(Holsenback and McGill 2007)*

In a research thesis by DeScioli and Byrnes (2001), calculations have been demonstrated on how to calculate the safety stock based on the service level in the mission statement of the organizations. The cost of a stock-out is implied by the targeted service level and required safety stock to achieve a service level such that:

$$SS * C_c = NS_O * CS_O,$$

where SS is the safety stock, C_c is the carry cost, NS_O is the number of stock-outs, and CS_O is the cost of a stock-out.

From this research by DeScioli and Byrnes (2001), the cost of a stock-out was estimated using the actual current practice in the organization. Assuming a target of 99% service level (which is the current

TABLE 15.1

Different Inventory Models and Safety Stock Formulations

		Lead Time		Key
		Constant	**Variable**	
Demand	Constant	I No safety stock	II $R_L = RL$ $\sigma_L = \sqrt{R_2 s^2{}_L}$ $SS = F^{-1}{}_s(CSL)\,\sigma_L$	R = Average demand per period L = Average lead time for replenishment SS = Safety stock
	Variable	III $R_L = RL$ $\sigma_L = \sqrt{\sigma^2{}_R L}$ $SS = F^{-1}{}_s(CSL)\,\sigma_L$	IV $R_L = RL$ $\sigma_L = \sqrt{(\sigma^2{}_R L + R^2\,S^2{}_L)}$ $SS = F^{-1}{}_s(CSL)\,\sigma_L$	σ_L = Standard deviation of demand per period S_L = Standard deviation for lead time $F^{-1}{}_s$ = Inverse normal CSL = Cycle service level R_L = Reorder point

Source: Talluri et al. (2004).

level obtained by organization), a stock-out has an implied cost of $77.75. This analysis assumed the majority of inventory with no demand was slow moving inventory and hence used $3.6 million as the average inventory rather than the $1.9 million that was actually included in the generated demand model.

15.2.1.3 Obsolete and Excessive Inventory

Obsolete inventory has become a prominent phenomenon in most of the organizations. Many organizations are striving to avoid obsolete inventory and are also trying to avoid excessive inventory. There have been many articles in the literature that identify the best practices to control obsolete and excessive inventory.

The items when become obsolete are unusable, and they do not yield any value to the services, and in turn they consume valuable storage space in the warehouses; added are the taxes. These excessive costs may yield to increase in the overall facility costs. The organizations must implement steps and methods that can help inventory managers identify the excessive inventory and make use of the excessive inventory before it turns out to be obsolete. There have been many research articles that help in designing steps to avoid obsolete inventory. Having excessive inventory can be attributed as the primary cause of obsolete inventory. A literature review on inventory control and reduction of inventory shows that it is common to all the organizations that excess inventory translates to more dollars spent. Tony Wild (2002) suggests "more inventory means worse delivery time".

Mark Williams, in his article about ways to reduce inventory, shows that carrying costs account to 20%–36% of the annual inventory costs (2009). In this article, Williams formulates ten key ways of inventory reduction. Reducing obsolete inventory, implementing ABC inventory management strategies, and reducing lead times are the main areas that have been briefly discussed in this research article. A significant amount of investment can be saved when organizations have no obsolete and excessive inventory. Any decrease in these numbers can reduce the operational costs, and most importantly taxes paid due to inventory stored in the warehouse will also decrease. Gary Gossard has statistics on percentage reduction in inventory when certain ways to reduce operating inventories are adopted (2003). According to Gossard, conducting reviews reduced the inventories by 65%. The use of the ABC approach to reduce the inventory will, most likely, save money invested to buy 37% of the total inventory. Nicholson et al. (2004) explains a case study and has a detailed literature review of inventory management in healthcare industry and pharmaceutical industry.

A detailed explanation and analysis of ABC analysis has been explained in a case study done at a hospital by Larry (1983). The case study was done to implement a computerized ABC/EOQ inventory system. The primary objectives were:

- To design an inventory system that would can consider the operational cost as an integral part of ordering process
- To develop management indices of inventory performance and develop a decision factors for interpreting the indices
- To create a purchasing strategy to comply with the ABC/EOQ model.

The results of implementing the inventory system based on ABC analysis were found to increase the turnovers, decrease inventory stock-outs, and reduce inventory on hand. This article provides an ABC analysis. The details have been explained in Table 15.2. ABC analysis categorizes the inventory into three categories. It is based on Pareto 80/20 rule, i.e., 10%–15% of the items consume 70%–80% of the investment denoted as "A" items, and 65%–70% of the items consume 20%–25% of the investment. These are categorized as "B" items. The remaining 10%–15% items that consume 10%–20% are denoted as "C" items.

TABLE 15.2

An Example of ABC Analysis

Category	% of Items	% of Inventory Investment	Monthly Purchases ($)
A	10–15	70–80	100
B	20–25	15–20	25–100
C	60–70	10–15	25

TABLE 15.3

Decision Rules for Evaluation of Inventory Simulation Model

Incident	Decision Rule
Stock-outs	More than two stock-out episodes in 1 month require an increase in order point
Overstocks	Two consecutive months of overstocks require a reduction in the order point and interpretation of applicability of the EOQ model to the A item
Price increases	All price increases are assessed for alternate source of supply, bid authorization through prime vendor, quantity purchase instead of EOQ purchase
Returned for credit	More than one episode monthly suggests reassessment of EOQ model item or change in physician mix in the institution

An EOQ simulation scenario explained in Larry (1983) lists the decision rules for inventory management. Table 15.3 has been explained in Larry (1983).

Major costs of high inventory include increased rent expense and handling costs, greater product damage, more frequent product obsolescence, and longer delay in noticing quality errors. For most products, the annual carrying cost of inventory is an astounding 20%–40% of the materials cost.

15.2.2 Best Practices of Reducing Inventory

Reducing lead times, reducing obsolete inventory, using ABC analysis, increasing the inventory turns ratios can help the organizations in effective inventory management, thus saving investment in maintaining inventory. Table 15.4 shows the percentage reduction in inventory with the implementation of each of these methodologies.

Consider the detailed aspects of reducing inventory and also reducing inventory costs. From Table 15.4, the top seven methods of reducing excessive inventory can be incorporated in one comprehensive inventory management technique. The Inventory Quality Ratio (IQR) is a simple, straightforward way of measuring inventory performance, managing inventory dollars, and identifying inventory reduction opportunities. The IQR logic was developed collectively by the materials managers of 35 companies. It was used by them to reduce inventories a total of $500 million (25% average reduction) while improving on-time deliveries. It has since been used by planners and buyers in manufacturing and distribution companies worldwide to reduce inventories 20%–40% (Gossard 2003).

The IQR logic first divides inventory into three groups: items with future requirements, items with no future requirements but with recent past usage, and items with neither. The items in these groups are then stratified into typical ABC-type classifications based on their future dollar requirements, their past dollar usage, or their current dollar balances, respectively. A target inventory level expressed in days' supply is set for each item based on its classification. The balance on hand of each item is compared to the target,

TABLE 15.4

Top Ten Inventory Reduction Practices

Top Ten Inventory Reduction Practices	Percentage Reduction
Conduct periodic reviews	65
Analyze usage and lead times	50
Reduce safety stocks	42
Use ABC approach (80/20 rule)	37
Improve cycle counting	37
Shift ownership to suppliers	34
Redetermine order quantities	31
Improve forecast of A and B items	23
Give schedules to suppliers	22
Implement new inventory software	21

Source: Gossard (2003).

and the dollars of each item are categorized as either Active (A1, A2), Excess (E1, E2), Slow Moving or Obsolete (SM1, SM2). These are called the inventory quality categories. The IQR is the ratio of the active inventory dollars to total inventory dollars. In a theoretically perfect situation (i.e., with no Excess, Slow Moving, or Obsolete inventories), the IQR would be 100%.

The IQR incorporates the best practices of periodic reviews and ABC analysis with forward-looking days' supply and user-defined parameters. It provides inventory managers with a dynamic methodology to review and reassess lead times, safety stocks, order quantities, and replenishment cycles on a weekly or monthly basis. The IQR also enhances existing MRP systems by adding a dollar focus to prioritize current reduction opportunities.

$$\text{Inventory Quality Ratio (IQR)}$$

$$= \left(\text{Active Inventory Dollars}\right) / \left(\text{Total Inventory Dollars}\right)$$

$$IQR = \frac{A1 + A2}{A1 + A2 + E1 + E2 + E3 + SM1 + SM2}$$

15.2.2.1 Eliminating Obsolete Inventory

Many business owners have difficulty throwing away products they paid good money for. But holding on to obsolete products just burns up even more investments. Eliminate obsolete stock promptly, and use the cash and space you save for something more profitable.

Review on how obsolete stock can be eliminated by creating a "red tag" program to identify old inventory has been widely cited in the literature. Tag old inventory with large red stickers. Note on the sticker the date tagged, person doing the tagging, and a review date. Move these products into a quarantined area of your warehouse. If the warehouses have not used the products by the review date, cut the losses and liquidate the merchandise. Red tagging of obsolete items is something that originated with Japanese automakers. Examples such as Toyota's Red Tag sales events are common. These companies are just moving out old stock to make room for newer, more profitable inventories. Many companies empower employees to red tag items themselves. Red tagging works for anything in your warehouse, not just consumable inventories. Gather a small group of employees and do a 1-h red tag "blitz" in an area. Items that appear as though they don't belong in the work area are placed in a pile. This might include items such as jigs and fixtures, tools, or personal belongings. Next, items in the pile are offered back to the employees in an auction-style format. Unclaimed items are tagged and moved to the red tag quarantine area and then discarded if not claimed by the review date.

Table 15.5 shows the various industrial metrics followed in order to attain improvement. Table 15.5 indicates the customer perspective and organization for each metric and also shows the measurement criteria.

15.2.3 SC Models

The layout of the SC as in Figures 15.1 and 15.2 shows the flow of the products moving from suppliers to manufacturers, distributors, retailers, and finally to the customer. The initial starting point of any SC would be the need of a product, i.e., the demand of the product and ending point of the SC would be the delivery of the product to the customer. The different stages of SC in which the product is handled are called echelons. Figure 15.4 is the layout of the two-echelon SC.

The effectiveness of the SC depends on the level of uncertainty of the product availability. Lesser the uncertainty, the more efficient is the SC. The level of uncertainty in the SC has been widely discussed, in terms of resolving the problem of SC in the community of lean construction (Ballard and Howell 1995). 'Similar to manufacturing, the researchers have endeavored to develop Supply chain ideas over a more dynamic construction environment (Tommelein 1997; Mecca 2000). We would limit our discussion to two-echelon and one-echelon SC models only. The complexity increases as the number of echelons in the SC increases.

TABLE 15.5

Industrial Bench Marking Metrics

Inventory Metrics	Customer Perspective	Forecast Accuracy
Turnover Inventory turns	In-stock percent at point of sale	Sales forecast accuracy Track actual sales vs. forecasted sales variances Forecasting utilization of inventory assets The higher the inventory turns, the better the firm uses its inventory assets
Inventory levels Dollars and/or units at various points in SC	Purchase order fill rate percent Percent shipped on time Percent delivered on time	Order forecast accuracy
Order quantity Order processing/setup cost, inventory carrying cost, back order cost, excess, and obsolete stock cost	Reliability Stock-out percentages, delays, loss, and paperwork involved	Order forecast accuracy
Critical inventory Average inventory, EOQ Space utilization and layout % space utilized (cum.)	Stock-out percentage Percentage of orders fulfilled	Maintaining proper inventory levels Determining method for reordering inventory Forecasting storage space and lead times involved
Stock to sales ratios Weeks/days of supply	Lost sales analysis Evaluate actual/potential lost sales due to lack of inventory	Track actual order qty. vs. forecasted order qty. variances at critical times that could influence production Includes non-compliant orders with frequency and volume as two options
Industry ratio Comparison with others	Part count accuracy percentage Quality-percentage defects Price of non-conformance	Percent variability in lead time
Engineering changes per month	Communication effectiveness Measure collaborative cycle Time/issue resolution time	Customer satisfaction

Source: Raghuram.

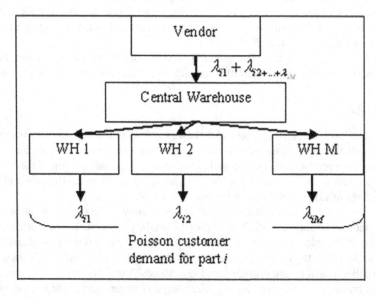

FIGURE 15.4 Two-echelon supply inventory model.

15.2.3.1 Two-Echelon Model

The discussion in Caglar et al.'s (2003) model about optimizing two-echelon inventory models has been cited by many research articles. Caglar developed a model to minimize the system-wide inventory holding costs while meeting a service constraint at each of the field depots. The service constraint considered was based on the average response time. It was defined as the average time it takes a customer to receive a spare part after a failure is reported. The model was verified by using several cases referred to in his original article. A two-echelon multi-consumable goods inventory system consisting of a central distribution center and multiple customers that require service is investigated. The system is illustrated in Figure 15.4.

Each secondary warehouse acts as a smaller warehouse. These secondary warehouses in turn supply to many customers and maintain a stock level S_{iM} for each item. So each secondary warehouse consists of a set i of n items that are used with a mean rate λ. When an item is used by a customer, the customer replenishes itself by taking item i from the secondary warehouse M and supply stock if the item is in stock. If the item is not in stock, the item is back ordered, and the customer has to wait for the item to become available at the secondary warehouse.

There has been some related research to understand the characteristics of multi-echelon inventory model and the dynamics of a two-echelon SC in particular. The conclusion from these studies states that over 65% of most companies do not compute inventory carrying costs; they calculate carrying cost based on rough estimates. Leading researchers and logistics experts place the cost of carrying inventory between 18% per year and 75% of total SC costs per year depending on the type of products and business. The standard "rule of thumb" for inventory carrying cost is 25% of total inventory value on hand. The cost of capital is the leading factor in determining the percentage of carrying cost.

If all supply and demand variabilities for a particular product were known, then the holding cost for inventory could be minimized. An important technique to reduce inventory costs is to reduce supply variability by including suppliers in demand planning activities. This leads to improved lead times and can result in up to 25% reduction in inventory carrying costs (Holsenback and McGill 2007).

The objective of our research was to make a decision of SC type based on basic purchasing and holding cost information, while maintaining an average response time that will not negatively impact the customers. This may include the elimination of the primary warehouse.

Caglar et al.'s (2003) optimization equation for minimizing total inventory costs subject to a time constraint, which also sets the percent availability for items available to a customer, could be used to determine proper stocking levels at each secondary and primary warehouse. Caglar et al.'s (2003) response time equation was used to quantify expected response time.

Minimize

$$\sum_{i\in I} h_i \bar{I}_i(S_{i0}) + \sum_{i\in I}\sum_{i\in I} h_i \bar{I}_i(S_{ij},S_{i0})$$

$$W_j \le \tau_j, (j\in J),$$

where

$$0 \le S_{ij} \le \hat{S}_{ij}, \quad S_{ij} \text{ integer } (i\in I; j\in J),$$

$$0 \le S_{i0} \le \hat{S}_{i0}, \quad S_{i0} \text{ integer } (i\in I),$$

τ_j = customer expectation for maximum expected response time and W_j is calculated using response time equation and Little's law from Caglar et al. (2003).

According to Little's law in queuing theory of stochastic processes, $L=\lambda W$, where L is the mean number in the system and W_j is the mean response time in the context of this paper. However, even though this model is very good at optimizing a two-echelon SC, it requires a large amount of data and assumptions. The model was developed in Caglar et al. (2003) in a way that it would provide an approximate distribution for inventory on-hand and also provide information on back orders at each depot for a two-echelon system.

15.2.3.2 The One-Echelon Model

The one-echelon model is a one-warehouse model with JIT system. The JIT requires better planning of demand from customers, and additional procurement cost per unit is higher due to high variation in demand. There are many cases where the elimination or significant downsizing of a warehouse can save money without sacrificing service to the customer. The layout of one-echelon supply is shown in Figure 15.5.

JIT is a concept widely used by many Japanese manufacturers and is now becoming popular in the western world. The theory of JIT is suppliers deliver items when the item is needed. If implemented properly, this lowers inventory levels for the customer and drives down the cost of maintaining inventories but may sometimes increase the procurement costs.

To compare the total cost of a one-echelon JIT system to all other systems, the same service level W_j was used. Also, the system turns into a one-echelon inventory problem. This simplified the model, as there were fewer levels for the system to queue from.

The JIT system in this model works by items ordered going directly from the vendor to the secondary warehouse, where a smaller stock level is used versus the primary warehouse. One-echelon systems do not have an intermediary warehouse between the vendors and the secondary warehouse. This system is shown in Figure 15.5.

Costs associated with the JIT system contained all of the fixed costs of the system as well as additional costs of requiring more service from vendors. In some instances, per unit price of a product can remain constant by ordering large quantity orders or several small quantity orders. However, shipping rates for the several smaller orders may increase. Due to this, it may be important to select vendors that are close to the secondary warehouses.

Once again, in many situations, the data needed to optimize may not be available in the time frame. This is where carrying cost ratio can provide a decision to move to a two-echelon model.

15.3 Research Objective

15.3.1 Research Question

From the literature review rationale, there has been limited research on how to measure the efficiency of warehouses. The previous research describes optimizing the warehouse and SC operations based on complex equation and hard to collect data. There has been lack of measurement criteria or metric that can identify the reasons for warehouse to perform below average. The objective of this research is to provide a useful decision support tool that allows management to make more effective decisions about inventory policy.

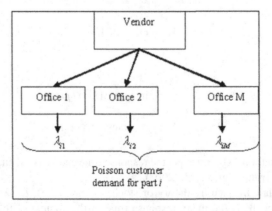

FIGURE 15.5 One-echelon SC model.

The proposed research model seeks to provide decision criteria for the organizations whether to continue the operations of the warehouse or to close the warehouse based on the calculations based on easy to collect data related to facility costs, procurement costs, and distribution costs.

The carrying cost ratio model was used to compare the total cost of the purchasing inventory from retail operators to the amount of money spent on receiving, stocking, and delivering it to a warehouse. The objective of this research is to provide a methodology for reducing cost incurred over the SC process from the time an inventory item is loaded on a truck from the original vendor to the time the individual secondary warehouse sells/makes use of the item for their business. The merits of understanding these incurred costs include

- An understanding of the cost of items
- Knowledge of the cost the operation would be required to overcome these costs
- Guidelines for what actions an operation can take to decrease the cost/dollar spent ratio.

The current research objective of this model seeks to evaluate the two-echelon SC models, calculate the carrying cost of inventory, and develop a modified carrying cost ratio for the evaluation of all the secondary warehouses. The ratio would identify warehouses that have more facility costs than inventory. Calculate the inventory turns/year to identify the warehouses that have excessive inventory and store obsolete inventory.

This research has been designed to study the following hypothesis. The proposed hypothesis of this research is as follows.

- *Hypothesis:* We hypothesize that the metric and the methodology that is based upon inventory control theory can be used in a consistent manner to effectively manage inventory.

15.3.2 Specific Objectives

The specific objectives of this research were to analyze the present SC and develop an effective SC to reduce the overall costs associated with storing the product in the warehouse to the point of time product was actually delivered to the end user/point of care.

In order to meet our research objective, the model has to satisfy three specific objectives:

- *Specific Objective #1:* Demonstrate how the suggested metric compares to other commonly used inventory control metrics.
- *Specific Objective #2:* Develop an "easy to use" inventory control methodology.
- *Specific Objective #3:* Demonstrate a methodology for applying the metric for management.

15.3.3 Intellectual Merit

The intellectual merits in meeting the specific objectives are

- A tested inventory control metric that extends theoretical inventory control methods
- An introduction of a methodology that provides a useful approach for practitioners
- Comparison of the usage of this metric and method against previous theoretical inventory control models.

15.4 Research Methodology

The research methodology describes our approach on evaluating the aforementioned inventory SC models. The decision criterion is based upon total cost of the purchasing, storing, and delivering items to the customer. The model can determine which system has a better chance of success based upon the weighting of the inventory holding costs. The next sections describe a comparison of two-echelon, one-echelon, and the proposed modified carrying cost ratio.

We used the assumptions listed below:

- The consumable goods network consists of the primary warehouse, secondary warehouses, and the customers.
- The shipment time between the primary warehouse and the secondary warehouse j is stochastic with mean T_j.
- The travel time from a secondary to a customer is negligible, as they are in the same building.
- In the JIT analysis, ordering costs will be included in the negotiated JIT contract.
- The secondary warehouses will review base stock policy based on an ABC analysis with the base stock level for item i at secondary warehouse j set at S_{ij}, which cannot exceed a limit $\hat{S}_{ij}$ specified by management.
- Every item is crucial for the customers to function properly. For example, dentists cannot serve clients without toothpaste.
- When a part is ordered from a secondary and it is available at the primary, a vehicle is sent immediately, and the response time for that action is zero.
- We assume K_j, the number of customers served by the secondary warehouse j, is large, and we model the demand rate for item i at secondary j as a Poisson arrival process with rate $\lambda_{ij} = K_j l_i$. However, this assumption is typically violated whenever an order is made by the customer; it is common in the literature (Graves 1985) when dealing with machine failure rates.
- Lateral shipments between secondary warehouses are not allowed.

The notations used in research are listed in Table 15.6 for all of the illustrated models.

TABLE 15.6

Notation of Terminology

Notation	Description
A_w	Annual fixed cost of warehouse operation
C_I	Total cost of holding inventory
C_{Lj}	Labor cost at warehouse j
C_V	Cost of vehicles and maintenance at office j
C_{Uj}	Cost of utilities at office j
C_W	Lease price or depreciation and cost of capitol of warehouse
C_{Mj}	Annual property maintenance for warehouse j
$J = \{1, 2, ..., M\}$	Set of offices
K_j	Customer at office j
l_i	Demand rate of item i
L_{JITij}	JIT lead time for an expedited order of item i at office j
$\lambda_{ij} = K_j l_i$	Demand rate for item i at office j
θ_c	Organization's cost of capital
θ_{Oij}	Obsolescence rate for item i at office j
θ_S	Shrinkage rate based on total inventory in system
P_{Wi}	Purchase price using warehouse system of item i
P_{JITi}	Negotiated JIT purchase price for item i
S_{ij}	Base stock level for item i at office j
SS_{ij}	Safety stock of item i at office j
V_{Wj}	Value of warehouse j
W_{ij}	Waiting time for a customer ordering item i from office j
W_j	Waiting time for a customer ordering from office j

15.4.1 Two-Echelon Model

In 2003, Caglar et al. presented a two-echelon SC model that we consider very useful in making cost-effective decisions about warehouse inventory levels. We utilize this model to demonstrate the current two-echelon SC in practice by the city department. First, we will consider a two-echelon multi-consumable goods inventory system consisting of a central distribution center and multiple customers that require service as illustrated in Figure 15.5.

Each service center office acts as a smaller warehouse. This is because they each supply many customers and maintain a stock level S_{CM} for each item. Therefore, each office consists of a set I of n items that are used at a mean rate. When an item is used by a customer, the customer replenishes itself by taking item i from office M. If the item is not in stock, the item is back-ordered, and the customer has to wait for the the item to become available at the office. The decision criteria of SC is based on basic purchasing and holding cost information, while maintaining an average response time that will not negatively affect the customers. This may include the elimination of the central warehouse.

Using the notation in Table 15.6, a model of the cost of operating a warehouse and implementing a JIT system was derived. This information can then be used to determine if the organization benefits from operating the warehouse. There are many operating costs associated with warehouse management. These operating costs include fixed costs such as racking, utilities, labor, vehicle fleet maintenance, property maintenance, property depreciation, and a lease or any other tied up capital. The costs included can be variable and fixed, and it depends on the organization. Let Aw be all periodic fixed costs that the savings of purchasing in large quantities have to justify in order to minimize the total cost of the operation. For this model, we will use annual costs.

$$A_w = \sum_{j \in J} C_{Wj} + C_{Uj} + C_{Lj} + C_{Vj} + C_{Mj} + \theta_c * V_{Wj} \tag{15.1}$$

These fixed costs in addition to item-associated costs make up the total cost of having a warehouse in operation. Many of these costs are hidden and are frequently overlooked when procurement managers decide the level of quantities to purchase. Shrinkage in the form of lost items, stolen items, or damaged items; obsolescence; and the cost of capital on the inventory is typically among these hidden costs. These costs can be modeled as a percentage of the total inventory on hand.

15.4.2 One-Echelon Model

The second model used for reference is the common one-echelon JIT system. JIT requires better planning of demand from customers and can sometimes make management feel uneasy about the extra procurement cost of items on a per unit basis.

But there are many cases where the elimination or significant downsizing of a warehouse operation can save money without sacrificing service to the customer. In the JIT system depicted in this model, ordered items go directly from the vendor to the office, where a smaller stock level is used versus the warehouse. One-echelon systems will differ in that there is no intermediary between the vendors and the offices (Wang et al. 2000; Caglar et al. 2003; Lee 2003). This system is shown based on a simplification of Caglar et al.'s model in Figure 15.5.

The JIT contracts that will need to be made with the vendors is established based upon demand rate λ_{ij}. We determine the expected time of back orders of item i in office j by the following:

$$W_{ij} = E\left[L(S_{ij})\right] = \sum_{j \in J} \sum_{i \in I}\left(L_{JITij} * \left(1 - \sum_{i=0}^{SS_{ij}}\left(\frac{\lambda_{ij} L_{JITij}}{n!}\right)^n \exp(\lambda_{ij} L_{JITij})\right)\right) \tag{15.2}$$

In this case, items are delivered to the offices at the same rate the items are being used. The symbol t_{ij} represents time between deliveries for item i at office j. Therefore, by substitution, $\lambda_{ij} t_{ij}$ is also the order quantity.

$$S_{ij} = \lambda_{ij} t_{ij} + SS_{ij} \tag{15.3}$$

Keeping the expected wait time for the customer for each system the same will allow for a comparison of costs without changing the response time to the customer. Costs associated with the JIT system contain all of the fixed costs of the system as well as any additional costs of requiring more service from vendors. In some instances, the unit price can remain constant by ordering a couple of large quantity orders or several small quantity orders. However, shipping rates for the smaller orders may increase. Due to this, it may be important to select vendors that are near to the offices. After factoring in a possible increase in purchase and shipping prices, we suggest that the total cost for the JIT system will be as follows:

$$C_{JIT} = \sum_{i \in I} \sum_{j \in J} P_{JITi} \lambda_{ij} + C_I \tag{15.4}$$

where

$$C_I = \sum_{i \in I} \sum_{j \in J} \left(I_{ij} * (\theta_C + \theta_S + \theta_{Oij}) \right) \tag{15.5}$$

Once again, in many situations the data needed to use this optimization may not be available in the time allotted to the project. This is where our simplified carrying cost ratio model simplifies the decision to move to a two-echelon system.

15.4.3 Model Description of Modified Carrying Cost Ratio

The proposed carrying cost ratio model focuses on comparing the two systems and selecting the best choice of operational model. As long as the total cost for purchasing, storing, and delivering items to the customer can be derived, we can determine which system is a better economic choice with our decision model. The ratio compares the total cost of the purchased inventory to the amount of money spent holding and delivering it to the offices. This cost ratio has been developed to evaluate and analyze SC costs for operations relying on inventory delivery from a supplier. The purpose is to provide a methodology for determining cost incurred over the SC process from the time an inventory item is loaded on a truck from the original vendor to the time an operation buys or requisitions the item for use in their business. The merits of understanding these incurred costs include

- An understanding of the cost of each item
- Knowledge of the cost the operation would be required to overcome
- Guidelines for which actions an operation can take to decrease the cost/dollar spent ratio.

The carrying cost model takes into account the importance of the inventory turns ratio and also the carrying cost ratio. In most of the models, we only take inventory turns as a decision tool. We hypothesize that the cost of inventory plus the fixed costs comprise the total cost of the warehouse operation, given by the equation below. The research methodology is to determine whether cost of inventory plus the fixed costs make up the total cost of the warehouse operation.

$$\text{Total Warehouse Cost} = A_w + C_I \tag{15.6}$$

We suggest that after identifying the stock levels using the aforementioned formulas or current accounting information, the next step would be to use our ratio to determine which system is better for the operation. We present the ratio as a calculation that can be used in operations—the ratio of the total cost of maintaining the inventory divided by the total inventory purchase price.

After identifying the stock levels using the above-mentioned formulas or current accounting information, the next step was to develop a ratio to determine which system is better for the operation. This model developed in this research is used as a metric in analyzing and comparing the one-echelon and two-echelon inventory models. The metric μ_w used in the decision making is a ratio of the total cost of maintaining the inventory and the total inventory purchase price.

$$\mu_W = \frac{A_W + C_I}{\sum_{i \in I} C_{Wi}}, \tag{15.7}$$

where all costs are annual and $\sum_{i \in I} C_{Wi}$ = total dollars purchased.

The decision to be adopted for the SC based on a scale is shown in Table 15.7. The range of ratio between 0.1 and 0.2 has been regarded as the best possible SC to reduce the overall costs. The range between 0.2 and 0.4 has been considered as acceptable to accommodate the additional costs that are the result of the improving the SC and to accommodate any changes in the SC based on procurement. The range of ratio above 0.4 needs improvement and must be reduced in order to reduce the overall costs.

The above relationship provides a baseline for the financial efficiency of the operation. This unitless number is a ratio of total dollars spent maintaining inventory to the total purchase price of all the items in the inventory. Industrial practices include the additional costs due to JIT contracts that are in the range of 15%–25% increase. Thus, if an organization's carrying cost ratio is above this target, JIT one-echelon options need to be considered such as buying directly from the retailer.

15.4.3.1 Impact of Holding Cost

A research survey conducted by J. E. Holsenback in 2007 demonstrated the necessity of accurately measuring and monitoring inventory holding cost. The study further demonstrated that knowledge of the underlying statistical pattern of supply and demand variations can significantly improve forecasting and impact the appropriate levels of safety stock inventory in a variety of industries.

> Inventory holding cost/carrying cost assumes that it is linearly proportional to the amount of inventory held, when the rate itself very well may decay (or increase) with increasing quantities. In fact, holding cost may change from one accounting period to the next. Failure to accurately determine the holding cost and use this cost to make decisions fails to recognize that inventory can represent one-third to one-half of a company's assets. For instance a company with a 36% holding cost will pay for the inventory twice in slightly more than two years: once to purchase it, and a second time to carry it for about 25 months. So, it seems problematic that nearly one half of companies do not use holding cost to make their inventory management decisions. This holding affects profitability, and may affect a company's business plan in terms of make-buy, or make-to-order/make-to-stock, as well as other top-level decisions.
>
> *(IOMA, Dec. 2002)*

Table 15.8 shows a widely cited breakdown of holding costs associated with warehousing merchandise (Johnson et al. 1999). So, if the ratio is above this baseline for any particular contribution, focus can be turned to that area. In the event that the storage facilities are above the baseline, lowering facilities cost by elimination of facilities in conjunction with a JIT system is recommended.

The equation in the calculation of modified carrying cost ratio defines the total cost determined over the course of the SC. It combines the cost of delivering an item with the cost incurred during the process of holding that item in inventory. This equation is the ratio of warehouse cost per item to purchase price

TABLE 15.7

Decision Tool for Operating Warehouses

Ratio	Range	Decision
μ_W	0.1–0.2	Best possible SC
μ_W	0.2–0.4	Adopt this solution for reduced SC costs
μ_W	0.4–0.6	Needs minor improvements
μ_W	0.6–0.9	Needs rapid improvements
μ_W	>1	Change the components of SC

TABLE 15.8

General Handling Cost

Cost Source	% of Purchase Price
Insurance	0.25
Storage facilities	0.25
Taxes	0.50
Transportation	0.50
Handling	2.50
Depreciation	5.00
Interest	6.00
Obsolescence	10.00
Total	25.00

Source: REM Associates.

per item. This effectively demonstrates the ratio of money a supplier spends storing and shipping an item to the actual monetary investment put in to each inventory item, represented by the ratio $(C_{System})/C_P$. This ratio, when combined with holding cost, can be extremely effective in determining the efficiency of an SC as well as providing an indicator of the inventory turn rate for the entire system. For this project, our primary focus was the eventual calculation of this ratio. In this case study, we shall consider five secondary warehouses for our analysis.

15.4.3.2 Impact of Inventory Turns

Inventory turns have a significant impact on the warehouse operations. The turns assist the inventory manager to identify the items that are fast moving and need continuous monitoring. The inventory turnover ratio measures the efficiency of the business in managing and selling its inventory. This ratio gauges the liquidity of the firm's inventory.

The proposed model doesn't directly depend on the inventory turns, but the variables involved in the calculation of inventory turns directly relate to the proposed model to reduce obsolete inventory. The expression below explains the calculation of inventory turns ratio

$$\text{Inventory turnover rate} = \frac{\text{Cost of Goods Sold from}}{\text{Average Inventory}} \tag{15.8}$$

Generally, a high inventory ratio means that the company is efficiently managing and selling its inventory. The faster the inventory sells, the fewer funds the company has tied up. Companies have to be careful if they have a high inventory turnover as they are subject to stock-outs.

If a company has a low inventory turnover ratio, then there is a risk they are holding obsolete inventory which is difficult to sell. This may erode a company's profit. However, the company may be holding a lot of inventory for legitimate reasons. They may be preparing for a holiday season in the case of the retail industry or preparing for a strike, among other reasons.

From the description above about inventory turns ratio, the effectiveness of the proposed model would depend on the inventory turns of the warehouses. The calculation related to inventory turns has been explained in results section.

15.4.3.2.1 Impact of Obsolete Inventory

Obsolete inventory as explained in the earlier section can be due to the inventory that has low turnover ratio. The proposed model has been developed to reduce obsolete inventory and increase the inventory turnover ratio.

The literature review section earlier has explained in detail about the ways to reduce the obsolete inventory. From the ABC analysis, the items that are labeled as C items or otherwise called slow moving items. These slow moving items can impact the holding cost, and these items have significant impact on the proposed model. In the denominator of carrying cost expression as shown earlier, the average inventory increases as the obsolete inventory increases, and thus the inventory turns reduce. In the calculation of the carrying cost ratio, the total dollars purchased keeps increasing as the warehouses procure products that have low turnover ratios.

15.5 Model Validation

15.5.1 Case Study: Description

A large city health department in United States had a trend of increasing operational costs, and decrease in overall performance of the warehouses was observed. The city managed primary warehouses, and these primary warehouses distributed supplies throughout the city at different points of care. These points of care act as secondary warehouses. Preliminary analysis of the warehouses indicated that warehouses procured higher levels of products than required.

The health department followed a two-echelon SC inventory model. Detailed explanation about the two-echelon SC inventory model is included in the literature review section. A sample schematic of a two-echelon model in Figure 15.6 shows a two-echelon SC inventory model would be similar to the one that was in practice for the healthcare organizations.

The performance metric for warehouses was the decrease in percentage of obsolete inventory. Best industry practice is to have excessive inventory in the range of 3%–6% of total inventory. Secondary performance metric used in this research was SC inventory turns. Best industry practice was to have inventory turns above 1.2. The warehouse has been experiencing stock-outs of supplies, thus resulting in unhappy customers.

The expected result from this research was that the introduction of new SC model would reduce holding/ storing excessive inventory products and also reduce obsolete inventory. These organizations had central warehouses that would deliver the requested products to the warehouse in the organization.

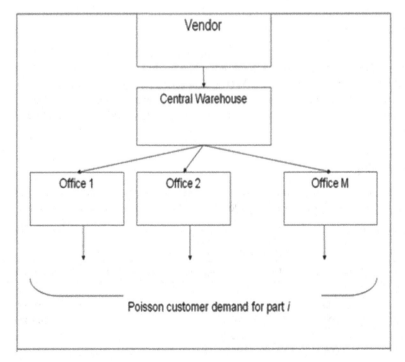

FIGURE 15.6 Two-echelon SC model.

Thus, the need to improve the operational SC aims to reduce the obsolete inventory and help organizations in generating revenues by reducing obsolete inventory and avoiding expired supplies to be distributed to the points of care. The health department had a two-echelon SC. Figure 15.6 shows the schematic layout of the two-echelon SC model.

The research methodology was used in the analysis of the warehouse and inventory management systems of "City of X" health and human services (CoXHHS) department that had its own distribution network to service five secondary warehouses. An analysis was then done to determine inefficiencies in the SC (slow inventory turn items), and the information was then used to perform a cash flow analysis for which actions would be useful in reducing cost/dollar purchased. The methodology can be very beneficial in determining which actions yielded the most positive results in reducing costs and/or increasing net profits for an organization.

15.5.2 Data Collection

From the annual reports, the organization had an inventory value of $500,000.

Data relating to SC costs was gathered from the annual reports, and the subsections of SC costs as explained were collected. Holding costs would be calculated by the addition of cost of allocating space for storage and cost of procurement of products (C_P).

Space cost (C_s) would include costs related to utilities, labor (picking, packing, and shipping). The expressions for calculating holding costs are shown below:

$$\text{Holding costs} = C_s + C_p$$

$$\text{Space cost} = C_s$$

Procurement costs (C_P) would include cost of items, inbound trucking delivery to warehouse, opportunity cost of tied up money. Customer service or delivery costs (C_d) would include fleet maintenance costs and cost of delivery (such as cost per mile for pick-up or use of courier services such as UPS).

15.5.3 Facilities Costs

The facility cost calculation involved compiling the total facilities cost for each of the warehouses involved in the operation's SC. The data about individual facility costs is included in Table 15.9.

Additionally, CoXHHS was leasing the WH 2, at a cost of $78,000 a year. This cost of lease was incremental price and led to a possibility of elimination of the warehouse, since all the other warehouse facilities were owned by the city. Factors such as extra lease cost would be crucial in decisions yielding from the model.

15.5.4 Purchasing Costs

Schnetzler et al. (2007) note that in trying to achieve lower inventories and shorter lead times, operational costs are affected. With facilities costs in Table 15.10 and individual warehouse turn rates shown, it was

TABLE 15.9

Facility Costs for Secondary Warehouses

WH *j*	Labor Cost	Utilities and Supplies	Lease Cost	Facility Total Cost
WH 1	123,000	356,000	0	480,000
WH 2	30,000	50,000	78,000	158,000
WH 3	26,000	74,000	0	100,000
WH 4	26,000	62,000	0	89,000
WH 5	12,000	28,000	0	40,000
Total	217,000	570,000	78,000	867,000

TABLE 15.10

Inventory Turns Ratio for Secondary Warehouses

Warehouse #	Turns/Year	Total Receipts
WH 1	0.36	$48,065.62
WH 2	2.18	$501,062.43
WH 3	0.07	$34,541.00
WH 4	0.49	$531,931.75
WH 5	0.15	$25,475.21
Total Purchases		$1,141,076.01

possible to proceed to a more in depth analysis of the data. The first step was to calculate an average turn rate for each facility in the CoXHHS SC. The desired result is that each facility would have at least a turn rate of 1.0, indicating that the inventory in each warehouse was overturned once a year. The results are summarized in Table 15.10.

Table 15.10 shows that the only facility which demonstrated a desired average turn rate was warehouse 2. The other buildings, especially warehouse 3, featured extremely low turn rates. The most likely cause of low inventory turns ratio was the high inventory costs in the form of obsolete or excess inventory stored in the facility, to explain in detail the warehouse had inventory supplies stored for longer periods of time. The longer the time supplies were stored in the primary warehouse the more expensive it gets to hold the inventory in the form of handling storage spaces, security, and other costs explained in the earlier sections. Figure 15.7 shows the investments in dollars that were received by warehouse 2 for a period of 1 year. The graph shows that warehouse 2 had good history of inventory receipts and inventory issues. Hence, warehouse 2 had the highest inventory turns ratio. Similarly, warehouse 4 was among the warehouses that had significantly lower inventory turnover ratios. Figure 15.8 indicates that warehouse 1 had almost same distribution history as that of warehouse 2, but it had high ending balances of inventory resulting in high holding costs for storing excess inventory. The remaining distribution of warehouses has been included in Appendix A.

The low receipts for the WH 5 show that they were not ordering any items, a fact that is consistent with its role as an intermediary building in the SC. Thus, their low turn rate is acceptable given the building's role. However, the facilities each sent out a large number of orders but experienced an unacceptably low turn rate.

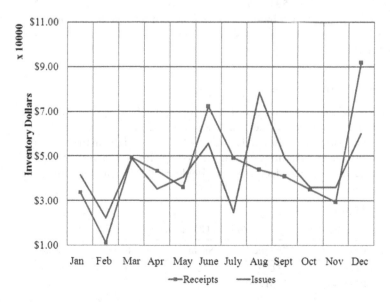

FIGURE 15.7 Distribution of warehouse 2.

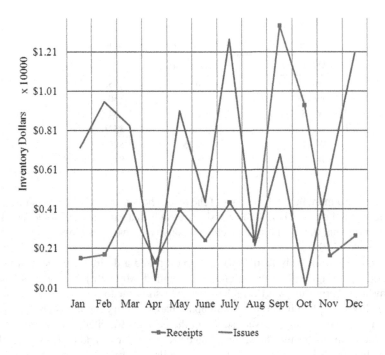

FIGURE 15.8 Distribution of warehouse 1.

15.5.5 The Carrying Cost Ratio

The total cost incurred per item was calculated for the entire CoXHHS SC and compared to the total purchase cost, resulting in the warehouse cost per dollar spent on holding the inventory in the warehouse. This calculated value was also exceptionally high, netting an average of $0.95 per dollar purchased being spent to store and transport each inventory item. Lowering this ratio could be accomplished through a variety of methods including consolidating inventory, increasing efficiency by standardizing procedures and optimizing storage use, and most importantly through elimination of obsolete inventory items from each facility. Table 15.11 shows the calculations for the CoXHHS modified carrying cost ratio. The shrinkage was included by the organization, and no specific information was available on this. Fleet costs are the transportation costs. We assume that shrinkage and fleet costs are same for all the warehouses in this study.

15.5.6 Inventory Turn Analysis

Secondary research metric was the average SC inventory turns. The objective was to increase the average inventory turns from the present 0.775 per year to a 2.0 per year. The range of present inventory turns was as high as 2.18 and as low as 0.07. Best industrial practices are usually in the range of 1.2–2.4.

The ratio showed that the facilities cost of the system was well above 25% of the total purchase price. So, in order to eliminate facilities and implement JIT inventory turns, data was needed.

TABLE 15.11

Modified Carrying Cost Ratio of COXHHS

Costs	Facilities	Shrinkage	Fleet	Sum
Annual	867,000	127,000	87,000	1,081,000
Purchases	$1,141,076			$1,141,076
			$\mu = 0.95$	

Inventory turns are defined as the average number of items kept in stock divided by the annual usage of the item.

$$T = \frac{S_{ij} + S_{i0}}{\lambda_{ij}}$$

From the above expression, Table 15.12 shows the sample calculations for calculating the inventory turns for warehouse 2. The calculation of inventory turns for all the warehouses has been included in Appendix B (Table 15.13).

The ABC analysis compares all the items ordered and prioritizes them according to use. Results of an ABC analysis are indicated in Table 15.14 for the primary warehouse of CoXHHS. Category "D" items were extremely slow moving items, and it was observed that none of the "D" items had at least one issue in the past 1 year. The high percentage of "D" category items accounted for the entire obsolete inventory in the primary warehouse.

ABC analysis classifies all the supplies by the percent of total dollars invested in purchasing the supplies. ABC analysis of secondary warehouse 2 as shown in Table 15.15 shows that 80% of all the investment in inventory accounts to 8% of the supplies (referred to items in A category) and 15% of the investment accounts to 10% of the supplies (referred to items in B category) and 5% of the

TABLE 15.12

Calculation of Inventory Turns for Warehouse 2

Month	Receipts	Issues	Ending Balance	Inventory Turns Projected Rate
Jan	$33,743.97	$41,396.82	$241,814.45	2.05
Feb	$10,996.46	$22,098.34	$214,561.54	1.24
Mar	$49,052.13	$48,812.51	$207,328.94	2.83
Apr	$43,417.58	$35,162.41	$220,699.94	1.91
May	$35,934.11	$40,559.21	$256,198.47	1.9
June	$72,153.98	$55,617.79	$256,099.58	2.61
July	$49,097.26	$24,727.25	$301,216.67	0.99
Aug	$43,699.36	$78,316.46	$230,303.09	4.08
Sept	$40,814.80	$48,988.60	$243,880.23	2.41
Oct	$35,104.14	$35,950.06	$239,340.29	1.8
Nov	$29,170.13	$35,932.18	$226,527.14	1.9
Dec	$91,622.48	$60,019.94	$260,678.96	2.76

TABLE 15.13

Average Inventory Turns for Warehouse 2

Total Receipts	Total Issues	Avg. Ending Balance	Inventory Turn Rate	Total Adjustments
$501,062.43	$527,581.55	$241,554.11	2.18	$11,351.78

TABLE 15.14

ABC Analysis of Primary Warehouse

Category	# of Items	% of Items
A	104	3.5
B	150	5.0
C	476	15.9
D	2263	75.6
Total	2992	100.0

TABLE 15.15

ABC Analysis of Secondary Warehouse 2

Category	# of Items	% of Items	Inventory Value	% of Inventory Value
A	36	8	367,035.6	80
B	49	10	68,698.59	15
C	384	82	24,859.63	5
Total	469	100	460,593.82	100

investment inventory accounts to 82% of the supplies (referred to items in C category). ABC analysis of warehouse 2 with results is indicated in Table 15.15. ABC analysis of other warehouses has been included in the Appendix A.

Order policy for each type of movers is set by movement category. Items that are deemed as "A" movers were placed on continual review for reordering. "B" movers have a review quarterly. "C" movers can be reviewed annually.

15.5.7 The Decision

After determining that the current carrying cost ratio for the CoXHHS was above the expected 15%–25% procurement cost increase, a decision was made to switch from a two-echelon system to a one-echelon system. The switch had Earnings Before Interest and Taxes (EBIT) of $250,000 with a payback period of just over 1 year. Ordering policies were simplified and managed by each secondary warehouse, eliminating the need for a centralized logistics system. The carrying cost ratio was reduced from 0.95 to 0.39. From the series of iterations as shown in Table 15.16 and referring back to the table for decision criterion, consolidating WH 1 and WH 3 would reduce the overall SC costs. Though the WH 5 also had low inventory turnover ratio, the carrying cost model considers the impact of inventory turnover ratio and carrying cost ratio. So, the ratio is 0.39 when WH 1 and WH 3 are consolidated with other warehouses. Ordering policies were simplified and managed by each secondary, thus eliminating the primary warehouse. Most of the savings were due to lowering the total volume of the obsolete inventory in the SC. The reduction in obsolete inventory produced a 75% reduction in racking requirements.

TABLE 15.16

Carrying Cost Ratio Iterations for Decision

Iteration	Carrying Cost Ratio	Decision Criterion
1	0.51	When WH 1 is consolidated with other warehouses
2	1.38	When WH 2 is consolidated with other warehouses
3	1.63	When WH 3 is consolidated with other warehouses
4	1.56	When WH 4 is consolidated with other warehouses
5	0.89	When WH 5 is consolidated with other warehouses
6	0.60	When WH 1 and WH 2 are consolidated with other warehouses
7	0.39	When WH 1 and WH 3 are consolidated with other warehouses
8	0.76	When WH 1 and WH 4 are consolidated with other warehouses
9	0.45	When WH 1 and WH 5 are consolidated with other warehouses
10	1.22	When WH 3 and WH 2 are consolidated with other warehouses
11	6.92	When WH 4 and WH 2 are consolidated with other warehouses
12	1.30	When WH 5 and WH 2 are consolidated with other warehouses
13	1.40	When WH 3 and WH 4 are consolidated with other warehouses
14	0.79	When WH 3 and WH 5 are consolidated with other warehouses
15	1.48	When WH 4 and WH 5 are consolidated with other warehouses

The carrying cost ratio criterion of decision helps mangers to make strategic and tactical decisions so that the decision can reduce the overall costs of the SC. The organization has consolidated WH 1 and WH 3 with other warehouses. From Table 15.16, no other iteration had carrying cost ratio in the acceptable range.

15.6 Conclusion

Many organizations operate warehouses in order to reduce costs. Oftentimes in governmental operations, if not carefully managed these warehouse operations become bloated with inventory that is no longer needed or is needed at a much lower demand. Unless managers periodically analyze the contents of their warehouses, the carrying cost of all items purchased can outweigh savings from procurement when purchasing in bulk.

Decrease in carrying cost ratio demonstrates consolidating commodities into fewer facilities will lower costs. Allow cost justification and priority quantification on which facilities should be eliminated and in what order. Secondary metric/goal to increase SC inventory turns has been achieved with the increase in inventory turns to 1.2 after the implementation of recommendations from this research.

In today's fast-paced business world, the time to evaluate business operations is not available, and quick decisions need to be made. This modified carrying cost ratio, based on easily found data, shows when a warehouse's operations are inefficient and not cost-effective. This model speeds up the process and thereby speeds change and cost savings in a company.

Our results from the analysis of the model include the evaluation of warehouses using carrying costs ratio, identification of obsolete inventory in warehouses resulting in low inventory turns ratio. Current research model describes decision criteria for the inventory managers in terms of stocking importance of fast moving items and slow moving items. The future benefits for the current organization include reduced building and facility costs, decrease in annual operating budgets, reduced warehouse operational cost, improved labor productivity, improved warehouse space utilization, established performance measures.

15.6.1 Limitations

However, there are some limitations to this model. One limitation would be very large systems where JIT contracts would be too complicated. Organizations with a large service range such as a regional or larger retailer may not benefit from this ratio as is. But, for a smaller company or a city, this model can be very effective at recognizing overcapacity or inefficiencies in an SC. The data was collected from accounting records, and hence any errors in the accounting can change the outcome of this case study.

15.6.1.1 Contribution to Body of Knowledge

The model developed in this research would provide researchers and practitioners a method to calculate the efficiency of warehouse in terms of reducing inventory and avoiding obsolete inventory. The research model develops a carrying cost ratio that can be calculated easily from easy to find data. This model can help managers estimate how inefficient warehousing can become if inventory is not periodically checked for obsolescence. The decision tool from this research can be used for tactical and for making strategic decision. As a model to calculate the efficiency of warehouses in terms of reducing inventory and avoiding obsolete inventory, the model can help managers estimate how inefficient warehousing can become if inventory is not periodically checked for obsolescence, and this research develops a carrying cost ratio.

Appendix 15.A

See Figures 15.9 and 15.10.

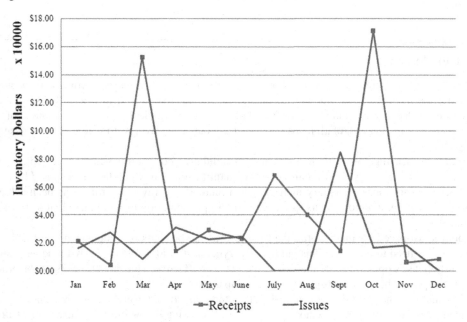

FIGURE 15.9   Distribution of warehouse 4.

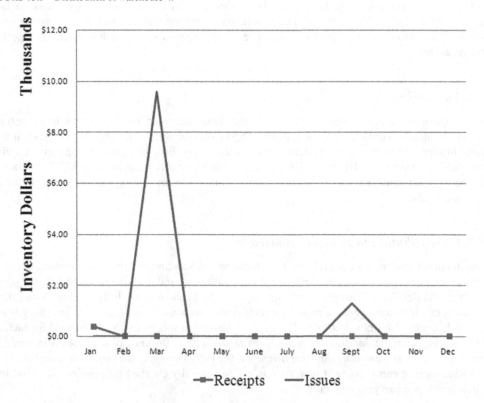

FIGURE 15.10   Distribution of warehouse 3.

Appendix 15.B

See Tables 15.17–15.22.

TABLE 15.17

Calculation of Inventory Turns for Warehouse 1

Month	Receipts	Issues	Ending Balance	Inventory Turns Projected Rate
Jan	$1,568.36	$7,236.51	$202,869.62	0.43
Feb	1,761.13	9,551.05	195,812.47	0.59
Mar	4,287.56	8,331.95	202,217.92	0.49
Apr	1,376.41	481.05	203,421.35	0.03
May	4,036.50	9,081.41	204,298.67	0.53
June	2,511.46	4,442.58	200,335.48	0.27
July	4,409.40	12,733.49	201,053.26	0.76
Aug	2,475.40	2,232.99	191,966.22	0.14
Sept	13,410.46	6,882.61	255,630.13	0.32
Oct	9,355.39	207.81	264,354.49	0.01
Nov	1,725.00	6,002.56	265,309.89	0.27
Dec	2,716.90	12,102.76	256,821.40	0.57

TABLE 15.18

Average Inventory Turns for Warehouse 1

Total Receipts	Total Issues	Avg. Ending Balance	Inventory Turn Rate
$48,065.62	$79,286.77	$220,340.91	0.36

TABLE 15.19

Calculations for Inventory Turns for Warehouse 3

Month	Receipts	Issues	Ending Balance	Inventory Turns Projected Rate
Jan	$380.50	$0.00	$176,160.86	0.00
Feb	0.00	0.00	176,160.86	0.00
Mar	0.00	9,574.71	166,586.12	0.69
Apr	0.00	0.00	166,586.12	0.00
May	0.00	0.00	166,586.12	0.00
June	0.00	0.00	166,586.12	0.00
July	0.00	0.00	166,586.12	0.00
Aug	0.00	0.00	166,586.12	0.00
Sept	0.00	1,285.27	165,300.85	0.09
Oct	0.00	0.00	165,300.85	0.00
Nov	0.00	0.00	135,890.72	0.00
Dec	0.00	0.00	135,890.72	0.00

TABLE 15.20

Average Inventory Turns for Warehouse 3

Total Receipts	Total Issues	Avg. Ending Balance	Inventory Turn Rate
$0.00	$10,859.99	$162,851.80	0.07

TABLE 15.21

Calculation of Inventory Turns for Warehouse 4

Month	Receipts	Issues	Ending Balance	Inventory Turns Projected Rate
Jan	$21,064.40	$16,068.08	$551,494.86	0.35
Feb	4,285.37	27,255.85	528,864.35	0.62
Mar	152,430.30	8,551.39	477,191.54	0.22
Apr	14,224.90	30,906.12	480,220.13	0.77
May	29,101.65	22,447.35	485,137.98	0.56
June	23,086.43	24,459.24	444,811.66	0.66
July	68,153.57	0.00	505,870.59	0.00
Aug	40,169.52	0.00	558,767.55	0.00
Sept	14,358.71	84,839.63	455,376.68	2.24
Oct	171,228.53	16,379.99	548,123.65	0.36
Nov	6,281.58	18,284.57	508,378.06	0.43
Dec	8,611.20	0.00	516,703.66	0.00

TABLE 15.22

Average Inventory Turns for Warehouse 4

Total Receipts	Total Issues	Avg. Ending Balance	Inventory Turn Rate
$531,931.75	$249,192.21	$505,078.39	0.49

REFERENCES

Ballard, G., and Howell, G. (1995). Toward construction JIT. *Proceedings of the 1995 ARCOM Conference, Association of Researchers in Construction Management*, Sheffield.

Caglar, D., Li, C.L., and Simchi-Levi, C. (2003). Two-echelon spare parts inventory system subject to a service constraint. *IIE Transactions*, 36, 655–666.

DeScioli, D.T., and Byrnes, L.S. (2001). Differentiating the hospital supply chain for enhanced performance. Master's Thesis, Rutgers University, New Brunswick, NJ.

Gossard, Gary. (2003). Best practices for inventory reduction, supply chain market. 13 Jan. 2003 Web 23 Mar. 2010.

Graves, S.C. (1985). A multi-echelon inventory model for a repairable item with one-for-one replenishment. *Management Science*, 31, 1247–1256.

Holsenback, E.J., and McGill, H.J. (2007). A survey of inventory holding cost assessment and safety stock allocation. *Academy of Accounting and Financial Studies Journal*, 11(1), 111–120.

IOMA: Managing Logistics (2002). Inventory carrying costs: Is there a "right" way to calculate them?

Johnson, J.C., Wood, D.F., Wardlow, D.L., and Murphy, P.R., Jr. (1999). *Contemporary Logistics*, 7th Edition. Prentice Hall, Upper Saddle River, NJ.

Larry, P.V. (1983). System to maximize inventory performance in a small hospital. *American Journal of Hospital Pharmacy*, 40(1), 70–73.

Lee, C.B. (2003). Multi-echelon inventory optimization. Evant White Paper Series. www.stanford.edu/group/scforum/Welcome/white%20Papers/Multi-Echelon%20%Inventory720Optimization%20-%20Evant%20white%20paper.pdf. Accessed: August 30, 2007.

Mecca, S. (2000). As sequences flow: Proposal of organizational rules for lean construction management. *IGLC-&7 Proceedings*, Brighton.

Nicholson, L., Vakharia, A.J., and Erenguc, S.S. (2004). Outsourcing inventory management decisions in healthcare: Models and application. *European Journal of Operational Research*, 154, 271–290.

Piasecki, D. (2001). Optimizing economic order quantity. *IIE Solutions*.

Raghuram. Inventory metrics. 6 Apr. 2010. http://www2.egr.uh.edu/~araguram/INVENTORY+METRICS-sachin1.htm.

REM Associates. (n.d.). *Methodology of Calculating Inventory Carrying Costs*. Princeton, NJ.

Rogers, D. F. and Tsubakitani, S. (1991). Newsboy-style results for multi-echelon inventory problems: Backorders optimization with intermediate delays. *Journal of Operational Research Society*, 42(1), 57–68.

Schnetzler, M.J., Sennheiser, A., and Schonsleben, P. (2007). A Decomposition-based approach for the development of a supply chain strategy. *International Journal of Production Economics*, 105, 21–42.

Schonberger, E., and Andriessen, L. (1982). The Apollonian Clockwork: Tempo (New Series), 3, 3–21.

Sinha, D., and Matta, K.F. (1991). Multi-echelon (R, S) inventory model. *Decision Sciences*, 22(3), 484–499.

Talluri, S., Cetin, K., and Gardner, A.J. (2004). Integrating demand and supply variability into safety stock evaluations. *International Journal of Physical Distribution & Logistics Management*, 31(1), 62–69.

Tommelein, I.D. (1997). Discrete-event simulation of lean construction process. *IGLC-5 Proceedings*, University of California, Berkeley, CA, 121–123.

Wang, Y., Cohen, M.A., and Zheng, Y.S. (2000). A two-echelon repairable system with the restocking-center-dependent depot replenishment lead times. *Management Science*, 46, 1441–1453.

Wild, T. (2002). *Best Practices in Inventory Management*. John Wiley & Sons, New York.

Williams, M. (2009). 10 keys to inventory reduction. The Williams Supply Chain Group, Inc. 18 Nov. Web. 23 Mar. 2010.

Wilson, R.H. (1934). A scientific routine for stock control. *Harvard Business Review*, 12, 116–128

16

Manufacturing Feasibility Evaluation of RFID Chips Embedded in Artificial Organs

Maurice Cavitt, Erick C. Jones, and Deijing Kong

16.1 Introduction

Radio frequency identification (RFID) technology has the ability to operate without the restrictions of line of sight. RFID systems are very popular and useful tools in manufacturing, supply chain management, and inventory control. RFID systems consist of two main components: the radio frequency (RF) tags (transponders) and the RF reader (transceivers). The RFID tag reader interrogates the tag providing information, which is stored on the digital memory chip, which contains detailed descriptions such as location, price, color, date, and age by beaconing a specific RF signal. The RF tags respond to this signal by transmitting back a unique serial number or electronic product code. RFID tags have numerous advantages such as reasonable data storage capacity, read/write/rewrite capability, ability to operate in harsh environments, and high scan rates. Since RFID tags are equipped with microchips embedded inside of them, their functionality can range from integrated sensors, to read/write storage, to supporting encryption and access control.

RFID memory chip can provide a channel to communicate with the staff, which cannot be accessed after implanting an RFID tag. After the artificial organ is embedded in the living body, the activities and condition of the embedded artificial organ is critical for the life of the patient. For this reason, the functionalities and condition of the artificial organ has much interest by researchers and doctors. The utilization of RFID system embedded inside artificial organ presents an effectual and feasible solution.

In a current publication, Jones et al. describe the advantages and limitations of utilizing RFID technology to track pharmaceutical drugs. They begin from the manufacture lot and continue through distribution to the point of interest within the patient's body. Jones et al. also demonstrate medical tracking strategies for patients, staff members, equipment, and information that could be implemented to increase the efficiency of healthcare, as well as facilitate better patient outcomes. Studies have been performed to demonstrate the opportunity for resource utilization and efficiency increases when equipment location is facilitated with an RFID system [1]. Sangwan [2] proposes an RFID system for patients, charts, and equipment location within a multi-level hospital setting. This system includes an alert system to notify staff members when a tracked item is removed from defined boundaries. Cypack has embedded RFID chips into pharmaceutical packaging to track patient compliance by monitoring when the package is opened, but has not integrated it into the actual medication [3]. For surgical procedures, RFID tags have been tested for tracking and tracing surgical sponges in order to eliminate errors due to manual counting at the completion of a procedure [4]. It is envisioned that the same concept and technology can be utilized to address the concept of integrating RFID technology in artificial organs. The overall goal of the pending research is to utilize the same concepts addressed above which has the ability to lead to the development of a biocompatible RFID tag for use, beginning with the manufacturer and continuing through distribution to the point of interest within the patient's body.

In Choi et al.'s research [5], an RFID tag system was created to store biological information by body signal detection.

It displays an integrated circuitry tag chip which is composed of a seven block system consisting of analog front end, digital controller, Electrical Erasable Programmable Read-Only Memory abbreviated as EEPROM, heartbeat sensor interface, blood pressure sensor, and blood sugar sensor. The tag has the ability to detect vital information pertaining to heartbeats, blood pressure, and blood sugar levels by the way of sensors. Once captured, the information is stored inside an embedded memory component. From this point, the information can be transmitted from the tag to the reader. There are two critical components that the RFID tag builds upon; these components are known as the data transaction block and sensor interfaces. The data transaction circuitry which specifically describes an event contains a command interpreter, error detection, and collision avoidance circuits, while the sensor interface comprises resistance deviation-to-pulse width converter and interface circuit. The command interpreter application confines stored data inside the flash memory; the error detection has the ability to recognize transmission errors during the activity of data exchange between the RFID reader and the tags; the collision avoidance circuitry application is to reduce the chance of data shortages when the tags are in the process of transmitting a Unique Item Identifier (UID) to a reader at the same time. The resistance deviation-to-pulse width converter in the sensor interface has the ability to detect minor resistance change of the resistive sensors having a high fixed offset resistance, while the sensor interface circuit with RFID tag is to transfer generated Pulse Width Modulation (PWM) signals to the RFID tag system.

After implementation, it was proved that the novel RFID tag system with sensors can detect and store vital information such as blood pressure and body temperature. In addition, the novel tag can be expanded to obtain other bio-information by adding more sensors. The size of this type of chips is $4.5\,\text{mm} \times 4.5\,\text{mm}$ using Hynix 0.18-μm CMOS, and the size is regular and normal.

The RFID systems utilized in the embedded artificial organ must be small enough to be ignored by the living body except storing the bio-information. As lectured by Hitachi, micro-RFID tag (wireless tag) IC measuring only $0.05 \times 0.05 \times 0.005\,\text{mm}$ was achieved in 2007 [6]. The IC was manufactured using 90-nm CMOS technology using Silicon on Insulator (SOI) substrates. The size of CMOS used in Hitachi micro-RFID tag IC is as small as 1/2 in Choi's research, and the size of tag IC is much smaller than Choi's. Hitachi super micro-RFID tag IC features a three-layer metal wiring layer and a $21 \times 32\,\mu\text{m}$ memory chip capable of recording 128-bit data, but the antenna is separated with the tag IC, and maximum communication range with the reader is $300\,\text{mm}$.

16.2 Methods

This chapter discusses biocompatible concerns such as how a micro-RFID system can be designed and incorporated into an artificial organ to provide critical information of the device. This chapter also discusses concerns such as how RFID technology integrated into an artificial organ can provide accurate information for doctors and nurses assisting patients in critical need or regular checkups to make sure the device is operating correctly.

Reducing the size of the RFID tag and antenna by using micro-manufacturing technology and providing a cost effective manufacturing process will be a feasible solution for reducing the cost and increasing the performance. Some researchers believe that manufacturing of electrostatic devices such as antennas may not be prudent at levels of 40 nm and below because serious miniaturization problems may be expected in the next six to ten years [7]. The testing and design at the proposed 100 micron meter level is cost effective and prudent to test RFID technologies.

The long-term research objective is to design a reliable RFID system that can be manufactured at the micro-scale level to provide better performance and feasibility to be integrated inside artificial organs. The research objective is to test and evaluate the manufacturing design of antennas for RFID tags at the micro-scale level. These effects can be evaluated after testing of antennas designed from micro-manufactured process such as Electro Discharge Machining (EDM).

16.3 Discussion and Conclusion

By literature research, the design of RFID system for detecting and storing biological information and micro-RFID tag IC has been developed by predecessors. The concept of using RFID tags implanted in the artificial organ to detect and store biological information and the organ's description is feasible, which can make the jobs and task of doctors easier when assisting a patient, as well as to check for any internal abnormal conditions.

The best design for micro-RFID system is to make the tag and antenna together as one single cell to reduce its size, and micro-manufacturing needs to be utilized in the process. This research intends to meet the proposed objectives by completing the following specific objectives:

Specific Objective #1: Evaluate manufacturing processes that reduce RFID passive tag size. Incorporate a new antenna design to reduce the size of the tag without sacrificing the performances. These tags can be utilized for tagging individual items at the item level and in the future to promote less obtrusive tagging in small items such as microprocessors

Specific Objective #2: Evaluate processes that reduce RFID passive tag cost. Develop a manufacturing methodology to make the RFID tags at reduced cost. This development process will identify the manufacturing issues of the new antenna designed from Specific Objective #1 and select a set of efficient manufacturing techniques and the process sequence.

Specific Objective #3: Evaluate and test micro-RFID chip. Manufacture an RFID chip imbedded in artificial organs to provide doctors and nurses critical information to better serve patients. A unique chip that has the correct polarization and tag reflection is novel for an integrated RFID chip. The goal is to develop a chip that supports this critical information.

Acknowledgment

We would like to acknowledge the University of Nebraska-Lincoln Radio Frequency Supply Chain and Logistics (RfSCL) Laboratory for their support and time with the work of this chapter.

REFERENCES

1. I. K. Mun, A. B. Kantrowitz, P. W. Carmel, K. P. Mason, and D. W. Engels. Active RFID System Augmented with 2D Barcode for Asset Management in a Hospital Setting. *IEEE International Conference on RFID Gaylord Texan Resort.* Grapevine, TX, March 2007.
2. R. S. Sangwan, R. G. Qiu, and D. Jessen. Using RFID Tags for Tracking Patients, Charts and Medical Equipment within an Integrated Health Delivery Network. *IEEE Networking, Sensing and Control, ICNSC2005*, p. 1070, March 2005.
3. J. Emigh. Supply Chain Management/Logistics. *eweek.com*, August 2004. August 2010. www.eweek.com/c/a/Supply-Chain-Management-and-Logistics/Merger-Creates-65M-EPharmacy-with-RFID/.
4. A. Rogers, E. Jones, and D. Oleyniknov. Radio Frequency Identification (RFID) Applied to Surgical Sponges. *Surgical Endoscopy*, 3, 1235–1237, 2007.
5. Y. L. Choi, S. M. Kim, S. H. Son, and K. R. Cho. Design of the RFID for Storage of Biological Information. *Journal of Systemics, Cybernetics and Informatics*, 7.
6. T. Nozawa. Hitachi Achieves 0.05-mm Square Super Micro RFID Tag, Further Size Reductions in Mind. *Tech-On!* February 2007. August 2010. http://techon.nikkeibp.co.jp/english/NEWS_EN/20070220/127959
7. L. B. Kish. End of Moore's Law: Thermal (Noise) Death of Integration in Micro and Nano Electronics. Texas A&M University, Department of Electrical Engineering, College Station, TX 2002.

Part 5

New Trends in Global Supply Chain Engineering

17

Embedding Integrated RFID Sensors into Fiber Reinforced Plastics During the Manufacturing Process

Billy Joe Gray, Felicia Jefferson, and Erick C. Jones

Great things are done by a series of small things brought together.

Vincent Van Gough

17.1 Introduction

The introduction begins the discussion of the topics of embedding electronic sensors into fiber reinforced polymers (FRPs) and the use of radio frequency identification (RFID) in order to satisfy wireless communication with these sensors. The chapter discusses the reasons why material sensing is necessary, how wireless sensing falls back into manufacturing, how sensing would be used in manufacturing, and how sensing enables smart materials. The research purpose, executive summary, and the organization of the dissertation are all set up in the introduction.

17.1.1 Sensing in Materials

There are several reasons why researchers and engineers are interested in sensing capabilities inside of materials. First, in the manufacture of FRPs, many designs utilize material structures that are larger than necessary due to known deficiencies in the manufacturing process. These deficiencies include voids in the resin from entrapped air pockets, inconsistencies in the catalyst resin mix, incomplete saturation between the resin and the fiber reinforcement, and a list of other possible defects (Loyola, Zhao, Loh, & La Saponara, 2013; Mason Al-Ali, & Gerhardt, 2006; Philipp, Winkler, & Reinhart, 2013; Strong, 2008). Sensing in the material during the manufacturing processes allows the researchers and engineers to understand what types of stresses occur during these processes and what physical properties are in a specific batch (Merilampi, Björninen, Ukkonen, Ruuskanen, & Sydänheimo, 2011). The inclusion of sensing can lead to higher quality manufacturing processes that create better materials and the ability for designers and manufacturers to reduce weight and thickness. According to Mason Al-Ali, & Gerhardt (2006), most engineers add extra thicknesses to FRP designs to allow for these defects in the manufacturing process. These thicker parts cause higher material costs for the manufacturer and increased weight in the part, and possibly pass cost inefficiencies on to the consumer of the part.

A second reason for researchers and engineers to want to sense material conditions falls back to manufacturing. Manufacturers know what the intended cure rates are supposed to be in composite manufacturing. They also know that parts do not always cure evenly throughout the part which can cause built up stresses in the part (Strong, 2008). Many of these stresses can affect the bond between the resin and the reinforcement resulting in loads that are translated through the resin onto the reinforcement in an optimal manner. Once the parts are manufactured, they are often tested to ensure that the material will meet the design requirements. With embedded sensing, manufacturers will be able to tell what stresses the part experiences during manufacturing and whether the part cured correctly. Because this can be performed real time, extra materials may not have to be manufactured for testing thereby reducing costs in manufacturing. Coupled with the designer's improved efficiencies mentioned before, composite manufacturing can become more cost efficient, which aides in making composites a more economically viable option. The more efficient costs also play into more possible adoptions of composites over other material types.

A third reason why researchers and engineers are interested in the ability to sense inside of materials is for the development of cyber-physical sensing. Dumstorff, Paul, and Lang explained cyber-physical sensing as "… computational elements (cyber) collaborate and even merge with the physical elements" (2014). The integration of sensing into materials leads researchers back into cybernetics and smart materials where the sensors embedded into the material can feedback information about what physical properties the structure is being exposed to. The sensing capabilities allow for materials to identify damage and provide input about their condition (Arronche, La Saponara, Yesil, & Bayram, 2013). An example of this approach can be viewed from the perspective of damage control from catastrophic events where the structure can only provide further use in a limited capacity such as limiting an aircraft's maneuverability based on a damaged wing structure. Another view of this approach can be from a maintenance perspective where the sensor-enabled material identifies when it needs to be serviced based on its actual use instead of a specified time interval.

17.1.2 Why Is There a Need for Integrated Sensing?

The need for integrated sensing is so large that the Department of Energy (DoE) listed it as one of their four key technologies in the Enabling Technologies category at their Fiber Reinforced Polymer Composite Manufacturing Workshop in January 2014. This need was identified from the standpoint that "Sensors are not well integrated with data or manufacturing processes" ("Fiber Reinforced Polymer Composite Manufacturing Workshop: Summary Report," 2014). The workshop also noted the lack of use of intelligent sensors. From the workshop's perspective, the necessary "distributed sensors linked to data and physics, integrated with manufacturing and embedded in structures is an area of opportunity" ("Fiber Reinforced Polymer Composite Manufacturing Workshop: Summary Report," 2014). Included in these areas of opportunity are self-diagnostic materials, "sensing technologies, especially for joints", "nondestructive testing at the point of manufacture", and data informatics and data mining at the material level of manufacturing ("Fiber Reinforced Polymer Composite Manufacturing Workshop: Summary Report," 2014). One of the outcomes from the workshop was to identify the need of using actual processing data to produce design data needed to design new structures. The DoE viewed the design data as a manner in which designers could reduce the need for models and simulations that they currently build in order to determine the strength and behavior of structures built with these materials. They also noted the belief that the use of integrated sensors would lead to being able to predict the life of composite parts and components which would advance the use of composites in different applications ("Fiber Reinforced Polymer Composite Manufacturing Workshop: Summary Report," 2014). This includes using the sensor and nondestructive tools to monitor the material's life.

17.2 Purpose for this Research

Unfortunately, researchers and engineers typically only measure the first few products to ensure that the process will yield what they believe is an acceptable product. Sensing is discontinued after the first few products, usually because the first products would have to be destroyed in order to determine material strength. Most sensors currently in use need an interface to the outside world in order to communicate sensor data. This is often in the form of leads or wires. It would also be useful for a number of reasons to be able to sense in the material during their end use. Wired sensors would be somewhat prohibitive in these applications. RFID, however, enables the ability to wirelessly communicate information, and its use is the focus of this study.

17.2.1 Polymers during Cure Processes

Though an older concept, the monitoring of the cure process of high-value FRP components has traditionally relied on wired leads to provide power and feedback to computers so that the process can be monitored. This results in the measurements being taken in a cutout or on a scarf edge, locations that will be removed from the final product. This also yields stress points in these areas due to the protrusion of the electrical leads that lead from the sensors back to the computer equipment. By utilizing RFID tags, it is postulated that the sensing of the cure cycle could be easily monitored without inducing defects in the areas of the part that they are embedded in.

One of the methods engineers utilize when designing FRP parts is to increase the thickness of the part by a safety margin. They make the parts thicker than they may need to be in order to offset any inconsistencies in the materials that cause weakness or premature fatigue. This is done primarily because of variation and difficulties in monitoring every part that is manufactured. Variations in conditions, including temperature and humidity, can affect the stress in the part. Too high a temperature can lead to creep in the resin. Too low a temperature inhibits the polymer's crosslinking. Both feed into the quality and strength of the FRP (Jeon, Muliana, and La Saponara, 2014; Miyano, Nakada, and Cai, 2008; Nakada and Miyano, 2009). In order to know how the FRP part is processed, researchers have developed techniques and equipment that will allow them to monitor the cure process in real time.

In order to monitor FRP development, sensors are embedded into the layers of reinforcement of the FRP. Some sensors include fiber optics, which are woven into the fiber reinforcements and act as a part of the reinforcement matrix as well as sense stress throughout the part. Other sensors include dielectric sensing which utilizes electric current flow to detect when crosslinking occurs in the resin. Current will flow while the resin remains viscous but will decrease as the resin continues to crosslink. This allows the observer to know the precise time that the part is actually done. Though there are other methods, all have the same recurring theme of having to have wired leads that run from the sensor to a multiplexer or industrial computer to actually interpret the sensor and record the data. Even in the case of fiber optics, where the fiber optic sensor can remain in the FRP, the leads that run to the computer create a defect resulting in that part of the FRP to be removed from the final part. In some instances, this is acceptable if the leads protrude in a cut out region, but it may be that extra material has to be added to the part to attach the sensor to the leads. Mason states: "During part development, cure can be reliably characterized, in general terms, using these variables. Cure rates, however, vary from part to part, even when parts are meant to be identical" (2006).

Mason continues:

> Without a way to directly measure the progress of crosslinking, fabricators of thermoset composites traditionally have had to build a safety margin into cure times in order to avoid the damage that premature demolding can do to tools and undercured parts. While this ensures that sufficient crosslinking occurs, it lengthens cycle time and processing costs beyond what might otherwise be required. Additionally, there is the risk of overcuring, which can reduce ductility, making a part brittle.

(2006)

17.3 Research Objectives

The objective of this research is to develop a methodology, test the results, and evaluate the use of the sensor-enabled RFID tags to wirelessly monitor and communicate the physical stresses that an FRP part sees during the manufacturing and end use of that part. This portion of the research evaluates how the RFID tag affects the mechanical structure of the FRP part. The research objectives associated with this project are shown in Table 17.2 and are defined below. The outline of the research is shown in Figure 17.1.

Research Objective 1: Evaluate the impact of embedded RFID tags on the mechanical properties of a composite structure. The methods and approach to be used for this research are to evaluate which factors are necessary to measure a structure's mechanical properties, determine the feasibility of finite element methodology (FEM) as a modeling tool to predict the stresses on a structure, test and evaluate the necessary factors using finite element analysis (FEA), perform visual inspection on composite parts to validate materials are free from defects, and test parts to the applicable American Society for Testing and Materials (ASTM) specifications.

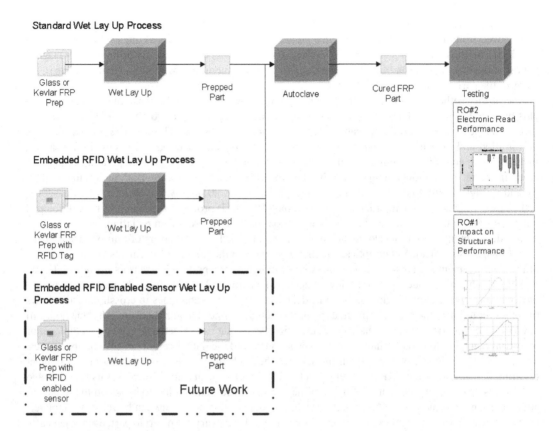

FIGURE 17.1   RFID-enabled sensing in FRPs.

Research Objective 2: Evaluate the impact of embedded RFID tags on electronic transmission read-ability performance. The methods and approach for this component of the research are to look at how to determine the performance factors for measuring the electronic transmission readability performance factors of the embedded RFID tags, test and evaluate the embedded RFID tag performance factors on electronic transmission readability, and determine the economic viability of embedding RFID tags into a composite material.

Research Objective 3: Evaluate the impact of embedded RFID tags on life cycle analysis (LCA) sustainability parameters. The methods and approach envisioned in this portion of the research are to determine the LCA sustainability parameters and test and evaluate the LCA sustainability parameters.

The intellectual merit of this research is that it yields a wireless tool that can be used to measure real-time conditions of an FRP's physical characteristics during the cure process. Current techniques require that the sensors are physically tethered to the computer. The broader impact of this research is an embedded method that allows for monitoring an FRP during further processing and use.

17.4 Organization of this Dissertation

The dissertation follows a five-point engineering format of introduction, background, methodology, results, and conclusion.

In this chapter, the information regarding why this research is being performed is introduced. The section describes the topic of physical sensing in FRPs and why there is a need for FRPs in wireless sensing. It also explains the purpose of this dissertation and the need for mechanical testing of embedded electronics.

Chapter 2 discusses the literature review of RFID technologies, FRPs, and embedded sensing. The background also discusses recent, relevant funded research.

Part 3 defines the methodology used in this research. This includes the specific objectives, the research methodology, and the tools used to validate or dispute the hypotheses.

Part 4 discusses and interprets the results of the experiments. Computer simulations, statistical data, and economic expectations are included in the chapter.

Part 5 is the conclusion of the research and provides a summary of the experiments conducted. It includes the limitations of the research and describes the next steps in the sequence of the research.

17.5 Background

In the background, definitions used in the research along with others' work that influenced this line of research are defined. Similar research that was previously funded through the National Science Foundation (NSF), the DoE, and through industry is identified and discussed. The chapter concludes with information on life cycle costing (LCC) and LCA.

17.5.1 RFID as a Technology

17.5.1.1 Radio Frequency Identification (RFID)

RFID is a technology that has been in existence in some form since the 1930s. One of the earliest practical uses of utilizing radio frequency (RF) to identify an object was in the form of radio detection and ranging (RADAR) (Jones & Chung, 2008, 2011; Balasubramanian, Jones, Gray, & Armstrong, 2015). Further advances led to RFID becoming more commonplace. The Dallas North Toll Road opened up in the 1960s and utilized RFID tags to identify the different vehicles on the toll road (Jones & Chung, 2008, 2011; Balasubramanian, Jones, Gray, & Armstrong, 2015). RFID tags were first used in cattle ear tags to track cattle as they moved from lot to lot. Further advances continued as electronics became smaller. RFID tags are small enough now that they can be implanted in a human or swallowed in a pill (Balasubramanian, Jones, Gray, & Armstrong, 2015).

17.5.1.2 RFID Theory of Operation

RFID works on the principles of electromagnetic frequencies. An electromagnetic wave is emitted from an antenna. Tags in the range of transmissions are energized and transmit back their recorded data. The antenna sends the tag signals to a reader that interprets the signal into data. Figure 17.2 shows a diagram of how RFID works.

The distance that a tag will operate at is impacted by the environment, the frequency, the power of the original signal, and the type of tag that is being used. There are several environmental factors to consider when RF signals are transmitted. Liquids and metallic objects can shield or block the RF transmissions. Many materials may reduce the signal strength but do not block it.

There are also several RF frequencies that can be used. These range from the high frequency 13.57 MHz up to the ultrahigh frequency 2.4 GHz. The signal strength can also be varied by changing the power of the signal (Balasubramanian, Jones, Gray, & Armstrong, 2015). There are two main types of tags that are used: passive and active.

17.5.1.3 Passive Tags

A passive RFID Tag is a tag that does not contain an integrated power source such as a battery. Passive tags are able to harvest the electrical energy they need to operate from the radio frequencies transmitted from the reader's antenna. Because these tags do not need an integrated power source, they have a more simplistic design that entails the RFID chip, the RFID antenna, and a backing material that the antenna and chip are adhered to.

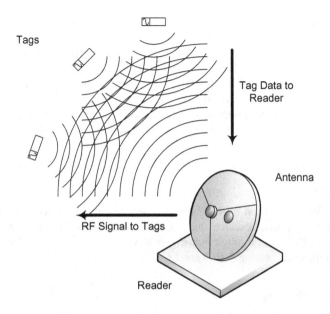

FIGURE 17.2   RFID theory of operation.

One of the biggest advantages the passive tag holds is the unlimited shelf life of the tag. Unless the tag is damaged through mechanical or environmental abuse, it should be able to respond to interrogation from a reader for an indefinite time period. Another advantage is the cost of the tag. Depending on volume, these tags can run as low as $0.05 per tag. It is still somewhat more expensive than printing on a barcode, but the additional benefits over barcodes make this tag economically attractive. Table 17.1 shows some of the advantages and disadvantages between RFID and barcode technologies. One of the drawbacks with passive tags is their read range. Compared to active tags, passive tags have a much smaller read range and can only reflect the energy that they receive from the reader antenna.

17.5.1.4 Active Tags

Active tags differ from passive tags in that they contain an integrated power source, normally a battery. The battery is used to operate the circuitry of the tag as well as provide a power source for the antenna. Active tags can also be connected with other devices such as global positioning systems (GPSs) or sensors in order to provide communication and input into a multimodal system. Active tags are larger and more expensive than passive tags. Their main advantage is the distances that they can transmit and receive signals.

TABLE 17.1

Advantages and Disadvantages of Barcode and RFID Technologies

	Barcode	**RFID**
Advantages	Indefinite lifespan depending on environment	Indefinite lifespan
	Inexpensive to produce	Readable through different materials
		Read many tags at once
		Reusable
		Can integrate with other devices
Disadvantages	Requires line of sight to operate	Costs are comparably higher
	Readable one at a time	
	Sensitive to handling	
	Sensitive to environment	
	Degrades over time	

Source: Balasubramanian, Jones, Gray, and Armstrong (2015).

17.5.1.5 Semi-Active Tags

Semi-active tags use technologies from both active and passive tags. They utilize an internal power source to operate internal circuitry and sensors. The communication of the tag still occurs through scavenged energy from the RF signal from the reader antenna. This allows for a tag that operates even after the battery dies on the sensors.

17.5.2 Fiber Reinforced Polymers

17.5.2.1 Manufacturing Processes

17.5.2.1.1 Wet Layup

The wet layup process is a method commonly used to build composite materials (Strong, 2008). This process allows for a variety of shapes and sizes to be built though it is commonly utilized more in large volume manufacturing of engineering composites than in advanced composites (Strong, 2008). One aspect of this method that is similar to many processes is that because of its manual nature, it is a good solution for small production runs where it would not be feasible to incorporate an automated solution.

The wet layup process lends itself to many types of resins that can be utilized. Most resins are shipped to the end user in the "neat" form where the end user will add any fillers or reinforcements that they desire in the end product. This results in resins from the low-cost polyesters up to the more expensive epoxies and bismaleimides as possible resin solutions.

The initiators and catalysts used in wet layup are typically chosen based on two criteria: cure temperature and resin type (Strong, 2008). Some resin/catalyst mixes can completely cure at room temperature (i.e., polyester/MEKP), while others need to be cured in an oven or autoclave. This affects the pot life of the mixes and the amount that can be mixed at one time. Depending on the accuracy of the measurements of the two components, the ratios and temperatures can induce variations from part to part.

Wet layup can utilize a variety of forms of reinforcement. These reinforcements can be anything from "mats, woven cloths, knits, or any other kind of common textile goods" (Strong, 2008). Reinforcements that lend themselves to this type of process include glass fiber, aramid fiber (Kevlar™), and carbon fiber. The reinforcements are laid upon the tool, and the resin/catalyst mix is applied and worked into the reinforcement. Depending on the strengths and mechanical properties that are to be attained, the reinforcements may be applied in different orientations. This assures that the final part will function in a manner according to the engineering specifications.

Though wet layup is a valid solution, it can potentially contribute problems to the part being manufactured. The problems, as defined by Strong (2008), include

- difficulty in aligning the fibers in exactly the directions desired
- difficulty in optimizing the amount of fibers to achieve the highest properties possible
- difficulty in controlling the fiber/resin ratio
- difficulty in getting full fiber wet-out
- difficulty in reducing the void content
- potential problems in mixing the resin and hardener (including emission and toxicity problems.

(p. 389)

17.5.3 Embedded Sensing

There have been multiple instances where sensors have been embedded into materials. The common goal is the ability to sense what the materials are exposed to in terms of stress or temperatures. In some cases, the sensor is a part of the structure in the material such as in the use of fiber optics. In other cases, the sensor is a defect in the material's structure, thereby degrading the strength of the material. In most of these implementations, a major problem has been the protrusion of electrical leads through the surface of the material. As a result, manufacturers can only sense in areas of the material that will be removed or do not factor in to the load on the structure.

Some newer developments in the sensing embedded into materials is the use of carbon nanotubes to determine impact and stress. The University of California at Davis has used this methodology in their labs over the past several years. What they have done involves using a matrix of Multi-Walled Carbon Nanotubes (MWCNs). They measure the electrical resistance and how it changes upon being influenced by an outside force. This allows them to measure the effects of stress on the surface of a material. One of the drawbacks is again the need for electrical leads that protrude from the part.

Another method of sensing is to embed fiber optic filaments into the structure. With fiber reinforced composites, the filament is included in the reinforcement. Researchers measure how the light is distorted while a stress is applied to the part in order to determine how the part is loaded. Again, this method requires that the filament is physically connected to leads in order to interface with the sensor.

Schaaf (2008) evaluated the use of embedded electronics in fiber reinforced composites for her dissertation. She utilized piezoelectronics but established a test protocol that was similar to that used in this research. What her research found is that depending on the variation of the sensor embedded into the composite some sensors worked with little difference in the structural strength of the part while other sensors negatively affected the structure of the material.

In the work by La Saponara, Horsley, and Lestari (2011), piezoelectric materials have been embedded into load-bearing composite structures in order to determine the stresses enacted upon that material. The electronic devices have been embedded into monolithic and sandwich structures as well as surface mounted onto the structures in order to monitor the structural health of those structures. This method is one of the methods envisioned as a nondestructive testing of finished materials by allowing the physical properties of the material to be known without destroying the part. In their series of research, La Saponara, Horsley, and Lestari (2011) utilized fatigue testing to cause failures in their test specimens. This allowed them to determine how the part would read and fail over time.

Tang, Winkelmann, Lestari, and La Saponara (2011) worked on fatigue testing of piezoelectronics in fiberglass. They utilized a control part absent of any electronics and compared it against the specimens that they built with electronics embedded into different layers in the part. They loaded the part at different frequencies in order to induce and evaluate the stresses put on to the parts over different simulated loads. What they found was that their embedded specimens broke where the leads protruded through the materials while the specimen that had surface mount sensor broke in an area away from the sensors.

Jeon, Muliana, and La Saponara (2014) continued the use of piezoelectronics to determine mechanical and thermal stresses that act on an FRP. In this research, the authors are utilizing the electronics to read stress applied to the material due to changes in temperature. Their use of the piezoelectronics is geared more toward an indirect measurement of the temperature through mechanical stress. Their research utilized their models that were developed and tracked the models' performance against the known coefficient of thermal expansion and the measured stresses.

One of the concerns with most of the embedded sensors used to determine stresses on a part is the need for power. There has been some investigation into the use of RFID as a method to monitor fiber reinforced composites. Early work started with utilizing active tags inside of concrete structures to measure stresses on the structure.

Pille (2010) discusses integrating sensing into cast parts. One comment made by Pille that specifically shows the need for embedded sensing is "Integrated sensors detect mechanical and thermal stress or deformation as well as vibration inside the casting...". He further mentions the ability to use the sensor data to monitor real time and provide information regarding stresses that have or could cause damage to a part or assembly. Pille promotes the idea of utilizing the sensors to also aid in the manufacturing process by self-identifying and instructing where that casting should be routed (Pille, 2010). Though Pille's work was with cast metals, he did identify methods that may be useful when other RFID prohibitive materials such as carbon fiber need to be used. These methods included the frequency type of RFID tags to use, the placement of the tags in the material vs. on the surface of the material, and insulation of the tag from the prohibitive material.

Dumstorff, Paul, and Lang (2014) evaluated the challenge of integrating the inlay of the RFID tag into the resin/reinforcement matrix of an FRP. They performed FEA and simulated what stresses the tag would create in the part. They simulated with the tag being a harder structure than the matrix, and they simulated the matrix being a harder structure than the tag. Their simulations included tensile and bending stresses that were applied to the part and the effects that occurred between the part and the tag. Dumstorff, Paul, and Lang identified that the RFID tag does alleviate many of the problems typically seen with embedded sensing, predominately the problem of wired leads protruding through the part. They also noted the need for investigation of whether the electronics in the RFID tag would survive the manufacturing process for the FRP. Though their investigation did not address a solution, they identified the need to determine how to introduce electronics into the layers of the FRP without causing delamination in the material.

17.5.4 Life Cycle Analysis (LCA)

LCA is the estimation of the costs of the environmental impacts from a product's life cycle. These include refinement of the base materials needed to manufacture the subcomponents, the transportation costs, the assembly costs, the distribution costs, and the disposal costs along with traditional processes necessary to manufacture the product (EEA, 2014; USEPA, 2006). The main components when developing an LCA include the life cycle inventory (LCI) and the life cycle impact assessment (LCIA). The LCI quantifies energy and raw material requirements as well as atmospheric and waterborne emissions, solid wastes, and other releases that occur over the life of the product, process, or activity (USEPA, 2006). LCIA evaluates the potential impacts on human health and the environment based on the resources and emissions identified in the LCI (USEPA, 2006).

LCA is a widely used tool to evaluate environmental impacts. It has been performed by a number of people and organizations since the 1970s (Williams, 2004). There are differing frameworks that exist through the different organizations that look at different concepts such as cradle to cradle and cradle to grave. Some approaches look at economic input–output (IO), while others look at process sum or the energy consumption. Formalized standards exist within the Environmental Protection Agency (EPA), the International Organization for Standardization (ISO) and through various research groups.

Though there are numerous variations, the idea is that there is a framework followed that identifies areas to evaluate for the different products. In this research, three areas are identified in LCA: material production and manufacturing, useful life, and end of life. The different components in each of these areas are evaluated for their impact on the environment.

17.5.5 Life Cycle Costing

Life cycle costing (LCC) is an analysis tool used to assign costs to the different components determined in the LCA. It looks at initial production costs as well as the in use and the end of life costs associated with the life cycle of the product. With some extra effort, the tool can include the costs associated with environmental damage from chemicals, greenhouse gases, etc. This allows the toll more encompassing of the complete system instead of just evaluating the products value stream (Kendall, Keoleian, & Lepech, 2008).

LCC has not been around as long as LCA. The first appearances seem to be in the 1990s. Since then, it has been swept up into the ISO 14040 series of standards that address Environmental Management.

LCC follows along the same lines as the life cycle assessment. Costs are associated with the different processes and activities needed to manufacture a product, the impact that the product has on society and the environment during its useful life and at its end of life.

The LCA is important because it evaluates the impact of adding electronics to the composite. The research goal is to become more efficient in our design and manufacturing processes, but the efficiency does need to offset the material consumption in traditional design and manufacturing processes.

Multiple methods can be used to perform LCA and LCC. The Tiered Hybrid Analysis model, as defined by Suh and Huppes (2005), requires data for the commodity items used in manufacturing the product and evaluates the environmental costs for each process and during the three phases that will be evaluated: material production and manufacturing, useful life, and end of life.

There are other methods that can be used. LCA based on process analysis can be performed using the Process Flow Diagram approach or the Matrix Representation approach. LCA can also be performed using the IO approach. These three methods can give environmental impacts (Process Flow and Matrix) or economic impacts (IO), but they do not provide both. Hybrid approaches have been developed that allow for both environmental and economic impacts to be evaluated. The three approaches are the Tiered Hybrid Analysis, IO-based Hybrid Analysis, and Integrated Hybrid Analysis. The main differences between the approaches are tied to the availability of data and the geographical system boundaries. According to Suh and Huppes (2005), the Tiered Hybrid Analysis is not as complex as the other two, and most of the analysis can be performed in Excel.

The analysis of the data can be performed locally using a laptop computer, the internet, and Microsoft Excel. The chief concern and costs will be centered on the databases that will need to be accessed. These databases define the impact costs associated with the subcomponents and end products that make up the product that is under analysis.

17.5.6 Previous Relevant Funded Research

17.5.6.1 National Science Foundation

The original work behind this research began in response to the National Science Foundation (NSF) Division of Civil, Mechanical and Manufacturing Innovation (CMMI), in the Advanced Manufacturing Cluster, Manufacturing Machines and Equipment (MME) Program, PD 13–1468.

17.5.6.2 Department of Energy

In January 2014, the DoE's Advanced Manufacturing Office hosted the Fiber Reinforced Polymer Composite Manufacturing Workshop with the goal of working toward low-cost FRPs. The workshop focused on identifying concerns with the manufacturing process technologies, enabling technologies and approaches, and recycled and emerging materials. The three agencies that attended the workshop were the Advanced Manufacturing National Program Office, the Defense Advanced Research Projects Agency (DARPA), and the National Aeronautics and Space Agency (NASA). Some of the chief concerns were "building confidence in materials through a technology insertion program" and "increasing bonded composite confidence". Though the focus of material selection for designs has been predominately carbon fiber, the workshop indicated that "other fiber reinforced materials and integrated approaches that can meet the performance and cost targets could be acceptable" (Department of Energy, 2014).

One of the comments out of the enabling technologies and approaches group was the discussion of sensing and measurement. The group commented heavily on intelligent sensing from self-diagnosis and testing of materials to lifetime analysis of the material. Their comments showed that they believed that this may be the only manner in which the proliferation of FRPs could occur.

17.5.6.3 Industry

Bernhard, Dräger, Grabowski, Sotriffer, and Philipp (2011) evaluated embedding RFID tags into FRPs in order to track the materials through a company's production, inspection, and shipping processes. They evaluated the impact of readability of RFID in different types of FRPs, predominately in glass- and carbon-based FRPs. They found that they could read easily through glass FRPs but that the low-frequency RFID tags would work at a reduced distance through carbon FRPs. They also experimented with where in the composite layers they placed the RFID tags. One of their main concerns with embedding RFID into the composites was how it would affect the mechanical properties of the FRP's structure.

Research performed by Dumstorff, Paul, and Lang (2014) evaluated FRPs and the impact that an embedded RFID tag would have on the mechanical properties of the materials. Their evaluation centered on FEM simulation to determine how the tag and FRP would respond to different types of loads (shear, tensile, and compression). Their research showed that the polymer exhibited greater flexibility in the matrix than what the RFID tag was capable of. Though the research helps to show how the material would behave under different loads, all work was performed through the simulation software. There is no follow-up study that shows physical mechanical testing and the results of a production part.

17.5.7 Methodology

The research objectives are expanded upon in this section in order to define the specific tasks that were performed in the research. The specific methods, actions, and equipment that were taken to build, test, and evaluate the embedded RFID tags are outlined along with the methods used to collect the data from the tests.

17.5.7.1 Research Objectives and Specific Tasks

Table 17.2 shows the research objectives and tasks used in this research. The following sections will define the methodology used for each research objective and the corresponding tasks with each objective.

Research Objective 1: Evaluate the impact of embedded RFID tags on the mechanical properties of a composite structure.

Task 1—Evaluate the necessary factors to measure a structure's mechanical properties.

The first step was to identify the necessary tests and criteria to ensure that the materials' structures can be tested to determine what impact embedding the RFID tags would have.

Literature review identified several methods that others have used to validate structural integrity. Many of the researchers utilized the ASTM specifications as a basis for testing materials. The three most common test specifications used were the compression test (ASTM D695-02), the tensile test (ASTM D638-14), and the short-beam shear test (ASTM D2344/D2344M-13). The original proposal for this research called for tensile testing, but because the tensile test is predominately utilized to identify the strength of the fiber and not the bond between the fiber and the resin, it was decided that the test was not necessary for the research.

Loads and stresses are commonly subjected onto a part to determine if embedding a device results in a defect. Common measurements on the parts include their width, length, and thickness. These measurements were used to determine the part's volume. Once the part was loaded up and a failure occurred, the load was divided by the volume to determine the stress on the part.

Task 2—Determine the feasibility of FEM as a modeling tool to predict the stresses on a structure.

FEM was evaluated as a tool for identifying potential problems with embedding RFID into FRPs.

In order to model the composite parts for FEM, a software package needed to be identified that could perform the calculations necessary for the FEM. Based on availability, AutoDesk's Mechanical

TABLE 17.2

Research Objectives and Tasks

Research Objective 1: Evaluate the impact of embedded RFID tags on the mechanical properties of a composite structure.
Task 1—Evaluate the necessary factors to measure a structure's mechanical properties.
Task 2—Determine the feasibility of FEM as a modeling tool to predict the stresses on a structure.
Task 3—Test and evaluate factors using FEM.
Task 4—Perform visual inspection on composite parts to validate if materials are free from defects.
Task 5—Test composite parts per ASTM D-2344 for short-beam test and ASTM D695-02 for the compression test
Research Objective 2: Evaluate the impact of embedded RFID tags on electronic transmission readability performance.
Task 6—Determine the performance factors for measuring the electronic transmission readability performance factors of the embedded RFID tags.
Task 7—Test and evaluate the embedded RFID tag performance factors on electronic transmission readability.
Task 8—Determine the economic viability of embedding RFID tags into a composite material.
Research Objective 3: Evaluate the impact of embedded RFID tags on LCA sustainability parameters.
Task 9—Determine the LCA sustainability parameters.
Task 10—Test and evaluate the LCA sustainability parameters.

Simulation 2015 package was used. This package included the correct materials for the composites and the RFID tags that were to be used in the simulation. The output of the software provided both mechanical movement of the part while under stress as well as a simulated stress depending on the load that was applied to the simulation.

Task 3—Test and evaluate factors using FEM.

Once the simulation software was determined, the next step was to build the FEM models in the simulation package and determine where the parts would break and under what stresses the parts would break.

Parts were modeled in AutoDesk's AutoCAD Inventor 2015. Because of how the laminations behave once they are bonded with the epoxy resin, the layers of 15 plies and 5 plies were modeled as two separate pieces instead of 20 separate pieces. This is allowable under lamination theory which theorizes that because the parts are bonded, they will behave mechanically as a whole piece instead of separate pieces. The reason behind the 15 plies and 5 plies is that the shear stresses would build up in the middle of the part or between 10 plies and 10 plies. If the tags were placed there, then it would be unclear if the part failed naturally at that point or if the part failed due to the inclusion of the tag. By offsetting which layers the tags are placed in, the failure would be more likely attributed to the tag instead of the material. The interest in the calculations is the bond between the composite material and the RFID tag. The use of lamination theory also simplifies the calculations that need to be made and speeds the simulation up without sacrificing the accuracy of the calculations. Once the separate pieces of the composite materials and the RFID tag are modeled and assembled in Inventor, the model can be passed to the Mechanical Simulation package in order to perform the FEM.

Simulations of the parts in compression and in shear were run. The outputs of the simulations contain multiple scenarios of how the parts will be stressed under load. In these simulations, a load of 1,200 pounds was specified. All parts were constrained in the manner in which they would be during actual testing. The simulations provided different results based on which scenarios were most probable. The outputs also show the stresses and movements of the parts in a color spectrum along with numerical readouts of the stress in pounds per square inch (psi) and movement in inches. Animations of the simulations are also available so that the load up of stresses and movements in part can be seen over a defined time period.

Task 4—Perform visual inspection on composite parts to validate materials are free from defects.

Upon manufacture of the FRP parts with and without embedded electronics, the parts were inspected to ensure that there were no visible or known defects in the parts prior to testing.

Parts were manufactured using the wet layup method. This is a manual process that is commonly used for prototyping and low-volume production. The process is applicable for both glass fiber and Kevlar fiber. The following are the processes used for each material type.

17.5.7.1.1 Manufacturing Methods for Glass FRPs

The glass parts were manufactured on an 18" × 18" × ¼" aluminum plate layup tool. The parts had sets of tags embedded in them, arranged in a manner that allowed for the test specimens defined in the test methodology to be cut of the parts. The glass parts were manufactured at a thickness of approximately 1/8". This allowed the specimens for all tests to be produced. Each part built contained at least one of each of the tag types as well as allowed space for an untagged test specimen. The parts were built using 20 plies with a $[0/45/90/-45/0]_4$ orientation. The tags are embedded in between the first two layers (or plies 5 and 6) closest to the tool side.

The specific manufacturing process is as follows:

a. Clean the layup tool to remove any residual materials from previous use. Cleaning processes may include scraping with steel wool and/or wiping down with acetone.

b. Treat the surface of the layup tool with a non-silicone-based wax. Apply one coat of wax. Once the wax has set, buff the wax using a cloth rag. Ensure that all wax is removed as failing to do so will result in surface defects.

c. Spray the tool with polyvinyl alcohol (PVA). Wipe off a 1" perimeter on the tool to allow for the bagging tape to adhere later. Wait for the PVA to dry.

d. For the glass part, a volume of $8\,in.^3$ ($8" \times 8" \times 1/8"$) will need to be filled. Part of this volume will be fabric, and part will be the epoxy resin. The void volume is assumed to be zero.

e. Cut out three pieces of peel ply at a size of $15" \times 15"$.

f. Cut out three pieces of breather material at a size of $15" \times 18"$ a one piece at a size of $4" \times 12"$.

g. Cut out one piece of bagging at a size of $22" \times 26"$.

h. Cut out 12 pieces of glass fabric at a size of $8" \times 8"$ with a fiber orientation of $0°$.

i. Cut out eight pieces of Glass fabric at a size of $8" \times 8"$ with a fiber orientation of $45°$.

j. Pour out $220\,g$ of epoxy resin and $60\,g$ of hardener.

k. Mix the epoxy and resin. Try to not entrain air into the mixture but make sure that the mixture is evenly mixed. The hardener is a darker color than the resin, so it will be somewhat evident in regards to the mixture. The final solution should be in amber/honey color. Streaks of the hardener in the resin should not be present in the mixture. Once the resin and hardener have been mixed, there will be approximately $2\,h$ until the resin begins to harden.

l. Apply resin to the tool surface. Cover an area approximately $10" \times 10"$. This will be the tool side of the part.

m. Add in a layer of glass with a fiber orientation of $0°$. Using a brush, press the glass into the resin so that the fabric lays flat onto the resin. Add additional resin to the glass, working it in from the middle of the part to the outside edges. Add in a second piece of the glass fabric with a $45°$ orientation. Repeat adding resin and fabric until the next $0°$ ply is added.

n. Add in the RFID tags onto the part. One of each tag type is to be added with a $1"$ space between each tag. All tags should lie in the $90°$ orientation plane.

o. Repeat adding glass in the following orientations: $[0/45/90/-45/0]_3$.

p. After the last layer is added, add the bagging tape around the edges of the tool. Do not remove the protection from the top of the bagging tape.

q. Add the peel ply layers to the top of the part. Make sure that the peel ply covers the resin.

r. Add the three pieces of $15" \times 18"$ breather material. Any excess breather should be folded under to help manage the material.

s. Fold the $4" \times 12"$ piece of breather into thirds, and place it on the edge of the tool. Set the base of the vacuum port onto this piece of breather.

t. Peel off the protective tape from the tape on one edge of the tool. Apply the edge of the vacuum bag to the tape.

u. Peel the protection from the bagging tape on the two adjacent sides approximately ¾ of the length of the tape. Apply the edges of the vacuum bag to the tape.

v. Peel off the protection from the tape on opposite side and apply the vacuum bag. There will be excess bag on both adjacent sides of the tool.

w. Measure out approximately $4"$ of bagging tape. Apply it to the folds in the vacuum bag to create pleats. Peel off the rest of the protection from the tape, and attach the last open parts of the vacuum bag.

x. Cut a slit into the center of the port, and attach the other half of the vacuum port.

y. Place the tool into the oven, and attach the vacuum line.

z. Start the vacuum. Check for leaks in the bagging, and seal with bagging tape.

aa. Start the oven. The temperature ramp rate is $5°F/min$. The cure temperature is $300°F$ for $1\,h$. The cooling temperature rate is $5°F/min$.

bb. Once the part is cooled, it can be removed from the tool for further processing.

17.5.7.1.2 Manufacturing Methods for Kevlar FRPs

The Kevlar parts were manufactured on an $18" \times 18" \times ¼"$ aluminum plate layup tool. The parts had sets of tags embedded in them, arranged in a manner that allowed for the test specimens defined in the test methodology to be cut of the parts. The Kevlar parts were manufactured at a thickness of approximately ¼". This allowed the specimens for all tests to be produced. Each part built contained at least one of each of the tag types as well as allowed space for an untagged test specimen. The part was built using 20 plies with a $[0/45/90/-45/0]_4$ orientation. The tags were embedded in between the first two layers closest to the tool side.

The specific process is as follows:

a. Clean the layup tool to remove any residual materials from previous use. Cleaning processes may include scraping with steel wool and/or wiping down with acetone.

b. Treat the surface of the layup tool with a non-silicone-based wax. Apply one coat of wax. Once the wax has set, buff the wax using a cloth rag. Ensure that all wax is removed as failing to do so will result in surface defects.

c. Spray the tool with PVA. Wipe off a 1" perimeter on the tool to allow for the bagging tape to adhere later. Wait for the PVA to dry.

d. For the Kevlar part, a volume of 16 in.^{3} (8" × 8" × ¼") will need to be filled. Part of this volume will be fabric, and part will be the epoxy resin. The void volume is assumed to be zero.

e. Cut out three pieces of peel ply at a size of 15" × 15".

f. Cut out three pieces of breather material at a size of 15" × 18" and one piece at a size of 4" × 12".

g. Cut out one piece of bagging at a size of 22" × 26".

h. Cut out 12 pieces of Kevlar fabric at a size of 8" × 8" with a fiber orientation of 0°.

i. Cut out eight pieces of Kevlar at a size of 8" × 8" with a fiber orientation of 45°.

j. Pour out 220 g of epoxy resin and 60 g of hardener.

k. Mix the epoxy and resin. Try to not entrain air into the mixture, but make sure that the mixture is evenly mixed. The hardener is a darker color than the resin, so it will be somewhat evident in regards to the mixture. The final solution should be in amber/honey color. Streaks of the hardener in the resin should not be prevalent in the mixture. Once the resin and hardener have been mixed, there will be approximately 2 h until the resin begins to harden.

l. Apply resin to the tool surface. Cover an area approximately 10" × 10". This will be the tool side of the part.

m. Add in a layer of Kevlar with a fiber orientation of 0°. Using a brush, press the Kevlar into the resin so that the fabric lays flat onto the resin. Add additional resin to the Kevlar, working it in from the middle of the part to the outside edges. Add in the second piece of the Kevlar fabric with a 45° orientation. Repeat adding resin and fabric until the next 0° ply is added.

n. Add in the RFID tags onto the part. One of each tag type is to be added with a 1" space between each tag. All tags should lie in the 90° orientation plane.

o. Repeat adding Kevlar in the following orientations: $[0/45/90/-45/0]_3$.

p. After the last layer is added, add in the bagging tape around the edges of the tool. Do not remove the protection from the top of the tape.

q. Add the peel ply layers to the top of the part. Make sure that the peel ply covers the resin.

r. Add the three pieces of 15" × 18" breather material. Any excess breather should be folded under to help manage the material.

s. Fold the 4" × 12" piece of breather into thirds, and place it on the edge of the tool. Set the base of the vacuum port onto this piece of breather.

t. Peel off the protective tape from the tape on one edge of the tool. Apply the edge of the vacuum bag to the tape.

u. Peel off the protection from the tape on the two adjacent sides approximately ¾ of the length of the bagging tape. Apply the edges of the vacuum bag to the tape.

v. Peel off the protection from the tape on opposite side and apply the vacuum bag. There will be excess bag on both adjacent sides of the tool.

w. Measure out approximately 4" of bagging tape. Apply it to the folds in the vacuum bag to create pleats. Peel off the rest of the protection from the tape, and attach the last open parts of the vacuum bag.

x. Cut a slit into the center of the port, and attach the other half of the vacuum port.

y. Place the tool into the oven, and attach the vacuum line.

z. Start the vacuum. Check for leaks in the bagging, and seal with bagging tape.

aa. Start the oven. The temperature ramp rate is 5°F/min. The cure temperature is 300°F for 1 h. The cooling temperature rate is 5°F/min.

bb. Once the part is cooled, it can be removed from the tool for further processing.

17.5.7.1.3 Modification of the RFID Tags

There were six variations of the RFID tags used in the experiments. All tags used were made from Alien's Higgs-3 part number ALN-9640. These modifications are listed as

0 = no tag included (control)

1 = perforated tag—holes were punched into the inlay of the RFID tag to try and allow the resin to bond through the tag

2 = complete tag—off the shelf RFID tag

3 = skeletonized tag—the inlay of the tag is cut down to reduce the footprint of the tag

4 = feathered tag—slits were cut into the inlay of the tag to try and allow resin to bond through the tag

5 = abraded tag—the complete tag was sanded to try and increase the surface area that the epoxy could bond to.

Visual inspection of the parts helped to ensure that the parts would fail based on the inclusion of the RFID tag and not because of a known manufacturing defect. Defects that were inspected for were voids caused by entrained air in the resin, incomplete bonds between the resin and the fibers due to contamination, and defects in the surface of the parts caused by the presence of silicon on the mold surface.

Task 5—Test composite parts per ASTM D-2344 for short-beam test and ASTM D695-02 for the compression test.

Mechanical testing of the FRP test specimens determined the impact of the tag on the structure of the part.

For the compression and shear tests, a 2 × 2 factorial Design of Experiments (DoE) was set up for each test. The following sections define the DoE for each test.

17.5.7.2 DoE for Compression Testing

17.5.7.2.1 Problem Description

In the compression test, the objective was to determine how the fibers of the reinforcement buckle with a given load. This test helped define the strength between resin and the fiber and determine if there are any voids and defects in the resin (Strong, 2008). In this research, the RFID tag that was embedded in the layers of the composite is viewed as a defect. The purpose of using this test was to see if the RFID tag caused the part being tested to fail at a lower load than the control part that does not contain a tag.

The same Alien ALN-9640 Higgs 3 tag was used in the same configurations as before. The materials are again Kevlar and glass fiber reinforcement with an epoxy resin.

The experimental design is a 2 × 2 factorial with two factors for material and six factors for tags.

17.5.7.2.2 Experimental Units

Five samples of Kevlar reinforced polymer for each tag type

Five samples of glass reinforced polymer for each tag type

Factor A: Tag modification with levels

     0 = no tag included (control)

     1 = perforated tag

     2 = complete tag

     3 = skeletonized tag

     4 = feathered tag

     5 = abraded tag

Factor B: Reinforcement type with levels

     K = Kevlar

     G = glass

17.5.7.2.3 Treatments

The treatments are the factor-level combinations. In this section of the experiments, the sets of treatments are K0, K1, K2, K3, K4, K5 and G0, G1, G2, G3, G4, G5. K and G correspond to Factor B: Reinforcement types, and 0, 1, 2, 3, 4, and 5 correspond to Factor A: Tag types.

17.5.7.2.4 Response

Compression strength (in psi).

17.5.7.2.5 Goal

To determine at each tag level for each material type if the failure of the samples with embedded tags is significantly different from the control.

17.5.7.2.6 Design

The total number of treatments is $6 \times 2 = 12$. We performed five replications for each treatment for a total of 60 parts that needed to be run. The five replications requirement was based on the test specifications. Each specimen was numbered in order to maintain traceability of the part.

     Data was collected off of the test specimen. All dimensional measurements were taken in inches, and all loads were measured in pounds. The stresses on the specimen were then calculated using the average width and thickness measurements and the observed peak load at failure. The calculation used to determine shear stress is

$$F^{\text{compress}} = \frac{P_m}{b \times h} \text{ as defined by the ASTM specification D695-02a,}$$

where

     F^{compress} = short-beam strength, MPa (psi)

     P_m = maximum load observed during the test, N (lbf)

     b = measured specimen width, mm (in.)

     h = measured specimen thickness, mm (in.)

Parts are manufactured with five tags in each part, one of each tag type, and room for a control part to be cut from the part. After the material was cured, the test specimens were cut from the parts and measured. The test specimens were determined randomly so that there were five of each type of tag. The randomization occurred through the randomization function = randbetween(0, 100000) in Excel. The numbers as assigned to the treatments were sorted least to greatest in order to randomize the treatments.

     The first set of statistics calculated were the mean, standard deviations, coefficient of variation, and the number of specimens for each material type and each tag type. In addition to the descriptive statistics, the analysis of variance (ANOVA), time series plot, normal probability plot, and residuals vs. fitted value plots will be performed. Any abnormal data points were explored in order to define the abnormality.

17.5.7.3 Test Method for Compression Testing

The compression test was run based on the ASTM D695-02a Standard Test Method for Compressive Properties for Rigid Plastics. Test specimens were prepared to achieve width × thickness × length dimensions of 0.50" × 0.20" × 1.50" for the Kevlar parts and 0.50" × 0.12" × 1.50" for the glass parts. Conditions at the time of test were at 67°F ± 10°F and at 50% ± 10% relative humidity. Test specimens were conditioned at this temperature and humidity for 24 h prior to testing. The compressive strength was calculated from the tests. The stress–strain calculations in the test procedure will be omitted due to the lack of a compressometer. The following steps are based on sections 10 and 11 of ASTM D695-02a.

10.1 Measure the width and thickness of the specimen to the nearest 0.01 mm (0.001 in.) at several points along its length. Calculate and record the average value of the cross-sectional area. Measure the length of the specimen and record the value.

10.2 Place the test specimen between the surfaces of the compression tool, taking care to align the centerline of the plunger and to ensure that the ends of the specimen are parallel with the surface of the compression tool. Adjust the crosshead of the testing machine until it just contacts the top of the compression tool plunger.

10.3 Place the specimens in the fixture so that they are flushed with the base and centered. The screws in the fixture are to be tightened finger tight.

10.4 Set the speed control at 0.050 in./min.

10.5 Record the maximum load carried by the specimen during the test. This should be the load at the moment of rupture.

11.1 Calculate compressive strength by dividing the maximum compressive load carried by the specimen during the test by the original average cross-sectional area of the specimen. Express the result in pounds-force per square inch, and report it to three significant digits.

17.5.7.4 Design of Experiments for Shear Testing

17.5.7.4.1 Problem Description

In the shear test, the objective is to determine if the layers of the matrix and reinforcement would shear in between the layers. This test helps define the strength between resin and the fiber (Strong, 2008). In this research, the RFID tag embedded in the layers of the composite is viewed as a defect. The purpose of using this test is to see if the RFID tag caused the part being tested to fail at a lower load than the control part that did not contain a tag.

The same Alien ALN-9640 Higgs 3 tag was used in the same configurations as before. The materials are again Kevlar and glass fiber reinforcement with an epoxy resin.

The experimental design is a 2 × 2 factorial with two factors for material and six factors for tags.

17.5.7.4.2 Experimental Units

Five samples of Kevlar reinforced polymer for each tag type
Five samples of glass reinforced polymer for each tag type

Factor A: Tag modification with levels
0 = no tag included (control)
1 = perforated tag
2 = complete tag
3 = skeletonized tag
4 = feathered tag
5 = abraded tag

Factor B: Reinforcement type with levels
   K = Kevlar
   G = glass

17.5.7.4.3 Treatments

The treatments are the factor-level combinations. In this section of the experiments, the sets of treatments are K0, K1, K2, K3, K4, K5 and G0, G1, G2, G3, G4, G5. K and G correspond to Factor B: Reinforcement types, and 0, 1, 2, 3, 4, and 5 correspond to Factor A: Tag types.

17.5.7.4.4 Response

Shear strength (in psi).

17.5.7.4.5 Goal

To determine at each tag level for each material type if the failure of the samples with embedded tags is significantly different from the controls.

17.5.7.4.6 Design

The total number of treatments is $6 \times 2 = 12$. Five replications were performed for each treatment for a total of 60 parts that needed to be run. The five replications requirement is based on the test specifications. Each specimen was numbered in order to maintain traceability of the part.

Data was collected off of the test specimen. All dimensional measurements were taken in inches, and all loads were measured in pounds. The stress on the specimen was then calculated using the average width and thickness measurements and the observed peak load at failure. The calculation used to determine shear stress is

$$F^{sbs} = 0.75 \times \frac{P_m}{b \times h}$$ as defined by the ASTM specification D2344/D2344M-13,

where
   F^{sbs} = short-beam strength, MPa (psi)
   P_m = maximum load observed during the test, N (lbf)
   b = measured specimen width, mm (in.)
   h = measured specimen thickness, mm (in.)

Parts were manufactured with five tags in each part, one of each tag type, and room to for a control part to be cut from the part. After the material was cured, the test specimens were cut from the parts and measured. The test specimens were determined randomly so that there are five of each type of tag. The randomization occurred through the randomization function = randbetween(0, 100000) in Excel. The numbers as assigned to the treatments were sorted least to greatest in order to randomize the treatments.

The first set of statistics calculated were the mean, standard deviations, coefficient of variation, and the number of specimens for each material type and each tag type. In addition to the descriptive statistics, the ANOVA, time series plot, normal probability plot, and residuals vs. fitted value plots were performed. Any abnormal data points were explored in order to define the abnormality.

17.5.7.5 Test Method for Short-Beam Strength

The short-beam shear test was run based on the ASTM D2344/D2344M-13 Standard Test Method for Short-Beam Strength of Polymer Matrix Composite Materials and Their Laminates. Test specimens were prepared to achieve width × thickness × length dimensions of 0.50" × 0.12" × 1.50" for the glass parts and 0.50" × 0.20" × 1.50" for the Kevlar parts. Conditions at the time of test shall be 67°F ± 10°F and 50% ± 10% relative humidity. Test specimens are conditioned at this temperature and humidity for 24h prior to testing. The short-beam (shear) strength was calculated from the tests. The following procedure is based on sections 11 and 12 of ASTM D2344/D2344M-13.

11.1 Measure the width and thickness of the specimen to the nearest 0.01 mm (0.001 in.) at several points along its length. Calculate and record the average value of the cross-sectional area. Measure the length of the specimen and record the value.

11.2 Set the speed control at 0.050 in./min.

11.3 Insert the test specimen into the test fixture. Align and center the specimen so that the edges are equally supported and that the longitudinal axis is perpendicular to the loading nose and side supports. The loading nose should be equidistant between the supports. The span length should be approximately 0.80" for the Kevlar and 0.48" for the glass to meet the 4:1 ratio when compared to the thickness of the parts. Because of this ratio requirement and the thicknesses of the glass and Kevlar parts being different, the two material types must be run during two separate setups.

11.4 Apply the load to the specimen until a load drop-off of 30% occurs, there is a two-piece specimen failure, or the head travel exceeds the specimen nominal thickness.

11.5 Record the load vs. crosshead displacement data throughout the test method. Record the maximum load, final load, and the load at any obvious discontinuities in the load–displacement data.

11.6 Record the failure mode and location of failure.

12.1 Calculate the short-beam strength using the equation

$$F^{sbs} = 0.75 \times \frac{P_m}{b \times h},$$

where

F^{sbs} = short-beam strength (psi)
P_m = maximum load observed during the test (lbf)
b = measured specimen width, (in.)
h = measured specimen thickness (in.)

Research Objective 2: Evaluate the impact of embedded RFID tags on electronic transmission readability performance.

Task 6—Determine the performance factors for measuring the electronic transmission readability performance factors of the embedded RFID tags.

Determine at which read distances the electronic readability transmission tests can be performed.

The area was constrained to 100 ft in distance. The area was cleared of any obstructions and marked off from 0 to 100 ft in 10 ft increments.

Task 7—Test and evaluate the embedded RFID tag performance factors on electronic transmission readability.

Perform the readability tests for the glass and Kevlar materials for all tag types.

Tags were moved away from the reader's antenna until the tags reached 100 ft or the tag had zero reads over a 5 s period.

17.5.7.6 Design of Experiments for Read Distance Testing

17.5.7.6.1 Problem Description

In the read distance test, the objective was to determine if the RFID tags can be read by the reader after the manufacturing process has occurred. This test helps define the ability to utilize RFID tags in composite material manufacturing. The RFID tag embedded in the layers of the composite was activated in order to determine how far away the tag can be read. The purpose of using this test was to see if the RFID tag is damaged by the modification or manufacturing processes.

The same Alien ALN-9640 Higgs 3 tag is used in the same configurations as before. The materials are again Kevlar and glass fiber reinforcement with an epoxy resin.

The experimental design is a 2×2 factorial with two factors for material and five factors for tags.

17.5.7.6.2 Experimental Units

Five samples of Kevlar reinforced polymer for each tag type
  Five samples of glass reinforced polymer for each tag type

  Factor A: Tag modification with levels
    1 = perforated tag
    2 = complete tag
    3 = skeletonized tag
    4 = feathered tag
    5 = abraded tag
  Factor B: Reinforcement type with levels
    K = Kevlar
    G = glass

17.5.7.6.3 Treatments

The treatments are the factor-level combinations. In this section of the experiments, the sets of treatments are K1, K2, K3, K4, K5 and G1, G2, G3, G4, G5. K and G correspond to Factor B: Reinforcement types, and 0, 1, 2, 3, 4, and 5 correspond to Factor A: Tag types.

17.5.7.6.4 Response

Read Distance (in ft).

17.5.7.6.5 Goal

To determine at each tag level for each material type if the read distance of the samples with embedded tags are significantly different from each other.

17.5.7.6.6 Design

The total number of treatments is $5 \times 2 = 10$. Eight replications were performed for each treatment for a total of 80 parts that need to be run. The eight replications were determined because of the number of samples that were available to be run. Each specimen was numbered in order to maintain traceability of the part.

Data was collected off from the RFID tag in the test specimen. The only recorded data was the RFID tag read distance based on one successful read within 5 s at each distance.

The test specimens come from the parts made for the compression and shear tests before they are destroyed.

The first set of statistics calculated were the mean, standard deviations, coefficient of variation, and the number of specimens for each material type and each tag type. In addition to the descriptive statistics, the ANOVA, time series plot, normal probability plot, and residuals vs. fitted value plots were performed. Any abnormal data points were explored in order to define the abnormality.

Task 8—Determine the economic viability of embedding RFID tags into a composite material.

Determine the costs incurred to set up an RFID-enabled system to monitor the tags embedded into the FRP parts.

Costs are accumulated in the project in order to determine how much costs would be incurred to replicate the setup for this project. Major cost items include the readers, antennas, and tags. Other costs that are accounted for include the programming time for the reader and the programming of the tags.

Research Objective 3: Evaluate the impact of embedded RFID tags on LCA sustainability parameters.

Task 9—Determine the LCA sustainability parameters.

Determine the appropriate LCA tools, and understand the various aspects necessary to perform LCA.

Utilizing literature and previous studies on composites and on electronics, the aspects needed to perform this type of analysis were better understood. The first step was to determine which type of analysis needed to be performed. Out of the several types of analyses available, the Tiered Hybrid method was

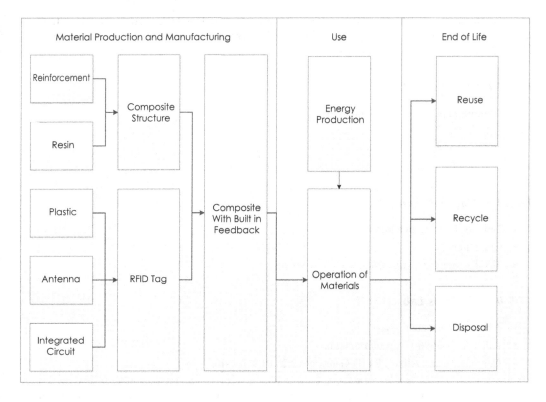

FIGURE 17.3 Material layout for LCA.

selected due to the complexity it would allow for and the ability to include not only environmental costs (environmental and energy impact) but also costs of the entire supply chain (SC) and costs during useful life. Most of these costs fall into three main areas. Material Production and Manufacturing contains all information regarding the origination of the base materials, the manufacturing and assembly of the products, and all transportation and energy associated with the manufacture of these products. The Use contains the energy and costs associated with deploying the products, the costs of operating those products, and transportation of those products to their end use stations. The End of Life associates the energies and costs of transporting, disposing, recycling, or reusing the products once they've completed their initial useful life (Figure 17.3).

Task 10—Test and evaluate the LCA sustainability parameters.

Perform LCA on the glass and Kevlar FRPs and on the glass and Kevlar FRPs with embedded RFID tags.

For this project, the open source program openLCA was utilized to build the LCA. Free databases were also utilized to cover items in the analysis such as transportation and for some of the materials. Other sources of data were estimated due to the lack of available and existing data needed for the full analysis.

All base materials are built into the LCA program. This includes defining the materials, their origination, their destination, the method of transportation, the energy needed to convert the material from one step to the next, the quantities produced and transported, the energy consumed during each process, and the environmental costs of the materials and processes. Because most of this data is not readily available, the interactions between the different parts of the life cycle and their costs were defined.

17.5.8 Location of Experiments and Equipment Used

All manufacturing and testing of parts occurred at Tarleton State University in the Engineering Technology labs. The labs used were the composites lab, where the manufacturing of the test parts occurred, the materials lab, where the curing and testing occurred, and the controls lab where the tags were programmed and signal strengths were observed. There is a variety of equipment used in each lab, which will be defined in the following sections.

17.5.8.1 Composites Lab

- Aluminum plate used as layup tools
- Kiln
- Vacuum pump
- Consumable materials.

17.5.8.2 Materials Lab

- Universal testing machine
- Computer
- Test fixtures for compression and shear testing.

17.5.8.3 Controls Lab

- Alien 9600+ reader
- Alien ALR-8696-C circular antenna
- Computer using Alien's RFID Gateway v2.23.01 software.

Data analysis for the experiments occurred at both Tarleton and at the University of Texas Arlington using Excel, Minitab, and SAS.

17.6 Results

This chapter discusses the analysis performed on the data from the experiments. The first section discusses the simulations that were performed for compression and then evaluates the actual mechanical testing performed on the parts. The second section looks at the simulations and mechanical testing performed for the shear testing. The simulations provided a likely location for the failure in the materials during the tests. The tests defined how the embedded electronics affected the FRP's structure. The third section evaluates the impact that the tags and the materials had on the RFID tags' read distances. The last section discusses the work performed on the LCA. This research sets up what the flowchart for the SC processes looks like.

17.6.1 Mechanical Analysis Simulation

17.6.1.1 Compression Test

The compression simulation for the glass reinforced epoxy shows the maximum movement of the material (Figure 17.4). This information signifies where the break in the material can be expected to occur as indicated in this simulation as the green area. The displacement of the material is approximately 0.40 in. at the defined location (Figure 17.5).

The compression simulation for the Kevlar reinforced epoxy also shows the maximum movement of the material. This information signifies where the break in the material can be expected to occur as indicated in this simulation as the red area. Of interest is the amount of movement in the material compared to the glass simulation. The Kevlar under the same load will displace up to 1 in. Most of this can be explained due to the properties that Kevlar exhibits, specifically the elastic property being better than glass (Figures 17.6 and 17.7).

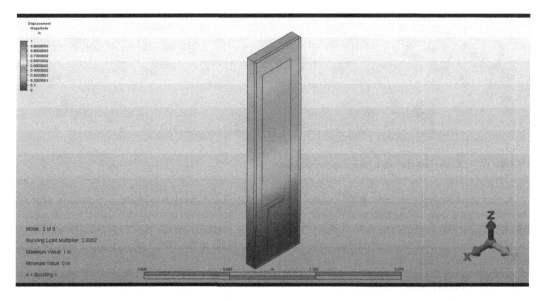

FIGURE 17.4 Compression simulation of glass reinforced epoxy.

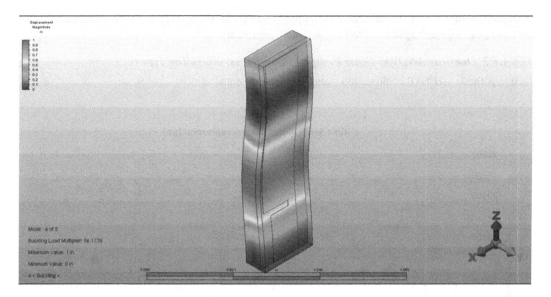

FIGURE 17.5 Compression simulation of Kevlar reinforced epoxy.

FIGURE 17.6 Glass test specimen from compression tests.

FIGURE 17.7   Kevlar test specimen from compression tests.

During the compression tests, parts typically failed at the location shown in the simulations. One of the interesting results of the tests that did not show up in the simulation run was that the failure occurred between the RFID tag and the polyethylene (PET) backing material on the tag. This leads to the belief from the compression tests and simulations that the epoxy bond to the RFID tag is not the biggest contributor to failure during the tests.

17.6.1.1.1 Compression Testing

The random jaggedness of the time series plot shows that there are no trends in the data (Figure 17.8; Table 17.3). This shows that the data is random and that there is not a serial correlation between the data points. The mean data shows that two of the specimens with embedded tags had a higher compression strength than the control. These were the perforated and feathered tags. The control specimen that did not have an embedded tag seemed to be tested more repeatedly.

17.6.1.1.2 One-way ANOVA: Glass Compression (psi) vs. Glass Tag Type

Null hypothesis—H_0: All compression strength means are equal.

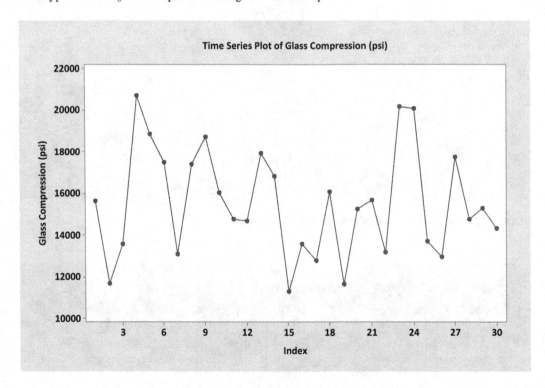

FIGURE 17.8   Time series plot of glass fiber reinforced epoxy.

TABLE 17.3

Descriptive Statistics for Glass Fiber Reinforced Epoxy

Variable	Glass Tag Type	Total Count	Mean	Standard Deviation	Coefficient of Variance
Glass compression (psi)	0	5	15469	487	3.15
	1	5	17857	1099	6.15
	2	5	13429	1228	9.15
	3	5	14732	3183	21.60
	4	5	18508	1779	9.61
	5	5	13092	1410	10.77

Alternative hypothesis—H_a: At least one mean is different.

Significance level $\alpha = 0.05$.

Upon evaluating the *F*-value, the ANOVA yields a value of 8.32 (Tables 17.4 and 17.5). This is larger than the values from the *F* distribution of 2.62. This results in rejecting the null hypothesis and shows that at least one of the means is different. The *p*-value reinforces the rejection of the null hypothesis since the 0.000 in the ANOVA is less than the α of 0.05. This also means that constant variance is not satisfied in the data.

Table 17.6 identifies the R2 of the model. Because the value is somewhat low, it can be assumed that the derived model does not define the data very well.

The box plot of the data from the compression test is shown in Figure 17.9. The box plot shows the means and the quartiles of the results for each tag type. Tags 1 and 4 appear to be different from the other three tags and the control (Table 17.7).

Tukey Pairwise Comparisons (Table 17.8)

Means that do not share a letter are significantly different.

The Tukey confidence intervals identify which tag types can be grouped with each other. In this analysis, tags 4, 1, and 0 are similar; tags 1, 0, and 3 are similar; and tags 0, 3, 2, and 5 are similar (Figure 17.10). This indicates not only that there are different means, but also that these means are most closely associated with each other (Figure 17.11).

TABLE 17.4

Factor Information for RFID Tags in Glass Fiber Reinforced Epoxy

Factor	Levels	Values
Glass tag type	6	0, 1, 2, 3, 4, 5

TABLE 17.5

Compression Test ANOVA for Glass Fiber Reinforced Epoxy

Source	DF	Adj SS	Adj MS	F-Value	p-Value
Glass tag type	5	126398637	25279727	8.32	0.000
Error	24	72934581	3038941		
Total	29	199333217			

TABLE 17.6

Model Summary

S	R-sq	R-sq(adj)	R-sq(pred)
1743.26	63.41%	55.79%	42.83%

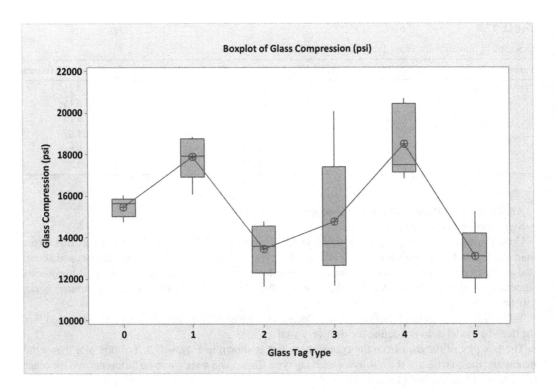

FIGURE 17.9   Box plot of glass compression test data.

TABLE 17.7

Glass Compression Data Means

Glass Tag Type	N	Mean	Standard Deviation	95% CI
0	5	15469	487	(13860, 17078)
1	5	17857	1099	(16248, 19466)
2	5	13429	1228	(11820, 15038)
3	5	14732	3183	(13123, 16341)
4	5	18508	1779	(16899, 20117)
5	5	13092	1410	(11483, 14701)

TABLE 17.8

Grouping Information Using the Tukey Method at 95% Confidence

Glass Tag Type	N	Mean	Grouping
4	5	18508	A
1	5	17857	AB
0	5	15469	ABC
3	5	14732	BC
2	5	13429	C
5	5	13092	C

The normal probability plot shows that the data is somewhat normally distributed. There is one data point that appears to be significantly different from the other data points. It will be evaluated as an outlier though it did not register as one during the box plot (Figure 17.12).

The residuals vs. fitted values plot shows mostly constant variance in the data. One point appears as an outlier and needs to be evaluated further (Figure 17.13; Table 17.9).

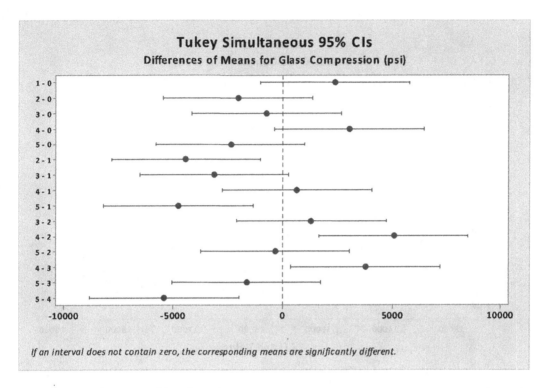

FIGURE 17.10 Tukey 95% confidence interval.

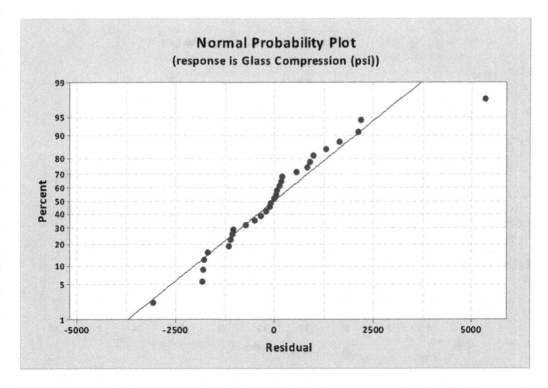

FIGURE 17.11 Normal probability plot for glass compression data.

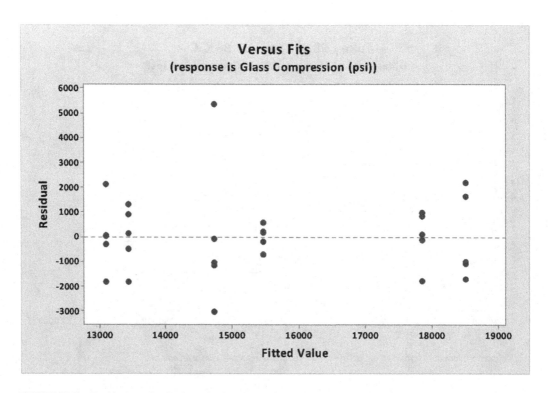

FIGURE 17.12   Residuals vs. fitted values plot for glass compression.

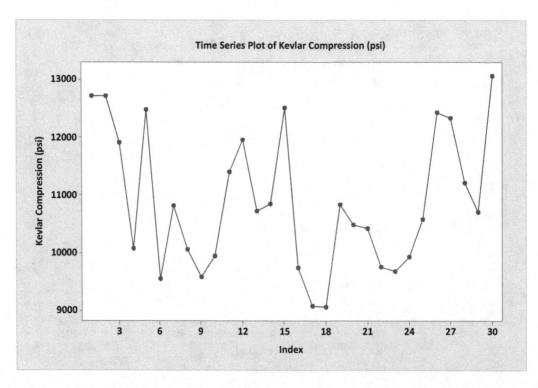

FIGURE 17.13   Time series plot of Kevlar fiber reinforced epoxy.

TABLE 17.9

Descriptive Statistics for Kevlar Fiber Reinforced Epoxy

Variable	Glass Tag Type	Total Count	Mean	Standard Deviation	Coefficient of Variance
Kevlar compression (psi)	0	5	10501	478	4.55
	1	5	12603	288	2.28
	2	5	10128	794	7.84
	3	5	10186	845	8.29
	4	5	12043	584	4.85
	5	5	9812	187	1.91

TABLE 17.10

Factor Information for RFID Tags in Kevlar Fiber Reinforced Epoxy

Factor	Levels	Values
Kevlar tag type	6	0, 1, 2, 3, 4, 5

TABLE 17.11

Compression Test ANOVA for Kevlar Fiber Reinforced Epoxy

Source	DF	Adj SS	Adj MS	F-Value	p-Value
Kevlar tag type	5	33268423	6653685	19.66	0.000
Error	24	8123900	338496		
Total	29	41392324			

TABLE 17.12

Model Summary

S	R-sq	R-sq(adj)	R-sq(pred)
581.804	80.37%	76.28%	69.33%

The Kevlar fiber reinforced epoxy also shows random jaggedness and a lack of serial correlation between the data points. The means appear to be somewhat consistent with each other though the means for specimens 1 and 4 are higher.

17.6.1.1.3 One-way ANOVA: Kevlar Compression (psi) vs. Kevlar Tag Type

Null hypothesis: All means are equal.

Alternative hypothesis: At least one mean is different.

Significance level $\alpha = 0.05$.

Evaluating the *F*-value in the ANOVA yields a value of 19.66 (Tables 17.10 and 17.11). This is larger than the values from the *F* distribution of 2.62. Because of this, the null hypothesis is rejected, and at least one of the means is different. The *p*-value of 0.000 is less than the α of 0.05, so the null hypothesis is again rejected, and the constant variance is not satisfied in the data (Table 17.12).

The *R*-sq value for the Kevlar reinforced data is at 80%. The model is a decent indicator of the data points.

In Figure 17.14, tags 1 and 4 appear to be considerably different from the other tags. In this case, they have a higher compression strength than the control and the other three tag types (Table 17.13).

Tukey Pairwise Comparisons (Table 17.14)

Means that do not share a letter are significantly different.

In the Kevlar analysis, tags 4 and 1are similar to each other while tags 0, 3, 2, and 5 are similar to one another (Figure 17.15). This validates what was assumed when the means were looked at earlier in the results. It is also interesting that tags 0, 3, 2, and 5 were similar in the data analysis for the RFID tags embedded in glass.

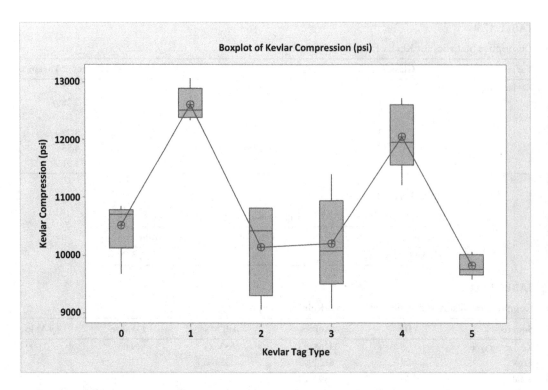

FIGURE 17.14   Box plot of Kevlar fiber reinforced epoxy.

TABLE 17.13

Kevlar Compression Data Means

Kevlar Tag Type	N	Mean	Standard Deviation	95% CI
0	5	10501	478	(9964, 11038)
1	5	12603	288	(12066, 13140)
2	5	10128	794	(9591, 10665)
3	5	10186	845	(9649, 10723)
4	5	12043	584	(11506, 12580)
5	5	9812	187	(9275, 10349)

TABLE 17.14

Grouping Information Using the Tukey Method at 95% Confidence

Kevlar Tag Type	N	Mean	Grouping
1	5	12603	A
4	5	12043	A
0	5	10501	B
3	5	10186	B
2	5	10128	B
5	5	9812	B

The normal probability plot shows that the data is normally distributed. All points lie linearly along the reference line (Figure 17.16).

The residuals vs. fitted values plot appears to show non-constant variance in the data. Because of this, the Box-Cox transformation is performed (Figure 17.17). A $\lambda = 3$ is calculated and yields the graph. It exhibits a smaller funnel effect than the initial plot, but upon evaluation of the transformed ANOVA,

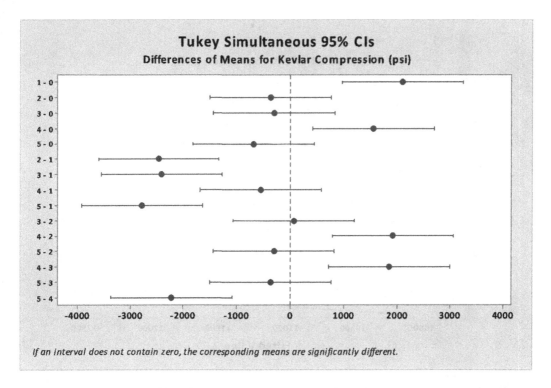

FIGURE 17.15 Tukey 95% confidence interval.

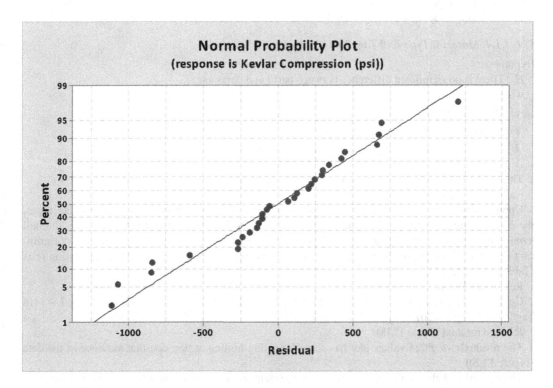

FIGURE 17.16 Normal probability plot for Kevlar compression data.

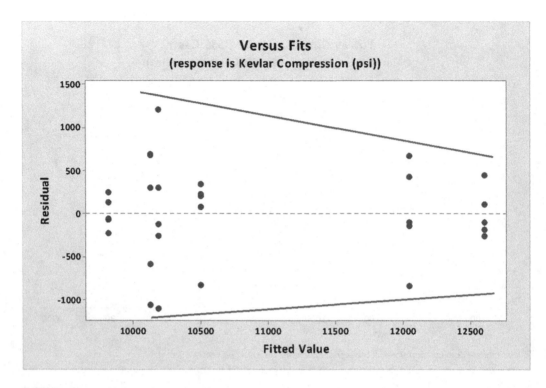

FIGURE 17.17   Residuals vs. fitted values plot for Kevlar compression.

our F-value is still greater than the 2.62, and the p-value is still less than the α of 0.05. This results in the need to still reject the H_0 and shows that the means of the Kevlar Tag Types are different (Figure 17.18).

17.6.1.1.4 Material Type and Tag Type Compression Strengths

Hypothesis:

H_0: There is no significant difference between part i and parameter j,
where

i is the material type

j is the compression strength

H_a: There is a significant difference between part i and parameter j.

The hypothesis will be tested at $\alpha = 0.30$ (Figure 17.19)

Categorical predictor coding (−1, 0, +1)

Upon evaluating the ANOVA for the compression strengths of material types and the tag types, the F-values are higher than the F distribution value of 1.25 (Table 17.15). In this instance, the null hypothesis is rejected, and the alternative hypothesis is used. For these calculations, there is a significant difference between the material types and at least one of the tag types in the compression tests (Tables 17.16 and 17.17).

Regression Equation

Compression Strength (psi) = 13197 + 2318 Glass − 2318 Kevlar − 212 Tag 0 + 2033 Tag 1 − 1418 Tag 2 − 738 Tag 3 + 2079 Tag 4 − 1745 Tag 5

R Large residual (Table 17.18)

The residuals vs. fitted values plot has some funneling hinting at non-constant variance in the data (Figure 17.20).

The normal probability plot has a short tail on the right side exhibiting a standard uniform distribution (Figure 17.21).

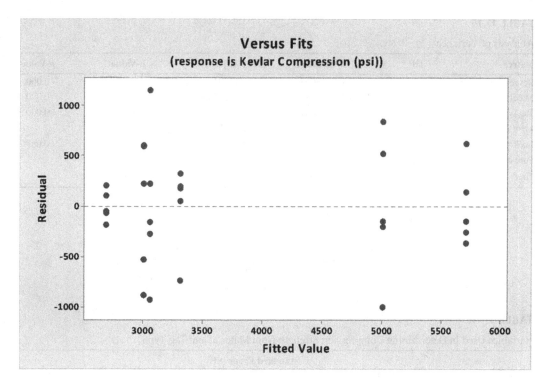

FIGURE 17.18 Transformed residuals vs. fitted values plot.

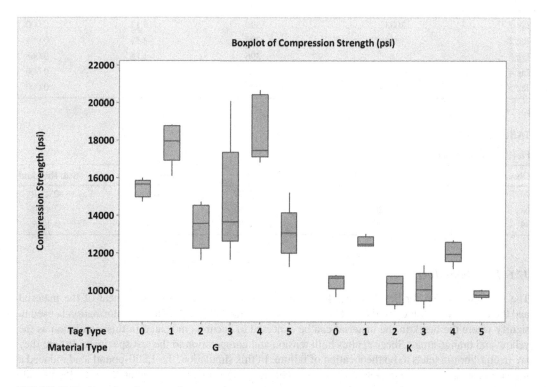

FIGURE 17.19 Box plot of compression strengths.

TABLE 17.15

Analysis of Variance

Source	DF	Adj SS	Adj MS	F-Value	p-Value
Regression	6	463387093	77231182	41.05	0.000
Material type	1	322381432	322381432	171.34	0.000
Tag type	5	141005661	28201132	14.99	0.000
Error	53	99719880	1881507		
Lack-of-fit	5	18661398	3732280	2.21	0.069
Pure error	48	81058481	1688718		
Total	59	563106973			

TABLE 17.16

Model Summary

S	R-sq	R-sq(adj)	R-sq(pred)
1371.68	82.29%	80.29%	77.30%

TABLE 17.17

Variables Used in Determining Compression Strength from Material and Tag Type

Variable	Coefficient	Standard Error (SE) Coefficient	T	p-Value
Constant	13197	177	74.52	0.000
Glass	2318	177	13.09	0.000
Kevlar	−809.5	177	13.09	0.000
Tag 0	−212	396	−0.53	0.595
Tag 1	2033	396	5.13	0.000
Tag 2	−1418	396	−3.58	0.001
Tag 3	−738	396	−1.86	0.068
Tag 4	2079	396	5.25	0.000
Tag 5	−1745	99.4	−4.41	0.000

TABLE 17.18

Fits and Diagnostics for Unusual Observations

Observation	Shear Strength (psi)	Fit	Residual	Std. Residual
4	11676	14777	−3101	−2.41 R
6	20696	17594	3102	2.41 R
49	20090	14777	5313	4.12 R

17.6.1.2 Shear Test

The shear simulation for the glass reinforced epoxy shows the maximum movement of the material and the total forces built up in the part during loading (Figure 17.22). Again, this information is used to signify where the break in the material can be expected to occur as indicated in this simulation as the yellow and orange areas. Shear applies both tension and compression to the test specimen. Where they are in equilibrium tends to be the location of failure. In this simulation, the 1,200-pound load induced a maximum stress of approximately 343,400 psi. The actual test specimen failed at closer to 350 pounds and only saw up to approximately 5,100 psi.

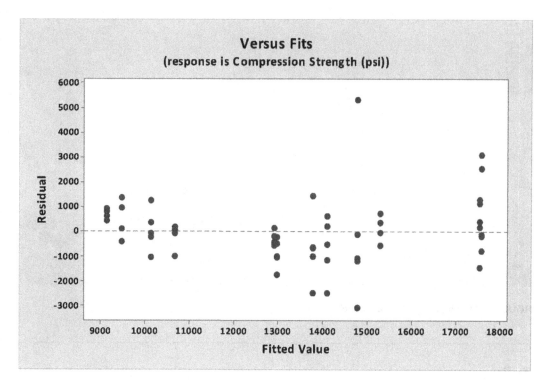

FIGURE 17.20   Residuals vs. fitted values plot.

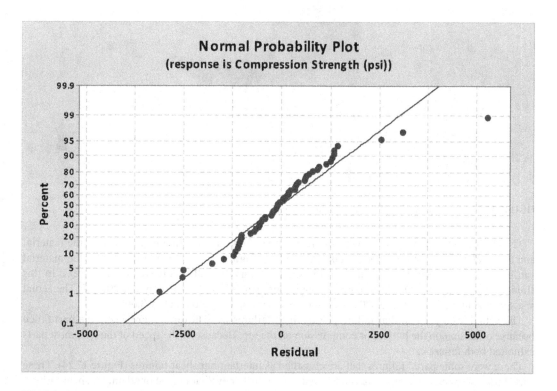

FIGURE 17.21   Normal probability plot.

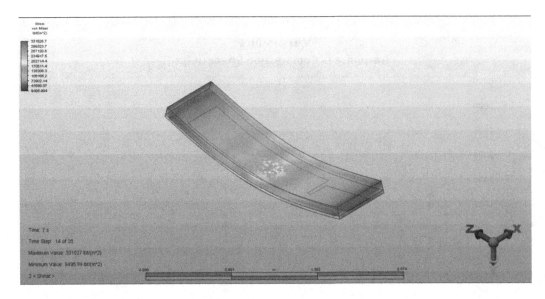

FIGURE 17.22   Shear simulation of glass reinforced epoxy.

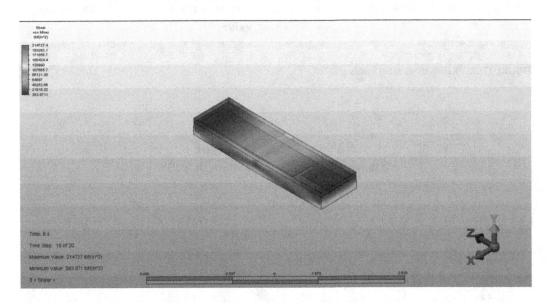

FIGURE 17.23   Shear simulation of Kevlar reinforced epoxy.

The shear simulation for the Kevlar reinforced epoxy shows the maximum movement of the material and the total forces built up in the part during loading (Figure 17.23). Where the break in the material can be expected to occur is indicated in this simulation as the yellow, orange, and red areas. In this simulation, the 1,200-pound load induced a maximum stress of approximately 201,200 psi. The actual test specimen failed at closer to 370 pounds and only saw up to approximately 3,000 psi.

The actual tests yield similar failure points. Most failures were flexure failure where the part failed because of tension on the bottom or compression on the top. Because of the speed of the test, most parts exhibited both failures.

There were some parts' failures that are classified as interlaminar shear failures (Figure 17.24). These parts failed between the layers of reinforcement. Upon further evaluation, the interlaminar shear failures

FIGURE 17.24 Fluxure failure in glass fiber reinforced epoxy.

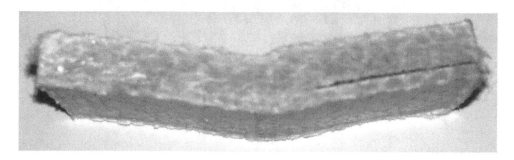

FIGURE 17.25 Interlaminar shear failure in Kevlar reinforced epoxy.

occurred within the RFID tag and the PET backing material. This proves that the epoxy to tag bond was not the weakest bond in the material.

For the glass specimen, the control yielded an average shear strength of 4,996.1 psi (Figures 17.25 and 17.26; Table 17.19). This appears to be considerably higher than the test specimen that had the RFID tag included in the material. The standard deviation and the coefficient of variation are also considerably smaller than the other test specimen which leads to the belief that the measurements were more consistent (Figure 17.27).

17.6.1.2.1 One-way ANOVA: Glass Shear Strength (psi) vs. Tag Family

Null hypothesis: All means are equal.

Alternative hypothesis: At least one mean is different.

Significance level $\alpha = 0.05$ (Figure 17.28; Tables 17.20–17.23).

Tukey Pairwise Comparisons (Table 17.24)

Means that do not share a letter are significantly different.

The pairwise comparisons show that the control specimen is statistically different than the specimen with tags. All specimens with tags are statistically the same (Figures 17.29 and 17.30).

The normal probability plot is somewhat straight hinting at normally distributed data (Figure 17.31).

The residuals vs. fitted values plot shows non-constant variance with the fitted values for the control much higher than the data for the parts embedded with RFID tags (Table 17.25).

For the Kevlar specimen, the control yielded an average shear strength of 2,968.9 psi. This appears to be somewhat higher than the test specimen that had the RFID tag included in the

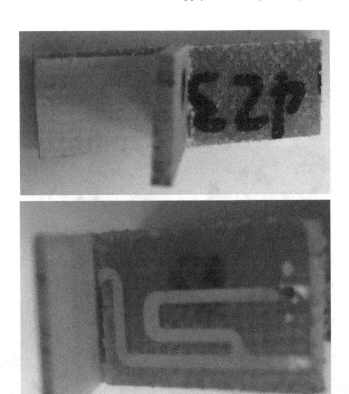

FIGURE 17.26   Detailed view of interlaminar shear at the RFID tag location.

TABLE 17.19

Descriptive Statistics for Glass Fiber Reinforced Epoxy

Variable	Glass Tag Type	Total Count	Mean	Standard Deviation	Coefficient of Variance
Glass shear strength (psi)	0	5	4996.1	171.5	3.43
	1	5	3564	403	11.32
	2	5	3776	609	16.13
	3	5	3951	558	14.12
	4	5	3816	485	12.71
	5	5	3712	349	9.40

material. One specimen, specimen 3, though of lower strength, is closer to the control than the other specimen types. The standard deviation and the coefficient of variation are also smaller than the other test specimens though some of the test specimens, such as specimen 4, are similar to the control (Figure 17.32).

17.6.1.2.2 One-way ANOVA: Kevlar Shear Strength (psi) vs. Kevlar Tag Family

Null hypothesis: All means are equal.

   Alternative hypothesis: At least one mean is different.

   Significance level $\alpha = 0.05$ (Figure 17.33; Tables 17.26–17.29).

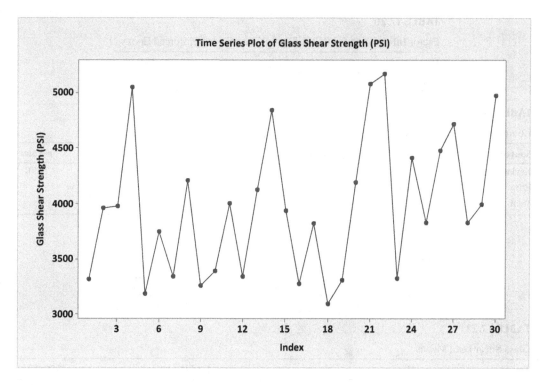

FIGURE 17.27 Time series plot of glass fiber reinforced epoxy.

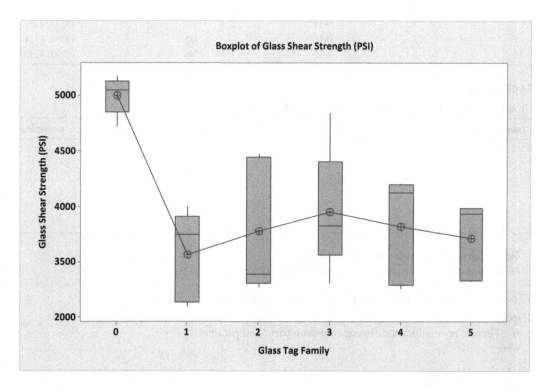

FIGURE 17.28 Box plot of glass shear test data.

TABLE 17.20

Factor Information for RFID Tags in Glass Fiber Reinforced Epoxy

Factor	Levels	Values
Glass tag type	6	0, 1, 2, 3, 4, 5

TABLE 17.21

Compression Test ANOVA for Glass Fiber Reinforced Epoxy

Source	DF	Adj SS	Adj MS	F-Value	p-Value
Kevlar tag type	5	6729905	1345981	6.56	0.001
Error	24	4924456	205186		
Total	29	11654361			

TABLE 17.22

Model Summary

S	R-sq	R-sq(adj)	R-sq(pred)
452.974	57.75%	48.94%	33.98%

TABLE 17.23

Glass Shear Data Means

Tag Type	N	Mean	Standard Deviation	95% CI
0	5	4996	171	(4578, 5414)
1	5	3564	403	(3146, 3982)
2	5	3776	609	(3358, 4194)
3	5	3951	558	(3533, 4369)
4	5	3816	485	(3398, 4234)
5	5	3712	349	(3293, 4130)

TABLE 17.24

Grouping Information Using the Tukey Method at 95% Confidence

Glass Tag Type	N	Mean	Grouping
0	5	15276	A
3	5	15230	B
4	5	12985	B
2	5	12459	B
5	5	11779	B
1	5	11452	B

Tukey Pairwise Comparisons (Table 17.30)

Means that do not share a letter are significantly different (Figures 17.34–17.36).

17.6.1.2.3 Material Type and Tag Type Shear Strengths

Hypothesis:

H_0: There is no significant difference between part i and parameter j, where

i is the material type

j is the mechanical property

H_A: There is a significant difference between part i and parameter j.

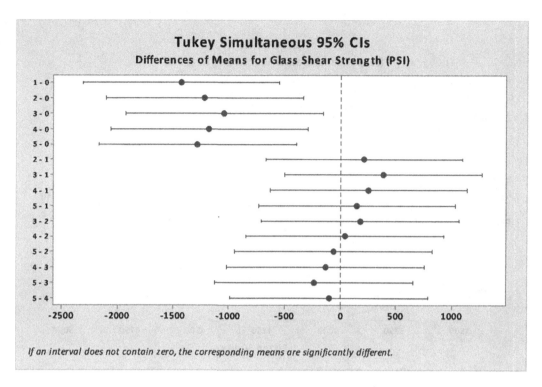

FIGURE 17.29 Tukey 95% confidence interval.

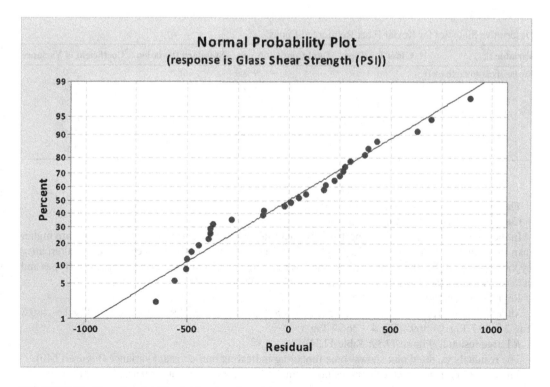

FIGURE 17.30 Normal probability plot for glass shear data.

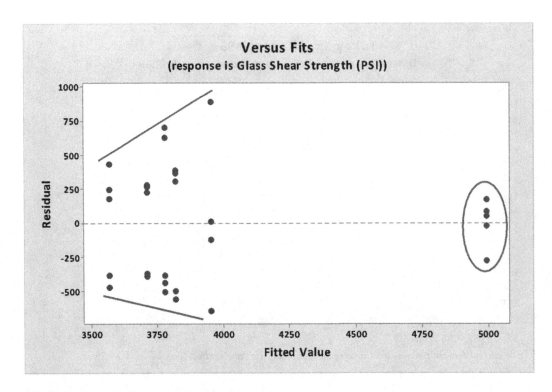

FIGURE 17.31   Residuals vs. fitted values plot for glass shear.

TABLE 17.25

Descriptive Statistics for Kevlar Fiber Reinforced Epoxy

Variable	Glass Tag Type	Total Count	Mean	Standard Deviation	Coefficient of Variance
Kevlar shear strength (psi)	0	5	2968.9	68.5	2.31
	1	5	2164	273	12.60
	2	5	2181.3	204.7	9.38
	3	5	2547.9	155.0	6.08
	4	5	2164.2	85.5	3.95
	5	5	2074.2	148.4	7.16

The hypothesis will be tested at $\alpha = 0.30$ (Figure 17.37).

Categorical predictor coding (−1, 0, +1)

In the ANOVA for the shear strengths of the material types and the tag types, the F-values are higher than the F distribution value of 1.25 (Table 17.31). The null hypothesis is rejected, and the alternative hypothesis is used. For these calculations, there is a significant difference between the material types and at least one of the tag types in the shear tests (Tables 17.32 and 17.33).

Regression Equation (Figure 17.38)

Shear Strength (psi) = 3159.6 + 809.5 Glass − 809.5 Kevlar + 822.9 Tag 0 − 295.7 Tag 1 − 180.8 Tag 2 + 89.7 Tag 3 − 169.4 Tag 4 − 266.7 Tag 5

R Large residual (Figure 17.39; Table 17.34)

The residuals vs. fitted plot shows some funneling indicating non-constant variance (Figure 17.40).

The normal probability plot shows a straight line indicating that the data is normally distributed.

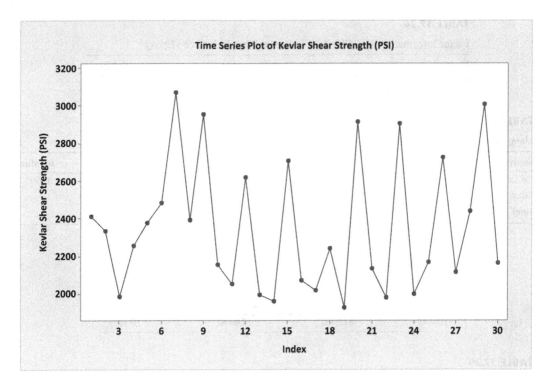

FIGURE 17.32 Time series plot of Kevlar fiber reinforced epoxy.

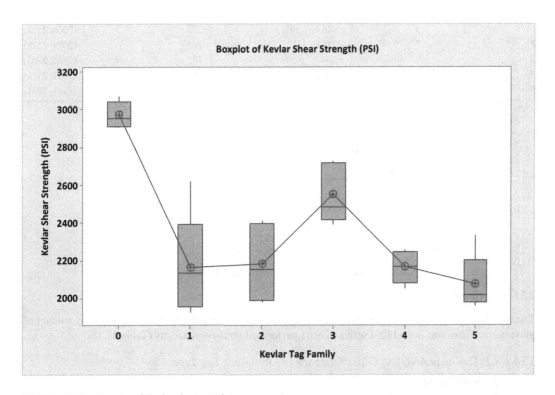

FIGURE 17.33 Box plot of Kevlar shear test data.

TABLE 17.26

Factor Information for RFID Tags in Kevlar Fiber Reinforced Epoxy

Factor	Levels	Values
Kevlar tag type	6	0, 1, 2, 3, 4, 5

TABLE 17.27

Shear Test ANOVA for Kevlar Fiber Reinforced Epoxy

Source	DF	Adj SS	Adj MS	F-Value	p-Value
Kevlar Tag Type	5	2979958	595992	20.51	0.000
Error	24	697274	29053		
Total	29	3677232			

TABLE 17.28

Model Summary

S	R-sq	R-sq(adj)	R-sq(pred)
170.450	81.04%	77.09%	70.37%

TABLE 17.29

Kevlar Shear Data Means

Tag Type	N	Mean	Standard Deviation	95% CI
0	5	2969	68	(2812, 3126)
1	5	2164	273	(2006, 2321)
2	5	2181	204	(2024, 2338)
3	5	2547	155	(2390, 2705)
4	5	2164	85	(2007, 2321)
5	5	2074	148	(1917, 2231)

TABLE 17.30

Grouping Information Using the Tukey Method at 95% Confidence

Kevlar Tag Type	N	Mean	Grouping
0	5	2968.9	A
3	5	2547.9	B
2	5	2181.3	C
4	5	2164.2	C
1	5	2164	C
5	5	2074.2	C

17.6.1.3 Read Distance Testing

The read distances occurred in batches of parts. A series of Kevlar parts were run followed by a series of glass parts. There was not a blind series of tests performed on these data sets (Table 17.35).

17.6.1.3.1 One-way ANOVA: Glass Distance (ft) vs. Glass Tag Type

Null hypothesis: All means are equal.
　Alternative hypothesis: At least one mean is different.
　Significance level $\alpha = 0.05$.

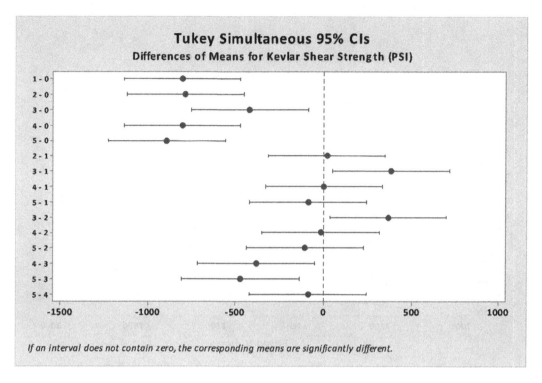

FIGURE 17.34 Tukey 95% confidence interval.

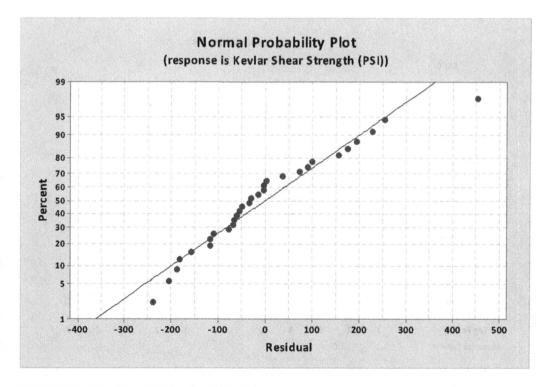

FIGURE 17.35 Normal probability plot for Kevlar shear data.

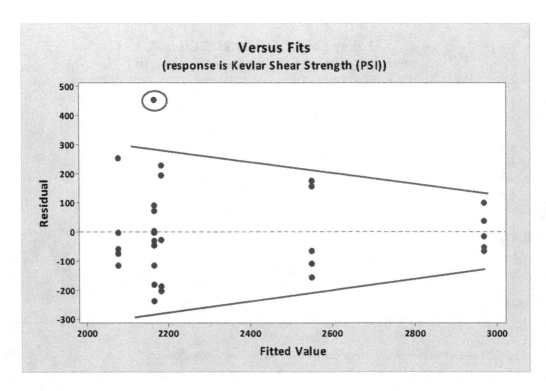

FIGURE 17.36   Residuals vs. fitted values plot for Kevlar shear.

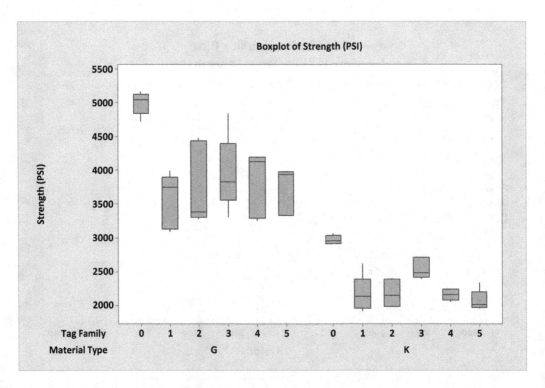

FIGURE 17.37   Box plot of shear strengths.

TABLE 17.31

Analysis of Variance

Source	DF	Adj SS	Adj MS	F-Value	p-Value
Regression	6	48372339	8062056	68.04	0.000
Material type	1	39320432	39320432	331.86	0.000
Tag family	5	9051907	1810381	15.28	0.000
Error	53	6279685	118485		
Lack-of-fit	5	657956	131591	1.12	0.361
Pure error	48	5621729	117119		
Total	59	54652024			

TABLE 17.32

Model Summary

S	R-sq	R-sq(adj)	R-sq(pred)
344.216	88.51%	87.21%	85.27%

TABLE 17.33

Variables Used in Determining Shear Strength from Material and Tag Type

Variable	Coefficient	SE Coefficient	T	p-Value
Constant	3159.6	44.4	71.10	0.000
Glass	809.5	44.4	18.22	0.000
Kevlar	−809.5	44.4	−18.22	0.000
Tag 0	822.9	99.4	8.28	0.000
Tag 1	−295.7	99.4	−2.98	0.004
Tag 2	−180.8	99.4	−1.82	0.074
Tag 3	89.7	99.4	0.90	0.371
Tag 4	−169.4	99.4	−1.70	0.094
Tag 5	−266.7	99.4	−2.68	0.010

The F-value from the ANOVA is less than the 2.09 value listed in the F distribution causing a fail-to-reject scenario for the H_0 that all means are equal (Tables 17.36 and 17.37). The p-value is also higher than α meaning that the mean is not statistically significant.

The R-sq value of 17.25% shows that the models do not adequately represent the data points (Figure 17.41; Table 17.38).

The box plot shows two outliers in the data for the read distance of the tags embedded in glass fiber. Tag 4 is the feathered tag and was most likely damaged during modification of the tag. This failure point is due to the tag having some limited read range which may be affected by the continuity in the antenna. If the antenna was cut, then it would lose much of its effectiveness. The second outlier is in the tag 5 parts. Tag 5 is the abraded tag, so the likelihood of damage to the tag through modification is very small. This tag may have had some defect to begin with or was adversely affected by the heat in the cure cycle.

The box plot does show that tag 4 has a high amount of variability. The outlier and its magnitude are contributing to this non-constant variation (Table 17.39).

Tukey Pairwise Comparisons (Table 17.40)

Means that do not share a letter are significantly different (Figure 17.42).

For the tags embedded in glass, all tags are similar to each other meaning that the tags all read to approximately the same distances (Figure 17.43).

The normal probability plot shows an s-curve in the residuals. The abnormality of this plot is caused by the way the data was collected and the large number of samples that read out to 100 ft (Figure 17.44).

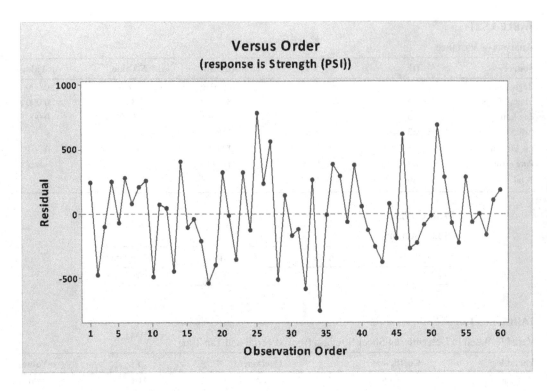

FIGURE 17.38   Observation orders.

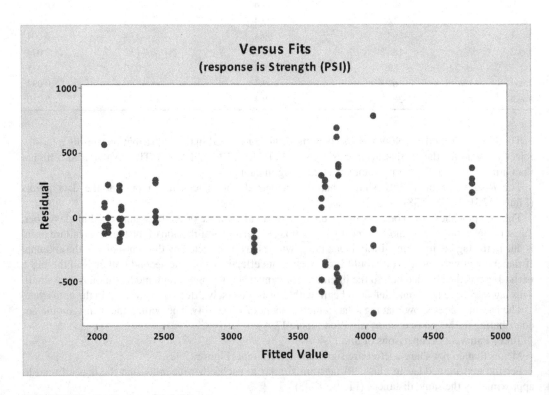

FIGURE 17.39   Residuals vs. fitted plot.

TABLE 17.34

Fits and Diagnostics for Unusual Observations

Observation	Shear Strength (psi)	Fit	Residual	Std. Residual
25	4841	4059	782	2.42 R
34	3301	4059	−758	−2.34 R
51	4476	3788	688	2.13 R

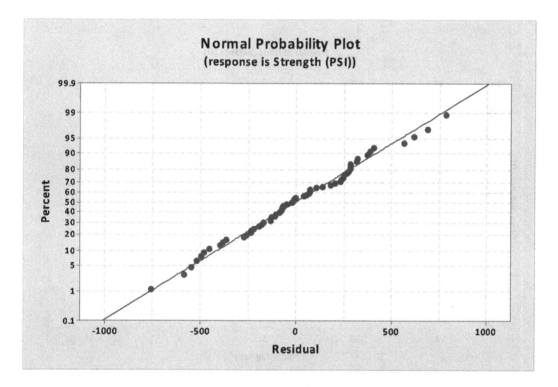

FIGURE 17.40 Normal probability plot.

TABLE 17.35

Descriptive Statistics for Read Distance Testing

Variable	Glass Tag Type	Total Count	Mean	Standard Deviation	Coefficient of Variance
Glass read distance (psi)	1	8	100.00	0	0
	2	8	100.00	0	0
	3	8	100.00	0	0
	4	8	85.3	29.9	35.05
	5	8	98.13	3.94	4.02

TABLE 17.36

Factor Information for RFID Tags in Glass Fiber Reinforced Epoxy

Factor	Levels	Values
Glass tag type	5	1, 2, 3, 4, 5

TABLE 17.37

Read Distance Test ANOVA for Glass Fiber Reinforced Epoxy

Source	DF	Adj SS	Adj MS	F-Value	p-Value
Glass tag type	4	1326	331.6	1.83	0.146
Error	35	6358	181.7		
Total	39	7685			

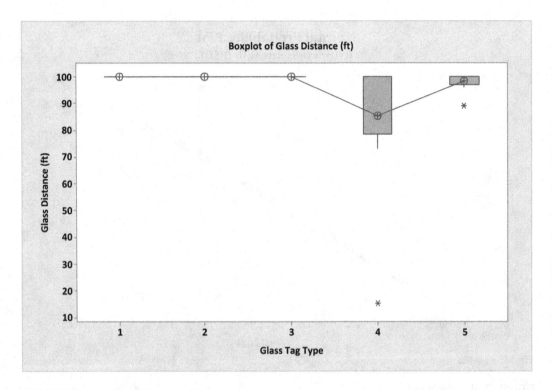

FIGURE 17.41   Box plot of glass read distance test data.

TABLE 17.38

Model Summary

S	R-sq	R-sq(adj)	R-sq(pred)
13.4784	17.26%	7.80%	0.00%

TABLE 17.39

Glass Read Distance Data Means

Tag Type	N	Mean	Standard Deviation	95% CI
1	8	100.0	0	(90.3, 109.7)
2	8	100.0	0	(90.3, 109.7)
3	8	100.0	0	(90.3, 109.7)
4	8	85.3	29.9	(75.6, 94.9)
5	8	98.13	3.94	(88.45, 107.80)

TABLE 17.40

Grouping Information Using the Tukey Method at 95% Confidence

Glass Tag Type	N	Mean	Grouping
3	8	100.0	A
2	8	100.0	A
1	8	100.0	A
5	8	98.13	A
4	8	85.3	A

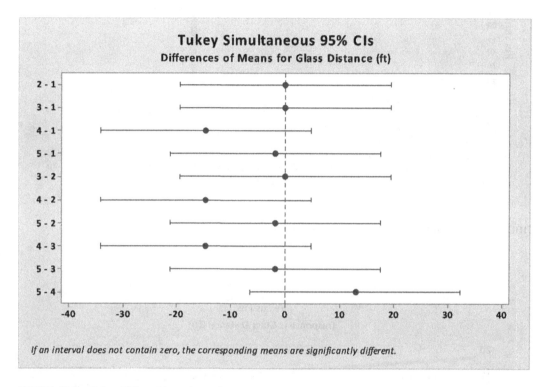

FIGURE 17.42   Tukey 95% confidence interval.

Once the outlier is removed from the residuals vs. fitted values plot, the data exhibits a slight non-constant variance. Again, the large number of data points that read at 100 ft has an effect on the plot.

Descriptive Statistics: Kevlar Distance (ft) (Table 17.41)

17.6.1.3.2 One-way ANOVA: Kevlar Distance (ft) vs. Kevlar Tag Type

Null hypothesis: All means are equal.

Alternative hypothesis: At least one mean is different.

Significance level $\alpha = 0.05$.

The F-value from the ANOVA is less than the 2.09 value listed in the F distribution causing a fail-to-reject scenario for the H_0 that all means are equal (Tables 17.42 and 17.43). The p-value is also much higher than α resulting in the mean being not statistically significant (Table 17.44).

The R-sq of 3.16% shows that the data is not represented by the model (Figure 17.45).

The box plot for the Kevlar tags shows one outlier in tag 2. Tag 2 is the unmodified tag. Because this tag read so much shorter than the other tags in the data set, it is assumed that there was a problem with the tag from either the manufacturer or a problem that propagated during the manufacturing of the Kevlar part.

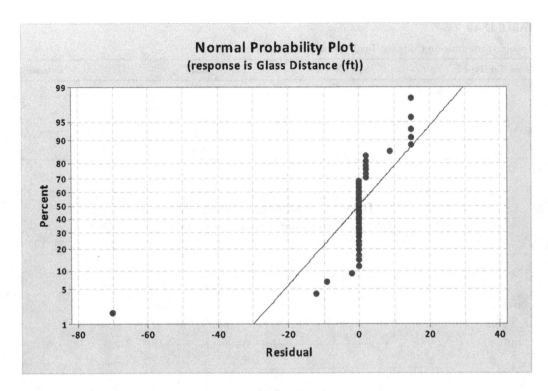

FIGURE 17.43   Normal probability plot for glass read distances data.

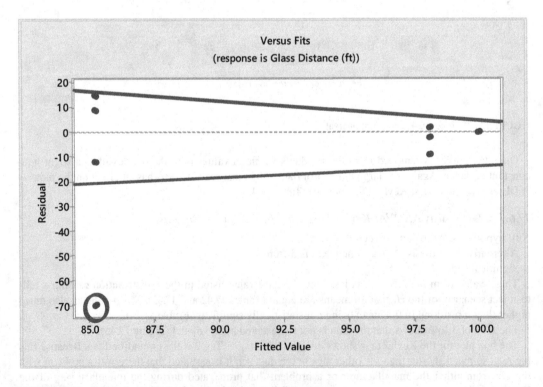

FIGURE 17.44   Residuals vs. fitted values plot for glass read distances.

TABLE 17.41

Descriptive Statistics for Kevlar Read Distances

Variable	Glass Tag Type	Total Count	Mean	Standard Deviation	Coefficient of Variance
Kevlar read distance (psi)	1	8	69.25	25.71	37.12
	2	8	80.13	18.34	22.89
	3	8	79.88	24.58	30.78
	4	8	71.3	31.5	44.22
	5	8	79.5	36.6	46.08

TABLE 17.42

Factor Information for RFID Tags in Kevlar Fiber Reinforced Epoxy

Factor	Levels	Values
Kevlar tag type	5	1, 2, 3, 4, 5

TABLE 17.43

Read Distance ANOVA for Kevlar Fiber Reinforced Epoxy

Source	DF	Adj SS	Adj MS	F-Value	p-Value
Kevlar tag type	4	899.3	224.8	0.29	0.885
Error	35	27556.7	787.3		
Total	39	28456.0			

TABLE 17.44

Model Summary

S	R-sq	R-sq(adj)	R-sq(pred)
28.0595	3.16%	0.00%	0.00%

All Kevlar parts had a reduced read range compared to the glass FRP parts. It is postulated that the Kevlar material does have a slight impact on the transmission of RF signals transmitted to and from the RFID tags (Table 17.45).

Tukey Pairwise Comparisons (Table 17.46)

Means that do not share a letter are significantly different (Figure 17.46).

In the read distances for the Kevlar, all means for the different tags are statistically the same (Figure 17.47).

The normal probability plot shows upper tail on the right side. This points to a more exponential distribution of the data instead of normal distribution (Figure 17.48).

The residuals vs. fitted values plot is mostly constant and does not exhibit any funneling in the data.

17.6.1.3.3 Material Type and Tag Type Read Distances

Hypothesis:

H_0: There is no significant difference between part i and the electronic transmission readability performance factor K,

where

i is the material type

K is the electronic transmission readability performance factor.

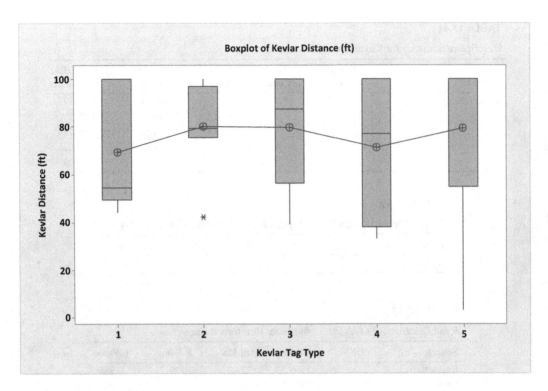

FIGURE 17.45   Box plot of Kevlar read distance.

TABLE 17.45

Kevlar Read Distance Data Means

Tag Type	N	Mean	Standard Deviation	95% CI
1	8	69.25	25.71	(49.11, 89.39)
2	8	80.13	18.34	(59.99, 100.26)
3	8	79.88	24.58	(59.74, 100.01)
4	8	71.3	31.5	(51.1, 91.4)
5	8	79.5	36.6	(59.4, 99.6)

TABLE 17.46

Grouping Information Using the Tukey Method at 95% Confidence

Kevlar Tag Type	N	Mean	Grouping
2	8	80.13	A
3	8	79.88	A
5	8	79.5	A
4	8	71.3	A
1	8	69.25	A

H_A: There is a significant difference between part i and the electronic transmission readability performance factor K.

An $\alpha = 0.30$ will be used.

Categorical predictor coding $(-1, 0, +1)$

In the ANOVA for the read distances, the F-value for the material type is higher than the F distribution value of 1.25, whereas the F-value for the tag family is lower than the F distribution value of 1.09

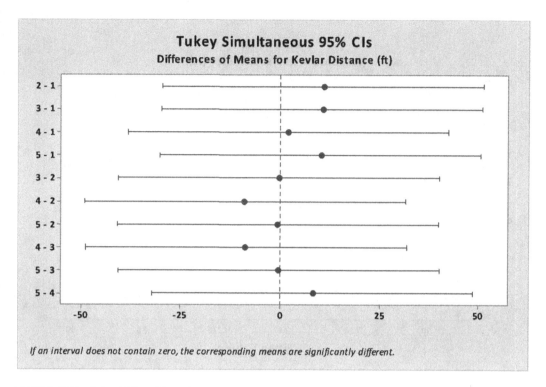

FIGURE 17.46 Tukey 95% confidence interval.

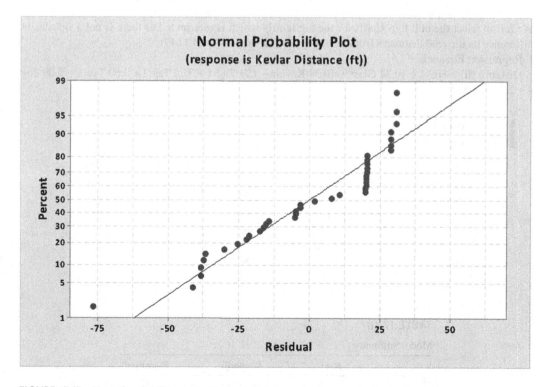

FIGURE 17.47 Normal probability plot for Kevlar read distances

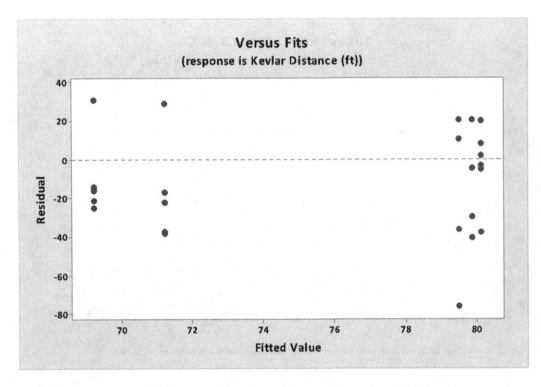

FIGURE 17.48 Residuals vs. fitted values plot for Kevlar read distances.

(Table 17.47). The null hypothesis is rejected for the material type, and the alternative hypothesis is used. For these calculations, there is a significant difference between the material types in the read distances. We fail to reject the null hypothesis for the tag family which is interpreted as there is not a significant difference on the read distances from the tag types (Tables 17.48 and 17.49).

Regression Equation

Distance (ft) = 86.34 + 10.34 Glass − 10.34 Kevlar − 1.71 Tag 1 + 3.72 Tag 2 + 3.60 Tag 3 − 8.09 Tag 4 + 2.47 Tag 5

TABLE 17.47

ANOVA

Source	DF	Adj SS	Adj MS	F-Value	p-Value
Regression	5	10169.9	2034.0	4.36	0.002
Material type	1	8549.1	8549.1	11.33	0.000
Tag family	4	1620.8	405.2	0.87	0.487
Error	74	34519.9	466.5		
Lack-of-fit	4	604.8	151.2	0.31	0.869
Pure error	70	33915.1	484.5		
Total	79	44689.9			

TABLE 17.48

Model Summary

S	R-sq	R-sq(adj)	R-sq(pred)
21.5983	22.76%	17.54%	9.72%

TABLE 17.49

Variables Used in Determining Shear Strength from Material and Tag Type

Variable	Coefficient	SE Coefficient	T	p-Value
Constant	86.34	2.41	35.75	0.000
Glass	10.34	2.41	4.28	0.000
Kevlar	−10.34	2.41	−4.28	0.000
Tag 1	−1.71	4.83	−0.35	0.724
Tag 2	3.72	4.83	0.77	0.443
Tag 3	3.60	4.83	0.75	0.458
Tag 4	−8.09	4.83	−1.65	0.098
Tag 5	2.47	4.83	0.51	0.610

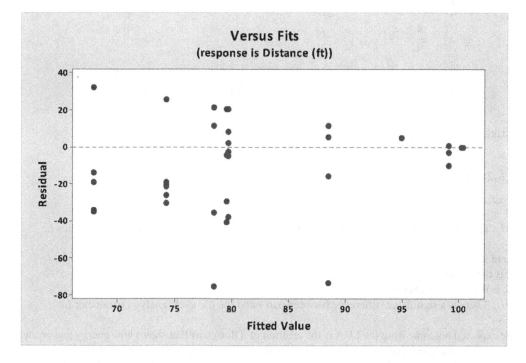

FIGURE 17.49 Residuals vs. fitted values plot.

TABLE 17.50

Fits and Diagnostics for Unusual Observations

Observation	Shear Strength (psi)	Fit	Residual	Std. Residual
12	3.00	78.47	−75.47	−3.63 R
75	15.00	88.59	−73.59	−3.54 R

R Large residual (Figure 17.49; Table 17.50)

The residuals vs. fitted plot shows non-constant variance due to the funneling effect of the data (Figure 17.50).

The normal probability plot exhibits some curvature in the data. There may be a slight exponential distribution in the data.

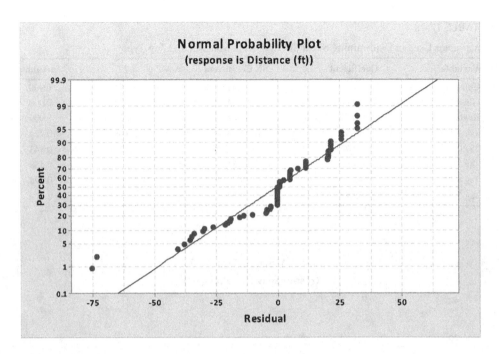

FIGURE 17.50   Normal probability plot.

17.6.2 Life Cycle Analysis

Hypotheses

H_0: There is not a significant difference between part i and the life cycle analysis parameter L,

where
  i is the material type
  L is the LCA parameter.
  H_A: There is a significant difference between part i and the life cycle analysis parameter L.

One expected outcome from the LCA is the creation of a flowchart that shows how energy and products interact. The complexity of the LCA grows rapidly depending on the product. This flowchart is of a water bottle. Due to restrictions in the data, the method for performing the LCA for the FRPs and the FRPs with embedded electronics is only defined in the methodology.

17.7 Conclusions and Discussions

The conclusion describes the outcomes of the research based on the results along with which recommendations are made based on those results. The discussion in the conclusion lists out the limitations of the research and defines what the future work will include. Figure 17.51 shows where this work applies and where future work will contribute.

17.7.1 Conclusions

17.7.1.1 Simulation Testing

The FEM simulations can be successful once additional information is known from actual testing. The location was identified in the simulations as movement in the part was very near the actual breaks in the

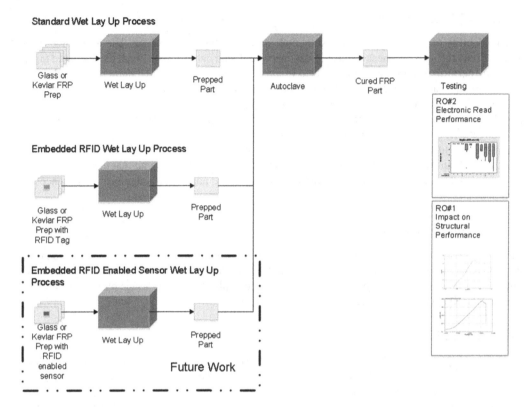

FIGURE 17.51 RFID-enabled sensing in FRPs.

mechanical tests. The stresses encountered in this research were not always very close to the simulated stresses. We believe that although the correct materials in the simulations were used, the values for these materials may need to be redefined. We also know that the simulations will only show the stress build up in the simulated part and that they will not simulate the actual break.

17.7.1.2 Mechanical Testing

The compression tests showed where the breaking point of the material is and allowed identification of the failure mode. In the compression test, the typical failure occurred in a region that contained the tag. All of these failures occurred on the tag side of the laminations and never between two layers of fabric. Upon evaluating the hypothesis that there is no significant difference in the compression strength between the materials and the tags, it was found that there are differences between the materials and there are differences between the tags.

The shear tests also showed the failure points in the materials and are much more interesting and somewhat more relevant to actual use. The shear tests did not always fail because of the tag causing delamination in the part. Some of the failures were in the materials themselves. Fortunately, the failures in the materials were at a higher load than the failures of the tag. Upon dissecting the failures of the parts with delamination, the failure did not occur between the tag and the resin. All of these failures occurred in the tag where the antenna was pulled from the inlay. This indicated that the tag used in the experiments caused the failure because of its construction, not necessarily because of the RFID tag being a defect in the layers of the FRP. In fact, the epoxy seemed to bond well with both the PET inlay and with the antenna. The mechanical testing also showed that there may be something to reducing the footprint of the tag in the FRP though more testing needs to take place. Evaluating the hypothesis, it was found that there is a significant difference between the material types and there is a significant difference between the tags.

17.7.1.3 Electrical Testing

The readability of the tags is influenced by embedding the tag into the FRP. The glass FRP did not greatly affect the read distances as most of the tags would read out to 100 ft. Tag 4, the feathered tag, had the worst performance of the tags embedded in glass. All of the Kevlar FRP parts influenced the read distance as the read distances ranged from 3 ft out to 100 ft. On average, the read distances of the Kevlar are only 75% of the read distances seen in the glass. This suggests that the Kevlar, though still able to pass RF, does negatively affect the transmission of RF. The possibility of the manufacturing process affecting the Kevlar tags is ruled out since both the glass and Kevlar parts are manufactured in the same manner. It would have made more sense that the glass would have been affected more by the heat since it is thinner than the Kevlar. When the hypothesis was evaluated, it was found that there is a significant difference in the read distances in the materials, but the tags do not exhibit a significant difference in the read distances.

17.7.1.4 Life Cycle Analysis

The LCA proved much more difficult to obtain than originally thought. The environmental and energy costs for the various points of manufacturing and transport are much more in depth and difficult to obtain. The flowchart of the processes does indicate a complicated energy usage problem regardless of whether the RFID tag is embedded or not.

17.7.2 Limitations

One of the biggest limitations to the research has been the costs associated with the LCA. The literature does a good job of discussing these issues, but there is a big hole in data, especially when trying to dig down at the chemical component level.

From the testing standpoint, there needs to be a more precise method of placing the tags into the FRPs. All tags are placed in the FRP, but there is a margin of error as to the orientation of the tag. This can be alleviated to some extent with the use of the pre-preg materials, but it will remain a problem to some extent.

17.7.3 Contribution to the Body of Knowledge

This work has helped by showing how RFID affects the strength of a composite material when it is embedded into that material. It has also shown that RFID can transmit through the FRP materials and depending on the setup of the RFID tag, RFID may be able to be used as an energy source to power small sensors attached to it. The biggest impact that this research has had on the body of knowledge is the mechanical testing of the materials with the tag embedded into the material. In this research, an off the shelf tag was used, and though it did not work entirely as planned, it still showed that the tag construction, or the bond between the antenna and the inlay, is weaker than the bond between the epoxy resin and the tag.

17.7.4 Future Work

There is more work to be done. The next step is to go forward with the tensile tests to ensure that there is not an effect on the fibers due to the inclusion of the RFID tag. This will require a better manufacturing method in order to precisely lay the tag into the FRP layers. Another step is to re-evaluate the tag used in the testing and replace the current tag with one that does not have an inlay. An alternative to this is to print an RFID tag onto a different material such as Tefzel or onto glass or Kevlar fiber so that it becomes more of the structure of the part.

Another step for the future work is to expand into other manufacturing processes such as working with pre-preg materials, working with resin infusion transfer, and working with the pultrusion process. This would expand the usability of the tool and increase the likelihood of adoption. It would also be interesting to see how the RFID tag would affect those structures since they are mechanically different.

The third future work area would be to include RFID into shaped structures that do not have flat faces. Curved parts or irregularly shaped parts would be needed to be tested since there are a large number of FRP parts that are not square.

The fourth area for future work is the integration of sensors into the RFID tags. There are existing strain-enabled RFID tags, but more work needs to be done in the area with these tags.

17.7.5 Related Coursework

There are several courses taken at the University of Texas at Arlington (UTA) and taught at Tarleton State University that have contributed to this dissertation.

At UTA, many of the courses required are factored into this dissertation. The first is IE 5300 RFID and Logistics. From this course, the main topic of RFID played heavily into the research as the embedded electronics used are RFID tags. The second class is IE 6302 Facility Planning. From this course, the use of standard practices helped with the manufacture of parts, but the logistics of how people and items move through the SC helped more with the LCA piece of the research. IE 5339 and IE 5346 helped with determining how to implement new technology as well as determining and resolving problems related to manufacturing, reliability, and testing of these new technologies. IE 5304 Engineering Economy helped with justifying different options during the research. It was especially helpful with the life cycle costs and determining economic feasibility.

At Tarleton, being thrust into teaching ENGT 3325 Thermoset Manufacturing contributed to the knowledge needed to build and manipulate the reinforcement fibers used in this research. The class also provided valuable manpower and the ability to validate the manufacturing processes with students before working on the actual parts and performing the tests.

REFERENCES

Arronche, L., La Saponara, V., Yesil, S., & Bayram, G. (2013). Impact damage sensing of multiscale composites through epoxy matrix containing carbon nanotubes. *Journal of Applied Polymer Science, 128*(5), 2797–2806.

ASTM D2344 / D2344M-13, Standard test method for short-beam strength of polymer matrix composite materials and their laminates. (2013). West Conshohocken, PA: ASTM International.

ASTM D638-14, Standard test method for tensile properties of plastics. (2014). West Conshoshoken, PA: ASTM International.

Balasubramanian, S., Jones, E.C., Gray, B., Armstrong, H., & Samdurkar, R. (March 2015). Evaluating six sigma implementation effectiveness through statistical process control. *Strategic Management Quarterly, 3*(1), 49–70.

Bernhard, J., Dräger, T., Grabowski, C., Sotriffer, I., & Philipp, T. (2011). Integrating RFID in fibre-reinforced plastics. *Paper presented at the Proceedings of RFID SysTech 2011; 7th European Workshop on Smart Objects: Systems, Technologies and Applications.*

Department of Energy: www.solarpowerworldonline.com/2014/05/department-energy-2014-year-csp/.

Dumstorff, G., Paul, S., & Lang, W. (2014). Integration without Disruption: the Basic Challenge of Sensor Integration. *Sensors Journal, IEEE, 14*(7), 2102–2111.

EEA: www.eea.europa.eu/publications/air-quality-in-europe-2018.

Fiber Reinforced Polymer Composite Manufacturing Workshop: Summary Report (E. E. a. R. E. A. M. Office, Trans.). (2014) (p. 25). Department of Energy.

Jeon, J., Muliana, A., & La Saponara, V. (2014). Thermal stress and deformation analyses in fiber reinforced polymer composites undergoing heat conduction and mechanical loading. *Composite Structures, 111*, 31–44.

Jones, E.C., & Chung, C. (August 2008). Education in modern solutions: RFID is a must in the industrial engineering curriculum. *Industrial Engineer, 40*(No. 8), 29–33.

Jones, E. C., & Chung, C. A. (2011). RFID and auto-ID in planning and logistics: a practical guide for military UID applications (pp. 1 online resource (xxix, 392 pp)). Retrieved from http://lib-ezproxy.tamu.edu:2048/login?url=http://proquest.safaribooksonline.com/?uiCode=tamucollst&xmlId=9781420094282.

Kendall, A., Keoleian, G. A., & Lepech, M. D. (2008). Materials design for sustainability through life cycle modeling of engineered cementitious composites. *Materials and Structures, 41*(6), 1117–1131.

La Saponara, V., Horsley, D. A., & Lestari, W. (2011). Structural health monitoring of glass/epoxy composite plates using PZT and PMN-PT transducers. *Journal of Engineering Materials and Technology, 133*(1), 011011.

Loyola, B. R., Zhao, Y., Loh, K. J., & La Saponara, V. (2013). The electrical response of carbon nanotube-based thin film sensors subjected to mechanical and environmental effects. *Smart Materials and Structures, 22*(2), 025010.

Mason, G., Al-Ali, A., & Gerhardt, T.J. (10 January 2006). Flex circuit shielded optical sensor. U.S. Patent No. 6,985,764.

Merilampi, S., Björninen, T., Ukkonen, L., Ruuskanen, P., & Sydänheimo, L. (2011). Embedded wireless strain sensors based on printed RFID tag. *Sensor Review, 31*(1), 32–40.

Miyano, Y., Nakada, M., & Cai, H. (2008). Formulation of long-term creep and fatigue strengths of polymer composites based on accelerated testing methodology. *Journal of Composite Materials, 42*(18), 1897–1919.

Nakada, M., & Miyano, Y. (2009). Accelerated testing for long-term fatigue strength of various FRP laminates for marine use. *Composites Science and Technology, 69*(6), 805–813.

Pille, C. (2010). In-Process Embedding of Piezo Sensors and Rfid Transponders into Cast Parts for Autonomous Manufacturing Logistics. *Proceedings of the Smart Systems Integration*, Como, Italy.

Schaaf, K. L. (2008). Composite materials with integrated embedded sensing networks.

Strong, A.B. (2008). *Fundamentals of Composites Manufacturing: Materials, Methods and Applications.* Dearborn, MI: Society of Manufacturing Engineers.

Suh, S., & Huppes, G. (2005). Methods for life cycle inventory of a product. *Journal of Cleaner Production, 13*(7), 687–697.

Tang, H.-Y., Winkelmann, C., Lestari, W., & La Saponara, V. (2011). Composite structural health monitoring through use of embedded PZT sensors. *Journal of Intelligent Material Systems and Structures.* DOI:10.1177/1045389X11406303.

US EPA: https://www3.epa.gov/ttn/naaqs/standards/pm/s_pm_cr.html.

Williams, E. (2004). Energy intensity of computer manufacturing: hybrid assessment combining process and economic input-output methods. *Environmental Science & Technology, 38*(22), 6166–6174.

18

Secure Documents with RFID and Potential Blockchain Implications

Erick C. Jones

The EOQ model at it's core can validate or invalidate Quality management theories.

Erick C. Jones

18.1 Secure Document RFID Applications

18.1.1 Introduction

Perhaps the most sensitive radio frequency identification (RFID) application to date involves the use of RFID technology with government passports. The issuance of the U.S. Electronic E-Passport began on August 14, 2006. E-Passports contain the same information as conventional passports but also include an RFID chip in the rear cover of the passport. Since the first E-Passports were issued, a great deal of public criticism has arisen. Some tests by independent parties indicate that it is possible to overcome the built in security and privacy measures incorporated into E-Passports. However, whether or not these potential weaknesses can be illegally exploited by illegal aliens and terrorist groups has yet to be determined. In this chapter, we will begin with a basic description of how the E-Passport functions and continue with a discussion of security issues.

18.1.2 Basic Passport Background

Passports are issued by virtually all nations. They are usually required for identification purposes for entry into most nations. The few exceptions to this requirement that do exist are slowly being eliminated. For example, the Intelligence Reform and Terrorism Prevention Act of 2004 required the U.S. Department of Homeland Security and the U.S. State Department to develop and implement a plan whereby all travelers need a document such as a passport for identification purposes on entry into the United States. As a result of the act, since January 23, 2007, all persons, including U.S. citizens traveling by air are required to have a passport or similar documentation for entry from Mexico and the Caribbean. As early as January 1, 2008, these requirements may be extended to both land and sea.

The passport currently being issued by the Department of State is the E-Passport.

Note that the page contains a photograph, the passport number, the individual's name, date of birth, birth place, sex, and passport issue and expiration dates. The E-Passport also contains an RFID chip on the inside back cover of the passport. The inside back cover is illustrated in the following Figure 18.1.

Since the passport issuing period is 10 years, it will be a number of years before all of the passports in circulation will be required to be renewed. Until then, it is anticipated that all of the non-E-Passports in circulation will continue to be valid.

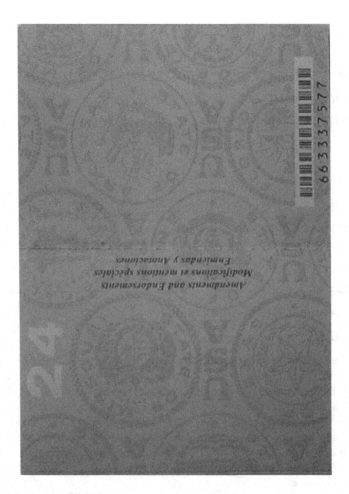

FIGURE 18.1   Inside back cover of E-Passport.

18.1.3 E-Passport RFID Chip

The E-Passport RFID chip contains 64K of encrypted data. Publicly accessible sources indicate that the chip holds the same information that is available on the picture page of the E-Passport. As we stated earlier, this includes the passport number, the individual's name, date of birth, birth place, sex, and passport issue and expiration dates. The chip also includes a digital photograph of the passport holder. The presence of the digital photograph allows for the possibility of incorporating biometric identification systems at some future point in time. This means that an individual may be digitally scanned at the point of entry. The real-time scan would then be biometrically compared to the digital photo contained in the RFID chip. The exact contents of the chip are governed by the International Civil Aviation Organization (ICAO), which we will discuss in the next section.

18.1.4 ICAO Protocol

The E-Passport follows the standards indicated by the ICAO. These standards are available from their website at www.icao.int/mrtd/download/technical.cfm [1]. One of the significant components of this protocol is that the E-Passport is only supposed to be readable from very short distances. This is officially reported as 4 in. However, there are some claims that E-Passports can be read as far as a few feet away. The unauthorized reading of passports by unknown individuals has been termed as "skimming".

To combat successful skimming, the U.S. State Department has incorporated a multi-layered security system to help prevent the unauthorized access of E-Passport data. The first layer of protection consists of electronic shielding built into the cover of the E-Passport. This is intended to block signals from any RFID readers attempting to energize the E-Passport and read the resulting signal [5].

The second level of security is what is known as Basic Access Control. This begins with a sequence of machine-readable characters physically printed on the E-Passport. This sequence of numbers is an encryption key. When the passport control officer scans the E-Passport, the RFID reader uses the encryption key to communicate and decode the data from the RFID chip [4]. In theory, this means that the only way to obtain and decode the data on the E-Passport is to first open up the passport and obtain the encryption key.

Critics of the Basic Access Control system are not so optimistic. In the summer of 2006, German hackers succeeded in successfully accessing ICAO-based passport data. By reading the publicly available ICAO documents, the hacker determined that the encryption key was based on information contained on the passport photo page [2]. The hacker was then able to crack an electronic passport and download the information to a smart memory card. By inserting the smart card into a physical passport, the hacker was able to present different physical and RFID passports.

An additional security measure used with E-Passports is known as a Public Key Infrastructure (PKI). The mechanics behind the PKI are beyond the scope of this chapter. However, it should be understood that the purpose of the PKI is to help insure that the data in the E-Passport RFID chip cannot be altered. It is in essence, a digital signature. In the event that the data is altered, the digital signature created with the PKI will indicate that tampering has occurred. For the individual, this also means that any change in name or other data will require that an entirely new passport be obtained. To help minimize the potential burden to citizens, the U.S. Department of State is allowing new passports to be obtained without charge for 1 year.

Another security problem associated with E-Passports is known as "eavesdropping". This is the electronic monitoring of the signals between the RFID reader and the E-Passport. The possibility of this has also been demonstrated as a group of Dutch hackers successfully eavesdropped on an RFID transmission and within 2 h successfully decrypted a digitized fingerprint, photograph, and other text information from an E-Passport in February of 2006 [3]. Since the Dutch E-Passport is based on the ICAO standards, it is presumed that this may also be performed on other ICAO standards-based E-Passports. The current government response to this potential weakness is to maintain electronic eavesdropping detection equipment at ports of entry.

18.1.5 Other Developments

Late in 2006, the Department of State announced the possibility of augmenting E-Passports with a Passport Card. The passport card is intended to simplify travel between the United States, Mexico, Canada, and the Caribbean. Like the E-Passport, the Passport Card will incorporate an RFID chip. However, at this time, the Passport Card is not expected to incorporate personal information in the same manner as the E-Passport. Instead, the Passport Card will be linked to a central database which contains the individual's photograph and biographical data. The Passport Card will also be more convenient and significantly cheaper to acquire than an E-Passport.

18.1.6 Deployment

It will likely be some time in the future before E-Passports outnumber the number of conventional passports in circulation. In addition to replacing the conventional passports with E-Passports, the Port of Entry facilities must also have the optical scanners and RFID readers that the E-Passport RFID chips need to operate. As this equipment is installed, the access lanes will be marked with the special international E-Passport symbol illustrated in Figure 18.2. This will allow travelers to properly take advantage of the increased capabilities of their E-Passports. It is expected that this will help speed the processing of travelers.

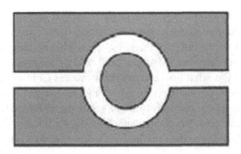

FIGURE 18.2   E-Passport lane symbol.

18.1.7 Summary

The use of E-Passports offers potentially faster processing of individuals through port of entry facilities. Faster processing is possible as the same information that is available on the picture page of the passport is also stored in the RFID chip. When the passport is optically scanned, the RFID chip transmits this information to the control point. The immigration agent can then check the passport record against immigration records and watch lists.

The technology inherent in RFID chips have led to a number of concerns with respect to the data security of E-Passports based on the ICAO standards. Independent tests have indicated that RFID E-Passport data can be both cloned as well as eavesdropped on by unauthorized parties. However, the issuance of E-Passports is still proceeding. Proponents of the use of E-Passports dismiss these security concerns, stating that the use of RFID technology is intended as an additional security measure rather than a replacement to the function of a conventional non-RFID passport.

REFERENCES

[1] International Civil Aviation Organization Protocol. www.icao.int/mrtd/download/technical.cfm
[2] Miller, P. German Hackers Clone RFID Passports. www.engadget.com/2006/08/03/german-hackers-clone-rfid-e-passports/
[3] Ricker, T. Dutch RFID E-Passport Cracked—U.S. Next. www.engadget.com/2006/02/03/dutch-rfid-e-passport-cracked-us-next/
[4] Schneider, B. RFID Passport Security Revisited. www.schneier.com/blog/archives/2005/08/rfid_passport_s_1.html
[5] Department of State Begins Issuing Electronic Passports to the Public. https://2001-2009.state.gov/r/pa/prs/ps/2006/70433.htm

19

Evaluating the Impact of Sleep Disruptions in Women through Automated Analysis

Shalini Gupta, Felicia Jefferson, and Erick C. Jones

19.1 Introduction

19.1.1 Prevalence of Sleep Disruption in U.S. and Relevant Expenditures

Most of the women have faced issues to get proper sleep, and this problem can be due to many reasons such as social, biological, physical, psychological, etc. [4]. But, if these extraneous factors persist, they may lead to serious health issues and sleep disorders [2].

Sleep disorders may cause more detrimental effects on overall health. Symptoms such as poor performance level, emotional imbalance, and health ailments have been attributed primarily to lack of quality sleep [28]. Nowadays, sleep has been regarded as a standard measure of perfect health because people with good health get sufficient sleep, whereas those facing sleep deprivation issues, often, need to be treated for major or minor health problems [6].

Radio frequency identification (RFID)/automated technology can provide real-life data and solutions to track the sleeping patterns such as how long and deeply an individual rests, how often an individual gets up, and even heart and respiration rates [42]. Sleeping well is imperative for a healthy body as well as for a bright mind [3]. However, persistent disturbance can affect our mood, energy level, and capability to face stressful situations [14]. Neglecting sleep relevant issues may cause serious health ailment, risk of accidents, reduced productivity, and impaired relationships [13]. To resolve the sleep impairment issue, we need to measure sleep disorder symptoms and sleep patterns.

19.1.1.1 Problem Statement

As per the previous research on sleep issues, the level of sleep disruption problem has been increased worldwide [1]. Based on the analysis conducted in the previous years, we have observed that sleep disruption issue has prevailed at a faster rate in developed countries such as U.S., China, and U.K. [26]. The sleep disruption issue is causing many health problems related to mental and social issues [20]. In fact, sleep disorder is a root cause behind major chronical diseases. Moreover, sleep disruption affects overall quality of life which is a combination of physical, mental, emotional, and social aspects and causes disturbance in positive factors of healthy life [10]. Thus, sleep disruption causes further issues related to life satisfaction and positive emotions. It has been observed that women with sleep disruption have depicted short temper attitude as well as higher risk of mood swing. Many factors are associated with sleep disruption [19]. In fact, researchers have proved that insufficient sleep has played a major role in obesity in women, children, and young adults [15]. Moreover, perinatal factors and genetic factors also get affected by insufficient sleep. From the biological standpoint of view, sleep disruption is triggered mainly due to imbalanced diet intake, stress, workload, metabolism, and hormonal imbalance [11] (Figure 19.1).

Sleep disorders become more chronical as age increases, but with proper awareness, the effects of chronical sleep disorders can be suppressed to a great extent [16]. Mostly women are more sensitive to age-related changes, and these kinds of changes make a significant impact not only on the sleeping time but also on the awakening states [34]. However, by accumulating prior information about the sleep

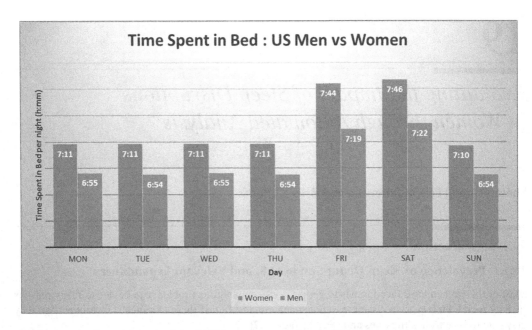

FIGURE 19.1 Estimated time spent in bed: U.S. men vs. women, January 2016.

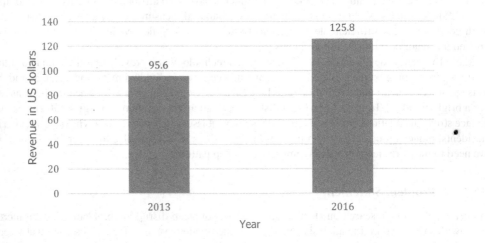

FIGURE 19.2 Sleep diagnostic device market revenue in U.S. and Europe (in million U.S. $).

performance such as brain aging, in particular neuronal loss information can help us taking preventive actions for the sleep disorders [41] (Figure 19.2).

19.1.1.2 Research Significance

The proposed research suggests a solution for sleep disruption by using automated/RFID analytics and attempts improving our understanding of sleep disruption physiology [43]. Sleep disruption monitoring is gaining attention among sleep monitoring devices that provide the opportunity for tracking sleep disruption consistently [42]. Automated technology allows repeated measurements, evaluation of sleep patterns, and suggestions [9]. However, facts revealed by clinical studies and research have the strong standpoint to measure sleep disruption records, and this may be helpful in treating sleep disorders [38]. Moreover, this analysis can also be useful for prescribing individual treatment and hence improvised individual health optimization [54]. In fact, some of the health tracking electronic gadgets assist individuals to track their own sleep performance [17]. Conceptually, the developed analytics provides models and correlation between variables such as electromyography (EMG), electrocardiogram (ECG), electrooculography (EOG), electroencephalograph (EEG), etc. By modeling sleeping data analytics, we may provide sleep performance. Accordingly, changes may be made to daytime habits and bedtime routine. This research aims at evaluating the impacts of sleep deprivation using RFID technology.

19.1.1.3 Research Questions and Hypotheses

There are two primary research questions. We believe that these questions must be answered in order to meet our research objectives.

> *Research Question 1*: What are impacts of implementing RFID-enabled (Smart) technologies embedded in linen-based beauty products to monitor sleep patterns on minimizing the negative impacts of sleep disorders on women?
>
> *Research Question 2*: What are the benefits of the proposed Shalini Jones Smart Linen (SJSL) framework that impact and improve sleep performance?

The research evaluated whether or not the implementation of SJSL framework will have a significant impact on health systems engineering research that investigates female sleep and human brain wave monitoring. SJSL refers to the Shalini Jones Smart Linen. "Smart" refers to the automated transmissions enabled by RFID technologies. We use SJ to refer to the models developed by her, and we use "Smart Linen" because others have labeled technologies "Smart", and we use the SJSL for convenience in the document.

To address these two research questions further, we have introduced two sets of hypotheses which assist to explore the research questions. As per the statistical hypothesis testing, null hypothesis and alternative hypothesis need to be compared (Table 19.1).

These two hypotheses statements are stated as follows:

Hypothesis Statement for Objective # 1

　Null Hypothesis

　　H_0: The implementation of AutoID/RFID technology will not have impact on measuring sleep disorders accurately.

　Alternative Hypothesis

　　H_a: The implementation of AutoID/RFID technology will have impact on measuring sleep disorders accurately.

　Decision Rule

　　Reject H_0: If the cost associated with AutoID/RFID-based sleep monitoring system is greater than 15% of the currently available systems.

TABLE 19.1

Hypothesis Statements

Hypothesis Statement	Null Hypothesis	Alternative Hypothesis	Decision Rule
Question # 1	H_0: The implementation of AutoID/RFID technology will not have impact on measuring sleep disorders accurately.	H_a: The implementation of AutoID/RFID technology will have impact on measuring sleep disorders accurately.	Reject H_0: If the cost associated with AutoID/RFID-based sleep monitoring system is greater than 15% of the currently available systems.
Question # 2	H_0: The developed framework will not effectively address the critical sleep disorders monitoring requirements.	H_a: The developed framework effectively addresses the critical sleep disorders monitoring requirements.	Reject H_0: If the sleep performance provided by AutoID/RFID-based sleep monitoring system is less than 5% counts.

Hypothesis Statement for Objective # 2
    Null Hypothesis
        H_0: The developed framework will not effectively address the critical sleep disorders' mon-
        itoring requirements.
    Alternative Hypothesis
        H_a: The developed framework effectively addresses the critical sleep disorders' monitoring
        requirements.
    Decision Rule
        Reject H_0: If the sleep performance provided by AutoID/RFID-based sleep monitoring
        system is less than 5% counts.

In this research, we will attempt to answer the research questions by meeting our overall research objective of evaluating the impacts of sleep disruptions through RFID/AutoID technology implementation.
We research the overall objective by using the following three specific objectives.

Specific Objective 1: Identify the factors affecting sleep disruptions, and evaluate the model suit-
    ability for sleep performance.
Specific Objective 2: Evaluate and identify the suitable automated analysis technique for sleep
    disorder measurement.
Specific Objective 3: Develop a software for monitoring sleep disruption in women, and evaluate
    the impact of proposed framework for sleep disruption performance measurement.

19.2 Research Purpose

The main purpose of this research is to demonstrate the wireless RFID-technology-based sleep disruption monitoring system [8]. The proposed system is an application-based technology that is able to use
radio frequency (RF) power from an RF transmitter and use it to transfer EEG signals to the RF-enabled
receivers. Sleep disruption monitoring by using RFID technology is a unique way to provide sleep performance [12]. Conceptually, the major advantage of using RFID technology is that it does not require
high sampling rates for analysis [36]. In this research, the suggested distance between the subject and
RFID-based system should be less than 1 meter to gain the expected level of reading accuracy.

Overall, the results of these research experiments demonstrate the feasibility of multiple linear regression (MLR) analysis and analytical hierarchy process (AHP) in the acquirement of EEG signals for
automated analysis [97]. In particular, the analysis was performed to analyze EEG sleep data for developing the analytics for automated sleep disruption monitoring research. However, available methods
also produce effective results, but the lack of an RF-based EEG recording-based self-sleep monitoring
device has attracted researchers' attention in this area. The analysis performed in this research shows
that the level of accuracy can be maintained by statistical analysis for signal synthesis and refinement
techniques. Based on the suggested framework, we can achieve better accuracy and produce effective
results. However, the sensor complexity and severe power constraints forced on EEG capturing systems
provide the designer of EEG recording systems a compromise [76]. Appropriate modification can be
made to the device features, and the power quality concern can also be balanced with signal quality.
These achievements can compensate for power consumption limitations and provide many benefits.

19.3 Organization of This Dissertation

The dissertation contains a five-point engineering format of introduction, background, methodology,
results, and conclusion.

Section 19.1 is the introduction and contains information regarding why this research is being performed. The section describes the topic of prevalence of sleep disruption in U. S. and relevant and

TABLE 19.2

Organization of Dissertation

Number	Name of Chapters	Description
1	Introduction	• Topic of prevalence of sleep disruption in U.S. • Relevant • Problem statement • Research significance • Purpose of this dissertation
2	Background and relevant research	• Discusses the dissertation's background. • Literature review of sleep disorders • Definition of sleep • Sleep disorders in women • Importance of good sleep • Common sleep problems in women • Sleep assessment methods • Roles of brain waves in sleepiness • Purpose of brain waves
3	Methodology	• Defines the methodology • Specific objectives to be researched • The three-phase research methodology
4	Results	• Discusses and interprets the results of the experiments • Analysis using MLR • Analysis using AHP • Results obtained by the developed software for monitoring sleep disruption
5	Contribution to the body of knowledge	• Conclusion • Findings • Recommendations • Limitations of the research • Future work

problem statement and research significance. It also explains the purpose of this dissertation and the need for developing RFID- and AutoID-enabled sleep disruption monitoring systems for women.

Section 19.4 discusses the dissertation's background. This is the literature review of sleep disorders, definition of sleep, sleep disorders in women, and importance of good sleep. Also, the section discusses common sleep problems in women and sleep assessment methods. The section also discusses roles of brain waves in sleepiness and purpose of brain waves.

Section 19.5 defines the methodology used in the dissertation. This includes the specific objectives to be researched and the three-phase research methodology to be employed.

Section 19.6 discusses and interprets the results of the experiments: analysis and results provided by MLR analysis, AHP, and finally, the results obtained by the developed software.

Section 19.7 of the dissertation provides a conclusion, findings, and recommendations. It includes discussing limitations of the research and describes the next steps in the sequence of the research (Table 19.2).

19.4 Background

19.4.1 Common Sleep Problems in Women

More than 50 million of Americans admit that they are facing sleep disorder although women are more sensitive to get affected than men [11]. Latest research studies suggest that sleep disorder needs special attention. A proper tailored treatment should be recommended according to women's sleep experiences [2].

19.4.1.1 Insomnia

Insomnia is the most usual sleep problem [10]. In America, most of the women have been reporting insomnia issue as compared to men [26]. In terms of percentage, studies show that insomnia affects 63% women and 54% men. Most of the women face this issue because of menstruation, pregnancy, or menopause and feel uneasiness. However, sleep improving approaches such as exercise, well-maintained diet, good ambiance, meditation, and a well-disciplined routine can be practiced by oneself [66]. In case self-practiced approaches don't lead to significant improvements, then proper treatments should be taken from a physician. In some instances, there could be some inherent causes, such as hereditary aspects, depression, stress level, uneasiness, reflux, bladder problems, or pain. However, all these problems can also be treated by appropriate medications [116].

19.4.1.2 Narcolepsy

Daytime sleepiness or feeling unenergetic may imply that this kind of issues should also be taken seriously [21]. These types of problems may be considered as narcolepsy, a neurological disorder with a probability of 0.0002 [64]. This disorder affects mostly teenagers; it causes sometimes "sleep attacks", excessive sleep urge, and lose of strength, and it also affects nighttime sleep [52].

19.4.1.3 Nocturnal Sleep-Related Eating Disorder

In this problem, the patient notices an intense urge of eating food in night while they feel asleep. In this disorder, a particular part of brain that controls memory partially gets inactive, so people with this disorder forget nighttime eating [98]. Previous studies show that majority of women get affected by this disorder. This issue may happen even during somnambulating as well.

19.4.1.4 Post-traumatic stress disorder (PTSD) and Sleep

The National Comorbidity Survey demonstrates a high prevalence of PTSD in the general population with a lifespan rate of 7.8% [6]. A recent survey from the National Epidemiologic Survey on Alcohol and Related Conditions (NESARC) showed that the lifetime rate of PTSD in individuals 18 or older is 4.8% [14]. Women have an increased lifetime prevalence of PTSD, with 10% of women developing the disorder compared to 5% of men [14]. Additionally, women are more at risk of developing PTSD after experiencing trauma, with statistics showing 13%–20% of women compared to 6%–8% of men developing the disorder [6]. One study focused on new mothers' PTSD symptoms after an earthquake. Results from the study revealed that women with increased earthquake exposure had a higher likelihood of having PTSD and depression than women who did not experience an earthquake [11]. Depression and PTSD were significantly correlated with sleep quality, education, income, and employment [48]. Unemployed women, in addition to women with a lower monthly household income, had an increased risk of having PTSD and depression if they had poor sleep quality [85].

Previous researchers show that majority of women face pain during nighttime; 25% women accept that they cannot sleep well because of pain or uneasiness, quite often three nights in a week [6]. Pain could be because of stress, headaches, migraine, arthritis, and rheumatism as well as heartburn. Because of pain, women feel tired and find difficulty in getting up on time [11]. Many remedies such as meditation, relaxation techniques, biofeedback, cognitive therapy, and proper medication can also be very helpful to overcome pain [85]. Most of the remedies are used to treat pain, sleep issue, or both.

19.4.2 Sleep Disorders

19.4.2.1 Definition of Sleep

Sleep has been defined in different ways, but every definition emphasizes more over a particular fact that a restorative process of mutually dependent qualitative and quantitative functions can be defined as sleep [114]. The functionalities of sleep process vary as age increases, and this leads to more fragmented

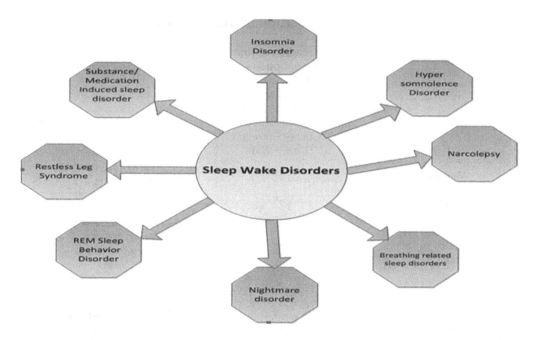

FIGURE 19.3 Types of sleep disorders.

sleep, unusual awakening times, external factors, and short sleep cycles. Sleep performance can be basically judged by measuring the extent of changes in normal sleep [112]. Conceptually, we try to measure the degree of deviation between normal sleep performances and sleep fragmentations in order to capture multifactorial sleep disturbances. However, sleep disturbances have been described as obstructive (obstructive sleep apnea (OSA)), periodic limb movements (PLMs) and restless legs syndrome (RLS), other medical illnesses, psychological conditions, etc. An extensive research revealed that excessive daytime sleep increases the chances of severe sleep disorder (Figure 19.3).

19.4.2.2 Sleep Disorders in Women

Most of the major attributes of sleep demonstrate that changes in the sleep occur mainly when women get older [34]. All these changes could be in any form such as short sleeping cycle, often getting disturbed by noise and light, taking longer time to fall asleep, irregular sleep cycles, etc. [38]. However, sleep performance recording methods have been very useful to capture the disturbances occurring during the sleep [39]. An extensive study conducted over 3,577 subjects reveals that the quality of sleep deteriorates with increased age [45]. During the fragmented sleep hours, higher level of disturbances and more fragmented sleep records have been captured during the last phase (latter part of night) of sleep, and this causes difficulty in getting up easily [46]. Sometimes, in more severe cases, the subject gets headache and drowsiness throughout the day. Also, we can say even throughout the sleep the total awake time tend to last longer and more frequently. This is a major reason behind decreased sleep efficiency [52] (Figure 19.4).

19.4.2.3 Importance of Good Sleep

Good sleep is as necessary as good diet and proper exercise. Even during the rest, we are active mentally while the body stays inactive [52]. Proper sleep is a major factor behind the healthy day. However, optimal hours of sleep depend on age group, gender, health status, and level of workload [58]. In fact, most people prefer to sleep for 7–9 h so that they can be productive. A poll conducted by the National Sleep Foundation (NSF) in 1998, *Women and Sleep*, observed that an average woman aged between the years 30 and 60 sleeps only 6 h and 41 min during the work week [74].

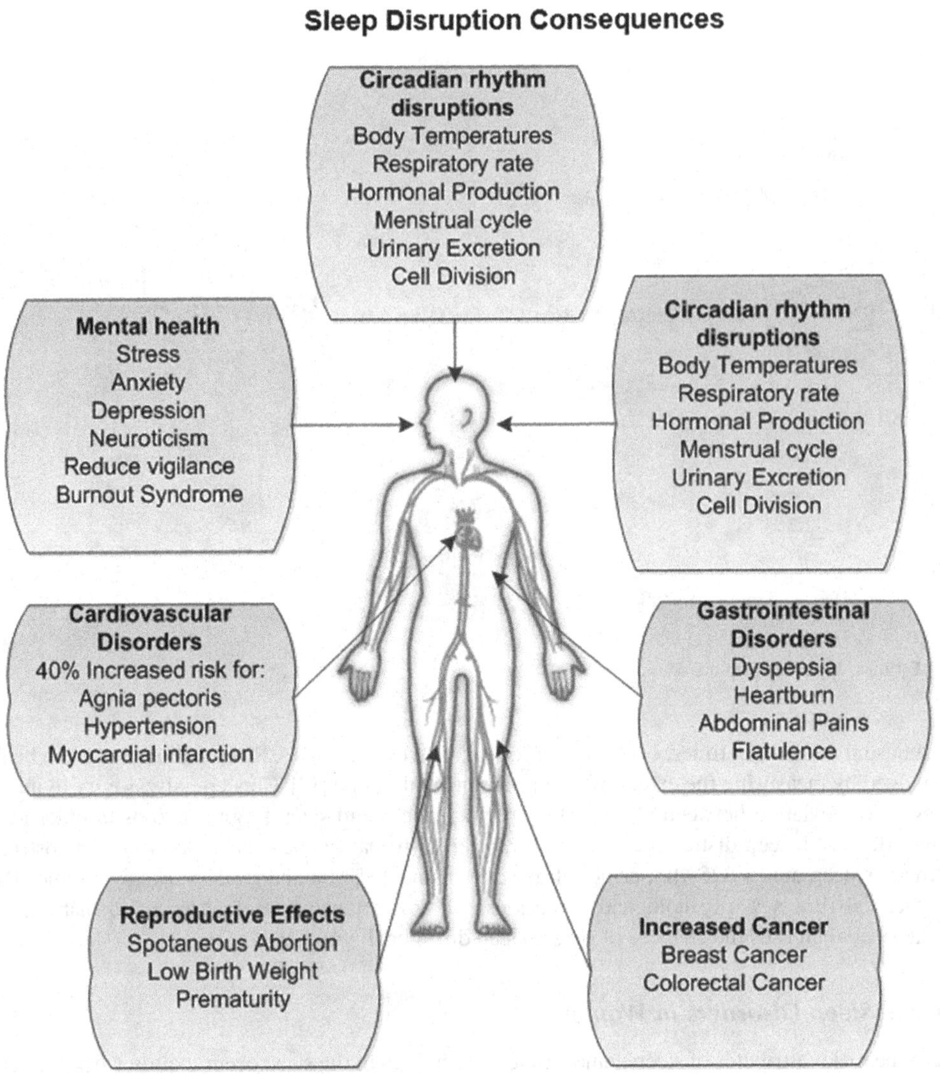

Sleep Disruption Consequences

FIGURE 19.4 Consequences of sleep disruptions.

Previous studies conducted by NSF depict that woman face more difficulty than men to get proper sleep, and this causes daytime sleepiness, problems, mood swing, higher risks of accidents, poor performance, and sickness as well as other health issues [66].

Having adequate hours of sleep is essential, but at the same time, quality of sleep also matters for achieving healthy biological conditions, especially in women [72]. Many other physical and mental health concerns can also get affected because of lack of proper sleep. The persistent sleep disruption may cause hormonal imbalance and affect lifestyle habits as well [20].

19.4.2.4 RLS and PLMD

More than 12 million Americans are suffering from RLS and PLMD issues [72]. In this type of disorder, uneasiness can be relieved by movement. Due to this type of problem, women face mood swings, daytime sleepiness, anxiety, and depression [108]. However, the exact reason of RLS has not been identified yet, but latest studies show that due to iron deficiency, this kind of problems can occur [64]. For treating this disorder, proper medications containing vitamin and iron should be prescribed. Among 85% of those with RLS also have PLMD issue or leg twitching or jerking movements during sleep that can persist for 30–40 s [85]. Due to this issue, bed partner can also get disturbance, but this issue can also be managed.

19.4.2.5 Shift Work

Early studies have found that shift workers tend to experience higher level of job stress, more alcohol use, more emotional problems, and poor sleep quality compared to non-shift workers [30]. Female shift workers also reported problems in their social life and an increased use of sleeping pill and tranquilizer [30]. Compared to day shifts, night shifts were found to be associated with higher risk of sleep and digestive disorders as well as disrupted social life [62]. The fact that a large segment of the modern western workforce work on non-standard schedules such as night shifts and rotating shifts has driven an increased volume of clinical and psychology studies on the effect of shift work on workers' physical and psychological well-being for the past few decades [78]. It has been identified that shift work affects workers in various ways by causing sleep disturbance and circadian rhythm disruption [111].

In America, 20% of the people work in odd times typically, not between 9 a.m. and 5 p.m. In this kind of situation, sleep disruption causes health issues [30]. Because of irregular routine and daytime sleeping hours, women get difficulty in getting quality sleep. In fact, studies show that women working in the night shift are hypersensitive toward mental and physical health issues, and this leads to more illnesses and accidents [62]. However, women working on the night shifts find it uneasy to fulfill their responsibilities and get less time for family and social activities. All these aspects cause irregular menstrual cycles, infertility, breast cancer, pregnancy issues, critical risks associated with miscarriages, and premature births [78]. However, most of the women working in night shift/non-traditional shifts do not observe any kind of typical issues in their babies [111].

19.4.2.6 Shift Work and Sleep Disturbance

Sleep disturbance is among the most important problems of shift work that lasts a long period of time [28]. Workers who currently work during irregular hours reported the highest rates of having difficulties in falling asleep and early awakening compared to former shift workers and non-shift workers, with former shift workers falling in between [30]. Even after people resume to normal work hours, the sleep disturbance caused by previous shift work experience does not simply go away [33].

Current shift workers are affected the most by sleep disturbance and have high risk of work-related accidents [62]. Specifically, it was found that compared to rotating daytime shift, fixed nighttime shift, and fixed daytime shift, workers on rotating daytime shift have the highest rate of work-related accidents and sick leave, followed by fixed nighttime shift workers, and with the fixed daytime shift the least prone to accidents [69]. The U.S. National Transportation Safety Board reported that 19%–30% of all transportation accidents with injury are due to fatigue, which is one of the most common results of sleep disturbance [78]. In their population-based study among Canadians, Kling found the highest increased risk for work injury associated with trouble sleeping among women who work on rotating shifts [89]. Consistent findings have suggested that among all work schedules, rotating shift affects work performance and work safety the most, with changes in relevant variables including higher level of fatigue, loss of concentration, higher rates of heavy smoking, coffee/tea consumption, constipation, job stress, and poor sexual performance [111].

The effect of shift work varies a lot from individual to individual [28]. Factors such as gender, age, morningness/eveningness, circadian flexibility/languidity, and resilience against environmental stressors all play a role in how shift work affects individuals [30]. Indeed, the effect of shift work shows trait-like qualities and parallels the effect of OSA, with the subjective experience of individuals differing significantly in correspondence to their personal traits [33].

Some shift workers exhibit enough symptoms to be diagnosed with shift work disorder (SWD), which is characterized by sleepiness and insomnia due to work schedule. Flo found that about one-third of nurses reported symptoms that meet the criteria of SWD, which is significantly higher than the prevalence found within community sample by Drake and colleagues [62]. This might be partially explained by the interaction between gender and work stress. Past research has identified female gender, hectic work, and physically strenuous work as the shared predictors of sleep disturbance and fatigue, suggesting that women, especially those who have stressful and physically demanding job, are more susceptible to sleep disturbance and fatigue [4]. As nurses are still predominantly female, they fall exactly into this category and are therefore more likely to have SWD than the overall shift worker population [62]. In addition, while non-night shift work is also associated with increased risk of SWD, there is a positive correlation between the number of night shifts and risk of SWD among nurses. Thus, the researchers recommended putting a limit on the total number of night shifts per year as a way to protect nurses from SWD [111].

19.4.2.7 Shift Work and Cognitive Impairment

Sleep problem and circadian rhythm disruption are both identified to have detrimental effect on cognitive functioning. As mentioned in the effect of OSA, sleep disturbance can cause deficits in executive functions, working memory, long-term memory, attention, etc. [41]. Current shift workers were found to have lower scores in cognitive speed, selective attention, and memory than workers who had never worked on shift [41]. However, the researchers argued that the reduced cognitive efficiency may be due to the circadian rhythm disruption alone rather than together with sleep disturbance, because no association was found between subjective sleep quality and cognitive performance among the male shift workers assessed [41]. The lack of the association between sleep disturbance and cognitive functioning in this study may be partially due to the effect of gender, since males are less likely to report sleepiness and fatigue compared to females. Another explanation may be that the instrument used to assess subjective sleep quality is not comprehensive enough to capture the sleep problem of those shift workers, and the strong effect of circadian rhythm disruption on cognitive functioning made the effect of the less severe sleep problems undetectable [82].

Studies on jet lag have identified alteration of brain structure that paralleled the memory deficits due to circadian rhythm disruption. Reduced cognitive performance, significantly higher salivary cortisol, and smaller volume of the right temporal were observed among flight attendants with more than 3 years of job experience. It was also found that former shift workers who have resumed to normal work schedule for more than 4 years showed increased cognitive performance, which may suggest the reversibility of cognitive impairment due to shift work [89]. At the cellular level, Gibson observed reduction in hippocampal cell proliferation and neurogenesis that paralleled jet-lag-induced memory deficits, suggesting that circadian rhythm disruption impairs cognitive functioning by impeding the birth and maturation of new cells [82].

19.4.2.8 Sleep Apnea

OSA is a common sleep disorder that is caused by complete or partial functional impairment of the upper airway dilator muscle, which leads to apnea/hypopnea-induced oxygen desaturation, repetitive micro-arousals, and disturbed sleep [3]. Thus, OSA patients suffer from sleep fragmentation and chronic sleep deprivation, with common symptoms of daytime sleepiness, tiredness, snoring, etc. [6]. When adequate apnea and hypopnea episodes are present together with these symptoms, OSA is labeled as obstructive sleep apnea syndrome (OSAS) [16]. Various factors have been identified as predictors of OSA including oropharyngeal narrowing, neck circumference, and BMI. In general, factors that predispose individuals to increased collapsibility of the upper airway are major risk factors for OSA [20]. Among all of them, obesity is the greatest risk factor for OSA due to its high prevalence [21]. Clinical diagnosis of OSA requires baseline polysomnography (PSG) of patients and a Continuous Positive Airway Pressure (CPAP) titration study, while home studies are increasingly being used as screening tests [34].

19.4.2.9 Detrimental Health Effects of OSA

In the past decade, studies on OSA have identified associations between OSA and various cardiovascular complications, metabolic disturbances, and neuropsychologic deficits [39]. The effect of OSA on cardiovascular systems is a major topic in OSA studies where converging results have been found [46].

Atrial fibrillation is often observed after elective cardioversion in untreated OSA patients [52]. Although sleep apnea only happens during sleep, its effects extend into daytime body functioning [58]. OSA is recognized as a treatable cause of hypertension by the Seventh Joint National Committee of Hypertension guidelines [62]. Both enhanced sympathetic tone and genetic factors contribute to this causation between OSA and hypertension [64]. Conduction abnormalities such as sinoatrial block, sinus arrest, Atrioventricular (AV) conduction abnormalities, and asystole also occur during apnea in OSA patients [66]. The association between OSA and cerebrovascular events is also well studied [72]. OSA has been identified as a risk factor of cerebrovascular disease due to the high prevalence of pre-existing OSA among patients with stroke [77].

Patients with OSA have a higher risk of metabolic syndrome than people without OSA controlling the factor of BMI [79]. As the association between OSA and specific components of metabolic syndrome such as insulin resistance is well recognized, some even argue that OSA can be considered a component of metabolic syndrome [80]. OSA also plays a role in neurologic disorders, for example, the onset and worsening of seizure [82]. Besides its detrimental effects on physical health, OSA is also associated with mood disturbance: the most common symptom reported is depression [83]. Among patients with relatively severe OSA, about half of them meet the clinical diagnosis criteria of depression [84].

19.4.2.10 OSA and Gender

OSA is a prevalent sleep disorder that that affects people across age groups, but it affects males in middle age the most [86]. Among the population of 25 years old and over, 4% men are affected by OSA, which is twice the chance of women having OSA [87]. Female sex hormones such as progesterone affect respiratory control and correlate with upper airway stability and thus may have protective effect against OSA [88].

Besides the gender difference in the prevalence of OSA, the symptoms of OSA are also gender-specific [92]. Women with OSA are more likely to report fatigue, and men with OSA are more likely to report sleepiness, while men and women without OSA have similar level of fatigue and sleepiness [95]. The finding suggests the importance of assessing fatigue in order to capture the experience of women with OSA [96]. Nonetheless, unlike the widely endorsed sleepiness evaluation, the assessment of fatigue has not yet been included in recent clinical guideline for the diagnosis and control of OSA [98]. Furthermore, it is suggested that sleepiness and fatigue are two independent symptoms that patients with similar severity of OSA may experience both or either or none of the two [99]. In addition, women have been found to prefer describing their experience of sleep-disordered breathing (SDB) using terms like fatigue and lack of energy than sleepiness [100]. The under-recognition of OSA in women also has socioeconomic impact [101]. The Centers for Medicare and Medicaid Services (CMS) consider CPAP therapy necessary for patients with mild OSA when appropriate symptoms are present, which include sleepiness but not fatigue [102]. As CMS also set the standard for Medicare coverage which is adopted by other insurance providers, patients with mild OSA but experiencing fatigue rather than sleepiness may not get appropriate allowance from their insurance providers for CPAP treatment [103]. It is possible that some of the patients with mild OSA that expresses as fatigue, most likely women, will choose not to get CPAP therapy and thus suffer from the detrimental physical health effect and cognitive impairment due to OSA [105]. As mentioned before, night shift promotes the development of OSA symptoms [107]. Therefore, certain occupations that require night shift and rotating shift may have greater need of CPAP treatment [108]. The inappropriate documentation of OSA symptoms and the insufficient insurance allowance because of that may affect these occupations more, such as nurses, who are still predominately women and work in shifts [110].

It is mentioned earlier that more severe OSA episodes happen during REM sleep and patients with OSA also have significantly reduced REM sleep [115]. Recent study took a close look at the relationship between REM sleep and OSA and found significant gender differences. Women with OSA experienced significantly less REM sleep and longer latency to the onset of REM sleep compared to men with OSA [116].

The particularly strong interaction between OSA and REM sleep among women may be related to female sex hormone. Netzer found an association between female sex hormone reduction and higher risk of SDB [118]. Specifically, significantly lower levels of progesterone, estradiol, and 17-OH progesterone have been found in women with obstructive sleep apnea/hypopnea syndrome (OSAHS). Therefore, hormone therapy may be an option to treat OSA and abnormalities in REM sleep [54].

19.4.2.11 Sleep Apnea

In the case of sleep apnea, a person suffers by snoring, breathing interruption, and daytime sleepiness [112]. More than 20 million Americans have sleep apnea problem, and particularly 25% of women over 50 years of age admit this issue [102]. The main reason behind sleep apnea is overweight and abdominal fat during menopause [115]. This causes a decrease in progesterone and further leads to higher risks of fluctuating blood pressure and cardiovascular disease and stroke [113]. However, a number of suitable treatments are available to manage this disorder.

19.4.3 Sleep Assessment Methods

Sleep is a complex phenomenon that could be described mainly in terms of two aspects: firstly behavioral aspects that suggest relative lack of movements, awareness, and responsiveness and secondly brain aspects that can be observed through EEG activity [16]. Proper sleep can be assessed in terms of duration and by its distribution throughout the day as well as sleep quality [23]. Sleep quality can be measured as consolidated vs. fragmented. Various methods have been developed to measure the quality of sleep [26]. In this section of research, we are attempting to provide a brief description over sleep quality recording methods which are already available in market such as PSG, video sonography, actigraphy, direct observations, sleep diaries, and questionnaire [77]. However, we need to know the pros and cons associated with each method to realize their importance in order to get better sleep records [43]. Especially, considerable attention has emerged in women toward the role of sleep. The best way to understand the quality of sleep is relevant to the degree of sleep performance. Additionally, the degree of performance can be described in terms of various dimensions such as sleep duration, sleep quality, level of brain activity patterns, schedule or circadian aspects, etc. [77] (Figure 19.5).

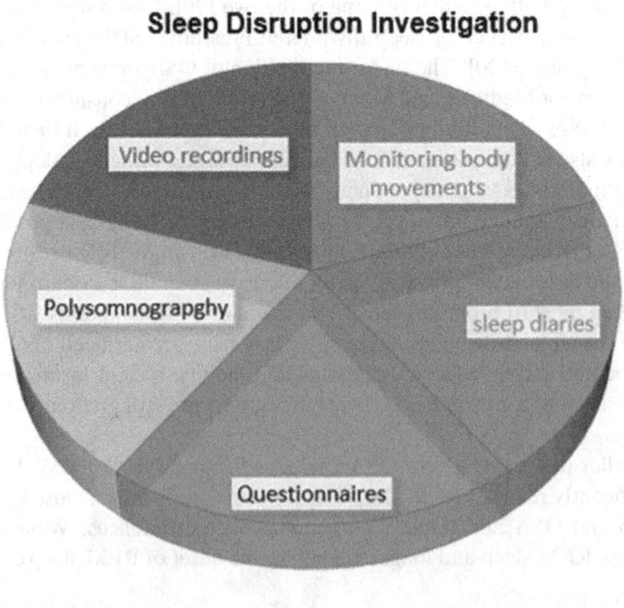

Sleep Disruption Investigation

FIGURE 19.5 Investigating sleep disruptions.

19.4.3.1 Polysomnography

This method has been considered as the best method in terms of fulfilling the standards [77]. In this method, observations are recorded on laboratory or ambulatory recordings and mainly associated with different functions of the body and mind such as electrical brain activity EEG, muscle activation EMG, eye movement EOG, breathing flow, oxygen saturation sensors (oximetry), video recording, and additional observations as per the research requirements [77]. In this method, sensors and electrodes are attached to different parts of body before sleeping and EEG signals were recorded [77]. This method is useful to provide comprehensive information about patterns of brain signals, sleep style, stages associated with sleep, qualitative and quantitative aspects of sleep, breathing pattern, oxygen absorption, eye movements, and leg movements during sleep [92]. The information we record by this method is very useful in order to measure the variety of sleep disorders such as sleep apnea, periodic movements in sleep, parasomnia, narcolepsy ERM sleep disorders, insomnia, and daytime sleeping habits. In terms of accuracy and details, this method is an objective method used to incorporate information that can be essential for brain and sleep research. A variety of sleep disorders cannot be scrutinized without having specific information [77]. However, laboratory setup, standardized situation, and supervision are essential to perform this test [99]. Moreover, it required the subject to tolerate the unusual laboratory environment, attached electrodes, and sensors which can be uncomfortable to get proper normal sleep. This is an expensive test, so it cannot be performed on regular basis [77].

19.4.3.2 Videosomnography

In this method, video recordings are done during sleep in a natural environment. One or more cameras are used to understand the sleeping patterns as well as subject's behavior during nighttime [77]. Anders and colleagues have developed this method. Even direct depiction of activities such as excessive sweating, repetitive behaviors, REM (Rapid Eye Movement) behavior disorders, and other parasomnias [111]. The best aspect of this procedure is that it provides sleep information captured in comfortable natural environment unlike PSG [77]. However, camera's position, installation, signal interference, and harmonics may impose some limitations. Additionally, some women feel that this can compromise their privacy [77].

19.4.3.3 Direct Behavioral Observation

The pattern capturing procedure in this method depends directly on REM random eye movements [77]. This method needs skillful and trained observers who can provide sleep rating and wakefulness states over a given period of time [41]. This method cannot be performed overnight since it requires consistent observations. In this method, REM and respiration are recorded, for respiration recording pressure sensitive sensor pad placed, and the sleep record provides information such as alert, non-alert waking, fuss, cry, drowse, daze or sleep–wake transition, active sleep, quiet sleep as well as active sleep–wake transition [54]. The whole procedure can be performed either at home or in other sleep setting environment; thus, it makes this method very convenient and provides detailed information about sleep states, as well as other behaviors. Due to labor-intensive behavior and limited time period for conducting study, this method cannot be usually preferred and seems impractical [104].

19.4.3.4 Actigraphy

This method uses a portable tool that enables us to record body movement and sleep–wake patterns. Initially, this method was used to record crib movements [77]. A wristwatch-like instrument is required to record activity data for a long period of time. Further, this data need to be scrutinized to understand sleep pattern [41]. In the first year of measurement period, we can identify active and quiet sleep patterns as well. Previous research has depicted that actigraphy method reveals significant difference among reports prepared by various sources [54]. However, there is a set of standard guidelines for performing this test. Specifically, actigraphy is a strong tool to assess sleep disorder schedules as this test can be useful to monitor the subject for a long period of time. Sleep records for disorders such as insomnia can also be measured by this procedure [104].

19.4.4 Roles of Brain Waves in Sleepiness

As per the mental health studies, brain waves can be captured in five different types of patterns; these patterns are in the form of electrical signals containing different ranges of frequencies [104]. These five types of brain waves are across the cortex and arranged from the highest frequency (lowest amplitude) to the lowest frequency (highest amplitude) as gamma, beta, alpha, theta, and delta [107]. The observatory procedure to record these waves is mainly through "EEG" recording system [1] (Figure 19.6).

Conceptually, by analyzing these electrical waves, we can measure the sleep performance as well as degree of mental functioning [1]. The frequency range associated with each brain wave plays a vital role in understanding how well we sleep [100]. However, analysis of these brain waves reveals more about capability to manage stress, focusing power, mental aptness, etc. [95]. However, a proper balance is required for all five brain waves as overproduction or underproduction of any of these electrical signals may cause severe consequences to overall health [72]. This concept makes us realize that all five brain waves are equally important and can't consider any one of these as superior than others [104].

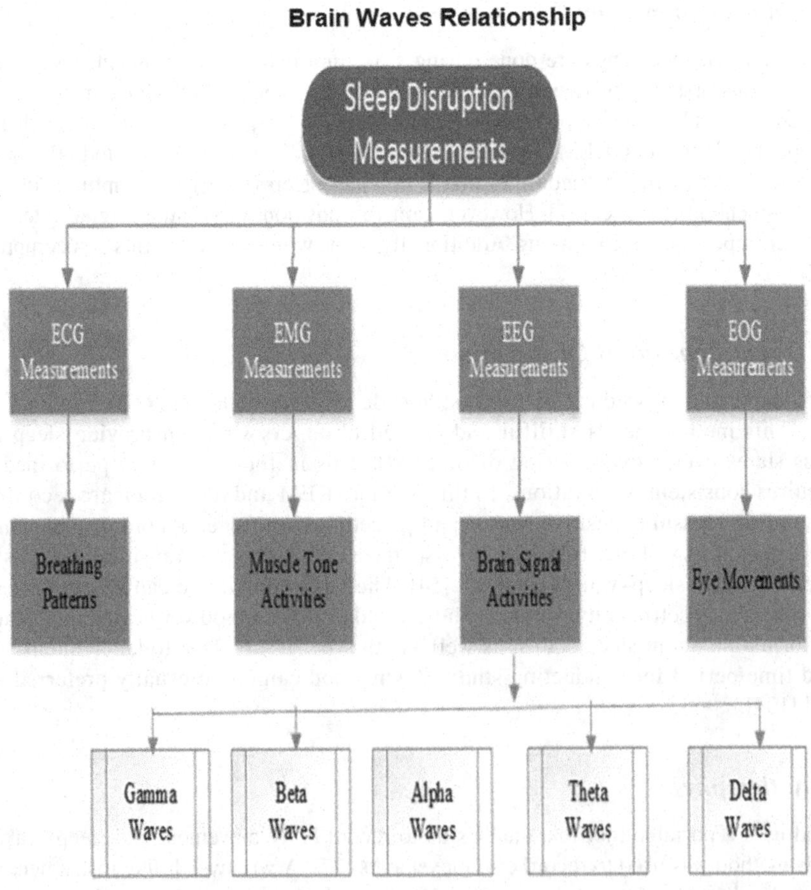

Brain Waves Relationship

FIGURE 19.6   Brain waves relationship diagram.

19.4.5 Purpose of Brain Waves

Each individual wave has a unique purpose and contribution to various tasks such as processing, grasping power, control over emotions, etc. To understand the functioning of each wave, a little description is required [77].

As per the studies conducted earlier, gamma waves depict learning, memory, and information processing capability associated with cognitive functioning, and higher processing tasks require 40 Hz gamma waves for achieving needed level of perception and grasping power [1]. In particular, below average level of gamma wave causes mental disability and slow learning disorders [2]. However, beta waves are high-frequency and low-amplitude waves that can be in the awakening state of brain. They are commonly associated with conscious thoughts, logical thinking and demonstrate stimulating effect [101].

An adequate level of beta waves helps us focus on studies and perform well over work – related activities [1]. However, excessive generation of beta waves causes higher level of stress and anxiety. Higher levels of beta frequencies are generated in the proportional level of arousal. By drinking caffeine or another stimulant, the beta wave generation can be enhanced naturally [2].

These brain waves are fast brain waves that could be observed throughout the day and help us accomplish conscious tasks recognized as critical thinking, writing, reading, and making harmonious social relationship [2]. In fact, alpha brain waves cause transition from our conscious thinking and subconscious mind. The frequency ranges for these waves lie between beta and theta. Mostly, the state of deep relaxation and calming down when expected can be attained due to adequate level of alpha brain waves [104].

There is an evident phenomenon called "alpha blocking" caused because of excessive stress level, wherein there is a higher level of beta activity and lower level of alpha brain wave. Actually, the beta waves are dominant over alpha waves as they electrify at a faster rate. The next wave is theta wave, associated with daydreaming and sleep [77]. This wave causes us to feel emotions, and higher level of theta waves is responsible for an intensified session of depression. However, some benefits have also been observed in theta waves such as improved level of intuition, creativity, and deep relaxation and inclined us toward natural state of brain [97]. Most importantly, theta waves cause restorative sleep, but excessive production of theta waves in waking state may have unfavorable effects [116].

Last brain wave is delta wave, involved with regulating heartbeat, digestion, deepest level of relaxation, restorative and alleviating sleep. Delta sleep has the slowest recorded waves mainly in infants and young children. Enough quantity of delta wave generation makes us feel fresh after waking up. However, overgeneration or undergeneration of delta waves or brain injuries affects learning ability, and more severe consequences may create difficulty in conscious awareness [118] (Table 19.3).

19.5 Research Methodology

19.5.1 Research Objective and Hypothesis

In this research, we have developed a framework directing three-phase strategy to evaluate sleep disorders in women. This research explores a unique procedure for measuring sleep disruption in women by using RFID and AutoID technology. A software was developed to provide the sleep performance of individual user and also display overall degree of sleep criticality (Figure 19.7).

There are two primary research questions that we have to achieve in this section:

Research Question 1: What are impacts of implementing RFID-enabled (Smart) technologies embedded in linen-based beauty products to monitor sleep patterns on minimizing the negative impacts of sleep disorders on women?

Research Question 2: What are the benefits of the proposed SJSL framework that impact and improve sleep performance?

TABLE 19.3

Comparative Analysis among Five Major Brain Waves Recorded through EEG Measurement

No.	Brain Wave	Frequency Ranges	Symptoms Above Average	Symptoms Below Average	Optimal	Remedies
1	Gamma waves	40–100 Hz (highest)	Anxiety, high arousal, stress	Attention-Deficit/ Hyperactivity Disorder (ADHD), depression, learning disabilities	Binding senses, cognition, information processing, learning, perception, REM sleep	Meditation
2	Beta waves	12–40 Hz (high)	Adrenaline, anxiety, high arousal, inability to relax, stress	ADHD, daydreaming, depression, poor cognition	Conscious focus, memory, problem solving	Coffee, energy drinks, various stimulants
3	Alpha waves	8–12 Hz (moderate)	Daydreaming, inability to focus, too relaxed	Anxiety, high stress, insomnia, Obsessive-Compulsive Disorder (OCD)	Relaxation	Alcohol, marijuana, relaxants, some antidepressants
4	Theta waves	4–8 Hz (slow)	ADHD, depression, hyperactivity, impulsivity, inattentiveness	Anxiety, poor emotional awareness, stress	Creativity, emotional connection, intuition, relaxation	Depressants
5	Delta waves	0–4 Hz (slowest)	Brain injuries, learning problems, inability to think, severe ADHD	Inability to rejuvenate body, inability to revitalize the brain, poor sleep	Immune system, natural healing, restorative/ deep sleep	Depressants, sleep

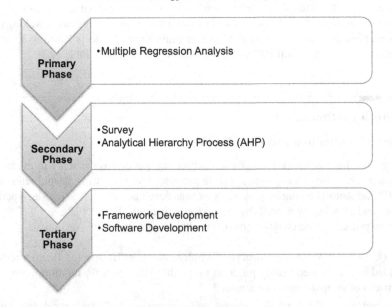

Three Phase Strategy to Evaluate Sleep Disorder

Primary Phase
- Multiple Regression Analysis

Secondary Phase
- Survey
- Analytical Hierarchy Process (AHP)

Tertiary Phase
- Framework Development
- Software Development

FIGURE 19.7   Three-phase strategy to evaluate sleep disorders in woman.

TABLE 19.4

Hypothesis Statements

Hypothesis Statement	Null Hypothesis	Alternative Hypothesis	Decision Rule
Objective # 1	H_0: The implementation of AutoID/RFID technology will not have impact on measuring sleep disorders accurately	H_a: The implementation of AutoID/RFID technology will have impact on measuring sleep disorders accurately	Reject H_0: If the cost associated with AutoID/RFID-based sleep monitoring system is greater than 15% of the currently available systems
Objective # 2	H_0: The developed framework will not effectively address the critical sleep disorders monitoring requirements	H_a: The developed framework effectively addresses the critical sleep disorders monitoring requirements	Reject H_0: If the sleep performance provided by AutoID/RFID-based sleep monitoring system is less than 5% counts

The research evaluated whether or not the implementation of SJSL framework will have a significant impact on health systems engineering research that investigate female sleep and human brain wave monitoring. (Table 19.4).

These two hypotheses statements are stated as follows:

Hypothesis Statement for Objective # 1

Null Hypothesis

H_0: The implementation of AutoID/RFID technology will not have impact on measuring sleep disorders accurately.

Alternative Hypothesis

H_a: The implementation of AutoID/RFID technology will have impact on measuring sleep disorders accurately.

Decision Rule

Reject H_0: If the cost associated with AutoID/RFID-based sleep monitoring system is greater than 15% of the currently available systems.

Hypothesis Statement for Objective # 2

Null Hypothesis

H_0: The developed framework will not effectively address the critical sleep disorders' monitoring requirements.

Alternative Hypothesis

H_a: The developed framework effectively addresses the critical sleep disorders' monitoring requirements.

Decision Rule

Reject H_0: If the sleep performance provided by AutoID/RFID-based sleep monitoring system is less than 5% counts.

In this research, we will attempt to analyze the following research objective, "Evaluating the impacts of sleep disruptions through RFID/AutoID technology implementation". We research the main objective by using the following three sub-objectives.

19.5.2 Research Criteria and Approach

In this research, step-by-step procedure was suggested to achieve research objectives. We have introduced three specific objective and associated steps for accomplishing the research aim.

Long-Term Research Objective

Specific Objective 1: Identify the factors affecting sleep disruptions, and evaluate the model suitability for sleep performance.

Specific Objective 2: Evaluate and identify the suitable automated analysis technique for sleep disorders measurement.

Specific Objective 3: Develop a software for monitoring sleep disruption in women, and evaluate the impact of proposed framework for sleep disruption performance measurement.

To satisfy the above three specific objectives, we approach several steps.

19.5.2.1 Phase 1

This particular phase will help us in understanding the steps required to achieve Specific Objective 1—"Identify the factors affecting sleep disruptions, and evaluate the model suitability for sleep performance" (Table 19.5).

Step 1—Identify the ways to measure sleep disruption in women.

Step 2—Evaluate the predicted model for the sleep disruption analysis.

Step 3—Determine how the developed analytics provide significant insights into sleep disruption monitoring system.

Step 4—Propose the model suitable for measuring sleep disruption in women.

Step 5—Perform preliminary analysis by using multiple regression analysis to validate the proposed model.

Step 6—Obtain the results from a preliminary analysis of all critical variables for sleep monitoring method.

Step 7—The results obtained by preliminary analysis will direct further research phases.

19.5.2.2 Phase 2

In this phase, we introduce steps to achieve Specific Objective 2: "Evaluate and identify the suitable feature oriented automated analysis technique for sleep disorders measurement" (Table 19.6).

Step 1—Questionnaire development
    Conduct a survey to observe different types of issues and problems associated with women during sleep.

TABLE 19.5

Steps Involved in Phase 1

Phase 1	
Step 1	Identify the ways to measure sleep disruption in women
Step 2	Evaluate the predicted model for the sleep disruption analysis
Step 3	Determine how the developed analytics provide significant insights into sleep disruption monitoring system
Step 4	Propose the model suitable for measuring sleep disruption in women
Step 5	Perform preliminary analysis by using multiple regression analysis to validate the proposed model
Step 6	Obtain the results from a preliminary analysis of all critical variables for sleep monitoring method
Step 7	The results obtained by preliminary analysis will direct further research phases

TABLE 19.6

Steps Involved in Phase 2

Phase 2	
Step 1	Questionnaire development
Step 2	Conduct a detailed study for issues and symptoms to understand the critical sleep disruption issues
Step 3	Evaluate the performance level of AutoID technology and also type of features to design appropriate AutoID technology
Step 4	Monitor the feedback provided by detailed study
Step 5	Development of strategy to find out the weights of various problems
Step 6	Administering the questionnaires to the experts
Step 7	Specify weights for relevant criteria, and rank the factors and sub-factors by AHP
Step 8	Analysis and reporting of the results

SLEEP DISRUPTION SURVEY FORM

NAME

AGE

GENDER

DEGREE OF SLEEP DISRUPTION   1   2   3   4   5
(Note: 1 is for low and 5 is for high)

ADDITIONAL ISSUES

ADDITIONAL COMMENTS

- Identify the major issues/problems causing sleep disruption in women. From the survey, we know the critical problems and rate them in terms of degree of seriousness.
- The sleep disruption performance rating can be set by setting up a threshold level. The level of threshold in this research is 65%.

Step 2—Conduct a detailed study for issues and symptoms observed by women during sleep and implement AHP to understand the critical sleep disruption issues.

Step 3—Evaluate the performance level of AutoID technology. From the survey, evaluate the type of features required to design appropriate AutoID technology for sleep disruption monitoring.

Step 4—Monitor the feedback provided by detailed study and conducted survey in order to address objective 2.

Step 5—Development of strategy to find out the weights of various problems associated with sleeping women.

Step 6—Administering the questionnaires to the experts/women related to the relevant field.

Step 7—Specify weights for relevant criteria, and rank the factors and sub-factors by AHP.

Step 8—Analysis and reporting of the results would help us design a software system and AutoID-enabled pillowcase/scarf for monitoring sleep disruption in women.

19.5.2.3 Phase 3

This phase will address the steps to achieve Specific Objective 3: "Develop a software for monitoring sleep disruption in women and evaluate the impact of proposed framework for sleep disruption performance measurement" (Table 19.7).

Step 1—Evaluate the different sleep monitoring methods, and provide a comparative analysis among different methods for improving the efficiency of sleep disruption monitoring system.
For collecting data for understanding sleep disruptions, we choose a medical hospital for collecting data.

Step 2—Brian signals' capturing
We have collected different sets of sleep data for monitoring sleep disruption in women. Different sleep stages can also be recognized by types of brain signals captured by EEG process.

Step 3—Design a suitable algorithm prior to designing a software for monitoring sleep disruption especially for women.

Step 4—Develop a suitable framework for sleep disruption monitoring in women (Figure 19.8).

TABLE 19.7

Steps Involved in Phase 3

Phase 3	
Step 1	Evaluate the different sleep monitoring methods and provide a comparative analysis among different methods
Step 2	Brain signals' capturing
Step 3	Design a suitable algorithm prior to designing a software for monitoring sleep disruption especially for women
Step 4	Develop a suitable framework for sleep disruption monitoring in women

Proposed Sleep Disruption Monitoring System

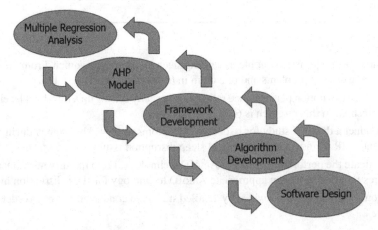

FIGURE 19.8 Sleep disorder monitoring system in proposed methodology.

The proposed sleep disruption monitoring system developed in this research is based on a major observation that sleep disorders prevailed at a faster rate due to avoidance and lack of proper attention at an early stage. First, we record EEG signals by using a wearable scarf which consists of a set of EEG detection sensors. With the help of EEG signals detection, we are able to monitor brain waves and transmit that data using RFID. The principal is that we have sensors monitoring brain wave activity, and these sensors then relay their information to the RFID tags, and the RFID tags then send their information to the antenna/reader so it can be read out by the computer. Then, the computer synthesizes it. We need to attach sensors to the scarf having direct contact with head, but the system should also need to be comfortable. Afterward, EEG signal pattern analysis is used for identifying critical sleep stages for further analysis. These systems provide a self-assessment sleep performance at a high level of accuracy, the developed instrumented sleep disruption monitoring system provides a subjective way as well as an objective way to analyze the sleep status trends and period when major disruption causes disturbance on a regular basis. However, in this research, we attempt to focus on addressing the analytics development part of the process.

Step 5—Data Collection

Sleep disruption data are collected from different valid organizations such as Bombay Medical Hospital, National Sleep Foundation, Public Databases, the U.S. Sleep Foundation Data Bank. Data sets contain EEG, EMG, ECG, and EOG data and also contain alpha, beta, gamma, theta, and delta waves.

Step 6—Economic Analysis

Economic analysis was performed, and the estimated cost of this research project was calculated by using standard assumptions and valid data records. We have used Microsoft Excel software for calculations and finding total cost for overall project including design and implementation of RFID/AutoID-based systems for monitoring sleep disruption in women (Figure 19.9).

19.6 Results

A software package, sleep status monitoring software has been developed to assist in various decision-making stages of the research. In the developed software package, the user can directly provide the input by using an RFID/AutoID-enabled scarf/pillowcase. The software explores its utility suited for a variety of program modules mutually incorporated to form an integrated software package. The complexity of the data and information flow generated in the developed software system is extremely high. They are driven by such frequent events as attempts to identify sleep status, associated sleep disruptions, and integration of different features. The information synthesis is required to handle large data volume and is manageable with user-friendly software features. In this research, we seek to investigate the feasibility of a software-based sleep disruption monitoring that continuously and autonomously captures sleep data and synthesizes data handling processes. The purpose of this research is to investigate an RFID/AutoID-based sleep disruption monitoring status application for mobile devices, including smartphones (such as iPhone, Android, Microsoft Mobile Phone, HTC smartphone, Blackberry, etc.) and the other handheld smart devices (such as iPad and some light/portable TabletPC), exchanging real-time information through the AutoID technology which is being used to make near-optimal decisions and send back information for required time period. Further, development of a mobile application of such data intensive operations necessitates exclusive multiple regression data manipulating techniques to provide the most critical information for decision makers. Also, we have implemented AHP for evaluating the critical features required to develop the software. The major impact of this research is the enhancement of mobile user capabilities driving improved productivity.

The integrated software package has specific modules that can be used to support the decision making for the case under consideration. The results provided by software module is obtained by the analysis of

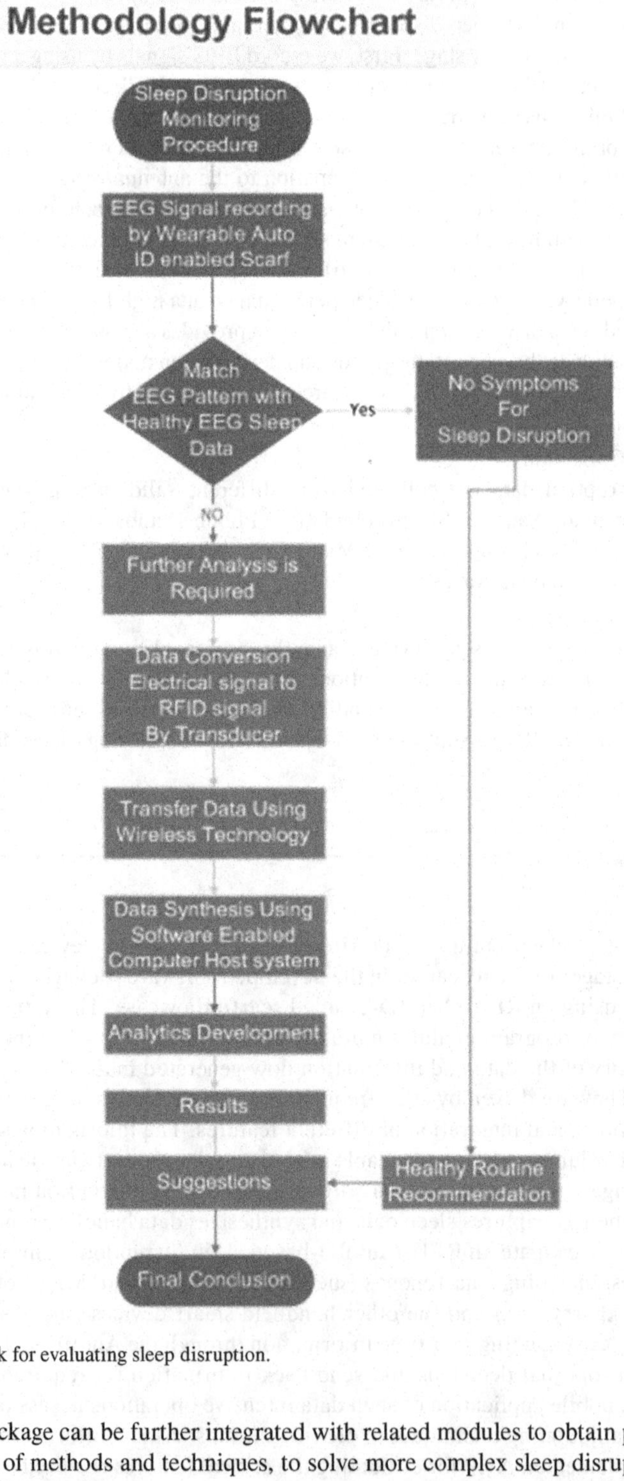

Methodology Flowchart

FIGURE 19.9 Framework for evaluating sleep disruption.

sleep patterns. This package can be further integrated with related modules to obtain parallel solutions, based on a wide range of methods and techniques, to solve more complex sleep disruption problems of different women of various age groups.

The aim of this research is to develop sleep disruption monitoring system that can be used wirelessly and also evaluates the EEG signal patterns, the experimental phase involved capturing the brain activities by using a wearable RFID/AutoID-enabled head scarf/pillowcase. For preliminary testing, the designed RFID/AutoID-enabled head scarf/pillowcase was placed around the head of object to provide the required amount of comfort. By considering the effect of distance on the data transferring rate, the antennas of the wireless sensor nodes were placed at an optimal distance of 2 m from the RF transmitter. The setup will be coupled with the software-enabled computer to synthesize the data capture and display the sleep status. The software code was prepared using Dot Net and Visual Basic platforms. The device will record the brain activities in the form of EEG signals and capture several episodes of sleep. The waveform pattern of sleep can be seen; also the major ripples in the waveforms suggest the cause of sleep disruption as it doesn't follow a normal pattern. Moreover, some distraction can be observed because of RF transmitter.

19.6.1 Phase 1 Analysis and Results—MLR

Sleep disruption can be improvised by implementing RFID technology which will track sleep quality and its respective pretreatment medication and posttreatment medication, thus reducing the risk of wrong medication and also decreasing unnecessary costs. This tracking can be implemented after analyzing EEG, EMG, EOG, and ECG data. Sleep disruption can be monitored by developing a sensor and RFID-enabled application. With the help of these devices, individual records can be stored, so as to reduce the chances of prescribing expensive treatment which would result in cost savings. Tracking of sleep performance with the help of comprehensive analysis of EEG, EMG, EOG, and ECG signals can be done, so as to suggest appropriate treatment to avoid the risk of severe sleep relevant disorders.

For creating initial data analytics, mainly, we are required to measure four types of signals. Firstly, we need to capture EEG signals. This task can be done by using RFID sensor which can be used to measure electrical activities. Since electrical activities measured during sleep show different characteristics than the active state, EEG signals reveal different stages of sleep. In the traditional procedure, medical technicians attach electrodes to the head to measure signals. Secondly, we need to measure EMG signals, and this particular signal is used to capture muscle tone activities, and these signals as well show different records during the sleep. A final observation is for EOG; it shows the movement of eye during deep sleep, particularly when we dream. In fact, this aspect helps us understand REM. Conceptually, eyeball movement nature indicates deep sleep. This type of measurement is considered as PSG (Figure 19.10).

For this analysis, we have implemented the MLR. In this procedure, significance of four predictor variables was analyzed, i.e., EEG, EMG, ECG, and EOG. This analysis is useful to understand sleep performance. Public data were used for 18 patients, and the analysis was done with four factor variables and one response variable. In this analysis, we will attempt to determine the effects of multiple predictor variables. The response variable is the sleep performance, and the four predictor variables are as follows: (1) EEG, (2) EMG, (3) EOG, and (4) ECG. We have assumed 0.01 as the statistical significance level. Initially, we need to check whether the MLR model is suitable for this analysis or not. To understand this, we have performed a preliminary correlation analysis of all three variables for each sleep monitoring method.

We can observe that there is a good correlation between sleep performance and EEG, EMG, EOG, and ECG, but there is a lower correlation between sleep performance and EOG. In fact, these results could be valuable as they add value to our final model (Tables 19.8 and 19.9).

Below are the results of an MLR of the RFID-enabled sleep disruption monitoring system.

Let

$\hat{y}$ = Sleep performance

X_i = Signals

X_1 = EEG

X_2 = EMG

X_3 = EOG

X_4 = ECG

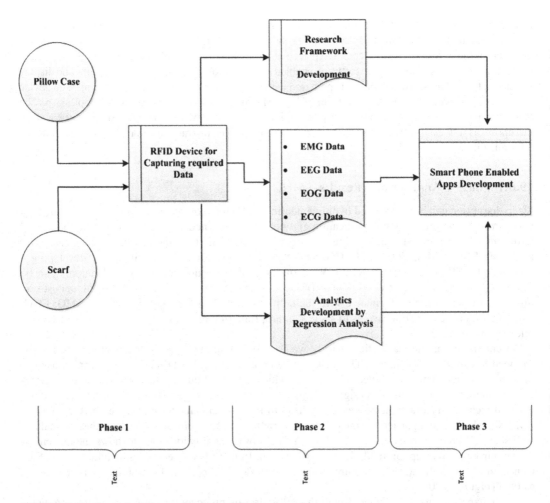

FIGURE 19.10 Conceptual diagram for sleep monitoring research.

TABLE 19.8

Analysis of SAS Output

Variable	N	Mean	Std. Dev.	Sum	Min.	Max.
Sleep performance	18	9.069	4.237	163.250	2.500	20.000
EEG	18	4.616	5.367	83.089	0.330	18.014
EMG	18	2418	1573	43525	500.00	5500
EOG	18	20.461	21.311	368.300	1.700	90.900
ECG	18	0.553	0.243	9.950	0.100	0.850

TABLE 19.9

Analysis of SAS Output

	EEG	EMG	EOG	ECG
EEG	1.000	0.816	0.258	−0.0748
EMG	0.816	1.000	0.398	0.1607
EOG	0.258	0.3989	1.000	−0.0377
ECG	−0.074	0.1607	−0.037	1.000

Regress $\hat{y}$ vs. X_1, X_2, X_3, and X_4 to get the p-values for independent variables X_1, X_2, X_3, and X_4. Below is the ANOVA table after regressing $\hat{y}$ with X_1 and X_2. The assumptions for the preliminary model have been checked, and we found that diagnostics have been performed and verified. Hence, we can move forward to develop this model.

The preliminary model is

$$\hat{y} = 4.15175 + 0.57105X_1 + 0.00052319X_2 + 0.00482X_3 + 0.01762X_4$$

In an MLR model, a single response measurement $\hat{y}$ is related to multiple predictor variables. In the equation, we have derived the value of intercept is 4.15175, and the values of beta coefficients are 0.57105, 0.00052319, 0.00482, and 0.01762, respectively. The regression beta coefficient is the slope of the response line. The sufficient (positive) value of beta coefficient indicates that the interpretation suggests that for a substantial increase in the predictor variable, the dependent variable will also increase by the beta coefficient value. In order to address the research, equation contains the value of beta associated with first predictor variable EEG signal is 0.57105; this suggests that for every unit increment in the value of EEG signal, the sleep performance will also increase by the beta value 0.57105. The equation implies that the sleep performance $\hat{y}$ can be determined by analyzing EEG, ECG, EOG, and EMG signals. This equation provides the information about how the sleep performance varies around its mean values. This leads to a model in the form of an equation (Tables 19.10 and 19.11).

The values in the correlation matrix are the values for the correlations between predictors. We are using 0.70 as our cutoff value for serious multicollinearity. EEG and ECG are two predictor variables with serious multicollinearity. The value represents the increase in the parameters due to the correlation between the predictors.

We have tested the significance of the regression as the final test on the preliminary model for $\alpha = 0.01$.

H_0: $B_k = 0$ if $F^* > F (\alpha - 1, p - 1, n - p)$. Reject H_0
H_i: $B_k \neq 0$
F^* = mean square due to regression (MSR)/mean square due to error (MSE) = 60.00981/5.01434 = 11.9676
$F (1 - \alpha, 5 - 1, 18 - 5) = F(0.99, 4, 13) = 5.21$

$F^* > F$; therefore, we reject H_0 and determine the regression is significant. We wanted to create a model that would be easy to use, and we believe that requirement has been met. We have created a model which indicates the feasibility of future developments and satisfies requirements. With the help of this research, it could be considered that the analysis will be useful for creating an RFID-enabled sleep monitoring package.

TABLE 19.10

ANOVA Analysis

		ANOVA			
Source	DF	Sum of Squares	Mean Square	F-Value	Pr > F
Model	4	240.03924	60.00981	11.97	0.0003
Error	13	65.18646	5.01434		
Corrected total	17	305.22569			

TABLE 19.11

ANOVA Analysis

Root MSE	2.23927	R-Sq	0.7864
Dependent mean	9.06944	Adj R-Sq	0.7207
Coefficient of variance	24.69030		

19.6.2 Phase 2 Analysis and Results—AHP

19.6.2.1 Weight–Age Evaluation of Various Broad Measures, Factors, and Sub-factors

The data shown here is the average of the data collected from the women of different age groups. In this section, the weights of various factors, sub-factors, and broad performance measures are specified as output. Also, the consistency index and eigenvalues of each of the matrices are evaluated.

19.6.2.2 Measure: Overall Broad Factors

Sleep disorder major factors (Tables 19.12–19.20)

TABLE 19.12

Interaction Matrix for Broad Factors of Sleep Disruption in Women

	A	B	C	D	E	F	G	H	Weights
A	1	1.67	2.12	3.56	3.72	1.5	3.2	3.67	0.309249
B	0.59	1	1.55	2.5	3.8	0.88	2.55	2.66	0.237297
C	0.47	0.64	1	2.12	2.35	0.45	1.67	2.8	0.16401
D	0.28	0.4	0.47	1	1.8	0.67	1.56	1.33	0.114786
E	0.26	0.263	0.42	0.55	1	0.263	0.47	0.74	0.064095
F	0.67	1.14	2.2	1.49	3.8	1	2.5	3.2	0.248393
G	0.31	0.39	0.59	0.64	2.1	0.4	1	1.8	0.112616
H	0.27	0.37	0.36	0.75	1.34	0.31	0.55	1	0.079287

TABLE 19.13

Interaction Matrix for Sub-factors of Sleep Disruption in Women

	A	B	C	D	E	Weights
A	1	1.24	1.67	2.34	2.88	0.30177
B	0.8	1	1.45	2.67	2.78	0.27388
C	0.59	0.68	1	1.67	2.74	0.19955
D	0.42	0.37	0.59	1	3.2	0.14608
E	0.34	0.35	0.36	0.312	1	0.07870

TABLE 19.14

Interaction Matrix for Sub-factors of Sleep Disruption in Women

	A	B	C	D	E	Weights
A	1	0.71	1.8	2.3	2.9	0.26883
B	1.4	1	1.6	2.1	2.8	0.29436
C	0.56	0.63	1	2.5	3.1	0.21690
D	0.44	0.47	0.4	1	3.4	0.14483
E	0.34	0.35	0.32	0.29	1	0.07506

TABLE 19.15

Interaction Matrix for Sub-factors of Sleep Disruption in Women

	A	B	C	D	Weights
A	1	1.12	2.5	1.6	0.34327
B	0.89	1	2.1	1.8	0.31888
C	0.4	0.47	1	0.89	0.15087
D	0.625	0.56	1.12	1	0.18697

TABLE 19.16

Interaction Matrix for Sub-factors of Sleep Disruption in Women

	A	B	C	D	Weights
A	1	0.47	2.8	1.67	0.27240
B	2.1	1	2.9	2.46	0.43742
C	0.35	0.344	1	0.67	0.11990
D	0.59	0.4	1.49	1	0.17026

TABLE 19.17

Interaction Matrix for Sub-factors of Sleep Disruption in Women

	A	B	C	D	E	F	G	Weights
A	1	3.5	1.56	1.8	1.96	2.8	3.1	0.25544
B	0.28	1	0.26	0.39	0.47	0.68	0.74	0.05992
C	0.64	3.78	1	1.6	1.82	2.4	3.2	0.21563
D	0.55	2.56	0.625	1	1.67	2.89	3.54	0.18157
E	0.51	2.12	0.54	0.59	1	1.67	2.56	0.12879
F	0.35	1.45	0.42	0.34	0.59	1	3.34	0.09772
G	0.32	1.34	0.312	0.34	0.39	0.29	1	0.06089

TABLE 19.18

Interaction Matrix for Sub-factors of Sleep Disruption in Women

	A	B	C	D	E	F	Weights
A	1	1.89	1.55	2.41	2.89	3.6	0.28846
B	0.53	1	0.41	1.67	2.43	2.96	0.16622
C	0.66	2.45	1	2.67	2.89	3.78	0.26859
D	0.414	0.59	0.37	1	2.71	2.86	0.13774
E	0.34	0.42	0.35	0.36	1	1.56	0.07976
F	0.27	0.34	0.26	0.34	0.64	1	0.05924

TABLE 19.19

Interaction Matrix for Sub-factors of Sleep Disruption in Women

	A	B	C	D	E	Weights
A	1	0.3	0.4	0.83	0.29	0.08489
B	3.25	1	2.46	3.1	1.5	0.34981
C	2.5	0.4	1	2.61	0.38	0.17953
D	1.21	0.33	0.38	1	0.58	0.10939
E	3.4	0.67	2.67	1.67	1	0.27636

TABLE 19.20

Interaction Matrix for Sub-factors of Sleep Disruption in Women

	A	B	C	D	Weights
A	1	0.31	0.35	0.625	0.09849
B	3.2	1	1.78	2.56	0.35558
C	2.83	0.56	1	1.56	0.23477
D	1.6	0.39	0.64	1	0.14770

Broad factors:

   A. Sleep incompatibleness (waking activities)

   B. Sleep–wake sensitivity

   C. Irregular sleep habits

   D. Effective coping skills

   E. Wake system disengagement

   F. Sleep hygiene

   G. Wake–sleep attribution

   H. Efforts to sleep

Max eigenvalue = 8.75, Consistency ratio = 0.047 (Acceptable)

Sub-factors: Sleep incompatibleness (waking activities)

   A. Reading

   B. Watching TV

   C. Eating

   D. Talking

   E. Problem solving

Max eigenvalue = 5.09, Consistency ratio = 0.055 (Acceptable)

Sub-factors: Sleep–wake sensitivity

   A. Environment latitude

   B. Wake behaviors

   C. Lying awake in bed (pre-sleep or upon wakening)

   D. Sleeping in the day

   E. Sleeping elsewhere than in bed

Max eigenvalue = 5.33, Consistency ratio = 0.0054 (Acceptable)

Sub-factors: Irregular sleep habits

   A. Variable patterns

   B. Changing times for retiring and rising

   C. Extending time in bed to catch up on sleep

   D. Sleeping in at weekends

Max eigenvalue = 4.03, Consistency ratio = 0.0039 (Acceptable)

Sub-factors: Effective coping skills

   A. Experiencing time pressure

   B. Problems relaxing

   C. Worry, frustration, and low mood

   D. Active late in the evening

Max eigenvalue = 4.0504, Consistency ratio = 0.0034 (Acceptable)

Sub-factors: Wake system disengagement

   A. Active thinking

   B. Self-monitoring of internal (bodily and mental) cues

C. Hypervigilance
D. Poor sleep hygiene
E. Anxiety
F. Trying too hard to sleep

Max eigenvalue = 7.8095, Consistency ratio = 0.0898 (Acceptable)

Sub-factors: Sleep hygiene
A. Stimulants (e.g., caffeine, nicotine) in excess/near bedtime
B. Alcohol withdrawal symptoms during the night
C. Active exercise late evening
D. Bedroom stuffy
E. Bed uncomfortable
F. Bedroom temperature

Max eigenvalue = 6.299815, Consistency ratio = 0.0037 (Acceptable)

Sub-factors: Wake–sleep attribution
A. Attribution of impaired daytime mood
B. Attention
C. Performance to quality of sleep
D. Fatigue
E. Perception of self as insomniac

Max eigenvalue = 5.673, Consistency ratio = 0.00663 (Acceptable)

Sub-factors: Efforts to sleep
A. Attempts to suppress thoughts/suppress affect
B. Self-monitoring of alert/sleepiness state
C. Performance effort to fall asleep
D. Performance anxiety

Max eigenvalue = 4.1355, Consistency ratio = 0.00838 (Acceptable)

19.6.3 Phase 3 Analysis and Results—Software

A software package for monitoring sleep disruption has been developed to assist in various decision-making stages of this research. Software provides the functions and utility suited for a variety of decisions associated with sleep disruptions in women. In the developed software package, the user is able to provide input information. The developed software consists of different program modules. This software has significant level of flexibility of application and fulfills the system requirements. Also, the software module produces the independent records of individual patient to assist in decision making associated with the sleep disruption monitoring purpose. This software has integrated modules and provides an overall assessment of patient sleep record. The result provided by the developed software contains data synthesizing procedure and parallel solutions.

The developed software package incorporates the following different modules:

- Initial screen
- EEG input screen
- Patient/user detail screen

- EEG signal graphs initialization screen
- EEG signal graphs captured by different sensors
- Port selection and baud rate selection
- Database server authentication
- Different waveform plots
- Enlarged view of signals captured by different sensors
- Recorded data in tabulated form
- Final output screen of sleep record analysis.

From the phase 1 analysis, we found that the major analysis would be performed by analyzing EEG signals, and the phase 2 analysis helps us understand the critical problems faced mainly by majority of women. Based on the information we found from these two phases, a software module was prepared to display sleep performance.

The software requires an installer that sets up the supporting files on the system. The password is 123. The main executable file needs to be run to use the software, and an introductory screen appears as shown in Figure 19.11.

In the next step, the sensor information will need to be entered in the EEG 1 through 8. Also, we enter the Mac address information for executing software. In this software module, we can upload the logo/image as per our wish. I have uploaded University of Texas-Arlington logo as a reference for screen display. All the information we entered should be saved in order to keep it in the record file. The screenshot is shown in Figure 19.12.

The required information of EEG and Mac addresses is shown in the screenshot in Figure 19.12. Mac addresses on backplane of the RF transmitter module are 40D8D637 for Mac address 1 and 40E792EA for Mac address 2. The screenshot is shown in Figure 19.13.

In the next step, the patient details need to be entered such as name, patient ID, age, gender, sleep disorder—previous records, remarks—additional details, and then the information can be saved. We can see four different options for addressing different functions. The Get detail option helps software extract the complete information saved in the system for individual user. Delete entry enables us to update the records by deleting past and unused records of a patient. The data option provides the data record and relevant waveforms captured by different EEG sensors and other sensors such as temperature sensor and accelerometer sensor for capturing body temperature and body motion record during sleeping stage. Comma-separated values (CSV) file provides complete information of any particular user and their respective brain activity information.

The software is coupled with AutoID/RFID system and calculates sleep performance, extracts the data records by clicking on "display them" on the screen, as shown in Figure 19.14. The final result

FIGURE 19.11   Screenshot of initial screen.

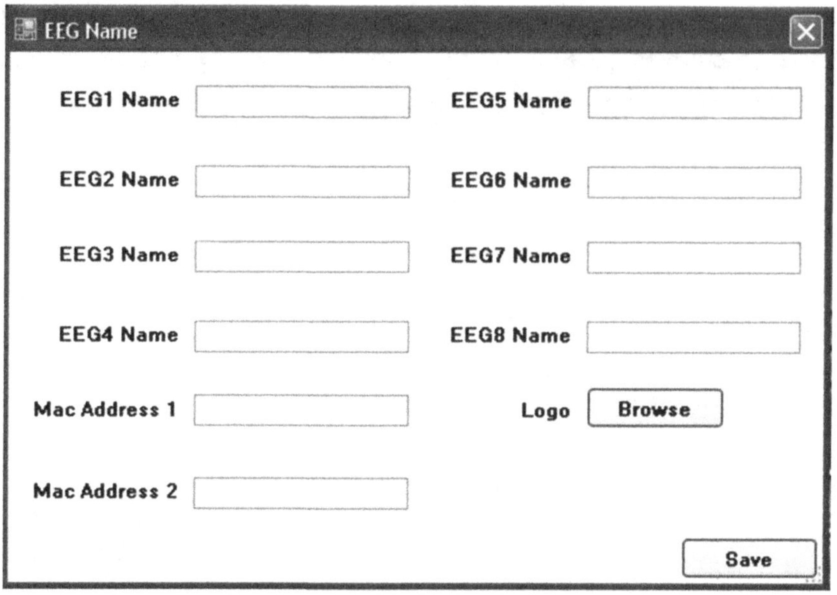

FIGURE 19.12 Screenshot of EEG input screen.

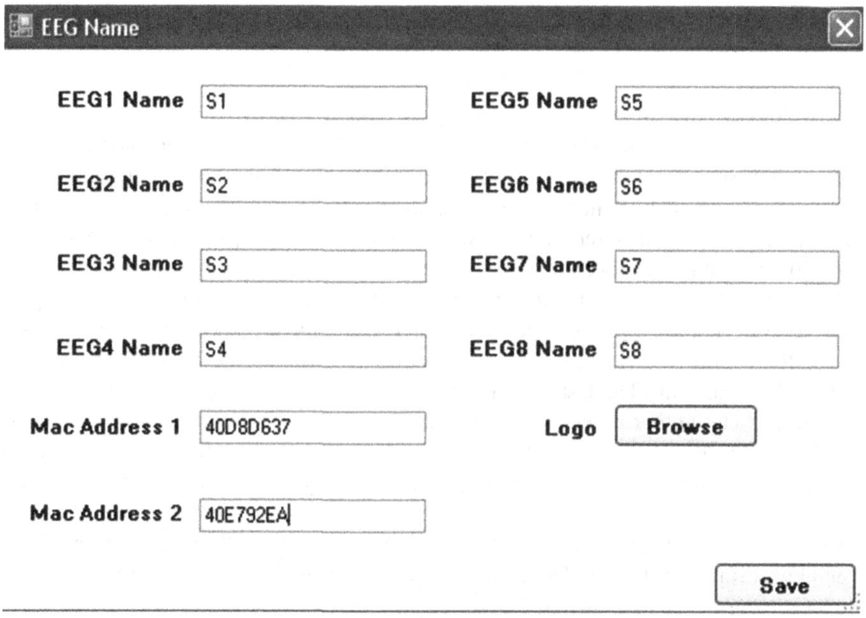

FIGURE 19.13 Screenshot of EEG screen with input information.

"Sleep Performance" is displayed which reveals whether the user is attaining appropriate sleep or not. In this system, we have attempted to incorporate different ways to analyze sleep records. The systems developed in the past mostly focus on EEG signal measuring procedure. However, we have developed a system which contains eight sensors: four EEG signal sensors, three accelerometer sensors, and one sensor for measuring body temperature. The function of accelerometer sensor is to measure the frequency of body movement during sleeping stage. The device developed to record and transfer the captured signals consists of two sets of transmitters and sensors. First transmitter coupled with four sensors captures and

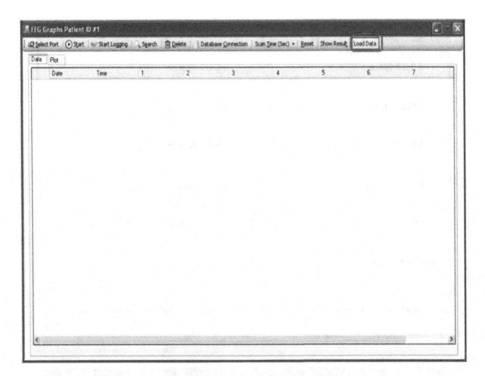

FIGURE 19.14   Screenshot of EEG signal graphs initialization screen.

transmits only EEG signals, and the other transmitter coupled with four sensors records and transmits temperature and frequency of body movement information. There is an RF-enabled receiver which is coupled with computer system and uses software for synthesizing data records. The transmitter can be placed 10 feet away from receiver and computer system in order to maintain optimum level of data transferring. This screen contains different options such as port selection option, start option for recording data, start logging option for saving data, search option for extracting user information, delete for removing data information if not significant to user record. Moreover, database connection option provides the detailed database information for individual user. Scan time option provides the time period selected for recording signals and brain activities. Also, "reset" option will clear all the information and provide data capturing from the beginning. The last option is "show result", which displays the sleep status in terms of threshold limits. The higher percentage of threshold indicates more chances to have critical sleep disruptions. The screenshot in Figure 19.14 shows when there is no connection between transmitters and receiver. Also, by choosing the "load data" option, we can directly upload the patient data file for analysis (Figure 19.14).

The subsequent screenshot (Figure 19.15) shows the plot screen as well. In the plot screen, we can set the upper and lower limits of threshold level for each sensor separately. Since there is no connection, the waveform plot screen will be as shown in Figure 19.15.

In the "select port" option, we need to enter the information of a computer port of which device is connected. The computer ports are identified as COM1, COM2, COM3, etc. The baud rate is 9,600 which shows the data transferring rate between the receiver and the transmitter. The screenshot is shown in Figure 19.16.

Moreover, the database selection requires additional information related to server host, username, and password. The same password 123 has been used for this screen as well. The purpose of this screen is to show the interface of the system with current and past database records of individual user. The screenshot is shown in Figure 19.17.

In the next step, the software then extracts input information of the patient from the RFID/AutoID-enabled scarf/pillowcase; these EEG signals recorded by the device will be synthesized by software

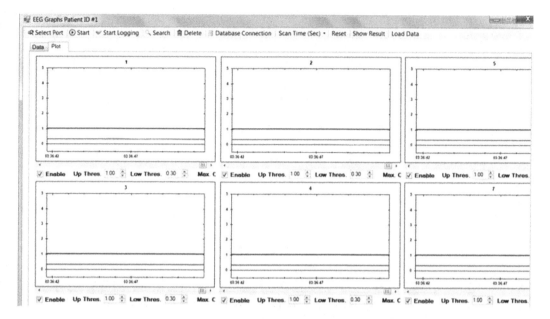

FIGURE 19.15 Screenshot of EEG signal graphs captured by different sensors.

Date	Time	1	2	3	4	5	6	7
08/07/2016	10:00:00	001.00	004.00	005.00	001.00	001.00	004.00	005.00
08/07/2016	10:00:01	002.00	034.00	004.00	002.00	002.00	034.00	004.00
08/07/2016	10:00:02	003.00	005.40	005.00	003.00	003.00	005.40	005.00
08/07/2016	10:00:03	004.00	002.20	007.00	004.00	004.00	002.20	007.00
08/07/2016	10:00:04	005.00	212.00	002.00	005.00	005.00	212.00	002.00
08/07/2016	10:00:05	006.00	005.50	051.00	006.00	006.00	005.50	051.00
08/07/2016	10:00:06	007.00	051.00	002.00	007.00	007.00	051.00	002.00
08/07/2016	10:00:07	008.00	021.00	005.00	008.00	008.00	021.00	005.00
08/07/2016	10:00:08	009.00	023.00	004.00	009.00	009.00	023.00	004.00
08/07/2016	10:00:09	010.00	065.00	002.00	010.00	010.00	065.00	002.00
08/07/2016	10:00:10	011.00	043.00	006.00	011.00	011.00	043.00	006.00
08/07/2016	10:00:11	012.00	076.00	613.00	012.00	012.00	076.00	613.00
08/07/2016	10:00:12	013.00	054.00	005.00	013.00	013.00	054.00	005.00
08/07/2016	10:00:13	014.00	065.00	012.00	014.00	014.00	065.00	012.00
08/07/2016	10:00:14	015.00	043.00	051.00	015.00	015.00	043.00	051.00

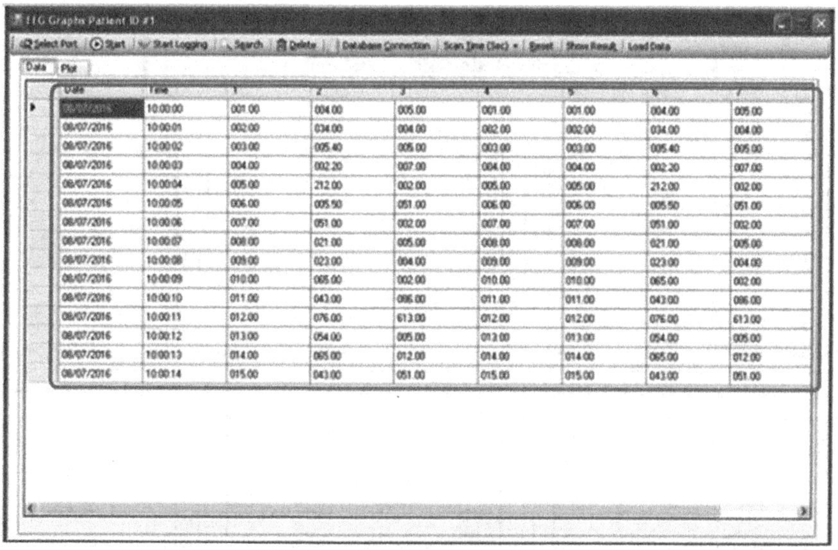

FIGURE 19.16 Screenshot of data uploading.

program. Each waveform can be seen in the screenshot provided below, and it also shows the waveforms respective to data recorded by each sensor. The screenshot is shown in Figure 19.18.

Each screen can be enlarged by clicking twice. The enlarged view of the waveforms is recorded through S2 and S4 sensors and is shown in Figures 19.19 and 19.20.

The screenshot shown in Figure 19.21 provides information of recorded database for a user. The system will record the time period in seconds and provide the data recorded by all the sensors (Figure 19.21).

The program now synthesizes the signals recorded by different sensors and thus provides an overall analysis by "average count screen". The user might be having more critical sleep disorders. If the percentage calculated in the screen is close to 100, the user needs to consult a physician. Normal sleeping

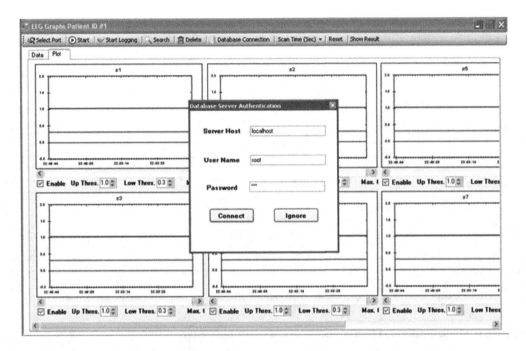

FIGURE 19.17   Screenshot of database server authentication.

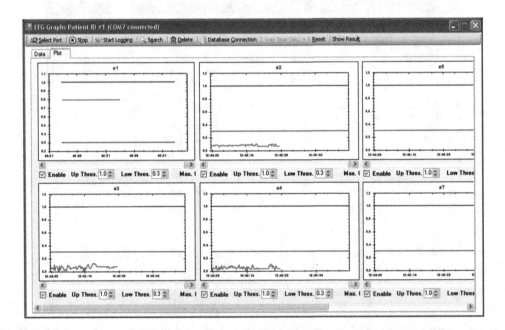

FIGURE 19.18   Screenshot of different waveform plots.

record will have the percentage close to 0. According to the concept of this technique, the software will synthesize and analyze the frequency levels of alpha, beta, delta, and gamma waves and match the recorded data with standard pattern of normal user who is of the same age group maintaining similar lifestyle. The normal user sleep records depict sleep records of women attaining optimum hours of sleep. Finally, the "calculate" button depicts the sleep performance status. The data record can be saved in a separate file to be viewed later on. The final output screenshot is shown in Figure 19.22.

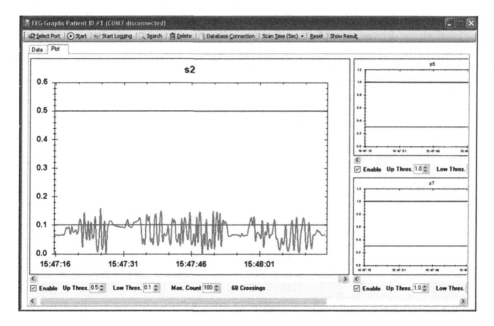

FIGURE 19.19   Screenshot of enlarged view of signals captured by S2 sensor.

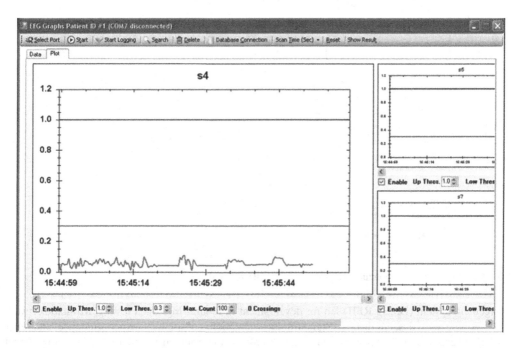

FIGURE 19.20   Screenshot of enlarged view of signals captured by S4 sensor.

19.6.4 Economic Analysis

In order to perform the economic analysis, the cost and budget plan associated with sleep disruption monitoring research project was calculated. This research needs different resources. The main resources are as follows: equipment, manpower, machine, RFID tags, scarf/pillowcase, EEG recording sensors, reader antenna, scanner, software-based app, RFID software-enabled computer systems, data

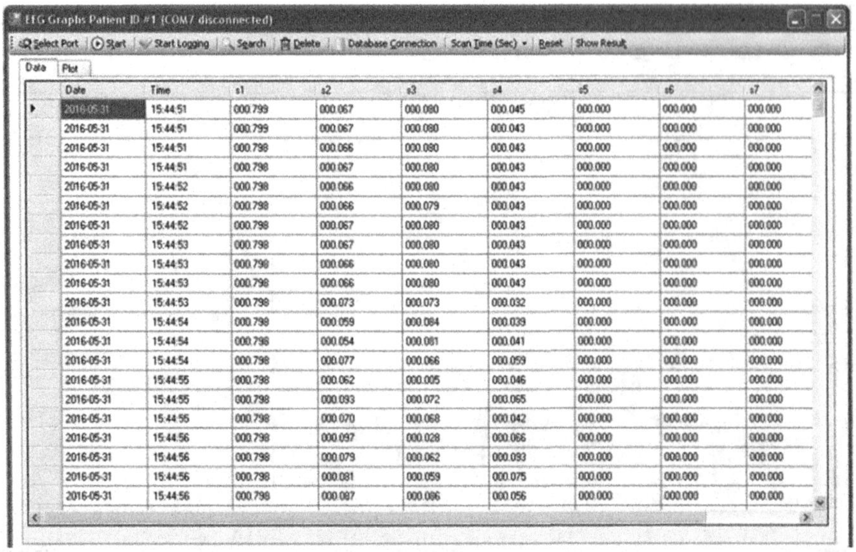

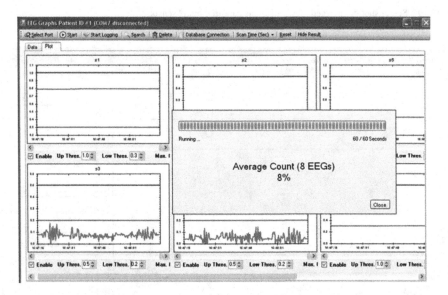

FIGURE 19.21   Screenshot of recorded data in tabulated form.

FIGURE 19.22   Screenshot depicting final output screen of sleep record analysis.

management system (DMS), RFID lab for development & monitoring, linen testing, Minitab software for developing analytics, engineering standard documentation, consultancy–expert guidance, and other services. The cost associated with each resource has been considered in order to prepare the budget plan for this research. The proposed sleep disruption monitoring system developed in this dissertation is based on a major observation that sleep disorders prevailed at a faster rate due to avoidance and lack of proper attention at an early stage. The RFID-enabled sleep disruption monitoring system is expensive and demands an investment of approximately $600,000. The payback period is five years (Table 19.21).

After the initial consultation period, step-by-step procedure and systematic analysis were performed to prepare the budgetary restrictions $583,607 and interlinking. Table 19.21 shows the costs and savings associated with this research project. The next steps present the summary of costs/benefits per project year plus other years project will be evaluated over and the net present value (NPV) summary.

TABLE 19.21

Presented are Details of All Costs and Benefits from Project Inception to End of Evaluation Period

No.	Name of Resource	Quantity	Cost	Extended Cost
1	RFID tags	100	$0.10	$100
2	Scarf/pillowcase	1	$15–$80	$80
3	EEG recording sensors	7	$395	$2,765
4	Reader antenna	4	$125	$500
5	Scanner	1	$1,700	$1,700
6	Software-based app	1	$2.00	$2.00
7	RFID software-enabled computer systems	1	$500	$500
8	DMS software	1	$299 per month	$3,588
9	RFID lab	4	$250 per day	$91,250
10	Man power (technically trained)	6	$100 per day	$213,600
11	Linen testing	4	$10,000 per tag set	$40,000
12	Minitab software for developing analytics	1	6682 per year for 10 user	$6,682
13	Engineering standard documentation	1	12000 per year	$12,000
14	Consultancy–expert guidance	1	300 per hour (8 h/week)	$124,800 per year
15	Service cost	1	35040 per year	$35,040
16	Miscellaneous	1	$50,000	$50,000
	Total cost			$583,607

A required rate of return of 7% was used. Based on the positive NPV, the decision was made to move forward with the project.

Additionally, to truly understand the savings of this research, the issue has to be evaluated in subsequent years to gauge the savings to other improvements and to the long-term profitability and stability. Although there are numerous other savings that are too difficult to evaluate within the scope of this research, the NPV is calculated based on a required return of 7%. The case inflows and outflows for five years are calculated for the required rate of return. The NPV > 0, so this project was deemed worthy.

19.7 Contribution to the Body of Knowledge

19.7.1 Conclusion

This research entitled "Evaluating the Impacts of Sleep Disruptions in Women through Automated Analysis" is an endeavor to study the significant analysis of sleep disruptions in women and capture the degree of sleep disorders with a view to map them using the AutoID techniques and RFID-based techniques in a more responsive manner. In the process of analysis, the following steps have been performed:

- Identification of the current techniques and the existing techniques.
- Identification of factors affecting sleep especially in women.
- Review of the possibilities and opportunities available with better responses as well as diverse viewpoints on fulfillment of accuracy requirements.
- In the selection of sleep disruption monitoring model, regression and AHP were used, and an analytics assessment software was developed to narrow down the sleep disruption causing parameters and the factors which are more critical so as to assess the process of sleep disruption monitoring. The outcomes of survey conducted among women of different age groups have been used to understand the problems associated with sleep.

- The use of AHP provides a relative criticality of sleep-related problems that provides direction for arriving at an optimum decision in regard to evaluating sleep disruptions.
- The feasibility of applying the regression model to evolve a unique factor affecting sleep disruption monitoring process, which is comparatively accurate and efficient, and scrutinize the sleep disruption monitoring process.
- The use of sensor-enabled scarf/pillowcase measures brain waves and developed software analyzes the role of brain waves for capturing sleep disruption's degree of seriousness. The experiments were conducted in RFID and AutoID laboratory.
- To arrive at the optimum decision and better accuracy, the developed system has been useful extensively.
- The entire approach of sleep disruption monitoring has been explored by using regression modeling approach, AHP, EEG capturing sensors-enabled scarf/pillowcase, and data synthesizing software which is a unique procedure provides detailed and accurate data analytics for sleep disruption monitoring.
- The entire process has been viewed from an integrated perspective to make the overall system more responsive and vibrant.

19.7.2 Hypothesis Conclusions

I met my research objective by investigating the specific aims and step-by-step procedures associated with each phase of analysis. There are some significant expected results from this research objectives and hypothesis.

- I met the *specific aim #1* – Identify the factors affecting sleep disruptions and evaluate the model suitability for sleep performance. By performing the MLR analysis, I have identified the critical factor, i.e., EEG signal for carrying out the further analysis. Also, the AHP was useful to figure out the major sleep disruption issues and their associated sub-factors for understanding the model suitability. Moreover, consistency index was used for validating the results obtained by the survey. So, overall procedure and steps in the first phase helped us to achieve specific objective #1.
- I met the *specific aim #2* – Evaluate and identify the suitable automated analysis technique for sleep disorders measurement. By investigating the different types of procedures available to monitor sleep disruption, we could figure out that RFID/AutoID-enabled technique would provide significant results in terms of accuracy. The procedure and steps associated with phase two was important to achieve specific objective #2.
- I met the *specific aim #3* – Develop a software for monitoring sleep disruption in women and evaluate the impact of proposed framework for sleep disruption performance measurement. In order to achieve specific objective #3, I have developed a software package that provides overall sleep assessment in terms of an average count level. Also, the screenshots included in the results section guides the step-by-step procedure for installing and running the software system.
- We expected to reject our H_0 with respect to the predefined hypothesis for the first objective that the implementation of AutoID/RFID technology will have impact on measuring sleep disorders accurately. Also, the decision rule concerned with the first objective states that if the cost associated with AutoID/RFID-based sleep monitoring system is greater than 15% of the currently available systems, then we will reject the null hypothesis for the first objective.
- As we have performed the analysis and developed a software system for data synthesis, so we found that the cost of proposed system is lesser than the available techniques in the market that prompts us to reject null hypothesis for the first objective.
- The null hypothesis concerned with the second research objective states that we expected the developed framework effectively addresses the critical sleep disorders monitoring requirements.

Also, the decision rule for objective two mentioned clearly that if the sleep performance provided by AutoID/RFID-based sleep monitoring system is less than 5% counts, then the null hypothesis for objective two will be rejected.

- The results obtained by the developed software help us comprehend the typical nature of sleep disruption monitoring and also provide a systematic procedure for monitoring sleep disruption.

19.7.3 Findings and Recommendations

The modeling of the sleep disruption monitoring process is relatively new in the field of technology and biomedical science. The reluctance to change and predominantly medical practices have not permitted any innovative thinking on the subject. The data management procedure for this system is extensive and requires the highest level of accuracy. The challenges and issues associated with this procedure encourage us to delve into further studies, and hence there is immense scope to use advanced-level technical knowledge and experiments. The data management is lethargic not only due to the extensive range and depth but also because of procedural inadequacies.

For this analysis, we have implemented the MLR. In this procedure, significance of four predictor variables was analyzed, i.e., EEG, EMG, ECG, and EOG. This analysis is useful to understand sleep performance. Data was collected for patients of different age groups, and the analysis was done with four factor variables and one response variable. In this analysis, we attempted to determine the effects of multiple predictor variables. The response variable is the sleep performance, and the four predictor variables are as follows: (1) EEG, (2) EMG, (3) EOG, and (4) ECG. We have assumed 0.01 as the statistical significance level. Initially, we need to check whether the MLR model is suitable for this analysis or not. To understand this, we have performed a preliminary correlation analysis of all four variables for each sleep monitoring method. In fact, the results could be valuable as they add value to our final model. The research will show the benefits of RFID implementation in sleep monitoring and its increasing need in the business prospectus of the commercial and hospital industry. Thus, there is a vast scope in the use of such technology to convert the sleep monitoring into a more easy process and money saving technology. Use of RFID to improve sleep monitoring service, patient safety, cost reduction, real-time data management, timely service, and process improvement can be deployed to make the tracking efficient.

The expected results obtained by this research would suggest the progressive and beneficial nature of the project in the next five years for the commercial purpose. The suggested analytics offers manifold reasons to address the challenges confronted by the healthcare organization, especially by utilizing the advantages of RFID application, economic analysis, and application package development. We can recognize this system as a very cost-effective tool to monitor sleep performance with points of sale solutions and serves sleep monitoring system globally from anywhere and at the very time. The analytics developed among four critical factors provides significant insights into how the sleep disruption monitoring and the RFID implementation impact the overall sleep tracking characteristics and the quality of sleep.

The major conclusions from this study are summarized below:

1. Better evaluation implies better management of benefits, costs, and risks.
2. There is a need for better tools of evaluation to assess process and product.
3. There is a need to understand the bottlenecks in sleep disruption monitoring procedure.

This research attempts to accomplish the above objective. This research proposed a systematic and flexible approach to solve the complex sleep disruption monitoring problem for women efficiently and effectively. It acquires the relationships by using AHP-based technique, which enables the inclusion of both quantitative and qualitative factors in the decision process. These factors are based on the current research experience in the sleep disorder monitoring fields. The presented approach discussed in this research has the ability to propose sleep disruption monitoring effectively. This approach is exemplified to provide a feasible quality solution and is to be applied to the real-world application easily and expeditiously. In addition, it is very flexible, which permits to add more participators which are located in different geographical locations.

The focus of this research was mainly on the implementation of AutoID/RFID in healthcare system. This includes scenarios where the RFID devices are used for data capture. The tags are attached to a scarf or pillowcase and can thus be close to the patient's head where they can measure the sleep disruption. The second theme of the research is to maintain the flow of patient EEG, ECG, EOG, and EMG data during the sleep using the RFID devices and transducers. The data captured will be stored on the tag and can be read off whenever the reader comes into contact with it. The third topic is about the management of RFID in hospitals that use the RFID-enabled pillowcase/scarf. We will specifically look into measuring sleep disruptions, treatment costs, improving efficiency of tracking, and the effects of RFID on humans. The design and implementation of RFID tags into linen is rather simple. Linen tags currently exist, and all that is required will be for them to be attached into pillowcases/scarves at the manufacturing level. Hospital-specific phone applications can be built in order to maintain security and mishandling of the equipment for the procedure.

Sleep disorders become more chronical as age increases, but with proper awareness, the effects of chronical sleep disorders can be suppressed up to a great extent. Mostly women are more sensitive to age-related changes, and these kinds of changes make a significant impact not only on the sleeping time but also on the awakening states. However, by accumulating prior information about the sleep performance such as brain aging, in particular neuronal loss information can help us to take preventive actions for the sleep disorders. Overall, the results of this research experiments demonstrate the feasibility of analysis and statistical analytics in the acquirement of EEG signals for automated analysis. In particular, the analysis was performed to analyze EEG sleep data for developing the analytics for automated sleep disruption monitoring research. However, available methods for sleep monitoring also produce effective results, but the lack of a RF-based EEG recording-based self-sleep monitoring devices has attracted researchers' attention in this area. The analysis performed in this research shows that the level of accuracy can be maintained by statistical analysis for signal synthesis and refinement. Based on the suggested framework, we can achieve better accuracy and produce effective results. However, the sensor complexity and severe power constraints forced on EEG capturing systems provide the designer of EEG recording systems a compromise though the appropriate modification can be made to the device features and the power quality concern can also be balanced with signal quality. These achievements can compensate for power consumption limitations and provide many benefits.

19.7.4 Limitation

Although the study supports key findings, there are some limitations associated with the RFID-enabled sleep monitoring system in tracking real-time information, data, sleep disruption, & monitoring speed. The integration of ECG, EMG, EOG, EEG, and RFID-enabled sleep monitoring system is very helpful to suggest appropriate corrective actions by providing accessibility and data visibility. In fact, the sleep disruption can be accurately tracked. The RFID implementation acts as a paradigm of technology changeover to the dynamic data flow. One more thing that can be focused on in future in order to drive the efficiency of sleep monitoring system is the use of RFID-enabled system to increase the ability to learn overall sleep performance. These RFID-enabled system leads to increasing in overall effectiveness of the healthcare organizations. So, it has been predicted that with the implementation of RFID technology, there can be expected benefits of

1. Increased sleep monitoring quality and accuracy
2. Real-time performance visibility
3. Faster in recording real-time data.

These can lead to an increase in overall efficiency, quality, and safety. A serious thought can be put into this to evaluate the economic impacts. Despite all the benefits touted for RFID, both within healthcare and other industries, there are many detractors to its implementation.

Although the uses of RFID enable a higher rate of patient safety and increased cost benefits, there are still some fundamental challenges faced to be able to utilize to its zenith. They include some implementation and ethical issues primarily. For example, for enabling RFID readers in pillows/scarves, it is required to have a consistent electrical supply, and patient safety could be called into question. Also, there have been patient and staff concerns about privacy, as RFID enables users to capture the sleep data. It is a genuine concern which needs to be addressed, so that the technology can be improved. RFID must also be evaluated so that policy regulations are not violated in terms of privacy. To maintain patient safety and privacy, there should be clear guidelines about its usage, and information should be provided to the patient about how they can track their sleep by the system. It is vital to encourage the suppliers to include RFID in their products so that the flow of data is smooth. Failure to have an effective RFID system might result in serious issues in a sleep disruption monitoring system and will thus not help in improving of data capturing.

The main limitations of the project is the number of women under consideration. As mentioned in the research, we can record the sleep monitoring data in systematic manner for providing sleep performance. Depending on the manner in which we measure EEG signals, the sensors may not be able to perform as effectively. We feel confident with the ability of electronics transducers, but, depending on the complexity of the circuits needed for the EEG recording, we may not be able to build a sensor that has a good level of resolution.

19.7.5 Future Work

This research is seen as a three-step process. The developed method using sensors and AutoID/RFID-enabled scarf/pillowcase provides a unique way to evaluate the sleep disruption monitoring and also suggests us a procedure to show how to develop the DMS for this system. In order to better understand the sleep performance, the future scope will be to take this understanding of the EEG signal recording process and begin incorporating additional memory into the sensors so that they can carry large number of data for systematic data management. We also expect this research to open up additional opportunities in the area of sleep disorder monitoring.

Appendix 19.A: Software Code

19.A.1 EEGNameForm.vb (when this software is running for first time on machine)

19.A.1.1 Gets data entered by user in text boxes

```
' Browse button action to choose logo file (png, jpg, jpeg) '
    Private Sub BrowseButton_Click(ByVal sender As System.Object, ByVal e As
System.EventArgs) Handles BrowseButton.Click
        'OpenFileDialog1.Filter = "(*.png)|*.png; |*.jpg; |*.jpeg"
        OpenFileDialog1.Filter = "PNG Image(*.png) |*.png|JPG Image(*.jpg)
|*.jpg|JPEG Image (*.jpeg)|*.jpeg|All Files (*.*) |*.*"
        OpenFileDialog1.FileName = ""
        If OpenFileDialog1.ShowDialog = Windows.Forms.DialogResult.OK Then
            PatientDetailForm.LogoImagePath = OpenFileDialog1.FileName
        End If
    End Sub
```

19.A.1.2 Save the data (prob name and MAC address) in EEGNames.txt file

```
Private Sub SaveButton_Click(ByVal sender As System.Object, ByVal e As
System.EventArgs) Handles SaveButton.Click
        If IsEntriesCompleted() = False Then
            MessageBox.Show(Me, "Please fill all entries", "Information",
MessageBoxButtons.OK, MessageBoxIcon.Information)
            Exit Sub
        End If
```

```
        Dim FilePath As String = Application.StartupPath + "\EEGNames.txt"
        SaveFileEEGNames(FilePath)
        NextForm = True
        Me.Close()
    End Sub


Private Sub SaveFileEEGNames(ByVal FilePath As String)
      Try
          Dim FileString As New StringBuilder
          FileString.AppendLine(EEGName1.Text)
          FileString.AppendLine(EEGName2.Text)
          FileString.AppendLine(EEGName3.Text)
          FileString.AppendLine(EEGName4.Text)
          FileString.AppendLine(EEGName5.Text)
          FileString.AppendLine(EEGName6.Text)
          FileString.AppendLine(EEGName7.Text)
          FileString.AppendLine(EEGName8.Text)
          FileString.AppendLine(MAC1.Text)
          FileString.AppendLine(MAC2.Text)
          FileString.AppendLine(PatientDetailForm.LogoImagePath)
          Dim FileWriter As New StreamWriter(FilePath)
          FileWriter.Write(FileString.ToString)
          FileWriter.Close()
      Catch ex As Exception
          File.Delete(FilePath)
          MessageBox.Show(Me, ex.Message, "Error", MessageBoxButtons.OK,
MessageBoxIcon.Error)
      End Try
    End Sub
```

19.A.2. PatientDetailForm.vb—contains code for patient details entry and save

19.A.2.1 Initial settings

```
Public SQLconnection As MySqlConnection
    Public SQLreader As MySqlDataReader
    Public SQLcommand As MySqlCommand

    ' Connection string which contains user name, password, server (localhost
or other), database to initially connect with database '
    Public Shared SQLConnectionString, SQLInitConnectionString As String
    Public Shared DatabaseName As String

    ' EEG prob names of all 8 channel; this name is entered by the user if he
is running the software for the first time '
    Public Shared EEGName1, EEGName2, EEGName3, EEGName4, EEGName5, EEGName6,
EEGName7, EEGName8 As String

    ' MAC address of the sensor nodes which connects wireless to base station '
    Public Shared MacAddress1, MacAddress2 As String

    ' Path selected by user when running software first time '
    Public Shared LogoImagePath As String


    Private Sub Form1_Load(ByVal sender As System.Object, ByVal e As System.
EventArgs) Handles MyBase.Load
        SQLconnection = New MySqlConnection
        LoadFileConnectionString()
```

```
        TestDatabaseConnection()
        CreateDatabase()
        LoadFileNames()
        GenderComboBox.SelectedIndex = 0
    End Sub


    Private Sub LoadFileConnectionString()
        Dim FilePath As String = Application.StartupPath +
"\SQLConnectionString.txt"
        Try
            If System.IO.File.Exists(FilePath) Then
                Dim FileReader As New System.IO.StreamReader(FilePath)
                SQLConnectionString = FileReader.ReadLine()
                FileReader.Close()
                SQLInitConnectionString =
SQLConnectionString.Substring(SQLConnectionString.IndexOf(";") + 1)
                DatabaseName = SQLConnectionString.
Substring(SQLConnectionString.IndexOf("=") + 1)
                DatabaseName = DatabaseName.Substring(0,
DatabaseName.IndexOf(";"))
            Else
                'MessageBox.Show(Me, "File SQLConnectionString.txt doesn't
exist", "Error", MessageBoxButtons.OK, MessageBoxIcon.Error)
                System.IO.File.Create(FilePath)
                DatabaseName = "SleepDisorder_1v0"
            End If
        Catch ex As Exception
            MessageBox.Show(Me, ex.Message, "Error", MessageBoxButtons.OK,
MessageBoxIcon.Error)
        End Try
    End Sub


    Private Sub TestDatabaseConnection()
        SQLconnection.ConnectionString = SQLInitConnectionString
        Try
            SQLconnection.Open()
        Catch ex As Exception
            ' If connection string from file contains incorrect password then
it display a dialog box to enter proper password '
            If ex.Message.Contains("Access denied") Then
                DatabaseConnection.ShowDialog()
            End If
        End Try
        SQLconnection.Close()
    End Sub


    Private Sub CreateDatabase()
        SQLconnection.ConnectionString = SQLInitConnectionString
        Try
            SQLconnection.Open()
            SQLcommand = New MySqlCommand("Create database " + DatabaseName,
SQLconnection)
            SQLcommand.ExecuteReader()
            SQLcommand.Dispose()
            SQLconnection.Close()
        Catch
```

```
        Finally
            SQLconnection.Close()
        End Try
        SQLconnection.ConnectionString = SQLConnectionString
        Try
            SQLconnection.Open()
            SQLcommand = New MySqlCommand("Create table " + DatabaseName +
".Patient_Detail(ID int,Name char(20),Gender char,Age int,Disorder char,
Remark char(30));", SQLconnection)
            SQLcommand.ExecuteReader()
        Catch
        End Try
        SQLcommand.Dispose()
        SQLconnection.Close()
        Try
            SQLconnection.Open()
            SQLcommand = New MySqlCommand("Create table " + DatabaseName +
".EEG(datetime datetime,ID int, Data1 double, Data2 double, Data3 double, Data4
double, Data5 double, Data6 double, Data7 double, Data8 double);", SQLconnection)
            SQLcommand.ExecuteReader()
        Catch
        End Try
        SQLcommand.Dispose()
        SQLconnection.Close()
        Try
            SQLconnection.Open()
            SQLcommand = New MySqlCommand("Create table " + DatabaseName +
".EEG_CSV(ID int, Data1 double, Data2 double, Data3 double, Data4 double,
Data5 double, Data6 double, Data7 double, Data8 double);", SQLconnection)
            SQLcommand.ExecuteReader()
        Catch
        End Try
        SQLcommand.Dispose()
        SQLconnection.Close()
    End Sub


    Private Sub LoadFileNames()
        Dim FilePath As String = Application.StartupPath + "\EEGNames.txt"
        If File.Exists(FilePath) = False Then
            EEGNameForm.ShowDialog()
        End If
        If File.Exists(FilePath) Then
            Dim FileReader As New StreamReader(FilePath)
            EEGName1 = FileReader.ReadLine()
            EEGName2 = FileReader.ReadLine()
            EEGName3 = FileReader.ReadLine()
            EEGName4 = FileReader.ReadLine()
            EEGName5 = FileReader.ReadLine()
            EEGName6 = FileReader.ReadLine()
            EEGName7 = FileReader.ReadLine()
            EEGName8 = FileReader.ReadLine()
            MacAddress1 = FileReader.ReadLine()
            MacAddress2 = FileReader.ReadLine()
            LogoImagePath = FileReader.ReadLine()
            LogoPictureBox.Image = Image.FromFile(LogoImagePath)
            FileReader.Close()
        End If
    End Sub
```

19.A.2.2 Gets data entered by user in text boxes

19.A.2.3 New Form

```
      Private Sub NewFormButton_Click(ByVal sender As System.Object, ByVal e
As System.EventArgs) Handles NewFormButton.Click
        NameTextBox.ReadOnly = False
        NameTextBox.Text = ""
        IDTextBox.ReadOnly = False
        IDTextBox.Text = ""
        AgeTextBox.ReadOnly = False
        AgeTextBox.Text = ""
        GenderComboBox.Enabled = True
        GenderComboBox.SelectedIndex = 0
        YesRadioButton.Enabled = True
        NoRadioButton.Enabled = True
        YesRadioButton.Checked = True
        OthersTextBox.ReadOnly = False
        OthersTextBox.Text = ""
        SaveButton.Text = "Save"
    End Sub


    Private Sub PatientIDTextBox_KeyDown(ByVal sender As Object, ByVal e As
System.Windows.Forms.KeyEventArgs) Handles PatientIDTextBox.KeyDown
        If e.KeyValue = Keys.Enter Then
            GetDetailsButton_Click(Nothing, Nothing)
        End If
    End Sub
```

19.A.2.4 Saves the data over MySQL data base at localhost (localPC)

```
 Private Sub SaveButton_Click(ByVal sender As System.Object, ByVal e As
System.EventArgs) Handles SaveButton.Click
        If IsValidEntries() = False Then
            MessageBox.Show(Me, "Please fill proper entires", "Information",
MessageBoxButtons.OK, MessageBoxIcon.Information)
            Exit Sub
        End If
        Dim dt As String = ""
        dt = DateTime.Now().ToString("yyyy-MM-dd HH:mm:ss")
        Try
            SQLconnection.ConnectionString = SQLConnectionString
            SQLconnection.Open()
            Dim Gender As String = ""
            If GenderComboBox.SelectedIndex = 0 Then Gender = "M" Else
Gender = "F"
            Dim Disorder As String = ""
            If YesRadioButton.Checked Then Disorder = "Y" Else
Disorder = "N"
            Dim sql As String = ""
            sql = "insert into Patient_Detail (ID,Name,Gender,Age,
Disorder,Remark) values(" + IDTextBox.Text + ",'" + NameTextBox.Text +
"','" + Gender + "'," + AgeTextBox.Text + ",'" + Disorder + "','" +
OthersTextBox.Text + "');"
            SQLcommand = New MySqlCommand(sql, SQLconnection)
            SQLcommand.ExecuteReader()
        Catch ex As Exception
            MessageBox.Show(Me, ex.Message, "Error", MessageBoxButtons.OK,
MessageBoxIcon.Error)
```

```
      End Try
      SQLcommand.Dispose()
      SQLconnection.Close()
   End Sub
```

19.A.2.5 Gets the entry when requested

```
 Private Sub GetDetailsButton_Click(ByVal sender As System.Object, ByVal e As
System.EventArgs) Handles GetDetailsButton.Click
      If PatientIDTextBox.Text = "" Then
          MessageBox.Show(Me, "Please enter patient ID", "Patient Details",
MessageBoxButtons.OK, MessageBoxIcon.Information)
          Exit Sub
      End If
      Try
          Dim test As Integer = CInt(PatientIDTextBox.Text)
      Catch ex As Exception
          MessageBox.Show(Me, "Please enter valid ID", "Patient Details",
MessageBoxButtons.OK, MessageBoxIcon.Information)
          Exit Sub
      End Try
      NewFormButton_Click(Nothing, Nothing)
      SQLconnection.ConnectionString = SQLConnectionString
      SQLconnection.Open()
      Dim SQLQuery As String = ""
      Dim Gender, Disorder As String
      SQLQuery = "select * from Patient_Detail where ID=" +
PatientIDTextBox.Text + ";"
      SQLcommand = New MySqlCommand(SQLQuery, SQLconnection)
      SQLcommand.CommandTimeout = 0
      SQLreader = SQLcommand.ExecuteReader()
      While SQLreader.Read
          IDTextBox.Text = SQLreader.GetString(0)
          IDTextBox.ReadOnly = True
          NameTextBox.Text = SQLreader.GetString(1)
          NameTextBox.ReadOnly = True
          Gender = SQLreader.GetString(2)
          If Gender = "M" Then GenderComboBox.SelectedIndex = 0 Else
GenderComboBox.SelectedIndex = 1
          GenderComboBox.Enabled = False
          AgeTextBox.Text = SQLreader.GetString(3)
          AgeTextBox.ReadOnly = True
          Disorder = SQLreader.GetString(4)
          If Disorder = "Y" Then YesRadioButton.Checked = True Else
NoRadioButton.Checked = True
          YesRadioButton.Enabled = False
          NoRadioButton.Enabled = False
          OthersTextBox.Text = SQLreader.GetString(5)
          OthersTextBox.ReadOnly = True
      End While
      SQLcommand.Dispose()
      SQLconnection.Close()
   End Sub
```

19.A.2.6 EEG plot from CSV file

```
      Private Sub EEGButton_Click(ByVal sender As System.Object, ByVal e As
System.EventArgs) Handles EEGButton.Click
          If PatientIDTextBox.Text = "" Then
```

```
            MessageBox.Show(Me, "Please enter patient ID", "EEG Plotting",
MessageBoxButtons.OK, MessageBoxIcon.Information)
            Exit Sub
        End If
        Try
            Dim test As Integer = CInt(PatientIDTextBox.Text)
        Catch ex As Exception
            MessageBox.Show(Me, "Please enter valid ID", "Patient Details",
MessageBoxButtons.OK, MessageBoxIcon.Information)
            Exit Sub
        End Try
        'Dim GraphsForm As EEGForm = New EEGForm
        'GraphsForm.PatientID = PatientIDTextBox.Text
        'GraphsForm.Show()
        EEGForm.PatientID = PatientIDTextBox.Text
        EEGForm.Show()
    End Sub

    Private Sub DeleteEntryButton_Click(ByVal sender As System.Object, ByVal
e As System.EventArgs) Handles DeleteEntryButton.Click
        If PatientIDTextBox.Text = "" Then
            MessageBox.Show(Me, "Please enter patient ID", "Patient Details",
MessageBoxButtons.OK, MessageBoxIcon.Information)
            Exit Sub
        End If
        Try
            Dim test As Integer = CInt(PatientIDTextBox.Text)
        Catch ex As Exception
            MessageBox.Show(Me, "Please enter valid ID", "Patient Details",
MessageBoxButtons.OK, MessageBoxIcon.Information)
            Exit Sub
        End Try
        NewFormButton_Click(Nothing, Nothing)
        Try
            SQLconnection.ConnectionString = SQLConnectionString
            SQLconnection.Open()
            Dim SQLQuery As String = ""
            SQLQuery = "delete from Patient_Detail where ID=" +
PatientIDTextBox.Text + ";"
            SQLcommand = New MySqlCommand(SQLQuery, SQLconnection)
            SQLcommand.CommandTimeout = 0
            SQLcommand.ExecuteReader()
        Catch ex As Exception
            MessageBox.Show(Me, ex.Message, "Error", MessageBoxButtons.OK,
MessageBoxIcon.Error)
        End Try
        SQLcommand.Dispose()
        SQLconnection.Close()

        Try
            SQLconnection.Open()
            Dim SQLQuery = "delete from eeg where ID=" + PatientIDTextBox.
Text + ";"
            SQLcommand = New MySqlCommand(SQLQuery, SQLconnection)
            SQLcommand.CommandTimeout = 0
            SQLcommand.ExecuteReader()
        Catch ex As Exception
            MessageBox.Show(Me, ex.Message, "Error", MessageBoxButtons.OK,
MessageBoxIcon.Error)
```

```
        End Try
        SQLcommand.Dispose()
        SQLconnection.Close()
    End Sub


    Private Sub OpenCSVButton_Click(ByVal sender As System.Object, ByVal e As
System.EventArgs) Handles OpenCSVButton.Click
        EEG_CSVForm.PatientID = PatientIDTextBox.Text
        EEG_CSVForm.Show()
    End Sub
```

19.A.2.7 *Delete Entry*

```
 Private Sub DeleteEntryButton_Click(ByVal sender As System.Object, ByVal e
As System.EventArgs) Handles DeleteEntryButton.Click
        If PatientIDTextBox.Text = "" Then
            MessageBox.Show(Me, "Please enter patient ID", "Patient Details",
MessageBoxButtons.OK, MessageBoxIcon.Information)
            Exit Sub
        End If
        Try
            Dim test As Integer = CInt(PatientIDTextBox.Text)
        Catch ex As Exception
            MessageBox.Show(Me, "Please enter valid ID", "Patient Details",
MessageBoxButtons.OK, MessageBoxIcon.Information)
            Exit Sub
        End Try
        NewFormButton_Click(Nothing, Nothing)
        Try
            SQLconnection.ConnectionString = SQLConnectionString
            SQLconnection.Open()
            Dim SQLQuery As String = ""
            SQLQuery = "delete from Patient_Detail where ID=" +
PatientIDTextBox.Text + ";"
            SQLcommand = New MySqlCommand(SQLQuery, SQLconnection)
            SQLcommand.CommandTimeout = 0
            SQLcommand.ExecuteReader()
        Catch ex As Exception
            MessageBox.Show(Me, ex.Message, "Error", MessageBoxButtons.OK,
MessageBoxIcon.Error)
        End Try
        SQLcommand.Dispose()
        SQLconnection.Close()


        Try
            SQLconnection.Open()
            Dim SQLQuery = "delete from eeg where ID=" + PatientIDTextBox.
Text + ";"
            SQLcommand = New MySqlCommand(SQLQuery, SQLconnection)
            SQLcommand.CommandTimeout = 0
            SQLcommand.ExecuteReader()
        Catch ex As Exception
            MessageBox.Show(Me, ex.Message, "Error", MessageBoxButtons.OK,
MessageBoxIcon.Error)
        End Try
        SQLcommand.Dispose()
        SQLconnection.Close()
    End Sub
```

19.A.3. EEGForm—contains code for receiving sensor data (via serial port) and saving to MySQL server

19.A.3.1 *Initial Settings*

```
Private Sub Form1_Load(ByVal sender As System.Object, ByVal e As System.
EventArgs) Handles MyBase.Load
        Me.Text = "EEG Graphs Patient ID #" + PatientID
        'Form7.ShowInTaskbar = True
        'Form7.ShowDialog()
        'If (Form7.authen = False) Then
        ' Me.Close()
        ' End If
        ' Form7.ShowInTaskbar = False
        'init()
        'test()
        'createdb()
        'createtable()
        'PatientDetailForm.ShowDialog()
        Dim mypane As GraphPane = ZedGraphControl1.GraphPane
        mycurve1 = mypane.AddCurve("IO1", list1, Color.Red, SymbolType.None)
        Graph(ZedGraphControl1, ZedGraphControl1.GraphPane, mycurve1, "EEG
1", 50)


        mypane = ZedGraphControl2.GraphPane
        mycurve2 = mypane.AddCurve("IO2", list2, Color.Red, SymbolType.None)
        Graph(ZedGraphControl2, ZedGraphControl2.GraphPane, mycurve2, "EEG
2", 50)


        mypane = ZedGraphControl3.GraphPane
        mycurve3 = mypane.AddCurve("IO3", list3, Color.Red, SymbolType.None)
        Graph(ZedGraphControl3, ZedGraphControl3.GraphPane, mycurve3, "EEG
3", 50)


        mypane = ZedGraphControl4.GraphPane
        mycurve4 = mypane.AddCurve("IO4", list4, Color.Red, SymbolType.None)
        Graph(ZedGraphControl4, ZedGraphControl4.GraphPane, mycurve4, "EEG
4", 50)


        mypane = ZedGraphControl5.GraphPane
        mycurve5 = mypane.AddCurve("IO5", list5, Color.Red, SymbolType.None)
        Graph(ZedGraphControl5, ZedGraphControl5.GraphPane, mycurve5, "EEG
5", 50)


        mypane = ZedGraphControl6.GraphPane
        mycurve6 = mypane.AddCurve("IO6", list5, Color.Red, SymbolType.None)
        Graph(ZedGraphControl6, ZedGraphControl6.GraphPane, mycurve6, "EEG
6", 50)


        mypane = ZedGraphControl7.GraphPane
        mycurve7 = mypane.AddCurve("IO7", list7, Color.Red, SymbolType.None)
        Graph(ZedGraphControl7, ZedGraphControl7.GraphPane, mycurve7, "EEG
7", 50)


        mypane = ZedGraphControl8.GraphPane
        mycurve8 = mypane.AddCurve("IO8", list8, Color.Red, SymbolType.None)
        Graph(ZedGraphControl8, ZedGraphControl8.GraphPane, mycurve8, "EEG
8", 50)
```

```
ZedGraphControl1.GraphPane.Title.Text = PatientDetailForm.EEGName1
ZedGraphControl2.GraphPane.Title.Text = PatientDetailForm.EEGName2
ZedGraphControl3.GraphPane.Title.Text = PatientDetailForm.EEGName3
ZedGraphControl4.GraphPane.Title.Text = PatientDetailForm.EEGName4
ZedGraphControl5.GraphPane.Title.Text = PatientDetailForm.EEGName5
ZedGraphControl6.GraphPane.Title.Text = PatientDetailForm.EEGName6
ZedGraphControl7.GraphPane.Title.Text = PatientDetailForm.EEGName7
ZedGraphControl8.GraphPane.Title.Text = PatientDetailForm.EEGName8

table.Columns.Item(2).HeaderText = PatientDetailForm.EEGName1
table.Columns.Item(3).HeaderText = PatientDetailForm.EEGName2
table.Columns.Item(4).HeaderText = PatientDetailForm.EEGName3
table.Columns.Item(5).HeaderText = PatientDetailForm.EEGName4
table.Columns.Item(6).HeaderText = PatientDetailForm.EEGName5
table.Columns.Item(7).HeaderText = PatientDetailForm.EEGName6
table.Columns.Item(8).HeaderText = PatientDetailForm.EEGName7
table.Columns.Item(9).HeaderText = PatientDetailForm.EEGName8
End Sub


'Public Sub loadaddress()
'    Dim FILE_NAME As String = Application.StartupPath + "\address.txt"
'    Dim T(10) As String
'    Dim i As Integer = 0
'    If System.IO.File.Exists(FILE_NAME) = True Then
'        Dim objReader As New System.IO.StreamReader(FILE_NAME)
'        Do While i <> 10
'            T(i) = objReader.ReadLine()
'            address(i) = T(i)
'            i = i + 1
'        Loop
'        objReader.Close()
'    Else
'        MessageBox.Show(Me, "File 'address.txt' Does Not Exist",
"Error", MessageBoxButtons.OK, MessageBoxIcon.Error)
'    End If
'End Sub


Public Sub setgraph(ByVal zed As ZedGraphControl, ByVal mypane As
GraphPane, ByVal mycurve As LineItem, ByVal adc As String, ByVal range As
Integer)
    mypane.Title.Text = adc + " vs Time"
    mypane.YAxis.Title.Text = adc
    mycurve.Label.Text = adc
    mypane.YAxis.Scale.Max = range
End Sub


Public Sub Graph(ByVal zed As ZedGraphControl, ByVal mypane As GraphPane,
ByVal mycurve As LineItem, ByVal ADC As String, ByVal range As Integer)
    'Dim myPane As GraphPane = ZedGraphControl1.GraphPane
    mypane.Title.FontSpec.FontColor = Color.Black
    mypane.Legend.Position = ZedGraph.LegendPos.Bottom
    mypane.Legend.FontSpec.Size = 16
    mypane.Legend.FontSpec.IsBold = True
    'myPane.CurveList.Clear()
    mypane.Title.Text = ADC + " vs Time"
    mypane.XAxis.Title.Text = "Time"
```

```
        mypane.YAxis.Title.Text = ADC
        set_scale(mypane, range)

        'myCurve = myPane.AddCurve("ADC1", list1, Color.Red, SymbolType.None)
        'set_line(myCurve)
        mycurve.Label.Text = ADC
        set_line(mycurve)

        zed.IsAutoScrollRange = False
        zed.IsShowHScrollBar = True
        zed.IsSynchronizeXAxes = True
        zed.IsSynchronizeYAxes = True
        'ZedGraphControl1.IsAntiAlias = True
        zed.Refresh()
        zed.AxisChange()
    End Sub


    Private Sub set_scale(ByVal grph As GraphPane, ByVal range As Integer)
        With grph
            .XAxis.Title.Text = "Time"
            .XAxis.Type = AxisType.Date
            .XAxis.Scale.Format = "HH:mm:ss"
            .XAxis.Scale.MajorUnit = DateUnit.Hour
            .XAxis.Scale.MinorUnit = DateUnit.Second
            .XAxis.Scale.MinorStep = 1
            '.XAxis.Scale.MajorStep = 1
            '.XAxis.Scale.Min = New XDate(DateTime.Now)
            '.XAxis.Scale.Max = New XDate(DateTime.Now.AddHours(24))
            '.XAxis.MajorTic.IsBetweenLabels = True
            '.XAxis.MinorTic.Size = 0
            '.XAxis.MajorTic.IsInside = False
            '.XAxis.MajorTic.IsOutside = True
            .XAxis.Scale.FontSpec.IsBold = True
            .XAxis.Scale.FontSpec.Size = 14
            '.XAxis.Scale.Min = 0
            '.XAxis.Scale.Max = 100
            .YAxis.Scale.Min = -5
            .YAxis.Scale.Max = range
            '.YAxis.Scale.MajorStep = 10
            .YAxis.Scale.MinorStep = 1
            .Title.FontSpec.Size = 18

            .Title.FontSpec.IsBold = True
            .YAxis.Scale.FontSpec.IsBold = True
            .YAxis.Scale.FontSpec.Size = 14
        End With
    End Sub


    Private Sub set_line(ByVal lne As LineItem)
        With lne.Line
            ''.IsAntiAlias = True
            .IsSmooth = True
            .Width = 2.0
        End With
    End Sub
```

19.A.3.2 *Receive the data from serial port in a string format*

```
Private Sub SerialPort1_DataReceived1(ByVal sender As Object, ByVal e As
System.IO.Ports.SerialDataReceivedEventArgs) Handles SerialPort1.DataReceived
        Dim str As String = SerialPort1.ReadExisting
        System.Windows.Forms.Form.CheckForIllegalCrossThreadCalls = False
        'Display(str)
        'Dim str1 As String
        'str1 = StrToHex(str)
        'TextBox7.AppendText(str)
        ReceivedString = ReceivedString + StrToHex(str)
        Dim t As String
        Dim Len As Integer = 100
        Dim iii As Integer = ReceivedString.IndexOf("7E")
        If run Then
            If (iii >= 0) Then
                If (ReceivedString.Substring(iii).Length >= 6) Then
                    Dim tempstr As String = ReceivedString.Substring(iii)
                    If tempstr.StartsWith("7E") Then
                        Len = Integer.Parse(ReceivedString.Substring(iii + 2, 4),
Globalization.NumberStyles.HexNumber) + 4
                    Else
                        ReceivedString = ""
                        Exit Sub
                    End If
                End If
                If (ReceivedString.Substring(iii).Length >= Len * 2) Then
                    Display(ReceivedString.Substring(iii, Len * 2))
                    ReceivedString = ""
                    Len = 100
                End If
                If (ReceivedString.Length > 200) Then ReceivedString = ""
            End If
        End If
    End Sub
```

19.A.3.3 *Break the data to get analog data to display and plot the values (eight channels)*

```
        Public Sub Display(ByVal ReceivedString As String)
        CheckForIllegalCrossThreadCalls = False
        Dim addstring As String = ""
        addstring = ReceivedString.Substring(16, 8)
        If addstring = PatientDetailForm.MacAddress1 Then
            Try
                ADC1 = (CDbl(Long.Parse(ReceivedString.Substring(38, 4),
Globalization.NumberStyles.HexNumber)) * 1.2) / 1023
                ADC2 = (CDbl(Long.Parse(ReceivedString.Substring(42, 4),
Globalization.NumberStyles.HexNumber)) * 1.2) / 1023
                ADC3 = (CDbl(Long.Parse(ReceivedString.Substring(46, 4),
Globalization.NumberStyles.HexNumber)) * 1.2) / 1023
                ADC4 = (CDbl(Long.Parse(ReceivedString.Substring(50, 4),
Globalization.NumberStyles.HexNumber)) * 1.2) / 1023
            Catch
            End Try
        ElseIf addstring = PatientDetailForm.MacAddress2 Then
            Try
                ADC5 = (CDbl(Long.Parse(ReceivedString.Substring(38, 4),
Globalization.NumberStyles.HexNumber)) * 1.2) / 1023
```

```
                ADC6 = (CDbl(Long.Parse(ReceivedString.Substring(42, 4),
Globalization.NumberStyles.HexNumber)) * 1.2) / 1023
                ADC7 = (CDbl(Long.Parse(ReceivedString.Substring(46, 4),
Globalization.NumberStyles.HexNumber)) * 1.2) / 1023
                ADC8 = (CDbl(Long.Parse(ReceivedString.Substring(50, 4),
Globalization.NumberStyles.HexNumber)) * 1.2) / 1023
            Catch
            End Try
        End If

        If log Then
            storetosql(ADC1, ADC2, ADC3, ADC4, ADC5, ADC6, ADC7, ADC8)
        End If
        Dim temp As String = Format(DateTime.Now, "yyyy-MM-dd HH:mm:ss").
ToString
        Try
            If Me.InvokeRequired Then
                Me.BeginInvoke(New invokedelegate(AddressOf tablefill))
            Else
                table.Rows.Add(temp.Substring(0, 10), temp.Substring(10),
ADC1.ToString("000.000"), ADC2.ToString("000.000"), ADC3.ToString("000.000"),
ADC4.ToString("000.000"), ADC5.ToString("000.000"), ADC6.ToString("000.000"),
ADC7.ToString("000.000"), ADC8.ToString("000.000"))
            End If
            Dim tt As XDate = New XDate(DateTime.Now)
            list1.Add(CDbl(tt), CDbl(ADC1))
            list2.Add(CDbl(tt), CDbl(ADC2))
            list3.Add(CDbl(tt), CDbl(ADC3))
            list4.Add(CDbl(tt), CDbl(ADC4))
            list5.Add(CDbl(tt), CDbl(ADC5))
            list6.Add(CDbl(tt), CDbl(ADC6))
            list7.Add(CDbl(tt), CDbl(ADC7))
            list8.Add(CDbl(tt), CDbl(ADC8))
            ZedGraphControl1.AxisChange()
            ZedGraphControl1.Refresh()
            ZedGraphControl2.AxisChange()
            ZedGraphControl2.Refresh()
            ZedGraphControl3.AxisChange()
            ZedGraphControl3.Refresh()
            ZedGraphControl4.AxisChange()
            ZedGraphControl4.Refresh()
            ZedGraphControl5.AxisChange()
            ZedGraphControl5.Refresh()
            ZedGraphControl6.AxisChange()
            ZedGraphControl6.Refresh()
            ZedGraphControl7.AxisChange()
            ZedGraphControl7.Refresh()
            ZedGraphControl8.AxisChange()
            ZedGraphControl8.Refresh()
        Catch ex As Exception
        End Try
    End Sub


    Public Sub tablefill()
        CheckForIllegalCrossThreadCalls = False
        Dim temp As String = Format(DateTime.Now, "yyyy-MM-dd HH:mm:ss").
ToString
```

```
        table.Rows.Add(temp.Substring(0, 10), temp.Substring(10), ADC1.
ToString("000.000"), ADC2.ToString("000.000"), ADC3.ToString("000.000"),
ADC4.ToString("000.000"), ADC5.ToString("000.000"), ADC6.ToString("000.000"),
ADC7.ToString("000.000"), ADC8.ToString("000.000"))
    End Sub
```

19.A.3.4 *Stores the data over MySQL DBMS to localhost (local PC)*

```
        Private Sub storetosql(ByVal a1 As Double, ByVal a2 As Double, ByVal
a3 As Double, ByVal a4 As Double, ByVal a5 As Double, ByVal a6 As Double,
ByVal a7 As Double, ByVal a8 As Double)
        OleDbConnection = New MySqlConnection
        OleDbConnection.ConnectionString = PatientDetailForm.
SQLConnectionString '"Database=vga;Data Source=localhost;User
Id=root;Password=parmar;Allow User Variables=True;"
        Try
            OleDbConnection.Open()
            Dim dt As String = Format(DateTime.Now, "yyyy-MM-dd HH:mm:ss").
ToString()
            Dim sql As String = "insert into EEG(datetime, ID, Data1, Data2,
Data3, Data4, Data5, Data6, Data7, Data8) values('" & dt & "'," & PatientID &
"," & a1.ToString("0.00") & "," & a2.ToString("0.00") & "," &
a3.ToString("0.00") & "," & a4.ToString("0.00") & "," & a5.ToString("0.00") &
"," & a6.ToString("0.00") & "," & a7.ToString("0.00") & "," &
a8.ToString("0.00") & ");"
            Dim objCmd As New MySqlCommand
            objCmd = New MySqlCommand(sql, OleDbConnection)
            objCmd.ExecuteReader()
        Catch ex As Exception
            MessageBox.Show(Me, ex.Message, "Error", MessageBoxButtons.OK,
MessageBoxIcon.Error)
            log = 0
            LoggingMenu.Image = My.Resources.log_start
            LoggingMenu.Text = "Start &Logging"
        End Try
        OleDbConnection.Close()
    End Sub
```

19.A.4 SearchForm.vb—Search the old data stores over MySQL DBMS of specific data and time

19.A.4.1 *Initial Settings*

```
        Private Sub Form4_Load(ByVal sender As System.Object, ByVal e As
System.EventArgs) Handles MyBase.Load
        mypane = ZedGraphControl1.GraphPane
        myCurve1 = mypane.AddCurve("IO1", list1, Color.Red, SymbolType.None)
        Graph(ZedGraphControl1, ZedGraphControl1.GraphPane, myCurve1, "IO1", 50)

        mypane = ZedGraphControl2.GraphPane
        myCurve2 = mypane.AddCurve("IO2", list2, Color.Red, SymbolType.None)
        Graph(ZedGraphControl2, ZedGraphControl2.GraphPane, myCurve2, "IO2", 50)

        mypane = ZedGraphControl3.GraphPane
        myCurve3 = mypane.AddCurve("IO3", list3, Color.Red, SymbolType.None)
        Graph(ZedGraphControl3, ZedGraphControl3.GraphPane, myCurve3, "IO3", 50)

        mypane = ZedGraphControl4.GraphPane
```

```
        myCurve4 = mypane.AddCurve("IO4", list4, Color.Red, SymbolType.None)
        Graph(ZedGraphControl4, ZedGraphControl4.GraphPane, myCurve4, "IO4", 50)

        mypane = ZedGraphControl5.GraphPane
        myCurve5 = mypane.AddCurve("IO5", list5, Color.Red, SymbolType.None)
        Graph(ZedGraphControl5, ZedGraphControl5.GraphPane, myCurve5, "IO5", 50)

        mypane = ZedGraphControl6.GraphPane
        myCurve6 = mypane.AddCurve("IO6", list6, Color.Red, SymbolType.None)
        Graph(ZedGraphControl6, ZedGraphControl6.GraphPane, myCurve6, "IO6", 50)

        mypane = ZedGraphControl7.GraphPane
        myCurve7 = mypane.AddCurve("IO7", list7, Color.Red, SymbolType.None)
        Graph(ZedGraphControl7, ZedGraphControl7.GraphPane, myCurve7, "IO7", 50)

        mypane = ZedGraphControl8.GraphPane
        myCurve8 = mypane.AddCurve("IO8", list8, Color.Red, SymbolType.None)
        Graph(ZedGraphControl8, ZedGraphControl8.GraphPane, myCurve8, "IO8", 50)

        fromdatebox.Text = ""
        todatebox.Text = ""
        filterbox.Items.Add("Data/Second")
        filterbox.Items.Add("Data/Minute")
        filterbox.Items.Add("Data/Hour")
        filterbox.Items.Add("Data/Day")
        filterbox.SelectedIndex = 0

        TabPage2.Text = PatientDetailForm.EEGName1
        TabPage3.Text = PatientDetailForm.EEGName2
        TabPage4.Text = PatientDetailForm.EEGName3
        TabPage5.Text = PatientDetailForm.EEGName4
        TabPage6.Text = PatientDetailForm.EEGName5
        TabPage7.Text = PatientDetailForm.EEGName6
        TabPage8.Text = PatientDetailForm.EEGName7
        TabPage9.Text = PatientDetailForm.EEGName8

        table.Columns.Item(2).HeaderText = PatientDetailForm.EEGName1
        table.Columns.Item(3).HeaderText = PatientDetailForm.EEGName2
        table.Columns.Item(4).HeaderText = PatientDetailForm.EEGName3
        table.Columns.Item(5).HeaderText = PatientDetailForm.EEGName4
        table.Columns.Item(6).HeaderText = PatientDetailForm.EEGName5
        table.Columns.Item(7).HeaderText = PatientDetailForm.EEGName6
        table.Columns.Item(8).HeaderText = PatientDetailForm.EEGName7
        table.Columns.Item(9).HeaderText = PatientDetailForm.EEGName8
    End Sub

    Public Sub Graph(ByVal zed As ZedGraphControl, ByVal mypane As GraphPane,
ByVal mycurve As LineItem, ByVal ADC As String, ByVal range As Integer)
        mypane.Title.FontSpec.FontColor = Color.Black
        myPane.Legend.Position = ZedGraph.LegendPos.Bottom
        myPane.Legend.FontSpec.Size = 16
        myPane.Legend.FontSpec.IsBold = True
        'myPane.CurveList.Clear()
        mypane.Title.Text = ADC + " vs Time"
        mypane.XAxis.Title.Text = "Time"
        mypane.YAxis.Title.Text = ADC
        set_scale(mypane, range)

        'myCurve = myPane.AddCurve("ADC1", list1, Color.Red, SymbolType.None)
```

```
        'set_line(myCurve)
        mycurve.Label.Text = ADC
        set_line(mycurve)

        zed.IsAutoScrollRange = False
        zed.IsShowHScrollBar = True
        zed.IsSynchronizeXAxes = True
        zed.IsSynchronizeYAxes = True
        'ZedGraphControl1.IsAntiAlias = True
        zed.Refresh()
        zed.AxisChange()
    End Sub


    Private Sub set_scale(ByVal grph As GraphPane, ByVal range As Integer)
        With grph
            .XAxis.Title.Text = "Time"
            .XAxis.Type = AxisType.Date
            .XAxis.Scale.Format = "HH:mm:ss"
            .XAxis.Scale.MajorUnit = DateUnit.Hour
            .XAxis.Scale.MinorUnit = DateUnit.Second
            .XAxis.Scale.MinorStep = 1
            '.XAxis.Scale.MajorStep = 1
            '.XAxis.Scale.Min = New XDate(DateTime.Now)
            '.XAxis.Scale.Max = New XDate(DateTime.Now.AddHours(24))
            '.XAxis.MajorTic.IsBetweenLabels = True
            '.XAxis.MinorTic.Size = 0
            '.XAxis.MajorTic.IsInside = False
            '.XAxis.MajorTic.IsOutside = True
            .XAxis.Scale.FontSpec.IsBold = True
            .XAxis.Scale.FontSpec.Size = 14
            '.XAxis.Scale.Min = 0
            '.XAxis.Scale.Max = 100
            .YAxis.Scale.Min = -5
            .YAxis.Scale.Max = range
            '.YAxis.Scale.MajorStep = 10
            .YAxis.Scale.MinorStep = 1
            .Title.FontSpec.Size = 18

            .Title.FontSpec.IsBold = True
            .YAxis.Scale.FontSpec.IsBold = True
            .YAxis.Scale.FontSpec.Size = 14
        End With
    End Sub

    Private Sub set_line(ByVal lne As LineItem)
        With lne.Line
            ''.IsAntiAlias = True
            .IsSmooth = True
            .Width = 2.0
        End With
    End Sub


    Public Sub setgraph(ByVal zed As ZedGraphControl, ByVal mypane As
GraphPane, ByVal mycurve As LineItem, ByVal adc As String, ByVal range As
Integer)
        mypane.Title.Text = adc + " vs Time"
        mypane.YAxis.Title.Text = adc
```

```
        mycurve.Label.Text = adc
        mypane.YAxis.Scale.Max = range
    End Sub
```

19.A.4.2 *Select the data of date entered by user and display it in graphical and tabular format*

```
        Private Sub SearchButton_Click(ByVal sender As System.Object,
ByVal e As System.EventArgs) Handles SearchButton.Click

        Dim ttemp1 As String = ""
        Dim ttemp2 As String = ""
        Dim dtemp1 As String = ""
        Dim dtemp2 As String = ""

        Try
            dtemp1 = DateTime.Parse(fromdatebox.Text).ToString("yyyy-MM-dd")
            dtemp2 = DateTime.Parse(todatebox.Text).ToString("yyyy-MM-dd")
            If fromtxtbox.Text <> "  :  :" Then DateTime.Parse(fromtxtbox.
Text)
            If totxtbox.Text <> "  :  :" Then DateTime.Parse(totxtbox.Text)
        Catch
            MessageBox.Show(Me, "Please enter valid date and time", "Invalid
Expression", MessageBoxButtons.OK, MessageBoxIcon.Error)
            Exit Sub
        End Try

        If totxtbox.Text = "  :  :" Then
            ttemp2 = " 23:59:59"
        Else
            ttemp2 = " " + totxtbox.Text
        End If

        If fromtxtbox.Text = "  :  :" Then
            ttemp1 = " 00:00:00"
        Else
            ttemp1 = " " + fromtxtbox.Text
        End If

        Try
            'Dim filter As String = "0"
            If filterbox.SelectedIndex = 0 Then
                sql1 = "select * from EEG where datetime>='" + dtemp1 + ttemp1 +
"' and datetime<='" + dtemp2 + ttemp2 + "'"
            ElseIf filterbox.SelectedIndex = 1 Then
                sql1 = "select * from EEG where datetime>='" + dtemp1 + ttemp1 +
"' and datetime<='" + dtemp2 + ttemp2 + "' and second(time(datetime))=0"
            ElseIf filterbox.SelectedIndex = 2 Then
                sql1 = "select * from EEG where datetime>='" + dtemp1 + ttemp1 +
"' and datetime<='" + dtemp2 + ttemp2 + "' and minute(time(datetime))=0 and
second(time(datetime))=0"
            ElseIf filterbox.SelectedIndex = 3 Then
                sql1 = "select * from EEG where datetime>='" + dtemp1 + ttemp1 +
"' and datetime<='" + dtemp2 + ttemp2 + "'"
            End If

            If filterbox.SelectedIndex = 3 Then
                sql1 += " and ID like '" + EEGForm.PatientID.ToString + "'
group by date(datetime);"
```

```
                Else
                sql1 += " and ID like '" + EEGForm.PatientID.ToString + "';"
                End If

        Catch ex As Exception
                MessageBox.Show(Me, ex.Message, "Error", MessageBoxButtons.OK,
MessageBoxIcon.Error)
        End Try
        Dim fromstring As String = ""
        Dim tostring As String = ""
        Try
                fromstring = dtemp1.Substring(8, 2) + " " + MonthName(dtemp1.
Substring(5, 2)) + " " + dtemp1.Substring(0, 4)
                tostring = dtemp2.Substring(8, 2) + " " + MonthName(dtemp2.
Substring(5, 2)) + " " + dtemp2.Substring(0, 4)
        Catch
        End Try

        If dtemp1 = dtemp2 Then
                ZedGraphControl1.GraphPane.Title.Text = fromstring
                ZedGraphControl2.GraphPane.Title.Text = fromstring
                ZedGraphControl3.GraphPane.Title.Text = fromstring
                ZedGraphControl4.GraphPane.Title.Text = fromstring
                ZedGraphControl5.GraphPane.Title.Text = fromstring
                ZedGraphControl6.GraphPane.Title.Text = fromstring
                ZedGraphControl7.GraphPane.Title.Text = fromstring
                ZedGraphControl8.GraphPane.Title.Text = fromstring
        Else
                ZedGraphControl1.GraphPane.Title.Text = fromstring + " - " +
tostring
                ZedGraphControl2.GraphPane.Title.Text = fromstring + " - " +
tostring
                ZedGraphControl3.GraphPane.Title.Text = fromstring + " - " +
tostring
                ZedGraphControl4.GraphPane.Title.Text = fromstring + " - " +
tostring
                ZedGraphControl5.GraphPane.Title.Text = fromstring + " - " +
tostring
                ZedGraphControl6.GraphPane.Title.Text = fromstring + " - " +
tostring
                ZedGraphControl7.GraphPane.Title.Text = fromstring + " - " +
tostring
                ZedGraphControl8.GraphPane.Title.Text = fromstring + " - " +
tostring
        End If

        table.Rows.Clear()
        list1.Clear()
        list2.Clear()
        list3.Clear()
        list4.Clear()
        list5.Clear()
        list6.Clear()
        list7.Clear()
        list8.Clear()
        OleDbConnection = New MySqlConnection
        OleDbConnection.ConnectionString = PatientDetailForm.
SQLConnectionString  '"Database=vga;Data Source=localhost;User
Id=root;Password=parmar;Allow User Variables=True;"
```

```
        If dtemp1 <> dtemp2 Then
            ZedGraphControl1.GraphPane.XAxis.Scale.Format = "dd/MM/yyyy
HH:mm:ss"
            ZedGraphControl2.GraphPane.XAxis.Scale.Format = "dd/MM/yyyy
HH:mm:ss"
            ZedGraphControl3.GraphPane.XAxis.Scale.Format = "dd/MM/yyyy
HH:mm:ss"
            ZedGraphControl4.GraphPane.XAxis.Scale.Format = "dd/MM/yyyy
HH:mm:ss"
            ZedGraphControl5.GraphPane.XAxis.Scale.Format = "dd/MM/yyyy
HH:mm:ss"
            ZedGraphControl6.GraphPane.XAxis.Scale.Format = "dd/MM/yyyy
HH:mm:ss"
            ZedGraphControl7.GraphPane.XAxis.Scale.Format = "dd/MM/yyyy
HH:mm:ss"
            ZedGraphControl8.GraphPane.XAxis.Scale.Format = "dd/MM/yyyy
HH:mm:ss"
        Else
            ZedGraphControl1.GraphPane.XAxis.Scale.Format = "HH:mm:ss"
            ZedGraphControl2.GraphPane.XAxis.Scale.Format = "HH:mm:ss"
            ZedGraphControl3.GraphPane.XAxis.Scale.Format = "HH:mm:ss"
            ZedGraphControl4.GraphPane.XAxis.Scale.Format = "HH:mm:ss"
            ZedGraphControl5.GraphPane.XAxis.Scale.Format = "HH:mm:ss"
            ZedGraphControl6.GraphPane.XAxis.Scale.Format = "HH:mm:ss"
            ZedGraphControl7.GraphPane.XAxis.Scale.Format = "HH:mm:ss"
            ZedGraphControl8.GraphPane.XAxis.Scale.Format = "HH:mm:ss"
        End If
        LoadingProgressBar.Style = ProgressBarStyle.Marquee
        LoadingProgressBar.MarqueeAnimationSpeed = 30
        WaitPanel.Visible = True
        SearchThread = New Thread(AddressOf Search)
        SearchThread.IsBackground = True
        SearchThread.Start()
    End Sub


    Dim SearchThread As Thread
    Private Sub Search()
        CheckForIllegalCrossThreadCalls = False
        Try
            OleDbConnection.Open()
            Dim objCmd As New MySqlCommand
            objCmd = New MySqlCommand(sql1, OleDbConnection)
            objCmd.CommandTimeout = 0
            reader = objCmd.ExecuteReader()
            While reader.Read
                If Me.InvokeRequired Then Me.Invoke(New
UpdateUIDelegate(AddressOf UpdateUI))
            End While
        Catch ex As Exception
        End Try
        OleDbConnection.Close()
        ZedGraphControl1.AxisChange()
        ZedGraphControl1.Refresh()
        ZedGraphControl2.AxisChange()
        ZedGraphControl2.Refresh()
        ZedGraphControl3.AxisChange()
        ZedGraphControl3.Refresh()
        ZedGraphControl4.AxisChange()
```

```
        ZedGraphControl4.Refresh()
        ZedGraphControl5.AxisChange()
        ZedGraphControl5.Refresh()
        ZedGraphControl6.AxisChange()
        ZedGraphControl6.Refresh()
        ZedGraphControl7.AxisChange()
        ZedGraphControl7.Refresh()
        ZedGraphControl8.AxisChange()
        ZedGraphControl8.Refresh()
        WaitPanel.Visible = False
    End Sub


    Private Delegate Sub UpdateUIDelegate()
    Private Sub UpdateUI()
        table.Rows.Add(DateTime.Parse(reader.GetString(0)).ToString("yyyy-
MM-dd"), DateTime.Parse(reader.GetString(0)).ToString("HH:mm:ss"), reader.
GetString(2), reader.GetString(3), reader.GetString(4), reader.GetString(5),
reader.GetString(6), reader.GetString(7), reader.GetString(8), reader.
GetString(9))
        Dim tt As DateTime
        If fromtxtbox.Text <> totxtbox.Text Then
            tt = DateTime.Parse(reader.GetDateTime(0).ToString("yyyy-MM-dd
HH:mm:ss"))
        Else
            tt = DateTime.Parse(reader.GetDateTime(0).ToString("HH:mm:ss"))
        End If
        list1.Add(tt.ToOADate(), CDbl(reader.GetString(2)))
        list2.Add(tt.ToOADate(), CDbl(reader.GetString(3)))
        list3.Add(tt.ToOADate(), CDbl(reader.GetString(4)))
        list4.Add(tt.ToOADate(), CDbl(reader.GetString(5)))
        list5.Add(tt.ToOADate(), CDbl(reader.GetString(6)))
        list6.Add(tt.ToOADate(), CDbl(reader.GetString(7)))
        list7.Add(tt.ToOADate(), CDbl(reader.GetString(8)))
        list8.Add(tt.ToOADate(), CDbl(reader.GetString(9)))
    End Sub
```

19.A.5 Data Analysis

```
Dim ScanTime As Integer = 60
    Private Sub ScanTimeTextBox_TextChanged(ByVal sender As Object, ByVal e
As System.EventArgs) Handles ScanTimeTextBox.TextChanged
        Try
            ScanTime = CInt(ScanTimeTextBox.Text)
            If ScanTime < 10 Then Throw New Exception("Data not in range")
            ScanTimeTextBox.BackColor = Color.White
        Catch ex As Exception
            ScanTime = 60
            ScanTimeTextBox.BackColor = Color.Red
        End Try
    End Sub


    Dim ScanCount As Integer = 0
    Private Sub ScanTimer_Tick(ByVal sender As System.Object, ByVal e As
System.EventArgs) Handles ScanTimer.Tick
        ScanCount += 1
```

```
            If ScanCount >= ScanTime Then
                run = True
                StartStopMenu_Click(Nothing, Nothing)
            End If
            ScanProgressBar.Value = ScanCount
            TimeLabel.Text = ScanCount & " / " & ScanTime & " Second"
            TimeLabel.Left = ScanProgressBar.Right - TimeLabel.Width
            If ScanCount > 1 Then TimeLabel.Text += "s"
        End Sub



    Private Sub CalculateResult()
            Dim AverageCount As Integer = 0
            Dim TotalEEGEnabled As Integer = 0
            Dim TempEEGGraph As EEGGraph.EEGGraph
            For i = 1 To 8
                TempEEGGraph = CType(plot.Controls("EegGraph" & i), EEGGraph.
    EEGGraph)
                If TempEEGGraph.IsEnabled = True Then
                    AverageCount += TempEEGGraph.CountPercentage
                    TotalEEGEnabled += 1
                End If
            Next
            Dim EEGString As String = "EEG"
            If TotalEEGEnabled > 1 Then EEGString += "s"
            AverageCount = AverageCount / TotalEEGEnabled
            AverageCountLabel.Text = "Average Count (" & TotalEEGEnabled & " " +
    EEGString + ")" + Environment.NewLine & AverageCount & "%"
            AverageCountLabel.Left = ResultPanel.Width / 2 - AverageCountLabel.
    Width / 2
        End Sub



    Dim PreviousYValue As Double
        Dim xMin, xMax As Double
        Public Sub AddPoint(ByVal x As Double, ByVal y As Double)
            If x > ZedGraphControl1.GraphPane.XAxis.Scale.Max Then
                xMin = DateTime.Now.ToOADate()
                xMax = DateTime.Now.AddMinutes(1).ToOADate()
                ZedGraphControl1.GraphPane.XAxis.Scale.Min = xMin
                ZedGraphControl1.GraphPane.XAxis.Scale.Max = xMax
                LpThLineItem.Clear()
                LpThLineItem.AddPoint(ZedGraphControl1.GraphPane.XAxis.Scale.Min,
    LThUpDown.Value)
                LpThLineItem.AddPoint(ZedGraphControl1.GraphPane.XAxis.Scale.Max,
    LThUpDown.Value)
                UpThLineItem.Clear()
                UpThLineItem.AddPoint(ZedGraphControl1.GraphPane.XAxis.Scale.Min,
    UThUpDown.Value)
                UpThLineItem.AddPoint(ZedGraphControl1.GraphPane.XAxis.Scale.Max,
    UThUpDown.Value)
            End If
            'ZedGraphControl1.GraphPane.XAxis.Scale.Min = DateTime.Now.ToOADate()
            'ZedGraphControl1.GraphPane.XAxis.Scale.Max =
    DateTime.Now.AddMinutes(1).ToOADate()
            If (y >= UThUpDown.Value And PreviousYValue <= UThUpDown.Value) Or
    (y <= UThUpDown.Value And PreviousYValue >= UThUpDown.Value) Then
                Crossed += 1
```

```
        End If
        If (y >= LThUpDown.Value And PreviousYValue <= LThUpDown.Value) Or
(y <= LThUpDown.Value And PreviousYValue >= LThUpDown.Value) Then
            Crossed += 1
        End If
        CrossingLabel.Text = Crossed & " Crossings"
        MyLineItem.AddPoint(x, y)
        ZedGraphControl1.RestoreScale(ZedGraphControl1.GraphPane)
        ZedGraphControl1.GraphPane.XAxis.Scale.Format = "HH:mm:ss"
        ZedGraphControl1.GraphPane.XAxis.Scale.Min = xMin
        ZedGraphControl1.GraphPane.XAxis.Scale.Max = xMax
        ZedGraphControl1.Refresh()
        PreviousYValue = y
    End Sub
```

Appendix 19.B: Sensors Data

Date	Time	S1	S2	S3	S4	S5	S6	S7	S8
6/5/2016	21:54:00	0.833	0.052	0.12	0.07	0.673	0.629	0.606	0.643
6/5/2016	21:54:00	0.833	0.052	0.118	0.073	0.604	0.643	0.663	0.663
6/5/2016	21:54:01	0.833	0.049	0.116	0.069	0.603	0.644	0.663	0.659
6/5/2016	21:54:01	0.833	0.052	0.118	0.074	0.601	0.652	0.676	0.642
6/5/2016	21:54:01	0.833	0.052	0.118	0.073	0.664	0.678	0.633	0.596
6/5/2016	21:54:01	0.833	0.052	0.118	0.073	0.659	0.676	0.639	0.605
6/5/2016	21:54:02	0.833	0.052	0.12	0.069	0.692	0.637	0.617	0.624
6/5/2016	21:54:02	0.833	0.052	0.12	0.073	0.622	0.619	0.656	0.692
6/5/2016	21:54:02	0.833	0.052	0.121	0.074	0.653	0.672	0.643	0.609
6/5/2016	21:54:03	0.833	0.052	0.12	0.074	0.662	0.624	0.608	0.65
6/5/2016	21:54:03	0.834	0.052	0.121	0.074	0.619	0.658	0.684	0.632
6/5/2016	21:54:03	0.833	0.052	0.12	0.074	0.686	0.63	0.606	0.637
6/5/2016	21:54:03	0.833	0.052	0.12	0.074	0.599	0.651	0.673	0.644
6/5/2016	21:54:03	0.833	0.052	0.12	0.074	0.664	0.678	0.635	0.598
6/5/2016	21:54:04	0.833	0.052	0.118	0.073	0.658	0.623	0.61	0.651
6/5/2016	21:54:04	0.833	0.052	0.12	0.073	0.601	0.652	0.677	0.642
6/5/2016	21:54:04	0.833	0.052	0.12	0.072	0.696	0.637	0.613	0.628
6/5/2016	21:54:04	0.833	0.052	0.12	0.072	0.601	0.645	0.666	0.655
6/5/2016	21:54:05	0.833	0.05	0.12	0.073	0.684	0.643	0.618	0.611
6/5/2016	21:54:05	0.833	0.05	0.12	0.072	0.63	0.605	0.64	0.669
6/5/2016	21:54:05	0.834	0.05	0.12	0.072	0.624	0.66	0.682	0.629
6/5/2016	21:54:05	0.833	0.052	0.12	0.073	0.693	0.633	0.61	0.632
6/5/2016	21:54:06	0.833	0.052	0.12	0.073	0.605	0.642	0.663	0.664
6/5/2016	21:54:06	0.833	0.052	0.12	0.073	0.667	0.674	0.63	0.587
6/5/2016	21:54:06	0.833	0.052	0.118	0.073	0.633	0.608	0.638	0.665
6/5/2016	21:54:06	0.833	0.052	0.12	0.073	0.642	0.664	0.658	0.616
6/5/2016	21:54:07	0.833	0.052	0.12	0.073	0.694	0.637	0.615	0.628
6/5/2016	21:54:07	0.833	0.052	0.12	0.073	0.624	0.609	0.651	0.684
6/5/2016	21:54:07	0.833	0.052	0.12	0.073	0.653	0.674	0.642	0.608
6/5/2016	21:54:07	0.833	0.052	0.12	0.073	0.656	0.623	0.611	0.652
6/5/2016	21:54:08	0.834	0.052	0.12	0.073	0.609	0.656	0.682	0.637
6/5/2016	21:54:08	0.834	0.052	0.12	0.073	0.682	0.645	0.619	0.605
6/5/2016	21:54:08	0.833	0.052	0.12	0.074	0.625	0.606	0.649	0.682

(Continued)

Date	Time	S1	S2	S3	S4	S5	S6	S7	S8
6/5/2016	21:54:09	0.834	0.052	0.12	0.073	0.645	0.665	0.652	0.613
6/5/2016	21:54:09	0.834	0.052	0.12	0.073	0.692	0.633	0.611	0.632
6/5/2016	21:54:09	0.833	0.052	0.12	0.073	0.605	0.642	0.663	0.664
6/5/2016	21:54:09	0.833	0.052	0.118	0.073	0.673	0.657	0.623	0.587
6/5/2016	21:54:09	0.834	0.05	0.118	0.072	0.63	0.605	0.64	0.667
6/5/2016	21:54:10	0.833	0.053	0.121	0.072	0.646	0.666	0.65	0.612
6/5/2016	21:54:10	0.833	0.052	0.124	0.075	0.657	0.624	0.61	0.652
6/5/2016	21:54:10	0.833	0.05	0.124	0.076	0.628	0.66	0.68	0.626
6/5/2016	21:54:11	0.834	0.055	0.126	0.081	0.687	0.631	0.608	0.636
6/5/2016	21:54:11	0.834	0.055	0.126	0.081	0.601	0.644	0.665	0.656
6/5/2016	21:54:11	0.833	0.053	0.126	0.077	0.67	0.667	0.626	0.582
6/5/2016	21:54:11	0.834	0.053	0.127	0.076	0.629	0.603	0.644	0.672
6/5/2016	21:54:12	0.834	0.053	0.122	0.075	0.642	0.664	0.659	0.616
6/5/2016	21:54:12	0.834	0.053	0.122	0.075	0.665	0.625	0.606	0.648
6/5/2016	21:54:12	0.834	0.052	0.116	0.073	0.598	0.646	0.667	0.651
6/5/2016	21:54:12	0.833	0.059	0.122	0.063	0.69	0.642	0.617	0.618
6/5/2016	21:54:13	0.834	0.059	0.135	0.067	0.624	0.606	0.65	0.682
6/5/2016	21:54:13	0.833	0.059	0.134	0.072	0.655	0.674	0.642	0.606
6/5/2016	21:54:13	0.833	0.059	0.134	0.072	0.643	0.618	0.628	0.659
6/5/2016	21:54:13	0.833	0.057	0.13	0.074	0.635	0.662	0.672	0.622
6/5/2016	21:54:13	0.834	0.054	0.129	0.073	0.692	0.633	0.61	0.633
6/5/2016	21:54:14	0.834	0.054	0.13	0.07	0.656	0.624	0.611	0.652
6/5/2016	21:54:14	0.834	0.054	0.13	0.07	0.623	0.61	0.651	0.685
6/5/2016	21:54:14	0.833	0.055	0.129	0.073	0.677	0.65	0.622	0.599
6/5/2016	21:54:14	0.834	0.053	0.133	0.072	0.616	0.633	0.659	0.684
6/5/2016	21:54:15	0.834	0.057	0.126	0.07	0.657	0.674	0.64	0.606
6/5/2016	21:54:15	0.834	0.055	0.128	0.074	0.623	0.612	0.652	0.687
6/5/2016	21:54:15	0.834	0.055	0.129	0.072	0.652	0.67	0.644	0.61
6/5/2016	21:54:16	0.833	0.057	0.133	0.075	0.678	0.626	0.604	0.642
6/5/2016	21:54:16	0.834	0.06	0.128	0.072	0.615	0.635	0.659	0.683
6/5/2016	21:54:16	0.834	0.06	0.128	0.072	0.648	0.666	0.649	0.612
6/5/2016	21:54:16	0.834	0.055	0.128	0.073	0.635	0.61	0.636	0.664
6/5/2016	21:54:16	0.834	0.063	0.127	0.073	0.66	0.679	0.637	0.601
6/5/2016	21:54:17	0.834	0.049	0.129	0.07	0.638	0.613	0.633	0.662
6/5/2016	21:57:57	0.835	0.086	0.134	0.107	0.677	0.65	0.621	0.599
6/5/2016	21:57:58	0.835	0.087	0.133	0.107	0.622	0.615	0.653	0.691
6/5/2016	21:57:58	0.835	0.087	0.133	0.107	0.667	0.659	0.623	0.582
6/5/2016	21:57:58	0.835	0.087	0.134	0.107	0.617	0.629	0.658	0.687
6/5/2016	21:57:58	0.835	0.086	0.134	0.107	0.665	0.677	0.63	0.59
6/5/2016	21:57:58	0.835	0.087	0.134	0.107	0.642	0.617	0.628	0.66
6/5/2016	21:57:59	0.835	0.087	0.134	0.107	0.63	0.66	0.678	0.623
6/5/2016	21:57:59	0.835	0.087	0.134	0.107	0.652	0.622	0.612	0.655
6/5/2016	21:57:59	0.835	0.087	0.134	0.108	0.645	0.666	0.649	0.611
6/5/2016	21:57:59	0.835	0.087	0.134	0.107	0.645	0.619	0.623	0.658
6/5/2016	21:58:00	0.835	0.087	0.134	0.107	0.625	0.659	0.683	0.626
6/5/2016	21:58:00	0.835	0.087	0.134	0.107	0.679	0.628	0.602	0.64
6/5/2016	21:58:00	0.835	0.087	0.134	0.107	0.598	0.645	0.666	0.651
6/5/2016	21:58:00	0.835	0.086	0.134	0.107	0.67	0.666	0.624	0.581
6/5/2016	21:58:01	0.835	0.087	0.134	0.108	0.624	0.605	0.65	0.683
6/5/2016	21:58:01	0.835	0.087	0.134	0.108	0.644	0.664	0.651	0.612

(Continued)

Date	Time	S1	S2	S3	S4	S5	S6	S7	S8
6/5/2016	21:58:01	0.835	0.087	0.134	0.107	0.648	0.621	0.619	0.657
6/5/2016	21:58:01	0.835	0.087	0.134	0.107	0.635	0.66	0.672	0.619
6/5/2016	21:58:01	0.835	0.087	0.133	0.107	0.666	0.625	0.603	0.648
6/5/2016	21:58:02	0.835	0.087	0.134	0.107	0.612	0.656	0.684	0.633
6/5/2016	21:58:02	0.835	0.087	0.134	0.108	0.655	0.623	0.61	0.653
6/5/2016	21:58:02	0.835	0.087	0.134	0.107	0.638	0.662	0.666	0.617
6/5/2016	21:58:03	0.835	0.087	0.134	0.107	0.646	0.621	0.621	0.657
6/5/2016	21:58:03	0.835	0.087	0.134	0.107	0.633	0.66	0.673	0.621
6/5/2016	21:58:03	0.835	0.087	0.134	0.107	0.664	0.624	0.604	0.649
6/5/2016	21:58:03	0.835	0.087	0.134	0.107	0.615	0.657	0.684	0.632
6/5/2016	21:58:04	0.835	0.087	0.134	0.107	0.685	0.63	0.604	0.638
6/5/2016	21:58:04	0.835	0.086	0.134	0.108	0.598	0.649	0.672	0.643
6/5/2016	21:58:04	0.835	0.087	0.134	0.107	0.655	0.623	0.609	0.652
6/5/2016	21:58:04	0.835	0.087	0.134	0.107	0.597	0.648	0.669	0.648
6/5/2016	21:58:05	0.835	0.087	0.134	0.107	0.677	0.648	0.619	0.599
6/5/2016	21:58:05	0.835	0.087	0.134	0.107	0.618	0.626	0.658	0.69
6/5/2016	21:58:05	0.835	0.087	0.134	0.107	0.664	0.679	0.632	0.594
6/5/2016	21:58:05	0.835	0.087	0.134	0.107	0.623	0.606	0.65	0.684
6/5/2016	21:58:06	0.835	0.087	0.134	0.107	0.667	0.671	0.626	0.582
6/5/2016	21:58:06	0.835	0.087	0.134	0.107	0.625	0.604	0.648	0.679
6/5/2016	21:58:06	0.835	0.087	0.134	0.108	0.651	0.671	0.643	0.608
6/5/2016	21:58:07	0.836	0.087	0.133	0.107	0.649	0.621	0.618	0.657
6/5/2016	21:58:07	0.835	0.087	0.134	0.107	0.601	0.652	0.676	0.64
6/5/2016	21:58:07	0.835	0.087	0.134	0.107	0.693	0.636	0.612	0.628
6/5/2016	21:58:07	0.835	0.086	0.134	0.108	0.599	0.65	0.673	0.643
6/5/2016	21:58:07	0.835	0.087	0.134	0.107	0.687	0.631	0.605	0.637
6/5/2016	21:58:08	0.835	0.087	0.134	0.107	0.598	0.65	0.672	0.643
6/5/2016	21:58:08	0.835	0.087	0.133	0.107	0.673	0.628	0.602	0.645
6/5/2016	21:58:08	0.835	0.087	0.134	0.107	0.625	0.659	0.682	0.626
6/5/2016	21:58:09	0.835	0.087	0.134	0.107	0.656	0.623	0.609	0.652
6/5/2016	21:58:09	0.835	0.087	0.134	0.107	0.604	0.653	0.679	0.638
6/5/2016	21:58:09	0.835	0.087	0.134	0.107	0.679	0.629	0.602	0.642
6/5/2016	21:58:09	0.835	0.087	0.134	0.108	0.601	0.652	0.677	0.64
6/5/2016	21:58:10	0.835	0.087	0.133	0.107	0.685	0.643	0.617	0.615
6/5/2016	21:58:10	0.835	0.087	0.133	0.107	0.623	0.606	0.65	0.683
6/5/2016	21:58:10	0.835	0.087	0.134	0.107	0.662	0.679	0.635	0.598
6/5/2016	21:58:10	0.835	0.086	0.134	0.107	0.625	0.603	0.646	0.678
6/5/2016	21:58:11	0.836	0.087	0.134	0.107	0.669	0.666	0.624	0.581
6/5/2016	21:58:11	0.835	0.087	0.133	0.107	0.637	0.611	0.633	0.663
6/5/2016	21:58:11	0.835	0.087	0.133	0.107	0.643	0.664	0.653	0.612
6/5/2016	21:58:11	0.835	0.087	0.133	0.107	0.642	0.617	0.628	0.66
6/5/2016	21:58:12	0.835	0.087	0.133	0.107	0.663	0.678	0.631	0.591
6/5/2016	21:58:12	0.835	0.087	0.134	0.107	0.621	0.617	0.655	0.692
6/5/2016	21:58:12	0.835	0.087	0.134	0.107	0.677	0.65	0.621	0.599
6/5/2016	21:58:13	0.835	0.087	0.134	0.107	0.602	0.642	0.663	0.659
6/5/2016	21:58:13	0.835	0.087	0.134	0.107	0.67	0.664	0.624	0.581
6/5/2016	21:58:13	0.835	0.087	0.134	0.107	0.646	0.619	0.621	0.657
6/5/2016	21:58:13	0.835	0.087	0.134	0.107	0.629	0.659	0.679	0.624
6/5/2016	21:58:14	0.835	0.087	0.134	0.107	0.693	0.635	0.611	0.631
6/5/2016	21:58:14	0.835	0.087	0.133	0.107	0.615	0.632	0.659	0.683

(Continued)

Date	Time	S1	S2	S3	S4	S5	S6	S7	S8
6/5/2016	21:58:14	0.836	0.087	0.134	0.107	0.669	0.666	0.625	0.581
6/5/2016	21:58:14	0.836	0.087	0.134	0.108	0.631	0.604	0.639	0.667
6/5/2016	21:58:15	0.836	0.087	0.134	0.108	0.644	0.674	0.639	0.605
6/5/2016	21:58:15	0.835	0.086	0.134	0.107	0.632	0.608	0.637	0.665
6/5/2016	21:58:15	0.835	0.087	0.133	0.107	0.636	0.662	0.669	0.618
6/5/2016	21:58:15	0.835	0.088	0.135	0.106	0.651	0.622	0.613	0.655
6/5/2016	21:58:15	0.835	0.088	0.135	0.106	0.622	0.658	0.683	0.629
6/5/2016	21:58:16	0.835	0.087	0.134	0.107	0.672	0.653	0.621	0.588
6/5/2016	21:58:16	0.835	0.087	0.135	0.106	0.622	0.612	0.652	0.689
6/5/2016	21:58:16	0.836	0.087	0.134	0.106	0.663	0.678	0.632	0.594
6/5/2016	21:58:16	0.835	0.088	0.135	0.106	0.64	0.616	0.629	0.66
6/5/2016	21:58:17	0.836	0.089	0.134	0.106	0.638	0.662	0.664	0.617
6/5/2016	21:58:17	0.836	0.087	0.134	0.106	0.649	0.622	0.617	0.656
6/5/2016	21:58:17	0.835	0.088	0.135	0.107	0.629	0.659	0.679	0.625
6/5/2016	21:58:18	0.835	0.088	0.135	0.107	0.679	0.628	0.603	0.64
6/5/2016	21:58:18	0.836	0.088	0.134	0.102	0.599	0.65	0.672	0.643
6/5/2016	21:58:18	0.836	0.083	0.133	0.103	0.689	0.639	0.616	0.622
6/5/2016	21:58:18	0.835	0.083	0.134	0.106	0.619	0.624	0.657	0.691
6/5/2016	21:58:19	0.836	0.084	0.137	0.108	0.662	0.679	0.635	0.597
6/5/2016	21:58:19	0.836	0.084	0.137	0.108	0.623	0.611	0.652	0.687
6/5/2016	21:58:19	0.836	0.091	0.136	0.103	0.655	0.673	0.64	0.606
6/5/2016	21:58:35	0.836	0.083	0.136	0.103	0.673	0.626	0.602	0.644
6/5/2016	21:58:35	0.836	0.083	0.136	0.103	0.603	0.653	0.678	0.638
6/5/2016	21:58:36	0.836	0.084	0.136	0.103	0.692	0.636	0.612	0.628
6/5/2016	21:58:36	0.836	0.086	0.134	0.106	0.629	0.658	0.68	0.625
6/5/2016	21:58:36	0.836	0.087	0.135	0.104	0.638	0.613	0.631	0.662
6/5/2016	21:58:36	0.836	0.087	0.135	0.104	0.642	0.663	0.655	0.613
6/5/2016	21:58:37	0.836	0.089	0.134	0.104	0.685	0.629	0.604	0.637
6/5/2016	21:58:37	0.836	0.088	0.14	0.102	0.609	0.655	0.682	0.636
6/5/2016	21:58:37	0.836	0.087	0.14	0.1	0.69	0.632	0.606	0.635
6/5/2016	21:58:37	0.836	0.081	0.129	0.101	0.603	0.652	0.678	0.639
6/5/2016	21:59:03	0.836	0.086	0.135	0.104	0.669	0.656	0.622	0.584
6/5/2016	21:59:03	0.836	0.086	0.135	0.106	0.616	0.631	0.659	0.684
6/5/2016	21:59:03	0.836	0.086	0.135	0.106	0.671	0.659	0.623	0.584
6/5/2016	21:59:03	0.836	0.086	0.135	0.104	0.598	0.645	0.667	0.649
6/5/2016	21:59:04	0.836	0.086	0.135	0.104	0.692	0.635	0.61	0.631
6/5/2016	21:59:04	0.838	0.086	0.135	0.106	0.618	0.626	0.657	0.69
6/5/2016	21:59:04	0.836	0.086	0.135	0.104	0.673	0.652	0.621	0.594
6/5/2016	21:59:04	0.836	0.086	0.135	0.106	0.601	0.642	0.664	0.657
6/5/2016	21:59:05	0.836	0.086	0.135	0.104	0.691	0.638	0.615	0.625
6/5/2016	21:59:05	0.836	0.086	0.135	0.104	0.598	0.648	0.67	0.646
6/5/2016	21:59:05	0.836	0.086	0.136	0.106	0.689	0.639	0.616	0.621
6/5/2016	21:59:05	0.836	0.086	0.135	0.106	0.606	0.653	0.68	0.637
6/5/2016	21:59:06	0.836	0.086	0.135	0.104	0.656	0.623	0.609	0.652
6/5/2016	21:59:06	0.836	0.086	0.135	0.104	0.644	0.664	0.651	0.612
6/5/2016	21:59:06	0.836	0.086	0.135	0.104	0.625	0.604	0.648	0.679
6/5/2016	21:59:06	0.836	0.087	0.135	0.104	0.666	0.673	0.628	0.584
6/5/2016	21:59:06	0.836	0.086	0.135	0.104	0.605	0.64	0.663	0.662
6/5/2016	21:59:07	0.836	0.086	0.135	0.104	0.69	0.632	0.608	0.635
6/5/2016	21:59:07	0.836	0.086	0.135	0.104	0.598	0.648	0.67	0.646

(Continued)

Date	Time	S1	S2	S3	S4	S5	S6	S7	S8
6/5/2016	21:59:07	0.836	0.086	0.135	0.106	0.69	0.632	0.606	0.635
6/5/2016	21:59:07	0.836	0.087	0.135	0.104	0.598	0.648	0.67	0.646
6/5/2016	21:59:08	0.836	0.086	0.135	0.106	0.678	0.644	0.618	0.604
6/5/2016	21:59:08	0.836	0.086	0.135	0.106	0.617	0.63	0.659	0.686
6/5/2016	21:59:08	0.836	0.086	0.135	0.106	0.677	0.648	0.619	0.602
6/5/2016	21:59:08	0.836	0.086	0.135	0.104	0.626	0.602	0.644	0.673
6/5/2016	21:59:09	0.838	0.086	0.136	0.106	0.667	0.667	0.625	0.581
6/5/2016	21:59:09	0.836	0.086	0.135	0.104	0.602	0.642	0.664	0.657
6/5/2016	21:59:09	0.836	0.086	0.135	0.104	0.678	0.645	0.618	0.603
6/5/2016	21:59:09	0.836	0.086	0.135	0.106	0.617	0.629	0.658	0.687
6/5/2016	21:59:09	0.836	0.086	0.135	0.106	0.674	0.65	0.621	0.597
6/5/2016	21:59:10	0.838	0.087	0.135	0.104	0.612	0.636	0.66	0.677
6/5/2016	21:59:10	0.838	0.087	0.135	0.104	0.68	0.645	0.619	0.606
6/5/2016	21:59:10	0.836	0.086	0.135	0.106	0.692	0.635	0.609	0.632
6/5/2016	21:59:10	0.836	0.086	0.136	0.106	0.601	0.651	0.676	0.64
6/5/2016	21:59:11	0.836	0.086	0.135	0.104	0.686	0.631	0.604	0.637
6/5/2016	21:59:11	0.836	0.086	0.135	0.104	0.626	0.659	0.682	0.625
6/5/2016	21:59:11	0.836	0.086	0.135	0.104	0.69	0.632	0.608	0.633
6/5/2016	21:59:11	0.836	0.086	0.135	0.106	0.601	0.651	0.677	0.64
6/5/2016	21:59:12	0.836	0.086	0.135	0.104	0.652	0.622	0.612	0.655
6/5/2016	21:59:12	0.836	0.087	0.135	0.104	0.638	0.662	0.666	0.617
6/5/2016	21:59:12	0.836	0.087	0.135	0.104	0.648	0.621	0.619	0.657
6/5/2016	21:59:12	0.838	0.086	0.135	0.106	0.642	0.663	0.656	0.613
6/5/2016	21:59:12	0.836	0.086	0.135	0.104	0.669	0.625	0.603	0.646
6/5/2016	21:59:13	0.836	0.086	0.135	0.106	0.625	0.658	0.683	0.626
6/5/2016	21:59:13	0.838	0.086	0.135	0.104	0.649	0.621	0.617	0.657
6/5/2016	21:59:13	0.838	0.086	0.135	0.104	0.649	0.669	0.645	0.61
6/5/2016	21:59:13	0.838	0.086	0.135	0.106	0.621	0.622	0.656	0.691
6/5/2016	21:59:14	0.836	0.084	0.135	0.104	0.671	0.658	0.622	0.585
6/5/2016	21:59:14	0.838	0.086	0.134	0.106	0.622	0.613	0.653	0.69
6/5/2016	21:59:14	0.838	0.086	0.134	0.106	0.646	0.666	0.648	0.61
6/5/2016	21:59:14	0.838	0.087	0.135	0.106	0.645	0.619	0.623	0.658
6/5/2016	21:59:15	0.838	0.086	0.133	0.106	0.635	0.66	0.673	0.619
6/5/2016	21:59:15	0.836	0.086	0.137	0.106	0.642	0.617	0.628	0.66
6/5/2016	21:59:15	0.838	0.086	0.135	0.106	0.655	0.674	0.64	0.605
6/5/2016	21:59:15	0.838	0.086	0.135	0.106	0.625	0.603	0.646	0.678
6/5/2016	21:59:15	0.836	0.086	0.135	0.106	0.664	0.677	0.63	0.588
6/5/2016	21:59:16	0.836	0.084	0.133	0.107	0.623	0.606	0.651	0.685
6/5/2016	21:59:16	0.838	0.086	0.135	0.104	0.659	0.679	0.636	0.601
6/5/2016	21:59:16	0.838	0.086	0.135	0.104	0.637	0.611	0.633	0.663
6/5/2016	21:59:17	0.838	0.087	0.136	0.106	0.651	0.671	0.643	0.608
6/5/2016	21:59:17	0.838	0.086	0.135	0.104	0.619	0.624	0.657	0.691
6/5/2016	21:59:17	0.838	0.083	0.134	0.106	0.678	0.648	0.619	0.603
6/5/2016	21:59:17	0.838	0.086	0.135	0.106	0.61	0.637	0.662	0.672
6/5/2016	21:59:17	0.838	0.086	0.135	0.106	0.66	0.678	0.636	0.599
6/5/2016	21:59:18	0.838	0.084	0.131	0.108	0.651	0.621	0.612	0.655
6/5/2016	21:59:18	0.838	0.086	0.133	0.107	0.598	0.645	0.667	0.649
6/5/2016	21:59:18	0.836	0.087	0.137	0.106	0.685	0.63	0.604	0.637
6/5/2016	21:59:18	0.836	0.087	0.137	0.106	0.606	0.655	0.682	0.637
6/5/2016	21:59:19	0.838	0.086	0.135	0.107	0.692	0.637	0.613	0.628

(Continued)

Date	Time	S1	S2	S3	S4	S5	S6	S7	S8
6/5/2016	21:59:19	0.836	0.088	0.133	0.106	0.605	0.653	0.68	0.637
6/5/2016	21:59:19	0.836	0.088	0.135	0.107	0.684	0.63	0.603	0.638
6/5/2016	21:59:19	0.838	0.086	0.134	0.107	0.605	0.64	0.663	0.664
6/5/2016	21:59:20	0.838	0.086	0.134	0.107	0.673	0.652	0.621	0.592
6/5/2016	21:59:20	0.836	0.086	0.134	0.107	0.621	0.617	0.655	0.692
6/5/2016	21:59:20	0.838	0.086	0.134	0.106	0.658	0.677	0.638	0.602
6/5/2016	21:59:43	0.838	0.047	0.109	0.075	0.637	0.612	0.632	0.663
6/5/2016	21:59:43	0.838	0.049	0.109	0.076	0.642	0.664	0.653	0.612
6/5/2016	21:59:43	0.838	0.048	0.113	0.081	0.632	0.606	0.637	0.665
6/5/2016	21:59:44	0.838	0.048	0.113	0.081	0.663	0.679	0.631	0.591
6/5/2016	21:59:44	0.838	0.05	0.103	0.077	0.621	0.622	0.657	0.692
6/5/2016	21:59:44	0.838	0.043	0.103	0.069	0.69	0.64	0.617	0.622
6/5/2016	21:59:44	0.838	0.046	0.115	0.073	0.604	0.653	0.679	0.638
6/5/2016	21:59:45	0.838	0.047	0.122	0.072	0.683	0.629	0.602	0.638
6/5/2016	21:59:45	0.838	0.047	0.122	0.072	0.64	0.662	0.659	0.615
6/5/2016	21:59:45	0.838	0.043	0.116	0.066	0.63	0.604	0.639	0.669
6/5/2016	21:59:45	0.838	0.053	0.116	0.073	0.659	0.679	0.637	0.601
6/5/2016	21:59:45	0.838	0.046	0.116	0.075	0.636	0.61	0.635	0.663
6/5/2016	21:59:46	0.838	0.046	0.116	0.075	0.665	0.674	0.628	0.584
6/5/2016	21:59:46	0.838	0.052	0.115	0.062	0.628	0.602	0.643	0.672
6/5/2016	21:59:46	0.838	0.048	0.111	0.077	0.652	0.672	0.642	0.606
6/5/2016	21:59:46	0.838	0.047	0.115	0.077	0.633	0.608	0.636	0.665
6/5/2016	21:59:47	0.838	0.05	0.116	0.073	0.655	0.674	0.64	0.605
6/5/2016	21:59:47	0.838	0.05	0.116	0.073	0.646	0.619	0.621	0.658
6/5/2016	21:59:47	0.838	0.054	0.127	0.059	0.648	0.667	0.646	0.61
6/5/2016	21:59:47	0.838	0.041	0.106	0.063	0.624	0.605	0.649	0.682
6/5/2016	22:01:17	0.834	0.049	0.114	0.081	0.667	0.624	0.605	0.648
6/5/2016	22:01:17	0.834	0.048	0.114	0.08	0.596	0.646	0.667	0.651
6/5/2016	22:01:17	0.834	0.048	0.114	0.08	0.694	0.632	0.609	0.631
6/5/2016	22:01:17	0.835	0.048	0.113	0.081	0.608	0.656	0.683	0.637
6/5/2016	22:01:18	0.835	0.05	0.113	0.081	0.657	0.623	0.611	0.652
6/5/2016	22:01:18	0.835	0.05	0.114	0.081	0.626	0.66	0.682	0.626
6/5/2016	22:01:18	0.835	0.05	0.114	0.081	0.677	0.626	0.603	0.644
6/5/2016	22:01:18	0.834	0.05	0.113	0.081	0.596	0.648	0.67	0.648
6/5/2016	22:01:40	0.835	0.049	0.115	0.08	0.598	0.651	0.674	0.644
6/5/2016	22:01:40	0.835	0.049	0.115	0.08	0.679	0.649	0.621	0.597
6/5/2016	22:01:40	0.835	0.05	0.115	0.08	0.597	0.648	0.67	0.649
6/5/2016	22:01:41	0.835	0.048	0.114	0.08	0.685	0.644	0.618	0.608
6/5/2016	22:01:41	0.835	0.049	0.117	0.077	0.599	0.643	0.665	0.657
6/5/2016	22:01:41	0.835	0.049	0.117	0.077	0.69	0.642	0.617	0.615
6/5/2016	22:01:41	0.835	0.049	0.115	0.079	0.605	0.639	0.663	0.667
6/5/2016	22:01:42	0.835	0.049	0.115	0.079	0.673	0.658	0.624	0.584
6/5/2016	22:01:42	0.835	0.048	0.115	0.077	0.63	0.603	0.642	0.671
6/5/2016	22:01:42	0.835	0.049	0.115	0.079	0.658	0.678	0.639	0.603
6/5/2016	22:01:42	0.835	0.049	0.115	0.079	0.64	0.613	0.631	0.662
6/5/2016	22:01:42	0.835	0.05	0.115	0.079	0.655	0.674	0.642	0.606
6/5/2016	22:01:43	0.835	0.05	0.115	0.079	0.636	0.609	0.636	0.664
6/5/2016	22:01:43	0.835	0.049	0.115	0.079	0.651	0.671	0.645	0.609
6/5/2016	22:01:43	0.835	0.049	0.115	0.079	0.624	0.606	0.65	0.684
6/5/2016	22:01:43	0.835	0.05	0.114	0.079	0.665	0.679	0.632	0.591

(Continued)

Date	Time	S1	S2	S3	S4	S5	S6	S7	S8
6/5/2016	22:01:44	0.835	0.05	0.115	0.079	0.635	0.608	0.637	0.665
6/5/2016	22:01:44	0.835	0.049	0.115	0.079	0.644	0.665	0.653	0.613
6/5/2016	22:01:44	0.835	0.049	0.115	0.079	0.646	0.619	0.625	0.658
6/5/2016	22:01:44	0.835	0.049	0.115	0.079	0.649	0.669	0.648	0.61
6/5/2016	22:01:45	0.835	0.049	0.115	0.079	0.64	0.613	0.631	0.662
6/5/2016	22:01:45	0.835	0.049	0.114	0.077	0.665	0.679	0.632	0.591
6/5/2016	22:01:45	0.835	0.049	0.115	0.079	0.622	0.616	0.655	0.692
6/5/2016	22:01:45	0.835	0.049	0.115	0.079	0.657	0.676	0.64	0.605
6/5/2016	22:01:45	0.835	0.049	0.114	0.077	0.622	0.615	0.655	0.692
6/5/2016	22:01:46	0.835	0.05	0.115	0.079	0.67	0.669	0.626	0.579
6/5/2016	22:01:46	0.835	0.049	0.115	0.077	0.622	0.617	0.656	0.692
6/5/2016	22:01:46	0.835	0.049	0.115	0.079	0.67	0.667	0.626	0.579
6/5/2016	22:01:46	0.835	0.049	0.115	0.079	0.612	0.635	0.66	0.68
6/5/2016	22:01:47	0.835	0.05	0.114	0.079	0.696	0.635	0.612	0.63
6/5/2016	22:01:47	0.835	0.049	0.115	0.077	0.598	0.651	0.674	0.644
6/5/2016	22:01:47	0.835	0.049	0.115	0.079	0.694	0.639	0.615	0.621
6/5/2016	22:01:47	0.835	0.049	0.115	0.079	0.601	0.652	0.678	0.642
6/5/2016	22:01:48	0.835	0.049	0.114	0.079	0.697	0.637	0.613	0.624
6/5/2016	22:01:48	0.835	0.049	0.115	0.077	0.605	0.639	0.663	0.667
6/5/2016	22:01:48	0.835	0.049	0.115	0.079	0.687	0.644	0.618	0.611
6/5/2016	22:01:48	0.835	0.049	0.114	0.077	0.596	0.648	0.67	0.649
6/5/2016	22:01:48	0.835	0.049	0.114	0.077	0.687	0.643	0.617	0.612
6/5/2016	22:01:49	0.835	0.05	0.115	0.079	0.613	0.633	0.66	0.683
6/5/2016	22:01:49	0.835	0.05	0.114	0.077	0.68	0.65	0.621	0.598
6/5/2016	22:01:49	0.835	0.05	0.114	0.077	0.599	0.644	0.666	0.656
6/5/2016	22:01:50	0.835	0.05	0.114	0.077	0.694	0.639	0.615	0.622
6/5/2016	22:01:50	0.835	0.05	0.115	0.079	0.625	0.659	0.682	0.628
6/5/2016	22:01:50	0.835	0.049	0.115	0.077	0.665	0.624	0.606	0.649
6/5/2016	22:01:50	0.835	0.05	0.115	0.077	0.649	0.667	0.648	0.611
6/5/2016	22:01:51	0.835	0.049	0.115	0.079	0.646	0.619	0.624	0.658
6/5/2016	22:01:51	0.835	0.049	0.115	0.079	0.636	0.662	0.671	0.621
6/5/2016	22:01:51	0.835	0.049	0.114	0.077	0.635	0.608	0.637	0.665
6/5/2016	22:01:51	0.835	0.048	0.115	0.077	0.658	0.678	0.639	0.603
6/5/2016	22:01:51	0.835	0.048	0.114	0.077	0.615	0.633	0.66	0.683
6/5/2016	22:01:52	0.835	0.048	0.114	0.077	0.694	0.64	0.617	0.621
6/5/2016	22:01:52	0.835	0.05	0.115	0.08	0.635	0.66	0.672	0.621
6/5/2016	22:01:52	0.835	0.05	0.115	0.077	0.643	0.616	0.629	0.66
6/5/2016	22:01:52	0.835	0.05	0.115	0.079	0.658	0.677	0.64	0.604
6/5/2016	22:01:53	0.835	0.049	0.114	0.077	0.621	0.622	0.657	0.692
6/5/2016	22:01:53	0.835	0.049	0.114	0.077	0.694	0.635	0.612	0.63
6/5/2016	22:01:53	0.835	0.049	0.114	0.077	0.601	0.652	0.677	0.642
6/5/2016	22:01:54	0.835	0.049	0.115	0.079	0.691	0.631	0.605	0.635
6/5/2016	22:01:54	0.835	0.049	0.115	0.079	0.597	0.65	0.672	0.646
6/5/2016	22:01:54	0.835	0.049	0.115	0.077	0.682	0.628	0.603	0.64
6/5/2016	22:01:54	0.835	0.049	0.114	0.077	0.633	0.66	0.674	0.623
6/5/2016	22:01:54	0.835	0.049	0.115	0.077	0.653	0.622	0.615	0.655
6/5/2016	22:01:55	0.835	0.05	0.111	0.076	0.629	0.66	0.679	0.625
6/5/2016	22:01:55	0.835	0.05	0.111	0.076	0.638	0.611	0.635	0.663
6/5/2016	22:01:55	0.835	0.049	0.115	0.073	0.672	0.663	0.624	0.581
6/5/2016	22:01:55	0.835	0.053	0.115	0.079	0.628	0.602	0.644	0.673

(Continued)

Date	Time	S1	S2	S3	S4	S5	S6	S7	S8
6/5/2016	22:01:56	0.835	0.049	0.114	0.075	0.645	0.666	0.652	0.612
6/5/2016	22:01:56	0.835	0.049	0.114	0.075	0.669	0.625	0.606	0.648
6/5/2016	22:01:56	0.835	0.055	0.116	0.073	0.624	0.659	0.683	0.629
6/5/2016	22:01:56	0.835	0.055	0.114	0.063	0.666	0.625	0.606	0.649
6/5/2016	22:01:56	0.835	0.057	0.107	0.06	0.626	0.659	0.682	0.628
6/5/2016	22:01:57	0.835	0.053	0.109	0.056	0.653	0.622	0.616	0.655
6/5/2016	22:01:57	0.835	0.053	0.109	0.056	0.623	0.659	0.683	0.629
6/5/2016	22:01:57	0.835	0.053	0.107	0.054	0.694	0.637	0.615	0.623
6/5/2016	22:01:57	0.835	0.054	0.103	0.05	0.61	0.637	0.662	0.676
6/5/2016	22:01:58	0.835	0.054	0.103	0.053	0.68	0.649	0.621	0.598
6/5/2016	22:01:58	0.835	0.054	0.103	0.053	0.61	0.656	0.684	0.636
6/5/2016	22:01:58	0.835	0.053	0.104	0.05	0.653	0.622	0.616	0.655
6/5/2016	22:01:58	0.835	0.053	0.104	0.05	0.635	0.662	0.673	0.622
6/5/2016	22:01:59	0.835	0.055	0.103	0.05	0.694	0.632	0.609	0.632
6/5/2016	22:01:59	0.835	0.042	0.104	0.039	0.63	0.66	0.678	0.625
6/5/2016	22:01:59	0.835	0.042	0.104	0.039	0.642	0.615	0.631	0.66
6/5/2016	22:01:59	0.835	0.053	0.11	0.081	0.644	0.665	0.653	0.613
6/5/2016	22:02:00	0.835	0.047	0.114	0.076	0.656	0.622	0.613	0.653
6/5/2016	22:02:00	0.835	0.047	0.113	0.074	0.63	0.66	0.678	0.624
6/5/2016	22:02:00	0.835	0.047	0.113	0.074	0.665	0.624	0.608	0.649
6/5/2016	22:02:00	0.835	0.049	0.111	0.074	0.624	0.659	0.683	0.629
6/5/2016	22:02:00	0.835	0.049	0.113	0.074	0.693	0.631	0.606	0.635
6/5/2016	22:02:01	0.835	0.048	0.114	0.074	0.601	0.652	0.677	0.643
6/5/2016	22:02:01	0.835	0.049	0.111	0.073	0.693	0.639	0.615	0.619
6/5/2016	22:02:01	0.835	0.049	0.111	0.073	0.598	0.65	0.674	0.645
6/5/2016	22:02:01	0.835	0.049	0.113	0.073	0.687	0.629	0.604	0.638
6/5/2016	22:02:02	0.835	0.048	0.114	0.073	0.605	0.64	0.663	0.667
6/5/2016	22:02:02	0.835	0.049	0.113	0.073	0.683	0.646	0.619	0.603
6/5/2016	22:02:02	0.835	0.049	0.113	0.073	0.624	0.609	0.651	0.686
6/5/2016	22:02:02	0.835	0.05	0.113	0.073	0.671	0.665	0.625	0.579
6/5/2016	22:02:02	0.835	0.048	0.113	0.072	0.615	0.632	0.66	0.684
6/5/2016	22:02:03	0.835	0.05	0.111	0.07	0.696	0.639	0.616	0.623
6/5/2016	22:02:03	0.835	0.048	0.111	0.07	0.609	0.637	0.662	0.674
6/5/2016	22:02:03	0.835	0.048	0.111	0.07	0.66	0.678	0.638	0.601
6/5/2016	22:02:03	0.835	0.054	0.108	0.068	0.649	0.621	0.622	0.657
6/5/2016	22:02:04	0.835	0.042	0.104	0.04	0.63	0.66	0.678	0.624
6/5/2016	22:02:04	0.835	0.057	0.102	0.055	0.642	0.615	0.63	0.66
6/5/2016	22:02:04	0.835	0.057	0.102	0.055	0.664	0.68	0.633	0.594
6/5/2016	22:02:04	0.835	0.054	0.102	0.052	0.626	0.602	0.645	0.676
6/5/2016	22:02:05	0.835	0.053	0.103	0.053	0.646	0.666	0.651	0.612
6/5/2016	22:02:05	0.835	0.054	0.102	0.053	0.644	0.617	0.629	0.66
6/5/2016	22:03:56	0.838	0.06	0.129	0.089	0.618	0.625	0.659	0.693
6/5/2016	22:03:56	0.838	0.06	0.129	0.089	0.667	0.68	0.632	0.59
6/5/2016	22:03:57	0.838	0.06	0.129	0.089	0.638	0.611	0.635	0.663
6/5/2016	22:03:57	0.838	0.06	0.129	0.089	0.657	0.676	0.643	0.605
6/5/2016	22:03:57	0.838	0.06	0.129	0.09	0.625	0.605	0.65	0.684
6/5/2016	22:03:57	0.838	0.06	0.129	0.09	0.664	0.682	0.636	0.596
6/5/2016	22:03:58	0.838	0.06	0.129	0.09	0.63	0.603	0.643	0.671
6/5/2016	22:03:58	0.838	0.06	0.129	0.09	0.676	0.658	0.624	0.583
6/5/2016	22:03:58	0.838	0.06	0.129	0.089	0.612	0.633	0.662	0.684

(Continued)

Date	Time	S1	S2	S3	S4	S5	S6	S7	S8
6/5/2016	22:03:58	0.838	0.06	0.129	0.088	0.676	0.658	0.624	0.583
6/5/2016	22:03:59	0.838	0.06	0.129	0.089	0.619	0.621	0.657	0.694
6/5/2016	22:03:59	0.838	0.06	0.129	0.089	0.676	0.658	0.624	0.583
6/5/2016	22:03:59	0.838	0.06	0.129	0.09	0.613	0.633	0.662	0.684
6/5/2016	22:03:59	0.838	0.061	0.129	0.089	0.694	0.632	0.61	0.633
6/5/2016	22:03:59	0.838	0.06	0.129	0.089	0.596	0.651	0.674	0.646
6/5/2016	22:04:00	0.838	0.06	0.129	0.089	0.694	0.631	0.606	0.635
6/5/2016	22:04:00	0.838	0.06	0.13	0.09	0.64	0.663	0.663	0.617
6/5/2016	22:04:00	0.838	0.06	0.129	0.09	0.657	0.622	0.613	0.653
6/5/2016	22:04:52	0.838	0.06	0.129	0.089	0.63	0.662	0.679	0.625
6/5/2016	22:04:52	0.838	0.06	0.129	0.09	0.699	0.637	0.613	0.624
6/5/2016	22:04:52	0.838	0.061	0.129	0.089	0.597	0.651	0.676	0.645
6/5/2016	22:04:52	0.838	0.061	0.13	0.09	0.645	0.617	0.629	0.66
6/5/2016	22:04:52	0.838	0.06	0.13	0.086	0.652	0.671	0.646	0.61
6/5/2016	22:04:52	0.838	0.06	0.13	0.086	0.628	0.602	0.645	0.676
6/5/2016	22:04:53	0.838	0.06	0.13	0.086	0.662	0.68	0.639	0.601
6/5/2016	22:04:54	0.838	0.059	0.13	0.089	0.635	0.608	0.637	0.665
6/5/2016	22:04:54	0.838	0.06	0.129	0.09	0.65	0.67	0.649	0.61
6/5/2016	22:04:55	0.838	0.06	0.129	0.089	0.638	0.61	0.636	0.664
6/5/2016	22:04:55	0.838	0.06	0.129	0.089	0.666	0.682	0.633	0.59
6/5/2016	22:04:55	0.838	0.06	0.129	0.09	0.624	0.606	0.652	0.687
6/5/2016	22:04:55	0.838	0.06	0.129	0.09	0.672	0.67	0.626	0.578
6/5/2016	22:04:56	0.838	0.06	0.128	0.089	0.599	0.643	0.666	0.659
6/5/2016	22:04:56	0.838	0.06	0.129	0.09	0.7	0.637	0.613	0.625
6/5/2016	22:04:56	0.838	0.06	0.128	0.089	0.611	0.636	0.662	0.68
6/5/2016	22:04:56	0.838	0.06	0.129	0.09	0.687	0.646	0.619	0.605
6/5/2016	22:04:57	0.838	0.06	0.129	0.09	0.612	0.635	0.662	0.683
6/5/2016	22:04:57	0.838	0.061	0.131	0.089	0.697	0.633	0.61	0.632
6/5/2016	22:04:57	0.838	0.062	0.131	0.089	0.623	0.66	0.684	0.629
6/5/2016	22:04:57	0.838	0.061	0.131	0.087	0.683	0.628	0.604	0.642
6/5/2016	22:04:58	0.838	0.061	0.131	0.087	0.597	0.646	0.667	0.655
6/5/2016	22:04:58	0.838	0.061	0.131	0.089	0.69	0.644	0.618	0.609
6/5/2016	22:04:58	0.838	0.06	0.13	0.088	0.61	0.636	0.662	0.679
6/5/2016	22:04:59	0.838	0.06	0.13	0.088	0.685	0.648	0.619	0.602
6/5/2016	22:04:59	0.838	0.06	0.131	0.088	0.622	0.616	0.656	0.693
6/5/2016	22:04:59	0.838	0.061	0.13	0.088	0.67	0.677	0.63	0.583
6/5/2016	22:04:59	0.838	0.061	0.131	0.088	0.605	0.639	0.664	0.67
6/5/2016	22:05:00	0.838	0.061	0.131	0.088	0.666	0.625	0.608	0.649
6/5/2016	22:05:00	0.838	0.061	0.131	0.089	0.653	0.672	0.645	0.609
6/5/2016	22:05:00	0.838	0.061	0.131	0.089	0.626	0.603	0.648	0.679
6/5/2016	22:05:01	0.838	0.061	0.13	0.089	0.673	0.663	0.625	0.579
6/5/2016	22:05:01	0.838	0.061	0.13	0.089	0.616	0.63	0.66	0.689
6/5/2016	22:05:01	0.838	0.06	0.131	0.089	0.676	0.66	0.624	0.581
6/5/2016	22:05:01	0.838	0.061	0.129	0.088	0.621	0.619	0.657	0.694
6/5/2016	22:05:02	0.838	0.061	0.129	0.089	0.671	0.673	0.628	0.579
6/5/2016	22:05:02	0.838	0.061	0.129	0.089	0.624	0.606	0.652	0.687
6/5/2016	22:05:02	0.838	0.061	0.131	0.089	0.666	0.68	0.633	0.59
6/5/2016	22:05:02	0.838	0.061	0.129	0.088	0.623	0.609	0.653	0.691
6/5/2016	22:05:02	0.838	0.061	0.13	0.088	0.669	0.678	0.63	0.584
6/5/2016	22:05:03	0.838	0.061	0.13	0.088	0.622	0.612	0.655	0.692

(Continued)

Date	Time	S1	S2	S3	S4	S5	S6	S7	S8
6/5/2016	22:05:03	0.838	0.061	0.13	0.088	0.674	0.663	0.624	0.579
6/5/2016	22:05:03	0.838	0.061	0.13	0.088	0.603	0.64	0.664	0.667
6/5/2016	22:05:03	0.838	0.061	0.13	0.089	0.659	0.623	0.613	0.653
6/5/2016	22:05:04	0.838	0.061	0.131	0.089	0.66	0.678	0.64	0.603
6/5/2016	22:05:04	0.838	0.061	0.131	0.089	0.626	0.602	0.646	0.678
6/5/2016	22:05:04	0.838	0.061	0.13	0.089	0.683	0.649	0.621	0.599
6/5/2016	22:05:04	0.838	0.061	0.13	0.089	0.621	0.621	0.657	0.694
6/5/2016	22:05:05	0.838	0.061	0.13	0.088	0.687	0.645	0.619	0.606
6/5/2016	22:05:05	0.838	0.061	0.13	0.088	0.597	0.645	0.667	0.656
6/5/2016	22:05:05	0.838	0.061	0.13	0.088	0.692	0.643	0.617	0.611
6/5/2016	22:05:05	0.838	0.061	0.13	0.089	0.617	0.63	0.66	0.69
6/5/2016	22:05:05	0.838	0.061	0.13	0.088	0.684	0.649	0.621	0.601
6/5/2016	22:05:06	0.838	0.061	0.13	0.089	0.621	0.618	0.657	0.694
6/5/2016	22:05:06	0.838	0.061	0.13	0.089	0.676	0.658	0.624	0.583
6/5/2016	22:05:06	0.838	0.061	0.13	0.089	0.597	0.651	0.676	0.645
6/5/2016	22:05:06	0.838	0.061	0.13	0.089	0.655	0.622	0.616	0.655
6/5/2016	22:05:07	0.838	0.06	0.13	0.089	0.65	0.67	0.648	0.61
6/5/2016	22:05:07	0.838	0.06	0.13	0.089	0.644	0.617	0.629	0.66
6/5/2016	22:05:07	0.838	0.06	0.13	0.089	0.651	0.671	0.648	0.61
6/5/2016	22:05:07	0.838	0.061	0.13	0.089	0.624	0.609	0.652	0.689
6/5/2016	22:05:08	0.838	0.061	0.13	0.089	0.672	0.67	0.626	0.577
6/5/2016	22:05:08	0.838	0.061	0.13	0.089	0.621	0.618	0.657	0.694
6/5/2016	22:05:08	0.838	0.061	0.13	0.089	0.664	0.682	0.637	0.598
6/5/2016	22:05:08	0.838	0.061	0.13	0.089	0.628	0.602	0.648	0.678
6/5/2016	22:05:08	0.838	0.061	0.129	0.088	0.672	0.67	0.626	0.577
6/5/2016	22:05:09	0.838	0.06	0.13	0.089	0.625	0.603	0.65	0.682
6/5/2016	22:05:09	0.838	0.061	0.13	0.089	0.68	0.652	0.622	0.594
6/5/2016	22:05:09	0.838	0.061	0.13	0.089	0.619	0.623	0.658	0.694
6/5/2016	22:05:09	0.838	0.061	0.13	0.089	0.674	0.662	0.624	0.579
6/5/2016	22:05:10	0.838	0.06	0.129	0.088	0.618	0.626	0.659	0.692
6/5/2016	22:05:10	0.838	0.061	0.13	0.089	0.671	0.674	0.629	0.581
6/5/2016	22:05:10	0.838	0.061	0.13	0.089	0.617	0.629	0.659	0.691
6/5/2016	22:05:10	0.838	0.061	0.13	0.089	0.699	0.638	0.616	0.623
6/5/2016	22:05:11	0.838	0.06	0.13	0.089	0.615	0.631	0.66	0.687
6/5/2016	22:05:11	0.838	0.06	0.13	0.089	0.691	0.644	0.619	0.611
6/5/2016	22:05:11	0.838	0.061	0.13	0.088	0.613	0.633	0.662	0.685
6/5/2016	22:05:11	0.838	0.061	0.13	0.088	0.674	0.664	0.625	0.578
6/5/2016	22:05:11	0.838	0.06	0.13	0.089	0.618	0.625	0.659	0.693
6/5/2016	22:05:12	0.838	0.059	0.13	0.089	0.696	0.642	0.618	0.617
6/5/2016	22:05:12	0.838	0.06	0.129	0.088	0.609	0.637	0.663	0.677
6/5/2016	22:05:13	0.838	0.06	0.129	0.088	0.685	0.648	0.619	0.601
6/5/2016	22:05:13	0.838	0.06	0.13	0.089	0.606	0.639	0.663	0.673
6/5/2016	22:05:13	0.838	0.061	0.13	0.089	0.678	0.655	0.623	0.587
6/5/2016	22:05:35	0.838	0.055	0.122	0.091	0.599	0.653	0.677	0.644
6/5/2016	22:05:36	0.838	0.055	0.122	0.091	0.676	0.662	0.624	0.579
6/5/2016	22:05:36	0.838	0.055	0.122	0.09	0.625	0.604	0.65	0.683
6/5/2016	22:05:36	0.838	0.055	0.121	0.09	0.667	0.68	0.632	0.59
6/5/2016	22:05:36	0.838	0.055	0.121	0.09	0.643	0.616	0.63	0.66
6/5/2016	22:05:37	0.838	0.055	0.12	0.09	0.625	0.66	0.683	0.629
6/5/2016	22:05:37	0.838	0.055	0.121	0.09	0.694	0.631	0.608	0.635

(Continued)

Date	Time	S1	S2	S3	S4	S5	S6	S7	S8
6/5/2016	22:05:37	0.838	0.055	0.12	0.09	0.597	0.646	0.667	0.655
6/5/2016	22:05:37	0.838	0.055	0.12	0.09	0.676	0.659	0.624	0.581
6/5/2016	22:05:38	0.838	0.056	0.12	0.089	0.621	0.619	0.657	0.693
6/5/2016	22:05:38	0.838	0.055	0.118	0.089	0.667	0.68	0.633	0.591
6/5/2016	22:05:38	0.838	0.054	0.118	0.09	0.629	0.602	0.645	0.676
6/5/2016	22:05:38	0.838	0.054	0.118	0.09	0.669	0.678	0.631	0.585
6/5/2016	22:05:39	0.838	0.054	0.12	0.09	0.632	0.604	0.64	0.669
6/5/2016	22:05:39	0.838	0.054	0.12	0.09	0.638	0.664	0.666	0.618
6/5/2016	22:05:39	0.838	0.054	0.118	0.09	0.696	0.632	0.609	0.632
6/5/2016	22:05:40	0.838	0.054	0.118	0.09	0.611	0.636	0.662	0.68
6/5/2016	22:05:40	0.838	0.054	0.118	0.089	0.689	0.644	0.619	0.609
6/5/2016	22:05:40	0.838	0.055	0.118	0.089	0.608	0.638	0.663	0.674
6/5/2016	22:05:40	0.838	0.053	0.12	0.09	0.682	0.651	0.622	0.595
6/5/2016	22:05:41	0.838	0.053	0.12	0.09	0.618	0.629	0.659	0.69
6/5/2016	22:05:41	0.838	0.054	0.118	0.09	0.673	0.664	0.625	0.578
6/5/2016	22:05:41	0.838	0.055	0.12	0.091	0.628	0.603	0.646	0.678
6/5/2016	22:05:41	0.838	0.054	0.12	0.09	0.669	0.678	0.631	0.585
6/5/2016	22:05:42	0.838	0.054	0.12	0.09	0.626	0.603	0.648	0.679
6/5/2016	22:05:42	0.838	0.054	0.118	0.09	0.644	0.666	0.656	0.615
6/5/2016	22:05:42	0.838	0.054	0.118	0.09	0.686	0.629	0.605	0.639
6/5/2016	22:05:43	0.838	0.054	0.118	0.09	0.605	0.64	0.663	0.67
6/5/2016	22:05:43	0.838	0.054	0.118	0.09	0.682	0.65	0.622	0.595
6/5/2016	22:05:43	0.838	0.054	0.118	0.089	0.626	0.603	0.648	0.679
6/5/2016	22:05:43	0.838	0.053	0.12	0.09	0.662	0.68	0.638	0.601
6/5/2016	22:05:43	0.838	0.054	0.118	0.09	0.643	0.616	0.63	0.66
6/5/2016	22:05:44	0.838	0.054	0.118	0.09	0.644	0.665	0.656	0.615
6/5/2016	22:05:44	0.838	0.055	0.12	0.089	0.689	0.629	0.606	0.638
6/5/2016	22:05:44	0.838	0.053	0.121	0.09	0.601	0.653	0.678	0.643
6/5/2016	22:05:44	0.838	0.054	0.117	0.09	0.699	0.636	0.612	0.628
6/5/2016	22:05:45	0.838	0.052	0.117	0.086	0.601	0.653	0.678	0.643
6/5/2016	22:05:45	0.838	0.052	0.117	0.086	0.692	0.643	0.617	0.612
6/5/2016	22:05:45	0.838	0.06	0.118	0.09	0.619	0.626	0.659	0.692
6/5/2016	22:05:45	0.838	0.055	0.12	0.09	0.65	0.669	0.649	0.611
6/5/2016	22:05:46	0.838	0.055	0.121	0.091	0.676	0.625	0.606	0.645
6/5/2016	22:05:46	0.838	0.055	0.121	0.091	0.621	0.622	0.657	0.693
6/5/2016	22:05:46	0.838	0.056	0.121	0.091	0.648	0.667	0.651	0.612
6/5/2016	22:05:46	0.838	0.052	0.121	0.09	0.663	0.624	0.611	0.651
6/5/2016	22:05:46	0.838	0.054	0.127	0.081	0.635	0.662	0.676	0.623
6/5/2016	22:05:47	0.838	0.062	0.131	0.081	0.655	0.623	0.617	0.655
6/5/2016	22:05:47	0.838	0.062	0.131	0.081	0.639	0.663	0.665	0.618
6/5/2016	22:05:47	0.838	0.066	0.134	0.08	0.662	0.624	0.61	0.651
6/5/2016	22:05:47	0.838	0.061	0.131	0.089	0.597	0.646	0.667	0.656
6/5/2016	22:05:48	0.838	0.063	0.131	0.084	0.678	0.655	0.623	0.587
6/5/2016	22:05:48	0.838	0.063	0.131	0.084	0.631	0.604	0.642	0.669
6/5/2016	22:05:48	0.838	0.062	0.133	0.088	0.643	0.665	0.659	0.616
6/5/2016	22:05:49	0.838	0.061	0.133	0.088	0.696	0.632	0.609	0.632
6/5/2016	22:05:49	0.838	0.061	0.133	0.088	0.608	0.639	0.663	0.673
6/5/2016	22:05:49	0.838	0.061	0.133	0.088	0.666	0.68	0.636	0.596
6/5/2016	22:05:49	0.838	0.062	0.131	0.088	0.656	0.622	0.616	0.655
6/5/2016	22:05:49	0.838	0.061	0.131	0.088	0.596	0.648	0.67	0.652

(Continued)

Date	Time	S1	S2	S3	S4	S5	S6	S7	S8
6/5/2016	22:05:50	0.838	0.062	0.131	0.088	0.687	0.645	0.619	0.606
6/5/2016	22:05:50	0.838	0.062	0.131	0.088	0.628	0.603	0.646	0.677
6/5/2016	22:05:50	0.838	0.062	0.131	0.088	0.637	0.663	0.671	0.621
6/5/2016	22:05:51	0.838	0.062	0.131	0.088	0.677	0.626	0.605	0.644
6/5/2016	22:05:51	0.838	0.061	0.133	0.088	0.608	0.639	0.663	0.674
6/5/2016	22:05:51	0.838	0.061	0.133	0.088	0.672	0.672	0.629	0.581
6/5/2016	22:05:51	0.838	0.062	0.131	0.088	0.646	0.618	0.626	0.658
6/5/2016	22:05:52	0.838	0.062	0.133	0.088	0.597	0.646	0.667	0.656
6/5/2016	22:07:23	0.836	0.061	0.131	0.093	0.672	0.67	0.628	0.579
6/5/2016	22:07:23	0.836	0.062	0.13	0.09	0.615	0.632	0.66	0.686
6/5/2016	22:07:24	0.836	0.062	0.13	0.089	0.67	0.678	0.631	0.585
6/5/2016	22:07:24	0.836	0.061	0.131	0.09	0.629	0.602	0.645	0.674
6/5/2016	22:07:24	0.836	0.061	0.131	0.089	0.639	0.664	0.667	0.619
6/5/2016	22:07:24	0.836	0.061	0.131	0.089	0.699	0.633	0.61	0.63
6/5/2016	22:07:25	0.836	0.061	0.131	0.089	0.597	0.645	0.667	0.657
6/5/2016	22:07:25	0.836	0.062	0.13	0.089	0.673	0.67	0.626	0.579
6/5/2016	22:07:25	0.836	0.061	0.131	0.09	0.63	0.602	0.643	0.671
6/5/2016	22:07:25	0.836	0.061	0.13	0.09	0.657	0.676	0.644	0.606
6/5/2016	22:07:26	0.836	0.061	0.13	0.09	0.622	0.616	0.656	0.693
6/5/2016	22:07:26	0.836	0.062	0.13	0.09	0.67	0.677	0.63	0.584
6/5/2016	22:07:26	0.836	0.062	0.131	0.09	0.626	0.603	0.648	0.679
6/5/2016	22:07:27	0.836	0.062	0.131	0.09	0.644	0.665	0.657	0.615
6/5/2016	22:07:27	0.836	0.061	0.13	0.089	0.666	0.624	0.609	0.65
6/5/2016	22:07:27	0.836	0.061	0.13	0.09	0.601	0.655	0.68	0.642
6/5/2016	22:07:28	0.836	0.062	0.13	0.089	0.65	0.621	0.623	0.657
6/5/2016	22:07:28	0.836	0.062	0.13	0.089	0.665	0.682	0.636	0.597
6/5/2016	22:07:28	0.836	0.062	0.13	0.089	0.625	0.605	0.651	0.684
6/5/2016	22:07:28	0.836	0.062	0.131	0.09	0.666	0.682	0.633	0.592
6/5/2016	22:07:28	0.836	0.061	0.13	0.089	0.629	0.602	0.645	0.673
6/5/2016	22:07:29	0.836	0.061	0.13	0.089	0.672	0.671	0.628	0.578
6/5/2016	22:07:29	0.836	0.061	0.13	0.09	0.61	0.637	0.663	0.677
6/5/2016	22:07:29	0.836	0.061	0.13	0.089	0.682	0.652	0.622	0.592
6/5/2016	22:07:29	0.836	0.061	0.13	0.09	0.608	0.639	0.663	0.673
6/5/2016	22:07:30	0.836	0.061	0.131	0.089	0.674	0.666	0.626	0.579
6/5/2016	22:07:30	0.836	0.061	0.131	0.089	0.624	0.61	0.653	0.69
6/5/2016	22:07:30	0.836	0.061	0.13	0.09	0.66	0.678	0.64	0.603
6/5/2016	22:07:30	0.836	0.062	0.13	0.089	0.624	0.61	0.653	0.69
6/5/2016	22:07:31	0.836	0.062	0.13	0.089	0.682	0.651	0.622	0.595
6/5/2016	22:07:32	0.836	0.061	0.13	0.089	0.605	0.64	0.664	0.67
6/5/2016	22:07:32	0.836	0.061	0.13	0.09	0.685	0.648	0.621	0.601
6/5/2016	22:07:32	0.836	0.061	0.131	0.089	0.599	0.644	0.666	0.659
6/5/2016	22:07:32	0.836	0.061	0.13	0.089	0.7	0.636	0.612	0.629
6/5/2016	22:07:33	0.836	0.062	0.131	0.089	0.595	0.649	0.671	0.651
6/5/2016	22:07:33	0.836	0.062	0.131	0.089	0.693	0.631	0.606	0.636
6/5/2016	22:07:33	0.836	0.061	0.13	0.089	0.618	0.659	0.685	0.632
6/5/2016	22:07:33	0.836	0.061	0.13	0.089	0.699	0.633	0.61	0.631
6/5/2016	22:07:34	0.836	0.062	0.13	0.089	0.613	0.635	0.662	0.684
6/5/2016	22:07:34	0.836	0.062	0.13	0.089	0.68	0.653	0.622	0.591
6/5/2016	22:07:34	0.836	0.061	0.131	0.089	0.603	0.642	0.664	0.666
6/5/2016	22:07:35	0.836	0.062	0.13	0.089	0.699	0.638	0.616	0.623

(Continued)

Date	Time	S1	S2	S3	S4	S5	S6	S7	S8
6/5/2016	22:07:35	0.836	0.062	0.13	0.089	0.596	0.648	0.669	0.653
6/5/2016	22:07:35	0.836	0.063	0.13	0.09	0.697	0.632	0.609	0.633
6/5/2016	22:07:36	0.836	0.065	0.13	0.089	0.637	0.663	0.672	0.621
6/5/2016	22:07:36	0.836	0.065	0.13	0.089	0.692	0.63	0.606	0.637
6/5/2016	22:07:37	0.836	0.062	0.131	0.09	0.596	0.649	0.671	0.65
6/5/2016	22:07:38	0.836	0.063	0.13	0.091	0.674	0.665	0.625	0.579
6/5/2016	22:07:38	0.836	0.062	0.131	0.09	0.63	0.603	0.643	0.671
6/5/2016	22:07:39	0.836	0.062	0.131	0.09	0.674	0.663	0.625	0.581
6/5/2016	22:07:39	0.836	0.062	0.131	0.09	0.61	0.637	0.663	0.677
6/5/2016	22:07:40	0.836	0.062	0.131	0.089	0.686	0.646	0.621	0.603
6/5/2016	22:07:40	0.836	0.062	0.131	0.09	0.616	0.631	0.66	0.689
6/5/2016	22:07:41	0.836	0.062	0.131	0.09	0.689	0.645	0.619	0.609
6/5/2016	22:07:41	0.836	0.062	0.131	0.089	0.608	0.657	0.684	0.638
6/5/2016	22:07:41	0.836	0.062	0.133	0.089	0.663	0.624	0.61	0.651
6/5/2016	22:07:42	0.836	0.062	0.133	0.089	0.651	0.671	0.648	0.611
6/5/2016	22:07:42	0.836	0.062	0.131	0.089	0.63	0.602	0.644	0.673
6/5/2016	22:07:42	0.836	0.062	0.131	0.089	0.671	0.674	0.629	0.581
6/5/2016	22:07:42	0.836	0.062	0.131	0.089	0.615	0.632	0.662	0.686
6/5/2016	22:07:43	0.836	0.062	0.131	0.089	0.684	0.65	0.621	0.599
6/5/2016	22:07:43	0.836	0.063	0.134	0.084	0.618	0.628	0.659	0.691
6/5/2016	22:07:43	0.836	0.063	0.134	0.084	0.673	0.669	0.626	0.578
6/5/2016	22:07:44	0.836	0.063	0.134	0.084	0.621	0.623	0.658	0.694
6/5/2016	22:07:44	0.836	0.063	0.135	0.084	0.677	0.658	0.624	0.584
6/5/2016	22:07:44	0.836	0.063	0.134	0.084	0.622	0.618	0.657	0.694
6/5/2016	22:07:45	0.836	0.063	0.134	0.084	0.676	0.662	0.625	0.581
6/5/2016	22:07:45	0.836	0.063	0.134	0.084	0.633	0.606	0.639	0.666
6/5/2016	22:07:45	0.836	0.062	0.134	0.084	0.659	0.679	0.64	0.604
6/5/2016	22:07:46	0.836	0.063	0.134	0.084	0.63	0.603	0.643	0.672
6/5/2016	22:07:46	0.836	0.063	0.134	0.086	0.665	0.682	0.636	0.596
6/5/2016	22:07:47	0.836	0.063	0.134	0.086	0.626	0.603	0.649	0.68
6/5/2016	22:07:47	0.836	0.062	0.134	0.086	0.67	0.677	0.63	0.583
6/5/2016	22:07:47	0.836	0.062	0.134	0.086	0.623	0.612	0.655	0.692
6/5/2016	22:07:47	0.836	0.062	0.131	0.088	0.669	0.679	0.631	0.588
6/5/2016	22:07:48	0.836	0.062	0.131	0.088	0.629	0.602	0.645	0.674
6/5/2016	22:07:48	0.836	0.062	0.131	0.089	0.667	0.68	0.632	0.588
6/5/2016	22:07:48	0.836	0.062	0.131	0.088	0.608	0.638	0.663	0.674
6/5/2016	22:07:49	0.836	0.062	0.133	0.088	0.692	0.643	0.618	0.612
6/5/2016	22:07:49	0.836	0.062	0.133	0.088	0.598	0.652	0.677	0.644
6/5/2016	22:07:49	0.836	0.062	0.131	0.088	0.692	0.63	0.606	0.637
6/5/2016	22:07:50	0.836	0.062	0.133	0.089	0.615	0.658	0.685	0.633
6/5/2016	22:07:50	0.836	0.062	0.133	0.089	0.645	0.618	0.629	0.659
6/5/2016	22:07:50	0.836	0.062	0.133	0.088	0.63	0.662	0.679	0.625
6/5/2016	22:07:50	0.836	0.062	0.131	0.088	0.676	0.626	0.606	0.645
6/5/2016	22:07:51	0.836	0.062	0.131	0.088	0.628	0.66	0.682	0.626
6/5/2016	22:07:51	0.836	0.062	0.131	0.088	0.68	0.628	0.605	0.644
6/5/2016	22:07:51	0.836	0.063	0.131	0.088	0.648	0.666	0.652	0.613
6/5/2016	22:07:51	0.836	0.062	0.131	0.089	0.643	0.615	0.631	0.662
6/5/2016	22:07:52	0.836	0.062	0.133	0.089	0.643	0.665	0.659	0.616
6/5/2016	22:07:52	0.836	0.062	0.133	0.089	0.637	0.61	0.636	0.664
6/5/2016	22:07:52	0.836	0.062	0.133	0.089	0.657	0.677	0.643	0.606

(Continued)

Date	Time	S1	S2	S3	S4	S5	S6	S7	S8
6/5/2016	22:07:53	0.836	0.062	0.131	0.089	0.626	0.604	0.65	0.683
6/5/2016	22:07:53	0.836	0.062	0.131	0.088	0.682	0.651	0.622	0.598
6/5/2016	22:07:53	0.836	0.062	0.131	0.088	0.608	0.639	0.663	0.673
6/5/2016	22:07:53	0.836	0.061	0.133	0.089	0.679	0.653	0.623	0.591
6/5/2016	22:07:53	0.836	0.062	0.131	0.088	0.612	0.635	0.662	0.683
6/5/2016	22:07:54	0.836	0.062	0.131	0.088	0.697	0.64	0.617	0.619
6/5/2016	22:07:54	0.836	0.062	0.131	0.088	0.617	0.63	0.66	0.689
6/5/2016	22:07:54	0.836	0.062	0.131	0.088	0.673	0.669	0.626	0.578
6/5/2016	22:07:55	0.836	0.062	0.131	0.088	0.621	0.621	0.657	0.693
6/5/2016	22:07:55	0.836	0.063	0.131	0.088	0.684	0.649	0.621	0.601
6/5/2016	22:07:55	0.836	0.063	0.131	0.088	0.597	0.646	0.669	0.655
6/5/2016	22:08:06	0.836	0.063	0.135	0.084	0.665	0.682	0.636	0.596
6/5/2016	22:08:06	0.836	0.063	0.135	0.084	0.63	0.602	0.643	0.672
6/5/2016	22:08:06	0.836	0.063	0.135	0.084	0.66	0.679	0.639	0.602
6/5/2016	22:08:06	0.836	0.063	0.134	0.084	0.631	0.604	0.64	0.669
6/5/2016	22:08:07	0.836	0.063	0.135	0.084	0.665	0.683	0.635	0.595
6/5/2016	22:08:07	0.836	0.063	0.134	0.084	0.629	0.602	0.644	0.673
6/5/2016	22:08:07	0.836	0.063	0.134	0.084	0.642	0.665	0.66	0.616
6/5/2016	22:08:08	0.836	0.063	0.134	0.084	0.652	0.622	0.619	0.657
6/5/2016	22:08:08	0.836	0.063	0.134	0.084	0.595	0.649	0.67	0.652
6/5/2016	22:08:08	0.836	0.063	0.134	0.084	0.686	0.646	0.619	0.602
6/5/2016	22:08:09	0.836	0.063	0.134	0.084	0.597	0.651	0.676	0.645
6/5/2016	22:08:09	0.836	0.063	0.134	0.084	0.7	0.636	0.612	0.628
6/5/2016	22:08:09	0.836	0.063	0.134	0.084	0.616	0.63	0.66	0.69
6/5/2016	22:08:09	0.836	0.062	0.134	0.084	0.698	0.64	0.618	0.621
6/5/2016	22:08:10	0.836	0.062	0.134	0.084	0.613	0.658	0.685	0.633
6/5/2016	22:08:10	0.836	0.063	0.134	0.084	0.686	0.629	0.605	0.64
6/5/2016	22:08:10	0.836	0.063	0.134	0.084	0.605	0.657	0.683	0.638
6/5/2016	22:08:10	0.836	0.063	0.134	0.086	0.674	0.626	0.606	0.646
6/5/2016	22:08:11	0.836	0.063	0.134	0.086	0.596	0.648	0.669	0.653
6/5/2016	22:09:05	0.835	0.062	0.134	0.086	0.662	0.68	0.638	0.602
6/5/2016	22:09:05	0.835	0.063	0.134	0.086	0.644	0.618	0.63	0.662
6/5/2016	22:09:06	0.835	0.063	0.134	0.086	0.64	0.664	0.664	0.618
6/5/2016	22:09:06	0.835	0.063	0.134	0.086	0.677	0.629	0.608	0.646
6/5/2016	22:09:07	0.835	0.063	0.134	0.086	0.598	0.648	0.669	0.652
6/5/2016	22:09:07	0.835	0.062	0.134	0.086	0.687	0.645	0.619	0.613
6/5/2016	22:09:08	0.835	0.062	0.135	0.086	0.626	0.606	0.65	0.682
6/5/2016	22:09:08	0.835	0.062	0.135	0.086	0.662	0.68	0.639	0.603
6/5/2016	22:09:08	0.835	0.062	0.134	0.086	0.638	0.612	0.637	0.665
6/5/2016	22:09:09	0.835	0.063	0.134	0.086	0.646	0.666	0.655	0.615
6/5/2016	22:09:09	0.835	0.062	0.134	0.086	0.689	0.631	0.609	0.64
6/5/2016	22:09:09	0.835	0.063	0.134	0.086	0.615	0.636	0.662	0.683
6/5/2016	22:09:10	0.835	0.063	0.134	0.086	0.655	0.672	0.645	0.611
6/5/2016	22:09:10	0.835	0.062	0.134	0.086	0.672	0.628	0.608	0.649
6/5/2016	22:09:10	0.835	0.063	0.134	0.086	0.598	0.65	0.671	0.65
6/5/2016	22:09:11	0.835	0.063	0.134	0.086	0.679	0.652	0.623	0.598
6/5/2016	22:09:11	0.835	0.063	0.134	0.086	0.625	0.61	0.653	0.687
6/5/2016	22:09:13	0.835	0.062	0.134	0.086	0.663	0.68	0.638	0.602
6/5/2016	22:09:13	0.835	0.062	0.134	0.086	0.655	0.623	0.616	0.657
6/5/2016	22:09:14	0.835	0.066	0.131	0.088	0.605	0.656	0.682	0.64

(Continued)

Date	Time	S1	S2	S3	S4	S5	S6	S7	S8
6/5/2016	22:09:14	0.835	0.066	0.131	0.088	0.678	0.653	0.623	0.595
6/5/2016	22:09:15	0.835	0.066	0.134	0.09	0.632	0.606	0.642	0.67
6/5/2016	22:09:15	0.835	0.066	0.134	0.09	0.601	0.653	0.676	0.644
6/5/2016	22:09:35	0.835	0.067	0.135	0.089	0.664	0.68	0.638	0.602
6/5/2016	22:09:35	0.835	0.067	0.135	0.089	0.628	0.606	0.65	0.682
6/5/2016	22:09:36	0.835	0.066	0.135	0.089	0.639	0.664	0.671	0.621
6/5/2016	22:09:36	0.835	0.066	0.135	0.089	0.679	0.63	0.606	0.646
6/5/2016	22:09:37	0.835	0.066	0.135	0.089	0.605	0.644	0.665	0.664
6/5/2016	22:09:37	0.835	0.066	0.135	0.089	0.677	0.656	0.624	0.591
6/5/2016	22:09:37	0.835	0.066	0.135	0.089	0.631	0.606	0.644	0.672
6/5/2016	22:09:38	0.835	0.066	0.135	0.088	0.628	0.662	0.684	0.628
6/5/2016	22:09:38	0.835	0.066	0.135	0.088	0.685	0.646	0.622	0.61
6/5/2016	22:09:38	0.835	0.066	0.135	0.089	0.623	0.623	0.658	0.694
6/5/2016	22:09:38	0.835	0.066	0.136	0.089	0.642	0.664	0.669	0.619
6/5/2016	22:09:39	0.835	0.066	0.135	0.089	0.676	0.629	0.606	0.648
6/5/2016	22:09:39	0.835	0.066	0.135	0.089	0.612	0.658	0.685	0.637
6/5/2016	22:09:39	0.835	0.066	0.135	0.089	0.685	0.646	0.622	0.612
6/5/2016	22:09:40	0.835	0.066	0.136	0.09	0.622	0.625	0.659	0.693
6/5/2016	22:09:40	0.835	0.066	0.135	0.089	0.65	0.669	0.651	0.613
6/5/2016	22:09:40	0.835	0.066	0.135	0.089	0.696	0.639	0.618	0.628
6/5/2016	22:09:40	0.835	0.066	0.135	0.089	0.622	0.625	0.659	0.693
6/5/2016	22:09:41	0.835	0.066	0.135	0.089	0.666	0.68	0.635	0.596
6/5/2016	22:09:41	0.835	0.066	0.135	0.089	0.637	0.611	0.639	0.666
6/5/2016	22:09:42	0.835	0.066	0.135	0.089	0.611	0.658	0.684	0.637
6/5/2016	22:09:42	0.835	0.066	0.135	0.089	0.677	0.657	0.624	0.59
6/5/2016	22:09:43	0.835	0.066	0.135	0.089	0.631	0.606	0.644	0.671
6/5/2016	22:09:43	0.835	0.065	0.136	0.089	0.649	0.667	0.652	0.615
6/5/2016	22:09:44	0.835	0.066	0.135	0.089	0.648	0.623	0.625	0.66
6/5/2016	22:09:44	0.835	0.066	0.135	0.089	0.604	0.645	0.665	0.664
6/5/2016	22:09:45	0.835	0.066	0.135	0.089	0.665	0.68	0.638	0.601
6/5/2016	22:09:46	0.835	0.066	0.135	0.089	0.628	0.606	0.651	0.682
6/5/2016	22:09:46	0.835	0.066	0.135	0.089	0.656	0.673	0.645	0.611
6/5/2016	22:09:46	0.835	0.066	0.135	0.09	0.642	0.617	0.633	0.664
6/5/2016	22:09:47	0.835	0.066	0.135	0.09	0.622	0.66	0.685	0.631
6/5/2016	22:09:47	0.835	0.066	0.135	0.089	0.669	0.678	0.632	0.591
6/5/2016	22:09:47	0.835	0.065	0.135	0.089	0.653	0.624	0.617	0.658
6/5/2016	22:09:48	0.835	0.065	0.135	0.089	0.621	0.629	0.659	0.692
6/5/2016	22:09:48	0.835	0.067	0.135	0.089	0.659	0.678	0.642	0.608
6/5/2016	22:09:48	0.835	0.066	0.135	0.089	0.638	0.612	0.638	0.665
6/5/2016	22:09:49	0.835	0.066	0.135	0.089	0.599	0.652	0.673	0.646
6/5/2016	22:09:49	0.835	0.066	0.135	0.089	0.671	0.674	0.63	0.587
6/5/2016	22:09:49	0.835	0.066	0.135	0.089	0.662	0.626	0.61	0.653
6/5/2016	22:09:49	0.835	0.067	0.134	0.089	0.608	0.642	0.664	0.67
6/5/2016	22:09:50	0.835	0.066	0.135	0.089	0.672	0.666	0.628	0.584
6/5/2016	22:09:51	0.835	0.066	0.135	0.089	0.629	0.605	0.648	0.676
6/5/2016	22:09:51	0.835	0.066	0.135	0.089	0.616	0.659	0.685	0.636
6/5/2016	22:09:52	0.835	0.066	0.135	0.089	0.676	0.657	0.625	0.591
6/5/2016	22:09:53	0.835	0.066	0.135	0.089	0.632	0.606	0.643	0.671
6/5/2016	22:09:53	0.835	0.066	0.135	0.089	0.645	0.666	0.657	0.617
6/5/2016	22:09:53	0.835	0.066	0.135	0.089	0.687	0.631	0.608	0.643

(Continued)

Date	Time	S1	S2	S3	S4	S5	S6	S7	S8
6/5/2016	22:09:54	0.835	0.066	0.135	0.089	0.625	0.611	0.653	0.687
6/5/2016	22:09:54	0.835	0.066	0.135	0.09	0.642	0.664	0.666	0.619
6/5/2016	22:09:54	0.835	0.065	0.135	0.089	0.684	0.631	0.606	0.644
6/5/2016	22:09:54	0.835	0.066	0.135	0.088	0.621	0.629	0.659	0.692
6/5/2016	22:09:55	0.835	0.066	0.135	0.088	0.658	0.677	0.643	0.608
6/5/2016	22:09:55	0.835	0.066	0.135	0.089	0.65	0.623	0.623	0.659
6/5/2016	22:09:55	0.835	0.066	0.135	0.089	0.601	0.655	0.677	0.644
6/5/2016	22:09:55	0.835	0.066	0.135	0.089	0.671	0.672	0.629	0.585
6/5/2016	22:09:56	0.835	0.066	0.135	0.089	0.643	0.618	0.632	0.663
6/5/2016	22:09:56	0.835	0.066	0.135	0.089	0.633	0.663	0.68	0.625
6/5/2016	22:09:57	0.835	0.066	0.135	0.089	0.694	0.64	0.619	0.625
6/5/2016	22:09:57	0.835	0.066	0.135	0.089	0.618	0.632	0.66	0.69
6/5/2016	22:09:57	0.835	0.066	0.135	0.089	0.663	0.678	0.64	0.605
6/5/2016	22:09:57	0.835	0.066	0.135	0.089	0.669	0.628	0.608	0.651
6/5/2016	22:09:58	0.835	0.066	0.135	0.089	0.601	0.651	0.672	0.649
6/5/2016	22:09:58	0.835	0.065	0.135	0.09	0.67	0.676	0.631	0.589
6/5/2016	22:09:58	0.835	0.066	0.135	0.089	0.644	0.619	0.631	0.663
6/5/2016	22:09:58	0.835	0.066	0.135	0.089	0.601	0.652	0.674	0.646
6/5/2016	22:09:59	0.835	0.066	0.135	0.089	0.676	0.659	0.625	0.588
6/5/2016	22:09:59	0.835	0.066	0.135	0.089	0.635	0.609	0.642	0.669
6/5/2016	22:10:00	0.835	0.066	0.135	0.089	0.617	0.66	0.685	0.635
6/5/2016	22:10:00	0.835	0.066	0.135	0.089	0.684	0.648	0.622	0.609
6/5/2016	22:10:00	0.835	0.065	0.136	0.089	0.628	0.606	0.65	0.68
6/5/2016	22:10:01	0.835	0.067	0.134	0.088	0.662	0.68	0.639	0.604
6/5/2016	22:10:01	0.835	0.067	0.135	0.088	0.645	0.621	0.629	0.662
6/5/2016	22:10:01	0.835	0.067	0.135	0.088	0.63	0.662	0.683	0.628
6/5/2016	22:10:02	0.835	0.066	0.136	0.087	0.682	0.649	0.623	0.605
6/5/2016	22:10:02	0.835	0.066	0.136	0.087	0.636	0.611	0.639	0.667
6/5/2016	22:10:02	0.835	0.066	0.134	0.089	0.642	0.664	0.666	0.619
6/5/2016	22:10:03	0.835	0.067	0.133	0.089	0.693	0.64	0.619	0.626
6/5/2016	22:11:14	0.834	0.059	0.129	0.089	0.67	0.676	0.631	0.588
6/5/2016	22:11:14	0.834	0.062	0.129	0.09	0.639	0.616	0.636	0.665
6/5/2016	22:11:14	0.834	0.066	0.135	0.093	0.631	0.663	0.683	0.628
6/5/2016	22:11:14	0.834	0.066	0.135	0.093	0.687	0.633	0.61	0.642
6/5/2016	22:11:15	0.834	0.065	0.135	0.09	0.621	0.631	0.66	0.692
6/5/2016	22:11:15	0.834	0.065	0.133	0.089	0.67	0.677	0.631	0.588
6/5/2016	22:11:15	0.834	0.065	0.133	0.089	0.657	0.626	0.613	0.657
6/5/2016	22:11:16	0.834	0.065	0.134	0.09	0.602	0.653	0.676	0.645
6/5/2016	22:11:16	0.834	0.065	0.133	0.09	0.673	0.667	0.628	0.584
6/5/2016	22:11:16	0.834	0.065	0.134	0.091	0.64	0.618	0.633	0.664
6/5/2016	22:11:17	0.834	0.065	0.134	0.091	0.64	0.664	0.672	0.621
6/5/2016	22:11:17	0.834	0.066	0.134	0.091	0.67	0.629	0.608	0.651
6/5/2016	22:11:17	0.834	0.065	0.134	0.09	0.611	0.642	0.664	0.674
6/5/2016	22:11:18	0.834	0.065	0.134	0.09	0.67	0.676	0.631	0.588
6/5/2016	22:11:18	0.834	0.066	0.134	0.09	0.637	0.613	0.638	0.666
6/5/2016	22:11:18	0.834	0.065	0.133	0.09	0.655	0.672	0.648	0.612
6/5/2016	22:11:19	0.834	0.065	0.133	0.09	0.638	0.613	0.638	0.666
6/5/2016	22:11:19	0.834	0.065	0.134	0.09	0.652	0.671	0.649	0.613
6/5/2016	22:11:19	0.834	0.065	0.134	0.09	0.649	0.624	0.623	0.66
6/5/2016	22:11:20	0.834	0.065	0.134	0.09	0.601	0.652	0.672	0.649

(Continued)

Date	Time	S1	S2	S3	S4	S5	S6	S7	S8
6/5/2016	22:11:20	0.834	0.065	0.133	0.089	0.672	0.671	0.629	0.585
6/5/2016	22:11:21	0.834	0.065	0.134	0.09	0.636	0.611	0.64	0.667
6/5/2016	22:11:22	0.834	0.066	0.135	0.087	0.656	0.676	0.645	0.611
6/5/2016	22:11:23	0.834	0.065	0.135	0.088	0.644	0.621	0.63	0.663
6/5/2016	22:11:23	0.834	0.065	0.135	0.088	0.599	0.65	0.671	0.652
6/5/2016	22:11:24	0.834	0.066	0.134	0.088	0.671	0.673	0.63	0.587
6/5/2016	22:11:24	0.834	0.066	0.135	0.088	0.652	0.624	0.618	0.659
6/5/2016	22:11:25	0.834	0.065	0.135	0.088	0.609	0.657	0.682	0.639
6/5/2016	22:11:26	0.834	0.065	0.135	0.088	0.666	0.68	0.637	0.599
6/5/2016	22:11:27	0.834	0.066	0.135	0.088	0.683	0.632	0.61	0.643
6/5/2016	22:11:28	0.834	0.066	0.135	0.088	0.619	0.632	0.662	0.69
6/5/2016	22:16:40	0.832	0.065	0.134	0.091	0.64	0.664	0.665	0.617
6/5/2016	22:16:41	0.832	0.065	0.134	0.09	0.657	0.623	0.613	0.655
6/5/2016	22:16:41	0.832	0.065	0.134	0.09	0.648	0.667	0.652	0.613
6/5/2016	22:16:42	0.832	0.066	0.134	0.091	0.698	0.632	0.611	0.633
6/5/2016	22:39:01	0.836	0.06	0.133	0.08	0.667	0.625	0.603	0.646
6/5/2016	22:39:02	0.836	0.061	0.131	0.08	0.629	0.659	0.68	0.624
6/5/2016	22:39:02	0.836	0.061	0.131	0.08	0.674	0.626	0.601	0.643
6/5/2016	22:39:03	0.836	0.06	0.131	0.08	0.606	0.655	0.68	0.637
6/5/2016	22:39:03	0.836	0.06	0.133	0.08	0.678	0.628	0.603	0.642
6/5/2016	22:39:03	0.836	0.06	0.133	0.08	0.623	0.658	0.683	0.628
6/5/2016	22:39:04	0.836	0.06	0.133	0.08	0.648	0.621	0.619	0.657
6/5/2016	22:39:04	0.836	0.06	0.133	0.08	0.651	0.671	0.643	0.608
6/5/2016	22:39:05	0.836	0.061	0.131	0.081	0.616	0.632	0.659	0.683
6/5/2016	22:39:05	0.836	0.061	0.133	0.08	0.69	0.639	0.617	0.622
6/5/2016	22:39:05	0.836	0.061	0.133	0.08	0.602	0.642	0.663	0.658
6/5/2016	22:39:06	0.838	0.06	0.133	0.08	0.667	0.67	0.626	0.582
6/5/2016	22:39:06	0.838	0.06	0.133	0.081	0.623	0.606	0.65	0.685
6/5/2016	22:39:07	0.836	0.06	0.133	0.08	0.664	0.679	0.631	0.592
6/5/2016	22:39:07	0.836	0.061	0.133	0.081	0.623	0.61	0.652	0.689
6/5/2016	22:39:08	0.838	0.06	0.133	0.08	0.677	0.649	0.619	0.601
6/5/2016	22:39:08	0.838	0.06	0.131	0.08	0.597	0.648	0.67	0.645
6/5/2016	22:39:09	0.838	0.06	0.131	0.08	0.692	0.638	0.615	0.625
6/5/2016	22:39:09	0.836	0.06	0.131	0.084	0.612	0.656	0.684	0.633
6/5/2016	22:39:10	0.838	0.059	0.13	0.084	0.665	0.625	0.603	0.649
6/5/2016	22:39:10	0.838	0.06	0.13	0.084	0.635	0.66	0.673	0.621
6/5/2016	22:39:10	0.838	0.06	0.131	0.084	0.658	0.623	0.606	0.651
6/5/2016	22:39:11	0.838	0.06	0.131	0.086	0.637	0.66	0.666	0.617
6/5/2016	22:39:12	0.838	0.06	0.131	0.084	0.667	0.625	0.603	0.648
6/5/2016	22:39:12	0.838	0.06	0.131	0.084	0.616	0.657	0.684	0.632
6/5/2016	22:39:12	0.838	0.06	0.131	0.084	0.66	0.624	0.605	0.65
6/5/2016	22:39:12	0.838	0.06	0.13	0.084	0.643	0.664	0.652	0.612
6/5/2016	22:39:13	0.838	0.06	0.13	0.084	0.63	0.603	0.64	0.669
6/5/2016	22:39:13	0.838	0.06	0.131	0.082	0.671	0.657	0.622	0.585
6/5/2016	22:39:13	0.838	0.061	0.131	0.081	0.621	0.619	0.656	0.692
6/5/2016	23:32:11	0.838	0.05	0.104	0.06	0.666	0.625	0.609	0.649
6/5/2016	23:32:11	0.839	0.05	0.104	0.06	0.599	0.646	0.667	0.655
6/5/2016	23:32:11	0.839	0.05	0.104	0.06	0.672	0.669	0.628	0.582
6/5/2016	23:32:12	0.839	0.05	0.104	0.06	0.637	0.611	0.637	0.664
6/5/2016	23:32:12	0.839	0.05	0.103	0.06	0.642	0.664	0.663	0.617

(Continued)

Date	Time	S1	S2	S3	S4	S5	S6	S7	S8
6/5/2016	23:32:12	0.838	0.049	0.104	0.06	0.69	0.631	0.609	0.637
6/5/2016	23:32:13	0.839	0.05	0.104	0.06	0.625	0.61	0.652	0.686
6/5/2016	23:32:13	0.839	0.05	0.104	0.06	0.642	0.664	0.662	0.617
6/5/2016	23:32:22	0.838	0.049	0.104	0.061	0.662	0.625	0.611	0.651
6/5/2016	23:32:22	0.839	0.05	0.103	0.06	0.623	0.659	0.684	0.63
6/5/2016	23:32:23	0.839	0.049	0.104	0.06	0.679	0.629	0.606	0.644
6/5/2016	23:32:23	0.839	0.05	0.104	0.06	0.613	0.636	0.66	0.682
6/5/2016	23:32:23	0.839	0.05	0.104	0.06	0.665	0.68	0.635	0.595
6/5/2016	23:32:23	0.838	0.05	0.104	0.06	0.644	0.617	0.63	0.659
6/5/2016	23:32:24	0.838	0.05	0.104	0.06	0.643	0.665	0.658	0.616
6/5/2016	23:32:24	0.838	0.05	0.106	0.06	0.642	0.616	0.632	0.66
6/5/2016	23:32:24	0.838	0.05	0.106	0.06	0.638	0.663	0.67	0.621
6/5/2016	23:32:25	0.838	0.05	0.104	0.06	0.693	0.632	0.61	0.635
6/5/2016	23:32:25	0.838	0.049	0.106	0.061	0.601	0.652	0.676	0.643
6/5/2016	23:44:08	0.838	0.052	0.107	0.059	0.686	0.629	0.606	0.637
6/5/2016	23:44:08	0.838	0.052	0.106	0.057	0.606	0.64	0.663	0.669
6/5/2016	23:44:08	0.838	0.052	0.106	0.059	0.646	0.666	0.652	0.612
6/5/2016	23:44:08	0.838	0.052	0.106	0.059	0.678	0.651	0.622	0.592
6/5/2016	23:44:09	0.838	0.05	0.106	0.059	0.597	0.649	0.673	0.646
6/5/2016	23:44:09	0.838	0.052	0.106	0.059	0.643	0.664	0.657	0.615
6/5/2016	23:44:09	0.838	0.052	0.104	0.057	0.686	0.644	0.618	0.608
6/5/2016	23:44:09	0.838	0.052	0.104	0.057	0.596	0.648	0.67	0.65
6/5/2016	23:44:10	0.838	0.052	0.106	0.057	0.689	0.63	0.605	0.637
6/5/2016	23:44:10	0.838	0.052	0.106	0.059	0.602	0.643	0.664	0.662
6/5/2016	23:44:10	0.838	0.052	0.106	0.057	0.662	0.678	0.638	0.601
6/5/2016	23:44:11	0.838	0.052	0.106	0.057	0.698	0.635	0.612	0.629
6/5/2016	23:44:11	0.838	0.052	0.106	0.057	0.633	0.608	0.638	0.666
6/5/2016	23:44:11	0.838	0.052	0.104	0.057	0.697	0.637	0.615	0.628
6/5/2016	23:44:11	0.838	0.05	0.106	0.059	0.637	0.611	0.635	0.663
6/5/2016	23:44:12	0.838	0.05	0.106	0.059	0.655	0.673	0.643	0.608
6/5/2016	23:44:12	0.838	0.052	0.104	0.056	0.696	0.639	0.617	0.622
6/5/2016	23:44:12	0.838	0.05	0.106	0.057	0.638	0.612	0.633	0.663
6/5/2016	23:44:12	0.838	0.05	0.106	0.059	0.601	0.655	0.678	0.64
6/5/2016	23:44:13	0.838	0.05	0.106	0.059	0.689	0.643	0.617	0.612
6/5/2016	23:44:13	0.838	0.052	0.106	0.057	0.638	0.613	0.633	0.663
6/5/2016	23:44:13	0.838	0.052	0.106	0.057	0.597	0.646	0.667	0.653
6/5/2016	23:44:13	0.838	0.053	0.104	0.057	0.69	0.643	0.617	0.612
6/5/2016	23:44:14	0.838	0.053	0.104	0.057	0.602	0.642	0.665	0.662
6/5/2016	23:44:14	0.838	0.052	0.104	0.057	0.693	0.642	0.617	0.616
6/5/2016	23:44:14	0.838	0.052	0.106	0.057	0.657	0.624	0.613	0.653
6/5/2016	23:44:15	0.838	0.052	0.106	0.057	0.61	0.637	0.662	0.677
6/5/2016	23:44:15	0.838	0.052	0.106	0.057	0.642	0.664	0.662	0.616
6/5/2016	23:44:15	0.838	0.052	0.106	0.059	0.698	0.637	0.613	0.626
6/5/2016	23:44:15	0.838	0.05	0.106	0.059	0.622	0.613	0.653	0.691
6/5/2016	23:44:15	0.838	0.05	0.106	0.057	0.619	0.659	0.684	0.631
6/5/2016	23:44:16	0.838	0.05	0.106	0.057	0.67	0.674	0.629	0.584
6/5/2016	23:44:16	0.838	0.052	0.106	0.057	0.698	0.636	0.613	0.626
6/5/2016	23:44:16	0.838	0.052	0.106	0.057	0.601	0.643	0.665	0.659
6/5/2016	23:44:17	0.838	0.052	0.104	0.057	0.694	0.639	0.617	0.621
6/5/2016	23:44:17	0.838	0.052	0.104	0.057	0.631	0.605	0.639	0.667

(Continued)

Date	Time	S1	S2	S3	S4	S5	S6	S7	S8
6/5/2016	23:44:17	0.838	0.05	0.106	0.059	0.652	0.672	0.644	0.609
6/5/2016	23:44:17	0.838	0.052	0.106	0.057	0.642	0.615	0.631	0.662
6/5/2016	23:44:18	0.838	0.05	0.106	0.059	0.653	0.672	0.645	0.609
6/5/2016	23:44:18	0.838	0.05	0.106	0.059	0.693	0.632	0.609	0.633
6/5/2016	23:44:18	0.838	0.052	0.106	0.057	0.608	0.656	0.684	0.637
6/5/2016	23:44:18	0.838	0.05	0.106	0.057	0.657	0.674	0.642	0.606
6/5/2016	23:44:19	0.838	0.052	0.106	0.057	0.689	0.629	0.606	0.637
6/5/2016	23:44:19	0.838	0.052	0.106	0.057	0.625	0.605	0.649	0.682
6/5/2016	23:44:19	0.838	0.052	0.104	0.057	0.633	0.662	0.674	0.622
6/5/2016	23:44:19	0.838	0.05	0.106	0.057	0.682	0.646	0.621	0.601
6/5/2016	23:44:20	0.838	0.052	0.106	0.057	0.64	0.615	0.631	0.662
6/5/2016	23:44:20	0.838	0.052	0.106	0.057	0.644	0.666	0.653	0.613
6/5/2016	23:44:20	0.838	0.052	0.106	0.057	0.683	0.629	0.606	0.639
6/5/2016	23:44:21	0.838	0.052	0.106	0.057	0.604	0.642	0.663	0.665
6/5/2016	23:44:21	0.838	0.05	0.106	0.059	0.697	0.639	0.616	0.622
6/5/2016	23:44:21	0.838	0.05	0.106	0.059	0.606	0.656	0.683	0.638
6/5/2016	23:44:21	0.838	0.052	0.104	0.057	0.678	0.626	0.604	0.644
6/5/2016	23:44:21	0.838	0.05	0.106	0.059	0.613	0.636	0.66	0.682
6/5/2016	23:44:51	0.838	0.049	0.102	0.059	0.678	0.655	0.622	0.588
6/5/2016	23:44:51	0.838	0.049	0.102	0.059	0.639	0.613	0.633	0.663
6/5/2016	23:44:52	0.838	0.048	0.104	0.067	0.596	0.651	0.672	0.646
6/5/2016	23:44:52	0.838	0.041	0.091	0.072	0.69	0.63	0.605	0.637
6/5/2016	23:44:52	0.838	0.05	0.102	0.087	0.604	0.656	0.682	0.638
6/5/2016	23:44:52	0.838	0.052	0.075	0.086	0.678	0.655	0.622	0.589
6/5/2016	23:44:52	0.838	0.052	0.075	0.086	0.66	0.624	0.611	0.652
6/5/2016	23:44:53	0.838	0.053	0.081	0.082	0.619	0.622	0.657	0.693
6/5/2016	23:44:53	0.838	0.05	0.083	0.083	0.679	0.652	0.622	0.595
6/5/2016	23:44:53	0.838	0.052	0.083	0.084	0.597	0.646	0.669	0.653
6/5/2016	23:44:53	0.838	0.052	0.083	0.084	0.674	0.659	0.624	0.582
6/5/2016	23:44:54	0.838	0.052	0.082	0.084	0.617	0.63	0.66	0.689
6/5/2016	23:44:54	0.838	0.053	0.082	0.083	0.683	0.65	0.621	0.599
6/5/2016	23:44:54	0.838	0.052	0.082	0.083	0.604	0.64	0.664	0.666
6/5/2016	23:44:54	0.838	0.053	0.082	0.083	0.698	0.635	0.612	0.63
6/5/2016	23:44:55	0.838	0.053	0.082	0.083	0.606	0.639	0.663	0.671
6/5/2016	23:44:55	0.838	0.052	0.082	0.083	0.673	0.667	0.625	0.578
6/5/2016	23:44:55	0.838	0.053	0.082	0.083	0.637	0.61	0.636	0.664
6/5/2016	23:44:55	0.838	0.053	0.082	0.083	0.665	0.68	0.633	0.592
6/5/2016	23:44:56	0.838	0.053	0.082	0.083	0.619	0.622	0.658	0.693
6/5/2016	23:44:56	0.838	0.052	0.081	0.083	0.672	0.67	0.626	0.579
6/5/2016	23:44:56	0.838	0.053	0.082	0.084	0.619	0.623	0.658	0.693
6/5/2016	23:44:57	0.838	0.052	0.082	0.084	0.699	0.638	0.616	0.625
6/5/2016	23:44:57	0.838	0.052	0.082	0.084	0.616	0.658	0.685	0.632
6/5/2016	23:44:57	0.838	0.053	0.082	0.084	0.686	0.629	0.604	0.64
6/5/2016	23:44:57	0.838	0.052	0.082	0.084	0.623	0.659	0.684	0.629
6/5/2016	23:44:57	0.838	0.053	0.082	0.084	0.659	0.623	0.612	0.652
6/5/2016	23:44:58	0.838	0.053	0.082	0.084	0.639	0.663	0.665	0.617
6/5/2016	23:44:58	0.838	0.053	0.081	0.084	0.656	0.622	0.615	0.655
6/5/2016	23:44:58	0.838	0.053	0.081	0.083	0.631	0.662	0.678	0.624
6/5/2016	23:44:59	0.838	0.053	0.081	0.084	0.69	0.631	0.608	0.637
6/5/2016	23:44:59	0.838	0.053	0.081	0.084	0.633	0.608	0.638	0.666

(Continued)

Date	Time	S1	S2	S3	S4	S5	S6	S7	S8
6/5/2016	23:44:59	0.838	0.052	0.081	0.083	0.667	0.679	0.631	0.587
6/5/2016	23:44:59	0.838	0.053	0.081	0.083	0.626	0.602	0.646	0.678
6/5/2016	23:45:00	0.838	0.053	0.081	0.084	0.66	0.679	0.638	0.601
6/5/2016	23:45:00	0.838	0.053	0.081	0.084	0.633	0.606	0.638	0.666
6/5/2016	23:45:00	0.838	0.053	0.081	0.083	0.643	0.665	0.657	0.615
6/5/2016	23:45:00	0.838	0.053	0.081	0.083	0.643	0.617	0.629	0.66

REFERENCES

1. (May 20, 2016). Retrieved from sleepfoundation.org/sleep-topics/women-and-sleep.
2. (May 20, 2016). Retrieved from www.sleepio.com/articles/sleep-science/how-do-you-measure-sleep 2–22.
3. Aguiar, I. C., et al. (2014). Obstructive sleep apnea and pulmonary function in patients with severe obesity before and after bariatric surgery: A randomized clinical trial. *Multidisciplinary Respiratory Medicine.* 9(1): 43.
4. Akerstedt, T., Fredlund, P., Gillberg, M., & Jansson, B. (2002). Work load and work hours in relation to disturbed sleep and fatigue in a large representative sample. *Journal of Psychosomatic Research.* 53, 585–588.
5. Angelo, S. (1997). The hospital as an enterprise: Management strategies. *Tropical Medicine and International Health* (2nd ed., pp. 278–283).
6. Arnetz, B. B., Templin, T., Saudi, W., & Jamil, H. (2012). Obstructive sleep apnea, posttraumatic stress disorder, and health in immigrants. *Psychosomatic Medicine.* 74(8), 824–831. doi:10.1097/PSY.0b013e31826bf1ec.
7. Ayre, L. (2012). *RFID in Libraries: A Step Toward Interoperability.* American Library Association.
8. Barcoding Hospital Data Capture Solutions. (May 20, 2016). Retrieved from www.barcoding.com/hospital-acute-care-facility-data-capture-solutions.shtml.
9. Bendavida, Y., & Boeck, H. (2011). Using RFID to improve hospital supply chain management for high value and consignment items. *Procedia Computer Science.* 5, 849–856. doi:10.1016/j.procs.2011.07.117.
10. Bjornsdottir, E., et al. (2012). Insomnia in untreated sleep apnea patients compared to controls. *Journal of Sleep Research.* 21(2): 131–138.
11. Blanco, C., Xu, Y., Brady, K., Perez, F. G., & Okuda, M., & Wang, S. Comorbidity of posttraumatic stress disorder with alcohol dependence among US adults: Results from national epidemiological survey on alcohol and related conditions. *Drug and Alcohol Dependence.* 132, 630–638.
12. Bowerson, D. J. (1990). The strategic benefits of logistics. *Harvard Business Review.* 24–29.
13. Bradley, T. D. Y., Strohl, T. B., & Spry, K. (1998). American Thoracic Society. Statement on health outcomes research in sleep apnea. *American Journal of Respiratory and Critical Care Medicine.* 157, 335–341.
14. Calhoun, P. S., Wiley, M., Dennis, M. F., Means, M. K., Edinger, J. D., & Beckham, J. C. (2007). Objective evidence of sleep disturbance in women with posttraumatic stress disorder. *Journal of Traumatic Stress.* 20, 1009–1018.
15. Campos-Rodríguez, F., Martínez-García, M. A., & Montserrat, J. M. (2012). Gender differences in treatment recommendations for sleep apnea. *Clinical Practice.* 9: 565–578.
16. Canadian Agency for Drugs and Technologies in Health. (2010). Diagnosis of snoring and obstructive sleep apnea: A review of the accuracy. *CADTH Technology Overviews.* 1(1): e0108.
17. Correa, F. A., Gil, M. J. A., & Redin, L. B. (2007). RFID and health management: Is it a good tool against system inefficiencies. *International Journal of Healthcare Technology and Management.* 8(3/4), 268–297.
18. Duri, E. A. (1997). *World Journal of Modeling and Simulation.* 3, 196–201.
19. Dursunoglu, N., Ozkurt, S., & Sarikaya S. (2009). Is the clinical presentation different between men and women admitting to the sleep laboratory? *Sleep and Breathing.* 3: 295–598.
20. Eckert, D. J., & Malhotra, A. (2008). Pathophysiology of adult obstructive sleep apnea. *Proceedings of the American Thoracic Society.* 5(2): 144–153.
21. Eckert, D. J., et al. (2009). The influence of obstructive sleep apnea and gender on genioglossus activity during rapid eye movement sleep. *Chest.* 135(4): 957–964.

22. Eliasson, A. H., Kashani, M. D., Howard, R. S., Vernalis, M. N., & Modlin, R. E. (2014). Fatigued on Venus, sleepy on Mars-gender and racial differences in symptoms of sleep apnea. *Sleep and Breathing*. 19(1), 99–107. doi:10.1007/s11325-014-0968-y.

23. Elizabeth, M. (2010). Emerging technologies in healthcare: Navigating risks, evaluating rewards. *Journal of Healthcare Management*. 55, 353–365.

24. Engleman, H., & Joffe, D. (1999). Neuropsychological function in obstructive sleep apnoea. *Sleep Medicine Reviews*. 3(1), 59–78. doi:10.1016/S1087-0792(99)90014-X.

25. Erdem, E., Zeng, H., Zhou, J., Shi, J., & Wells, D. L. (2011). Investigation of RFID tag readability for pharmaceutical products at item level RFID tag readability for pharmaceutical products. *Drug Development and Industrial Pharmacy*. 35(11), 1312–1324. doi:10.3109/03639040902902393.

26. Espie, C. A. (2002). INSOMNIA: Conceptual issues in the development, persistence, and treatment of sleep disorder in adults. *Annual Review of Psychology*. 53(215), 243.

27. Evans, J. R., & Lindsay, W. M. (2002). *The Management and Control of Quality* (5th ed., pp. 344–387). Thomson Learning, South-Western Division.

28. Fido, A., & Ghali, A. (2008). Detrimental effects of variable work shifts on quality of sleep, general health and work performance. *Medical Principles and Practice*. 17(6), 453–457. doi:10.1159/000151566.

29. Figueroa, A. L., et al. (2012). Distribution of inflammation within carotid atherosclerotic plaques with high-risk morphological features: A comparison between positron emission tomography activity, plaque morphology, and histopathology. *Circulation: Cardiovascular Imaging*. 5(1): 69–77.

30. Flo, E., Pallesen, S., Magerøy, N., Moen, B. E., Grønli, J., Nordhus, I. H., & Bjorvatn, B. (2012). Shift work disorder in nurses – assessment, prevalence and related health problems. *PLoS One*. doi:10.1371/journal.pone.0033981.

31. Gardner-Thorpe, J., et al. (2003). Angiogenesis in tissue-engineered small intestine. *Tissue Engineering*. 9(6): 1255–1261.

32. Gibson, E. M., Wang, C., Tjho, S., Khattar, N., & Kriegsfeld, L. J. (2010). Experimental 'jet lag' inhibits adult neurogenesis and produces long-term cognitive deficits in female hamsters. *PLoS One*. 5(12) doi:10.1371/journal.pone.0015267.

33. Gordon, N. P., Cleary, P. D., Parker, C. E., & Czeisler, C. A. (1986). The prevalence and health impact of shiftwork. *American Journal of Public Health*. 76, 1225–1228.

34. Guilleminault, C., et al. (1988). Women and the obstructive sleep apnea syndrome. *Chest*. 93(1): 104–109.

35. Gulemetova, R., Drolet, G., & Kinkead, R. (2013). Neonatal stress augments the hypoxic chemoreflex of adult male rats by increasing AMPA receptor-mediated modulation. *Experimental Physiology*. 98(8): 1312–1324.

36. Gupta, S., & Jones, E. C. (2014). Optimizing supply chain distribution using cloud based autonomous information. *International Journal of Supply Chain Management*. 3(4).

37. Harland, C. (1998). Supply network strategy: Observations on structure, infrastructure and operations (pp. 248–267). *Proceedings of the P'World Wide Symposium on Purchasing and Supply Chain Management*.

38. Hedner, J., et al. (2006). Hypertension prevalence in obstructive sleep apnoea and sex: A population-based case-control study. *European Respiratory Journal*. 27(3): 564–570.

39. Henry, D., & Rosenthal, L. (2013). "Listening for his breath:" The significance of gender and partner reporting on the diagnosis, management, and treatment of obstructive sleep apnea. *Social Science and Medicine*. 79: 48–56.

40. Jain, S. P., Jones, E. C., Gupta, S., & Okate, S. I. (2014). Evaluating the impact of sustainability and pipeline quality on global crude oil supply chain efficiency. *International Journal of Supply Chain Management*. 3(4).

41. Jefferson, F. A., Paul, K. N., & Clark, K. (2013). Sex differences in the REM sleep response to OSA. *Gordon Research Conference on Sleep Regulation and Function* [Abstr #2–22].

42. Jones, E. C., & Chung, C. A. (2008). RFID in logistics.

43. Jones, E. C., Gray, B., Okate, S. I., & Armstrong, H. (2014). What you should know about invisible monitoring and security.

44. Jones, E. C., Gupta, S., Jefferson, F., Rogers, J., Choi, J. B., Bolton, J., & Cochran, D. (2015). Chipped pharmaceuticals from production to in VIVO (in body) drug delivery becoming reality. *International Journal of Supply Chain Management*. 4(1).

45. Jordan, A. S., et al. (2004). The influence of gender and upper airway resistance on the ventilatory response to arousal in obstructive sleep apnoea in humans. *Journal of Physiology.* 558(Pt 3): 993–1004.

46. Kapsimalis, F., & Kryger, M. H. (2002). Gender and obstructive sleep apnea syndrome, Part 1: Clinical features. *Sleep.* 25(4): 412–419.

47. Kapur, V., et al. (1999). The medical cost of undiagnosed sleep apnea. *Sleep.* 22(6): 749–755.

48. Kessler, R. C., Sonnega, A., Bromet, F., Hughes, M., & Nelson, C. B. (1995). Posttraumatic stress disorder in the national comorbidity survey. *Archives of General Psychiatry.* 52, 1048–1060.

49. Khosla, R., & Chowdhury, B. (2007). RFID based real-time patient management system.

50. Kinkead, R., Guertin, P. A., & Gulemetova, R. (2013). Sex, stress and their influence on respiratory regulation. *Current Pharmaceutical Design.* 19(24): 4471–4484.

51. Kling, R. N., McLeod, C. B., & Koehoorn, M. (2010). Sleep problems and workplace injuries in Canada. *Sleep.* 33, 611–618.

52. Kloepfer, C., Riemann, D., Nofzinger, E. A., Feige, B., Unterrainer, J., O'Hara, R., Sorichter, S., & Nissen, C. (2009). Memory before and after sleep in patients with moderate obstructive sleep apnea. *Journal of Clinical Sleep Medicine.* 5(6), 540–548.

53. Koehl, M., Battle, S., & Meerlo, P. (2006). Sex differences in sleep: The response to sleep deprivation and restraint stress in mice. *Sleep.* 29(9): 1224–1231.

54. Koo, B. B., Dostal, J., Ioachimescu, O., & Budur, K. (2008). The effects of gender and age on REM-related sleep-disordered breathing. *Sleep & Breathing.* 12(3), 259–264. doi:10.1007/s11325-007-0161-7.

55. Krakow, B., & Ulibarri, V. A. (2013). Prevalence of sleep breathing complaints reported by treatment-seeking chronic insomnia disorder patients on presentation to a sleep medical center: A preliminary report. *Sleep & Breathing.* 17(1): 317–322.

56. Krishnan, V., & Collop, N. A. (2006) Gender differences in sleep disorders. *Current Opinion in Pulmonary Medicine.* 12(6): 383–389.

57. Krishnan, V., et al. (2008). Sleep quality and health-related quality of life in idiopathic pulmonary fibrosis. *Chest.* 134(4): 693–698.

58. Krishnan, V., Collop, N. A., & Scherr, S. C. (2008). An evaluation of a titration strategy for prescription of oral appliances for obstructive sleep apnea. *Chest.* 133(5): 1135–1141.

59. Kumar, S., Livermont, G., & McKewan, G. (2010). Stage implementation of RFID in hospitals. *Technology and Health Care.* 18, 31–46.

60. Kumar, S., Swanson, E., & Tran, T. (2009). RFID in the healthcare supply chain: Usage and application. *International Journal of Health Care Quality Assurance.* 22(1), 67–81.

61. Larsson, L. G., Lindberg, A., Franklin, K. A., & Lundbäck, B. (2003). Gender differences in symptoms related to sleep apnea in a general population and in relation to referral to sleep clinic. *Chest.* 124: 201–211.

62. Laudencka, A., Klawe, J. J., Tafil-Klawe, M., & Złomańczuk, P. (2007). Does night-shift work induce apnea events in obstructive sleep apnea patients? *Journal of Physiology and Pharmacology.* 58, 345–347.

63. Lee, I., & Lee, B. C. (2012). Measuring the value of RFID investment: Focusing on RFID budget allocation. *IEEE Transactions on Engineering Management.* 59, 67–81.

64. Lee, M. H., et al. (2014). Gender differences in the effect of comorbid insomnia symptom on depression, anxiety, fatigue, and daytime sleepiness in patients with obstructive sleep apnea. *Sleep and Breathing.* 18(1): 111–117.

65. Leonord, L., & Davis, C. (2010). Supply chain replenishment: Before-and-after EDI implementation. *Supply Chain Management: An International Journal.* 11, 225–232.

66. Lichstein, K. L., et al. (2013). Co-occurring insomnia and obstructive sleep apnea. *Sleep Medicine.* 14(9): 824–829.

67. Lin, C. C., Lin, P. Y., Lu, P. K., Hsieh, G. Y., Lee, W. L., & Lee, R. G. (2008). A healthcare integration system for disease assessment and safety monitoring of dementia patients. *IEEE Transactions on Information Technology in Biomedicine.* 12(5), 579–586.

68. Lin, S. H., Fong, L. S., & Sheng, C. W. (2012). RFID medicine management system. *International Conference on Machine Learning and Cybernetics,* 15–17.

69. Marquié, J. C., & Foret, J. (1999). Sleep, age, and shiftwork experience. *Journal of Sleep Research.* 8(4), 297–304.

70. Matos, G., et al. (2013). More than hormones: Sex differences in cardiovascular parameters after sleep loss in rats. *Programs in Neuropsychopharmacology and Biological Psychiatry.* 44: 34–38.

71. Mehmet, B. (2006). RFID and corporate responsibility: Hidden costs in RFID implementation. *Business and Society Review*. 111, 287–303.
72. Mermigkis, C., et al. (2012). CRP evolution pattern in CPAP-treated obstructive sleep apnea patients. Does gender play a role? *Sleep & Breathing*. 16(3): 813–819.
73. Mohensin, V. (2001). Gender differences in the expression of sleep-disordered breathing. *Chest*. 120: 1442–1447.
74. Morrish, E., Shneerson, J. M., & Smith, I. E. (2008). Why does gender influence survival in obstructive sleep apnoea? *Respiratory Medicine*. 102(9): 1231–1236.
75. Munoz, A., Mayoralas, L. R., Barbe, F., Pericas, J., & Agusti, A. G. N. (2000). Long-term effects of CPAP on daytime functioning in patients with sleep apnea syndrome. *The European Respiratory Journal*. 15(4), 676–681.
76. Ngai, E. W. T., et al. (2010). RFID systems implementation: A comprehensive framework and a case study. *International Journal of Production Research*. 11, 2583–2612.
77. O'Connor, C., Thornley, K. S., & Hanly, P. J. (2000). Gender differences in the polysomnographic features of obstructive sleep apnea. *American Journal of Respiratory and Critical Care Medicine*. 161: 1465–1472.
78. Ohayon, M., Lemoine, P., Arnaud, B. V., & Dreyfus, M. (2002). Prevalence and consequences of sleep disorders in a shift worker population. *Journal of Psychosomatic Research*. 53, 577–583.
79. Ozeke, O., et al. (2011). Chronic intermittent hypoxia caused by obstructive sleep apnea may play an important role in explaining the morbidity-mortality paradox of obesity. *Medical Hypotheses*. 76(1): 61–63.
80. Ozeke, O., et al. (2011). Influence of the severity of obstructive sleep apnea on nocturnal heart rate indices and its association with hypertension. *Anadolu Kardiyoloji Dergisi*. 11(6): 509–514.
81. Paul, K. N., Turek, F. W., & Kryger, M. H. (2008). Influence of sex on sleep regulatory mechanisms. *Journal of Women's Health (Larchmt)*. 17(7): 1201–1208.
82. Pedrosa, R. P., et al. (2011). Recent advances of the impact of obstructive sleep apnea on systemic hypertension. *Arquivos Brasileiros de Cardiologia*. 97(2): 40–47.
83. Pellegrino R., Mazzotti, D., Guindalini, C., Santos-Silva, R., Bittencourt, L. R., & Tufik, S. (2011). Apolipoprotein E polymorphisms and sleep quality in obstructive sleep apnea syndrome. *Clinica Chimica Acta*. 412: 23–24.
84. Punjabi, N. M. (2008). The epidemiology of adult obstructive sleep apnea. *Proceedings of the American Thoracic Society*. 5(2): 136–143.
85. Qu, Z., Wang, X., Tian, D., Zhao, Y., Zhang, Q., He, H., Zhang, X., Xu, F., & Guo, S. (2012). Posttraumatic stress disorder and depression among new mothers at 8 months later of the 2008 Sichuan earthquake in China. *Archives of Women's Mental Health*. 15, 49–55.
86. Quintana-Gallego, E., et al. (2004). Gender differences in obstructive sleep apnea syndrome: A clinical study of 1166 patients. *Respiratory Medicine*. 98(10): 984–989.
87. Rajagopalan, N. (2011). Obstructive sleep apnea: Not just a sleep disorder. *Journal of Postgraduate Medicine*. 27(2), 168–175. doi:10.4103/0022-3859.81866.
88. Ralls, F. M., & Grigg-Damberger, M. (2012). Roles of gender, age, race/ethnicity, and residential socioeconomics in obstructive sleep apnea syndromes. *Current Opinion in Pulmonary Medicine*. 18(6): 568–573.
89. Rouch, I., Wild, P., Ansiau, D., & Marquié, J. (2005). Shiftwork experience, age and cognitive performance. *Ergonomics*. 48(10), 1282–1293. doi:10.1080/00140130500241670.
90. Runyon J. J., Maislin, G., & Schwab, R. J., (2001). Gender differences in symptoms associated with sleep apnea. *Sleep Review*.
91. Saaty, T. L. (1990). *The Analytic Hierarchy Process: Planning, Priority Setting, Resource Allocation* (pp. 266–278). RWS Publication.
92. Sampaio, R., Pereira, M. G., & Winck, J. C. 2012, Psychological morbidity, illness representations, and quality of life in female and male patients with obstructive sleep apnea syndrome. *Psychology, Health and Medicine*. 17(2): 136–149.
93. Schneider, S., Fulda, S., & Schulz, H. (2004). Daytime variation in performance and tiredness/sleepiness ratings in patients with insomnia, narcolepsy, sleep apnea and normal controls. *Journal of Sleep Research*. 13(4), 373–383.

94. Sforza, E., et al. (2011). Sex differences in obstructive sleep apnoea in an elderly French population. *European Respiratory Journal*. 37(5): 1137–1143.

95. Shepertycky, M. R., Banno, K., & Kryger M. H. (2004). Differences between men and women in the clinical presentation of patients diagnosed with obstructive sleep apnea disorder. *Sleep*. 28: 309–313.

96. Shepertycky, M. R., Banno, K., & Kryger, M. H. (2005). Differences between men and women in the clinical presentation of patients diagnosed with obstructive sleep apnea syndrome. *Sleep*. 28(3): 309–314.

97. Simchi-Levi, D., Wu, D. S., & Shen, Z. M. (1996). *Handbook of Quantitative Supply Chain Analysis* (pp. 134–140). Kluwer Academic Publishers.

98. Simpson, L., et al. (2010). Sex differences in the association of regional fat distribution with the severity of obstructive sleep apnea. *Sleep*. 33(4): 467–474.

99. Smith, S. S., et al. (2006). Associations between the use of common medications and sleep architecture in patients with untreated obstructive sleep apnea. *Journal of Clinical Sleep Medicine*. 2(2): 156–162.

100. Subramanian, S., et al. (2013). Gender and age influence the effects of slow-wave sleep on respiration in patients with obstructive sleep apnea. *Sleep and Breathing*. 17(1): 51–56.

101. Subramanian, S., et al. (2012). Influence of gender and anthropometric measures on severity of obstructive sleep apnea. *Sleep and Breathing*. 16(4): 1091–1095.

102. Tarasiuk, A., & Reuveni, H. (2013). The economic impact of obstructive sleep apnea. *Current Opinion in Pulmonary Medicine*. 19(6): 639–644.

103. Mohsenin, V. (2003). Effects of gender on upper airway collapsibility and severity of obstructive sleep apnea. *Sleep Medicine*. 4: 523–529.

104. Vaananen, V., et al. (2003). Air concentrations and urinary metabolites of polycyclic aromatic hydrocarbons among paving and remixing workers. *Journal of Environmental Monitoring*. 5(5): 739–746.

105. Vagiakis, E., Kapsimalis, F., Lagogianni, I., Perraki, H., Minaritzoglou, A., Alexandropoulou, K., Roussos, C., & Kryger, M. (2006). Gender differences on polysomnographic findings in Greek subjects with obstructive sleep apnea syndrome. *Sleep Medicine*. 5: 424–430.

106. Valipour, A., Lothaller, H., Rauscher, H., Zwich, H., Burghuber, O. C., & Lavie, P. (2007). Gender-related differences in symptoms of patients with suspected breathing disorders in sleep: A clinical population study using the sleep disorders questionnaire. *Sleep*. 30: 312–319.

107. Veasey, S. C. (2012). Piecing together phenotypes of brain injury and dysfunction in obstructive sleep apnea. *Frontiers in Neurology*. doi:10.3389/fneur.2012.00139.

108. Veasey, S. C., et al. (2006). Medical therapy for obstructive sleep apnea: A review by the Medical Therapy for Obstructive Sleep Apnea Task Force of the Standards of Practice Committee of the American Academy of Sleep Medicine. *Sleep*. 29(8): 1036–1044.

109. Vinson, D. C., et al. (2010). Alcohol and sleep problems in primary care patients: A report from the AAFP National Research Network. *Annals of Family Medicine*. 8(6): 484–492.

110. Wali, S. O. (1997). Long-term compliance with continuous positive airway pressure in patients with obstructive sleep apnea syndrome. *Annals of Saudi Medicine*. 17(6): 616–618.

111. Walia, H. K., et al. (2012). Clinical presentation of shift workers to a sleep clinic. *Sleep and Breathing*. 16(2): 543–547.

112. Walker, R. P., et al. (2001). Preoperative differences between male and female patients with sleep apnea. *Laryngoscope*. 111(9): 1501–1505.

113. Ware, J. C., McBrayer, R. H., & Scott, J. A. (2000). Influence of sex and age on duration and frequency of sleep apnea events. *Sleep*. 23(2): 165–170.

114. White, D. P., et al. (1985). Pharyngeal resistance in normal humans: Influence of gender, age, and obesity. *Journal of Applied Physiology*. 58(2): 365–371.

115. Yardim-Akaydin, S., et al. (2014). Influence of gender on C-reactive protein, fibrinogen, and erythrocyte sedimentation rate in obstructive sleep apnea. *Antiinflammatory and Antiallergy Agents in Medicinal Chemistry*. 13(1): 56–63.

116. Ye, L., et al. (2009). Gender differences in obstructive sleep apnea and treatment response to continuous positive airway pressure. *Journal of Clinical Sleep Medicine*. 5(6): 512–518.

117. Young T., & Finn, L. (1998). Epidemiological insights into the public health burden of sleep disordered breathing: Sex differences in survival among sleep clinic patients. *Thorax*. 58: S16–S19.

118. Young, T., Peppard, P. E., & Gottlieb, D. J. (2002). Epidemiology of obstructive sleep apnea: A population health perspective. *American Journal of Respiratory and Critical Care Medicine*. 165(9): 1217–1239.

20

Evaluating the Impact of Sustainability Incentives to Optimize the Indonesian to the United States Crude Oil Supply Chain

Restu P. Suanarto and Erick C. Jones

20.1 Introduction

The *New York Times* explained that the United States increased its dependence on oil from Saudi Arabia by more than 20% last year (Krauss 2012). However, according to the United States of Energy Information Administration (U.S. EIA), the net imported oil of the United States has declined since peaking in 2005—see Figure 20.1 ("Oil: Explained" 2012). Krauss described that the increase in oil imports from Saudi Arabia began last summer for a number of reasons:

> Saudi Arabia increased oil production and exportation to all countries including the U.S. to keep oil prices stable, because Iran is exporting less oil due to sanctions imposed by the U.S. which gives some fear to make nuclear weapons; several domestic oil refining companies in the U.S. have found it necessary to buy more crude oil from Saudi Arabia to make up for declining production from Mexico and Venezuela; Canadian oil production has been increasing rapidly in recent years, unfortunately, there is not enough pipeline capacity; and there are also echoes from the disastrous British Petroleum (BP) well explosion and spill in 2010, which led to yearlong drilling moratorium in the Gulf Mexico.

(2012)

The U.S. EIA stated that the United States consumed an estimated 18.8 million barrels per day (MMbd) of petroleum products and produced 10.4 MMbd of crude oil and petroleum products during 2011 ("Oil: Explained" 2012). Therefore, the U.S. net imports of crude oil and petroleum products equaled 8.4 MMbd, making the United States dependent on foreign oil—see Figure 12.1 ("Oil: Explained" 2012).

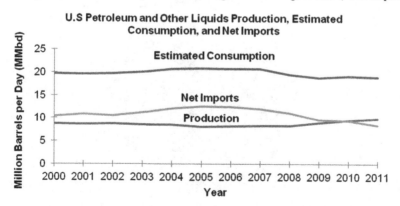

FIGURE 20.1 U.S. petroleum and other liquids production, estimated consumption, and net imports from 2000 to 2011. Preliminary data: U.S. EIA, October 21, 2012, Web.

The Western hemisphere including North, South, and Central America, the Caribbean, and the U.S. territories; and the Persian Gulf countries such as Iraq, Kuwait, Qatar, Saudi Arabia, and United Arab Emirates exported 52% and 22%, respectively, of crude oil and petroleum products to the United States in 2011 ("Oil: Explained" 2012). Oil from Canada (a Western hemisphere country) and Saudi Arabia (a Persian Gulf country) was accounted for 29% and 14%, respectively, of the U.S. crude oil and petroleum products, which made those countries as the top two foreign oil sources for the United States in 2011—see Figure 20.2 ("Oil: Explained" 2012). This is problematic due to the fact that 14% of the U.S. net crude oil and petroleum products imports come from one country, Saudi Arabia, which leaves the United States susceptible to Middle Eastern manipulation and homeland security.

What happens to the U.S. economy when Saudi Arabia manipulates demand and possibly stops exporting oil to the United States? Over the decades, there has been disbelief that the U.S. dependence on foreign oil has presented strategic challenges and has shown effects on the nation's economy and national security. However, this dependency also helps to shape the U.S. foreign policy and influences international relations. Today, the debate lies in the issues of which foreign oil dependence is more challenging and what steps should be taken by the U.S. government to help ease these issues. The significance of this research is to seek impacts of the U.S. dependency on foreign oil problems by introducing a mixed-integer programming (MIP) model that identifies how other nations such as Indonesia can supply some of crude oil imports with respect to the trade-off between crude oil supply chain quality, sustainable environmental incentives, and supply chain costs. According to the U.S. EIA, oil from Indonesia was accounted for only 0.24% of the U.S. crude oil and petroleum products in 2011—see Figure 20.2 ("Oil: Explained" 2012). Furthermore, the broader impact is investments into other countries crude oil supply chains can be quantified and optimized, and countries such as Indonesia can be identified as possible candidates for investment for future global crude oil needs.

The U.S. government, crude oil refining companies, and other stakeholders find that it is necessary to invest infrastructure and to buy crude oil from other nations. Therefore, this research strives to answer the research question of "When is it economically beneficial to invest in the supply chain quality of crude oil from a given nation?", hypothesizes that the crude oil supply chain quality will impact the crude oil supply chain costs and the environmental sustainability will have an impact on crude oil supply chain, and suggests that the crude oil supply chains in each of these countries will dictate their ability to provide crude oil.

The goal of most companies is to maximize profit and shareholder value. Pirog explained that companies can accomplish this goal through several activities such as organize production so that the company can make profit in the current time frame as well as in the future, make investment decisions to raise the company's rate of return, and motivate employees to increase productivity, decrease costs, and hence

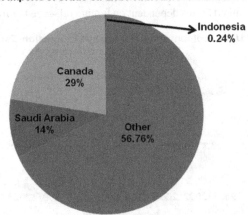

FIGURE 20.2 U.S. net imports of crude oil and petroleum products from Saudi Arabia, Canada, and Indonesia in 2011. Preliminary data: U.S. EIA, October 21, 2012, Web.

enhance profitability (2007, CRS-5). Those activities assure that the goods or services have high quality and are available at the lowest price consistent with demand and supply factors which benefit customers.

In oil industry, resources optimization through managing exploration, production, and development activities will maximize the shareholder value to guarantee a functioning market. Therefore, reserve replacement and the ability to expand production and sales to meet demand are necessary to ensure long-term viability of the oil companies. Pirog also stated that the efficiency in all parts of the supply chain leads to cost minimization, improvements in product performance, and environmental integrity (2007, CRS-5).

A majority of governments own their national oil companies; thus, the companies do not follow the maximization of shareholder value. However, they might have to compete with other government's objectives in order to maximize the shareholder value. The amount of a government's influence on its national oil companies varies widely. In the developed nations, the national oil companies such as Statoil of Norway and PETRONAS of Malaysia tend to follow "a commercial-oriented strategy" (Pirog 2007, CRS-6). In the less developed nations, the national oil companies such as Nigerian National Petroleum Co. of Nigeria, Petroleos de Venezuela of the Bolivarian Republic of Venezuela, and PERTAMINA of Indonesia, often the government objectives supersede commercial objectives. Additionally, the government applies more pressure to those companies to maximize the flow of funds to national treasuries.

With the aim of answering the research question and decreasing the U.S. dependency on foreign oil only from one or two countries, this research has an overall objective to investigate an MIP model that supports decisions about providing economic and environmental incentives to improve the supply chain quality of crude oil in Indonesia so that it becomes more cost-effective for the United States to import crude oil from Indonesia as opposed to other global sources and helps PERTAMINA to contribute more funds to the Indonesia's national treasuries as well.

Unlike other nations, the United States does not own a national oil company. Pirog explained that if the United States owned a national oil company, it would be established based on a "non-market strategy" policy and would have some potential advantages that other companies do not share such as acting to offset other national oil companies similar to how other nations' national oil companies behave, the oil company directly responding to and implementing national energy policy (2007, CRS-15). On the other hand, Pirog also argued some potential disadvantages such that if the United States had disagreements with a host nation, that country may be more willing to remove the U.S. national oil company vs. a privatized international oil company because international politics play a larger role, and international private oil companies are generally more efficient and productive, especially in terms of gaining access to drilling areas (2007, CRS-16).

There are several examples of unsuccessful deals between national oil companies in which the outcomes failed to meet expectations such as China and Iran as well as China and Saudi Arabia. Unlike with those countries, Indonesia has had a successful history working with the United States both domestically and with exporting crude oil. For these reasons, the United States would find it beneficial to increase its oil imports from Indonesia. The objective of this research is to evaluate the effectiveness of an MIP model that demonstrates the trade-off between crude oil supply chain qualities on profits in Indonesia. In order to meet this objective, three specific objectives are investigated such as evaluating the supply chain factors that determine supply chain quality of crude oil production, evaluating sampling plans that balances the trade-offs among various economic and environmental incentives for crude oil suppliers in Indonesia, and evaluating the economic impacts of inspection tools (quality) and environmental incentives (sustainability) tools on operational strategies in supplier networks.

20.2 Background

The world's most important sources of energy are petroleum, coal, natural gas, nuclear, and renewable energy. The Organization of Petroleum Exporting Countries (OPEC) stated that petroleum contributed to 35% of the world's energy source in 2010—see Figure 20.3 ("World Oil Outlook" 2012). The U.S. EIA stated that Americans utilized petroleum products for about 36% (35.3 quadrillion Btu) of the U.S. total energy use (97.5 quadrillion Btu) and 93% of transportation relied on those petroleum products in 2011 ("Energy Source" 2012). This shows that the transportation sector is the primary customer of total energy use in the U.S. Transportation moves both products and people from point A to B; thus, it is important to the economy. Industries must have access to get raw materials and distribute products, while people must go to work. Therefore, oil is critical to the economic growth, and demand for petroleum products from the transportation sector definitely drives the value of oil.

Reynolds envisioned that one of the side effects of the U.S. dependency on foreign oil is that only a few Americans could afford transportation due to an increase in oil price that leads to an increase in prices for all products (2010, 1). There are many misunderstandings regarding the relationship between crude oil prices and petroleum products such as gasoline prices. One can tell that the change in gasoline prices is related to a change in crude oil prices—see Figure 20.4. The American Petroleum Institute (API) explained three important points on how crude oil prices affect petroleum products prices:

> First, crude oil and petroleum products are global commodities which supply and demand factors on a global marketplace (see Figure 5) determine both crude oil and petroleum products prices. Second, the price paid for petroleum products is determined by crude oil prices. Third, worldwide markets, to a great extent, determine prices taking in account both current and future expected supply and demand conditions.

("Today's Crude Oil" 2006)

World Energy Sources in 2010

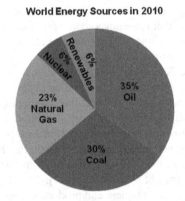

FIGURE 20.3 World energy sources in 2010. Preliminary data: OPEC World Oil Outlook 2012, January 14, 2013, Web.

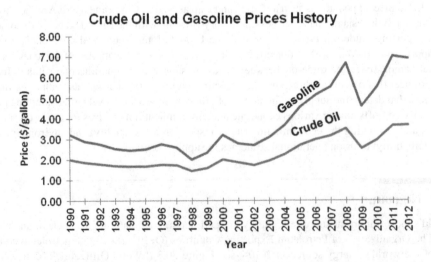

FIGURE 20.4 Crude oil and gasoline prices history from 1990 to 2012. Preliminary data: U.S. EIA, February 18, 2013, Web.

In the oil industry, the supply chain occurs within a global marketplace. It is an international chain that links producers, refiners, marketers, brokers, traders, and customers who sell and buy crude oil and petroleum products. Thus, the global oil marketplace facilitates oil movement from where it is produced, to where it is refined into petroleum products and to where those products are ultimately sold to customers ("Today's Crude Oil" 2006). The existing global marketplace reflects both sellers and buyers to the market in order to get the lowest transportation costs from sellers to buyers for each type of crude oil. As a result, trade flows in the global marketplace are the customers' preferences for different qualities of crude oil with the minimum transportation costs. However, this does not make trade flows to evaluate supply and demand or crude oil pricing. As an example, if an oil source cuts off its supply, whether or not that oil flows to the United States, then competition from buyers for the world's remaining supplies would drive up all crude oil prices because those supplies would find new buyers who would release their existing purchases to the market. Alternatively, if a nation decides to cut off its shipments of crude oil to the United States but maintained its production, then long-term impact on price would exist.

The API explained that the crude oil price increases because demand increases in response to global economic growth. Additionally, the increase in demand is also a result of the world's spare capacity reduction. This reduction is described by a supply that has not fully kept pace with the growing demand because it takes time to bring significant new products into the market. Politics play roles to the spare capacity reduction; hence, the global marketplace faces uncertainty in the oil supply. There are some examples of supply uncertainty due to geopolitical issues such as the supplies lost due to war in Iraq, civil unrest in Nigeria and Venezuela, and ongoing exports uncertainty from Iran ("Today's Crude Oil" 2006).

The oil global marketplace has been transforming over the last 25 years in its contractual structures of purchasing and selling the crude oil. Formerly, the market structure was based on rigid long-term and commercially arranged agreements. Today's market structure is more efficient that it allows greater flexibility for buyers and sellers to establish commercial relationships and meet their respective needs.

The refining sector of the oil industry has significantly affected the crude oil global marketplace due to the demand growth of petroleum products. Refineries affect the marketplace in terms of the utilization rate of refinery. As the petroleum products demand increases, the demand for conversion capacity increases. The reduction in spare refining capacity has affected the oil global marketplace because refineries are being utilized more for producing petroleum products which are seen as more valuable than the heavier crude oils. The reason refining places a relatively higher value on lighter, sweeter (light sweet) crudes than on heavier, more sour (heavy sour) crudes because light sweet require less production processes for a given volume of higher-valued products. The refined petroleum products have similar global marketplace and international flows as the crude oils.

The prices of petroleum products are a consequence of the world economy's growth regardless of the diminished excess capacity and increased supply uncertainty. This economy's growth increases the petroleum products demand that, in turn, increases the crude oil demand which outpaced the near-term ability to provide more supplies. Subsequently, the crude oil prices increased as a result of tightness in the global oil marketplace. In the production sector, as demand for petroleum products increased, the demand for the refinery capacity to convert crude oil into saleable products increased as well. Additionally, as the utilization rate of the world's refineries increased, demand for light sweet crudes increased relatively to heavy sour crudes. Moreover, these changes in oil global supply and demand increase the prices paid by retailers and, ultimately, by the customers.

Chopra and Meindl define a supply chain as "all parties involved, directly and indirectly, in fulfilling a customer request" (2007). This definition implies that the objective of a supply chain is then to maximize customer service. A customer, by definition, is an output's user of a process. For a company that focuses on customer service, a customer's customer is also very important. Thus, this company will link the upstream suppliers to the downstream distributors in its supply chain. The goal of a business is to make money or profit. In order to maximize profit, a company must minimize costs. Chima stated that all benefits and costs must be weighed on each decision that a company makes along its supply chain (2007, 27).

Over the years, there has been an apprehension that oil industry has a very scarce resources challenge. Studies have shown that oil resources are not the constraints in oil supply chain. Moreover, oil companies will still be able to sustain their current production levels for more than 50 years. However, in reality, Chima explained that the challenge lies on putting oil reserves into production and delivering

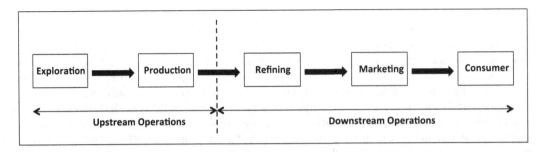

FIGURE 20.5 Supply chain model in the oil industry.

final products to customers at the lowest cost possible for most oil companies (2007, 28). Therefore, oil companies must have a solid supply chain model to maximize profits.

The oil industry involvement in global supply chain includes domestic and international transportation, order visibility among suppliers and customers, import or export facilitation, and information technology. Thus, this industry requires a solid model to implement its supply chain. Chima described that an oil supply chain consists of exploration, production, refining, marketing, and consumer—see Figure 20.5 (2007, 28). The link represents oil flow through the supply chain. This oil supply chain exists whenever the oil companies' suppliers keep their systems continuously resupplied. There are many activities involved within each sector of the supply chain.

A typical supply chain model in oil industry comprises of two main activities such as upstream and downstream operations. Upstream operations deal with exploration and production of the industry, while downstream operations deal with refining and processing of crude oil products, marketing, and distribution of crude oil products to customers. An oil company may fully integrate which has both upstream and downstream operations, or may concentrate on a particular sector such as exploration and production as well as refining and marketing.

Typically, oil exploration and production processes are comprised of five main activities: geologic survey, exploratory drilling, appraisal, production, and decommissioning (E-Tech International 2012). Refining simply is a process that transforms crude oil into petroleum products such as gasoline, kerosene, engine oil, diesel, and jet fuel. However, the oil refinery production process is one of the most complex processes because it involves many different processes with various connections in the supply chain. Marketing includes distribution and retail sale which involves movement of those refined products from refineries to end customers.

Most oil companies need to plan all significant operations in advance and manage their costs throughout the entire supply chain to enhance the profit margin. In the oil industry, the exploration and production sectors produce the same petroleum products for all competing companies, due to a narrow product differentiation. As a result, oil companies cannot introduce an exciting new product to distinguish themselves from one another. However, the companies must have the ability to adapt a solid supply chain model that can economically locate and produce oil efficiently to set apart themselves from their competitors.

20.3 Methodology

The Emerald Group has been publishing many international journals in the areas of supply chain management (SCM). There are two journals published by the group that relate to this research such as Bjorklund (2012) and Platts and Song (2010). Bjorklund (2012) outlined important aspects to consider in the design of environmental performance measurements in SCM. Platts and Song (2010) suggested measuring the actual total acquisition costs to gain profitability in supply chain network. Additionally, this research follows the same method as Rodrigo et al. (2010) which provided a set of objectives that were forming Pareto efficient frontiers. However, in order to optimize the profit and quality objective function, this research utilizes an MIP model, while Rodrigo et al. (2010) used a ε-constrained method.

As mentioned earlier, the significance of this research is to seek impacts of the U.S. dependency on foreign oil problems by introducing an MIP model that identifies how other nations such as Indonesia can supply some of the crude oil imports with respect to the trade-off between crude oil supply chain quality, sustainable environmental incentives, and supply chain costs. Furthermore, the broader impact is investments into other countries crude oil supply chains can be quantified and optimized, and countries such as Indonesia can be identified as possible candidates for investment for future global crude oil needs. This research strives to answer the research question of "When is it economically beneficial to invest in the supply chain quality of crude oil from a given nation?", hypothesizes that the crude oil supply chain quality will impact the crude oil supply chain costs and the environmental sustainability will have an impact on crude oil supply chain costs, and suggests that the crude oil supply chains each of these countries will dictate their ability to provide crude oil. The overall objective is to investigate an MIP model that supports decisions about providing economic and environmental incentives to improve the supply chain quality of crude oil in Indonesia so that it becomes more cost-effective for the United States to import crude oil from Indonesia as opposed to other global sources and helps PERTAMINA to contribute more funds to the Indonesia's national treasuries as well.

Most companies must decide on conflicting strategies of maximizing short-term profits or seeking long-term sustainability through high-quality standards. Usually, supply chain decisions are evaluated by analysis that considers the logistics costs and the quality initiatives independently. This independent decision-making process does not effectively determine the impacts of quality defects and can lead to ineffective strategic decisions that do not comprehensively account for the complexity of the problem. The objective of this research is to address that phenomenon by introducing an MIP model that identifies how other nations such as Indonesia can supply some of the crude oil imports with respect to the trade-off between crude oil supply chain quality, sustainable environmental incentives, and supply chain costs. In addition, most optimization decisions are based on forecasts that by definition have some degree of uncertainty. Consequently, the model should take into account uncertainty for robustness and consistency.

A hypothesis statement by definition is an educated guess of a proposed answer to a question that can be verified or rejected through a test statistic. This research proposes two answers of whether or not the crude oil supply chain quality and the environment sustainability will impact the supply chain costs from the research question. These two hypothesis statements are stated as follows:

Hypothesis Statement #1

H_0: The crude oil supply chain quality will not impact the supply chain costs.
H_1: The crude oil supply chain quality will impact the supply chain costs.

Hypothesis Statement #2

H_0: The environment sustainability will not impact the crude oil supply chain costs.
H_1: The environment sustainability will impact the crude oil supply chain costs.

A statistic test is conducted to determine whether or not the H_0 is verified or rejected for both of the hypothesis statements. The rejection region lies if both supply chain quality and environment sustainability metrics change the supply chain costs by 20%.

The goal of a business is to make money or profit. In order to maximize profit, a company must minimize costs. Chima stated that all benefits and costs must be weighed on each decision that a company makes along its supply chain (2007, 27). Most oil companies are facing the same challenge which lies on putting oil reserves into production and delivering final products to customers at the lowest cost possible (Chima 2007, 28). In the oil industry, the exploration and production sectors produce the same petroleum products for all competing companies, due to a narrow product differentiation. As a result, oil companies cannot introduce an exciting new product to distinguish themselves from one another. However, the companies must have the ability to adapt a solid supply chain model that can economically locate and produce oil efficiently to set apart themselves from their competitors. Thus, oil companies need to plan all significant operations in advance and manage their costs throughout the entire supply chain to enhance the profit margin. This research considers that the exploration, production, and refinery processes take place in Indonesia while distribution, marketing, and customer in the United States.

In general, every business requires two types of costs in producing its products or services such as fixed and variable costs. Fixed costs are expenses that are always fixed. These costs do not vary with the amount of the product produced and are independent regardless of the outcome of the operation. In the oil industry, fixed costs that occur on its each supply chain node include equipment leasing and operation costs. On the other hand, variable costs are dependent on sales. An increase in the quantity of products produced means an increase in the variable costs. Since the variable costs are usually the amount spent in producing a certain product, the selling price should be higher than the variable costs. The profit obtained in sales will contribute in recovering the value spent in the fixed costs. It is important to distinguish between fixed and variable costs in order to make a right decision in pricing and to know which costs should be accounted for. Fixed costs do not vary; thus, they are often ignored. This research focuses on the variable costs, especially transportation costs because they vary on the demand and distance traveled.

Transportation refers to the movement of product from one location to another as it makes its way from the beginning of a supply chain to the customer. Transportation is an important supply chain driver because products are rarely produced and consumed in the same location. Transportation is also a significant component of the costs incurred by most supply chain. Chopra and Meindl stated that transportation activity represented more than 10% of the Gross Domestic Product (GDP) of the United States in 2002 (2007). The role of transportation is even more significant in the oil industry because the supply chain occurs within a global marketplace, which facilitates oil movement from where it is produced, to where it is refined into petroleum products and to where those products are ultimately sold to customers ("Today's Crude Oil" 2006). Moreover, the existing global marketplace reflects both sellers and buyers to the market in order to get the lowest transportation costs from sellers to buyers for each type of crude oil.

Transportation sector is the primary customer of total energy use in the United States and definitely drives the value of oil. There are several types of transportation modes in the oil industry such as pipelines, trucks, railroad, and barges. Pipelines are the primary players in the U.S. transportation mode. Petroleum products cannot reach their millions of customers across the country without pipelines. Oil sellers and buyers prefer to use pipelines due to the economic costs. Trucking is the most expensive transportation mode in the oil industry because trucking costs increase with distance. Railroad prices are competitive with pipeline prices. However, railroads are sometimes limited geographically. Considering all transportation modes such as pipelines, trucks, railroads, and barges, pipelines are the most cost-effective method; this mode has the greatest impact on oil supply chain cost.

Quality by definition is meeting customer's expectations in terms of fitness for use, delivery, and price. Many organizations emphasize quality as a means to stay competitive in the marketplace over the long run. They view having a reputation of high quality as representing future market share for new customers and maintaining market share for existing customers over their lifetime. Further, improving quality can provide long-term financial savings. In order for a supply chain to remain profitable, quality from suppliers must be considered on the decision-making process. Competing strategies of increasing profit as opposed to increasing quality will require many trade-offs. Thus, quality is important all along the supply chain because the main objective of supply chain is to maximize customer service.

There are three quality metrics that are considered for pipelines performance. The first metric is the failure of a pipeline segment. This involved a complete loss of a particular segment of a pipeline to transport crude oil. Possible causes include unplanned maintenance, accidental excavation damage, or sabotage. The second metric is the loss of crude oil transmission compressor. This focuses on partial reductions in deliverability due to removal from service of one or more crude oil compressor. Possible causes include forced outage of a compressor driver, an explosion or fire in the compressor station, or the failure of ancillary systems. The third metric is the loss of deliverability from storage facilities. This includes the loss of deliverability from one or more of the major underground storage fields.

The United States of Environmental Protection Agency (EPA) classifies two types of wastes in the case of crude oil: exempt and non-exempt wastes. EPA defines exempt wastes as follows:

> Wastes that are generated before the end point of primary field operations are exempt. The term end point of initial product separation means the point at which crude oil leaves the last vessel in the tank battery associated with the wells. This tank battery separates crude oil from the produced water and/or gas.

(1993)

Pipelines are not part of primary field operations; thus, oil wastes that are generated by pipelines are non-exempt. Failure of a pipeline segment caused by accidental excavation damage is an example of non-exempt wastes, which will result in costing oil companies to pay fines to the EPA as well as settlement to the surrounding environment. This pipeline segment failure is chosen as the sampling plan of supply chain quality-level performance.

Globalization has resulted in pressure on multinational firms to improve environmental performance. In order to achieve improvement in environmental performance, a company must integrate its environmental management strategies, while maintaining production quality and cost goals, into the supply chain which includes all of the operational life cycle stages such as unique partnerships with suppliers. Environmental sustainability has been defined as "meeting the needs of the present without compromising the ability of the future generations to meet their needs".

For oil companies, the concept of sustainability is most appropriately used when evaluating their business strategies. Sustainability of a business concerns the degree to which they not only reduce negative impacts on the natural environment through their operations, but also invest in business practices that promote policies to make wide-reaching progress toward sustainable development. In the industry, the operations of oil companies are examined for their impact on the surrounding environment annually. To distinguish from the above definition of sustainability, environmentally conscious operations refer to green operations. However, green operations are not necessarily sustainable in the long run, but minimizing the negative impact of operational processes is still environmentally conscious. Company operations deal with energy usage necessary for operating refineries, emissions, and waste. Meanwhile, sustainability of the products deals with oil, natural gas, and possible alternatives to fossil fuels.

In the oil industry exploration and production processes, sustainability involves the products, and as such, the petroleum industry itself is environmentally unsustainable because like all fossil fuels, oil is a limited resource. Additionally, drilling in previously undisturbed areas requires clearing vegetation in order to build roads, to haul in equipment, and to construct wells. Wildlife is displaced. All of these actions are temporary and when the oil field reservoir is depleted, the area could be restored to its pre-developed condition. Indirect permanent effect comes from exhaust gases emitted by construction and haul vehicles. Also, drilling in the ocean has the potential for accidents as in the case of Deepwater Horizon explosion in the Gulf of Mexico. The subsequent oil spill killed an unknown numbers of fish and birds. This was the largest spill in history and caused a great harm to the environment. It was a single event which can be recovered from. At this time, any permanent impacts to sustainability are not fully known, but history shows that over time, in some instances decades, nature recovers. In the refining process, sustainability deals with the company operations which involve in energy usage necessary for operating refineries, emissions, and waste. For example, refinery produces waste gases that cannot be recaptured and are emitted into the atmosphere. This is an instance of an unsustainable practice. Both above and below ground sustainability involved in pipelines have the potential to break and spill petroleum during transport into the surrounding environment. Some risks of accidental spills of oil have the potential to pollute water, contaminate soil, harm species, and affect livelihoods.

Both types of sustainability that deal with either oil companies' processes or products will have positive and negative impacts on the supply chain costs. An example of the negative impact is definitely the disastrous British Petroleum (BP) drill explosion and oil spill in 2010 which impacted wildlife in the Gulf of Mexico. This accident resulted in damaging the environment as well as costing BP a settlement of billions of dollars. Contrary, an example of the positive impact is the ability to be able to preserve the productivity of oil itself as a natural resource asset which leads to supply chain costs savings.

Unlike the quality metrics which focused on pipelines performance, this research considers refining process as a good candidate to determine its sustainability metrics. Refinery is a complex process. In this process, crude oil is heated and broken down into its components. Then, the conversion process transforms lower-valued products into higher-valued products by removing impurities. This conversion process dictates the different types of crude oil, thus distinguishing the differences in refineries. The refining sector of the oil industry has significantly affected the crude oil global marketplace due to the demand growth of petroleum products. As the petroleum products demand increases, the demand for conversion capacity increases. Refineries affect supply chain profit margin such that refineries' variable costs vary on the petroleum products demand.

There are two sustainability metrics that are considered for refineries performance. The first metric is the refining operations which deal with energy usage necessary for operating refineries, emissions, and waste. The second metric is the refining products which deal with oil to fossil fuels. Refining processes that deal with energy usage are chosen as environmental sustainability according to the performance sampling plan.

This research establishes an MIP baseline models and an efficient frontier curve, which incorporate both sampling plans of pipeline quality and refinery sustainability performance to evaluate the economic impacts of inspection tools (quality) and environmental incentives (sustainability) tools on operational strategies in supplier networks. This research utilizes SAS Statistical software and MATLAB®/Excel/Lindo Optimization. Crude oil supply chain quality data are collected from the OPEC public databases, the U.S. EIA website, and the Indonesia Directorate General of Oil and Gas (MIGAS) website. Data involve in sustainability are collected from the U.S. EIA website and the U.S. EPA website.

20.3.1 Expected Results

There are three expected results from this research. First, we expect to reject our null hypothesis in favor of our hypothesis that the crude oil supply chain quality and sustainability impact crude oil supply chain costs. Second, we expect the crude oil supply chain quality metrics such as to impact the supply chain cost model by more than 20%. Finally third, we expect the crude oil supply chain sustainability factor which based on to impact nodes of the supply chain by more than 20%.

20.3.2 Limitations and Broader Impacts

There are some expected limitations for this research such as the availability of data and scope of the research. The U.S. EIA provides numerous useful data for the U.S. oil industry. Meanwhile, there are limitations concerning the data collection of the Indonesia oil industry due to lack of information. The scope of this research is only the Indonesia oil industry as well as the U.S. oil industry. This scope is already broad enough considering the nature of supply chain activities on both countries. Future work can be conducted as the continuation of this research which uses the proposed model that includes other countries.

The intellectual merit of the proposed research is a model that demonstrates the trade-offs between quality and supply chain profit for Indonesia that can be expanded to other nations. The broader impacts of the proposed research are investments into other countries crude oil supply chains can be quantified and optimized; and countries such as Indonesia can be identified as possible candidates for investment for future global crude oil needs.

REFERENCES

Abraham, J.N., and K.S. Rao. Integration of Generative and Evaluative Models for Production Scheduling of Lube Oil Plants in a Petroleum Refinery. *Applied Mathematical Modelling* 33 (2009): 1213–1227. Print.

Al-Qahtani, K., and A. Elkamel. Multisite Facility Network Integration Design and Coordination: An Application to the Refining Industry. *Computers & Chemical Engineering* 32 (2008): 2189–2202. Print.

Al-Qahtani, K., and A. Elkamel. Multisite Refinery and Petrochemical Network Design: Optimal Integration and Coordination. *Industrial & Engineering Chemistry Research* 48 (2009): 814–826. Print.

Anthony, R.N. Planning and Control Systems: A Framework for Analysis Working Paper. Harvard University, Graduate School of Business Administration, 1965. Web.

Austria. Organization of the Petroleum Exporting Countries (OPEC). World Oil Outlook 2012. Vienna: WOO, 2012. Web.

Azaron, A., et al. A Multi-Objective Stochastic Programming Approach for Supply Chain Design Considering Risk. *International Journal of Production Economics* 116 (2008): 129–138. Web.

Bjorklund, M., et al. Performance Measurements in the Greening of Supply Chains. *Supply Chain Management: An International Journal* 17.1 (2012): 29–39. Print.

Blackburn, J. Designing and Managing Sustainable Closed-Loop Supply Chains. Ongoing project funded by the National Science Foundation (NSF). Award Abstract: 0531661. 1 July 2005–31 December 2005.

Cafaro, D.C., and J. Cerda. Efficient Tool for the Scheduling of Multiproduct Pipelines and Terminal Operations. *Industrial & Engineering Chemistry Research* 47 (2008): 9941–9956. Print.

Cafaro, D.C., and J. Cerda. Optimal Scheduling of Multiproduct Pipeline Systems using a Non-Discrete MILP Formulation. *Computers & Chemical Engineering* 28 (2004): 2053–2068. Print.

Cafaro, D.C., and J. Cerda. Optimal Scheduling of Refined Products Pipelines with Multiple Sources. *Industrial & Engineering Chemistry Research* 48 (2009): 6675–6689. Print.

Carneiro, M.C., et al. Risk Management in the Oil Supply Chain: A CVaR Approach. *Industrial & Engineering Chemistry Research* 49 (2010): 3286–3294. Print.

Carvalho, M.C.A., and J.M. Pinto. An MILP Model and Solution Technique for the Planning of Infrastructure in Offshore Oil Fields. *Journal of Petroleum Science and Engineering* 51 (2006): 97–110. Print.

Chen, C.L., et al. Multi-Objective Optimization for a Multi-Enterprise Supply Chain Network. *Industrial and Engineering Chemistry Research* 42 (2003): 1879–1889. Web.

Chima, C.M. Supply-Chain Management Issues in the Oil and Gas Industry. *Journal of Business & Economics Research* 5.6 (2007): 27–36. Print. 1 November 2012.

Chopra, S., and P. Meindl. *Supply Chain Management: Strategy, Planning, & Operation*. Upper Saddle River, NJ: Prentice Hall, 2007. Print.

Cornillier, F., et al. A Heuristic for the Multiperiod Petrol Station Replenishment Problem. *European Journal of Operational Research* 191 (2008): 295–305. Print.

Cornillier, F., et al. The Petrol Station Replenishment Problem with Time Windows. *Computers & Operations Research* 36 (2009): 919–935. Print.

Eksioglu, S. Models for Supply Chain Design and Logistics Management of Biofuels. *Ongoing Project Funded by the National Science Foundation (NSF)*. Award Abstract: 1052671. 1 August 2011–31 July 2016.

Geffen, C.A., and S. Rothenberg. Suppliers and Environmental Innovation: The Automotive Paint Process. *International Journal of Operations & Production Management* 20.2 (2000): 166–186. Web.

Goel, V., and I.E. Grossmann. A Stochastic Programming Approach to Planning of Offshore Gas Field Developments under Uncertainty in Reserves. *Computers & Chemical Engineering* 28 (2004): 1409–1429. Print.

Gullen, G., et al. Multi-Objective Supply Chain Design under Uncertainty. *Chemical Engineering Science* 60 (2005): 1535–1553. Web.

Handfield, R.B., et al. Green Value Chain Practices in the Furniture Industry. *Journal of Operations Management* 15.4 (1997): 293–315. Web.

Herran, A., et al. A Mathematical Model for Planning Transportation of Multiple Petroleum Products in a Multipipeline System. *Computers & Chemical Engineering* 34 (2010): 401–413. Print.

Hertzmark, D.I. Pertamina Indonesia's State – Owned Oil Company. *The James A. Baker III Institute for Public Policy Rice University*, 2007, 1–68. Web. 13 January, 2012.

Hong, W. Optimal Sampling Plans in Supply Chains with Endogenous Product Quality. Ongoing Project Funded by the National Science Foundation (NSF). Award Abstract: 1030233. 15 August 2010–31 July 2013.

Indonesia. Direktorat Jendral (DitJen) MIGAS. *PERTAMINA*. Jakarta: Badan PERTAMINA, 2012. Web.

Jetlund, A.S., and I.A. Karimi. Improving the Logistics of Multicompartment Chemical Tankers. *Computers & Chemical Engineering* 28 (2004): 1267–1283. Print.

Julka, N., et al. Agent – Based Supply Chain Management – 1: Framework. *Computers & Chemical Engineering* 26 (2002): 1755–1769. Print.

Krauss, C. U.S. Reliance on Oil From Saudi Arabia Is Growing Again. The New York Times 16 August 2012: Energy & Environment. Print.

Meixell, M.J. and V.B. Gargeya. Global Supply Chain Design: A Literature Review and Critique, Transportation Research Part E. *Logistics and Transportation Review* 41 (2005): 531–550. Print. 18 January 2012.

MirHassani, S.A. An Operational Planning Model for Petroleum Products Logistics under Uncertainty. *Applied Mathematics and Computation* 196 (2008): 744–751. Print.

MirHassani, S.A., and M. Ghorbanalizadeh. The Multiproduct Pipeline Scheduling System. *Applied Mathematics and Computation* 56 (2008): 891–897. Print.

Muriel, A., and D. Simchi-Levi. *Supply Chain Design and Planning—Applications of Optimization Techniques for Strategic and Tactical Models.* North Holland: Design, Coordination and Operation, 2004. Print.

Murty, M.N., and S. Kumar. Win-win Opportunities and Environmental Regulation: Testing for Porter Hypothesis for Indian Manufacturing Industries. *Journal of Environmental Management* 67.2 (2003): 139–144. Web.

Nishi, T., et al. An Augmented Lagrangian Approach for Distributed Supply Chain Planning for Multiple Companies. *IEEE Transactions on Automation Science and Engineering* 5 (2008): 259–274. Print.

Painter, D.S. Oil and the American Century. *The Journal of American History* (2012): 24–39. Print. 15 January 2012.

Persson, J.A., and M. Gothe-Lundgren. Shipment Planning at Oil Refineries using Column Generation and Valid Inequalities. *European Journal of Operational Research* 163 (2005): 631–652. Print.

Pirog, R. The Role of National Oil Companies in the International Oil Market. Congressional Research Service (CRS), 21 August 2007, 1–17. Print. 23 October 2010.

Pitty, S., et al. Decision Support for Integrated Refinery Supply Chains. Part 1. Dynamic Simulation. *Computers & Chemical Engineering* 32 (2008): 2767–2786. Print.

Platts, K.W., and N. Song. Overseas Sourcing Decisions – The Total Cost of Sourcing from China. *Supply Chain Management: An International Journal* 15.4 (2010): 320–331. Print.

Rejowski, R., and J.M. Pinto. A Novel Continuous Time Representation for Scheduling of Pipeline Systems with Pumping Yield Rate Constraints. *Computers & Chemical Engineering* 32 (2008): 1042–1066. Print.

Rejowski, R., and J.M. Pinto. An MILP Formulation for the Scheduling of Multiproduct Pipeline Systems. *Brazilian Journal of Chemical Engineering* 19 (2002): 467–474. Print.

Rejowski, R., and J.M. Pinto. Efficient MILP Formulations and Valid Cuts for Multiproduct Pipeline Scheduling. *Computers & Chemical Engineering* 28 (2004): 1511–1528. Print.

Rejowski, R., and J.M. Pinto. Scheduling of a Multiproduct Pipeline Systems. *Computers & Chemical Engineering* 27 (2003): 1229–1246. Print.

Reynolds, L. Seven Dangerous (and Surprising) Side Effects of the U.S. Dependency on Foreign Oil. *The American Surveyor: A Foot in the Past…An Eye to the Future.* 4 August 2010, 1. Print.

Rodrigo, B.F., et al. Multi-Objective Stochastic Supply Chain Modeling to Evaluate Tradeoffs between Profit and Quality. *International Journals Production Economics* 127 (2010): 292–299. Print.

Sanchez, C.M., and W. McKinley. Environmental Regulatory Influence and Product Innovation: The Contingency Effects of Organizational Characteristics. *Journal of Engineering and Technology Management* 15.4 (1998): 257–278. Web.

Shapiro, J.F. *Modeling the Supply Chain.* Belmont, CA: Thomson Higher Education, 2007. Print.

Szidarovszky, F., et al. Techniques for Multi-Objective Decision Making in Systems Management. 1st Ed., Vol. 2. West Lafayette, IN: Elsevier. 1986. Web.

Tarhan, B., et al. Stochastic Programming Approach for the Planning of Offshore Oil or Gas Field Infrastructure under Decision – Dependent Uncertainty. *Industrial & Engineering Chemistry Research* 48 (2009): 3078–3097. Print.

Trench, C.J. How Pipelines Make the Oil Market Work – Their Networks, Operation and Regulation. Association of Oil Pipe Lines and American Petroleum Institute Pipeline Committee, 2001, 1–20. Print.

United States. E-Tech International. *Overview of the Oil and Gas Exploration and Production Process.* New Mexico: Environmental Management in Oil and Gas Exploration and Production, 2012. Print.

United States. Environmental Protection Agency (EPA). *Exemption of Oil and Gas Exploration and Production Wastes from Federal Hazardous Waste Regulation.* Renton, WA: Oil Pipeline, 1993. Web.

United States. The American Petroleum Institute (API). *Pipeline 101.* Washington, DC: Crude Oil, 2006. Print.

United States. The American Petroleum Institute (API). *Understanding Today's Crude Oil and Product Markets.* Washington, DC: Crude Oil, 2006. Print.

United States. The American Petroleum Institute (API). *Voluntary Sustainability Reporting Guidance 2010.* Washington, DC: Environmental Performance, 2010. Web.

United States. The National Energy Education Development (NEED) Project. Petroleum. Manassas, VA: Petroleum, 2012. Print.

United States. U.S. Energy Information Administration (U.S.EIA). Indonesia. Washington, DC: Frequently Asked Questions, 2012. Print.

United States. U.S. Energy Information Administration (U.S.EIA). Oil: Crude and Petroleum Products Explained. Washington, DC: GPO, 2012. Print.

United States. U.S. Energy Information Administration (U.S.EIA). OPEC Countries. Washington, DC: Frequently Asked Questions, 2012. Print.

United States. U.S. Energy Information Administration (U.S.EIA). PADD Regions Enable Regional Analysis of Petroleum Product Supply and Movement. Washington, DC: Frequently Asked Questions, 2012. Print.

United States. U.S. Energy Information Administration (U.S.EIA). What are the Major Sources and Users of Energy in the United States? Washington, DC: Frequently Asked Questions, 2012. Print.

United States. U.S. Energy Information Administration (U.S.EIA). What are the Products and Uses of Petroleum? Washington, DC: Frequently Asked Questions, 2012. Print.

United States. U.S. Energy Information Administration (U.S.EIA). World Oil Transit Chokepoints. Washington, DC: Frequently Asked Questions, 2012. Print.

Van den Heever, S.A. and I.E. Grossmann. An Iterative Aggregation/Disaggregation Approach for the Solution of a Mixed-Integer Non Linear Oil Field Infrastructure Planning Model. *Industrial & Engineering Chemistry Research* 39 (2000): 1955–1971. Print.

Wall, B.H., et al. *Growth in a Changing Environment: A History of Standard Oil Company.* Annandale, NJ: Exxon Corporation, 1988. Print.

Williams, E., et al. Environmental, social and economic implications of global reuse and recycling of personal computers. *Environmental Science & Technology* 42 (2008): 6446. Web.

Zhu, Q., and R.P. Cote. Integrating Green Supply Chain Management into an Embryonic Eco-Industrial Development: A Case Study of the Guitang Group. *Journal of Cleaner Production* 12.8 (2004): 1025–1035. Web.

21

Using Six Sigma to Evaluate Automatic Identification Technologies to Optimize Broken-Case Warehousing Operations

Christopher A. Chung and Erick C. Jones

The continuous exploration of what is required the processes that impact system performance over sub-optimizing parts of a system leads to true innovation success.

Erick C. Jones

21.1 Introduction

This project was conducted by a team of professors and students from the University of Texas in Arlington as well as Tecnológico de Monterrey, Campus Querétaro. The Principal Investigator was Dr. Erick C. Jones, an Industrial and Manufacturing Engineering Professor at the University of Texas at Arlington as well as the Director of RAID labs. This project was also supported by Dr. Beatriz Murrieta, an Industrial Engineering Professor at Tecnológico de Monterrey, Campus Querétaro as well as the Department Chair. Support and project input was also given by Dr. Vettrivel Gnaneswaran, the Assistant Director of the RAID labs.

The project leads for this investigation include Jose Sanchez Gonzalez, Mackenzie Dacres, and Rayanne Macnee. Jose Sanchez Gonzalez is a Graduate MSIE Student at the University of Texas at Arlington. Mackenzie Dacres is an Industrial Engineering Undergraduate Student at the University of Texas. Rayanne Macnee is a Nursing Undergraduate Student. Support was also given by Walter Muflur and Cynthia Vinueza-Garcia, both Undergraduate Industrial Engineering Students at the University of Texas at Arlington.

21.1.1 Radio Frequency Identification and Auto ID Lab

The Radio Frequency Identification and Auto ID (RAID) Labs were established in 2011 by the Principal Investigator Dr. Erick Jones. The vision of the lab is that everything will be tracked wirelessly in 10 years. The mission of the lab is to provide integrated solutions in logistics and other data-driven environments through automatic data capture, real-world prototypes, and analysis. It is the goal of the RAID Lab to support the marriage of industries supply chain needs for automation identification technology with academia's theoretical applications. The purpose of the facility is to support project initiatives such as radio frequency identification (RFID), logistics, manufacturing, and information technology. The RAID Lab has had six major projects fully funded within the 1 year it has been established and has five more upcoming.

21.1.2 The National Science Foundation—International Research Experiences for Students (IRES)

The National Science Foundation (NSF) is an independent federal agency that was established in 1950 by Congress. It has an annual budget of $6.9 billion, all of which goes towards the progression of science, national health, prosperity, and welfare. That $6.9 billion currently funds approximately 20% of all federally supported basic research. The International Research Experience for Students Program is funded to support the development of worldwide research and interaction. It seeks to increase students' comfort level when working with people from different cultures by exposing them to the technological, cultural, economic, and socio-political aspects of Mexican society. The outcomes are as follows: an increase in research skills, cultural awareness, and a student's abilities in research methods and problem-solving skills.

21.2 Background

21.2.1 Company Background

Research was conducted at a large food product distribution center in Latin America. Problem Statement is as follows:

The information associated with a stretch wrapped full pallet License Plate Number (LPN) is lost when a "full" pallet has to be broken or taken apart to fulfill orders with individual cases on that pallet. The cases associated with the full pallet do not have the information such as lot, expiration date, or other relevant information that was included with the original LPN. This is causing customer returns of cases that are approximated at 15% of the outbound volume. It is expected that the volume of "broken" pallet case picking will be increasing in the near future with which the current methods may lead increase labor hours, high turnover, and lower worker productivity.

21.3 Research Objective

21.3.1 Research Question

In developing a research objective, the team narrowed the focus of the project down to three specific research questions. These questions include the following: Can RFID impact the number of outbound cases without LPN information? Can engineering work process redesign (EWPR) impact the incident ratio (IR)? And can RFID and EWPR impact the proposed future labor hours? We will explore these questions through the course of this chapter.

21.3.2 Relationship to Business Problem

These research questions are closely tied to the business problem faced by employees at Company XYZ's. By investigating RFID technologies, we will gain insights to the "broken pallet" case picking process and will be able to evaluate the impacts of pallet LPN information transfer to cases as well as future workflow and workstation redesign for increased worker optimization and improved safety conditions if RFID is implemented and if broken pallet case volume increases.

Research Hypothesis:

In conducting our research, we developed three test metrics. These metrics are listed as follows:

Test Metrics:
1. The number of outbound cases without LPN information (NCLPN)
2. The incident ratio
3. The projected number of future labor hours (PNLH).

In addition to three test metrics, three hypotheses were created.

Null Hypothesis:

(H_{01}): RFID technologies do NOT reduce the NCLPN Alternative Hypothesis (H_a): RFID technologies do reduce NCLPN.

(H_{02}): RFID technologies and EWPR do NOT reduce the IR.

(H_{03}): RFID technologies and EWPR do NOT reduce the PNLH.

The Rejection Criteria:

H_{01} is that if the NCLPN can be reduced by 10% then we cannot reject the H_{01}.

H_{02} is that if the IR can be reduced by 10% then we cannot reject the H_{02}.

H_{03} is that if the PNLH can be reduced by 10% then we cannot reject the H_{03}.

21.3.3 Research Methodology

We will employ design for Six Sigma research approach (DFSS-R), developed by Jones (2006). DFSS-R is a research methodology focused on reducing variability, removing defects, and getting rid of wastes from processes, products, and transactions. The approach utilizes quality tools and optimization techniques with effective cost justification (Figure 21.1).

The design for Six Sigma research-based approach contains seven different levels, where the problem defined needs to be measurable followed by the definition of metrics.

Research Methodology with Steps:

This section describes the different actions that need to be done under each specific phase.

Figure 21.2 outlines the seven phases of DFSS-R methodology and the corresponding steps with each phase. In the first stage "Plan", we define and measure the problem. In the second stage "Predict", we measure, analyze, design, and identify. In this project, the last phase "Perform" which uses Optimize and Verify was not utilized due to time constraints.

Table 21.1 elaborates specifically on the tools the team utilized for this project. Specific tools are listed, and examples of these strategies are provided in Figures 21.3–21.5. Figure 21.3 provides an example of a sample flow chart and how it might be utilized to solve a problem. Figure 21.4 displays the organizational structure of a fishbone diagram. Figure 21.5 illustrates how by using Pareto analysis, one can identify 20% of the causes to 80% of the problem. These tools were all utilized through the course of the project to come to our conclusions.

The team also conducted through data collection through plant visits, interviews, and observations. Listed below is a summary of the various plant visits as well as the major accomplishments for each visit.

21.3.4 Research Approach

As mentioned before, the research approach used by the team was the DFSS-R methodology. We utilized the Define, Measure, Analyze, Design, and Identify phases. In the Define phase, we identified the company business problem and narrowed the scope of the research project. Utilizing the results of the previous phase, now we will identify the metrics for the business problem statements in the Measure phase. Using the results of the previous phase, we analyzed the impacts of the current operations on the

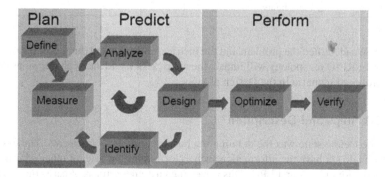

FIGURE 21.1   DFSS-R research methodology. (Jones 2006.)

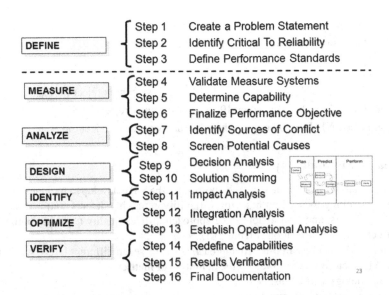

DEFINE	Step 1	Create a Problem Statement
	Step 2	Identify Critical To Reliability
	Step 3	Define Performance Standards
MEASURE	Step 4	Validate Measure Systems
	Step 5	Determine Capability
	Step 6	Finalize Performance Objective
ANALYZE	Step 7	Identify Sources of Conflict
	Step 8	Screen Potential Causes
DESIGN	Step 9	Decision Analysis
	Step 10	Solution Storming
IDENTIFY	Step 11	Impact Analysis
OPTIMIZE	Step 12	Integration Analysis
	Step 13	Establish Operational Analysis
VERIFY	Step 14	Redefine Capabilities
	Step 15	Results Verification
	Step 16	Final Documentation

FIGURE 21.2 Phases of DFSS-R.

TABLE 21.1

Tools Used within the DFSS-R Methodology

Define	Measure	Analyze	Design	Identify	Optimize	Verify
Interview process/ observations	Hypothesis testing	Fishbone	Scenarios	Cost-benefit analysis	Factorial design of experiments	Control plans
Language processing	Analysis of variance	Pareto analysis	Fractional factorials	Visual systems	Theory of constraints	TPM
Prioritization matrix	Quality function deployment	Process mapping	Data mining	5-S	Response surface methodology	Multiple response optimization
System map	Flowchart	Multi-vari chart	Blocking	TPM	Blocking	Visual systems
Stakeholder analysis	Measurement system analysis	Chi-square	Response surface methodology	Mistake-proofing	Data mining	SPC/APC
Thought process map	Graphical methods	Regression	Multiple response optimization	SPC/APC	Multiple response optimization	Mistake-proofing
Value stream mapping	Process behavior charts	Buffered tolerance limits	Theory of constraints	ROI analysis	Fractional factorials	Continuous improvement

metrics defined. We identified the problem and the metrics, and analyzed the metrics. Now we are going to identify how the RFID technology will impact the metrics. In the Identify phase, we evaluate the cost-benefit of the proposed scenario in the Design phase.

21.3.5 DFSS-R Steps and Description

The results of the Define state was the defining the business problem statements. The cases associated with the full pallet do not have the information such as lot, expiration date, or other relevant information that was included with the original LPN. This is causing customer returns of cases that is approximated at 15% of the outbound volume.

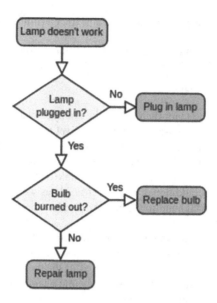

FIGURE 21.3 Sample flow chart.

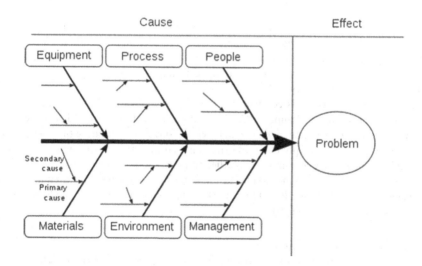

FIGURE 21.4 Sample fishbone diagram.

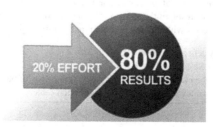

FIGURE 21.5 Pareto analysis.

After conducting the Measure phase, the team was able to determine the following metrics:

Metric No. 1: Number of outbound cases without LPN Information.
Metric No. 2: Incident ratio
Metric No. 3: Future number of labor hours (FNLH).

After determining the metrics, the team then began the Analyze phase of DFSS-R. The results of the Facility Layout Analysis were two floor-level conveyors travel to the outbound shipping transportation area. The pallets are staged in front of the conveyor so that they can be "broken" pallet case picked. Then, the workers unload the pallet onto floor conveyor where the pallets have a designated location.

This would indicate that fixed location designs are possible. However, integrating barcodes or additional RFID labels would require additional manpower needs as well as equipment for the operation. Based on the observation of material handling techniques used, worker productivity may be impacted by the calculation of incidence rate.

The flowchart was also analyzed, and it demonstrates that the current operation of integrating automation for transferring LPN information from pallets to cases will require new operating procedures. This future state analysis will impact several areas of the current flowchart. These areas include managing forklift traffic, staging pallets to be picked, labeling operation, and staging operation. In addition, worker procedures need to be analyzed for excessive exertion, and better ergonomic postures must be considered.

The results of the fishbone diagram are that the current LPN is linked only to the pallet label. The information from this LPN would have to be linked at the case level. This is due to the fact that the conveyor scanner does not determine non-LPN information for broken-case pallets. However, the conveyor scanner may be able to use RFID LPNs in the future with strategic location. The current barcodes on the cases can only be used for the final end customer and are not being manipulated for distribution center use. Possible manipulation of this system may be a solution. Lastly, the current employee working capability may contribute to the overall work productivity. Educating employee on proper working postures may also impact worker productivity and overall distribution center efficiency.

The results of the Pareto Analysis confirm that the biggest impact for lost LPN information would come from a variety of solutions. Company XYZ's should consider linking the LPN to the cases, utilizing the conveyor scanner to automate manual counts on the conveyor, evaluating the manipulation of the customer's barcode to connect supply chain information, and modifying working postures, and lifting techniques employed by the workers may be modified to impact work productivity.

After thorough analysis, the team moved into the Design phase where we came up with three different scenarios: Scenario 1: Passive Gen 2 RFID System (RFID), Scenario 2: EWPR, and Scenario 3: Passive Gen 2 RFID System and EWPR (REWPR).

Scenario 1: Passive Gen 2 RFID System (RFID)
In this picture, we can see the first scenario where the employee is attaching the passive RFID levels to the cases. These labels contain LPN information that will help keep track of the cases. Fixed or handheld readers are used by the employees to write, read, and verify the information in the Virtual Memory System (VMS).

Scenario 2: Engineering Work Process Redesign
In the second option, we will redesign some of the process based on improving worker productivity. It will imply the change of the conveyor's height. As a result of the adjustments, the employee work methods will be affected with the goal to optimize the worker movements with training with minimal facility upgrades.

Scenario 3: Passive Gen 2 RFID System and EWPR (REWPR)
The implementation of RFID Gen 2 System and the EWPR.
These changes will impact the way the employees load the cases on the conveyor belts. In addition, the organization will be able to keep track of the cases that are shipped from the distribution center

---

Summary: Consider using RFID for case-level LPN tracking; consider facility changes for higher worker productivity: Scenarios—passive Gen 2 RFID System, EWPR, and passive Gen 2 RFID System and EWPR.

Identify: In this phase, we evaluate the cost-benefits of the proposed scenarios in the Design phase. This will be done through the calculation of the return of investment as well as the payback period.

21.4 Results

We created three different scenarios in the Identify phase of DFSS-R phase.

Scenario 1 involves the implementation of a Passive Gen 2 RFID System (RFID). This would call for a large initial investment. With this scenario, every employee would be provided a barcode (RF) scanner. There is, however, an estimated investment rate of 31.4% with an estimated payback period of 0.43 years.

Scenario 2 involves the implementation of an EWPR. This scenario would call for an initial investment and would involve providing braces to increase the conveyor height. It is estimated that there will be an estimated savings return of 29.3% with a payback period estimated at 1.27 years.

Scenario 3 involves both the implantation of a Passive Gen 2 RFID System and EWPR (RfEWPR). This would call for an initial investment rate of 31.4% and a payback period of 0.44 years.

21.5 Discussion

21.5.1 Rejection of Hypothesis

In addition, we also rejected all three of our null hypothesizes. We found that RFID technologies do reduce the number of outbound cases without LPN information. We also found that RFID technologies and EWPR do reduce the IR. Lastly, we also found that RFID technologies and EWPR reduce the PNLH.

21.5.2 Limitation

The results and recommendations calculated during this project may not be accurate because of a variety of limitations we encountered. These limitations include the fact that the team was only able to observe operation for a limited time period given the duration of the research project. In addition, the team used mostly observations and limitation for the analysis. Also, a small sample set was used in all data collection. In order to validate results and give a serious evaluation, more data collection is needed. Lastly, it is recommended that the last phase of DFSS-R including steps optimize and verify is performed to insure that the technologies recommended are tested and are the proper solution for the given environment.

21.5.3 Conclusion

In conclusion, we are grateful to the National Science Foundation for the opportunity to be a part of this NSF-IRES in Mexico UT Arlington program. Because of their funding, we had the opportunity to enhance our Spanish language skills and experience the Mexican culture.

We also appreciate the opportunity for working with a research team and learning a scientific research approach using RFID and logistics technologies.

Acknowledgments

This case study utilized Six Sigma to improve warehousing operations at international distribution center. The project was funded by the National Science Foundation International Research Program. The students involved on the project included Jose Sanchez Gonzalez, Mackenzie Dacres, and Rayanne Macnee, and this text and the author acknowledge their contribution to this manuscript.

REFERENCES

"Company XYZ's Official Website | Breakfast, Snacks, Recipes, Cereal." *Company XYZ's Official Website | Breakfast, Snacks, Recipes, Cereal.* Company XYZ's, n.d. Web. 2 July 2012. www.CompanyXYZ.com/en_US/home.html.

"Nsf.gov—National Science Foundation—US National Science Foundation (NSF)." *Nsf.gov – National Science Foundation – US National Science Foundation (NSF).* National Science Foundation, n.d. Web. 2 July 2012. www.nsf.gov/index.jsp.

"The University of Texas at Arlington." *Fast Facts.* UTA College of Engineering, n.d. Web. 2 July 2012. www.uta.edu/engineering/about/fast-facts.php.

Jones, E.C., and Chung, C.A. *RFID and Auto-ID in Planning and Logistics. A Practical Guide for Military UID Applications.* Boca Raton, FL: CRC Press, 2017.

Konsynsk, B., and Smith, H.A. Developments in practice X: Radio frequency identification (RFID) – An internet for physical objects. *Communications of the Association for Information Systems* 12 (2003). doi:10.17705/1CAIS.01219.

Ngai, E.W.T., To, C.K.M., Moon, K.K.L., Chan, L.K., Yeung, P.K.W., and Lee, M.C.M. RFID systems implementation: A comprehensive framework and a case study. *International Journal of Production Research* 48, no. 9 (2010), 2583–2612.

Ustundag, A. Evaluating RFID investment on a supply chain using tagging cost sharing factor. *International Journal of Production Research* 48, no. 9 (1 May 2010), 2549–2562.

Whitaker, M., Mithas, S., and Krishnan, M.S. A field study of RFID deployment and return expectations. *Production and Operations Management* 16, no.5 (2007), 599–612.

22

Railroad Car Tracking by an RFID System to Organize Traffic Flow

Erick C. Jones, Mehmet Eren, and James R. Bubbels

There is one quality which one must possess to win, and that is definiteness of purpose, the knowledge of what one wants, and a burning desire to possess it.

Napolean Hill

22.1 Introduction

Almost every driver who has come across a railroad crossing and has had to wait for the train to pass has probably wondered to themselves: what if they had been warned of the oncoming train? If they had known about it blocking their path, would they have gone another way? Since not every railroad crossing has an overpass to allow traffic to freely pass, traffic can get backed up during busy times causing potential delays. With a warning system somewhere along their route, drivers will be able to take alternate routes and potentially save time.

Several issues can result from a traffic buildup with safety being the largest. The Southwest Research Institute recently presented the Texas Department of Transportation TransGuide with a system design document that looked right into the heart of the subject matter. The system is called AWARD or Advance Warning to Avoid Railroad Delays. This system would notify oncoming traffic of an oncoming train and that they would need to take an alternate route to avoid this train or expect a delay waiting for the train to pass.

The system, however, does not use radio frequency identification (RFID) as a tool.

RFID has been around for a long time, but until recently, it has not been really been utilized as well as it could potentially be. The RFID Certification Handbook[1] not only talks about RFID in general, but also gives insight as to where it could and already is used. An RFID system consists of a tag (either passive or active), reader, antenna, edgeware, middleware, and some sort of IT system. The RFID system can be set up to desired settings if the appropriate components are being used. In this particular case, the RFID system can be used not only to set up a warning system for oncoming traffic, but also to tell what the train is carrying, where it has been, and even how fast the train is currently traveling. This is why it would be interesting to see if an RFID system would potentially work in this particular situation. Information is invaluable to every component of a supply chain, and RFID could potentially provide it readily and in real time.

Another aspect that needs some attention in this project is the traffic signalization and specifics regarding what can be done at an intersection or section of railroad. The book, *Traffic Engineering*,[2] goes into these specifics. Although the specifics are not in great detail, they certainly are very helpful when tackling this particular task. The signalization times, design standards and regulations, and basic ideas to help create an ideal warning system are listed in this book.

When it comes to ideas on how to communicate with the drivers of the vehicles, the book *Intelligent Transportation Primer*[3] has a lot of good ideas. There is everything from a simple LCD display sign

---

[1] Harold and Jones 2006.
[2] Roess, Prassas, and McShane 2004.
[3] The Institute of Transportation Engineers 2000.

strategically located along the route, to simply having the driver tune his or her radio to a particular radio station which updates them with the information they need to know. Although there are many options, RFID may limit the ones that can be used and the ones cannot be used.

In the article *Safety Warning Based on Highway Sensor Networks*,[4] the authors go on to talk about a proposed system in which various sensors would be used to record and send information to inform drivers of what is happening ahead. They go on to say how and when a driver should be warned. Their proposed system is not limited to only railroad crossings, but can also be utilized for any traffic problem. The whole concept behind this system is not only safety but to also eliminate any unnecessary delays.

22.1.1 Current Problem

Railroad crossings cause delays in traffic. In most places, an approaching train cannot be seen from a far enough distance that drivers are able choose an alternative route. Instead, they head to the crossing and are forced to wait. In many situations, cars get trapped with no way out.

Freight trains generally have more cars and are much longer than passenger trains. Their speed tends to also be relatively low. They are the biggest part of the train network in the United States. Most freight trains have 100 cars on average, and each car is 51.51 ft (15.70 m). For safety purposes and certain laws, trains lower their speed when they get close to a crossing which creates longer times for the cars to wait at the crossing. The average passing time through a crossing for freight trains is about 4.5 min. In some crossings, this time can be up to 12 min due to weather and conditions of the trains.

Many railroad crossing accidents are caused by the cars and pedestrians who get to a closed railroad gate and do not obey the traffic signalization for various reasons. Nearly half of the total crossing accidents are caused at the railroad crossings which have warning devices like the stop signs, advance warning signs, and pavement markings. Many of these accidents occur when the lighting is poor and the people cannot visually see the train coming or they simply misjudge its location. Even with many new devices and methods being tested, accidents are still regularly occurring and a need for a new system is evident.

22.1.2 Reason for Improvement

The objective of the proposed system is to provide a warning system to traffic and prevent unnecessary delays. RFID can be used in place of other proposed systems, such as using radar sensors and underground sensors. These systems do not allow for flexibility and sometimes do not provide accurate information to the control center. Radar systems tend to be sensitive to the environment. Very cold weather or heavy rain can alter its functionality.

RFID eliminates this issue and provides extended information to the control center. This allows them to organize the traffic flow more efficiently. In doing this, not only does it organize traffic, but it also eliminates the unwanted backups at the crossings.

Another possibility, besides being a tool in a warning system, RFID may also be used for nationwide railcar tracking network to follow the movement of any train equipped with RFID system. There is also a possibility to use RFID for tracking passenger trains and for providing their expected arrivals–departures. This information can be updated on Internet, so the people who are going to use the train will be informed by using the website.

Being able to track railcars in real time opens the door to better supply chain management. Information about the location of supplies or finished goods could potentially speed up the entire production process and provide better customer service. This concept is not limited to only railcar tracking. It can also be applied to trucks, airplanes, and any other means of transporting goods.

The RFID tracking systems, like every system, have pluses and minuses. When all these are taking into consideration, RFID comes out on top as a great tool to solve the problem of traffic backups considering its other potential uses.

---

[4] Xing, Ding, Cheng, and Rotenstreich 2005.

22.1.3 Strategy

The proposed RFID system would use active tags to send and record any necessary information. The rest of the RFID system would need to be task oriented and specific.

The reader which reads the signal of the active tag mounted on the train needs to send the tag data to traffic signal control center. This task could be accomplished in a few different ways. First, a copper-twisted pair cable line can be used to connect the reader to the control center. By using the cable, the cost would be more reasonable in the long term, in comparison to other methods. Also, communication cutoffs would be minimized due to the cable's reliability. However, this method requires setting the cable underground which would take a lot of time, and it does not provide any flexibility for any kind of system changes if some conflict would arise.

Another possible method of communicating with the control center to consider is using a wireless technology. Bluetooth 802.11 technology is a wireless technology that connects the electronic devices wirelessly. Low required power can allow using sunlight as energy source for this method, but because of current distance limitations of the Bluetooth 802.11 technology, it would not be suitable for this application.

This leads to another possibility, a Global Positioning System (GPS). The current space-based tele-communications environment is characterized by satellites orbiting the earth at various distances. The signals can be transmitted and received with GPS devices by using the satellites. This kind of communi-cation is expensive, and it requires the user to be registered in the network all the time. This potentially rules GPS out as an option for the final system design.

The final option is broadcasting the signal from the reader to the control center. A radio station uses a small portion of the radio spectrum for broadcasting audible data. Radio data systems use a portion of the unused spectrum called a subcarrier to transmit information. An radio data systems (RDS) receiver receives the signal and then decodes it, or translates the information to text or audio information. This makes broadcasting a feasible option for the proposed system.

22.2 Methodology

22.2.1 Testing the Active Tags

The experiment consisted of a RF Code Mobile Reader installed in a HP Palm Pilot, RF Code active tags with a frequency of 303 MHz, and a car. The idea was to test the reader's ability to read while the tags were in motion much like a train would be. If the tags read consistently, then the system would be feasible. The test consisted of five active tags placed on the car at selected locations. Then, the car would drive past the stationary reader, and the data could be recorded for various speeds of the car.

22.2.2 Test Results

The car was tested at speeds of 0, 10, 20, 30, 40, and 50 miles/h. Each time the reader would capture certain tags based upon their location and also the speed of the car. The tag placed on the nose of the car proved to be the only tag that read every single time. The tags placed on other locations read based on the speed. The tags were numbered 1 through 5 with Tag 1 being the tag on the nose of the car. Tags 2, 3, and 4 were placed on the car's windshield, and Tag 5 was located inside the car. Since there was always one tag reading every single test, it can be concluded that speed is not a factor and that using active tags in the system is feasible.

22.2.3 Finding a Practical Way to Send Data to the Control Center

As mentioned before, each RFID reader placed around the crossings needs to communicate with the traf-fic control center. This can be established by wire or wireless communication. In the case of placing the readers around the crossing and assuming the traffic control center is to be not more than 4 miles away from the reader location, a radio transmitter or radio modem would be a good solution. The fact that the readers are placed outside and they communicate with the control center in open environment with no line of sight requirement makes the process easier. The frequency of 458 MHz allows a communication range up to 20 km in free space. A transmitter and receiver with that frequency are recommended to connect the RFID to the control center.

22.2.4 Determining the Appropriate Layout to Set the Devices

Since the connection from the reader to the control center can be made wirelessly, a certain tolerance for the distance of placing the readers must be considered. This tolerance allows the control center to organize the routes properly for specific cases. For the proposed system, RFID readers are to be placed about 1.5 miles away from the crossing.

22.3 Simulation Results

To demonstrate a case regarding the wait time of the cars, SIMUL8 software is used. In the simulation,

4,000 unit = 1 min
66.667 unit = 1 s
Average passing time for a train = 5 min[5] (default)
Train speed = 30 mph (default)
Average wait time for a car due to closed crossing = 3.8 min
Average number of cars waiting = 73.6

From this result, each car loses 3.8 min depending on the time of the day, and there are approximately 74 cars involved this loss. Therefore, each time the crossing is closed, the average total time lost is 4.29 h. This might not represent any variable that can be used in the calculations, but it makes sense if some of the drivers are in duty and using their working time.

There are also some accidents which occur concerning railroad crossings. These accidents can be caused by signalization errors or the cars that do not obey the signalizations. An early warning system might be able to reduce these accidents. The idea is to divert traffic so that there are fewer backups. If traffic is diverted, there is less of a chance of an accident caused by a driver not being alert or impatient.

22.3.1 Cost Analysis

The essential equipment for an RFID system is the reader and a tag. As mentioned earlier, the recommended tags need to be active, which are more expensive than passive tags. The range for active tags is $35–$142. The tag that has the highest read range of 100 ft is about $140. Each train requires one of these active tags costing $140.

Because of the environment, the reader has to be durable, but at the same time, it should not be costly. There are many kinds of active readers in the market that cost anywhere between $1,200 and $7,000. The reader chosen for the proposed system costs $1,480.

If we look at the average total cost for a crossing including the other equipment required, the following are found:

The reader: $1,200–$7,000
Active tags: $35–$142
Transmitter – Receiver: $300–$800

---

[5] Based on the interview with Bhaven Naik, PhD std.- Mid America Transportation Dept.

Electronic sign: $80–$600

Labor: $700

Average total for the proposed system: $4,100 (two readers—tags not included)

Periodic cost: $350 each year (maintenance)

Total cost for 5 years: $5,850

If the system were to be implemented at every intersection not including tag cost,

280,000 crossings*$5,850 = $1,638,000,000

22.3.2 Recommendations

RFID readers can be connected up to four antennas. Taking advantage of this fact, instead of using a reader at each crossing, a reader antenna can be placed by itself at certain crossings. If two or three crossings are close enough to each other, only one reader would be necessary with the use of antennas. In this case, the communication can be established via special antenna cables which vary depending on the kind of the reader. This would in turn affect the cost analysis depending on what gets implemented.

An alternative solution could be to connect the reader directly to the traffic signs. This system would bypass the control center. Each warning sign in this case needs to have a radio transmitter to get the information from the reader directly. Despite a cheaper alternative, this solution would take away from some of the benefits that RFID could create.

22.4 Conclusion

A RFID-based system can replace existing sensor systems with affordable cost and more effectiveness. The proposed RFID system has capability of sending more information about the train other than basic data such as the trains speed. The main question before the experiment is can the readers read tags in motion. The test results show that active tags are able to be read when they are at twice the expected speed of a passing train at an intersection. This makes the usage of RFID in a system a reality. A radio transmitter for communication between the reader and control center or directly to the electronic signs is the ideal recommendation for the proposed RFID system.

The primary concern of this study is saving time and avoiding backups. However, there is the definite possibility that the proposed system may help to prevent accidents. The total cost for the proposed system per crossing is $5,850. The system could be paid for in several ways depending on who is using it. In terms of a warning system, if it can prevent accidents from happening or even save the right person time, the potential savings begin to add up. In terms of the other possibilities, if a train can be tracked in real time, then supply chain management becomes faster. Also RFID may be able to help increase passenger traffic on passenger trains if a person could check the train's status in real time. The possibilities are endless, and a warning system using RFID is only the beginning. The initial cost may be large, but the potential savings and usage help tip the scale back into the proposed systems favor.

REFERENCES

Coleman, F., R.W. Eck, and E.R. Russell. Railroad-highway grade crossings. A look forward. Committee on Railroad-Highway Grade Crossings, 2000.

Harold, G.C., and E.C. Jones. *RFID Certification Textbook*. Houston, TX: PWD Group Inc., 2006.

Roess, R. P., E. S. Prassas, and W. R. McShane. *Traffic Engineering*, 2rd Edition. Upper Saddle River, NJ: Pearson Prentice Hall, 2004.

Siegemund, F., and C. Florkemeier. Interaction in pervasive computing settings using bluetooth-enabled active tags and passive RFID technology together with mobile phones. *Proceedings of the First IEEE International Conference on Pervasive Computing and Communications, 2003. (PerCom 2003)*, Fort Worth, TX, 2003.

Singh, J.P., N. Bambos, B. Srinivasan and D. Clawin. Wireless LAN performance under varied stress conditions in vehicular traffic scenarios. *Proceedings IEEE 56th Vehicular Technology Conference*, Vancouver, BC, 2002.

The Institute of Transportation Engineers. Intelligent Transportation Primer. Library of Congress, 2000.

TransGuide. Southwest Research Institute, Railroad Delay Advance Warning System. Texas Department of Transportation, 25/3/1998.

Xing, K., M. Ding, X. Cheng, and S. Rotenstreich. Safety warning based on highway sensor networks. *IEEE Wireless Communications and Networking Conference*, New Orleans, LA, 2005.

23

Logistics Ecosystems

Juan Marcos Castillo

All anyone asks for is a chance to work with pride.

Deming

There is an important discussion about ecosystems in business. Starting from the Basole et al. (2016) construction that says: "adapted from the biological/ecological sciences, the ecosystem perspective is based on the premise that industries consist of a heterogeneous and continuously evolving set of constituents that are interconnected through a complex, global network of relationships, co-create value, and are codependent for survival". According to biological ecosystem definition: "An ecosystem is a community of interacting organisms and the physical environment in which they live. Ecosystems are not just assemblages of species; they are systems combined of organic and inorganic matter and natural forces that interact and change". In addition, Moore describes business ecosystems as: "communities of customers, suppliers, lead producers, and other stakeholders interacting with one another to produce goods and services and coevolving capabilities". Furthermore, a logistics ecosystem is not complete without the definition of the term "Logistics", which is:

> "the movement and transmittal of goods, services and information". This is not a lite definition, since Lummus et al. (2001) took a series of historical definitions to conclude the presented definition. Thus, the discussion about ecosystems and how they are related with Logistics can give us the following definition from the authors: "Logistics ecosystems are the community of organizations from end to end of the supply chain collaborating to move and transmit goods, services and information."

23.1 Smart Logistic Hubs

The mention of ubiquitous computing by Wiser in 1996 was the start of the discussion about smart products and services that has the main purpose to deliver the humanity of unnecessary work. In contrast, there is some mention that those concepts were based on just one-on-one relationships and not complex systems such as Artificial Intelligence (AI) and Internet of Things (IoT). The reality is that in the past 10 years, the inclusion of AI and IoT is directly connected when the logistics experts describe the future of Smart Logistics.

Smart Logistics Setup (SLS) was presented in 2007 by Stefansson and Sternberg as a proposed model to understand Smart Logistics. The discussion about Smart Logistics continued by Uckelman (2012) when he presents the concept of Smart logistics in his documentation and the actual definition of it. Smart Logistics is defined by:

> Smart Logistics (SL) embrace smart services and smart products within Logistics, SL is derived from technology driven approach, and thereby subject to change, SL frees humans from activities that can be delegated to Smart Products and Services, SL are invisible and calm and can therefore be described as transparent, SL are connected, thus communicating and possibly

> interacting with environment, SL facilitate state-of-the-art data processing, integrates existing logistic technologies, such as material handling systems, and enable these to react and act in a correspondingly smart manner, and include state-of-the-art billing, payment or licensing as integral component.
>
> *Uckelman (2012)*

However, after the 10 years of discussion about Smart Logistics, it is still not a full reality in complex systems like logistics hubs. There are pilot projects from some companies about block chain, which is one of the approaches to achieve Smart Logistics. However, it is not a reality in terms of full implementation in logistics ecosystems where there is more than one transportation system included and multiple logistics stakeholders involve.

This concept of Smart Logistics is the dream of Europe, Asia, and America, and further studies are being conceptualized to convert the idea of not just Smart Logistics, but Smart Logistics hubs or clusters.

The following topic to describe is logistics hub or cluster, well defined by Sheffi (2013) as follows:

> Logistics intensive clusters are agglomerations of several types of firms and operations: (i) firms providing logistics services, such as 3PLs, transportation, warehousing and forwarders, (ii) the logistics operations of industrial firms, such as the distribution operations of retailers, manufacturers (in many cases after-market parts) and distributors and (iii) the operations of companies for whom logistics is a large part of their business. Such logistics clusters also include firms that service logistics companies, such as truck maintenance operations, software providers, specialized law firms, international financial services providers, etc.

Thus, the authors believe that Smart Logistics hub is going to be more common for sustainable operations, because the tracking in the operation can help in the optimization and reduction in routing that permits minimization of waste and CO_2 emissions.

23.2 Value-Added Logistics Services: The Panama Canal Example

After years of studies and observations about logistics Ecosystems, the Value-Added Logistics Services (VALS) is going to be one of the key factors of success to ensure the movement of cargo through that hub.

In addition, logistics has become more important in the last two decades, because it constitutes a significant source of cost for companies. Logistics total cost equals to 13%–16% of a company's sales. Nevertheless, logistics has also become a source of competitive advantage, because it allows a company to be more efficient in its operations, in terms of quality, cost, and/or time, and therefore offer a higher value and a better experience to its customers.

Despite the fact that adding value to products or services leveraging logistics/distribution capabilities to increase the loyalty of the customers was a hot topic in the 1990s, the origin of this idea is older than that. The discussion may start with the concept of Servicisation of Business introduced by Vandermerwe and Rada or with the work of Langley and Holcomb which presented the concept of "logistics customer value". The origin of the value-added services is not that clear, since the concept of add value goes back in the 1800s, in the beginning of the age of industrialization, and the logistics is as old as humanity itself. What is clear is that the relationship between logistics and value-added services was a powerful marketing strategy used by multinationals to strengthen relationships with customers since the 1990s.

In order to define VALS, the core topic of this chapter, it is necessary to examine other related concepts first. The first definition to evaluate is the one provided by Rutner and Langley who stated that the value of logistics is to meet customer service requirements and minimize the costs of the supply chain and maximizing the profitability of the shareholders. The second concept to consider is "global value chains", which were defined by Gereffi and Fernandez as the full range of activities that firms and workers do to bring a product from its conception to its end use. Recognizing that these activities integrate the value chain. They can be contained within a single firm or divided among different firms. The third definition to examine was also provided by Rutner and Langley, who define value-added services as creating a business experience that exceeds customer requirements and expectations that not only will be repeated by the customer but will also be shared throughout the community business. The latter definition is not far from the concept of quality, which according to Besterfield is a product or service that fulfills or exceeds customers' expectations based on the intended use and selling price. Other authors have stated that value-adding services (VAS) are related to doing things or offering some kind of activities to customers rather than the total creation of tangible products. They are additional services to complement other major services and typically connote customized and extra special services beyond the basics.

Consequently, VALS represent supplementary or additional logistics services, which complement the core offers of a firm. In other words, VALS give the product or offering a differential "plus" over competitive offerings that includes a higher level of quality during the logistics processes. Furthermore, the VALS key relies on the segmentation of the benefits that the customer requires.

VALS can take place in the warehouse, the distribution center, or an intermediate facility. For example, as products spend time in distribution centers, companies have an opportunity to add value to these products by labeling, packaging, preparing for retail display, and performing postponed operations before the products are moved into the retail channels. Those activities mentioned above are examples of typical VALS conducted by third-party logistics (3PL) providers. Several frameworks for categorizing 3PL service offerings have been devised, where the major categorization criteria have been asset-based vs. non-asset-based, service vs. solution or support, discrete vs. integrated, back-office oriented vs. front-office oriented, and coordination vs. adaptation. Table 23.1 shows some of the most common VALS provided to international cargo.

Previous studies were aimed at identifying the most important selection criteria for 3PL selection. The authors found that at the top level, performance, cost, and service, in sequence, are the three criterion groups with the greatest influence on selection, while at the detail level, value-added services provision, problem-solving capability, continuous cost reduction, and document accuracy are the most remarkable features.

According to Gulc, logistics service quality (LQS) is one of the crucial factors determining customers' satisfaction and position of logistics enterprises on the competitive market. In addition, Mentzer and Flint stated that LQS has become a powerful source of competitive differentiation in several marketing offers of world-class companies. Nevertheless, scholars and practitioners in logistics have never agreed to a universal approach to the definition of the concept of quality in logistics service and its associated dimensions. This is due to the specificity and multi-attribute character of service, but also because of the different understanding of service quality by the organization and by customer.

Gulc also stated that most common approach to evaluate the quality of logistics services (QLS) is the user-based approach. It is based on individual customers' opinion of perceived quality. In addition, Gulc said that the most widespread methods to measure QLS are the subjective ones, which focus on client's perception and can be sorted into three groups:

- Multi-attribute measurement methods, which assume that the total assessment of service quality is the sum of individual perception of each client.
- Incident research methods, which depends on the assumption that the clients' assessment of service quality depends on their experience.
- Measurement of complaints.

According to Mentzer and others, one of the most difficult tasks of providing services is often the determination of what the customer truly values. Consequently, Mentzer and others proposed to use the means-end value hierarchy model (MEVHM), which could help logistics managers to understand more fully what their customers' value, not just their satisfaction with the attributes the company has traditionally measured. The MEVHM has been used in the marketing discipline (particularly in consumer research) to explain how customers perceive and evaluate their product/service use experiences, and what product/service attributes and benefits are sought by customers and why. Consequently, this research uses the MEVHM as Mentzer and others proposed, as it will be detailed in the methodology section, since the purpose of our research is to evaluate VALS in Panama, from the perspective of companies (that could be seen as customers) that acquire these services.

TABLE 23.1

VALS Offered to International Cargo

VALS	Service Offered
Labeling	Print and stick labels on the product or its packaging. This include country of origin labels, brand labels, bar codes, unique ID labels, price stickers, and other promotional labeling
Marking	Add information about the characteristics of the product or the packaging. Symbols, pictograms, graphics, logos, text, or numbers are directly printed or engraved on the product or on its case
Packaging	Pack goods into consolidated containers, cartons, or store displays
Repackaging	Repackaging of damaged boxes into new outer cartons or country-specific, customer-specific, or language-specific packages
Maquila	Manufacturing operation, where factories import certain material and equipment on a duty-free and tariff-free basis for assembly, processing, or manufacturing and then export the assembled, processed, and/or manufactured products
Inserting	Attaching instructions for use, catalogues, flyers, or any other marketing material, in the respective languages required
Light assembly	Assembling partially finished products to transform it to a finished product
Sub-assembly	Pre-assembling parts and components by hand or with special tools, to reduce the number of assembly steps required at the factory
Repairing	Valuable test and repair services tailored to each client's unique requirements
Storage	Keeping the products in a suitable place so that their conditions are preserved until they are required
Programming	Programming of electronic devices
Promotion and advertisement support	Kit Building, price labeling, attaching marketing material
Instruction	Some logistics centers have also become involved in education and instruction and turned themselves into similar customer service centers for end users
Quality control	Conducting quality inspections to ensure that products are free from defects and in a suitable condition
Transport	Movement of export/import goods to and from the ports
Kitting	Sorting different materials into store-ready kits, bundles, bags, or packages
Order picking	Taking and collecting articles in a specified quantity before shipment to satisfy customers' orders
Distribution	Delivering goods to customers
Dealing with customs and phytosanitary procedures	Ensuring compliance of customs and phytosanitary procedures
Transloading or transshipment	Transferring a shipment from one transportation mode to another
Returns handling (reverse logistics)	Receiving, inspection, and re-shipment or disposal of items returned by customers

Source: The authors based on VALS offered by several 3PLs such as DHL, APL logistics.

In most developed countries, the role of ship terminals (cruise and cargo) has expanded beyond receiving storing and delivering cargos to becoming an integral node connecting to global logistics chains. Several authors have suggested that ports form part of a value-driven chain, and as such, they can add value to the goods passing through them. In addition, ESCAP stated that the commercial success of a port could stem from a productivity advantage in traditional cargo-handling service, from value-added service, or from a combination of the two. The latter adds value to different operations, services, and capabilities that take place in a port environment. This includes capacity to handle different types of cargo and a variety of services in intermodal operations, capacity to convey cargo through the most diversified routes/modes at the least possible time to end-users premises, and capacity to deliver tailored services to different market segments and to act as collaborative intermodal hub networks. It is evident that the competition among and between ports has increased, and VAS is a powerful way for ports to build a sustainable competitive advantage and have the potential to attract port users and retain them. In some circumstances, ports could offer the services directly, and in others, ports outsource or provide the necessary facilities for 3PL companies to offer the VAS.

According to Pinnock and others, the Panama Canal expansion places on the table a new opportunity for Caribbean countries to develop a competitive logistics infrastructure, which could compete with Panama in adding value to the global chain. For this to happen, the weaknesses and the lack of connectivity between infrastructure, regulations, and processes need to be addressed. It also requires specialized skills, knowledge, and competence of a flexible and agile workforce.

The Panama Canal has a diversification of the services provided, based on the master plan of the Oceanic Zone development (2017). The relevance of VALS for Panamanian government and logistics private sector is evidenced in documents such as PenLog or the Logistics Strategic Plan of Panama to 2030 (2017). The Marketing and Commercial Department of the Panama Canal started the discussion in 2004. Later, in 2016, Yossi Sheffi (from CTL MIT) insisted on the relevance of this diversification of the services provided by the Canal, when he proposed a VALS hub. In fact, the Government is evaluating a multipurpose hub in the Canal that included VALS currently.

This whole context gives more relevance to our research, since it contributes to analyze the current situation of VALS industry in Panama.

23.3 Data Analytics to Optimize Decision-Making Processes

The application of data analytics tools can give great benefits when further research is required to understand factors that affect complex systems, especially in transportation networks in logistics Ecosystems. That is the case of the studies of the authors in air transportation which is totally adaptable to other type of transportation systems.

The authors propose them a model as a way to approach this kind of routing optimization based on historical data. The authors present this approach as a way to solve in a simple, but not heuristic approach to the routing problematic, always trying to achieve based on network problems, clustering, and dynamic programming by the regular Operation Research approaches (Figure 23.1).

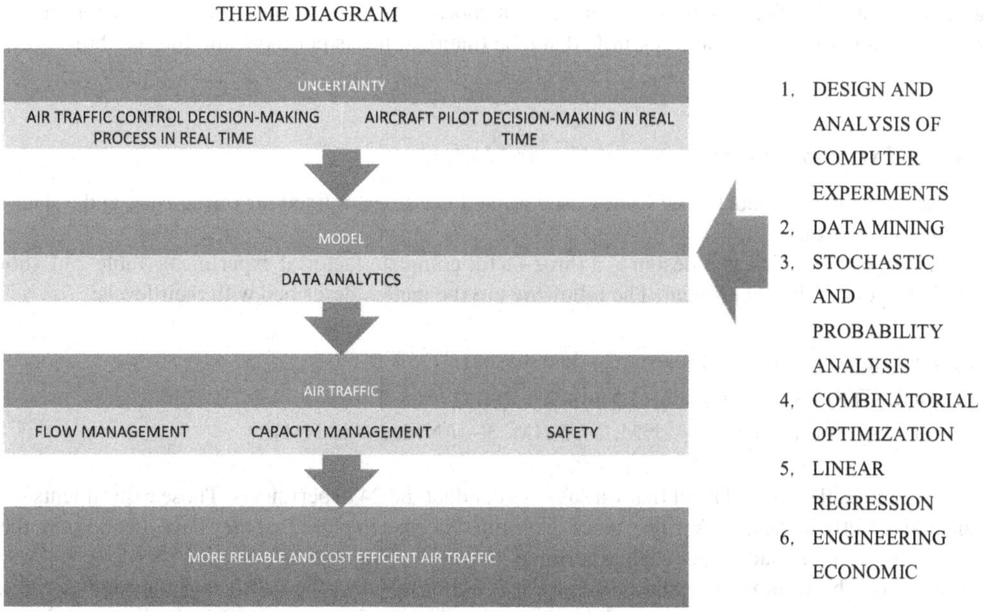

FIGURE 23.1 Statistical meta-model diagram.

23.4 Design and Analysis of Computer Experiments for Simulation

The following is the example of Design and Analysis of Computer Experiments (DACE) applied in an airspace optimization model based on simulation. The methodology and the model are defined with the final objective to understand using statistics more than just the compare and contrast comparison between transportation layouts using complex simulation models.

23.4.1 Design and Model Definition

23.4.1.1 Factors

23.4.1.1.1 Itinerary

The itinerary is a database which includes type of aircraft, license plate, origin, destiny, departure time, and arrival time. Each row of the database is a flight.

23.4.1.1.2 Ground Traffic Rules

The ground traffic rules (GTRules) is a time distance between aircraft during the arrival, which is between 1 and 2 min.

23.4.1.1.3 Air Traffic Rules

The air traffic rule is the distance in nautical miles between aircraft during the approximation to the airport which lies between 3 NM as a minimum and 10 NM.

Consequently, the data set of itinerary is a factor with two levels (high season data set, low season data set), the GTRules is a factor with three levels (1, 1.5, and 2 min), and the air traffic rule is a factor with four levels (3, 5, 7, and 10 NM).

23.4.1.2 Response Variables

When Copa airlines use to run the simulation, they obtain five outputs as response variables per each model. The key performance indicators for the air traffic management in Panama are the sequencing actions (number of interactions per day), the airborne conflicts (number of conflicts per day), the flight time (hours per day), the track mile distance (nautical miles per day), and the fuel burn (gallon per day).

23.4.1.3 Experimental Design and Linear Model

The first experiment conducted by COPA used a fixed GTRules, a fixed air traffic rule, and a data set from the high season.

Therefore, our experimental design is a three-factor complete factorial experiment. Table 23.1 shows the coded layout of the experiment. The following are the factors described with their levels:

   Factor 1: Itinerary (1—high season, 2—low season)
   Factor 2: GTRules (1—1 min, 2—1.5 min, 3—2 min)
   Factor 3: Air traffic rules (1—3 NM, 2—5 NM, 3—7 NM, 4—10 NM).

Table 23.2 shows the coded layout that was used to conduct the 24 experiments. Those experiments were conducted directly in the COPA office, since the limited license in place that they have. In addition, there is just one replication made it per each experiment.

In order to achieve flexibility and efficiency, it is better to select the full factorial design to run the experiments. This kind of design was originally used in design of experiments for physical experiments, but it is suitable to apply in computer experiments as well [17].

TABLE 23.2

Layout Coded of the Three Factor Complete Factorial Design

Factor 1	Factor 2	Factor 3	Factor 1	Factor 2	Factor 3
1	1	1	2	1	1
1	1	2	2	1	2
1	1	3	2	1	3
1	1	4	2	1	4
1	2	1	2	2	1
1	2	2	2	2	2
1	2	3	2	2	3
1	2	4	2	2	4
1	3	1	2	3	1
1	3	2	2	3	2
1	3	3	2	3	3
1	3	4	2	3	4

The linear model formulation per each response variable is as follows:

$$Y_{ijkt} = \mu_{...} + \alpha_i + \beta_j + \gamma_k + (\alpha\beta)_{ij} + (\alpha\gamma)_{ik} + (\beta\gamma)_{jk} + (\alpha\beta\gamma)_{ijk} + \varepsilon_{ijkt} \qquad (23.1)$$

for $i = 1, \ldots, a, j = 1, \ldots, b, k = 1, \ldots, c$, and $t = 1, \ldots, r$.

where

ε_{ijkt} are iid $N(0, \sigma^2)$

Y_{ijkt} is the t-th response observed for $trt(i, j, k)$

$\mu_{...}$ is the overall mean

α_i is the effect on the response due to the ith level of factor 1.

β_j is the effect on the response due to the jth level of factor 2.

γ_k is the effect on the response due to the kth level of factor 3.

$(\alpha\beta)_{ij}$ is the interaction effect in ith and jth of factors 1 and 2.

$(\alpha\gamma)_{ik}$ is the interaction effect in the ith and kth of factors 1 and 3.

$(\beta\gamma)_{jk}$ is the interaction effect in the jth and kth of factors 2 and 3.

$(\alpha\beta\gamma)_{ijk}$ is the interaction effect in ith, jth, and kth of factors 1, 2, and 3.

COPA mentioned that there is a way to obtain the probabilistic data, but the analyst asked us to run the model without stochastic data, since they made the previous experiments using deterministic output. Consequently, the mathematical model is going to suffer a modification, since it will not consider any interaction effect with the three factors in conjunction.

The linear model formulation per each response variable is given as follows:

$$Y_{ijkt} = \mu_{...} + \alpha_i + \beta_j + \gamma_k + (\alpha\beta)_{ij} + (\alpha\gamma)_{ik} + (\beta\gamma)_{jk} + \varepsilon_{ijkt} \qquad (23.2)$$

for $i = 1, \ldots, a, j = 1, \ldots, b, k = 1, \ldots, c$, and $t = 1, \ldots, r$.

where

ε_{ijkt} are iid $N(0, \sigma^2)$.

Y_{ijkt} is the t-th response observed for $trt(i, j, k)$.

$\mu_{...}$ is the overall mean.

α_i is the effect on the response due to the ith level of factor 1.

β_j is the effect on the response due to the jth level of factor 2.

γ_k is the effect on the response due to the kth level of factor 3.

$(\alpha\beta)_{ij}$ is the interaction effect in ith and jth of factors 1 and 2.

$(\alpha\gamma)_{ik}$ is the interaction effect in the ith and kth of factors 1 and 3.

$(\beta\gamma)_{jk}$ is the interaction effect in the jth and kth of factors 2 and 3.

23.4.1.4 The Simulation Model

23.4.1.4.1 The Simulation Software

The Total Airspace & Airport Modeler (TAAM) is a fast-time gate-to-gate simulator of airport and airspace operations. This software can simulate 4D and 3D. TAAM enables the analyst to identify the system benefits of such changes in the airport layout for gates, taxiways, and runways.

Some of the features are the 3D multi-color models of airports and aircrafts, 4D full airspace and flight profile calculations, detailed ground functionality, detailed airside functionality, a flexible rule base to accommodate different modeling requirements, statistical data generated in a wide variety of report forms, direct output to spreadsheet, and database tools for further in-depth analysis [18].

23.4.1.5 The Simulation Model

The simulation model consists in set the static files (in our case, the itineraries), the parameter setting, and the rules (air traffic rules and GTRules for this experiment).

There exist other parameters that must keep standard, such as airport layout (32 gates), two runways, three taxiways, and the airport geolocation [19]. The airport with the specifications must be drawn in AutoCAD and uploaded in the software. In addition, there is an airspace design, so the regions of the airspace and the air ways must be drawn.

23.4.1.6 The Itinerary Samples

In order to obtain the sample, the Department of Operation Efficiency of COPA analyzed the air traffic flow from 1 January to 7 July and took two days: one from the high season and another from the low season. Then, COPA took, using another software called AIMS, the itinerary for each day. However, the procedure says that it is required to take at a minimum of three days. This is necessary since they need to take from the 05:00 a.m. of the actual day to the 05:00 a.m. of the day after the actual day. This is necessary to keep the continuity of the simulation in terms of time. As an explanation, COPA takes the 05:00 as a reference, since is the hour zone of Panama based on the Greenwich Meridian.

As we mentioned before, the itineraries contain the type of aircraft, the license plate, the origin, the destiny, the departure time, and the arrival time. This information is per flight.

23.4.1.7 Simulation Output

In order to obtain the output, it is necessary to use the sample itinerary which is part of the input information. Then, it is important to change some of the air traffic rules and the GTRules in two windows and in the map of the air space. The areas of the map are changed for approximation to the Tocumen Airport. In other words, these rules affect in some ways the departure, if the runways have no conflict in the departure, and these rules affect all the arrival queues in the air space of Panama.

Therefore, the simulation is going to run per five days, just to check any outlier and maintain the continuity. However, the model has a rule to stop in some point (which is 05:00 a.m. as we mentioned before) to record the information for the main in study. There is another rule to stop at 05:00 a.m. the next day to stop the recording; this process recording is manual. After the model stop, it is necessary to run the three different queries, and two of them were customized by COPA for the previous analysis.

In addition, the output of time is in seconds and the fuel consumption is kilograms, so it is necessary to convert those. The flight time is converted in hours of flight and the fuel burn changes in gallons.

23.4.2 Statistical Analysis

For the statistical analysis, it presents each response variable separately in order to analyze the effect of each factor which their levels. The objective is to know how the factors and the levels affect each response variable separately. For this analysis, the software used is SAS. Therefore, the analysis shows the ANOVA table with the main factors and the interaction effects. However, it does not include the full interaction with the three factors since there are no replications. The model does not include the full interaction effect between the three factors, since the simulation model is deterministic. Furthermore, the interaction plot and the "Tukey" comparison per each model are presented with the followed discussion.

23.4.2.1 Analysis of Variance

The analysis of variance (ANOVA) conducted presents the results per each response variable. Therefore, we are working with five different models and five different analyses. Significance level used for the ANOVA is 0.1 as an alpha value.

Consequently, the hypothesis for the linear model stands as

H_0: no difference in the treatments/full model is not statistically significant.

H_1: at least two treatments are different/full model is statistically significant.

So, the p-value must be less than the alpha value 0.1 to reject H_0. Then, the model is statistically significant.
  The hypotheses analyzed based on the ANOVA tables for interaction effects are

H_0^{12}: factor 1 and factor 2 interaction is negligible.

H_1^{12}: factor 1 and factor 2 interaction is not negligible.

H_0^{13}: factor 1 and factor 3 interaction is negligible.

H_1^{13}: factor 1 and factor 3 interaction is not negligible.

H_0^{23}: factor 2 and factor 3 interaction is negligible.

H_1^{23}: factor 2 and factor 3 interaction is not negligible.

The decision rule for those hypotheses is that the p-value must be less than the alpha value 0.1 to reject H_0.
  The evaluation of the five models using the ANOVA approach concludes that at 0.1 level of significance, all the linear models are statistically significant. So, we reject H_0 in our first hypothesis analysis. However, the interactions between factor 2 and the other factors are greater than 0.1 as an alpha value, which means we fail to reject H_0 in the interaction hypothesis. In contrast, the interaction between factor 1 and factor 3 is significant, and we can reject H_0.
  The hypotheses analyzed based on the ANOVA table for the main effects are

H_0^2: main effect for factor 2 is negligible.

H_1^2: main effect for factor 2 is not negligible.

The decision rule for this hypothesis is that the p-value must be less than the alpha value of 0.1 to reject H_0.
  The GTRules or factor 2 is not significant at 0.1 level, since the three-way ANOVA shows the p-value of GTRules (factor 2). So, we fail to reject H_0 and the main effect of factor 2 is negligible. There is no necessity to test the other main effects since the interaction between factors 1 and 3 is not negligible (Figure 23.2).

Source	DF	Sum of Squares	Mean Square	F Value	Pr > F
Model	17	22519.16667	1324.65686	195.44	<.0001
Error	6	40.66667	6.77778		
Corrected Total	23	22559.83333			

R-Square	Coeff Var	Root MSE	Sact Mean
0.998197	1.577032	2.603417	165.0833

Source	DF	Type I SS	Mean Square	F Value	Pr > F
Iti	1	7561.50000	7561.50000	1115.63	<.0001
GTRules	2	4.33333	2.16667	0.32	0.7380
ATRules	3	14345.83333	4781.94444	705.53	<.0001
Iti*GTRules	2	37.00000	18.50000	2.73	0.1436
Iti*ATRules	3	517.83333	172.61111	25.47	0.0008
GTRules*ATRules	6	52.66667	8.77778	1.30	0.3808

Source	DF	Type III SS	Mean Square	F Value	Pr > F
Iti	1	7561.50000	7561.50000	1115.63	<.0001
GTRules	2	4.33333	2.16667	0.32	0.7380
ATRules	3	14345.83333	4781.94444	705.53	<.0001
Iti*GTRules	2	37.00000	18.50000	2.73	0.1436
Iti*ATRules	3	517.83333	172.61111	25.47	0.0008
GTRules*ATRules	6	52.66667	8.77778	1.30	0.3808

FIGURE 23.2 ANOVA table for sequence actions as a dependent variable.

Figure 23.3 shows that the p-value of GTRules is 0.738 when the number of sequence actions is a response variable. Figure 23.4 shows that the p-value of GTRules is 0.2776 when the response variable is the number of conflicts. Figure 23.5 shows that the p-value of GTRules is 0.7511 when the response variable is the flight time. Figure 23.6 presents that the p-value of GTRules is 0.7026 when the track mile distance is the response variable. Figure 23.7 presents that the p-value of GTRules is 0.7382 when the fuel burn is the response variable. In other words, the GTRules has no significant effect in the dependent variables or air traffic key performance indicator (KPIs).

As it is mentioned before, the "Iti" or itinerary and the ATRules or air traffic rules are statistically significant at 0.1 level. So, ATRules and itinerary have an effect over the air traffic KPIs. Therefore, the following analysis of interaction plots and Tukey pairwise comparison is going to be considering only between those two factors.

23.4.2.2 Interaction Plots

The objective of the interaction plots is to understand how the interaction can affect each response variable.

Table 23.3 shows the interaction plot for itinerary and air traffic rules using the response variable as sequence actions, and the same type of plots using the response variable as the number of conflicts. The plots of sequence actions show that the air traffic rule level 1, which is 3 NM miles, minimizes the numbers of sequence actions. In contrast, the plots of numbers of conflicts present that the air traffic rule level 3, which is 7 NM miles, minimizes the numbers of conflicts and the level 1 of "ATRules" is the worst for this purpose.

Source	DF	Sum of Squares	Mean Square	F Value	Pr > F
Model	17	3835.833333	225.637255	26.72	0.0003
Error	6	50.666667	8.444444		
Corrected Total	23	3886.500000			

R-Square	Coeff Var	Root MSE	Cflict Mean
0.986963	7.597209	2.905933	38.25000

Source	DF	Type I SS	Mean Square	F Value	Pr > F
Iti	1	864.000000	864.000000	102.32	<.0001
GTRules	2	27.000000	13.500000	1.60	0.2776
ATRules	3	2723.500000	907.833333	107.51	<.0001
Iti*GTRules	2	3.000000	1.500000	0.18	0.8415
Iti*ATRules	3	192.333333	64.111111	7.59	0.0182
GTRules*ATRules	6	26.000000	4.333333	0.51	0.7815

Source	DF	Type III SS	Mean Square	F Value	Pr > F
Iti	1	864.000000	864.000000	102.32	<.0001
GTRules	2	27.000000	13.500000	1.60	0.2776
ATRules	3	2723.500000	907.833333	107.51	<.0001
Iti*GTRules	2	3.000000	1.500000	0.18	0.8415
Iti*ATRules	3	192.333333	64.111111	7.59	0.0182
GTRules*ATRules	6	26.000000	4.333333	0.51	0.7815

FIGURE 23.3 ANOVA table for number of conflicts as a dependent variable.

In addition, Table 23.3 shows the interaction plot for itinerary and air traffic rules using the response variable the flight time and the same kind of plot using the response variable—the track mile distance. The plots of flight time and track mile distance show the same. The air traffic rule at level 1 minimizes both response variables.

Finally, Table 23.3 shows the interaction plot for itinerary and air traffic rules using the response variable—the fuel burn. This plot shows that the level 1 of air traffic rules minimizes the fuel burn. Therefore, there is an issue between the interaction plot results from the number of conflict and the other interaction plots, since the level 1 of air traffic rules minimizes all the response variables except the number of conflict, which is maximized.

23.4.2.3 Pairwise Tukey Comparison

In order to conduct the corresponding family of tests of the form,

$H_o: D = 0$
$H_1: D \neq 0$.

The objective is to find the significance of the comparison. So, if 0 is included in the confidence interval, it means that it is not statistically significant.

23.4.2.3.1 Sequence Actions

Figure 23.8 shows the 36 pairwise comparisons of Tukey. Consequently, Figure 23.8 shows the following information.

All the comparisons are statistically significant, except

Source	DF	Sum of Squares	Mean Square	F Value	Pr > F
Model	17	216612.1440	12741.8908	3714.94	<.0001
Error	6	20.5794	3.4299		
Corrected Total	23	216632.7234			

R-Square	Coeff Var	Root MSE	FTime Mean
0.999905	0.151742	1.851999	1220.496

Source	DF	Type I SS	Mean Square	F Value	Pr > F
Iti	1	181381.1840	181381.1840	52882.3	<.0001
GTRules	2	2.0598	1.0299	0.30	0.7511
ATRules	3	32100.5313	10700.1771	3119.67	<.0001
Iti*GTRules	2	1.9931	0.9965	0.29	0.7578
Iti*ATRules	3	3102.3106	1034.1035	301.50	<.0001
GTRules*ATRules	6	24.0652	4.0109	1.17	0.4271

Source	DF	Type III SS	Mean Square	F Value	Pr > F
Iti	1	181381.1840	181381.1840	52882.3	<.0001
GTRules	2	2.0598	1.0299	0.30	0.7511
ATRules	3	32100.5313	10700.1771	3119.67	<.0001
Iti*GTRules	2	1.9931	0.9965	0.29	0.7578
Iti*ATRules	3	3102.3106	1034.1035	301.50	<.0001
GTRules*ATRules	6	24.0652	4.0109	1.17	0.4271

FIGURE 23.4 ANOVA table for flight time as a dependent variable.

1. The comparison between sequencing actions when the interaction is high season itinerary and 5 NM as air traffic rule and the sequencing actions when the interaction is high season itinerary and 10 NM.
2. The comparison between sequencing actions when the interaction is low season itinerary and 5 NM as air traffic rule and the sequencing actions when the interaction is low season itinerary and 7 NM.
3. The comparison between sequencing actions when the interaction is low season itinerary and 7 NM and the sequencing actions when the interaction is low season itinerary and 10 NM as air traffic rule.

23.4.2.3.2 Number of Conflicts

Figure 23.9 shows that the majority of the comparisons are significant because they are not including 0 in the Tukey confidence interval. The following are the exceptions:

1. High season itinerary with 3 NM vs. high season itinerary with 5 NM.
2. High season itinerary with 5 NM vs. low season itinerary with 3 NM.
3. High season itinerary with 7 NM vs. high season itinerary with 10 NM.
4. High season itinerary with 7 NM vs. low season itinerary with 5 NM.
5. High season itinerary with 7 NM vs. low season itinerary with 7 NM.
6. High season itinerary with 7 NM vs. low season itinerary with 10 NM.

Source	DF	Sum of Squares	Mean Square	F Value	Pr > F
Model	17	34949883849	2055875521	3248.03	<.0001
Error	6	3797769	632961		
Corrected Total	23	34953681618			

R-Square	Coeff Var	Root MSE	TMDist Mean
0.999891	0.159594	795.5888	498508.5

Source	DF	Type I SS	Mean Square	F Value	Pr > F
Iti	1	29912584945	29912584945	47258.1	<.0001
GTRules	2	474151	237076	0.37	0.7026
ATRules	3	4560621424	1520207141	2401.74	<.0001
Iti*GTRules	2	287703	143852	0.23	0.8033
Iti*ATRules	3	471737542	157245847	248.43	<.0001
GTRules*ATRules	6	4178084	696347	1.10	0.4554

Source	DF	Type III SS	Mean Square	F Value	Pr > F
Iti	1	29912584945	29912584945	47258.1	<.0001
GTRules	2	474151	237076	0.37	0.7026
ATRules	3	4560621424	1520207141	2401.74	<.0001
Iti*GTRules	2	287703	143852	0.23	0.8033
Iti*ATRules	3	471737542	157245847	248.43	<.0001
GTRules*ATRules	6	4178084	696347	1.10	0.4554

FIGURE 23.5 ANOVA table for track mile distance as a dependent variable.

7. High season itinerary with 10 NM vs. low season itinerary with 5 NM.
8. High season itinerary with 10 NM vs. low season itinerary with 10 NM.
9. Low season itinerary with 5 NM vs. low season itinerary with 10 NM.
10. Low season itinerary with 5 NM vs. low season itinerary with 10 NM.

23.4.2.3.3 Flight Time, Track Mile Distance, and Fuel Burn

Figures 23.9a–c shows that none of the comparison includes 0 in the interval, so all of them are statistically significant.

As a conclusion, the three factors' complete factorial design linear model is statistically significant at 0.1 level of significance. However, the GTRules are not significant at 0.1 level of significance, so it has no effect in the air traffic KPIs.

The main objective of the simulation model is to minimize the air traffic KPIs, so the interaction plots show that the level 1 of air traffic rules is the best in order to minimize the number of sequence actions, the flight time, the track mile distance, and the fuel burn, but not number of conflicts. The number of conflicts is reduced by the level 3, and the level 1 has the worst impact on it.

Based on the Tukey pairwise comparison, the analysis when the number of conflicts is the response variable appears to have 10 over 36 comparisons as not statistically significant, which include four of the eight comparisons using the level 3 of air traffic rules. The level 3 of air traffic rules is the one which minimizes the number of conflicts based on the interaction plots.

Source	DF	Sum of Squares	Mean Square	F Value	Pr > F
Model	17	1.6263486E13	956675650912	2099.05	<.0001
Error	6	2734594642	455765773.67		
Corrected Total	23	1.6266221E13			

R-Square	Coeff Var	Root MSE	FuelB Mean
0.999832	0.177819	21348.67	12005824

Source	DF	Type I SS	Mean Square	F Value	Pr > F
Iti	1	1.3020771E13	1.3020771E13	28569.0	<.0001
GTRules	2	206192953.04	103096476.52	0.23	0.8041
ATRules	3	2.9608878E12	986962604521	2165.50	<.0001
Iti*GTRules	2	291163925.63	145581962.82	0.32	0.7382
Iti*ATRules	3	278828016005	92942672002	203.93	<.0001
GTRules*ATRules	6	2502124108	417020684.67	0.91	0.5416

Source	DF	Type III SS	Mean Square	F Value	Pr > F
Iti	1	1.3020771E13	1.3020771E13	28569.0	<.0001
GTRules	2	206192953.04	103096476.52	0.23	0.8041
ATRules	3	2.9608878E12	986962604521	2165.50	<.0001
Iti*GTRules	2	291163925.63	145581962.82	0.32	0.7382
Iti*ATRules	3	278828016005	92942672002	203.93	<.0001
GTRules*ATRules	6	2502124108	417020684.67	0.91	0.5416

FIGURE 23.6 ANOVA table for fuel burn as a dependent variable.

		Least Squares Means for Effect Iti*ATRules					Least Squares Means for Effect Iti*ATRules		
i	j	Difference Between Means	Simultaneous 90% Confidence Limits for LSMean(i)-LSMean(j)		i	j	Difference Between Means	Simultaneous 90% Confidence Limits for LSMean(i)-LSMean(j)	
1	2	-66.333333	-74.101787	-58.564879	3	5	77.333333	69.564879	85.101787
1	3	-46.000000	-53.768454	-38.231546	3	6	29.666667	21.898213	37.435121
1	4	-63.000000	-70.768454	-55.231546	3	7	24.666667	16.898213	32.435121
1	5	31.333333	23.564879	39.101787	3	8	19.000000	11.231546	26.768454
1	6	-16.333333	-24.101787	-8.564879	4	5	94.333333	86.564879	102.101787
1	7	-21.333333	-29.101787	-13.564879	4	6	46.666667	38.898213	54.435121
1	8	-27.000000	-34.768454	-19.231546	4	7	41.666667	33.898213	49.435121
2	3	20.333333	12.564879	28.101787	4	8	36.000000	28.231546	43.768454
2	4	3.333333	-4.435121	11.101787	5	6	-47.666667	-55.435121	-39.898213
2	5	97.666667	89.898213	105.435121	5	7	-52.666667	-60.435121	-44.898213
2	6	50.000000	42.231546	57.768454	5	8	-58.333333	-66.101787	-50.564879
2	7	45.000000	37.231546	52.768454	6	7	-5.000000	-12.768454	2.768454
2	8	39.333333	31.564879	47.101787	6	8	-10.666667	-18.435121	-2.898213
3	4	-17.000000	-24.768454	-9.231546	7	8	-5.666667	-13.435121	2.101787

FIGURE 23.7 Pairwise Tukey comparison for sequence actions.

TABLE 23.3

Interaction Plot Summary

Plot	Plot Description
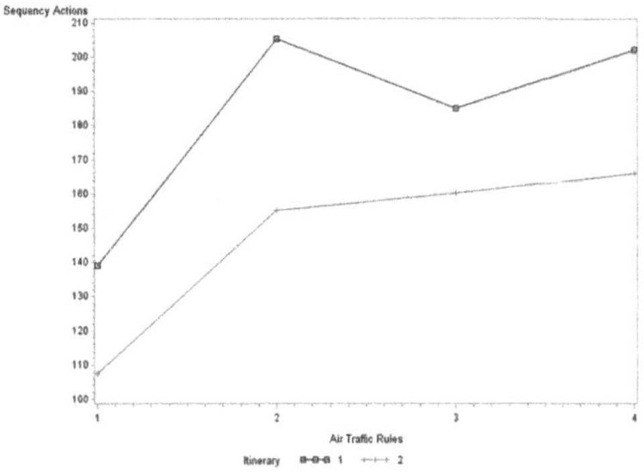	Interaction plot of sequence actions as a response variable by air traffic rule
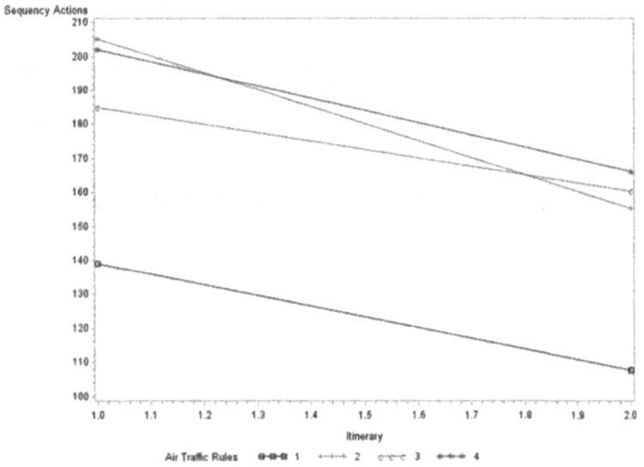	Interaction plot of sequence actions as a response variable by itinerary
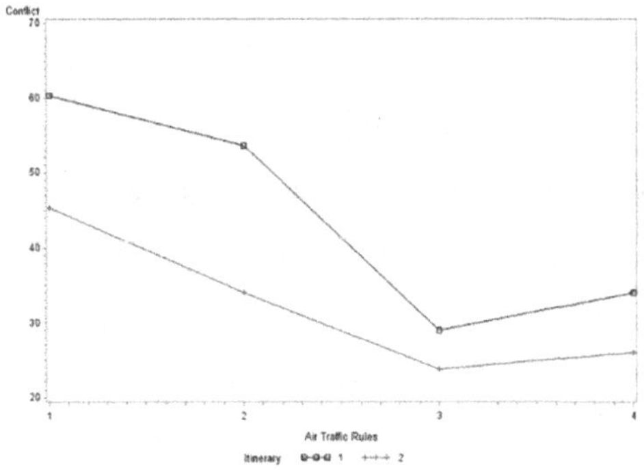	Interaction plot of number of conflicts as a response variable by air traffic rule
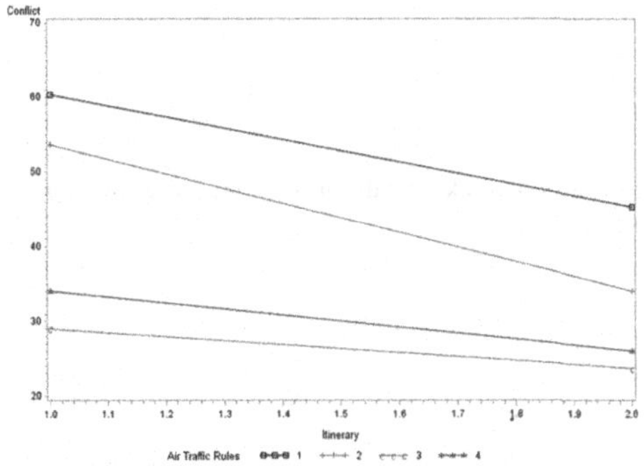	Interaction plot of number of conflicts as a response variable by itinerary

(Continued)

TABLE 23.3 (*Continued*)

Interaction Plot Summary

Plot	Plot Description
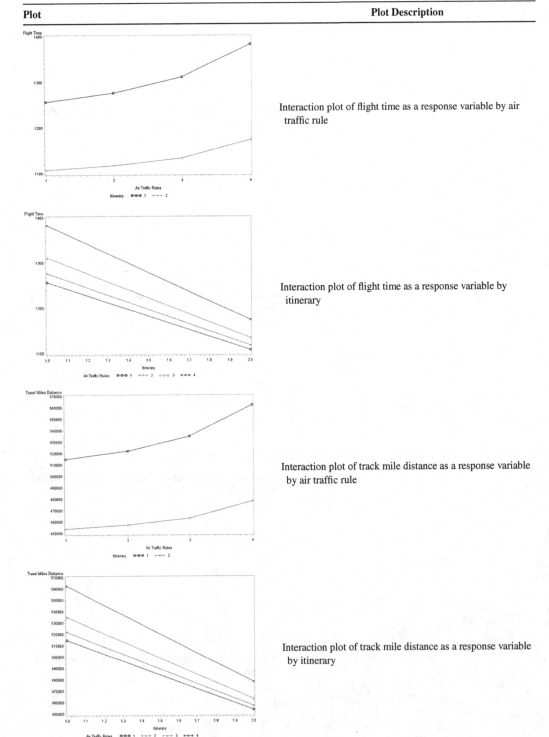	Interaction plot of flight time as a response variable by air traffic rule
	Interaction plot of flight time as a response variable by itinerary
	Interaction plot of track mile distance as a response variable by air traffic rule
	Interaction plot of track mile distance as a response variable by itinerary

(Continued)

TABLE 23.3 (*Continued*)

Interaction Plot Summary

Plot	Plot Description
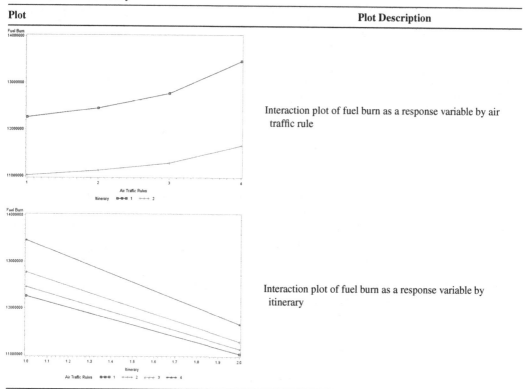	Interaction plot of fuel burn as a response variable by air traffic rule
	Interaction plot of fuel burn as a response variable by itinerary

		Least Squares Means for Effect Iti*ATRules				Least Squares Means for Effect Iti*ATRules	
		Difference Between Means	Simultaneous 90% Confidence Limits for LSMean(i)-LSMean(j)			Difference Between Means	Simultaneous 90% Confidence Limits for LSMean(i)-LSMean(j)
i	j			i	j		
1	2	6.666667	-2.004479	15.337812	3	5	-16.333333	-25.004479	-7.662188
1	3	31.333333	22.662188	40.004479	3	6	-5.000000	-13.671146	3.671146
1	4	26.333333	17.662188	35.004479	3	7	5.333333	-3.337812	14.004479
1	5	15.000000	6.328854	23.671146	3	8	3.000000	-5.671146	11.671146
1	6	26.333333	17.662188	35.004479	4	5	-11.333333	-20.004479	-2.662188
1	7	36.666667	27.995521	45.337812	4	6	0	-8.671146	8.671146
1	8	34.333333	25.662188	43.004479	4	7	10.333333	1.662188	19.004479
2	3	24.666667	15.995521	33.337812	4	8	8.000000	-0.671146	16.671146
2	4	19.666667	10.995521	28.337812	5	6	11.333333	2.662188	20.004479
2	5	8.333333	-0.337812	17.004479	5	7	21.666667	12.995521	30.337812
2	6	19.666667	10.995521	28.337812	5	8	19.333333	10.662188	28.004479
2	7	30.000000	21.328854	38.671146	6	7	10.333333	1.662188	19.004479
2	8	27.666667	18.995521	36.337812	6	8	8.000000	-0.671146	16.671146
3	4	-5.000000	-13.671146	3.671146	7	8	-2.333333	-11.004479	6.337812

FIGURE 23.8 Pairwise Tukey comparison for number of conflicts.

(a)

Least Squares Means for Effect Iti*ATRules					Least Squares Means for Effect Iti*ATRules				
i	j	Difference Between Means	Simultaneous 90% Confidence Limits for LSMean(i)-LSMean(j)		i	j	Difference Between Means	Simultaneous 90% Confidence Limits for LSMean(i)-LSMean(j)	
1	2	-19.803333	-25.329599	-14.277068	3	5	203.566667	198.040401	209.092932
1	3	-54.110000	-59.636266	-48.583734	3	6	193.786667	188.260401	199.312932
1	4	-125.900000	-131.426266	-120.373734	3	7	177.260000	171.733734	182.786266
1	5	149.456667	143.930401	154.982932	3	8	137.486667	131.960401	143.012932
1	6	139.676667	134.150401	145.202932	4	5	275.356667	269.830401	280.882932
1	7	123.150000	117.623734	128.676266	4	6	265.576667	260.050401	271.102932
1	8	83.376667	77.850401	88.902932	4	7	249.050000	243.523734	254.576266
2	3	-34.306667	-39.832932	-28.780401	4	8	209.276667	203.750401	214.802932
2	4	-106.096667	-111.622932	-100.570401	5	6	-9.780000	-15.306266	-4.253734
2	5	169.260000	163.733734	174.786266	5	7	-26.306667	-31.832932	-20.780401
2	6	159.480000	153.953734	165.006266	5	8	-66.080000	-71.606266	-60.553734
2	7	142.953333	137.427068	148.479599	6	7	-16.526667	-22.052932	-11.000401
2	8	103.180000	97.653734	108.706266	6	8	-56.300000	-61.826266	-50.773734
3	4	-71.790000	-77.316266	-66.263734	7	8	-39.773333	-45.299599	-34.247068

(b)

Least Squares Means for Effect Iti*ATRules					Least Squares Means for Effect Iti*ATRules				
i	j	Difference Between Means	Simultaneous 90% Confidence Limits for LSMean(i)-LSMean(j)		i	j	Difference Between Means	Simultaneous 90% Confidence Limits for LSMean(i)-LSMean(j)	
1	2	-7177.333333	-9551.327122	-4803.339545	3	5	81404	79030	83778
1	3	-20115	-22489	-17741	3	6	77747	75373	80121
1	4	-47727	-50101	-45353	3	7	71850	69476	74224
1	5	61289	58915	63663	3	8	56870	54496	59244
1	6	57632	55258	60006	4	5	109017	106643	111391
1	7	51735	49361	54109	4	6	105359	102985	107733
1	8	36755	34381	39129	4	7	99462	97088	101836
2	3	-12938	-15312	-10564	4	8	84482	82108	86856
2	4	-40550	-42924	-38176	5	6	-3657.333333	-6031.327122	-1283.339545
2	5	68467	66093	70841	5	7	-9554.666667	-11929	-7180.672878
2	6	64809	62435	67183	5	8	-24535	-26909	-22161
2	7	58912	56538	61286	6	7	-5897.333333	-8271.327122	-3523.339545
2	8	43932	41558	46306	6	8	-20877	-23251	-18503
3	4	-27612	-29986	-25238	7	8	-14980	-17354	-12606

FIGURE 23.9 (a) Pairwise Tukey comparison for flight time. (b) Pairwise Tukey comparison for track mile distance. (c) Pairwise Tukey comparison for fuel burn.

(*Continued*)

(c)

		Least Squares Means for Effect Iti*ATRules		
i	j	Difference Between Means	Simultaneous 90% Confidence Limits for LSMean(i)-LSMean(j)	
1	2	-199774	-263477	-136071
1	3	-516002	-579705	-452299
1	4	-1209758	-1273462	-1146055
1	5	1246276	1182573	1309979
1	6	1138233	1074530	1201936
1	7	979001	915298	1042704
1	8	603498	539795	667201
2	3	-316228	-379932	-252525
2	4	-1009984	-1073688	-946281
2	5	1446050	1382347	1509753
2	6	1338007	1274304	1401710
2	7	1178775	1115071	1242478
2	8	803272	739569	866975
3	4	-693756	-757459	-630053

		Least Squares Means for Effect Iti*ATRules		
i	j	Difference Between Means	Simultaneous 90% Confidence Limits for LSMean(i)-LSMean(j)	
3	5	1762278	1698575	1825982
3	6	1654235	1590532	1717938
3	7	1495003	1431300	1558706
3	8	1119500	1055797	1183203
4	5	2456034	2392331	2519738
4	6	2347991	2284288	2411695
4	7	2188759	2125056	2252462
4	8	1813256	1749553	1876960
5	6	-108043	-171746	-44340
5	7	-267275	-330979	-203572
5	8	-642778	-706481	-579075
6	7	-158232	-222935	-95529
6	8	-534735	-598438	-471032
7	8	-375503	-439206	-311799

FIGURE 23.9 (CONTINUED) (a) Pairwise Tukey comparison for flight time. (b) Pairwise Tukey comparison for track mile distance. (c) Pairwise Tukey comparison for fuel burn.

REFERENCES

Basole, R.C., Huntamaki, J., Still, K., &, Russell, M. (2016). Visual decision support for business ecosystem analysis. *Journal of Expert Systems with applications*, 65, 271–282. doi:10.1016/j.eswa.2016.08.041.

Castillo, J.M. (2018) Dissertation topic: "Statistical meta-model for air traffic flow and capacity management based on airspace optimization-simulation: The continuous challenge of the hub of the America congestion". University of Texas at Arlington.

Castillo, J.M., Guerra de Castillo, Z.Y., Arosemena, P.A., & Kelso, A.C. (2019) Chapter 5: Value-added logistics services after Panama Canal expansion. In: Yoshizaki, H.T.Y.; Martinez, J.C.V.; Argueta, C.M. (eds.), *The Book Supply Chain Management and Logistics in Latin America: A Multi-Country Perspective.* Emerald Publishing Ltd., Bingley.

Castillo, J.M., Jones, E., Chen, V., &, Guerra de Castillo, Z. (2018) Design and analysis of computer experiments based on a simulation model of air traffic flow optimization in Panama. *Journal of Traffic and Transportation Engineering* 6, 205–222. doi:10.17265/2328-142/2018.05.001.

Lummus, R.R., Krumwiede, D.W., Vokurka, R.J. (2001) The relationship of logistics to supply chain management: Developing a common industry definition. *Industrial Management & Data Systems*, 101(8), 426–432. doi:10.1108/02635570110406730.

Sheffi, Y. (2013) Logistics-intensive clusters: Global competitiveness and regional growth. In: Bookbinder, J. (eds.), *Handbook of Global Logistics. International Series in Operations Research & Management Science*, Vol. 181. Springer, New York. doi:10.1007/978-1-4419-6132-7_19.

Stefansson, G., & Lumsden, K. (2008) Performance issues of smart transportation management systems. *International Journal of Productivity and Performance Management*, 58(1), 55–70. doi:10.1108/17410400910921083.

Uckelman, D. (2012) A definition approach to smart logistics. In: *Next Generation Teletraffic and Wired/Wireless Advanced Networking. 8th International Conference, NEW2AN and 1st Russian Conference on Smart Sapces, ruSMART 2008*, St. Petersburg, Russia, September 2008.

Index

Printed in the United States
by Baker & Taylor Publisher Services